COLLINS
POCKET
THESAURUS

COLLINS
POCKET
THESAURUS

Collins

An Imprint of HarperCollinsPublishers

First Edition 1992

New Edition 2000

Latest reprint 2000

10 9 8 7 6 5 4 3 2

© HarperCollins Publishers 1992, 2000

ISBN 0-00-472397-X

Collins® and Bank of English® are registered trademarks
of HarperCollins Publishers Limited

The HarperCollins website address is
www.**fire**and**water**.com

A catalogue record for this book is available from the British Library.

Corpus Acknowledgments
We would like to thank those authors and publishers
who kindly gave permission for copyright material to be used in the
Bank of English. We would also like to thank Times Newspapers Ltd
for providing valuable data.

Typeset by Stewart C. Russell

Printed and bound in Great Britain by Omnia Books Limited, Glasgow

This thesaurus has been compiled by referring to the Bank of English, a unique database of the English language with examples of over 323 million words enabling Collins lexicographers to analyse how English is actually used today and how it is changing. This is the evidence on which the changes in this thesaurus are based.

The Bank of English was set up as a joint initiative by HarperCollins Publishers and Birmingham University to be a resource for language research and lexicography. It contains a very wide range of material from books, newspapers, radio, TV, magazines, letters and talks reflecting the whole spectrum of English today. Its size and range make it an unequalled resource and the purpose-built software for its analysis is unique to Collins Dictionaries.

This ensures that Collins Dictionaries accurately reflect English as it is used today in a way that is most helpful to the dictionary user as well as including the full range of rarer and historical words and meanings.

EDITORIAL STAFF

Editorial Director
Diana Treffry

Managing Editor
Sheila Ferguson

Senior Lexicographer
Elspeth Summers

Lexicographers
Lorna Gilmour
Ian Brookes
Andrew Holmes
Mary O'Neill

Computing Staff
John Podbielski
Stewart C. Russell
Jane Creevy

FOREWORD

Collins Pocket Thesaurus, which was first published in 1992, has proved to be an immensely popular language resource. It allows you to look up a word and find a wide selection of alternatives that can replace it. It is, therefore, tremendously helpful when you are trying to find different ways of expressing yourself, as well as being an invaluable aid for crosswords and puzzles.

The A-Z arrangement of main entry words lets you go straight to any word without having to use an index, just as if you were looking up a word in a dictionary. In addition, all main entry words are printed in red so that they are quick and easy to find. In the new **Pocket Thesaurus**, the number of entries has been increased, thus giving you an even greater chance of finding the word you want. At the same time, the list of alternative words (synonyms) for each main entry word has been reviewed to give the widest possible choice of the most helpful alternatives. The new edition also takes account of recent changes in the language, with new terms like *gridlock*, *nerd* and *Internet* included as main entries, and words like *wannabe*, *stakeholder* and *luvvie* being found among the synonyms.

As part of an innovative design, the most helpful synonyms have been underlined and placed first in each list. This layout lets you see immediately which sense of the word is referred to. It also gives you an idea of which synonym is the closest alternative to the word you have looked up.

These features mean that the **Collins Pocket Thesaurus** provides the user with a treasury of useful words arranged in the most helpful format possible.

FEATURES OF THE BOOK

thirst, yearning, yen (*informal*)

Entry Word ————————— **crawl** *verb* **1** <u>creep</u>, advance
slowly, inch, slither, worm one's
way, wriggle, writhe **2** <u>grovel</u>,

Synonym ————————— creep, fawn, humble oneself,
toady **3** <u>be full of</u>, be alive, be
overrun (*slang*), swarm, teem

Most Helpful Synonym ————— **craze** *noun* <u>fad</u>, enthusiasm,
fashion, infatuation, mania, rage,
trend, vogue

Part of Speech ————————— **crazy** *adjective* **1** *Informal*
<u>ridiculous</u>, absurd, foolish,
idiotic, ill-conceived, ludicrous,
nonsensical, preposterous,
senseless **2** <u>fanatical</u>, devoted,
enthusiastic, infatuated, mad,

Usage Label ————————— passionate, wild (*informal*)
3 <u>insane</u>, crazed, demented,
deranged, mad, nuts (*slang*), out

Idiom ————————— of one's mind, unbalanced

creak *verb* <u>squeak</u>, grate, grind,
groan, scrape, scratch, screech

cream *noun* **1** <u>lotion</u>, cosmetic,
emulsion, essence, liniment, oil,
ointment, paste, salve, unguent

Foreign Word/Phrase ————— **2** <u>best</u>, *crème de la crème*, elite,
flower, pick, prime ◆ *adjective*
3 <u>off-white</u>, yellowish-white

creamy *adjective* <u>smooth</u>,
buttery, milky, rich, soft, velvety

Sense Number ————————— **crease** *noun* **1** <u>line</u>, corrugation,
fold, groove, ridge, wrinkle
◆ *verb* **2** <u>wrinkle</u>, corrugate,
crumple, double up, fold,
rumple, screw up

create *verb* **1** <u>make</u>, compose,
devise, formulate, invent,
originate, produce, spawn
2 <u>cause</u>, bring about, lead to,
occasion **3** <u>appoint</u>, constitute,
establish, install, invest, make,

Phrasal Verb ————————— set up

creation *noun* **1** <u>making</u>,
conception, formation,

A a

abandon *verb* **1** <u>leave</u>, desert, forsake, strand **2** <u>give up</u>, relinquish, surrender, yield ◆ *noun* **3** <u>wildness</u>, recklessness

abandonment *noun* <u>leaving</u>, dereliction, desertion, forsaking

abashed *adjective* <u>embarrassed</u>, ashamed, chagrined, disconcerted, dismayed, humiliated, mortified, shamefaced, taken aback

abate *verb* <u>decrease</u>, decline, diminish, dwindle, fade, lessen, let up, moderate, relax, slacken, subside, weaken

abbey *noun* <u>monastery</u>, convent, friary, nunnery, priory

abbreviate *verb* <u>shorten</u>, abridge, compress, condense, contract, cut, reduce, summarize

abbreviation *noun* <u>shortening</u>, abridgment, contraction, reduction, summary, synopsis

abdicate *verb* <u>give up</u>, abandon, quit, relinquish, renounce, resign, step down (*informal*)

abdication *noun* <u>giving up</u>, abandonment, quitting, renunciation, resignation, retirement, surrender

abduct *verb* <u>kidnap</u>, carry off, seize, snatch (*slang*)

abduction *noun* <u>kidnapping</u>, carrying off, seizure

aberration *noun* <u>oddity</u>, abnormality, anomaly, defect, irregularity, lapse, peculiarity, quirk

abet *verb* <u>help</u>, aid, assist, connive at, support

abeyance *noun* **in abeyance** <u>shelved</u>, hanging fire, on ice (*informal*), pending, suspended

abhor *verb* <u>hate</u>, abominate, detest, loathe, shrink from, shudder at

abhorrent *adjective* <u>hateful</u>, abominable, disgusting, distasteful, hated, horrid, loathsome, offensive, repulsive

abide *verb* <u>tolerate</u>, accept, bear, endure, put up with, stand, suffer

abide by *verb* <u>obey</u>, agree to, comply with, conform to, follow, observe, submit to

abiding *adjective* <u>everlasting</u>, continuing, enduring, lasting, permanent, persistent, unchanging

ability *noun* <u>skill</u>, aptitude, capability, competence, expertise, proficiency, talent

abject *adjective* **1** <u>miserable</u>, deplorable, forlorn, hopeless, pitiable, wretched **2** <u>servile</u>, cringing, degraded, fawning, grovelling, submissive

ablaze *adjective* <u>on fire</u>, aflame, alight, blazing, burning, fiery, flaming, ignited, lighted

able *adjective* <u>capable</u>, accomplished, competent, efficient, proficient, qualified, skilful

able-bodied *adjective* <u>strong</u>, fit, healthy, robust, sound, sturdy

abnormal *adjective* <u>unusual</u>, atypical, exceptional, extraordinary, irregular, odd, peculiar, strange, uncommon

abnormality noun <u>oddity</u>, deformity, exception, irregularity, peculiarity, singularity, strangeness

abode noun <u>home</u>, domicile, dwelling, habitat, habitation, house, lodging, pad (slang), quarters, residence

abolish verb <u>do away with</u>, annul, cancel, destroy, eliminate, end, eradicate, put an end to, quash, rescind, revoke, stamp out

abolition noun <u>ending</u>, cancellation, destruction, elimination, end, extermination, termination, wiping out

abominable adjective <u>terrible</u>, despicable, detestable, disgusting, hateful, horrible, horrid, repulsive, revolting, vile

abort verb **1** <u>terminate</u> (a pregnancy), miscarry **2** <u>stop</u>, arrest, axe (informal), call off, check, end, fail, halt, terminate

abortion noun <u>termination</u>, deliberate miscarriage, miscarriage

abortive adjective <u>failed</u>, fruitless, futile, ineffectual, miscarried, unsuccessful, useless, vain

abound verb <u>be plentiful</u>, flourish, proliferate, swarm, swell, teem, thrive

abounding adjective <u>plentiful</u>, abundant, bountiful, copious, full, profuse, prolific, rich

about preposition **1** <u>regarding</u>, as regards, concerning, dealing with, on, referring to, relating to **2** <u>near</u>, adjacent to, beside, circa (used with dates), close to, nearby

♦ adverb **3** <u>nearly</u>, almost, approaching, approximately, around, close to, more or less, roughly

above preposition <u>over</u>, beyond, exceeding, higher than, on top of, upon

abrasion noun Medical <u>graze</u>, chafe, scrape, scratch, scuff, surface injury

abrasive adjective **1** <u>unpleasant</u>, caustic, cutting, galling, grating, irritating, rough, sharp **2** <u>rough</u>, chafing, grating, scraping, scratchy

abreast adjective **1** <u>alongside</u>, beside, side by side **2** **abreast of** <u>informed about</u>, acquainted with, au courant with, au fait with, conversant with, familiar with, in the picture about, in touch with, keeping one's finger on the pulse of, knowledgeable about, up to date with, up to speed with

abridge verb <u>shorten</u>, abbreviate, condense, cut, decrease, reduce, summarize

abroad adverb <u>overseas</u>, in foreign lands, out of the country

abrupt adjective **1** <u>sudden</u>, precipitate, quick, surprising, unexpected **2** <u>curt</u>, brusque, gruff, impatient, rude, short, terse

abscond verb <u>flee</u>, clear out, disappear, escape, make off, run off, steal away

absence noun **1** <u>nonattendance</u>, absenteeism, truancy **2** <u>lack</u>, deficiency, need, omission, unavailability, want

absent adjective **1** <u>missing</u>, away, elsewhere, gone, nonexistent,

out, unavailable
2 <u>absent-minded</u>, blank, distracted, inattentive, oblivious, preoccupied, vacant, vague
♦ *verb* 3 **absent oneself** <u>stay away</u>, keep away, play truant, withdraw

absent-minded *adjective* <u>vague</u>, distracted, dreaming, forgetful, inattentive, preoccupied, unaware

absolute *adjective* 1 <u>total</u>, complete, outright, perfect, pure, sheer, thorough, utter 2 <u>supreme</u>, full, sovereign, unbounded, unconditional, unlimited, unrestricted

absolutely *adverb* <u>totally</u>, completely, entirely, fully, one hundred per cent, perfectly, utterly, wholly

absolution *noun* <u>forgiveness</u>, deliverance, exculpation, exoneration, mercy, pardon, release

absolve *verb* <u>forgive</u>, deliver, exculpate, excuse, let off, pardon, release, set free

absorb *verb* 1 <u>soak up</u>, consume, digest, imbibe, incorporate, receive, suck up, take in 2 <u>preoccupy</u>, captivate, engage, engross, fascinate, rivet

absorbed *adjective*
1 <u>preoccupied</u>, captivated, engrossed, fascinated, immersed, involved, lost, rapt, riveted, wrapped up 2 <u>digested</u>, assimilated, incorporated, received, soaked up

absorbent *adjective* <u>permeable</u>, porous, receptive, spongy

absorbing *adjective* <u>fascinating</u>, captivating, engrossing, gripping, interesting, intriguing, riveting, spellbinding

absorption *noun* 1 <u>soaking up</u>, assimilation, consumption, digestion, incorporation, sucking up 2 <u>concentration</u>, fascination, immersion, intentness, involvement, preoccupation

abstain *verb* <u>refrain</u>, avoid, decline, deny (oneself), desist, fast, forbear, forgo, give up, keep from

abstemious *adjective* self-denying, ascetic, austere, frugal, moderate, sober, temperate

abstention *noun* <u>refusal</u>, abstaining, abstinence, avoidance, forbearance, refraining, self-control, self-denial, self-restraint

abstinence *noun* <u>self-denial</u>, abstemiousness, avoidance, forbearance, moderation, self-restraint, soberness, teetotalism, temperance

abstinent *adjective* <u>self-denying</u>, abstaining, abstemious, forbearing, moderate, self-controlled, sober, temperate

abstract *adjective* 1 <u>theoretical</u>, abstruse, general, hypothetical, indefinite, notional, recondite
♦ *noun* 2 <u>summary</u>, abridgment, digest, epitome, outline, précis, résumé, synopsis ♦ *verb*
3 <u>summarize</u>, abbreviate, abridge, condense, digest, epitomize, outline, précis, shorten 4 <u>remove</u>, detach, extract, isolate, separate, take away, take out, withdraw

abstraction *noun* 1 <u>idea</u>, concept, formula, generalization, hypothesis, notion, theorem,

theory, thought
2 <u>absent-mindedness</u>, absence, dreaminess, inattention, pensiveness, preoccupation, remoteness, woolgathering

abstruse *adjective* <u>obscure</u>, arcane, complex, deep, enigmatic, esoteric, recondite, unfathomable, vague

absurd *adjective* <u>ridiculous</u>, crazy (*informal*), farcical, foolish, idiotic, illogical, inane, incongruous, irrational, ludicrous, nonsensical, preposterous, senseless, silly, stupid, unreasonable

absurdity *noun* <u>ridiculousness</u>, farce, folly, foolishness, incongruity, joke, nonsense, silliness, stupidity

abundance *noun* <u>plenty</u>, affluence, bounty, copiousness, exuberance, fullness, profusion

abundant *adjective* <u>plentiful</u>, ample, bountiful, copious, exuberant, filled, full, luxuriant, profuse, rich, teeming

abuse *noun* **1** <u>ill-treatment</u>, damage, exploitation, harm, hurt, injury, maltreatment, manhandling **2** <u>insults</u>, blame, castigation, censure, defamation, derision, disparagement, invective, reproach, scolding, vilification **3** <u>misuse</u>, misapplication ♦ *verb* **4** <u>ill-treat</u>, damage, exploit, harm, hurt, injure, maltreat, misuse, take advantage of **5** <u>insult</u>, castigate, curse, defame, disparage, malign, scold, vilify

abusive *adjective* **1** <u>insulting</u>, censorious, defamatory, disparaging, libellous, offensive,

reproachful, rude, scathing
2 <u>harmful</u>, brutal, cruel, destructive, hurtful, injurious, rough

abysmal *adjective* <u>terrible</u>, appalling, awful, bad, dire, dreadful

abyss *noun* <u>pit</u>, chasm, crevasse, fissure, gorge, gulf, void

academic *adjective* **1** <u>scholarly</u>, bookish, erudite, highbrow, learned, literary, studious
2 <u>hypothetical</u>, abstract, conjectural, impractical, notional, speculative, theoretical ♦ *noun*
3 <u>scholar</u>, academician, don, fellow, lecturer, master, professor, tutor

accede *verb* **1** <u>agree</u>, accept, acquiesce, admit, assent, comply, concede, concur, consent, endorse, grant
2 <u>inherit</u>, assume, attain, come to, enter upon, succeed, succeed to (*as heir*)

accelerate *verb* <u>speed up</u>, advance, expedite, further, hasten, hurry, quicken

acceleration *noun* <u>speeding up</u>, hastening, hurrying, quickening, stepping up (*informal*)

accent *noun* **1** <u>pronunciation</u>, articulation, brogue, enunciation, inflection, intonation, modulation, tone **2** <u>emphasis</u>, beat, cadence, force, pitch, rhythm, stress, timbre ♦ *verb*
3 <u>emphasize</u>, accentuate, stress, underline, underscore

accentuate *verb* <u>emphasize</u>, accent, draw attention to, foreground, highlight, stress, underline, underscore

accept *verb* **1** <u>receive</u>, acquire,

gain, get, obtain, secure, take
2 <u>agree to</u>, admit, approve,
believe, concur with, consent to,
cooperate with, recognize

acceptable *adjective* <u>satisfactory</u>,
adequate, admissible, all right,
fair, moderate, passable, tolerable

acceptance *noun* **1** <u>accepting</u>,
acquiring, gaining, getting,
obtaining, receipt, securing,
taking **2** <u>agreement</u>,
acknowledgment, acquiescence,
admission, adoption, approval,
assent, concurrence, consent,
cooperation, recognition

accepted *adjective* <u>agreed</u>,
acknowledged, approved,
common, conventional,
customary, established, normal,
recognized, traditional

access *noun* <u>entrance</u>, admission,
admittance, approach, entry,
passage, path, road

accessibility *noun* **1** <u>handiness</u>,
availability, nearness, possibility,
readiness **2** <u>approachability</u>,
affability, cordiality, friendliness,
informality **3** <u>openness</u>,
susceptibility

accessible *adjective* **1** <u>handy</u>,
achievable, at hand, attainable,
available, near, nearby,
obtainable, reachable
2 <u>approachable</u>, affable,
available, cordial, friendly,
informal **3** <u>open</u>, exposed, liable,
susceptible, vulnerable,
wide-open

accessory *noun* **1** <u>addition</u>,
accompaniment, adjunct,
adornment, appendage,
attachment, decoration, extra,
supplement, trimming
2 <u>accomplice</u>, abettor, assistant,

associate (*in crime*), colleague,
confederate, helper, partner

accident *noun* **1** <u>misfortune</u>,
calamity, collision, crash,
disaster, misadventure, mishap
2 <u>chance</u>, fate, fluke, fortuity,
fortune, hazard, luck

accidental *adjective*
<u>unintentional</u>, casual, chance,
fortuitous, haphazard,
inadvertent, incidental, random,
unexpected, unforeseen,
unlooked-for, unplanned

accidentally *adverb*
<u>unintentionally</u>, by accident, by
chance, fortuitously,
haphazardly, inadvertently,
incidentally, randomly,
unwittingly

acclaim *verb* **1** <u>praise</u>, applaud,
approve, celebrate, cheer, clap,
commend, exalt, hail, honour,
salute ♦ *noun* **2** <u>praise</u>,
acclamation, applause, approval,
celebration, commendation,
honour, kudos

acclamation *noun* <u>praise</u>,
acclaim, adulation, approval,
ovation, plaudit, tribute

acclimatization *noun*
<u>adaptation</u>, adjustment,
habituation, inurement,
naturalization

acclimatize *verb* <u>adapt</u>,
accommodate, accustom, adjust,
get used to, habituate, inure,
naturalize

accolade *noun* <u>praise</u>, acclaim,
applause, approval,
commendation, compliment,
ovation, recognition, tribute

accommodate *verb* **1** <u>house</u>,
cater for, entertain, lodge, put
up, shelter **2** <u>help</u>, aid, assist,

oblige, serve **3** <u>adapt</u>, adjust, comply, conform, fit, harmonize, modify, reconcile, settle

accommodating *adjective* <u>helpful</u>, considerate, cooperative, friendly, hospitable, kind, obliging, polite, unselfish, willing

accommodation *noun* <u>housing</u>, board, digs (*Brit. informal*), house, lodging(s), quarters, shelter

accompaniment *noun* **1** <u>supplement</u>, accessory, companion, complement **2** <u>backing music</u>, backing

accompany *verb* **1** <u>go with</u>, attend, chaperon, conduct, convoy, escort, hold (someone's) hand **2** <u>occur with</u>, belong to, come with, follow, go together with, supplement

accompanying *adjective* <u>additional</u>, associated, attached, attendant, complementary, related, supplementary

accomplice *noun* <u>helper</u>, abettor, accessory, ally, assistant, associate, collaborator, colleague, henchman, partner

accomplish *verb* <u>do</u>, achieve, attain, bring about, carry out, complete, effect, execute, finish, fulfil, manage, perform, produce

accomplished *adjective* <u>skilled</u>, expert, gifted, masterly, polished, practised, proficient, talented

accomplishment *noun* **1** <u>completion</u>, bringing about, carrying out, conclusion, execution, finishing, fulfilment, performance **2** <u>achievement</u>, act, coup, deed, exploit, feat, stroke, triumph

accord *noun* **1** <u>agreement</u>, conformity, correspondence, harmony, rapport, sympathy, unison ♦ *verb* **2** <u>fit</u>, agree, conform, correspond, harmonize, match, suit, tally

accordingly *adverb* **1** <u>appropriately</u>, correspondingly, fitly, properly, suitably **2** <u>consequently</u>, as a result, ergo, hence, in consequence, so, therefore, thus

according to *adverb* **1** <u>as stated by</u>, as believed by, as maintained by, in the light of, on the authority of, on the report of **2** <u>in keeping with</u>, after, after the manner of, consistent with, in accordance with, in compliance with, in line with, in the manner of

accost *verb* <u>approach</u>, buttonhole, confront, greet, hail

account *noun* **1** <u>description</u>, explanation, narrative, report, statement, story, tale, version **2** *Commerce* <u>statement</u>, balance, bill, books, charge, invoice, reckoning, register, score, tally **3** <u>importance</u>, consequence, honour, note, significance, standing, value, worth ♦ *verb* **4** <u>consider</u>, count, estimate, judge, rate, reckon, regard, think, value

accountability *noun* <u>responsibility</u>, answerability, chargeability, culpability, liability

accountable *adjective* <u>responsible</u>, amenable, answerable, charged with, liable, obligated, obliged

accountant *noun* <u>auditor</u>, bean counter (*informal*), book-keeper

account for *verb* explain, answer for, clarify, clear up, elucidate, illuminate, justify, rationalize

accredited *adjective* authorized, appointed, certified, empowered, endorsed, guaranteed, licensed, official, recognized

accrue *verb* increase, accumulate, amass, arise, be added, build up, collect, enlarge, flow, follow, grow

accumulate *verb* collect, accrue, amass, build up, gather, hoard, increase, pile up, store

accumulation *noun* collection, build-up, gathering, heap, hoard, increase, mass, pile, stack, stock, stockpile, store

accuracy *noun* exactness, accurateness, authenticity, carefulness, closeness, correctness, fidelity, precision, strictness, truthfulness, veracity

accurate *adjective* exact, authentic, close, correct, faithful, precise, scrupulous, spot-on (*Brit. informal*), strict, true, unerring

accurately *adverb* exactly, authentically, closely, correctly, faithfully, precisely, scrupulously, strictly, to the letter, truly, unerringly

accursed *adjective* 1 cursed, bewitched, condemned, damned, doomed, hopeless, ill-fated, ill-omened, jinxed, unfortunate, unlucky, wretched 2 hateful, abominable, despicable, detestable, execrable, hellish, horrible

accusation *noun* charge, allegation, complaint, denunciation, incrimination, indictment, recrimination

accuse *verb* charge, blame, censure, denounce, impeach, impute, incriminate, indict

accustom *verb* adapt, acclimatize, acquaint, discipline, exercise, familiarize, train

accustomed *adjective* 1 usual, common, conventional, customary, established, everyday, expected, habitual, normal, ordinary, regular, traditional 2 used, acclimatized, acquainted, adapted, familiar, familiarized, given to, in the habit of, trained

ace *noun* 1 *Cards, dice, etc.* one, single point 2 *Informal* expert, champion, dab hand (*Brit. informal*), master, star, virtuoso, wizard (*informal*) ♦ *adjective* 3 *Informal* excellent, awesome (*slang*), brilliant, fine, great, outstanding, superb

ache *verb* 1 hurt, pain, pound, smart, suffer, throb, twinge ♦ *noun* 2 pain, hurt, pang, pounding, soreness, suffering, throbbing

achieve *verb* attain, accomplish, acquire, bring about, carry out, complete, do, execute, fulfil, gain, get, obtain, perform

achievement *noun* accomplishment, act, deed, effort, exploit, feat, feather in one's cap, stroke

acid *adjective* 1 sour, acerbic, acrid, pungent, tart, vinegary 2 sharp, biting, bitter, caustic, cutting, harsh, trenchant, vitriolic

acidity *noun* 1 sourness, acerbity, pungency, tartness 2 sharpness, bitterness, harshness

acknowledge verb 1 <u>accept</u>, admit, allow, concede, confess, declare, grant, own, profess, recognize, yield 2 <u>greet</u>, address, hail, notice, recognize, salute 3 <u>reply to</u>, answer, notice, react to, recognize, respond to, return

acknowledged adjective <u>accepted</u>, accredited, approved, confessed, declared, professed, recognized, returned

acknowledgment noun 1 <u>acceptance</u>, admission, allowing, confession, declaration, profession, realization, yielding 2 <u>greeting</u>, addressing, hail, hailing, notice, recognition, salutation, salute 3 <u>appreciation</u>, answer, credit, gratitude, reaction, recognition, reply, response, return, thanks

acquaint verb <u>tell</u>, disclose, divulge, enlighten, familiarize, inform, let (someone) know, notify, reveal

acquaintance noun 1 <u>associate</u>, colleague, contact 2 <u>knowledge</u>, awareness, experience, familiarity, fellowship, relationship, understanding

acquainted with adjective <u>familiar with</u>, alive to, apprised of, au fait with, aware of, conscious of, experienced in, informed of, knowledgeable about, versed in

acquiesce verb <u>agree</u>, accede, accept, allow, approve, assent, comply, concur, conform, consent, give in, go along with, submit, yield

acquiescence noun <u>agreement</u>, acceptance, approval, assent, compliance, conformity, consent, giving in, obedience, submission, yielding

acquire verb <u>get</u>, amass, attain, buy, collect, earn, gain, gather, obtain, receive, secure, win

acquisition noun 1 <u>possession</u>, buy, gain, prize, property, purchase 2 <u>acquiring</u>, attainment, gaining, procurement

acquisitive adjective <u>greedy</u>, avaricious, avid, covetous, grabbing, grasping, predatory, rapacious

acquit verb 1 <u>clear</u>, discharge, free, liberate, release, vindicate 2 <u>behave</u>, bear, comport, conduct, perform

acquittal noun <u>clearance</u>, absolution, deliverance, discharge, exoneration, liberation, release, relief, vindication

acrid adjective <u>pungent</u>, bitter, caustic, harsh, sharp, vitriolic

acrimonious adjective <u>bitter</u>, caustic, irascible, petulant, rancorous, spiteful, splenetic, testy

acrimony noun <u>bitterness</u>, harshness, ill will, irascibility, rancour, virulence

act noun 1 <u>deed</u>, accomplishment, achievement, action, exploit, feat, performance, undertaking 2 <u>law</u>, bill, decree, edict, enactment, measure, ordinance, resolution, statute 3 <u>performance</u>, routine, show, sketch, turn 4 <u>pretence</u>, affectation, attitude, front, performance, pose, posture, show ♦ verb 5 <u>do</u>, carry out, enact, execute, function, operate, perform, take effect, work 6 <u>perform</u>, act out, impersonate, mimic, play, play *or* take the part of, portray, represent

act for *verb* <u>stand in for</u>, cover for, deputize for, fill in for, replace, represent, substitute for, take the place of

acting *noun* 1 <u>performance</u>, characterization, impersonation, performing, playing, portrayal, stagecraft, theatre ♦ *adjective* 2 <u>temporary</u>, interim, pro tem, provisional, substitute, surrogate

action *noun* 1 <u>deed</u>, accomplishment, achievement, act, exploit, feat, performance 2 <u>lawsuit</u>, case, litigation, proceeding, prosecution, suit 3 <u>energy</u>, activity, force, liveliness, spirit, vigour, vim, vitality 4 <u>movement</u>, activity, functioning, motion, operation, process, working 5 <u>battle</u>, clash, combat, conflict, contest, encounter, engagement, fight, skirmish, sortie

activate *verb* <u>start</u>, arouse, energize, galvanize, initiate, mobilize, move, rouse, set in motion, stir

active *adjective* 1 <u>busy</u>, bustling, hard-working, involved, occupied, on the go (*informal*), on the move, strenuous 2 <u>energetic</u>, alert, animated, industrious, lively, quick, sprightly, spry, vigorous 3 <u>in operation</u>, acting, at work, effectual, in action, in force, operative, working

activist *noun* <u>militant</u>, organizer, partisan

activity *noun* 1 <u>action</u>,

animation, bustle, exercise, exertion, hustle, labour, motion, movement 2 <u>pursuit</u>, hobby, interest, pastime, project, scheme

actor *noun* <u>performer</u>, actress, luvvie (*informal*), player, Thespian

actress *noun* <u>performer</u>, actor, leading lady, player, starlet, Thespian

actual *adjective* <u>definite</u>, concrete, factual, physical, positive, real, substantial, tangible

actually *adverb* <u>really</u>, as a matter of fact, indeed, in fact, in point of fact, in reality, in truth, literally, truly

acumen *noun* <u>judgment</u>, astuteness, cleverness, ingenuity, insight, intelligence, perspicacity, shrewdness

acute *adjective* 1 <u>serious</u>, critical, crucial, dangerous, grave, important, severe, urgent 2 <u>sharp</u>, excruciating, fierce, intense, piercing, powerful, severe, shooting, violent 3 <u>perceptive</u>, astute, clever, insightful, keen, observant, sensitive, sharp, smart

acuteness *noun* 1 <u>seriousness</u>, gravity, importance, severity, urgency 2 <u>perceptiveness</u>, astuteness, cleverness, discrimination, insight, perspicacity, sharpness

adamant *adjective* <u>determined</u>, firm, fixed, obdurate, resolute, stubborn, unbending, uncompromising

adapt *verb* <u>adjust</u>, acclimatize, accommodate, alter, change, conform, convert, modify, remodel, tailor

adaptability noun <u>flexibility</u>, changeability, resilience, versatility

adaptable adjective <u>flexible</u>, adjustable, changeable, compliant, easy-going, plastic, pliant, resilient, versatile

adaptation noun
1 <u>acclimatization</u>, familiarization, naturalization 2 <u>conversion</u>, adjustment, alteration, change, modification, transformation, variation, version

add verb 1 <u>count up</u>, add up, compute, reckon, total, tot up 2 <u>include</u>, adjoin, affix, append, attach, augment, supplement

addendum noun <u>addition</u>, appendage, appendix, attachment, extension, extra, postscript, supplement

addict noun 1 <u>junkie</u> (informal), fiend (informal), freak (informal) 2 <u>fan</u>, adherent, buff (informal), devotee, enthusiast, follower, nut (slang)

addicted adjective <u>hooked</u> (slang), absorbed, accustomed, dedicated, dependent, devoted, habituated

addiction noun <u>dependence</u>, craving, enslavement, habit, obsession

addition noun 1 <u>inclusion</u>, adding, amplification, attachment, augmentation, enlargement, extension, increasing 2 <u>extra</u>, addendum, additive, appendage, appendix, extension, gain, increase, increment, supplement 3 <u>counting up</u>, adding up, computation, totalling, totting up 4 **in addition (to)** <u>as well (as)</u>,

additionally, also, besides, into the bargain, moreover, over and above, to boot, too

additional adjective <u>extra</u>, added, fresh, further, new, other, spare, supplementary

address noun 1 <u>location</u>, abode, dwelling, home, house, residence, situation, whereabouts 2 <u>speech</u>, discourse, dissertation, lecture, oration, sermon, talk ♦ verb 3 <u>speak to</u>, approach, greet, hail, talk to 4 **address (oneself) to** <u>concentrate on</u>, apply (oneself) to, attend to, devote (oneself) to, engage in, focus on, take care of

add up verb <u>count up</u>, add, compute, count, reckon, total, tot up

adept adjective 1 <u>skilful</u>, able, accomplished, adroit, expert, practised, proficient, skilled, versed ♦ noun 2 <u>expert</u>, dab hand (Brit. informal), genius, hotshot (informal), master

adequacy noun <u>sufficiency</u>, capability, competence, fairness, suitability, tolerability

adequate adjective <u>enough</u>, competent, fair, satisfactory, sufficient, tolerable, up to scratch (informal)

adhere verb <u>stick</u>, attach, cleave, cling, fasten, fix, glue, hold fast, paste

adherent noun <u>supporter</u>, admirer, devotee, disciple, fan, follower, upholder

adhesive adjective 1 <u>sticky</u>, clinging, cohesive, gluey, glutinous, tenacious ♦ noun 2 <u>glue</u>, cement, gum, paste

adieu noun <u>goodbye</u>, farewell, leave-taking, parting, valediction

adjacent adjective <u>next</u>, adjoining, beside, bordering, cheek by jowl, close, near, neighbouring, next door, touching

adjoin verb <u>connect</u>, border, join, link, touch

adjoining adjective <u>connecting</u>, abutting, adjacent, bordering, neighbouring, next door, touching

adjourn verb <u>postpone</u>, defer, delay, discontinue, interrupt, put off, suspend

adjournment noun <u>postponement</u>, delay, discontinuation, interruption, putting off, recess, suspension

adjudicate verb <u>judge</u>, adjudge, arbitrate, decide, determine, mediate, referee, settle, umpire

adjudication noun <u>judgment</u>, arbitration, conclusion, decision, finding, pronouncement, ruling, settlement, verdict

adjust verb <u>alter</u>, accustom, adapt, make conform, modify

adjustable adjective <u>alterable</u>, adaptable, flexible, malleable, modifiable, movable

adjustment noun 1 <u>alteration</u>, adaptation, modification, redress, regulation, tuning 2 <u>acclimatization</u>, orientation, settling in

ad-lib verb <u>improvise</u>, busk, extemporize, make up, speak off the cuff, wing it (informal)

administer verb 1 <u>manage</u>, conduct, control, direct, govern, handle, oversee, run, supervise

2 <u>give</u>, apply, dispense, impose, mete out, perform, provide

administration noun <u>management</u>, application, conduct, control, direction, government, running, supervision

administrative adjective <u>managerial</u>, directorial, executive, governmental, organizational, regulatory, supervisory

administrator noun <u>manager</u>, bureaucrat, executive, official, organizer, supervisor

admirable adjective <u>excellent</u>, commendable, exquisite, fine, laudable, praiseworthy, wonderful, worthy

admiration noun <u>regard</u>, amazement, appreciation, approval, esteem, praise, respect, wonder

admire verb 1 <u>respect</u>, appreciate, approve, esteem, look up to, praise, prize, think highly of, value 2 <u>marvel at</u>, appreciate, delight in, take pleasure in, wonder at

admirer noun 1 <u>suitor</u>, beau, boyfriend, lover, sweetheart, wooer 2 <u>fan</u>, devotee, disciple, enthusiast, follower, partisan, supporter

admissible adjective <u>permissible</u>, acceptable, allowable, passable, tolerable

admission noun 1 <u>entrance</u>, acceptance, access, admittance, entrée, entry, initiation, introduction 2 <u>confession</u>, acknowledgment, allowance, declaration, disclosure, divulgence, revelation

admit verb **1** <u>confess</u>, acknowledge, declare, disclose, divulge, own, reveal **2** <u>allow</u>, agree, grant, let, permit, recognize **3** <u>let in</u>, accept, allow, give access, initiate, introduce, receive, take in

admonish verb <u>reprimand</u>, berate, chide, rebuke, scold, slap on the wrist, tell off (*informal*)

adolescence noun **1** <u>youth</u>, boyhood, girlhood, minority, teens **2** <u>youthfulness</u>, childishness, immaturity

adolescent adjective **1** <u>young</u>, boyish, girlish, immature, juvenile, puerile, teenage, youthful ♦ noun **2** <u>youth</u>, juvenile, minor, teenager, youngster

adopt verb **1** <u>foster</u>, take in **2** <u>choose</u>, assume, espouse, follow, maintain, take up

adoption noun **1** <u>fostering</u>, adopting, taking in **2** <u>choice</u>, appropriation, assumption, embracing, endorsement, espousal, selection, taking up

adorable adjective <u>lovable</u>, appealing, attractive, charming, cute, dear, delightful, fetching, pleasing

adore verb <u>love</u>, admire, cherish, dote on, esteem, exalt, glorify, honour, idolize, revere, worship

adoring adjective <u>loving</u>, admiring, affectionate, devoted, doting, fond

adorn verb <u>decorate</u>, array, embellish, festoon

adornment noun <u>decoration</u>, accessory, embellishment, festoon, frill, frippery, ornament, supplement, trimming

adrift adjective **1** <u>drifting</u>, afloat, unanchored, unmoored **2** <u>aimless</u>, directionless, goalless, purposeless ♦ adverb **3** <u>wrong</u>, amiss, astray, off course

adroit adjective <u>skilful</u>, adept, clever, deft, dexterous, expert, masterful, neat, proficient, skilled

adulation noun <u>worship</u>, fawning, fulsome praise, servile flattery, sycophancy

adult noun **1** <u>grown-up</u>, grown or grown-up person (man or woman), person of mature age ♦ adjective **2** <u>fully grown</u>, full grown, fully developed, grown-up, mature, of age, ripe

advance verb **1** <u>progress</u>, come forward, go on, hasten, make inroads, proceed, speed **2** <u>benefit</u>, further, improve, prosper **3** <u>suggest</u>, offer, present, proffer, put forward, submit **4** <u>lend</u>, pay beforehand, supply on credit ♦ noun **5** <u>progress</u>, advancement, development, forward movement, headway, inroads, onward movement **6** <u>improvement</u>, breakthrough, gain, growth, progress, promotion, step **7** <u>loan</u>, credit, deposit, down payment, prepayment, retainer **8 advances** <u>overtures</u>, approach, approaches, moves, proposals, proposition ♦ adjective **9** <u>prior</u>, beforehand, early, forward, in front **10 in advance** <u>beforehand</u>, ahead, earlier, previously

advanced adjective <u>foremost</u>, ahead, avant-garde, forward, higher, leading, precocious, progressive

advancement *noun* promotion, betterment, gain, improvement, preferment, progress, rise

advantage *noun* benefit, ascendancy, dominance, good, help, lead, precedence, profit, superiority, sway

advantageous *adjective* **1** beneficial, convenient, expedient, helpful, of service, profitable, useful, valuable, worthwhile **2** superior, dominant, dominating, favourable

adventure *noun* escapade, enterprise, experience, exploit, incident, occurrence, undertaking, venture

adventurer *noun* **1** mercenary, charlatan, fortune-hunter, gambler, opportunist, rogue, speculator **2** hero, daredevil, heroine, knight-errant, traveller, voyager

adventurous *adjective* daring, bold, daredevil, enterprising, intrepid, reckless

adversary *noun* opponent, antagonist, competitor, contestant, enemy, foe, rival

adverse *adjective* unfavourable, contrary, detrimental, hostile, inopportune, negative, opposing

adversity *noun* hardship, affliction, bad luck, disaster, distress, hard times, misfortune, reverse, trouble

advert *noun Brit. informal* advertisement, ad (*informal*), announcement, blurb, commercial, notice, plug (*informal*), poster

advertise *verb* publicize,

announce, inform, make known, notify, plug (*informal*), promote, tout

advertisement *noun* advert (*Brit. informal*), ad (*informal*), announcement, blurb, commercial, notice, plug (*informal*), poster

advice *noun* guidance, counsel, help, opinion, recommendation, suggestion

advisability *noun* wisdom, appropriateness, aptness, desirability, expediency, fitness, propriety, prudence, suitability

advisable *adjective* wise, appropriate, desirable, expedient, fitting, politic, prudent, recommended, seemly, sensible

advise *verb* **1** recommend, admonish, caution, commend, counsel, prescribe, suggest, urge **2** notify, acquaint, apprise, inform, make known, report, tell, warn

adviser *noun* guide, aide, confidant, consultant, counsellor, helper, mentor, right-hand man

advisory *adjective* advising, consultative, counselling, helping, recommending

advocate *verb* **1** recommend, advise, argue for, campaign for, champion, commend, encourage, promote, propose, support, uphold ♦ *noun* **2** supporter, campaigner, champion, counsellor, defender, promoter, proponent, spokesman, upholder **3** *Law* lawyer, attorney, barrister, counsel, solicitor

affable *adjective* friendly, amiable,

amicable, approachable, congenial, cordial, courteous, genial, pleasant, sociable, urbane

affair noun **1** event, activity, business, episode, happening, incident, matter, occurrence **2** relationship, amour, intrigue, liaison, romance

affect[1] verb **1** influence, act on, alter, bear upon, change, concern, impinge upon, relate to **2** move, disturb, overcome, perturb, stir, touch, upset

affect[2] verb put on, adopt, aspire to, assume, contrive, feign, imitate, pretend, simulate

affectation noun pretence, act, artificiality, assumed manners, façade, insincerity, pose, pretentiousness, show

affected adjective pretended, artificial, contrived, feigned, insincere, mannered, phoney or phony (informal), put-on, unnatural

affecting adjective moving, pathetic, pitiful, poignant, sad, touching

affection noun fondness, attachment, care, feeling, goodwill, kindness, liking, love, tenderness, warmth

affectionate adjective fond, attached, caring, devoted, doting, friendly, kind, loving, tender, warm-hearted

affiliate verb join, ally, amalgamate, associate, band together, combine, incorporate, link, unite

affinity noun **1** attraction, fondness, inclination, leaning, liking, partiality, rapport, sympathy **2** similarity, analogy, closeness, connection, correspondence, kinship, likeness, relationship, resemblance

affirm verb declare, assert, certify, confirm, maintain, pronounce, state, swear, testify

affirmation noun declaration, assertion, certification, confirmation, oath, pronouncement, statement, testimony

affirmative adjective agreeing, approving, assenting, concurring, confirming, consenting, corroborative, favourable, positive

afflict verb torment, distress, grieve, harass, hurt, oppress, pain, plague, trouble

affliction noun suffering, adversity, curse, disease, hardship, misfortune, ordeal, plague, scourge, torment, trial, trouble, woe

affluence noun wealth, abundance, fortune, opulence, plenty, prosperity, riches

affluent adjective wealthy, loaded (slang), moneyed, opulent, prosperous, rich, well-heeled (informal), well-off, well-to-do

afford verb **1** As in can afford spare, bear, manage, stand, sustain **2** give, offer, produce, provide, render, supply, yield

affordable adjective inexpensive, cheap, economical, low-cost, moderate, modest, reasonable

affront noun **1** insult, offence, outrage, provocation, slap in the face (informal), slight, slur ♦ verb

2 offend, anger, annoy, displease, insult, outrage, provoke, slight

aflame *adjective* burning, ablaze, alight, blazing, fiery, flaming, lit, on fire

afoot *adverb* going on, abroad, brewing, current, happening, in preparation, in progress, on the go (*informal*), up (*informal*)

afraid *adjective* 1 scared, apprehensive, cowardly, faint-hearted, fearful, frightened, nervous 2 sorry, regretful, unhappy

afresh *adverb* again, anew, newly, once again, once more, over again

after *adverb* following, afterwards, behind, below, later, subsequently, succeeding, thereafter

aftermath *noun* effects, aftereffects, consequences, end result, outcome, results, sequel, upshot, wake

again *adverb* 1 once more, afresh, anew, another time 2 also, besides, furthermore, in addition, moreover

against *preposition* 1 beside, abutting, facing, in contact with, on, opposite to, touching, upon 2 opposed to, anti (*informal*), averse to, hostile to, in defiance of, in opposition to, resisting, versus 3 in preparation for, in anticipation of, in expectation of, in provision for

age *noun* 1 time, date, day(s), duration, epoch, era, generation, lifetime, period, span 2 old age, advancing years, decline (*of life*), majority, maturity, senescence,

senility, seniority ♦ *verb* 3 grow old, decline, deteriorate, mature, mellow, ripen

aged *adjective* old, ancient, antiquated, antique, elderly, getting on, grey

agency *noun* 1 business, bureau, department, office, organization 2 *Old-fashioned* medium, activity, means, mechanism

agenda *noun* list, calendar, diary, plan, programme, schedule, timetable

agent *noun* 1 representative, envoy, go-between, negotiator, rep (*informal*), surrogate 2 worker, author, doer, mover, operator, performer 3 force, agency, cause, instrument, means, power, vehicle

aggravate *verb* 1 make worse, exacerbate, exaggerate, increase, inflame, intensify, magnify, worsen 2 *Informal* annoy, bother, get on one's nerves (*informal*), irritate, nettle, provoke

aggravation *noun* 1 worsening, exacerbation, exaggeration, heightening, increase, inflaming, intensification, magnification 2 *Informal* annoyance, exasperation, gall, grief (*informal*), hassle (*informal*), irritation, provocation

aggregate *noun* 1 total, accumulation, amount, body, bulk, collection, combination, mass, pile, sum, whole ♦ *adjective* 2 total, accumulated, collected, combined, composite, cumulative, mixed ♦ *verb* 3 combine, accumulate, amass, assemble, collect, heap, mix, pile

aggression *noun* 1 hostility,

antagonism, belligerence, destructiveness, pugnacity 2 <u>attack</u>, assault, injury, invasion, offensive, onslaught, raid

aggressive adjective 1 <u>hostile</u>, belligerent, destructive, offensive, pugnacious, quarrelsome 2 <u>forceful</u>, assertive, bold, dynamic, energetic, enterprising, militant, pushy (informal), vigorous

aggressor noun <u>attacker</u>, assailant, assaulter, invader

aggrieved adjective <u>hurt</u>, afflicted, distressed, disturbed, harmed, injured, unhappy, wronged

aghast adjective <u>horrified</u>, amazed, appalled, astonished, astounded, awestruck, confounded, shocked, startled, stunned

agile adjective 1 <u>nimble</u>, active, brisk, lithe, quick, sprightly, spry, supple, swift 2 <u>acute</u>, alert, bright (informal), clever, lively, quick-witted, sharp

agility noun <u>nimbleness</u>, litheness, liveliness, quickness, suppleness, swiftness

agitate verb 1 <u>upset</u>, disconcert, distract, excite, fluster, perturb, trouble, unnerve, worry 2 <u>stir</u>, beat, convulse, disturb, rouse, shake, toss

agitation noun 1 <u>turmoil</u>, clamour, commotion, confusion, disturbance, excitement, ferment, trouble, upheaval 2 <u>turbulence</u>, convulsion, disturbance, shaking, stirring, tossing

agitator noun <u>troublemaker</u>, agent provocateur, firebrand,

instigator, rabble-rouser, revolutionary, stirrer (informal)

agog adjective <u>eager</u>, avid, curious, enthralled, enthusiastic, excited, expectant, impatient, in suspense

agonize verb <u>suffer</u>, be distressed, be in agony, be in anguish, go through the mill, labour, strain, struggle, worry

agony noun <u>suffering</u>, anguish, distress, misery, pain, throes, torment, torture

agree verb 1 <u>consent</u>, assent, be of the same opinion, comply, concur, see eye to eye 2 <u>get on (together)</u>, coincide, conform, correspond, match, tally

agreeable adjective 1 <u>pleasant</u>, delightful, enjoyable, gratifying, likable or likeable, pleasing, satisfying, to one's taste 2 <u>consenting</u>, amenable, approving, complying, concurring, in accord, onside (informal), sympathetic, well-disposed, willing

agreement noun 1 <u>assent</u>, agreeing, compliance, concord, concurrence, consent, harmony, union, unison 2 <u>correspondence</u>, compatibility, conformity, congruity, consistency, similarity 3 <u>contract</u>, arrangement, bargain, covenant, deal (informal), pact, settlement, treaty, understanding

agricultural adjective <u>farming</u>, agrarian, country, rural, rustic

agriculture noun <u>farming</u>, cultivation, culture, husbandry, tillage

aground adverb <u>beached</u>, ashore, foundered, grounded, high and dry, on the rocks, stranded, stuck

ahead *adverb* in front, at an advantage, at the head, before, in advance, in the lead, leading, to the fore, winning

aid *noun* 1 help, assistance, benefit, encouragement, favour, promotion, relief, service, support ♦ *verb* 2 help, assist, encourage, favour, promote, serve, subsidize, support, sustain

aide *noun* assistant, attendant, helper, right-hand man, second, supporter

ailing *adjective* ill, indisposed, infirm, poorly, sick, under the weather (*informal*), unwell, weak

ailment *noun* illness, affliction, complaint, disease, disorder, infirmity, malady, sickness

aim *verb* 1 intend, attempt, endeavour, mean, plan, point, propose, seek, set one's sights on, strive, try ♦ *noun* 2 intention, ambition, aspiration, desire, goal, objective, plan, purpose, target

aimless *adjective* purposeless, directionless, pointless, random, stray

air *noun* 1 atmosphere, heavens, sky 2 wind, breeze, draught, zephyr 3 manner, appearance, atmosphere, aura, demeanour, impression, look, mood 4 tune, aria, lay, melody, song ♦ *verb* 5 publicize, circulate, display, exhibit, express, give vent to, make known, make public, reveal, voice 6 ventilate, aerate, expose, freshen

airborne *adjective* flying, floating, gliding, hovering, in flight, in the air, on the wing

airing *noun* 1 ventilation, aeration, drying, freshening 2 exposure, circulation, display, dissemination, expression, publicity, utterance, vent

airless *adjective* stuffy, close, heavy, muggy, oppressive, stifling, suffocating, sultry

airs *plural noun* affectation, arrogance, haughtiness, hauteur, pomposity, pretensions, superciliousness, swank (*informal*)

airy *adjective* 1 well-ventilated, fresh, light, open, spacious, uncluttered 2 light-hearted, blithe, cheerful, high-spirited, jaunty, lively, sprightly

aisle *noun* passageway, alley, corridor, gangway, lane, passage, path

alacrity *noun* eagerness, alertness, enthusiasm, promptness, quickness, readiness, speed, willingness, zeal

alarm *noun* 1 fear, anxiety, apprehension, consternation, fright, nervousness, panic, scare, trepidation 2 danger signal, alarm bell, alert, bell, distress signal, hooter, siren, warning ♦ *verb* 3 frighten, daunt, dismay, distress, give (someone) a turn (*informal*), panic, scare, startle, unnerve

alarming *adjective* frightening, daunting, distressing, disturbing, scaring, shocking, startling, unnerving

alcoholic *noun* 1 drunkard, dipsomaniac, drinker, drunk, inebriate, tippler, toper, wino (*informal*) ♦ *adjective* 2 intoxicating, brewed, distilled, fermented, hard, strong

alcove noun <u>recess</u>, bay, compartment, corner, cubbyhole, cubicle, niche, nook

alert adjective 1 <u>watchful</u>, attentive, awake, circumspect, heedful, observant, on guard, on one's toes, on the lookout, vigilant, wide-awake ♦ noun 2 <u>warning</u>, alarm, signal, siren ♦ verb 3 <u>warn</u>, alarm, forewarn, inform, notify, signal

alertness noun <u>watchfulness</u>, attentiveness, heedfulness, liveliness, vigilance

alias adverb 1 <u>also known as</u>, also called, otherwise, otherwise known as ♦ noun 2 <u>pseudonym</u>, assumed name, nom de guerre, nom de plume, pen name, stage name

alibi noun <u>excuse</u>, defence, explanation, justification, plea, pretext, reason

alien adjective 1 <u>foreign</u>, exotic, incongruous, strange, unfamiliar ♦ noun 2 <u>foreigner</u>, newcomer, outsider, stranger

alienate verb <u>set against</u>, disaffect, estrange, make unfriendly, turn away

alienation noun <u>setting against</u>, disaffection, estrangement, remoteness, separation, turning away

alight[1] verb 1 <u>get off</u>, descend, disembark, dismount, get down 2 <u>land</u>, come down, come to rest, descend, light, perch, settle, touch down

alight[2] adjective 1 <u>on fire</u>, ablaze, aflame, blazing, burning, fiery, flaming, lighted, lit 2 <u>lit up</u>, bright, brilliant, illuminated, shining

align verb 1 <u>ally</u>, affiliate, agree, associate, cooperate, join, side, sympathize 2 <u>line up</u>, even up, order, range, regulate, straighten

alignment noun 1 <u>alliance</u>, affiliation, agreement, association, cooperation, sympathy, union 2 <u>lining up</u>, adjustment, arrangement, evening up, order, straightening up

alike adjective 1 <u>similar</u>, akin, analogous, corresponding, identical, of a piece, parallel, resembling, the same ♦ adverb 2 <u>similarly</u>, analogously, correspondingly, equally, evenly, identically, uniformly

alive adjective 1 <u>living</u>, animate, breathing, in the land of the living (informal), subsisting 2 <u>in existence</u>, active, existing, extant, functioning, in force, operative 3 <u>lively</u>, active, alert, animated, energetic, full of life, vital, vivacious

all adjective 1 <u>the whole of</u>, every bit of, the complete, the entire, the sum of, the totality of, the total of 2 <u>every</u>, each, each and every, every one of, every single 3 <u>complete</u>, entire, full, greatest, perfect, total, utter ♦ adverb 4 <u>completely</u>, altogether, entirely, fully, totally, utterly, wholly ♦ noun 5 <u>whole amount</u>, aggregate, entirety, everything, sum total, total, totality, utmost

allegation noun <u>claim</u>, accusation, affirmation, assertion, charge, declaration, statement

allege verb <u>claim</u>, affirm, assert, charge, declare, maintain, state

alleged adjective 1 <u>stated</u>,

affirmed, asserted, declared, described, designated
2 supposed, doubtful, dubious, ostensible, professed, purported, so-called, unproved

allegiance noun loyalty, constancy, devotion, faithfulness, fidelity, obedience

allegorical adjective symbolic, emblematic, figurative, symbolizing

allegory noun symbol, fable, myth, parable, story, symbolism, tale

allergic adjective sensitive, affected by, hypersensitive, susceptible

allergy noun sensitivity, antipathy, hypersensitivity, susceptibility

alleviate verb ease, allay, lessen, lighten, moderate, reduce, relieve, soothe

alley noun passage, alleyway, backstreet, lane, passageway, pathway, walk

alliance noun union, affiliation, agreement, association, coalition, combination, confederation, connection, federation, league, marriage, pact, partnership, treaty

allied adjective united, affiliated, associated, combined, connected, in league, linked, related

allocate verb assign, allot, allow, apportion, budget, designate, earmark, mete, set aside, share out

allocation noun assignment, allotment, allowance, lot, portion, quota, ration, share

allot verb assign, allocate, apportion, budget, designate, earmark, mete, set aside, share out

allotment noun **1** plot, kitchen garden, patch, tract
2 assignment, allocation, allowance, grant, portion, quota, ration, share, stint

all-out adjective total, complete, exhaustive, full, full-scale, maximum, thoroughgoing, undivided, unremitting, unrestrained

allow verb **1** permit, approve, authorize, enable, endure, let, sanction, stand, suffer, tolerate
2 give, allocate, allot, assign, grant, provide, set aside, spare
3 acknowledge, admit, concede, confess, grant, own

allowable adjective permissible, acceptable, admissible, all right, appropriate, suitable, tolerable

allowance noun **1** portion, allocation, amount, grant, lot, quota, ration, share, stint
2 concession, deduction, discount, rebate, reduction

allow for verb take into account, consider, make allowances for, make concessions for, make provision for, plan for, provide for, take into consideration

alloy noun **1** mixture, admixture, amalgam, blend, combination, composite, compound, hybrid
♦ verb **2** mix, amalgamate, blend, combine, compound, fuse

all right adjective **1** satisfactory, acceptable, adequate, average, fair, O.K. or okay (informal), standard, up to scratch (informal)
2 O.K. or okay (informal),

healthy, safe, sound, unharmed, uninjured, well, whole

allude *verb* <u>refer</u>, hint, imply, intimate, mention, suggest, touch upon

allure *noun* **1** <u>attractiveness</u>, appeal, attraction, charm, enchantment, enticement, glamour, lure, persuasion, seductiveness, temptation ♦ *verb* **2** <u>attract</u>, captivate, charm, enchant, entice, lure, persuade, seduce, tempt, win over

alluring *adjective* <u>attractive</u>, beguiling, captivating, come-hither, fetching, glamorous, seductive, tempting

allusion *noun* <u>reference</u>, casual remark, hint, implication, innuendo, insinuation, intimation, mention, suggestion

ally *noun* **1** <u>partner</u>, accomplice, associate, collaborator, colleague, friend, helper ♦ *verb* **2** <u>unite</u>, associate, collaborate, combine, join, join forces, unify

almighty *adjective* **1** <u>all-powerful</u>, absolute, invincible, omnipotent, supreme, unlimited **2** *Informal* <u>great</u>, enormous, excessive, intense, loud, severe, terrible

almost *adverb* <u>nearly</u>, about, approximately, close to, just about, not quite, on the brink of, practically, virtually

alone *adjective* <u>by oneself</u>, apart, detached, isolated, lonely, only, on one's tod (*slang*), separate, single, solitary, unaccompanied

aloof *adjective* <u>distant</u>, detached, haughty, remote, standoffish, supercilious, unapproachable, unfriendly

aloud *adverb* <u>out loud</u>, audibly, clearly, distinctly, intelligibly, plainly

already *adverb* <u>before now</u>, at present, before, by now, by then, even now, heretofore, just now, previously

also *adverb* <u>too</u>, additionally, and, as well, besides, further, furthermore, in addition, into the bargain, moreover, to boot

alter *verb* <u>change</u>, adapt, adjust, amend, convert, modify, reform, revise, transform, turn, vary

alteration *noun* <u>change</u>, adaptation, adjustment, amendment, conversion, difference, modification, reformation, revision, transformation, variation

alternate *verb* **1** <u>change</u>, act reciprocally, fluctuate, interchange, oscillate, rotate, substitute, take turns ♦ *adjective* **2** <u>every other</u>, alternating, every second, interchanging, rotating

alternative *noun* **1** <u>choice</u>, option, other (*of two*), preference, recourse, selection, substitute ♦ *adjective* **2** <u>different</u>, alternate, another, other, second, substitute

alternatively *adverb* <u>or</u>, as an alternative, if not, instead, on the other hand, otherwise

although *conjunction* <u>though</u>, albeit, despite the fact that, even if, even though, notwithstanding, while

altogether *adverb* **1** <u>completely</u>, absolutely, fully, perfectly, quite, thoroughly, totally, utterly, wholly **2** <u>on the whole</u>, all in all, all things considered, as a whole,

collectively, generally, in general
3 in total, all told, everything
included, in all, in sum, taken
together

altruistic adjective selfless,
benevolent, charitable, generous,
humanitarian, philanthropic,
public-spirited, self-sacrificing,
unselfish

always adverb continually,
consistently, constantly,
eternally, evermore, every time,
forever, invariably, perpetually,
repeatedly, without exception

amalgamate verb combine, ally,
blend, fuse, incorporate,
integrate, merge, mingle, unite

amalgamation noun
combination, blend, coalition,
compound, fusion, joining,
merger, mixture, union

amass verb collect, accumulate,
assemble, compile, gather,
hoard, pile up

amateur noun nonprofessional,
dabbler, dilettante, layman

amateurish adjective
unprofessional, amateur,
bungling, clumsy, crude,
inexpert, unaccomplished

amaze verb astonish, alarm,
astound, bewilder, dumbfound,
shock, stagger, startle, stun,
surprise

amazement noun astonishment,
admiration, bewilderment,
confusion, perplexity, shock,
surprise, wonder

amazing adjective astonishing,
astounding, breathtaking,
eye-opening, overwhelming,
staggering, startling, stunning,
surprising

ambassador noun
representative, agent, consul,
deputy, diplomat, envoy, legate,
minister

ambiguity noun vagueness,
doubt, dubiousness,
equivocation, obscurity,
uncertainty

ambiguous adjective unclear,
dubious, enigmatic, equivocal,
inconclusive, indefinite,
indeterminate, obscure, vague

ambition noun **1** enterprise,
aspiration, desire, drive,
eagerness, longing, striving,
yearning, zeal **2** goal, aim,
aspiration, desire, dream, hope,
intent, objective, purpose, wish

ambitious adjective enterprising,
aspiring, avid, eager, hopeful,
intent, purposeful, striving,
zealous

ambivalent adjective undecided,
contradictory, doubtful,
equivocal, in two minds,
uncertain, wavering

amble verb stroll, dawdle,
meander, mosey (informal),
ramble, saunter, walk, wander

ambush noun **1** trap, lying in
wait, waylaying ♦ verb **2** trap,
attack, bushwhack (U.S.),
ensnare, surprise, waylay

amenable adjective receptive,
able to be influenced,
acquiescent, agreeable, open,
persuadable, responsive,
susceptible

amend verb change, alter,
correct, fix, improve, mend,
modify, reform, remedy, repair,
revise

amendment noun **1** change,

alteration, correction, emendation, improvement, modification, reform, remedy, repair, revision **2** <u>alteration</u>, addendum, addition, attachment, clarification

amends *plural noun As in* **make amends for** <u>compensation</u>, atonement, recompense, redress, reparation, restitution, satisfaction

amenity *noun* <u>facility</u>, advantage, comfort, convenience, service

amiable *adjective* <u>pleasant</u>, affable, agreeable, charming, congenial, engaging, friendly, genial, likable *or* likeable, lovable

amicable *adjective* <u>friendly</u>, amiable, civil, cordial, courteous, harmonious, neighbourly, peaceful, sociable

amid, amidst *preposition* <u>in the middle of</u>, among, amongst, in the midst of, in the thick of, surrounded by

amiss *adverb* **1** <u>wrongly</u>, erroneously, improperly, inappropriately, incorrectly, mistakenly, unsuitably **2** *As in* **take (something) amiss** <u>as an insult</u>, as offensive, out of turn, wrongly ♦ *adjective* **3** <u>wrong</u>, awry, faulty, incorrect, mistaken, untoward

ammunition *noun* <u>munitions</u>, armaments, explosives, powder, rounds, shells, shot

amnesty *noun* <u>general pardon</u>, absolution, dispensation, forgiveness, immunity, remission (*of penalty*), reprieve

amok, amuck *adverb As in* **run amok** <u>madly</u>, berserk, destructively, ferociously, in a frenzy, murderously, savagely,

uncontrollably, violently, wildly

among, amongst *preposition* **1** <u>in the midst of</u>, amid, amidst, in the middle of, in the thick of, surrounded by, together with, with **2** <u>in the group of</u>, in the class of, in the company of, in the number of, out of **3** <u>to each of</u>, between

amorous *adjective* <u>loving</u>, erotic, impassioned, in love, lustful, passionate, tender

amount *noun* <u>quantity</u>, expanse, extent, magnitude, mass, measure, number, supply, volume

amount to *verb* <u>add up to</u>, become, come to, develop into, equal, mean, total

ample *adjective* <u>plenty</u>, abundant, bountiful, copious, expansive, extensive, full, generous, lavish, plentiful, profuse

amplify *verb* **1** <u>explain</u>, develop, elaborate, enlarge, expand, flesh out, go into detail **2** <u>increase</u>, enlarge, expand, extend, heighten, intensify, magnify, strengthen, widen

amply *adverb* <u>fully</u>, abundantly, completely, copiously, generously, profusely, richly

amputate *verb* <u>cut off</u>, curtail, lop, remove, separate, sever, truncate

amuck *see* AMOK

amuse *verb* <u>entertain</u>, charm, cheer, delight, interest, please, tickle

amusement *noun* **1** <u>entertainment</u>, cheer, enjoyment, fun, merriment, mirth, pleasure **2** <u>entertainment</u>, diversion, game, hobby, joke, pastime, recreation, sport

amusing *adjective* <u>funny</u>, comical, droll, enjoyable, entertaining, humorous, interesting, witty

anaemic *adjective* <u>pale</u>, ashen, colourless, feeble, pallid, sickly, wan, weak

anaesthetic *noun* 1 <u>painkiller</u>, analgesic, anodyne, narcotic, opiate, sedative, soporific
♦ *adjective* 2 <u>pain-killing</u>, analgesic, anodyne, deadening, dulling, numbing, sedative, soporific

analogy *noun* <u>similarity</u>, comparison, correlation, correspondence, likeness, parallel, relation, resemblance

analyse *verb* 1 <u>examine</u>, evaluate, investigate, research, test, work over 2 <u>break down</u>, dissect, divide, resolve, separate, think through

analysis *noun* <u>examination</u>, breakdown, dissection, inquiry, investigation, scrutiny, sifting, test

analytic, analytical *adjective* <u>rational</u>, inquiring, inquisitive, investigative, logical, organized, problem solving, systematic

anarchic *adjective* <u>lawless</u>, chaotic, disorganized, rebellious, riotous, ungoverned

anarchist *noun* <u>revolutionary</u>, insurgent, nihilist, rebel, terrorist

anarchy *noun* <u>lawlessness</u>, chaos, confusion, disorder, disorganization, revolution, riot

anatomy *noun* 1 <u>examination</u>, analysis, dissection, division, inquiry, investigation, study

2 <u>structure</u>, build, composition, frame, framework, make-up

ancestor *noun* <u>forefather</u>, forebear, forerunner, precursor, predecessor

ancient *adjective* <u>old</u>, aged, antique, archaic, old-fashioned, primeval, primordial, timeworn

ancillary *adjective* <u>supplementary</u>, additional, auxiliary, extra, secondary, subordinate, subsidiary, supporting

and *conjunction* <u>also</u>, along with, as well as, furthermore, in addition to, including, moreover, plus, together with

anecdote *noun* <u>story</u>, reminiscence, short story, sketch, tale, urban legend, yarn

angel *noun* 1 <u>divine messenger</u>, archangel, cherub, seraph
2 *Informal* <u>dear</u>, beauty, darling, gem, jewel, paragon, saint, treasure

angelic *adjective* 1 <u>pure</u>, adorable, beautiful, entrancing, lovely, saintly, virtuous
2 <u>heavenly</u>, celestial, cherubic, ethereal, seraphic

anger *noun* 1 <u>rage</u>, annoyance, displeasure, exasperation, fury, ire, outrage, resentment, temper, wrath ♦ *verb* 2 <u>madden</u>, annoy, displease, enrage, exasperate, gall, incense, infuriate, outrage, rile, vex

angle[1] *noun* 1 <u>intersection</u>, bend, corner, crook, edge, elbow, nook, point 2 <u>point of view</u>, approach, aspect, outlook, perspective, position, side, slant, standpoint, viewpoint

angle[2] *verb* <u>fish</u>, cast

angry *adjective* <u>furious</u>, annoyed, cross, displeased, enraged, exasperated, incensed, infuriated, irate, mad (*informal*), outraged, resentful

angst *noun* <u>anxiety</u>, apprehension, unease, worry

anguish *noun* <u>suffering</u>, agony, distress, grief, heartache, misery, pain, sorrow, torment, woe

animal *noun* **1** <u>creature</u>, beast, brute **2** *Applied to a person* <u>brute</u>, barbarian, beast, monster, savage, wild man ◆ *adjective* **3** <u>physical</u>, bestial, bodily, brutish, carnal, gross, sensual

animate *verb* **1** <u>enliven</u>, energize, excite, fire, inspire, invigorate, kindle, move, stimulate ◆ *adjective* **2** <u>living</u>, alive and kicking, breathing, live, moving

animated *adjective* <u>lively</u>, ebullient, energetic, enthusiastic, excited, passionate, spirited, vivacious

animation *noun* <u>liveliness</u>, ebullience, energy, enthusiasm, excitement, fervour, passion, spirit, verve, vivacity, zest

animosity *noun* <u>hostility</u>, acrimony, antipathy, bitterness, enmity, hatred, ill will, malevolence, malice, rancour, resentment

annals *plural noun* <u>records</u>, accounts, archives, chronicles, history

annex *verb* **1** <u>seize</u>, acquire, appropriate, conquer, occupy, take over **2** <u>join</u>, add, adjoin, attach, connect, fasten

annihilate *verb* <u>destroy</u>, abolish, eradicate, exterminate, extinguish, obliterate, wipe out

announce *verb* <u>make known</u>, advertise, broadcast, declare, disclose, proclaim, report, reveal, tell

announcement *noun* <u>statement</u>, advertisement, broadcast, bulletin, communiqué, declaration, proclamation, report, revelation

announcer *noun* <u>presenter</u>, broadcaster, commentator, master of ceremonies, newscaster, newsreader, reporter

annoy *verb* <u>irritate</u>, anger, bother, displease, disturb, exasperate, get on one's nerves (*informal*), hassle (*informal*), madden, molest, pester, plague, trouble, vex

annoyance *noun* **1** <u>irritation</u>, anger, bother, hassle (*informal*), nuisance, trouble **2** <u>nuisance</u>, bore, bother, drag (*informal*), pain (*informal*)

annoying *adjective* <u>irritating</u>, disturbing, exasperating, maddening, troublesome

annual *adjective* <u>yearly</u>, once a year, yearlong

annually *adverb* <u>yearly</u>, by the year, once a year, per annum, per year

annul *verb* <u>invalidate</u>, abolish, cancel, declare *or* render null and void, negate, nullify, repeal, retract

anoint *verb* <u>consecrate</u>, bless, hallow, sanctify

anomalous *adjective* <u>unusual</u>, abnormal, eccentric, exceptional, incongruous, inconsistent, irregular, odd, peculiar

anomaly noun <u>irregularity</u>, abnormality, eccentricity, exception, incongruity, inconsistency, oddity, peculiarity

anonymous adjective <u>unnamed</u>, incognito, nameless, unacknowledged, uncredited, unidentified, unknown, unsigned

answer verb 1 <u>reply</u>, explain, react, resolve, respond, retort, return, solve ♦ noun 2 <u>reply</u>, comeback, defence, explanation, reaction, rejoinder, response, retort, return, riposte, solution

answerable adjective, usually with for or to <u>responsible</u>, accountable, amenable, chargeable, liable, subject, to blame

answer for verb <u>be responsible for</u>, be accountable for, be answerable for, be chargeable for, be liable for, be to blame for

antagonism noun <u>hostility</u>, antipathy, conflict, discord, dissension, friction, opposition, rivalry

antagonist noun <u>opponent</u>, adversary, competitor, contender, enemy, foe, rival

antagonistic adjective <u>hostile</u>, at odds, at variance, conflicting, incompatible, in dispute, opposed, unfriendly

antagonize verb <u>annoy</u>, anger, get on one's nerves (informal), hassle (informal), irritate, offend

anthem noun 1 <u>hymn</u>, canticle, carol, chant, chorale, psalm 2 <u>song of praise</u>, paean

anthology noun <u>collection</u>, compendium, compilation,

miscellany, selection, treasury

anticipate verb <u>expect</u>, await, foresee, foretell, hope for, look forward to, predict, prepare for

anticipation noun <u>expectation</u>, expectancy, foresight, forethought, premonition, prescience

anticlimax noun <u>disappointment</u>, bathos, comedown (informal), letdown

antics plural noun <u>clowning</u>, escapades, horseplay, mischief, playfulness, pranks, tomfoolery, tricks

antidote noun <u>cure</u>, countermeasure, remedy

antipathy noun <u>hostility</u>, aversion, bad blood, dislike, enmity, hatred, ill will

antiquated adjective <u>obsolete</u>, antique, archaic, dated, old-fashioned, out-of-date, passé

antique noun 1 <u>period piece</u>, bygone, heirloom, relic ♦ adjective 2 <u>vintage</u>, antiquarian, classic, olden 3 <u>old-fashioned</u>, archaic, obsolete, outdated

antiquity noun 1 <u>old age</u>, age, ancientness, elderliness, oldness 2 <u>distant past</u>, ancient times, olden days, time immemorial

antiseptic adjective 1 <u>hygienic</u>, clean, germ-free, pure, sanitary, sterile, uncontaminated ♦ noun 2 <u>disinfectant</u>, germicide, purifier

antisocial adjective 1 <u>unsociable</u>, alienated, misanthropic, reserved, retiring, uncommunicative, unfriendly, withdrawn 2 <u>disruptive</u>, antagonistic, belligerent, disorderly, hostile, menacing, rebellious, uncooperative

antithesis noun opposite, contrary, contrast, converse, inverse, reverse

anxiety noun uneasiness, angst, apprehension, concern, foreboding, misgiving, nervousness, tension, trepidation, worry

anxious adjective 1 uneasy, apprehensive, concerned, fearful, in suspense, nervous, on tenterhooks, tense, troubled, worried 2 eager, desirous, impatient, intent, itching, keen, yearning

apart adverb 1 to pieces, asunder, in bits, in pieces, to bits 2 separate, alone, aside, away, by oneself, isolated, to one side 3 apart from except for, aside from, besides, but, excluding, not counting, other than, save

apartment noun room, accommodation, flat, living quarters, penthouse, quarters, rooms, suite

apathetic adjective uninterested, cool, indifferent, passive, phlegmatic, unconcerned

apathy noun lack of interest, coolness, indifference, inertia, nonchalance, passivity, torpor, unconcern

apex noun highest point, crest, crown, culmination, peak, pinnacle, point, summit, top

apiece adverb each, for each, from each, individually, respectively, separately, to each

aplomb noun self-possession, calmness, composure, confidence, level-headedness, poise, sang-froid, self-assurance, self-confidence

apocryphal adjective dubious, doubtful, legendary, mythical, questionable, unauthenticated, unsubstantiated

apologetic adjective regretful, contrite, penitent, remorseful, rueful, sorry

apologize verb say sorry, ask forgiveness, beg pardon, express regret

apology noun 1 defence, acknowledgment, confession, excuse, explanation, justification, plea 2 As in an apology for mockery, caricature, excuse, imitation, travesty

apostle noun 1 evangelist, herald, messenger, missionary, preacher 2 supporter, advocate, champion, pioneer, propagandist, proponent

apotheosis noun deification, elevation, exaltation, glorification, idealization, idolization

appal verb horrify, alarm, daunt, dishearten, dismay, frighten, outrage, shock, unnerve

appalling adjective horrifying, alarming, awful, daunting, dreadful, fearful, frightful, horrible, shocking, terrifying

apparatus noun 1 equipment, appliance, contraption (informal), device, gear, machinery, mechanism, tackle, tools 2 organization, bureaucracy, chain of command, hierarchy, network, setup (informal), structure, system

apparent adjective 1 obvious,

discernible, distinct, evident, manifest, marked, unmistakable, visible 2 seeming, ostensible, outward, superficial

apparently adverb it appears that, it seems that, on the face of it, ostensibly, outwardly, seemingly, superficially

apparition noun ghost, chimera, phantom, spectre, spirit, wraith

appeal verb 1 plead, ask, beg, call upon, entreat, pray, request 2 attract, allure, charm, entice, fascinate, interest, please, tempt ♦ noun 3 plea, application, entreaty, petition, prayer, request, supplication 4 attraction, allure, beauty, charm, fascination

appealing adjective attractive, alluring, charming, desirable, engaging, winsome

appear verb 1 come into view, be present, come out, come to light, crop up (informal), emerge, occur, show up (informal), surface, turn up 2 look (like or as if), occur, seem, strike one as

appearance noun 1 arrival, coming, emergence, introduction, presence 2 look, demeanour, expression, figure, form, looks, manner, mien (literary) 3 impression, front, guise, illusion, image, outward show, pretence, semblance

appease verb 1 pacify, calm, conciliate, mollify, placate, quiet, satisfy, soothe 2 ease, allay, alleviate, calm, relieve, soothe

appeasement noun 1 pacification, accommodation, compromise, concession, conciliation, mollification,

placation 2 easing, alleviation, lessening, relieving, soothing

appendage noun attachment, accessory, addition, supplement

appendix noun supplement, addendum, addition, adjunct, appendage, postscript

appetite noun desire, craving, demand, hunger, liking, longing, passion, relish, stomach, taste, yearning

appetizing adjective delicious, appealing, inviting, mouthwatering, palatable, succulent, tasty, tempting

applaud verb clap, acclaim, approve, cheer, commend, compliment, encourage, extol, praise

applause noun ovation, accolade, approval, big hand, cheers, clapping, hand, praise

appliance noun device, apparatus, gadget, implement, instrument, machine, mechanism, tool

applicable adjective appropriate, apt, fitting, pertinent, relevant, suitable, useful

applicant noun candidate, claimant, inquirer

application noun 1 request, appeal, claim, inquiry, petition, requisition 2 effort, commitment, dedication, diligence, hard work, industry, perseverance

apply verb 1 request, appeal, claim, inquire, petition, put in, requisition 2 use, bring to bear, carry out, employ, exercise, exert, implement, practise, utilize 3 put on, cover with, lay

on, paint, place, smear, spread
on 4 <u>be relevant</u>, be applicable,
be appropriate, bear upon, be
fitting, fit, pertain, refer, relate
5 **apply oneself** <u>try</u>, be diligent,
buckle down (*informal*), commit
oneself, concentrate, dedicate
oneself, devote oneself,
persevere, work hard

appoint *verb* 1 <u>assign</u>, choose,
commission, delegate, elect,
name, nominate, select
2 <u>decide</u>, allot, arrange, assign,
choose, designate, establish, fix,
set 3 <u>equip</u>, fit out, furnish,
provide, supply

appointed *adjective* 1 <u>assigned</u>,
chosen, delegated, elected,
named, nominated, selected
2 <u>decided</u>, allotted, arranged,
assigned, chosen, designated,
established, fixed, set
3 <u>equipped</u>, fitted out,
furnished, provided, supplied

appointment *noun* 1 <u>meeting</u>,
arrangement, assignation, date,
engagement, interview,
rendezvous 2 <u>selection</u>,
assignment, choice, election,
naming, nomination 3 <u>job</u>,
assignment, office, place,
position, post, situation
4 **appointments** <u>fittings</u>, fixtures,
furnishings, gear, outfit,
paraphernalia, trappings

apportion *verb* <u>divide</u>, allocate,
allot, assign, dispense, distribute,
dole out, ration out, share

apportionment *noun* <u>division</u>,
allocation, allotment,
assignment, dispensing,
distribution, doling out,
rationing out, sharing

apposite *adjective* <u>appropriate</u>,

applicable, apt, fitting, pertinent,
relevant, suitable, to the point

appraisal *noun* <u>assessment</u>,
estimate, estimation, evaluation,
judgment, opinion

appraise *verb* <u>assess</u>, estimate,
evaluate, gauge, judge, rate,
review, value

appreciable *adjective* <u>significant</u>,
considerable, definite,
discernible, evident, marked,
noticeable, obvious,
pronounced, substantial

appreciate *verb* 1 <u>value</u>, admire,
enjoy, like, prize, rate highly,
respect, treasure 2 <u>be aware of</u>,
perceive, realize, recognize,
sympathize with, take account
of, understand 3 <u>be grateful for</u>,
be appreciative, be indebted, be
obliged, be thankful for, give
thanks for 4 <u>increase</u>, enhance,
gain, grow, improve, rise

appreciation *noun* 1 <u>gratitude</u>,
acknowledgment, gratefulness,
indebtedness, obligation,
thankfulness, thanks
2 <u>awareness</u>, admiration,
comprehension, enjoyment,
perception, realization,
recognition, sensitivity,
sympathy, understanding
3 <u>increase</u>, enhancement, gain,
growth, improvement, rise

appreciative *adjective* 1 <u>grateful</u>,
beholden, indebted, obliged,
thankful 2 <u>aware</u>, admiring,
enthusiastic, respectful,
responsive, sensitive,
sympathetic, understanding

apprehend *verb* 1 <u>arrest</u>,
capture, catch, nick (*slang, chiefly
Brit.*), seize, take prisoner
2 <u>understand</u>, comprehend,

conceive, get the picture, grasp, perceive, realize, recognize

apprehension noun 1 anxiety, alarm, concern, dread, fear, foreboding, suspicion, trepidation, worry 2 arrest, capture, catching, seizure, taking 3 awareness, comprehension, grasp, perception, understanding

apprehensive adjective anxious, concerned, foreboding, nervous, uneasy, worried

apprentice noun trainee, beginner, learner, novice, probationer, pupil, student

approach verb 1 move towards, come close, come near, draw near, near, reach 2 make a proposal to, appeal to, apply to, make overtures to, sound out 3 set about, begin work on, commence, embark on, enter upon, make a start, undertake ♦ noun 4 coming, advance, arrival, drawing near, nearing 5 often plural proposal, advance, appeal, application, invitation, offer, overture, proposition 6 access, avenue, entrance, passage, road, way 7 way, manner, means, method, style, technique 8 likeness, approximation, semblance

approachable adjective 1 friendly, affable, congenial, cordial, open, sociable 2 accessible, attainable, reachable

appropriate adjective 1 suitable, apt, befitting, fitting, pertinent, relevant, to the point, well-suited ♦ verb 2 seize, commandeer, confiscate, impound, take possession of, usurp 3 steal, embezzle, filch, misappropriate,

pilfer, pocket 4 set aside, allocate, allot, apportion, assign, devote, earmark

approval noun 1 consent, agreement, assent, authorization, blessing, endorsement, permission, recommendation, sanction 2 favour, acclaim, admiration, applause, appreciation, esteem, good opinion, praise, respect

approve verb 1 favour, admire, commend, have a good opinion of, like, praise, regard highly, respect 2 agree to, allow, assent to, authorize, consent to, endorse, pass, permit, recommend, sanction

approximate adjective 1 close, near 2 rough, estimated, inexact, loose ♦ verb 3 come close, approach, border on, come near, reach, resemble, touch, verge on

approximately adverb almost, about, around, circa (used with dates), close to, in the region of, just about, more or less, nearly, roughly

approximation noun guess, conjecture, estimate, estimation, guesswork, rough calculation, rough idea

apron noun pinny (informal), pinafore

apt adjective 1 inclined, disposed, given, liable, likely, of a mind, prone, ready 2 appropriate, fitting, pertinent, relevant, suitable, to the point 3 gifted, clever, quick, sharp, smart, talented

aptitude noun 1 tendency, inclination, leaning, predilection, proclivity, propensity 2 <u>gift</u>, ability, capability, faculty, intelligence, proficiency, talent

arable *adjective* <u>productive</u>, farmable, fertile, fruitful

arbiter *noun* 1 <u>judge</u>, adjudicator, arbitrator, referee, umpire 2 <u>authority</u>, controller, dictator, expert, governor, lord, master, pundit, ruler

arbitrary *adjective* <u>random</u>, capricious, chance, erratic, inconsistent, personal, subjective, whimsical

arbitrate *verb* <u>settle</u>, adjudicate, decide, determine, judge, mediate, pass judgment, referee, umpire

arbitration *noun* <u>settlement</u>, adjudication, decision, determination, judgment

arbitrator *noun* <u>judge</u>, adjudicator, arbiter, referee, umpire

arc *noun* <u>curve</u>, arch, bend, bow, crescent, half-moon

arcade *noun* <u>gallery</u>, cloister, colonnade, portico

arcane *adjective* <u>mysterious</u>, esoteric, hidden, occult, recondite, secret

arch¹ *noun* 1 <u>curve</u>, archway, dome, span, vault 2 <u>curve</u>, arc, bend, bow, hump, semicircle ♦ *verb* 3 <u>curve</u>, arc, bend, bow, bridge, span

arch² *adjective* <u>playful</u>, frolicsome, mischievous, pert, roguish, saucy, sly, waggish

archaic *adjective* 1 <u>old</u>, ancient, antique, bygone, <u>olden</u> (*archaic*), primitive 2 <u>old-fashioned</u>, antiquated, behind the times, obsolete, outmoded, out of date, passé

archetypal *adjective* 1 <u>typical</u>, classic, ideal, model, standard 2 <u>original</u>, prototypic *or* prototypical

archetype *noun* 1 <u>standard</u>, model, paradigm, pattern, prime example 2 <u>original</u>, prototype

architect *noun* <u>designer</u>, master builder, planner

architecture *noun* 1 <u>design</u>, building, construction, planning 2 <u>structure</u>, construction, design, framework, make-up, style

archive *noun* 1 <u>record office</u>, museum, registry, repository 2 **archives** <u>records</u>, annals, chronicles, documents, papers, rolls

arctic *adjective Informal* <u>freezing</u>, chilly, cold, frigid, frozen, glacial, icy

Arctic *adjective* <u>polar</u>, far-northern, hyperborean

ardent *adjective* 1 <u>passionate</u>, amorous, hot-blooded, impassioned, intense, lusty 2 <u>enthusiastic</u>, avid, eager, keen, zealous

ardour *noun* 1 <u>passion</u>, fervour, intensity, spirit, vehemence, warmth 2 <u>enthusiasm</u>, avidity, eagerness, keenness, zeal

arduous *adjective* <u>difficult</u>, exhausting, fatiguing, gruelling, laborious, onerous, punishing, rigorous, strenuous, taxing, tiring

area *noun* 1 <u>region</u>, district, locality, neighbourhood, zone 2 <u>part</u>, portion, section, sector 3 <u>field</u>, department, domain, province, realm, sphere, territory

arena noun 1 <u>ring</u>, amphitheatre, bowl, enclosure, field, ground, stadium 2 <u>sphere</u>, area, domain, field, province, realm, sector, territory

argue verb 1 <u>discuss</u>, assert, claim, debate, dispute, maintain, reason, remonstrate 2 <u>quarrel</u>, bicker, disagree, dispute, fall out (informal), fight, squabble

argument noun 1 <u>quarrel</u>, clash, controversy, disagreement, dispute, feud, fight, row, squabble 2 <u>discussion</u>, assertion, claim, debate, dispute, plea, questioning, remonstration 3 <u>reason</u>, argumentation, case, defence, dialectic, ground(s), line of reasoning, logic, polemic, reasoning

argumentative adjective <u>quarrelsome</u>, belligerent, combative, contentious, contrary, disputatious, litigious, opinionated

arid adjective 1 <u>dry</u>, barren, desert, parched, sterile, torrid, waterless 2 <u>boring</u>, dreary, dry, dull, tedious, tiresome, uninspired, uninteresting

arise verb 1 <u>happen</u>, begin, emerge, ensue, follow, occur, result, start, stem 2 Old-fashioned <u>get up</u>, get to one's feet, go up, rise, stand up, wake up

aristocracy noun <u>upper class</u>, elite, gentry, nobility, patricians, peerage, ruling class

aristocrat adjective <u>noble</u>, aristo (informal), grandee, lady, lord, patrician, peer, peeress

aristocratic noun <u>upper-class</u>, blue-blooded, elite, gentlemanly, lordly, noble, patrician, titled

arm¹ noun <u>upper limb</u>, appendage, limb

arm² verb Especially with weapons <u>equip</u>, accoutre, array, deck out, furnish, issue with, provide, supply

armada noun <u>fleet</u>, flotilla, navy, squadron

armaments plural noun <u>weapons</u>, ammunition, arms, guns, materiel, munitions, ordnance, weaponry

armed adjective <u>carrying weapons</u>, equipped, fitted out, primed, protected

armistice noun <u>truce</u>, ceasefire, peace, suspension of hostilities

armour noun <u>protection</u>, armour plate, covering, sheathing, shield

armoured adjective <u>protected</u>, armour-plated, bombproof, bulletproof, ironclad, mailed, steel-plated

arms plural noun 1 <u>weapons</u>, armaments, firearms, guns, instruments of war, ordnance, weaponry 2 <u>heraldry</u>, blazonry, crest, escutcheon, insignia

army noun 1 <u>soldiers</u>, armed force, legions, military force, soldiery, troops 2 <u>vast number</u>, array, horde, host, multitude, pack, swarm, throng

aroma noun <u>scent</u>, bouquet, fragrance, odour, perfume, redolence, savour, smell

aromatic adjective <u>fragrant</u>, balmy, perfumed, pungent, redolent, savoury, spicy, sweet-scented, sweet-smelling

around preposition 1 <u>surrounding</u>, about, encircling, enclosing, encompassing, on all sides of,

on every side of
2 <u>approximately</u>, about, circa
(*used with dates*), roughly
♦ *adverb* **3** <u>everywhere</u>, about, all
over, here and there, in all
directions, on all sides,
throughout, to and fro **4** <u>near</u>,
at hand, close, close at hand,
nearby, nigh (*archaic or dialect*)

arouse *verb* **1** <u>stimulate</u>, excite,
incite, instigate, provoke, spur,
stir up, summon up, whip up
2 <u>awaken</u>, rouse, waken, wake up

arrange *verb* **1** <u>plan</u>, construct,
contrive, devise, fix up, organize,
prepare **2** <u>agree</u>, adjust, come to
terms, compromise, determine,
settle **3** <u>put in order</u>, classify,
group, line up, order, organize,
position, sort **4** <u>adapt</u>,
instrument, orchestrate, score

arrangement *noun* **1** *often plural*
<u>plan</u>, organization, planning,
preparation, provision, schedule
2 <u>agreement</u>, adjustment,
compact, compromise, deal,
settlement, terms **3** <u>order</u>,
alignment, classification, form,
organization, structure, system
4 <u>adaptation</u>, instrumentation,
interpretation, orchestration,
score, version

array *noun* **1** <u>arrangement</u>,
collection, display, exhibition,
formation, line-up, parade,
show, supply **2** *Poetic* <u>clothing</u>,
apparel, attire, clothes, dress,
finery, garments, regalia ♦ *verb*
3 <u>arrange</u>, display, exhibit,
group, parade, range, show
4 <u>dress</u>, adorn, attire, clothe,
deck, decorate, festoon

arrest *verb* **1** <u>capture</u>,
apprehend, catch, detain, nick

(*slang, chiefly Brit.*), seize, take
prisoner **2** <u>stop</u>, block, delay,
end, inhibit, interrupt, obstruct,
slow, suppress **3** <u>grip</u>, absorb,
engage, engross, fascinate, hold,
intrigue, occupy ♦ *noun*
4 <u>capture</u>, bust (*informal*), cop
(*slang*), detention, seizure
5 <u>stopping</u>, blockage, delay,
end, hindrance, interruption,
obstruction, suppression

arresting *adjective* <u>striking</u>,
engaging, impressive, noticeable,
outstanding, remarkable,
stunning, surprising

arrival *noun* **1** <u>coming</u>, advent,
appearance, arriving, entrance,
happening, occurrence, taking
place **2** <u>newcomer</u>, caller,
entrant, incomer, visitor

arrive *verb* **1** <u>come</u>, appear,
enter, get to, reach, show up
(*informal*), turn up **2** *Informal*
<u>succeed</u>, become famous, make
good, make it (*informal*), make
the grade (*informal*)

arrogance *noun* <u>conceit</u>,
disdainfulness, haughtiness,
high-handedness, insolence,
pride, superciliousness, swagger

arrogant *adjective* <u>conceited</u>,
disdainful, haughty,
high-handed, overbearing,
proud, scornful, supercilious

arrow *noun* **1** <u>dart</u>, bolt, flight,
quarrel, shaft (*archaic*) **2** <u>pointer</u>,
indicator

arsenal *noun* <u>armoury</u>,
ammunition dump, arms depot,
ordnance depot, stockpile, store,
storehouse, supply

art *noun* <u>skill</u>, craft, expertise,
ingenuity, mastery, virtuosity

artful *adjective* <u>cunning</u>, clever,

crafty, shrewd, sly, smart, wily

article *noun* **1** piece,
composition, discourse, essay,
feature, item, paper, story,
treatise **2** thing, commodity,
item, object, piece, substance,
unit **3** clause, item, paragraph,
part, passage, point, portion,
section

articulate *adjective* **1** expressive,
clear, coherent, eloquent, fluent,
lucid, well-spoken ♦ *verb*
2 express, enunciate, pronounce,
say, speak, state, talk, utter, voice

artifice *noun* **1** trick, contrivance,
device, machination, manoeuvre,
stratagem, subterfuge, tactic
2 cleverness, ingenuity,
inventiveness, skill

artificial *adjective* **1** synthetic,
man-made, manufactured,
non-natural, plastic **2** fake,
bogus, counterfeit, imitation,
mock, sham, simulated
3 insincere, affected, contrived,
false, feigned, forced, phoney *or*
phony (*informal*), unnatural

artillery *noun* big guns, battery,
cannon, cannonry, gunnery,
ordnance

artisan *noun* craftsman,
journeyman, mechanic, skilled
workman, technician

artistic *adjective* creative,
aesthetic, beautiful, cultured,
elegant, refined, sophisticated,
stylish, tasteful

artistry *noun* skill, brilliance,
craftsmanship, creativity, finesse,
mastery, proficiency, virtuosity

artless *adjective*
1 straightforward, frank,
guileless, open, plain **2** natural,
plain, pure, simple, unadorned,

unaffected, unpretentious

as *conjunction* **1** when, at the
time that, during the time that,
just as, while **2** in the way that,
in the manner that, like **3** what,
that which **4** since, because,
considering that, seeing that
5 for instance, like, such as
♦ *preposition* **6** being, in the
character of, in the role of,
under the name of

ascend *verb* move up, climb, go
up, mount, scale

ascent *noun* **1** rise, ascending,
ascension, climb, mounting,
rising, scaling, upward
movement **2** upward slope,
gradient, incline, ramp, rise,
rising ground

ascertain *verb* find out, confirm,
determine, discover, establish,
learn

ascetic *noun* **1** monk, abstainer,
hermit, nun, recluse ♦ *adjective*
2 self-denying, abstinent,
austere, celibate, frugal,
puritanical, self-disciplined

ascribe *verb* attribute, assign,
charge, credit, impute, put
down, refer, set down

ashamed *adjective* embarrassed,
distressed, guilty, humiliated,
mortified, remorseful,
shamefaced, sheepish, sorry

ashen *adjective* pale, colourless,
grey, leaden, like death warmed
up (*informal*), pallid, wan, white

ashore *adverb* on land, aground,
landwards, on dry land, on the
beach, on the shore,
shorewards, to the shore

aside *adverb* **1** to one side, apart,
beside, on one side, out of the

way, privately, separately, to the side ♦ *noun* 2 <u>interpolation</u>, parenthesis

asinine *adjective* <u>stupid</u>, fatuous, foolish, idiotic, imbecilic, moronic, senseless

ask *verb* 1 <u>inquire</u>, interrogate, query, question, quiz 2 <u>request</u>, appeal, beg, demand, plead, seek 3 <u>invite</u>, bid, summon

askew *adverb* 1 <u>crookedly</u>, aslant, awry, obliquely, off-centre, to one side ♦ *adjective* 2 <u>crooked</u>, awry, cockeyed (*informal*), lopsided, oblique, off-centre, skewwhiff (*Brit. informal*)

asleep *adjective* <u>sleeping</u>, dormant, dozing, fast asleep, napping, slumbering, snoozing (*informal*), sound asleep

aspect *noun* 1 <u>feature</u>, angle, facet, side 2 <u>position</u>, outlook, point of view, prospect, scene, situation, view 3 <u>appearance</u>, air, attitude, bearing, condition, demeanour, expression, look, manner

asphyxiate *verb* <u>suffocate</u>, choke, smother, stifle, strangle, strangulate, throttle

aspiration *noun* <u>aim</u>, ambition, desire, dream, goal, hope, objective, wish

aspire *verb* <u>aim</u>, desire, dream, hope, long, seek, set one's heart on, wish

aspiring *adjective* <u>hopeful</u>, ambitious, eager, longing, wannabe (*informal*), would-be

ass *noun* 1 <u>donkey</u>, moke (*slang*) 2 <u>fool</u>, blockhead, halfwit, idiot, jackass, numbskull *or* numskull,

oaf, twit (*informal, chiefly Brit.*)

assail *verb* <u>attack</u>, assault, fall upon, lay into (*informal*), set upon

assailant *noun* <u>attacker</u>, aggressor, assailer, assaulter, invader

assassin *noun* <u>murderer</u>, executioner, hatchet man (*slang*), hit man (*slang*), killer, liquidator, slayer

assassinate *verb* <u>murder</u>, eliminate (*slang*), hit (*slang*), kill, liquidate, slay, take out (*slang*)

assault *noun* 1 <u>attack</u>, charge, invasion, offensive, onslaught ♦ *verb* 2 <u>attack</u>, beset, fall upon, lay into (*informal*), set about, set upon, strike at

assemble *verb* 1 <u>gather</u>, amass, bring together, call together, collect, come together, congregate, meet, muster, rally 2 <u>put together</u>, build up, connect, construct, fabricate, fit together, join, piece together, set up

assembly *noun* 1 <u>gathering</u>, collection, company, conference, congress, council, crowd, group, mass, meeting 2 <u>putting together</u>, building up, connecting, construction, piecing together, setting up

assent *noun* 1 <u>agreement</u>, acceptance, approval, compliance, concurrence, consent, permission, sanction ♦ *verb* 2 <u>agree</u>, allow, approve, consent, grant, permit

assert *verb* 1 <u>state</u>, affirm, declare, maintain, profess, pronounce, swear 2 <u>insist upon</u>, claim, defend, press, put forward, stand up for, stress, uphold **3 assert oneself** <u>be forceful</u>, exert one's influence, make one's presence felt, put oneself forward, put one's foot down (*informal*)

assertion *noun* **1** <u>statement</u>, claim, declaration, pronouncement **2** <u>insistence</u>, maintenance, stressing

assertive *adjective* <u>confident</u>, aggressive, domineering, emphatic, feisty (*informal, chiefly U.S. & Canad.*), forceful, insistent, positive, pushy (*informal*), strong-willed

assess *verb* **1** <u>judge</u>, appraise, estimate, evaluate, rate, size up (*informal*), value, weigh **2** <u>evaluate</u>, fix, impose, levy, rate, tax, value

assessment *noun* **1** <u>judgment</u>, appraisal, estimate, evaluation, rating, valuation **2** <u>evaluation</u>, charge, fee, levy, rating, toll, valuation

asset *noun* **1** <u>benefit</u>, advantage, aid, blessing, boon, feather in one's cap, help, resource, service **2 assets** <u>property</u>, capital, estate, funds, goods, money, possessions, resources, wealth

assiduous *adjective* <u>diligent</u>, hard-working, indefatigable, industrious, persevering, persistent, unflagging

assign *verb* **1** <u>select</u>, appoint, choose, delegate, designate, name, nominate **2** <u>give</u>, allocate, allot, apportion, consign, distribute, give out, grant **3** <u>attribute</u>, accredit, ascribe, put down

assignation *noun* **1** <u>secret</u> meeting, clandestine meeting, illicit meeting, rendezvous, tryst (*archaic*) **2** <u>selection</u>, appointment, assignment, choice, delegation, designation, nomination

assignment *noun* <u>task</u>, appointment, commission, duty, job, mission, position, post, responsibility

assimilate *verb* **1** <u>learn</u>, absorb, digest, incorporate, take in **2** <u>adjust</u>, adapt, blend in, mingle

assist *verb* <u>help</u>, abet, aid, cooperate, lend a helping hand, serve, support

assistance *noun* <u>help</u>, aid, backing, cooperation, helping hand, support

assistant *noun* <u>helper</u>, accomplice, aide, ally, colleague, right-hand man, second, supporter

associate *verb* **1** <u>connect</u>, ally, combine, identify, join, link, lump together **2** <u>mix</u>, accompany, consort, hobnob, mingle, socialize ♦ *noun* **3** <u>partner</u>, collaborator, colleague, confederate, co-worker **4** <u>friend</u>, ally, companion, comrade, mate (*informal*)

association *noun* **1** <u>group</u>, alliance, band, club, coalition, federation, league, organization, society **2** <u>connection</u>, blend, combination, joining, juxtaposition, mixture, pairing, union

assorted *adjective* <u>various</u>, different, diverse, miscellaneous, mixed, motley, sundry, varied

assortment *noun* <u>variety</u>, array,

choice, collection, jumble,
medley, mixture, selection

assume verb **1** take for granted,
believe, expect, fancy, imagine,
infer, presume, suppose,
surmise, think **2** take on, accept,
enter upon, put on, shoulder,
take over **3** put on, adopt,
affect, feign, imitate,
impersonate, mimic, pretend to,
simulate

assumed adjective **1** false, bogus,
counterfeit, fake, fictitious,
made-up, make-believe **2** taken
for granted, accepted, expected,
hypothetical, presumed,
presupposed, supposed, surmised

assumption noun
1 presumption, belief,
conjecture, guess, hypothesis,
inference, supposition, surmise
2 taking on, acceptance,
acquisition, adoption, entering
upon, putting on, shouldering,
takeover, taking up **3** taking,
acquisition, appropriation,
seizure, takeover

assurance noun **1** assertion,
declaration, guarantee, oath,
pledge, promise, statement,
vow, word **2** confidence,
boldness, certainty, conviction,
faith, nerve, poise, self-confidence

assure verb **1** promise, certify,
confirm, declare confidently,
give one's word to, guarantee,
pledge, swear, vow **2** convince,
comfort, embolden, encourage,
hearten, persuade, reassure
3 make certain, clinch,
complete, confirm, ensure,
guarantee, make sure, seal,
secure

assured adjective **1** confident,

certain, poised, positive,
self-assured, self-confident, sure
of oneself **2** certain, beyond
doubt, confirmed, ensured,
fixed, guaranteed, in the bag
(slang), secure, settled, sure

astonish verb amaze, astound,
bewilder, confound, daze,
dumbfound, stagger, stun,
surprise

astonishing adjective amazing,
astounding, bewildering,
breathtaking, brilliant,
sensational (informal), staggering,
stunning, surprising

astonishment noun amazement,
awe, bewilderment, confusion,
consternation, surprise, wonder,
wonderment

astounding adjective amazing,
astonishing, bewildering,
breathtaking, brilliant,
impressive, sensational (informal),
staggering, stunning, surprising

astray adjective, adverb off the
right track, adrift, amiss, lost, off,
off course, off the mark, off the
subject

astute adjective intelligent, canny,
clever, crafty, cunning,
perceptive, sagacious, sharp,
shrewd, subtle

asylum noun **1** refuge, harbour,
haven, preserve, retreat, safety,
sanctuary, shelter **2** Old-fashioned
mental hospital, hospital,
institution, madhouse (informal),
psychiatric hospital

atheism noun nonbelief,
disbelief, godlessness,
heathenism, infidelity, irreligion,
paganism, scepticism, unbelief

atheist noun nonbeliever,
disbeliever, heathen, infidel,

pagan, sceptic, unbeliever

athlete noun sportsperson, competitor, contestant, gymnast, player, runner, sportsman, sportswoman

athletic adjective fit, active, energetic, muscular, powerful, strapping, strong, sturdy

athletics plural noun sports, contests, exercises, gymnastics, races, track and field events

atmosphere noun 1 air, aerosphere, heavens, sky 2 feeling, ambience, character, climate, environment, mood, spirit, surroundings, tone

atom noun particle, bit, dot, molecule, speck, spot, trace

atone verb, usually with **for** make amends, compensate, do penance, make redress, make reparation, make up for, pay for, recompense, redress

atonement noun amends, compensation, penance, recompense, redress, reparation, restitution

atrocious adjective 1 cruel, barbaric, brutal, fiendish, infernal, monstrous, savage, vicious, wicked 2 Informal shocking, appalling, detestable, grievous, horrible, horrifying, terrible

atrocity noun 1 cruelty, barbarity, brutality, fiendishness, horror, savagery, viciousness, wickedness 2 act of cruelty, abomination, crime, evil, horror, outrage

attach verb 1 connect, add, couple, fasten, fix, join, link, secure, stick, tie 2 put, ascribe,

assign, associate, attribute, connect

attached adjective 1 spoken for, accompanied, engaged, married, partnered 2 **attached to** fond of, affectionate towards, devoted to, full of regard for

attachment noun 1 fondness, affection, affinity, attraction, liking, regard 2 accessory, accoutrement, extension, extra, fitting, fixture, supplement

attack verb 1 assault, invade, lay into (informal), raid, set upon, storm, strike (at) 2 criticize, abuse, blame, censure, have a go (at) (informal), put down, vilify ◆ noun 3 assault, campaign, charge, foray, incursion, invasion, offensive, onslaught, raid, strike 4 criticism, abuse, blame, censure, denigration, stick (slang), vilification 5 bout, convulsion, fit, paroxysm, seizure, spasm, stroke

attacker noun assailant, aggressor, assaulter, intruder, invader, raider

attain verb achieve, accomplish, acquire, complete, fulfil, gain, get, obtain, reach

attainment noun achievement, accomplishment, completion, feat

attempt verb 1 try, endeavour, seek, strive, undertake, venture ◆ noun 2 try, bid, crack (informal), effort, go (informal), shot (informal), stab (informal), trial

attend verb 1 be present, appear, frequent, go to, haunt, put in an appearance, show oneself, turn up, visit 2 look after, care for, mind, minister to, nurse, take care of, tend **3** <u>pay attention</u>, hear, heed, listen, mark, note, observe, pay heed **4 attend to** <u>apply oneself to</u>, concentrate on, devote oneself to, get to work on, look after, occupy oneself with, see to, take care of

attendance noun **1** <u>presence</u>, appearance, attending, being there **2** <u>turnout</u>, audience, crowd, gate, house, number present

attendant noun **1** <u>assistant</u>, aide, companion, escort, follower, guard, helper, servant ◆ adjective **2** <u>accompanying</u>, accessory, associated, concomitant, consequent, related

attention noun **1** <u>concentration</u>, deliberation, heed, intentness, mind, scrutiny, thinking, thought **2** <u>notice</u>, awareness, consciousness, consideration, observation, recognition, regard **3** <u>care</u>, concern, looking after, ministration, treatment

attentive adjective **1** <u>intent</u>, alert, awake, careful, concentrating, heedful, mindful, observant, studious, watchful **2** <u>considerate</u>, courteous, helpful, kind, obliging, polite, respectful, thoughtful

attic noun <u>loft</u>, garret

attire noun <u>clothes</u>, apparel, costume, dress, garb, garments, outfit, robes, wear

attitude noun **1** <u>disposition</u>, approach, frame of mind, mood, opinion, outlook, perspective, point of view, position, stance **2** <u>position</u>, pose, posture, stance

attract verb <u>appeal to</u>, allure, charm, draw, enchant, entice, lure, pull (informal), tempt

attraction noun <u>appeal</u>, allure, charm, enticement, fascination, lure, magnetism, pull (informal), temptation

attractive adjective <u>appealing</u>, alluring, charming, fair, fetching, good-looking, handsome, inviting, lovely, pleasant, pretty, tempting

attribute verb **1** <u>ascribe</u>, assign, charge, credit, put down to, refer, set down to, trace to ◆ noun **2** <u>quality</u>, aspect, character, characteristic, facet, feature, peculiarity, property, trait

attune verb <u>accustom</u>, adapt, adjust, familiarize, harmonize, regulate

audacious adjective **1** <u>daring</u>, bold, brave, courageous, fearless, intrepid, rash, reckless **2** <u>cheeky</u>, brazen, defiant, impertinent, impudent, insolent, presumptuous, shameless

audacity noun **1** <u>daring</u>, boldness, bravery, courage, fearlessness, nerve, rashness, recklessness **2** <u>cheek</u>, chutzpah (U.S. & Canad. informal), effrontery, impertinence, impudence, insolence, nerve

audible adjective <u>clear</u>, detectable, discernible, distinct, hearable, perceptible

audience noun **1** <u>spectators</u>, assembly, crowd, gallery, gathering, listeners, onlookers, turnout, viewers **2** <u>interview</u>, consultation, hearing, meeting, reception

aura noun <u>air</u>, ambience, atmosphere, feeling, mood, quality, tone

auspicious *adjective* <u>favourable</u>, bright, encouraging, felicitous, hopeful, promising

austere *adjective* **1** <u>stern</u>, forbidding, formal, serious, severe, solemn, strict **2** <u>ascetic</u>, abstemious, puritanical, self-disciplined, sober, solemn, strait-laced, strict **3** <u>plain</u>, bleak, harsh, simple, spare, Spartan, stark

austerity *noun* **1** <u>sternness</u>, formality, inflexibility, rigour, seriousness, severity, solemnity, stiffness, strictness **2** <u>asceticism</u>, puritanism, self-denial, self-discipline, sobriety **3** <u>plainness</u>, simplicity, starkness

authentic *adjective* <u>genuine</u>, actual, authoritative, bona fide, legitimate, pure, real, true-to-life, valid

authenticity *noun* <u>genuineness</u>, accuracy, certainty, faithfulness, legitimacy, purity, truthfulness, validity

author *noun* **1** <u>writer</u>, composer, creator **2** <u>creator</u>, architect, designer, father, founder, inventor, originator, producer

authoritarian *adjective* **1** <u>strict</u>, autocratic, dictatorial, doctrinaire, dogmatic, severe, tyrannical ♦ *noun* **2** <u>disciplinarian</u>, absolutist, autocrat, despot, dictator, tyrant

authoritative *adjective* **1** <u>reliable</u>, accurate, authentic, definitive, dependable, trustworthy, valid **2** <u>commanding</u>, assertive, imperious, imposing, masterly, self-assured

authority *noun* **1** <u>power</u>, command, control, direction, influence, supremacy, sway, weight **2** *usually plural* <u>powers that be</u>, administration, government, management, officialdom, police, the Establishment **3** <u>expert</u>, connoisseur, judge, master, professional, specialist

authorization *noun* <u>permission</u>, a blank cheque, approval, leave, licence, permit, warrant

authorize *verb* **1** <u>empower</u>, accredit, commission, enable, entitle, give authority **2** <u>permit</u>, allow, approve, give authority for, license, sanction, warrant

autocracy *noun* <u>dictatorship</u>, absolutism, despotism, tyranny

autocrat *noun* <u>dictator</u>, absolutist, despot, tyrant

autocratic *adjective* <u>dictatorial</u>, absolute, all-powerful, despotic, domineering, imperious, tyrannical

automatic *adjective* **1** <u>mechanical</u>, automated, mechanized, push-button, self-propelling **2** <u>involuntary</u>, instinctive, mechanical, natural, reflex, spontaneous, unconscious, unwilled

autonomous *adjective* <u>self-ruling</u>, free, independent, self-determining, self-governing, sovereign

autonomy *noun* <u>independence</u>, freedom, home rule, self-determination, self-government, self-rule, sovereignty

auxiliary *adjective* **1** <u>supplementary</u>, back-up, emergency, fall-back, reserve, secondary, subsidiary, substitute

2 <u>supporting</u>, accessory, aiding, ancillary, assisting, helping ♦ *noun* **3** <u>backup</u>, reserve **4** <u>helper</u>, assistant, associate, companion, subordinate, supporter

avail *verb* **1** <u>benefit</u>, aid, assist, be of advantage, be useful, help, profit ♦ *noun* **2** <u>benefit</u>, advantage, aid, good, help, profit, use

availability *noun* <u>accessibility</u>, attainability, handiness, readiness

available *adjective* <u>accessible</u>, at hand, at one's disposal, free, handy, on tap, ready, to hand

avalanche *noun* **1** <u>snow-slide</u>, landslide, landslip **2** <u>flood</u>, barrage, deluge, inundation, torrent

avant-garde *adjective* <u>progressive</u>, experimental, ground-breaking, innovative, pioneering, unconventional

avarice *noun* <u>greed</u>, covetousness, meanness, miserliness, niggardliness, parsimony, stinginess

avaricious *adjective* <u>grasping</u>, covetous, greedy, mean, miserly, niggardly, parsimonious, stingy

avenge *verb* <u>get revenge for</u>, get even for (*informal*), get one's own back, hit back, punish, repay, retaliate

avenue *noun* <u>street</u>, approach, boulevard, course, drive, passage, path, road, route, way

average *noun* **1** <u>usual</u>, mean, medium, midpoint, norm, normal, par, standard **2 on average** <u>usually</u>, as a rule, for the most part, generally,

normally, typically ♦ *adjective* **3** <u>usual</u>, commonplace, fair, general, normal, ordinary, regular, standard, typical **4** <u>mean</u>, intermediate, median, medium, middle ♦ *verb* **5** <u>make on average</u>, balance out to, be on average, do on average, even out to

averse *adjective* <u>opposed</u>, disinclined, hostile, ill-disposed, loath, reluctant, unwilling

aversion *noun* <u>hatred</u>, animosity, antipathy, disinclination, dislike, hostility, revulsion, unwillingness

avert *verb* **1** <u>turn away</u>, turn aside **2** <u>ward off</u>, avoid, fend off, forestall, frustrate, preclude, prevent, stave off

aviator *noun* <u>pilot</u>, aeronaut, airman, flyer

avid *adjective* **1** <u>enthusiastic</u>, ardent, devoted, eager, fanatical, intense, keen, passionate, zealous **2** <u>insatiable</u>, grasping, greedy, hungry, rapacious, ravenous, thirsty, voracious

avoid *verb* **1** <u>refrain from</u>, dodge, duck (out of) (*informal*), eschew, fight shy of, shirk **2** <u>prevent</u>, avert **3** <u>keep away from</u>, bypass, dodge, elude, escape, evade, shun, steer clear of

avoidance *noun* <u>evasion</u>, dodging, eluding, escape, keeping away, shunning, steering clear

avowed *adjective* **1** <u>declared</u>, open, professed, self-proclaimed, sworn **2** <u>confessed</u>, acknowledged, admitted

await *verb* **1** <u>wait for</u>, abide, anticipate, expect, look for, look forward to, stay for **2** <u>be in store</u>

for, attend, be in readiness for, be prepared for, be ready for, wait for

awake adjective **1** not sleeping, aroused, awakened, aware, conscious, wakeful, wide-awake **2** alert, alive, attentive, aware, heedful, observant, on the lookout, vigilant, watchful ♦ verb **3** wake up, awaken, rouse, wake **4** alert, arouse, kindle, provoke, revive, stimulate, stir up

awaken verb **1** awake, arouse, revive, rouse, wake **2** alert, kindle, provoke, stimulate, stir up

awakening noun waking up, arousal, revival, rousing, stimulation, stirring up

award verb **1** give, bestow, confer, endow, grant, hand out, present ♦ noun **2** prize, decoration, gift, grant, trophy

aware adjective **1** aware of, knowing about, acquainted with, conscious of, conversant with, familiar with, mindful of **2** informed, enlightened, in the picture, knowledgeable

awareness noun knowledge, consciousness, familiarity, perception, realization, recognition, understanding

away adverb **1** off, abroad, elsewhere, from here, from home, hence **2** at a distance, apart, far, remote **3** aside, out of the way, to one side **4** continuously, incessantly, interminably, relentlessly, repeatedly, uninterruptedly, unremittingly ♦ adjective **5** not present, abroad, absent, elsewhere, gone, not at home, not here, out

awe noun **1** wonder, admiration, amazement, astonishment, dread, fear, horror, respect, reverence, terror ♦ verb **2** impress, amaze, astonish, frighten, horrify, intimidate, stun, terrify

awesome adjective awe-inspiring, amazing, astonishing, breathtaking, formidable, impressive, intimidating, stunning

awful adjective **1** terrible, abysmal, appalling, deplorable, dreadful, frightful, ghastly, horrendous **2** Obsolete awe-inspiring, awesome, fearsome, majestic, solemn

awfully adverb **1** badly, disgracefully, dreadfully, reprehensibly, unforgivably, unpleasantly, woefully, wretchedly **2** Informal very, dreadfully, exceedingly, exceptionally, extremely, greatly, immensely, terribly

awkward adjective **1** clumsy, gauche, gawky, inelegant, lumbering, uncoordinated, ungainly **2** unmanageable, clunky (informal), cumbersome, difficult, inconvenient, troublesome, unwieldy **3** embarrassing, delicate, difficult, ill at ease, inconvenient, uncomfortable

awkwardness noun **1** clumsiness, gawkiness, inelegance, ungainliness **2** unwieldiness, difficulty, inconvenience **3** embarrassment, delicacy, difficulty, inconvenience

axe noun **1** hatchet, adze, chopper **2** the axe Informal the sack (informal), dismissal, termination, the boot (*slang*), the chop (*slang*) ◆ *verb* 3 *Informal* <u>cut back</u>, cancel, dismiss, dispense with, eliminate, fire (*informal*), get rid of, remove, sack (*informal*)

axiom *noun* <u>principle</u>, adage, aphorism, dictum, maxim, precept, truism

axiomatic *adjective* <u>self-evident</u>, accepted, assumed, certain, given, granted, manifest, understood

axis *noun* <u>pivot</u>, axle, centre line, shaft, spindle

axle *noun* <u>shaft</u>, axis, pin, pivot, rod, spindle

B b

babble *verb* 1 <u>gabble</u>, burble, chatter, jabber, prattle, waffle (*informal, chiefly Brit.*) 2 <u>gibber</u>, gurgle ◆ *noun* 3 <u>gabble</u>, burble, drivel, gibberish, waffle (*informal, chiefly Brit.*)

baby *noun* 1 <u>infant</u>, babe, babe in arms, bairn (*Scot.*), child, newborn child ◆ *adjective* 2 <u>small</u>, little, mini, miniature, minute, teeny-weeny, tiny, wee

babyish *adjective* <u>childish</u>, foolish, immature, infantile, juvenile, puerile, sissy, spoiled

back *noun* 1 <u>rear</u>, end, far end, hind part, hindquarters, reverse, stern, tail end 2 **behind one's back** <u>secretly</u>, covertly, deceitfully, sneakily, surreptitiously ◆ *verb* 3 <u>move back</u>, back off, backtrack, go back, retire, retreat, reverse, turn tail, withdraw 4 <u>support</u>,

advocate, assist, champion, endorse, promote, sponsor ◆ *adjective* 5 <u>rear</u>, end, hind, hindmost, posterior, tail 6 <u>previous</u>, delayed, earlier, elapsed, former, overdue, past

backbiting *noun* <u>slander</u>, bitchiness (*slang*), cattiness (*informal*), defamation, disparagement, gossip, malice, scandalmongering, spitefulness

backbone *noun* 1 *Medical* <u>spinal column</u>, spine, vertebrae, vertebral column 2 <u>strength of character</u>, character, courage, determination, fortitude, grit, nerve, pluck, resolution

backbreaking *adjective* <u>exhausting</u>, arduous, crushing, gruelling, hard, laborious, punishing, strenuous

back down *verb* <u>give in</u>, accede, admit defeat, back-pedal, concede, surrender, withdraw, yield

backer *noun* <u>supporter</u>, advocate, angel (*informal*), benefactor, patron, promoter, second, sponsor, subscriber

backfire *verb* <u>fail</u>, boomerang, disappoint, flop (*informal*), miscarry, rebound, recoil

background *noun* <u>history</u>, circumstances, culture, education, environment, grounding, tradition, upbringing

backing *noun* <u>support</u>, aid, assistance, encouragement, endorsement, moral support, patronage, sponsorship

backlash *noun* <u>reaction</u>, counteraction, recoil, repercussion, resistance, response, retaliation

backlog noun <u>build-up</u>, accumulation, excess, hoard, reserve, stock, supply

back out verb, often with **of** <u>withdraw</u>, abandon, cancel, give up, go back on, resign, retreat

backslide verb <u>relapse</u>, go astray, go wrong, lapse, revert, slip, stray, weaken

backslider noun <u>relapser</u>, apostate, deserter, recidivist, recreant, renegade, turncoat

back up verb <u>support</u>, aid, assist, bolster, confirm, corroborate, reinforce, second, stand by, substantiate

backward adjective <u>slow</u>, behind, dull, retarded, subnormal, underdeveloped, undeveloped

backwards, backward adverb <u>towards the rear</u>, behind, in reverse, rearward

bacteria plural noun <u>microorganisms</u>, bacilli, bugs (slang), germs, microbes, pathogens, viruses

bad adjective 1 <u>inferior</u>, defective, faulty, imperfect, inadequate, poor, substandard, unsatisfactory 2 <u>harmful</u>, damaging, dangerous, deleterious, detrimental, hurtful, ruinous, unhealthy 3 <u>evil</u>, corrupt, criminal, immoral, mean, sinful, wicked, wrong 4 <u>naughty</u>, disobedient, mischievous, unruly 5 <u>rotten</u>, decayed, mouldy, off, putrid, rancid, sour, spoiled 6 <u>unfavourable</u>, adverse, distressing, gloomy, grim, troubled, unfortunate, unpleasant

badge noun <u>mark</u>, brand, device, emblem, identification, insignia, sign, stamp, token

badger verb <u>pester</u>, bully, goad, harass, hound, importune, nag, plague, torment

badinage noun <u>wordplay</u>, banter, mockery, pleasantry, repartee, teasing

badly adverb 1 <u>poorly</u>, carelessly, imperfectly, inadequately, incorrectly, ineptly, wrongly 2 <u>unfavourably</u>, unfortunately, unsuccessfully 3 <u>severely</u>, deeply, desperately, exceedingly, extremely, greatly, intensely, seriously

baffle verb <u>puzzle</u>, bewilder, confound, confuse, flummox, mystify, nonplus, perplex, stump

bag noun 1 <u>container</u>, receptacle, sac, sack ♦ verb 2 <u>catch</u>, acquire, capture, kill, land, shoot, trap

baggage noun <u>luggage</u>, accoutrements, bags, belongings, equipment, gear, paraphernalia, suitcases, things

baggy adjective <u>loose</u>, bulging, droopy, floppy, ill-fitting, oversize, roomy, sagging, slack

bail noun law <u>security</u>, bond, guarantee, pledge, surety, warranty

bail out see BALE OUT

bait noun 1 <u>lure</u>, allurement, attraction, decoy, enticement, incentive, inducement, snare, temptation ♦ verb 2 <u>tease</u>, annoy, bother, harass, hassle (informal), hound, irritate, persecute, torment, wind up (Brit. slang)

baked adjective <u>dry</u>, arid, desiccated, parched, scorched, seared, sun-baked, torrid

balance noun 1 <u>stability</u>,

composure, equanimity, poise, self-control, self-possession, steadiness 2 **equilibrium**, correspondence, equity, equivalence, evenness, parity, symmetry 3 **remainder**, difference, residue, rest, surplus ♦ verb 4 **stabilize**, level, match, parallel, steady 5 **compare**, assess, consider, deliberate, estimate, evaluate, weigh 6 Accounting **calculate**, compute, settle, square, tally, total

balcony noun 1 **terrace**, veranda 2 **upper circle**, gallery, gods

bald adjective 1 **hairless**, baldheaded, depilated 2 **plain**, blunt, direct, forthright, straightforward, unadorned, unvarnished

balderdash noun **nonsense**, claptrap (informal), drivel, garbage (informal), gibberish, hogwash, hot air (informal), rubbish

baldness noun 1 **hairlessness**, alopecia (Pathology), baldheadedness 2 **plainness**, austerity, bluntness, severity, simplicity

bale out, bail out verb 1 Informal **help**, aid, relieve, rescue, save (someone's) bacon (informal, chiefly Brit.) 2 **escape**, quit, retreat, withdraw

balk, baulk verb 1 **recoil**, evade, flinch, hesitate, jib, refuse, resist, shirk, shrink from 2 **foil**, check, counteract, defeat, frustrate, hinder, obstruct, prevent, thwart

ball noun **sphere**, drop, globe, globule, orb, pellet, spheroid

ballast noun **counterbalance**, balance, counterweight,

equilibrium, sandbag, stability, stabilizer, weight

balloon verb **swell**, billow, blow up, dilate, distend, expand, grow rapidly, inflate, puff out

ballot noun **vote**, election, poll, polling, voting

ballyhoo noun Informal **fuss**, babble, commotion, hubbub, hue and cry, hullabaloo, noise, racket, to-do

balm noun 1 **ointment**, balsam, cream, embrocation, emollient, lotion, salve, unguent 2 **comfort**, anodyne, consolation, curative, palliative, restorative, solace

balmy adjective **mild**, clement, pleasant, summery, temperate

bamboozle verb Informal 1 **cheat**, con (informal), deceive, dupe, fool, hoodwink, swindle, trick 2 **puzzle**, baffle, befuddle, confound, confuse, mystify, perplex, stump

ban verb 1 **prohibit**, banish, bar, block, boycott, disallow, disqualify, exclude, forbid, outlaw ♦ noun 2 **prohibition**, boycott, disqualification, embargo, restriction, taboo

banal adjective **unoriginal**, hackneyed, humdrum, mundane, pedestrian, stale, stereotyped, trite, unimaginative

band[1] noun 1 **ensemble**, combo, group, orchestra 2 **gang**, body, company, group, party, posse (informal)

band[2] noun **strip**, belt, bond, chain, cord, ribbon, strap

bandage noun 1 **dressing**, compress, gauze, plaster ♦ verb 2 **dress**, bind, cover, swathe

bandit noun <u>robber</u>, brigand, desperado, highwayman, marauder, outlaw, thief

bane noun <u>plague</u>, bête noire, curse, nuisance, pest, ruin, scourge, torment

bang noun 1 <u>explosion</u>, clang, clap, clash, pop, slam, thud, thump 2 <u>blow</u>, bump, cuff, knock, punch, smack, stroke, whack ♦ verb 3 <u>hit</u>, belt (*informal*), clatter, knock, slam, strike, thump 4 <u>explode</u>, boom, clang, resound, thump, thunder ♦ adverb 5 <u>hard</u>, abruptly, headlong, noisily, suddenly 6 <u>straight</u>, precisely, slap, smack

banish verb 1 <u>expel</u>, deport, eject, evict, exile, outlaw 2 <u>get rid of</u>, ban, cast out, discard, dismiss, oust, remove

banishment noun <u>expulsion</u>, deportation, exile, expatriation, transportation

banisters plural noun <u>railing</u>, balusters, balustrade, handrail, rail

bank[1] noun 1 <u>storehouse</u>, depository, repository 2 <u>store</u>, accumulation, fund, hoard, reserve, reservoir, savings, stock, stockpile ♦ verb 3 <u>save</u>, deposit, keep

bank[2] noun 1 <u>mound</u>, banking, embankment, heap, mass, pile, ridge 2 <u>side</u>, brink, edge, margin, shore ♦ verb 3 <u>pile</u>, amass, heap, mass, mound, stack 4 <u>tilt</u>, camber, cant, heel, incline, pitch, slant, slope, tip

bank[3] noun <u>row</u>, array, file, group, line, rank, sequence, series, succession

bankrupt adjective <u>insolvent</u>, broke (*informal*), destitute, impoverished, in queer street, in the red, ruined, wiped out (*informal*)

bankruptcy noun <u>insolvency</u>, disaster, failure, liquidation, ruin

banner noun <u>flag</u>, colours, ensign, pennant, placard, standard, streamer

banquet noun <u>feast</u>, dinner, meal, repast, revel, treat

banter verb 1 <u>joke</u>, jest, kid (*informal*), rib (*informal*), taunt, tease ♦ noun 2 <u>joking</u>, badinage, jesting, kidding (*informal*), repartee, teasing, wordplay

baptism noun Christianity <u>christening</u>, immersion, purification, sprinkling

baptize verb Christianity <u>purify</u>, cleanse, immerse

bar noun 1 <u>rod</u>, paling, palisade, pole, rail, shaft, stake, stick 2 <u>obstacle</u>, barricade, barrier, block, deterrent, hindrance, impediment, obstruction, stop 3 <u>public house</u>, boozer (*Brit., Austral. & N Z, informal*), canteen, counter, inn, pub (*informal, chiefly Brit.*), saloon, tavern, watering hole (*facetious slang*) ♦ verb 4 <u>fasten</u>, barricade, bolt, latch, lock, secure 5 <u>obstruct</u>, hinder, prevent, restrain 6 <u>exclude</u>, ban, black, blackball, forbid, keep out, prohibit

Bar noun **the Bar** Law <u>barristers</u>, body of lawyers, counsel, court, judgment, tribunal

barb noun 1 <u>dig</u>, affront, cut, gibe, insult, sarcasm, scoff, sneer 2 <u>point</u>, bristle, prickle, prong, quill, spike, spur, thorn

barbarian noun **1** <u>savage</u>, brute, yahoo **2** <u>lout</u>, bigot, boor, philistine

barbaric adjective **1** <u>uncivilized</u>, primitive, rude, wild **2** <u>brutal</u>, barbarous, coarse, crude, cruel, fierce, inhuman, savage

barbarism noun <u>savagery</u>, coarseness, crudity

barbarous adjective **1** <u>uncivilized</u>, barbarian, brutish, primitive, rough, rude, savage, uncouth, wild **2** <u>brutal</u>, barbaric, cruel, ferocious, heartless, inhuman, monstrous, ruthless, vicious

barbed adjective **1** <u>cutting</u>, critical, hostile, hurtful, nasty, pointed, scathing, unkind **2** <u>spiked</u>, hooked, jagged, prickly, spiny, thorny

bare adjective **1** <u>naked</u>, nude, stripped, unclad, unclothed, uncovered, undressed, without a stitch on (informal) **2** <u>plain</u>, bald, basic, sheer, simple, stark, unembellished **3** <u>simple</u>, austere, spare, spartan, unadorned, unembellished

barefaced adjective **1** <u>obvious</u>, blatant, flagrant, open, transparent, unconcealed **2** <u>shameless</u>, audacious, bold, brash, brazen, impudent, insolent

barely adverb <u>only just</u>, almost, at a push, by the skin of one's teeth, hardly, just, scarcely

bargain noun **1** <u>agreement</u>, arrangement, contract, pact, pledge, promise **2** <u>good buy</u>, (cheap) purchase, discount, giveaway, good deal, reduction, snip (informal), steal (informal) ♦ verb **3** <u>negotiate</u>, agree, contract, covenant, promise,

stipulate, transact

barge noun <u>canal boat</u>, flatboat, lighter, narrow boat

bark[1] noun, verb <u>yap</u>, bay, growl, howl, snarl, woof, yelp

bark[2] noun <u>covering</u>, casing, cortex (Anatomy, botany), crust, husk, rind, skin

barmy adjective Slang <u>insane</u>, crazy, daft (informal), foolish, idiotic, nuts (slang), out of one's mind, stupid

barracks plural noun <u>camp</u>, billet, encampment, garrison, quarters

barrage noun **1** <u>torrent</u>, burst, deluge, hail, mass, onslaught, plethora, stream **2** Military <u>bombardment</u>, battery, cannonade, fusillade, gunfire, salvo, shelling, volley

barren adjective **1** <u>infertile</u>, childless, sterile **2** <u>unproductive</u>, arid, desert, desolate, dry, empty, unfruitful, waste

barricade noun **1** <u>barrier</u>, blockade, bulwark, fence, obstruction, palisade, rampart, stockade ♦ verb **2** <u>bar</u>, block, blockade, defend, fortify, obstruct, protect, shut in

barrier noun **1** <u>barricade</u>, bar, blockade, boundary, fence, obstacle, obstruction, wall **2** <u>hindrance</u>, difficulty, drawback, handicap, hurdle, obstacle, restriction, stumbling block

barter verb <u>trade</u>, bargain, drive a hard bargain, exchange, haggle, sell, swap, traffic

base[1] noun **1** <u>bottom</u>, bed, foot, foundation, pedestal, rest, stand, support **2** <u>basis</u>, core, essence,

heart, key, origin, root, source
3 <u>centre</u>, camp, headquarters,
home, post, settlement, starting
point, station ♦ *verb* 4 <u>found</u>,
build, construct, depend, derive,
establish, ground, hinge 5 <u>place</u>,
locate, post, station

base² *adjective* 1 <u>dishonourable</u>,
contemptible, despicable,
disreputable, evil, immoral,
shameful, sordid, wicked
2 <u>counterfeit</u>, alloyed, debased,
fake, forged, fraudulent, impure

baseless *adjective* <u>unfounded</u>,
groundless, unconfirmed,
uncorroborated, ungrounded,
unjustified, unsubstantiated,
unsupported

bash *verb* 1 *Informal* <u>hit</u>, belt
(*informal*), smash, sock (*slang*),
strike, wallop (*informal*) ♦ *noun*
2 *Informal* <u>attempt</u>, crack
(*informal*), go (*informal*), shot
(*informal*), stab (*informal*), try

bashful *adjective* <u>shy</u>, blushing,
coy, diffident, reserved, reticent,
retiring, timid

basic *adjective* <u>essential</u>,
elementary, fundamental, key,
necessary, primary, vital

basically *adverb* <u>essentially</u>, at
heart, fundamentally, inherently,
in substance, intrinsically,
mostly, primarily

basics *plural noun* <u>essentials</u>,
brass tacks (*informal*),
fundamentals, nitty-gritty
(*informal*), nuts and bolts
(*informal*), principles, rudiments

basis *noun* <u>foundation</u>, base,
bottom, footing, ground,
groundwork, support

bask *verb* <u>lie in</u>, laze, loll, lounge,
relax, sunbathe, swim in

bass *adjective* <u>deep</u>, deep-toned,
low, low-pitched, resonant,
sonorous

bastard *noun* 1 *Informal, offensive*
<u>rogue</u>, blackguard, miscreant,
reprobate, scoundrel, villain,
wretch 2 <u>illegitimate child</u>, love
child, natural child

bastion *noun* <u>stronghold</u>,
bulwark, citadel, defence,
fortress, mainstay, prop, rock,
support, tower of strength

bat *noun, verb* <u>hit</u>, bang, smack,
strike, swat, thump, wallop
(*informal*), whack

batch *noun* <u>group</u>, amount,
assemblage, bunch, collection,
crowd, lot, pack, quantity, set

bath *noun* 1 <u>wash</u>, cleansing,
douche, scrubbing, shower,
soak, tub ♦ *verb* 2 <u>wash</u>, bathe,
clean, douse, scrub down,
shower, soak

bathe *verb* 1 <u>swim</u> 2 <u>wash</u>,
cleanse, rinse 3 <u>cover</u>, flood,
immerse, steep, suffuse

baton *noun* <u>stick</u>, club, crook,
mace, rod, sceptre, staff,
truncheon, wand

batten *verb, usually with* **down**
<u>fasten</u>, board up, clamp down,
cover up, fix, nail down, secure,
tighten

batter *verb* <u>beat</u>, buffet, clobber
(*slang*), pelt, pound, pummel,
thrash, wallop (*informal*)

battery *noun* <u>artillery</u>, cannon,
cannonry, gun emplacements,
guns

battle *noun* 1 <u>fight</u>, action,
attack, combat, encounter,
engagement, hostilities, skirmish
2 <u>conflict</u>, campaign, contest,

crusade, dispute, struggle ♦ *verb*
3 struggle, argue, clamour,
dispute, fight, lock horns, strive,
war

battlefield *noun* battleground,
combat zone, field, field of
battle, front

battleship *noun* warship,
gunboat, man-of-war

batty *adjective* crazy, daft
(*informal*), dotty (*slang, chiefly
Brit.*), eccentric, mad, odd,
peculiar, potty (*Brit. informal*),
touched

bauble *noun* trinket, bagatelle,
gewgaw, gimcrack, knick-knack,
plaything, toy, trifle

baulk *see* BALK

bawdy *adjective* rude, coarse,
dirty, indecent, lascivious,
lecherous, lewd, ribald, salacious,
smutty

bawl *verb* 1 cry, blubber, sob,
wail, weep 2 shout, bellow, call,
clamour, howl, roar, yell

bay¹ *noun* inlet, bight, cove, gulf,
natural harbour, sound

bay² *noun* recess, alcove,
compartment, niche, nook,
opening

bay³ *verb* howl, bark, clamour,
cry, growl, yelp

bazaar *noun* 1 fair,
bring-and-buy, fête, sale of work
2 market, exchange, marketplace

be *verb* exist, be alive, breathe,
inhabit, live

beach *noun* shore, coast, sands,
seashore, seaside, water's edge

beached *adjective* stranded,
abandoned, aground, ashore,
deserted, grounded, high and
dry, marooned, wrecked

beacon *noun* signal, beam,
bonfire, flare, lighthouse, sign,
watchtower

bead *noun* drop, blob, bubble,
dot, droplet, globule, pellet, pill

beady *adjective* bright, gleaming,
glinting, glittering, sharp, shining

beak *noun* 1 bill, mandible, neb
(*archaic or dialect*), nib 2 *Slang*
nose, proboscis, snout

beam *noun* 1 smile, grin 2 ray,
gleam, glimmer, glint, glow,
shaft, streak, stream 3 rafter,
girder, joist, plank, spar, support,
timber ♦ *verb* 4 smile, grin
5 radiate, glare, gleam, glitter,
glow, shine 6 send out,
broadcast, emit, transmit

bear *verb* 1 support, have, hold,
maintain, possess, shoulder,
sustain, uphold 2 carry, bring,
convey, hump (*Brit. slang*),
move, take, transport 3 produce,
beget, breed, bring forth,
engender, generate, give birth
to, yield 4 tolerate, abide, allow,
brook, endure, permit, put up
with (*informal*), stomach, suffer

bearable *adjective* tolerable,
admissible, endurable,
manageable, passable,
sufferable, supportable,
sustainable

bearer *noun* carrier, agent,
conveyor, messenger, porter,
runner, servant

bearing *noun* 1 *usually with on or*
upon relevance, application,
connection, import, pertinence,
reference, relation, significance
2 manner, air, aspect, attitude,
behaviour, demeanour,
deportment, posture

bearings *plural noun* position,

aim, course, direction, location, orientation, situation, track, way, whereabouts

bear out verb <u>support</u>, confirm, corroborate, endorse, justify, prove, substantiate, uphold, vindicate

beast noun 1 <u>animal</u>, brute, creature 2 <u>brute</u>, barbarian, fiend, monster, ogre, sadist, savage, swine

beastly adjective <u>unpleasant</u>, awful, disagreeable, horrid, mean, nasty, rotten

beat verb 1 <u>hit</u>, bang, batter, buffet, knock, pound, strike, thrash 2 <u>flap</u>, flutter 3 <u>throb</u>, palpitate, pound, pulsate, quake, thump, vibrate 4 <u>defeat</u>, conquer, outdo, overcome, overwhelm, surpass, vanquish
♦ noun 5 <u>throb</u>, palpitation, pulsation, pulse 6 <u>route</u>, circuit, course, path, rounds, way 7 <u>rhythm</u>, accent, cadence, metre, stress, time

beaten adjective 1 <u>stirred</u>, blended, foamy, frothy, mixed, whipped, whisked 2 <u>defeated</u>, cowed, overcome, overwhelmed, thwarted, vanquished

beat up verb Informal <u>assault</u>, attack, batter, beat the living daylights out of (informal), knock about or around, thrash

beau noun 1 Chiefly U.S. <u>boyfriend</u>, admirer, fiancé, lover, suitor, sweetheart 2 <u>dandy</u>, coxcomb, fop, gallant, ladies' man

beautiful adjective <u>attractive</u>, charming, delightful, exquisite, fair, fine, gorgeous, handsome, lovely, pleasing

beautify verb <u>make beautiful</u>, adorn, decorate, embellish, festoon, garnish, glamorize, ornament

beauty noun 1 <u>attractiveness</u>, charm, comeliness, elegance, exquisiteness, glamour, grace, handsomeness, loveliness 2 <u>belle</u>, good-looker, lovely (slang), stunner (informal)

becalmed adjective <u>still</u>, motionless, settled, stranded, stuck

because conjunction <u>since</u>, as, by reason of, in that, on account of, owing to, thanks to

beckon verb <u>gesture</u>, bid, gesticulate, motion, nod, signal, summon, wave at

become verb 1 <u>come to be</u>, alter to, be transformed into, change into, develop into, grow into, mature into, ripen into 2 <u>suit</u>, embellish, enhance, fit, flatter, set off

becoming adjective 1 <u>appropriate</u>, compatible, fitting, in keeping, proper, seemly, suitable, worthy 2 <u>flattering</u>, attractive, comely, enhancing, graceful, neat, pretty, tasteful

bed noun 1 <u>bedstead</u>, berth, bunk, cot, couch, divan 2 <u>plot</u>, area, border, garden, patch, row, strip 3 <u>bottom</u>, base, foundation, groundwork

bedevil verb 1 <u>torment</u>, afflict, distress, harass, plague, trouble, vex, worry 2 <u>confuse</u>, confound

bedlam noun <u>pandemonium</u>, chaos, commotion, confusion, furore, tumult, turmoil, uproar

bedraggled *adjective* <u>messy</u>, dirty, dishevelled, disordered, muddied, unkempt, untidy

bedridden *adjective* <u>confined to bed</u>, confined, flat on one's back, incapacitated, laid up (*informal*)

bedrock *noun* 1 <u>bottom</u>, bed, foundation, rock bottom, substratum, substructure 2 <u>basics</u>, basis, core, essentials, fundamentals, nuts and bolts (*informal*), roots

beefy *adjective Informal* <u>brawny</u>, bulky, hulking, muscular, stocky, strapping, sturdy, thickset

befall *verb Archaic or literary* <u>happen</u>, chance, come to pass, fall, occur, take place, transpire (*informal*)

befitting *adjective* <u>appropriate</u>, apposite, becoming, fit, fitting, proper, right, seemly, suitable

before *preposition* 1 <u>ahead of</u>, in advance of, in front of 2 <u>earlier than</u>, in advance of, prior to 3 <u>in the presence of</u>, in front of ♦ *adverb* 4 <u>previously</u>, ahead, earlier, formerly, in advance, sooner 5 <u>in front</u>, ahead

beforehand *adverb* <u>in advance</u>, ahead of time, already, before, earlier, in anticipation, previously, sooner

befriend *verb* <u>help</u>, aid, assist, back, encourage, side with, stand by, support, welcome

beg *verb* 1 <u>scrounge</u>, cadge, seek charity, solicit charity, sponge on, touch (someone) for (*slang*) 2 <u>implore</u>, beseech, entreat, petition, plead, request, solicit

beggar *noun* <u>tramp</u>, bag lady (*chiefly U.S.*), bum (*informal*), down-and-out, pauper, vagrant

beggarly *adjective* <u>poor</u>, destitute, impoverished, indigent, needy, poverty-stricken

begin *verb* 1 <u>start</u>, commence, embark on, initiate, instigate, institute, prepare, set about 2 <u>happen</u>, appear, arise, come into being, emerge, originate, start

beginner *noun* <u>novice</u>, amateur, apprentice, learner, neophyte, starter, trainee, tyro

beginning *noun* 1 <u>start</u>, birth, commencement, inauguration, inception, initiation, onset, opening, origin, outset 2 <u>seed</u>, fount, germ, root

begrudge *verb* <u>resent</u>, be jealous, be reluctant, be stingy, envy, grudge

beguile *verb* 1 <u>fool</u>, cheat, deceive, delude, dupe, hoodwink, mislead, take for a ride (*informal*), trick 2 <u>charm</u>, amuse, distract, divert, engross, entertain, occupy

beguiling *adjective* <u>charming</u>, alluring, attractive, bewitching, captivating, enchanting, enthralling, intriguing

behave *verb* 1 <u>act</u>, function, operate, perform, run, work 2 <u>conduct oneself properly</u>, act correctly, keep one's nose clean, mind one's manners

behaviour *noun* 1 <u>conduct</u>, actions, bearing, demeanour, deportment, manner, manners, ways 2 <u>action</u>, functioning, operation, performance

behind *preposition* 1 <u>after</u>, at the

back of, at the heels of, at the rear of, following, later than **2** causing, at the bottom of, initiating, instigating, responsible for **3** supporting, backing, for, in agreement, on the side of
♦ *adverb* **4** after, afterwards, following, in the wake (of), next, subsequently **5** overdue, behindhand, in arrears, in debt
♦ *noun* **6** *Informal* bottom, butt (*U.S. & Canad. informal*), buttocks, posterior

behold *verb Archaic or literary* look at, observe, perceive, regard, survey, view, watch, witness

beholden *adjective* indebted, bound, grateful, obliged, owing, under obligation

being *noun* **1** existence, life, reality **2** nature, entity, essence, soul, spirit, substance **3** creature, human being, individual, living thing

belated *adjective* late, behindhand, behind time, delayed, late in the day, overdue, tardy

belch *verb* **1** burp (*informal*), hiccup **2** emit, discharge, disgorge, erupt, give off, spew forth, vent

beleaguered *adjective* **1** harassed, badgered, hassled (*informal*), persecuted, pestered, plagued, put upon, vexed **2** besieged, assailed, beset, blockaded, hemmed in, surrounded

belief *noun* **1** trust, assurance, confidence, conviction, feeling, impression, judgment, notion, opinion **2** faith, credo, creed, doctrine, dogma, ideology,

principles, tenet

believable *adjective* credible, authentic, imaginable, likely, plausible, possible, probable, trustworthy

believe *verb* **1** accept, be certain of, be convinced of, credit, depend on, have faith in, rely on, swear by, trust **2** think, assume, gather, imagine, judge, presume, reckon, speculate, suppose

believer *noun* follower, adherent, convert, devotee, disciple, supporter, upholder, zealot

belittle *verb* disparage, decry, denigrate, deprecate, deride, scoff at, scorn, sneer at

belligerent *adjective* **1** aggressive, bellicose, combative, hostile, pugnacious, unfriendly, warlike, warring
♦ *noun* **2** fighter, combatant, warring nation

bellow *noun, verb* shout, bawl, cry, howl, roar, scream, shriek, yell

belly *noun* **1** stomach, abdomen, corporation (*informal*), gut, insides (*informal*), paunch, potbelly, tummy ♦ *verb* **2** swell out, billow, bulge, fill, spread, swell

bellyful *noun* surfeit, enough, excess, glut, plateful, plenty, satiety, too much

belonging *noun* relationship, acceptance, affinity, association, attachment, fellowship, inclusion, loyalty, rapport

belongings *plural noun* possessions, accoutrements, chattels, effects, gear, goods, paraphernalia, personal property, stuff, things

belong to verb 1 <u>be the property of</u>, be at the disposal of, be held by, be owned by 2 <u>be a member of</u>, be affiliated to, be allied to, be associated with, be included in

beloved adjective <u>dear</u>, admired, adored, darling, loved, pet, precious, prized, treasured, worshipped

below preposition 1 <u>lesser</u>, inferior, subject, subordinate 2 <u>less than</u>, lower than ♦ adverb 3 <u>lower</u>, beneath, down, under, underneath

belt noun 1 <u>waistband</u>, band, cummerbund, girdle, girth, sash 2 Geography <u>zone</u>, area, district, layer, region, stretch, strip, tract

bemoan verb <u>lament</u>, bewail, deplore, grieve for, mourn, regret, rue, weep for

bemused adjective <u>puzzled</u>, at sea, bewildered, confused, flummoxed, muddled, nonplussed, perplexed

bench noun 1 <u>seat</u>, form, pew, settle, stall 2 <u>worktable</u>, board, counter, table, trestle table, workbench 3 **the bench** <u>court</u>, courtroom, judges, judiciary, magistrates, tribunal

benchmark noun <u>reference point</u>, criterion, gauge, level, measure, model, norm, par, standard, yardstick

bend verb 1 <u>curve</u>, arc, arch, bow, lean, turn, twist, veer ♦ noun 2 <u>curve</u>, angle, arc, arch, bow, corner, loop, turn, twist

beneath preposition 1 <u>under</u>, below, lower than, underneath 2 <u>inferior to</u>, below, less than 3 <u>unworthy of</u>, unbefitting ♦ adverb 4 <u>underneath</u>, below, in a lower place

benefactor noun <u>supporter</u>, backer, donor, helper, patron, philanthropist, sponsor, well-wisher

beneficial adjective <u>helpful</u>, advantageous, benign, favourable, profitable, useful, valuable, wholesome

beneficiary noun <u>recipient</u>, heir, inheritor, payee, receiver

benefit noun 1 <u>help</u>, advantage, aid, asset, assistance, favour, good, profit ♦ verb 2 <u>help</u>, aid, assist, avail, enhance, further, improve, profit

benevolent adjective <u>kind</u>, altruistic, benign, caring, charitable, generous, philanthropic

benign adjective 1 <u>kindly</u>, amiable, friendly, genial, kind, obliging, sympathetic 2 Medical <u>harmless</u>, curable, remediable

bent adjective 1 <u>curved</u>, angled, arched, bowed, crooked, hunched, stooped, twisted 2 **bent on** <u>determined to</u>, disposed to, fixed on, inclined to, insistent on, predisposed to, resolved on, set on ♦ noun 3 <u>inclination</u>, ability, aptitude, leaning, penchant, preference, propensity, tendency

bequeath verb <u>leave</u>, bestow, endow, entrust, give, grant, hand down, impart, pass on, will

bequest noun <u>legacy</u>, bestowal, endowment, estate, gift, inheritance, settlement

berate verb scold, castigate, censure, chide, criticize, harangue, rebuke, reprimand, reprove, tell off (informal), upbraid

bereavement noun loss, affliction, death, deprivation, misfortune, tribulation

bereft adjective deprived, devoid, lacking, parted from, robbed of, wanting

berserk adverb crazy, amok, enraged, frantic, frenzied, mad, raging, wild

berth noun 1 bunk, bed, billet, hammock 2 Nautical anchorage, dock, harbour, haven, pier, port, quay, wharf ♦ verb 3 Nautical anchor, dock, drop anchor, land, moor, tie up

beseech verb beg, ask, call upon, entreat, implore, plead, pray, solicit

beset verb plague, bedevil, harass, pester, trouble

beside preposition 1 next to, abreast of, adjacent to, alongside, at the side of, close to, near, nearby, neighbouring 2 beside oneself distraught, apoplectic, at the end of one's tether, demented, desperate, frantic, frenzied, out of one's mind, unhinged

besides adverb 1 too, also, as well, further, furthermore, in addition, into the bargain, moreover, otherwise, what's more ♦ preposition 2 apart from, barring, excepting, excluding, in addition to, other than, over and above, without

besiege verb 1 surround, blockade, encircle, hem in, lay siege to, shut in 2 harass, badger, harry, hassle (informal), hound, nag, pester, plague

besotted adjective infatuated, doting, hypnotized, smitten, spellbound

best adjective 1 finest, foremost, leading, most excellent, outstanding, pre-eminent, principal, supreme, unsurpassed ♦ adverb 2 most highly, extremely, greatly, most deeply, most fully ♦ noun 3 finest, cream, crème de la crème, elite, flower, pick, prime, top

bestial adjective brutal, barbaric, beastly, brutish, inhuman, savage, sordid

bestow verb present, award, commit, give, grant, hand out, impart, lavish

bet noun 1 gamble, long shot, risk, speculation, stake, venture, wager ♦ verb 2 gamble, chance, hazard, risk, speculate, stake, venture, wager

betoken verb indicate, bode, denote, promise, represent, signify, suggest

betray verb 1 be disloyal, be treacherous, be unfaithful, break one's promise, double-cross (informal), inform on or against, sell out (informal), stab in the back 2 give away, disclose, divulge, expose, let slip, reveal, uncover, unmask

betrayal noun 1 disloyalty, deception, double-cross (informal), sell-out (informal), treachery, treason, trickery 2 giving away, disclosure, divulgence, revelation

better adjective 1 superior,

excelling, finer, greater, higher-quality, more desirable, preferable, surpassing 2 <u>well</u>, cured, fully recovered, on the mend (*informal*), recovering, stronger ♦ *adverb* 3 <u>in a more excellent manner</u>, in a superior way, more advantageously, more attractively, more competently, more effectively 4 <u>to a greater degree</u>, more completely, more thoroughly ♦ *verb* 5 <u>improve</u>, enhance, further, raise

between *preposition* <u>amidst</u>, among, betwixt, in the middle of, mid

beverage *noun* <u>drink</u>, liquid, liquor, refreshment

bevy *noun* <u>group</u>, band, bunch (*informal*), collection, company, crowd, gathering, pack, troupe

bewail *verb* <u>lament</u>, bemoan, cry over, deplore, grieve for, moan, mourn, regret

beware *verb* <u>be careful</u>, be cautious, be wary, guard against, heed, look out, mind, take heed, watch out

bewilder *verb* <u>confound</u>, baffle, bemuse, confuse, flummox, mystify, nonplus, perplex, puzzle

bewildered *adjective* <u>confused</u>, at a loss, at sea, baffled, flummoxed, mystified, nonplussed, perplexed, puzzled

bewitch *verb* <u>enchant</u>, beguile, captivate, charm, enrapture, entrance, fascinate, hypnotize

bewitched *adjective* <u>enchanted</u>, charmed, entranced, fascinated, mesmerized, spellbound, under a spell

beyond *preposition* 1 <u>past</u>, above, apart from, at a distance, away from, over 2 <u>exceeding</u>, out of reach of, superior to, surpassing

bias *noun* 1 <u>prejudice</u>, favouritism, inclination, leaning, partiality, tendency ♦ *verb* 2 <u>prejudice</u>, distort, influence, predispose, slant, sway, twist, warp, weight

biased *adjective* <u>prejudiced</u>, distorted, one-sided, partial, slanted, weighted

bicker *verb* <u>quarrel</u>, argue, disagree, dispute, fight, row (*informal*), squabble, wrangle

bid *verb* 1 <u>offer</u>, proffer, propose, submit, tender 2 <u>say</u>, call, greet, tell, wish 3 <u>tell</u>, ask, command, direct, instruct, order, require ♦ *noun* 4 <u>offer</u>, advance, amount, price, proposal, sum, tender 5 <u>attempt</u>, crack (*informal*), effort, go (*informal*), stab (*informal*), try

bidding *noun* <u>order</u>, beck and call, command, direction, instruction, request, summons

big *adjective* 1 <u>large</u>, enormous, extensive, great, huge, immense, massive, substantial, vast 2 <u>important</u>, eminent, influential, leading, main, powerful, prominent, significant 3 <u>grown-up</u>, adult, elder, grown, mature 4 <u>generous</u>, altruistic, benevolent, gracious, magnanimous, noble, unselfish

bighead *noun Informal* <u>boaster</u>, braggart, know-all (*informal*)

bigheaded *adjective* <u>boastful</u>, arrogant, cocky, conceited, egotistic, immodest, overconfident, swollen-headed

bigot *noun* <u>fanatic</u>, racist,

sectarian, zealot

bigoted adjective <u>intolerant</u>, biased, dogmatic, narrow-minded, opinionated, prejudiced, sectarian

bigotry noun <u>intolerance</u>, bias, discrimination, dogmatism, fanaticism, narrow-mindedness, prejudice, sectarianism

bigwig noun Informal <u>important person</u>, big shot (informal), celebrity, dignitary, mogul, personage, somebody, V.I.P.

bill¹ noun 1 <u>charges</u>, account, invoice, reckoning, score, statement, tally 2 <u>proposal</u>, measure, piece of legislation, projected law 3 <u>advertisement</u>, bulletin, circular, handbill, handout, leaflet, notice, placard, poster 4 <u>list</u>, agenda, card, catalogue, inventory, listing, programme, roster, schedule ◆ verb 5 <u>charge</u>, debit, invoice 6 <u>advertise</u>, announce, give advance notice of, post

bill² noun <u>beak</u>, mandible, neb (archaic or dialect), nib

billet verb 1 <u>quarter</u>, accommodate, berth, station ◆ noun 2 <u>quarters</u>, accommodation, barracks, lodging

billow noun 1 <u>wave</u>, breaker, crest, roller, surge, swell, tide ◆ verb 2 <u>surge</u>, balloon, belly, puff up, rise up, roll, swell

bind verb 1 <u>secure</u>, fasten, hitch, lash, stick, strap, tie, wrap 2 <u>oblige</u>, compel, constrain, engage, force, necessitate, require ◆ noun 3 Informal <u>nuisance</u>, bore, difficulty, dilemma, drag (informal), pain in

the neck (informal), quandary, spot (informal)

binding adjective <u>compulsory</u>, indissoluble, irrevocable, mandatory, necessary, obligatory, unalterable

binge noun Informal <u>bout</u>, bender (informal), feast, fling, orgy, spree

biography noun <u>life story</u>, account, curriculum vitae, CV, life, memoir, profile, record

birth noun 1 <u>childbirth</u>, delivery, nativity, parturition 2 <u>ancestry</u>, background, blood, breeding, lineage, parentage, pedigree, stock

bisect verb <u>cut in two</u>, cross, cut across, divide in two, halve, intersect, separate, split

bit¹ noun <u>piece</u>, crumb, fragment, grain, morsel, part, scrap, speck

bit² noun <u>curb</u>, brake, check, restraint, snaffle

bitchy adjective Informal <u>spiteful</u>, backbiting, catty (informal), mean, nasty, snide, vindictive

bite verb 1 <u>cut</u>, chew, gnaw, nip, pierce, pinch, snap, tear, wound ◆ noun 2 <u>wound</u>, nip, pinch, prick, smarting, sting, tooth marks 3 <u>snack</u>, food, light meal, morsel, mouthful, piece, refreshment, taste

biting adjective 1 <u>piercing</u>, bitter, cutting, harsh, penetrating, sharp 2 <u>sarcastic</u>, caustic, cutting, incisive, mordant, scathing, stinging, trenchant, vitriolic

bitter adjective 1 <u>sour</u>, acid, acrid, astringent, harsh, sharp, tart, unsweetened, vinegary 2 <u>resentful</u>, acrimonious, begrudging, hostile, sore, sour, sullen **3** <u>freezing</u>, biting, fierce, intense, severe, stinging

bitterness *noun* **1** <u>sourness</u>, acerbity, acidity, sharpness, tartness **2** <u>resentment</u>, acrimony, animosity, asperity, grudge, hostility, rancour, sarcasm

bizarre *adjective* <u>strange</u>, eccentric, extraordinary, fantastic, freakish, ludicrous, outlandish, peculiar, unusual, weird, zany

blab *verb* <u>tell</u>, blurt out, disclose, divulge, give away, let slip, let the cat out of the bag, reveal, spill the beans (*informal*)

black *adjective* **1** <u>dark</u>, dusky, ebony, jet, raven, sable, swarthy **2** <u>hopeless</u>, depressing, dismal, foreboding, gloomy, ominous, sad, sombre **3** <u>angry</u>, furious, hostile, menacing, resentful, sullen, threatening **4** <u>wicked</u>, bad, evil, iniquitous, nefarious, villainous ♦ *verb* **5** <u>boycott</u>, ban, bar, blacklist

blacken *verb* **1** <u>darken</u>, befoul, begrime, cloud, dirty, make black, smudge, soil **2** <u>discredit</u>, defame, denigrate, malign, slander, smear, smirch, vilify

blackguard *noun* <u>scoundrel</u>, bastard (*offensive*), bounder (*old-fashioned Brit. slang*), rascal, rogue, swine, villain

blacklist *verb* <u>exclude</u>, ban, bar, boycott, debar, expel, reject, snub

black magic *noun* <u>witchcraft</u>, black art, diabolism, necromancy, sorcery, voodoo, wizardry

blackmail *noun* **1** <u>threat</u>, extortion, hush money (*slang*), intimidation, ransom ♦ *verb* **2** <u>threaten</u>, coerce, compel, demand, extort, hold to ransom, intimidate, squeeze

blackness *noun* <u>darkness</u>, duskiness, gloom, murkiness, swarthiness

blackout *noun* **1** <u>unconsciousness</u>, coma, faint, loss of consciousness, oblivion, swoon **2** <u>noncommunication</u>, censorship, radio silence, secrecy, suppression, withholding news

black sheep *noun* <u>disgrace</u>, bad egg (*old-fashioned informal*), dropout, ne'er-do-well, outcast, prodigal, renegade, reprobate, wastrel

blame *verb* **1** <u>hold responsible</u>, accuse, censure, chide, condemn, criticize, find fault with, reproach ♦ *noun* **2** <u>responsibility</u>, accountability, culpability, fault, guilt, liability, onus

blameless *adjective* <u>innocent</u>, above suspicion, clean, faultless, guiltless, immaculate, impeccable, irreproachable, perfect, unblemished, virtuous

blameworthy *adjective* <u>reprehensible</u>, discreditable, disreputable, indefensible, inexcusable, iniquitous, reproachable, shameful

bland *adjective* <u>dull</u>, boring, flat, humdrum, insipid, tasteless, unexciting, uninspiring, vapid

blank *adjective* **1** <u>unmarked</u>, bare, clean, clear, empty, plain, void, white **2** <u>expressionless</u>, deadpan, empty, impassive, poker-faced

(*informal*), vacant, vague ♦ *noun*
3 <u>empty space</u>, emptiness, gap,
nothingness, space, vacancy,
vacuum, void

blanket *noun* 1 <u>cover</u>, coverlet,
rug 2 <u>covering</u>, carpet, cloak,
coat, layer, mantle, sheet ♦ *verb*
3 <u>cover</u>, cloak, coat, conceal,
hide, mask, obscure, suppress

blare *verb* <u>sound out</u>, blast,
clamour, clang, resound, roar,
scream, trumpet

blarney *noun* <u>flattery</u>,
blandishment, cajolery, coaxing,
soft soap (*informal*), spiel, sweet
talk (*informal*), wheedling

blasé *adjective* <u>indifferent</u>,
apathetic, lukewarm,
nonchalant, offhand,
unconcerned

blaspheme *verb* <u>curse</u>, abuse,
damn, desecrate, execrate,
profane, revile, swear

blasphemous *adjective*
<u>irreverent</u>, godless, impious,
irreligious, profane, sacrilegious,
ungodly

blasphemy *noun* <u>irreverence</u>,
cursing, desecration, execration,
impiety, profanity, sacrilege,
swearing

blast *noun* 1 <u>explosion</u>, bang,
burst, crash, detonation,
discharge, eruption, outburst,
salvo, volley 2 <u>gust</u>, gale, squall,
storm, strong breeze, tempest
3 <u>blare</u>, blow, clang, honk, peal,
scream, toot, wail ♦ *verb* 4 <u>blow
up</u>, break up, burst, demolish,
destroy, explode, put paid to,
ruin, shatter

blastoff *noun* <u>launch</u>, discharge,
expulsion, firing, launching,
liftoff, projection, shot

blatant *adjective* <u>obvious</u>, brazen,
conspicuous, flagrant, glaring,
obtrusive, ostentatious, overt

blaze *noun* 1 <u>fire</u>, bonfire,
conflagration, flames 2 <u>glare</u>,
beam, brilliance, flare, flash,
gleam, glitter, glow, light,
radiance ♦ *verb* 3 <u>burn</u>, fire,
flame 4 <u>shine</u>, beam, flare, flash,
glare, gleam, glow

bleach *verb* <u>whiten</u>, blanch, fade,
grow pale, lighten, wash out

bleak *adjective* 1 <u>exposed</u>, bare,
barren, desolate, unsheltered,
weather-beaten, windswept
2 <u>dismal</u>, cheerless, depressing,
discouraging, dreary, gloomy,
grim, hopeless, joyless, sombre

bleary *adjective* <u>dim</u>, blurred,
blurry, foggy, fuzzy, hazy,
indistinct, misty, murky

bleed *verb* 1 <u>lose blood</u>, flow,
gush, ooze, run, shed blood,
spurt 2 <u>draw or take blood</u>,
extract, leech 3 *Informal* <u>extort</u>,
drain, exhaust, fleece, milk,
squeeze

blemish *noun* 1 <u>mark</u>, blot,
defect, disfigurement, fault, flaw,
imperfection, smudge, stain,
taint ♦ *verb* 2 <u>stain</u>, damage,
disfigure, impair, injure, mar,
mark, spoil, sully, taint, tarnish

blend *verb* 1 <u>mix</u>, amalgamate,
combine, compound, merge,
mingle, unite 2 <u>go well</u>,
complement, fit, go with,
harmonize, suit ♦ *noun*
3 <u>mixture</u>, alloy, amalgamation,
combination, compound,
concoction, mix, synthesis, union

bless *verb* 1 <u>sanctify</u>, anoint,
consecrate, dedicate, exalt,
hallow, ordain 2 <u>grant</u>, bestow,

favour, give, grace, provide

blessed *adjective* <u>holy</u>, adored, beatified, divine, hallowed, revered, sacred, sanctified

blessing *noun* **1** <u>benediction</u>, benison, commendation, consecration, dedication, grace, invocation, thanksgiving **2** <u>approval</u>, backing, consent, favour, good wishes, leave, permission, sanction, support **3** <u>benefit</u>, favour, gift, godsend, good fortune, help, kindness, service, windfall

blight *noun* **1** <u>curse</u>, affliction, bane, contamination, corruption, evil, plague, pollution, scourge, woe **2** <u>disease</u>, canker, decay, fungus, infestation, mildew, pest, pestilence, rot ♦ *verb* **3** <u>frustrate</u>, crush, dash, disappoint, mar, ruin, spoil, undo, wreck

blind *adjective* **1** <u>sightless</u>, eyeless, unseeing, unsighted, visionless **2** <u>unaware of</u>, careless, heedless, ignorant, inattentive, inconsiderate, indifferent, insensitive, oblivious, unconscious of **3** <u>unreasoning</u>, indiscriminate, prejudiced ♦ *noun* **4** <u>cover</u>, camouflage, cloak, façade, feint, front, mask, masquerade, screen, smoke screen

blindly *adverb* **1** <u>thoughtlessly</u>, carelessly, heedlessly, inconsiderately, recklessly, senselessly **2** <u>aimlessly</u>, at random, indiscriminately, instinctively

blink *verb* **1** <u>wink</u>, bat, flutter **2** <u>flicker</u>, flash, gleam, glimmer, shine, twinkle, wink ♦ *noun* **3 on the blink** *Slang* <u>not working</u>

(properly), faulty, malfunctioning, out of action, out of order, playing up

bliss *noun* <u>joy</u>, beatitude, blessedness, blissfulness, ecstasy, euphoria, felicity, gladness, happiness, heaven, nirvana, paradise, rapture

blissful *adjective* <u>joyful</u>, ecstatic, elated, enraptured, euphoric, happy, heavenly (*informal*), rapturous

blister *noun* <u>sore</u>, abscess, boil, carbuncle, cyst, pimple, pustule, swelling

blithe *adjective* <u>heedless</u>, careless, casual, indifferent, nonchalant, thoughtless, unconcerned, untroubled

blitz *noun* <u>attack</u>, assault, blitzkrieg, bombardment, campaign, offensive, onslaught, raid, strike

blizzard *noun* <u>snowstorm</u>, blast, gale, squall, storm, tempest

bloat *verb* <u>puff up</u>, balloon, blow up, dilate, distend, enlarge, expand, inflate, swell

blob *noun* <u>drop</u>, ball, bead, bubble, dab, droplet, globule, lump, mass

bloc *noun* <u>group</u>, alliance, axis, coalition, faction, league, union

block *noun* **1** <u>piece</u>, bar, brick, chunk, hunk, ingot, lump, mass **2** <u>obstruction</u>, bar, barrier, blockage, hindrance, impediment, jam, obstacle ♦ *verb* **3** <u>obstruct</u>, bung up (*informal*), choke, clog, close, plug, stem the flow, stop up **4** <u>stop</u>, bar, check, halt, hinder, impede, obstruct, thwart

blockade noun <u>stoppage</u>, barricade, barrier, block, hindrance, impediment, obstacle, obstruction, restriction, siege

blockage noun <u>obstruction</u>, block, impediment, occlusion, stoppage

blockhead noun <u>idiot</u>, chump (informal), dunce, fool, nitwit, numbskull or numskull, thickhead, twit (informal, chiefly Brit.)

bloke noun Informal <u>man</u>, chap, character (informal), fellow, guy (informal), individual, person

blond, blonde adjective <u>fair</u>, fair-haired, fair-skinned, flaxen, golden-haired, light, tow-headed

blood noun 1 <u>lifeblood</u>, gore, vital fluid 2 <u>family</u>, ancestry, birth, descent, extraction, kinship, lineage, relations

bloodcurdling adjective <u>terrifying</u>, appalling, chilling, dreadful, fearful, frightening, hair-raising, horrendous, horrifying, scaring, spine-chilling

bloodshed noun <u>killing</u>, blood bath, blood-letting, butchery, carnage, gore, massacre, murder, slaughter, slaying

bloodthirsty adjective <u>cruel</u>, barbarous, brutal, cut-throat, ferocious, gory, murderous, savage, vicious, warlike

bloody adjective 1 <u>bloodstained</u>, bleeding, blood-soaked, blood-spattered, gaping, raw 2 <u>cruel</u>, ferocious, fierce, sanguinary, savage

bloom noun 1 <u>flower</u>, blossom, blossoming, bud, efflorescence,

opening (of flowers) 2 <u>prime</u>, beauty, flourishing, freshness, glow, health, heyday, lustre, radiance, vigour ♦ verb 3 <u>blossom</u>, blow, bud, burgeon, open, sprout 4 <u>flourish</u>, develop, fare well, grow, prosper, succeed, thrive, wax

blossom noun 1 <u>flower</u>, bloom, bud, floret, flowers ♦ verb 2 <u>flower</u>, bloom, burgeon 3 <u>grow</u>, bloom, develop, flourish, mature, progress, prosper, thrive

blot noun 1 <u>spot</u>, blotch, mark, patch, smear, smudge, speck, splodge 2 <u>stain</u>, blemish, defect, fault, flaw, scar, spot, taint ♦ verb 3 <u>stain</u>, disgrace, mark, smirch, smudge, spoil, spot, sully, tarnish 4 <u>soak up</u>, absorb, dry, take up 5 <u>blot out</u> a <u>obliterate</u>, darken, destroy, eclipse, efface, obscure, shadow b <u>erase</u>, cancel, expunge

blow[1] verb 1 <u>carry</u>, buffet, drive, fling, flutter, move, sweep, waft 2 <u>exhale</u>, breathe, pant, puff 3 <u>play</u>, blare, mouth, pipe, sound, toot, trumpet, vibrate

blow[2] noun 1 <u>knock</u>, bang, clout (informal), punch, smack, sock (slang), stroke, thump, wallop (informal), whack 2 <u>setback</u>, bombshell, calamity, catastrophe, disappointment, disaster, misfortune, reverse, shock

blow out verb 1 <u>put out</u>, extinguish, snuff 2 <u>burst</u>, erupt, explode, rupture, shatter

blow up verb 1 <u>explode</u>, blast, blow sky-high, bomb, burst, detonate, rupture, shatter

2 <u>inflate</u>, bloat, distend, enlarge, expand, fill, puff up, pump up, swell 3 *Informal* <u>lose one's temper</u>, become angry, erupt, fly off the handle (*informal*), hit the roof (*informal*), rage, see red (*informal*)

bludgeon *noun* 1 <u>club</u>, cosh (*Brit.*), cudgel, truncheon ◆ *verb* 2 <u>club</u>, beat up, cosh (*Brit.*), cudgel, knock down, strike 3 <u>bully</u>, bulldoze (*informal*), coerce, force, railroad (*informal*), steamroller

blue *adjective* 1 <u>azure</u>, cerulean, cobalt, cyan, navy, sapphire, sky-coloured, ultramarine 2 <u>depressed</u>, dejected, despondent, downcast, low, melancholy, sad, unhappy 3 <u>smutty</u>, indecent, lewd, obscene, risqué, X-rated (*informal*)

blueprint *noun* <u>plan</u>, design, draft, outline, pattern, pilot scheme, prototype, sketch

blues *plural noun* <u>depression</u>, doldrums, dumps (*informal*), gloom, low spirits, melancholy, unhappiness

bluff¹ *verb* 1 <u>deceive</u>, con, delude, fake, feign, mislead, pretend, pull the wool over someone's eyes ◆ *noun* 2 <u>deception</u>, bluster, bravado, deceit, fraud, humbug, pretence, sham, subterfuge

bluff² *noun* 1 <u>precipice</u>, bank, cliff, crag, escarpment, headland, peak, promontory, ridge ◆ *adjective* 2 <u>hearty</u>, blunt, blustering, genial, good-natured, open, outspoken, plain-spoken

blunder *noun* 1 <u>mistake</u>, bloomer (*Brit. informal*), clanger (*informal*), faux pas, gaffe, howler (*informal*), indiscretion 2 <u>error</u>, fault, inaccuracy, mistake, oversight, slip, slip-up (*informal*) ◆ *verb* 3 <u>make a mistake</u>, botch, bungle, err, put one's foot in it (*informal*), slip up (*informal*) 4 <u>stumble</u>, bumble, flounder

blunt *adjective* 1 <u>dull</u>, dulled, edgeless, pointless, rounded, unsharpened 2 <u>forthright</u>, bluff, brusque, frank, outspoken, plain-spoken, rude, straightforward, tactless ◆ *verb* 3 <u>dull</u>, dampen, deaden, numb, soften, take the edge off, water down, weaken

blur *verb* 1 <u>make indistinct</u>, cloud, darken, make hazy, make vague, mask, obscure ◆ *noun* 2 <u>indistinctness</u>, confusion, fog, haze, obscurity

blurt out *verb* <u>exclaim</u>, disclose, let the cat out of the bag, reveal, spill the beans (*informal*), tell all, utter suddenly

blush *verb* 1 <u>turn red</u>, colour, flush, go red (as a beetroot), redden, turn scarlet ◆ *noun* 2 <u>reddening</u>, colour, flush, glow, pink tinge, rosiness, rosy tint, ruddiness

bluster *verb* 1 <u>roar</u>, bully, domineer, hector, rant, storm ◆ *noun* 2 <u>hot air</u> (*informal*), bluff, bombast, bravado

blustery *adjective* <u>gusty</u>, boisterous, inclement, squally, stormy, tempestuous, violent, wild, windy

board *noun* 1 <u>plank</u>, panel, piece of timber, slat, timber 2 <u>directors</u>, advisers, committee,

conclave, council, panel, trustees
3 <u>meals</u>, daily meals, provisions, victuals ♦ *verb* **4** <u>get on</u>, embark, enter, mount **5** <u>lodge</u>, put up, quarter, room

boast *verb* **1** <u>brag</u>, blow one's own trumpet, crow, strut, swagger, talk big (*slang*), vaunt **2** <u>possess</u>, be proud of, congratulate oneself on, exhibit, flatter oneself, pride oneself on, show off ♦ *noun* **3** <u>brag</u>, avowal

boastful *adjective* <u>bragging</u>, cocky, conceited, crowing, egotistical, full of oneself, swaggering, swollen-headed, vaunting

bob *verb* <u>duck</u>, bounce, hop, nod, oscillate, waggle, wobble

bode *verb* <u>portend</u>, augur, be an omen of, forebode, foretell, predict, signify, threaten

bodily *adjective* <u>physical</u>, actual, carnal, corporal, corporeal, material, substantial, tangible

body *noun* **1** <u>physique</u>, build, figure, form, frame, shape **2** <u>torso</u>, trunk **3** <u>corpse</u>, cadaver, carcass, dead body, remains, stiff (*slang*) **4** <u>organization</u>, association, band, bloc, collection, company, confederation, congress, corporation, society **5** <u>main part</u>, bulk, essence, mass, material, matter, substance

boffin *noun Brit. informal* <u>expert</u>, brainbox, egghead, genius, intellectual, inventor, mastermind

bog *noun* <u>marsh</u>, fen, mire, morass, quagmire, slough, swamp, wetlands

bogey *noun* <u>bugbear</u>, bête noire, bugaboo, nightmare

bogus *adjective* <u>fake</u>, artificial, counterfeit, false, forged, fraudulent, imitation, phoney *or* phony (*informal*), sham

bohemian *adjective*
1 <u>unconventional</u>, alternative, artistic, arty (*informal*), left bank, nonconformist, offbeat, unorthodox ♦ *noun*
2 <u>nonconformist</u>, beatnik, dropout, hippy, iconoclast

boil[1] *verb* <u>bubble</u>, effervesce, fizz, foam, froth, seethe

boil[2] *noun* <u>pustule</u>, blister, carbuncle, gathering, swelling, tumour, ulcer

boisterous *adjective* <u>unruly</u>, disorderly, loud, noisy, riotous, rollicking, rowdy, unrestrained, vociferous, wild

bold *adjective* **1** <u>fearless</u>, adventurous, audacious, brave, courageous, daring, enterprising, heroic, intrepid, valiant **2** <u>impudent</u>, barefaced, brazen, cheeky, confident, forward, insolent, rude, shameless

bolster *verb* <u>support</u>, augment, boost, help, reinforce, shore up, strengthen

bolt *noun* **1** <u>bar</u>, catch, fastener, latch, lock, sliding bar **2** <u>pin</u>, peg, rivet, rod ♦ *verb* **3** <u>run away</u>, abscond, dash, escape, flee, fly, make a break (for it), run for it **4** <u>lock</u>, bar, fasten, latch, secure **5** <u>gobble</u>, cram, devour, gorge, gulp, guzzle, stuff, swallow whole, wolf

bomb *noun* **1** <u>explosive</u>, device, grenade, mine, missile, projectile, rocket, shell, torpedo ♦ *verb* **2** <u>blow up</u>, attack, blow sky-high, bombard, destroy, shell, strafe, torpedo

bombard verb **1** <u>bomb</u>, assault, blitz, fire upon, open fire, pound, shell, strafe **2** <u>attack</u>, assail, beset, besiege, harass, hound, pester

bombardment noun <u>bombing</u>, assault, attack, barrage, blitz, fusillade, shelling

bombastic adjective <u>grandiloquent</u>, grandiose, high-flown, inflated, pompous, verbose, wordy

bona fide adjective <u>genuine</u>, actual, authentic, honest, kosher (informal), legitimate, real, true

bond noun **1** <u>fastening</u>, chain, cord, fetter, ligature, manacle, shackle, tie **2** <u>tie</u>, affiliation, affinity, attachment, connection, link, relation, union **3** <u>agreement</u>, contract, covenant, guarantee, obligation, pledge, promise, word ♦ verb **4** <u>hold together</u>, bind, connect, fasten, fix together, glue, paste

bondage noun <u>slavery</u>, captivity, confinement, enslavement, imprisonment, subjugation

bonus noun <u>extra</u>, dividend, gift, icing on the cake, plus, premium, prize, reward

bony adjective <u>thin</u>, emaciated, gaunt, lean, scrawny, skin and bone, skinny

book noun **1** <u>work</u>, publication, title, tome, tract, volume **2** <u>notebook</u>, album, diary, exercise book, jotter, pad ♦ verb **3** <u>reserve</u>, arrange for, charter, engage, make reservations, organize, programme, schedule **4** <u>note</u>, enter, list, log, mark down, put down, record,

register, write down

booklet noun <u>brochure</u>, leaflet, pamphlet

boom verb **1** <u>bang</u>, blast, crash, explode, resound, reverberate, roar, roll, rumble, thunder **2** <u>flourish</u>, develop, expand, grow, increase, intensify, prosper, strengthen, swell, thrive ♦ noun **3** <u>bang</u>, blast, burst, clap, crash, explosion, roar, rumble, thunder **4** <u>expansion</u>, boost, development, growth, improvement, increase, jump, upsurge, upswing, upturn

boon noun <u>benefit</u>, advantage, blessing, favour, gift, godsend, manna from heaven, windfall

boorish adjective <u>loutish</u>, churlish, coarse, crude, oafish, uncivilized, uncouth, vulgar

boost noun **1** <u>help</u>, encouragement, praise, promotion **2** <u>rise</u>, addition, expansion, improvement, increase, increment, jump ♦ verb **3** <u>increase</u>, add to, amplify, develop, enlarge, expand, heighten, raise **4** <u>advertise</u>, encourage, foster, further, hype, plug (informal), praise, promote

boot verb <u>kick</u>, drive, drop-kick, knock, punt, put the boot in(to) (slang), shove

booty noun <u>plunder</u>, gains, haul, loot, prey, spoils, swag (slang), takings, winnings

border noun **1** <u>frontier</u>, borderline, boundary, line, march **2** <u>edge</u>, bounds, brink, limits, margin, rim, verge ♦ verb **3** <u>edge</u>, bind, decorate, fringe, hem, rim, trim

bore¹ verb <u>drill</u>, burrow, gouge

out, mine, penetrate, perforate, pierce, sink, tunnel

bore² verb 1 <u>tire</u>, be tedious, fatigue, jade, pall on, send to sleep, wear out, weary ♦ noun 2 <u>nuisance</u>, anorak (informal), pain (informal), yawn (informal)

bored adjective <u>fed up</u>, listless, tired, uninterested, wearied

boredom noun <u>tedium</u>, apathy, ennui, flatness, monotony, sameness, tediousness, weariness, world-weariness

boring adjective <u>uninteresting</u>, dull, flat, humdrum, mind-numbing, monotonous, tedious, tiresome

borrow verb 1 <u>take on loan</u>, cadge, scrounge (informal), touch (someone) for (slang), use temporarily 2 <u>steal</u>, adopt, copy, obtain, plagiarize, take, usurp

bosom noun 1 <u>breast</u>, bust, chest ♦ adjective 2 <u>intimate</u>, boon, cherished, close, confidential, dear, very dear

boss¹ noun <u>head</u>, chief, director, employer, gaffer (informal, chiefly Brit.), leader, manager, master, supervisor

boss² noun <u>stud</u>, knob, point, protuberance, tip

boss around verb Informal <u>domineer</u>, bully, dominate, oppress, order, push around (slang)

bossy adjective <u>domineering</u>, arrogant, authoritarian, autocratic, dictatorial, hectoring, high-handed, imperious, overbearing, tyrannical

botch verb 1 <u>spoil</u>, blunder, bungle, cock up (Brit. slang),

make a pig's ear of (informal), mar, mess up, screw up (informal) ♦ noun 2 <u>mess</u>, blunder, bungle, cock-up (Brit. slang), failure, hash, pig's ear (informal)

bother verb 1 <u>trouble</u>, alarm, concern, disturb, harass, hassle (informal), inconvenience, pester, plague, worry ♦ noun 2 <u>trouble</u>, difficulty, fuss, hassle (informal), inconvenience, irritation, nuisance, problem, worry

bottleneck noun <u>hold-up</u>, block, blockage, congestion, impediment, jam, obstacle, obstruction, snarl-up (informal, chiefly Brit.)

bottle up verb <u>suppress</u>, check, contain, curb, keep back, restrict, shut in, trap

bottom noun 1 <u>lowest part</u>, base, bed, depths, floor, foot, foundation 2 <u>underside</u>, lower side, sole, underneath 3 <u>buttocks</u>, backside, behind (informal), posterior, rear, rump, seat ♦ adjective 4 <u>lowest</u>, last

bottomless adjective <u>unlimited</u>, boundless, deep, fathomless, immeasurable, inexhaustible, infinite, unfathomable

bounce verb 1 <u>rebound</u>, bob, bound, jump, leap, recoil, ricochet, spring ♦ noun 2 Informal <u>life</u>, dynamism, energy, go (informal), liveliness, vigour, vivacity, zip (informal) 3 <u>springiness</u>, elasticity, give, recoil, resilience, spring

bound¹ adjective 1 <u>tied</u>, cased, fastened, fixed, pinioned, secured, tied up 2 <u>certain</u>, destined, doomed, fated, sure

3 obliged, beholden, committed, compelled, constrained, duty-bound, forced, pledged, required

bound² verb limit, confine, demarcate, encircle, enclose, hem in, restrain, restrict, surround

bound³ verb, noun leap, bob, bounce, gambol, hurdle, jump, skip, spring, vault

boundary noun limits, barrier, border, borderline, brink, edge, extremity, fringe, frontier, margin

boundless adjective unlimited, endless, immense, incalculable, inexhaustible, infinite, unconfined, untold, vast

bounds plural noun boundary, border, confine, edge, extremity, limit, rim, verge

bountiful adjective Literary **1** plentiful, abundant, ample, bounteous, copious, exuberant, lavish, luxuriant, prolific **2** generous, liberal, magnanimous, open-handed, prodigal, unstinting

bounty noun Literary **1** generosity, benevolence, charity, kindness, largesse or largess, liberality, philanthropy **2** reward, bonus, gift, present

bouquet noun **1** bunch of flowers, buttonhole, corsage, garland, nosegay, posy, spray, wreath **2** aroma, fragrance, perfume, redolence, savour, scent

bourgeois adjective middle-class, conventional, hidebound, materialistic, traditional

bout noun **1** period, fit, spell, stint, term, turn **2** fight, boxing

match, competition, contest, encounter, engagement, match, set-to, struggle

bow¹ verb **1** bend, bob, droop, genuflect, nod, stoop **2** give in, acquiesce, comply, concede, defer, kowtow, relent, submit, succumb, surrender, yield ♦ noun **3** bending, bob, genuflexion, kowtow, nod, obeisance

bow² noun Nautical prow, beak, fore, head, stem

bowels plural noun **1** guts, entrails, innards (informal), insides (informal), intestines, viscera, vitals **2** depths, belly, core, deep, hold, inside, interior

bowl¹ noun basin, dish, vessel

bowl² verb throw, fling, hurl, pitch

box¹ noun **1** container, carton, case, casket, chest, pack, package, receptacle, trunk ♦ verb **2** pack, package, wrap

box² verb fight, exchange blows, spar

boxer noun fighter, prizefighter, pugilist, sparring partner

boy noun lad, fellow, junior, schoolboy, stripling, youngster, youth

boycott verb embargo, ban, bar, black, exclude, outlaw, prohibit, refuse, reject

boyfriend noun sweetheart, admirer, beau, date, lover, man, suitor

boyish adjective youthful, adolescent, childish, immature, juvenile, puerile, young

brace noun **1** support, bolster, bracket, buttress, prop, reinforcement, stay, strut, truss ♦ verb **2** support, bolster, buttress, fortify, reinforce, steady, strengthen

bracing adjective <u>refreshing</u>, brisk, crisp, exhilarating, fresh, invigorating, stimulating

brag verb <u>boast</u>, blow one's own trumpet, bluster, crow, swagger, talk big (slang), vaunt

braggart noun <u>boaster</u>, bigmouth (slang), bragger, show-off (informal)

braid verb <u>interweave</u>, entwine, interlace, intertwine, lace, plait, twine, weave

brainless adjective <u>stupid</u>, foolish, idiotic, inane, mindless, senseless, thoughtless, witless

brains plural noun <u>intelligence</u>, intellect, sense, understanding

brainwave noun <u>idea</u>, bright idea, stroke of genius, thought

brainy adjective Informal <u>intelligent</u>, bright, brilliant, clever, smart

brake noun 1 <u>control</u>, check, constraint, curb, rein, restraint ♦ verb 2 <u>slow</u>, check, decelerate, halt, moderate, reduce speed, slacken, stop

branch noun 1 <u>bough</u>, arm, limb, offshoot, shoot, spray, sprig 2 <u>division</u>, chapter, department, office, part, section, subdivision, subsection, wing

brand noun 1 <u>label</u>, emblem, hallmark, logo, mark, marker, sign, stamp, symbol, trademark 2 <u>kind</u>, cast, class, grade, make, quality, sort, species, type, variety ♦ verb 3 <u>mark</u>, burn, burn in, label, scar, stamp 4 <u>stigmatize</u>, censure, denounce, discredit, disgrace, expose, mark

brandish verb <u>wave</u>, display, exhibit, flaunt, flourish, parade, raise, shake, swing, wield

brash adjective <u>bold</u>, brazen, cocky, impertinent, impudent, insolent, pushy (informal), rude

bravado noun <u>swagger</u>, bluster, boastfulness, boasting, bombast, swashbuckling, vaunting

brave adjective 1 <u>courageous</u>, bold, daring, fearless, heroic, intrepid, plucky, resolute, valiant ♦ verb 2 <u>confront</u>, defy, endure, face, stand up to, suffer, tackle, withstand

bravery noun <u>courage</u>, boldness, daring, fearlessness, fortitude, heroism, intrepidity, mettle, pluck, spirit, valour

brawl noun 1 <u>fight</u>, affray (Law), altercation, clash, dispute, fracas, fray, melee or mêlée, punch-up (Brit. informal), rumpus, scuffle, skirmish ♦ verb 2 <u>fight</u>, scrap (informal), scuffle, tussle, wrestle

brawn noun <u>muscle</u>, beef (informal), might, muscles, power, strength, vigour

brawny adjective <u>muscular</u>, beefy (informal), hefty (informal), lusty, powerful, strapping, strong, sturdy, well-built

brazen adjective <u>bold</u>, audacious, barefaced, brash, defiant, impudent, insolent, shameless, unabashed, unashamed

breach noun 1 <u>nonobservance</u>, contravention, infraction, infringement, noncompliance, transgression, trespass, violation 2 <u>crack</u>, cleft, fissure, gap, opening, rift, rupture, split

bread noun 1 <u>food</u>, fare,

nourishment, sustenance **2** *Slang* money, cash, dough (*slang*)

breadth *noun* **1** <u>width</u>, broadness, latitude, span, spread, wideness **2** <u>extent</u>, compass, expanse, range, scale, scope

break *verb* **1** <u>separate</u>, burst, crack, destroy, disintegrate, fracture, fragment, shatter, smash, snap, split, tear **2** <u>disobey</u>, breach, contravene, disregard, infringe, renege on, transgress, violate **3** <u>reveal</u>, announce, disclose, divulge, impart, inform, let out, make public, proclaim, tell **4** <u>stop</u>, abandon, cut, discontinue, give up, interrupt, pause, rest, suspend **5** <u>weaken</u>, demoralize, dispirit, subdue, tame, undermine **6** *Of a record, etc.* <u>beat</u>, better, exceed, excel, go beyond, outdo, outstrip, surpass, top ♦ *noun* **7** <u>division</u>, crack, fissure, fracture, gap, hole, opening, split, tear **8** <u>rest</u>, breather (*informal*), hiatus, interlude, intermission, interruption, interval, let-up (*informal*), lull, pause, respite **9** *Informal* <u>stroke of luck</u>, advantage, chance, fortune, opening, opportunity

breakable *adjective* <u>fragile</u>, brittle, crumbly, delicate, flimsy, frail, frangible, friable

breakdown *noun* <u>collapse</u>, disintegration, disruption, failure, mishap, stoppage

break down *verb* **1** <u>collapse</u>, come unstuck, fail, seize up, stop, stop working **2** <u>be overcome</u>, crack up (*informal*),

go to pieces

break-in *noun* <u>burglary</u>, breaking and entering, robbery

break off *verb* **1** <u>detach</u>, divide, part, pull off, separate, sever, snap off, splinter **2** <u>stop</u>, cease, desist, discontinue, end, finish, halt, pull the plug on, suspend, terminate

break out *verb* <u>begin</u>, appear, arise, commence, emerge, happen, occur, set in, spring up, start

breakthrough *noun* <u>development</u>, advance, discovery, find, invention, leap, progress, quantum leap, step forward

break up *verb* **1** <u>separate</u>, dissolve, divide, divorce, part, scatter, sever, split **2** <u>stop</u>, adjourn, disband, dismantle, end, suspend, terminate

breast *noun* <u>bosom</u>, bust, chest, front, teat, udder

breath *noun* <u>respiration</u>, breathing, exhalation, gasp, gulp, inhalation, pant, wheeze

breathe *verb* **1** <u>inhale and exhale</u>, draw in, gasp, gulp, pant, puff, respire, wheeze **2** <u>whisper</u>, murmur, sigh

breather *noun* *Informal* <u>rest</u>, break, breathing space, halt, pause, recess, respite

breathless *adjective* **1** <u>out of breath</u>, gasping, gulping, panting, short-winded, spent, wheezing **2** <u>excited</u>, eager, on tenterhooks, open-mouthed, with bated breath

breathtaking *adjective* <u>amazing</u>, astonishing, awe-inspiring, exciting, impressive, magnificent, sensational, stunning (*informal*), thrilling

breed *verb* 1 <u>reproduce</u>, bear, bring forth, hatch, multiply, procreate, produce, propagate 2 <u>bring up</u>, cultivate, develop, nourish, nurture, raise, rear 3 <u>produce</u>, arouse, bring about, cause, create, generate, give rise to, stir up ♦ *noun* 4 <u>variety</u>, pedigree, race, species, stock, strain, type 5 <u>kind</u>, brand, sort, stamp, type, variety

breeding *noun* 1 <u>upbringing</u>, ancestry, cultivation, development, lineage, nurture, raising, rearing, reproduction, training 2 <u>refinement</u>, conduct, courtesy, cultivation, culture, polish, sophistication, urbanity

breeze *noun* 1 <u>light wind</u>, air, breath of wind, current of air, draught, gust, waft, zephyr ♦ *verb* 2 <u>move briskly</u>, flit, glide, hurry, pass, sail, sweep

breezy *adjective* 1 <u>windy</u>, airy, blowy, blustery, fresh, gusty, squally 2 <u>carefree</u>, blithe, casual, easy-going, free and easy, jaunty, light-hearted, lively, sprightly

brevity *noun* 1 <u>shortness</u>, briefness, impermanence, transience, transitoriness 2 <u>conciseness</u>, crispness, curtness, economy, pithiness, succinctness, terseness

brew *verb* 1 <u>make</u> (*beer*), boil, ferment, infuse (*tea*), soak, steep, stew 2 <u>develop</u>, foment, form, gather, start, stir up ♦ *noun* 3 <u>drink</u>, beverage, blend, concoction, infusion, liquor, mixture, preparation

bribe *verb* 1 <u>buy off</u>, corrupt, grease the palm *or* hand of (*slang*), pay off (*informal*), reward, suborn ♦ *noun* 2 <u>inducement</u>, allurement, backhander (*slang*), enticement, kickback (*U.S.*), pay-off (*informal*), sweetener (*slang*)

bribery *noun* <u>buying off</u>, corruption, inducement, palm-greasing (*slang*), payola (*informal*)

bric-a-brac *noun* <u>knick-knacks</u>, baubles, curios, ornaments, trinkets

bridal *adjective* <u>matrimonial</u>, conjugal, connubial, marital, marriage, nuptial, wedding

bridge *noun* 1 <u>arch</u>, flyover, overpass, span, viaduct ♦ *verb* 2 <u>connect</u>, join, link, span

bridle *noun* 1 <u>curb</u>, check, control, rein, restraint ♦ *verb* 2 <u>get angry</u>, be indignant, bristle, draw (oneself) up, get one's back up, raise one's hackles, rear up

brief *adjective* 1 <u>short</u>, ephemeral, fleeting, momentary, quick, short-lived, swift, transitory ♦ *noun* 2 <u>summary</u>, abridgment, abstract, digest, epitome, outline, précis, sketch, synopsis ♦ *verb* 3 <u>inform</u>, advise, explain, fill in (*informal*), instruct, keep posted, prepare, prime, put (someone) in the picture (*informal*)

briefing *noun* <u>instructions</u>, conference, directions, guidance, information, preparation, priming, rundown

briefly *adverb* <u>shortly</u>, concisely,

hastily, hurriedly, in a nutshell, in brief, momentarily, quickly

brigade *noun* group, band, company, corps, force, organization, outfit, squad, team, troop, unit

brigand *noun* bandit, desperado, freebooter, gangster, highwayman, marauder, outlaw, plunderer, robber

bright *adjective* 1 shining, brilliant, dazzling, gleaming, glowing, luminous, lustrous, radiant, shimmering, vivid 2 intelligent, astute, aware, clever, inventive, quick-witted, sharp, smart, wide-awake 3 sunny, clear, cloudless, fair, limpid, lucid, pleasant, translucent, transparent, unclouded

brighten *verb* make brighter, gleam, glow, illuminate, lighten, light up, shine

brightness *noun* 1 shine, brilliance, glare, incandescence, intensity, light, luminosity, radiance, vividness 2 intelligence, acuity, cleverness, quickness, sharpness, smartness

brilliance, brilliancy *noun* 1 brightness, dazzle, intensity, luminosity, lustre, radiance, sparkle, vividness 2 talent, cleverness, distinction, excellence, genius, greatness, inventiveness, wisdom 3 splendour, éclat, glamour, grandeur, illustriousness, magnificence

brilliant *adjective* 1 shining, bright, dazzling, glittering, intense, luminous, radiant, sparkling, vivid 2 splendid,

celebrated, famous, glorious, illustrious, magnificent, notable, outstanding, superb 3 intelligent, clever, expert, gifted, intellectual, inventive, masterly, penetrating, profound, talented

brim *noun* 1 rim, border, brink, edge, lip, margin, skirt, verge ♦ *verb* 2 be full, fill, fill up, hold no more, overflow, run over, spill, well over

bring *verb* 1 take, bear, carry, conduct, convey, deliver, escort, fetch, guide, lead, transfer, transport 2 cause, contribute to, create, effect, inflict, occasion, produce, result in, wreak

bring about *verb* cause, accomplish, achieve, create, effect, generate, give rise to, make happen, produce

bring off *verb* accomplish, achieve, carry off, execute, perform, pull off, succeed

bring up *verb* 1 rear, breed, develop, educate, form, nurture, raise, support, teach, train 2 mention, allude to, broach, introduce, move, propose, put forward, raise

brink *noun* edge, border, boundary, brim, fringe, frontier, limit, lip, margin, rim, skirt, threshold, verge

brisk *adjective* lively, active, bustling, busy, energetic, quick, sprightly, spry, vigorous

briskly *adverb* quickly, actively, apace, efficiently, energetically, promptly, rapidly, readily, smartly

bristle *noun* 1 hair, barb, prickle, spine, stubble, thorn, whisker ♦ *verb* 2 stand up, rise, stand on end **3** <u>be angry</u>, bridle, flare up, rage, see red, seethe

bristly adjective <u>hairy</u>, prickly, rough, stubbly

brittle adjective <u>fragile</u>, breakable, crisp, crumbling, crumbly, delicate, frail, frangible, friable

broach verb **1** <u>bring up</u>, introduce, mention, open up, propose, raise the subject, speak of, suggest, talk of, touch on **2** <u>open</u>, crack, draw off, pierce, puncture, start, tap, uncork

broad adjective **1** <u>wide</u>, ample, expansive, extensive, generous, large, roomy, spacious, vast, voluminous, widespread **2** <u>general</u>, all-embracing, comprehensive, encyclopedic, inclusive, sweeping, wide, wide-ranging

broadcast noun **1** <u>transmission</u>, programme, show, telecast ♦ verb **2** <u>transmit</u>, air, beam, cable, put on the air, radio, relay, show, televise **3** <u>make public</u>, advertise, announce, circulate, proclaim, publish, report, spread

broaden verb <u>expand</u>, develop, enlarge, extend, increase, spread, stretch, supplement, swell, widen

broad-minded adjective <u>tolerant</u>, free-thinking, indulgent, liberal, open-minded, permissive, unbiased, unbigoted, unprejudiced

broadside noun <u>attack</u>, assault, battering, bombardment, censure, criticism, denunciation, diatribe

brochure noun <u>booklet</u>, advertisement, circular, folder,

handbill, hand-out, leaflet, mailshot, pamphlet

broke adjective Informal <u>penniless</u>, bankrupt, bust (informal), down and out, impoverished, insolvent, in the red, ruined, short, skint (Brit. slang)

broken adjective **1** <u>smashed</u>, burst, fractured, fragmented, ruptured, separated, severed, shattered **2** <u>interrupted</u>, discontinuous, erratic, fragmentary, incomplete, intermittent, spasmodic **3** <u>not working</u>, defective, imperfect, kaput (informal), on the blink (slang), out of order **4** <u>imperfect</u>, disjointed, halting, hesitating, stammering

brokenhearted adjective <u>heartbroken</u>, desolate, devastated, disconsolate, grief-stricken, inconsolable, miserable, sorrowful, wretched

broker noun <u>dealer</u>, agent, factor, go-between, intermediary, middleman, negotiator

bronze adjective <u>reddish-brown</u>, brownish, chestnut, copper, rust, tan

brood noun **1** <u>offspring</u>, clutch, family, issue, litter, progeny ♦ verb **2** <u>think upon</u>, agonize, dwell upon, mope, mull over, muse, ponder, ruminate

brook noun <u>stream</u>, beck, burn, rill, rivulet, watercourse

brother noun **1** <u>sibling</u>, blood brother, kin, kinsman, relation, relative **2** <u>monk</u>, cleric, friar

brotherhood noun **1** <u>fellowship</u>, brotherliness, camaraderie, companionship, comradeship,

friendliness, kinship
2 association, alliance, community, fraternity, guild, league, order, society, union

brotherly adjective kind, affectionate, altruistic, amicable, benevolent, cordial, fraternal, friendly, neighbourly, philanthropic, sympathetic

browbeat verb bully, badger, coerce, dragoon, hector, intimidate, ride roughshod over, threaten, tyrannize

brown adjective 1 brunette, auburn, bay, bronze, chestnut, chocolate, coffee, dun, hazel, sunburnt, tan, tanned, tawny, umber ♦ verb 2 fry, cook, grill, sauté, seal, sear

browse verb 1 skim, dip into, examine cursorily, flip through, glance at, leaf through, look round, look through, peruse, scan, survey 2 graze, eat, feed, nibble

bruise verb 1 discolour, damage, injure, mar, mark, pound ♦ noun 2 discoloration, black mark, blemish, contusion, injury, mark, swelling

brunt noun full force, burden, force, impact, pressure, shock, strain, stress, thrust, violence

brush¹ noun 1 broom, besom, sweeper 2 encounter, clash, conflict, confrontation, skirmish, tussle ♦ verb 3 clean, buff, paint, polish, sweep, wash 4 touch, flick, glance, graze, kiss, scrape, stroke, sweep

brush² noun shrubs, brushwood, bushes, copse, scrub, thicket, undergrowth

brush off verb Slang ignore, disdain, dismiss, disregard, reject, repudiate, scorn, snub, spurn

brush up verb revise, bone up (informal), cram, go over, polish up, read up, refresh one's memory, relearn, study

brusque adjective curt, abrupt, discourteous, gruff, impolite, sharp, short, surly, terse

brutal adjective 1 cruel, bloodthirsty, heartless, inhuman, ruthless, savage, uncivilized, vicious 2 harsh, callous, gruff, impolite, insensitive, rough, rude, severe

brutality noun cruelty, atrocity, barbarism, bloodthirstiness, ferocity, inhumanity, ruthlessness, savagery, viciousness

brute noun 1 savage, barbarian, beast, devil, fiend, monster, sadist, swine 2 animal, beast, creature, wild animal ♦ adjective 3 mindless, bodily, carnal, fleshly, instinctive, physical, senseless, unthinking

bubble noun 1 air ball, bead, blister, blob, drop, droplet, globule ♦ verb 2 foam, boil, effervesce, fizz, froth, percolate, seethe, sparkle 3 gurgle, babble, burble, murmur, ripple, trickle

bubbly adjective 1 lively, animated, bouncy, elated, excited, happy, merry, sparky 2 frothy, carbonated, effervescent, fizzy, foamy, sparkling

buccaneer noun pirate, corsair, freebooter, privateer, sea-rover

buckle noun 1 fastener, catch, clasp, clip, hasp ♦ verb 2 fasten, clasp, close, hook, secure

3 <u>distort</u>, bend, bulge, cave in, collapse, contort, crumple, fold, twist, warp

bud noun **1** <u>shoot</u>, embryo, germ, sprout ♦ verb **2** <u>develop</u>, burgeon, burst forth, grow, shoot, sprout

budding adjective <u>developing</u>, beginning, burgeoning, embryonic, fledgling, growing, incipient, nascent, potential, promising

budge verb <u>move</u>, dislodge, push, shift, stir

budget noun **1** <u>allowance</u>, allocation, cost, finances, funds, means, resources ♦ verb **2** <u>plan</u>, allocate, apportion, cost, estimate, ration

buff[1] adjective **1** <u>yellowish-brown</u>, sandy, straw, tan, yellowish ♦ verb **2** <u>polish</u>, brush, burnish, rub, shine, smooth

buff[2] noun Informal <u>expert</u>, addict, admirer, aficionado, connoisseur, devotee, enthusiast, fan

buffer noun <u>safeguard</u>, bulwark, bumper, cushion, fender, intermediary, screen, shield, shock absorber

buffet[1] noun <u>snack bar</u>, brasserie, café, cafeteria, refreshment counter, sideboard

buffet[2] verb <u>batter</u>, beat, bump, knock, pound, pummel, strike, thump, wallop (informal)

buffoon noun <u>clown</u>, comedian, comic, fool, harlequin, jester, joker, wag

bug noun **1** Informal <u>illness</u>, disease, infection, lurgy (informal), virus **2** <u>fault</u>, defect, error, flaw, glitch, gremlin ♦ verb

3 Informal <u>annoy</u>, bother, disturb, get on one's nerves (informal), hassle (informal), irritate, pester, vex **4** <u>tap</u>, eavesdrop, listen in, spy

bugbear noun <u>pet hate</u>, bane, bête noire, bogey, dread, horror, nightmare

build verb **1** <u>construct</u>, assemble, erect, fabricate, form, make, put up, raise ♦ noun **2** <u>physique</u>, body, figure, form, frame, shape, structure

building noun <u>structure</u>, domicile, dwelling, edifice, house

build-up noun <u>increase</u>, accumulation, development, enlargement, escalation, expansion, gain, growth

bulbous adjective <u>bulging</u>, bloated, convex, rounded, swelling, swollen

bulge noun **1** <u>swelling</u>, bump, hump, lump, projection, protrusion, protuberance **2** <u>increase</u>, boost, intensification, rise, surge ♦ verb **3** <u>swell out</u>, dilate, distend, expand, project, protrude, puff out, stick out

bulk noun **1** <u>size</u>, dimensions, immensity, largeness, magnitude, substance, volume, weight **2** <u>main part</u>, better part, body, lion's share, majority, mass, most, nearly all, preponderance

bulky adjective <u>large</u>, big, cumbersome, heavy, hulking, massive, substantial, unwieldy, voluminous, weighty

bulldoze verb <u>demolish</u>, flatten, level, raze

bullet noun <u>projectile</u>, ball,

missile, pellet, shot, slug

bulletin noun <u>announcement</u>, account, communication, communiqué, dispatch, message, news flash, notification, report, statement

bully noun 1 <u>persecutor</u>, browbeater, bully boy, coercer, intimidator, oppressor, ruffian, tormentor, tough ♦ verb 2 <u>persecute</u>, browbeat, coerce, domineer, hector, intimidate, oppress, push around (slang), terrorize, tyrannize

bulwark noun 1 <u>fortification</u>, bastion, buttress, defence, embankment, partition, rampart 2 <u>defence</u>, buffer, guard, mainstay, safeguard, security, support

bumbling adjective <u>clumsy</u>, awkward, blundering, bungling, incompetent, inefficient, inept, maladroit, muddled

bump verb 1 <u>knock</u>, bang, collide (with), crash, hit, slam, smash into, strike 2 <u>jerk</u>, bounce, jolt, rattle, shake ♦ noun 3 <u>knock</u>, bang, blow, collision, crash, impact, jolt, thud, thump 4 <u>lump</u>, bulge, contusion, hump, nodule, protuberance, swelling

bumper adjective <u>exceptional</u>, abundant, bountiful, excellent, jumbo (informal), massive, whopping (informal)

bumpkin noun <u>yokel</u>, country bumpkin, hick (informal, chiefly U.S. & Canad.), hillbilly, peasant, rustic

bumptious adjective <u>cocky</u>, arrogant, brash, conceited, forward, full of oneself, overconfident, pushy (informal), self-assertive

bumpy adjective <u>rough</u>, bouncy, choppy, jarring, jerky, jolting, rutted, uneven

bunch noun 1 <u>number</u>, assortment, batch, bundle, clump, cluster, collection, heap, lot, mass, pile 2 <u>group</u>, band, crowd, flock, gang, gathering, party, team ♦ verb 3 <u>group</u>, assemble, bundle, cluster, collect, huddle, mass, pack

bundle noun 1 <u>bunch</u>, assortment, batch, collection, group, heap, mass, pile, stack ♦ verb 2 with **out, off, into**, etc. <u>push</u>, hurry, hustle, rush, shove, throw, thrust

bundle up verb <u>wrap up</u>, swathe

bungle verb <u>mess up</u>, blow (slang), blunder, botch, foul up, make a mess of, muff, ruin, spoil

bungling adjective <u>incompetent</u>, blundering, cack-handed (informal), clumsy, ham-fisted (informal), inept, maladroit

bunk, bunkum noun Informal <u>nonsense</u>, balderdash, baloney (informal), garbage (informal), hogwash, hot air (informal), moonshine, poppycock (informal), rubbish, stuff and nonsense, twaddle

buoy noun 1 <u>marker</u>, beacon, float, guide, signal ♦ verb 2 **buoy up** <u>encourage</u>, boost, cheer, cheer up, hearten, keep afloat, lift, raise, support, sustain

buoyancy noun 1 <u>lightness</u>, weightlessness 2 <u>cheerfulness</u>, animation, bounce (informal), good humour, high spirits, liveliness

buoyant adjective 1 floating, afloat, light, weightless 2 cheerful, carefree, chirpy (informal), happy, jaunty, light-hearted, upbeat (informal)

burden noun 1 load, encumbrance, weight 2 trouble, affliction, millstone, onus, responsibility, strain, weight, worry ♦ verb 3 weigh down, bother, handicap, load, oppress, saddle with, tax, worry

bureau noun 1 office, agency, branch, department, division, service 2 desk, writing desk

bureaucracy noun 1 government, administration, authorities, civil service, corridors of power, officials, the system 2 red tape, officialdom, regulations

bureaucrat noun official, administrator, civil servant, functionary, mandarin, officer, public servant

burglar noun housebreaker, cat burglar, filcher, pilferer, robber, sneak thief, thief

burglary noun breaking and entering, break-in, housebreaking, larceny, robbery, stealing, theft, thieving

burial noun interment, entombment, exequies, funeral, obsequies

buried adjective 1 interred, entombed, laid to rest 2 hidden, concealed, private, sequestered, tucked away

burlesque noun 1 parody, caricature, mockery, satire, send-up (Brit. informal), spoof (informal), takeoff (informal), travesty ♦ verb 2 satirize, ape,

caricature, exaggerate, imitate, lampoon, make a monkey out of, make fun of, mock, parody, ridicule, send up (Brit. informal), spoof (informal), take off (informal), take the piss out of (taboo slang), travesty

burly adjective brawny, beefy (informal), big, bulky, hefty, hulking, stocky, stout, sturdy, thickset, well-built

burn verb 1 be on fire, be ablaze, blaze, flame, flare, glow, go up in flames, smoke 2 set on fire, char, ignite, incinerate, kindle, light, parch, scorch, sear, singe, toast 3 be passionate, be angry, be aroused, be inflamed, fume, seethe, simmer, smoulder

burning adjective 1 intense, ardent, eager, fervent, impassioned, passionate, vehement 2 crucial, acute, compelling, critical, essential, important, pressing, significant, urgent, vital 3 blazing, fiery, flaming, flashing, gleaming, glowing, illuminated, scorching, smouldering

burnish verb polish, brighten, buff, furbish, glaze, rub up, shine, smooth

burrow noun 1 hole, den, lair, retreat, shelter, tunnel ♦ verb 2 dig, delve, excavate, hollow out, scoop out, tunnel

burst verb 1 explode, blow up, break, crack, puncture, rupture, shatter, split, tear apart 2 rush, barge, break, break out, erupt, gush forth, run, spout ♦ noun 3 explosion, bang, blast, blowout, break, crack, discharge, rupture, split 4 rush, gush, gust, outbreak, outburst, outpouring, spate, spurt, surge, torrent ♦ *adjective* **5** ruptured, flat, punctured, rent, split

bury *verb* **1** inter, consign to the grave, entomb, inhume, lay to rest **2** embed, engulf, submerge **3** hide, conceal, cover, enshroud, secrete, stow away

bush *noun* **1** shrub, hedge, plant, shrubbery, thicket **2 the bush** the wild, backwoods, brush, scrub, scrubland, woodland

bushy *adjective* thick, bristling, fluffy, fuzzy, luxuriant, rough, shaggy, unruly

busily *adverb* actively, assiduously, briskly, diligently, energetically, industriously, purposefully, speedily, strenuously

business *noun* **1** trade, bargaining, commerce, dealings, industry, manufacturing, selling, transaction **2** establishment, company, concern, corporation, enterprise, firm, organization, venture **3** profession, career, employment, function, job, line, occupation, trade, vocation, work **4** concern, affair, assignment, duty, pigeon (*informal*), problem, responsibility, task

businesslike *adjective* efficient, methodical, orderly, organized, practical, professional, systematic, thorough, well-ordered

businessman *noun* executive, capitalist, employer, entrepreneur, financier, industrialist, merchant, tradesman, tycoon

bust¹ *noun* bosom, breast, chest, front, torso

bust² *Informal* ♦ *verb* **1** break, burst, fracture, rupture **2** arrest, catch, raid, search ♦ *adjective* **3 go bust** go bankrupt, become insolvent, be ruined, fail

bustle *verb* **1** hurry, fuss, hasten, rush, scamper, scurry, scuttle ♦ *noun* **2** activity, ado, commotion, excitement, flurry, fuss, hurly-burly, stir, to-do

bustling *adjective* busy, active, buzzing, crowded, full, humming, lively, swarming, teeming

busy *adjective* **1** occupied, active, employed, engaged, hard at work, industrious, on duty, rushed off one's feet, working **2** lively, energetic, exacting, full, hectic, hustling ♦ *verb* **3** occupy, absorb, employ, engage, engross, immerse, interest

busybody *noun* nosy parker (*informal*), gossip, meddler, snooper, stirrer (*informal*), troublemaker

but *conjunction* **1** however, further, moreover, nevertheless, on the contrary, on the other hand, still, yet ♦ *preposition* **2** except, bar, barring, excepting, excluding, notwithstanding, save, with the exception of ♦ *adverb* **3** only, just, merely, simply, singly, solely

butcher *noun* **1** murderer, destroyer, killer, slaughterer, slayer ♦ *verb* **2** slaughter, carve, clean, cut, cut up, dress, joint, prepare **3** kill, assassinate, cut down, destroy, exterminate, liquidate, massacre, put to the sword, slaughter, slay

butt[1] *noun* **1** end, haft, handle, hilt, shaft, shank, stock **2** <u>stub</u>, fag end (*informal*), leftover, tip

butt[2] *noun* <u>target</u>, Aunt Sally, dupe, laughing stock, victim

butt[3] *verb, noun* **1** *With or of the head or horns* <u>knock</u>, bump, poke, prod, push, ram, shove, thrust ♦ *verb* **2 butt in** <u>interfere</u>, chip in (*informal*), cut in, interrupt, intrude, meddle, put one's oar in, stick one's nose in

butt[4] *noun* <u>cask</u>, barrel

buttonhole *verb* <u>detain</u>, accost, bore, catch, grab, importune, take aside, waylay

buttress *noun* **1** <u>support</u>, brace, mainstay, prop, reinforcement, stanchion, strut ♦ *verb* **2** <u>support</u>, back up, bolster, prop up, reinforce, shore up, strengthen, sustain, uphold

buxom *adjective* <u>plump</u>, ample, bosomy, busty, curvaceous, healthy, voluptuous, well-rounded

buy *verb* **1** <u>purchase</u>, acquire, get, invest in, obtain, pay for, procure, shop for ♦ *noun* **2** <u>purchase</u>, acquisition, bargain, deal

by *preposition* **1** <u>via</u>, by way of, over **2** <u>through</u>, through the agency of **3** <u>near</u>, along, beside, close to, next to, past ♦ *adverb* **4** <u>near</u>, at hand, close, handy, in reach **5** <u>past</u>, aside, away, to one side

bygone *adjective* <u>past</u>, antiquated, extinct, forgotten, former, lost, of old, olden

bypass *verb* <u>go round</u>, avoid, circumvent, depart from, detour round, deviate from, get round, give a wide berth to, pass round

bystander *noun* <u>onlooker</u>, eyewitness, looker-on, observer, passer-by, spectator, viewer, watcher, witness

byword *noun* <u>saying</u>, adage, maxim, motto, precept, proverb, slogan

C c

cab *noun* <u>taxi</u>, hackney carriage, minicab, taxicab

cabal *noun* **1** <u>clique</u>, caucus, conclave, faction, league, party, set **2** <u>plot</u>, conspiracy, intrigue, machination, scheme

cabin *noun* **1** <u>room</u>, berth, compartment, quarters **2** <u>hut</u>, chalet, cottage, lodge, shack, shanty, shed

cabinet *noun* <u>cupboard</u>, case, chiffonier, closet, commode, dresser, escritoire, locker

Cabinet *noun* <u>council</u>, administration, assembly, counsellors, ministry

cad *noun Old-fashioned, informal* <u>scoundrel</u>, bounder (*old-fashioned Brit. slang*), heel (*slang*), rat (*informal*), rotter (*slang, chiefly Brit.*)

caddish *adjective* <u>ungentlemanly</u>, despicable, ill-bred, low, unmannerly

café *noun* <u>snack bar</u>, brasserie, cafeteria, coffee bar, coffee shop, lunchroom, restaurant, tearoom

cage *noun* <u>enclosure</u>, pen, pound

cagey, cagy *adjective Informal*

wary, careful, cautious, chary, discreet, guarded, noncommittal, shrewd, wily

cajole *verb* persuade, coax, flatter, seduce, sweet-talk (*informal*), wheedle

cake *noun* 1 block, bar, cube, loaf, lump, mass, slab ♦ *verb* 2 encrust, bake, coagulate, congeal, solidify

calamitous *adjective* disastrous, cataclysmic, catastrophic, deadly, devastating, dire, fatal, ruinous, tragic

calamity *noun* disaster, cataclysm, catastrophe, misadventure, misfortune, mishap, ruin, tragedy, tribulation

calculate *verb* 1 work out, compute, count, determine, enumerate, estimate, figure, reckon 2 plan, aim, design, intend

calculated *adjective* deliberate, considered, intended, intentional, planned, premeditated, purposeful

calculating *adjective* scheming, crafty, cunning, devious, Machiavellian, manipulative, sharp, shrewd, sly

calculation *noun* 1 working out, answer, computation, estimate, forecast, judgment, reckoning, result 2 planning, contrivance, deliberation, discretion, foresight, forethought, precaution

calibre *noun* 1 worth, ability, capacity, distinction, merit, quality, stature, talent 2 diameter, bore, gauge, measure

call *verb* 1 name, christen,

describe as, designate, dub, entitle, label, style, term 2 cry, arouse, hail, rouse, shout, yell 3 phone, ring up (*informal, chiefly Brit.*), telephone 4 summon, assemble, convene, gather, muster, rally ♦ *noun* 5 cry, hail, scream, shout, signal, whoop, yell 6 summons, appeal, command, demand, invitation, notice, order, plea, request 7 need, cause, excuse, grounds, justification, occasion, reason

call for *verb* 1 require, demand, entail, involve, necessitate, need, occasion, suggest 2 fetch, collect, pick up

calling *noun* profession, career, life's work, mission, trade, vocation

call on *verb* visit, drop in on, look in on, look up, see

callous *adjective* heartless, cold, hard-bitten, hardened, hardhearted, insensitive, uncaring, unfeeling

callow *adjective* inexperienced, green, guileless, immature, naive, raw, unsophisticated

calm *adjective* 1 cool, collected, composed, dispassionate, relaxed, sedate, self-possessed, unemotional 2 still, balmy, mild, quiet, serene, smooth, tranquil, windless ♦ *noun* 3 peacefulness, hush, peace, quiet, repose, serenity, stillness ♦ *verb* 4 quieten, hush, mollify, placate, relax, soothe

calmness *noun* 1 coolness, composure, cool (*slang*), equanimity, impassivity, poise, sang-froid, self-possession 2 peacefulness, calm, hush, quiet, repose, restfulness, serenity, stillness, tranquillity

camouflage noun 1 <u>disguise</u>, blind, cloak, concealment, cover, mask, masquerade, screen, subterfuge ♦ verb 2 <u>disguise</u>, cloak, conceal, cover, hide, mask, obfuscate, obscure, screen, veil

camp¹ noun <u>camp site</u>, bivouac, camping ground, encampment, tents

camp² adjective Informal <u>effeminate</u>, affected, artificial, mannered, ostentatious, posturing

campaign noun <u>operation</u>, attack, crusade, drive, expedition, movement, offensive, push

canal noun <u>waterway</u>, channel, conduit, duct, passage, watercourse

cancel verb 1 <u>call off</u>, abolish, abort, annul, delete, do away with, eliminate, erase, expunge, obliterate, repeal, revoke 2 **cancel out** <u>make up for</u>, balance out, compensate for, counterbalance, neutralize, nullify, offset

cancellation noun <u>abandonment</u>, abolition, annulment, deletion, elimination, repeal, revocation

cancer noun <u>growth</u>, corruption, malignancy, pestilence, sickness, tumour

candid adjective <u>honest</u>, blunt, forthright, frank, open, outspoken, plain, straightforward, truthful

candidate noun <u>contender</u>,

applicant, claimant, competitor, contestant, entrant, nominee, runner

candour noun <u>honesty</u>, directness, forthrightness, frankness, openness, outspokenness, straightforwardness, truthfulness

canker noun <u>disease</u>, bane, blight, cancer, corruption, infection, rot, scourge, sore, ulcer

cannon noun <u>gun</u>, big gun, field gun, mortar

canny adjective <u>shrewd</u>, astute, careful, cautious, clever, judicious, prudent, wise

canon noun 1 <u>rule</u>, criterion, dictate, formula, precept, principle, regulation, standard, statute, yardstick 2 <u>list</u>, catalogue, roll

canopy noun <u>awning</u>, covering, shade, sunshade

cant¹ noun 1 <u>hypocrisy</u>, humbug, insincerity, lip service, pretence, pretentiousness, sanctimoniousness 2 <u>jargon</u>, argot, lingo, patter, slang, vernacular

cant² verb <u>tilt</u>, angle, bevel, incline, rise, slant, slope

cantankerous adjective <u>bad-tempered</u>, choleric, contrary, disagreeable, grumpy, irascible, irritable, testy, waspish

canter noun 1 <u>jog</u>, amble, dogtrot, lope ♦ verb 2 <u>jog</u>, amble, lope

canvass verb 1 <u>campaign</u>, electioneer, solicit, solicit votes 2 <u>poll</u>, examine, inspect, investigate, scrutinize, study ♦ noun 3 <u>poll</u>, examination, investigation, scrutiny, survey, tally

cap verb Informal <u>beat</u>, better, crown, eclipse, exceed, outdo, outstrip, surpass, top, transcend

capability noun <u>ability</u>, capacity, competence, means, potential, power, proficiency, qualification(s), wherewithal

capable adjective <u>able</u>, accomplished, competent, efficient, gifted, proficient, qualified, talented

capacious adjective <u>spacious</u>, broad, commodious, expansive, extensive, roomy, sizable or sizeable, substantial, vast, voluminous, wide

capacity noun **1** <u>size</u>, amplitude, compass, dimensions, extent, magnitude, range, room, scope, space, volume **2** <u>ability</u>, aptitude, aptness, capability, competence, facility, genius, gift **3** <u>function</u>, office, position, post, province, role, sphere

cape noun <u>headland</u>, head, peninsula, point, promontory

caper noun **1** <u>escapade</u>, antic, high jinks, jape, lark (informal), mischief, practical joke, prank, stunt ♦verb **2** <u>dance</u>, bound, cavort, frolic, gambol, jump, skip, spring, trip

capital noun **1** <u>money</u>, assets, cash, finances, funds, investment(s), means, principal, resources, wealth, wherewithal ♦ adjective **2** <u>principal</u>, cardinal, major, prime, vital **3** Old-fashioned <u>first-rate</u>, excellent, fine, splendid, sterling, superb

capitalism noun <u>private</u>

<u>enterprise</u>, free enterprise, laissez faire or laisser faire, private ownership

capitalize on verb <u>take advantage of</u>, benefit from, cash in on (informal), exploit, gain from, make the most of, profit from

capitulate verb <u>give in</u>, come to terms, give up, relent, submit, succumb, surrender, yield

caprice noun <u>whim</u>, fad, fancy, fickleness, impulse, inconstancy, notion, whimsy

capricious adjective <u>unpredictable</u>, changeful, erratic, fickle, fitful, impulsive, inconsistent, inconstant, mercurial, variable, wayward, whimsical

capsize verb <u>overturn</u>, invert, keel over, tip over, turn over, turn turtle, upset

capsule noun **1** <u>pill</u>, lozenge, tablet **2** Botany <u>pod</u>, case, receptacle, seed case, sheath, shell, vessel

captain noun <u>leader</u>, boss, chief, commander, head, master, skipper

captivate verb <u>charm</u>, allure, attract, beguile, bewitch, enchant, enrapture, enthral, entrance, fascinate, infatuate, mesmerize

captive noun **1** <u>prisoner</u>, convict, detainee, hostage, internee, prisoner of war, slave ♦ adjective **2** <u>confined</u>, caged, enslaved, ensnared, imprisoned, incarcerated, locked up, penned, restricted, subjugated

captivity noun <u>confinement</u>,

bondage, custody, detention, imprisonment, incarceration, internment, slavery

capture verb 1 <u>catch</u>, apprehend, arrest, bag, collar (*informal*), secure, seize, take, take prisoner ♦ noun 2 <u>catching</u>, apprehension, arrest, imprisonment, seizure, taking, taking captive, trapping

car noun 1 <u>vehicle</u>, auto (*U.S.*), automobile, jalopy (*informal*), machine, motor, motorcar, wheels (*informal*) 2 *U.S. & Canad.* <u>(railway) carriage</u>, buffet car, cable car, coach, dining car, sleeping car, van

carcass noun <u>body</u>, cadaver (*Medical*), corpse, dead body, framework, hulk, remains, shell, skeleton

cardinal adjective <u>principal</u>, capital, central, chief, essential, first, fundamental, key, leading, main, paramount, primary

care verb 1 <u>be concerned</u>, be bothered, be interested, mind ♦ noun 2 <u>caution</u>, attention, carefulness, consideration, forethought, heed, management, pains, prudence, vigilance, watchfulness 3 <u>protection</u>, charge, control, custody, guardianship, keeping, management, supervision 4 <u>worry</u>, anxiety, concern, disquiet, perplexity, pressure, responsibility, stress, trouble

career noun 1 <u>occupation</u>, calling, employment, life's work, livelihood, pursuit, vocation ♦ verb 2 <u>rush</u>, barrel (along) (*informal, chiefly U.S. & Canad.*), bolt, dash, hurtle, race, speed, tear

care for verb 1 <u>look after</u>, attend, foster, mind, minister to, nurse, protect, provide for, tend, watch over 2 <u>like</u>, be fond of, desire, enjoy, love, prize, take to, want

carefree adjective <u>untroubled</u>, blithe, breezy, cheerful, easy-going, halcyon, happy-go-lucky, light-hearted

careful adjective 1 <u>cautious</u>, chary, circumspect, discreet, prudent, scrupulous, thoughtful, thrifty 2 <u>thorough</u>, conscientious, meticulous, painstaking, particular, precise

careless adjective 1 <u>slapdash</u>, cavalier, inaccurate, irresponsible, lackadaisical, neglectful, offhand, slipshod, sloppy (*informal*) 2 <u>negligent</u>, absent-minded, forgetful, hasty, remiss, thoughtless, unthinking 3 <u>nonchalant</u>, artless, casual, unstudied

carelessness noun <u>negligence</u>, indiscretion, irresponsibility, laxity, neglect, omission, slackness, sloppiness (*informal*), thoughtlessness

caress verb 1 <u>stroke</u>, cuddle, embrace, fondle, hug, kiss, neck (*informal*), nuzzle, pet ♦ noun 2 <u>stroke</u>, cuddle, embrace, fondling, hug, kiss, pat

caretaker noun <u>warden</u>, concierge, curator, custodian, janitor, keeper, porter, superintendent, watchman

cargo noun <u>load</u>, baggage, consignment, contents, freight, goods, merchandise, shipment

caricature noun 1 <u>parody</u>, burlesque, cartoon, distortion, farce, lampoon, satire, send-up

(*Brit. informal*), takeoff (*informal*), travesty ♦ *verb* **2** parody, burlesque, distort, lampoon, mimic, mock, ridicule, satirize, send up (*Brit. informal*), take off (*informal*)

carnage *noun* slaughter, blood bath, bloodshed, butchery, havoc, holocaust, massacre, mass murder, murder, shambles

carnal *adjective* sexual, erotic, fleshly, lascivious, lewd, libidinous, lustful, sensual

carnival *noun* festival, celebration, fair, fête, fiesta, gala, holiday, jamboree, jubilee, merrymaking, revelry

carol *noun* song, chorus, ditty, hymn, lay

carp *verb* find fault, cavil, complain, criticize, pick holes, quibble, reproach

carpenter *noun* joiner, cabinet-maker, woodworker

carriage *noun* **1** vehicle, cab, coach, conveyance **2** bearing, air, behaviour, comportment, conduct, demeanour, deportment, gait, manner, posture

carry *verb* **1** transport, bear, bring, conduct, convey, fetch, haul, lug, move, relay, take, transfer **2** win, accomplish, capture, effect, gain, secure

carry on *verb* **1** continue, endure, keep going, last, maintain, perpetuate, persevere, persist **2** *Informal* make a fuss, create (*slang*), misbehave, raise Cain

carry out *verb* perform, accomplish, achieve, carry through, effect, execute, fulfil, implement, realize

carton *noun* box, case, container, pack, package, packet

cartoon *noun* **1** drawing, caricature, comic strip, lampoon, parody, satire, sketch, takeoff (*informal*) **2** animation, animated cartoon, animated film

cartridge *noun* **1** shell, charge, round **2** container, capsule, case, cassette, cylinder, magazine

carve *verb* cut, chip, chisel, engrave, etch, hew, mould, sculpt, slice, whittle

cascade *noun* **1** waterfall, avalanche, cataract, deluge, downpour, falls, flood, fountain, outpouring, shower, torrent ♦ *verb* **2** flow, descend, fall, flood, gush, overflow, pitch, plunge, pour, spill, surge, teem, tumble

case¹ *noun* **1** instance, example, illustration, occasion, occurrence, specimen **2** situation, circumstance(s), condition, context, contingency, event, position, state **3** *Law* lawsuit, action, dispute, proceedings, suit, trial

case² *noun* **1** container, box, canister, carton, casket, chest, crate, holder, receptacle, suitcase, tray **2** covering, capsule, casing, envelope, jacket, sheath, shell, wrapper

cash *noun* money, brass (*Northern English dialect*), coinage, currency, dough (*slang*), funds, notes, ready money, silver

cashier¹ *noun* teller, bank clerk, banker, bursar, clerk, purser, treasurer

cashier² verb <u>dismiss</u>, discard, discharge, drum out, expel, give the boot to (slang)

casket noun <u>box</u>, case, chest, coffer, jewel box

cast noun **1** <u>actors</u>, characters, company, dramatis personae, players, troupe **2** <u>type</u>, complexion, manner, stamp, style ♦ verb **3** <u>choose</u>, allot, appoint, assign, name, pick, select **4** <u>give out</u>, bestow, deposit, diffuse, distribute, emit, radiate, scatter, shed, spread **5** <u>form</u>, found, model, mould, set, shape **6** <u>throw</u>, fling, hurl, launch, pitch, sling, thrust, toss

caste noun <u>class</u>, estate, grade, order, rank, social order, status, stratum

castigate verb <u>reprimand</u>, berate, censure, chastise, criticize, lambast(e), rebuke, scold

cast-iron adjective <u>certain</u>, copper-bottomed, definite, established, fixed, guaranteed, settled

castle noun <u>fortress</u>, chateau, citadel, keep, palace, stronghold, tower

cast-off adjective **1** <u>unwanted</u>, discarded, rejected, scrapped, surplus to requirements, unneeded, useless ♦ noun **2** <u>reject</u>, discard, failure, outcast, second

castrate verb <u>neuter</u>, emasculate, geld

casual adjective **1** <u>careless</u>, blasé, cursory, lackadaisical, nonchalant, offhand, relaxed, unconcerned **2** <u>occasional</u>, accidental, chance, incidental, irregular, random, unexpected

3 <u>informal</u>, non-dressy, sporty

casualty noun <u>victim</u>, death, fatality, loss, sufferer, wounded

cat noun <u>feline</u>, kitty (informal), moggy (slang), puss (informal), pussy (informal), tabby

catacombs plural noun <u>vault</u>, crypt, tomb

catalogue noun **1** <u>list</u>, directory, gazetteer, index, inventory, record, register, roll, roster, schedule ♦ verb **2** <u>list</u>, accession, alphabetize, classify, file, index, inventory, register, tabulate

catapult noun **1** <u>sling</u>, slingshot (U.S.) ♦ verb **2** <u>shoot</u>, heave, hurl, pitch, plunge, propel

catastrophe noun <u>disaster</u>, adversity, calamity, cataclysm, fiasco, misfortune, tragedy, trouble

catcall noun <u>jeer</u>, boo, gibe, hiss, raspberry, whistle

catch verb **1** <u>seize</u>, clutch, get, grab, grasp, grip, lay hold of, snatch, take **2** <u>capture</u>, apprehend, arrest, ensnare, entrap, snare **3** <u>discover</u>, catch in the act, detect, expose, find out, surprise, take unawares, unmask **4** <u>contract</u>, develop, get, go down with, incur, succumb to, suffer from **5** <u>make out</u>, comprehend, discern, get, grasp, hear, perceive, recognize, sense, take in ♦ noun **6** <u>fastener</u>, bolt, clasp, clip, latch **7** Informal <u>drawback</u>, disadvantage, fly in the ointment, hitch, snag, stumbling block, trap, trick

catching adjective <u>infectious</u>, communicable, contagious, transferable, transmittable

catch on verb Informal
<u>understand</u>, comprehend, find
out, get the picture, grasp, see,
see through, twig (Brit. informal)

catchword noun <u>slogan</u>, byword,
motto, password, watchword

catchy adjective <u>memorable</u>,
captivating, haunting, popular

categorical adjective <u>absolute</u>,
downright, emphatic, explicit,
express, positive, unambiguous,
unconditional, unequivocal,
unqualified, unreserved

category noun <u>class</u>,
classification, department,
division, grade, grouping,
heading, section, sort, type

cater verb <u>provide</u>, furnish, outfit,
purvey, supply

cattle plural noun <u>cows</u>, beasts,
bovines, livestock, stock

catty adjective <u>spiteful</u>,
backbiting, bitchy (informal),
malevolent, malicious, rancorous,
shrewish, snide, venomous

cause noun 1 <u>origin</u>, agent,
beginning, creator, genesis,
mainspring, maker, producer,
root, source, spring 2 <u>reason</u>,
basis, grounds, incentive,
inducement, justification,
motivation, motive, purpose
3 <u>aim</u>, belief, conviction,
enterprise, ideal, movement,
principle ♦ verb 4 <u>produce</u>, bring
about, create, generate, give rise
to, incite, induce, lead to, result
in

caustic adjective 1 <u>burning</u>, acrid,
astringent, biting, corroding,
corrosive, mordant, vitriolic
2 <u>sarcastic</u>, acrimonious, cutting,
pungent, scathing, stinging,
trenchant, virulent, vitriolic

caution noun 1 <u>care</u>, alertness,
carefulness, circumspection,
deliberation, discretion,
forethought, heed, prudence,
vigilance, watchfulness
2 <u>warning</u>, admonition, advice,
counsel, injunction ♦ verb
3 <u>warn</u>, admonish, advise, tip
off, urge

cautious adjective <u>careful</u>, cagey
(informal), chary, circumspect,
guarded, judicious, prudent,
tentative, wary

cavalcade noun <u>parade</u>, array,
march-past, procession,
spectacle, train

cavalier adjective <u>haughty</u>,
arrogant, disdainful, lofty, lordly,
offhand, scornful, supercilious

cavalry noun <u>horsemen</u>, horse,
mounted troops

cave noun <u>hollow</u>, cavern, cavity,
den, grotto

cavern noun <u>cave</u>, hollow,
pothole

cavernous adjective <u>deep</u>,
hollow, sunken, yawning

cavity noun <u>hollow</u>, crater, dent,
gap, hole, pit

cease verb <u>stop</u>, break off,
conclude, discontinue, end,
finish, halt, leave off, refrain,
terminate

ceaseless adjective <u>continual</u>,
constant, endless, eternal,
everlasting, incessant,
interminable, never-ending,
nonstop, perpetual, unremitting

cede verb <u>surrender</u>, concede,
hand over, make over,
relinquish, renounce, resign,
transfer, yield

celebrate verb 1 <u>rejoice</u>,

commemorate, drink to, keep, kill the fatted calf, observe, put the flags out, toast 2 _perform_, bless, honour, solemnize

celebrated _adjective_ well-known, acclaimed, distinguished, eminent, famous, illustrious, notable, popular, prominent, renowned

celebration _noun_ 1 _party_, festival, festivity, gala, jubilee, merrymaking, red-letter day, revelry 2 _performance_, anniversary, commemoration, honouring, observance, remembrance, solemnization

celebrity _noun_ 1 _personality_, big name, big shot (_informal_), dignitary, luminary, star, superstar, V.I.P. 2 _fame_, distinction, notability, prestige, prominence, renown, reputation, repute, stardom

celestial _adjective_ heavenly, angelic, astral, divine, ethereal, spiritual, sublime, supernatural

celibacy _noun_ chastity, continence, purity, virginity

cell _noun_ 1 _room_, cavity, chamber, compartment, cubicle, dungeon, stall 2 _unit_, caucus, core, coterie, group, nucleus

cement _noun_ 1 _mortar_, adhesive, glue, gum, paste, plaster, sealant ♦ _verb_ 2 _stick together_, attach, bind, bond, combine, glue, join, plaster, seal, unite, weld

cemetery _noun_ graveyard, burial ground, churchyard, God's acre, necropolis

censor _verb_ cut, blue-pencil, bowdlerize, expurgate

censorious _adjective_ critical, captious, carping, cavilling, condemnatory, disapproving, disparaging, fault-finding, hypercritical, scathing, severe

censure _noun_ 1 _disapproval_, blame, condemnation, criticism, obloquy, rebuke, reprimand, reproach, reproof, stick (_slang_) ♦ _verb_ 2 _criticize_, blame, castigate, condemn, denounce, rap over the knuckles, rebuke, reprimand, reproach, scold, slap on the wrist

central _adjective_ 1 _middle_, inner, interior, mean, median, mid 2 _main_, chief, essential, focal, fundamental, key, primary, principal

centralize _verb_ unify, concentrate, condense, incorporate, rationalize, streamline

centre _noun_ 1 _middle_, core, focus, heart, hub, kernel, midpoint, nucleus, pivot ♦ _verb_ 2 _focus_, cluster, concentrate, converge, revolve

ceremonial _adjective_ 1 _ritual_, formal, liturgical, ritualistic, solemn, stately ♦ _noun_ 2 _ritual_, ceremony, formality, rite, solemnity

ceremonious _adjective_ formal, civil, courteous, deferential, dignified, punctilious, solemn, stately, stiff

ceremony _noun_ 1 _ritual_, commemoration, function, observance, parade, rite, service, show, solemnities 2 _formality_, ceremonial, decorum, etiquette, niceties, pomp, propriety, protocol

certain _adjective_ 1 _sure_, assured,

confident, convinced, positive,
satisfied 2 <u>known</u>, conclusive,
incontrovertible, irrefutable, true,
undeniable, unequivocal
3 <u>inevitable</u>, bound, definite,
destined, fated, inescapable, sure
4 <u>fixed</u>, decided, definite,
established, settled

certainly *adverb* <u>definitely</u>,
assuredly, indisputably,
indubitably, surely, truly,
undeniably, undoubtedly,
without doubt

certainty *noun* 1 <u>sureness</u>,
assurance, confidence,
conviction, faith, positiveness,
trust, validity 2 <u>fact</u>, reality, sure
thing (*informal*), truth

certificate *noun* <u>document</u>,
authorization, credential(s),
diploma, licence, testimonial,
voucher, warrant

certify *verb* <u>confirm</u>, assure,
attest, authenticate, declare,
guarantee, testify, validate, verify

chafe *verb* 1 <u>rub</u>, abrade, rasp,
scrape, scratch 2 <u>be annoyed</u>, be
impatient, fret, fume, rage, worry

chaff[1] *noun* <u>waste</u>, dregs, husks,
refuse, remains, rubbish, trash

chaff[2] *verb* <u>tease</u>, mock, rib
(*informal*), ridicule, scoff, taunt

chain *noun* 1 <u>link</u>, bond,
coupling, fetter, manacle,
shackle 2 <u>series</u>, progression,
sequence, set, string, succession,
train ♦ *verb* 3 <u>bind</u>, confine,
enslave, fetter, handcuff,
manacle, restrain, shackle, tether

chairman *noun* <u>director</u>,
chairperson, chairwoman, master
of ceremonies, president,
speaker, spokesman

challenge *noun* 1 <u>test</u>,
confrontation, provocation,
question, trial, ultimatum ♦ *verb*
2 <u>test</u>, confront, defy, dispute,
object to, question, tackle, throw
down the gauntlet

chamber *noun* 1 <u>room</u>,
apartment, bedroom,
compartment, cubicle,
enclosure, hall 2 <u>council</u>,
assembly, legislative body,
legislature

champion *noun* 1 <u>winner</u>,
conqueror, hero, title holder,
victor 2 <u>defender</u>, backer,
guardian, patron, protector,
upholder ♦ *verb* 3 <u>support</u>,
advocate, back, commend,
defend, encourage, espouse,
fight for, promote, uphold

chance *noun* 1 <u>probability</u>,
likelihood, odds, possibility,
prospect 2 <u>opportunity</u>,
occasion, opening, time 3 <u>luck</u>,
accident, coincidence, destiny,
fate, fortune, providence 4 <u>risk</u>,
gamble, hazard, jeopardy,
speculation, uncertainty ♦ *verb*
5 <u>risk</u>, endanger, gamble,
hazard, jeopardize, stake, try,
venture, wager

change *noun* 1 <u>alteration</u>,
difference, innovation,
metamorphosis, modification,
mutation, revolution,
transformation, transition
2 <u>variety</u>, break (*informal*),
departure, diversion, novelty,
variation 3 <u>exchange</u>,
conversion, interchange,
substitution, swap, trade ♦ *verb*
4 <u>alter</u>, convert, modify, mutate,
reform, reorganize, restyle, shift,
transform, vary 5 <u>exchange</u>,
barter, convert, interchange,

replace, substitute, swap, trade

changeable *adjective* variable, erratic, fickle, inconstant, irregular, mobile, mutable, protean, shifting, unsettled, unstable, volatile, wavering

channel *noun* 1 route, approach, artery, avenue, course, means, medium, path, way 2 passage, canal, conduit, duct, furrow, groove, gutter, route, strait ◆ *verb* 3 direct, conduct, convey, guide, transmit

chant *verb* 1 sing, carol, chorus, descant, intone, recite, warble ◆ *noun* 2 song, carol, chorus, melody, psalm

chaos *noun* disorder, anarchy, bedlam, confusion, disorganization, lawlessness, mayhem, pandemonium, tumult

chaotic *adjective* disordered, anarchic, confused, deranged, disorganized, lawless, riotous, topsy-turvy, tumultuous, uncontrolled

chap *noun Informal* fellow, bloke (*Brit. informal*), character, guy (*informal*), individual, man, person

chaperone *noun* 1 escort, companion ◆ *verb* 2 escort, accompany, attend, protect, safeguard, shepherd, watch over

chapter *noun* section, clause, division, episode, part, period, phase, stage, topic

character *noun* 1 nature, attributes, calibre, complexion, disposition, personality, quality, temperament, type 2 reputation, honour, integrity, rectitude, strength, uprightness 3 role, part, persona, portrayal

4 eccentric, card (*informal*), oddball (*informal*), original 5 symbol, device, figure, hieroglyph, letter, mark, rune, sign

characteristic *noun* 1 feature, attribute, faculty, idiosyncrasy, mark, peculiarity, property, quality, quirk, trait ◆ *adjective* 2 typical, distinctive, distinguishing, idiosyncratic, individual, peculiar, representative, singular, special, symbolic, symptomatic

characterize *verb* identify, brand, distinguish, indicate, mark, represent, stamp, typify

charade *noun* pretence, fake, farce, pantomime, parody, travesty

charge *verb* 1 accuse, arraign, blame, impeach, incriminate, indict 2 rush, assail, assault, attack, stampede, storm 3 fill, load 4 *Formal* command, bid, commit, demand, entrust, instruct, order, require ◆ *noun* 5 price, amount, cost, expenditure, expense, outlay, payment, rate, toll 6 accusation, allegation, imputation, indictment 7 rush, assault, attack, onset, onslaught, sortie, stampede 8 care, custody, duty, office, responsibility, safekeeping, trust 9 ward 10 instruction, command, demand, direction, injunction, mandate, order, precept

charisma *noun* charm, allure, attraction, lure, magnetism, personality

charismatic *adjective* charming, alluring, attractive, enticing, influential, magnetic

charitable *adjective* **1** <u>tolerant</u>, considerate, favourable, forgiving, humane, indulgent, kindly, lenient, magnanimous, sympathetic, understanding **2** <u>generous</u>, beneficent, benevolent, bountiful, kind, lavish, liberal, philanthropic

charity *noun* **1** <u>donations</u>, assistance, benefaction, contributions, endowment, fund, gift, hand-out, help, largesse *or* largess, philanthropy, relief **2** <u>kindness</u>, altruism, benevolence, compassion, fellow feeling, generosity, goodwill, humanity, indulgence

charlatan *noun* <u>fraud</u>, cheat, con man (*informal*), fake, impostor, phoney *or* phony (*informal*), pretender, quack, sham, swindler

charm *noun* **1** <u>attraction</u>, allure, appeal, fascination, magnetism **2** <u>spell</u>, enchantment, magic, sorcery **3** <u>talisman</u>, amulet, fetish, trinket ♦ *verb* **4** <u>attract</u>, allure, beguile, bewitch, captivate, delight, enchant, enrapture, entrance, fascinate, mesmerize, win over

charming *adjective* <u>attractive</u>, appealing, captivating, cute, delightful, fetching, likable *or* likeable, pleasing, seductive, winsome

chart *noun* **1** <u>table</u>, blueprint, diagram, graph, map, plan ♦ *verb* **2** <u>plot</u>, delineate, draft, map out, outline, shape, sketch

charter *noun* **1** <u>document</u>, contract, deed, licence, permit, prerogative ♦ *verb* **2** <u>hire</u>, commission, employ, lease, rent

3 <u>authorize</u>, sanction

chase *verb* **1** <u>pursue</u>, course, follow, hunt, run after, track **2** <u>drive away</u>, drive, expel, hound, put to flight ♦ *noun* **3** <u>pursuit</u>, hunt, hunting, race

chasm *noun* <u>gulf</u>, abyss, crater, crevasse, fissure, gap, gorge, ravine

chaste *adjective* <u>pure</u>, immaculate, innocent, modest, simple, unaffected, undefiled, virtuous

chasten *verb* <u>subdue</u>, chastise, correct, discipline, humble, humiliate, put in one's place, tame

chastise *verb* **1** <u>scold</u>, berate, castigate, censure, correct, discipline, upbraid **2** *Old-fashioned* <u>beat</u>, flog, lash, lick (*informal*), punish, scourge, whip

chastity *noun* <u>purity</u>, celibacy, continence, innocence, maidenhood, modesty, virginity, virtue

chat *noun* **1** <u>talk</u>, chatter, chinwag (*Brit. informal*), conversation, gossip, heart-to-heart, natter, tête-à-tête ♦ *verb* **2** <u>talk</u>, chatter, gossip, jaw (*slang*), natter

chatter *noun* **1** <u>prattle</u>, babble, blather, chat, gab (*informal*), gossip, natter ♦ *verb* **2** <u>prattle</u>, babble, blather, chat, gab (*informal*), gossip, natter, rabbit (on) (*Brit. informal*), schmooze (*slang*)

cheap *adjective* **1** <u>inexpensive</u>, bargain, cut-price, economical, keen, low-cost, low-priced, reasonable, reduced **2** <u>inferior</u>, common, poor, second-rate, shoddy, tatty, tawdry, two a penny, worthless **3** *Informal* despicable, contemptible, mean

cheapen *verb* degrade, belittle, debase, demean, denigrate, depreciate, devalue, discredit, disparage, lower

cheat *verb* **1** deceive, beguile, con (*informal*), defraud, double-cross (*informal*), dupe, fleece, fool, mislead, rip off (*slang*), swindle, trick ♦ *noun* **2** deceiver, charlatan, con man (*informal*), double-crosser (*informal*), shark, sharper, swindler, trickster **3** deception, deceit, fraud, rip-off (*slang*), scam (*slang*), swindle, trickery

check *verb* **1** examine, inquire into, inspect, investigate, look at, make sure, monitor, research, scrutinize, study, test, vet **2** stop, delay, halt, hinder, impede, inhibit, limit, obstruct, restrain, retard ♦ *noun* **3** examination, inspection, investigation, once-over (*informal*), research, scrutiny, test **4** stoppage, constraint, control, curb, damper, hindrance, impediment, limitation, obstacle, obstruction, restraint

cheek *noun Informal* impudence, audacity, chutzpah (*U.S. & Canad. informal*), disrespect, effrontery, impertinence, insolence, lip (*slang*), nerve, temerity

cheeky *adjective* impudent, audacious, disrespectful, forward, impertinent, insolent, insulting, pert, saucy

cheer *verb* **1** applaud, acclaim, clap, hail **2** cheer up, brighten, buoy up, comfort, encourage, gladden, hearten, uplift ♦ *noun* **3** applause, acclamation, ovation, plaudits

cheerful *adjective* happy, buoyant, cheery, chirpy (*informal*), enthusiastic, jaunty, jolly, light-hearted, merry, optimistic, upbeat (*informal*)

cheerfulness *noun* happiness, buoyancy, exuberance, gaiety, geniality, good cheer, good humour, high spirits, jauntiness, light-heartedness

cheerless *adjective* gloomy, bleak, desolate, dismal, drab, dreary, forlorn, miserable, sombre, woeful

cheer up *verb* **1** comfort, encourage, enliven, gladden, hearten, jolly along (*informal*) **2** take heart, buck up (*informal*), perk up, rally

cheery *adjective* cheerful, breezy, carefree, chirpy (*informal*), genial, good-humoured, happy, jovial, upbeat (*informal*)

chemist *noun* pharmacist, apothecary (*obsolete*), dispenser

cherish *verb* **1** cling to, cleave to, encourage, entertain, foster, harbour, hold dear, nurture, prize, sustain, treasure **2** care for, comfort, hold dear, love, nurse, shelter, support

chest *noun* box, case, casket, coffer, crate, strongbox, trunk

chew *verb* bite, champ, chomp, crunch, gnaw, grind, masticate, munch

chewy *adjective* tough, as tough as old boots, leathery

chic adjective stylish, elegant, fashionable, smart, trendy (Brit. informal)

chide verb Old-fashioned scold, admonish, berate, censure, criticize, lecture, rebuke, reprimand, reproach, reprove, tell off (informal)

chief noun 1 head, boss (informal), captain, commander, director, governor, leader, manager, master, principal, ruler ◆ adjective 2 primary, foremost, highest, key, leading, main, predominant, pre-eminent, premier, prime, principal, supreme, uppermost

chiefly adverb 1 especially, above all, essentially, primarily, principally 2 mainly, in general, in the main, largely, mostly, on the whole, predominantly, usually

child noun youngster, babe, baby, bairn (Scot.), infant, juvenile, kid (informal), offspring, toddler, tot

childbirth noun child-bearing, confinement, delivery, labour, lying-in, parturition, travail

childhood noun youth, boyhood or girlhood, immaturity, infancy, minority, schooldays

childish adjective immature, boyish or girlish, foolish, infantile, juvenile, puerile, young

childlike adjective innocent, artless, guileless, ingenuous, naive, simple, trusting

chill noun 1 cold, bite, coldness, coolness, crispness, frigidity, nip, rawness, sharpness ◆ verb 2 cool, freeze, refrigerate 3 dishearten, dampen, deject, depress, discourage, dismay ◆ adjective

4 cold, biting, bleak, chilly, freezing, frigid, raw, sharp, wintry

chilly adjective 1 cool, brisk, crisp, draughty, fresh, nippy, penetrating, sharp 2 unfriendly, frigid, hostile, unresponsive, unsympathetic, unwelcoming

chime verb, noun ring, clang, jingle, peal, sound, tinkle, toll

china noun pottery, ceramics, crockery, porcelain, service, tableware, ware

chink noun opening, aperture, cleft, crack, cranny, crevice, fissure, gap

chip noun 1 scratch, fragment, nick, notch, shard, shaving, sliver, wafer ◆ verb 2 nick, chisel, damage, gash, whittle

chirp verb chirrup, cheep, peep, pipe, tweet, twitter, warble

chivalrous adjective courteous, bold, brave, courageous, gallant, gentlemanly, honourable, valiant

chivalry noun courtesy, courage, gallantry, gentlemanliness, knight-errantry, knighthood, politeness

choice noun 1 option, alternative, pick, preference, say 2 selection, range, variety ◆ adjective 3 best, elite, excellent, exclusive, prime, rare, select

choke verb 1 strangle, asphyxiate, gag, overpower, smother, stifle, suffocate, suppress, throttle 2 block, bar, bung, clog, congest, constrict, obstruct, stop

choose verb pick, adopt, designate, elect, opt for, prefer, select, settle upon

choosy adjective Informal fussy,

discriminating, faddy, fastidious, finicky, particular, picky (*informal*), selective

chop verb <u>cut</u>, cleave, fell, hack, hew, lop, sever

chore noun <u>task</u>, burden, duty, errand, job

chortle verb, noun <u>chuckle</u>, cackle, crow, guffaw

chorus noun 1 <u>choir</u>, choristers, ensemble, singers, vocalists 2 <u>refrain</u>, burden, response, strain 3 <u>unison</u>, accord, concert, harmony

christen verb 1 <u>baptize</u> 2 <u>name</u>, call, designate, dub, style, term, title

Christmas noun <u>festive season</u>, Noel, Xmas (*informal*), Yule (*archaic*), Yuletide (*archaic*)

chronicle noun 1 <u>record</u>, account, annals, diary, history, journal, narrative, register, story ◆ verb 2 <u>record</u>, enter, narrate, put on record, recount, register, relate, report, set down, tell

chubby adjective <u>plump</u>, buxom, flabby, podgy, portly, rotund, round, stout, tubby

chuck verb Informal <u>throw</u>, cast, fling, heave, hurl, pitch, sling, toss

chuckle verb <u>laugh</u>, chortle, crow, exult, giggle, snigger, titter

chum noun Informal <u>friend</u>, companion, comrade, crony, mate (*informal*), pal (*informal*)

chunk noun <u>piece</u>, block, dollop (*informal*), hunk, lump, mass, nugget, portion, slab

churlish adjective <u>rude</u>, brusque, harsh, ill-tempered, impolite, sullen, surly, uncivil

churn verb <u>stir up</u>, agitate, beat, convulse, swirl, toss

cinema noun <u>films</u>, big screen (*informal*), flicks (*slang*), motion pictures, movies, pictures

cipher noun 1 <u>code</u>, cryptograph 2 <u>nobody</u>, nonentity

circle noun 1 <u>ring</u>, disc, globe, orb, sphere 2 <u>group</u>, clique, club, company, coterie, set, society ◆ verb 3 <u>go round</u>, circumnavigate, circumscribe, encircle, enclose, envelop, ring, surround

circuit noun <u>course</u>, journey, lap, orbit, revolution, route, tour, track

circuitous adjective <u>indirect</u>, labyrinthine, meandering, oblique, rambling, roundabout, tortuous, winding

circular adjective 1 <u>round</u>, ring-shaped, rotund, spherical 2 <u>orbital</u>, circuitous, cyclical ◆ noun 3 <u>advertisement</u>, notice

circulate verb 1 <u>spread</u>, broadcast, disseminate, distribute, issue, make known, promulgate, publicize, publish 2 <u>flow</u>, gyrate, radiate, revolve, rotate

circulation noun 1 <u>bloodstream</u> 2 <u>flow</u>, circling, motion, rotation 3 <u>distribution</u>, currency, dissemination, spread, transmission

circumference noun <u>boundary</u>, border, edge, extremity, limits, outline, perimeter, periphery, rim

circumstance noun <u>event</u>, accident, condition, contingency, happening, incident, occurrence, particular, respect, situation

circumstances *plural noun* <u>situation</u>, means, position, state, state of affairs, station, status

cistern *noun* <u>tank</u>, basin, reservoir, sink, vat

citadel *noun* <u>fortress</u>, bastion, fortification, keep, stronghold, tower

cite *verb* <u>quote</u>, adduce, advance, allude to, enumerate, extract, mention, name, specify

citizen *noun* <u>inhabitant</u>, denizen, dweller, resident, subject, townsman

city *noun* <u>town</u>, conurbation, metropolis, municipality

civic *adjective* <u>public</u>, communal, local, municipal

civil *adjective* 1 <u>civic</u>, domestic, municipal, political 2 <u>polite</u>, affable, courteous, obliging, refined, urbane, well-mannered

civilization *noun* 1 <u>culture</u>, advancement, cultivation, development, education, enlightenment, progress, refinement, sophistication 2 <u>society</u>, community, nation, people, polity

civilize *verb* <u>cultivate</u>, educate, enlighten, refine, sophisticate, tame

civilized *adjective* <u>cultured</u>, educated, enlightened, humane, polite, sophisticated, tolerant, urbane

claim *verb* 1 <u>assert</u>, allege, challenge, insist, maintain, profess, uphold 2 <u>demand</u>, ask, call for, insist, need, require ♦ *noun* 3 <u>assertion</u>, affirmation, allegation, pretension, privilege,

protestation 4 <u>demand</u>, application, call, petition, request, requirement 5 <u>right</u>, title

clairvoyant *noun* 1 <u>psychic</u>, diviner, fortune-teller, visionary ♦ *adjective* 2 <u>psychic</u>, extrasensory, second-sighted, telepathic, visionary

clamber *verb* <u>climb</u>, claw, scale, scrabble, scramble, shin

clammy *adjective* <u>moist</u>, close, damp, dank, sticky, sweaty

clamour *noun* <u>noise</u>, commotion, din, hubbub, outcry, racket, shouting, uproar

clamp *noun* 1 <u>vice</u>, bracket, fastener, grip, press ♦ *verb* 2 <u>fasten</u>, brace, fix, make fast, secure

clan *noun* <u>family</u>, brotherhood, faction, fraternity, group, society, tribe

clandestine *adjective* <u>secret</u>, cloak-and-dagger, concealed, covert, furtive, private, stealthy, surreptitious, underground

clap *verb* <u>applaud</u>, acclaim, cheer

clarification *noun* <u>explanation</u>, elucidation, exposition, illumination, interpretation, simplification

clarify *verb* <u>explain</u>, clear up, elucidate, illuminate, interpret, make plain, simplify, throw *or* shed light on

clarity *noun* <u>clearness</u>, definition, limpidity, lucidity, precision, simplicity, transparency

clash *verb* 1 <u>conflict</u>, cross swords, feud, grapple, lock horns, quarrel, war, wrangle 2 <u>crash</u>, bang, clang, clank, clatter, jangle, jar, rattle ♦ *noun*

3 <u>conflict</u>, brush, collision, confrontation, difference of opinion, disagreement, fight, showdown (*informal*)

clasp *noun* 1 <u>fastening</u>, brooch, buckle, catch, clip, fastener, grip, hook, pin 2 <u>grasp</u>, embrace, grip, hold, hug ◆ *verb* 3 <u>grasp</u>, clutch, embrace, grip, hold, hug, press, seize, squeeze 4 <u>fasten</u>, connect

class *noun* 1 <u>group</u>, category, division, genre, kind, set, sort, type ◆ *verb* 2 <u>classify</u>, brand, categorize, designate, grade, group, label, rank, rate

classic *adjective* 1 <u>definitive</u>, archetypal, exemplary, ideal, model, quintessential, standard 2 <u>typical</u>, characteristic, regular, standard, time-honoured, usual 3 <u>best</u>, consummate, finest, first-rate, masterly, world-class 4 <u>lasting</u>, abiding, ageless, deathless, enduring, immortal, undying ◆ *noun* 5 <u>standard</u>, exemplar, masterpiece, model, paradigm, prototype

classical *adjective* <u>pure</u>, elegant, harmonious, refined, restrained, symmetrical, understated, well-proportioned

classification *noun* <u>categorization</u>, analysis, arrangement, grading, sorting, taxonomy

classify *verb* <u>categorize</u>, arrange, catalogue, grade, pigeonhole, rank, sort, systematize, tabulate

classy *adjective* Informal <u>high-class</u>, elegant, exclusive, posh (*informal, chiefly Brit.*), stylish, superior, top-drawer, up-market

clause *noun* <u>section</u>, article, chapter, condition, paragraph, part, passage

claw *noun* 1 <u>nail</u>, pincer, talon, tentacle ◆ *verb* 2 <u>scratch</u>, dig, lacerate, maul, rip, scrape, tear

clean *adjective* 1 <u>pure</u>, flawless, fresh, immaculate, impeccable, spotless, unblemished, unsullied 2 <u>hygienic</u>, antiseptic, decontaminated, purified, sterile, sterilized, uncontaminated, unpolluted 3 <u>moral</u>, chaste, decent, good, honourable, innocent, pure, respectable, upright, virtuous 4 <u>complete</u>, conclusive, decisive, entire, final, perfect, thorough, total, unimpaired, whole ◆ *verb* 5 <u>cleanse</u>, disinfect, launder, purge, purify, rinse, sanitize, scour, scrub, wash

cleanse *verb* <u>clean</u>, absolve, clear, purge, purify, rinse, scour, scrub, wash

cleanser *noun* <u>detergent</u>, disinfectant, purifier, scourer, soap, solvent

clear *adjective* 1 <u>certain</u>, convinced, decided, definite, positive, resolved, satisfied, sure 2 <u>obvious</u>, apparent, blatant, comprehensible, conspicuous, distinct, evident, manifest, palpable, plain, pronounced, recognizable, unmistakable 3 <u>transparent</u>, crystalline, glassy, limpid, pellucid, see-through, translucent 4 <u>bright</u>, cloudless, fair, fine, light, luminous, shining, sunny, unclouded 5 <u>unobstructed</u>, empty, free, open, smooth, unhindered, unimpeded 6 <u>unblemished</u>, clean, immaculate, innocent, pure, untarnished ♦ *verb* **7** <u>unblock</u>, disentangle, extricate, free, loosen, open, rid, unload **8** <u>pass over</u>, jump, leap, miss, vault **9** <u>brighten</u>, break up, lighten **10** <u>clean</u>, cleanse, erase, purify, refine, sweep away, tidy (up), wipe **11** <u>absolve</u>, acquit, excuse, exonerate, justify, vindicate **12** <u>gain</u>, acquire, earn, make, reap, secure

clear-cut *adjective* <u>straightforward</u>, black-and-white, cut-and-dried (*informal*), definite, explicit, plain, precise, specific, unambiguous, unequivocal

clearly *adverb* <u>obviously</u>, beyond doubt, distinctly, evidently, markedly, openly, overtly, undeniably, undoubtedly

clergy *noun* <u>priesthood</u>, churchmen, clergymen, clerics, holy orders, ministry, the cloth

clergyman *noun* <u>minister</u>, chaplain, cleric, man of God, man of the cloth, padre, parson, pastor, priest, vicar

clever *adjective* <u>intelligent</u>, bright, gifted, ingenious, knowledgeable, quick-witted, resourceful, shrewd, smart, talented

cleverness *noun* <u>intelligence</u>, ability, brains, ingenuity, quick wits, resourcefulness, shrewdness, smartness

cliché *noun* <u>platitude</u>, banality, commonplace, hackneyed phrase, stereotype, truism

client *noun* <u>customer</u>, applicant, buyer, consumer, patient, patron, shopper

clientele *noun* <u>customers</u>,

business, clients, following, market, patronage, regulars, trade

cliff *noun* <u>rock face</u>, bluff, crag, escarpment, overhang, precipice, scar, scarp

climactic *adjective* <u>crucial</u>, critical, decisive, paramount, peak

climate *noun* <u>weather</u>, temperature

climax *noun* <u>culmination</u>, height, highlight, high point, peak, summit, top, zenith

climb *verb* <u>ascend</u>, clamber, mount, rise, scale, shin up, soar, top

climb down *verb* **1** <u>descend</u>, dismount **2** <u>back down</u>, eat one's words, retract, retreat

clinch *verb* <u>settle</u>, conclude, confirm, decide, determine, seal, secure, set the seal on, sew up (*Informal*)

cling *verb* <u>stick</u>, adhere, clasp, clutch, embrace, grasp, grip, hug

clinical *adjective* <u>unemotional</u>, analytic, cold, detached, dispassionate, impersonal, objective, scientific

clip[1] *verb* **1** <u>trim</u>, crop, curtail, cut, pare, prune, shear, shorten, snip ♦ *noun, verb* **2** *Informal* <u>smack</u>, clout (*informal*), cuff, knock, punch, strike, thump, wallop (*informal*), whack

clip[2] *verb* <u>attach</u>, fasten, fix, hold, pin, staple

clique *noun* <u>group</u>, cabal, circle, coterie, faction, gang, set

cloak *noun* **1** <u>cape</u>, coat, mantle, wrap ♦ *verb* **2** <u>cover</u>, camouflage, conceal, disguise, hide, mask, obscure, screen, veil

clog verb obstruct, block, congest, hinder, impede, jam

close[1] verb **1** shut, bar, block, lock, plug, seal, secure, stop up **2** end, cease, complete, conclude, finish, shut down, terminate, wind up **3** connect, come together, couple, fuse, join, unite ♦ noun **4** end, completion, conclusion, culmination, denouement, ending, finale, finish

close[2] adjective **1** near, adjacent, adjoining, at hand, cheek by jowl, handy, impending, nearby, neighbouring, nigh **2** intimate, attached, confidential, dear, devoted, familiar, inseparable, loving **3** careful, detailed, intense, minute, painstaking, rigorous, thorough **4** compact, congested, crowded, dense, impenetrable, jam-packed, packed, tight **5** stifling, airless, heavy, humid, muggy, oppressive, stuffy, suffocating, sweltering **6** secretive, private, reticent, secret, taciturn, uncommunicative **7** mean, miserly, stingy

closed adjective **1** shut, fastened, locked, out of service, sealed **2** exclusive, restricted **3** finished, concluded, decided, ended, over, resolved, settled, terminated

cloth noun fabric, material, textiles

clothe verb dress, array, attire, cover, drape, equip, fit out, garb, robe, swathe

clothes plural noun clothing, apparel, attire, costume, dress, garb, garments, gear (informal), outfit, wardrobe, wear

clothing noun clothes, apparel, attire, costume, dress, garb, garments, gear (informal), outfit, wardrobe, wear

cloud noun **1** mist, gloom, haze, murk, vapour ♦ verb **2** obscure, becloud, darken, dim, eclipse, obfuscate, overshadow, shade, shadow, veil **3** confuse, disorient, distort, impair, muddle, muddy the waters

cloudy adjective **1** dull, dim, gloomy, leaden, louring or lowering, overcast, sombre, sunless **2** opaque, muddy, murky

clout Informal ♦ noun **1** influence, authority, power, prestige, pull, weight ♦ verb **2** hit, clobber (slang), punch, sock (slang), strike, thump, wallop (informal)

clown noun **1** comedian, buffoon, comic, fool, harlequin, jester, joker, prankster ♦ verb **2** play the fool, act the fool, jest, mess about

club noun **1** association, company, fraternity, group, guild, lodge, set, society, union **2** stick, bat, bludgeon, cosh (Brit.), cudgel, truncheon ♦ verb **3** beat, bash, batter, bludgeon, cosh (Brit.), hammer, pummel, strike

clue noun indication, evidence, hint, lead, pointer, sign, suggestion, suspicion, trace

clueless adjective stupid, dim, dozy (Brit. informal), dull, half-witted, simple, slow, thick, unintelligent, witless

clump noun **1** cluster, bunch, bundle, group, mass ♦ verb **2** stomp, lumber, plod, thud, thump, tramp

clumsy adjective awkward,

bumbling, gauche, gawky, ham-fisted (*informal*), lumbering, maladroit, ponderous, uncoordinated, ungainly, unwieldy

cluster *noun* 1 <u>gathering</u>, assemblage, batch, bunch, clump, collection, group, knot ◆ *verb* 2 <u>gather</u>, assemble, bunch, collect, flock, group

clutch *verb* <u>seize</u>, catch, clasp, cling to, embrace, grab, grasp, grip, snatch

clutches *plural noun* <u>power</u>, claws, control, custody, grasp, grip, hands, keeping, possession, sway

clutter *verb* 1 <u>litter</u>, scatter, strew ◆ *noun* 2 <u>untidiness</u>, confusion, disarray, disorder, hotchpotch, jumble, litter, mess, muddle

coach *noun* 1 <u>bus</u>, car, carriage, charabanc, vehicle 2 <u>instructor</u>, handler, teacher, trainer, tutor ◆ *verb* 3 <u>instruct</u>, drill, exercise, prepare, train, tutor

coalesce *verb* <u>blend</u>, amalgamate, combine, fuse, incorporate, integrate, merge, mix, unite

coalition *noun* <u>alliance</u>, amalgamation, association, bloc, combination, confederation, conjunction, fusion, merger, union

coarse *adjective* 1 <u>rough</u>, crude, homespun, impure, unfinished, unpolished, unprocessed, unpurified, unrefined 2 <u>vulgar</u>, earthy, improper, indecent, indelicate, ribald, rude, smutty

coarseness *noun* 1 <u>roughness</u>, crudity, unevenness 2 <u>vulgarity</u>, bawdiness, crudity, earthiness,

indelicacy, ribaldry, smut, uncouthness

coast *noun* 1 <u>shore</u>, beach, border, coastline, seaboard, seaside ◆ *verb* 2 <u>cruise</u>, drift, freewheel, glide, sail, taxi

coat *noun* 1 <u>fur</u>, fleece, hair, hide, pelt, skin, wool 2 <u>layer</u>, coating, covering, overlay ◆ *verb* 3 <u>cover</u>, apply, plaster, smear, spread

coax *verb* <u>persuade</u>, allure, cajole, entice, prevail upon, sweet-talk (*informal*), talk into, wheedle

cocktail *noun* <u>mixture</u>, blend, combination, mix

cocky *adjective* <u>overconfident</u>, arrogant, brash, cocksure, conceited, egotistical, full of oneself, swaggering, vain

code *noun* 1 <u>cipher</u>, cryptograph 2 <u>principles</u>, canon, convention, custom, ethics, etiquette, manners, maxim, regulations, rules, system

cogent *adjective* <u>convincing</u>, compelling, effective, forceful, influential, potent, powerful, strong, weighty

cogitate *verb* <u>think</u>, consider, contemplate, deliberate, meditate, mull over, muse, ponder, reflect, ruminate

coherent *adjective* 1 <u>consistent</u>, logical, lucid, meaningful, orderly, organized, rational, reasoned, systematic 2 <u>intelligible</u>, articulate, comprehensible

coil *verb* <u>wind</u>, curl, loop, snake, spiral, twine, twist, wreathe, writhe

coin *noun* 1 <u>money</u>, cash,

change, copper, silver, specie
♦ *verb* 2 invent, create, fabricate, forge, make up, mint, mould, originate

coincide *verb* 1 occur simultaneously, be concurrent, coexist, synchronize 2 agree, accord, concur, correspond, harmonize, match, square, tally

coincidence *noun* 1 chance, accident, fluke, happy accident, luck, stroke of luck 2 coinciding, concurrence, conjunction, correlation, correspondence

coincidental *adjective* chance, accidental, casual, fluky (*informal*), fortuitous, unintentional, unplanned

cold *adjective* 1 chilly, arctic, bleak, cool, freezing, frigid, frosty, frozen, icy, wintry 2 unfriendly, aloof, distant, frigid, indifferent, reserved, standoffish ♦ *noun* 3 coldness, chill, frigidity, frostiness, iciness

cold-blooded *adjective* callous, dispassionate, heartless, ruthless, steely, stony-hearted, unemotional, unfeeling

collaborate *verb* 1 work together, cooperate, join forces, participate, play ball (*informal*), team up 2 conspire, collude, cooperate, fraternize

collaboration *noun* teamwork, alliance, association, cooperation, partnership

collaborator *noun* 1 co-worker, associate, colleague, confederate, partner, team-mate 2 traitor, fraternizer, quisling, turncoat

collapse *verb* 1 fall down, cave in, crumple, fall, fall apart at the

seams, give way, subside 2 fail, come to nothing, fold, founder, go belly-up (*informal*) ♦ *noun* 3 falling down, cave-in, disintegration, falling apart, ruin, subsidence 4 failure, downfall, flop, slump 5 faint, breakdown, exhaustion, prostration

collar *verb Informal* seize, apprehend, arrest, capture, catch, grab, nab (*informal*), nail (*informal*)

colleague *noun* fellow worker, ally, assistant, associate, collaborator, comrade, helper, partner, team-mate, workmate

collect *verb* 1 assemble, cluster, congregate, convene, converge, flock together, rally 2 gather, accumulate, amass, assemble, heap, hoard, save, stockpile

collected *adjective* calm, composed, cool, poised, self-possessed, serene, unperturbed, unruffled

collection *noun* 1 accumulation, anthology, compilation, heap, hoard, mass, pile, set, stockpile, store 2 group, assembly, assortment, cluster, company, crowd 3 contribution, alms, offering, offertory

collective *adjective* combined, aggregate, composite, corporate, cumulative, joint, shared, unified, united

collide *verb* 1 crash, clash, come into collision, meet head-on 2 conflict, clash

collision *noun* 1 crash, accident, bump, impact, pile-up (*informal*), prang (*informal*), smash 2 conflict, clash, confrontation, encounter, opposition, skirmish

colloquial *adjective* informal, conversational, demotic, everyday, familiar, idiomatic, vernacular

colony *noun* settlement, community, dependency, dominion, outpost, possession, province, satellite state, territory

colossal *adjective* huge, enormous, gigantic, immense, mammoth, massive, monumental, prodigious, vast

colour *noun* **1** hue, colorant, dye, paint, pigment, shade, tint ♦ *verb* **2** paint, dye, stain, tinge, tint **3** blush, flush, redden

colourful *adjective* **1** bright, brilliant, multicoloured, psychedelic, variegated **2** interesting, distinctive, graphic, lively, picturesque, rich, vivid

colourless *adjective* **1** drab, achromatic, anaemic, ashen, bleached, faded, wan, washed out **2** uninteresting, characterless, dreary, dull, insipid, lacklustre, vapid

column *noun* **1** pillar, obelisk, post, shaft, support, upright **2** line, cavalcade, file, procession, rank, row

coma *noun* unconsciousness, oblivion, stupor, trance

comb *verb* **1** untangle, arrange, dress, groom **2** search, forage, hunt, rake, ransack, rummage, scour, sift

combat *noun* **1** fight, action, battle, conflict, contest, encounter, engagement, skirmish, struggle, war, warfare ♦ *verb* **2** fight, defy, do battle with, oppose, resist, withstand

combatant *noun* fighter, adversary, antagonist, enemy, opponent, soldier, warrior

combination *noun* **1** mixture, amalgamation, blend, coalescence, composite, connection, mix **2** association, alliance, coalition, confederation, consortium, federation, syndicate, union

combine *verb* join together, amalgamate, blend, connect, integrate, link, merge, mix, pool, unite

come *verb* **1** move towards, advance, approach, draw near, near **2** arrive, appear, enter, materialize, reach, show up (*informal*), turn up (*informal*) **3** happen, fall, occur, take place **4** result, arise, emanate, emerge, flow, issue, originate **5** reach, extend **6** be available, be made, be offered, be on offer, be produced

come about *verb* happen, arise, befall, come to pass, occur, result, take place, transpire (*informal*)

come across *verb* find, bump into (*informal*), chance upon, discover, encounter, meet, notice, stumble upon, unearth

comeback *noun* **1** *Informal* return, rally, rebound, recovery, resurgence, revival, triumph **2** response, rejoinder, reply, retaliation, retort, riposte

come back *verb* return, reappear, recur, re-enter

comedian *noun* comic, card (*informal*), clown, funny man, humorist, jester, joker, wag, wit

comedown *noun* **1** decline,

deflation, demotion, reverse
2 *Informal* <u>disappointment</u>,
anticlimax, blow, humiliation,
letdown

comedy *noun* <u>humour</u>, farce,
fun, hilarity, jesting, joking, light
entertainment

comeuppance *noun* *Informal*
<u>punishment</u>, chastening, deserts,
due reward, recompense,
retribution

comfort *noun* **1** <u>luxury</u>, cosiness,
ease, opulence, snugness,
wellbeing **2** <u>relief</u>, compensation,
consolation, help, succour,
support ◆ *verb* **3** <u>console</u>,
commiserate with, hearten,
reassure, soothe

comfortable *adjective* **1** <u>relaxing</u>,
agreeable, convenient, cosy,
homely, pleasant, restful, snug
2 <u>happy</u>, at ease, at home,
contented, gratified, relaxed,
serene **3** *Informal* <u>well-off</u>,
affluent, in clover (*informal*),
prosperous, well-to-do

comforting *adjective* <u>consoling</u>,
cheering, consolatory,
encouraging, heart-warming,
reassuring, soothing

comic *adjective* **1** <u>funny</u>, amusing,
comical, droll, farcical,
humorous, jocular, witty ◆ *noun*
2 <u>comedian</u>, buffoon, clown,
funny man, humorist, jester,
wag, wit

comical *adjective* <u>funny</u>, amusing,
comic, droll, farcical, hilarious,
humorous, priceless, side-splitting

coming *adjective* **1** <u>approaching</u>,
at hand, forthcoming, imminent,
impending, in store, near, nigh
◆ *noun* **2** <u>arrival</u>, advent, approach

command *verb* **1** <u>order</u>, bid,

charge, compel, demand, direct,
require **2** <u>have authority over</u>,
control, dominate, govern,
handle, head, lead, manage,
rule, supervise ◆ *noun* **3** <u>order</u>,
commandment, decree,
demand, directive, instruction,
requirement, ultimatum
4 <u>authority</u>, charge, control,
government, management,
mastery, power, rule, supervision

commandeer *verb* <u>seize</u>,
appropriate, confiscate,
requisition, sequester, sequestrate

commander *noun* <u>officer</u>, boss,
captain, chief, commanding
officer, head, leader, ruler

commanding *adjective*
<u>controlling</u>, advantageous,
decisive, dominant, dominating,
superior

commemorate *verb* <u>remember</u>,
celebrate, honour, immortalize,
pay tribute to, salute

commemoration *noun*
<u>remembrance</u>, ceremony,
honouring, memorial service,
tribute

commence *verb* <u>begin</u>, embark
on, enter upon, initiate, upon,
originate, start

commend *verb* <u>praise</u>, acclaim,
applaud, approve, compliment,
extol, recommend, speak highly
of

commendable *adjective*
<u>praiseworthy</u>, admirable,
creditable, deserving, estimable,
exemplary, laudable,
meritorious, worthy

commendation *noun* <u>praise</u>,
acclaim, acclamation,
approbation, approval, credit,
encouragement, good opinion,

panegyric, recommendation

comment noun 1 <u>remark</u>, observation, statement 2 <u>note</u>, annotation, commentary, explanation, exposition, illustration ♦ verb 3 <u>remark</u>, mention, note, observe, point out, say, utter 4 <u>annotate</u>, elucidate, explain, interpret

commentary noun 1 <u>narration</u>, description, voice-over 2 <u>notes</u>, analysis, critique, explanation, review, treatise

commentator noun 1 <u>reporter</u>, special correspondent, sportscaster 2 <u>critic</u>, annotator, interpreter

commerce noun <u>trade</u>, business, dealing, exchange, traffic

commercial adjective 1 <u>mercantile</u>, trading 2 <u>materialistic</u>, mercenary, profit-making

commiserate verb <u>sympathize</u>, console, feel for, pity

commission noun 1 <u>duty</u>, errand, mandate, mission, task 2 <u>fee</u>, cut, percentage, rake-off (*slang*), royalties 3 <u>committee</u>, board, commissioners, delegation, deputation, representatives ♦ verb 4 <u>appoint</u>, authorize, contract, delegate, depute, empower, engage, nominate, order, select

commit verb 1 <u>do</u>, carry out, enact, execute, perform, perpetrate 2 <u>put in custody</u>, confine, imprison

commitment noun 1 <u>dedication</u>, devotion, involvement, loyalty 2 <u>responsibility</u>, duty, engagement, liability, obligation, tie

common adjective 1 <u>average</u>, commonplace, conventional, customary, everyday, familiar, frequent, habitual, ordinary, regular, routine, standard, stock, usual 2 <u>popular</u>, accepted, general, prevailing, prevalent, universal, widespread 3 <u>collective</u>, communal, popular, public, social 4 <u>vulgar</u>, coarse, inferior, plebeian

commonplace adjective 1 <u>everyday</u>, banal, common, humdrum, mundane, obvious, ordinary, run-of-the-mill, widespread ♦ noun 2 <u>cliché</u>, banality, platitude, truism

common sense noun <u>good sense</u>, gumption (*Brit. informal*), horse sense, level-headedness, native intelligence, prudence, sound judgment, wit

commotion noun <u>disturbance</u>, disorder, excitement, furore, fuss, hue and cry, rumpus, tumult, turmoil, upheaval, uproar

communal adjective <u>public</u>, collective, general, joint, shared

commune noun <u>community</u>, collective, cooperative, kibbutz

commune with verb <u>contemplate</u>, meditate on, muse on, ponder, reflect on

communicate verb <u>make known</u>, convey, declare, disclose, impart, inform, pass on, proclaim, transmit

communication noun 1 <u>passing on</u>, contact, conversation, correspondence, dissemination, link, transmission 2 <u>message</u>, announcement, disclosure, dispatch, information, news, report, statement, word

communicative *adjective* talkative, chatty, expansive, forthcoming, frank, informative, loquacious, open, outgoing, voluble

Communism *noun* socialism, Bolshevism, collectivism, Marxism, state socialism

Communist *noun* socialist, Bolshevik, collectivist, Marxist, Red (*informal*)

community *noun* society, brotherhood, commonwealth, company, general public, people, populace, public, residents, state

commuter *noun* daily traveller, straphanger (*informal*), suburbanite

compact[1] *adjective* 1 closely packed, compressed, condensed, dense, pressed together, solid, thick 2 brief, compendious, concise, succinct, terse, to the point ◆ *verb* 3 pack closely, compress, condense, cram, stuff, tamp

compact[2] *noun* agreement, arrangement, bargain, bond, contract, covenant, deal, pact, treaty, understanding

companion *noun* 1 friend, accomplice, ally, associate, colleague, comrade, consort, mate (*informal*), partner 2 escort, aide, assistant, attendant, chaperon, squire

companionship *noun* fellowship, camaraderie, company, comradeship, conviviality, esprit de corps, friendship, rapport, togetherness

company *noun* 1 business, association, concern, corporation, establishment, firm, house, partnership, syndicate 2 group, assembly, band, collection, community, crowd, gathering, party, set 3 guests, callers, party, visitors

comparable *adjective* 1 on a par, a match for, as good as, commensurate, equal, equivalent, in a class with, proportionate, tantamount 2 similar, akin, alike, analogous, cognate, corresponding, cut from the same cloth, of a piece, related

comparative *adjective* relative, by comparison, qualified

compare *verb* 1 weigh, balance, contrast, juxtapose, set against 2 *usually with* with be on a par with, approach, bear comparison, be in the same class as, be the equal of, compete with, equal, hold a candle to, match 3 **compare to** liken to, correlate to, equate to, identify with, mention in the same breath as, parallel, resemble

comparison *noun* 1 contrast, distinction, juxtaposition 2 similarity, analogy, comparability, correlation, likeness, resemblance

compartment *noun* section, alcove, bay, berth, booth, carriage, cubbyhole, cubicle, locker, niche, pigeonhole

compass *noun* range, area, boundary, circumference, extent, field, limit, reach, realm, scope

compassion *noun* sympathy, condolence, fellow feeling, humanity, kindness, mercy, pity, sorrow, tender-heartedness, tenderness, understanding

compassionate *adjective*
<u>sympathetic</u>, benevolent, charitable, humane, humanitarian, kind-hearted, merciful, pitying, tender-hearted, understanding

compatibility *noun* <u>harmony</u>, affinity, agreement, concord, empathy, like-mindedness, rapport, sympathy

compatible *adjective*
<u>harmonious</u>, adaptable, congruous, consistent, in harmony, in keeping, suitable

compel *verb* <u>force</u>, coerce, constrain, dragoon, impel, make, oblige, railroad (*informal*)

compelling *adjective*
1 <u>fascinating</u>, enchanting, enthralling, gripping, hypnotic, irresistible, mesmeric, spellbinding **2** <u>pressing</u>, binding, coercive, imperative, overriding, peremptory, unavoidable, urgent **3** <u>convincing</u>, cogent, conclusive, forceful, irrefutable, powerful, telling, weighty

compensate *verb* **1** <u>recompense</u>, atone, make amends, make good, refund, reimburse, remunerate, repay **2** <u>cancel (out)</u>, balance, counteract, counterbalance, make up for, offset, redress

compensation *noun*
<u>recompense</u>, amends, atonement, damages, reimbursement, remuneration, reparation, restitution, satisfaction

compete *verb* <u>contend</u>, be in the running, challenge, contest, fight, strive, struggle, vie

competence *noun* <u>ability</u>,

capability, capacity, expertise, fitness, proficiency, skill, suitability

competent *adjective* <u>able</u>, adequate, capable, fit, proficient, qualified, suitable

competition *noun* **1** <u>rivalry</u>, opposition, strife, struggle **2** <u>contest</u>, championship, event, head-to-head, puzzle, quiz, tournament **3** <u>opposition</u>, challengers, field, rivals

competitive *adjective*
1 <u>cut-throat</u>, aggressive, antagonistic, at odds, dog-eat-dog, opposing, rival **2** <u>ambitious</u>, combative

competitor *noun* <u>contestant</u>, adversary, antagonist, challenger, opponent, rival

compilation *noun* <u>collection</u>, accumulation, anthology, assemblage, assortment, treasury

compile *verb* <u>put together</u>, accumulate, amass, collect, cull, garner, gather, marshal, organize

complacency *noun*
<u>self-satisfaction</u>, contentment, satisfaction, smugness

complacent *adjective*
<u>self-satisfied</u>, contented, pleased with oneself, resting on one's laurels, satisfied, serene, smug, unconcerned

complain *verb* <u>find fault</u>, bemoan, bewail, carp, deplore, groan, grouse, grumble, lament, moan, whine, whinge (*informal*)

complaint *noun* **1** <u>criticism</u>, charge, grievance, gripe (*informal*), grouse, grumble, lament, moan, protest **2** <u>illness</u>, affliction, ailment, disease, disorder, malady, sickness, upset

complement noun
1 completion, companion, consummation, counterpart, finishing touch, rounding-off, supplement 2 total, aggregate, capacity, entirety, quota, totality, wholeness ♦ verb 3 complete, cap (informal), crown, round off, set off

complementary adjective completing, companion, corresponding, interdependent, interrelating, matched, reciprocal

complete adjective 1 total, absolute, consummate, outright, perfect, thorough, thoroughgoing, utter 2 finished, accomplished, achieved, concluded, ended 3 entire, all, faultless, full, intact, plenary, unbroken, whole ♦ verb 4 finish, close, conclude, crown, end, finalize, round off, settle, wrap up (informal)

completely adverb totally, absolutely, altogether, entirely, every inch, fully, hook, line and sinker, in full, lock, stock and barrel, one hundred per cent, perfectly, thoroughly, utterly, wholly

completion noun finishing, bitter end, close, conclusion, culmination, end, fruition, fulfilment

complex adjective 1 compound, composite, heterogeneous, manifold, multifarious, multiple 2 complicated, convoluted, elaborate, intricate, involved, labyrinthine, tangled, tortuous ♦ noun 3 structure, aggregate, composite, network, organization, scheme, system

4 Informal obsession, fixation, fixed idea, idée fixe, phobia, preoccupation

complexion noun 1 skin, colour, colouring, hue, pigmentation, skin tone 2 nature, appearance, aspect, character, guise, light, look, make-up

complexity noun complication, elaboration, entanglement, intricacy, involvement, ramification

complicate verb make difficult, confuse, entangle, involve, muddle, ravel

complicated adjective 1 difficult, involved, perplexing, problematic, puzzling, troublesome 2 involved, complex, convoluted, elaborate, intricate, labyrinthine

complication noun
1 complexity, confusion, entanglement, intricacy, web 2 problem, difficulty, drawback, embarrassment, obstacle, snag

compliment noun 1 praise, bouquet, commendation, congratulations, eulogy, flattery, honour, tribute ♦ verb 2 praise, commend, congratulate, extol, flatter, pay tribute to, salute, speak highly of

complimentary adjective
1 flattering, appreciative, approving, commendatory, congratulatory, laudatory 2 free, courtesy, donated, gratis, gratuitous, honorary, on the house

compliments plural noun greetings, good wishes, regards, remembrances, respects, salutation

comply verb <u>obey</u>, abide by, acquiesce, adhere to, conform to, follow, observe, submit, toe the line

component noun 1 <u>part</u>, constituent, element, ingredient, item, piece, unit ♦ adjective 2 <u>constituent</u>, inherent, intrinsic

compose verb 1 <u>put together</u>, build, comprise, constitute, construct, fashion, form, make, make up 2 <u>create</u>, contrive, devise, invent, produce, write 3 <u>calm</u>, collect, control, pacify, placate, quiet, soothe 4 <u>arrange</u>, adjust

composed adjective <u>calm</u>, at ease, collected, cool, level-headed, poised, relaxed, sedate, self-possessed, serene, unflappable

composition noun 1 <u>creation</u>, compilation, fashioning, formation, formulation, making, production, putting together 2 <u>design</u>, arrangement, configuration, formation, layout, make-up, organization, structure 3 <u>essay</u>, exercise, literary work, opus, piece, treatise, work

composure noun <u>calmness</u>, aplomb, equanimity, poise, sang-froid, self-assurance, self-possession, serenity

compound noun 1 <u>combination</u>, alloy, amalgam, blend, composite, fusion, medley, mixture, synthesis ♦ verb 2 <u>combine</u>, amalgamate, blend, intermingle, mix, synthesize, unite 3 <u>intensify</u>, add to, aggravate, augment, complicate, exacerbate, heighten, magnify, worsen ♦ adjective 4 <u>complex</u>,

composite, intricate, multiple

comprehend verb <u>understand</u>, apprehend, conceive, fathom, grasp, know, make out, perceive, see, take in

comprehensible adjective <u>understandable</u>, clear, coherent, conceivable, explicit, intelligible, plain

comprehension noun <u>understanding</u>, conception, discernment, grasp, intelligence, perception, realization

comprehensive adjective <u>broad</u>, all-embracing, all-inclusive, blanket, complete, encyclopedic, exhaustive, full, inclusive, thorough

compress verb <u>squeeze</u>, abbreviate, concentrate, condense, contract, crush, press, shorten, squash

comprise verb 1 <u>be composed of</u>, consist of, contain, embrace, encompass, include, take in 2 <u>make up</u>, compose, constitute, form

compromise noun 1 <u>give-and-take</u>, accommodation, adjustment, agreement, concession, settlement, trade-off ♦ verb 2 <u>meet halfway</u>, adjust, agree, concede, give and take, go fifty-fifty (informal), settle, strike a balance 3 <u>dishonour</u>, discredit, embarrass, expose, jeopardize, prejudice, weaken

compulsion noun 1 <u>urge</u>, drive, necessity, need, obsession, preoccupation 2 <u>force</u>, coercion, constraint, demand, duress, obligation, pressure, urgency

compulsive adjective <u>irresistible</u>,

compelling, driving, neurotic, obsessive, overwhelming, uncontrollable, urgent

compulsory adjective <u>obligatory</u>, binding, de rigueur, forced, imperative, mandatory, required, requisite

compute verb <u>calculate</u>, add up, count, enumerate, figure out, reckon, tally, total

comrade noun <u>companion</u>, ally, associate, colleague, co-worker, fellow, friend, partner

con Informal ♦ noun 1 <u>swindle</u>, deception, fraud, scam (slang), sting (informal), trick ♦ verb 2 <u>swindle</u>, cheat, deceive, defraud, double-cross (informal), dupe, hoodwink, rip off (slang), trick

concave adjective <u>hollow</u>, indented

conceal verb <u>hide</u>, bury, camouflage, cover, disguise, mask, obscure, screen

concede verb 1 <u>admit</u>, accept, acknowledge, allow, confess, grant, own 2 <u>give up</u>, cede, hand over, relinquish, surrender, yield

conceit noun 1 <u>self-importance</u>, arrogance, egotism, narcissism, pride, swagger, vanity 2 Archaic <u>fancy</u>, fantasy, image, whim, whimsy

conceited adjective <u>self-important</u>, arrogant, bigheaded (informal), cocky, egotistical, full of oneself, immodest, narcissistic, too big for one's boots or breeches, vain

conceivable adjective <u>imaginable</u>, believable, credible, possible, thinkable

conceive verb 1 <u>imagine</u>, believe, comprehend, envisage, fancy, suppose, think, understand 2 <u>think up</u>, contrive, create, design, devise, formulate 3 <u>become pregnant</u>, become impregnated

concentrate verb 1 <u>focus one's attention on</u>, be engrossed in, put one's mind to, rack one's brains 2 <u>focus</u>, bring to bear, centre, cluster, converge 3 <u>gather</u>, accumulate, cluster, collect, congregate, huddle

concentrated adjective 1 <u>intense</u>, all-out (informal), deep, hard, intensive 2 <u>condensed</u>, boiled down, evaporated, reduced, rich, thickened, undiluted

concentration noun 1 <u>single-mindedness</u>, absorption, application, heed 2 <u>focusing</u>, bringing to bear, centralization, centring, consolidation, convergence, intensification 3 <u>convergence</u>, accumulation, aggregation, cluster, collection, horde, mass

concept noun <u>idea</u>, abstraction, conception, conceptualization, hypothesis, image, notion, theory, view

conception noun 1 <u>idea</u>, concept, design, image, notion, plan 2 <u>impregnation</u>, fertilization, germination, insemination

concern noun 1 <u>worry</u>, anxiety, apprehension, burden, care, disquiet, distress 2 <u>importance</u>, bearing, interest, relevance 3 <u>business</u>, affair, interest, job, responsibility, task 4 <u>business</u>, company, corporation, enterprise, establishment, firm, organization ♦ *verb* **5** <u>worry</u>, bother, disquiet, distress, disturb, make anxious, perturb, trouble **6** <u>be relevant to</u>, affect, apply to, bear on, interest, involve, pertain to, regard, touch

concerned *adjective* **1** <u>involved</u>, active, implicated, interested, mixed up, privy to **2** <u>worried</u>, anxious, bothered, distressed, disturbed, troubled, uneasy, upset

concerning *preposition* <u>regarding</u>, about, apropos of, as regards, on the subject of, re, relating to, respecting, touching, with reference to

concession *noun* **1** <u>grant</u>, adjustment, allowance, boon, compromise, indulgence, permit, privilege, sop **2** <u>conceding</u>, acknowledgment, admission, assent, confession, surrender, yielding

conciliate *verb* <u>pacify</u>, appease, clear the air, mediate, mollify, placate, reconcile, soothe, win over

conciliation *noun* <u>pacification</u>, appeasement, mollification, placation, reconciliation, soothing

conciliatory *adjective* <u>pacifying</u>, appeasing, mollifying, pacific, peaceable, placatory

concise *adjective* <u>brief</u>, compendious, condensed, laconic, pithy, short, succinct, terse

conclude *verb* **1** <u>decide</u>, assume, deduce, gather, infer, judge, surmise, work out **2** <u>end</u>, cease, close, complete, finish, round

off, terminate, wind up **3** <u>accomplish</u>, bring about, carry out, effect, pull off

conclusion *noun* **1** <u>decision</u>, conviction, deduction, inference, judgment, opinion, verdict **2** <u>end</u>, bitter end, close, completion, ending, finale, finish, result, termination **3** <u>outcome</u>, consequence, culmination, end result, result, upshot

conclusive *adjective* <u>decisive</u>, clinching, convincing, definite, final, irrefutable, ultimate, unanswerable

concoct *verb* <u>make up</u>, brew, contrive, devise, formulate, hatch, invent, prepare, think up

concoction *noun* <u>mixture</u>, blend, brew, combination, compound, creation, preparation

concrete *adjective* **1** <u>specific</u>, definite, explicit **2** <u>real</u>, actual, factual, material, sensible, substantial, tangible

concur *verb* <u>agree</u>, acquiesce, assent, consent

condemn *verb* **1** <u>disapprove</u>, blame, censure, damn, denounce, reproach, reprove, upbraid **2** <u>sentence</u>, convict, damn, doom, pass sentence on

condemnation *noun* **1** <u>disapproval</u>, blame, censure, denunciation, reproach, reproof, stricture **2** <u>sentence</u>, conviction, damnation, doom, judgment

condensation *noun* **1** <u>distillation</u>, liquefaction, precipitate, precipitation **2** <u>abridgment</u>, contraction, digest, précis, synopsis **3** <u>concentration</u>, compression,

consolidation, crystallization,
curtailment, reduction

condense verb 1 abridge,
abbreviate, compress,
concentrate, epitomize, shorten,
summarize 2 concentrate, boil
down, reduce, thicken

condensed adjective 1 abridged,
compressed, concentrated,
shortened, shrunken,
slimmed-down, summarized
2 concentrated, boiled down,
reduced, thickened

condescend verb 1 patronize,
talk down to 2 lower oneself,
bend, deign, humble or demean
oneself, see fit, stoop

condescending adjective
patronizing, disdainful, lofty,
lordly, snobbish, snooty
(informal), supercilious, superior,
toffee-nosed (slang, chiefly Brit.)

condition noun 1 state,
circumstances, lie of the land,
position, shape, situation, state
of affairs 2 requirement,
limitation, prerequisite, proviso,
qualification, restriction, rider,
stipulation, terms 3 health,
fettle, fitness, kilter, order, shape,
state of health, trim 4 ailment,
complaint, infirmity, malady,
problem, weakness ♦ verb
5 accustom, adapt, equip,
prepare, ready, tone up, train,
work out

conditional adjective dependent,
contingent, limited, provisional,
qualified, subject to, with
reservations

conditions plural noun
circumstances, environment,
milieu, situation, surroundings,
way of life

condone verb overlook, excuse,
forgive, let pass, look the other
way, make allowance for,
pardon, turn a blind eye to

conduct noun 1 behaviour,
attitude, bearing, demeanour,
deportment, manners, ways
2 management, administration,
control, direction, guidance,
handling, organization, running,
supervision ♦ verb 3 carry out,
administer, control, direct,
handle, manage, organize,
preside over, run, supervise
4 behave, acquit, act, carry,
comport, deport 5 accompany,
convey, escort, guide, lead,
steer, usher

confederacy noun union,
alliance, coalition, confederation,
federation, league

confer verb 1 discuss, consult,
converse, deliberate, discourse,
talk 2 grant, accord, award,
bestow, give, hand out, present

conference noun meeting,
colloquium, congress,
consultation, convention,
discussion, forum, seminar,
symposium

confess verb 1 admit,
acknowledge, come clean
(informal), concede, confide,
disclose, divulge, own up
2 declare, affirm, assert, confirm,
profess, reveal

confession noun admission,
acknowledgment, disclosure,
exposure, revelation, unbosoming

confidant, confidante noun
close friend, alter ego, bosom
friend, crony, familiar, intimate

confide verb 1 tell, admit,
confess, disclose, divulge,

impart, reveal, whisper 2 *Formal* entrust, commend, commit, consign

confidence *noun* 1 trust, belief, credence, dependence, faith, reliance 2 self-assurance, aplomb, assurance, boldness, courage, firmness, nerve, self-possession 3 **in confidence** in secrecy, between you and me (and the gatepost), confidentially, privately

confident *adjective* 1 certain, convinced, counting on, positive, satisfied, secure, sure 2 self-assured, assured, bold, dauntless, fearless, self-reliant

confidential *adjective* secret, classified, hush-hush (*informal*), intimate, off the record, private, privy

confidentially *adverb* in secret, behind closed doors, between ourselves, in camera, in confidence, personally, privately, sub rosa

confine *verb* restrict, cage, enclose, hem in, hold back, imprison, incarcerate, intern, keep, limit, shut up

confinement *noun* 1 imprisonment, custody, detention, incarceration, internment, porridge (*slang*) 2 childbirth, childbed, labour, lying-in, parturition

confines *plural noun* limits, boundaries, bounds, circumference, edge, precincts

confirm *verb* 1 prove, authenticate, bear out, corroborate, endorse, ratify, substantiate, validate, verify 2 strengthen, buttress, establish,

fix, fortify, reinforce

confirmation *noun* 1 proof, authentication, corroboration, evidence, substantiation, testimony, validation, verification 2 sanction, acceptance, agreement, approval, assent, endorsement, ratification

confirmed *adjective* long-established, chronic, dyed-in-the-wool, habitual, hardened, ingrained, inveterate, seasoned

confiscate *verb* seize, appropriate, commandeer, impound, sequester, sequestrate

confiscation *noun* seizure, appropriation, forfeiture, impounding, sequestration, takeover

conflict *noun* 1 opposition, antagonism, difference, disagreement, discord, dissension, friction, hostility, strife 2 battle, clash, combat, contest, encounter, fight, strife, war ◆ *verb* 3 be incompatible, be at variance, clash, collide, differ, disagree, interfere

conflicting *adjective* incompatible, antagonistic, clashing, contradictory, contrary, discordant, inconsistent, opposing, paradoxical

conform *verb* 1 comply, adapt, adjust, fall in with, follow, obey, toe the line 2 agree, accord, correspond, harmonize, match, suit, tally

conformist *noun* traditionalist, stick-in-the-mud (*informal*), yes man

conformity *noun* compliance, conventionality, observance, orthodoxy, traditionalism

confound verb <u>bewilder</u>, astound, baffle, confuse, dumbfound, flummox, mystify, nonplus, perplex

confront verb <u>face</u>, accost, challenge, defy, encounter, oppose, stand up to, tackle

confrontation noun <u>conflict</u>, contest, encounter, fight, head-to-head, set-to (informal), showdown (informal)

confuse verb 1 <u>mix up</u>, disarrange, disorder, jumble, mingle, muddle, ravel 2 <u>bewilder</u>, baffle, bemuse, faze, flummox, mystify, nonplus, perplex, puzzle 3 <u>disconcert</u>, discompose, disorient, fluster, rattle (informal), throw off balance, unnerve, upset

confused adjective 1 <u>bewildered</u>, at sea, baffled, disorientated, flummoxed, muddled, nonplussed, perplexed, puzzled, taken aback 2 <u>disordered</u>, chaotic, disorganized, higgledy-piggledy (informal), in disarray, jumbled, mixed up, topsy-turvy, untidy

confusing adjective <u>bewildering</u>, baffling, contradictory, disconcerting, misleading, perplexing, puzzling, unclear

confusion noun 1 <u>bewilderment</u>, disorientation, mystification, perplexity, puzzlement 2 <u>disorder</u>, chaos, commotion, jumble, mess, muddle, shambles, turmoil, untidiness, upheaval

congenial adjective 1 <u>pleasant</u>, affable, agreeable, companionable, favourable, friendly, genial, kindly

2 <u>compatible</u>, kindred, like-minded, sympathetic, well-suited

congenital adjective <u>inborn</u>, immanent, inbred, inherent, innate, natural

congested adjective 1 <u>overcrowded</u>, crowded, teeming 2 <u>clogged</u>, blocked-up, crammed, jammed, overfilled, overflowing, packed, stuffed

congestion noun 1 <u>overcrowding</u>, crowding 2 <u>clogging</u>, bottleneck, jam, surfeit

congratulate verb <u>compliment</u>, pat on the back, wish joy to

congratulations plural noun, interjection <u>good wishes</u>, best wishes, compliments, felicitations, greetings

congregate verb <u>come together</u>, assemble, collect, convene, converge, flock, gather, mass, meet

congregation noun <u>assembly</u>, brethren, crowd, fellowship, flock, multitude, throng

congress noun <u>meeting</u>, assembly, conclave, conference, convention, council, legislature, parliament

conjecture noun 1 <u>guess</u>, hypothesis, shot in the dark, speculation, supposition, surmise, theory ♦verb 2 <u>guess</u>, hypothesize, imagine, speculate, suppose, surmise, theorize

conjugal adjective <u>marital</u>, bridal, connubial, married, matrimonial, nuptial, wedded

conjure verb <u>perform tricks</u>, juggle

conjure up *verb* <u>bring to mind</u>, contrive, create, evoke, produce as if by magic, recall, recollect

conjuror, conjurer *noun* <u>magician</u>, illusionist, sorcerer, wizard

connect *verb* <u>link</u>, affix, attach, couple, fasten, join, unite

connected *adjective* <u>linked</u>, affiliated, akin, allied, associated, combined, coupled, joined, related, united

connection *noun* **1** <u>association</u>, affinity, bond, liaison, link, relationship, relevance, tie-in **2** <u>link</u>, alliance, association, attachment, coupling, fastening, junction, tie, union **3** <u>contact</u>, acquaintance, ally, associate, friend, sponsor

connivance *noun* <u>collusion</u>, abetting, complicity, conspiring, tacit consent

connive *verb* **1** <u>conspire</u>, collude, cook up (*informal*), intrigue, plot, scheme **2 connive at** <u>turn a blind eye to</u>, abet, disregard, let pass, look the other way, overlook, wink at

connoisseur *noun* <u>expert</u>, aficionado, appreciator, authority, buff (*informal*), devotee, judge

conquer *verb* **1** <u>defeat</u>, beat, crush, get the better of, master, overcome, overpower, overthrow, quell, subjugate, vanquish **2** <u>seize</u>, acquire, annex, obtain, occupy, overrun, win

conqueror *noun* <u>winner</u>, conquistador, defeater, master, subjugator, vanquisher, victor

conquest *noun* **1** <u>defeat</u>, mastery, overthrow, rout, triumph, victory **2** <u>takeover</u>, annexation, coup, invasion, occupation, subjugation

conscience *noun* <u>principles</u>, moral sense, scruples, sense of right and wrong, still small voice

conscientious *adjective* <u>thorough</u>, careful, diligent, exact, faithful, meticulous, painstaking, particular, punctilious

conscious *adjective* **1** <u>aware</u>, alert, alive to, awake, responsive, sensible, sentient **2** <u>deliberate</u>, calculated, intentional, knowing, premeditated, self-conscious, studied, wilful

consciousness *noun* <u>awareness</u>, apprehension, knowledge, realization, recognition, sensibility

consecrate *verb* <u>sanctify</u>, dedicate, devote, hallow, ordain, set apart, venerate

consecutive *adjective* <u>successive</u>, in sequence, in turn, running, sequential, succeeding, uninterrupted

consensus *noun* <u>agreement</u>, assent, common consent, concord, general agreement, harmony, unanimity, unity

consent *noun* **1** <u>agreement</u>, acquiescence, approval, assent, compliance, go-ahead (*informal*), O.K. *or* okay (*informal*), permission, sanction ♦ *verb* **2** <u>agree</u>, acquiesce, allow, approve, assent, concur, permit

consequence *noun* **1** <u>result</u>, effect, end result, issue, outcome, repercussion, sequel, upshot **2** <u>importance</u>, account, concern, import, moment, significance, value, weight

consequent *adjective* <u>following</u>, ensuing, resultant, resulting, subsequent, successive

consequently *adverb* <u>as a result</u>, accordingly, ergo, hence, subsequently, therefore, thus

conservation *noun* <u>protection</u>, guardianship, husbandry, maintenance, preservation, safeguarding, safekeeping, saving, upkeep

conservative *adjective*
1 <u>traditional</u>, cautious, conventional, die-hard, hidebound, reactionary, sober
♦ *noun* 2 <u>traditionalist</u>, reactionary, stick-in-the-mud (*informal*)

Conservative *adjective* 1 <u>Tory</u>, right-wing ♦ *noun* 2 <u>Tory</u>, right-winger

conserve *verb* <u>protect</u>, hoard, husband, keep, nurse, preserve, save, store up, take care of, use sparingly

consider *verb* 1 <u>think</u>, believe, deem, hold to be, judge, rate, regard as 2 <u>think about</u>, cogitate, contemplate, deliberate, meditate, ponder, reflect, ruminate, turn over in one's mind, weigh 3 <u>bear in mind</u>, keep in view, make allowance for, reckon with, remember, respect, take into account

considerable *adjective* <u>large</u>, appreciable, goodly, great, marked, noticeable, plentiful, sizable *or* sizeable, substantial

considerably *adverb* <u>greatly</u>, appreciably, markedly, noticeably, remarkably,

significantly, substantially, very much

considerate *adjective* <u>thoughtful</u>, attentive, concerned, kindly, mindful, obliging, patient, tactful, unselfish

consideration *noun* 1 <u>thought</u>, analysis, deliberation, discussion, examination, reflection, review, scrutiny 2 <u>factor</u>, concern, issue, point 3 <u>thoughtfulness</u>, concern, considerateness, kindness, respect, tact 4 <u>payment</u>, fee, recompense, remuneration, reward, tip

considering *preposition* <u>taking into account</u>, in the light of, in view of

consignment *noun* <u>shipment</u>, batch, delivery, goods

consist *verb* 1 **consist of** <u>be made up of</u>, amount to, be composed of, comprise, contain, embody, include, incorporate, involve 2 **consist in** <u>lie in</u>, be expressed by, be found *or* contained in, inhere in, reside in

consistency *noun* 1 <u>texture</u>, compactness, density, firmness, thickness, viscosity 2 <u>constancy</u>, evenness, regularity, steadfastness, steadiness, uniformity

consistent *adjective*
1 <u>unchanging</u>, constant, dependable, persistent, regular, steady, true to type, undeviating
2 <u>agreeing</u>, coherent, compatible, congruous, consonant, harmonious, logical

consolation *noun* <u>comfort</u>, cheer, encouragement, help, relief, solace, succour, support

console *verb* <u>comfort</u>, calm,

cheer, encourage, express sympathy for, soothe

consolidate verb 1 <u>strengthen</u>, fortify, reinforce, secure, stabilize 2 <u>combine</u>, amalgamate, federate, fuse, join, unite

consort verb 1 <u>associate</u>, fraternize, go around with, hang about, around or out with, keep company, mix ♦ noun 2 <u>spouse</u>, companion, husband, partner, wife

conspicuous adjective 1 <u>obvious</u>, blatant, clear, evident, noticeable, patent, salient 2 <u>noteworthy</u>, illustrious, notable, outstanding, prominent, remarkable, salient, signal, striking

conspiracy noun <u>plot</u>, collusion, intrigue, machination, scheme, treason

conspirator noun <u>plotter</u>, conspirer, intriguer, schemer, traitor

conspire verb 1 <u>plot</u>, contrive, intrigue, machinate, manoeuvre, plan, scheme 2 <u>work together</u>, combine, concur, contribute, cooperate, tend

constant adjective 1 <u>continuous</u>, ceaseless, incessant, interminable, nonstop, perpetual, sustained, unrelenting 2 <u>unchanging</u>, even, fixed, invariable, permanent, stable, steady, uniform, unvarying 3 <u>faithful</u>, devoted, loyal, stalwart, staunch, true, trustworthy, trusty

constantly adverb <u>continuously</u>, all the time, always, continually, endlessly, incessantly, interminably, invariably,

nonstop, perpetually

consternation noun <u>dismay</u>, alarm, anxiety, distress, dread, fear, trepidation

constituent noun 1 <u>voter</u>, elector 2 <u>component</u>, element, factor, ingredient, part, unit ♦ adjective 3 <u>component</u>, basic, elemental, essential, integral

constitute verb <u>make up</u>, compose, comprise, establish, form, found, set up

constitution noun 1 <u>health</u>, build, character, disposition, physique 2 <u>structure</u>, composition, form, make-up, nature

constitutional adjective 1 <u>statutory</u>, chartered, vested ♦ noun 2 <u>walk</u>, airing, stroll, turn

constrain verb 1 <u>force</u>, bind, coerce, compel, impel, necessitate, oblige, pressurize 2 <u>restrict</u>, check, confine, constrict, curb, restrain, straiten

constraint noun 1 <u>restriction</u>, check, curb, deterrent, hindrance, limitation, rein 2 <u>force</u>, coercion, compulsion, necessity, pressure, restraint

construct verb <u>build</u>, assemble, compose, create, fashion, form, make, manufacture, put together, shape

construction noun 1 <u>building</u>, composition, creation, edifice 2 Formal <u>interpretation</u>, explanation, inference, reading, rendering

constructive adjective <u>helpful</u>, positive, practical, productive, useful, valuable

consult verb <u>ask</u>, compare notes,

confer, pick (someone's) brains, question, refer to, take counsel, turn to

consultant noun <u>specialist</u>, adviser, authority

consultation noun <u>seminar</u>, appointment, conference, council, deliberation, dialogue, discussion, examination, hearing, interview, meeting, session

consume verb 1 <u>eat</u>, devour, eat up, gobble (up), put away, swallow 2 <u>use up</u>, absorb, dissipate, exhaust, expend, spend, squander, waste 3 <u>destroy</u>, annihilate, demolish, devastate, lay waste, ravage 4 often passive <u>obsess</u>, absorb, dominate, eat up, engross, monopolize, preoccupy

consumer noun <u>buyer</u>, customer, purchaser, shopper, user

consummate verb 1 <u>complete</u>, accomplish, conclude, crown, end, finish, fulfil ◆ adjective 2 <u>skilled</u>, accomplished, matchless, perfect, polished, practised, superb, supreme 3 <u>complete</u>, absolute, conspicuous, extreme, supreme, total, utter

consumption noun 1 <u>using up</u>, depletion, diminution, dissipation, exhaustion, expenditure, loss, waste 2 Old-fashioned <u>tuberculosis</u>, T.B.

contact noun 1 <u>communication</u>, association, connection 2 <u>touch</u>, contiguity 3 <u>acquaintance</u>, connection ◆ verb 4 <u>get</u> or be in touch with, approach, call, communicate with, reach, speak to, write to

contagious adjective <u>infectious</u>,

catching, communicable, spreading, transmissible

contain verb 1 <u>hold</u>, accommodate, enclose, have capacity for, incorporate, seat 2 <u>include</u>, comprehend, comprise, consist of, embody, embrace, involve 3 <u>restrain</u>, control, curb, hold back, hold in, keep a tight rein on, repress, stifle

container noun <u>holder</u>, receptacle, repository, vessel

contaminate verb <u>pollute</u>, adulterate, befoul, corrupt, defile, infect, stain, taint, tarnish

contamination noun <u>pollution</u>, contagion, corruption, defilement, impurity, infection, poisoning, taint

contemplate verb 1 <u>think about</u>, consider, deliberate, meditate, muse over, ponder, reflect upon, ruminate (upon) 2 <u>consider</u>, envisage, expect, foresee, intend, plan, think of 3 <u>look at</u>, examine, eye up, gaze at, inspect, regard, stare at, study, survey, view

contemporary adjective 1 <u>coexisting</u>, concurrent, contemporaneous 2 <u>modern</u>, à la mode, current, newfangled, present, present-day, recent, up-to-date ◆ noun 3 <u>peer</u>, fellow

contempt noun <u>scorn</u>, derision, disdain, disregard, disrespect, mockery, neglect, slight

contemptible adjective <u>despicable</u>, detestable, ignominious, measly, paltry, pitiful, shameful, worthless

contemptuous adjective <u>scornful</u>, arrogant,

condescending, derisive, disdainful, haughty, sneering, supercilious, withering

contend verb 1 <u>compete</u>, clash, contest, fight, jostle, strive, struggle, vie 2 <u>argue</u>, affirm, allege, assert, dispute, hold, maintain

content[1] noun 1 <u>meaning</u>, essence, gist, significance, substance 2 <u>amount</u>, capacity, load, measure, size, volume

content[2] adjective 1 <u>satisfied</u>, agreeable, at ease, comfortable, contented, fulfilled, willing to accept ♦ verb 2 <u>satisfy</u>, appease, humour, indulge, mollify, placate, please ♦ noun 3 <u>satisfaction</u>, comfort, contentment, ease, gratification, peace of mind, pleasure

contented adjective <u>satisfied</u>, comfortable, content, glad, gratified, happy, pleased, serene, thankful

contentious adjective <u>argumentative</u>, bickering, captious, cavilling, disputatious, quarrelsome, querulous, wrangling

contentment noun <u>satisfaction</u>, comfort, content, ease, equanimity, fulfilment, happiness, peace, pleasure, serenity

contents plural noun <u>constituents</u>, elements, ingredients, load

contest noun 1 <u>competition</u>, game, match, tournament, trial 2 <u>struggle</u>, battle, combat, conflict, controversy, dispute, fight ♦ verb 3 <u>dispute</u>, argue, call in or into question, challenge,

debate, doubt, object to, oppose, question 4 <u>compete</u>, contend, fight, strive, vie

contestant noun <u>competitor</u>, candidate, contender, entrant, participant, player

context noun 1 <u>circumstances</u>, ambience, conditions, situation 2 <u>frame of reference</u>, background, connection, framework, relation

contingency noun <u>possibility</u>, accident, chance, emergency, event, eventuality, happening, incident

continual adjective <u>constant</u>, frequent, incessant, interminable, recurrent, regular, repeated, unremitting

continually adverb <u>constantly</u>, all the time, always, forever, incessantly, interminably, nonstop, persistently, repeatedly

continuation noun 1 <u>continuing</u>, perpetuation, prolongation, resumption 2 <u>addition</u>, extension, furtherance, postscript, sequel, supplement

continue verb 1 <u>remain</u>, abide, carry on, endure, last, live on, persist, stay, survive 2 <u>keep on</u>, carry on, go on, maintain, persevere, persist in, stick at, sustain 3 <u>resume</u>, carry on, pick up where one left off, proceed, recommence, return to, take up

continuing adjective <u>lasting</u>, enduring, in progress, ongoing, sustained

continuity noun <u>sequence</u>, cohesion, connection, flow, progression, succession

continuous adjective <u>constant</u>,

extended, prolonged, unbroken, unceasing, undivided, uninterrupted

contraband noun **1** smuggling, black-marketing, bootlegging, trafficking ♦ adjective **2** smuggled, banned, bootleg, forbidden, hot (informal), illegal, illicit, prohibited, unlawful

contract noun **1** agreement, arrangement, bargain, commitment, covenant, pact, settlement ♦ verb **2** agree, bargain, come to terms, commit oneself, covenant, negotiate, pledge **3** shorten, abbreviate, curtail, diminish, dwindle, lessen, narrow, reduce, shrink, shrivel **4** catch, acquire, be afflicted with, develop, get, go down with, incur

contraction noun shortening, abbreviation, compression, narrowing, reduction, shrinkage, shrivelling, tightening

contradict verb deny, be at variance with, belie, challenge, controvert, fly in the face of, negate, rebut

contradiction noun denial, conflict, contravention, incongruity, inconsistency, negation, opposite

contradictory adjective inconsistent, conflicting, contrary, incompatible, opposed, opposite, paradoxical

contraption noun Informal device, apparatus, contrivance, gadget, instrument, mechanism

contrary noun **1** opposite, antithesis, converse, reverse ♦ adjective **2** opposed, adverse, clashing, contradictory, counter,

discordant, hostile, inconsistent, opposite, paradoxical **3** perverse, awkward, cantankerous, difficult, disobliging, intractable, obstinate, stroppy (Brit. slang), unaccommodating

contrast noun **1** difference, comparison, disparity, dissimilarity, distinction, divergence, foil, opposition ♦ verb **2** differentiate, compare, differ, distinguish, oppose, set in opposition, set off

contribute verb **1** give, add, bestow, chip in (informal), donate, provide, subscribe, supply **2** contribute to be partly responsible for, be conducive to, be instrumental in, help, lead to, tend to

contribution noun gift, addition, donation, grant, input, offering, subscription

contributor noun giver, donor, patron, subscriber, supporter

contrite adjective sorry, chastened, conscience-stricken, humble, penitent, regretful, remorseful, repentant, sorrowful

contrivance noun **1** device, apparatus, appliance, contraption, gadget, implement, instrument, invention, machine, mechanism **2** plan, intrigue, machination, plot, ruse, scheme, stratagem, trick

contrive verb **1** bring about, arrange, effect, manage, manoeuvre, plan, plot, scheme, succeed **2** devise, concoct, construct, create, design, fabricate, improvise, invent, manufacture

contrived adjective forced,

artificial, elaborate, laboured, overdone, planned, strained, unnatural

control noun 1 <u>power</u>, authority, charge, command, guidance, management, oversight, supervision, supremacy 2 <u>restraint</u>, brake, check, curb, limitation, regulation ♦ verb 3 <u>have power over</u>, administer, command, direct, govern, handle, have charge of, manage, manipulate, supervise 4 <u>restrain</u>, check, constrain, contain, curb, hold back, limit, repress, subdue

controls plural noun <u>instruments</u>, console, control panel, dash, dashboard, dials

controversial adjective <u>disputed</u>, at issue, contentious, debatable, disputable, open to question, under discussion

controversy noun <u>argument</u>, altercation, debate, dispute, quarrel, row, squabble, wrangling

convalescence noun <u>recovery</u>, improvement, recuperation, rehabilitation, return to health

convalescent adjective <u>recovering</u>, getting better, improving, mending, on the mend, recuperating

convene verb <u>gather</u>, assemble, bring together, call, come together, congregate, convoke, meet, summon

convenience noun 1 <u>availability</u>, accessibility, advantage, appropriateness, benefit, fitness, suitability, usefulness, utility 2 <u>appliance</u>, amenity, comfort, facility, help, labour-saving device

convenient adjective 1 <u>useful</u>, appropriate, fit, handy, helpful,

labour-saving, serviceable, suitable, timely 2 <u>nearby</u>, accessible, at hand, available, close at hand, handy, just round the corner, within reach

convention noun 1 <u>custom</u>, code, etiquette, practice, propriety, protocol, tradition, usage 2 <u>agreement</u>, bargain, contract, pact, protocol, treaty 3 <u>assembly</u>, conference, congress, convocation, council, meeting

conventional adjective 1 <u>ordinary</u>, accepted, customary, normal, orthodox, regular, standard, traditional, usual 2 <u>unoriginal</u>, banal, hackneyed, prosaic, routine, run-of-the-mill, stereotyped

converge verb <u>come together</u>, coincide, combine, gather, join, meet, merge

conversation noun <u>talk</u>, chat, conference, dialogue, discourse, discussion, gossip, tête-à-tête

converse[1] verb <u>talk</u>, chat, commune, confer, discourse, exchange views

converse[2] noun 1 <u>opposite</u>, antithesis, contrary, obverse, other side of the coin, reverse ♦ adjective 2 <u>opposite</u>, contrary, counter, reverse, reversed, transposed

conversion noun 1 <u>change</u>, metamorphosis, transformation 2 <u>adaptation</u>, alteration, modification, reconstruction, remodelling, reorganization

convert verb 1 <u>change</u>, alter, transform, transpose, turn 2 <u>adapt</u>, apply, customize, modify, remodel, reorganize, restyle, revise 3 <u>reform</u>, convince, proselytize ♦ *noun* 4 <u>neophyte</u>, disciple, proselyte

convex *adjective* <u>rounded</u>, bulging, gibbous, protuberant

convey *verb* 1 <u>communicate</u>, disclose, impart, make known, relate, reveal, tell 2 <u>carry</u>, bear, bring, conduct, fetch, guide, move, send, transport

convict *verb* 1 <u>find guilty</u>, condemn, imprison, pronounce guilty, sentence ♦ *noun* 2 <u>prisoner</u>, criminal, culprit, felon, jailbird, lag (*slang*)

conviction *noun* 1 <u>belief</u>, creed, faith, opinion, persuasion, principle, tenet, view 2 <u>confidence</u>, assurance, certainty, certitude, firmness, reliance

convince *verb* <u>persuade</u>, assure, bring round, prevail upon, satisfy, sway, win over

convincing *adjective* <u>persuasive</u>, cogent, conclusive, credible, impressive, plausible, powerful, telling

convulse *verb* <u>shake</u>, agitate, churn up, derange, disorder, disturb, twist, work

convulsion *noun* <u>spasm</u>, contraction, cramp, fit, paroxysm, seizure

cool *adjective* 1 <u>cold</u>, chilled, chilly, nippy, refreshing 2 <u>calm</u>, collected, composed, relaxed, sedate, self-controlled, self-possessed, unemotional, unruffled 3 <u>unfriendly</u>, aloof, distant, indifferent, lukewarm, offhand, standoffish, unenthusiastic, unwelcoming ♦ *verb* 4 <u>chill</u>, cool off, freeze,

lose heat, refrigerate ♦ *noun* 5 *Slang* <u>calmness</u>, composure, control, poise, self-control, self-discipline, self-possession, temper

cooperate *verb* <u>work together</u>, collaborate, combine, conspire, coordinate, join forces, pool resources, pull together

cooperation *noun* <u>teamwork</u>, collaboration, combined effort, esprit de corps, give-and-take, unity

cooperative *adjective* 1 <u>helpful</u>, accommodating, obliging, onside (*informal*), responsive, supportive 2 <u>shared</u>, collective, combined, joint

coordinate *verb* <u>bring together</u>, harmonize, integrate, match, organize, synchronize, systematize

cope *verb* 1 <u>manage</u>, carry on, get by (*informal*), hold one's own, make the grade, struggle through, survive 2 <u>cope with</u> <u>deal with</u>, contend with, grapple with, handle, struggle with, weather, wrestle with

copious *adjective* <u>abundant</u>, ample, bountiful, extensive, full, lavish, plentiful, profuse

copy *noun* 1 <u>reproduction</u>, counterfeit, duplicate, facsimile, forgery, imitation, likeness, model, replica ♦ *verb* 2 <u>reproduce</u>, counterfeit, duplicate, replicate, transcribe 3 <u>imitate</u>, ape, emulate, follow, mimic, mirror, repeat

cord *noun* <u>rope</u>, line, string, twine

cordial *adjective* <u>warm</u>, affable, agreeable, cheerful, congenial, friendly, genial, hearty, sociable

cordon noun 1 <u>chain</u>, barrier, line, ring ♦ verb 2 **cordon off** <u>surround</u>, close off, encircle, enclose, fence off, isolate, picket, separate

core noun <u>centre</u>, crux, essence, gist, heart, kernel, nub, nucleus, pith

corner noun 1 <u>angle</u>, bend, crook, joint 2 <u>space</u>, hideaway, hide-out, nook, retreat ♦ verb 3 <u>trap</u>, run to earth 4 As in **corner the market** <u>monopolize</u>, dominate, engross, hog (slang)

corny adjective Slang <u>unoriginal</u>, hackneyed, old-fashioned, old hat, stale, stereotyped, trite

corporation noun 1 <u>business</u>, association, corporate body, society 2 <u>town council</u>, civic authorities, council, municipal authorities 3 Informal <u>paunch</u>, beer belly (informal), middle-age spread (informal), potbelly, spare tyre (Brit. slang), spread (informal)

corps noun <u>team</u>, band, company, detachment, division, regiment, squadron, troop, unit

corpse noun <u>body</u>, cadaver, carcass, remains, stiff (slang)

correct adjective 1 <u>true</u>, accurate, exact, faultless, flawless, O.K. or okay (informal), precise, right 2 <u>proper</u>, acceptable, appropriate, fitting, kosher (informal), O.K. or okay (informal), seemly, standard ♦ verb 3 <u>rectify</u>, adjust, amend, cure, emend, redress, reform, remedy, right 4 <u>punish</u>, admonish, chasten, chastise, chide, discipline, rebuke, reprimand, reprove

correction noun 1 <u>rectification</u>, adjustment, alteration, amendment, emendation, improvement, modification 2 <u>punishment</u>, admonition, castigation, chastisement, discipline, reformation, reproof

correctly adverb <u>rightly</u>, accurately, perfectly, precisely, properly, right

correctness noun 1 <u>truth</u>, accuracy, exactitude, exactness, faultlessness, fidelity, preciseness, precision, regularity 2 <u>decorum</u>, civility, good breeding, propriety, seemliness

correspond verb 1 <u>be consistent</u>, accord, agree, conform, fit, harmonize, match, square, tally 2 <u>communicate</u>, exchange letters, keep in touch, write

correspondence noun 1 <u>letters</u>, communication, mail, post, writing 2 <u>relation</u>, agreement, coincidence, comparison, conformity, correlation, harmony, match, similarity

correspondent noun 1 <u>letter writer</u>, pen friend or pal 2 <u>reporter</u>, contributor, journalist

corresponding adjective <u>related</u>, analogous, answering, complementary, equivalent, matching, reciprocal, similar

corridor noun <u>passage</u>, aisle, alley, hallway, passageway

corroborate verb <u>support</u>, authenticate, back up, bear out, confirm, endorse, ratify, substantiate, validate

corrode verb <u>eat away</u>, consume, corrupt, erode, gnaw, oxidize, rust, wear away

corrosive adjective <u>corroding</u>,

caustic, consuming, erosive, virulent, vitriolic, wasting, wearing

corrupt adjective **1** dishonest, bent (slang), bribable, crooked (informal), fraudulent, unprincipled, unscrupulous, venal **2** depraved, debased, degenerate, dissolute, profligate, vicious **3** distorted, altered, doctored, falsified ♦ verb **4** bribe, buy off, entice, fix (informal), grease (someone's) palm (slang), lure, suborn **5** debauch, pervert, subvert **6** distort, doctor, tamper with

corruption noun **1** dishonesty, bribery, extortion, fraud, shady dealings (informal), unscrupulousness, venality **2** depravity, decadence, evil, immorality, perversion, vice, wickedness **3** distortion, doctoring, falsification

corset noun girdle, belt, bodice

cosmetic adjective beautifying, nonessential, superficial, surface

cosmic adjective universal, stellar

cosmopolitan adjective **1** sophisticated, broad minded, catholic, open-minded, universal, urbane, well-travelled, worldly-wise ♦ noun **2** man or woman of the world, jet-setter, sophisticate

cost noun **1** price, amount, charge, damage (informal), expense, outlay, payment, worth **2** loss, damage, detriment, expense, harm, hurt, injury, penalty, sacrifice, suffering ♦ verb **3** sell at, come to, command a price of, set (someone) back (informal) **4** lose, do disservice

to, harm, hurt, injure

costly adjective **1** expensive, dear, exorbitant, extortionate, highly-priced, steep (informal), stiff **2** damaging, catastrophic, deleterious, disastrous, harmful, loss-making, ruinous

costs plural noun expenses, budget, outgoings, overheads

costume noun outfit, apparel, attire, clothing, dress, ensemble, garb, livery, uniform

cosy adjective snug, comfortable, comfy (informal), homely, intimate, sheltered, tucked up, warm

cottage noun cabin, chalet, hut, lodge, shack

cough noun **1** frog or tickle in one's throat, bark, hack ♦ verb **2** clear one's throat, bark, hack

council noun governing body, assembly, board, cabinet, committee, conference, congress, convention, panel, parliament

counsel noun **1** advice, direction, guidance, information, recommendation, suggestion, warning **2** legal adviser, advocate, attorney, barrister, lawyer, solicitor ♦ verb **3** advise, advocate, exhort, instruct, recommend, urge, warn

count verb **1** add (up), calculate, compute, enumerate, number, reckon, tally, tot up **2** matter, be important, carry weight, rate, signify, tell, weigh **3** consider, deem, judge, look upon, rate, regard, think **4** take into account or consideration, include, number among ♦ noun **5** calculation, computation, enumeration, numbering, poll, reckoning, sum, tally

counter *verb* **1** retaliate, answer, hit back, meet, oppose, parry, resist, respond, ward off ♦ *adverb* **2** opposite to, against, at variance with, contrariwise, conversely, in defiance of, versus

counteract *verb* act against, foil, frustrate, negate, neutralize, offset, resist, thwart

counterbalance *verb* offset, balance, compensate, make up for, set off

counterfeit *adjective* **1** fake, bogus, false, forged, imitation, phoney *or* phony (*informal*), sham, simulated ♦ *noun* **2** fake, copy, forgery, fraud, imitation, phoney *or* phony (*informal*), reproduction, sham ♦ *verb* **3** fake, copy, fabricate, feign, forge, imitate, impersonate, pretend, sham, simulate

countermand *verb* cancel, annul, override, repeal, rescind, retract, reverse, revoke

counterpart *noun* opposite number, complement, equal, fellow, match, mate, supplement, tally, twin

countless *adjective* innumerable, endless, immeasurable, incalculable, infinite, legion, limitless, myriad, numberless, untold

count on *or* **upon** *verb* depend on, bank on, believe (in), lean on, pin one's faith on, reckon on, rely on, take for granted, take on trust, trust

country *noun* **1** nation, commonwealth, kingdom, people, realm, state **2** territory, land, region, terrain **3** people, citizens, community, inhabitants, nation, populace, public, society **4** countryside, backwoods, farmland, green belt, outback (*Austral. & N.Z.*), provinces, sticks (*informal*)

countryside *noun* country, farmland, green belt, outback (*Austral. & N.Z.*), outdoors, sticks (*informal*)

count up *verb* add, reckon up, sum, tally, total

county *noun* province, shire

coup *noun* masterstroke, accomplishment, action, deed, exploit, feat, manoeuvre, stunt

couple *noun* **1** pair, brace, duo, two, twosome ♦ *verb* **2** link, connect, hitch, join, marry, pair, unite, wed, yoke

coupon *noun* slip, card, certificate, ticket, token, voucher

courage *noun* bravery, daring, fearlessness, gallantry, heroism, mettle, nerve, pluck, resolution, valour

courageous *adjective* brave, bold, daring, fearless, gallant, gritty, intrepid, lion-hearted, stouthearted, valiant

courier *noun* **1** guide, representative **2** messenger, bearer, carrier, envoy, runner

course *noun* **1** classes, curriculum, lectures, programme, schedule **2** progression, development, flow, movement, order, progress, sequence, unfolding **3** route, direction, line, passage, path, road, track, trajectory, way **4** racecourse, cinder track, circuit

5 <u>procedure</u>, behaviour, conduct, manner, method, mode, plan, policy, programme **6** <u>period</u>, duration, lapse, passage, passing, sweep, term, time **7 of course** <u>naturally</u>, certainly, definitely, indubitably, needless to say, obviously, undoubtedly, without a doubt ◆ *verb* **8** run, flow, gush, race, speed, stream, surge **9** <u>hunt</u>, chase, follow, pursue

court *noun* **1** <u>law court</u>, bar, bench, tribunal **2** <u>courtyard</u>, cloister, piazza, plaza, quad (*informal*), quadrangle, square, yard **3** <u>palace</u>, hall, manor **4** <u>royal household</u>, attendants, cortege, entourage, retinue, suite, train ◆ *verb* **5** <u>woo</u>, date, go (out) with, run after, serenade, set one's cap at, take out, walk out with **6** <u>cultivate</u>, curry favour with, fawn upon, flatter, pander to, seek, solicit **7** <u>invite</u>, attract, bring about, incite, prompt, provoke, seek

courteous *adjective* <u>polite</u>, affable, attentive, civil, gallant, gracious, refined, respectful, urbane, well-mannered

courtesy *noun* **1** <u>politeness</u>, affability, civility, courteousness, gallantry, good manners, graciousness, urbanity **2** <u>favour</u>, indulgence, kindness

courtier *noun* <u>attendant</u>, follower, squire

courtly *adjective* <u>ceremonious</u>, chivalrous, dignified, elegant, formal, gallant, polished, refined, stately, urbane

courtyard *noun* <u>yard</u>, enclosure, quad, quadrangle

cove *noun* <u>bay</u>, anchorage, inlet, sound

covenant *noun* **1** <u>promise</u>, agreement, arrangement, commitment, contract, pact, pledge ◆ *verb* **2** <u>promise</u>, agree, contract, pledge, stipulate, undertake

cover *verb* **1** <u>clothe</u>, dress, envelop, put on, wrap **2** <u>overlay</u>, coat, daub, encase, envelop **3** <u>submerge</u>, engulf, flood, overrun, wash over **4** <u>conceal</u>, cloak, disguise, enshroud, hide, mask, obscure, shroud, veil **5** <u>travel over</u>, cross, pass through *or* over, traverse **6** <u>protect</u>, defend, guard, shield **7** <u>report</u>, describe, investigate, narrate, relate, tell of, write up ◆ *noun* **8** <u>covering</u>, canopy, case, coating, envelope, jacket, lid, top, wrapper **9** <u>disguise</u>, façade, front, mask, pretext, screen, smoke screen, veil **10** <u>protection</u>, camouflage, concealment, defence, guard, shelter, shield **11** <u>insurance</u>, compensation, indemnity, protection, reimbursement

covering *adjective* **1** <u>explanatory</u>, accompanying, descriptive, introductory ◆ *noun* **2** <u>cover</u>, blanket, casing, coating, layer, wrapping

cover-up *noun* <u>concealment</u>, complicity, conspiracy, front, smoke screen, whitewash (*informal*)

cover up *verb* <u>conceal</u>, draw a veil over, hide, hush up, suppress, sweep under the carpet, whitewash (*informal*)

covet *verb* <u>long for</u>, aspire to,

crave, desire, envy, lust after, set one's heart on, yearn for

covetous *adjective* <u>envious</u>, acquisitive, avaricious, close-fisted, grasping, greedy, jealous, rapacious, yearning

coward *noun* <u>wimp</u> (*informal*), chicken (*slang*), scaredy-cat (*informal*), yellow-belly (*slang*)

cowardice *noun* <u>faint-heartedness</u>, fearfulness, spinelessness, weakness

cowardly *adjective* <u>faint-hearted</u>, chicken (*slang*), craven, fearful, scared, soft, spineless, timorous, weak, yellow (*informal*)

cowboy *noun* <u>cowhand</u>, cattleman, drover, gaucho (*S. American*), herdsman, rancher, stockman

cower *verb* <u>cringe</u>, draw back, flinch, grovel, quail, shrink, tremble

coy *adjective* <u>shy</u>, bashful, demure, modest, reserved, retiring, shrinking, timid

crack *verb* 1 <u>break</u>, burst, cleave, fracture, snap, splinter, split 2 <u>snap</u>, burst, crash, detonate, explode, pop, ring 3 <u>give in</u>, break down, collapse, give way, go to pieces, lose control, succumb, yield 4 *Informal* <u>hit</u>, clip (*informal*), clout (*informal*), cuff, slap, smack, whack 5 <u>solve</u>, decipher, fathom, get the answer to, work out ◆ *noun* 6 <u>snap</u>, burst, clap, crash, explosion, pop, report 7 <u>break</u>, chink, cleft, cranny, crevice, fissure, fracture, gap, rift 8 *Informal* <u>blow</u>, clip (*informal*), clout (*informal*), cuff, slap, smack, whack 9 *Informal* <u>joke</u>,

dig, funny remark, gag (*informal*), jibe, quip, wisecrack, witticism ◆ *adjective* 10 *Slang* <u>first-class</u>, ace, choice, elite, excellent, first-rate, hand-picked, superior, world-class

crackdown *noun* <u>suppression</u>, clampdown, crushing, repression

cracked *adjective* <u>broken</u>, chipped, damaged, defective, faulty, flawed, imperfect, split

cradle *noun* 1 <u>crib</u>, bassinet, cot, Moses basket 2 <u>birthplace</u>, beginning, fount, fountainhead, origin, source, spring, wellspring ◆ *verb* 3 <u>hold</u>, lull, nestle, nurse, rock, support

craft *noun* 1 <u>occupation</u>, business, employment, handicraft, pursuit, trade, vocation, work 2 <u>skill</u>, ability, aptitude, art, artistry, expertise, ingenuity, know-how (*informal*), technique, workmanship 3 <u>vessel</u>, aircraft, boat, plane, ship, spacecraft

craftsman *noun* <u>skilled worker</u>, artisan, maker, master, smith, technician, wright

craftsmanship *noun* <u>workmanship</u>, artistry, expertise, mastery, technique

crafty *adjective* <u>cunning</u>, artful, calculating, devious, sharp, shrewd, sly, subtle, wily

crag *noun* <u>rock</u>, bluff, peak, pinnacle, tor

cram *verb* 1 <u>stuff</u>, compress, force, jam, pack in, press, shove, squeeze 2 <u>overeat</u>, glut, gorge, satiate, stuff 3 <u>study</u>, bone up (*informal*), mug up (*slang*), revise, swot

cramp[1] noun <u>spasm</u>, ache, contraction, convulsion, pain, pang, stitch, twinge

cramp[2] verb <u>restrict</u>, constrain, hamper, handicap, hinder, impede, inhibit, obstruct

cramped adjective <u>closed in</u>, confined, congested, crowded, hemmed in, overcrowded, packed, uncomfortable

cranny noun <u>crevice</u>, chink, cleft, crack, fissure, gap, hole, opening

crash noun 1 <u>collision</u>, accident, bump, pile-up (*informal*), prang (*informal*), smash, wreck 2 <u>smash</u>, bang, boom, clang, clash, clatter, din, racket, thunder 3 <u>collapse</u>, debacle, depression, downfall, failure, ruin ♦ verb 4 <u>collide</u>, bump (into), crash-land (*an aircraft*), drive into, have an accident, hit, plough into, wreck 5 <u>collapse</u>, be ruined, fail, fold, fold up, go belly up (*informal*), go bust (*informal*), go to the wall, go under 6 <u>hurtle</u>, fall headlong, give way, lurch, overbalance, plunge, topple

crass adjective <u>insensitive</u>, boorish, gross, indelicate, oafish, stupid, unrefined, witless

crate noun <u>container</u>, box, case, packing case, tea chest

crater noun <u>hollow</u>, depression, dip

crave verb 1 <u>long for</u>, desire, hanker after, hope for, lust after, want, yearn for 2 *Informal* <u>beg</u>, ask, beseech, entreat, implore, petition, plead for, pray for, seek, solicit, supplicate

craving noun <u>longing</u>, appetite, desire, hankering, hope, hunger, thirst, yearning, yen (*informal*)

crawl verb 1 <u>creep</u>, advance slowly, inch, slither, worm one's way, wriggle, writhe 2 <u>grovel</u>, creep, fawn, humble oneself, toady 3 <u>be full of</u>, be alive, be overrun (*slang*), swarm, teem

craze noun <u>fad</u>, enthusiasm, fashion, infatuation, mania, rage, trend, vogue

crazy adjective 1 *Informal* <u>ridiculous</u>, absurd, foolish, idiotic, ill-conceived, ludicrous, nonsensical, preposterous, senseless 2 <u>fanatical</u>, devoted, enthusiastic, infatuated, mad, passionate, wild (*informal*) 3 <u>insane</u>, crazed, demented, deranged, mad, nuts (*slang*), out of one's mind, unbalanced

creak verb <u>squeak</u>, grate, grind, groan, scrape, scratch, screech

cream noun 1 <u>lotion</u>, cosmetic, emulsion, essence, liniment, oil, ointment, paste, salve, unguent 2 <u>best</u>, crème de la crème, elite, flower, pick, prime ♦ adjective 3 <u>off-white</u>, yellowish-white

creamy adjective <u>smooth</u>, buttery, milky, rich, soft, velvety

crease noun 1 <u>line</u>, corrugation, fold, groove, ridge, wrinkle ♦ verb 2 <u>wrinkle</u>, corrugate, crumple, double up, fold, rumple, screw up

create verb 1 <u>make</u>, compose, devise, formulate, invent, originate, produce, spawn 2 <u>cause</u>, bring about, lead to, occasion 3 <u>appoint</u>, constitute, establish, install, invest, make, set up

creation noun 1 <u>making</u>, conception, formation,

generation, genesis, procreation
2 <u>setting up</u>, development, establishment, formation, foundation, inception, institution, production **3** <u>invention</u>, achievement, brainchild (*informal*), concoction, handiwork, magnum opus, *pièce de résistance*, production **4** <u>universe</u>, cosmos, nature, world

creative *adjective* <u>imaginative</u>, artistic, clever, gifted, ingenious, inspired, inventive, original, visionary

creativity *noun* <u>imagination</u>, cleverness, ingenuity, inspiration, inventiveness, originality

creator *noun* <u>maker</u>, architect, author, designer, father, inventor, originator, prime mover

creature *noun* **1** <u>living thing</u>, animal, beast, being, brute **2** <u>person</u>, human being, individual, man, mortal, soul, woman

credentials *plural noun* <u>certification</u>, authorization, document, licence, papers, passport, reference(s), testimonial

credibility *noun* <u>believability</u>, integrity, plausibility, reliability, trustworthiness

credible *adjective* **1** <u>believable</u>, conceivable, imaginable, likely, plausible, possible, probable, reasonable, thinkable **2** <u>reliable</u>, dependable, honest, sincere, trustworthy, trusty

credit *noun* **1** <u>praise</u>, acclaim, acknowledgment, approval, commendation, honour, kudos, recognition, tribute **2** *As in* **be a credit to** <u>source of satisfaction *or* pride</u>, feather in one's cap,

honour **3** <u>prestige</u>, esteem, good name, influence, position, regard, reputation, repute, standing, status **4** <u>belief</u>, confidence, credence, faith, reliance, trust **5** **on credit** <u>on account</u>, by deferred payment, by instalments, on hire-purchase, on (the) H.P., on the slate (*informal*), on tick (*informal*) ♦ *verb* **6** <u>believe</u>, accept, have faith in, rely on, trust **7** **credit with** <u>attribute to</u>, ascribe to, assign to, impute to

creditable *adjective* <u>praiseworthy</u>, admirable, commendable, honourable, laudable, reputable, respectable, worthy

credulity *noun* <u>gullibility</u>, blind faith, credulousness, naïveté

creed *noun* <u>belief</u>, articles of faith, catechism, credo, doctrine, dogma, principles

creek *noun* **1** <u>inlet</u>, bay, bight, cove, firth *or* frith (*Scot.*) **2** *U.S., Canad., Austral., & N.Z.* <u>stream</u>, bayou, brook, rivulet, runnel, tributary, watercourse

creep *verb* **1** <u>sneak</u>, approach unnoticed, skulk, slink, steal, tiptoe **2** <u>crawl</u>, glide, slither, squirm, wriggle, writhe ♦ *noun* **3** *Slang* <u>bootlicker</u> (*informal*), crawler (*slang*), sneak, sycophant, toady

creeper *noun* <u>climbing plant</u>, rambler, runner, trailing plant, vine (*chiefly U.S.*)

creeps *plural noun* **give one the creeps** *Informal* <u>disgust</u>, frighten, make one's hair stand on end, make one squirm, repel, repulse, scare

creepy *adjective Informal*

<u>disturbing</u>, eerie, frightening, hair-raising, macabre, menacing, scary (*informal*), sinister

crescent *noun* <u>meniscus</u>, new moon, sickle

crest *noun* 1 <u>top</u>, apex, crown, highest point, peak, pinnacle, ridge, summit 2 <u>tuft</u>, comb, crown, mane, plume 3 <u>emblem</u>, badge, bearings, device, insignia, symbol

crestfallen *adjective* <u>disappointed</u>, dejected, depressed, despondent, discouraged, disheartened, downcast, downhearted

crevice *noun* <u>gap</u>, chink, cleft, crack, cranny, fissure, hole, opening, slit

crew *noun* 1 <u>(ship's) company</u>, hands, (ship's) complement 2 <u>team</u>, corps, gang, posse, squad 3 *Informal* <u>crowd</u>, band, bunch (*informal*), gang, horde, mob, pack, set

crib *noun* 1 *Informal* <u>translation</u>, key 2 <u>cradle</u>, bassinet, bed, cot 3 <u>manger</u>, rack, stall ♦ *verb* 4 *Informal* <u>copy</u>, cheat, pirate, plagiarize, purloin, steal

crime *noun* 1 <u>offence</u>, felony, misdeed, misdemeanour, transgression, trespass, unlawful act, violation 2 <u>lawbreaking</u>, corruption, illegality, misconduct, vice, wrongdoing

criminal *noun* 1 <u>lawbreaker</u>, convict, crook (*informal*), culprit, felon, offender, sinner, villain ♦ *adjective* 2 <u>unlawful</u>, corrupt, crooked (*informal*), illegal, illicit, immoral, lawless, wicked, wrong 3 *Informal* <u>disgraceful</u>, deplorable, foolish, preposterous,

ridiculous, scandalous, senseless

cringe *verb* 1 <u>shrink</u>, cower, draw back, flinch, recoil, shy, wince 2 <u>grovel</u>, bootlick (*informal*), crawl, creep, fawn, kowtow, pander to, toady

cripple *verb* 1 <u>disable</u>, hamstring, incapacitate, lame, maim, paralyse, weaken 2 <u>damage</u>, destroy, impair, put out of action, put paid to, ruin, spoil

crippled *adjective* <u>disabled</u>, handicapped, incapacitated, laid up (*informal*), lame, paralysed

crisis *noun* 1 <u>critical point</u>, climax, crunch (*informal*), crux, culmination, height, moment of truth, turning point 2 <u>emergency</u>, deep water, dire straits, meltdown (*informal*), panic stations (*informal*), plight, predicament, trouble

crisp *adjective* 1 <u>crunchy</u>, brittle, crispy, crumbly, firm, fresh 2 <u>clean</u>, neat, smart, spruce, tidy, trim, well-groomed, well-pressed 3 <u>bracing</u>, brisk, fresh, invigorating, refreshing

criterion *noun* <u>standard</u>, benchmark, gauge, measure, principle, rule, test, touchstone, yardstick

critic *noun* 1 <u>judge</u>, analyst, authority, commentator, connoisseur, expert, pundit, reviewer 2 <u>fault-finder</u>, attacker, detractor, knocker (*informal*)

critical *adjective* 1 <u>crucial</u>, all-important, decisive, pivotal, precarious, pressing, serious, urgent, vital 2 <u>disparaging</u>, captious, censorious, derogatory, disapproving, fault-finding, nagging, nit-picking (*informal*), scathing 3 <u>analytical</u>, discerning, discriminating, fastidious, judicious, penetrating, perceptive

criticism noun **1** <u>fault-finding</u>, bad press, censure, character assassination, disapproval, disparagement, flak (informal), stick (slang) **2** <u>analysis</u>, appraisal, appreciation, assessment, comment, commentary, critique, evaluation, judgment

criticize verb <u>find fault with</u>, carp, censure, condemn, disapprove of, disparage, knock (informal), put down, slate (informal)

croak verb <u>squawk</u>, caw, grunt, utter or speak huskily, wheeze

crook noun Informal <u>criminal</u>, cheat, racketeer, robber, rogue, shark, swindler, thief, villain

crooked adjective **1** <u>bent</u>, curved, deformed, distorted, hooked, irregular, misshapen, out of shape, twisted, warped, zigzag **2** <u>at an angle</u>, askew, awry, lopsided, off-centre, skewwhiff (Brit. informal), slanting, squint, uneven **3** Informal <u>dishonest</u>, bent (slang), corrupt, criminal, fraudulent, illegal, shady (informal), underhand, unlawful

croon verb <u>sing</u>, hum, purr, warble

crop noun **1** <u>produce</u>, fruits, gathering, harvest, reaping, vintage, yield ♦ verb **2** <u>cut</u>, clip, lop, pare, prune, shear, snip, trim **3** <u>graze</u>, browse, nibble

crop up verb Informal <u>happen</u>, appear, arise, emerge, occur, spring up, turn up

cross verb **1** <u>go across</u>, bridge, cut across, extend over, move across, pass over, span, traverse **2** <u>intersect</u>, crisscross, intertwine **3** <u>oppose</u>, block, impede, interfere, obstruct, resist **4** <u>interbreed</u>, blend, crossbreed, cross-fertilize, cross-pollinate, hybridize, intercross, mix, mongrelize ♦ noun **5** <u>crucifix</u>, rood **6** <u>crossroads</u>, crossing, intersection, junction **7** <u>mixture</u>, amalgam, blend, combination **8** <u>trouble</u>, affliction, burden, grief, load, misfortune, trial, tribulation, woe, worry ♦ adjective **9** <u>angry</u>, annoyed, grumpy, ill-tempered, in a bad mood, irascible, put out, short **10** <u>transverse</u>, crosswise, diagonal, intersecting, oblique

cross-examine verb <u>question</u>, grill (informal), interrogate, pump, quiz

cross out or **off** verb <u>strike off or out</u>, blue-pencil, cancel, delete, eliminate, score off or out

crouch verb <u>bend down</u>, bow, duck, hunch, kneel, squat, stoop

crow verb <u>gloat</u>, blow one's own trumpet, boast, brag, exult, strut, swagger, triumph

crowd noun **1** <u>multitude</u>, army, horde, host, mass, mob, pack, swarm, throng **2** <u>group</u>, bunch (informal), circle, clique, lot, set **3** <u>audience</u>, attendance, gate, house, spectators ♦ verb **4** <u>flock</u>, congregate, gather, mass, stream, surge, swarm, throng **5** <u>squeeze</u>, bundle, congest, cram, pack, pile

crowded adjective <u>packed</u>, busy, congested, cramped, full, jam-packed, swarming, teeming

crown noun **1** <u>coronet</u>, circlet, diadem, tiara **2** <u>laurel wreath</u>, garland, honour, laurels, prize, trophy, wreath **3** high point, apex, crest, pinnacle, summit, tip, top ♦ *verb* **4** honour, adorn, dignify, festoon **5** cap, be the climax *or* culmination of, complete, finish, perfect, put the finishing touch to, round off, top **6** *Slang* strike, belt (*informal*), biff (*slang*), box, cuff, hit over the head, punch

Crown *noun* **1** monarchy, royalty, sovereignty **2** monarch, emperor *or* empress, king *or* queen, ruler, sovereign

crucial *adjective* **1** *Informal* vital, essential, high-priority, important, momentous, pressing, urgent **2** critical, central, decisive, pivotal

crucify *verb* execute, persecute, torment, torture

crude *adjective* **1** primitive, clumsy, makeshift, rough, rough-and-ready, rudimentary, unpolished **2** vulgar, coarse, dirty, gross, indecent, obscene, smutty, tasteless, uncouth **3** unrefined, natural, raw, unprocessed

crudely *adverb* vulgarly, bluntly, coarsely, impolitely, roughly, rudely, tastelessly

crudity *noun* **1** roughness, clumsiness, crudeness **2** vulgarity, coarseness, impropriety, indecency, indelicacy, obscenity, smuttiness

cruel *adjective* **1** brutal, barbarous, callous, hard-hearted, heartless, inhumane, malevolent, sadistic, spiteful, unkind, vicious **2** merciless, pitiless, ruthless, unrelenting

cruelly *adverb* **1** brutally, barbarously, callously, heartlessly, in cold blood, mercilessly, pitilessly, sadistically, spitefully **2** bitterly, deeply, fearfully, grievously, monstrously, severely

cruelty *noun* brutality, barbarity, callousness, depravity, fiendishness, inhumanity, mercilessness, ruthlessness, spitefulness

cruise *noun* **1** sail, boat trip, sea trip, voyage ♦ *verb* **2** sail, coast, voyage **3** travel along, coast, drift, keep a steady pace

crumb *noun* bit, fragment, grain, morsel, scrap, shred, soupçon

crumble *verb* **1** disintegrate, collapse, decay, degenerate, deteriorate, fall apart, go to pieces, go to wrack and ruin, tumble down **2** crush, fragment, granulate, grind, pound, powder, pulverize

crumple *verb* **1** crush, crease, rumple, screw up, scrumple, wrinkle **2** collapse, break down, cave in, fall, give way, go to pieces

crunch *verb* **1** chomp, champ, chew noisily, grind, munch ♦ *noun* **2** *Informal* critical point, crisis, crux, emergency, moment of truth, test

crusade *noun* campaign, cause, drive, movement, push

crush *verb* **1** squash, break, compress, press, pulverize, squeeze **2** overcome, conquer, overpower, overwhelm, put down, quell, stamp out, subdue **3** humiliate, abash, mortify, put down (*slang*), quash, shame

♦ *noun* **4** <u>crowd</u>, huddle, jam

crust *noun* <u>layer</u>, coating, covering, shell, skin, surface

crusty *adjective* **1** <u>crispy</u>, hard **2** <u>irritable</u>, cantankerous, cross, gruff, prickly, short-tempered, testy

cry *verb* **1** <u>weep</u>, blubber, shed tears, snivel, sob **2** <u>shout</u>, bawl, bellow, call out, exclaim, howl, roar, scream, shriek, yell ♦ *noun* **3** <u>weeping</u>, blubbering, snivelling, sob, sobbing, weep **4** <u>shout</u>, bellow, call, exclamation, howl, roar, scream, screech, shriek, yell **5** <u>appeal</u>, plea

cry off *verb Informal* <u>back out</u>, excuse oneself, quit, withdraw

cub *noun* <u>young</u>, offspring, whelp

cuddle *verb* <u>hug</u>, bill and coo, cosset, embrace, fondle, pet, snuggle

cudgel *noun* <u>club</u>, baton, bludgeon, cosh (*Brit.*), stick, truncheon

cue *noun* <u>signal</u>, catchword, hint, key, prompting, reminder, sign, suggestion

cul-de-sac *noun* <u>dead end</u>, blind alley

culminate *verb* <u>end up</u>, climax, close, come to a climax, come to a head, conclude, finish, wind up

culmination *noun* <u>climax</u>, acme, conclusion, consummation, finale, peak, pinnacle, zenith

culpable *adjective* <u>blameworthy</u>, at fault, found wanting, guilty, in the wrong, to blame, wrong

culprit *noun* <u>offender</u>, criminal, evildoer, felon, guilty party,

miscreant, transgressor, wrongdoer

cult *noun* **1** <u>sect</u>, clique, faction, religion, school **2** <u>devotion</u>, idolization, worship

cultivate *verb* **1** <u>farm</u>, plant, plough, tend, till, work **2** <u>develop</u>, foster, improve, promote, refine **3** <u>court</u>, dance attendance upon, run after, seek out

cultivation *noun* **1** <u>farming</u>, gardening, husbandry, planting, ploughing, tillage **2** <u>development</u>, encouragement, fostering, furtherance, nurture, patronage, promotion, support

cultural *adjective* <u>artistic</u>, civilizing, edifying, educational, enlightening, enriching, humane, liberal

culture *noun* **1** <u>civilization</u>, customs, lifestyle, mores, society, way of life **2** <u>refinement</u>, education, enlightenment, good taste, sophistication, urbanity **3** <u>farming</u>, cultivation, husbandry

cultured *adjective* <u>refined</u>, educated, enlightened, highbrow, sophisticated, urbane, well-informed, well-read

culvert *noun* <u>drain</u>, channel, conduit, gutter, watercourse

cumbersome *adjective* <u>awkward</u>, bulky, burdensome, heavy, unmanageable, unwieldy, weighty

cunning *adjective* **1** <u>crafty</u>, artful, devious, Machiavellian, sharp, shifty, sly, wily **2** <u>skilful</u>, imaginative, ingenious ♦ *noun* **3** <u>craftiness</u>, artfulness, deviousness, guile, slyness, trickery **4** <u>skill</u>, artifice, cleverness, ingenuity, subtlety

cup noun 1 <u>mug</u>, beaker, bowl, chalice, goblet, teacup 2 <u>trophy</u>

cupboard noun <u>cabinet</u>, press

curb noun 1 <u>restraint</u>, brake, bridle, check, control, deterrent, limitation, rein ♦ verb 2 <u>restrain</u>, check, control, hinder, impede, inhibit, restrict, retard, suppress

cure verb 1 <u>make better</u>, correct, ease, heal, mend, relieve, remedy, restore 2 <u>preserve</u>, dry, pickle, salt, smoke ♦ noun 3 <u>remedy</u>, antidote, medicine, nostrum, panacea, treatment

curiosity noun 1 <u>inquisitiveness</u>, interest, nosiness (informal), prying, snooping (informal) 2 <u>oddity</u>, freak, novelty, phenomenon, rarity, sight, spectacle, wonder

curious adjective 1 <u>inquiring</u>, inquisitive, interested, questioning, searching 2 <u>inquisitive</u>, meddling, nosy (informal), prying 3 <u>unusual</u>, bizarre, extraordinary, mysterious, novel, odd, peculiar, rare, strange, unexpected

curl verb 1 <u>twirl</u>, bend, coil, curve, loop, spiral, turn, twist, wind ♦ noun 2 <u>twist</u>, coil, kink, ringlet, spiral, whorl

curly adjective <u>curling</u>, crinkly, curled, frizzy, fuzzy, wavy, winding

currency noun 1 <u>money</u>, coinage, coins, notes 2 <u>acceptance</u>, circulation, exposure, popularity, prevalence, vogue

current adjective 1 <u>present</u>, contemporary, fashionable, in fashion, in vogue, present-day, trendy (Brit. informal), up-to-date 2 <u>prevalent</u>, accepted, common, customary, in circulation, popular, topical, widespread ♦ noun 3 <u>flow</u>, course, draught, jet, progression, river, stream, tide, undertow 4 <u>mood</u>, atmosphere, feeling, tendency, trend, undercurrent

curse verb 1 <u>swear</u>, blaspheme, cuss (informal), take the Lord's name in vain 2 <u>damn</u>, anathematize, excommunicate ♦ noun 3 <u>oath</u>, blasphemy, expletive, obscenity, swearing, swearword 4 <u>denunciation</u>, anathema, ban, excommunication, hoodoo (informal), jinx 5 <u>affliction</u>, bane, hardship, plague, scourge, torment, trouble

cursed adjective <u>damned</u>, accursed, bedevilled, doomed, ill-fated

curt adjective <u>short</u>, abrupt, blunt, brief, brusque, gruff, monosyllabic, succinct, terse

curtail verb <u>cut short</u>, cut back, decrease, diminish, dock, lessen, reduce, shorten, truncate

curtain noun <u>hanging</u>, drape (chiefly U.S.)

curve noun 1 <u>bend</u>, arc, curvature, loop, trajectory, turn ♦ verb 2 <u>bend</u>, arc, arch, coil, hook, spiral, swerve, turn, twist, wind

curved adjective <u>bent</u>, arched, bowed, rounded, serpentine, sinuous, twisted

cushion noun 1 <u>pillow</u>, beanbag, bolster, hassock, headrest, pad ♦ verb 2 <u>soften</u>, dampen, deaden, muffle, stifle, suppress

cushy adjective Informal easy,
comfortable, soft, undemanding

custody noun 1 safekeeping,
care, charge, keeping,
protection, supervision
2 imprisonment, confinement,
detention, incarceration

custom noun 1 tradition,
convention, policy, practice,
ritual, rule, usage 2 habit,
practice, procedure, routine,
way, wont 3 customers,
patronage, trade

customary adjective usual,
accepted, accustomed, common,
conventional, established,
normal, ordinary, routine,
traditional

customer noun client, buyer,
consumer, patron, purchaser,
regular (informal), shopper

customs plural noun duty, import
charges, tariff, tax, toll

cut verb 1 penetrate, chop,
pierce, score, sever, slash, slice,
slit, wound 2 divide, bisect,
dissect, slice, split 3 trim, clip,
hew, lop, mow, pare, prune,
shave, snip 4 abridge,
abbreviate, condense, curtail,
delete, shorten 5 reduce,
contract, cut back, decrease,
diminish, lower, slash, slim
(down) 6 shape, carve, chisel,
engrave, fashion, form, sculpt,
whittle 7 hurt, insult, put down,
snub, sting, wound 8 Informal
ignore, avoid, cold-shoulder,
slight, spurn, turn one's back on
♦ noun 9 incision, gash,
laceration, nick, slash, slit, stroke,
wound 10 reduction, cutback,
decrease, fall, lowering, saving

11 Informal share, percentage,
piece, portion, section, slice
12 style, fashion, look, shape

cutback noun reduction, cut,
decrease, economy, lessening,
retrenchment

cut down verb 1 fell, hew, level,
lop 2 reduce, decrease, lessen,
lower

cute adjective appealing,
attractive, charming, delightful,
engaging, lovable, sweet,
winning, winsome

cut in verb interrupt, break in,
butt in, intervene, intrude

cut off verb 1 separate, isolate,
sever 2 interrupt, disconnect,
intercept

cut out verb stop, cease, give up,
refrain from

cutthroat adjective
1 competitive, dog-eat-dog,
fierce, relentless, ruthless,
unprincipled ♦ noun 2 murderer,
assassin, butcher, executioner,
hit man (slang), killer

cutting adjective hurtful,
acrimonious, barbed, bitter,
caustic, malicious, sarcastic,
scathing, vitriolic, wounding

cycle noun era, circle, period,
phase, revolution, rotation

cynic noun sceptic, doubter,
misanthrope, misanthropist,
pessimist, scoffer

cynical adjective sceptical,
contemptuous, derisive,
distrustful, misanthropic,
mocking, pessimistic, scoffing,
scornful, unbelieving

cynicism noun scepticism,
disbelief, doubt, misanthropy,
pessimism

D d

dab verb 1 <u>pat</u>, daub, stipple, tap, touch ♦ noun 2 <u>spot</u>, bit, drop, pat, smudge, speck 3 <u>pat</u>, flick, stroke, tap, touch

dabble verb 1 <u>play at</u>, dip into, potter, tinker, trifle (with) 2 <u>splash</u>, dip

daft adjective Informal, chiefly Brit. 1 <u>foolish</u>, absurd, asinine, crackpot (informal), crazy, idiotic, silly, stupid, witless 2 <u>crazy</u>, crackers (Brit. slang), demented, deranged, insane, nuts (slang), touched, unhinged

dagger noun <u>knife</u>, bayonet, dirk, stiletto

daily adjective 1 <u>everyday</u>, diurnal, quotidian ♦ adverb 2 <u>every day</u>, day by day, once a day

dainty adjective <u>delicate</u>, charming, elegant, exquisite, fine, graceful, neat, petite, pretty

dam noun 1 <u>barrier</u>, barrage, embankment, obstruction, wall ♦ verb 2 <u>block up</u>, barricade, hold back, obstruct, restrict

damage verb 1 <u>harm</u>, hurt, impair, injure, ruin, spoil, weaken, wreck ♦ noun 2 <u>harm</u>, destruction, detriment, devastation, hurt, injury, loss, suffering 3 Informal <u>cost</u>, bill, charge, expense

damages plural noun Law <u>compensation</u>, fine, reimbursement, reparation, satisfaction

damaging adjective <u>harmful</u>, deleterious, detrimental, disadvantageous, hurtful, injurious, ruinous

dame noun <u>noblewoman</u>, baroness, dowager, grande dame, lady, peeress

damn verb 1 <u>condemn</u>, blast, censure, criticize, denounce, put down 2 <u>sentence</u>, condemn, doom

damnation noun <u>condemnation</u>, anathema, damning, denunciation, doom

damned adjective 1 <u>doomed</u>, accursed, condemned, lost 2 Slang <u>detestable</u>, confounded, hateful, infernal, loathsome

damp adjective 1 <u>moist</u>, clammy, dank, dewy, drizzly, humid, soggy, sopping, wet ♦ noun 2 <u>moisture</u>, dampness, dankness, drizzle ♦ verb 3 <u>moisten</u>, dampen, wet 4 **damp down** <u>reduce</u>, allay, check, curb, diminish, inhibit, pour cold water on, stifle

dampen verb 1 <u>reduce</u>, check, dull, lessen, moderate, restrain, stifle 2 <u>moisten</u>, make damp, spray, wet

damper noun As in **put a damper on** <u>discouragement</u>, cold water (informal), hindrance, restraint, wet blanket (informal)

dance verb 1 <u>prance</u>, hop, jig, skip, sway, trip, whirl ♦ noun 2 <u>ball</u>, disco, discotheque, hop (informal), knees-up (Brit. informal), social

dancer noun <u>ballerina</u>, Terpsichorean

danger noun <u>peril</u>, hazard, jeopardy, menace, pitfall, risk, threat, vulnerability

dangerous adjective <u>perilous</u>, breakneck, chancy (informal), hazardous, insecure, precarious, risky, unsafe, vulnerable

dangerously adverb <u>perilously</u>, alarmingly, hazardously, precariously, recklessly, riskily, unsafely

dangle verb 1 <u>hang</u>, flap, hang down, sway, swing, trail 2 <u>wave</u>, brandish, flaunt, flourish

dapper adjective <u>neat</u>, natty (informal), smart, soigné or soignée, spruce, spry, trim, well-groomed, well turned out

dare verb 1 <u>risk</u>, hazard, make bold, presume, venture 2 <u>challenge</u>, defy, goad, provoke, taunt, throw down the gauntlet ◆ noun 3 <u>challenge</u>, provocation, taunt

daredevil noun 1 <u>adventurer</u>, desperado, exhibitionist, madcap, show-off (informal), stunt man ◆ adjective 2 <u>daring</u>, adventurous, audacious, bold, death-defying, madcap, reckless

daring adjective 1 <u>brave</u>, adventurous, audacious, bold, daredevil, fearless, intrepid, reckless, venturesome ◆ noun 2 <u>bravery</u>, audacity, boldness, bottle (Brit. slang), courage, fearlessness, nerve (informal), pluck, temerity

dark adjective 1 <u>dim</u>, dingy, murky, shadowy, shady, sunless, unlit 2 <u>black</u>, dark-skinned, dusky, ebony, sable, swarthy 3 <u>gloomy</u>, bleak, dismal, grim, morose, mournful, sad, sombre 4 <u>evil</u>, foul, infernal, sinister, vile, wicked 5 <u>secret</u>, concealed,

hidden, mysterious ◆ noun 6 <u>darkness</u>, dimness, dusk, gloom, murk, obscurity, semi-darkness 7 <u>night</u>, evening, nightfall, night-time, twilight

darken verb <u>make dark</u>, blacken, dim, obscure, overshadow

darkness noun <u>dark</u>, blackness, duskiness, gloom, murk, nightfall, shade, shadows

darling noun 1 <u>beloved</u>, dear, dearest, love, sweetheart, truelove ◆ adjective 2 <u>beloved</u>, adored, cherished, dear, precious, treasured

darn verb 1 <u>mend</u>, cobble up, patch, repair, sew up, stitch ◆ noun 2 <u>mend</u>, invisible repair, patch, reinforcement

dart verb <u>dash</u>, fly, race, run, rush, shoot, spring, sprint, tear

dash verb 1 <u>rush</u>, bolt, fly, hurry, race, run, speed, sprint, tear 2 <u>throw</u>, cast, fling, hurl, slam, sling 3 <u>crash</u>, break, destroy, shatter, smash, splinter 4 <u>frustrate</u>, blight, foil, ruin, spoil, thwart, undo ◆ noun 5 <u>rush</u>, dart, race, run, sortie, sprint, spurt 6 <u>little</u>, bit, drop, hint, pinch, soupçon, sprinkling, tinge, touch 7 <u>style</u>, brio, élan, flair, flourish, panache, spirit, verve

dashing adjective 1 <u>bold</u>, debonair, gallant, lively, spirited, swashbuckling 2 <u>stylish</u>, elegant, flamboyant, jaunty, showy, smart, sporty

data noun <u>information</u>, details, facts, figures, statistics

date noun 1 <u>time</u>, age, epoch, era, period, stage 2 <u>appointment</u>, assignation, engagement, meeting, rendezvous, tryst **3** <u>partner</u>, escort, friend ♦ *verb* **4** <u>put a date on</u>, assign a date to, fix the period of **5** <u>become old-fashioned</u>, be dated, show one's age **6** <u>date from</u> *or* <u>date back to</u> <u>come from</u>, bear a date of, belong to, exist from, originate in

dated *adjective* <u>old-fashioned</u>, obsolete, old hat, outdated, outmoded, out of date, passé, unfashionable

daub *verb* <u>smear</u>, coat, cover, paint, plaster, slap on (*informal*)

daunting *adjective* <u>intimidating</u>, alarming, demoralizing, disconcerting, discouraging, disheartening, frightening, off-putting (*Brit. informal*), unnerving

dauntless *adjective* <u>fearless</u>, bold, doughty, gallant, indomitable, intrepid, resolute, stouthearted, undaunted, unflinching

dawdle *verb* <u>waste time</u>, dally, delay, drag one's feet *or* heels, hang about, idle, loaf, loiter, trail

dawn *noun* **1** <u>daybreak</u>, aurora (*poetic*), cockcrow, crack of dawn, daylight, morning, sunrise, sunup **2** <u>beginning</u>, advent, birth, emergence, genesis, origin, rise, start ♦ *verb* **3** <u>grow light</u>, break, brighten, lighten **4** <u>begin</u>, appear, develop, emerge, originate, rise, unfold **5** **dawn on** *or* **upon** <u>hit</u>, become apparent, come into one's head, come to mind, occur, register (*informal*), strike

day *noun* **1** <u>twenty-four hours</u>, daylight, daytime **2** <u>point in</u> time, date, time **3** <u>time</u>, age, epoch, era, heyday, period, zenith

daybreak *noun* <u>dawn</u>, break of day, cockcrow, crack of dawn, first light, morning, sunrise, sunup

daydream *noun* **1** <u>fantasy</u>, dream, fancy, imagining, pipe dream, reverie, wish ♦ *verb* **2** <u>fantasize</u>, dream, envision, fancy, imagine, muse

daylight *noun* <u>sunlight</u>, light of day, sunshine

daze *verb* **1** <u>stun</u>, benumb, numb, paralyse, shock, stupefy ♦ *noun* **2** <u>shock</u>, bewilderment, confusion, distraction, stupor, trance, trancelike state

dazed *adjective* <u>shocked</u>, bewildered, confused, disorientated, dizzy, muddled, punch-drunk, staggered, stunned

dazzle *verb* **1** <u>impress</u>, amaze, astonish, bowl over (*informal*), overpower, overwhelm, take one's breath away **2** <u>blind</u>, bedazzle, blur, confuse, daze ♦ *noun* **3** <u>splendour</u>, brilliance, glitter, magnificence, razzmatazz (*slang*), sparkle

dazzling *adjective* <u>splendid</u>, brilliant, glittering, glorious, scintillating, sensational (*informal*), sparkling, stunning, virtuoso

dead *adjective* **1** <u>deceased</u>, defunct, departed, extinct, late, passed away, perished **2** <u>not working</u>, inactive, inoperative, stagnant, unemployed, useless **3** <u>numb</u>, inert, paralysed **4** <u>total</u>, absolute, complete, outright, thorough, unqualified, utter

5 *Informal* <u>exhausted</u>, dead beat
(*informal*), spent, tired, worn out
6 <u>boring</u>, dull, flat, uninteresting
♦ *noun* **7** <u>middle</u>, depth, midst
♦ *adverb* **8** *Informal* <u>exactly</u>,
absolutely, completely, directly,
entirely, totally

deaden *verb* <u>reduce</u>, alleviate,
blunt, cushion, diminish, dull,
lessen, muffle, smother, stifle,
suppress, weaken

deadline *noun* <u>time limit</u>, cutoff
point, limit, target date

deadlock *noun* <u>impasse</u>, dead
heat, draw, gridlock, stalemate,
standoff, standstill, tie

deadlocked *adjective* <u>even</u>,
equal, level, neck and neck

deadly *adjective* **1** <u>lethal</u>,
dangerous, death-dealing,
deathly, fatal, malignant, mortal
2 *Informal* <u>boring</u>, dull,
mind-numbing, monotonous,
tedious, tiresome, uninteresting,
wearisome

deadpan *adjective* <u>expressionless</u>,
blank, impassive, inexpressive,
inscrutable, poker-faced,
straight-faced

deaf *adjective* **1** <u>hard of hearing</u>,
stone deaf, without hearing
2 <u>oblivious</u>, indifferent,
unconcerned, unhearing,
unmoved

deafen *verb* <u>make deaf</u>, din,
drown out, split *or* burst the
eardrums

deafening *adjective* <u>ear-piercing</u>,
booming, ear-splitting,
overpowering, piercing,
resounding, ringing, thunderous

deal *noun* **1** *Informal* <u>agreement</u>,
arrangement, bargain, contract,

pact, transaction, understanding
2 <u>amount</u>, degree, extent,
portion, quantity, share ♦ *verb*
3 <u>sell</u>, bargain, buy and sell, do
business, negotiate, stock, trade,
traffic

dealer *noun* <u>trader</u>, merchant,
purveyor, supplier, tradesman,
wholesaler

deal out *verb* <u>distribute</u>, allot,
apportion, assign, dispense, dole
out, give, mete out, share

deal with *verb* **1** <u>handle</u>, attend
to, cope with, get to grips with,
manage, see to, take care of,
treat **2** <u>be concerned with</u>,
consider

dear *noun* **1** <u>beloved</u>, angel,
darling, loved one, precious,
treasure ♦ *adjective* **2** <u>beloved</u>,
cherished, close, favourite,
intimate, precious, prized,
treasured **3** <u>expensive</u>, at a
premium, costly, high-priced,
overpriced, pricey (*informal*)

dearly *adverb* **1** <u>very much</u>,
extremely, greatly, profoundly
2 <u>at great cost</u>, at a high price

dearth *noun* <u>scarcity</u>, deficiency,
inadequacy, insufficiency, lack,
paucity, poverty, shortage, want

death *noun* **1** <u>dying</u>, demise,
departure, end, exit, passing
2 <u>destruction</u>, downfall,
extinction, finish, ruin, undoing

deathly *adjective* <u>deathlike</u>,
ghastly, grim, pale, pallid, wan

debacle *noun* <u>disaster</u>,
catastrophe, collapse, defeat,
fiasco, reversal, rout

debase *verb* <u>degrade</u>, cheapen,
devalue, lower, reduce

debatable *adjective* <u>doubtful</u>,

arguable, controversial, dubious, moot, problematical, questionable, uncertain

debate noun 1 <u>discussion</u>, argument, contention, controversy, dispute ♦ verb 2 <u>discuss</u>, argue, dispute, question 3 <u>consider</u>, deliberate, ponder, reflect, ruminate, weigh

debauchery noun <u>depravity</u>, dissipation, dissoluteness, excess, indulgence, intemperance, lewdness, overindulgence

debonair adjective <u>elegant</u>, charming, courteous, dashing, refined, smooth, suave, urbane, well-bred

debrief verb <u>interrogate</u>, cross-examine, examine, probe, question, quiz

debris noun <u>remains</u>, bits, detritus, fragments, rubble, ruins, waste, wreckage

debt noun 1 <u>debit</u>, commitment, liability, obligation 2 **in debt** <u>owing</u>, in arrears, in the red (informal), liable

debtor noun <u>borrower</u>, mortgagor

debunk verb Informal <u>expose</u>, cut down to size, deflate, disparage, mock, ridicule, show up

debut noun <u>introduction</u>, beginning, bow, coming out, entrance, first appearance, initiation, presentation

decadence noun <u>degeneration</u>, corruption, decay, decline, deterioration, dissipation, dissolution

decadent adjective <u>degenerate</u>, corrupt, decaying, declining, dissolute, immoral, self-indulgent

decapitate verb <u>behead</u>, execute, guillotine

decay verb 1 <u>decline</u>, crumble, deteriorate, disintegrate, dwindle, shrivel, wane, waste away, wither 2 <u>rot</u>, corrode, decompose, perish, putrefy ♦ noun 3 <u>decline</u>, collapse, degeneration, deterioration, fading, failing, wasting, withering 4 <u>rot</u>, caries, decomposition, gangrene, putrefaction

decease noun Formal <u>death</u>, demise, departure, dying, release

deceased adjective <u>dead</u>, defunct, departed, expired, former, late, lifeless

deceit noun <u>dishonesty</u>, cheating, chicanery, deception, fraud, lying, pretence, treachery, trickery

deceitful adjective <u>dishonest</u>, deceptive, false, fraudulent, sneaky, treacherous, two-faced, untrustworthy

deceive verb <u>take in</u> (informal), cheat, con (informal), dupe, fool, hoodwink, mislead, swindle, trick

deceiver noun <u>liar</u>, cheat, con man (informal), double-dealer, fraud, impostor, swindler, trickster

decency noun <u>respectability</u>, civility, correctness, courtesy, decorum, etiquette, modesty, propriety

decent adjective 1 <u>reasonable</u>, adequate, ample, fair, passable, satisfactory, sufficient, tolerable 2 <u>respectable</u>, chaste, decorous, modest, proper, pure 3 <u>proper</u>, appropriate, becoming, befitting, fitting, seemly, suitable 4 Informal <u>kind</u>, accommodating, courteous, friendly, generous, gracious, helpful, obliging, thoughtful

deception noun **1** trickery, cunning, deceit, fraud, guile, legerdemain, treachery **2** trick, bluff, decoy, hoax, illusion, lie, ruse, subterfuge

deceptive adjective misleading, ambiguous, deceitful, dishonest, false, fraudulent, illusory, unreliable

decide verb reach or come to a decision, adjudge, adjudicate, choose, conclude, determine, make up one's mind, resolve

decidedly adverb definitely, clearly, distinctly, downright, positively, unequivocally, unmistakably

decimate verb devastate, ravage, wreak havoc on

decipher verb figure out (informal), crack, decode, deduce, interpret, make out, read, solve

decision noun **1** judgment, arbitration, conclusion, finding, resolution, ruling, sentence, verdict **2** decisiveness, determination, firmness, purpose, resolution, resolve, strength of mind or will

decisive adjective **1** influential, conclusive, critical, crucial, fateful, momentous, significant **2** resolute, decided, determined, firm, forceful, incisive, strong-minded, trenchant

deck verb decorate, adorn, array, beautify, clothe, dress, embellish, festoon

declaim verb **1** orate, harangue,

hold forth, lecture, proclaim, rant, recite, speak **2** declaim **against** protest against, attack, decry, denounce, inveigh, rail

declaration noun **1** statement, acknowledgment, affirmation, assertion, avowal, disclosure, protestation, revelation, testimony **2** announcement, edict, notification, proclamation, profession, pronouncement

declare verb **1** state, affirm, announce, assert, claim, maintain, proclaim, profess, pronounce, swear, utter **2** make known, confess, disclose, reveal, show

decline verb **1** lessen, decrease, diminish, dwindle, ebb, fade, fall off, shrink, sink, wane **2** deteriorate, decay, degenerate, droop, languish, pine, weaken, worsen **3** refuse, abstain, avoid, reject, say 'no', turn down ♦ noun **4** lessening, downturn, drop, dwindling, falling off, recession, slump **5** deterioration, decay, degeneration, failing, weakening, worsening

decode verb decipher, crack, decrypt, interpret, solve, unscramble, work out

decompose verb rot, break up, crumble, decay, fall apart, fester, putrefy

decor noun decoration, colour scheme, furnishing style, ornamentation

decorate verb **1** adorn, beautify, embellish, festoon, grace, ornament, trim **2** do up (informal), colour, furbish, paint, paper, renovate, wallpaper **3** pin a medal on, cite, confer an honour on *or* upon

decoration *noun* 1 adornment, beautification, elaboration, embellishment, enrichment, ornamentation, trimming 2 ornament, bauble, frill, garnish, trimmings 3 medal, award, badge, ribbon, star

decorative *adjective* ornamental, beautifying, fancy, nonfunctional, pretty

decorous *adjective* proper, becoming, correct, decent, dignified, fitting, polite, seemly, well-behaved

decorum *noun* propriety, decency, dignity, etiquette, good manners, politeness, protocol, respectability

decoy *noun* 1 lure, bait, enticement, inducement, pretence, trap ♦ *verb* 2 lure, deceive, ensnare, entice, entrap, seduce, tempt

decrease *verb* 1 lessen, cut down, decline, diminish, drop, dwindle, lower, reduce, shrink, subside ♦ *noun* 2 lessening, contraction, cutback, decline, dwindling, falling off, loss, reduction, subsidence

decree *noun* 1 law, act, command, edict, order, proclamation, ruling, statute ♦ *verb* 2 order, command, demand, ordain, prescribe, proclaim, pronounce, rule

decrepit *adjective* 1 weak, aged, doddering, feeble, frail, infirm 2 worn-out, battered, beat-up (*informal*), broken-down, dilapidated, ramshackle, rickety, run-down, tumbledown, weather-beaten

decry *verb* condemn, belittle, criticize, denigrate, denounce, discredit, disparage, put down, run down

dedicate *verb* 1 devote, commit, give over to, pledge, surrender 2 inscribe, address

dedicated *adjective* devoted, committed, enthusiastic, purposeful, single-minded, wholehearted, zealous

dedication *noun* 1 devotion, adherence, allegiance, commitment, faithfulness, loyalty, single-mindedness, wholeheartedness 2 inscription, address, message

deduce *verb* conclude, draw, gather, glean, infer, reason, take to mean, understand

deduct *verb* subtract, decrease by, knock off (*informal*), reduce by, remove, take away, take off

deduction *noun* 1 subtraction, decrease, diminution, discount, reduction, withdrawal 2 conclusion, assumption, finding, inference, reasoning, result

deed *noun* 1 action, achievement, act, exploit, fact, feat, performance 2 *Law* document, contract, title

deep *adjective* 1 wide, bottomless, broad, far, profound, unfathomable, yawning 2 mysterious, abstract, abstruse, arcane, esoteric, hidden, obscure, recondite, secret 3 intense, extreme, grave, great, profound, serious (*informal*), unqualified 4 absorbed, engrossed, immersed, lost, preoccupied, rapt **5** dark, intense, rich, strong, vivid **6** low, bass, booming, low-pitched, resonant, sonorous ♦ *noun* **7 the deep** *Poetic* ocean, briny (*informal*), high seas, main, sea

deepen *verb* intensify, grow, increase, magnify, reinforce, strengthen

deeply *adverb* **1** thoroughly, completely, gravely, profoundly, seriously, severely, to the core, to the heart, to the quick **2** intensely, acutely, affectingly, distressingly, feelingly, mournfully, movingly, passionately, sadly

deface *verb* vandalize, damage, deform, disfigure, mar, mutilate, spoil, tarnish

de facto *adverb* **1** in fact, actually, in effect, in reality, really ♦ *adjective* **2** actual, existing, real

defame *verb* slander, bad-mouth (*slang, chiefly U.S. & Canad.*), cast aspersions on, denigrate, discredit, disparage, knock (*informal*), libel, malign, smear

default *noun* **1** failure, deficiency, dereliction, evasion, lapse, neglect, nonpayment, omission ♦ *verb* **2** fail, dodge, evade, neglect

defeat *verb* **1** beat, conquer, crush, master, overwhelm, rout, trounce, vanquish, wipe the floor with (*informal*) **2** frustrate, baffle, balk, confound, foil, get the better of, ruin, thwart ♦ *noun* **3** conquest, beating, overthrow, pasting (*slang*), rout **4** frustration, failure, rebuff, reverse, setback, thwarting

defeatist *noun* **1** pessimist, prophet of doom, quitter ♦ *adjective* **2** pessimistic

defect *noun* **1** imperfection, blemish, blotch, error, failing, fault, flaw, spot, taint ♦ *verb* **2** desert, abandon, change sides, go over, rebel, revolt, walk out on (*informal*)

defection *noun* desertion, apostasy, rebellion

defective *adjective* faulty, broken, deficient, flawed, imperfect, not working, on the blink (*slang*), out of order

defector *noun* deserter, apostate, renegade, turncoat

defence *noun* **1** protection, cover, guard, immunity, resistance, safeguard, security, shelter **2** shield, barricade, bulwark, buttress, fortification, rampart **3** argument, excuse, explanation, justification, plea, vindication **4** *Law* plea, alibi, denial, rebuttal, testimony

defenceless *adjective* helpless, exposed, naked, powerless, unarmed, unguarded, unprotected, vulnerable, wide open

defend *verb* **1** protect, cover, guard, keep safe, preserve, safeguard, screen, shelter, shield **2** support, champion, endorse, justify, speak up for, stand up for, stick up for (*informal*), uphold, vindicate

defendant *noun* the accused, defence, offender, prisoner at the bar, respondent

defender *noun* **1** protector, bodyguard, escort, guard **2** supporter, advocate, champion, sponsor

defensive *adjective* on guard, on the defensive, protective, uptight (*informal*), watchful

defer[1] *verb* postpone, delay, hold over, procrastinate, put off, put on ice, shelve, suspend

defer[2] *verb* comply, accede, bow, capitulate, give in, give way to, submit, yield

deference *noun* respect, attention, civility, consideration, courtesy, honour, politeness, regard, reverence

deferential *adjective* respectful, ingratiating, obedient, obeisant, obsequious, polite, reverential, submissive

defiance *noun* resistance, confrontation, contempt, disobedience, disregard, insolence, insubordination, opposition, rebelliousness

defiant *adjective* resisting, audacious, bold, daring, disobedient, insolent, insubordinate, mutinous, provocative, rebellious

deficiency *noun* 1 lack, absence, dearth, deficit, scarcity, shortage 2 failing, defect, demerit, fault, flaw, frailty, imperfection, shortcoming, weakness

deficient *adjective* 1 lacking, inadequate, insufficient, meagre, scant, scarce, short, skimpy, wanting 2 unsatisfactory, defective, faulty, flawed, impaired, imperfect, incomplete, inferior, weak

deficit *noun* shortfall, arrears, deficiency, loss, shortage

define *verb* 1 describe,

characterize, designate, explain, expound, interpret, specify, spell out 2 mark out, bound, circumscribe, delineate, demarcate, limit, outline

definite *adjective* 1 clear, black-and-white, cut-and-dried (*informal*), exact, fixed, marked, particular, precise, specific 2 certain, assured, decided, guaranteed, positive, settled, sure

definitely *adverb* certainly, absolutely, categorically, clearly, positively, surely, undeniably, unmistakably, unquestionably, without doubt

definition *noun* 1 explanation, clarification, elucidation, exposition, statement of meaning 2 sharpness, clarity, contrast, distinctness, focus, precision

definitive *adjective* 1 final, absolute, complete, conclusive, decisive 2 authoritative, exhaustive, perfect, reliable, ultimate

deflate *verb* 1 collapse, empty, exhaust, flatten, puncture, shrink 2 humiliate, chasten, disconcert, dispirit, humble, mortify, put down (*slang*), squash 3 *Economics* reduce, depress, devalue, diminish

deflect *verb* turn aside, bend, deviate, diverge, glance off, ricochet, swerve, veer

deflection *noun* deviation, bend, divergence, swerve

deform *verb* 1 distort, buckle, contort, gnarl, mangle, misshape, twist, warp 2 disfigure, deface, maim, mar, mutilate, ruin, spoil

deformity noun <u>abnormality</u>, defect, disfigurement, malformation

defraud verb <u>cheat</u>, con (*informal*), diddle (*informal*), embezzle, fleece, pilfer, rip off (*slang*), swindle, trick

deft adjective <u>skilful</u>, adept, adroit, agile, dexterous, expert, neat, nimble, proficient

defunct adjective **1** <u>dead</u>, deceased, departed, extinct, gone **2** <u>obsolete</u>, bygone, expired, inoperative, invalid, nonexistent, out of commission

defy verb <u>resist</u>, brave, confront, disregard, flout, scorn, slight, spurn

degenerate adjective **1** <u>depraved</u>, corrupt, debauched, decadent, dissolute, immoral, low, perverted ◆ verb **2** <u>worsen</u>, decay, decline, decrease, deteriorate, fall off, lapse, sink, slip

degradation noun **1** <u>disgrace</u>, discredit, dishonour, humiliation, ignominy, mortification, shame **2** <u>deterioration</u>, decline, degeneration, demotion, downgrading

degrade verb **1** <u>disgrace</u>, debase, demean, discredit, dishonour, humble, humiliate, shame **2** <u>demote</u>, downgrade, lower

degrading adjective <u>demeaning</u>, dishonourable, humiliating, infra dig (*informal*), shameful, undignified, unworthy

degree noun <u>stage</u>, grade, notch, point, rung, step, unit

deity noun <u>god</u>, divinity, goddess, godhead, idol, immortal, supreme being

dejected adjective <u>downhearted</u>, crestfallen, depressed, despondent, disconsolate, disheartened, downcast, glum, miserable, sad

dejection noun <u>low spirits</u>, depression, despair, despondency, doldrums, downheartedness, gloom, melancholy, sadness, sorrow, unhappiness

de jure adverb <u>legally</u>, by right, rightfully

delay verb **1** <u>put off</u>, defer, hold over, postpone, procrastinate, shelve, suspend **2** <u>hold up</u>, bog down, detain, hinder, hold back, impede, obstruct, set back, slow up ◆ noun **3** <u>putting off</u>, deferment, postponement, procrastination, suspension **4** <u>hold-up</u>, hindrance, impediment, interruption, interval, setback, stoppage, wait

delegate noun **1** <u>representative</u>, agent, ambassador, commissioner, deputy, envoy, legate ◆ verb **2** <u>entrust</u>, assign, consign, devolve, give, hand over, pass on, transfer **3** <u>appoint</u>, accredit, authorize, commission, depute, designate, empower, mandate

delegation noun **1** <u>deputation</u>, commission, contingent, embassy, envoys, legation, mission **2** <u>devolution</u>, assignment, commissioning, committal

delete verb <u>remove</u>, cancel, cross out, efface, erase, expunge, obliterate, rub out, strike out

deliberate adjective **1** <u>intentional</u>,

calculated, conscious, planned, prearranged, premeditated, purposeful, wilful 2 <u>unhurried</u>, careful, cautious, circumspect, measured, methodical, ponderous, slow, thoughtful ♦ verb 3 <u>consider</u>, cogitate, consult, debate, discuss, meditate, ponder, reflect, think, weigh

deliberately adverb <u>intentionally</u>, by design, calculatingly, consciously, in cold blood, knowingly, on purpose, wilfully, wittingly

deliberation noun 1 <u>consideration</u>, calculation, circumspection, forethought, meditation, reflection, thought 2 <u>discussion</u>, conference, consultation, debate

delicacy noun 1 <u>fineness</u>, accuracy, daintiness, elegance, exquisiteness, lightness, precision, subtlety 2 <u>fragility</u>, flimsiness, frailty, slenderness, tenderness, weakness 3 <u>treat</u>, dainty, luxury, savoury, titbit 4 <u>fastidiousness</u>, discrimination, finesse, purity, refinement, sensibility, taste 5 <u>sensitivity</u>, sensitiveness, tact

delicate adjective 1 <u>fine</u>, deft, elegant, exquisite, graceful, precise, skilled, subtle 2 <u>subtle</u>, choice, dainty, delicious, fine, savoury, tender 3 <u>fragile</u>, flimsy, frail, slender, slight, tender, weak 4 <u>considerate</u>, diplomatic, discreet, sensitive, tactful

delicately adverb 1 <u>finely</u>, daintily, deftly, elegantly, exquisitely, gracefully, precisely, skilfully, subtly 2 <u>tactfully</u>,

diplomatically, sensitively

delicious adjective <u>delectable</u>, appetizing, choice, dainty, mouthwatering, savoury, scrumptious (informal), tasty, toothsome

delight noun 1 <u>pleasure</u>, ecstasy, enjoyment, gladness, glee, happiness, joy, rapture ♦ verb 2 <u>please</u>, amuse, charm, cheer, enchant, gratify, thrill 3 **delight in** <u>take pleasure in</u>, appreciate, enjoy, feast on, like, love, relish, revel in, savour

delighted adjective <u>pleased</u>, ecstatic, elated, enchanted, happy, joyous, jubilant, overjoyed, thrilled

delightful adjective <u>pleasant</u>, agreeable, charming, delectable, enchanting, enjoyable, pleasurable, rapturous, thrilling

delinquent noun <u>criminal</u>, culprit, lawbreaker, miscreant, offender, villain, wrongdoer

delirious adjective 1 <u>mad</u>, crazy, demented, deranged, incoherent, insane, raving, unhinged 2 <u>ecstatic</u>, beside oneself, carried away, excited, frantic, frenzied, hysterical, wild

delirium noun 1 <u>madness</u>, derangement, hallucination, insanity, raving 2 <u>frenzy</u>, ecstasy, fever, hysteria, passion

deliver verb 1 <u>carry</u>, bear, bring, cart, convey, distribute, transport 2 <u>hand over</u>, commit, give up, grant, make over, relinquish, surrender, transfer, turn over, yield 3 <u>give</u>, announce, declare, present, read, utter 4 <u>release</u>, emancipate, free, liberate, loose, ransom, rescue, save 5 <u>strike</u>, administer, aim, deal, direct, give, inflict, launch

deliverance noun <u>release</u>, emancipation, escape, liberation, ransom, redemption, rescue, salvation

delivery noun **1** <u>handing over</u>, consignment, conveyance, dispatch, distribution, surrender, transfer, transmission **2** <u>speech</u>, articulation, elocution, enunciation, intonation, utterance **3** <u>childbirth</u>, confinement, labour, parturition

delude verb <u>deceive</u>, beguile, dupe, fool, hoodwink, kid (*informal*), mislead, take in (*informal*), trick

deluge noun **1** <u>flood</u>, cataclysm, downpour, inundation, overflowing, spate, torrent **2** <u>rush</u>, avalanche, barrage, flood, spate, torrent ♦ *verb* **3** <u>flood</u>, douse, drench, drown, inundate, soak, submerge, swamp **4** <u>overwhelm</u>, engulf, inundate, overload, overrun, swamp

delusion noun <u>misconception</u>, error, fallacy, false impression, fancy, hallucination, illusion, misapprehension, mistake

de luxe adjective <u>luxurious</u>, costly, exclusive, expensive, grand, opulent, select, special, splendid, superior

delve verb <u>research</u>, burrow, explore, ferret out, forage, investigate, look into, probe, rummage, search

demagogue noun <u>agitator</u>, firebrand, rabble-rouser

demand verb **1** <u>request</u>, ask, challenge, inquire, interrogate, question **2** <u>require</u>, call for, cry out for, entail, involve, necessitate, need, want **3** <u>claim</u>, exact, expect, insist on, order ♦ *noun* **4** <u>request</u>, inquiry, order, question, requisition **5** <u>need</u>, call, claim, market, requirement, want

demanding adjective <u>difficult</u>, challenging, exacting, hard, taxing, tough, trying, wearing

demarcation noun <u>delimitation</u>, differentiation, distinction, division, separation

demean verb <u>lower</u>, abase, debase, degrade, descend, humble, stoop

demeanour noun <u>behaviour</u>, air, bearing, carriage, comportment, conduct, deportment, manner

demented adjective <u>mad</u>, crazed, crazy, deranged, frenzied, insane, maniacal, unbalanced, unhinged

demise noun **1** <u>failure</u>, collapse, downfall, end, fall, ruin **2** *Euphemistic* <u>death</u>, decease, departure

democracy noun <u>self-government</u>, commonwealth, republic

democratic adjective <u>self-governing</u>, autonomous, egalitarian, popular, populist, representative

demolish verb **1** <u>knock down</u>, bulldoze, destroy, dismantle, flatten, level, raze, tear down **2** <u>defeat</u>, annihilate, destroy, overthrow, overturn, undo, wreck

demolition noun <u>knocking down</u>, bulldozing, destruction, explosion, levelling, razing, tearing down, wrecking

demon noun **1** evil spirit, devil, fiend, ghoul, goblin, malignant spirit **2** wizard, ace (*informal*), fiend, master

demonic, demoniac, demoniacal adjective **1** devilish, diabolic, diabolical, fiendish, hellish, infernal, satanic **2** frenzied, crazed, frantic, frenetic, furious, hectic, maniacal, manic

demonstrable adjective provable, evident, irrefutable, obvious, palpable, self-evident, unmistakable, verifiable

demonstrate verb **1** prove, display, exhibit, indicate, manifest, show, testify to **2** show how, describe, explain, illustrate, make clear, teach **3** march, parade, picket, protest, rally

demonstration noun **1** march, mass lobby, parade, picket, protest, rally, sit-in **2** explanation, description, exposition, presentation, test, trial **3** proof, confirmation, display, evidence, exhibition, expression, illustration, testimony

demoralize verb dishearten, deject, depress, discourage, dispirit, undermine, unnerve, weaken

demote verb downgrade, degrade, kick downstairs (*slang*), lower in rank, relegate

demur verb **1** object, balk, dispute, hesitate, protest, refuse, take exception, waver ♦ noun **2** As in **without demur** objection, compunction, dissent, hesitation, misgiving, protest, qualm

demure adjective shy, diffident, modest, reserved, reticent, retiring, sedate, unassuming

den noun **1** lair, cave, cavern, haunt, hide-out, hole, shelter **2** Chiefly U.S. study, cubbyhole, hideaway, retreat, sanctuary, sanctum

denial noun **1** negation, contradiction, dissent, renunciation, repudiation, retraction **2** refusal, prohibition, rebuff, rejection, repulse, veto

denigrate verb disparage, bad-mouth (*slang, chiefly U.S. & Canad.*), belittle, knock (*informal*), malign, rubbish (*informal*), run down, slander, vilify

denomination noun **1** religious group, belief, creed, persuasion, school, sect **2** unit, grade, size, value

denote verb indicate, betoken, designate, express, imply, mark, mean, show, signify

denounce verb condemn, accuse, attack, censure, denunciate, revile, stigmatize, vilify

dense adjective **1** thick, close-knit, compact, condensed, heavy, impenetrable, opaque, solid **2** Informal stupid, dozy (*Brit. informal*), dull, obtuse, slow-witted, stolid, thick

density noun tightness, bulk, compactness, consistency, denseness, impenetrability, mass, solidity, thickness

dent noun **1** hollow, chip, crater, depression, dimple, dip, impression, indentation, pit ♦ verb **2** make a dent in, gouge, hollow, press in, push in

deny verb 1 <u>contradict</u>, disagree with, disprove, rebuff, rebut, refute 2 <u>refuse</u>, begrudge, disallow, forbid, reject, turn down, withhold 3 <u>renounce</u>, disclaim, disown, recant, repudiate, retract

depart verb 1 <u>leave</u>, absent (oneself), disappear, exit, go, go away, quit, retire, retreat, withdraw 2 <u>deviate</u>, differ, digress, diverge, stray, swerve, turn aside, vary, veer

department noun <u>section</u>, branch, bureau, division, office, station, subdivision, unit

departure noun 1 <u>leaving</u>, exit, exodus, going, going away, leave-taking, removal, retirement, withdrawal 2 <u>divergence</u>, deviation, digression, variation 3 <u>shift</u>, change, difference, innovation, novelty, whole new ball game (informal)

depend verb 1 <u>trust in</u>, bank on, count on, lean on, reckon on, rely upon, turn to 2 <u>be determined by</u>, be based on, be contingent on, be subject to, be subordinate to, hang on, hinge on, rest on, revolve around

dependable adjective <u>reliable</u>, faithful, reputable, responsible, staunch, steady, sure, trustworthy, trusty, unfailing

dependant noun <u>relative</u>, child, minor, protégé, subordinate

dependent adjective 1 <u>relying on</u>, defenceless, helpless, reliant, vulnerable, weak 2 **dependent on** or **upon** <u>determined by</u>, conditional on, contingent on, depending on, influenced by, subject to

depict verb 1 <u>draw</u>, delineate, illustrate, outline, paint, picture, portray, sketch 2 <u>describe</u>, characterize, narrate, outline, represent

depiction noun <u>representation</u>, delineation, description, picture, portrayal, sketch

deplete verb <u>use up</u>, consume, drain, empty, exhaust, expend, impoverish, lessen, reduce

deplorable adjective 1 <u>regrettable</u>, grievous, lamentable, pitiable, sad, unfortunate, wretched 2 <u>disgraceful</u>, dishonourable, reprehensible, scandalous, shameful

deplore verb <u>disapprove of</u>, abhor, censure, condemn, denounce, object to, take a dim view of

deploy verb <u>position</u>, arrange, set out, station, use, utilize

deployment noun <u>position</u>, arrangement, organization, spread, stationing, use, utilization

deport verb 1 <u>expel</u>, banish, exile, expatriate, extradite, oust 2 **deport oneself** <u>behave</u>, acquit oneself, act, bear oneself, carry oneself, comport oneself, conduct oneself, hold oneself

depose verb 1 <u>remove from office</u>, demote, dethrone, dismiss, displace, oust 2 Law <u>testify</u>, avouch, declare, make a deposition

deposit verb 1 <u>put</u>, drop, lay, locate, place 2 <u>store</u>, bank, consign, entrust, lodge ♦ noun 3 <u>down payment</u>, instalment, part payment, pledge, retainer, security, stake **4** <u>sediment</u>, accumulation, dregs, lees, precipitate, silt

depot noun **1** <u>storehouse</u>, depository, repository, warehouse **2** Chiefly U.S. & Canad. <u>bus station</u>, garage, terminus

depraved adjective <u>corrupt</u>, degenerate, dissolute, evil, immoral, sinful, vicious, vile, wicked

depravity noun <u>corruption</u>, debauchery, evil, immorality, sinfulness, vice, wickedness

depreciate verb **1** <u>devalue</u>, decrease, deflate, lessen, lose value, lower, reduce **2** <u>disparage</u>, belittle, denigrate, deride, detract, run down, scorn, sneer at

depreciation noun
1 <u>devaluation</u>, deflation, depression, drop, fall, slump
2 <u>disparagement</u>, belittlement, denigration, deprecation, detraction

depress verb **1** <u>sadden</u>, deject, discourage, dishearten, dispirit, make despondent, oppress, weigh down **2** <u>lower</u>, cheapen, depreciate, devalue, diminish, downgrade, lessen, reduce **3** <u>press down</u>, flatten, level, lower, push down

depressed adjective
1 <u>low-spirited</u>, blue, dejected, despondent, discouraged, dispirited, downcast, downhearted, fed up, sad, unhappy **2** <u>poverty-stricken</u>, deprived, disadvantaged, needy, poor, run-down **3** <u>lowered</u>,

cheapened, depreciated, devalued, weakened **4** <u>sunken</u>, concave, hollow, indented, recessed

depressing adjective <u>bleak</u>, discouraging, disheartening, dismal, dispiriting, gloomy, harrowing, sad, saddening

depression noun **1** <u>low spirits</u>, dejection, despair, despondency, downheartedness, dumps (informal), gloominess, melancholy, sadness, the blues **2** <u>recession</u>, economic decline, hard or bad times, inactivity, slump, stagnation **3** <u>hollow</u>, bowl, cavity, dent, dimple, dip, indentation, pit, valley

deprivation noun **1** <u>withholding</u>, denial, dispossession, expropriation, removal, withdrawal **2** <u>want</u>, destitution, distress, hardship, need, privation

deprive verb <u>withhold</u>, bereave, despoil, dispossess, rob, strip

deprived adjective <u>poor</u>, bereft, destitute, disadvantaged, down at heel, in need, lacking, needy

depth noun **1** <u>deepness</u>, drop, extent, measure **2** <u>insight</u>, astuteness, discernment, penetration, profoundness, profundity, sagacity, wisdom

deputation noun <u>delegation</u>, commission, embassy, envoys, legation

deputize verb <u>stand in for</u>, act for, take the place of, understudy

deputy noun <u>substitute</u>, delegate, legate, lieutenant, number two, proxy, representative, second-in-command, surrogate

deranged adjective <u>mad</u>, crazed,

crazy, demented, distracted,
insane, irrational, unbalanced,
unhinged

derelict *adjective* 1 abandoned,
deserted, dilapidated, discarded,
forsaken, neglected, ruined
♦ *noun* 2 tramp, bag lady,
down-and-out, outcast, vagrant

deride *verb* mock, disdain,
disparage, insult, jeer, ridicule,
scoff, scorn, sneer, taunt

derisory *adjective* ridiculous,
contemptible, insulting,
laughable, ludicrous, outrageous,
preposterous

derivation *noun* origin,
beginning, foundation, root,
source

derive from *verb* come from,
arise from, emanate from, flow
from, issue from, originate from,
proceed from, spring from, stem
from

derogatory *adjective* disparaging,
belittling, defamatory, offensive,
slighting, uncomplimentary,
unfavourable, unflattering

descend *verb* 1 move down,
drop, fall, go down, plummet,
plunge, sink, subside, tumble
2 slope, dip, incline, slant
3 lower oneself, degenerate,
deteriorate, stoop 4 be
descended originate, be handed
down, be passed down, derive,
issue, proceed, spring 5 descend
on attack, arrive, invade, raid,
swoop

descent *noun* 1 coming down,
drop, fall, plunge, swoop
2 slope, declivity, dip, drop,
incline, slant 3 ancestry,
extraction, family tree,
genealogy, lineage, origin,

parentage 4 decline,
degeneration, deterioration

describe *verb* 1 relate, depict,
explain, express, narrate,
portray, recount, report, tell
2 trace, delineate, draw, mark
out, outline

description *noun* 1 account,
depiction, explanation, narrative,
portrayal, report, representation,
sketch 2 kind, brand, category,
class, order, sort, type, variety

descriptive *adjective* graphic,
detailed, explanatory, expressive,
illustrative, pictorial, picturesque,
vivid

desert[1] *noun* wilderness, solitude,
waste, wasteland, wilds

desert[2] *verb* abandon, abscond,
forsake, jilt, leave, leave
stranded, maroon, quit, strand,
walk out on (*informal*)

deserted *adjective* abandoned,
derelict, desolate, empty,
forsaken, neglected, unoccupied,
vacant

deserter *noun* defector,
absconder, escapee, fugitive,
renegade, runaway, traitor, truant

desertion *noun* abandonment,
absconding, apostasy, betrayal,
defection, dereliction, escape,
evasion, flight, relinquishment

deserve *verb* merit, be entitled
to, be worthy of, earn, justify,
rate, warrant

deserved *adjective* well-earned,
due, earned, fitting, justified,
merited, proper, rightful,
warranted

deserving *adjective* worthy,
commendable, estimable,
laudable, meritorious,

praiseworthy, righteous

design verb 1 plan, draft, draw, outline, sketch, trace 2 create, conceive, fabricate, fashion, invent, originate, think up 3 intend, aim, mean, plan, propose, purpose ♦ noun 4 plan, blueprint, draft, drawing, model, outline, scheme, sketch 5 arrangement, construction, form, organization, pattern, shape, style 6 intention, aim, end, goal, object, objective, purpose, target

designate verb 1 name, call, dub, entitle, label, style, term 2 appoint, assign, choose, delegate, depute, nominate, select

designation noun name, description, label, mark, title

designer noun creator, architect, deviser, inventor, originator, planner

desirable adjective 1 worthwhile, advantageous, advisable, beneficial, good, preferable, profitable 2 attractive, adorable, alluring, fetching, glamorous, seductive, sexy (Informal)

desire verb 1 want, crave, hanker after, hope for, long for, set one's heart on, thirst for, wish for, yearn for ♦ noun 2 wish, aspiration, craving, hankering, hope, longing, thirst, want 3 lust, appetite, libido, passion

desist verb stop, break off, cease, discontinue, end, forbear, leave off, pause, refrain from

desolate adjective 1 uninhabited, bare, barren, bleak, dreary, godforsaken, solitary, wild 2 miserable, dejected,

despondent, disconsolate, downcast, forlorn, gloomy, wretched ♦ verb 3 lay waste, depopulate, despoil, destroy, devastate, lay low, pillage, plunder, ravage, ruin 4 deject, depress, discourage, dishearten, dismay, distress, grieve

desolation noun 1 ruin, destruction, devastation, havoc 2 bleakness, barrenness, isolation, solitude 3 misery, anguish, dejection, despair, distress, gloom, sadness, woe, wretchedness

despair noun 1 despondency, anguish, dejection, depression, desperation, gloom, hopelessness, misery, wretchedness ♦ verb 2 lose hope, give up, lose heart

despairing adjective hopeless, dejected, desperate, despondent, disconsolate, frantic, grief-stricken, inconsolable, miserable, wretched

despatch see DISPATCH

desperado noun criminal, bandit, lawbreaker, outlaw, villain

desperate adjective 1 reckless, audacious, daring, frantic, furious, risky 2 grave, drastic, extreme, urgent

desperately adverb 1 gravely, badly, dangerously, perilously, seriously, severely 2 hopelessly, appallingly, fearfully, frightfully, shockingly

desperation noun 1 recklessness, foolhardiness, frenzy, impetuosity, madness, rashness 2 misery, agony, anguish, despair, hopelessness, trouble, unhappiness, worry

despicable *adjective* <u>contemptible</u>, detestable, disgraceful, hateful, mean, shameful, sordid, vile, worthless, wretched

despise *verb* <u>look down on</u>, abhor, detest, loathe, revile, scorn

despite *preposition* <u>in spite of</u>, against, even with, in the face of, in the teeth of, notwithstanding, regardless of, undeterred by

despondency *noun* <u>dejection</u>, depression, despair, desperation, gloom, low spirits, melancholy, misery, sadness

despondent *adjective* <u>dejected</u>, depressed, disconsolate, disheartened, dispirited, downhearted, glum, in despair, sad, sorrowful

despot *noun* <u>tyrant</u>, autocrat, dictator, oppressor

despotic *adjective* <u>tyrannical</u>, authoritarian, autocratic, dictatorial, domineering, imperious, oppressive

despotism *noun* <u>tyranny</u>, autocracy, dictatorship, oppression, totalitarianism

destination *noun* <u>journey's end</u>, haven, resting-place, station, stop, terminus

destined *adjective* <u>fated</u>, bound, certain, doomed, intended, meant, predestined

destiny *noun* <u>fate</u>, doom, fortune, karma, kismet, lot, portion

destitute *adjective* <u>penniless</u>, down and out, impoverished, indigent, insolvent, moneyless, penurious, poor, poverty-stricken

destroy *verb* <u>ruin</u>, annihilate, crush, demolish, devastate, eradicate, shatter, wipe out, wreck

destruction *noun* <u>ruin</u>, annihilation, demolition, devastation, eradication, extermination, havoc, slaughter, wreckage

destructive *adjective* <u>damaging</u>, calamitous, catastrophic, deadly, devastating, fatal, harmful, lethal, ruinous

detach *verb* <u>separate</u>, cut off, disconnect, disengage, divide, remove, sever, tear off, unfasten

detached *adjective* **1** <u>separate</u>, disconnected, discrete, unconnected **2** <u>uninvolved</u>, disinterested, dispassionate, impartial, impersonal, neutral, objective, reserved, unbiased

detachment *noun* **1** <u>indifference</u>, aloofness, coolness, nonchalance, remoteness, unconcern **2** <u>impartiality</u>, fairness, neutrality, objectivity **3** *Military* <u>unit</u>, body, force, party, patrol, squad, task force

detail *noun* **1** <u>point</u>, aspect, component, element, fact, factor, feature, particular, respect **2** <u>fine point</u>, nicety, particular, triviality **3** *Military* <u>party</u>, assignment, body, detachment, duty, fatigue, force, squad ♦ *verb* **4** <u>list</u>, catalogue, enumerate, itemize, recite, recount, rehearse, relate, tabulate **5** <u>appoint</u>, allocate, assign, charge, commission, delegate, send

detailed *adjective* <u>comprehensive</u>, blow-by-blow, exhaustive, full, intricate, minute, particular, thorough

detain verb 1 <u>delay</u>, check, hinder, hold up, impede, keep back, retard, slow up (or down) 2 <u>hold</u>, arrest, confine, intern, restrain

detect verb 1 <u>notice</u>, ascertain, identify, note, observe, perceive, recognize, spot 2 <u>discover</u>, find, track down, uncover, unmask

detective noun <u>investigator</u>, cop (slang), gumshoe (U.S. slang), private eye, private investigator, sleuth (informal)

detention noun <u>imprisonment</u>, confinement, custody, incarceration, quarantine

deter verb <u>discourage</u>, dissuade, frighten, inhibit from, intimidate, prevent, put off, stop, talk out of

detergent noun <u>cleaner</u>, cleanser

deteriorate verb <u>decline</u>, degenerate, go downhill (informal), lower, slump, worsen

determination noun <u>tenacity</u>, dedication, doggedness, fortitude, perseverance, persistence, resolve, single mindedness, steadfastness, willpower

determine verb 1 <u>settle</u>, conclude, decide, end, finish, ordain, regulate 2 <u>find out</u>, ascertain, detect, discover, learn, verify, work out 3 <u>decide</u>, choose, elect, make up one's mind, resolve

determined adjective <u>resolute</u>, dogged, firm, intent, persevering, persistent, single-minded, steadfast, tenacious, unwavering

deterrent noun <u>discouragement</u>, check, curb, disincentive, hindrance, impediment, obstacle, restraint

detest verb <u>hate</u>, abhor, abominate, despise, dislike intensely, loathe, recoil from

detonate verb <u>explode</u>, blast, blow up, discharge, set off, trigger

detour noun <u>diversion</u>, bypass, indirect course, roundabout way

detract verb <u>lessen</u>, devaluate, diminish, lower, reduce, take away from

detriment noun <u>damage</u>, disadvantage, disservice, harm, hurt, impairment, injury, loss

detrimental adjective <u>damaging</u>, adverse, deleterious, destructive, disadvantageous, harmful, prejudicial, unfavourable

devastate verb <u>destroy</u>, demolish, lay waste, level, ravage, raze, ruin, sack, wreck

devastating adjective <u>overwhelming</u>, cutting, overpowering, savage, trenchant, vitriolic, withering

devastation noun <u>destruction</u>, demolition, desolation, havoc, ruin

develop verb 1 <u>advance</u>, evolve, flourish, grow, mature, progress, prosper, ripen 2 <u>form</u>, breed, establish, generate, invent, originate 3 <u>expand</u>, amplify, augment, broaden, elaborate, enlarge, unfold, work out

development noun 1 <u>growth</u>, advance, evolution, expansion, improvement, increase, progress, spread 2 <u>event</u>, happening, incident, occurrence, result, turn of events, upshot

deviant *adjective* 1 <u>perverted</u>, kinky (*slang*), sick (*informal*), twisted, warped ♦ *noun* 2 <u>pervert</u>, freak, misfit

deviate *verb* <u>differ</u>, depart, diverge, stray, swerve, veer, wander

deviation *noun* <u>departure</u>, digression, discrepancy, disparity, divergence, inconsistency, irregularity, shift, variation

device *noun* 1 <u>gadget</u>, apparatus, appliance, contraption, implement, instrument, machine, tool 2 <u>ploy</u>, gambit, manoeuvre, plan, scheme, stratagem, trick, wile

devil *noun* 1 **the Devil** <u>Satan</u>, Beelzebub, Evil One, Lucifer, Mephistopheles, Old Nick (*informal*), Prince of Darkness 2 <u>brute</u>, beast, demon, fiend, monster, ogre, terror 3 <u>scamp</u>, rascal, rogue, scoundrel 4 <u>person</u>, beggar, creature, thing, wretch

devilish *adjective* <u>fiendish</u>, atrocious, damnable, detestable, diabolical, hellish, infernal, satanic, wicked

devious *adjective* 1 <u>sly</u>, calculating, deceitful, dishonest, double-dealing, insincere, scheming, surreptitious, underhand, wily 2 <u>indirect</u>, circuitous, rambling, roundabout

devise *verb* <u>work out</u>, conceive, construct, contrive, design, dream up, formulate, invent, think up

devoid *adjective* <u>lacking</u>, bereft, deficient, destitute, empty, free from, wanting, without

devote *verb* <u>dedicate</u>, allot, apply, assign, commit, give, pledge, reserve, set apart

devoted *adjective* <u>dedicated</u>, ardent, committed, constant, devout, faithful, loyal, staunch, steadfast, true

devotee *noun* <u>enthusiast</u>, adherent, admirer, aficionado, buff (*informal*), disciple, fan, fanatic, follower, supporter

devotion *noun* 1 <u>dedication</u>, adherence, allegiance, commitment, constancy, faithfulness, fidelity, loyalty 2 <u>love</u>, affection, attachment, fondness, passion 3 <u>devoutness</u>, godliness, holiness, piety, reverence, spirituality 4 **devotions** <u>prayers</u>, church service, divine office, religious observance

devour *verb* 1 <u>eat</u>, consume, gobble, gulp, guzzle, polish off (*informal*), swallow, wolf 2 <u>destroy</u>, annihilate, consume, ravage, waste, wipe out 3 <u>enjoy</u>, read compulsively *or* voraciously, take in

devout *adjective* <u>religious</u>, godly, holy, orthodox, pious, prayerful, pure, reverent, saintly

dexterity *noun* 1 <u>skill</u>, adroitness, deftness, expertise, finesse, nimbleness, proficiency, touch 2 <u>cleverness</u>, ability, aptitude, ingenuity

diabolical *adjective Informal* <u>dreadful</u>, abysmal, appalling, atrocious, hellish, outrageous, shocking, terrible

diagnose *verb* <u>identify</u>, analyse,

determine, distinguish, interpret, pinpoint, pronounce, recognize

diagnosis *noun* **1** examination, analysis, investigation, scrutiny **2** opinion, conclusion, interpretation, pronouncement

diagonal *adjective* slanting, angled, cross, crossways, crosswise, oblique

diagonally *adverb* aslant, at an angle, cornerwise, crosswise, obliquely

diagram *noun* plan, chart, drawing, figure, graph, representation, sketch

dialect *noun* language, brogue, idiom, jargon, patois, provincialism, speech, vernacular

dialogue *noun* conversation, communication, conference, discourse, discussion

diary *noun* journal, appointment book, chronicle, daily record, engagement book, Filofax (*Trademark*)

dicky *adjective Brit. informal* weak, fluttery, shaky, unreliable, unsound, unsteady

dictate *verb* **1** speak, read out, say, utter **2** order, command, decree, demand, direct, impose, lay down the law, pronounce ♦ *noun* **3** command, decree, demand, direction, edict, fiat, injunction, order **4** principle, code, law, rule

dictator *noun* absolute ruler, autocrat, despot, oppressor, tyrant

dictatorial *adjective* **1** absolute, arbitrary, autocratic, despotic, totalitarian, tyrannical, unlimited, unrestricted **2** domineering,

authoritarian, bossy (*informal*), imperious, oppressive, overbearing

dictatorship *noun* absolute rule, absolutism, authoritarianism, autocracy, despotism, totalitarianism, tyranny

diction *noun* pronunciation, articulation, delivery, elocution, enunciation, fluency, inflection, intonation, speech

dictionary *noun* wordbook, glossary, lexicon, vocabulary

die *verb* **1** pass away, breathe one's last, croak (*slang*), expire, give up the ghost, kick the bucket (*slang*), peg out (*informal*), perish, snuff it (*slang*) **2** dwindle, decay, decline, fade, sink, subside, wane, wilt, wither **3** stop, break down, fade out *or* away, fail, fizzle out, halt, lose power, peter out, run down **4 be dying** long, ache, be eager, desire, hunger, pine for, yearn

die-hard *noun* reactionary, fanatic, old fogey, stick-in-the-mud (*informal*)

diet¹ *noun* **1** food, fare, nourishment, nutriment, provisions, rations, sustenance, victuals **2** regime, abstinence, fast, regimen ♦ *verb* **3** slim, abstain, eat sparingly, fast, lose weight

diet² *noun* council, chamber, congress, convention, legislature, meeting, parliament

differ *verb* **1** be dissimilar, contradict, contrast, depart from, diverge, run counter to, stand apart, vary **2** disagree, clash, contend, debate, demur, dispute, dissent, oppose, take exception, take issue

difference *noun* 1 <u>dissimilarity</u>, alteration, change, contrast, discrepancy, disparity, diversity, variation, variety 2 <u>disagreement</u>, argument, clash, conflict, contretemps, debate, dispute, quarrel 3 <u>remainder</u>, balance, rest, result

different *adjective* 1 <u>unlike</u>, altered, changed, contrasting, disparate, dissimilar, divergent, inconsistent, opposed 2 <u>various</u>, assorted, diverse, miscellaneous, sundry, varied 3 <u>unusual</u>, atypical, distinctive, extraordinary, peculiar, singular, special, strange, uncommon

differentiate *verb* 1 <u>distinguish</u>, contrast, discriminate, make a distinction, mark off, separate, set off *or* apart, tell apart 2 <u>make different</u>, adapt, alter, change, convert, modify, transform

difficult *adjective* 1 <u>hard</u>, arduous, demanding, formidable, laborious, onerous, strenuous, uphill 2 <u>problematical</u>, abstruse, baffling, complex, complicated, intricate, involved, knotty, obscure 3 <u>hard to please</u>, demanding, fastidious, fussy, perverse, refractory, unaccommodating

difficulty *noun* 1 <u>laboriousness</u>, arduousness, awkwardness, hardship, strain, strenuousness, tribulation 2 <u>predicament</u>, dilemma, embarrassment, hot water (*informal*), jam (*informal*), mess, plight, quandary, trouble 3 <u>problem</u>, complication, hindrance, hurdle, impediment, obstacle, pitfall, snag, stumbling block

diffidence *noun* <u>shyness</u>, bashfulness, hesitancy, insecurity, modesty, reserve, self-consciousness, timidity

diffident *adjective* <u>shy</u>, bashful, doubtful, hesitant, insecure, modest, reserved, self-conscious, timid, unassertive, unassuming

dig *verb* 1 <u>excavate</u>, burrow, delve, hollow out, mine, quarry, scoop, tunnel 2 <u>investigate</u>, delve, dig down, go into, probe, research, search 3 *with* **out** *or* **up** <u>find</u>, discover, expose, uncover, unearth, uproot 4 <u>poke</u>, drive, jab, prod, punch, thrust ♦ *noun* 5 <u>poke</u>, jab, prod, punch, thrust 6 <u>cutting remark</u>, barb, crack (*slang*), gibe, insult, jeer, sneer, taunt, wisecrack (*informal*)

digest *verb* 1 <u>ingest</u>, absorb, assimilate, dissolve, incorporate 2 <u>take in</u>, absorb, consider, contemplate, grasp, study, understand ♦ *noun* 3 <u>summary</u>, abridgment, abstract, epitome, précis, résumé, synopsis

digestion *noun* <u>ingestion</u>, absorption, assimilation, conversion, incorporation, transformation

dignified *adjective* <u>distinguished</u>, formal, grave, imposing, noble, reserved, solemn, stately

dignitary *noun* <u>public figure</u>, bigwig (*informal*), high-up (*informal*), notable, personage, pillar of society, V.I.P., worthy

dignity *noun* 1 <u>decorum</u>, courtliness, grandeur, gravity, loftiness, majesty, nobility, solemnity, stateliness 2 <u>honour</u>, eminence, importance, rank, respectability, standing, status **3** self-importance, pride, self-esteem, self-respect

digress verb wander, depart, deviate, diverge, drift, get off the point or subject, go off at a tangent, ramble, stray

digression noun departure, aside, detour, deviation, divergence, diversion, straying, wandering

dilapidated adjective ruined, broken-down, crumbling, decrepit, in ruins, ramshackle, rickety, run-down, tumbledown

dilate verb enlarge, broaden, expand, puff out, stretch, swell, widen

dilatory adjective time-wasting, delaying, lingering, procrastinating, slow, sluggish, tardy, tarrying

dilemma noun predicament, difficulty, mess, plight, problem, puzzle, quandary, spot (informal)

dilettante noun amateur, aesthete, dabbler, trifler

diligence noun application, attention, care, industry, laboriousness, perseverance

diligent adjective hard-working, assiduous, attentive, careful, conscientious, industrious, painstaking, persistent, studious, tireless

dilute verb **1** water down, adulterate, cut, make thinner, thin (out), weaken **2** reduce, attenuate, decrease, diffuse, diminish, lessen, mitigate, temper, weaken

dim adjective **1** poorly lit, cloudy, dark, grey, overcast, shadowy, tenebrous **2** unclear, bleary, blurred, faint, fuzzy, ill-defined, indistinct, obscured, shadowy **3** Informal stupid, dense, dozy (Brit. informal), dull, dumb (informal), obtuse, slow on the uptake (informal), thick **4 take a dim view** disapprove, be displeased, be sceptical, look askance, reject, suspect, take exception, view with disfavour ♦ verb **5** dull, blur, cloud, darken, fade, obscure

dimension noun, often plural measurement, amplitude, bulk, capacity, extent, proportions, size, volume

diminish verb **1** decrease, curtail, cut, lessen, lower, reduce, shrink **2** dwindle, decline, die out, recede, subside, wane

diminutive adjective small, little, mini, miniature, minute, petite, tiny, undersized

din noun **1** noise, clamour, clatter, commotion, crash, pandemonium, racket, row, uproar ♦ verb **2 din (something) into (someone)** instil, drum into, go on at, hammer into, inculcate, instruct, teach

dine verb eat, banquet, feast, lunch, sup

dingy adjective dull, dark, dim, drab, dreary, gloomy, murky, obscure, sombre

dinner noun meal, banquet, feast, main meal, repast, spread (informal)

dip verb **1** plunge, bathe, douse, duck, dunk, immerse **2** slope, decline, descend, drop (down), fall, lower, sink, subside ♦ noun

3 <u>plunge</u>, douche, drenching, ducking, immersion, soaking
4 <u>bathe</u>, dive, plunge, swim
5 <u>hollow</u>, basin, concavity, depression, hole, incline, slope
6 <u>drop</u>, decline, fall, lowering, sag, slip, slump

dip into verb <u>sample</u>, browse, glance at, peruse, skim

diplomacy noun
1 <u>statesmanship</u>, international negotiation, statecraft 2 <u>tact</u>, artfulness, craft, delicacy, discretion, finesse, savoir-faire, skill, subtlety

diplomat noun <u>negotiator</u>, conciliator, go-between, mediator, moderator, politician, tactician

diplomatic adjective <u>tactful</u>, adept, discreet, polite, politic, prudent, sensitive, subtle

dire adjective 1 <u>disastrous</u>, awful, calamitous, catastrophic, horrible, ruinous, terrible, woeful 2 <u>desperate</u>, critical, crucial, drastic, extreme, now or never, pressing, urgent 3 <u>grim</u>, dismal, dreadful, fearful, gloomy, ominous, portentous

direct adjective 1 <u>straight</u>, nonstop, not crooked, shortest, through, unbroken, uninterrupted 2 <u>immediate</u>, face-to-face, first-hand, head-on, personal 3 <u>honest</u>, candid, frank, open, plain-spoken, straight, straightforward, upfront (informal) 4 <u>explicit</u>, absolute, blunt, categorical, downright, express, plain, point-blank, unambiguous, unequivocal ♦ verb 5 <u>control</u>, conduct, guide, handle, lead, manage, oversee, run, supervise 6 <u>order</u>, bid, charge, command, demand, dictate, instruct 7 <u>guide</u>, indicate, lead, point in the direction of, point the way, show 8 <u>address</u>, label, mail, route, send 9 <u>aim</u>, focus, level, point, train

direction noun 1 <u>way</u>, aim, bearing, course, line, path, road, route, track 2 <u>management</u>, administration, charge, command, control, guidance, leadership, order, supervision

directions plural noun <u>instructions</u>, briefing, guidance, guidelines, plan, recommendation, regulations

directive noun <u>order</u>, command, decree, edict, injunction, instruction, mandate, regulation, ruling

directly adverb 1 <u>straight</u>, by the shortest route, exactly, in a beeline, precisely, unswervingly, without deviation 2 <u>honestly</u>, openly, plainly, point-blank, straightforwardly, truthfully, unequivocally 3 <u>at once</u>, as soon as possible, forthwith, immediately, promptly, right away, straightaway

director noun <u>controller</u>, administrator, chief, executive, governor, head, leader, manager, supervisor

dirge noun <u>lament</u>, dead march, elegy, funeral song, requiem, threnody

dirt noun 1 <u>filth</u>, dust, grime, impurity, muck, mud 2 <u>soil</u>, clay, earth, loam 3 <u>obscenity</u>, indecency, pornography, sleaze, smut

dirty *adjective* **1** <u>filthy</u>, foul, grimy, grubby, messy, mucky, muddy, polluted, soiled, unclean **2** <u>dishonest</u>, crooked, fraudulent, illegal, treacherous, unfair, unscrupulous, unsporting **3** <u>obscene</u>, blue, indecent, pornographic, salacious, sleazy, smutty **4** *As in* **a dirty look** <u>angry</u>, annoyed, bitter, choked, indignant, offended, resentful, scorching ◆ *verb* **5** <u>soil</u>, blacken, defile, foul, muddy, pollute, smirch, spoil, stain

disability *noun* **1** <u>handicap</u>, affliction, ailment, complaint, defect, disorder, impairment, infirmity, malady **2** <u>incapacity</u>, inability, unfitness

disable *verb* **1** <u>handicap</u>, cripple, damage, enfeeble, immobilize, impair, incapacitate, paralyse **2** <u>disqualify</u>, invalidate, render *or* declare incapable

disabled *adjective* <u>handicapped</u>, crippled, incapacitated, infirm, lame, paralysed, weakened

disadvantage *noun* **1** <u>harm</u>, damage, detriment, disservice, hurt, injury, loss, prejudice **2** <u>drawback</u>, downside, handicap, inconvenience, nuisance, snag, trouble

disagree *verb* **1** <u>differ (in opinion)</u>, argue, clash, cross swords, dispute, dissent, object, quarrel, take issue with **2** <u>conflict</u>, be dissimilar, contradict, counter, differ, diverge, run counter to, vary **3** <u>make ill</u>, bother, discomfort, distress, hurt, nauseate, sicken, trouble, upset

disagreeable *adjective* **1** <u>nasty</u>,

disgusting, displeasing, distasteful, objectionable, obnoxious, offensive, repugnant, repulsive, unpleasant **2** <u>rude</u>, bad-tempered, churlish, difficult, disobliging, irritable, surly, unpleasant

disagreement *noun* **1** <u>incompatibility</u>, difference, discrepancy, disparity, dissimilarity, divergence, incongruity, variance **2** <u>argument</u>, altercation, clash, conflict, dispute, dissent, quarrel, row, squabble

disallow *verb* <u>reject</u>, disavow, dismiss, disown, rebuff, refuse, repudiate

disappear *verb* **1** <u>vanish</u>, evanesce, fade away, pass, recede **2** <u>cease</u>, die out, dissolve, evaporate, leave no trace, melt away, pass away, perish

disappearance *noun* <u>vanishing</u>, departure, eclipse, evanescence, evaporation, going, melting, passing

disappoint *verb* <u>let down</u>, disenchant, disgruntle, dishearten, disillusion, dismay, dissatisfy, fail

disappointed *adjective* <u>let down</u>, cast down, despondent, discouraged, disenchanted, disgruntled, dissatisfied, downhearted, frustrated

disappointing *adjective* <u>unsatisfactory</u>, depressing, disconcerting, discouraging, inadequate, insufficient, sad, sorry

disappointment *noun* **1** <u>frustration</u>, chagrin, discontent, discouragement, disenchantment, disillusionment, dissatisfaction, regret **2** <u>letdown</u>, blow, calamity, choker (*informal*), misfortune, setback

disapproval *noun* <u>displeasure</u>, censure, condemnation, criticism, denunciation, dissatisfaction, objection, reproach

disapprove *verb* <u>condemn</u>, deplore, dislike, find unacceptable, frown on, look down one's nose at (*informal*), object to, reject, take a dim view of, take exception to

disarm *verb* **1** <u>render defenceless</u>, disable **2** <u>win over</u>, persuade, set at ease **3** <u>demilitarize</u>, deactivate, demobilize, disband

disarmament *noun* <u>arms reduction</u>, arms limitation, de-escalation, demilitarization, demobilization

disarming *adjective* <u>charming</u>, irresistible, likable *or* likeable, persuasive, winning

disarrange *verb* <u>disorder</u>, confuse, disorganize, disturb, jumble (up), mess (up), scatter, shake (up), shuffle

disarray *noun* **1** <u>confusion</u>, disorder, disorganization, disunity, indiscipline, unruliness **2** <u>untidiness</u>, chaos, clutter, hotchpotch, jumble, mess, muddle, shambles

disaster *noun* <u>catastrophe</u>, adversity, calamity, cataclysm, misfortune, ruin, tragedy, trouble

disastrous *adjective* <u>terrible</u>, calamitous, cataclysmic, catastrophic, devastating, fatal, ruinous, tragic

disbelief *noun* <u>scepticism</u>, distrust, doubt, dubiety, incredulity, mistrust, unbelief

discard *verb* <u>get rid of</u>, abandon, cast aside, dispense with, dispose of, drop, dump (*informal*), jettison, reject, throw away *or* out

discharge *verb* **1** <u>release</u>, allow to go, clear, free, liberate, pardon, set free **2** <u>dismiss</u>, cashier, discard, expel, fire (*informal*), oust, remove, sack (*informal*) **3** <u>fire</u>, detonate, explode, let loose (*informal*), let off, set off, shoot **4** <u>pour forth</u>, dispense, emit, exude, give off, leak, ooze, release **5** <u>carry out</u>, accomplish, do, execute, fulfil, observe, perform **6** <u>pay</u>, clear, honour, meet, relieve, satisfy, settle, square up ♦ *noun* **7** <u>release</u>, acquittal, clearance, liberation, pardon **8** <u>dismissal</u>, demobilization, ejection **9** <u>firing</u>, blast, burst, detonation, explosion, report, salvo, shot, volley **10** <u>emission</u>, excretion, ooze, pus, secretion, seepage, suppuration

disciple *noun* <u>follower</u>, adherent, apostle, devotee, pupil, student, supporter

disciplinarian *noun* <u>authoritarian</u>, despot, martinet, stickler, taskmaster, tyrant

discipline *noun* **1** <u>training</u>, drill, exercise, method, practice, regimen, regulation **2** <u>punishment</u>, castigation, chastisement, correction **3** <u>self-control</u>, conduct, control, orderliness, regulation, restraint, strictness **4** <u>field of study</u>, area, branch of knowledge, course,

curriculum, speciality, subject
♦ *verb* 5 <u>train</u>, bring up, drill, educate, exercise, prepare
6 <u>punish</u>, bring to book, castigate, chasten, chastise, correct, penalize, reprimand, reprove

disclose *verb* 1 <u>make known</u>, broadcast, communicate, confess, divulge, let slip, publish, relate, reveal 2 <u>show</u>, bring to light, expose, lay bare, reveal, uncover, unveil

disclosure *noun* <u>revelation</u>, acknowledgment, admission, announcement, confession, declaration, divulgence, leak, publication

discolour *verb* <u>stain</u>, fade, mark, soil, streak, tarnish, tinge

discomfort *noun* 1 <u>pain</u>, ache, hurt, irritation, malaise, soreness
2 <u>uneasiness</u>, annoyance, distress, hardship, irritation, nuisance, trouble

disconcert *verb* <u>disturb</u>, faze, fluster, perturb, rattle (*informal*), take aback, unsettle, upset, worry

disconcerting *adjective* <u>disturbing</u>, alarming, awkward, bewildering, confusing, distracting, embarrassing, off-putting (*Brit. informal*), perplexing, upsetting

disconnect *verb* <u>cut off</u>, detach, disengage, divide, part, separate, sever, take apart, uncouple

disconnected *adjective* <u>illogical</u>, confused, disjointed, incoherent, jumbled, mixed-up, rambling, unintelligible

disconsolate *adjective* <u>inconsolable</u>, crushed, dejected, desolate, forlorn, grief-stricken,

heartbroken, miserable, wretched

discontent *noun* <u>dissatisfaction</u>, displeasure, envy, regret, restlessness, uneasiness, unhappiness

discontented *adjective* <u>dissatisfied</u>, disaffected, disgruntled, displeased, exasperated, fed up, unhappy, vexed

discontinue *verb* <u>stop</u>, abandon, break off, cease, drop, end, give up, quit, suspend, terminate

discord *noun* 1 <u>disagreement</u>, conflict, dissension, disunity, division, friction, incompatibility, strife 2 <u>disharmony</u>, cacophony, din, dissonance, harshness, jarring, racket, tumult

discordant *adjective*
1 <u>disagreeing</u>, at odds, clashing, conflicting, contradictory, contrary, different, incompatible
2 <u>inharmonious</u>, cacophonous, dissonant, grating, harsh, jarring, shrill, strident

discount *verb* 1 <u>leave out</u>, brush off (*slang*), disbelieve, disregard, ignore, overlook, pass over
2 <u>deduct</u>, lower, mark down, reduce, take off ♦ *noun*
3 <u>deduction</u>, concession, cut, rebate, reduction

discourage *verb* 1 <u>dishearten</u>, dampen, deject, demoralize, depress, dispirit, intimidate, overawe, put a damper on 2 <u>put off</u>, deter, dissuade, inhibit, prevent, talk out of

discouraged *adjective* <u>put off</u>, crestfallen, deterred, disheartened, dismayed, dispirited, downcast, down in the mouth, glum

discouragement noun 1 <u>loss of confidence</u>, dejection, depression, despair, despondency, disappointment, dismay, downheartedness 2 <u>deterrent</u>, damper, disincentive, hindrance, impediment, obstacle, opposition, setback

discouraging adjective <u>disheartening</u>, dampening, daunting, depressing, disappointing, dispiriting, off-putting (*Brit. informal*), unfavourable

discourse noun 1 <u>conversation</u>, chat, communication, dialogue, discussion, seminar, speech, talk 2 <u>speech</u>, dissertation, essay, homily, lecture, oration, sermon, treatise ♦ verb 3 <u>hold forth</u>, expatiate, speak, talk

discourteous adjective <u>rude</u>, bad-mannered, boorish, disrespectful, ill-mannered, impolite, insolent, offhand, ungentlemanly, ungracious

discourtesy noun 1 <u>rudeness</u>, bad manners, disrespectfulness, impertinence, impoliteness, incivility, insolence 2 <u>insult</u>, affront, cold shoulder, kick in the teeth (*slang*), rebuff, slight, snub

discover verb 1 <u>find</u>, come across, come upon, dig up, locate, turn up, uncover, unearth 2 <u>find out</u>, ascertain, detect, learn, notice, perceive, realize, recognize, uncover

discovery noun 1 <u>finding</u>, detection, disclosure, exploration, location, revelation, uncovering 2 <u>breakthrough</u>, find, innovation, invention, secret

discredit verb 1 <u>disgrace</u>, bring into disrepute, defame, dishonour, disparage, slander, smear, vilify 2 <u>doubt</u>, challenge, deny, disbelieve, discount, dispute, distrust, mistrust, question ♦ noun 3 <u>disgrace</u>, dishonour, disrepute, ignominy, ill-repute, scandal, shame, stigma

discreditable adjective <u>disgraceful</u>, dishonourable, ignominious, reprehensible, scandalous, shameful, unworthy

discreet adjective <u>tactful</u>, careful, cautious, circumspect, considerate, diplomatic, guarded, judicious, prudent, wary

discrepancy noun <u>disagreement</u>, conflict, contradiction, difference, disparity, divergence, incongruity, inconsistency, variation

discretion noun 1 <u>tact</u>, carefulness, caution, consideration, diplomacy, judiciousness, prudence, wariness 2 <u>choice</u>, inclination, pleasure, preference, volition, will

discriminate verb 1 <u>show prejudice</u>, favour, show bias, single out, treat as inferior, treat differently, victimize 2 <u>differentiate</u>, distinguish, draw a distinction, segregate, separate, tell the difference

discriminating adjective <u>discerning</u>, cultivated, fastidious, particular, refined, selective, tasteful

discrimination noun 1 <u>prejudice</u>, bias, bigotry, favouritism, intolerance, unfairness 2 <u>discernment</u>, judgment, perception, refinement, subtlety, taste

discuss verb talk about, argue, confer, consider, converse, debate, deliberate, examine

discussion noun talk, analysis, argument, conference, consultation, conversation, debate, deliberation, dialogue, discourse

disdain noun 1 contempt, arrogance, derision, haughtiness, scorn, superciliousness ◆ verb 2 scorn, deride, disregard, look down on, reject, slight, sneer at, spurn

disdainful adjective contemptuous, aloof, arrogant, derisive, haughty, proud, scornful, sneering, supercilious, superior

disease noun illness, affliction, ailment, complaint, condition, disorder, infection, infirmity, malady, sickness

diseased adjective sick, ailing, infected, rotten, sickly, unhealthy, unsound, unwell, unwholesome

disembark verb land, alight, arrive, get off, go ashore, step out of

disenchanted adjective disillusioned, cynical, disappointed, indifferent, jaundiced, let down, sick of, soured

disenchantment noun disillusionment, disappointment, disillusion, rude awakening

disengage verb release, disentangle, extricate, free, loosen, set free, unloose, untie

disentangle verb untangle, disconnect, disengage, extricate, free, loose, unravel

disfavour noun disapproval, disapprobation, dislike, displeasure

disfigure verb damage, blemish, deface, deform, distort, mar, mutilate, scar

disgorge verb vomit, discharge, eject, empty, expel

disgrace noun 1 shame, degradation, dishonour, disrepute, ignominy, infamy, odium, opprobrium 2 stain, blemish, blot, reproach, scandal, slur, stigma ◆ verb 3 bring shame upon, degrade, discredit, dishonour, humiliate, shame, sully, taint

disgraceful adjective shameful, contemptible, detestable, dishonourable, disreputable, ignominious, scandalous, shocking, unworthy

disgruntled adjective discontented, annoyed, displeased, dissatisfied, grumpy, irritated, peeved, put out, vexed

disguise verb 1 hide, camouflage, cloak, conceal, cover, mask, screen, shroud, veil 2 misrepresent, fake, falsify ◆ noun 3 costume, camouflage, cover, mask, screen, veil 4 façade, deception, dissimulation, front, pretence, semblance, trickery, veneer

disguised adjective in disguise, camouflaged, covert, fake, false, feigned, incognito, masked, undercover

disgust noun 1 loathing, abhorrence, aversion, dislike, distaste, hatred, nausea,

repugnance, repulsion, revulsion
♦ *verb* 2 <u>sicken</u>, displease, nauseate, offend, put off, repel, revolt

disgusted *adjective* <u>sickened</u>, appalled, nauseated, offended, repulsed, scandalized

disgusting *adjective* <u>sickening</u>, foul, gross, loathsome, nauseating, offensive, repellent, repugnant, revolting

dish *noun* 1 <u>bowl</u>, plate, platter, salver 2 <u>food</u>, fare, recipe

dishearten *verb* <u>discourage</u>, cast down, deject, depress, deter, dismay, dispirit, put a damper on

dishevelled *adjective* <u>untidy</u>, bedraggled, disordered, messy, ruffled, rumpled, tousled, uncombed, unkempt

dishonest *adjective* <u>deceitful</u>, bent (*slang*), cheating, corrupt, crooked (*informal*), disreputable, double-dealing, false, lying, treacherous

dishonesty *noun* <u>deceit</u>, cheating, chicanery, corruption, fraud, treachery, trickery, unscrupulousness

dishonour *verb* 1 <u>shame</u>, debase, debauch, defame, degrade, discredit, disgrace, sully ♦ *noun* 2 <u>shame</u>, discredit, disgrace, disrepute, ignominy, infamy, obloquy, reproach, scandal 3 <u>insult</u>, abuse, affront, discourtesy, indignity, offence, outrage, sacrilege, slight

dishonourable *adjective* 1 <u>shameful</u>, contemptible, despicable, discreditable, disgraceful, ignominious, infamous, scandalous 2 <u>untrustworthy</u>, blackguardly,

corrupt, disreputable, shameless, treacherous, unprincipled, unscrupulous

disillusioned *adjective* <u>disenchanted</u>, disabused, disappointed, enlightened, undeceived

disinclination *noun* <u>reluctance</u>, aversion, dislike, hesitance, objection, opposition, repugnance, resistance, unwillingness

disinclined *adjective* <u>reluctant</u>, averse, hesitating, loath, not in the mood, opposed, resistant, unwilling

disinfect *verb* <u>sterilize</u>, clean, cleanse, decontaminate, deodorize, fumigate, purify, sanitize

disinfectant *noun* <u>antiseptic</u>, germicide, sterilizer

disinherit *verb* Law <u>cut off</u>, disown, dispossess, oust, repudiate

disintegrate *verb* <u>break up</u>, break apart, crumble, fall apart, go to pieces, separate, shatter, splinter

disinterest *noun* <u>impartiality</u>, detachment, fairness, neutrality

disinterested *adjective* <u>impartial</u>, detached, dispassionate, even-handed, impersonal, neutral, objective, unbiased, unprejudiced

disjointed *adjective* <u>incoherent</u>, confused, disconnected, disordered, rambling

dislike *verb* 1 <u>be averse to</u>, despise, detest, disapprove, hate, loathe, not be able to bear *or* abide *or* stand, object to, take a dim view of ♦ *noun* **2** <u>aversion</u>, animosity, antipathy, disapproval, disinclination, displeasure, distaste, enmity, hostility, repugnance

dislodge *verb* <u>displace</u>, disturb, extricate, force out, knock loose, oust, remove, uproot

disloyal *adjective* <u>treacherous</u>, faithless, false, subversive, traitorous, two-faced, unfaithful, untrustworthy

disloyalty *noun* <u>treachery</u>, breach of trust, deceitfulness, double-dealing, falseness, inconstancy, infidelity, treason, unfaithfulness

dismal *adjective* <u>gloomy</u>, bleak, cheerless, dark, depressing, discouraging, dreary, forlorn, sombre, wretched

dismantle *verb* <u>take apart</u>, demolish, disassemble, strip, take to pieces

dismay *verb* **1** <u>alarm</u>, appal, distress, frighten, horrify, paralyse, scare, terrify, unnerve **2** <u>disappoint</u>, daunt, discourage, dishearten, disillusion, dispirit, put off ♦ *noun* **3** <u>alarm</u>, anxiety, apprehension, consternation, dread, fear, horror, trepidation **4** <u>disappointment</u>, chagrin, discouragement, disillusionment

dismember *verb* <u>cut into pieces</u>, amputate, dissect, mutilate, sever

dismiss *verb* **1** <u>sack</u> (*informal*), axe (*informal*), cashier, discharge, fire (*informal*), give notice to, give (someone) their marching orders, lay off, remove **2** <u>let go</u>, disperse, dissolve, free, release, send away **3** <u>put out of one's mind</u>, banish, discard, dispel,

disregard, lay aside, reject, set aside

dismissal *noun* <u>the sack</u> (*informal*), expulsion, marching orders (*informal*), notice, removal, the boot (*slang*), the push (*slang*)

disobedience *noun* <u>defiance</u>, indiscipline, insubordination, mutiny, noncompliance, nonobservance, recalcitrance, revolt, unruliness, waywardness

disobedient *adjective* <u>defiant</u>, contrary, disorderly, insubordinate, intractable, naughty, refractory, undisciplined, unruly, wayward

disobey *verb* <u>refuse to obey</u>, contravene, defy, disregard, flout, ignore, infringe, rebel, violate

disorder *noun* **1** <u>untidiness</u>, chaos, clutter, confusion, disarray, jumble, mess, muddle, shambles **2** <u>disturbance</u>, commotion, riot, turmoil, unrest, unruliness, uproar **3** <u>illness</u>, affliction, ailment, complaint, disease, malady, sickness

disorderly *adjective* **1** <u>untidy</u>, chaotic, confused, disorganized, higgledy-piggledy (*informal*), jumbled, messy, shambolic (*informal*) **2** <u>unruly</u>, disruptive, indisciplined, lawless, riotous, rowdy, tumultuous, turbulent, ungovernable

disorganized *adjective* <u>muddled</u>, chaotic, confused, disordered, haphazard, jumbled, unsystematic

disown *verb* <u>deny</u>, cast off, disavow, disclaim, reject, renounce, repudiate

disparage verb run down, belittle, denigrate, deprecate, deride, malign, put down, ridicule, slander, vilify

dispassionate adjective
1 unemotional, calm, collected, composed, cool, imperturbable, serene, unruffled **2** objective, detached, disinterested, fair, impartial, impersonal, neutral, unbiased, unprejudiced

dispatch, despatch verb
1 send, consign, dismiss, hasten **2** carry out, discharge, dispose of, finish, perform, settle **3** murder, assassinate, execute, kill, slaughter, slay ♦ noun **4** message, account, bulletin, communication, communiqué, news, report, story

dispel verb drive away, banish, chase away, dismiss, disperse, eliminate, expel

dispense verb **1** distribute, allocate, allot, apportion, assign, deal out, dole out, share **2** prepare, measure, mix, supply **3** administer, apply, carry out, discharge, enforce, execute, implement, operate **4** dispense with a do away with, abolish, brush aside, cancel, dispose of, get rid of b do without, abstain from, forgo, give up, relinquish

disperse verb **1** scatter, broadcast, diffuse, disseminate, distribute, spread, strew **2** break up, disband, dissolve, scatter, separate

dispirited adjective disheartened, crestfallen, dejected, depressed, despondent, discouraged, downcast, gloomy, glum, sad

displace verb **1** move, disturb, misplace, shift, transpose **2** replace, oust, succeed, supersede, supplant, take the place of

display verb **1** show, demonstrate, disclose, exhibit, expose, manifest, present, reveal **2** show off, flash (informal), flaunt, flourish, parade, vaunt ♦ noun **3** exhibition, array, demonstration, presentation, revelation, show **4** show, flourish, ostentation, pageant, parade, pomp, spectacle

displease verb annoy, anger, irk, irritate, offend, pique, put out, upset, vex

displeasure noun annoyance, anger, disapproval, dissatisfaction, distaste, indignation, irritation, resentment

disposable adjective
1 throwaway, biodegradable, nonreturnable **2** available, consumable, expendable

disposal noun **1** throwing away, discarding, dumping (informal), ejection, jettisoning, removal, riddance, scrapping **2** at one's disposal available, at one's service, consumable, expendable, free for use

dispose verb arrange, array, distribute, group, marshal, order, place, put

dispose of verb **1** get rid of, destroy, discard, dump (informal), jettison, scrap, throw out or away, unload **2** deal with, decide, determine, end, finish with, settle

disposition noun **1** character, constitution, make-up, nature, spirit, temper, temperament

2 <u>tendency</u>, bent, bias, habit, inclination, leaning, proclivity, propensity 3 <u>arrangement</u>, classification, distribution, grouping, ordering, organization, placement

disproportion noun <u>inequality</u>, asymmetry, discrepancy, disparity, imbalance, lopsidedness, unevenness

disproportionate adjective <u>unequal</u>, excessive, inordinate, out of proportion, unbalanced, uneven, unreasonable

disprove verb <u>prove false</u>, contradict, discredit, expose, give the lie to, invalidate, negate, rebut, refute

dispute noun 1 <u>disagreement</u>, altercation, argument, conflict, feud, quarrel 2 <u>argument</u>, contention, controversy, debate, discussion, dissension ◆ verb 3 <u>doubt</u>, challenge, contest, contradict, deny, impugn, question, rebut 4 <u>argue</u>, clash, cross swords, debate, quarrel, squabble

disqualification noun ban, elimination, exclusion, ineligibility, rejection

disqualified adjective ineligible, debarred, eliminated, knocked out, out of the running

disqualify verb <u>ban</u>, debar, declare ineligible, preclude, prohibit, rule out

disquiet noun 1 <u>uneasiness</u>, alarm, anxiety, concern, disturbance, foreboding, nervousness, trepidation, worry ◆ verb 2 <u>make uneasy</u>, bother, concern, disturb, perturb, trouble, unsettle, upset, worry

disregard verb 1 <u>ignore</u>, brush aside or away, discount, make light of, neglect, overlook, pass over, pay no heed to, turn a blind eye to ◆ noun 2 <u>inattention</u>, contempt, disdain, disrespect, indifference, neglect, negligence, oversight

disrepair noun <u>dilapidation</u>, collapse, decay, deterioration, ruination

disreputable adjective <u>discreditable</u>, dishonourable, ignominious, infamous, louche, notorious, scandalous, shady (informal), shameful

disrepute noun <u>discredit</u>, disgrace, dishonour, ignominy, ill repute, infamy, obloquy, shame, unpopularity

disrespect noun <u>contempt</u>, cheek, impertinence, impoliteness, impudence, insolence, irreverence, lack of respect, rudeness, sauce

disrespectful adjective <u>contemptuous</u>, cheeky, discourteous, impertinent, impolite, impudent, insolent, insulting, irreverent, rude

disrupt verb 1 <u>disturb</u>, confuse, disorder, disorganize, spoil, upset 2 <u>interrupt</u>, break up or into, interfere with, intrude, obstruct, unsettle, upset

disruption noun <u>disturbance</u>, interference, interruption, stoppage

disruptive adjective <u>disturbing</u>, disorderly, distracting, troublesome, unruly, unsettling, upsetting

dissatisfaction noun <u>discontent</u>, annoyance, chagrin, disappointment, displeasure, frustration, irritation, resentment, unhappiness

dissatisfied *adjective* <u>discontented</u>, disappointed, disgruntled, displeased, fed up, frustrated, unhappy, unsatisfied

dissect *verb* **1** <u>cut up *or* apart</u>, anatomize, dismember, lay open **2** <u>analyse</u>, break down, explore, inspect, investigate, research, scrutinize, study

disseminate *verb* <u>spread</u>, broadcast, circulate, disperse, distribute, publicize, scatter

dissension *noun* <u>disagreement</u>, conflict, discord, dispute, dissent, friction, quarrel, row, strife

dissent *verb* **1** <u>disagree</u>, differ, object, protest, refuse, withhold assent *or* approval ◆ *noun* **2** <u>disagreement</u>, discord, dissension, objection, opposition, refusal, resistance

dissenter *noun* <u>objector</u>, dissident, nonconformist

dissertation *noun* <u>thesis</u>, critique, discourse, disquisition, essay, exposition, treatise

disservice *noun* <u>bad turn</u>, harm, injury, injustice, unkindness, wrong

dissident *adjective* **1** <u>dissenting</u>, disagreeing, discordant, heterodox, nonconformist ◆ *noun* **2** <u>protester</u>, agitator, dissenter, rebel

dissimilar *adjective* <u>different</u>, disparate, divergent, diverse, heterogeneous, unlike, unrelated, various

dissipate *verb* **1** <u>squander</u>,

consume, deplete, expend, fritter away, run through, spend, waste **2** <u>disperse</u>, disappear, dispel, dissolve, drive away, evaporate, scatter, vanish

dissipation *noun* **1** <u>dispersal</u>, disappearance, disintegration, dissolution, scattering, vanishing **2** <u>debauchery</u>, dissoluteness, excess, extravagance, indulgence, intemperance, prodigality, profligacy, wantonness, waste

dissociate *verb* **1** <u>break away</u>, break off, part company, quit **2** <u>separate</u>, detach, disconnect, distance, divorce, isolate, segregate, set apart

dissolute *adjective* <u>immoral</u>, debauched, degenerate, depraved, dissipated, profligate, rakish, wanton, wild

dissolution *noun* **1** <u>breaking up</u>, disintegration, division, parting, separation **2** <u>adjournment</u>, discontinuation, end, finish, suspension, termination

dissolve *verb* **1** <u>melt</u>, deliquesce, fuse, liquefy, soften, thaw **2** <u>end</u>, break up, discontinue, suspend, terminate, wind up

dissuade *verb* <u>deter</u>, advise against, discourage, put off, remonstrate, talk out of, warn

distance *noun* **1** <u>space</u>, extent, gap, interval, length, range, span, stretch **2** <u>reserve</u>, aloofness, coldness, coolness, remoteness, restraint, stiffness **3 in the distance** <u>far off</u>, afar, far away, on the horizon, yonder ◆ *verb* **4 distance oneself** <u>separate oneself</u>, be distanced from, dissociate oneself

distant adjective 1 <u>far-off</u>, abroad, far, faraway, far-flung, outlying, out-of-the-way, remote 2 <u>apart</u>, dispersed, distinct, scattered, separate 3 <u>reserved</u>, aloof, cool, reticent, standoffish, unapproachable, unfriendly, withdrawn

distaste noun <u>dislike</u>, aversion, disgust, horror, loathing, odium, repugnance, revulsion

distasteful adjective <u>unpleasant</u>, disagreeable, objectionable, offensive, repugnant, repulsive, uninviting, unpalatable, unsavoury

distil verb <u>extract</u>, condense, purify, refine

distinct adjective 1 <u>different</u>, detached, discrete, individual, separate, unconnected 2 <u>definite</u>, clear, decided, evident, marked, noticeable, obvious, palpable, unmistakable, well-defined

distinction noun 1 <u>differentiation</u>, discernment, discrimination, perception, separation 2 <u>feature</u>, characteristic, distinctiveness, individuality, mark, particularity, peculiarity, quality 3 <u>difference</u>, contrast, differential, division, separation 4 <u>excellence</u>, eminence, fame, greatness, honour, importance, merit, prominence, repute

distinctive adjective <u>characteristic</u>, idiosyncratic, individual, original, peculiar, singular, special, typical, unique

distinctly adverb <u>definitely</u>, clearly, decidedly, markedly, noticeably, obviously, patently, plainly, unmistakably

distinguish verb 1 <u>differentiate</u>, ascertain, decide, determine, discriminate, judge, tell apart, tell the difference 2 <u>characterize</u>, categorize, classify, mark, separate, set apart, single out 3 <u>make out</u>, discern, know, perceive, pick out, recognize, see, tell

distinguished adjective <u>eminent</u>, acclaimed, celebrated, famed, famous, illustrious, noted, renowned, well-known

distort verb 1 <u>misrepresent</u>, bias, colour, falsify, pervert, slant, twist 2 <u>deform</u>, bend, buckle, contort, disfigure, misshape, twist, warp

distortion noun 1 <u>misrepresentation</u>, bias, falsification, perversion, slant 2 <u>deformity</u>, bend, buckle, contortion, crookedness, malformation, twist, warp

distract verb 1 <u>divert</u>, draw away, sidetrack, turn aside 2 <u>amuse</u>, beguile, engross, entertain, occupy

distracted adjective <u>agitated</u>, at sea, flustered, harassed, in a flap (*informal*), perplexed, puzzled, troubled

distraction noun 1 <u>diversion</u>, disturbance, interference, interruption 2 <u>entertainment</u>, amusement, diversion, pastime, recreation 3 <u>agitation</u>, bewilderment, commotion, confusion, discord, disorder, disturbance

distraught adjective <u>frantic</u>, agitated, beside oneself, desperate, distracted, distressed, out of one's mind, overwrought, worked-up

distress noun 1 <u>worry</u>, grief, heartache, misery, pain, sorrow, suffering, torment, wretchedness 2 <u>need</u>, adversity, difficulties, hardship, misfortune, poverty, privation, trouble ♦verb 3 <u>upset</u>, disturb, grieve, harass, sadden, torment, trouble, worry

distressed adjective 1 <u>upset</u>, agitated, distracted, distraught, tormented, troubled, worried, wretched 2 <u>poverty-stricken</u>, destitute, down at heel, indigent, needy, poor, straitened

distressing adjective <u>upsetting</u>, disturbing, harrowing, heart-breaking, painful, sad, worrying

distribute verb 1 <u>hand out</u>, circulate, convey, deliver, pass round 2 <u>share</u>, allocate, allot, apportion, deal, dispense, dole out

distribution noun 1 <u>delivery</u>, dealing, handling, mailing, transportation 2 <u>sharing</u>, allocation, allotment, apportionment, division 3 <u>classification</u>, arrangement, grouping, organization, placement

district noun <u>area</u>, locale, locality, neighbourhood, parish, quarter, region, sector, vicinity

distrust verb 1 <u>suspect</u>, be suspicious of, be wary of, disbelieve, doubt, mistrust, question, smell a rat (informal) ♦noun 2 <u>suspicion</u>, disbelief, doubt, misgiving, mistrust, question, scepticism, wariness

disturb verb 1 <u>interrupt</u>, bother,

butt in on, disrupt, interfere with, intrude on, pester 2 <u>upset</u>, alarm, distress, fluster, harass, perturb, trouble, unnerve, unsettle, worry 3 <u>muddle</u>, disarrange, disorder

disturbance noun 1 <u>interruption</u>, annoyance, bother, distraction, intrusion 2 <u>disorder</u>, brawl, commotion, fracas, fray, rumpus

disturbed adjective 1 Psychiatry <u>unbalanced</u>, disordered, maladjusted, neurotic, troubled, upset 2 <u>worried</u>, anxious, apprehensive, bothered, concerned, nervous, troubled, uneasy, upset

disturbing adjective <u>worrying</u>, alarming, disconcerting, distressing, frightening, harrowing, startling, unsettling, upsetting

disuse noun <u>neglect</u>, abandonment, decay, idleness

ditch noun 1 <u>channel</u>, drain, dyke, furrow, gully, moat, trench, watercourse ♦verb 2 Slang <u>get rid of</u>, abandon, discard, dispose of, drop, dump (informal), jettison, scrap, throw out or overboard

dither verb 1 Chiefly Brit. <u>vacillate</u>, faff about (Brit. informal), hesitate, hum and haw, shillyshally (informal), teeter, waver ♦noun 2 Chiefly Brit. <u>flutter</u>, flap (informal), fluster, tizzy (informal)

dive verb 1 <u>plunge</u>, descend, dip, drop, duck, nose-dive, plummet, swoop ♦noun 2 <u>plunge</u>, jump, leap, lunge, nose dive, spring

diverge verb 1 <u>separate</u>, branch, divide, fork, part, split, spread

2 <u>deviate</u>, depart, digress, meander, stray, turn aside, wander

diverse *adjective* 1 <u>various</u>, assorted, manifold, miscellaneous, of every description, several, sundry, varied 2 <u>different</u>, discrete, disparate, dissimilar, distinct, divergent, separate, unlike, varying

diversify *verb* <u>vary</u>, branch out, change, expand, have a finger in every pie, spread out

diversion *noun* 1 *Chiefly Brit.* <u>detour</u>, departure, deviation, digression 2 <u>pastime</u>, amusement, distraction, entertainment, game, recreation, relaxation, sport

diversity *noun* <u>difference</u>, distinctiveness, diverseness, heterogeneity, multiplicity, range, variety

divert *verb* 1 <u>redirect</u>, avert, deflect, switch, turn aside 2 <u>distract</u>, draw *or* lead away from, lead astray, sidetrack 3 <u>entertain</u>, amuse, beguile, delight, gratify, regale

diverting *adjective* <u>entertaining</u>, amusing, beguiling, enjoyable, fun, humorous, pleasant

divide *verb* 1 <u>separate</u>, bisect, cut (up), part, partition, segregate, split 2 <u>share</u>, allocate, allot, deal out, dispense, distribute 3 <u>cause to disagree</u>, break up, come between, estrange, split

dividend *noun* <u>bonus</u>, cut (*informal*), divvy (*informal*), extra, gain, plus, portion, share, surplus

divine *adjective* 1 <u>heavenly</u>, angelic, celestial, godlike, holy, spiritual, superhuman, supernatural 2 <u>sacred</u>, consecrated, holy, religious, sanctified, spiritual 3 *Informal* <u>wonderful</u>, beautiful, excellent, glorious, marvellous, perfect, splendid, superlative ♦ *verb* 4 <u>infer</u>, apprehend, deduce, discern, guess, perceive, suppose, surmise

divinity *noun* 1 <u>theology</u>, religion, religious studies 2 <u>god</u> *or* <u>goddess</u>, deity, guardian spirit, spirit 3 <u>godliness</u>, deity, divine nature, holiness, sanctity

divisible *adjective* <u>dividable</u>, separable, splittable

division *noun* 1 <u>separation</u>, cutting up, dividing, partition, splitting up 2 <u>sharing</u>, allotment, apportionment, distribution 3 <u>part</u>, branch, category, class, department, group, section 4 <u>disagreement</u>, difference of opinion, discord, rupture, split, variance

divorce *noun* 1 <u>separation</u>, annulment, dissolution, split-up ♦ *verb* 2 <u>separate</u>, disconnect, dissociate, dissolve (*marriage*), divide, part, sever, split up

divulge *verb* <u>make known</u>, confess, declare, disclose, let slip, proclaim, reveal, tell

dizzy *adjective* 1 <u>giddy</u>, faint, light-headed, off balance, reeling, shaky, swimming, wobbly, woozy (*informal*) 2 <u>confused</u>, at sea, befuddled, bemused, bewildered, dazed, dazzled, muddled

do *verb* 1 <u>perform</u>, accomplish, achieve, carry out, complete, execute 2 <u>be adequate</u>, be sufficient, cut the mustard, pass muster, satisfy, suffice **3** get ready, arrange, fix, look after, prepare, see to **4** solve, decipher, decode, figure out, puzzle out, resolve, work out **5** cause, bring about, create, effect, produce ♦ *noun* **6** *Informal, chiefly Brit. & N.Z.* event, affair, function, gathering, occasion, party

do away with *verb* **1** kill, exterminate, murder, slay **2** get rid of, abolish, discard, discontinue, eliminate, put an end to, put paid to, remove

docile *adjective* submissive, amenable, biddable, compliant, manageable, obedient, pliant

docility *noun* submissiveness, compliance, manageability, meekness, obedience

dock¹ *noun* **1** wharf, harbour, pier, quay, waterfront ♦ *verb* **2** moor, anchor, berth, drop anchor, land, put in, tie up **3** *Of spacecraft* link up, couple, hook up, join, rendezvous, unite

dock² *verb* **1** deduct, decrease, diminish, lessen, reduce, subtract, withhold **2** cut off, clip, crop, curtail, cut short, shorten

doctor *noun* **1** G.P., general practitioner, medic (*informal*), medical practitioner, physician ♦ *verb* **2** change, alter, disguise, falsify, misrepresent, pervert, tamper with **3** add to, adulterate, cut, dilute, mix with, spike, water down

doctrinaire *adjective* dogmatic, biased, fanatical, inflexible, insistent, opinionated, rigid

doctrine *noun* teaching, article of

faith, belief, conviction, creed, dogma, opinion, precept, principle, tenet

document *noun* **1** paper, certificate, record, report ♦ *verb* **2** support, authenticate, certify, corroborate, detail, substantiate, validate, verify

dodge *verb* **1** duck, dart, sidestep, swerve, turn aside **2** evade, avoid, elude, get out of, shirk ♦ *noun* **3** trick, device, ploy, ruse, scheme, stratagem, subterfuge, wheeze (*Brit. slang*)

dog *noun* **1** hound, canine, cur, man's best friend, pooch (*slang*) **2** **go to the dogs** *Informal* go to ruin, degenerate, deteriorate, go down the drain, go to pot ♦ *verb* **3** trouble, follow, haunt, hound, plague, pursue, track, trail

dogged *adjective* determined, indefatigable, obstinate, persistent, resolute, steadfast, stubborn, tenacious, unflagging, unshakable

dogma *noun* doctrine, belief, credo, creed, opinion, teachings

dogmatic *adjective* opinionated, arrogant, assertive, doctrinaire, emphatic, obdurate, overbearing

doldrums *noun* **the doldrums** inactivity, depression, dumps (*informal*), gloom, listlessness, malaise

dole *noun* **1** *Brit. & Austral. informal* benefit, allowance, gift, grant, handout ♦ *verb* **2** **dole out** give out, allocate, allot, apportion, assign, dispense, distribute, hand out

dollop *noun* lump, helping, portion, scoop, serving

dolt noun <u>idiot</u>, ass, blockhead, chump (*informal*), clot (*Brit. informal*), dope (*informal*), dunce, fool, oaf

domestic adjective **1** <u>home</u>, family, household, private **2** <u>home-loving</u>, domesticated, homely, housewifely, stay-at-home **3** <u>domesticated</u>, house-trained, pet, tame, trained **4** <u>native</u>, indigenous, internal ◆ noun **5** <u>servant</u>, char (*informal*), charwoman, daily, help, maid

dominant adjective **1** <u>controlling</u>, assertive, authoritative, commanding, governing, ruling, superior, supreme **2** <u>main</u>, chief, predominant, pre-eminent, primary, principal, prominent

dominate verb **1** <u>control</u>, direct, govern, have the whip hand over, monopolize, rule, tyrannize **2** <u>tower above</u>, loom over, overlook, stand head and shoulders above, stand over, survey

domination noun <u>control</u>, ascendancy, authority, command, influence, power, rule, superiority, supremacy

domineering adjective <u>overbearing</u>, arrogant, authoritarian, bossy (*informal*), dictatorial, high-handed, imperious, oppressive, tyrannical

dominion noun **1** <u>control</u>, authority, command, jurisdiction, power, rule, sovereignty, supremacy **2** <u>kingdom</u>, country, domain, empire, realm, territory

don verb <u>put on</u>, clothe oneself in, dress in, get into, pull on, slip on or into

donate verb <u>give</u>, contribute, make a gift of, present, subscribe

donation noun <u>contribution</u>, gift, grant, hand-out, offering, present, subscription

donor noun <u>giver</u>, benefactor, contributor, donator, philanthropist

doom noun **1** <u>destruction</u>, catastrophe, downfall, fate, fortune, ruin ◆ verb **2** <u>condemn</u>, consign, damn, destine, sentence

doomed adjective <u>condemned</u>, bewitched, cursed, fated, hopeless, ill-fated, ill-omened, luckless, star-crossed

door noun <u>opening</u>, doorway, entrance, entry, exit

dope noun **1** *Slang* <u>drug</u>, narcotic, opiate **2** *Informal* <u>idiot</u>, dimwit (*informal*), dunce, fool, nitwit (*informal*), numbskull or numskull, simpleton, twit (*informal, chiefly Brit.*) ◆ verb **3** <u>drug</u>, anaesthetize, knock out, narcotize, sedate, stupefy

dormant adjective <u>inactive</u>, asleep, hibernating, inert, inoperative, latent, sleeping, slumbering, suspended

dose noun <u>quantity</u>, dosage, draught, measure, portion, potion, prescription

dot noun **1** <u>spot</u>, fleck, jot, mark, point, speck, speckle **2** **on the dot** <u>on time</u>, exactly, on the button (*informal*), precisely, promptly, punctually, to the minute ◆ verb **3** <u>spot</u>, dab, dabble, fleck, speckle, sprinkle, stipple, stud

dotage noun <u>senility</u>, decrepitude, feebleness, imbecility, old age, second childhood, weakness

dote on *or* **upon** *verb* <u>adore</u>, admire, hold dear, idolize, lavish affection on, prize, treasure

doting *adjective* <u>adoring</u>, devoted, fond, foolish, indulgent, lovesick

double *adjective* **1** <u>twice</u>, coupled, dual, duplicate, in pairs, paired, twin, twofold ♦ *verb* **2** <u>multiply</u>, duplicate, enlarge, grow, increase, magnify ♦ *noun* **3** <u>twin</u>, clone, dead ringer (*slang*), Doppelgänger, duplicate, lookalike, replica, spitting image (*informal*) **4 at** *or* **on the double** <u>quickly</u>, at full speed, briskly, immediately, posthaste, without delay

double-cross *verb* <u>betray</u>, cheat, defraud, hoodwink, mislead, swindle, trick, two-time (*informal*)

doubt *noun* **1** <u>uncertainty</u>, hesitancy, hesitation, indecision, irresolution, lack of conviction, suspense **2** <u>suspicion</u>, apprehension, distrust, misgiving, mistrust, qualm, scepticism ♦ *verb* **3** <u>be uncertain</u>, be dubious, demur, fluctuate, hesitate, scruple, vacillate, waver **4** <u>suspect</u>, discredit, distrust, fear, lack confidence in, mistrust, query, question

doubtful *adjective* **1** <u>unlikely</u>, debatable, dubious, equivocal, improbable, problematic(al), questionable, unclear **2** <u>unsure</u>, distrustful, hesitating, in two minds (*informal*), sceptical, suspicious, tentative, uncertain, unconvinced, wavering

doubtless *adverb* **1** <u>certainly</u>, assuredly, indisputably, of

course, surely, undoubtedly, unquestionably, without doubt **2** <u>probably</u>, apparently, most likely, ostensibly, presumably, seemingly, supposedly

dour *adjective* <u>gloomy</u>, dismal, dreary, forbidding, grim, morose, sour, sullen, unfriendly

dowdy *adjective* <u>frumpy</u>, dingy, drab, frowzy, old-fashioned, shabby, unfashionable

do without *verb* <u>manage</u> <u>without</u>, abstain from, dispense with, forgo, get along without, give up, kick (*informal*)

down *adjective* **1** <u>depressed</u>, dejected, disheartened, downcast, low, miserable, sad, unhappy ♦ *verb* **2** *Informal* <u>swallow</u>, drain, drink (down), gulp, put away, toss off ♦ *noun* **3 have a down on** *Informal* <u>be</u> <u>antagonistic</u> *or* <u>hostile to</u>, bear a grudge towards, be prejudiced against, be set against, have it in for (*slang*)

down-and-out *noun* **1** <u>tramp</u>, bag lady, beggar, derelict, dosser (*Brit. slang*), pauper, vagabond, vagrant ♦ *adjective* **2** <u>destitute</u>, derelict, impoverished, on one's uppers (*informal*), penniless, short, without two pennies to rub together (*informal*)

downcast *adjective* <u>dejected</u>, crestfallen, depressed, despondent, disappointed, disconsolate, discouraged, disheartened, dismayed, dispirited

downfall *noun* <u>ruin</u>, collapse, comeuppance (*slang*), destruction, disgrace, fall, overthrow, undoing

downgrade verb demote, degrade, humble, lower or reduce in rank, take down a peg (informal)

downhearted adjective dejected, crestfallen, depressed, despondent, discouraged, disheartened, dispirited, downcast, sad, unhappy

downpour noun rainstorm, cloudburst, deluge, flood, inundation, torrential rain

downright adjective complete, absolute, out-and-out, outright, plain, thoroughgoing, total, undisguised, unqualified, utter

down-to-earth adjective sensible, matter-of-fact, no-nonsense, plain-spoken, practical, realistic, sane, unsentimental

downtrodden adjective oppressed, exploited, helpless, subjugated, subservient, tyrannized

downward adjective descending, declining, earthward, heading down, sliding, slipping

doze verb 1 nap, kip (Brit. slang), nod off (informal), sleep, slumber, snooze (informal) ◆ noun 2 nap, catnap, forty winks (informal), kip (Brit. slang), shuteye (slang), siesta, snooze (informal)

drab adjective dull, dingy, dismal, dreary, flat, gloomy, shabby, sombre

draft noun 1 outline, abstract, plan, rough, sketch, version 2 order, bill (of exchange), cheque, postal order ◆ verb 3 outline, compose, design, draw, draw up, formulate, plan, sketch

drag verb 1 pull, draw, haul, lug, tow, trail, tug 2 **drag on** or **out** last, draw out, extend, keep going, lengthen, persist, prolong, protract, spin out, stretch out ◆ noun 3 Slang nuisance, annoyance, bore, bother, pain (informal), pest

dragoon verb force, browbeat, bully, coerce, compel, constrain, drive, impel, intimidate, railroad (informal)

drain noun 1 pipe, channel, conduit, culvert, ditch, duct, sewer, sink, trench 2 reduction, depletion, drag, exhaustion, sap, strain, withdrawal ◆ verb 3 remove, bleed, draw off, dry, empty, pump off or out, tap, withdraw 4 flow out, effuse, exude, leak, ooze, seep, trickle, well out 5 drink up, finish, gulp down, quaff, swallow 6 exhaust, consume, deplete, dissipate, empty, sap, strain, use up

drama noun 1 play, dramatization, show, stage show 2 theatre, acting, dramaturgy, stagecraft 3 excitement, crisis, histrionics, scene, spectacle, turmoil

dramatic adjective 1 theatrical, dramaturgical, Thespian 2 powerful, expressive, impressive, moving, striking, vivid 3 exciting, breathtaking, climactic, electrifying, melodramatic, sensational, suspenseful, tense, thrilling

dramatist noun playwright, dramaturge, screenwriter, scriptwriter

dramatize verb exaggerate, lay it on (thick) (slang), overdo, overstate, play to the gallery

drape *verb* cover, cloak, fold, swathe, wrap

drastic *adjective* extreme, desperate, dire, forceful, harsh, radical, severe, strong

draught *noun* 1 breeze, current, flow, movement, puff 2 drink, cup, dose, potion, quantity

draw *verb* 1 sketch, depict, design, map out, mark out, outline, paint, portray, trace 2 pull, drag, haul, tow, tug 3 take out, extract, pull out 4 attract, allure, elicit, entice, evoke, induce, influence, invite, persuade 5 deduce, derive, infer, make, take ◆ *noun* 6 *Informal* attraction, enticement, lure, pull (*informal*) 7 tie, dead heat, deadlock, impasse, stalemate

drawback *noun* disadvantage, deficiency, difficulty, downside, flaw, handicap, hitch, snag, stumbling block

drawing *noun* picture, cartoon, depiction, illustration, outline, portrayal, representation, sketch, study

drawn *adjective* tense, haggard, pinched, stressed, tired, worn

draw on *verb* make use of, employ, exploit, extract, fall back on, have recourse to, rely on, take from, use

draw out *verb* extend, drag out, lengthen, make longer, prolong, protract, spin out, stretch, string out

draw up *verb* 1 draft, compose, formulate, frame, prepare, write out 2 halt, bring to a stop, pull up, stop

dread *verb* 1 fear, cringe at, have cold feet (*informal*), quail, shrink from, shudder, tremble ◆ *noun* 2 fear, alarm, apprehension, dismay, fright, horror, terror, trepidation

dreadful *adjective* terrible, abysmal, appalling, atrocious, awful, fearful, frightful, hideous, horrible, shocking

dream *noun* 1 vision, delusion, hallucination, illusion, imagination, trance 2 daydream, fantasy, pipe dream 3 ambition, aim, aspiration, desire, goal, hope, wish 4 delight, beauty, gem, joy, marvel, pleasure, treasure ◆ *verb* 5 have dreams, conjure up, envisage, fancy, hallucinate, imagine, think, visualize 6 daydream, build castles in the air *or* in Spain, fantasize, stargaze

dreamer *noun* idealist, daydreamer, escapist, fantasist, utopian, visionary, Walter Mitty

dreamy *adjective* 1 vague, absent, abstracted, daydreaming, faraway, pensive, preoccupied, with one's head in the clouds 2 impractical, airy-fairy, fanciful, imaginary, quixotic, speculative

dreary *adjective* dull, boring, drab, humdrum, monotonous, tedious, tiresome, uneventful, wearisome

dregs *plural noun* 1 sediment, deposit, dross, grounds, lees, residue, residuum, scum, waste 2 scum, good-for-nothings, rabble, ragtag and bobtail, riffraff

drench *verb* soak, drown, flood, inundate, saturate, souse, steep, swamp, wet

dress noun 1 <u>frock</u>, gown, outfit, robe 2 <u>clothing</u>, apparel, attire, clothes, costume, garb, garments, togs ♦ verb 3 <u>put on</u>, attire, change, clothe, don, garb, robe, slip on or into 4 <u>bandage</u>, bind up, plaster, treat 5 <u>arrange</u>, adjust, align, get ready, prepare, straighten

dressmaker noun <u>seamstress</u>, couturier, tailor

dribble verb 1 <u>run</u>, drip, drop, fall in drops, leak, ooze, seep, trickle 2 <u>drool</u>, drivel, slaver, slobber

drift verb 1 <u>float</u>, be carried along, coast, go (aimlessly), meander, stray, waft, wander 2 <u>pile up</u>, accumulate, amass, bank up, drive, gather ♦ noun 3 <u>pile</u>, accumulation, bank, heap, mass, mound 4 <u>meaning</u>, direction, gist, import, intention, purport, significance, tendency, thrust

drifter noun <u>wanderer</u>, beachcomber, bum (informal), hobo (U.S.), itinerant, rolling stone, vagrant

drill noun 1 <u>boring tool</u>, bit, borer, gimlet 2 <u>training</u>, discipline, exercise, instruction, practice, preparation, repetition ♦ verb 3 <u>bore</u>, penetrate, perforate, pierce, puncture, sink in 4 <u>train</u>, coach, discipline, exercise, instruct, practise, rehearse, teach

drink verb 1 <u>swallow</u>, gulp, guzzle, imbibe, quaff, sip, suck, sup 2 <u>booze</u> (informal), hit the bottle (informal), tipple, tope ♦ noun 3 <u>beverage</u>, liquid,

potion, refreshment 4 <u>alcohol</u>, booze (informal), hooch or hootch (informal, chiefly U.S. & Canad.), liquor, spirits, the bottle (informal) 5 <u>glass</u>, cup, draught

drip verb 1 <u>drop</u>, dribble, exude, plop, splash, sprinkle, trickle ♦ noun 2 <u>drop</u>, dribble, leak, trickle 3 Informal <u>weakling</u>, mummy's boy (informal), namby-pamby, softie (informal), weed (informal), wet (Brit. informal)

drive verb 1 <u>operate</u>, direct, guide, handle, manage, motor, ride, steer, travel 2 <u>goad</u>, coerce, constrain, force, press, prod, prompt, spur 3 <u>push</u>, herd, hurl, impel, propel, send, urge 4 <u>push</u>, hammer, ram, thrust ♦ noun 5 <u>run</u>, excursion, jaunt, journey, outing, ride, spin (informal), trip 6 <u>campaign</u>, action, appeal, crusade, effort, push (informal) 7 <u>initiative</u>, ambition, energy, enterprise, get-up-and-go (informal), motivation, vigour, zip (informal)

drivel noun 1 <u>nonsense</u>, garbage (informal), gibberish, hogwash, hot air (informal), poppycock (informal), rubbish, trash, twaddle, waffle (informal, chiefly Brit.) ♦ verb 2 <u>babble</u>, blether, gab (informal), prate, ramble, waffle (informal, chiefly Brit.)

driving adjective <u>forceful</u>, compelling, dynamic, energetic, sweeping, vigorous, violent

drizzle noun 1 <u>fine rain</u>, Scotch mist ♦ verb 2 <u>rain</u>, shower, spot or spit with rain, spray, sprinkle

droll adjective <u>amusing</u>, comical, entertaining, funny, humorous, jocular, waggish, whimsical

drone verb **1** <u>hum</u>, buzz, purr, thrum, vibrate, whirr **2 drone on** <u>speak monotonously</u>, be boring, chant, intone, spout, talk interminably ♦ noun **3** <u>hum</u>, buzz, murmuring, purr, thrum, vibration, whirring

drool verb **1** <u>dribble</u>, drivel, salivate, slaver, slobber, water at the mouth **2 drool over** <u>gloat over</u>, dote on, gush, make much of, rave about (informal)

droop verb <u>sag</u>, bend, dangle, drop, fall down, hang (down), sink

drop verb **1** <u>fall</u>, decline, descend, diminish, plummet, plunge, sink, tumble **2** <u>drip</u>, dribble, fall in drops, trickle **3** <u>discontinue</u>, axe (informal), give up, kick (informal), quit, relinquish ♦ noun **4** <u>droplet</u>, bead, bubble, drip, globule, pearl, tear **5** <u>dash</u>, mouthful, shot (informal), sip, spot, tot, trace, trickle **6** <u>decrease</u>, cut, decline, deterioration, downturn, fall-off, lowering, reduction, slump **7** <u>fall</u>, descent, plunge

drop off verb **1** <u>set down</u>, deliver, leave, let off **2** Informal <u>fall asleep</u>, doze (off), have forty winks (informal), nod (off), snooze (informal) **3** <u>decrease</u>, decline, diminish, dwindle, fall off, lessen, slacken

drop out verb <u>leave</u>, abandon, fall by the wayside, give up, quit, stop, withdraw

drought noun <u>dry spell</u>, aridity, dehydration, dryness

drove noun <u>herd</u>, collection, company, crowd, flock, horde, mob, multitude, swarm, throng

drown verb **1** <u>drench</u>, deluge, engulf, flood, go under, immerse, inundate, sink, submerge, swamp **2** <u>overpower</u>, deaden, muffle, obliterate, overcome, overwhelm, stifle, swallow up, wipe out

drowsy adjective <u>sleepy</u>, dopey (slang), dozy, half asleep, heavy, lethargic, somnolent, tired, torpid

drudge noun <u>menial</u>, dogsbody (informal), factotum, servant, skivvy (chiefly Brit.), slave, toiler, worker

drudgery noun <u>menial labour</u>, donkey-work, fag (informal), grind (informal), hard work, labour, skivvying (Brit.), slog, toil

drug noun **1** <u>medication</u>, medicament, medicine, physic, poison, remedy **2** <u>dope</u> (slang), narcotic, opiate, stimulant ♦ verb **3** <u>dose</u>, administer a drug, dope (slang), medicate, treat **4** <u>knock out</u>, anaesthetize, deaden, numb, poison, stupefy

drum verb **1** <u>beat</u>, pulsate, rap, reverberate, tap, tattoo, throb **2 drum into** <u>drive home</u>, din into, hammer away, harp on, instil into, reiterate

drunk adjective **1** <u>intoxicated</u>, drunken, inebriated, legless (informal), merry (Brit. informal), plastered (slang), tipsy, under the influence ♦ noun **2** <u>drunkard</u>, alcoholic, boozer (informal), inebriate, lush (slang), wino (informal)

drunkard noun <u>drinker</u>, alcoholic, dipsomaniac, drunk, lush (slang), tippler, wino (informal)

drunkenness noun <u>intoxication</u>,

alcoholism, bibulousness, dipsomania, inebriation, insobriety, intemperance

dry *adjective* **1** <u>dehydrated</u>, arid, barren, desiccated, dried up, parched, thirsty **2** <u>dull</u>, boring, dreary, monotonous, plain, tedious, tiresome, uninteresting **3** <u>sarcastic</u>, deadpan, droll, low-key, sly ♦ *verb* **4** <u>dehydrate</u>, dehumidify, desiccate, drain, make dry, parch, sear

dry out or **up** *verb* <u>become dry</u>, harden, shrivel up, wilt, wither, wizen

dual *adjective* <u>twofold</u>, binary, double, duplex, duplicate, matched, paired, twin

dubious *adjective* **1** <u>suspect</u>, fishy (*informal*), questionable, suspicious, unreliable, untrustworthy **2** <u>unsure</u>, doubtful, hesitant, sceptical, uncertain, unconvinced, undecided, wavering

duck *verb* **1** <u>bob</u>, bend, bow, crouch, dodge, drop, lower, stoop **2** <u>plunge</u>, dip, dive, douse, dunk, immerse, souse, submerge, wet **3** *Informal* <u>dodge</u>, avoid, escape, evade, shirk, shun, sidestep

dud *Informal* ♦ *noun* **1** <u>failure</u>, flop (*informal*), washout (*informal*) ♦ *adjective* **2** <u>useless</u>, broken, duff (*Brit. informal*), failed, inoperative, worthless

dudgeon *noun* **in high dudgeon** <u>indignant</u>, angry, choked, fuming, offended, resentful, vexed

due *adjective* **1** <u>expected</u>, scheduled **2** <u>payable</u>, in arrears, outstanding, owed, owing,

unpaid **3** <u>fitting</u>, appropriate, deserved, justified, merited, proper, rightful, suitable, well-earned ♦ *noun* **4** <u>right(s)</u>, comeuppance (*slang*), deserts, merits, privilege ♦ *adverb* **5** <u>directly</u>, dead, exactly, straight, undeviatingly

duel *noun* **1** <u>single combat</u>, affair of honour **2** <u>contest</u>, clash, competition, encounter, engagement, fight, head-to-head, rivalry ♦ *verb* **3** <u>fight</u>, clash, compete, contend, contest, lock horns, rival, struggle, vie with

dues *plural noun* <u>membership fee</u>, charge, charges, contribution, fee, levy

dull *adjective* **1** <u>boring</u>, dreary, flat, humdrum, monotonous, plain, run-of-the-mill, tedious, uninteresting **2** <u>stupid</u>, dense, dim-witted (*informal*), dozy (*Brit. informal*), slow, thick, unintelligent **3** <u>cloudy</u>, dim, dismal, gloomy, leaden, overcast **4** <u>lifeless</u>, apathetic, blank, indifferent, listless, passionless, unresponsive **5** <u>blunt</u>, blunted, unsharpened ♦ *verb* **6** <u>relieve</u>, allay, alleviate, blunt, lessen, moderate, soften, take the edge off

duly *adverb* **1** <u>properly</u>, accordingly, appropriately, befittingly, correctly, decorously, deservedly, fittingly, rightfully, suitably **2** <u>on time</u>, at the proper time, punctually

dumb *adjective* **1** <u>mute</u>, mum, silent, soundless, speechless, tongue-tied, voiceless, wordless **2** *Informal* <u>stupid</u>, asinine, dense, dim-witted (*informal*), dull, foolish, thick, unintelligent

dumbfounded *adjective* <u>amazed</u>, astonished, astounded, flabbergasted (*informal*), lost for words, nonplussed, overwhelmed, speechless, staggered, stunned

dummy *noun* 1 <u>model</u>, figure, form, manikin, mannequin 2 <u>copy</u>, counterfeit, duplicate, imitation, sham, substitute 3 *Slang* <u>fool</u>, blockhead, dunce, idiot, nitwit (*informal*), numbskull or numskull, oaf, simpleton ♦ *adjective* 4 <u>imitation</u>, artificial, bogus, fake, false, mock, phoney or phony (*informal*), sham, simulated

dump *verb* 1 <u>drop</u>, deposit, fling down, let fall, throw down 2 <u>get rid of</u>, dispose of, ditch (*slang*), empty out, jettison, scrap, throw away or out, tip, unload ♦ *noun* 3 <u>rubbish tip</u>, junkyard, refuse heap, rubbish heap, tip 4 *Informal* <u>pigsty</u>, hole (*informal*), hovel, mess, slum

dunce *noun* <u>simpleton</u>, blockhead, duffer (*informal*), dunderhead, ignoramus, moron, nincompoop, numbskull or numskull, thickhead

dungeon *noun* <u>prison</u>, cage, cell, oubliette, vault

duplicate *adjective* 1 <u>identical</u>, corresponding, matched, matching, twin, twofold ♦ *noun* 2 <u>copy</u>, carbon copy, clone, double, facsimile, photocopy, replica, reproduction ♦ *verb* 3 <u>copy</u>, clone, double, repeat, replicate, reproduce

durability *noun* <u>durableness</u>, constancy, endurance, imperishability, permanence, persistence

durable *adjective* <u>long-lasting</u>, dependable, enduring, hard-wearing, persistent, reliable, resistant, strong, sturdy, tough

duration *noun* <u>length</u>, extent, period, span, spell, stretch, term, time

duress *noun* <u>pressure</u>, coercion, compulsion, constraint, threat

dusk *noun* <u>twilight</u>, dark, evening, eventide, gloaming (*Scot. or poetic*), nightfall, sundown, sunset

dusky *adjective* 1 <u>dark</u>, dark-complexioned, sable, swarthy 2 <u>dim</u>, cloudy, gloomy, murky, obscure, shadowy, shady, tenebrous, twilit

dust *noun* 1 <u>grime</u>, grit, particles, powder ♦ *verb* 2 <u>sprinkle</u>, cover, dredge, powder, scatter, sift, spray, spread

dusty *adjective* <u>dirty</u>, grubby, sooty, unclean, unswept

dutiful *adjective* <u>conscientious</u>, devoted, obedient, respectful, reverential, submissive

duty *noun* 1 <u>responsibility</u>, assignment, function, job, obligation, role, task, work 2 <u>loyalty</u>, allegiance, deference, obedience, respect, reverence 3 <u>tax</u>, excise, levy, tariff, toll 4 <u>on duty</u> <u>at work</u>, busy, engaged, on active service

dwarf *verb* 1 <u>tower above or over</u>, diminish, dominate, overshadow ♦ *adjective* 2 <u>miniature</u>, baby, bonsai, diminutive, small, tiny, undersized ♦ *noun* **3** <u>midget</u>, Lilliputian, pygmy *or* pigmy, Tom Thumb

dwell *verb Formal, literary* <u>live</u>, abide, inhabit, lodge, reside

dwelling *noun Formal, literary* <u>home</u>, abode, domicile, habitation, house, lodging, quarters, residence

dwindle *verb* <u>lessen</u>, decline, decrease, die away, diminish, fade, peter out, shrink, subside, taper off, wane

dye *noun* **1** <u>colouring</u>, colorant, colour, pigment, stain, tinge, tint ♦ *verb* **2** <u>colour</u>, pigment, stain, tinge, tint

dying *adjective* <u>expiring</u>, at death's door, failing, *in extremis*, moribund, not long for this world

dynamic *adjective* <u>energetic</u>, forceful, go-ahead, go-getting (*informal*), high-powered, lively, powerful, vital

dynasty *noun* <u>empire</u>, government, house, regime, rule, sovereignty

E e

each *adjective* **1** <u>every</u> ♦ *pronoun* **2** <u>every one</u>, each and every one, each one, one and all ♦ *adverb* **3** <u>apiece</u>, for each, individually, per capita, per head, per person, respectively, to each

eager *adjective* <u>keen</u>, agog, anxious, athirst, avid, enthusiastic, fervent, hungry, impatient, longing

eagerness *noun* <u>keenness</u>, ardour, enthusiasm, fervour, hunger, impatience, thirst, yearning, zeal

ear *noun* <u>sensitivity</u>, appreciation, discrimination, taste

early *adjective* **1** <u>premature</u>, advanced, forward, untimely **2** <u>primitive</u>, primeval, primordial, undeveloped, young ♦ *adverb* **3** <u>too soon</u>, ahead of time, beforehand, in advance, in good time, prematurely

earmark *verb* <u>set aside</u>, allocate, designate, flag, label, mark out, reserve

earn *verb* **1** <u>make</u>, bring in, collect, gain, get, gross, net, receive **2** <u>deserve</u>, acquire, attain, be entitled to, be worthy of, merit, rate, warrant, win

earnest *adjective* **1** <u>serious</u>, grave, intent, resolute, resolved, sincere, solemn, thoughtful ♦ *noun* **2** *As in* **in earnest** <u>seriousness</u>, sincerity, truth

earnings *plural noun* <u>income</u>, pay, proceeds, profits, receipts, remuneration, salary, takings, wages

earth *noun* **1** <u>world</u>, globe, orb, planet, sphere **2** <u>soil</u>, clay, dirt, ground, land, turf

earthenware *noun* <u>crockery</u>, ceramics, pots, pottery, terracotta

earthly *adjective* **1** <u>worldly</u>, human, material, mortal, secular, temporal **2** *Informal* <u>possible</u>, conceivable, feasible, imaginable, likely, practical

earthy *adjective* <u>crude</u>, bawdy, coarse, raunchy (*slang*), ribald, robust, uninhibited, unsophisticated

ease noun 1 <u>easiness</u>, effortlessness, facility, readiness, simplicity 2 <u>content</u>, comfort, happiness, peace, peace of mind, quiet, serenity, tranquillity 3 <u>rest</u>, leisure, relaxation, repose, restfulness ◆ verb 4 <u>relieve</u>, alleviate, calm, comfort, lessen, lighten, relax, soothe 5 <u>move carefully</u>, edge, inch, manoeuvre, slide, slip

easily adverb <u>without difficulty</u>, comfortably, effortlessly, readily, smoothly, with ease, with one hand tied behind one's back

easy adjective 1 <u>not difficult</u>, a piece of cake (informal), child's play (informal), effortless, no trouble, painless, plain sailing, simple, straightforward, uncomplicated, undemanding 2 <u>carefree</u>, comfortable, cushy (informal), leisurely, peaceful, quiet, relaxed, serene, tranquil, untroubled 3 <u>tolerant</u>, easy-going, indulgent, lenient, mild, permissive, unoppressive

easy-going adjective <u>relaxed</u>, carefree, casual, easy, even-tempered, happy-go-lucky, laid-back (informal), nonchalant, placid, tolerant, undemanding

eat verb 1 <u>consume</u>, chew, devour, gobble, ingest, munch, scoff (slang), swallow 2 <u>have a meal</u>, dine, feed, take nourishment 3 <u>destroy</u>, corrode, decay, dissolve, erode, rot, waste away, wear away

eavesdrop verb <u>listen in</u>, earwig (informal), monitor, overhear, snoop (informal), spy

ebb verb 1 <u>flow back</u>, go out, recede, retire, retreat, subside,

wane, withdraw 2 <u>decline</u>, decrease, diminish, dwindle, fade away, fall away, flag, lessen, peter out ◆ noun 3 <u>flowing back</u>, going out, low tide, low water, retreat, subsidence, wane, withdrawal

eccentric adjective 1 <u>odd</u>, freakish, idiosyncratic, irregular, outlandish, peculiar, quirky, strange, unconventional ◆ noun 2 <u>crank</u> (informal), character (informal), nonconformist, oddball (informal), weirdo or weirdie (informal)

eccentricity noun <u>oddity</u>, abnormality, caprice, capriciousness, foible, idiosyncrasy, irregularity, peculiarity, quirk

ecclesiastic noun 1 <u>clergyman</u>, churchman, cleric, holy man, man of the cloth, minister, parson, pastor, priest ◆ adjective 2 Also **ecclesiastical** <u>clerical</u>, divine, holy, pastoral, priestly, religious, spiritual

echo noun 1 <u>repetition</u>, answer, reverberation 2 <u>copy</u>, imitation, mirror image, parallel, reflection, reiteration, reproduction ◆ verb 3 <u>repeat</u>, resound, reverberate 4 <u>copy</u>, ape, imitate, mirror, parallel, recall, reflect, resemble

eclipse noun 1 <u>obscuring</u>, darkening, dimming, extinction, shading ◆ verb 2 <u>surpass</u>, exceed, excel, outdo, outshine, put in the shade (informal), transcend

economic adjective 1 <u>financial</u>, commercial, industrial 2 <u>profitable</u>, money-making, productive, profit-making, remunerative, viable 3 Informal

Also **economical** <u>inexpensive</u>, cheap, low-priced, modest, reasonable

economical *adjective* **1** <u>thrifty</u>, careful, frugal, prudent, scrimping, sparing **2** <u>cost-effective</u>, efficient, money-saving, sparing, time-saving

economize *verb* <u>cut back</u>, be economical, be frugal, draw in one's horns, retrench, save, scrimp, tighten one's belt

economy *noun* <u>thrift</u>, frugality, husbandry, parsimony, prudence, restraint

ecstasy *noun* <u>rapture</u>, bliss, delight, elation, euphoria, fervour, joy, seventh heaven

ecstatic *adjective* <u>rapturous</u>, blissful, elated, enraptured, entranced, euphoric, in seventh heaven, joyous, on cloud nine (*informal*), overjoyed

eddy *noun* **1** <u>swirl</u>, counter-current, counterflow, undertow, vortex, whirlpool ♦ *verb* **2** <u>swirl</u>, whirl

edge *noun* **1** <u>border</u>, boundary, brink, fringe, limit, outline, perimeter, rim, side, verge **2** <u>sharpness</u>, bite, effectiveness, force, incisiveness, keenness, point **3** *As in* **have the edge on** <u>advantage</u>, ascendancy, dominance, lead, superiority, upper hand **4** **on edge** <u>nervous</u>, apprehensive, edgy, ill at ease, impatient, irritable, keyed up, on tenterhooks, tense ♦ *verb* **5** <u>border</u>, fringe, hem **6** <u>inch</u>, creep, ease, sidle, steal

edgy *adjective* <u>nervous</u>, anxious, ill at ease, irritable, keyed up, on

edge, on tenterhooks, restive, tense

edible *adjective* <u>eatable</u>, digestible, fit to eat, good, harmless, palatable, wholesome

edict *noun* <u>decree</u>, act, command, injunction, law, order, proclamation, ruling

edifice *noun* <u>building</u>, construction, erection, house, structure

edify *verb* <u>instruct</u>, educate, enlighten, guide, improve, inform, nurture, school, teach

edit *verb* <u>revise</u>, adapt, condense, correct, emend, polish, rewrite

edition *noun* <u>version</u>, copy, impression, issue, number, printing, programme (*TV, Radio*), volume

educate *verb* <u>teach</u>, civilize, develop, discipline, enlighten, improve, inform, instruct, school, train, tutor

educated *adjective* **1** <u>taught</u>, coached, informed, instructed, nurtured, schooled, tutored **2** <u>cultured</u>, civilized, cultivated, enlightened, knowledgeable, learned, refined, sophisticated

education *noun* <u>teaching</u>, development, discipline, enlightenment, instruction, nurture, schooling, training, tuition

educational *adjective* <u>instructive</u>, cultural, edifying, educative, enlightening, improving, informative

eerie *adjective* <u>frightening</u>, creepy (*informal*), ghostly, mysterious, scary (*informal*), spooky (*informal*), strange, uncanny, unearthly, weird

efface *verb* <u>obliterate</u>, blot out, cancel, delete, destroy, eradicate, erase, rub out, wipe out

effect *noun* 1 <u>result</u>, conclusion, consequence, end result, event, outcome, upshot 2 <u>operation</u>, action, enforcement, execution, force, implementation 3 <u>impression</u>, essence, impact, sense, significance, tenor ♦ *verb* 4 <u>bring about</u>, accomplish, achieve, complete, execute, fulfil, perform, produce

effective *adjective* 1 <u>efficient</u>, active, adequate, capable, competent, productive, serviceable, useful 2 <u>in operation</u>, active, current, in effect, in force, operative 3 <u>powerful</u>, cogent, compelling, convincing, forceful, impressive, persuasive, telling

effects *plural noun* <u>belongings</u>, gear, goods, paraphernalia, possessions, property, things

effeminate *adjective* <u>womanly</u>, camp (*informal*), feminine, sissy, soft, tender, unmanly, weak, womanish

effervescent *adjective* 1 <u>bubbling</u>, carbonated, fizzy, foaming, frothy, sparkling 2 <u>lively</u>, animated, bubbly, ebullient, enthusiastic, exuberant, irrepressible, vivacious

effete *adjective* <u>decadent</u>, dissipated, enfeebled, feeble, ineffectual, spoiled, weak

efficacious *adjective* <u>effective</u>, adequate, efficient, operative, potent, powerful, productive, successful, useful

efficiency *noun* <u>competence</u>, adeptness, capability, economy, effectiveness, power, productivity, proficiency

efficient *adjective* <u>competent</u>, businesslike, capable, economic, effective, organized, productive, proficient, well-organized, workmanlike

effigy *noun* <u>likeness</u>, dummy, figure, guy, icon, idol, image, picture, portrait, representation, statue

effluent *noun* <u>waste</u>, effluvium, pollutant, sewage

effort *noun* 1 <u>exertion</u>, application, elbow grease (*facetious*), endeavour, energy, pains, struggle, toil, trouble, work 2 <u>attempt</u>, endeavour, essay, go (*informal*), shot (*informal*), stab (*informal*), try

effortless *adjective* <u>easy</u>, painless, plain sailing, simple, smooth, uncomplicated, undemanding

effrontery *noun* <u>insolence</u>, arrogance, audacity, brazenness, cheek (*informal*), impertinence, impudence, nerve, presumption, temerity

effusive *adjective* <u>demonstrative</u>, ebullient, expansive, exuberant, gushing, lavish, unreserved, unrestrained

egg on *verb* <u>encourage</u>, exhort, goad, incite, prod, prompt, push, spur, urge

egocentric *adjective* <u>self-centred</u>, egoistic, egoistical, egotistic, egotistical, selfish

egotism, egoism *noun* <u>self-centredness</u>, conceitedness, narcissism, self-absorption, self-esteem, self-importance, self-interest, selfishness, vanity

egotist, egoist *noun* <u>egomaniac</u>, bighead (*informal*), boaster, braggart, narcissist

egotistic, egotistical, egoistic or **egoistical** *adjective* <u>self-centred</u>, boasting, conceited, egocentric, full of oneself, narcissistic, self-absorbed, self-important, vain

egress *noun Formal* <u>exit</u>, departure, exodus, way out, withdrawal

eject *verb* <u>throw out</u>, banish, drive out, evict, expel, oust, remove, turn out

ejection *noun* <u>expulsion</u>, banishment, deportation, eviction, exile, removal

eke out *verb* <u>be sparing with</u>, economize on, husband, stretch out

elaborate *adjective* 1 <u>detailed</u>, intricate, minute, painstaking, precise, studied, thorough 2 <u>complicated</u>, complex, fancy, fussy, involved, ornamented, ornate ♦ *verb* 3 <u>expand (upon)</u>, add detail, amplify, develop, embellish, enlarge, flesh out

elapse *verb* <u>pass</u>, glide by, go by, lapse, roll by, slip away

elastic *adjective* 1 <u>stretchy</u>, plastic, pliable, pliant, resilient, rubbery, springy, supple, tensile 2 <u>adaptable</u>, accommodating, adjustable, compliant, flexible, supple, tolerant, variable, yielding

elated *adjective* <u>joyful</u>, cock-a-hoop, delighted, ecstatic, euphoric, exhilarated, gleeful, jubilant, overjoyed

elation *noun* <u>joy</u>, bliss, delight, ecstasy, euphoria, exhilaration, glee, high spirits, jubilation, rapture

elbow *noun* 1 <u>joint</u>, angle ♦ *verb* 2 <u>push</u>, jostle, knock, nudge, shove

elbow room *noun* <u>scope</u>, freedom, latitude, leeway, play, room, space

elder *adjective* 1 <u>older</u>, first-born, senior ♦ *noun* 2 <u>older person</u>, senior

elect *verb* <u>choose</u>, appoint, determine, opt for, pick, prefer, select, settle on, vote

election *noun* <u>voting</u>, appointment, choice, judgment, preference, selection, vote

elector *noun* <u>voter</u>, constituent, selector

electric *adjective* <u>charged</u>, dynamic, exciting, rousing, stimulating, stirring, tense, thrilling

electrify *verb* <u>startle</u>, astound, excite, galvanize, invigorate, jolt, shock, stir, thrill

elegance *noun* <u>style</u>, dignity, exquisiteness, grace, gracefulness, grandeur, luxury, refinement, taste

elegant *adjective* <u>stylish</u>, chic, delicate, exquisite, fine, graceful, handsome, polished, refined, tasteful

element *noun* 1 <u>component</u>, constituent, factor, ingredient, part, section, subdivision, unit 2 *As in* **in one's element** <u>environment</u>, domain, field, habitat, medium, milieu, sphere

elementary *adjective* <u>simple</u>,

clear, easy, plain, rudimentary, straightforward, uncomplicated

elements *plural noun* **1** <u>basics</u>, essentials, foundations, fundamentals, nuts and bolts (*informal*), principles, rudiments **2** <u>weather conditions</u>, atmospheric conditions, powers of nature

elevate *verb* **1** <u>raise</u>, heighten, hoist, lift, lift up, uplift **2** <u>promote</u>, advance, aggrandize, exalt, prefer, upgrade

elevated *adjective* <u>high-minded</u>, dignified, exalted, grand, high-flown, inflated, lofty, noble, sublime

elevation *noun* **1** <u>promotion</u>, advancement, aggrandizement, exaltation, preferment, upgrading **2** <u>altitude</u>, height

elicit *verb* **1** <u>bring about</u>, bring forth, bring out, bring to light, call forth, cause, derive, evolve, give rise to **2** <u>obtain</u>, draw out, evoke, exact, extort, extract, wrest

eligible *adjective* <u>qualified</u>, acceptable, appropriate, desirable, fit, preferable, proper, suitable, worthy

eliminate *verb* <u>get rid of</u>, cut out, dispose of, do away with, eradicate, exterminate, remove, stamp out, take out

elite *noun* <u>best</u>, aristocracy, cream, *crème de la crème*, flower, nobility, pick, upper class

elitist *adjective* <u>snobbish</u>, exclusive, selective

elixir *noun* <u>panacea</u>, nostrum

elocution *noun* <u>diction</u>, articulation, declamation, delivery, enunciation, oratory, pronunciation, speech, speechmaking

elongate *verb* <u>make longer</u>, draw out, extend, lengthen, prolong, protract, stretch

elope *verb* <u>run away</u>, abscond, bolt, decamp, disappear, escape, leave, run off, slip away, steal away

eloquence *noun* <u>expressiveness</u>, expression, fluency, forcefulness, oratory, persuasiveness, rhetoric, way with words

eloquent *adjective*
1 <u>silver-tongued</u>, articulate, fluent, forceful, moving, persuasive, stirring, well-expressed **2** <u>expressive</u>, meaningful, suggestive, telling, vivid

elsewhere *adverb* <u>in *or* to another place</u>, abroad, away, hence (*archaic*), not here, somewhere else

elucidate *verb* <u>clarify</u>, clear up, explain, explicate, expound, illuminate, illustrate, make plain, shed *or* throw light upon, spell out

elude *verb* **1** <u>escape</u>, avoid, dodge, duck (*informal*), evade, flee, get away from, outrun **2** <u>baffle</u>, be beyond (someone), confound, escape, foil, frustrate, puzzle, stump, thwart

elusive *adjective* **1** <u>difficult to catch</u>, shifty, slippery, tricky **2** <u>indefinable</u>, fleeting, intangible, subtle, transient, transitory

emaciated *adjective* <u>skeletal</u>, cadaverous, gaunt, haggard, lean, pinched, scrawny, thin, undernourished, wasted

emanate verb <u>flow</u>, arise, come forth, derive, emerge, issue, originate, proceed, spring, stem

emancipate verb <u>free</u>, deliver, liberate, release, set free, unchain, unfetter

emancipation noun <u>freedom</u>, deliverance, liberation, liberty, release

embalm verb <u>preserve</u>, mummify

embargo noun 1 <u>ban</u>, bar, boycott, interdiction, prohibition, restraint, restriction, stoppage ♦ verb 2 <u>ban</u>, bar, block, boycott, prohibit, restrict, stop

embark verb 1 <u>go aboard</u>, board ship, take ship 2 **embark on** or **upon** <u>begin</u>, commence, enter, launch, plunge into, set about, set out, start, take up

embarrass verb <u>shame</u>, discomfit, disconcert, distress, fluster, humiliate, mortify, show up (informal)

embarrassed adjective <u>ashamed</u>, awkward, blushing, discomfited, disconcerted, humiliated, mortified, red-faced, self-conscious, sheepish

embarrassing adjective <u>humiliating</u>, awkward, compromising, discomfiting, disconcerting, mortifying, sensitive, shameful, toe-curling (informal), uncomfortable

embarrassment noun 1 <u>shame</u>, awkwardness, bashfulness, distress, humiliation, mortification, self-consciousness, showing up (informal) 2 <u>predicament</u>, bind (informal), difficulty, mess, pickle (informal), scrape (informal)

embellish verb <u>decorate</u>, adorn, beautify, elaborate, embroider, enhance, enrich, festoon, ornament

embellishment noun <u>decoration</u>, adornment, elaboration, embroidery, enhancement, enrichment, exaggeration, ornament, ornamentation

embezzle verb <u>misappropriate</u>, appropriate, filch, misuse, peculate, pilfer, purloin, rip off (slang), steal

embezzlement noun <u>misappropriation</u>, appropriation, filching, fraud, misuse, peculation, pilfering, stealing, theft

embittered adjective <u>resentful</u>, angry, bitter, disaffected, disillusioned, rancorous, soured, with a chip on one's shoulder (informal)

emblem noun <u>symbol</u>, badge, crest, image, insignia, mark, sign, token

embodiment noun <u>personification</u>, epitome, example, exemplar, expression, incarnation, representation, symbol

embody verb 1 <u>personify</u>, exemplify, manifest, represent, stand for, symbolize, typify 2 <u>incorporate</u>, collect, combine, comprise, contain, include

embolden verb <u>encourage</u>, fire, inflame, invigorate, rouse, stimulate, stir, strengthen

embrace verb 1 <u>hug</u>, clasp,

cuddle, envelop, hold, seize, squeeze, take or hold in one's arms **2** <u>accept</u>, adopt, espouse, seize, take on board, take up, welcome **3** <u>include</u>, comprehend, comprise, contain, cover, encompass, involve, take in ♦ *noun* **4** <u>hug</u>, clasp, clinch (*slang*), cuddle, squeeze

embroil *verb* <u>involve</u>, enmesh, ensnare, entangle, implicate, incriminate, mire, mix up

embryo *noun* <u>germ</u>, beginning, nucleus, root, rudiment

emend *verb* <u>revise</u>, amend, correct, edit, improve, rectify

emendation *noun* <u>revision</u>, amendment, correction, editing, improvement, rectification

emerge *verb* **1** <u>come into view</u>, appear, arise, come forth, emanate, issue, rise, spring up, surface **2** <u>become apparent</u>, become known, come out, come out in the wash, come to light, crop up, transpire

emergence *noun* <u>coming</u>, advent, appearance, arrival, development, materialization, rise

emergency *noun* <u>crisis</u>, danger, difficulty, extremity, necessity, plight, predicament, quandary, scrape (*informal*)

emigrate *verb* <u>move abroad</u>, migrate, move

emigration *noun* <u>departure</u>, exodus, migration

eminence *noun* <u>prominence</u>, distinction, esteem, fame, greatness, importance, note, prestige, renown, repute

eminent *adjective* <u>prominent</u>, celebrated, distinguished,

esteemed, famous, high-ranking, illustrious, noted, renowned, well-known

emission *noun* <u>giving off or out</u>, discharge, ejaculation, ejection, exhalation, radiation, shedding, transmission

emit *verb* <u>give off</u>, cast out, discharge, eject, emanate, exude, radiate, send out, transmit

emotion *noun* <u>feeling</u>, ardour, excitement, fervour, passion, sensation, sentiment, vehemence, warmth

emotional *adjective* **1** <u>sensitive</u>, demonstrative, excitable, hot-blooded, passionate, sentimental, temperamental **2** <u>moving</u>, affecting, emotive, heart-warming, poignant, sentimental, stirring, touching

emotive *adjective* <u>sensitive</u>, controversial, delicate, touchy

emphasis *noun* <u>stress</u>, accent, attention, force, importance, priority, prominence, significance, weight

emphasize *verb* <u>stress</u>, accentuate, dwell on, give priority to, highlight, lay stress on, play up, press home, underline

emphatic *adjective* <u>forceful</u>, categorical, definite, insistent, positive, pronounced, resounding, unequivocal, unmistakable, vigorous

empire *noun* <u>kingdom</u>, commonwealth, domain, realm

empirical, empiric *adjective* <u>first-hand</u>, experiential, experimental, observed, practical, pragmatic

employ verb 1 <u>hire</u>, commission, engage, enlist, retain, take on 2 <u>keep busy</u>, engage, fill, make use of, occupy, take up, use up 3 <u>use</u>, apply, bring to bear, exercise, exert, make use of, ply, put to use, utilize ♦ noun 4 As in **in the employ of** <u>service</u>, employment, engagement, hire

employed adjective <u>working</u>, active, busy, engaged, in a job, in employment, in work, occupied

employee noun <u>worker</u>, hand, job-holder, staff member, wage-earner, workman

employer noun <u>boss</u> (informal), company, firm, gaffer (informal, chiefly Brit.), owner, patron, proprietor

employment noun 1 <u>taking on</u>, engagement, enlistment, hire, retaining 2 <u>use</u>, application, exercise, exertion, utilization 3 <u>job</u>, line, occupation, profession, trade, vocation, work

emporium noun Old-fashioned <u>shop</u>, bazaar, market, mart, store, warehouse

empower verb <u>enable</u>, allow, authorize, commission, delegate, entitle, license, permit, qualify, sanction, warrant

emptiness noun 1 <u>bareness</u>, blankness, desolation, vacancy, vacuum, void, waste 2 <u>purposelessness</u>, banality, futility, hollowness, inanity, meaninglessness, senselessness, vanity, worthlessness 3 <u>insincerity</u>, cheapness, hollowness, idleness

empty adjective 1 <u>bare</u>, blank, clear, deserted, desolate, hollow,

unfurnished, uninhabited, unoccupied, vacant, void 2 <u>purposeless</u>, banal, fruitless, futile, hollow, inane, meaningless, senseless, vain, worthless 3 <u>insincere</u>, cheap, hollow, idle ♦ verb 4 <u>evacuate</u>, clear, drain, exhaust, pour out, unload, vacate, void

empty-headed adjective <u>scatterbrained</u>, brainless, dizzy (informal), featherbrained, harebrained, silly, vacuous

emulate verb <u>imitate</u>, compete with, copy, echo, follow, mimic, rival

enable verb <u>allow</u>, authorize, empower, entitle, license, permit, qualify, sanction, warrant

enact verb 1 <u>establish</u>, authorize, command, decree, legislate, ordain, order, proclaim, sanction 2 <u>perform</u>, act out, depict, play, play the part of, portray, represent

enamoured adjective <u>in love</u>, captivated, charmed, enraptured, fond, infatuated, smitten, taken

encampment noun <u>camp</u>, base, bivouac, camping ground, campsite, cantonment, quarters, tents

encapsulate verb <u>sum up</u>, abridge, compress, condense, digest, epitomize, précis, summarize

enchant verb <u>fascinate</u>, beguile, bewitch, captivate, charm, delight, enrapture, enthral, ravish

enchanter noun <u>sorcerer</u>, conjuror, magician, magus, necromancer, warlock, witch, wizard

enchanting *adjective* <u>fascinating</u>, alluring, attractive, bewitching, captivating, charming, delightful, entrancing, lovely, pleasant

enclose *verb* **1** <u>surround</u>, bound, encase, encircle, fence, hem in, shut in, wall in **2** <u>send with</u>, include, insert, put in

encompass *verb* **1** <u>surround</u>, circle, encircle, enclose, envelop, ring **2** <u>include</u>, admit, comprise, contain, cover, embrace, hold, incorporate, take in

encounter *verb* **1** <u>meet</u>, bump into (*informal*), chance upon, come upon, confront, experience, face, run across ◆ *noun* **2** <u>meeting</u>, brush, confrontation, rendezvous **3** <u>battle</u>, clash, conflict, contest, head-to-head, run-in (*informal*)

encourage *verb* **1** <u>inspire</u>, buoy up, cheer, comfort, console, embolden, hearten, reassure **2** <u>spur</u>, advocate, egg on, foster, promote, prompt, support, urge

encouragement *noun* <u>inspiration</u>, cheer, incitement, promotion, reassurance, stimulation, stimulus, support

encouraging *adjective* <u>promising</u>, bright, cheerful, comforting, good, heartening, hopeful, reassuring, rosy

encroach *verb* <u>intrude</u>, impinge, infringe, invade, make inroads, overstep, trespass, usurp

encumber *verb* <u>burden</u>, hamper, handicap, hinder, impede, inconvenience, obstruct, saddle, weigh down

end *noun* **1** <u>extremity</u>, boundary, edge, extent, extreme, limit, point, terminus, tip **2** <u>finish</u>, cessation, close, closure, ending, expiration, expiry, stop, termination **3** <u>conclusion</u>, culmination, denouement, ending, finale, resolution **4** <u>remnant</u>, butt, fragment, leftover, oddment, remainder, scrap, stub **5** <u>destruction</u>, death, demise, doom, extermination, extinction, ruin **6** <u>purpose</u>, aim, goal, intention, object, objective, point, reason ◆ *verb* **7** <u>finish</u>, cease, close, conclude, culminate, stop, terminate, wind up

endanger *verb* <u>put at risk</u>, compromise, imperil, jeopardize, put in danger, risk, threaten

endearing *adjective* <u>attractive</u>, captivating, charming, cute, engaging, lovable, sweet, winning

endearment *noun* <u>loving word</u>, sweet nothing

endeavour *Formal* ◆ *verb* **1** <u>try</u>, aim, aspire, attempt, labour, make an effort, strive, struggle, take pains ◆ *noun* **2** <u>effort</u>, attempt, enterprise, trial, try, undertaking, venture

ending *noun* <u>finish</u>, cessation, close, completion, conclusion, culmination, denouement, end, finale

endless *adjective* <u>eternal</u>, boundless, continual, everlasting, incessant, infinite, interminable, unlimited

endorse *verb* **1** <u>approve</u>, advocate, authorize, back, champion, promote, ratify, recommend, support **2** <u>sign</u>, countersign

endorsement *noun* **1** <u>approval</u>,

advocacy, approbation, authorization, backing, favour, ratification, recommendation, seal of approval, support
2 <u>signature</u>, countersignature

endow verb <u>provide</u>, award, bequeath, bestow, confer, donate, finance, fund, give

endowment noun <u>provision</u>, award, benefaction, bequest, donation, gift, grant, legacy

endurable adjective <u>bearable</u>, acceptable, sufferable, sustainable, tolerable

endurance noun 1 <u>staying power</u>, fortitude, patience, perseverance, persistence, resolution, stamina, strength, tenacity, toleration
2 <u>permanence</u>, continuity, durability, duration, longevity, stability

endure verb 1 <u>bear</u>, cope with, experience, stand, suffer, sustain, undergo, withstand 2 <u>last</u>, continue, live on, persist, remain, stand, stay, survive

enduring adjective <u>long-lasting</u>, abiding, continuing, lasting, perennial, persistent, steadfast, unfaltering, unwavering

enemy noun <u>foe</u>, adversary, antagonist, competitor, opponent, rival, the opposition, the other side

energetic adjective <u>vigorous</u>, active, animated, dynamic, forceful, indefatigable, lively, strenuous, tireless

energy noun <u>vigour</u>, drive, forcefulness, <u>get-up-and-go</u> (informal), liveliness, pep, stamina, verve, vitality

enforce verb <u>impose</u>, administer, apply, carry out, execute, implement, insist on, prosecute, put into effect

engage verb 1 <u>participate</u>, embark on, enter into, join, set about, take part, undertake
2 <u>occupy</u>, absorb, engross, grip, involve, preoccupy 3 <u>captivate</u>, arrest, catch, fix, gain 4 <u>employ</u>, appoint, enlist, enrol, hire, retain, take on 5 Military <u>begin battle with</u>, assail, attack, encounter, fall on, join battle with, meet, take on 6 <u>set going</u>, activate, apply, bring into operation, energize, switch on

engaged adjective 1 <u>betrothed</u> (archaic), affianced, pledged, promised, spoken for
2 <u>occupied</u>, busy, employed, in use, tied up, unavailable

engagement noun
1 <u>appointment</u>, arrangement, commitment, date, meeting
2 <u>betrothal</u>, troth (archaic)
3 <u>battle</u>, action, combat, conflict, encounter, fight

engaging adjective <u>charming</u>, agreeable, attractive, fetching (informal), likable or likeable, pleasing, winning, winsome

engender verb <u>produce</u>, breed, cause, create, generate, give rise to, induce, instigate, lead to

engine noun <u>machine</u>, mechanism, motor

engineer verb <u>bring about</u>, contrive, create, devise, effect, mastermind, plan, plot, scheme

engrave verb 1 <u>carve</u>, chisel, cut, etch, inscribe 2 <u>fix</u>, embed, impress, imprint, ingrain, lodge

engraving noun <u>carving</u>,

etching, inscription, plate, woodcut

engross verb absorb, engage, immerse, involve, occupy, preoccupy

engrossed adjective absorbed, caught up, enthralled, fascinated, gripped, immersed, lost, preoccupied, rapt, riveted

engulf verb immerse, envelop, inundate, overrun, overwhelm, submerge, swallow up, swamp

enhance verb improve, add to, boost, heighten, increase, lift, reinforce, strengthen, swell

enigma noun mystery, conundrum, problem, puzzle, riddle, teaser

enigmatic adjective mysterious, ambiguous, cryptic, equivocal, inscrutable, obscure, puzzling, unfathomable

enjoy verb 1 take pleasure in or from, appreciate, be entertained by, be pleased with, delight in, like, relish 2 have, be blessed or favoured with, experience, have the benefit of, own, possess, reap the benefits of, use

enjoyable adjective pleasurable, agreeable, delightful, entertaining, gratifying, pleasant, satisfying, to one's liking

enjoyment noun pleasure, amusement, delectation, delight, entertainment, fun, gratification, happiness, joy, relish

enlarge verb 1 increase, add to, amplify, broaden, expand, extend, grow, magnify, swell, widen 2 **enlarge on** expand on, descant on, develop, elaborate on, expatiate on, give further

details about

enlighten verb inform, advise, cause to understand, counsel, edify, educate, instruct, make aware, teach

enlightened adjective informed, aware, civilized, cultivated, educated, knowledgeable, open-minded, reasonable, sophisticated

enlightenment noun understanding, awareness, comprehension, education, insight, instruction, knowledge, learning, wisdom

enlist verb 1 join up, enrol, enter (into), join, muster, register, sign up, volunteer 2 obtain, engage, procure, recruit

enliven verb cheer up, animate, excite, inspire, invigorate, pep up, rouse, spark, stimulate, vitalize

enmity noun hostility, acrimony, animosity, bad blood, bitterness, hatred, ill will, malice

ennoble verb dignify, aggrandize, elevate, enhance, exalt, glorify, honour, magnify, raise

enormity noun 1 wickedness, atrocity, depravity, monstrousness, outrageousness, vileness, villainy 2 atrocity, abomination, crime, disgrace, evil, horror, monstrosity, outrage 3 Informal hugeness, greatness, immensity, magnitude, vastness

enormous adjective huge, colossal, gigantic, gross, immense, mammoth, massive, mountainous, tremendous, vast

enough adjective 1 sufficient,

abundant, adequate, ample, plenty ♦ *noun* **2** <u>sufficiency</u>, abundance, adequacy, ample supply, plenty, right amount ♦ *adverb* **3** <u>sufficiently</u>, abundantly, adequately, amply, reasonably, satisfactorily, tolerably

enquire *see* INQUIRE

enquiry *see* INQUIRY

enrage *verb* <u>anger</u>, exasperate, incense, inflame, infuriate, madden

enrich *verb* **1** <u>enhance</u>, augment, develop, improve, refine, supplement **2** <u>make rich</u>, make wealthy

enrol *verb* <u>enlist</u>, accept, admit, join up, recruit, register, sign up *or* on, take on

enrolment *noun* <u>enlistment</u>, acceptance, admission, engagement, matriculation, recruitment, registration

en route *adverb* <u>on *or* along the way</u>, in transit, on the road

ensemble *noun* **1** <u>whole</u>, aggregate, collection, entirety, set, sum, total, totality **2** <u>outfit</u>, costume, get-up (*informal*), suit **3** <u>group</u>, band, cast, chorus, company, troupe

ensign *noun* <u>flag</u>, banner, colours, jack, pennant, pennon, standard, streamer

ensue *verb* <u>follow</u>, arise, come next, derive, flow, issue, proceed, result, stem

ensure *verb* **1** <u>make certain</u>, certify, confirm, effect, guarantee, make sure, secure, warrant **2** <u>protect</u>, guard, make safe, safeguard, secure

entail *verb* <u>involve</u>, bring about,

call for, demand, give rise to, necessitate, occasion, require

entangle *verb* **1** <u>tangle</u>, catch, embroil, enmesh, ensnare, entrap, implicate, snag, snare, trap **2** <u>mix up</u>, complicate, confuse, jumble, muddle, perplex, puzzle

enter *verb* **1** <u>come *or* go in *or* into</u>, arrive, make an entrance, pass into, penetrate, pierce **2** <u>join</u>, commence, embark upon, enlist, enrol, set out on, start, take up **3** <u>record</u>, inscribe, list, log, note, register, set down, take down

enterprise *noun* **1** <u>firm</u>, business, company, concern, establishment, operation **2** <u>undertaking</u>, adventure, effort, endeavour, operation, plan, programme, project, venture **3** <u>initiative</u>, adventurousness, boldness, daring, drive, energy, enthusiasm, resourcefulness

enterprising *adjective* <u>resourceful</u>, adventurous, bold, daring, energetic, enthusiastic, go-ahead, intrepid, spirited

entertain *verb* **1** <u>amuse</u>, charm, cheer, delight, please, regale **2** <u>show hospitality to</u>, accommodate, be host to, harbour, have company, lodge, put up, treat **3** <u>consider</u>, conceive, contemplate, imagine, keep in mind, think about

entertaining *adjective* <u>enjoyable</u>, amusing, cheering, diverting, funny, humorous, interesting, pleasant, pleasurable

entertainment *noun* <u>enjoyment</u>, amusement, fun, leisure activity, pastime, pleasure, recreation, sport, treat

enthral *verb* <u>fascinate</u>, captivate, charm, enchant, enrapture, entrance, grip, mesmerize

enthusiasm *noun* <u>keenness</u>, eagerness, fervour, interest, passion, relish, zeal, zest

enthusiast *noun* <u>lover</u>, aficionado, buff (*informal*), devotee, fan, fanatic, follower, supporter

enthusiastic *adjective* <u>keen</u>, avid, eager, fervent, passionate, vigorous, wholehearted, zealous

entice *verb* <u>attract</u>, allure, cajole, coax, lead on, lure, persuade, seduce, tempt

entire *adjective* <u>whole</u>, complete, full, gross, total

entirely *adverb* <u>completely</u>, absolutely, altogether, fully, in every respect, thoroughly, totally, utterly, wholly

entitle *verb* **1** <u>give the right to</u>, allow, authorize, empower, enable, license, permit **2** <u>call</u>, christen, dub, label, name, term, title

entity *noun* <u>thing</u>, being, creature, individual, object, organism, substance

entourage *noun* <u>retinue</u>, associates, attendants, company, court, escort, followers, staff, train

entrails *plural noun* <u>intestines</u>, bowels, guts, innards (*informal*), insides (*informal*), offal, viscera

entrance[1] *noun* **1** <u>way in</u>, access, door, doorway, entry, gate, opening, passage **2** <u>appearance</u>, arrival, coming in, entry, introduction **3** <u>admission</u>, access,

admittance, entrée, entry, permission to enter

entrance[2] *verb* **1** <u>enchant</u>, bewitch, captivate, charm, delight, enrapture, enthral, fascinate **2** <u>mesmerize</u>, hypnotize, put in a trance

entrant *noun* <u>competitor</u>, candidate, contestant, entry, participant, player

entreaty *noun* <u>plea</u>, appeal, earnest request, exhortation, petition, prayer, request, supplication

entrenched *adjective* <u>fixed</u>, deep-rooted, deep-seated, ineradicable, ingrained, rooted, set, unshakable, well-established

entrepreneur *noun* <u>businessman or businesswoman</u>, impresario, industrialist, magnate, tycoon

entrust *verb* <u>give custody of</u>, assign, commit, confide, delegate, deliver, hand over, turn over

entry *noun* **1** <u>way in</u>, access, door, doorway, entrance, gate, opening, passage **2** <u>coming in</u>, appearance, entering, entrance, initiation, introduction **3** <u>admission</u>, access, entrance, entrée, permission to enter **4** <u>record</u>, account, item, listing, note

entwine *verb* <u>twist</u>, interlace, interweave, knit, plait, twine, weave, wind

enumerate *verb* <u>list</u>, cite, itemize, mention, name, quote, recite, recount, relate, spell out

enunciate *verb* **1** <u>pronounce</u>, articulate, enounce, say, sound, speak, utter, vocalize, voice

2 state, declare, proclaim, promulgate, pronounce, propound, publish

envelop verb enclose, cloak, cover, encase, encircle, engulf, shroud, surround, wrap

envelope noun wrapping, case, casing, cover, covering, jacket, wrapper

enviable adjective desirable, advantageous, favoured, fortunate, lucky, privileged, to die for (informal)

envious adjective covetous, green with envy, grudging, jealous, resentful

environment noun surroundings, atmosphere, background, conditions, habitat, medium, setting, situation

environmental adjective ecological, green

environmentalist noun conservationist, ecologist, green

environs plural noun surrounding area, district, locality, neighbourhood, outskirts, precincts, suburbs, vicinity

envisage verb **1** imagine, conceive (of), conceptualize, contemplate, fancy, picture, think up, visualize **2** foresee, anticipate, envision, predict, see

envoy noun messenger, agent, ambassador, courier, delegate, diplomat, emissary, intermediary, representative

envy noun **1** covetousness, enviousness, jealousy, resentfulness, resentment ♦ verb **2** covet, be envious (of), begrudge, be jealous (of), grudge, resent

ephemeral adjective brief, fleeting, momentary, passing, short-lived, temporary, transient, transitory

epidemic noun spread, contagion, growth, outbreak, plague, rash, upsurge, wave

epigram noun witticism, aphorism, bon mot, quip

epilogue noun conclusion, coda, concluding speech, postscript

episode noun **1** event, adventure, affair, escapade, experience, happening, incident, matter, occurrence **2** part, chapter, instalment, passage, scene, section

epistle noun letter, communication, message, missive, note

epitaph noun monument, inscription

epithet noun name, appellation, description, designation, moniker or monicker (slang), nickname, sobriquet, tag, title

epitome noun personification, archetype, embodiment, essence, quintessence, representation, type, typical example

epitomize verb typify, embody, exemplify, illustrate, personify, represent, symbolize

epoch noun era, age, date, period, time

equable adjective even-tempered, calm, composed, easy-going, imperturbable, level-headed, placid, serene, unflappable (informal)

equal adjective **1** identical, alike, corresponding, equivalent, the same, uniform **2** regular, symmetrical, uniform, unvarying **3** even, balanced, evenly matched, fifty-fifty (*informal*), level pegging (*Brit. informal*) **4** fair, egalitarian, even-handed, impartial, just, unbiased **5** **equal to** capable of, competent to, fit for, good enough for, ready for, strong enough, suitable for, up to ♦ *noun* **6** match, counterpart, equivalent, rival, twin ♦ *verb* **7** match, amount to, be tantamount to, correspond to, equate, level, parallel, tie with

equality *noun* **1** sameness, balance, correspondence, equivalence, evenness, identity, likeness, similarity, uniformity **2** fairness, egalitarianism, equal opportunity, parity

equalize *verb* make equal, balance, equal, even up, level, match, regularize, smooth, square, standardize

equate *verb* make or be equal, be commensurate, compare, correspond with or to, liken, mention in the same breath, parallel

equation *noun* equating, comparison, correspondence, parallel

equilibrium *noun* stability, balance, equipoise, evenness, rest, steadiness, symmetry

equip *verb* supply, arm, array, fit out, furnish, kit out, provide, stock

equipment *noun* tools, accoutrements, apparatus, gear, paraphernalia, stuff, supplies, tackle

equitable *adjective* fair,

even-handed, honest, impartial, just, proper, reasonable, unbiased

equivalence *noun* equality, correspondence, evenness, likeness, parity, sameness, similarity

equivalent *noun* **1** equal, counterpart, match, opposite number, parallel, twin ♦ *adjective* **2** equal, alike, commensurate, comparable, corresponding, interchangeable, of a piece, same, similar, tantamount

equivocal *adjective* ambiguous, evasive, indefinite, indeterminate, misleading, oblique, obscure, uncertain, vague

era *noun* age, date, day or days, epoch, generation, period, time

eradicate *verb* wipe out, annihilate, destroy, eliminate, erase, exterminate, extinguish, obliterate, remove, root out

erase *verb* wipe out, blot, cancel, delete, expunge, obliterate, remove, rub out

erect *verb* **1** build, construct, put up, raise, set up **2** found, create, establish, form, initiate, institute, organize, set up ♦ *adjective* **3** upright, elevated, perpendicular, pricked-up, stiff, straight, vertical

erode *verb* wear down or away, abrade, consume, corrode, destroy, deteriorate, disintegrate, eat away, grind down

erosion *noun* deterioration, abrasion, attrition, destruction, disintegration, eating away, grinding down, wearing down or away

erotic adjective <u>sexual</u>, amatory, carnal, lustful, seductive, sensual, sexy (informal), voluptuous

err verb <u>make a mistake</u>, blunder, go wrong, miscalculate, misjudge, mistake, slip up (informal)

errand noun <u>job</u>, charge, commission, message, mission, task

erratic adjective <u>unpredictable</u>, changeable, inconsistent, irregular, uneven, unreliable, unstable, variable, wayward

erroneous adjective <u>incorrect</u>, fallacious, false, faulty, flawed, invalid, mistaken, unsound, wrong

error noun <u>mistake</u>, bloomer (Brit. informal), blunder, howler (informal), miscalculation, oversight, slip, solecism

erstwhile adjective <u>former</u>, bygone, late, old, once, one-time, past, previous, sometime

erudite adjective <u>learned</u>, cultivated, cultured, educated, knowledgeable, scholarly, well-educated, well-read

erupt verb **1** <u>explode</u>, belch forth, blow up, burst out, gush, pour forth, spew forth or out, spout, throw off **2** Medical <u>break out</u>, appear

eruption noun **1** <u>explosion</u>, discharge, ejection, flare-up, outbreak, outburst **2** Medical <u>inflammation</u>, outbreak, rash

escalate verb <u>increase</u>, expand, extend, grow, heighten, intensify, mount, rise

escapade noun <u>adventure</u>, antic, caper, prank, scrape (informal), stunt

escape verb **1** <u>get away</u>, abscond, bolt, break free or out, flee, fly, make one's getaway, run away or off, slip away **2** <u>avoid</u>, dodge, duck, elude, evade, pass, shun, slip **3** <u>leak</u>, emanate, exude, flow, gush, issue, pour forth, seep ♦ noun **4** <u>getaway</u>, break, break-out, flight **5** <u>avoidance</u>, circumvention, evasion **6** <u>relaxation</u>, distraction, diversion, pastime, recreation **7** <u>leak</u>, emanation, emission, seepage

escort noun **1** <u>guard</u>, bodyguard, convoy, cortege, entourage, retinue, train **2** <u>companion</u>, attendant, beau, chaperon, guide, partner ♦ verb **3** <u>accompany</u>, chaperon, conduct, guide, lead, partner, shepherd, usher

especial adjective Formal <u>exceptional</u>, noteworthy, outstanding, principal, special, uncommon, unusual

especially adverb <u>exceptionally</u>, conspicuously, markedly, notably, outstandingly, remarkably, specially, strikingly, uncommonly, unusually

espionage noun <u>spying</u>, counter-intelligence, intelligence, surveillance, undercover work

espousal noun <u>support</u>, adoption, advocacy, backing, championing, defence, embracing, promotion, taking up

espouse verb <u>support</u>, adopt, advocate, back, champion, embrace, promote, stand up for, take up, uphold

essay noun **1** <u>composition</u>, article, discourse, dissertation, paper, piece, tract, treatise ♦ verb **2** Formal <u>attempt</u>, aim, endeavour, try, undertake

essence noun **1** <u>fundamental nature</u>, being, core, heart, nature, quintessence, soul, spirit, substance **2** <u>concentrate</u>, distillate, extract, spirits, tincture

essential adjective **1** <u>vital</u>, crucial, important, indispensable, necessary, needed, requisite **2** <u>fundamental</u>, basic, cardinal, elementary, innate, intrinsic, main, principal ♦ noun **3** <u>prerequisite</u>, basic, fundamental, must, necessity, rudiment, sine qua non

establish verb **1** <u>create</u>, constitute, form, found, ground, inaugurate, institute, settle, set up **2** <u>prove</u>, authenticate, certify, confirm, corroborate, demonstrate, substantiate, verify

establishment noun **1** <u>creation</u>, formation, foundation, founding, inauguration, installation, institution, organization, setting up **2** <u>organization</u>, business, company, concern, corporation, enterprise, firm, institution, outfit (informal) **3** **the Establishment** <u>the authorities</u>, ruling class, the powers that be, the system

estate noun **1** <u>lands</u>, area, domain, holdings, manor, property **2** Law <u>property</u>, assets, belongings, effects, fortune, goods, possessions, wealth

esteem noun **1** <u>respect</u>, admiration, credit, estimation, good opinion, honour, regard,

reverence, veneration ♦ verb **2** <u>respect</u>, admire, love, prize, regard highly, revere, think highly of, treasure, value **3** Formal <u>consider</u>, believe, deem, estimate, judge, reckon, regard, think, view

estimate verb **1** <u>calculate roughly</u>, assess, evaluate, gauge, guess, judge, number, reckon, value **2** <u>form an opinion</u>, believe, conjecture, consider, judge, rank, rate, reckon, surmise ♦ noun **3** <u>approximate calculation</u>, assessment, ballpark figure (informal), guess, guesstimate (informal), judgment, valuation **4** <u>opinion</u>, appraisal, assessment, belief, estimation, judgment

estimation noun <u>opinion</u>, appraisal, appreciation, assessment, belief, consideration, considered opinion, judgment, view

estuary noun <u>inlet</u>, creek, firth, fjord, mouth

et cetera adverb **1** <u>and so on</u>, and so forth ♦ noun **2** <u>and the rest</u>, and others, and the like, et al.

etch verb <u>cut</u>, carve, eat into, engrave, impress, imprint, inscribe, stamp

etching noun <u>print</u>, carving, engraving, impression, imprint, inscription

eternal adjective **1** <u>everlasting</u>, endless, immortal, infinite, never-ending, perpetual, timeless, unceasing, unending **2** <u>permanent</u>, deathless, enduring, immutable, imperishable, indestructible, lasting, unchanging

eternity *noun* 1 <u>infinity</u>, ages, endlessness, immortality, perpetuity, timelessness 2 *Theology* <u>the afterlife</u>, heaven, paradise, the hereafter, the next world

ethical *adjective* <u>moral</u>, conscientious, fair, good, honourable, just, principled, proper, right, upright, virtuous

ethics *plural noun* <u>moral code</u>, conscience, morality, moral philosophy, moral values, principles, rules of conduct, standards

ethnic, ethnical *adjective* <u>cultural</u>, folk, indigenous, national, native, racial, traditional

etiquette *noun* <u>good or proper behaviour</u>, civility, courtesy, decorum, formalities, manners, politeness, propriety, protocol

euphoria *noun* <u>elation</u>, ecstasy, exaltation, exhilaration, intoxication, joy, jubilation, rapture

evacuate *verb* <u>clear</u>, abandon, desert, forsake, leave, move out, pull out, quit, vacate, withdraw

evade *verb* 1 <u>avoid</u>, dodge, duck, elude, escape, get away from, sidestep, steer clear of 2 <u>avoid answering</u>, equivocate, fend off, fudge, hedge, parry

evaluate *verb* <u>assess</u>, appraise, calculate, estimate, gauge, judge, rate, reckon, size up (*informal*), weigh

evaporate *verb* 1 <u>dry up</u>, dehydrate, desiccate, dry, vaporize 2 <u>disappear</u>, dematerialize, dissolve, fade

away, melt away, vanish

evasion *noun* 1 <u>avoidance</u>, dodging, escape 2 <u>deception</u>, equivocation, evasiveness, prevarication

evasive *adjective* <u>deceptive</u>, cagey (*informal*), equivocating, indirect, oblique, prevaricating, shifty, slippery

eve *noun* 1 <u>night before</u>, day before, vigil 2 <u>brink</u>, edge, point, threshold, verge

even *adjective* 1 <u>level</u>, flat, horizontal, parallel, smooth, steady, straight, true, uniform 2 <u>regular</u>, constant, smooth, steady, unbroken, uniform, uninterrupted, unvarying, unwavering 3 <u>equal</u>, comparable, fifty-fifty (*informal*), identical, level, like, matching, neck and neck, on a par, similar, tied 4 <u>calm</u>, composed, cool, even-tempered, imperturbable, placid, unruffled, well-balanced 5 <u>get even (with)</u> *Informal* <u>pay back</u>, get one's own back, give tit for tat, reciprocate, repay, requite

evening *noun* <u>dusk</u>, gloaming (*Scot. or poetic*), twilight

event *noun* 1 <u>incident</u>, affair, business, circumstance, episode, experience, happening, occasion, occurrence 2 <u>competition</u>, bout, contest, game, tournament

even-tempered *adjective* <u>calm</u>, composed, cool, imperturbable, level-headed, placid, tranquil, unexcitable, unruffled

eventful *adjective* <u>exciting</u>, active, busy, dramatic, full, lively, memorable, remarkable

eventual adjective final, concluding, overall, ultimate

eventuality noun possibility, case, chance, contingency, event, likelihood, probability

eventually adverb in the end, after all, at the end of the day, finally, one day, some time, ultimately, when all is said and done

ever adverb 1 at any time, at all, at any period, at any point, by any chance, in any case, on any occasion 2 always, at all times, constantly, continually, evermore, for ever, perpetually

everlasting adjective eternal, endless, immortal, indestructible, never-ending, perpetual, timeless, undying

evermore adverb for ever, always, eternally, ever, to the end of time

every adjective each, all, each one

everybody pronoun everyone, all and sundry, each one, each person, every person, one and all, the whole world

everyday adjective common, customary, mundane, ordinary, routine, run-of-the-mill, stock, usual, workaday

everyone pronoun everybody, all and sundry, each one, each person, every person, one and all, the whole world

everything pronoun all, each thing, the lot, the whole lot

everywhere adverb to or in every place, all around, all over, far and wide or near, high and low, in every nook and cranny, the world over, ubiquitously

evict verb expel, boot out (informal), eject, kick out (informal), oust, remove, throw out, turf out (informal), turn out

evidence noun 1 proof, confirmation, corroboration, demonstration, grounds, indication, sign, substantiation, testimony ♦ verb 2 show, demonstrate, display, exhibit, indicate, prove, reveal, signify, witness

evident adjective obvious, apparent, clear, manifest, noticeable, perceptible, plain, unmistakable, visible

evidently adverb 1 obviously, clearly, manifestly, plainly, undoubtedly, unmistakably, without question 2 apparently, ostensibly, outwardly, seemingly, to all appearances

evil noun 1 wickedness, badness, depravity, malignity, sin, vice, villainy, wrongdoing 2 harm, affliction, disaster, hurt, ill, injury, mischief, misfortune, suffering, woe ♦ adjective 3 wicked, bad, depraved, immoral, malevolent, malicious, sinful, villainous 4 harmful, calamitous, catastrophic, destructive, dire, disastrous, pernicious, ruinous 5 offensive, foul, noxious, pestilential, unpleasant, vile

evoke verb recall, arouse, awaken, call, give rise to, induce, rekindle, stir up, summon up

evolution noun development, expansion, growth, increase, maturation, progress, unfolding, working out

evolve verb develop, expand,

grow, increase, mature, progress, unfold, work out

exact adjective **1** <u>accurate</u>, correct, definite, faultless, precise, right, specific, true, unerring ♦ verb **2** <u>demand</u>, claim, command, compel, extort, extract, force

exacting adjective <u>demanding</u>, difficult, hard, harsh, rigorous, severe, strict, stringent, taxing, tough

exactly adverb **1** <u>precisely</u>, accurately, correctly, explicitly, faithfully, scrupulously, truthfully, unerringly **2** <u>in every respect</u>, absolutely, indeed, precisely, quite, specifically, to the letter

exactness noun <u>precision</u>, accuracy, correctness, exactitude, rigorousness, scrupulousness, strictness, veracity

exaggerate verb <u>overstate</u>, amplify, embellish, embroider, enlarge, overemphasize, overestimate

exaggeration noun <u>overstatement</u>, amplification, embellishment, enlargement, hyperbole, overemphasis, overestimation

exalt verb **1** <u>praise</u>, acclaim, extol, glorify, idolize, set on a pedestal, worship **2** <u>raise</u>, advance, elevate, ennoble, honour, promote, upgrade

exaltation noun **1** <u>praise</u>, acclaim, glorification, idolization, reverence, tribute, worship **2** <u>rise</u>, advancement, elevation, ennoblement, promotion, upgrading

exalted adjective <u>high-ranking</u>, dignified, eminent, grand, honoured, lofty, prestigious

examination noun **1** <u>inspection</u>, analysis, exploration, interrogation, investigation, research, scrutiny, study, test **2** <u>questioning</u>, inquiry, inquisition, probe, quiz, test

examine verb **1** <u>inspect</u>, analyse, explore, investigate, peruse, scrutinize, study, survey **2** <u>question</u>, cross-examine, grill (informal), inquire, interrogate, quiz, test

example noun **1** <u>specimen</u>, case, illustration, instance, sample **2** <u>model</u>, archetype, ideal, paradigm, paragon, prototype, standard **3** <u>warning</u>, caution, lesson

exasperate verb <u>irritate</u>, anger, annoy, enrage, incense, inflame, infuriate, madden, pique

exasperation noun <u>irritation</u>, anger, annoyance, fury, pique, provocation, rage, wrath

excavate verb <u>dig out</u>, burrow, delve, dig up, mine, quarry, tunnel, uncover, unearth

exceed verb **1** <u>surpass</u>, beat, better, cap (informal), eclipse, outdo, outstrip, overtake, pass, top **2** <u>go over the limit of</u>, go over the top, overstep

exceedingly adverb <u>extremely</u>, enormously, exceptionally, extraordinarily, hugely, superlatively, surpassingly, unusually, very

excel verb **1** <u>be superior</u>, beat, eclipse, outdo, outshine, surpass, transcend **2** excel in or at <u>be good at</u>, be proficient in, be skilful at, be talented at, shine at, show talent in

excellence noun <u>high quality</u>, distinction, eminence, goodness, greatness, merit, pre-eminence, superiority, supremacy

excellent adjective <u>outstanding</u>, brilliant, exquisite, fine, first-class, first-rate, good, great, superb, superlative, world-class

except preposition 1 Also **except for** <u>apart from</u>, barring, besides, but, excepting, excluding, omitting, other than, saving, with the exception of ♦ verb 2 <u>exclude</u>, leave out, omit, pass over

exception noun 1 <u>special case</u>, anomaly, deviation, freak, inconsistency, irregularity, oddity, peculiarity 2 <u>exclusion</u>, leaving out, omission, passing over

exceptional adjective 1 <u>special</u>, abnormal, atypical, extraordinary, irregular, odd, peculiar, strange, unusual 2 <u>remarkable</u>, excellent, extraordinary, marvellous, outstanding, phenomenal, prodigious, special, superior

excerpt noun <u>extract</u>, fragment, part, passage, piece, quotation, section, selection

excess noun 1 <u>surfeit</u>, glut, overload, superabundance, superfluity, surplus, too much 2 <u>overindulgence</u>, debauchery, dissipation, dissoluteness, extravagance, intemperance, prodigality

excessive adjective <u>immoderate</u>, disproportionate, exaggerated, extreme, inordinate, overmuch, superfluous, too much, undue,

unfair, unreasonable

exchange verb 1 <u>interchange</u>, barter, change, convert into, swap, switch, trade ♦ noun 2 <u>interchange</u>, barter, quid pro quo, reciprocity, substitution, swap, switch, tit for tat, trade

excitable adjective <u>nervous</u>, emotional, highly strung, hot-headed, mercurial, quick-tempered, temperamental, volatile

excite verb <u>arouse</u>, animate, galvanize, inflame, inspire, provoke, rouse, stir up, thrill

excitement noun <u>agitation</u>, action, activity, animation, commotion, furore, passion, thrill

exciting adjective <u>stimulating</u>, dramatic, electrifying, exhilarating, rousing, sensational, stirring, thrilling

exclaim verb <u>cry out</u>, call out, declare, proclaim, shout, utter, yell

exclamation noun <u>cry</u>, call, interjection, outcry, shout, utterance, yell

exclude verb 1 <u>keep out</u>, ban, bar, boycott, disallow, forbid, prohibit, refuse, shut out 2 <u>leave out</u>, count out, eliminate, ignore, omit, pass over, reject, rule out, set aside

exclusion noun 1 <u>ban</u>, bar, boycott, disqualification, embargo, prohibition, veto 2 <u>elimination</u>, omission, rejection

exclusive adjective 1 <u>sole</u>, absolute, complete, entire, full, total, undivided, whole 2 <u>limited</u>, confined, peculiar, restricted, unique 3 <u>select</u>, chic, cliquish, fashionable, posh (*informal, chiefly Brit.*), restricted, snobbish, up-market

excommunicate *verb* expel, anathematize, ban, banish, cast out, denounce, exclude, repudiate

excruciating *adjective* agonizing, harrowing, insufferable, intense, piercing, severe, unbearable, violent

exculpate *verb* absolve, acquit, clear, discharge, excuse, exonerate, pardon, vindicate

excursion *noun* trip, day trip, expedition, jaunt, journey, outing, pleasure trip, ramble, tour

excusable *adjective* forgivable, allowable, defensible, justifiable, pardonable, permissible, understandable, warrantable

excuse *noun* 1 justification, apology, defence, explanation, grounds, mitigation, plea, reason, vindication ◆ *verb* 2 justify, apologize for, defend, explain, mitigate, vindicate 3 forgive, acquit, exculpate, exonerate, make allowances for, overlook, pardon, tolerate, turn a blind eye to 4 free, absolve, discharge, exempt, let off, release, relieve, spare

execute *verb* 1 put to death, behead, electrocute, guillotine, hang, kill, shoot 2 carry out, accomplish, administer, discharge, effect, enact, implement, perform, prosecute

execution *noun* 1 carrying out, accomplishment, administration, enactment, enforcement, implementation, operation, performance, prosecution

2 killing, capital punishment, hanging

executioner *noun* 1 hangman, headsman 2 killer, assassin, exterminator, hit man (*slang*), liquidator, murderer, slayer

executive *noun* 1 administrator, director, manager, official 2 administration, directorate, directors, government, hierarchy, leadership, management ◆ *adjective* 3 administrative, controlling, decision-making, directing, governing, managerial

exemplary *adjective* 1 ideal, admirable, commendable, excellent, fine, good, model, praiseworthy 2 warning, cautionary

exemplify *verb* show, demonstrate, display, embody, exhibit, illustrate, represent, serve as an example of

exempt *adjective* 1 immune, excepted, excused, free, not liable, released, spared ◆ *verb* 2 grant immunity, absolve, discharge, excuse, free, let off, release, relieve, spare

exemption *noun* immunity, absolution, discharge, dispensation, exception, exoneration, freedom, release

exercise *noun* 1 exertion, activity, effort, labour, toil, training, work, work-out 2 task, drill, lesson, practice, problem 3 use, application, discharge, fulfilment, implementation, practice, utilization ◆ *verb* 4 put to use, apply, bring to bear, employ, exert, use, utilize 5 train, practise, work out

exert *verb* 1 use, apply, bring to

bear, employ, exercise, make use of, utilize, wield **2 exert oneself** <u>make an effort</u>, apply oneself, do one's best, endeavour, labour, strain, strive, struggle, toil, work

exertion noun <u>effort</u>, elbow grease (*facetious*), endeavour, industry, strain, exercise, struggle, toil

exhaust verb **1** <u>tire out</u>, debilitate, drain, enervate, enfeeble, fatigue, sap, weaken, wear out **2** <u>use up</u>, consume, deplete, dissipate, expend, run through, spend, squander, waste

exhausted adjective **1** <u>worn out</u>, all in (*slang*), debilitated, done in (*informal*), drained, fatigued, knackered (*slang*), spent, tired out **2** <u>used up</u>, consumed, depleted, dissipated, expended, finished, spent, squandered, wasted

exhausting adjective <u>tiring</u>, backbreaking, debilitating, gruelling, laborious, punishing, sapping, strenuous, taxing

exhaustion noun **1** <u>tiredness</u>, debilitation, fatigue, weariness **2** <u>depletion</u>, consumption, emptying, using up

exhaustive adjective <u>thorough</u>, all-embracing, complete, comprehensive, extensive, full-scale, in-depth, intensive

exhibit verb <u>display</u>, demonstrate, express, indicate, manifest, parade, put on view, reveal, show

exhibition noun <u>display</u>, demonstration, exposition, performance, presentation, representation, show, spectacle

exhilarating adjective <u>exciting</u>, breathtaking, enlivening, invigorating, stimulating, thrilling

exhort verb *Formal* <u>urge</u>, advise, beseech, call upon, entreat, persuade, press, spur

exhume verb *Formal* <u>dig up</u>, disentomb, disinter, unearth

exigency, exigence noun <u>need</u>, constraint, demand, necessity, requirement

exile noun **1** <u>banishment</u>, deportation, expatriation, expulsion **2** <u>expatriate</u>, deportee, émigré, outcast, refugee ♦ verb **3** <u>banish</u>, deport, drive out, eject, expatriate, expel

exist verb **1** <u>be</u>, be present, endure, live, occur, survive **2** <u>survive</u>, eke out a living, get along or by, keep one's head above water, stay alive, subsist

existence noun <u>being</u>, actuality, life, subsistence

existent adjective <u>in existence</u>, alive, existing, extant, living, present, standing, surviving

exit noun **1** <u>way out</u>, door, gate, outlet **2** <u>departure</u>, exodus, farewell, going, goodbye, leave-taking, retreat, withdrawal ♦ verb **3** <u>depart</u>, go away, go offstage (*Theatre*), go out, leave, make tracks, retire, retreat, take one's leave, withdraw

exodus noun <u>departure</u>, evacuation, exit, flight, going out, leaving, migration, retreat, withdrawal

exonerate verb <u>clear</u>, absolve, acquit, discharge, exculpate, excuse, justify, pardon, vindicate

exorbitant adjective <u>excessive</u>, extortionate, extravagant, immoderate, inordinate, outrageous, preposterous, unreasonable

exorcise verb <u>drive out</u>, cast out, deliver (from), expel, purify

exotic adjective 1 <u>unusual</u>, colourful, fascinating, glamorous, mysterious, strange, striking, unfamiliar 2 <u>foreign</u>, alien, external, imported, naturalized

expand verb 1 <u>increase</u>, amplify, broaden, develop, enlarge, extend, grow, magnify, swell, widen 2 <u>spread (out)</u>, diffuse, stretch (out), unfold, unfurl, unravel, unroll 3 **expand on** <u>go into detail about</u>, amplify, develop, elaborate on, embellish, enlarge on, expatiate on, expound on, flesh out

expanse noun <u>area</u>, breadth, extent, range, space, stretch, sweep, tract

expansion noun <u>increase</u>, amplification, development, enlargement, growth, magnification, opening out, spread

expansive adjective 1 <u>wide</u>, broad, extensive, far-reaching, voluminous, wide-ranging, widespread 2 <u>talkative</u>, affable, communicative, effusive, friendly, loquacious, open, outgoing, sociable, unreserved

expatriate adjective 1 <u>exiled</u>, banished, emigrant, émigré ♦ noun 2 <u>exile</u>, emigrant, émigré, refugee

expect verb 1 <u>think</u>, assume, believe, imagine, presume, reckon, suppose, surmise, trust 2 <u>look forward to</u>, anticipate, await, contemplate, envisage,

hope for, predict, watch for 3 <u>require</u>, call for, demand, insist on, want

expectant adjective 1 <u>expecting</u>, anticipating, apprehensive, eager, hopeful, in suspense, ready, watchful 2 <u>pregnant</u>, expecting (informal), gravid

expectation noun 1 <u>probability</u>, assumption, belief, conjecture, forecast, likelihood, presumption, supposition 2 <u>anticipation</u>, apprehension, expectancy, hope, promise, suspense

expediency noun <u>suitability</u>, advisability, benefit, convenience, pragmatism, profitability, prudence, usefulness, utility

expedient noun 1 <u>means</u>, contrivance, device, makeshift, measure, method, resort, scheme, stopgap ♦ adjective 2 <u>advantageous</u>, appropriate, beneficial, convenient, effective, helpful, opportune, practical, suitable, useful

expedition noun <u>journey</u>, excursion, mission, quest, safari, tour, trek, voyage

expel verb 1 <u>drive out</u>, belch, cast out, discharge, eject, remove, spew 2 <u>dismiss</u>, ban, banish, drum out, evict, exclude, exile, throw out, turf out (informal)

expend verb Formal <u>spend</u>, consume, dissipate, exhaust, go through, pay out, use (up)

expendable adjective <u>dispensable</u>, inessential, nonessential, replaceable, unimportant, unnecessary

expenditure noun <u>spending</u>,

consumption, cost, expense, outgoings, outlay, output, payment

expense noun <u>cost</u>, charge, expenditure, loss, outlay, payment, spending

expensive adjective <u>dear</u>, costly, exorbitant, extravagant, high-priced, lavish, overpriced, steep (informal), stiff

experience noun 1 <u>knowledge</u>, contact, exposure, familiarity, involvement, participation, practice, training 2 <u>event</u>, adventure, affair, encounter, episode, happening, incident, occurrence ♦ verb 3 <u>undergo</u>, encounter, endure, face, feel, go through, live through, sample, taste

experienced adjective <u>knowledgeable</u>, accomplished, expert, practised, seasoned, tested, tried, veteran, well-versed

experiment noun 1 <u>test</u>, examination, experimentation, investigation, procedure, proof, research, trial, trial run ♦ verb 2 <u>test</u>, examine, investigate, put to the test, research, sample, try, verify

experimental adjective <u>test</u>, exploratory, pilot, preliminary, probationary, provisional, speculative, tentative, trial, trial-and-error

expert noun 1 <u>master</u>, authority, connoisseur, dab hand (Brit. informal), past master, professional, specialist, virtuoso ♦ adjective 2 <u>skilful</u>, adept, adroit, experienced, masterly, practised, professional, proficient, qualified, virtuoso

expertise noun <u>skill</u>, adroitness, command, facility, judgment, know-how (informal), knowledge, mastery, proficiency

expire verb 1 <u>finish</u>, cease, close, come to an end, conclude, end, lapse, run out, stop, terminate 2 <u>breathe out</u>, emit, exhale, expel 3 <u>die</u>, depart, kick the bucket (informal), pass away or on, perish

explain verb 1 <u>make clear or plain</u>, clarify, clear up, define, describe, elucidate, expound, resolve, teach 2 <u>account for</u>, excuse, give a reason for, justify

explanation noun 1 <u>reason</u>, account, answer, excuse, justification, motive, vindication 2 <u>description</u>, clarification, definition, elucidation, illustration, interpretation

explanatory adjective <u>descriptive</u>, illustrative, interpretive

explicit adjective <u>clear</u>, categorical, definite, frank, precise, specific, straightforward, unambiguous

explode verb 1 <u>blow up</u>, burst, detonate, discharge, erupt, go off, set off, shatter 2 <u>disprove</u>, debunk, discredit, give the lie to, invalidate, refute, repudiate

exploit verb 1 <u>take advantage of</u>, abuse, manipulate, milk, misuse, play on or upon 2 <u>make the best use of</u>, capitalize on, cash in on (informal), profit by or from, use, utilize ♦ noun 3 <u>feat</u>, accomplishment, achievement, adventure, attainment, deed, escapade, stunt

exploitation noun <u>misuse</u>, abuse, manipulation

exploration noun
1 <u>investigation</u>, analysis, examination, inquiry, inspection, research, scrutiny, search
2 <u>expedition</u>, reconnaissance, survey, tour, travel, trip

exploratory adjective <u>investigative</u>, experimental, fact-finding, probing, searching, trial

explore verb 1 <u>investigate</u>, examine, inquire into, inspect, look into, probe, research, search
2 <u>travel</u>, reconnoitre, scout, survey, tour

explosion noun 1 <u>bang</u>, blast, burst, clap, crack, detonation, discharge, report 2 <u>outburst</u>, eruption, fit, outbreak

explosive adjective 1 <u>unstable</u>, volatile 2 <u>violent</u>, fiery, stormy, touchy, vehement

exponent noun 1 <u>advocate</u>, backer, champion, defender, promoter, proponent, supporter, upholder 2 <u>performer</u>, player

expose verb 1 <u>uncover</u>, display, exhibit, present, reveal, show, unveil 2 <u>make vulnerable</u>, endanger, imperil, jeopardize, lay open, leave open, subject

exposed adjective 1 <u>unconcealed</u>, bare, on display, on show, on view, revealed, uncovered
2 <u>unsheltered</u>, open, unprotected 3 <u>vulnerable</u>, in peril, laid bare, susceptible, wide open

exposure noun <u>publicity</u>, display, exhibition, presentation, revelation, showing, uncovering, unveiling

expound verb <u>explain</u>, describe, elucidate, interpret, set forth, spell out, unfold

express verb 1 <u>state</u>, articulate, communicate, declare, phrase, put into words, say, utter, voice, word 2 <u>show</u>, convey, exhibit, indicate, intimate, make known, represent, reveal, signify, stand for, symbolize ♦ adjective
3 <u>explicit</u>, categorical, clear, definite, distinct, plain, unambiguous 4 <u>specific</u>, clear-cut, especial, particular, singular, special 5 <u>fast</u>, direct, high-speed, nonstop, rapid, speedy, swift

expression noun 1 <u>statement</u>, announcement, communication, declaration, utterance
2 <u>indication</u>, demonstration, exhibition, manifestation, representation, show, sign, symbol, token 3 <u>look</u>, air, appearance, aspect, countenance, face 4 <u>phrase</u>, idiom, locution, remark, term, turn of phrase, word

expressive adjective <u>vivid</u>, eloquent, moving, poignant, striking, telling

expressly adverb 1 <u>definitely</u>, categorically, clearly, distinctly, explicitly, in no uncertain terms, plainly, unambiguously
2 <u>specifically</u>, especially, particularly, specially

expulsion noun <u>ejection</u>, banishment, dismissal, eviction, exclusion, removal

exquisite adjective 1 <u>beautiful</u>, attractive, charming, comely, lovely, pleasing, striking 2 <u>fine</u>, beautiful, dainty, delicate, elegant, lovely, precious
3 <u>intense</u>, acute, keen, sharp

extempore *adverb, adjective* impromptu, ad lib, freely, improvised, offhand, off the cuff (*informal*), spontaneously, unpremeditated, unprepared

extend *verb* **1** make longer, drag out, draw out, lengthen, prolong, spin out, spread out, stretch **2** last, carry on, continue, go on **3** widen, add to, augment, broaden, enhance, enlarge, expand, increase, supplement **4** offer, confer, impart, present, proffer

extension *noun* **1** annexe, addition, appendage, appendix, supplement **2** lengthening, broadening, development, enlargement, expansion, increase, spread, widening

extensive *adjective* wide, broad, far-flung, far-reaching, large-scale, pervasive, spacious, vast, voluminous, widespread

extent *noun* size, amount, area, breadth, expanse, length, stretch, volume, width

extenuating *adjective* mitigating, justifying, moderating, qualifying

exterior *noun* **1** outside, coating, covering, façade, face, shell, skin, surface ♦ *adjective* **2** outside, external, outer, outermost, outward, surface

exterminate *verb* destroy, abolish, annihilate, eliminate, eradicate

external *adjective* **1** outer, exterior, outermost, outside, outward, surface **2** outside, alien, extrinsic, foreign

extinct *adjective* dead, defunct, gone, lost, vanished

extinction *noun* dying out, abolition, annihilation, destruction, eradication, extermination, obliteration, oblivion

extinguish *verb* **1** put out, blow out, douse, quench, smother, snuff out, stifle **2** destroy, annihilate, eliminate, end, eradicate, exterminate, remove, wipe out

extol *verb* praise, acclaim, commend, eulogize, exalt, glorify, sing the praises of

extort *verb* force, blackmail, bully, coerce, extract, squeeze

extortionate *adjective* exorbitant, excessive, extravagant, inflated, outrageous, preposterous, sky-high, unreasonable

extra *adjective* **1** additional, added, ancillary, auxiliary, further, more, supplementary **2** surplus, excess, leftover, redundant, spare, superfluous, unused ♦ *noun* **3** addition, accessory, attachment, bonus, extension, supplement ♦ *adverb* **4** exceptionally, especially, extraordinarily, extremely, particularly, remarkably, uncommonly, unusually

extract *verb* **1** pull out, draw, pluck out, pull, remove, take out, uproot, withdraw **2** derive, draw, elicit, glean, obtain ♦ *noun* **3** passage, citation, clipping, cutting, excerpt, quotation, selection **4** essence, concentrate, distillation, juice

extraneous *adjective* irrelevant, beside the point, immaterial, inappropriate, off the subject, unconnected, unrelated

extraordinary adjective unusual, amazing, exceptional, fantastic, outstanding, phenomenal, remarkable, strange, uncommon

extravagance noun 1 waste, lavishness, overspending, prodigality, profligacy, squandering, wastefulness 2 excess, exaggeration, outrageousness, preposterousness, wildness

extravagant adjective 1 wasteful, lavish, prodigal, profligate, spendthrift 2 excessive, outrageous, over the top (slang), preposterous, reckless, unreasonable

extreme adjective 1 maximum, acute, great, highest, intense, severe, supreme, ultimate, utmost 2 severe, drastic, harsh, radical, rigid, strict, uncompromising 3 excessive, fanatical, immoderate, radical 4 farthest, far off, most distant, outermost, remotest ◆ noun 5 limit, boundary, edge, end, extremity, pole

extremely adverb very, awfully (informal), exceedingly, exceptionally, extraordinarily, severely, terribly, uncommonly, unusually

extremist noun fanatic, die-hard, radical, zealot

extremity noun 1 limit, border, boundary, edge, extreme, frontier, pinnacle, tip 2 crisis, adversity, dire straits, disaster, emergency, exigency, trouble 3 extremities hands and feet, fingers and toes, limbs

extricate verb free, disengage, disentangle, get out, release, remove, rescue, wriggle out of

extrovert adjective outgoing, exuberant, gregarious, sociable

exuberance noun 1 high spirits, cheerfulness, ebullience, enthusiasm, liveliness, spirit, vitality, vivacity, zest 2 luxuriance, abundance, copiousness, lavishness, profusion

exuberant adjective 1 high-spirited, animated, cheerful, ebullient, energetic, enthusiastic, lively, spirited, vivacious 2 luxuriant, abundant, copious, lavish, plentiful, profuse

exult verb be joyful, be overjoyed, celebrate, jump for joy, rejoice

eye noun 1 eyeball, optic (informal) 2 appreciation, discernment, discrimination, judgment, perception, recognition, taste ◆ verb 3 look at, check out (informal), contemplate, inspect, study, survey, view, watch

eyesight noun vision, perception, sight

eyesore noun mess, blemish, blot, disfigurement, horror, monstrosity, sight (informal)

eyewitness noun observer, bystander, onlooker, passer-by, spectator, viewer, witness

F f

fable noun 1 story, allegory, legend, myth, parable, tale 2 fiction, fabrication, fantasy, invention, tall story (informal), urban legend, yarn (informal)

fabric noun 1 <u>cloth</u>, material, stuff, textile, web 2 <u>framework</u>, constitution, construction, foundations, make-up, organization, structure

fabricate verb 1 <u>make up</u>, concoct, devise, fake, falsify, feign, forge, invent, trump up 2 <u>build</u>, assemble, construct, erect, form, make, manufacture, shape

fabrication noun 1 <u>forgery</u>, concoction, fake, falsehood, fiction, invention, lie, myth 2 <u>construction</u>, assembly, building, erection, manufacture, production

fabulous adjective 1 Informal <u>wonderful</u>, brilliant, fantastic (informal), marvellous, out-of-this-world (informal), sensational (informal), spectacular, superb 2 <u>astounding</u>, amazing, breathtaking, inconceivable, incredible, phenomenal, unbelievable 3 <u>legendary</u>, apocryphal, fantastic, fictitious, imaginary, invented, made-up, mythical, unreal

façade noun <u>appearance</u>, exterior, face, front, guise, mask, pretence, semblance, show

face noun 1 <u>countenance</u>, features, mug (slang), visage 2 <u>expression</u>, appearance, aspect, look 3 <u>scowl</u>, frown, grimace, pout, smirk 4 <u>façade</u>, appearance, display, exterior, front, mask, show 5 <u>side</u>, exterior, front, outside, surface 6 <u>self-respect</u>, authority, dignity, honour, image, prestige, reputation, standing, status

◆ verb 7 <u>meet</u>, brave, come up against, confront, deal with, encounter, experience, oppose, tackle 8 <u>look onto</u>, be opposite, front onto, overlook 9 <u>coat</u>, clad, cover, dress, finish

faceless adjective <u>impersonal</u>, anonymous, remote

facet noun <u>aspect</u>, angle, face, part, phase, plane, side, slant, surface

facetious adjective <u>funny</u>, amusing, comical, droll, flippant, frivolous, humorous, jocular, playful, tongue in cheek

face up to verb <u>accept</u>, acknowledge, come to terms with, confront, cope with, deal with, meet head-on, tackle

facile adjective <u>superficial</u>, cursory, glib, hasty, shallow, slick

facilitate verb <u>promote</u>, expedite, forward, further, help, make easy, pave the way for, speed up

facility noun 1 <u>skill</u>, ability, adroitness, dexterity, ease, efficiency, effortlessness, fluency, proficiency 2 often plural <u>equipment</u>, advantage, aid, amenity, appliance, convenience, means, opportunity, resource

facsimile noun <u>copy</u>, carbon copy, duplicate, fax, photocopy, print, replica, reproduction, transcript

fact noun 1 <u>event</u>, act, deed, fait accompli, happening, incident, occurrence, performance 2 <u>truth</u>, certainty, reality

faction noun 1 <u>group</u>, bloc, cabal, clique, contingent, coterie, gang, party, set, splinter group 2 <u>dissension</u>, conflict, disagreement, discord, disunity, division, infighting, rebellion

factor noun <u>element</u>, aspect, cause, component, consideration, influence, item, part

factory noun <u>works</u>, mill, plant

factual adjective <u>true</u>, authentic, correct, exact, genuine, precise, real, true-to-life

faculties plural noun <u>powers</u>, capabilities, intelligence, reason, senses, wits

faculty noun 1 <u>ability</u>, aptitude, capacity, facility, power, propensity, skill 2 <u>department</u>, school

fad noun <u>craze</u>, fashion, mania, rage, trend, vogue, whim

fade verb 1 <u>pale</u>, bleach, discolour, lose colour, wash out 2 <u>dwindle</u>, decline, die away, disappear, dissolve, melt away, vanish, wane

faded adjective <u>discoloured</u>, bleached, dull, indistinct, pale, washed out

fading adjective <u>declining</u>, decreasing, disappearing, dying, on the decline, vanishing

fail verb 1 <u>be unsuccessful</u>, bite the dust, break down, come to grief, come unstuck, fall, fizzle out (informal), flop (informal), founder, miscarry, misfire 2 <u>disappoint</u>, abandon, desert, forget, forsake, let down, neglect, omit 3 <u>give out</u>, conk out (informal), cut out, die, peter out, stop working 4 <u>go bankrupt</u>, become insolvent, close down, fold (informal), go

broke (informal), go bust (informal), go into receivership, go out of business, go to the wall, go under ♦ noun 5 **without fail** <u>regularly</u>, conscientiously, constantly, dependably, like clockwork, punctually, religiously, without exception

failing noun 1 <u>weakness</u>, blemish, defect, deficiency, drawback, fault, flaw, imperfection, shortcoming ♦ preposition 2 <u>in the absence of</u>, in default of, lacking

failure noun 1 <u>defeat</u>, breakdown, collapse, downfall, fiasco, lack of success, miscarriage, overthrow 2 <u>loser</u>, black sheep, dead duck (slang), disappointment, dud (informal), flop (informal), nonstarter, washout (informal) 3 <u>bankruptcy</u>, crash, downfall, insolvency, liquidation, ruin

faint adjective 1 <u>dim</u>, distant, faded, indistinct, low, muted, soft, subdued, vague 2 <u>slight</u>, feeble, remote, unenthusiastic, weak 3 <u>dizzy</u>, exhausted, giddy, light-headed, muzzy, weak, woozy (informal) ♦ verb 4 <u>pass out</u>, black out, collapse, flake out (informal), keel over (informal), lose consciousness, swoon (literary) ♦ noun 5 <u>blackout</u>, collapse, swoon (literary), unconsciousness

faintly adverb 1 <u>softly</u>, feebly, in a whisper, indistinctly, weakly 2 <u>slightly</u>, a little, dimly, somewhat

fair[1] adjective 1 <u>unbiased</u>, above board, equitable, even-handed, honest, impartial, just, lawful,

legitimate, proper, unprejudiced
2 <u>light</u>, blond, blonde,
fair-haired, flaxen-haired,
towheaded **3** <u>respectable</u>,
adequate, average, decent,
moderate, O.K. or okay
(*informal*), passable, reasonable,
satisfactory, tolerable **4** <u>beautiful</u>,
bonny, comely, handsome,
lovely, pretty **5** <u>fine</u>, bright,
clear, cloudless, dry, sunny,
unclouded

fair² noun <u>carnival</u>, bazaar,
festival, fête, gala, show

fairly adverb **1** <u>moderately</u>,
adequately, pretty well, quite,
rather, reasonably, somewhat,
tolerably **2** <u>deservedly</u>, equitably,
honestly, impartially, justly,
objectively, properly, without
fear or favour **3** <u>positively</u>,
absolutely, really

fairness noun <u>impartiality</u>,
decency, disinterestedness,
equitableness, equity, justice,
legitimacy, rightfulness

fairy noun <u>sprite</u>, brownie, elf,
leprechaun, peri, pixie, Robin
Goodfellow

fairy tale or **fairy story** noun
1 <u>folk tale</u>, romance **2** <u>lie</u>,
cock-and-bull story (*informal*),
fabrication, fiction, invention, tall
story, untruth

faith noun **1** <u>confidence</u>,
assurance, conviction, credence,
credit, dependence, reliance,
trust **2** <u>religion</u>, belief, church,
communion, creed,
denomination, dogma,
persuasion **3** <u>allegiance</u>,
constancy, faithfulness, fidelity,
loyalty

faithful adjective **1** <u>loyal</u>,

constant, dependable, devoted,
reliable, staunch, steadfast, true,
trusty **2** <u>accurate</u>, close, exact,
precise, strict, true

faithless adjective <u>disloyal</u>, false,
fickle, inconstant, traitorous,
treacherous, unfaithful, unreliable

fake verb **1** <u>forge</u>, copy,
counterfeit, fabricate, feign,
pretend, put on, sham, simulate
♦ noun **2** <u>impostor</u>, charlatan,
copy, forgery, fraud, hoax,
imitation, reproduction, sham
♦ adjective **3** <u>artificial</u>, counterfeit,
false, forged, imitation, mock,
phoney or phony (*informal*), sham

fall verb **1** <u>descend</u>, cascade,
collapse, dive, drop, plummet,
plunge, sink, subside, tumble
2 <u>decrease</u>, decline, diminish,
drop, dwindle, go down, lessen,
slump, subside **3** <u>be overthrown</u>,
capitulate, pass into enemy
hands, succumb, surrender
4 <u>die</u>, be killed, meet one's end,
perish **5** <u>occur</u>, befall, chance,
come about, come to pass,
happen, take place **6** <u>slope</u>, fall
away, incline **7** <u>lapse</u>, err, go
astray, offend, sin, transgress,
trespass ♦ noun **8** <u>descent</u>, dive,
drop, nose dive, plummet,
plunge, slip, tumble **9** <u>decrease</u>,
cut, decline, dip, drop,
lessening, lowering, reduction,
slump **10** <u>collapse</u>, capitulation,
defeat, destruction, downfall,
overthrow, ruin **11** <u>lapse</u>, sin,
transgression

fallacy noun <u>error</u>, delusion,
falsehood, flaw,
misapprehension,
misconception, mistake, untruth

fallible adjective <u>imperfect</u>, erring,

frail, ignorant, uncertain, weak

fall out verb <u>argue</u>, clash, come to blows, differ, disagree, fight, quarrel, squabble

fallow adjective <u>uncultivated</u>, dormant, idle, inactive, resting, unplanted, unused

false adjective 1 <u>incorrect</u>, erroneous, faulty, inaccurate, inexact, invalid, mistaken, wrong 2 <u>untrue</u>, lying, unreliable, unsound, untruthful 3 <u>artificial</u>, bogus, counterfeit, fake, forged, imitation, sham, simulated 4 <u>deceptive</u>, deceitful, fallacious, fraudulent, hypocritical, misleading, trumped up

falsehood noun 1 <u>untruthfulness</u>, deceit, deception, dishonesty, dissimulation, mendacity 2 <u>lie</u>, fabrication, fib, fiction, story, untruth

falsify verb <u>forge</u>, alter, counterfeit, distort, doctor, fake, misrepresent, tamper with

falter verb <u>hesitate</u>, stammer, stumble, stutter, totter, vacillate, waver

faltering adjective <u>hesitant</u>, broken, irresolute, stammering, tentative, timid, uncertain, weak

fame noun <u>prominence</u>, celebrity, glory, honour, renown, reputation, repute, stardom

familiar adjective 1 <u>well-known</u>, accustomed, common, customary, frequent, ordinary, recognizable, routine 2 <u>friendly</u>, amicable, close, easy, intimate, relaxed 3 <u>disrespectful</u>, bold, forward, impudent, intrusive, presumptuous

familiarity noun 1 <u>acquaintance</u>, awareness, experience, grasp, understanding 2 <u>friendliness</u>, ease, informality, intimacy, openness, sociability 3 <u>disrespect</u>, boldness, forwardness, presumption

familiarize verb <u>accustom</u>, habituate, instruct, inure, school, season, train

family noun 1 <u>relations</u>, folk (informal), household, kin, kith and kin, one's nearest and dearest, one's own flesh and blood, relatives 2 <u>clan</u>, dynasty, house, race, tribe 3 <u>group</u>, class, genre, network, subdivision, system

famine noun <u>hunger</u>, dearth, scarcity, starvation

famished adjective <u>starving</u>, ravenous, voracious

famous adjective <u>well-known</u>, acclaimed, celebrated, distinguished, eminent, illustrious, legendary, noted, prominent, renowned

fan[1] noun 1 <u>blower</u>, air conditioner, ventilator ♦ verb 2 <u>blow</u>, air-condition, cool, refresh, ventilate

fan[2] noun <u>supporter</u>, admirer, aficionado, buff (informal), devotee, enthusiast, follower, lover

fanatic noun <u>extremist</u>, activist, bigot, militant, zealot

fanatical adjective <u>passionate</u>, bigoted, extreme, fervent, frenzied, immoderate, obsessive, overenthusiastic, wild, zealous

fanciful adjective <u>unreal</u>, imaginary, mythical, romantic, visionary, whimsical, wild

fancy *adjective* **1** <u>elaborate</u>, baroque, decorative, embellished, extravagant, intricate, ornamental, ornate ♦ *noun* **2** <u>whim</u>, caprice, desire, humour, idea, impulse, inclination, notion, thought, urge **3** <u>delusion</u>, chimera, daydream, dream, fantasy, vision ♦ *verb* **4** <u>suppose</u>, believe, conjecture, imagine, reckon, think, think likely **5** <u>wish for</u>, crave, desire, hanker after, hope for, long for, thirst for, yearn for **6** *Informal* <u>be attracted to</u>, be captivated by, like, lust after, take a liking to, take to

fantasize *verb* <u>daydream</u>, dream, envision, imagine

fantastic *adjective* **1** *Informal* <u>excellent</u>, awesome (*slang*), first-rate, marvellous, sensational (*informal*), superb, wonderful **2** <u>strange</u>, fanciful, grotesque, outlandish **3** <u>unrealistic</u>, extravagant, far-fetched, ludicrous, ridiculous, wild **4** <u>implausible</u>, absurd, cock-and-bull (*informal*), incredible, preposterous, unlikely

fantasy *noun* **1** <u>imagination</u>, creativity, fancy, invention, originality **2** <u>daydream</u>, dream, flight of fancy, illusion, mirage, pipe dream, reverie, vision

far *adverb* **1** <u>a long way</u>, afar, a good way, a great distance, deep, miles **2** <u>much</u>, considerably, decidedly, extremely, greatly, incomparably, very much ♦ *adjective* **3** <u>remote</u>, distant, faraway, far-flung, far-off, outlying, out-of-the-way

farce *noun* **1** <u>comedy</u>, buffoonery, burlesque, satire, slapstick **2** <u>mockery</u>, joke, nonsense, parody, sham, travesty

farcical *adjective* <u>ludicrous</u>, absurd, comic, derisory, laughable, nonsensical, preposterous, ridiculous, risible

fare *noun* **1** <u>charge</u>, price, ticket money **2** <u>food</u>, provisions, rations, sustenance, victuals ♦ *verb* **3** <u>get on</u>, do, get along, make out, manage, prosper

farewell *noun* <u>goodbye</u>, adieu, departure, leave-taking, parting, sendoff (*informal*), valediction

far-fetched *adjective* <u>unconvincing</u>, cock-and-bull (*informal*), fantastic, implausible, incredible, preposterous, unbelievable, unlikely, unrealistic

farm *noun* **1** <u>smallholding</u>, croft (*Scot.*), farmstead, grange, homestead, plantation, ranch (*chiefly North American*) ♦ *verb* **2** <u>cultivate</u>, plant, work

fascinate *verb* <u>intrigue</u>, absorb, beguile, captivate, engross, enthral, entrance, hold spellbound, rivet, transfix

fascinating *adjective* <u>gripping</u>, alluring, captivating, compelling, engaging, engrossing, enticing, intriguing, irresistible, riveting

fascination *noun* <u>attraction</u>, allure, charm, enchantment, lure, magic, magnetism, pull

fashion *noun* **1** <u>style</u>, craze, custom, fad, look, mode, rage, trend, vogue **2** <u>method</u>, manner, mode, style, way ♦ *verb* **3** <u>make</u>, construct, create, forge, form, manufacture, mould, shape

fashionable adjective popular, à la mode, chic, in (informal), in vogue, modern, stylish, trendy (Brit. informal), up-to-date, with it (informal)

fast¹ adjective 1 quick, brisk, fleet, flying, hasty, nippy (Brit. informal), rapid, speedy, swift 2 fixed, close, fastened, firm, immovable, secure, sound, steadfast, tight 3 dissipated, dissolute, extravagant, loose, profligate, reckless, self-indulgent, wanton, wild ♦ adverb 4 quickly, hastily, hurriedly, in haste, like lightning, rapidly, speedily, swiftly 5 soundly, deeply, firmly, fixedly, securely, tightly

fast² verb 1 go hungry, abstain, deny oneself, go without food ♦ noun 2 fasting, abstinence

fasten verb fix, affix, attach, bind, connect, join, link, secure, tie

fat adjective 1 overweight, corpulent, heavy, obese, plump, podgy, portly, rotund, stout, tubby 2 fatty, adipose, greasy, oily, oleaginous ♦ noun 3 fatness, blubber, bulk, corpulence, flab, flesh, obesity, paunch

fatal adjective 1 lethal, deadly, final, incurable, killing, malignant, mortal, terminal 2 ruinous, baleful, baneful, calamitous, catastrophic, disastrous

fatality noun death, casualty, loss, mortality

fate noun 1 destiny, chance, divine will, fortune, kismet, nemesis, predestination, providence 2 fortune, cup,

horoscope, lot, portion, stars

fated adjective destined, doomed, foreordained, inescapable, inevitable, predestined, preordained, sure, written

fateful adjective 1 crucial, critical, decisive, important, portentous, significant 2 disastrous, deadly, destructive, fatal, lethal, ominous, ruinous

father noun 1 daddy (informal), dad (informal), old man (informal), pa (informal), papa (old-fashioned informal), pater, pop (informal) 2 forefather, ancestor, forebear, predecessor, progenitor 3 founder, architect, author, creator, inventor, maker, originator, prime mover 4 priest, padre (informal), pastor ♦ verb 5 sire, beget, get, procreate

fatherland noun homeland, motherland, native land

fatherly adjective paternal, affectionate, benevolent, benign, kindly, patriarchal, protective, supportive

fathom verb understand, comprehend, get to the bottom of, grasp, interpret

fatigue noun 1 tiredness, heaviness, languor, lethargy, listlessness ♦ verb 2 tire, drain, exhaust, knacker (slang), take it out of (informal), weaken, wear out, weary

fatten verb 1 grow fat, expand, gain weight, put on weight, spread, swell, thicken 2 often with up feed up, build up, feed, nourish, overfeed, stuff

fatty adjective greasy, adipose, fat, oily, oleaginous, rich

fatuous *adjective* <u>foolish</u>, brainless, idiotic, inane, ludicrous, mindless, moronic, silly, stupid, witless

fault *noun* **1** <u>flaw</u>, blemish, defect, deficiency, failing, imperfection, shortcoming, weakness, weak point **2** <u>mistake</u>, blunder, error, indiscretion, lapse, oversight, slip **3** <u>responsibility</u>, accountability, culpability, liability **4 at fault** <u>guilty</u>, answerable, blamable, culpable, in the wrong, responsible, to blame **5 find fault with** <u>criticize</u>, carp at, complain, pick holes in, pull to pieces, quibble, take to task **6 to a fault** <u>excessively</u>, immoderately, in the extreme, overmuch, unduly ♦ *verb* **7** <u>criticize</u>, blame, censure, find fault with, hold (someone) responsible, impugn

faultless *adjective* <u>flawless</u>, correct, exemplary, foolproof, impeccable, model, perfect, unblemished

faulty *adjective* <u>defective</u>, broken, damaged, flawed, impaired, imperfect, incorrect, malfunctioning, out of order, unsound

favour *noun* **1** <u>approval</u>, approbation, backing, good opinion, goodwill, patronage, support **2** <u>good turn</u>, benefit, boon, courtesy, indulgence, kindness, service ♦ *verb* **3** <u>side with</u>, indulge, reward, smile upon **4** <u>advocate</u>, approve, champion, commend, encourage, incline towards, prefer, support

favourable *adjective* **1** <u>advantageous</u>, auspicious, beneficial, encouraging, helpful, opportune, promising, propitious, suitable **2** <u>positive</u>, affirmative, agreeable, approving, encouraging, enthusiastic, reassuring, sympathetic

favourably *adverb* **1** <u>advantageously</u>, auspiciously, conveniently, fortunately, opportunely, profitably, to one's advantage, well **2** <u>positively</u>, approvingly, enthusiastically, helpfully, with approval

favourite *adjective* **1** <u>preferred</u>, best-loved, choice, dearest, esteemed, favoured ♦ *noun* **2** <u>darling</u>, beloved, blue-eyed boy (*informal*), idol, pet, teacher's pet, the apple of one's eye

fawn[1] *verb, often with* **on** *or* **upon** <u>curry favour</u>, crawl, creep, cringe, dance attendance, flatter, grovel, ingratiate oneself, kowtow, pander to

fawn[2] *adjective* <u>beige</u>, buff, greyish-brown, neutral

fawning *adjective* <u>obsequious</u>, crawling, cringing, deferential, flattering, grovelling, servile, sycophantic

fear *noun* **1** <u>alarm</u>, apprehensiveness, dread, fright, horror, panic, terror, trepidation **2** <u>bugbear</u>, bête noire, bogey, horror, nightmare, spectre ♦ *verb* **3** <u>be afraid</u>, dread, shake in one's shoes, shudder at, take fright, tremble at **4 fear for** <u>worry about</u>, be anxious about, feel concern for

fearful *adjective* **1** <u>scared</u>, afraid, alarmed, frightened, jumpy, nervous, timid, timorous, uneasy **2** <u>frightful</u>, awful, dire, dreadful, gruesome, hair-raising, horrendous, horrific, terrible

fearfully *adverb* **1** <u>nervously</u>, apprehensively, diffidently, timidly, timorously, uneasily **2** <u>very</u>, awfully, exceedingly, excessively, frightfully, terribly, tremendously

fearless *adjective* <u>brave</u>, bold, courageous, dauntless, indomitable, intrepid, plucky, unafraid, undaunted, valiant

fearsome *adjective* <u>terrifying</u>, awe-inspiring, daunting, formidable, frightening, horrifying, menacing, unnerving

feasible *adjective* <u>possible</u>, achievable, attainable, likely, practicable, reasonable, viable, workable

feast *noun* **1** <u>banquet</u>, dinner, repast, spread (*informal*), treat **2** <u>festival</u>, celebration, fête, holiday, holy day, red-letter day, saint's day **3** <u>treat</u>, delight, enjoyment, gratification, pleasure ♦ *verb* **4** <u>eat one's fill</u>, gorge, gormandize, indulge, overindulge, pig out (*slang*), wine and dine

feat *noun* <u>accomplishment</u>, achievement, act, attainment, deed, exploit, performance

feathers *plural noun* <u>plumage</u>, down, plumes

feature *noun* **1** <u>aspect</u>, characteristic, facet, factor, hallmark, peculiarity, property, quality, trait **2** <u>highlight</u>, attraction, main item, speciality

3 <u>article</u>, column, item, piece, report, story ♦ *verb* **4** <u>spotlight</u>, emphasize, foreground, give prominence to, play up, present, star

features *plural noun* <u>face</u>, countenance, lineaments, physiognomy

feckless *adjective* <u>irresponsible</u>, good-for-nothing, hopeless, incompetent, ineffectual, shiftless, worthless

federation *noun* <u>union</u>, alliance, amalgamation, association, coalition, combination, league, syndicate

fed up *adjective* <u>dissatisfied</u>, bored, brassed off (*Brit. slang*), depressed, discontented, down in the mouth, glum, sick and tired (*informal*), tired

fee *noun* <u>charge</u>, bill, payment, remuneration, toll

feeble *adjective* **1** <u>weak</u>, debilitated, doddering, effete, frail, infirm, puny, sickly, weedy (*informal*) **2** <u>unconvincing</u>, flimsy, inadequate, insufficient, lame, paltry, pathetic, poor, tame, thin

feebleness *noun* <u>weakness</u>, effeteness, frailty, infirmity, languor, lassitude, sickliness

feed *verb* **1** <u>cater for</u>, nourish, provide for, provision, supply, sustain, victual, wine and dine **2** *sometimes with* **on** <u>eat</u>, devour, exist on, live on, partake of ♦ *noun* **3** <u>food</u>, fodder, pasturage, provender **4** *Informal* <u>meal</u>, feast, nosh (*slang*), repast, spread (*informal*)

feel *verb* **1** <u>touch</u>, caress, finger, fondle, handle, manipulate, paw, stroke **2** <u>experience</u>, be aware

of, notice, observe, perceive
3 <u>sense</u>, be convinced, intuit
4 <u>believe</u>, consider, deem, hold,
judge, think ◆ *noun* **5** <u>texture</u>,
finish, surface, touch
6 <u>impression</u>, air, ambience,
atmosphere, feeling, quality,
sense

feeler *noun* **1** <u>antenna</u>, tentacle,
whisker **2** <u>approach</u>, advance,
probe

feeling *noun* **1** <u>emotion</u>, ardour,
fervour, intensity, passion,
sentiment, warmth **2** <u>impression</u>,
hunch, idea, inkling, notion,
presentiment, sense, suspicion
3 <u>opinion</u>, inclination, instinct,
point of view, view **4** <u>sympathy</u>,
compassion, concern, empathy,
pity, sensibility, sensitivity,
understanding **5** <u>sense of touch</u>,
perception, sensation
6 <u>atmosphere</u>, air, ambience,
aura, feel, mood, quality

fell *verb* <u>cut down</u>, cut, demolish,
hew, knock down, level

fellow *noun* **1** <u>man</u>, bloke (*Brit.
informal*), chap (*informal*),
character, guy (*informal*),
individual, person **2** <u>associate</u>,
colleague, companion, comrade,
partner, peer

fellowship *noun* **1** <u>camaraderie</u>,
brotherhood, companionship,
sociability **2** <u>society</u>, association,
brotherhood, club, fraternity,
guild, league, order

feminine *adjective* <u>womanly</u>,
delicate, gentle, ladylike, soft,
tender

femme fatale *noun* <u>seductress</u>,
enchantress, siren, vamp
(*informal*)

fen *noun* <u>marsh</u>, bog, morass,

quagmire, slough, swamp

fence *noun* **1** <u>barrier</u>, barricade,
defence, hedge, palisade,
railings, rampart, wall ◆ *verb*
2 *often with* **in** *or* **off** <u>enclose</u>,
bound, confine, encircle, pen,
protect, surround **3** <u>evade</u>,
dodge, equivocate, flannel (*Brit.
informal*), parry

ferment *noun* <u>commotion</u>,
disruption, excitement, frenzy,
furore, stir, tumult, turmoil,
unrest, uproar

ferocious *adjective* **1** <u>fierce</u>,
predatory, rapacious, ravening,
savage, violent, wild **2** <u>cruel</u>,
bloodthirsty, brutal, ruthless,
vicious

ferocity *noun* <u>savagery</u>,
bloodthirstiness, brutality,
cruelty, fierceness, viciousness,
wildness

ferret out *verb* <u>track down</u>, dig
up, discover, elicit, root out,
search out, trace, unearth

ferry *noun* **1** <u>ferry boat</u>, packet,
packet boat ◆ *verb* **2** <u>carry</u>,
chauffeur, convey, run, ship,
shuttle, transport

fertile *adjective* <u>rich</u>, abundant,
fecund, fruitful, luxuriant,
plentiful, productive, prolific,
teeming

fertility *noun* <u>fruitfulness</u>,
abundance, fecundity,
luxuriance, productiveness,
richness

fertilizer *noun* <u>compost</u>,
dressing, dung, manure

fervent, fervid *adjective* <u>ardent</u>,
devout, earnest, enthusiastic,
heartfelt, impassioned, intense,
vehement

fervour *noun* <u>intensity</u>, ardour, enthusiasm, excitement, passion, vehemence, warmth, zeal

fester *verb* **1** <u>decay</u>, putrefy, suppurate, ulcerate **2** <u>intensify</u>, aggravate, smoulder

festival *noun* **1** <u>celebration</u>, carnival, entertainment, fête, gala, jubilee **2** <u>holy day</u>, anniversary, commemoration, feast, fête, fiesta, holiday, red-letter day, saint's day

festive *adjective* <u>celebratory</u>, cheery, convivial, happy, jovial, joyful, joyous, jubilant, merry

festivity *noun, often plural* <u>celebration</u>, entertainment, festival, party

festoon *verb* <u>decorate</u>, array, deck, drape, garland, hang, swathe, wreathe

fetch *verb* **1** <u>bring</u>, carry, convey, deliver, get, go for, obtain, retrieve, transport **2** <u>sell for</u>, bring in, earn, go for, make, realize, yield

fetching *adjective* <u>attractive</u>, alluring, captivating, charming, cute, enticing, winsome

fetish *noun* **1** <u>fixation</u>, mania, obsession, thing *(informal)* **2** <u>talisman</u>, amulet

feud *noun* **1** <u>hostility</u>, argument, conflict, disagreement, enmity, quarrel, rivalry, row, vendetta ♦ *verb* **2** <u>quarrel</u>, bicker, clash, contend, dispute, fall out, row, squabble, war

fever *noun* <u>excitement</u>, agitation, delirium, ferment, fervour, frenzy, restlessness

feverish *adjective* **1** <u>hot</u>, febrile, fevered, flushed, inflamed,

pyretic *(Medical)* **2** <u>excited</u>, agitated, frantic, frenetic, frenzied, overwrought, restless

few *adjective* <u>not many</u>, meagre, negligible, rare, scanty, scarcely any, sparse, sporadic

fiasco *noun* <u>debacle</u>, catastrophe, cock-up *(Brit. slang)*, disaster, failure, mess, washout *(informal)*

fib *noun* <u>lie</u>, fiction, story, untruth, white lie

fibre *noun* **1** <u>thread</u>, filament, pile, strand, texture, wisp **2** <u>essence</u>, nature, quality, spirit, substance **3** *As in* **moral fibre** <u>resolution</u>, stamina, strength, toughness

fickle *adjective* <u>changeable</u>, capricious, faithless, inconstant, irresolute, temperamental, unfaithful, variable, volatile

fiction *noun* **1** <u>tale</u>, fantasy, legend, myth, novel, romance, story, yarn *(informal)* **2** <u>lie</u>, cock and bull story *(informal)*, fabrication, falsehood, invention, tall story, untruth, urban legend

fictional *adjective* <u>imaginary</u>, invented, legendary, made-up, nonexistent, unreal

fictitious *adjective* <u>false</u>, bogus, fabricated, imaginary, invented, made-up, make-believe, mythical, untrue

fiddle *verb* **1** <u>fidget</u>, finger, interfere with, mess about *or* around, play, tamper with, tinker **2** *Informal* <u>cheat</u>, cook the books *(informal)*, diddle *(informal)*, fix, swindle, wangle *(informal)* ♦ *noun* **3** <u>violin</u> **4** *Informal* <u>fraud</u>, fix, racket, scam *(slang)*, swindle **5** **fit as a fiddle** <u>healthy</u>, bloomir•g, hale and hearty, in fine fettle, in good form, in good shape, in rude health, in the pink, sound, strong

fiddling *adjective* trivial, futile, insignificant, pettifogging, petty, trifling

fidelity *noun* 1 loyalty, allegiance, constancy, dependability, devotion, faithfulness, staunchness, trustworthiness 2 accuracy, closeness, correspondence, exactness, faithfulness, precision, scrupulousness

fidget *verb* 1 move restlessly, fiddle (*informal*), fret, squirm, twitch ♦ *noun* 2 **the fidgets** restlessness, fidgetiness, jitters (*informal*), nervousness, unease, uneasiness

fidgety *adjective* restless, impatient, jittery (*informal*), jumpy, nervous, on edge, restive, twitchy (*informal*), uneasy

field *noun* 1 meadow, grassland, green, lea (*poetic*), pasture 2 competitors, applicants, candidates, competition, contestants, entrants, possibilities, runners 3 speciality, area, department, discipline, domain, line, province, territory ♦ *verb* 4 retrieve, catch, pick up, return, stop 5 deal with, deflect, handle, turn aside

fiend *noun* 1 demon, devil, evil spirit 2 brute, barbarian, beast, ghoul, monster, ogre, savage 3 *Informal* enthusiast, addict, fanatic, freak (*informal*), maniac

fiendish *adjective* wicked, cruel, devilish, diabolical, hellish, infernal, malignant, monstrous, satanic, unspeakable

fierce *adjective* 1 wild, brutal, cruel, dangerous, ferocious, fiery, menacing, savage, vicious 2 strong, furious, howling, inclement, powerful, raging, stormy, tempestuous, violent 3 intense, cut-throat, keen, relentless, strong

fiercely *adverb* ferociously, furiously, passionately, savagely, tempestuously, tigerishly, tooth and nail, viciously, with no holds barred

fiery *adjective* 1 burning, ablaze, afire, aflame, blazing, flaming, on fire 2 excitable, fierce, hot-headed, impetuous, irascible, irritable, passionate

fight *verb* 1 battle, box, clash, combat, do battle, grapple, spar, struggle, tussle, wrestle 2 oppose, contest, defy, dispute, make a stand against, resist, stand up to, withstand 3 engage in, carry on, conduct, prosecute, wage ♦ *noun* 4 conflict, battle, clash, contest, dispute, duel, encounter, struggle, tussle 5 resistance, belligerence, militancy, pluck, spirit

fighter *noun* 1 soldier, fighting man, man-at-arms, warrior 2 boxer, prize fighter, pugilist

fight off *verb* repel, beat off, keep *or* hold at bay, repress, repulse, resist, stave off, ward off

figure *noun* 1 number, character, digit, numeral, symbol 2 amount, cost, price, sum, total, value 3 shape, body, build, frame, physique, proportions 4 diagram, design, drawing, illustration, pattern, representation, sketch

5 <u>character</u>, big name, celebrity, dignitary, personality ♦ *verb*
6 <u>calculate</u>, compute, count, reckon, tally, tot up, work out
7 *usually with* **in** <u>feature</u>, act, appear, be featured, contribute to, play a part

figurehead *noun* <u>front man</u>, mouthpiece, puppet, titular *or* nominal head

figure out *verb* **1** <u>calculate</u>, compute, reckon, work out **2** <u>understand</u>, comprehend, decipher, fathom, make out, see

filch *verb* <u>steal</u>, embezzle, misappropriate, pilfer, pinch (*informal*), take, thieve, walk off with

file¹ *noun* **1** <u>folder</u>, case, data, documents, dossier, information, portfolio **2** <u>line</u>, column, queue, row ♦ *verb* **3** <u>register</u>, document, enter, pigeonhole, put in place, record **4** <u>march</u>, parade, troop

file² *verb* <u>smooth</u>, abrade, polish, rasp, rub, scrape, shape

fill *verb* **1** <u>stuff</u>, cram, crowd, glut, pack, stock, supply, swell **2** <u>saturate</u>, charge, imbue, impregnate, pervade, suffuse **3** <u>plug</u>, block, bung, close, cork, seal, stop **4** <u>perform</u>, carry out, discharge, execute, fulfil, hold, occupy ♦ *noun* **5** **one's fill** <u>sufficient</u>, all one wants, ample, enough, plenty

filler *noun* <u>padding</u>, makeweight, stopgap

fill in *verb* **1** <u>complete</u>, answer, fill out (*U.S.*), fill up **2** *Informal* <u>inform</u>, acquaint, apprise, bring up to date, give the facts *or* background **3** <u>replace</u>, deputize, represent, stand in, sub,

substitute, take the place of

filling *noun* **1** <u>stuffing</u>, contents, filler, inside, insides, padding, wadding ♦ *adjective* **2** <u>satisfying</u>, ample, heavy, square, substantial

film *noun* **1** <u>movie</u>, flick (*slang*), motion picture **2** <u>layer</u>, coating, covering, dusting, membrane, skin, tissue ♦ *verb* **3** <u>photograph</u>, shoot, take, video, videotape

filter *noun* **1** <u>sieve</u>, gauze, membrane, mesh, riddle, strainer ♦ *verb* **2** <u>purify</u>, clarify, filtrate, refine, screen, sieve, sift, strain, winnow **3** <u>trickle</u>, dribble, escape, exude, leak, ooze, penetrate, percolate, seep

filth *noun* **1** <u>dirt</u>, excrement, grime, muck, refuse, sewage, slime, sludge, squalor **2** <u>obscenity</u>, impurity, indecency, pornography, smut, vulgarity

filthy *adjective* **1** <u>dirty</u>, foul, polluted, putrid, slimy, squalid, unclean **2** <u>muddy</u>, begrimed, blackened, grimy, grubby **3** <u>obscene</u>, corrupt, depraved, impure, indecent, lewd, licentious, pornographic, smutty

final *adjective* **1** <u>last</u>, closing, concluding, latest, terminal, ultimate **2** <u>definitive</u>, absolute, conclusive, decided, definite, incontrovertible, irrevocable, settled

finale *noun* <u>ending</u>, climax, close, conclusion, culmination, denouement, epilogue

finalize *verb* <u>complete</u>, clinch, conclude, decide, settle, tie up, work out, wrap up (*informal*)

finally *adverb* **1** <u>eventually</u>, at last, at length, at long last, in the end, lastly, ultimately **2** **in**

conclusion, in summary, to conclude

finance noun **1** economics, accounts, banking, business, commerce, investment, money ♦ verb **2** fund, back, bankroll (U.S.), guarantee, pay for, subsidize, support, underwrite

finances plural noun resources, affairs, assets, capital, cash, funds, money, wherewithal

financial adjective economic, fiscal, monetary, pecuniary

find verb **1** discover, come across, encounter, hit upon, locate, meet, recognize, spot, uncover **2** perceive, detect, discover, learn, note, notice, observe, realise ♦ noun **3** discovery, acquisition, asset, bargain, catch, good buy

find out verb **1** learn, detect, discover, note, observe, perceive, realize **2** detect, catch, disclose, expose, reveal, uncover, unmask

fine¹ adjective **1** excellent, accomplished, exceptional, exquisite, first-rate, magnificent, masterly, outstanding, splendid, superior **2** sunny, balmy, bright, clear, clement, cloudless, dry, fair, pleasant **3** satisfactory, acceptable, all right, convenient, good, O.K. or okay (informal), suitable **4** delicate, dainty, elegant, expensive, exquisite, fragile, quality **5** subtle, abstruse, acute, hairsplitting, minute, nice, precise, sharp **6** slender, diaphanous, flimsy, gauzy, gossamer, light, sheer, thin

fine² noun **1** penalty, damages, forfeit, punishment ♦ verb **2** penalize, mulct, punish

finery noun splendour, frippery, gear (informal), glad rags (informal), ornaments, showiness, Sunday best, trappings, trinkets

finesse noun skill, adeptness, adroitness, craft, delicacy, diplomacy, discretion, savoir-faire, sophistication, subtlety, tact

finger verb touch, feel, fiddle with (informal), handle, manipulate, maul, paw (informal), toy with

finish verb **1** stop, cease, close, complete, conclude, end, round off, terminate, wind up, wrap up (informal) **2** consume, devour, dispose of, eat, empty, exhaust, use up **3** destroy, bring down, defeat, dispose of, exterminate, overcome, put an end to, put paid to, rout, ruin **4** perfect, polish, refine **5** coat, gild, lacquer, polish, stain, texture, veneer, wax ♦ noun **6** end, cessation, close, completion, conclusion, culmination, denouement, finale, run-in **7** defeat, annihilation, curtains (informal), death, end, end of the road, ruin **8** surface, lustre, patina, polish, shine, smoothness, texture

finished adjective **1** polished, accomplished, perfected, professional, refined **2** over, closed, complete, done, ended, finalized, through **3** spent, done, drained, empty, exhausted, used up **4** ruined, defeated, done for (informal), doomed, lost, through, undone, wiped out

finite adjective limited, bounded, circumscribed, delimited, demarcated, restricted

fire noun **1** flames, blaze, combustion, conflagration, inferno **2** bombardment, barrage, cannonade, flak, fusillade, hail, salvo, shelling, sniping, volley **3** passion, ardour, eagerness, enthusiasm, excitement, fervour, intensity, sparkle, spirit, verve, vigour ♦ verb **4** shoot, detonate, discharge, explode, let off, pull the trigger, set off, shell **5** inspire, animate, enliven, excite, galvanize, impassion, inflame, rouse, stir **6** Informal dismiss, cashier, discharge, make redundant, sack (informal), show the door

firebrand noun rabble-rouser, agitator, demagogue, incendiary, instigator, tub-thumper

fireworks plural noun **1** pyrotechnics, illuminations **2** rage, hysterics, row, storm, trouble, uproar

firm[1] adjective **1** hard, dense, inflexible, rigid, set, solid, solidified, stiff, unyielding **2** secure, embedded, fast, fixed, immovable, rooted, stable, steady, tight, unshakable **3** definite, adamant, inflexible, resolute, resolved, set on, unbending, unshakable, unyielding

firm[2] noun company, association, business, concern, conglomerate, corporation, enterprise, organization, partnership

firmly adverb **1** securely, immovably, like a rock, steadily, tightly, unflinchingly, unshakably **2** resolutely, staunchly, steadfastly, unchangeably, unwaveringly

firmness noun **1** hardness, inelasticity, inflexibility, resistance, rigidity, solidity, stiffness **2** resolve, constancy, inflexibility, resolution, staunchness, steadfastness

first adjective **1** foremost, chief, head, highest, leading, pre-eminent, prime, principal, ruling **2** earliest, initial, introductory, maiden, opening, original, premier, primordial **3** elementary, basic, cardinal, fundamental, key, primary, rudimentary ♦ noun **4** As in **from the first** start, beginning, commencement, inception, introduction, outset, starting point ♦ adverb **5** beforehand, at the beginning, at the outset, firstly, initially, in the first place, to begin with, to start with

first-rate adjective excellent, crack (slang), elite, exceptional, first class, outstanding, superb, superlative, top-notch (Informal), world-class

fishy adjective **1** Informal suspicious, dodgy (Brit., Austral., & N.Z. informal), dubious, funny (informal), implausible, odd, questionable, suspect, unlikely **2** fishlike, piscatorial, piscatory, piscine

fissure noun crack, breach, cleft, crevice, fault, fracture, opening, rift, rupture, split

fit[1] verb **1** match, accord, belong, conform, correspond, meet, suit, tally **2** prepare, arm, equip, fit out, kit out, provide **3** adapt, adjust, alter, arrange, customize,

modify, shape, tweak (*informal*)
♦ *adjective* 4 <u>appropriate</u>, apt, becoming, correct, fitting, proper, right, seemly, suitable 5 <u>healthy</u>, able-bodied, hale, in good shape, robust, strapping, trim, well

fit² *noun* 1 <u>seizure</u>, attack, bout, convulsion, paroxysm, spasm 2 <u>outbreak</u>, bout, burst, outburst, spell

fitful *adjective* <u>irregular</u>, broken, desultory, disturbed, inconstant, intermittent, spasmodic, sporadic, uneven

fitness *noun* 1 <u>appropriateness</u>, aptness, competence, eligibility, propriety, readiness, suitability 2 <u>health</u>, good condition, good health, robustness, strength, vigour

fitting *adjective* 1 <u>appropriate</u>, apposite, becoming, correct, decent, proper, right, seemly, suitable ♦ *noun* 2 <u>accessory</u>, attachment, component, part, piece, unit

fix *verb* 1 <u>place</u>, embed, establish, implant, install, locate, plant, position, set 2 <u>fasten</u>, attach, bind, connect, link, secure, stick, tie 3 <u>decide</u>, agree on, arrange, arrive at, determine, establish, set, settle, specify 4 <u>repair</u>, correct, mend, patch up, put to rights, see to 5 <u>focus</u>, direct 6 *Informal* <u>manipulate</u>, fiddle (*informal*), influence, rig ♦ *noun* 7 *Informal* <u>predicament</u>, difficulty, dilemma, embarrassment, mess, pickle (*informal*), plight, quandary

fixation *noun* <u>preoccupation</u>, complex, hang-up (*informal*), idée

fixe, infatuation, mania, obsession, thing (*informal*)

fixed *adjective* 1 <u>permanent</u>, established, immovable, rigid, rooted, secure, set 2 <u>intent</u>, resolute, steady, unwavering 3 <u>agreed</u>, arranged, decided, definite, established, planned, resolved, settled

fix up *verb* 1 <u>arrange</u>, agree on, fix, organize, plan, settle, sort out 2 *often with* **with** <u>provide</u>, arrange for, bring about, lay on

fizz *verb* <u>bubble</u>, effervesce, fizzle, froth, hiss, sparkle, sputter

fizzy *adjective* <u>bubbly</u>, bubbling, carbonated, effervescent, gassy, sparkling

flabbergasted *adjective* <u>astonished</u>, amazed, astounded, dumbfounded, lost for words, overwhelmed, speechless, staggered, stunned

flabby *adjective* <u>limp</u>, baggy, drooping, flaccid, floppy, loose, pendulous, sagging

flag¹ *noun* 1 <u>banner</u>, colours, ensign, pennant, pennon, standard, streamer ♦ *verb* 2 <u>mark</u>, indicate, label, note 3 *sometimes with* **down** <u>hail</u>, signal, warn, wave

flag² *verb* <u>weaken</u>, abate, droop, fade, languish, peter out, sag, wane, weary, wilt

flagging *adjective* <u>fading</u>, declining, deteriorating, faltering, waning, weakening, wilting

flagrant *adjective* <u>outrageous</u>, barefaced, blatant, brazen, glaring, heinous, scandalous, shameless

flagstone *noun* <u>paving stone</u>, block, flag, slab

flail *verb* <u>thrash</u>, beat, thresh, windmill

flair *noun* 1 <u>ability</u>, aptitude, faculty, feel, genius, gift, knack, mastery, talent 2 <u>style</u>, chic, dash, discernment, elegance, panache, stylishness, taste

flake *noun* 1 <u>wafer</u>, layer, peeling, scale, shaving, sliver ♦ *verb* 2 <u>blister</u>, chip, peel (off)

flake out *verb* <u>collapse</u>, faint, keel over, pass out

flamboyant *adjective* 1 <u>extravagant</u>, dashing, elaborate, florid, ornate, ostentatious, showy, swashbuckling, theatrical 2 <u>colourful</u>, brilliant, dazzling, glamorous, glitzy (*slang*)

flame *noun* 1 <u>fire</u>, blaze, brightness, light 2 *Informal* <u>sweetheart</u>, beau, boyfriend, girlfriend, heart-throb (*Brit.*), lover ♦ *verb* 3 <u>burn</u>, blaze, flare, flash, glare, glow, shine

flaming *adjective* <u>burning</u>, ablaze, blazing, fiery, glowing, raging, red-hot

flank *noun* 1 <u>side</u>, hip, loin, thigh 2 <u>wing</u>, side

flap *verb* 1 <u>flutter</u>, beat, flail, shake, thrash, vibrate, wag, wave ♦ *noun* 2 <u>flutter</u>, beating, shaking, swinging, swish, waving 3 *Informal* <u>panic</u>, agitation, commotion, fluster, state (*informal*), sweat (*informal*), tizzy (*informal*)

flare *verb* 1 <u>blaze</u>, burn up, flicker, glare 2 <u>widen</u>, broaden, spread out ♦ *noun* 3 <u>flame</u>, blaze, burst, flash, flicker, glare

flare up *verb* <u>lose one's temper</u>, blow one's top (*informal*), boil over, explode, fly off the handle (*informal*), throw a tantrum

flash *noun* 1 <u>blaze</u>, burst, dazzle, flare, flicker, gleam, shimmer, spark, streak 2 <u>moment</u>, instant, jiffy (*informal*), second, split second, trice, twinkling of an eye ♦ *adjective* 3 *Informal* <u>ostentatious</u>, tacky (*informal*), tasteless, vulgar ♦ *verb* 4 <u>blaze</u>, flare, flicker, glare, gleam, shimmer, sparkle, twinkle 5 <u>speed</u>, dart, dash, fly, race, shoot, streak, whistle, zoom 6 <u>show</u>, display, exhibit, expose, flaunt, flourish

flashy *adjective* <u>showy</u>, flamboyant, garish, gaudy, glitzy (*slang*), jazzy (*informal*), ostentatious, snazzy (*informal*)

flat¹ *adjective* 1 <u>even</u>, horizontal, level, levelled, low, smooth 2 <u>dull</u>, boring, dead, lacklustre, lifeless, monotonous, tedious, tiresome, uninteresting 3 <u>absolute</u>, categorical, downright, explicit, out-and-out, positive, unequivocal, unqualified 4 <u>punctured</u>, blown out, burst, collapsed, deflated, empty ♦ *adverb* 5 <u>completely</u>, absolutely, categorically, exactly, point blank, precisely, utterly 6 **flat out** <u>at full speed</u>, all out, at full tilt, for all one is worth, hell for leather (*informal*)

flat² *noun* <u>apartment</u>, rooms

flatly *adverb* <u>absolutely</u>, categorically, completely, positively, unhesitatingly

flatness *noun* 1 <u>evenness</u>, smoothness, uniformity

2 <u>dullness</u>, monotony, tedium

flatten *verb* <u>level</u>, compress, even out, iron out, raze, smooth off, squash, trample

flatter *verb* 1 <u>praise</u>, butter up, compliment, pander to, soft-soap (*informal*), sweet-talk (*informal*), wheedle 2 <u>suit</u>, become, do something for, enhance, set off, show to advantage

flattering *adjective* 1 <u>becoming</u>, effective, enhancing, kind, well-chosen 2 <u>ingratiating</u>, adulatory, complimentary, fawning, fulsome, laudatory

flattery *noun* <u>obsequiousness</u>, adulation, blandishment, fawning, servility, soft-soap (*informal*), sweet-talk (*informal*), sycophancy

flaunt *verb* <u>show off</u>, brandish, display, exhibit, flash about, flourish, parade, sport (*informal*)

flavour *noun* 1 <u>taste</u>, aroma, flavouring, piquancy, relish, savour, seasoning, smack, tang, zest 2 <u>quality</u>, character, essence, feel, feeling, style, tinge, tone ♦ *verb* 3 <u>season</u>, ginger up, imbue, infuse, leaven, spice

flaw *noun* <u>weakness</u>, blemish, chink in one's armour, defect, failing, fault, imperfection, weak spot

flawed *adjective* <u>damaged</u>, blemished, defective, erroneous, faulty, imperfect, unsound

flawless *adjective* <u>perfect</u>, faultless, impeccable, spotless, unblemished, unsullied

flee *verb* <u>run away</u>, bolt, depart, escape, fly, make one's getaway, scarper (*Brit. slang*), take flight, take off (*informal*), take to one's heels, turn tail

fleet *noun* <u>navy</u>, armada, flotilla, task force

fleeting *adjective* <u>momentary</u>, brief, ephemeral, passing, short-lived, temporary, transient, transitory

flesh *noun* 1 <u>meat</u>, brawn, fat, tissue, weight 2 <u>human nature</u>, carnality, flesh and blood **3 one's own flesh and blood** <u>family</u>, blood, kin, kinsfolk, kith and kin, relations, relatives

flexibility *noun* <u>adaptability</u>, adjustability, elasticity, give (*informal*), pliability, pliancy, resilience, springiness

flexible *adjective* 1 <u>pliable</u>, elastic, lithe, plastic, pliant, springy, stretchy, supple 2 <u>adaptable</u>, adjustable, discretionary, open, variable

flick *verb* 1 <u>strike</u>, dab, flip, hit, tap, touch **2 flick through** <u>browse</u>, flip through, glance at, skim, skip, thumb

flicker *verb* 1 <u>twinkle</u>, flare, flash, glimmer, gutter, shimmer, sparkle 2 <u>flutter</u>, quiver, vibrate, waver ♦ *noun* 3 <u>glimmer</u>, flare, flash, gleam, spark 4 <u>trace</u>, breath, glimmer, iota, spark

flight¹ *noun* 1 **Of air travel** <u>journey</u>, trip, voyage 2 <u>aviation</u>, aeronautics, flying 3 <u>flock</u>, cloud, formation, squadron, swarm, unit

flight² *noun* <u>escape</u>, departure, exit, exodus, fleeing, getaway, retreat, running away

flimsy *adjective* 1 <u>fragile</u>, delicate,

frail, insubstantial, makeshift, rickety, shaky **2** <u>thin</u>, gauzy, gossamer, light, sheer, transparent **3** <u>unconvincing</u>, feeble, implausible, inadequate, pathetic, poor, unsatisfactory, weak

flinch *verb* <u>recoil</u>, cower, cringe, draw back, quail, shirk, shrink, shy away, wince

fling *verb* **1** <u>throw</u>, cast, catapult, heave, hurl, propel, sling, toss ♦ *noun* **2** <u>binge</u> (*informal*), bash, good time, party, rave-up (*Brit. slang*), spree

flip *verb, noun* <u>toss</u>, flick, snap, spin, throw

flippancy *noun* <u>frivolity</u>, impertinence, irreverence, levity, pertness, sauciness

flippant *adjective* <u>frivolous</u>, cheeky, disrespectful, glib, impertinent, irreverent, offhand, superficial

flirt *verb* **1** <u>lead on</u>, chat up (*informal*), make advances, make eyes at, make sheep's eyes at, philander **2** *usually with* **with** <u>toy with</u>, consider, dabble in, entertain, expose oneself to, give a thought to, play with, trifle with ♦ *noun* **3** <u>tease</u>, coquette, heart-breaker, philanderer

flirtatious *adjective* <u>teasing</u>, amorous, come-hither, coquettish, coy, enticing, flirty, provocative, sportive

float *verb* **1** <u>be buoyant</u>, hang, hover **2** <u>glide</u>, bob, drift, move gently, sail, slide, slip along **3** <u>launch</u>, get going, promote, set up

floating *adjective* **1** <u>buoyant</u>, afloat, buoyed up, sailing,

swimming **2** <u>fluctuating</u>, free, movable, unattached, variable, wandering

flock *noun* **1** <u>herd</u>, colony, drove, flight, gaggle, skein **2** <u>crowd</u>, collection, company, congregation, gathering, group, herd, host, mass ♦ *verb* **3** <u>gather</u>, collect, congregate, converge, crowd, herd, huddle, mass, throng

flog *verb* <u>beat</u>, flagellate, flay, lash, scourge, thrash, trounce, whack, whip

flood *noun* **1** <u>deluge</u>, downpour, inundation, overflow, spate, tide, torrent **2** <u>abundance</u>, flow, glut, profusion, rush, stream, torrent ♦ *verb* **3** <u>immerse</u>, drown, inundate, overflow, pour over, submerge, swamp **4** <u>engulf</u>, overwhelm, surge, swarm, sweep **5** <u>oversupply</u>, choke, fill, glut, saturate

floor *noun* **1** <u>tier</u>, level, stage, storey ♦ *verb* **2** <u>knock down</u>, deck (*slang*), prostrate **3** *Informal* <u>bewilder</u>, baffle, confound, defeat, disconcert, dumbfound, perplex, puzzle, stump, throw (*informal*)

flop *verb* **1** <u>fall</u>, collapse, dangle, droop, drop, sag, slump **2** *Informal* <u>fail</u>, come unstuck, fall flat, fold (*informal*), founder, go belly-up (*slang*), misfire ♦ *noun* **3** *Informal* <u>failure</u>, debacle, disaster, fiasco, nonstarter, washout (*informal*)

floppy *adjective* <u>droopy</u>, baggy, flaccid, limp, loose, pendulous, sagging, soft

floral *adjective* <u>flowery</u>, flower-patterned

florid *adjective* **1** <u>flushed</u>, blowsy, high-coloured, rubicund, ruddy **2** <u>flowery</u>, baroque, flamboyant, fussy, high-flown, ornate, overelaborate

flotsam *noun* <u>debris</u>, detritus, jetsam, junk, odds and ends, wreckage

flounder *verb* <u>fumble</u>, grope, struggle, stumble, thrash, toss

flourish *verb* **1** <u>prosper</u>, bloom, blossom, boom, flower, grow, increase, succeed, thrive **2** <u>wave</u>, brandish, display, flaunt, shake, wield ♦ *noun* **3** <u>wave</u>, display, fanfare, parade, show **4** <u>ornamentation</u>, curlicue, decoration, embellishment, plume, sweep

flourishing *adjective* <u>successful</u>, blooming, going places, in the pink, luxuriant, prospering, rampant, thriving

flout *verb* <u>defy</u>, laugh in the face of, mock, scoff at, scorn, sneer at, spurn

flow *verb* **1** <u>run</u>, circulate, course, move, roll **2** <u>pour</u>, cascade, flood, gush, rush, stream, surge, sweep **3** <u>result</u>, arise, emanate, emerge, issue, proceed, spring ♦ *noun* **4** <u>tide</u>, course, current, drift, flood, flux, outpouring, spate, stream

flower *noun* **1** <u>bloom</u>, blossom, efflorescence **2** <u>elite</u>, best, cream, *crème de la crème*, pick ♦ *verb* **3** <u>blossom</u>, bloom, flourish, mature, open, unfold

flowery *adjective* <u>ornate</u>, baroque, embellished, fancy, florid, high-flown

flowing *adjective* **1** <u>streaming</u>, falling, gushing, rolling, rushing, smooth, sweeping **2** <u>fluent</u>, continuous, easy, smooth, unbroken, uninterrupted

fluctuate *verb* <u>change</u>, alternate, oscillate, seesaw, shift, swing, vary, veer, waver

fluency *noun* <u>ease</u>, articulateness, assurance, command, control, facility, readiness, slickness, smoothness

fluent *adjective* <u>smooth</u>, articulate, easy, effortless, flowing, natural, voluble, well-versed

fluff *noun* **1** <u>fuzz</u>, down, nap, pile ♦ *verb* **2** *Informal* <u>spoil</u>, bungle, make a mess off, mess up (*informal*), muddle

fluffy *adjective* <u>soft</u>, downy, feathery, fleecy, fuzzy

fluid *noun* **1** <u>liquid</u>, liquor, solution ♦ *adjective* **2** <u>liquid</u>, flowing, liquefied, melted, molten, runny, watery

fluke *noun* <u>lucky break</u>, accident, chance, coincidence, quirk of fate, serendipity, stroke of luck

flurry *noun* **1** <u>commotion</u>, ado, bustle, disturbance, excitement, flutter, fuss, stir **2** <u>gust</u>, squall

flush[1] *verb* **1** <u>blush</u>, colour, glow, go red, redden **2** <u>rinse out</u>, cleanse, flood, hose down, wash out ♦ *noun* **3** <u>blush</u>, colour, glow, redness, rosiness

flush[2] *adjective* **1** <u>level</u>, even, flat, square, true **2** *Informal* <u>wealthy</u>, in the money (*informal*), moneyed, rich, well-heeled (*informal*), well-off

flushed *adjective* <u>blushing</u>, crimson, embarrassed, glowing, hot, red, rosy, ruddy

fluster verb 1 <u>upset</u>, agitate, bother, confuse, disturb, perturb, rattle (*informal*), ruffle, unnerve ♦ *noun* 2 <u>turmoil</u>, disturbance, dither (*chiefly Brit.*), flap (*informal*), flurry, flutter, furore, state (*informal*)

flutter verb 1 <u>beat</u>, flap, palpitate, quiver, ripple, tremble, vibrate, waver ♦ *noun* 2 <u>vibration</u>, palpitation, quiver, shiver, shudder, tremble, tremor, twitching 3 <u>agitation</u>, commotion, confusion, dither (*chiefly Brit.*), excitement, fluster, state (*informal*)

fly verb 1 <u>take wing</u>, flit, flutter, hover, sail, soar, wing 2 <u>pilot</u>, control, manoeuvre, operate 3 <u>display</u>, flap, float, flutter, show, wave 4 <u>pass</u>, elapse, flit, glide, pass swiftly, roll on, run its course, slip away 5 <u>rush</u>, career, dart, dash, hurry, race, shoot, speed, sprint, tear 6 <u>flee</u>, escape, get away, run for it, skedaddle (*informal*), take to one's heels

flying adjective <u>hurried</u>, brief, fleeting, hasty, rushed, short-lived, transitory

foam noun 1 <u>froth</u>, bubbles, head, lather, spray, spume, suds ♦ *verb* 2 <u>bubble</u>, boil, effervesce, fizz, froth, lather

focus noun 1 <u>centre</u>, focal point, heart, hub, target ♦ *verb* 2 <u>concentrate</u>, aim, centre, direct, fix, pinpoint, spotlight, zoom in

foe noun <u>enemy</u>, adversary, antagonist, opponent, rival

fog noun <u>mist</u>, gloom, miasma, murk, peasouper (*informal*), smog

foggy adjective <u>misty</u>, cloudy, dim, hazy, indistinct, murky, smoggy, vaporous

foil[1] verb <u>thwart</u>, balk, counter, defeat, disappoint, frustrate, nullify, stop

foil[2] noun <u>contrast</u>, antithesis, complement

foist verb <u>impose</u>, fob off, palm off, pass off, sneak in, unload

fold verb 1 <u>bend</u>, crease, double over 2 *Informal* <u>go bankrupt</u>, collapse, crash, fail, go bust (*informal*), go to the wall, go under, shut down ♦ *noun* 3 <u>crease</u>, bend, furrow, overlap, pleat, wrinkle

folder noun <u>file</u>, binder, envelope, portfolio

folk noun <u>people</u>, clan, family, kin, kindred, race, tribe

follow verb 1 <u>come after</u>, come next, succeed, supersede, supplant, take the place of 2 <u>pursue</u>, chase, dog, hound, hunt, shadow, stalk, track, trail 3 <u>accompany</u>, attend, escort, tag along 4 <u>obey</u>, be guided by, conform, heed, observe 5 <u>understand</u>, appreciate, catch on (*informal*), comprehend, fathom, grasp, realize, take in 6 <u>result</u>, arise, develop, ensue, flow, issue, proceed, spring 7 <u>be interested in</u>, cultivate, keep abreast of, support

follower noun <u>supporter</u>, adherent, apostle, devotee, disciple, fan, pupil

following adjective 1 <u>next</u>, consequent, ensuing, later, subsequent, succeeding, successive ♦ *noun* 2 <u>supporters</u>, clientele, coterie, entourage, fans, retinue, suite, train

folly noun <u>foolishness</u>, imprudence, indiscretion, lunacy, madness, nonsense, rashness, stupidity

fond adjective **1** <u>loving</u>, adoring, affectionate, amorous, caring, devoted, doting, indulgent, tender, warm **2** <u>foolish</u>, deluded, delusive, empty, naive, overoptimistic, vain **3 fond of** <u>keen on</u>, addicted to, attached to, enamoured of, having a soft spot for, hooked on, into (informal), partial to

fondle verb <u>caress</u>, cuddle, dandle, pat, pet, stroke

fondly adverb **1** <u>lovingly</u>, affectionately, dearly, indulgently, possessively, tenderly, with affection **2** <u>foolishly</u>, credulously, naively, stupidly, vainly

fondness noun **1** <u>liking</u>, attachment, fancy, love, partiality, penchant, soft spot, taste, weakness **2** <u>devotion</u>, affection, attachment, kindness, love, tenderness

food noun <u>nourishment</u>, cuisine, diet, fare, grub (slang), nutrition, rations, refreshment

fool noun **1** <u>simpleton</u>, blockhead, dunce, halfwit, idiot, ignoramus, imbecile (informal), numbskull or numskull, twit (informal, chiefly Brit.) **2** <u>dupe</u>, fall guy (informal), laughing stock, mug (Brit. slang), stooge (slang), sucker (slang) **3** <u>clown</u>, buffoon, harlequin, jester ◆ verb **4** <u>deceive</u>, beguile, con (informal), delude, dupe, hoodwink, mislead, take in, trick

foolhardy adjective <u>rash</u>, hot-headed, impetuous, imprudent, irresponsible, reckless

foolish adjective <u>unwise</u>, absurd, ill-judged, imprudent, injudicious, senseless, silly

foolishly adverb <u>unwisely</u>, idiotically, ill-advisedly, imprudently, injudiciously, mistakenly, stupidly

foolishness noun <u>stupidity</u>, absurdity, folly, imprudence, indiscretion, irresponsibility, silliness, weakness

foolproof adjective <u>infallible</u>, certain, guaranteed, safe, sure-fire (informal), unassailable, unbreakable

footing noun **1** <u>basis</u>, foundation, groundwork **2** <u>relationship</u>, grade, position, rank, standing, status

footling adjective <u>trivial</u>, fiddling, hairsplitting, insignificant, minor, petty, silly, trifling, unimportant

footstep noun <u>step</u>, footfall, tread

forage verb **1** <u>search</u>, cast about, explore, hunt, rummage, scour, seek ◆ noun **2** Cattle, etc. <u>fodder</u>, feed, food, provender

foray noun <u>raid</u>, incursion, inroad, invasion, sally, sortie, swoop

forbear verb <u>refrain</u>, abstain, cease, desist, hold back, keep from, restrain oneself, stop

forbearance noun <u>patience</u>, long-suffering, moderation, resignation, restraint, self-control, temperance, tolerance

forbearing adjective <u>patient</u>, forgiving, indulgent, lenient, long-suffering, merciful, moderate, tolerant

forbid *verb* <u>prohibit</u>, ban, disallow, exclude, outlaw, preclude, rule out, veto

forbidden *adjective* <u>prohibited</u>, banned, outlawed, out of bounds, proscribed, taboo, vetoed

forbidding *adjective* <u>threatening</u>, daunting, frightening, hostile, menacing, ominous, sinister, unfriendly

force *noun* **1** <u>power</u>, energy, impulse, might, momentum, pressure, strength, vigour **2** <u>compulsion</u>, arm-twisting (*informal*), coercion, constraint, duress, pressure, violence **3** <u>intensity</u>, emphasis, fierceness, vehemence, vigour **4** <u>army</u>, host, legion, patrol, regiment, squad, troop, unit **5** **in force: a** <u>valid</u>, binding, current, effective, in operation, operative, working **b** in great numbers, all together, in full strength ♦ *verb* **6** <u>compel</u>, coerce, constrain, dragoon, drive, impel, make, oblige, press, pressurize **7** <u>break open</u>, blast, prise, wrench, wrest **8** <u>push</u>, propel, thrust

forced *adjective* **1** <u>compulsory</u>, conscripted, enforced, involuntary, mandatory, obligatory **2** <u>false</u>, affected, artificial, contrived, insincere, laboured, stiff, strained, unnatural, wooden

forceful *adjective* <u>powerful</u>, cogent, compelling, convincing, dynamic, effective, persuasive

forcible *adjective* **1** <u>violent</u>, aggressive, armed, coercive, compulsory **2** <u>strong</u>,

compelling, energetic, forceful, potent, powerful, weighty

forebear *noun* <u>ancestor</u>, father, forefather, forerunner, predecessor

foreboding *noun* <u>dread</u>, anxiety, apprehension, apprehensiveness, chill, fear, misgiving, premonition, presentiment

forecast *verb* **1** <u>predict</u>, anticipate, augur, divine, foresee, foretell, prophesy ♦ *noun* **2** <u>prediction</u>, conjecture, guess, prognosis, prophecy

forefather *noun* <u>ancestor</u>, father, forebear, forerunner, predecessor

forefront *noun* <u>lead</u>, centre, fore, foreground, front, prominence, spearhead, vanguard

foregoing *adjective* <u>preceding</u>, above, antecedent, anterior, former, previous, prior

foreign *adjective* <u>alien</u>, exotic, external, imported, remote, strange, unfamiliar, unknown

foreigner *noun* <u>alien</u>, immigrant, incomer, stranger

foremost *adjective* <u>leading</u>, chief, highest, paramount, pre-eminent, primary, prime, principal, supreme

forerunner *noun* <u>precursor</u>, envoy, harbinger, herald, prototype

foresee *verb* <u>anticipate</u>, envisage, forecast, foretell, predict, prophesy

foreshadow *verb* <u>predict</u>, augur, forebode, indicate, portend, prefigure, presage, promise, signal

foresight *noun* <u>anticipation</u>, far-sightedness, forethought, precaution, preparedness, prescience, prudence

foretell verb <u>predict</u>, forecast, forewarn, presage, prognosticate, prophesy

forethought noun <u>anticipation</u>, far-sightedness, foresight, precaution, providence, provision, prudence

forever adverb 1 <u>evermore</u>, always, for all time, for keeps, in perpetuity, till Doomsday, till the cows come home (informal) 2 <u>constantly</u>, all the time, continually, endlessly, eternally, incessantly, interminably, perpetually, unremittingly

forewarn verb <u>caution</u>, advise, alert, apprise, give fair warning, put on guard, tip off

forfeit noun 1 <u>penalty</u>, damages, fine, forfeiture, loss, mulct ♦ verb 2 <u>lose</u>, be deprived of, be stripped of, give up, relinquish, renounce, say goodbye to, surrender

forge verb 1 <u>create</u>, construct, devise, fashion, form, frame, make, mould, shape, work 2 <u>falsify</u>, copy, counterfeit, fake, feign, imitate

forgery noun 1 <u>fraudulence</u>, coining, counterfeiting, falsification, fraudulent imitation 2 <u>fake</u>, counterfeit, falsification, imitation, phoney or phony (informal), sham

forget verb <u>neglect</u>, leave behind, lose sight of, omit, overlook

forgetful adjective <u>absent-minded</u>, careless, inattentive, neglectful, oblivious, unmindful, vague

forgive verb <u>excuse</u>, absolve, acquit, condone, exonerate, let bygones be bygones, let off (informal), pardon

forgiveness noun <u>pardon</u>, absolution, acquittal, amnesty, exoneration, mercy, remission

forgiving adjective <u>merciful</u>, clement, compassionate, forbearing, lenient, magnanimous, soft-hearted, tolerant

forgo verb <u>give up</u>, abandon, do without, relinquish, renounce, resign, surrender, waive, yield

forgotten adjective <u>left behind</u>, bygone, lost, omitted, past, past recall, unremembered

fork verb <u>branch</u>, bifurcate, diverge, divide, part, split

forked adjective <u>branching</u>, angled, bifurcate(d), branched, divided, pronged, split, zigzag

forlorn adjective <u>miserable</u>, disconsolate, down in the dumps (informal), helpless, hopeless, pathetic, pitiful, unhappy, woebegone, wretched

form noun 1 <u>shape</u>, appearance, configuration, formation, pattern, structure 2 <u>type</u>, kind, sort, style, variety 3 <u>condition</u>, fettle, fitness, health, shape, trim 4 <u>procedure</u>, convention, custom, etiquette, protocol 5 <u>document</u>, application, paper, sheet 6 <u>class</u>, grade, rank ♦ verb 7 <u>make</u>, build, construct, create, fashion, forge, mould, produce, shape 8 <u>arrange</u>, combine, draw up, organize 9 <u>take shape</u>, appear, become visible, come into being, crystallize, grow, materialize, rise 10 <u>develop</u>, acquire, contract, cultivate, pick up **11** <u>constitute</u>, compose, comprise, make up

formal *adjective* **1** <u>official</u>, ceremonial, ritualistic, solemn **2** <u>conventional</u>, affected, correct, precise, stiff, unbending

formality *noun* **1** <u>convention</u>, custom, procedure, red tape, rite, ritual **2** <u>correctness</u>, decorum, etiquette, protocol

format *noun* <u>style</u>, appearance, arrangement, construction, form, layout, look, make-up, plan, type

formation *noun* **1** <u>establishment</u>, constitution, development, forming, generation, genesis, manufacture, production **2** <u>pattern</u>, arrangement, configuration, design, grouping, structure

formative *adjective* <u>developmental</u>, influential

former *adjective* <u>previous</u>, earlier, erstwhile, one-time, prior

formerly *adverb* <u>previously</u>, at one time, before, lately, once

formidable *adjective* **1** <u>intimidating</u>, daunting, dismaying, fearful, frightful, menacing, terrifying, threatening **2** <u>impressive</u>, awesome, great, mighty, powerful, redoubtable, terrific, tremendous

formula *noun* <u>method</u>, blueprint, precept, principle, procedure, recipe, rule

formulate *verb* **1** <u>define</u>, detail, express, frame, give form to, set down, specify, systematize **2** <u>devise</u>, develop, forge, invent, map out, originate, plan, work out

forsake *verb* **1** <u>desert</u>, abandon, disown, leave in the lurch, strand **2** <u>give up</u>, forgo, relinquish, renounce, set aside, surrender, yield

forsaken *adjective* <u>deserted</u>, abandoned, disowned, forlorn, left in the lurch, marooned, outcast, stranded

fort *noun* **1** <u>fortress</u>, blockhouse, camp, castle, citadel, fortification, garrison, stronghold **2 hold the fort** <u>stand in</u>, carry on, keep things on an even keel, take over the reins

forte *noun* <u>speciality</u>, gift, long suit (*informal*), métier, strength, strong point, talent

forth *adverb* <u>forward</u>, ahead, away, onward, out, outward

forthcoming *adjective* **1** <u>approaching</u>, coming, expected, future, imminent, impending, prospective, upcoming **2** <u>accessible</u>, at hand, available, in evidence, obtainable, on tap (*informal*), ready **3** <u>communicative</u>, chatty, expansive, free, informative, open, sociable, talkative, unreserved

forthright *adjective* <u>outspoken</u>, blunt, candid, direct, frank, open, plain-spoken, straightforward, upfront (*informal*)

forthwith *adverb* <u>at once</u>, directly, immediately, instantly, quickly, right away, straightaway, without delay

fortification *noun* **1** <u>defence</u>, bastion, fastness, fort, fortress, protection, stronghold **2** <u>strengthening</u>, reinforcement

fortify *verb* <u>strengthen</u>, augment,

buttress, protect, reinforce, shore up, support

fortitude noun <u>courage</u>, backbone, bravery, fearlessness, grit, perseverance, resolution, strength, valour

fortress noun <u>castle</u>, citadel, fastness, fort, redoubt, stronghold

fortunate adjective **1** <u>lucky</u>, favoured, in luck, jammy (*Brit. slang*), successful, well-off **2** <u>favourable</u>, advantageous, convenient, expedient, felicitous, fortuitous, helpful, opportune, providential

fortunately adverb <u>luckily</u>, by a happy chance, by good luck, happily, providentially

fortune noun **1** <u>wealth</u>, affluence, opulence, possessions, property, prosperity, riches, treasure **2** <u>luck</u>, chance, destiny, fate, kismet, providence **3 fortunes** <u>destiny</u>, adventures, experiences, history, lot, success

forward adjective **1** <u>leading</u>, advance, first, foremost, front, head **2** <u>presumptuous</u>, bold, brash, brazen, cheeky, familiar, impertinent, impudent, pushy (*informal*) **3** <u>well-developed</u>, advanced, precocious, premature ◆ adverb **4** <u>ahead</u>, forth, on, onward ◆ verb **5** <u>promote</u>, advance, assist, expedite, further, hasten, hurry **6** <u>send</u>, dispatch, post, send on

foster verb **1** <u>promote</u>, cultivate, encourage, feed, nurture, stimulate, support, uphold **2** <u>bring up</u>, mother, nurse, raise, rear, take care of

foul adjective **1** <u>dirty</u>, fetid, filthy, malodorous, nauseating, putrid,

repulsive, squalid, stinking, unclean **2** <u>obscene</u>, abusive, blue, coarse, indecent, lewd, profane, scurrilous, vulgar **3** <u>offensive</u>, abhorrent, despicable, detestable, disgraceful, scandalous, shameful, wicked **4** <u>unfair</u>, crooked, dishonest, fraudulent, shady (*informal*), underhand, unscrupulous ◆ verb **5** <u>pollute</u>, besmirch, contaminate, defile, dirty, stain, sully, taint

found verb <u>establish</u>, constitute, create, inaugurate, institute, organize, originate, set up, start

foundation noun **1** <u>groundwork</u>, base, basis, bedrock, bottom, footing, substructure, underpinning **2** <u>setting up</u>, endowment, establishment, inauguration, institution, organization, settlement

founder[1] noun <u>initiator</u>, architect, author, beginner, father, inventor, originator

founder[2] verb **1** <u>sink</u>, be lost, go down, go to the bottom, submerge **2** <u>fail</u>, break down, collapse, come to grief, come unstuck, fall through, miscarry, misfire **3** <u>stumble</u>, lurch, sprawl, stagger, trip

foundling noun <u>stray</u>, orphan, outcast, waif

fountain noun **1** <u>jet</u>, font, fount, reservoir, spout, spray, spring, well **2** <u>source</u>, cause, derivation, fount, fountainhead, origin, wellspring

foyer noun <u>entrance hall</u>, antechamber, anteroom, lobby, reception area, vestibule

fracas noun <u>brawl</u>, affray (*Law*),

disturbance, melee or mêlée, riot, rumpus, scuffle, skirmish

fraction noun piece, part, percentage, portion, section, segment, share, slice

fractious adjective irritable, captious, cross, petulant, querulous, refractory, testy, tetchy, touchy

fracture noun 1 break, cleft, crack, fissure, opening, rift, rupture, split ◆ verb 2 break, crack, rupture, splinter, split

fragile adjective delicate, breakable, brittle, dainty, fine, flimsy, frail, frangible, weak

fragment noun 1 piece, bit, chip, particle, portion, scrap, shred, sliver ◆ verb 2 break, break up, come apart, come to pieces, crumble, disintegrate, shatter, splinter, split up

fragmentary adjective incomplete, bitty, broken, disconnected, incoherent, partial, piecemeal, scattered, scrappy, sketchy

fragrance noun scent, aroma, balm, bouquet, fragrancy, perfume, redolence, smell, sweet odour

fragrant adjective perfumed, aromatic, balmy, odorous, redolent, sweet-scented, sweet-smelling

frail adjective weak, delicate, feeble, flimsy, fragile, infirm, insubstantial, puny, vulnerable

frailty noun feebleness, fallibility, frailness, infirmity, susceptibility, weakness

frame noun 1 casing, construction, framework, shell,

structure 2 physique, anatomy, body, build, carcass 3 frame of mind mood, attitude, disposition, humour, outlook, state, temper ◆ verb 4 construct, assemble, build, make, manufacture, put together 5 draft, compose, devise, draw up, formulate, map out, sketch 6 mount, case, enclose, surround

framework noun structure, foundation, frame, groundwork, plan, shell, skeleton, the bare bones

frank adjective honest, blunt, candid, direct, forthright, open, outspoken, plain-spoken, sincere, straightforward, truthful

frankly adverb 1 honestly, candidly, in truth, to be honest 2 openly, bluntly, directly, freely, plainly, without reserve

frankness noun outspokenness, bluntness, candour, forthrightness, openness, plain speaking, truthfulness

frantic adjective 1 furious, at the end of one's tether, berserk, beside oneself, distracted, distraught, wild 2 hectic, desperate, fraught (Informal), frenetic, frenzied

fraternity noun 1 club, association, brotherhood, circle, company, guild, league, union 2 companionship, brotherhood, camaraderie, fellowship, kinship

fraternize verb associate, consort, cooperate, hobnob, keep company, mingle, mix, socialize

fraud noun 1 deception, chicanery, deceit, double-dealing, duplicity, sharp practice, swindling, treachery, trickery **2** impostor, charlatan, fake, fraudster, hoaxer, phoney or phony (*informal*), pretender, swindler

fraudulent *adjective* deceitful, crooked (*informal*), dishonest, double-dealing, duplicitous, sham, swindling, treacherous

fray *verb* wear thin, chafe, rub, wear

freak *noun* **1** oddity, aberration, anomaly, malformation, monstrosity, weirdo or weirdie (*informal*) **2** enthusiast, addict, aficionado, buff (*informal*), devotee, fan, fanatic, fiend (*informal*), nut (*slang*) ♦ *adjective* **3** abnormal, exceptional, unparalleled, unusual

free *adjective* **1** for nothing, complimentary, for free (*informal*), free of charge, gratis, gratuitous, on the house, unpaid, without charge **2** at liberty, at large, footloose, independent, liberated, loose, on the loose, unfettered **3** allowed, able, clear, permitted, unimpeded, unrestricted **4** available, empty, idle, spare, unemployed, unoccupied, unused, vacant **5** generous, lavish, liberal, unsparing, unstinting ♦ *verb* **6** release, deliver, let out, liberate, loose, set free, turn loose, unchain, untie **7** extricate, cut loose, disengage, disentangle, rescue

freedom *noun* **1** liberty, deliverance, emancipation, independence, release **2** opportunity, blank cheque, carte blanche, discretion, free rein, latitude, licence

free-for-all *noun* fight, brawl, dust-up (*informal*), fracas, melee or mêlée, riot, row, scrimmage

freely *adverb* **1** willingly, of one's own accord, of one's own free will, spontaneously, voluntarily, without prompting **2** openly, candidly, frankly, plainly, unreservedly, without reserve **3** abundantly, amply, copiously, extravagantly, lavishly, liberally, unstintingly

freeze *verb* **1** chill, harden, ice over or up, stiffen **2** suspend, fix, hold up, inhibit, peg, stop

freezing *adjective* icy, arctic, biting, bitter, chill, frosty, glacial, raw, wintry

freight *noun* **1** transportation, carriage, conveyance, shipment **2** cargo, burden, consignment, goods, load, merchandise, payload

French *adjective* Gallic

frenzied *adjective* furious, distracted, feverish, frantic, frenetic, rabid, uncontrolled, wild

frenzy *noun* fury, derangement, hysteria, paroxysm, passion, rage, seizure

frequent *adjective* **1** common, customary, everyday, familiar, habitual, persistent, recurrent, repeated, usual ♦ *verb* **2** visit, attend, be found at, hang out at (*informal*), haunt, patronize

frequently *adverb* often, commonly, habitually, many times, much, not infrequently, repeatedly

fresh *adjective* **1** new, different, modern, novel, original, recent,

up-to-date **2** <u>additional</u>, added,
auxiliary, extra, further, more,
other, supplementary
3 <u>invigorating</u>, bracing, brisk,
clean, cool, crisp, pure,
refreshing, unpolluted **4** <u>lively</u>,
alert, energetic, keen, refreshed,
sprightly, spry, vigorous
5 <u>natural</u>, unprocessed **6** *Informal*
<u>cheeky</u>, disrespectful, familiar,
forward, impudent, insolent,
presumptuous

freshen *verb* <u>refresh</u>, enliven,
freshen up, liven up, restore,
revitalize

freshness *noun* **1** <u>novelty</u>,
inventiveness, newness,
originality **2** <u>cleanness</u>,
brightness, clearness, glow,
shine, sparkle, vigour,
wholesomeness

fret *verb* <u>worry</u>, agonize, brood,
grieve, lose sleep over, upset *or*
distress oneself

fretful *adjective* <u>irritable</u>,
crotchety (*informal*), edgy,
fractious, querulous,
short-tempered, testy, touchy,
uneasy

friction *noun* **1** <u>rubbing</u>,
abrasion, chafing, grating,
rasping, resistance, scraping
2 <u>hostility</u>, animosity, bad blood,
conflict, disagreement, discord,
dissension, resentment

friend *noun* **1** <u>companion</u>, buddy
(*informal*), chum (*informal*),
comrade, mate (*informal*), pal,
playmate **2** <u>supporter</u>, ally,
associate, patron, well-wisher

friendliness *noun* <u>kindliness</u>,
affability, amiability,
congeniality, conviviality,
geniality, neighbourliness,

sociability, warmth

friendly *adjective* <u>sociable</u>,
affectionate, amicable, close,
familiar, helpful, intimate,
neighbourly, on good terms,
pally (*informal*), sympathetic,
welcoming

friendship *noun* <u>goodwill</u>,
affection, amity, attachment,
concord, familiarity, friendliness,
harmony, intimacy

fright *noun* <u>fear</u>, alarm,
consternation, dread, horror,
panic, scare, shock, trepidation

frighten *verb* <u>scare</u>, alarm,
intimidate, petrify, shock, startle,
terrify, terrorize, unnerve

frightened *adjective* <u>afraid</u>,
alarmed, petrified, scared, scared
stiff, startled, terrified, terrorized,
terror-stricken

frightening *adjective* <u>terrifying</u>,
alarming, fearful, fearsome,
horrifying, menacing, scary
(*informal*), shocking, unnerving

frightful *adjective* <u>terrifying</u>,
alarming, awful, dreadful, fearful,
ghastly, horrendous, horrible,
terrible, traumatic

frigid *adjective* **1** <u>cold</u>, arctic,
frosty, frozen, glacial, icy, wintry
2 <u>forbidding</u>, aloof, austere,
formal, unapproachable,
unfeeling, unresponsive

frills *plural noun* <u>trimmings</u>,
additions, bells and whistles,
embellishments, extras, frippery,
fuss, ornamentation, ostentation

fringe *noun* **1** <u>border</u>, edging,
hem, trimming **2** <u>edge</u>,
borderline, limits, margin,
outskirts, perimeter, periphery
♦ *adjective* **3** <u>unofficial</u>,

unconventional, unorthodox

frisk verb 1 <u>frolic</u>, caper, cavort, gambol, jump, play, prance, skip, trip 2 *Informal* <u>search</u>, check, inspect, run over, shake down (*U.S. slang*)

frisky adjective <u>lively</u>, coltish, frolicsome, high-spirited, kittenish, playful, sportive

fritter away verb <u>waste</u>, dissipate, idle away, misspend, run through, spend like water, squander

frivolity noun <u>fun</u>, flippancy, frivolousness, gaiety, levity, light-heartedness, silliness, superficiality, triviality

frivolous adjective 1 <u>flippant</u>, childish, foolish, idle, juvenile, puerile, silly, superficial 2 <u>trivial</u>, footling (*informal*), minor, petty, shallow, trifling, unimportant

frolic verb 1 <u>play</u>, caper, cavort, frisk, gambol, lark, make merry, romp, sport ♦ noun 2 <u>revel</u>, antic, game, lark, romp, spree

frolicsome adjective <u>playful</u>, coltish, frisky, kittenish, lively, merry, sportive

front noun 1 <u>exterior</u>, façade, face, foreground, frontage 2 <u>forefront</u>, front line, head, lead, vanguard 3 <u>disguise</u>, blind, cover, cover-up, façade, mask, pretext, show ♦ adjective 4 <u>first</u>, foremost, head, lead, leading, topmost ♦ verb 5 <u>face onto</u>, look over or onto, overlook

frontier noun <u>boundary</u>, borderline, edge, limit, perimeter, verge

frost noun <u>hoarfrost</u>, freeze, rime

frosty adjective 1 <u>cold</u>, chilly, frozen, icy, wintry 2 <u>unfriendly</u>, discouraging, frigid, off-putting (*Brit. informal*), standoffish, unenthusiastic, unwelcoming

froth noun 1 <u>foam</u>, bubbles, effervescence, head, lather, scum, spume, suds ♦ verb 2 <u>fizz</u>, bubble over, come to a head, effervesce, foam, lather

frothy adjective <u>foamy</u>, foaming, sudsy

frown verb 1 <u>scowl</u>, glare, glower, knit one's brows, look daggers, lour or lower 2 **frown on** <u>disapprove of</u>, discourage, dislike, look askance at, take a dim view of

frozen adjective <u>icy</u>, arctic, chilled, frigid, frosted, icebound, ice-cold, ice-covered, numb

frugal adjective <u>thrifty</u>, abstemious, careful, economical, niggardly, parsimonious, prudent, sparing

fruit noun 1 <u>produce</u>, crop, harvest, product, yield 2 <u>result</u>, advantage, benefit, consequence, effect, end result, outcome, profit, return, reward

fruitful adjective <u>useful</u>, advantageous, beneficial, effective, productive, profitable, rewarding, successful, worthwhile

fruition noun <u>maturity</u>, attainment, completion, fulfilment, materialization, perfection, realization, ripeness

fruitless adjective <u>useless</u>, futile, ineffectual, pointless, profitless, unavailing, unproductive, unprofitable, unsuccessful, vain

frustrate verb <u>thwart</u>, balk, block, check, counter, defeat, disappoint, foil, forestall, nullify, stymie

frustrated adjective <u>disappointed</u>, discouraged, disheartened, embittered, resentful

frustration noun 1 <u>obstruction</u>, blocking, circumvention, foiling, thwarting 2 <u>annoyance</u>, disappointment, dissatisfaction, grievance, irritation, resentment, vexation

fuddy-duddy noun <u>conservative</u>, (old) fogey, square (informal), stick-in-the-mud (informal), stuffed shirt (informal)

fudge verb <u>hedge</u>, equivocate, flannel (Brit. informal), stall

fuel noun <u>incitement</u>, ammunition, provocation

fugitive noun 1 <u>runaway</u>, deserter, escapee, refugee ♦ adjective 2 <u>momentary</u>, brief, ephemeral, fleeting, passing, short-lived, temporary, transient, transitory

fulfil verb 1 <u>achieve</u>, accomplish, carry out, complete, perform, realise, satisfy 2 <u>comply with</u>, answer, conform to, fill, meet, obey, observe

fulfilment noun <u>achievement</u>, accomplishment, attainment, completion, consummation, implementation, realization

full adjective 1 <u>saturated</u>, brimming, complete, filled, loaded, replete, satiated, stocked 2 <u>plentiful</u>, abundant, adequate, ample, comprehensive, exhaustive, extensive, generous 3 <u>rich</u>, clear, deep, distinct, loud, resonant, rounded 4 <u>plump</u>, buxom, curvaceous, rounded, voluptuous 5 <u>loose</u>, baggy,

capacious, large, puffy, voluminous ♦ noun 6 **in full** <u>completely</u>, in its entirety, in total, without exception

full-blooded adjective <u>vigorous</u>, hearty, lusty, red-blooded, virile

fullness noun 1 <u>plenty</u>, abundance, copiousness, fill, profusion, satiety, saturation, sufficiency 2 <u>richness</u>, clearness, loudness, resonance, strength

full-scale adjective <u>major</u>, all-out, comprehensive, exhaustive, in-depth, sweeping, thorough, thoroughgoing, wide-ranging

fully adverb <u>totally</u>, altogether, completely, entirely, in all respects, one hundred per cent, perfectly, thoroughly, utterly, wholly

fulsome adjective <u>insincere</u>, excessive, extravagant, immoderate, inordinate, sycophantic, unctuous

fumble verb <u>grope</u>, feel around, flounder, scrabble

fume verb <u>rage</u>, get hot under the collar (informal), rant, see red (informal), seethe, smoulder, storm

fumes plural noun <u>smoke</u>, exhaust, gas, pollution, smog, vapour

fumigate verb <u>disinfect</u>, clean out or up, cleanse, purify, sanitize, sterilize

fuming adjective <u>angry</u>, enraged, in a rage, incensed, on the warpath (informal), raging, seething, up in arms

fun noun 1 <u>enjoyment</u>, amusement, entertainment, jollity, merriment, mirth,

pleasure, recreation, sport
2 make fun of <u>mock</u>, lampoon, laugh at, parody, poke fun at, ridicule, satirize, send up (*Brit. informal*) ♦ *adjective* **3** <u>enjoyable</u>, amusing, convivial, diverting, entertaining, lively, witty

function *noun* **1** <u>purpose</u>, business, duty, job, mission, *raison d'être*, responsibility, role, task **2** <u>reception</u>, affair, do (*informal*), gathering, social occasion ♦ *verb* **3** <u>work</u>, act, behave, do duty, go, operate, perform, run

functional *adjective* **1** <u>practical</u>, hard-wearing, serviceable, useful, utilitarian **2** <u>working</u>, operative

fund *noun* **1** <u>reserve</u>, kitty, pool, stock, store, supply ♦ *verb* **2** <u>finance</u>, pay for, subsidize, support

fundamental *adjective*
1 <u>essential</u>, basic, cardinal, central, elementary, key, primary, principal, rudimentary, underlying **2** <u>noun</u> <u>principle</u>, axiom, cornerstone, law, rudiment, rule

fundamentally *adverb*
<u>essentially</u>, at bottom, at heart, basically, intrinsically, primarily, radically

funds *plural noun* <u>money</u>, capital, cash, finance, ready money, resources, savings, the wherewithal

funeral *noun* <u>burial</u>, cremation, inhumation, interment, obsequies

funnel *verb* <u>channel</u>, conduct, convey, direct, filter, move, pass, pour

funny *adjective* **1** <u>humorous</u>, amusing, comic, comical, droll,

entertaining, hilarious, riotous, side-splitting, witty **2** <u>peculiar</u>, curious, mysterious, odd, queer, strange, suspicious, unusual, weird

furious *adjective* **1** <u>angry</u>, beside oneself, enraged, fuming, incensed, infuriated, livid (*informal*), raging, up in arms **2** <u>violent</u>, fierce, intense, savage, turbulent, unrestrained, vehement

furnish *verb* **1** <u>decorate</u>, equip, fit out, stock **2** <u>supply</u>, give, grant, hand out, offer, present, provide

furniture *noun* <u>household goods</u>, appliances, fittings, furnishings, goods, possessions, things (*informal*)

furore *noun* <u>disturbance</u>, commotion, hullabaloo, outcry, stir, to-do, uproar

furrow *noun* **1** <u>groove</u>, channel, crease, hollow, line, rut, seam, trench, wrinkle ♦ *verb* **2** <u>wrinkle</u>, corrugate, crease, draw together, knit

further *adverb* **1** <u>in addition</u>, additionally, also, besides, furthermore, into the bargain, moreover, to boot ♦ *adjective* **2** <u>additional</u>, extra, fresh, more, new, other, supplementary ♦ *verb* **3** <u>promote</u>, advance, assist, encourage, forward, help, lend support to, work for

furthermore *adverb* <u>besides</u>, additionally, as well, further, in addition, into the bargain, moreover, to boot, too

furthest *adjective* <u>most distant</u>, extreme, farthest, furthermost, outmost, remotest, ultimate

furtive adjective sly, clandestine, conspiratorial, secretive, sneaky, stealthy, surreptitious, underhand, under-the-table

fury noun 1 anger, frenzy, impetuosity, madness, passion, rage, wrath 2 violence, ferocity, fierceness, force, intensity, savagery, severity, vehemence

fuss noun 1 bother, ado, commotion, excitement, hue and cry, palaver, stir, to-do 2 argument, complaint, furore, objection, row, squabble, trouble ♦ verb 3 worry, fidget, flap (informal), fret, get worked up, take pains

fussy adjective 1 hard to please, choosy (informal), difficult, fastidious, finicky, nit-picking (informal), particular, pernickety, picky (informal) 2 overelaborate, busy, cluttered, overworked, rococo

fusty adjective stale, airless, damp, mildewed, mouldering, musty, stuffy

futile adjective useless, fruitless, ineffectual, unavailing, unprofitable, unsuccessful, vain, worthless

futility noun uselessness, emptiness, hollowness, ineffectiveness

future noun 1 hereafter, time to come 2 outlook, expectation, prospect ♦ adjective 3 forthcoming, approaching, coming, fated, impending, later, subsequent, to come

fuzzy adjective 1 fluffy, downy, frizzy, woolly 2 indistinct, bleary, blurred, distorted, ill-defined, out of focus, unclear, vague

G g

gabble verb 1 prattle, babble, blabber, gibber, gush, jabber, spout ♦ noun 2 gibberish, babble, blabber, chatter, drivel, prattle, twaddle

gadabout noun pleasure-seeker, gallivanter, rambler, rover, wanderer

gadget noun device, appliance, contraption (informal), contrivance, gizmo (slang, chiefly U.S.), instrument, invention, thing, tool

gaffe noun blunder, bloomer (informal), clanger (informal), faux pas, howler, indiscretion, lapse, mistake, slip, solecism

gaffer noun 1 Informal manager, boss (informal), foreman, overseer, superintendent, supervisor 2 old man, granddad, greybeard, old boy (informal), old fellow, old-timer (U.S.)

gag¹ verb 1 suppress, curb, muffle, muzzle, quiet, silence, stifle, stop up 2 retch, heave, puke (slang), spew, throw up (informal), vomit

gag² noun joke, crack (slang), funny (informal), hoax, jest, wisecrack (informal), witticism

gaiety noun 1 cheerfulness, blitheness, exhilaration, glee, high spirits, jollity, light-heartedness, merriment, mirth 2 merrymaking, conviviality, festivity, fun, jollification, revelry

gaily adverb 1 cheerfully, blithely,

gleefully, happily, joyfully,
light-heartedly, merrily
2 <u>colourfully</u>, brightly, brilliantly,
flamboyantly, flashily, gaudily,
showily

gain verb **1** <u>obtain</u>, acquire,
attain, capture, collect, gather,
get, land, pick up, secure, win
2 <u>reach</u>, arrive at, attain, come
to, get to **3** gain on <u>get nearer</u>,
approach, catch up with, close,
narrow the gap, overtake ♦ noun
4 <u>profit</u>, advantage, benefit,
dividend, return, yield
5 <u>increase</u>, advance, growth,
improvement, progress, rise

gainful adjective <u>profitable</u>,
advantageous, beneficial, fruitful,
lucrative, productive,
remunerative, rewarding, useful,
worthwhile

gains plural noun <u>profits</u>,
earnings, prize, proceeds,
revenue, takings, winnings

gainsay verb <u>contradict</u>,
contravene, controvert, deny,
disagree with, dispute, rebut,
retract

gait noun <u>walk</u>, bearing, carriage,
pace, step, stride, tread

gala noun <u>festival</u>, carnival,
celebration, festivity, fête,
jamboree, pageant

gale noun **1** <u>storm</u>, blast, cyclone,
hurricane, squall, tempest,
tornado, typhoon **2** Informal
<u>outburst</u>, burst, eruption,
explosion, fit, howl, outbreak,
peal, shout, shriek

gall¹ noun **1** Informal <u>impudence</u>,
brazenness, cheek (informal),
chutzpah (U.S. & Canad.
informal), effrontery,
impertinence, insolence, nerve

(informal) **2** <u>bitterness</u>, acrimony,
animosity, bile, hostility, rancour

gall² verb **1** <u>scrape</u>, abrade, chafe,
irritate **2** <u>annoy</u>, exasperate, irk,
irritate, provoke, rankle, vex

gallant adjective **1** <u>brave</u>, bold,
courageous, heroic, honourable,
intrepid, manly, noble, valiant
2 <u>chivalrous</u>, attentive,
courteous, gentlemanly,
gracious, noble, polite

gallantry noun **1** <u>bravery</u>,
boldness, courage, heroism,
intrepidity, manliness, spirit,
valour **2** <u>attentiveness</u>, chivalry,
courteousness, courtesy,
gentlemanliness, graciousness,
nobility, politeness

galling adjective <u>annoying</u>, bitter,
exasperating, irksome, irritating,
provoking, vexatious

gallivant verb <u>wander</u>, gad
about, ramble, roam, rove

gallop verb <u>run</u>, bolt, career,
dash, hurry, race, rush, speed,
sprint

galore adverb <u>in abundance</u>, all
over the place, aplenty,
everywhere, in great quantity, in
numbers, in profusion, to spare

galvanize verb <u>stimulate</u>,
electrify, excite, inspire,
invigorate, jolt, provoke, spur, stir

gamble verb **1** <u>bet</u>, game, have a
flutter (informal), play, punt,
wager **2** <u>risk</u>, chance, hazard,
speculate, stick one's neck out
(informal), take a chance ♦ noun
3 <u>risk</u>, chance, leap in the dark,
lottery, speculation, uncertainty,
venture **4** <u>bet</u>, flutter (informal),
punt, wager

gambol verb **1** <u>frolic</u>, caper,

cavort, frisk, hop, jump, prance, skip ♦ *noun* **2** <u>frolic</u>, caper, hop, jump, prance, skip

game *noun* **1** <u>pastime</u>, amusement, distraction, diversion, entertainment, lark, recreation, sport **2** <u>match</u>, competition, contest, event, head-to-head, meeting, tournament **3** <u>wild animals</u>, prey, quarry **4** <u>scheme</u>, design, plan, plot, ploy, stratagem, tactic, trick ♦ *adjective* **5** <u>brave</u>, courageous, gallant, gritty, intrepid, persistent, plucky, spirited **6** <u>willing</u>, desirous, eager, interested, keen, prepared, ready

gamut *noun* <u>range</u>, area, catalogue, compass, field, scale, scope, series, sweep

gang *noun* <u>group</u>, band, clique, club, company, coterie, crowd, mob, pack, squad, team

gangling *adjective* <u>tall</u>, angular, awkward, lanky, rangy, rawboned, spindly

gangster *noun* <u>racketeer</u>, crook (*informal*), hood (*U.S. slang*), hoodlum (*chiefly U.S.*), mobster (*U.S. slang*)

gap *noun* **1** <u>opening</u>, break, chink, cleft, crack, hole, space **2** <u>interval</u>, breathing space, hiatus, interlude, intermission, interruption, lacuna, lull, pause, respite **3** <u>difference</u>, disagreement, disparity, divergence, inconsistency

gape *verb* **1** <u>stare</u>, gawk, gawp (*Brit. slang*), goggle, wonder **2** <u>open</u>, crack, split, yawn

gaping *adjective* <u>wide</u>, broad, cavernous, great, open, vast, wide open, yawning

garbage *noun* <u>rubbish</u>, refuse, trash (*chiefly U.S.*), waste

garbled *adjective* <u>jumbled</u>, confused, distorted, double-Dutch, incomprehensible, mixed up, unintelligible

garish *adjective* <u>gaudy</u>, brash, brassy, flashy, loud, showy, tacky (*informal*), tasteless, vulgar

garland *noun* **1** <u>wreath</u>, bays, chaplet, crown, festoon, honours, laurels ♦ *verb* **2** <u>adorn</u>, crown, deck, festoon, wreathe

garments *plural noun* <u>clothes</u>, apparel, attire, clothing, costume, dress, garb, gear (*slang*), outfit, uniform

garner *verb* <u>collect</u>, accumulate, amass, gather, hoard, save, stockpile, store, stow away

garnish *verb* **1** <u>decorate</u>, adorn, embellish, enhance, ornament, set off, trim ♦ *noun* **2** <u>decoration</u>, adornment, embellishment, enhancement, ornamentation, trimming

garrison *noun* **1** <u>troops</u>, armed force, command, detachment, unit **2** <u>fort</u>, base, camp, encampment, fortification, fortress, post, station, stronghold ♦ *verb* **3** <u>station</u>, assign, position, post, put on duty

garrulous *adjective* <u>talkative</u>, chatty, gossiping, loquacious, prattling, verbose, voluble

gash *verb* **1** <u>cut</u>, gouge, lacerate, slash, slit, split, tear, wound ♦ *noun* **2** <u>cut</u>, gouge, incision, laceration, slash, slit, split, tear, wound

gasp *verb* **1** <u>gulp</u>, blow, catch

one's breath, choke, pant, puff ♦ *noun* **2** <u>gulp</u>, exclamation, pant, puff, sharp intake of breath

gate *noun* <u>barrier</u>, door, entrance, exit, gateway, opening, passage, portal

gather *verb* **1** <u>assemble</u>, accumulate, amass, collect, garner, mass, muster, stockpile **2** <u>learn</u>, assume, conclude, deduce, hear, infer, surmise, understand **3** <u>pick</u>, cull, garner, glean, harvest, pluck, reap, select **4** <u>intensify</u>, deepen, expand, grow, heighten, increase, rise, swell, thicken **5** <u>fold</u>, pleat, tuck

gathering *noun* <u>assembly</u>, company, conclave, congress, convention, crowd, group, meeting

gauche *adjective* <u>awkward</u>, clumsy, ill-mannered, inelegant, tactless, unsophisticated

gaudy *adjective* <u>garish</u>, bright, flashy, loud, showy, tacky (*informal*), tasteless, vulgar

gauge *verb* **1** <u>measure</u>, ascertain, calculate, check, compute, count, determine, weigh **2** <u>judge</u>, adjudge, appraise, assess, estimate, evaluate, guess, rate, reckon, value ♦ *noun* **3** <u>indicator</u>, criterion, guide, guideline, measure, meter, standard, test, touchstone, yardstick

gaunt *adjective* <u>thin</u>, angular, bony, haggard, lean, pinched, scrawny, skinny, spare

gawky *adjective* <u>awkward</u>, clumsy, gauche, loutish, lumbering, maladroit, ungainly

gay *adjective* **1** <u>homosexual</u>, lesbian, queer (*informal, derogatory*) **2** <u>carefree</u>, blithe, cheerful, jovial, light-hearted, lively, merry, sparkling **3** <u>colourful</u>, bright, brilliant, flamboyant, flashy, rich, showy, vivid ♦ *noun* **4** <u>homosexual</u>, lesbian

gaze *verb* **1** <u>stare</u>, gape, look, regard, view, watch, wonder ♦ *noun* **2** <u>stare</u>, fixed look, look

gazette *noun* <u>newspaper</u>, journal, news-sheet, paper, periodical

gear *noun* **1** <u>cog</u>, cogwheel, gearwheel **2** <u>mechanism</u>, cogs, machinery, works **3** <u>equipment</u>, accoutrements, apparatus, instruments, paraphernalia, supplies, tackle, tools **4** <u>clothing</u>, clothes, costume, dress, garments, outfit, togs, wear ♦ *verb* **5** <u>equip</u>, adapt, adjust, fit

gelatinous *adjective* <u>jelly-like</u>, glutinous, gummy, sticky, viscous

gelid *adjective* <u>cold</u>, arctic, chilly, freezing, frigid, frosty, frozen, glacial, ice-cold, icy

gem *noun* **1** <u>precious stone</u>, jewel, stone **2** <u>prize</u>, jewel, masterpiece, pearl, treasure

general *adjective* **1** <u>common</u>, accepted, broad, extensive, popular, prevalent, public, universal, widespread **2** <u>imprecise</u>, approximate, ill-defined, indefinite, inexact, loose, unspecific, vague **3** <u>universal</u>, across-the-board, blanket, collective, comprehensive, indiscriminate, miscellaneous, sweeping, total

generally *adverb* **1** <u>usually</u>, as a rule, by and large, customarily, normally, on the whole, ordinarily, typically **2** commonly, extensively, popularly, publicly, universally, widely

generate *verb* produce, breed, cause, create, engender, give rise to, make, propagate

generation *noun* **1** production, creation, formation, genesis, propagation, reproduction **2** age group, breed, crop **3** age, epoch, era, period, time

generic *adjective* collective, blanket, common, comprehensive, general, inclusive, universal, wide

generosity *noun* **1** charity, beneficence, bounty, kindness, largesse *or* largess, liberality, munificence, open-handedness **2** unselfishness, goodness, high-mindedness, magnanimity, nobleness

generous *adjective* **1** charitable, beneficent, bountiful, hospitable, kind, lavish, liberal, open-handed, unstinting **2** unselfish, big hearted, good, high-minded, lofty, magnanimous, noble **3** plentiful, abundant, ample, copious, full, lavish, liberal, rich, unstinting

genesis *noun* beginning, birth, creation, formation, inception, origin, start

genial *adjective* cheerful, affable, agreeable, amiable, congenial, friendly, good-natured, jovial, pleasant, warm

geniality *noun* cheerfulness, affability, agreeableness, amiability, conviviality, cordiality, friendliness, good cheer, joviality, warmth

genius *noun* **1** master, brainbox,

expert, hotshot (*informal*), maestro, mastermind, virtuoso, whiz (*informal*) **2** brilliance, ability, aptitude, bent, capacity, flair, gift, knack, talent

genre *noun* type, category, class, group, kind, sort, species, style

genteel *adjective* refined, courteous, cultured, elegant, gentlemanly, ladylike, polite, respectable, urbane, well-mannered

gentle *adjective*
1 sweet-tempered, compassionate, humane, kindly, meek, mild, placid, tender **2** moderate, light, mild, muted, slight, soft, soothing **3** gradual, easy, imperceptible, light, mild, moderate, slight, slow **4** tame, biddable, broken, docile, manageable, placid, tractable

gentlemanly *adjective* polite, civil, courteous, gallant, genteel, honourable, refined, urbane, well-mannered

gentleness *noun* tenderness, compassion, kindness, mildness, softness, sweetness

gentry *noun* nobility, aristocracy, elite, upper class, upper crust (*informal*)

genuine *adjective* **1** authentic, actual, bona fide, legitimate, real, the real McCoy, true, veritable **2** sincere, candid, earnest, frank, heartfelt, honest, unaffected, unfeigned

germ *noun* **1** microbe, bacterium, bug (*informal*), microorganism, virus **2** beginning, embryo, origin, root, rudiment, seed, source, spark

germane adjective <u>relevant</u>, apposite, appropriate, apropos, connected, fitting, material, pertinent, related, to the point or purpose

germinate verb <u>sprout</u>, bud, develop, generate, grow, originate, shoot, swell, vegetate

gesticulate verb <u>signal</u>, gesture, indicate, make a sign, motion, sign, wave

gesture noun 1 <u>signal</u>, action, gesticulation, indication, motion, sign ♦ verb 2 <u>signal</u>, gesticulate, indicate, motion, sign, wave

get verb 1 <u>obtain</u>, acquire, attain, fetch, gain, land, net, pick up, procure, receive, secure, win 2 <u>contract</u>, catch, come down with, fall victim to, take 3 <u>capture</u>, grab, lay hold of, nab (informal), seize, take 4 <u>become</u>, come to be, grow, turn 5 <u>understand</u>, catch, comprehend, fathom, follow, perceive, see, take in, work out 6 <u>persuade</u>, convince, induce, influence, prevail upon 7 Informal <u>annoy</u>, bug (informal), gall, irritate, upset, vex

get across verb 1 <u>cross</u>, ford, negotiate, pass over, traverse 2 <u>communicate</u>, bring home to, convey, impart, make clear or understood, put over, transmit

get at verb 1 <u>gain access to</u>, acquire, attain, come to grips with, get hold of, reach 2 <u>imply</u>, hint, intend, lead up to, mean, suggest 3 <u>criticize</u>, attack, blame, find fault with, nag, pick on

getaway noun <u>escape</u>, break, break-out, flight

get by verb <u>manage</u>, cope, exist, fare, get along, keep one's head above water, make both ends meet, survive

get off verb <u>leave</u>, alight, depart, descend, disembark, dismount, escape, exit

get on verb 1 <u>board</u>, ascend, climb, embark, mount 2 <u>be friendly</u>, be compatible, concur, get along, hit it off (informal)

get over verb <u>recover from</u>, come round, get better, mend, pull through, rally, revive, survive

ghastly adjective <u>horrible</u>, dreadful, frightful, gruesome, hideous, horrendous, loathsome, shocking, terrible, terrifying

ghost noun 1 <u>spirit</u>, apparition, phantom, soul, spectre, spook (informal), wraith 2 <u>trace</u>, glimmer, hint, possibility, semblance, shadow, suggestion

ghostly adjective <u>supernatural</u>, eerie, ghostlike, phantom, spectral, spooky (informal), unearthly, wraithlike

ghoulish adjective <u>macabre</u>, disgusting, grisly, gruesome, morbid, sick (informal), unwholesome

giant noun 1 <u>ogre</u>, colossus, monster, titan ♦ adjective 2 <u>huge</u>, colossal, enormous, gargantuan, gigantic, immense, mammoth, titanic, vast

gibberish noun <u>nonsense</u>, babble, drivel, gobbledegook (informal), mumbo jumbo, twaddle

gibe, jibe verb 1 <u>taunt</u>, jeer, make fun of, mock, poke fun at, ridicule, scoff, scorn, sneer

♦ *noun* 2 <u>taunt</u>, barb, crack (*slang*), dig, jeer, sarcasm, scoffing, sneer

giddiness *noun* <u>dizziness</u>, faintness, light-headedness, vertigo

giddy *adjective* <u>dizzy</u>, dizzying, faint, light-headed, reeling, unsteady, vertiginous

gift *noun* 1 <u>donation</u>, bequest, bonus, contribution, grant, hand-out, legacy, offering, present 2 <u>talent</u>, ability, capability, capacity, flair, genius, knack, power

gifted *adjective* <u>talented</u>, able, accomplished, brilliant, capable, clever, expert, ingenious, masterly, skilled

gigantic *adjective* <u>enormous</u>, colossal, giant, huge, immense, mammoth, stupendous, titanic, tremendous

giggle *verb, noun* <u>laugh</u>, cackle, chortle, chuckle, snigger, titter, twitter

gild *verb* <u>embellish</u>, adorn, beautify, brighten, coat, dress up, embroider, enhance, ornament

gimmick *noun* <u>stunt</u>, contrivance, device, dodge, ploy, scheme

gingerly *adverb* <u>cautiously</u>, carefully, charily, circumspectly, hesitantly, reluctantly, suspiciously, timidly, warily

gird *verb* <u>surround</u>, encircle, enclose, encompass, enfold, hem in, ring

girdle *noun* 1 <u>belt</u>, band, cummerbund, sash, waistband ♦ *verb* 2 <u>surround</u>, bound, encircle, enclose, encompass, gird, ring

girl *noun* <u>female child</u>, damsel (*archaic*), daughter, lass, lassie (*informal*), maid (*archaic*), maiden (*archaic*), miss

girth *noun* <u>circumference</u>, bulk, measure, size

gist *noun* <u>point</u>, core, essence, force, idea, meaning, sense, significance, substance

give *verb* 1 <u>present</u>, award, contribute, deliver, donate, grant, hand over *or* out, provide, supply 2 <u>announce</u>, communicate, issue, notify, pronounce, transmit, utter 3 <u>concede</u>, grant, hand over, relinquish, surrender, yield 4 <u>produce</u>, cause, engender, make, occasion

give away *verb* <u>reveal</u>, betray, disclose, divulge, expose, leak, let out, let slip, uncover

give in *verb* <u>admit defeat</u>, capitulate, collapse, concede, quit, submit, succumb, surrender, yield

give off *verb* <u>emit</u>, discharge, exude, produce, release, send out, throw out

give out *verb* <u>emit</u>, discharge, exude, produce, release, send out, throw out

give up *verb* <u>abandon</u>, call it a day *or* night, cease, desist, leave off, quit, relinquish, renounce, stop, surrender

glad *adjective* 1 <u>happy</u>, contented, delighted, gratified, joyful, overjoyed, pleased 2 <u>pleasing</u>, cheerful, cheering, gratifying, pleasant

gladden verb please, cheer, delight, gratify, hearten

gladly adverb happily, cheerfully, freely, gleefully, readily, willingly, with pleasure

gladness noun happiness, cheerfulness, delight, gaiety, glee, high spirits, joy, mirth, pleasure

glamorous adjective elegant, attractive, dazzling, exciting, fascinating, glittering, glossy, prestigious, smart

glamour noun charm, allure, appeal, attraction, beauty, enchantment, fascination, prestige

glance verb 1 look, glimpse, peek, peep, scan, view 2 gleam, flash, glimmer, glint, glisten, glitter, reflect, shimmer, shine, twinkle ♦ noun 3 look, dekko (slang), glimpse, peek, peep, view

glare verb 1 scowl, frown, glower, look daggers, lour or lower 2 dazzle, blaze, flame, flare ♦ noun 3 scowl, black look, dirty look, frown, glower, lour or lower 4 dazzle, blaze, brilliance, flame, glow

glaring adjective 1 conspicuous, blatant, flagrant, gross, manifest, obvious, outrageous, unconcealed 2 dazzling, blazing, bright, garish, glowing

glassy adjective 1 transparent, clear, glossy, shiny, slippery, smooth 2 expressionless, blank, cold, dull, empty, fixed, glazed, lifeless, vacant

glaze verb 1 coat, enamel, gloss, lacquer, polish, varnish ♦ noun 2 coat, enamel, finish, gloss, lacquer, lustre, patina, polish,

shine, varnish

gleam noun 1 glow, beam, flash, glimmer, ray, sparkle 2 trace, flicker, glimmer, hint, inkling, suggestion ♦ verb 3 shine, flash, glimmer, glint, glisten, glitter, glow, shimmer, sparkle

glee noun delight, elation, exhilaration, exuberance, exultation, joy, merriment, triumph

gleeful adjective delighted, cock-a-hoop, elated, exuberant, exultant, joyful, jubilant, overjoyed, triumphant

glib adjective smooth, easy, fluent, insincere, plausible, quick, ready, slick, suave, voluble

glide verb slide, coast, drift, float, flow, roll, run, sail, skate, slip

glimmer verb 1 flicker, blink, gleam, glisten, glitter, glow, shimmer, shine, sparkle, twinkle ♦ noun 2 gleam, blink, flicker, glow, ray, shimmer, sparkle, twinkle 3 trace, flicker, gleam, hint, inkling, suggestion

glimpse noun 1 look, glance, peek, peep, sight, sighting ♦ verb 2 catch sight of, espy, sight, spot, spy, view

glint verb 1 gleam, flash, glimmer, glitter, shine, sparkle, twinkle ♦ noun 2 gleam, flash, glimmer, glitter, shine, sparkle, twinkle, twinkling

glisten verb gleam, flash, glance, glare, glimmer, glint, glitter, shimmer, shine, sparkle, twinkle

glitch noun problem, blip, difficulty, gremlin, hitch, interruption, malfunction, snag

glitter verb 1 shine, flash, glare,

gleam, glimmer, glint, glisten, shimmer, sparkle, twinkle ♦ *noun* **2** shine, brightness, flash, glare, gleam, radiance, sheen, shimmer, sparkle **3** glamour, display, gaudiness, pageantry, show, showiness, splendour, tinsel

gloat *verb* relish, crow, drool, exult, glory, revel in, rub it in (*informal*), triumph

global *adjective* **1** worldwide, international, universal, world **2** comprehensive, all-inclusive, exhaustive, general, total, unlimited

globe *noun* sphere, ball, earth, orb, planet, world

globule *noun* droplet, bead, bubble, drop, particle, pearl, pellet

gloom *noun* **1** darkness, blackness, dark, dusk, murk, obscurity, shade, shadow, twilight **2** depression, dejection, despondency, low spirits, melancholy, sorrow, unhappiness, woe

gloomy *adjective* **1** dark, black, dim, dismal, dreary, dull, grey, murky, sombre **2** depressing, bad, cheerless, disheartening, dispiriting, dreary, sad, sombre **3** miserable, crestfallen, dejected, dispirited, downcast, downhearted, glum, melancholy, morose, pessimistic, sad

glorify *verb* **1** enhance, aggrandize, dignify, elevate, ennoble, magnify **2** worship, adore, bless, exalt, honour, idolize, pay homage to, revere, venerate **3** praise, celebrate, eulogize, extol, sing *or* sound

the praises of

glorious *adjective* **1** famous, celebrated, distinguished, eminent, honoured, illustrious, magnificent, majestic, renowned **2** splendid, beautiful, brilliant, dazzling, gorgeous, shining, superb **3** delightful, excellent, fine, gorgeous, marvellous, wonderful

glory *noun* **1** honour, dignity, distinction, eminence, fame, praise, prestige, renown **2** splendour, grandeur, greatness, magnificence, majesty, nobility, pageantry, pomp ♦ *verb* **3** triumph, boast, exult, pride oneself, relish, revel, take delight

gloss¹ *noun* shine, brightness, gleam, lustre, patina, polish, sheen, veneer

gloss² *noun* **1** comment, annotation, commentary, elucidation, explanation, footnote, interpretation, note, translation ♦ *verb* **2** interpret, annotate, comment, elucidate, explain, translate

glossy *adjective* shiny, bright, glassy, glazed, lustrous, polished, shining, silky

glow *verb* **1** shine, brighten, burn, gleam, glimmer, redden, smoulder ♦ *noun* **2** light, burning, gleam, glimmer, luminosity, phosphorescence **3** radiance, brightness, brilliance, effulgence, splendour, vividness

glower *verb* **1** scowl, frown, give a dirty look, glare, look daggers, lour *or* lower ♦ *noun* **2** scowl, black look, dirty look, frown, glare, lour *or* lower

glowing *adjective* **1** <u>bright</u>, aglow, flaming, luminous, radiant **2** <u>complimentary</u>, adulatory, ecstatic, enthusiastic, laudatory, rave (*informal*), rhapsodic

glue *noun* **1** <u>adhesive</u>, cement, gum, paste ♦ *verb* **2** <u>stick</u>, affix, cement, fix, gum, paste, seal

glum *adjective* <u>gloomy</u>, crestfallen, dejected, doleful, low, morose, pessimistic, sullen

glut *noun* **1** <u>surfeit</u>, excess, oversupply, plethora, saturation, superfluity, surplus ♦ *verb* **2** <u>saturate</u>, choke, clog, deluge, flood, inundate, overload, oversupply

glutton *noun* <u>gourmand</u>, gannet (*slang*), pig (*informal*)

gluttonous *adjective* <u>greedy</u>, gormandizing, insatiable, piggish, ravenous, voracious

gluttony *noun* <u>greed</u>, gormandizing, greediness, voracity

gnarled *adjective* <u>twisted</u>, contorted, knotted, knotty, rough, rugged, weather-beaten, wrinkled

gnaw *verb* <u>bite</u>, chew, munch, nibble

go *verb* **1** <u>move</u>, advance, journey, make for, pass, proceed, set off, travel **2** <u>leave</u>, depart, make tracks, move out, slope off, withdraw **3** <u>function</u>, move, operate, perform, run, work **4** <u>contribute</u>, lead to, serve, tend, work towards **5** <u>harmonize</u>, agree, blend, chime, complement, correspond, fit, match, suit **6** <u>elapse</u>, expire, flow, lapse, pass, slip away

♦ *noun* **7** <u>attempt</u>, bid, crack (*informal*), effort, shot (*informal*), try, turn **8** *Informal* <u>energy</u>, drive, force, life, spirit, verve, vigour, vitality, vivacity

goad *verb* **1** <u>provoke</u>, drive, egg on, exhort, incite, prod, prompt, spur ♦ *noun* **2** <u>provocation</u>, impetus, incentive, incitement, irritation, spur, stimulus, urge

goal *noun* <u>aim</u>, ambition, end, intention, object, objective, purpose, target

gobble *verb* <u>devour</u>, bolt, cram, gorge, gulp, guzzle, stuff, swallow, wolf

gobbledegook *noun* <u>nonsense</u>, babble, cant, gabble, gibberish, hocus-pocus, jargon, mumbo jumbo, twaddle

go-between *noun* <u>intermediary</u>, agent, broker, dealer, mediator, medium, middleman

godforsaken *adjective* <u>desolate</u>, abandoned, bleak, deserted, dismal, dreary, forlorn, gloomy, lonely, remote, wretched

godlike *adjective* <u>divine</u>, celestial, heavenly, superhuman, transcendent

godly *adjective* <u>devout</u>, god-fearing, good, holy, pious, religious, righteous, saintly

godsend *noun* <u>blessing</u>, boon, manna, stroke of luck, windfall

go for *verb* **1** <u>favour</u>, admire, be attracted to, be fond of, choose, like, prefer **2** <u>attack</u>, assail, assault, launch oneself at, rush upon, set about *or* upon, spring upon

golden *adjective* **1** <u>yellow</u>, blond *or* blonde, flaxen **2** <u>successful</u>, flourishing, glorious, halcyon, happy, prosperous, rich **3** promising, excellent, favourable, opportune

gone adjective **1** finished, elapsed, ended, over, past **2** missing, absent, astray, away, lacking, lost, vanished

good adjective **1** pleasing, acceptable, admirable, excellent, fine, first-class, first-rate, great, satisfactory, splendid, superior **2** praiseworthy, admirable, ethical, honest, honourable, moral, righteous, trustworthy, upright, virtuous, worthy **3** expert, able, accomplished, adept, adroit, clever, competent, proficient, skilled, talented **4** beneficial, advantageous, convenient, favourable, fitting, helpful, profitable, suitable, useful, wholesome **5** kind, altruistic, benevolent, charitable, friendly, humane, kind-hearted, kindly, merciful, obliging **6** valid, authentic, bona fide, genuine, legitimate, proper, real, true **7** well-behaved, dutiful, obedient, orderly, polite, well-mannered **8** full, adequate, ample, complete, considerable, extensive, large, substantial, sufficient ♦ noun **9** benefit, advantage, gain, interest, profit, use, usefulness, welfare, wellbeing **10** virtue, excellence, goodness, merit, morality, rectitude, right, righteousness, worth **11** for good permanently, finally, for ever, irrevocably, once and for all

goodbye noun farewell, adieu, leave-taking, parting

good-for-nothing noun **1** layabout, black sheep, idler, ne'er-do-well, skiver (Brit. slang), slacker (informal), waster, wastrel ♦ adjective **2** worthless, feckless, idle, irresponsible, useless

goodly adjective considerable, ample, large, significant, sizable or sizeable, substantial, tidy (informal)

goodness noun **1** excellence, merit, quality, superiority, value, worth **2** kindness, benevolence, friendliness, generosity, goodwill, humaneness, kind-heartedness, kindliness, mercy **3** virtue, honesty, honour, integrity, merit, morality, probity, rectitude, righteousness, uprightness **4** benefit, advantage, salubriousness, wholesomeness

goods plural noun **1** property, belongings, chattels, effects, gear, paraphernalia, possessions, things, trappings **2** merchandise, commodities, stock, stuff, wares

goodwill noun friendliness, amity, benevolence, friendship, heartiness, kindliness

go off verb **1** explode, blow up, detonate, fire **2** leave, decamp, depart, go away, move out, part, quit, slope off **3** Informal rot, go bad, go stale

go out verb **1** leave, depart, exit **2** be extinguished, die out, expire, fade out

go over verb examine, inspect, rehearse, reiterate, review, revise, study, work over

gore¹ noun blood, bloodshed, butchery, carnage, slaughter

gore² verb pierce, impale, transfix, wound

gorge noun 1 <u>ravine</u>, canyon, chasm, cleft, defile, fissure, pass ◆ verb 2 <u>overeat</u>, cram, devour, feed, glut, gobble, gulp, guzzle, stuff, wolf

gorgeous adjective 1 <u>beautiful</u>, dazzling, elegant, magnificent, ravishing, splendid, stunning (informal), sumptuous, superb 2 Informal <u>pleasing</u>, delightful, enjoyable, exquisite, fine, glorious, good, lovely

gory adjective <u>bloodthirsty</u>, blood-soaked, bloodstained, bloody, murderous, sanguinary

gospel noun 1 <u>truth</u>, certainty, fact, the last word 2 <u>doctrine</u>, credo, creed, message, news, revelation, tidings

gossip noun 1 <u>idle talk</u>, blether, chinwag (Brit. informal), chitchat, hearsay, scandal, small talk, tittle-tattle 2 <u>busybody</u>, chatterbox (informal), chatterer, gossipmonger, scandalmonger, tattler, telltale ◆ verb 3 <u>chat</u>, blether, gabble, jaw (slang), prate, prattle, tattle

go through verb 1 <u>suffer</u>, bear, brave, endure, experience, tolerate, undergo, withstand 2 <u>examine</u>, check, explore, forage, hunt, look, search

gouge verb 1 <u>scoop</u>, chisel, claw, cut, dig (out), hollow (out) ◆ noun 2 <u>gash</u>, cut, furrow, groove, hollow, scoop, scratch, trench

gourmet noun <u>connoisseur</u>, bon vivant, epicure, foodie (informal), gastronome

govern verb 1 <u>rule</u>, administer, command, control, direct, guide, handle, lead, manage, order

2 <u>restrain</u>, check, control, curb, discipline, hold in check, master, regulate, subdue, tame

government noun 1 <u>rule</u>, administration, authority, governance, sovereignty, statecraft 2 <u>executive</u>, administration, ministry, powers-that-be, regime

governor noun <u>leader</u>, administrator, chief, commander, controller, director, executive, head, manager, ruler

gown noun <u>dress</u>, costume, frock, garb, garment, habit, robe

grab verb <u>snatch</u>, capture, catch, catch or take hold of, clutch, grasp, grip, pluck, seize, snap up

grace noun 1 <u>elegance</u>, attractiveness, beauty, charm, comeliness, ease, gracefulness, poise, polish, refinement, tastefulness 2 <u>goodwill</u>, benefaction, benevolence, favour, generosity, goodness, kindliness, kindness 3 <u>manners</u>, consideration, decency, decorum, etiquette, propriety, tact 4 <u>indulgence</u>, mercy, pardon, reprieve 5 <u>prayer</u>, benediction, blessing, thanks, thanksgiving ◆ verb 6 <u>honour</u>, adorn, decorate, dignify, embellish, enhance, enrich, favour, ornament, set off

graceful adjective <u>elegant</u>, beautiful, charming, comely, easy, pleasing, tasteful

gracious adjective <u>kind</u>, charitable, civil, considerate, cordial, courteous, friendly, polite, well-mannered

grade noun 1 <u>level</u>, category, class, degree, echelon, group, rank, stage ◆*verb* **2** classify, arrange, class, group, order, range, rank, rate, sort

gradient *noun* slope, bank, declivity, grade, hill, incline, rise

gradual *adjective* steady, gentle, graduated, piecemeal, progressive, regular, slow, unhurried

gradually *adverb* steadily, by degrees, gently, little by little, progressively, slowly, step by step, unhurriedly

graduate *verb* **1** mark off, calibrate, grade, measure out, proportion, regulate **2** classify, arrange, grade, group, order, rank, sort

graft *noun* **1** shoot, bud, implant, scion, splice, sprout ◆*verb* **2** transplant, affix, implant, ingraft, insert, join, splice

grain *noun* **1** cereals, corn **2** seed, grist, kernel **3** bit, fragment, granule, modicum, morsel, particle, piece, scrap, speck, trace **4** texture, fibre, nap, pattern, surface, weave **5** *As in* **go against the grain** inclination, character, disposition, humour, make-up, temper

grand *adjective* **1** impressive, dignified, grandiose, great, imposing, large, magnificent, regal, splendid, stately, sublime **2** excellent, fine, first-class, great (*informal*), outstanding, smashing (*informal*), splendid, wonderful

grandeur *noun* splendour, dignity, magnificence, majesty, nobility, pomp, stateliness, sublimity

grandiose *adjective*

1 pretentious, affected, bombastic, extravagant, flamboyant, high-flown, ostentatious, pompous, showy **2** imposing, grand, impressive, lofty, magnificent, majestic, monumental, stately

grant *verb* **1** consent to, accede to, agree to, allow, permit **2** give, allocate, allot, assign, award, donate, hand out, present **3** admit, acknowledge, concede ◆*noun* **4** award, allowance, donation, endowment, gift, hand-out, present, subsidy

granule *noun* grain, atom, crumb, fragment, molecule, particle, scrap, speck

graphic *adjective* **1** vivid, clear, detailed, explicit, expressive, lively, lucid, striking **2** pictorial, diagrammatic, visual

grapple *verb* **1** grip, clutch, grab, grasp, seize, wrestle **2** deal with, address oneself to, confront, get to grips with, struggle, tackle, take on

grasp *verb* **1** grip, catch, clasp, clinch, clutch, grab, grapple, hold, lay *or* take hold of, seize, snatch **2** understand, catch on, catch *or* get the drift of, comprehend, get, realize, see, take in ◆*noun* **3** grip, clasp, clutches, embrace, hold, possession, tenure **4** control, power, reach, scope **5** understanding, awareness, comprehension, grip, knowledge, mastery

grasping *adjective* greedy, acquisitive, avaricious, covetous, rapacious

grate verb 1 <u>shred</u>, mince, pulverize, triturate 2 <u>scrape</u>, creak, grind, rasp, rub, scratch 3 <u>annoy</u>, exasperate, get on one's nerves (*informal*), irritate, jar, rankle, set one's teeth on edge

grateful adjective <u>thankful</u>, appreciative, beholden, indebted, obliged

gratification noun <u>satisfaction</u>, delight, enjoyment, fulfilment, indulgence, pleasure, relish, reward, thrill

gratify verb <u>please</u>, delight, give pleasure, gladden, humour, requite, satisfy

grating[1] adjective <u>irritating</u>, annoying, discordant, displeasing, harsh, jarring, offensive, raucous, strident, unpleasant

grating[2] noun <u>grille</u>, grate, grid, gridiron, lattice, trellis

gratitude noun <u>thankfulness</u>, appreciation, gratefulness, indebtedness, obligation, recognition, thanks

gratuitous adjective 1 <u>free</u>, complimentary, gratis, spontaneous, unasked-for, unpaid, unrewarded, voluntary 2 <u>unjustified</u>, baseless, causeless, groundless, needless, superfluous, uncalled-for, unmerited, unnecessary, unwarranted, wanton

gratuity noun <u>tip</u>, bonus, donation, gift, largesse or largess, reward

grave[1] noun <u>burying place</u>, crypt, mausoleum, pit, sepulchre, tomb, vault

grave[2] adjective 1 <u>solemn</u>, dignified, dour, earnest, serious, sober, sombre, unsmiling 2 <u>important</u>, acute, critical, dangerous, pressing, serious, severe, threatening, urgent

graveyard noun <u>cemetery</u>, burial ground, charnel house, churchyard, necropolis

gravity noun 1 <u>importance</u>, acuteness, momentousness, perilousness, seriousness, severity, significance, urgency, weightiness 2 <u>solemnity</u>, dignity, earnestness, gravitas, seriousness, sobriety

graze[1] verb <u>feed</u>, browse, crop, pasture

graze[2] verb 1 <u>touch</u>, brush, glance off, rub, scrape, shave, skim 2 <u>scratch</u>, abrade, chafe, scrape, skin ♦ noun 3 <u>scratch</u>, abrasion, scrape

greasy adjective <u>fatty</u>, oily, oleaginous, slimy, slippery

great adjective 1 <u>large</u>, big, enormous, gigantic, huge, immense, prodigious, vast, voluminous 2 <u>important</u>, critical, crucial, momentous, serious, significant 3 <u>famous</u>, eminent, illustrious, noteworthy, outstanding, prominent, remarkable, renowned 4 *Informal* <u>excellent</u>, fantastic (*informal*), fine, marvellous (*informal*), superb, terrific (*informal*), tremendous (*informal*), wonderful

greatly adverb <u>very much</u>, considerably, enormously, exceedingly, hugely, immensely, remarkably, tremendously, vastly

greatness noun 1 <u>immensity</u>, enormity, hugeness, magnitude,

prodigiousness, size, vastness
2 importance, gravity,
momentousness, seriousness,
significance, urgency, weight
3 <u>fame</u>, celebrity, distinction,
eminence, glory, grandeur,
illustriousness, note, renown

greed, greediness *noun*
1 <u>gluttony</u>, edacity, esurience,
gormandizing, hunger, voracity
2 <u>avarice</u>, acquisitiveness,
avidity, covetousness, craving,
desire, longing, selfishness

greedy *adjective* 1 <u>gluttonous</u>,
gormandizing, hungry,
insatiable, piggish, ravenous,
voracious 2 <u>grasping</u>, acquisitive,
avaricious, avid, covetous,
craving, desirous, rapacious,
selfish

green *adjective* 1 <u>leafy</u>, grassy,
verdant 2 <u>ecological</u>,
conservationist,
environment-friendly,
non-polluting, ozone-friendly
3 <u>immature</u>, gullible,
inexperienced, naive, new, raw,
untrained, wet behind the ears
(*informal*) 4 <u>jealous</u>, covetous,
envious, grudging, resentful
♦ *noun* 5 <u>lawn</u>, common, sward,
turf

greet *verb* <u>welcome</u>, accost,
address, compliment, hail, meet,
receive, salute

greeting *noun* <u>welcome</u>, address,
reception, salutation, salute

gregarious *adjective* <u>outgoing</u>,
affable, companionable,
convivial, cordial, friendly,
sociable, social

grey *adjective* 1 <u>pale</u>, ashen,
pallid, wan 2 <u>dismal</u>, dark,
depressing, dim, drab, dreary,

dull, gloomy 3 <u>characterless</u>,
anonymous, colourless, dull

gridlock *noun* <u>standstill</u>,
deadlock, impasse, stalemate

grief *noun* <u>sadness</u>, anguish,
distress, heartache, misery,
regret, remorse, sorrow,
suffering, woe

grievance *noun* <u>complaint</u>, axe
to grind, gripe (*informal*), injury,
injustice

grieve *verb* 1 <u>mourn</u>, complain,
deplore, lament, regret, rue,
suffer, weep 2 <u>sadden</u>, afflict,
distress, hurt, injure, pain, wound

grievous *adjective* 1 <u>painful</u>,
dreadful, grave, harmful, severe
2 <u>deplorable</u>, atrocious, dreadful,
monstrous, offensive,
outrageous, shameful, shocking

grim *adjective* <u>forbidding</u>,
formidable, harsh, merciless,
ruthless, severe, sinister, stern,
terrible

grimace *noun* 1 <u>scowl</u>, face,
frown, sneer ♦ *verb* 2 <u>scowl</u>,
frown, lour *or* lower, make a face
or faces, sneer

grime *noun* <u>dirt</u>, filth, grot
(*slang*), smut, soot

grimy *adjective* <u>dirty</u>, filthy, foul,
grubby, soiled, sooty, unclean

grind *verb* 1 <u>crush</u>, abrade,
granulate, grate, mill, pound,
powder, pulverize, triturate
2 <u>smooth</u>, polish, sand, sharpen,
whet 3 <u>scrape</u>, gnash, grate
♦ *noun* 4 *Informal* <u>hard work</u>,
chore, drudgery, labour, sweat
(*informal*), toil

grip *noun* 1 <u>clasp</u>, hold 2 <u>control</u>,
clutches, domination, influence,
possession, power

3 understanding, command, comprehension, grasp, mastery ◆ *verb* **4** grasp, clasp, clutch, hold, seize, take hold of **5** engross, absorb, enthral, entrance, fascinate, hold, mesmerize, rivet

gripping *adjective* fascinating, compelling, engrossing, enthralling, entrancing, exciting, riveting, spellbinding, thrilling

grisly *adjective* gruesome, appalling, awful, dreadful, ghastly, horrible, macabre, shocking, terrifying

grit *noun* **1** gravel, dust, pebbles, sand **2** courage, backbone, determination, fortitude, guts (*informal*), perseverance, resolution, spirit, tenacity ◆ *verb* **3** grind, clench, gnash, grate

gritty *adjective* **1** rough, dusty, granular, gravelly, rasping, sandy **2** courageous, brave, determined, dogged, plucky, resolute, spirited, steadfast, tenacious

groan *noun* **1** moan, cry, sigh, whine **2** *Informal* complaint, gripe (*informal*), grouse, grumble, objection, protest ◆ *verb* **3** moan, cry, sigh, whine **4** *Informal* complain, bemoan, gripe (*informal*), grouse, grumble, lament, object

groggy *adjective* dizzy, confused, dazed, faint, shaky, unsteady, weak, wobbly

groom *noun* **1** stableman, hostler or ostler (*archaic*), stableboy ◆ *verb* **2** smarten up, clean, preen, primp, spruce up, tidy **3** rub down, brush, clean, curry, tend **4** train, coach, drill,

educate, make ready, nurture, prepare, prime, ready

groove *noun* indentation, channel, cut, flute, furrow, hollow, rut, trench, trough

grope *verb* feel, cast about, fish, flounder, forage, fumble, scrabble, search

gross *adjective* **1** fat, corpulent, hulking, obese, overweight **2** total, aggregate, before deductions, before tax, entire, whole **3** vulgar, coarse, crude, indelicate, obscene, offensive **4** blatant, flagrant, grievous, heinous, rank, sheer, unmitigated, utter ◆ *verb* **5** earn, bring in, make, rake in (*informal*), take

grotesque *adjective* unnatural, bizarre, deformed, distorted, fantastic, freakish, outlandish, preposterous, strange

ground *noun* **1** earth, dry land, land, soil, terra firma, terrain, turf **2** stadium, arena, field, park (*informal*), pitch **3** *often plural* land, estate, fields, gardens, terrain, territory **4** *usually plural* dregs, deposit, lees, sediment **5** grounds reason, basis, cause, excuse, foundation, justification, motive, occasion, pretext, rationale ◆ *verb* **6** base, establish, fix, found, set, settle **7** instruct, acquaint with, familiarize with, initiate, teach, train, tutor

groundless *adjective* unjustified, baseless, empty, idle, uncalled-for, unfounded, unwarranted

groundwork *noun* preliminaries, foundation, fundamentals, preparation, spadework, underpinnings

group noun 1 <u>set</u>, band, bunch, cluster, collection, crowd, gang, pack, party ♦ verb 2 <u>arrange</u>, bracket, class, classify, marshal, order, sort

grouse verb 1 <u>complain</u>, bellyache (slang), carp, gripe (informal), grumble, moan, whine, whinge (informal) ♦ noun 2 <u>complaint</u>, grievance, gripe (informal), grouch (informal), grumble, moan, objection, protest

grove noun <u>wood</u>, coppice, copse, covert, plantation, spinney, thicket

grovel verb <u>humble oneself</u>, abase oneself, bow and scrape, crawl, creep, cringe, demean oneself, fawn, kowtow, toady

grow verb 1 <u>increase</u>, develop, enlarge, expand, get bigger, multiply, spread, stretch, swell 2 <u>originate</u>, arise, issue, spring, stem 3 <u>improve</u>, advance, flourish, progress, prosper, succeed, thrive 4 <u>become</u>, come to be, get, turn 5 <u>cultivate</u>, breed, farm, nurture, produce, propagate, raise

grown-up adjective 1 <u>mature</u>, adult, fully-grown, of age ♦ noun 2 <u>adult</u>, man, woman

growth noun 1 <u>increase</u>, development, enlargement, expansion, multiplication, proliferation, stretching 2 <u>improvement</u>, advance, expansion, progress, prosperity, rise, success 3 Medical <u>tumour</u>, lump

grub noun 1 <u>larva</u>, caterpillar, maggot 2 Slang <u>food</u>, nosh

(slang), rations, sustenance, victuals ♦ verb 3 <u>dig up</u>, burrow, pull up, root (informal) 4 <u>search</u>, ferret, forage, hunt, rummage, scour, uncover, unearth

grubby adjective <u>dirty</u>, filthy, grimy, messy, mucky, scruffy, seedy, shabby, sordid, squalid, unwashed

grudge verb 1 <u>resent</u>, begrudge, complain, covet, envy, mind ♦ noun 2 <u>resentment</u>, animosity, antipathy, bitterness, dislike, enmity, grievance, rancour

gruelling adjective <u>exhausting</u>, arduous, backbreaking, demanding, laborious, punishing, severe, strenuous, taxing, tiring

gruesome adjective <u>horrific</u>, ghastly, grim, grisly, horrible, macabre, shocking, terrible

gruff adjective 1 <u>surly</u>, bad-tempered, brusque, churlish, grumpy, rough, rude, sullen, ungracious 2 <u>hoarse</u>, croaking, guttural, harsh, husky, low, rasping, rough, throaty

grumble verb 1 <u>complain</u>, bleat, carp, gripe (informal), grouch (informal), grouse, moan, whine, whinge (informal) 2 <u>rumble</u>, growl, gurgle, murmur, mutter, roar ♦ noun 3 <u>complaint</u>, grievance, gripe (informal), grouch (informal), grouse, moan, objection, protest 4 <u>rumble</u>, growl, gurgle, murmur, muttering, roar

grumpy adjective <u>irritable</u>, cantankerous, crotchety (informal), ill-tempered, peevish, sulky, sullen, surly, testy

guarantee noun 1 <u>assurance</u>,

bond, certainty, pledge, promise, security, surety, warranty, word of honour ♦ *verb* 2 make certain, assure, certify, ensure, pledge, promise, secure, vouch for, warrant

guard *verb* 1 watch over, defend, mind, preserve, protect, safeguard, secure, shield ♦ *noun* 2 protector, custodian, defender, lookout, picket, sentinel, sentry, warder, watch, watchman 3 protection, buffer, defence, safeguard, screen, security, shield 4 off guard unprepared, napping, unready, unwary 5 on guard prepared, alert, cautious, circumspect, on the alert, on the lookout, ready, vigilant, wary, watchful

guarded *adjective* cautious, cagey (*informal*), careful, circumspect, noncommittal, prudent, reserved, reticent, suspicious, wary

guardian *noun* keeper, champion, curator, custodian, defender, guard, protector, warden

guerrilla *noun* freedom fighter, partisan, underground fighter

guess *verb* 1 estimate, conjecture, hypothesize, predict, speculate, work out 2 suppose, believe, conjecture, fancy, imagine, judge, reckon, suspect, think ♦ *noun* 3 prediction, conjecture, hypothesis, shot in the dark, speculation, supposition, theory

guesswork *noun* speculation, conjecture, estimation, supposition, surmise, theory

guest *noun* visitor, boarder,

caller, company, lodger, visitant

guidance *noun* advice, counselling, direction, help, instruction, leadership, management, teaching

guide *noun* 1 escort, adviser, conductor, counsellor, leader, mentor, teacher, usher 2 model, example, ideal, inspiration, paradigm, standard 3 pointer, beacon, guiding light, landmark, lodestar, marker, sign, signpost 4 guidebook, Baedeker, catalogue, directory, handbook, instructions, key, manual ♦ *verb* 5 lead, accompany, conduct, direct, escort, shepherd, show the way, usher 6 steer, command, control, direct, handle, manage, manoeuvre 7 supervise, advise, counsel, influence, instruct, oversee, superintend, teach, train

guild *noun* society, association, brotherhood, club, company, corporation, fellowship, fraternity, league, lodge, order, organization, union

guile *noun* cunning, artifice, cleverness, craft, deceit, slyness, trickery, wiliness

guilt *noun* 1 culpability, blame, guiltiness, misconduct, responsibility, sinfulness, wickedness, wrongdoing 2 remorse, contrition, guilty conscience, regret, self-reproach, shame, stigma

guiltless *adjective* innocent, blameless, clean (*slang*), irreproachable, pure, sinless, spotless, squeaky-clean, untainted

guilty *adjective* 1 responsible, at fault, blameworthy, culpable, reprehensible, sinful, to blame, wrong **2** <u>remorseful</u>, ashamed, conscience-stricken, contrite, regretful, rueful, shamefaced, sheepish, sorry

guise noun <u>form</u>, appearance, aspect, demeanour, disguise, mode, pretence, semblance, shape

gulf noun **1** <u>bay</u>, bight, sea inlet **2** <u>chasm</u>, abyss, gap, opening, rift, separation, split, void

gullibility noun <u>credulity</u>, innocence, naïveté, simplicity

gullible adjective <u>naive</u>, born yesterday, credulous, innocent, simple, trusting, unsuspecting, wet behind the ears (*informal*)

gully noun <u>channel</u>, ditch, gutter, watercourse

gulp verb **1** <u>swallow</u>, devour, gobble, guzzle, quaff, swig (*informal*), swill, wolf **2** <u>gasp</u>, choke, swallow ♦ noun **3** <u>swallow</u>, draught, mouthful, swig (*informal*)

gum noun **1** <u>glue</u>, adhesive, cement, paste, resin ♦ verb **2** <u>stick</u>, affix, cement, glue, paste

gumption noun <u>resourcefulness</u>, acumen, astuteness, common sense, enterprise, initiative, mother wit, savvy (*slang*), wit(s)

gun noun <u>firearm</u>, handgun, piece (*slang*), shooter (*slang*)

gunman noun <u>terrorist</u>, bandit, gunslinger (*U.S. slang*), killer

gurgle verb **1** <u>murmur</u>, babble, bubble, lap, plash, purl, ripple, splash ♦ noun **2** <u>murmur</u>, babble, purl, ripple

guru noun <u>teacher</u>, authority, leader, master, mentor, sage,

Svengali, tutor

gush verb **1** <u>flow</u>, cascade, flood, pour, run, rush, spout, spurt, stream **2** <u>enthuse</u>, babble, chatter, effervesce, effuse, overstate, spout ♦ noun **3** <u>stream</u>, cascade, flood, flow, jet, rush, spout, spurt, torrent

gust noun **1** <u>blast</u>, blow, breeze, puff, rush, squall ♦ verb **2** <u>blow</u>, blast, squall

gusto noun <u>relish</u>, delight, enjoyment, enthusiasm, fervour, pleasure, verve, zeal

gut noun **1** Informal <u>paunch</u>, belly, potbelly, spare tyre (*Brit. slang*) **2 guts: a** <u>intestines</u>, belly, bowels, entrails, innards (*informal*), insides (*informal*), stomach, viscera **b** Informal <u>courage</u>, audacity, backbone, bottle (*slang*), daring, mettle, nerve, pluck, spirit ♦ verb **3** <u>disembowel</u>, clean **4** <u>ravage</u>, clean out, despoil, empty ♦ adjective **5** As in **gut reaction** <u>instinctive</u>, basic, heartfelt, intuitive, involuntary, natural, spontaneous, unthinking, visceral

gutsy adjective <u>brave</u>, bold, courageous, determined, gritty, indomitable, plucky, resolute, spirited

gutter noun <u>drain</u>, channel, conduit, ditch, sluice, trench, trough

guttural adjective <u>throaty</u>, deep, gravelly, gruff, hoarse, husky, rasping, rough, thick

guy noun Informal <u>man</u>, bloke (*Brit. informal*), chap, fellow, lad, person

guzzle verb <u>devour</u>, bolt, cram, drink, gobble, stuff (oneself), swill, wolf

Gypsy, Gipsy noun traveller, Bohemian, nomad, rambler, roamer, Romany, rover, wanderer

H h

habit noun 1 mannerism, custom, practice, proclivity, propensity, quirk, tendency, way 2 addiction, dependence

habitation noun 1 dwelling, abode, domicile, home, house, living quarters, lodging, quarters, residence 2 occupancy, inhabitance, occupation, tenancy

habitual adjective customary, accustomed, familiar, normal, regular, routine, standard, traditional, usual

hack¹ verb cut, chop, hew, lacerate, mangle, mutilate, slash

hack² noun 1 scribbler, literary hack, penny-a-liner 2 horse, crock, nag

hackneyed adjective unoriginal, clichéd, commonplace, overworked, stale, stereotyped, stock, threadbare, tired, trite

hag noun witch, crone, harridan

haggard adjective gaunt, careworn, drawn, emaciated, pinched, thin, wan

haggle verb bargain, barter, beat down

hail¹ noun 1 bombardment, barrage, downpour, rain, shower, storm, volley ◆ verb 2 rain down on, batter, beat down upon, bombard, pelt, rain, shower

hail² verb 1 greet, acclaim, acknowledge, applaud, cheer, honour, salute, welcome 2 flag down, signal to, wave down 3 **hail from** come from, be a native of, be born in, originate in

hair noun locks, head of hair, mane, mop, shock, tresses

hairdresser noun stylist, barber, coiffeur or coiffeuse

hair-raising adjective frightening, alarming, bloodcurdling, horrifying, scary, shocking, spine-chilling, terrifying

hairstyle noun haircut, coiffure, cut, hairdo, style

hairy adjective 1 shaggy, bushy, furry, hirsute, stubbly, unshaven, woolly 2 Slang dangerous, difficult, hazardous, perilous, risky

halcyon adjective 1 peaceful, calm, gentle, quiet, serene, tranquil, undisturbed 2 As in **halcyon days** happy, carefree, flourishing, golden, palmy, prosperous

hale adjective healthy, able-bodied, fit, flourishing, in the pink, robust, sound, strong, vigorous, well

half noun 1 equal part, fifty per cent, hemisphere, portion, section ◆ adjective 2 partial, halved, limited, moderate ◆ adverb 3 partially, in part, partly

half-baked adjective ill-judged, ill-conceived, impractical, poorly planned, short-sighted, unformed, unthought out or through

half-hearted adjective unenthusiastic, apathetic, indifferent, lacklustre, listless, lukewarm, perfunctory, tame

halfway adverb 1 <u>midway</u>, to or in the middle ♦ adjective 2 <u>midway</u>, central, equidistant, intermediate, mid, middle

halfwit noun <u>fool</u>, airhead (slang), dunderhead, idiot, imbecile (informal), moron, numbskull or numskull, simpleton, twit (informal, chiefly Brit.)

hall noun 1 <u>entrance hall</u>, corridor, entry, foyer, hallway, lobby, passage, passageway, vestibule 2 <u>meeting place</u>, assembly room, auditorium, chamber, concert hall

hallmark noun 1 <u>seal</u>, device, endorsement, mark, sign, stamp, symbol 2 <u>indication</u>, sure sign, telltale sign

hallucination noun <u>illusion</u>, apparition, delusion, dream, fantasy, figment of the imagination, mirage, vision

halo noun <u>ring of light</u>, aura, corona, nimbus, radiance

halt verb 1 <u>stop</u>, break off, cease, come to an end, desist, rest, stand still, wait 2 <u>end</u>, block, bring to an end, check, curb, cut short, nip in the bud, terminate ♦ noun 3 <u>stop</u>, close, end, pause, standstill, stoppage

halting adjective <u>faltering</u>, awkward, hesitant, laboured, stammering, stumbling, stuttering

halve verb <u>bisect</u>, cut in half, divide equally, share equally, split in two

hammer verb 1 <u>hit</u>, bang, beat, drive, knock, strike, tap 2 Informal <u>defeat</u>, beat, drub, run

rings around (informal), thrash, trounce, wipe the floor with (informal)

hamper verb <u>hinder</u>, frustrate, hamstring, handicap, impede, interfere with, obstruct, prevent, restrict

hand noun 1 <u>palm</u>, fist, mitt (slang), paw (informal) 2 <u>hired man</u>, artisan, craftsman, employee, labourer, operative, worker, workman 3 <u>penmanship</u>, calligraphy, handwriting, script 4 <u>ovation</u>, clap, round of applause 5 **at** or **on hand** <u>nearby</u>, at one's fingertips, available, close, handy, near, ready, within reach ♦ verb 6 <u>pass</u>, deliver, hand over

handbook noun <u>guidebook</u>, Baedeker, guide, instruction book, manual

handcuff verb <u>shackle</u>, fetter, manacle

handcuffs plural noun <u>shackles</u>, cuffs (informal), fetters, manacles

handful noun <u>few</u>, small number, smattering, sprinkling

handicap noun 1 <u>disadvantage</u>, barrier, drawback, hindrance, impediment, limitation, obstacle, restriction, stumbling block 2 <u>advantage</u>, head start 3 <u>disability</u>, defect, impairment ♦ verb 4 <u>restrict</u>, burden, encumber, hamper, hamstring, hinder, hold back, impede, limit

handicraft noun <u>craftsmanship</u>, art, craft, handiwork, skill, workmanship

handiwork noun <u>creation</u>, achievement, design, invention, product, production

handle noun 1 <u>grip</u>, haft, hilt, stock ♦ verb 2 <u>hold</u>, feel, finger, grasp, pick up, touch 3 <u>control</u>, direct, guide, manage, manipulate, manoeuvre 4 <u>deal with</u>, cope with, manage

hand-out noun 1 <u>charity</u>, alms, dole 2 <u>leaflet</u>, bulletin, circular, literature (informal), mailshot, press release

handsome adjective 1 <u>good-looking</u>, attractive, comely, dishy (informal, chiefly Brit.), elegant, gorgeous, personable, well-proportioned 2 <u>large</u>, abundant, ample, considerable, generous, liberal, plentiful, sizable or sizeable

handwriting noun <u>penmanship</u>, calligraphy, hand, scrawl, script

handy adjective 1 <u>available</u>, accessible, at hand, at one's fingertips, close, convenient, nearby, on hand, within reach 2 <u>useful</u>, convenient, easy to use, helpful, manageable, neat, practical, serviceable, user-friendly 3 <u>skilful</u>, adept, adroit, deft, dexterous, expert, proficient, skilled

hang verb 1 <u>suspend</u>, dangle, droop 2 <u>execute</u>, lynch, string up (informal) ♦ noun 3 <u>get the hang of</u> grasp, comprehend, understand

hang back verb <u>hesitate</u>, be reluctant, demur, hold back, recoil

hangdog adjective <u>guilty</u>, cowed, cringing, defeated, downcast, furtive, shamefaced, wretched

hangover noun <u>aftereffects</u>, crapulence, morning after (informal)

hang-up noun <u>preoccupation</u>, block, difficulty, inhibition, obsession, problem, thing (informal)

hank noun <u>coil</u>, length, loop, piece, roll, skein

hanker verb, with **for** or **after** <u>desire</u>, crave, hunger, itch, long, lust, pine, thirst, yearn

haphazard adjective <u>disorganized</u>, aimless, casual, hit or miss (informal), indiscriminate, slapdash

happen verb 1 <u>occur</u>, come about, come to pass, develop, result, take place, transpire (informal) 2 <u>chance</u>, turn out

happening noun <u>event</u>, affair, episode, experience, incident, occurrence, proceeding

happily adverb 1 <u>willingly</u>, freely, gladly, with pleasure 2 <u>joyfully</u>, blithely, cheerfully, gaily, gleefully, joyously, merrily 3 <u>luckily</u>, fortunately, opportunely, providentially

happiness noun <u>joy</u>, bliss, cheerfulness, contentment, delight, ecstasy, elation, jubilation, pleasure, satisfaction

happy adjective 1 <u>joyful</u>, blissful, cheerful, content, delighted, ecstatic, elated, glad, jubilant, merry, overjoyed, pleased, thrilled 2 <u>fortunate</u>, advantageous, auspicious, favourable, lucky, timely

happy-go-lucky adjective <u>carefree</u>, blithe, easy-going, light-hearted, nonchalant, unconcerned, untroubled

harangue verb 1 <u>rant</u>, address, declaim, exhort, hold forth,

lecture, spout (*informal*) ♦ *noun*
2 speech, address, declamation,
diatribe, exhortation, tirade

harass *verb* annoy, bother, harry,
hassle (*informal*), hound,
persecute, pester, plague,
trouble, vex

harassed *adjective* worried,
careworn, distraught, hassled
(*informal*), strained, tormented,
troubled, under pressure, vexed

harassment *noun* trouble,
annoyance, bother, hassle
(*informal*), irritation, nuisance,
persecution, pestering

harbour *noun* **1** port, anchorage,
haven ♦ *verb* **2** shelter, hide,
protect, provide refuge, shield
3 maintain, cling to, entertain,
foster, hold, nurse, nurture, retain

hard *adjective* **1** solid, firm,
inflexible, rigid, rocklike, stiff,
strong, tough, unyielding
2 strenuous, arduous,
backbreaking, exacting,
exhausting, laborious, rigorous,
tough **3** difficult, complicated,
intricate, involved, knotty,
perplexing, puzzling, thorny
4 unfeeling, callous, cold, cruel,
hardhearted, pitiless, stern,
unkind, unsympathetic **5** painful,
disagreeable, distressing,
grievous, intolerable, unpleasant
♦ *adverb* **6** energetically, fiercely,
forcefully, forcibly, heavily,
intensely, powerfully, severely,
sharply, strongly, vigorously,
violently, with all one's might,
with might and main
7 diligently, doggedly,
industriously, persistently,
steadily, untiringly

hard-bitten *or* **hard-boiled**

adjective tough, cynical,
hard-nosed (*informal*),
matter-of-fact, practical, realistic,
unsentimental

harden *verb* **1** solidify, anneal,
bake, cake, freeze, set, stiffen
2 accustom, habituate, inure,
season, train

hardened *adjective* **1** habitual,
chronic, incorrigible, inveterate,
shameless **2** accustomed,
habituated, inured, seasoned,
toughened

hard-headed *adjective* sensible,
level-headed, practical,
pragmatic, realistic, shrewd,
tough, unsentimental

hardhearted *adjective*
unsympathetic, callous, cold,
hard, heartless, insensitive,
uncaring, unfeeling

hardiness *noun* resilience,
resolution, robustness,
ruggedness, sturdiness, toughness

hardly *adverb* barely, just, only
just, scarcely, with difficulty

hardship *noun* suffering,
adversity, difficulty, misfortune,
need, privation, tribulation

hard up *adjective* poor, broke
(*informal*), impecunious,
impoverished, on the breadline,
out of pocket, penniless, short,
skint (*Brit. slang*), strapped for
cash (*informal*)

hardy *adjective* strong, robust,
rugged, sound, stout, sturdy,
tough

harm *verb* **1** injure, abuse,
damage, hurt, ill-treat, maltreat,
ruin, spoil, wound ♦ *noun*
2 injury, abuse, damage, hurt,
ill, loss, mischief, misfortune

harmful adjective destructive,
damaging, deleterious,
detrimental, hurtful, injurious,
noxious, pernicious

harmless adjective innocuous,
gentle, innocent, inoffensive,
nontoxic, safe, unobjectionable

harmonious adjective
1 melodious, agreeable,
concordant, consonant, dulcet,
mellifluous, musical,
sweet-sounding, tuneful
2 friendly, agreeable, amicable,
compatible, congenial, cordial,
sympathetic

harmonize verb blend, chime
with, cohere, coordinate,
correspond, match, tally, tone in
with

harmony noun 1 agreement,
accord, amicability,
compatibility, concord,
cooperation, friendship, peace,
rapport, sympathy 2 tunefulness,
euphony, melody, tune, unison

harness noun 1 equipment,
gear, tack, tackle ◆ verb
2 exploit, channel, control,
employ, mobilize, utilize

harrowing adjective distressing,
agonizing, disturbing,
heart-rending, nerve-racking,
painful, terrifying, tormenting,
traumatic

harry verb pester, badger,
bother, chivvy, harass, hassle
(informal), molest, plague

harsh adjective 1 raucous,
discordant, dissonant, grating,
guttural, rasping, rough, strident
2 severe, austere, cruel,
Draconian, drastic, pitiless,
punitive, ruthless, stern

harshly adverb severely, brutally,

cruelly, roughly, sternly, strictly

harshness noun severity,
asperity, austerity, brutality,
rigour, roughness, sternness

harvest noun 1 crop, produce,
yield ◆ verb 2 gather, mow, pick,
pluck, reap

hash noun **make a hash of**
Informal mess up, botch, bungle,
make a pig's ear of (informal),
mishandle, mismanage, muddle

hassle noun 1 argument,
bickering, disagreement, dispute,
fight, quarrel, row, squabble
2 trouble, bother, difficulty, grief
(informal), inconvenience,
problem ◆ verb 3 bother, annoy,
badger, bug (informal), harass,
hound, pester

haste noun 1 speed, alacrity,
quickness, rapidity, swiftness,
urgency, velocity 2 rush, hurry,
hustle, impetuosity

hasten verb rush, dash, fly, hurry
(up), make haste, race, scurry,
speed

hastily adverb 1 speedily,
promptly, quickly, rapidly
2 hurriedly, impetuously,
precipitately, rashly

hasty adjective 1 speedy, brisk,
hurried, prompt, rapid, swift,
urgent 2 impetuous, impulsive,
precipitate, rash, thoughtless

hatch verb 1 incubate, breed,
bring forth, brood 2 devise,
conceive, concoct, contrive,
cook up (informal), design,
dream up (informal), think up

hate verb 1 detest, abhor,
despise, dislike, loathe, recoil
from 2 be unwilling, be loath,
be reluctant, be sorry, dislike,

feel disinclined, shrink from
♦ *noun* 3 <u>dislike</u>, animosity,
antipathy, aversion, detestation,
enmity, hatred, hostility, loathing

hateful *adjective* <u>despicable</u>,
abhorrent, detestable, horrible,
loathsome, obnoxious, odious,
offensive, repellent, repugnant,
repulsive

hatred *noun* <u>dislike</u>, animosity,
antipathy, aversion, detestation,
enmity, hate, repugnance,
revulsion

haughty *adjective* <u>proud</u>,
arrogant, conceited,
contemptuous, disdainful,
imperious, scornful, snooty
(*informal*), stuck-up (*informal*),
supercilious

haul *verb* 1 <u>drag</u>, draw, heave,
lug, pull, tug ♦ *noun* 2 <u>gain</u>,
booty, catch, harvest, loot,
spoils, takings, yield

haunt *verb* 1 <u>plague</u>, obsess,
possess, prey on, recur, stay
with, torment, trouble, weigh on
♦ *noun* 2 <u>meeting place</u>, hangout
(*informal*), rendezvous, stamping
ground

haunted *adjective* 1 <u>possessed</u>,
cursed, eerie, ghostly, jinxed,
spooky (*informal*) 2 <u>preoccupied</u>,
obsessed, plagued, tormented,
troubled, worried

haunting *adjective* <u>poignant</u>,
evocative, nostalgic, persistent,
unforgettable

have *verb* 1 <u>possess</u>, hold, keep,
obtain, own, retain 2 <u>receive</u>,
accept, acquire, gain, get,
obtain, procure, secure, take
3 <u>experience</u>, endure, enjoy,
feel, meet with, suffer, sustain,
undergo 4 *Slang* <u>cheat</u>, deceive,

dupe, fool, outwit, swindle, take
in (*informal*), trick 5 <u>give birth</u>
<u>to</u>, bear, beget, bring forth,
deliver 6 **have to** <u>be obliged</u>, be
bound, be compelled, be forced,
have got to, must, ought, should

haven *noun* <u>sanctuary</u>, asylum,
refuge, retreat, sanctum, shelter

have on *verb* 1 <u>wear</u>, be clothed
in, be dressed in 2 <u>tease</u>,
deceive, kid (*informal*), pull
someone's leg, take the mickey,
trick, wind up (*Brit. slang*)

havoc *noun* <u>disorder</u>, chaos,
confusion, disruption, mayhem,
shambles

haywire *adjective* As in **go**
haywire <u>topsy-turvy</u>, chaotic,
confused, disordered,
disorganized, mixed up, out of
order, shambolic (*informal*)

hazard *noun* 1 <u>danger</u>, jeopardy,
peril, pitfall, risk, threat ♦ *verb*
2 <u>jeopardize</u>, endanger, expose,
imperil, risk, threaten 3 As in
hazard a guess <u>conjecture</u>,
advance, offer, presume, throw
out, venture, volunteer

hazardous *adjective* <u>dangerous</u>,
dicey (*informal, chiefly Brit.*),
difficult, insecure, perilous,
precarious, risky, unsafe

haze *noun* <u>mist</u>, cloud, fog,
obscurity, vapour

hazy *adjective* 1 <u>misty</u>, cloudy,
dim, dull, foggy, overcast
2 <u>vague</u>, fuzzy, ill-defined,
indefinite, indistinct, muddled,
nebulous, uncertain, unclear

head *noun* 1 <u>skull</u>, crown, loaf
(*slang*), nut (*slang*), pate
2 <u>leader</u>, boss (*informal*), captain,
chief, commander, director,
manager, master, principal,

supervisor **3** top, crest, crown, peak, pinnacle, summit, tip **4** brain, brains (*informal*), intellect, intelligence, mind, thought, understanding **5 go to one's head** excite, intoxicate, make conceited, puff up **6 head over heels** uncontrollably, completely, intensely, thoroughly, utterly, wholeheartedly ♦ *adjective* **7** chief, arch, first, leading, main, pre-eminent, premier, prime, principal, supreme ♦ *verb* **8** lead, be *or* go first, cap, crown, lead the way, precede, top **9** control, be in charge of, command, direct, govern, guide, lead, manage, run **10 make for**, aim, go to, make a beeline for, point, set off for, set out, start towards, steer, turn

headache *noun* **1** migraine, head (*informal*), neuralgia **2** problem, bane, bother, inconvenience, nuisance, trouble, vexation, worry

heading *noun* title, caption, headline, name, rubric

headlong *adverb, adjective* **1** headfirst, head-on ♦ *adverb* **2** hastily, heedlessly, helter-skelter, hurriedly, pell-mell, precipitately, rashly, thoughtlessly ♦ *adjective* **3** hasty, breakneck, dangerous, impetuous, impulsive, inconsiderate, precipitate, reckless, thoughtless

headstrong *adjective* obstinate, foolhardy, heedless, impulsive, perverse, pig-headed, self-willed, stubborn, unruly, wilful

headway *noun* progress, advance, improvement,

progression, way

heady *adjective* **1** inebriating, intoxicating, potent, strong **2** exciting, exhilarating, intoxicating, stimulating, thrilling

heal *verb* cure, make well, mend, regenerate, remedy, restore, treat

health *noun* **1** wellbeing, fitness, good condition, healthiness, robustness, soundness, strength, vigour **2** condition, constitution, fettle, shape, state

healthy *adjective* **1** well, active, fit, hale and hearty, in fine fettle, in good shape (*informal*), in the pink, robust, strong **2** wholesome, beneficial, hygienic, invigorating, nourishing, nutritious, salubrious, salutary

heap *noun* **1** pile, accumulation, collection, hoard, lot, mass, mound, stack **2** *often plural* a lot, great deal, load(s) (*informal*), lots (*informal*), mass, plenty, pot(s) (*informal*), stack(s), tons ♦ *verb* **3** pile, accumulate, amass, collect, gather, hoard, stack **4** confer, assign, bestow, load, shower upon

hear *verb* **1** listen to, catch, overhear **2** learn, ascertain, discover, find out, gather, get wind of (*informal*), pick up **3** *Law* try, examine, investigate, judge

hearing *noun* inquiry, industrial tribunal, investigation, review, trial

hearsay *noun* rumour, gossip, idle talk, report, talk, tittle-tattle, word of mouth

heart *noun* **1** nature, character, disposition, soul, temperament **2** bravery, courage, fortitude, pluck, purpose, resolution, spirit, will **3** <u>centre</u>, core, hub, middle, nucleus, quintessence **4 by heart** <u>by memory</u>, by rote, off pat, parrot-fashion (*informal*), pat, word for word

heartache *noun* <u>sorrow</u>, agony, anguish, despair, distress, grief, heartbreak, pain, remorse, suffering, torment, torture

heartbreak *noun* <u>grief</u>, anguish, desolation, despair, misery, pain, sorrow, suffering

heartbreaking *adjective* <u>tragic</u>, agonizing, distressing, harrowing, heart-rending, pitiful, poignant, sad

heartbroken *adjective* <u>miserable</u>, brokenhearted, crushed, desolate, despondent, disconsolate, dispirited, heartsick

heartfelt *adjective* <u>sincere</u>, deep, devout, earnest, genuine, honest, profound, unfeigned, wholehearted

heartily *adverb* <u>enthusiastically</u>, eagerly, earnestly, resolutely, vigorously, zealously

heartless *adjective* <u>cruel</u>, callous, cold, hard, hardhearted, merciless, pitiless, uncaring, unfeeling

heart-rending *adjective* <u>moving</u>, affecting, distressing, harrowing, heartbreaking, poignant, sad, tragic

hearty *adjective* **1** <u>friendly</u>, back-slapping, ebullient, effusive, enthusiastic, genial, jovial, warm **2** <u>substantial</u>, ample, filling, nourishing, sizable *or* sizeable, solid, square

heat *verb* **1** <u>warm up</u>, make hot,

reheat ♦ *noun* **2** <u>hotness</u>, high temperature, warmth **3** <u>intensity</u>, excitement, fervour, fury, passion, vehemence

heated *adjective* <u>angry</u>, excited, fierce, frenzied, furious, impassioned, intense, passionate, stormy, vehement

heathen *noun* **1** <u>unbeliever</u>, infidel, pagan ♦ *adjective* **2** <u>pagan</u>, godless, idolatrous, irreligious

heave *verb* **1** <u>lift</u>, drag (up), haul (up), hoist, pull (up), raise, tug **2** <u>throw</u>, cast, fling, hurl, pitch, send, sling, toss **3** <u>sigh</u>, groan, puff **4** <u>vomit</u>, be sick, gag, retch, spew, throw up (*informal*)

heaven *noun* **1** <u>paradise</u>, bliss, Elysium *or* Elysian fields (*Greek myth*), hereafter, life everlasting, next world, nirvana (*Buddhism, Hinduism*), Zion (*Christianity*) **2** <u>happiness</u>, bliss, ecstasy, paradise, rapture, seventh heaven, utopia **3 the heavens** <u>sky</u>, ether, firmament

heavenly *adjective* **1** <u>beautiful</u>, blissful, delightful, divine (*informal*), exquisite, lovely, ravishing, sublime, wonderful **2** <u>celestial</u>, angelic, blessed, divine, holy, immortal

heavily *adverb* **1** <u>ponderously</u>, awkwardly, clumsily, weightily **2** <u>densely</u>, closely, compactly, thickly **3** <u>considerably</u>, a great deal, copiously, excessively, to excess, very much

heaviness *noun* <u>weight</u>, gravity, heftiness, ponderousness

heavy *adjective* **1** <u>weighty</u>, bulky, hefty, massive, ponderous **2** <u>considerable</u>, abundant, copious, excessive, large, profuse

heckle verb jeer, barrack (*informal*), boo, disrupt, interrupt, shout down, taunt

hectic adjective frantic, animated, chaotic, feverish, frenetic, heated, turbulent

hedge noun 1 barrier, boundary, screen, windbreak ♦ verb 2 dodge, duck, equivocate, evade, flannel (*Brit. informal*), prevaricate, sidestep, temporize 3 insure, cover, guard, protect, safeguard, shield

heed noun 1 care, attention, caution, mind, notice, regard, respect, thought ♦ verb 2 pay attention to, bear in mind, consider, follow, listen to, note, obey, observe, take notice of

heedless adjective careless, foolhardy, inattentive, oblivious, thoughtless, unmindful

heel noun Slang swine, bounder (*old-fashioned Brit. slang*), cad (*Brit. informal*), rotter (*slang, chiefly Brit.*)

heel over verb lean over, keel over, list, tilt

hefty adjective strong, big, burly, hulking, massive, muscular, robust, strapping

height noun 1 altitude, elevation, highness, loftiness, stature, tallness 2 peak, apex, crest, crown, pinnacle, summit, top, zenith 3 culmination, climax, limit, maximum, ultimate

heighten verb intensify, add to, amplify, enhance, improve, increase, magnify, sharpen, strengthen

heir noun successor, beneficiary,

heiress (*fem.*), inheritor, next in line

hell noun 1 underworld, abyss, fire and brimstone, Hades (*Greek myth*), hellfire, inferno, nether world 2 torment, agony, anguish, misery, nightmare, ordeal, suffering, wretchedness

hellish adjective devilish, damnable, diabolical, fiendish, infernal

hello interjection welcome, good afternoon, good evening, good morning, greetings

helm noun 1 tiller, rudder, wheel 2 at the helm in charge, at the wheel, in command, in control, in the driving seat, in the saddle

help verb 1 aid, abet, assist, cooperate, lend a hand, succour, support 2 improve, alleviate, ameliorate, ease, facilitate, mitigate, relieve 3 refrain from, avoid, keep from, prevent, resist ♦ noun 4 assistance, advice, aid, cooperation, guidance, helping hand, support

helper noun assistant, adjutant, aide, ally, attendant, collaborator, helpmate, mate, right-hand man, second, supporter

helpful adjective 1 useful, advantageous, beneficial, constructive, practical, profitable, timely 2 cooperative, accommodating, considerate, friendly, kind, neighbourly, supportive, sympathetic

helping noun portion, dollop (*informal*), piece, plateful, ration, serving

helpless adjective weak, disabled, impotent, incapable, infirm, paralysed, powerless

helter-skelter *adjective*
1 <u>haphazard</u>, confused,
disordered, higgledy-piggledy
(*informal*), hit-or-miss, jumbled,
muddled, random, topsy-turvy
♦ *adverb* 2 <u>carelessly</u>, anyhow,
hastily, headlong, hurriedly,
pell-mell, rashly, recklessly, wildly

hem *noun* 1 <u>edge</u>, border, fringe,
margin, trimming ♦ *verb* 2 **hem
in** <u>surround</u>, beset, circumscribe,
confine, enclose, restrict, shut in

hence *conjunction* <u>therefore</u>, ergo,
for this reason, on that account,
thus

henchman *noun* <u>attendant</u>,
associate, bodyguard, follower,
minder (*slang*), right-hand man,
sidekick (*slang*), subordinate,
supporter

henpecked *adjective* <u>bullied</u>,
browbeaten, dominated, meek,
subjugated, timid

herald *noun* 1 <u>messenger</u>, crier
2 <u>forerunner</u>, harbinger,
indication, omen, precursor,
sign, signal, token ♦ *verb*
3 <u>indicate</u>, foretoken, portend,
presage, promise, show, usher in

herd *noun* 1 <u>multitude</u>,
collection, crowd, drove, flock,
horde, mass, mob, swarm,
throng ♦ *verb* 2 <u>congregate</u>,
assemble, collect, flock, gather,
huddle, muster, rally

hereafter *adverb* 1 <u>in future</u>,
from now on, hence,
henceforth, henceforward ♦ *noun*
2 <u>afterlife</u>, life after death, next
world

hereditary *adjective* 1 <u>genetic</u>,
inborn, inbred, inheritable,
transmissible 2 <u>inherited</u>,

ancestral, traditional

heredity *noun* <u>genetics</u>,
constitution, genetic make-up,
inheritance

heresy *noun* <u>dissidence</u>, apostasy,
heterodoxy, iconoclasm,
unorthodoxy

heretic *noun* <u>dissident</u>, apostate,
dissenter, nonconformist,
renegade, revisionist

heretical *adjective* <u>unorthodox</u>,
heterodox, iconoclastic,
idolatrous, impious, revisionist

heritage *noun* <u>inheritance</u>,
bequest, birthright, endowment,
legacy, tradition

hermit *noun* <u>recluse</u>, anchorite,
eremite, loner (*informal*), monk

hero *noun* 1 <u>idol</u>, champion,
conqueror, star, superstar, victor
2 <u>leading man</u>, protagonist

heroic *adjective* <u>courageous</u>,
brave, daring, fearless, gallant,
intrepid, lion-hearted, valiant

heroine *noun* <u>leading lady</u>, diva,
prima donna, protagonist

heroism *noun* <u>bravery</u>, courage,
courageousness, fearlessness,
gallantry, intrepidity, spirit, valour

hesitant *adjective* <u>uncertain</u>,
diffident, doubtful, half-hearted,
halting, irresolute, reluctant,
unsure, vacillating, wavering

hesitate *verb* 1 <u>waver</u>, delay,
dither (*chiefly Brit.*), doubt, hum
and haw, pause, vacillate, wait
2 <u>be reluctant</u>, balk, be
unwilling, demur, hang back,
scruple, shrink from, think twice

hesitation *noun* 1 <u>indecision</u>,
delay, doubt, hesitancy,
irresolution, uncertainty,
vacillation 2 <u>reluctance</u>,

misgiving(s), qualm(s), scruple(s), unwillingness

hew verb **1** <u>cut</u>, axe, chop, hack, lop, split **2** <u>carve</u>, fashion, form, make, model, sculpt, sculpture, shape, smooth

heyday noun <u>prime</u>, bloom, pink, prime of life, salad days

hiatus noun <u>pause</u>, break, discontinuity, gap, interruption, interval, respite, space

hidden adjective <u>concealed</u>, clandestine, covert, latent, secret, under wraps, unseen, veiled

hide[1] verb **1** <u>conceal</u>, secrete, stash (informal) **2** <u>go into hiding</u>, go to ground, go underground, hole up, lie low, take cover **3** <u>disguise</u>, camouflage, cloak, conceal, cover, mask, obscure, shroud, veil **4** <u>suppress</u>, draw a veil over, hush up, keep dark, keep secret, keep under one's hat, withhold

hide[2] noun <u>skin</u>, pelt

hidebound adjective <u>conventional</u>, narrow-minded, rigid, set in one's ways, strait-laced, ultraconservative

hideous adjective <u>ugly</u>, ghastly, grim, grisly, grotesque, gruesome, monstrous, repulsive, revolting, unsightly

hide-out noun <u>hideaway</u>, den, hiding place, lair, shelter

hiding noun <u>beating</u>, drubbing, licking (informal), spanking, thrashing, walloping (informal), whipping

hierarchy noun <u>grading</u>, pecking order, ranking

high adjective **1** <u>tall</u>, elevated,

lofty, soaring, steep, towering **2** <u>extreme</u>, excessive, extraordinary, great, intensified, sharp, strong **3** <u>important</u>, arch, chief, eminent, exalted, powerful, superior **4** Informal <u>intoxicated</u>, stoned (slang), tripping (informal) **5** <u>high-pitched</u>, acute, penetrating, piercing, piping, sharp, shrill, strident ♦ adverb **6** <u>aloft</u>, at great height, far up, way up

highbrow noun **1** <u>intellectual</u>, aesthete, egghead (informal), scholar ♦ adjective **2** <u>intellectual</u>, bookish, cultivated, cultured, sophisticated

high-flown adjective <u>extravagant</u>, elaborate, exaggerated, florid, grandiose, inflated, lofty, overblown, pretentious

high-handed adjective <u>dictatorial</u>, despotic, domineering, imperious, oppressive, overbearing, tyrannical, wilful

highlight noun **1** <u>feature</u>, climax, focal point, focus, high point, high spot, peak ♦ verb **2** <u>emphasize</u>, accent, accentuate, bring to the fore, show up, spotlight, stress, underline

highly adverb <u>extremely</u>, exceptionally, greatly, immensely, tremendously, vastly, very, very much

highly strung adjective <u>nervous</u>, edgy, excitable, neurotic, sensitive, stressed, temperamental, tense

hijack verb <u>seize</u>, commandeer, expropriate, take over

hike noun **1** <u>walk</u>, march, ramble, tramp, trek ♦ verb **2** <u>walk</u>, back-pack, ramble, tramp **3 hike up** raise, hitch up, jack up, lift, pull up

hilarious *adjective* funny, amusing, comical, entertaining, humorous, rollicking, side-splitting, uproarious

hilarity *noun* laughter, amusement, exhilaration, glee, high spirits, jollity, merriment, mirth

hill *noun* mount, fell, height, hillock, hilltop, knoll, mound, tor

hillock *noun* mound, hummock, knoll

hilly *adjective* mountainous, rolling, undulating

hilt *noun* handle, grip, haft, handgrip

hinder *verb* obstruct, block, check, delay, encumber, frustrate, hamper, handicap, hold up *or* back, impede, interrupt, stop

hindmost *adjective* last, final, furthest, furthest behind, rearmost, trailing

hindrance *noun* obstacle, barrier, deterrent, difficulty, drawback, handicap, hitch, impediment, obstruction, restriction, snag, stumbling block

hinge *verb* depend, be contingent, hang, pivot, rest, revolve around, turn

hint *noun* **1** indication, allusion, clue, implication, innuendo, insinuation, intimation, suggestion **2** advice, help, pointer, suggestion, tip **3** trace, dash, suggestion, suspicion, tinge, touch, undertone ♦ *verb* **4** suggest, imply, indicate,

insinuate, intimate

hippy *noun* bohemian, beatnik, dropout

hire *verb* **1** employ, appoint, commission, engage, sign up, take on **2** rent, charter, engage, lease, let ♦ *noun* **3** rental, charge, cost, fee, price, rent

hiss *noun* **1** sibilation, buzz, hissing **2** catcall, boo, jeer ♦ *verb* **3** whistle, sibilate, wheeze, whirr, whiz **4** jeer, boo, deride, hoot, mock

historic *adjective* significant, epoch-making, extraordinary, famous, ground-breaking, momentous, notable, outstanding, remarkable

historical *adjective* factual, actual, attested, authentic, documented, real

history *noun* **1** chronicle, account, annals, narrative, recital, record, story **2** the past, antiquity, olden days, yesterday, yesteryear

hit *verb* **1** strike, bang, beat, clout (*informal*), knock, slap, smack, thump, wallop (*informal*), whack **2** collide with, bang into, bump, clash with, crash against, run into, smash into **3** reach, accomplish, achieve, arrive at, attain, gain **4** affect, damage, devastate, impact on, influence, leave a mark on, overwhelm, touch **5 hit it off** *Informal* get on (well) with, be on good terms, click (*slang*), get on like a house on fire (*informal*) ♦ *noun* **6** stroke, belt (*informal*), blow, clout (*informal*), knock, rap, slap, smack, wallop (*informal*) **7** success, sensation, smash (*informal*), triumph, winner

hit-and-miss *adjective*
<u>haphazard</u>, aimless, casual, disorganized, indiscriminate, random, undirected, uneven

hitch *noun* 1 <u>problem</u>, catch, difficulty, drawback, hindrance, hold-up, impediment, obstacle, snag ♦ *verb* 2 <u>fasten</u>, attach, connect, couple, harness, join, tether, tie 3 *Informal* <u>hitchhike</u>, thumb a lift 4 **hitch up** <u>pull up</u>, jerk, tug, yank

hitherto *adverb* <u>previously</u>, heretofore, so far, thus far, until now

hit on *verb* <u>think up</u>, arrive at, discover, invent, light upon, strike upon, stumble on

hoard *noun* 1 <u>store</u>, accumulation, cache, fund, pile, reserve, stockpile, supply, treasure-trove ♦ *verb* 2 <u>save</u>, accumulate, amass, collect, gather, lay up, put by, stash away (*informal*), stockpile, store

hoarse *adjective* <u>raucous</u>, croaky, grating, gravelly, gruff, guttural, husky, rasping, rough, throaty

hoax *noun* 1 <u>trick</u>, con (*informal*), deception, fraud, practical joke, prank, spoof (*informal*), swindle ♦ *verb* 2 <u>deceive</u>, con (*slang*), dupe, fool, hoodwink, swindle, take in (*informal*), trick

hobby *noun* <u>pastime</u>, diversion, (leisure) activity, leisure pursuit, relaxation

hobnob *verb* <u>socialize</u>, associate, consort, fraternize, hang about, hang out (*informal*), keep company, mingle, mix

hoist *verb* 1 <u>raise</u>, elevate, erect,

heave, lift ♦ *noun* 2 <u>lift</u>, crane, elevator, winch

hold *verb* 1 <u>own</u>, have, keep, maintain, occupy, possess, retain 2 <u>grasp</u>, clasp, cling, clutch, cradle, embrace, enfold, grip 3 <u>restrain</u>, confine, detain, impound, imprison 4 <u>consider</u>, assume, believe, deem, judge, presume, reckon, regard, think 5 <u>convene</u>, call, conduct, preside over, run 6 <u>accommodate</u>, contain, have a capacity for, seat, take ♦ *noun* 7 <u>grip</u>, clasp, grasp 8 <u>foothold</u>, footing, support 9 <u>control</u>, influence, mastery

holder *noun* 1 <u>owner</u>, bearer, keeper, possessor, proprietor 2 <u>case</u>, container, cover

hold forth *verb* <u>speak</u>, declaim, discourse, go on, lecture, preach, spiel (*informal*), spout (*informal*)

hold-up *noun* 1 <u>delay</u>, bottleneck, hitch, setback, snag, stoppage, traffic jam, wait 2 <u>robbery</u>, mugging (*informal*), stick-up (*slang, chiefly U.S.*), theft

hold up *verb* 1 <u>delay</u>, detain, hinder, retard, set back, slow down, stop 2 <u>support</u>, prop, shore up, sustain 3 <u>rob</u>, mug (*informal*), waylay

hold with *verb* <u>approve of</u>, agree to *or* with, be in favour of, countenance, subscribe to, support

hole *noun* 1 <u>opening</u>, aperture, breach, crack, fissure, gap, orifice, perforation, puncture, tear, vent 2 <u>cavity</u>, cave, cavern, chamber, hollow, pit 3 <u>burrow</u>, den, earth, lair, shelter 4 *Informal*

hovel, dive (*slang*), dump
(*informal*), slum **5** *Informal*
predicament, dilemma, fix
(*informal*), hot water (*informal*),
jam (*informal*), mess, scrape
(*informal*), spot (*informal*), tight
spot

holiday *noun* **1** vacation, break,
leave, recess, time off **2** festival,
celebration, feast, fête, gala

holiness *noun* divinity, godliness,
piety, purity, righteousness,
sacredness, saintliness, sanctity,
spirituality

hollow *adjective* **1** empty,
unfilled, vacant, void
2 reverberant, deep, dull, low,
muted **3** worthless, fruitless,
futile, meaningless, pointless,
useless, vain ♦ *noun* **4** cavity,
basin, bowl, crater, depression,
hole, pit, trough **5** valley, dale,
dell, dingle, glen ♦ *verb* **6** scoop,
dig, excavate, gouge

holocaust *noun* genocide,
annihilation, conflagration,
destruction, devastation,
massacre

holy *adjective* **1** devout,
god-fearing, godly, pious, pure,
religious, righteous, saintly,
virtuous **2** sacred, blessed,
consecrated, hallowed,
sacrosanct, sanctified, venerable

homage *noun* respect, adoration,
adulation, deference, devotion,
honour, reverence, worship

home *noun* **1** house, abode,
domicile, dwelling, habitation,
pad (*slang*), residence
2 birthplace, home town **3 at
home: a** in, available, present **b**
at ease, comfortable, familiar,
relaxed **4 bring home to** make

clear, drive home, emphasize,
impress upon, press home
♦ *adjective* **5** domestic, familiar,
internal, local, native

homeland *noun* native land,
country of origin, fatherland,
mother country, motherland

homeless *adjective* **1** destitute,
displaced, dispossessed,
down-and-out ♦ *noun* **2 the
homeless** vagrants, squatters

homely *adjective* comfortable,
cosy, friendly, homespun,
modest, ordinary, plain, simple,
welcoming

homespun *adjective*
unsophisticated, coarse, homely,
home-made, plain, rough

homicidal *adjective* murderous,
deadly, lethal, maniacal, mortal

homicide *noun* **1** murder,
bloodshed, killing, manslaughter,
slaying **2** murderer, killer, slayer

homily *noun* sermon, address,
discourse, lecture, preaching

homogeneity *noun* uniformity,
consistency, correspondence,
sameness, similarity

homogeneous *adjective* uniform,
akin, alike, analogous,
comparable, consistent,
identical, similar, unvarying

hone *verb* sharpen, edge, file,
grind, point, polish, whet

honest *adjective* **1** trustworthy,
ethical, honourable, law-abiding,
reputable, scrupulous, truthful,
upright, virtuous **2** open, candid,
direct, forthright, frank, plain,
sincere, upfront (*informal*)

honestly *adverb* **1** ethically, by
fair means, cleanly, honourably,
lawfully, legally **2** frankly,

candidly, in all sincerity, plainly, straight (out), to one's face, truthfully

honesty noun **1** <u>integrity</u>, honour, incorruptibility, morality, probity, rectitude, scrupulousness, trustworthiness, truthfulness, uprightness, virtue **2** <u>frankness</u>, bluntness, candour, openness, outspokenness, sincerity, straightforwardness

honorary adjective <u>nominal</u>, complimentary, in name or title only, titular, unofficial, unpaid

honour noun **1** <u>glory</u>, credit, dignity, distinction, fame, prestige, renown, reputation **2** <u>tribute</u>, accolade, commendation, homage, praise, recognition **3** <u>fairness</u>, decency, goodness, honesty, integrity, morality, probity, rectitude **4** <u>privilege</u>, compliment, credit, pleasure ♦ verb **5** <u>respect</u>, adore, appreciate, esteem, prize, value **6** <u>fulfil</u>, be true to, carry out, discharge, keep, live up to, observe **7** <u>acclaim</u>, commemorate, commend, decorate, praise **8** <u>accept</u>, acknowledge, pass, pay, take

honourable adjective <u>respected</u>, creditable, estimable, reputable, respectable, virtuous

hoodwink verb <u>deceive</u>, con (informal), delude, dupe, fool, mislead, swindle, trick

hook noun **1** <u>fastener</u>, catch, clasp, link, peg ♦ verb **2** <u>fasten</u>, clasp, fix, secure **3** <u>catch</u>, ensnare, entrap, snare, trap

hooked adjective **1** <u>bent</u>, aquiline, curved, hook-shaped **2** <u>addicted</u>, devoted, enamoured, obsessed,

taken, turned on (slang)

hooligan noun <u>delinquent</u>, lager lout, ruffian, vandal, yob or yobbo (Brit. slang)

hooliganism noun <u>delinquency</u>, disorder, loutishness, rowdiness, vandalism, violence

hoop noun <u>ring</u>, band, circlet, girdle, loop, wheel

hoot noun **1** <u>cry</u>, call, toot **2** <u>catcall</u>, boo, hiss, jeer ♦ verb **3** <u>jeer</u>, boo, hiss, howl down

hop verb **1** <u>jump</u>, bound, caper, leap, skip, spring, trip, vault ♦ noun **2** <u>jump</u>, bounce, bound, leap, skip, spring, step, vault

hope verb **1** <u>desire</u>, aspire, cross one's fingers, long, look forward to, set one's heart on ♦ noun **2** <u>desire</u>, ambition, assumption, dream, expectation, longing

hopeful adjective **1** <u>optimistic</u>, buoyant, confident, expectant, looking forward to, sanguine **2** <u>promising</u>, auspicious, bright, encouraging, heartening, reassuring, rosy

hopefully adverb <u>optimistically</u>, confidently, expectantly

hopeless adjective <u>pointless</u>, futile, impossible, no-win, unattainable, useless, vain

horde noun <u>crowd</u>, band, drove, gang, host, mob, multitude, pack, swarm, throng

horizon noun <u>skyline</u>, vista

horizontal adjective <u>level</u>, flat, parallel

horrible adjective **1** <u>terrifying</u>, appalling, dreadful, frightful, ghastly, grim, grisly, gruesome, hideous, repulsive, revolting, shocking **2** <u>unpleasant</u>, awful, cruel, disagreeable, dreadful, horrid, mean, nasty, terrible

horrid *adjective* **1** <u>unpleasant</u>, awful, disagreeable, dreadful, horrible, terrible **2** *Informal* <u>unkind</u>, beastly (*informal*), cruel, mean, nasty

horrific *adjective* <u>terrifying</u>, appalling, awful, dreadful, frightful, ghastly, grisly, horrendous, horrifying, shocking

horrify *verb* **1** <u>terrify</u>, alarm, frighten, intimidate, make one's hair stand on end, petrify, scare **2** <u>shock</u>, appal, dismay, outrage, sicken

horror *noun* **1** <u>terror</u>, alarm, consternation, dread, fear, fright, panic **2** <u>hatred</u>, aversion, detestation, disgust, loathing, odium, repugnance, revulsion

horse *noun* <u>nag</u>, colt, filly, gee-gee (*slang*), mare, mount, stallion, steed (*archaic or literary*)

horseman *noun* <u>rider</u>, cavalier, cavalryman, dragoon, equestrian

horseplay *noun* <u>buffoonery</u>, clowning, fooling around, high jinks, pranks, romping, rough-and-tumble, skylarking (*informal*)

hospitable *adjective* <u>welcoming</u>, cordial, friendly, generous, gracious, kind, liberal, sociable

hospitality *noun* <u>welcome</u>, conviviality, cordiality, friendliness, neighbourliness, sociability, warmth

host[1] *noun* **1** <u>master of ceremonies</u>, entertainer, innkeeper, landlord or landlady, proprietor **2** <u>presenter</u>, anchorman or anchorwoman,

compere (*Brit.*) ♦ *verb* **3** <u>present</u>, compere (*Brit.*), front (*informal*), introduce

host[2] *noun* <u>multitude</u>, army, array, drove, horde, legion, myriad, swarm, throng

hostage *noun* <u>prisoner</u>, captive, pawn

hostile *adjective* **1** <u>opposed</u>, antagonistic, belligerent, contrary, ill-disposed, rancorous **2** <u>unfriendly</u>, adverse, inhospitable, unsympathetic, unwelcoming

hostilities *plural noun* <u>warfare</u>, conflict, fighting, war

hostility *noun* <u>opposition</u>, animosity, antipathy, enmity, hatred, ill will, malice, resentment, unfriendliness

hot *adjective* **1** <u>heated</u>, boiling, roasting, scalding, scorching, searing, steaming, sultry, sweltering, torrid, warm **2** <u>spicy</u>, biting, peppery, piquant, pungent, sharp **3** <u>fierce</u>, fiery, intense, passionate, raging, stormy, violent **4** <u>recent</u>, fresh, just out, latest, new, up to the minute **5** <u>popular</u>, approved, favoured, in demand, in vogue, sought-after

hot air *noun* <u>empty talk</u>, bombast, claptrap (*informal*), guff (*slang*), verbiage, wind

hot-blooded *adjective* <u>passionate</u>, ardent, excitable, fiery, impulsive, spirited, temperamental, wild

hotchpotch *noun* <u>mixture</u>, farrago, jumble, medley, *mélange*, mess, mishmash, potpourri

hot-headed *adjective* <u>rash</u>, fiery, foolhardy, hasty, hot-tempered, impetuous, quick-tempered, reckless, volatile

hound *verb* <u>harass</u>, badger, goad, harry, impel, persecute, pester, provoke

house *noun* 1 <u>home</u>, abode, domicile, dwelling, habitation, homestead, pad (*slang*), residence 2 <u>family</u>, household 3 <u>dynasty</u>, clan, tribe 4 <u>firm</u>, business, company, organization, outfit (*informal*) 5 <u>assembly</u>, Commons, legislative body, parliament 6 **on the house** <u>free</u>, for nothing, gratis ♦ *verb* 7 <u>accommodate</u>, billet, harbour, lodge, put up, quarter, take in 8 <u>contain</u>, cover, keep, protect, sheathe, shelter, store

household *noun* <u>family</u>, home, house

householder *noun* <u>occupant</u>, homeowner, resident, tenant

housing *noun* 1 <u>accommodation</u>, dwellings, homes, houses 2 <u>case</u>, casing, container, cover, covering, enclosure, sheath

hovel *noun* <u>hut</u>, cabin, den, hole, shack, shanty, shed

hover *verb* 1 <u>float</u>, drift, flutter, fly, hang 2 <u>linger</u>, hang about 3 <u>waver</u>, dither (*chiefly Brit.*), fluctuate, oscillate, vacillate

however *adverb* <u>nevertheless</u>, after all, anyhow, but, nonetheless, notwithstanding, still, though, yet

howl *noun* 1 <u>cry</u>, bawl, bay, clamour, groan, roar, scream, shriek, wail ♦ *verb* 2 <u>cry</u>, bawl, bellow, roar, scream, shriek, wail, weep, yell

howler *noun* <u>mistake</u>, bloomer (*Brit. informal*), blunder, boob (*Brit. slang*), clanger (*informal*), error, malapropism

hub *noun* <u>centre</u>, core, focal point, focus, heart, middle, nerve centre

huddle *verb* 1 <u>crowd</u>, cluster, converge, flock, gather, press, throng 2 <u>curl up</u>, crouch, hunch up ♦ *noun* 3 *Informal* <u>conference</u>, confab (*informal*), discussion, meeting, powwow

hue *noun* <u>colour</u>, dye, shade, tinge, tint, tone

hug *verb* 1 <u>clasp</u>, cuddle, embrace, enfold, hold close, squeeze, take in one's arms ♦ *noun* 2 <u>embrace</u>, bear hug, clasp, clinch (*slang*), squeeze

huge *adjective* <u>large</u>, colossal, enormous, gigantic, immense, mammoth, massive, monumental, tremendous, vast

hulk *noun* 1 <u>wreck</u>, frame, hull, shell, shipwreck 2 <u>oaf</u>, lout, lubber, lump (*informal*)

hull *noun* <u>frame</u>, body, casing, covering, framework

hum *verb* 1 <u>murmur</u>, buzz, drone, purr, throb, thrum, vibrate, whir 2 <u>be busy</u>, bustle, buzz, pulsate, pulse, stir

human *adjective* 1 <u>mortal</u>, manlike ♦ *noun* 2 <u>human being</u>, creature, individual, man *or* woman, mortal, person, soul

humane *adjective* <u>kind</u>, benign, compassionate, forgiving, good-natured, merciful, sympathetic, tender, understanding

humanitarian *adjective*

1 <u>compassionate</u>, altruistic, benevolent, charitable, humane, philanthropic, public-spirited
♦ *noun* **2** <u>philanthropist</u>, altruist, benefactor, Good Samaritan

humanity *noun* **1** <u>human race</u>, Homo sapiens, humankind, man, mankind, people **2** <u>human nature</u>, mortality **3** <u>sympathy</u>, charity, compassion, fellow feeling, kind-heartedness, kindness, mercy, philanthropy

humanize *verb* <u>civilize</u>, educate, enlighten, improve, soften, tame

humble *adjective* **1** <u>modest</u>, meek, self-effacing, unassuming, unostentatious, unpretentious **2** <u>lowly</u>, mean, modest, obscure, ordinary, plebeian, poor, simple, undistinguished ♦ *verb* **3** <u>humiliate</u>, chasten, crush, disgrace, put (someone) in their place, subdue, take down a peg (*informal*)

humbug *noun* **1** <u>fraud</u>, charlatan, con man (*informal*), faker, impostor, phoney *or* phony (*informal*), swindler, trickster **2** <u>nonsense</u>, baloney (*informal*), cant, claptrap (*informal*), hypocrisy, quackery, rubbish

humdrum *adjective* <u>dull</u>, banal, boring, dreary, monotonous, mundane, ordinary, tedious, tiresome, uneventful

humid *adjective* <u>damp</u>, clammy, dank, moist, muggy, steamy, sticky, sultry, wet

humidity *noun* <u>damp</u>, clamminess, dampness, dankness, moistness, moisture, mugginess, wetness

humiliate *verb* <u>embarrass</u>, bring low, chasten, crush, degrade, humble, mortify, put down, put (someone) in their place, shame

humiliating *adjective* <u>embarrassing</u>, crushing, degrading, humbling, ignominious, mortifying, shaming

humiliation *noun* <u>embarrassment</u>, degradation, disgrace, dishonour, humbling, ignominy, indignity, loss of face, mortification, put-down, shame

humility *noun* <u>modesty</u>, humbleness, lowliness, meekness, submissiveness, unpretentiousness

humorist *noun* <u>comedian</u>, card (*informal*), comic, funny man, jester, joker, wag, wit

humorous *adjective* <u>funny</u>, amusing, comic, comical, droll, entertaining, jocular, playful, waggish, witty

humour *noun* **1** <u>funniness</u>, amusement, comedy, drollery, facetiousness, fun, jocularity, ludicrousness **2** <u>joking</u>, comedy, farce, jesting, pleasantry, wisecracks (*informal*), wit, witticisms **3** <u>mood</u>, disposition, frame of mind, spirits, temper ♦ *verb* **4** <u>indulge</u>, accommodate, flatter, go along with, gratify, mollify, pander to

hump *noun* **1** <u>lump</u>, bulge, bump, mound, projection, protrusion, protuberance, swelling ♦ *verb* **2** *Slang* <u>carry</u>, heave, hoist, lug, shoulder

hunch *noun* **1** <u>feeling</u>, idea, impression, inkling, intuition, premonition, presentiment, suspicion ♦ *verb* **2** <u>draw in</u>, arch, bend, curve

hunger *noun* **1** <u>famine</u>, starvation

2 <u>appetite</u>, emptiness, hungriness, ravenousness **3** <u>desire</u>, ache, appetite, craving, itch, lust, thirst, yearning ♦ *verb* **4** <u>want</u>, ache, crave, desire, hanker, itch, long, thirst, wish, yearn

hungry *adjective* **1** <u>empty</u>, famished, peckish (*informal, chiefly Brit.*), ravenous, starved, starving, voracious **2** <u>eager</u>, athirst, avid, covetous, craving, desirous, greedy, keen, yearning

hunk *noun* <u>lump</u>, block, chunk, mass, nugget, piece, slab, wedge

hunt *verb* **1** <u>stalk</u>, chase, hound, pursue, track, trail **2** <u>search</u>, ferret about, forage, look, scour, seek ♦ *noun* **3** <u>search</u>, chase, hunting, investigation, pursuit, quest

hurdle *noun* **1** <u>fence</u>, barricade, barrier **2** <u>obstacle</u>, barrier, difficulty, handicap, hazard, hindrance, impediment, obstruction, stumbling block

hurl *verb* <u>throw</u>, cast, fling, heave, launch, let fly, pitch, propel, sling, toss

hurricane *noun* <u>storm</u>, cyclone, gale, tempest, tornado, twister (*U.S. informal*), typhoon

hurried *adjective* <u>hasty</u>, brief, cursory, perfunctory, quick, rushed, short, speedy, swift

hurry *verb* **1** <u>rush</u>, dash, fly, get a move on (*informal*), make haste, scoot, scurry, step on it (*informal*) ♦ *noun* **2** <u>urgency</u>, flurry, haste, quickness, rush, speed

hurt *verb* **1** <u>harm</u>, bruise, damage, disable, impair, injure, mar, spoil, wound **2** <u>ache</u>, be

sore, be tender, burn, smart, sting, throb **3** <u>sadden</u>, annoy, distress, grieve, pain, upset, wound ♦ *noun* **4** <u>distress</u>, discomfort, pain, pang, soreness, suffering ♦ *adjective* **5** <u>injured</u>, bruised, cut, damaged, harmed, scarred, wounded **6** <u>offended</u>, aggrieved, crushed, wounded

hurtful *adjective* <u>unkind</u>, cruel, cutting, damaging, destructive, malicious, nasty, spiteful, upsetting, wounding

hurtle *verb* <u>rush</u>, charge, crash, fly, plunge, race, shoot, speed, stampede, tear

husband *noun* **1** <u>partner</u>, better half (*humorous*), mate, spouse ♦ *verb* **2** <u>economize</u>, budget, conserve, hoard, save, store

husbandry *noun* **1** <u>farming</u>, agriculture, cultivation, tillage **2** <u>thrift</u>, economy, frugality

hush *verb* **1** <u>quieten</u>, mute, muzzle, shush, silence ♦ *noun* **2** <u>quiet</u>, calm, peace, silence, stillness, tranquillity

hush-hush *adjective* <u>secret</u>, classified, confidential, restricted, top-secret, under wraps

husky *adjective* **1** <u>hoarse</u>, croaky, gruff, guttural, harsh, raucous, rough, throaty **2** *Informal* <u>muscular</u>, burly, hefty, powerful, rugged, stocky, strapping, thickset

hustle *verb* <u>jostle</u>, elbow, force, jog, push, shove

hut *noun* <u>shed</u>, cabin, den, hovel, lean-to, shanty, shelter

hybrid *noun* <u>crossbreed</u>, amalgam, composite, compound, cross, half-breed, mixture, mongrel

hygiene *noun* <u>cleanliness</u>, sanitation

hygienic *adjective* <u>clean</u>, aseptic, disinfected, germ-free, healthy, pure, sanitary, sterile

hymn *noun* <u>anthem</u>, carol, chant, paean, psalm

hype *noun* <u>publicity</u>, ballyhoo (*informal*), brouhaha, plugging (*informal*), promotion, razzmatazz (*slang*)

hypnotic *adjective* <u>mesmeric</u>, mesmerizing, sleep-inducing, soothing, soporific, spellbinding

hypnotize *verb* <u>mesmerize</u>, put in a trance, put to sleep

hypocrisy *noun* <u>insincerity</u>, cant, deceitfulness, deception, duplicity, pretence

hypocrite *noun* <u>fraud</u>, charlatan, deceiver, impostor, phoney *or* phony (*informal*), pretender

hypocritical *adjective* <u>insincere</u>, canting, deceitful, duplicitous, false, fraudulent, phoney *or* phony (*informal*), sanctimonious, two-faced

hypothesis *noun* <u>assumption</u>, postulate, premise, proposition, supposition, theory, thesis

hypothetical *adjective* <u>theoretical</u>, academic, assumed, conjectural, imaginary, putative, speculative, supposed

hysteria *noun* <u>frenzy</u>, agitation, delirium, hysterics, madness, panic

hysterical *adjective* **1** <u>frenzied</u>, crazed, distracted, distraught, frantic, overwrought, raving **2** *Informal* <u>hilarious</u>, comical, side-splitting, uproarious

I i

icy *adjective* **1** <u>cold</u>, biting, bitter, chill, chilly, freezing, frosty, ice-cold, raw **2** <u>slippery</u>, glassy, slippy (*informal or dialect*) **3** <u>unfriendly</u>, aloof, cold, distant, frigid, frosty, unwelcoming

idea *noun* **1** <u>thought</u>, concept, impression, perception **2** <u>belief</u>, conviction, notion, opinion, teaching, view **3** <u>plan</u>, aim, intention, object, objective, purpose

ideal *adjective* **1** <u>perfect</u>, archetypal, classic, complete, consummate, model, quintessential, supreme ♦ *noun* **2** <u>model</u>, last word, paradigm, paragon, pattern, perfection, prototype, standard

idealist *noun* <u>romantic</u>, dreamer, Utopian, visionary

idealistic *adjective* <u>perfectionist</u>, impracticable, optimistic, romantic, starry-eyed, Utopian, visionary

idealize *verb* <u>romanticize</u>, apotheosize, ennoble, exalt, glorify, magnify, put on a pedestal, worship

ideally *adverb* <u>in a perfect world</u>, all things being equal, if one had one's way

identical *adjective* <u>alike</u>, duplicate, indistinguishable, interchangeable, matching, twin

identification *noun* **1** <u>recognition</u>, naming, pinpointing **2** <u>empathy</u>, association, connection, fellow feeling, involvement, rapport, relationship, sympathy

identify verb **1** <u>recognize</u>, diagnose, make out, name, pick out, pinpoint, place, put one's finger on (*informal*), spot **2 identify with** <u>relate to</u>, associate with, empathize with, feel for, respond to

identity noun **1** <u>existence</u>, individuality, personality, self **2** <u>sameness</u>, correspondence, unity

idiocy noun <u>foolishness</u>, asininity, fatuousness, imbecility, inanity, insanity, lunacy, senselessness

idiom noun **1** <u>phrase</u>, expression, turn of phrase **2** <u>language</u>, jargon, parlance, style, vernacular

idiosyncrasy noun <u>peculiarity</u>, characteristic, eccentricity, mannerism, oddity, quirk, trick

idiot noun <u>fool</u>, chump, cretin, dunderhead, halfwit, imbecile, moron, nincompoop, numbskull or numskull, simpleton, twit (*informal, chiefly Brit.*)

idiotic adjective <u>foolish</u>, asinine, crazy, daft (*informal*), foolhardy, harebrained, insane, moronic, senseless, stupid

idle adjective **1** <u>inactive</u>, redundant, unemployed, unoccupied, unused, vacant **2** <u>lazy</u>, good-for-nothing, indolent, lackadaisical, shiftless, slothful, sluggish **3** <u>useless</u>, fruitless, futile, groundless, ineffective, pointless, unavailing, unsuccessful, vain, worthless ♦ verb **4** often with **away** <u>laze</u>, dally, dawdle, kill time, loaf, loiter, lounge, potter

idleness noun **1** <u>inactivity</u>,

inaction, leisure, time on one's hands, unemployment **2** <u>laziness</u>, inertia, shiftlessness, sloth, sluggishness, torpor

idol noun **1** <u>graven image</u>, deity, god **2** <u>hero</u>, beloved, darling, favourite, pet, pin-up (*slang*)

idolatry noun <u>adoration</u>, adulation, exaltation, glorification

idolize verb <u>worship</u>, adore, dote upon, exalt, glorify, hero-worship, look up to, love, revere, venerate

idyllic adjective <u>idealized</u>, charming, halcyon, heavenly, ideal, picturesque, unspoiled

if conjunction <u>provided</u>, assuming, on condition that, providing, supposing

ignite verb **1** <u>catch fire</u>, burn, burst into flames, flare up, inflame, take fire **2** <u>set fire to</u>, kindle, light, set alight, torch

ignominious adjective <u>humiliating</u>, discreditable, disgraceful, dishonourable, indecorous, inglorious, shameful, sorry, undignified

ignominy noun <u>disgrace</u>, discredit, dishonour, disrepute, humiliation, infamy, obloquy, shame, stigma

ignorance noun <u>unawareness</u>, inexperience, innocence, unconsciousness, unfamiliarity

ignorant adjective **1** <u>uninformed</u>, benighted, inexperienced, innocent, oblivious, unaware, unconscious, unenlightened, uninitiated, unwitting **2** <u>uneducated</u>, illiterate **3** <u>insensitive</u>, crass, half-baked (*informal*), rude

ignore verb overlook, discount, disregard, neglect, pass over, reject, take no notice of, turn a blind eye to

ill adjective 1 unwell, ailing, diseased, indisposed, infirm, off-colour, poorly (*informal*), sick, under the weather (*informal*), unhealthy 2 harmful, bad, damaging, deleterious, detrimental, evil, foul, injurious, unfortunate ♦ *noun* 3 harm, affliction, hardship, hurt, injury, misery, misfortune, trouble, unpleasantness, woe ♦ *adverb* 4 badly, inauspiciously, poorly, unfavourably, unfortunately, unluckily 5 hardly, barely, by no means, scantily

ill-advised adjective misguided, foolhardy, ill-considered, ill-judged, imprudent, incautious, injudicious, rash, reckless, thoughtless, unwise

ill-disposed adjective unfriendly, antagonistic, disobliging, hostile, inimical, uncooperative, unwelcoming

illegal adjective unlawful, banned, criminal, felonious, forbidden, illicit, outlawed, prohibited, unauthorized, unlicensed

illegality noun crime, felony, illegitimacy, lawlessness, wrong

illegible adjective indecipherable, obscure, scrawled, unreadable

illegitimate adjective 1 unlawful, illegal, illicit, improper, unauthorized 2 born out of wedlock, bastard

ill-fated adjective doomed, hapless, ill-omened, ill-starred, luckless, star-crossed, unfortunate, unhappy, unlucky

illicit adjective 1 illegal, criminal, felonious, illegitimate, prohibited, unauthorized, unlawful, unlicensed 2 forbidden, clandestine, furtive, guilty, immoral, improper

illiterate adjective uneducated, ignorant, uncultured, untaught, untutored

ill-mannered adjective rude, badly behaved, boorish, churlish, discourteous, impolite, insolent, loutish, uncouth

illness noun disease, affliction, ailment, disorder, infirmity, malady, sickness

illogical adjective irrational, absurd, inconsistent, invalid, meaningless, senseless, unreasonable, unscientific, unsound

ill-treat verb abuse, damage, harm, injure, maltreat, mishandle, misuse, oppress

illuminate verb 1 light up, brighten 2 explain, clarify, clear up, elucidate, enlighten, interpret, make clear, shed light on

illuminating adjective informative, enlightening, explanatory, helpful, instructive, revealing

illumination noun 1 light, brightness, lighting, radiance 2 enlightenment, clarification, insight, revelation

illusion noun 1 fantasy, chimera, daydream, figment of the imagination, hallucination, mirage, will-o'-the-wisp 2 misconception, deception, delusion, error, fallacy, misapprehension

illusory *adjective* <u>unreal</u>, chimerical, deceptive, delusive, fallacious, false, hallucinatory, mistaken, sham

illustrate *verb* <u>demonstrate</u>, bring home, elucidate, emphasize, explain, point up, show

illustrated *adjective* <u>pictorial</u>, decorated, graphic

illustration *noun* 1 <u>example</u>, case, instance, specimen 2 <u>picture</u>, decoration, figure, plate, sketch

illustrious *adjective* <u>famous</u>, celebrated, distinguished, eminent, glorious, great, notable, prominent, renowned

ill will *noun* <u>hostility</u>, animosity, bad blood, dislike, enmity, hatred, malice, rancour, resentment, venom

image *noun* 1 <u>representation</u>, effigy, figure, icon, idol, likeness, picture, portrait, statue 2 <u>replica</u>, counterpart, (dead) ringer (*slang*), Doppelgänger, double, facsimile, spitting image (*informal*) 3 <u>concept</u>, idea, impression, mental picture, perception

imaginable *adjective* <u>possible</u>, believable, comprehensible, conceivable, credible, likely, plausible

imaginary *adjective* <u>fictional</u>, fictitious, hypothetical, illusory, imagined, invented, made-up, nonexistent, unreal

imagination *noun* 1 <u>creativity</u>, enterprise, ingenuity, invention, inventiveness, originality, resourcefulness, vision 2 <u>unreality</u>, illusion, supposition

imaginative *adjective* <u>creative</u>, clever, enterprising, ingenious, inspired, inventive, original

imagine *verb* 1 <u>envisage</u>, conceive, conceptualize, conjure up, picture, plan, think of, think up, visualize 2 <u>believe</u>, assume, conjecture, fancy, guess (*informal, chiefly U.S. & Canad.*), infer, suppose, surmise, suspect, take it, think

imbecile *noun* 1 <u>idiot</u>, chump, cretin, fool, halfwit, moron, numbskull or numskull, thickhead, twit (*informal, chiefly Brit.*) ♦ *adjective* 2 <u>stupid</u>, asinine, fatuous, feeble-minded, foolish, idiotic, moronic, thick, witless

imbibe *verb* 1 <u>drink</u>, consume, knock back (*informal*), quaff, sink (*informal*), swallow, swig (*informal*) 2 *Literary* <u>absorb</u>, acquire, assimilate, gain, gather, ingest, receive, take in

imbroglio *noun* <u>complication</u>, embarrassment, entanglement, involvement, misunderstanding, quandary

imitate *verb* <u>copy</u>, ape, echo, emulate, follow, mimic, mirror, repeat, simulate

imitation *noun* 1 <u>mimicry</u>, counterfeiting, duplication, likeness, resemblance, simulation 2 <u>replica</u>, fake, forgery, impersonation, impression, reproduction, sham, substitution ♦ *adjective* 3 <u>artificial</u>, dummy, ersatz, man-made, mock, phoney or phony (*informal*), reproduction, sham, simulated, synthetic

imitative *adjective* <u>derivative</u>, copycat (*informal*), mimetic, parrot-like, second-hand, simulated, unoriginal

imitator noun impersonator, copier, copycat (informal), impressionist, mimic, parrot

immaculate adjective 1 clean, neat, spick-and-span, spotless, spruce, squeaky-clean 2 flawless, above reproach, faultless, impeccable, perfect, unblemished, unexceptionable, untarnished

immaterial adjective irrelevant, extraneous, inconsequential, inessential, insignificant, of no importance, trivial, unimportant

immature adjective 1 young, adolescent, undeveloped, unformed, unripe 2 childish, callow, inexperienced, infantile, juvenile, puerile

immaturity noun 1 unripeness, greenness, imperfection, rawness, unpreparedness 2 childishness, callowness, inexperience, puerility

immediate adjective 1 instant, instantaneous 2 nearest, close, direct, near, next

immediately adverb at once, directly, forthwith, instantly, now, promptly, right away, straight away, this instant, without delay

immense adjective huge, colossal, enormous, extensive, gigantic, great, massive, monumental, stupendous, tremendous, vast

immensity noun size, bulk, enormity, expanse, extent, greatness, hugeness, magnitude, vastness

immerse verb 1 plunge, bathe, dip, douse, duck, dunk, sink, submerge 2 engross, absorb, busy, engage, involve, occupy, take up

immersion noun 1 dipping, dousing, ducking, dunking, plunging, submerging 2 involvement, absorption, concentration, preoccupation

immigrant noun settler, incomer, newcomer

imminent adjective near, at hand, close, coming, forthcoming, gathering, impending, in the pipeline, looming

immobile adjective stationary, at a standstill, at rest, fixed, immovable, motionless, rigid, rooted, static, still, stock-still, unmoving

immobility noun stillness, fixity, inertness, motionlessness, stability, steadiness

immobilize verb paralyse, bring to a standstill, cripple, disable, freeze, halt, stop, transfix

immoderate adjective excessive, exaggerated, exorbitant, extravagant, extreme, inordinate, over the top (slang), undue, unjustified, unreasonable

immoral adjective wicked, bad, corrupt, debauched, depraved, dissolute, indecent, sinful, unethical, unprincipled, wrong

immorality noun wickedness, corruption, debauchery, depravity, dissoluteness, sin, vice, wrong

immortal adjective 1 eternal, deathless, enduring, everlasting, imperishable, lasting, perennial, undying ♦ *noun* **2** god, goddess **3** great, genius, hero

immortality *noun* **1** eternity, everlasting life, perpetuity **2** fame, celebrity, glory, greatness, renown

immortalize *verb* commemorate, celebrate, exalt, glorify

immovable *adjective* **1** fixed, firm, immutable, jammed, secure, set, stable, stationary, stuck **2** inflexible, adamant, obdurate, resolute, steadfast, unshakable, unwavering, unyielding

immune *adjective* exempt, clear, free, invulnerable, proof (against), protected, resistant, safe, unaffected

immunity *noun* **1** exemption, amnesty, freedom, indemnity, invulnerability, licence, release **2** resistance, immunization, protection

immunize *verb* vaccinate, inoculate, protect, safeguard

imp *noun* **1** demon, devil, sprite **2** rascal, brat, minx, rogue, scamp

impact *noun* **1** collision, blow, bump, contact, crash, jolt, knock, smash, stroke, thump **2** effect, consequences, impression, influence, repercussions, significance ♦ *verb* **3** hit, clash, collide, crash, crush, strike

impair *verb* worsen, blunt, damage, decrease, diminish, harm, hinder, injure, lessen, reduce, undermine, weaken

impaired *adjective* damaged,

defective, faulty, flawed, imperfect, unsound

impart *verb* **1** communicate, convey, disclose, divulge, make known, pass on, relate, reveal, tell **2** give, accord, afford, bestow, confer, grant, lend, yield

impartial *adjective* neutral, detached, disinterested, equitable, even-handed, fair, just, objective, open-minded, unbiased, unprejudiced

impartiality *noun* neutrality, detachment, disinterestedness, dispassion, equity, even-handedness, fairness, objectivity, open-mindedness

impassable *adjective* blocked, closed, impenetrable, obstructed

impasse *noun* deadlock, dead end, stalemate, standoff, standstill

impassioned *adjective* intense, animated, fervent, fiery, heated, inspired, passionate, rousing, stirring

impatience *noun* **1** haste, impetuosity, intolerance, rashness **2** restlessness, agitation, anxiety, eagerness, edginess, fretfulness, nervousness, uneasiness

impatient *adjective* **1** hasty, demanding, hot-tempered, impetuous, intolerant **2** restless, eager, edgy, fretful, straining at the leash

impeach *verb* charge, accuse, arraign, indict

impeccable *adjective* faultless, blameless, flawless, immaculate, irreproachable, perfect, unblemished, unimpeachable

impecunious *adjective* poor,

broke (*informal*), destitute, down and out, indigent, insolvent, penniless, poverty-stricken

impede *verb* hinder, block, check, disrupt, hamper, hold up, obstruct, slow (down), thwart

impediment *noun* obstacle, barrier, difficulty, encumbrance, hindrance, obstruction, snag, stumbling block

impel *verb* force, compel, constrain, drive, induce, oblige, push, require

impending *adjective* looming, approaching, coming, forthcoming, gathering, imminent, in the pipeline, near, upcoming

impenetrable *adjective* 1 solid, dense, impassable, impermeable, impervious, inviolable, thick
2 incomprehensible, arcane, enigmatic, inscrutable, mysterious, obscure, unfathomable, unintelligible

imperative *adjective* urgent, crucial, essential, pressing, vital

imperceptible *adjective* undetectable, faint, indiscernible, microscopic, minute, slight, small, subtle, tiny

imperfect *adjective* flawed, damaged, defective, faulty, impaired, incomplete, limited, unfinished

imperfection *noun* fault, blemish, defect, deficiency, failing, flaw, frailty, shortcoming, taint, weakness

imperial *adjective* royal, kingly, majestic, princely, queenly, regal, sovereign

imperil *verb* endanger, expose,

jeopardize, risk

impersonal *adjective* remote, aloof, cold, detached, dispassionate, formal, inhuman, neutral

impersonate *verb* imitate, ape, do (*informal*), masquerade as, mimic, pass oneself off as, pose as (*informal*), take off (*informal*)

impersonation *noun* imitation, caricature, impression, mimicry, parody, takeoff (*informal*)

impertinence *noun* rudeness, brazenness, cheek (*informal*), disrespect, effrontery, front, impudence, insolence, nerve (*informal*), presumption

impertinent *adjective* rude, brazen, cheeky (*informal*), disrespectful, impolite, impudent, insolent, presumptuous

imperturbable *adjective* calm, collected, composed, cool, nerveless, self-possessed, serene, unexcitable, unflappable (*informal*), unruffled

impervious *adjective* 1 sealed, impassable, impenetrable, impermeable, resistant
2 unaffected, immune, invulnerable, proof against, unmoved, untouched

impetuosity *noun* haste, impulsiveness, precipitateness, rashness

impetuous *adjective* rash, hasty, impulsive, precipitate, unthinking

impetus *noun* 1 incentive, catalyst, goad, impulse, motivation, push, spur, stimulus
2 force, energy, momentum, power

impinge verb 1 <u>encroach</u>, infringe, invade, obtrude, trespass, violate 2 <u>affect</u>, bear upon, have a bearing on, impact, influence, relate to, touch

impious adjective <u>sacrilegious</u>, blasphemous, godless, irreligious, irreverent, profane, sinful, ungodly, unholy, wicked

impish adjective <u>mischievous</u>, devilish, puckish, rascally, roguish, sportive, waggish

implacable adjective <u>unyielding</u>, inflexible, intractable, merciless, pitiless, unbending, uncompromising, unforgiving

implant verb 1 <u>instil</u>, inculcate, infuse 2 <u>insert</u>, fix, graft

implement verb 1 <u>carry out</u>, bring about, complete, effect, enforce, execute, fulfil, perform, realize ♦ noun 2 <u>tool</u>, apparatus, appliance, device, gadget, instrument, utensil

implicate verb <u>incriminate</u>, associate, embroil, entangle, include, inculpate, involve

implication noun <u>suggestion</u>, inference, innuendo, meaning, overtone, presumption, significance

implicit adjective 1 <u>implied</u>, inferred, latent, tacit, taken for granted, undeclared, understood, unspoken 2 <u>absolute</u>, constant, firm, fixed, full, steadfast, unqualified, unreserved, wholehearted

implied adjective <u>unspoken</u>, hinted at, implicit, indirect, suggested, tacit, undeclared, unexpressed, unstated

implore verb <u>beg</u>, beseech, entreat, importune, plead with, pray

imply verb 1 <u>hint</u>, insinuate, intimate, signify, suggest 2 <u>entail</u>, indicate, involve, mean, point to, presuppose

impolite adjective <u>bad-mannered</u>, discourteous, disrespectful, ill-mannered, insolent, loutish, rude, uncouth

impoliteness noun <u>bad manners</u>, boorishness, churlishness, discourtesy, disrespect, insolence, rudeness

import verb 1 <u>bring in</u>, introduce ♦ noun 2 <u>meaning</u>, drift, gist, implication, intention, sense, significance, thrust 3 <u>importance</u>, consequence, magnitude, moment, significance, substance, weight

importance noun 1 <u>significance</u>, concern, consequence, import, interest, moment, substance, usefulness, value, weight 2 <u>prestige</u>, distinction, eminence, esteem, influence, prominence, standing, status

important adjective 1 <u>significant</u>, far-reaching, momentous, seminal, serious, substantial, urgent, weighty 2 <u>powerful</u>, eminent, high-ranking, influential, noteworthy, pre-eminent, prominent

importunate adjective <u>persistent</u>, demanding, dogged, insistent, pressing, urgent

impose verb 1 <u>establish</u>, decree, fix, institute, introduce, levy, ordain 2 <u>inflict</u>, appoint, enforce, saddle (someone) with

imposing adjective <u>impressive</u>, commanding, dignified, grand, majestic, stately, striking

imposition noun 1 <u>application</u>, introduction, levying 2 <u>intrusion</u>, liberty, presumption

impossibility noun <u>hopelessness</u>, impracticability, inability

impossible adjective
1 <u>unattainable</u>, impracticable, inconceivable, out of the question, unachievable, unobtainable, unthinkable
2 <u>absurd</u>, ludicrous, outrageous, preposterous, unreasonable

impostor noun <u>impersonator</u>, charlatan, deceiver, fake, fraud, phoney or phony (informal), pretender, sham, trickster

impotence noun <u>powerlessness</u>, feebleness, frailty, helplessness, inability, incapacity, incompetence, ineffectiveness, paralysis, uselessness, weakness

impotent adjective <u>powerless</u>, feeble, frail, helpless, incapable, incapacitated, incompetent, ineffective, paralysed, weak

impoverish verb 1 <u>bankrupt</u>, beggar, break, ruin 2 <u>diminish</u>, deplete, drain, exhaust, reduce, sap, use up, wear out

impoverished adjective <u>poor</u>, bankrupt, destitute, impecunious, needy, on one's uppers, penurious, poverty-stricken

impracticable adjective <u>unfeasible</u>, impossible, out of the question, unachievable, unattainable, unworkable

impractical adjective
1 <u>unworkable</u>, impossible, impracticable, inoperable, nonviable, unrealistic, wild

2 <u>idealistic</u>, romantic, starry-eyed, unrealistic

imprecise adjective <u>indefinite</u>, equivocal, hazy, ill-defined, indeterminate, inexact, inexplicit, loose, rough, vague, woolly

impregnable adjective <u>invulnerable</u>, impenetrable, indestructible, invincible, secure, unassailable, unbeatable, unconquerable

impregnate verb 1 <u>saturate</u>, infuse, permeate, soak, steep, suffuse 2 <u>fertilize</u>, inseminate, make pregnant

impress verb 1 <u>excite</u>, affect, inspire, make an impression, move, stir, strike, touch 2 <u>stress</u>, bring home to, emphasize, fix, inculcate, instil into 3 <u>imprint</u>, emboss, engrave, indent, mark, print, stamp

impression noun 1 <u>effect</u>, feeling, impact, influence, reaction 2 <u>idea</u>, belief, conviction, feeling, hunch, notion, sense, suspicion 3 <u>mark</u>, dent, hollow, imprint, indentation, outline, stamp
4 <u>imitation</u>, impersonation, parody, send-up (Brit. informal), takeoff (informal)

impressionable adjective <u>suggestible</u>, gullible, ingenuous, open, receptive, responsive, sensitive, susceptible, vulnerable

impressive adjective <u>grand</u>, awesome, dramatic, exciting, moving, powerful, stirring, striking

imprint noun 1 <u>mark</u>, impression, indentation, sign, stamp ♦ verb
2 <u>fix</u>, engrave, etch, impress, print, stamp

imprison verb jail, confine, detain, incarcerate, intern, lock up, put away, send down (informal)

imprisoned adjective jailed, behind bars, captive, confined, incarcerated, in jail, inside (slang), locked up, under lock and key

imprisonment noun custody, confinement, detention, incarceration, porridge (slang)

improbability noun doubt, dubiety, uncertainty, unlikelihood

improbable adjective doubtful, dubious, fanciful, far-fetched, implausible, questionable, unconvincing, unlikely, weak

impromptu adjective unprepared, ad-lib, extemporaneous, improvised, offhand, off the cuff (informal), spontaneous, unrehearsed, unscripted

improper adjective 1 indecent, risqué, smutty, suggestive, unbecoming, unseemly, untoward, vulgar 2 unwarranted, inappropriate, out of place, uncalled-for, unfit, unsuitable

impropriety noun indecency, bad taste, incongruity, vulgarity

improve verb 1 enhance, advance, better, correct, help, rectify, touch up, upgrade 2 progress, develop, make strides, pick up, rally, rise

improvement noun 1 enhancement, advancement, betterment 2 progress, development, rally, recovery, upswing

improvident adjective

imprudent, careless, negligent, prodigal, profligate, reckless, short-sighted, spendthrift, thoughtless, wasteful

improvisation noun 1 spontaneity, ad-libbing, extemporizing, invention 2 makeshift, ad-lib, expedient

improvise verb 1 extemporize, ad-lib, busk, invent, play it by ear (informal), speak off the cuff (informal), wing it (informal) 2 concoct, contrive, devise, throw together

imprudent adjective unwise, careless, foolhardy, ill-advised, ill-considered, ill-judged, injudicious, irresponsible, rash, reckless

impudence noun boldness, audacity, brazenness, cheek (informal), effrontery, impertinence, insolence, nerve (informal), presumption, shamelessness

impudent adjective bold, audacious, brazen, cheeky (informal), impertinent, insolent, presumptuous, rude, shameless

impulse noun urge, caprice, feeling, inclination, notion, whim, wish

impulsive adjective instinctive, devil-may-care, hasty, impetuous, intuitive, passionate, precipitate, rash, spontaneous

impunity noun security, dispensation, exemption, freedom, immunity, liberty, licence, permission

impure adjective 1 unrefined, adulterated, debased, mixed 2 contaminated, defiled, dirty, infected, polluted, tainted

3 immoral, corrupt, indecent, lascivious, lewd, licentious, obscene, unchaste

impurity noun contamination, defilement, dirtiness, infection, pollution, taint

imputation noun blame, accusation, aspersion, censure, insinuation, reproach, slander, slur

inability noun incapability, disability, disqualification, impotence, inadequacy, incapacity, incompetence, ineptitude, powerlessness

inaccessible adjective out of reach, impassable, out of the way, remote, unapproachable, unattainable, unreachable

inaccuracy noun error, defect, erratum, fault, lapse, mistake

inaccurate adjective incorrect, defective, erroneous, faulty, imprecise, mistaken, out, unreliable, unsound, wrong

inactive adjective unused, dormant, idle, inoperative, unemployed, unoccupied

inactivity noun immobility, dormancy, hibernation, inaction, passivity, unemployment

inadequacy noun **1** shortage, dearth, insufficiency, meagreness, paucity, poverty, scantiness **2** incompetence, deficiency, inability, incapacity, ineffectiveness **3** shortcoming, defect, failing, imperfection, weakness

inadequate adjective **1** insufficient, meagre, scant, sketchy, sparse **2** incompetent, deficient, faulty, found wanting,

incapable, not up to scratch (informal), unqualified

inadmissible adjective unacceptable, inappropriate, irrelevant, unallowable

inadvertently adverb unintentionally, accidentally, by accident, by mistake, involuntarily, mistakenly, unwittingly

inadvisable adjective unwise, ill-advised, impolitic, imprudent, inexpedient, injudicious

inane adjective senseless, empty, fatuous, frivolous, futile, idiotic, mindless, silly, stupid, vacuous

inanimate adjective lifeless, cold, dead, defunct, extinct, inert

inapplicable adjective irrelevant, inappropriate, unsuitable

inappropriate adjective unsuitable, improper, incongruous, out of place, unbecoming, unbefitting, unfitting, unseemly, untimely

inarticulate adjective faltering, halting, hesitant, poorly spoken

inattention noun neglect, absent-mindedness, carelessness, daydreaming, inattentiveness, preoccupation, thoughtlessness

inattentive adjective preoccupied, careless, distracted, dreamy, negligent, unobservant, vague

inaudible adjective indistinct, low, mumbling, out of earshot, stifled, unheard

inaugural adjective first, initial, introductory, maiden, opening

inaugurate verb **1** launch, begin, commence, get under way, initiate, institute, introduce, set in motion 2 <u>invest</u>, induct, install

inauguration noun 1 <u>launch</u>, initiation, institution, opening, setting up 2 <u>investiture</u>, induction, installation

inauspicious adjective <u>unpromising</u>, bad, discouraging, ill-omened, ominous, unfavourable, unfortunate, unlucky, unpropitious

inborn adjective <u>natural</u>, congenital, hereditary, inbred, ingrained, inherent, innate, instinctive, intuitive, native

inbred adjective <u>innate</u>, constitutional, deep-seated, ingrained, inherent, native, natural

incalculable adjective <u>countless</u>, boundless, infinite, innumerable, limitless, numberless, untold, vast

incantation noun <u>chant</u>, charm, formula, invocation, spell

incapable adjective 1 <u>incompetent</u>, feeble, inadequate, ineffective, inept, inexpert, insufficient, unfit, unqualified, weak 2 <u>unable</u>, helpless, impotent, powerless

incapacitate verb <u>disable</u>, cripple, immobilize, lay up (informal), paralyse, put out of action (informal)

incapacitated adjective <u>indisposed</u>, hors de combat, immobilized, laid up (informal), out of action (informal), unfit

incapacity noun <u>inability</u>, impotence, inadequacy, incapability, incompetency, ineffectiveness, powerlessness, unfitness, weakness

incarcerate verb <u>imprison</u>, confine, detain, impound, intern, jail or gaol, lock up, throw in jail

incarceration noun <u>imprisonment</u>, captivity, confinement, detention, internment

incarnate adjective <u>personified</u>, embodied, typified

incarnation noun <u>embodiment</u>, epitome, manifestation, personification, type

incense verb <u>anger</u>, enrage, inflame, infuriate, irritate, madden, make one's hackles rise, rile (informal)

incensed adjective <u>angry</u>, enraged, fuming, furious, indignant, infuriated, irate, maddened, steamed up (slang), up in arms

incentive noun <u>encouragement</u>, bait, carrot (informal), enticement, inducement, lure, motivation, spur, stimulus

inception noun <u>beginning</u>, birth, commencement, dawn, initiation, origin, outset, start

incessant adjective <u>endless</u>, ceaseless, constant, continual, eternal, interminable, never-ending, nonstop, perpetual, unceasing, unending

incessantly adverb <u>endlessly</u>, ceaselessly, constantly, continually, eternally, interminably, nonstop, perpetually, persistently

incident noun 1 <u>happening</u>, adventure, episode, event, fact, matter, occasion, occurrence 2 <u>disturbance</u>, clash, commotion, confrontation, contretemps, scene

incidental *adjective* <u>secondary</u>, ancillary, minor, nonessential, occasional, subordinate, subsidiary

incidentally *adverb* <u>parenthetically</u>, by the bye, by the way, in passing

incinerate *verb* <u>burn up</u>, carbonize, char, cremate, reduce to ashes

incipient *adjective* <u>beginning</u>, commencing, developing, embryonic, inchoate, nascent, starting

incision *noun* <u>cut</u>, gash, notch, opening, slash, slit

incisive *adjective* <u>penetrating</u>, acute, keen, perspicacious, piercing, trenchant

incite *verb* <u>provoke</u>, encourage, foment, inflame, instigate, spur, stimulate, stir up, urge, whip up

incitement *noun* <u>provocation</u>, agitation, encouragement, impetus, instigation, prompting, spur, stimulus

incivility *noun* <u>rudeness</u>, bad manners, boorishness, discourteousness, discourtesy, disrespect, ill-breeding, impoliteness

inclement *adjective* <u>stormy</u>, foul, harsh, intemperate, rough, severe, tempestuous

inclination *noun* **1** <u>tendency</u>, disposition, liking, partiality, penchant, predilection, predisposition, proclivity, proneness, propensity **2** <u>slope</u>, angle, gradient, incline, pitch, slant, tilt

incline *verb* **1** <u>predispose</u>, influence, persuade, prejudice,

sway **2** <u>slope</u>, lean, slant, tilt, tip, veer ♦ *noun* **3** <u>slope</u>, ascent, descent, dip, grade, gradient, rise

inclined *adjective* <u>disposed</u>, apt, given, liable, likely, minded, predisposed, prone, willing

include *verb* **1** <u>contain</u>, comprise, cover, embrace, encompass, incorporate, involve, subsume, take in **2** <u>introduce</u>, add, enter, insert

inclusion *noun* <u>addition</u>, incorporation, insertion

inclusive *adjective* <u>comprehensive</u>, across-the-board, all-embracing, blanket, general, global, sweeping, umbrella

incognito *adjective* <u>in disguise</u>, disguised, under an assumed name, unknown, unrecognized

incoherence *noun* <u>unintelligibility</u>, disjointedness, inarticulateness

incoherent *adjective* <u>unintelligible</u>, confused, disjointed, disordered, inarticulate, inconsistent, jumbled, muddled, rambling, stammering, stuttering

income *noun* <u>revenue</u>, earnings, pay, proceeds, profits, receipts, salary, takings, wages

incoming *adjective* <u>arriving</u>, approaching, entering, homeward, landing, new, returning

incomparable *adjective* <u>unequalled</u>, beyond compare, inimitable, matchless, peerless, superlative, supreme, transcendent, unmatched, unparalleled, unrivalled

incompatible *adjective*
<u>inconsistent</u>, conflicting, contradictory, incongruous, mismatched, unsuited

incompetence *noun* <u>ineptitude</u>, inability, inadequacy, incapability, incapacity, ineffectiveness, unfitness, uselessness

incompetent *adjective* <u>inept</u>, bungling, floundering, incapable, ineffectual, inexpert, unfit, useless

incomplete *adjective* <u>unfinished</u>, deficient, fragmentary, imperfect, partial, wanting

incomprehensible *adjective* <u>unintelligible</u>, baffling, beyond one's grasp, impenetrable, obscure, opaque, perplexing, puzzling, unfathomable

inconceivable *adjective* <u>unimaginable</u>, beyond belief, incomprehensible, incredible, mind-boggling (*informal*), out of the question, unbelievable, unheard-of, unthinkable

inconclusive *adjective* <u>indecisive</u>, ambiguous, indeterminate, open, unconvincing, undecided, up in the air (*informal*), vague

incongruity *noun* <u>inappropriateness</u>, conflict, discrepancy, disparity, incompatibility, inconsistency, unsuitability

incongruous *adjective* <u>inappropriate</u>, discordant, improper, incompatible, out of keeping, out of place, unbecoming, unsuitable

inconsiderable *adjective* <u>insignificant</u>, inconsequential, minor, negligible, slight, small, trifling, trivial, unimportant

inconsiderate *adjective* <u>selfish</u>, indelicate, insensitive, rude, tactless, thoughtless, unkind, unthinking

inconsistency *noun*
1 <u>incompatibility</u>, disagreement, discrepancy, disparity, divergence, incongruity, variance
2 <u>unreliability</u>, fickleness, instability, unpredictability, unsteadiness

inconsistent *adjective*
1 <u>incompatible</u>, at odds, conflicting, contradictory, discordant, incongruous, irreconcilable, out of step
2 <u>changeable</u>, capricious, erratic, fickle, unpredictable, unstable, unsteady, variable

inconsolable *adjective* <u>heartbroken</u>, brokenhearted, desolate, despairing

inconspicuous *adjective* <u>unobtrusive</u>, camouflaged, hidden, insignificant, ordinary, plain, unassuming, unnoticeable, unostentatious

incontrovertible *adjective* <u>indisputable</u>, certain, established, incontestable, indubitable, irrefutable, positive, sure, undeniable, unquestionable

inconvenience *noun* 1 <u>trouble</u>, awkwardness, bother, difficulty, disadvantage, disruption, disturbance, fuss, hindrance, nuisance ♦ *verb* 2 <u>trouble</u>, bother, discommode, disrupt, disturb, put out, upset

inconvenient *adjective* <u>troublesome</u>, awkward, bothersome, disadvantageous, disturbing, inopportune, unsuitable, untimely

incorporate *verb* include, absorb, assimilate, blend, combine, integrate, merge, subsume

incorrect *adjective* false, erroneous, faulty, flawed, inaccurate, mistaken, untrue, wrong

incorrigible *adjective* incurable, hardened, hopeless, intractable, inveterate, irredeemable, unreformed

incorruptible *adjective* **1** honest, above suspicion, straight, trustworthy, upright **2** imperishable, everlasting, undecaying

increase *verb* **1** grow, advance, boost, develop, enlarge, escalate, expand, extend, multiply, raise, spread, swell ♦ *noun* **2** growth, development, enlargement, escalation, expansion, extension, gain, increment, rise, upturn

increasingly *adverb* progressively, more and more

incredible *adjective* **1** implausible, beyond belief, far-fetched, improbable, inconceivable, preposterous, unbelievable, unimaginable, unthinkable **2** *Informal* amazing, astonishing, astounding, extraordinary, prodigious, sensational (*informal*), wonderful

incredulity *noun* disbelief, distrust, doubt, scepticism

incredulous *adjective* disbelieving, distrustful, doubtful, dubious, sceptical, suspicious, unbelieving, unconvinced

increment *noun* increase,

accrual, addition, advancement, augmentation, enlargement, gain, step up, supplement

incriminate *verb* implicate, accuse, blame, charge, impeach, inculpate, involve

incumbent *adjective* obligatory, binding, compulsory, mandatory, necessary

incur *verb* earn, arouse, bring (upon oneself), draw, expose oneself to, gain, meet with, provoke

incurable *adjective* fatal, inoperable, irremediable, terminal

indebted *adjective* grateful, beholden, in debt, obligated, obliged, under an obligation

indecency *noun* obscenity, immodesty, impropriety, impurity, indelicacy, lewdness, licentiousness, pornography, vulgarity

indecent *adjective* **1** lewd, crude, dirty, filthy, immodest, improper, impure, licentious, pornographic, salacious **2** unbecoming, in bad taste, indecorous, unseemly, vulgar

indecipherable *adjective* illegible, indistinguishable, unintelligible, unreadable

indecision *noun* hesitation, dithering (*chiefly Brit.*), doubt, indecisiveness, shilly-shallying (*informal*), uncertainty, vacillation, wavering

indecisive *adjective* hesitating, dithering (*chiefly Brit.*), faltering, in two minds (*informal*), tentative, uncertain, undecided, vacillating, wavering

indeed *adverb* really, actually,

certainly, in truth, truly, undoubtedly

indefensible *adjective* unforgivable, inexcusable, unjustifiable, unpardonable, untenable, unwarrantable, wrong

indefinable *adjective* inexpressible, impalpable, indescribable

indefinite *adjective* unclear, doubtful, equivocal, ill-defined, imprecise, indeterminate, inexact, uncertain, unfixed, vague

indefinitely *adverb* endlessly, ad infinitum, continually, for ever

indelible *adjective* permanent, enduring, indestructible, ineradicable, ingrained, lasting

indelicate *adjective* offensive, coarse, crude, embarrassing, immodest, risqué, rude, suggestive, tasteless, vulgar

indemnify *verb* 1 insure, guarantee, protect, secure, underwrite 2 compensate, reimburse, remunerate, repair, repay

indemnity *noun* 1 insurance, guarantee, protection, security 2 compensation, redress, reimbursement, remuneration, reparation, restitution

independence *noun* freedom, autonomy, liberty, self-reliance, self-rule, self-sufficiency, sovereignty

independent *adjective* 1 free, liberated, separate, unconstrained, uncontrolled 2 self-governing, autonomous, nonaligned, self-determining, sovereign 3 self-sufficient, liberated, self-contained,

self-reliant, self-supporting

independently *adverb* separately, alone, autonomously, by oneself, individually, on one's own, solo, unaided

indescribable *adjective* unutterable, beyond description, beyond words, indefinable, inexpressible

indestructible *adjective* permanent, enduring, everlasting, immortal, imperishable, incorruptible, indelible, indissoluble, lasting, unbreakable

indeterminate *adjective* uncertain, imprecise, indefinite, inexact, undefined, unfixed, unspecified, unstipulated, vague

indicate *verb* 1 signify, betoken, denote, imply, manifest, point to, reveal, suggest 2 point out, designate, specify 3 show, display, express, read, record, register

indication *noun* sign, clue, evidence, hint, inkling, intimation, manifestation, mark, suggestion, symptom

indicative *adjective* suggestive, pointing to, significant, symptomatic

indicator *noun* sign, gauge, guide, mark, meter, pointer, signal, symbol

indict *verb* charge, accuse, arraign, impeach, prosecute, summon

indictment *noun* charge, accusation, allegation, impeachment, prosecution, summons

indifference *noun* disregard,

aloofness, apathy, coldness, coolness, detachment, inattention, negligence, nonchalance, unconcern

indifferent *adjective*
1 <u>unconcerned</u>, aloof, callous, cold, cool, detached, impervious, inattentive, uninterested, unmoved, unsympathetic
2 <u>mediocre</u>, moderate, no great shakes (*informal*), ordinary, passable, so-so (*informal*), undistinguished

indigestion *noun* <u>heartburn</u>, dyspepsia, upset stomach

indignant *adjective* <u>resentful</u>, angry, disgruntled, exasperated, incensed, irate, peeved (*informal*), riled, scornful, up in arms (*informal*)

indignation *noun* <u>resentment</u>, anger, exasperation, pique, rage, scorn, umbrage

indignity *noun* <u>humiliation</u>, affront, dishonour, disrespect, injury, insult, opprobrium, slight, snub

indirect *adjective* 1 <u>circuitous</u>, long-drawn-out, meandering, oblique, rambling, roundabout, tortuous, wandering
2 <u>incidental</u>, secondary, subsidiary, unintended

indiscreet *adjective* <u>tactless</u>, impolitic, imprudent, incautious, injudicious, naive, rash, reckless, unwise

indiscretion *noun* <u>mistake</u>, error, faux pas, folly, foolishness, gaffe, lapse, slip

indiscriminate *adjective* <u>random</u>, careless, desultory, general, uncritical, undiscriminating, unsystematic, wholesale

indispensable *adjective* <u>essential</u>, crucial, imperative, key, necessary, needed, requisite, vital

indisposed *adjective* <u>ill</u>, ailing, poorly (*informal*), sick, under the weather, unwell

indisposition *noun* <u>illness</u>, ailment, ill health, sickness

indisputable *adjective* <u>undeniable</u>, beyond doubt, certain, incontestable, incontrovertible, indubitable, irrefutable, unquestionable

indistinct *adjective* <u>unclear</u>, blurred, faint, fuzzy, hazy, ill-defined, indeterminate, shadowy, undefined, vague

individual *adjective* 1 <u>personal</u>, characteristic, distinctive, exclusive, idiosyncratic, own, particular, peculiar, singular, special, specific, unique ♦ *noun*
2 <u>person</u>, being, character, creature, soul, unit

individualist *noun* <u>maverick</u>, freethinker, independent, loner, lone wolf, nonconformist, original

individuality *noun* <u>distinctiveness</u>, character, originality, personality, separateness, singularity, uniqueness

individually *adverb* <u>separately</u>, apart, independently, one at a time, one by one, singly

indoctrinate *verb* <u>train</u>, brainwash, drill, ground, imbue, initiate, instruct, school, teach

indoctrination *noun* <u>training</u>, brainwashing, drilling, grounding, inculcation, instruction, schooling

indolent *adjective* <u>lazy</u>, idle,

inactive, inert, languid, lethargic,
listless, slothful, sluggish, workshy

indomitable *adjective* invincible,
bold, resolute, staunch,
steadfast, unbeatable,
unconquerable, unflinching,
unyielding

indubitable *adjective* certain,
incontestable, incontrovertible,
indisputable, irrefutable, obvious,
sure, undeniable, unquestionable

induce *verb* 1 persuade,
convince, encourage, incite,
influence, instigate, prevail upon,
prompt, talk into 2 cause, bring
about, effect, engender,
generate, give rise to, lead to,
occasion, produce

inducement *noun* incentive,
attraction, bait, carrot (*informal*),
encouragement, incitement,
lure, reward

indulge *verb* 1 gratify, feed, give
way to, pander to, satisfy, yield
to 2 spoil, cosset, give in to, go
along with, humour,
mollycoddle, pamper

indulgence *noun* 1 gratification,
appeasement, fulfilment,
satiation, satisfaction 2 luxury,
extravagance, favour, privilege,
treat 3 tolerance, forbearance,
patience, understanding

indulgent *adjective* lenient,
compliant, easy-going,
forbearing, kindly, liberal,
permissive, tolerant,
understanding

industrialist *noun* capitalist, big
businessman, captain of
industry, magnate,
manufacturer, tycoon

industrious *adjective*
hard-working, busy,

conscientious, diligent,
energetic, persistent, purposeful,
tireless, zealous

industry *noun* 1 business,
commerce, manufacturing,
production, trade 2 effort,
activity, application, diligence,
labour, tirelessness, toil, zeal

inebriated *adjective* drunk,
half-cut (*informal*), intoxicated,
legless (*informal*), merry (*Brit.
informal*), paralytic (*informal*),
plastered (*slang*), tight (*informal*),
tipsy, under the influence
(*informal*)

ineffective *adjective* useless,
fruitless, futile, idle, impotent,
inefficient, unavailing,
unproductive, vain, worthless

ineffectual *adjective* weak,
feeble, impotent, inadequate,
incompetent, ineffective, inept

inefficiency *noun* incompetence,
carelessness, disorganization,
muddle, slackness, sloppiness

inefficient *adjective* incompetent,
disorganized, ineffectual, inept,
wasteful, weak

ineligible *adjective* unqualified,
disqualified, ruled out,
unacceptable, unfit, unsuitable

inept *adjective* incompetent,
bumbling, bungling, clumsy,
inexpert, maladroit

ineptitude *noun* incompetence,
clumsiness, inexpertness,
unfitness

inequality *noun* disparity, bias,
difference, disproportion,
diversity, irregularity, prejudice,
unevenness

inequitable *adjective* unfair,
biased, discriminatory,

one-sided, partial, partisan, preferential, prejudiced, unjust

inert adjective <u>inactive</u>, dead, dormant, immobile, lifeless, motionless, static, still, unreactive, unresponsive

inertia noun <u>inactivity</u>, apathy, immobility, lethargy, listlessness, passivity, sloth, unresponsiveness

inescapable adjective <u>unavoidable</u>, certain, destined, fated, ineluctable, inevitable, inexorable, sure

inestimable adjective <u>incalculable</u>, immeasurable, invaluable, precious, priceless, prodigious

inevitable adjective <u>unavoidable</u>, assured, certain, destined, fixed, ineluctable, inescapable, inexorable, sure

inevitably adverb <u>unavoidably</u>, as a result, automatically, certainly, necessarily, of necessity, perforce, surely, willy-nilly

inexcusable adjective <u>unforgivable</u>, indefensible, outrageous, unjustifiable, unpardonable, unwarrantable

inexorable adjective <u>unrelenting</u>, inescapable, relentless, remorseless, unbending, unyielding

inexpensive adjective <u>cheap</u>, bargain, budget, economical, modest, reasonable

inexperience noun <u>unfamiliarity</u>, callowness, greenness, ignorance, newness, rawness

inexperienced adjective <u>immature</u>, callow, green, new, raw, unpractised, untried, unversed

inexpert adjective <u>amateurish</u>, bungling, cack-handed (informal), clumsy, inept, maladroit, unpractised, unprofessional, unskilled

inexplicable adjective <u>unaccountable</u>, baffling, enigmatic, incomprehensible, insoluble, mysterious, mystifying, strange, unfathomable, unintelligible

inextricably adverb <u>inseparably</u>, indissolubly, indistinguishably, intricately, irretrievably, totally

infallibility noun <u>perfection</u>, impeccability, omniscience, supremacy, unerringness

infallible adjective <u>foolproof</u>, certain, dependable, reliable, sure, sure-fire (informal), trustworthy, unbeatable, unfailing

infamous adjective <u>notorious</u>, disreputable, ignominious, ill-famed

infancy noun <u>beginnings</u>, cradle, dawn, inception, origins, outset, start

infant noun <u>baby</u>, babe, bairn (Scot.), child, toddler, tot

infantile adjective <u>childish</u>, babyish, immature, puerile

infatuate verb <u>obsess</u>, besot, bewitch, captivate, enchant, enrapture, fascinate

infatuated adjective <u>obsessed</u>, besotted, bewitched, captivated, carried away, enamoured, enraptured, fascinated, possessed, smitten (informal), spellbound

infatuation noun <u>obsession</u>, crush (informal), fixation, madness, passion, thing (informal)

infect verb contaminate, affect, blight, corrupt, defile, poison, pollute, taint

infection noun contamination, contagion, corruption, defilement, poison, pollution, virus

infectious adjective catching, communicable, contagious, spreading, transmittable, virulent

infer verb deduce, conclude, derive, gather, presume, surmise, understand

inference noun deduction, assumption, conclusion, presumption, reading, surmise

inferior adjective 1 lower, lesser, menial, minor, secondary, subordinate, subsidiary ♦ noun 2 underling, junior, menial, subordinate

inferiority noun 1 inadequacy, deficiency, imperfection, insignificance, mediocrity, shoddiness, worthlessness 2 subservience, abasement, lowliness, subordination

infernal adjective devilish, accursed, damnable, damned, diabolical, fiendish, hellish, satanic

infertile adjective barren, sterile, unfruitful, unproductive

infertility noun sterility, barrenness, infecundity, unproductiveness

infest verb overrun, beset, invade, penetrate, permeate, ravage, swarm, throng

infested adjective overrun, alive, crawling, ravaged, ridden, swarming, teeming

infiltrate verb penetrate, filter

through, insinuate oneself, make inroads (into), percolate, permeate, pervade, sneak in (informal)

infinite adjective never-ending, boundless, eternal, everlasting, illimitable, immeasurable, inexhaustible, limitless, measureless, unbounded

infinitesimal adjective microscopic, insignificant, minuscule, minute, negligible, teeny, tiny, unnoticeable

infinity noun eternity, boundlessness, endlessness, immensity, vastness

infirm adjective frail, ailing, debilitated, decrepit, doddering, enfeebled, failing, feeble, weak

infirmity noun frailty, decrepitude, ill health, sickliness, vulnerability

inflame verb enrage, anger, arouse, excite, incense, infuriate, madden, provoke, rouse, stimulate

inflamed adjective sore, fevered, hot, infected, red, swollen

inflammable adjective flammable, combustible, incendiary

inflammation noun soreness, painfulness, rash, redness, tenderness

inflammatory adjective provocative, explosive, fiery, intemperate, like a red rag to a bull, rabble-rousing

inflate verb expand, bloat, blow up, dilate, distend, enlarge, increase, puff up or out, pump up, swell

inflated adjective exaggerated,

ostentatious, overblown, swollen

inflation noun expansion, enlargement, escalation, extension, increase, rise, spread, swelling

inflexibility noun obstinacy, intransigence, obduracy

inflexible adjective 1 obstinate, implacable, intractable, obdurate, resolute, set in one's ways, steadfast, stubborn, unbending, uncompromising 2 inelastic, hard, rigid, stiff, taut

inflict verb impose, administer, apply, deliver, levy, mete or deal out, visit, wreak

infliction noun imposition, administration, perpetration, wreaking

influence noun 1 effect, authority, control, domination, magnetism, pressure, weight 2 power, clout (informal), hold, importance, leverage, prestige, pull (informal) ♦ verb 3 affect, control, direct, guide, manipulate, sway

influential adjective important, authoritative, instrumental, leading, potent, powerful, significant, telling, weighty

influx noun arrival, incursion, inrush, inundation, invasion, rush

inform verb 1 tell, advise, communicate, enlighten, instruct, notify, teach, tip off 2 incriminate, betray, blow the whistle on (informal), denounce, grass (Brit. slang), inculpate, shop (slang, chiefly Brit.), squeal (slang)

informal adjective relaxed, casual, colloquial, cosy, easy, familiar, natural, simple, unofficial

informality noun familiarity, casualness, ease, naturalness, relaxation, simplicity

information noun facts, data, intelligence, knowledge, message, news, notice, report

informative adjective instructive, chatty, communicative, edifying, educational, enlightening, forthcoming, illuminating, revealing

informed adjective knowledgeable, enlightened, erudite, expert, familiar, in the picture, learned, up to date, versed, well-read

informer noun betrayer, accuser, Judas, sneak, stool pigeon

infrequent adjective occasional, few and far between, once in a blue moon, rare, sporadic, uncommon, unusual

infringe verb break, contravene, disobey, transgress, violate

infringement noun contravention, breach, infraction, transgression, trespass, violation

infuriate verb enrage, anger, exasperate, incense, irritate, madden, provoke, rile

infuriating adjective annoying, exasperating, galling, irritating, maddening, mortifying, provoking, vexatious

ingenious adjective creative, bright, brilliant, clever, crafty, inventive, original, resourceful, shrewd

ingenuity noun originality, cleverness, flair, genius, gift, inventiveness, resourcefulness, sharpness, shrewdness

ingenuous adjective naive,

artless, guileless, honest,
innocent, open, plain, simple,
sincere, trusting, unsophisticated

inglorious adjective
dishonourable, discreditable,
disgraceful, disreputable,
ignoble, ignominious, infamous,
shameful, unheroic

ingratiate verb pander to, crawl,
curry favour, fawn, flatter,
grovel, insinuate oneself, toady

ingratiating adjective
sycophantic, crawling, fawning,
flattering, humble, obsequious,
servile, toadying, unctuous

ingratitude noun ungratefulness,
thanklessness

ingredient noun component,
constituent, element, part

inhabit verb live, abide, dwell,
occupy, populate, reside

inhabitant noun dweller, citizen,
denizen, inmate, native,
occupant, occupier, resident,
tenant

inhabited adjective populated,
colonized, developed, occupied,
peopled, settled, tenanted

inhale verb breathe in, draw in,
gasp, respire, suck in

inherent adjective innate,
essential, hereditary, inborn,
inbred, inbuilt, ingrained,
inherited, intrinsic, native, natural

inherit verb be left, come into,
fall heir to, succeed to

inheritance noun legacy,
bequest, birthright, heritage,
patrimony

inhibit verb restrain, check,
constrain, curb, discourage,
frustrate, hinder, hold back or in,
impede, obstruct

inhibited adjective shy,
constrained, guarded, repressed,
reserved, reticent, self-conscious,
subdued

inhibition noun shyness, block,
hang-up (informal), reserve,
restraint, reticence,
self-consciousness

inhospitable adjective
1 unwelcoming, cool,
uncongenial, unfriendly,
unreceptive, unsociable,
xenophobic 2 bleak, barren,
desolate, forbidding,
godforsaken, hostile

inhuman adjective cruel,
barbaric, brutal, cold-blooded,
heartless, merciless, pitiless,
ruthless, savage, unfeeling

inhumane adjective cruel, brutal,
heartless, pitiless, unfeeling,
unkind, unsympathetic

inhumanity noun cruelty,
atrocity, barbarism, brutality,
heartlessness, pitilessness,
ruthlessness, unkindness

inimical adjective hostile, adverse,
antagonistic, ill-disposed,
opposed, unfavourable,
unfriendly, unwelcoming

inimitable adjective unique,
consummate, incomparable,
matchless, peerless, unparalleled,
unrivalled

iniquitous adjective wicked,
criminal, evil, immoral,
reprehensible, sinful, unjust

iniquity noun wickedness,
abomination, evil, injustice, sin,
wrong

initial adjective first, beginning,
incipient, introductory, opening,
primary

initially *adverb* at first, at *or* in the beginning, first, firstly, originally, primarily

initiate *verb* **1** begin, commence, get under way, kick off (*informal*), launch, open, originate, set in motion, start **2** induct, indoctrinate, introduce, invest **3** instruct, acquaint with, coach, familiarize with, teach, train ♦ *noun* **4** novice, beginner, convert, entrant, learner, member, probationer

initiation *noun* introduction, debut, enrolment, entrance, inauguration, induction, installation, investiture

initiative *noun* **1** first step, advantage, first move, lead **2** resourcefulness, ambition, drive, dynamism, enterprise, get-up-and-go (*informal*), leadership

inject *verb* **1** vaccinate, inoculate **2** introduce, bring in, infuse, insert, instil

injection *noun* **1** vaccination, inoculation, jab (*informal*), shot (*informal*) **2** introduction, dose, infusion, insertion

injudicious *adjective* unwise, foolish, ill-advised, ill-judged, impolitic, imprudent, incautious, inexpedient, rash, unthinking

injunction *noun* order, command, exhortation, instruction, mandate, precept, ruling

injure *verb* hurt, damage, harm, impair, ruin, spoil, undermine, wound

injured *adjective* hurt, broken, damaged, disabled, undermined, weakened, wounded

injury *noun* harm, damage, detriment, disservice, hurt, ill, trauma (*Pathology*), wound, wrong

injustice *noun* unfairness, bias, discrimination, inequality, inequity, iniquity, oppression, partisanship, prejudice, wrong

inkling *noun* suspicion, clue, conception, hint, idea, indication, intimation, notion, suggestion, whisper

inland *adjective* interior, domestic, internal, upcountry

inlet *noun* bay, bight, creek, firth *or* frith (*Scot.*), fjord, passage

inmost *or* **innermost** *adjective* deepest, basic, central, essential, intimate, personal, private, secret

innate *adjective* inborn, congenital, constitutional, essential, inbred, ingrained, inherent, instinctive, intuitive, native, natural

inner *adjective* **1** inside, central, interior, internal, inward, middle **2** private, hidden, intimate, personal, repressed, secret, unrevealed

innkeeper *noun* publican, host *or* hostess, hotelier, landlord *or* landlady, mine host

innocence *noun* **1** guiltlessness, blamelessness, clean hands, incorruptibility, probity, purity, uprightness, virtue **2** harmlessness, innocuousness, inoffensiveness **3** inexperience, artlessness, credulousness, gullibility, ingenuousness, naïveté, simplicity, unworldliness

innocent *adjective* **1** not guilty, blameless, guiltless, honest, in

the clear, uninvolved **2** <u>harmless</u>,
innocuous, inoffensive,
unobjectionable,
well-intentioned, well-meant
3 <u>naive</u>, artless, childlike,
credulous, gullible, ingenuous,
open, simple, unworldly

innovation noun <u>modernization</u>,
alteration, change, departure,
introduction, newness, novelty,
variation

innuendo noun <u>insinuation</u>,
aspersion, hint, implication,
imputation, intimation, overtone,
suggestion, whisper

innumerable adjective <u>countless</u>,
beyond number, incalculable,
infinite, multitudinous, myriad,
numberless, numerous,
unnumbered, untold

inoffensive adjective <u>harmless</u>,
innocent, innocuous, mild, quiet,
retiring, unobjectionable,
unobtrusive

inoperative adjective <u>out of
action</u>, broken, defective,
ineffective, invalid, null and void,
out of order, out of service,
useless

inopportune adjective
<u>inconvenient</u>, ill-chosen,
ill-timed, inappropriate,
unfavourable, unfortunate,
unpropitious, unseasonable,
unsuitable, untimely

inordinate adjective <u>excessive</u>,
disproportionate, extravagant,
immoderate, intemperate,
preposterous, unconscionable,
undue, unreasonable,
unwarranted

inorganic adjective <u>artificial</u>,
chemical, man-made

inquest noun <u>inquiry</u>, inquisition,
investigation, probe

inquire verb **1** <u>investigate</u>,
examine, explore, look into,
make inquiries, probe, research
2 Also **enquire** <u>ask</u>, query,
question

inquiry noun **1** <u>investigation</u>,
examination, exploration,
inquest, interrogation, probe,
research, study, survey **2** Also
enquiry <u>question</u>, query

inquisition noun <u>investigation</u>,
cross-examination, examination,
grilling (informal), inquest,
inquiry, questioning, third
degree (informal)

inquisitive adjective <u>curious</u>,
inquiring, nosy (informal),
probing, prying, questioning

insane adjective **1** <u>mad</u>, crazed,
crazy, demented, deranged,
mentally ill, out of one's mind,
unhinged **2** <u>stupid</u>, daft
(informal), foolish, idiotic,
impractical, irrational,
irresponsible, preposterous,
senseless

insanitary adjective <u>unhealthy</u>,
dirty, disease-ridden, filthy,
infested, insalubrious, polluted,
unclean, unhygienic

insanity noun **1** <u>madness</u>,
delirium, dementia, mental
disorder, mental illness
2 <u>stupidity</u>, folly, irresponsibility,
lunacy, senselessness

insatiable adjective
<u>unquenchable</u>, greedy,
intemperate, rapacious,
ravenous, voracious

inscribe verb <u>carve</u>, cut, engrave,
etch, impress, imprint

inscription noun <u>engraving</u>,

dedication, legend, words

inscrutable *adjective*
1 enigmatic, blank, deadpan, impenetrable, poker-faced (*informal*) 2 mysterious, hidden, incomprehensible, inexplicable, unexplainable, unfathomable, unintelligible

insecure *adjective* 1 anxious, afraid, uncertain, unsure 2 unsafe, defenceless, exposed, unguarded, unprotected, vulnerable, wide-open

insecurity *noun* anxiety, fear, uncertainty, worry

insensible *adjective* unaware, impervious, oblivious, unaffected, unconscious, unmindful

insensitive *adjective* unfeeling, callous, hardened, indifferent, thick-skinned, tough, uncaring, unconcerned

inseparable *adjective* 1 indivisible, indissoluble 2 devoted, bosom, close, intimate

insert *verb* enter, embed, implant, introduce, place, put, stick in

insertion *noun* inclusion, addition, implant, interpolation, introduction, supplement

inside *adjective* 1 inner, interior, internal, inward 2 confidential, classified, exclusive, internal, private, restricted, secret ♦ *adverb* 3 indoors, under cover, within ♦ *noun* 4 interior, contents 5 insides *Informal* stomach, belly, bowels, entrails, guts, innards (*informal*), viscera, vitals

insidious *adjective* stealthy, deceptive, sly, smooth, sneaking, subtle, surreptitious

insight *noun* understanding, awareness, comprehension, discernment, judgment, observation, penetration, perception, perspicacity, vision

insignia *noun* badge, crest, emblem, symbol

insignificance *noun* unimportance, inconsequence, irrelevance, meaninglessness, pettiness, triviality, worthlessness

insignificant *adjective* unimportant, inconsequential, irrelevant, meaningless, minor, nondescript, paltry, petty, trifling, trivial

insincere *adjective* deceitful, dishonest, disingenuous, duplicitous, false, hollow, hypocritical, lying, two-faced, untruthful

insincerity *noun* deceitfulness, dishonesty, dissimulation, duplicity, hypocrisy, pretence, untruthfulness

insinuate *verb* 1 imply, allude, hint, indicate, intimate, suggest 2 ingratiate, curry favour, get in with, worm or work one's way in

insinuation *noun* implication, allusion, aspersion, hint, innuendo, slur, suggestion

insipid *adjective* 1 bland, anaemic, characterless, colourless, prosaic, uninteresting, vapid, wishy-washy (*informal*) 2 tasteless, bland, flavourless, unappetizing, watery

insist *verb* 1 demand, lay down the law, put one's foot down (*informal*), require 2 assert, aver, claim, maintain, reiterate, repeat, swear, vow

insistence noun persistence, emphasis, importunity, stress

insistent adjective persistent, dogged, emphatic, importunate, incessant, persevering, unrelenting, urgent

insolence noun rudeness, boldness, cheek (informal), disrespect, effrontery, impertinence, impudence

insolent adjective rude, bold, contemptuous, impertinent, impudent, insubordinate, insulting

insoluble adjective inexplicable, baffling, impenetrable, indecipherable, mysterious, unaccountable, unfathomable, unsolvable

insolvency noun bankruptcy, failure, liquidation, ruin

insolvent adjective bankrupt, broke (informal), failed, gone bust (informal), gone to the wall, in receivership, ruined

insomnia noun sleeplessness, wakefulness

inspect verb examine, check, go over or through, investigate, look over, scrutinize, survey, vet

inspection noun examination, check, checkup, investigation, once-over (informal), review, scrutiny, search, survey

inspector noun examiner, censor, investigator, overseer, scrutinizer, superintendent, supervisor

inspiration noun 1 influence, muse, spur, stimulus
2 revelation, creativity, illumination, insight

inspire verb 1 stimulate, animate, encourage, enliven, galvanize, influence, spur 2 arouse, enkindle, excite, give rise to, produce

inspired adjective 1 brilliant, dazzling, impressive, memorable, outstanding, superlative, thrilling, wonderful 2 uplifted, elated, enthused, exhilarated, stimulated

inspiring adjective uplifting, exciting, exhilarating, heartening, moving, rousing, stimulating, stirring

instability noun unpredictability, changeableness, fickleness, fluctuation, impermanence, inconstancy, insecurity, unsteadiness, variability, volatility

install verb 1 set up, fix, lay, lodge, place, position, put in, station 2 induct, establish, inaugurate, institute, introduce, invest 3 settle, ensconce, position

installation noun 1 setting up, establishment, fitting, instalment, placing, positioning 2 induction, inauguration, investiture 3 equipment, machinery, plant, system

instalment noun portion, chapter, division, episode, part, repayment, section

instance noun 1 example, case, illustration, occasion, occurrence, situation ♦ verb 2 quote, adduce, cite, mention, name, specify

instant noun 1 second, flash, jiffy (informal), moment, split second, trice, twinkling of an eye (informal) 2 juncture, moment, occasion, point, time ♦ adjective

3 immediate, direct, instantaneous, on-the-spot, prompt, quick, split-second
4 precooked, convenience, fast, ready-mixed

instantaneous *adjective* immediate, direct, instant, on-the-spot, prompt

instantaneously *adverb* immediately, at once, instantly, in the twinkling of an eye (*informal*), on the spot, promptly, straight away

instantly *adverb* immediately, at once, directly, instantaneously, now, right away, straight away, this minute

instead *adverb* **1** rather, alternatively, in lieu, in preference, on second thoughts, preferably **2** instead of in place of, in lieu of, rather than

instigate *verb* provoke, bring about, incite, influence, initiate, prompt, set off, start, stimulate, trigger

instigation *noun* prompting, behest, bidding, encouragement, incitement, urging

instigator *noun* ringleader, agitator, leader, motivator, prime mover, troublemaker

instil *verb* introduce, engender, imbue, implant, inculcate, infuse, insinuate

instinct *noun* intuition, faculty, gift, impulse, knack, predisposition, proclivity, talent, tendency

instinctive *adjective* inborn, automatic, inherent, innate, intuitive, involuntary, natural, reflex, spontaneous, unpremeditated, visceral

instinctively *adverb* intuitively, automatically, by instinct, involuntarily, naturally, without thinking

institute *noun* **1** society, academy, association, college, foundation, guild, institution, school ♦ *verb* **2** establish, fix, found, initiate, introduce, launch, organize, originate, pioneer, set up, start

institution *noun* **1** establishment, academy, college, foundation, institute, school, society **2** custom, convention, law, practice, ritual, rule, tradition

institutional *adjective* conventional, accepted, established, formal, orthodox

instruct *verb* **1** order, bid, charge, command, direct, enjoin, tell **2** teach, coach, drill, educate, ground, school, train, tutor

instruction *noun* **1** teaching, coaching, education, grounding, guidance, lesson(s), schooling, training, tuition **2** order, command, demand, directive, injunction, mandate, ruling

instructions *plural noun* orders, advice, directions, guidance, information, key, recommendations, rules

instructive *adjective* informative, edifying, educational, enlightening, helpful, illuminating, revealing, useful

instructor *noun* teacher, adviser, coach, demonstrator, guide, mentor, trainer, tutor

instrument noun **1** <u>tool</u>, apparatus, appliance, contraption (*informal*), device, gadget, implement, mechanism **2** <u>means</u>, agency, agent, mechanism, medium, organ, vehicle

instrumental adjective <u>active</u>, contributory, helpful, influential, involved, useful

insubordinate adjective <u>disobedient</u>, defiant, disorderly, mutinous, rebellious, recalcitrant, refractory, undisciplined, ungovernable, unruly

insubordination noun <u>disobedience</u>, defiance, indiscipline, insurrection, mutiny, rebellion, recalcitrance, revolt

insubstantial adjective <u>flimsy</u>, feeble, frail, poor, slight, tenuous, thin, weak

insufferable adjective <u>unbearable</u>, detestable, dreadful, impossible, insupportable, intolerable, unendurable

insufficient adjective <u>inadequate</u>, deficient, incapable, lacking, scant, short

insular adjective <u>narrow-minded</u>, blinkered, circumscribed, inward-looking, limited, narrow, parochial, petty, provincial

insulate verb <u>isolate</u>, close off, cocoon, cushion, cut off, protect, sequester, shield

insult verb **1** <u>offend</u>, abuse, affront, call names, put down, slander, slight, snub ♦ noun **2** <u>abuse</u>, affront, aspersion, insolence, offence, put-down, slap in the face (*informal*), slight, snub

insulting adjective <u>offensive</u>, abusive, contemptuous, degrading, disparaging, insolent, rude, scurrilous

insuperable adjective <u>insurmountable</u>, impassable, invincible, unconquerable

insupportable adjective **1** <u>intolerable</u>, insufferable, unbearable, unendurable **2** <u>unjustifiable</u>, indefensible, untenable

insurance noun <u>protection</u>, assurance, cover, guarantee, indemnity, safeguard, security, warranty

insure verb <u>protect</u>, assure, cover, guarantee, indemnify, underwrite, warrant

insurgent noun **1** <u>rebel</u>, insurrectionist, mutineer, revolutionary, rioter ♦ adjective **2** <u>rebellious</u>, disobedient, insubordinate, mutinous, revolting, revolutionary, riotous, seditious

insurmountable adjective <u>insuperable</u>, hopeless, impassable, impossible, invincible, overwhelming, unconquerable

insurrection noun <u>rebellion</u>, coup, insurgency, mutiny, revolt, revolution, riot, uprising

intact adjective <u>undamaged</u>, complete, entire, perfect, sound, unbroken, unharmed, unimpaired, unscathed, whole

integral adjective <u>essential</u>, basic, component, constituent, fundamental, indispensable, intrinsic, necessary

integrate verb <u>combine</u>,

amalgamate, assimilate, blend, fuse, incorporate, join, merge, unite

integration *noun* <u>assimilation</u>, amalgamation, blending, combining, fusing, incorporation, mixing, unification

integrity *noun* 1 <u>honesty</u>, goodness, honour, incorruptibility, principle, probity, purity, rectitude, uprightness, virtue 2 <u>unity</u>, coherence, cohesion, completeness, soundness, wholeness

intellect *noun* <u>intelligence</u>, brains (*informal*), judgment, mind, reason, sense, understanding

intellectual *adjective* 1 <u>scholarly</u>, bookish, cerebral, highbrow, intelligent, studious, thoughtful
♦ *noun* 2 <u>thinker</u>, academic, egghead (*informal*), highbrow

intelligence *noun*
1 <u>understanding</u>, acumen, brain power, brains (*informal*), cleverness, comprehension, intellect, perception, sense
2 <u>information</u>, data, facts, findings, knowledge, news, notification, report

intelligent *adjective* <u>clever</u>, brainy (*informal*), bright, enlightened, perspicacious, quick-witted, sharp, smart, well-informed

intelligentsia *noun* <u>intellectuals</u>, highbrows, literati

intelligible *adjective* <u>understandable</u>, clear, comprehensible, distinct, lucid, open, plain

intemperate *adjective* <u>excessive</u>, extreme, immoderate, profligate, self-indulgent, unbridled, unrestrained, wild

intend *verb* <u>plan</u>, aim, have in mind *or* view, mean, propose, purpose

intense *adjective* 1 <u>extreme</u>, acute, deep, excessive, fierce, great, powerful, profound, severe 2 <u>passionate</u>, ardent, fanatical, fervent, fierce, heightened, impassioned, vehement

intensify *verb* <u>increase</u>, add to, aggravate, deepen, escalate, heighten, magnify, redouble, reinforce, sharpen, strengthen

intensity *noun* <u>force</u>, ardour, emotion, fanaticism, fervour, fierceness, passion, strength, vehemence

intensive *adjective* <u>concentrated</u>, comprehensive, demanding, exhaustive, in-depth, thorough, thoroughgoing

intent *noun* 1 <u>intention</u>, aim, design, end, goal, meaning, object, objective, plan, purpose
♦ *adjective* 2 <u>attentive</u>, absorbed, determined, eager, engrossed, preoccupied, rapt, resolved, steadfast, watchful

intention *noun* <u>purpose</u>, aim, design, end, goal, idea, object, objective, point, target

intentional *adjective* <u>deliberate</u>, calculated, intended, meant, planned, premeditated, wilful

intentionally *adverb* <u>deliberately</u>, designedly, on purpose, wilfully

inter *verb* <u>bury</u>, entomb, lay to rest

intercede *verb* <u>mediate</u>, arbitrate, intervene, plead

intercept *verb* <u>seize</u>, block,

catch, cut off, head off, interrupt, obstruct, stop

interchange verb 1 switch, alternate, exchange, reciprocate, swap ♦ noun 2 junction, intersection

interchangeable adjective identical, equivalent, exchangeable, reciprocal, synonymous

intercourse noun 1 communication, commerce, contact, dealings 2 sexual intercourse, carnal knowledge, coitus, copulation, sex (informal)

interest noun 1 curiosity, attention, concern, notice, regard 2 hobby, activity, diversion, pastime, preoccupation, pursuit 3 advantage, benefit, good, profit 4 stake, claim, investment, right, share ♦ verb 5 intrigue, attract, catch one's eye, divert, engross, fascinate

interested adjective 1 curious, attracted, drawn, excited, fascinated, keen 2 involved, concerned, implicated

interesting adjective intriguing, absorbing, appealing, attractive, compelling, engaging, engrossing, gripping, stimulating, thought-provoking

interface noun connection, border, boundary, frontier, link

interfere verb 1 intrude, butt in, intervene, meddle, stick one's oar in (informal), tamper 2 often with with conflict, clash, hamper, handicap, hinder, impede, inhibit, obstruct

interference noun 1 intrusion, intervention, meddling, prying

2 conflict, clashing, collision, obstruction, opposition

interim adjective temporary, acting, caretaker, improvised, makeshift, provisional, stopgap

interior noun 1 inside, centre, core, heart ♦ adjective 2 inside, inner, internal, inward 3 mental, hidden, inner, intimate, personal, private, secret, spiritual

interloper noun trespasser, gate-crasher (informal), intruder, meddler

interlude noun interval, break, breathing space, delay, hiatus, intermission, pause, respite, rest, spell, stoppage

intermediary noun mediator, agent, broker, go-between, middleman

intermediate adjective middle, halfway, in-between (informal), intervening, mid, midway, transitional

interment noun burial, funeral

interminable adjective endless, ceaseless, everlasting, infinite, long-drawn-out, long-winded, never-ending, perpetual, protracted

intermingle verb mix, blend, combine, fuse, interlace, intermix, interweave, merge

intermission noun interval, break, interlude, pause, recess, respite, rest, stoppage

intermittent adjective periodic, broken, fitful, irregular, occasional, spasmodic, sporadic

intern verb imprison, confine, detain, hold, hold in custody

internal adjective 1 inner, inside, interior 2 domestic, civic, home, in-house, intramural

international *adjective* <u>universal</u>, cosmopolitan, global, intercontinental, worldwide

Internet *noun* <u>information superhighway</u>, cyberspace, the net (*informal*), the web (*informal*), World Wide Web

interpose *verb* <u>interrupt</u>, insert, interject, put one's oar in

interpret *verb* <u>explain</u>, construe, decipher, decode, elucidate, make sense of, render, translate

interpretation *noun* <u>explanation</u>, analysis, clarification, elucidation, exposition, portrayal, rendition, translation, version

interpreter *noun* <u>translator</u>, commentator

interrogate *verb* <u>question</u>, cross-examine, examine, grill (*informal*), investigate, pump, quiz

interrogation *noun* <u>questioning</u>, cross-examination, examination, grilling (*informal*), inquiry, inquisition, third degree (*informal*)

interrupt *verb* 1 <u>intrude</u>, barge in (*informal*), break in, butt in, disturb, heckle, interfere (with) 2 <u>suspend</u>, break off, cut short, delay, discontinue, hold up, lay aside, stop

interruption *noun* <u>stoppage</u>, break, disruption, disturbance, hitch, intrusion, pause, suspension

intersection *noun* <u>junction</u>, crossing, crossroads, interchange

interval *noun* <u>break</u>, delay, gap, interlude, intermission, pause, respite, rest, space, spell

intervene *verb* 1 <u>involve oneself</u>, arbitrate, intercede, interfere,

intrude, mediate, step in (*informal*), take a hand (*informal*) 2 <u>happen</u>, befall, come to pass, ensue, occur, take place

intervention *noun* <u>mediation</u>, agency, interference, intrusion

interview *noun* 1 <u>meeting</u>, audience, conference, consultation, dialogue, press conference, talk ♦ *verb* 2 <u>question</u>, examine, interrogate, talk to

interviewer *noun* <u>questioner</u>, examiner, interrogator, investigator, reporter

intestines *plural noun* <u>guts</u>, bowels, entrails, innards (*informal*), insides (*informal*), viscera

intimacy *noun* <u>familiarity</u>, closeness, confidentiality

intimate[1] *adjective* 1 <u>close</u>, bosom, confidential, dear, near, thick (*informal*) 2 <u>personal</u>, confidential, private, secret 3 <u>detailed</u>, deep, exhaustive, first-hand, immediate, in-depth, profound, thorough 4 <u>snug</u>, comfy (*informal*), cosy, friendly, warm ♦ *noun* 5 <u>friend</u>, close friend, confidant *or* confidante, (constant) companion, crony

intimate[2] *verb* 1 <u>suggest</u>, hint, imply, indicate, insinuate 2 <u>announce</u>, communicate, declare, make known, state

intimately *adverb* 1 <u>confidingly</u>, affectionately, confidentially, familiarly, personally, tenderly, warmly 2 <u>in detail</u>, fully, inside out, thoroughly, very well

intimation *noun* 1 <u>hint</u>, allusion, indication, inkling, insinuation, reminder, suggestion, warning

2 <u>announcement</u>, communication, declaration, notice

intimidate *verb* <u>frighten</u>, browbeat, bully, coerce, daunt, overawe, scare, subdue, terrorize, threaten

intimidation *noun* <u>bullying</u>, arm-twisting (*informal*), browbeating, coercion, menaces, pressure, terrorization, threat(s)

intolerable *adjective* <u>unbearable</u>, excruciating, impossible, insufferable, insupportable, painful, unendurable

intolerance *noun* <u>narrow-mindedness</u>, bigotry, chauvinism, discrimination, dogmatism, fanaticism, illiberality, prejudice

intolerant *adjective* <u>narrow-minded</u>, bigoted, chauvinistic, dictatorial, dogmatic, fanatical, illiberal, prejudiced, small-minded

intone *verb* <u>recite</u>, chant

intoxicated *adjective* 1 <u>drunk</u>, drunken, inebriated, legless (*informal*), paralytic (*informal*), plastered (*slang*), tipsy, under the influence 2 <u>euphoric</u>, dizzy, elated, enraptured, excited, exhilarated, high (*informal*)

intoxicating *adjective* 1 <u>alcoholic</u>, strong 2 <u>exciting</u>, exhilarating, heady, thrilling

intoxication *noun* 1 <u>drunkenness</u>, inebriation, insobriety, tipsiness 2 <u>excitement</u>, delirium, elation, euphoria, exhilaration

intransigent *adjective* <u>uncompromising</u>, hardline,

intractable, obdurate, obstinate, stiff-necked, stubborn, unbending, unyielding

intrepid *adjective* <u>fearless</u>, audacious, bold, brave, courageous, daring, gallant, plucky, stouthearted, valiant

intricacy *noun* <u>complexity</u>, complication, convolutions, elaborateness

intricate *adjective* <u>complicated</u>, complex, convoluted, elaborate, fancy, involved, labyrinthine, tangled, tortuous

intrigue *verb* 1 <u>interest</u>, attract, fascinate, rivet, titillate 2 <u>plot</u>, connive, conspire, machinate, manoeuvre, scheme ♦ *noun* 3 <u>plot</u>, chicanery, collusion, conspiracy, machination, manoeuvre, scheme, stratagem, wile 4 <u>affair</u>, amour, intimacy, liaison, romance

intriguing *adjective* <u>interesting</u>, beguiling, compelling, diverting, exciting, fascinating, tantalizing, titillating

intrinsic *adjective* <u>inborn</u>, basic, built-in, congenital, constitutional, essential, fundamental, inbred, inherent, native, natural

introduce *verb* 1 <u>present</u>, acquaint, familiarize, make known 2 <u>bring in</u>, establish, found, initiate, institute, launch, pioneer, set up, start 3 <u>bring up</u>, advance, air, broach, moot, put forward, submit 4 <u>insert</u>, add, inject, put in, throw in (*informal*)

introduction *noun* 1 <u>launch</u>, establishment, inauguration, institution, pioneering 2 <u>opening</u>, foreword, intro (*informal*), lead-in, preamble, preface, prelude, prologue

introductory *adjective* preliminary, first, inaugural, initial, opening, preparatory

introspective *adjective* inward-looking, brooding, contemplative, introverted, meditative, pensive

introverted *adjective* introspective, inner-directed, inward-looking, self-contained, withdrawn

intrude *verb* interfere, butt in, encroach, infringe, interrupt, meddle, push in, trespass

intruder *noun* trespasser, gate-crasher (*informal*), infiltrator, interloper, invader, prowler

intrusion *noun* invasion, encroachment, infringement, interference, interruption, trespass

intrusive *adjective* interfering, impertinent, importunate, meddlesome, nosy (*informal*), presumptuous, pushy (*informal*), uncalled-for, unwanted

intuition *noun* instinct, hunch, insight, perception, presentiment, sixth sense

intuitive *adjective* instinctive, innate, spontaneous, untaught

inundate *verb* flood, drown, engulf, immerse, overflow, overrun, overwhelm, submerge, swamp

invade *verb* 1 attack, assault, burst in, descend upon, encroach, infringe, make inroads, occupy, raid, violate 2 infest, overrun, permeate, pervade, swarm over

invader *noun* attacker, aggressor, plunderer, raider, trespasser

invalid[1] *adjective* 1 disabled, ailing, bedridden, frail, ill, infirm, sick ♦ *noun* 2 patient, convalescent, valetudinarian

invalid[2] *adjective* null and void, fallacious, false, illogical, inoperative, irrational, unfounded, unsound, void, worthless

invalidate *verb* nullify, annul, cancel, overthrow, undermine, undo

invaluable *adjective* precious, inestimable, priceless, valuable, worth one's *or* its weight in gold

invariably *adverb* consistently, always, customarily, day in, day out, habitually, perpetually, regularly, unfailingly, without exception

invasion *noun* 1 attack, assault, campaign, foray, incursion, inroad, offensive, onslaught, raid 2 intrusion, breach, encroachment, infraction, infringement, usurpation, violation

invective *noun* abuse, censure, denunciation, diatribe, tirade, tongue-lashing, vilification, vituperation

invent *verb* 1 create, coin, conceive, design, devise, discover, formulate, improvise, originate, think up 2 make up, concoct, cook up (*informal*), fabricate, feign, forge, manufacture, trump up

invention *noun* 1 creation, brainchild (*informal*), contraption, contrivance, design, device, discovery, gadget,

instrument 2 <u>creativity</u>, genius, imagination, ingenuity, inventiveness, originality, resourcefulness **3** <u>fiction</u>, fabrication, falsehood, fantasy, forgery, lie, untruth, yarn

inventive *adjective* <u>creative</u>, fertile, imaginative, ingenious, innovative, inspired, original, resourceful

inventor *noun* <u>creator</u>, architect, author, coiner, designer, maker, originator

inventory *noun* <u>list</u>, account, catalogue, file, record, register, roll, roster

inverse *adjective* <u>opposite</u>, contrary, converse, reverse, reversed, transposed

invert *verb* <u>overturn</u>, reverse, transpose, upset, upturn

invest *verb* **1** <u>spend</u>, advance, devote, lay out, put in, sink **2** <u>empower</u>, authorize, charge, license, sanction, vest

investigate *verb* <u>examine</u>, explore, go into, inquire into, inspect, look into, probe, research, study

investigation *noun* <u>examination</u>, exploration, inquest, inquiry, inspection, probe, review, search, study, survey

investigator *noun* <u>examiner</u>, inquirer, (private) detective, private eye (*informal*), researcher, sleuth

investiture *noun* <u>installation</u>, enthronement, inauguration, induction, ordination

investment *noun* **1** <u>transaction</u>, speculation, venture **2** <u>stake</u>, ante (*informal*), contribution

inveterate *adjective* <u>long-standing</u>, chronic, confirmed, deep-seated, dyed-in-the-wool, entrenched, habitual, hardened, incorrigible, incurable

invidious *adjective* <u>undesirable</u>, hateful

invigilate *verb* <u>watch over</u>, conduct, keep an eye on, oversee, preside over, run, superintend, supervise

invigorate *verb* <u>refresh</u>, energize, enliven, exhilarate, fortify, galvanize, liven up, revitalize, stimulate

invincible *adjective* <u>unbeatable</u>, impregnable, indestructible, indomitable, insuperable, invulnerable, unassailable, unconquerable

inviolable *adjective* <u>sacrosanct</u>, hallowed, holy, inalienable, sacred, unalterable

inviolate *adjective* <u>intact</u>, entire, pure, unbroken, undefiled, unhurt, unpolluted, unsullied, untouched, whole

invisible *adjective* <u>unseen</u>, imperceptible, indiscernible

invitation *noun* <u>request</u>, call, invite (*informal*), summons

invite *verb* **1** <u>request</u>, ask, beg, bid, summon **2** <u>encourage</u>, ask for (*informal*), attract, court, entice, provoke, tempt, welcome

inviting *adjective* <u>tempting</u>, alluring, appealing, attractive, enticing, mouthwatering, seductive, welcoming

invocation *noun* <u>appeal</u>, entreaty, petition, prayer, supplication

invoke verb 1 <u>call upon</u>, appeal to, beg, beseech, entreat, implore, petition, pray, supplicate 2 <u>apply</u>, implement, initiate, put into effect, resort to, use

involuntary adjective <u>unintentional</u>, automatic, instinctive, reflex, spontaneous, unconscious, uncontrolled, unthinking

involve verb 1 <u>entail</u>, imply, mean, necessitate, presuppose, require 2 <u>concern</u>, affect, draw in, implicate, touch

involved adjective 1 <u>complicated</u>, complex, confusing, convoluted, elaborate, intricate, labyrinthine, tangled, tortuous 2 <u>concerned</u>, caught (up), implicated, mixed up in or with, participating, taking part

involvement noun <u>connection</u>, association, commitment, interest, participation

invulnerable adjective <u>safe</u>, impenetrable, indestructible, insusceptible, invincible, proof against, secure, unassailable

inward adjective 1 <u>incoming</u>, entering, inbound, ingoing 2 <u>internal</u>, inner, inside, interior 3 <u>private</u>, confidential, hidden, inmost, innermost, personal, secret

inwardly adverb <u>privately</u>, at heart, deep down, inside, secretly

irate adjective <u>angry</u>, annoyed, cross, enraged, furious, incensed, indignant, infuriated, livid

irksome adjective <u>irritating</u>, annoying, bothersome, disagreeable, exasperating, tiresome, troublesome, trying,

vexing, wearisome

iron adjective 1 <u>ferrous</u>, chalybeate, ferric 2 <u>inflexible</u>, adamant, hard, implacable, indomitable, rigid, steely, strong, tough, unbending, unyielding

ironic, ironical adjective 1 <u>sarcastic</u>, double-edged, mocking, sardonic, satirical, with tongue in cheek, wry 2 <u>paradoxical</u>, incongruous

iron out verb <u>settle</u>, clear up, get rid of, put right, reconcile, resolve, smooth over, sort out, straighten out

irony noun 1 <u>sarcasm</u>, mockery, satire 2 <u>paradox</u>, incongruity

irrational adjective <u>illogical</u>, absurd, crazy, nonsensical, preposterous, unreasonable

irrefutable adjective <u>undeniable</u>, certain, incontestable, incontrovertible, indisputable, indubitable, sure, unquestionable

irregular adjective 1 <u>variable</u>, erratic, fitful, haphazard, occasional, random, spasmodic, sporadic, unsystematic 2 <u>unconventional</u>, abnormal, exceptional, extraordinary, peculiar, unofficial, unorthodox, unusual 3 <u>uneven</u>, asymmetrical, bumpy, crooked, jagged, lopsided, ragged, rough

irregularity noun 1 <u>uncertainty</u>, desultoriness, disorganization, haphazardness 2 <u>abnormality</u>, anomaly, oddity, peculiarity, unorthodoxy 3 <u>unevenness</u>, asymmetry, bumpiness, jaggedness, lopsidedness, raggedness, roughness

irrelevant adjective <u>unconnected</u>, beside the point, extraneous, immaterial, impertinent, inapplicable, inappropriate, neither here nor there, unrelated

irreparable *adjective* <u>beyond repair</u>, incurable, irremediable, irretrievable, irreversible

irrepressible *adjective* <u>ebullient</u>, boisterous, buoyant, effervescent, unstoppable

irreproachable *adjective* <u>blameless</u>, beyond reproach, faultless, impeccable, innocent, perfect, pure, unimpeachable

irresistible *adjective* <u>overwhelming</u>, compelling, compulsive, overpowering, urgent

irresponsible *adjective* <u>immature</u>, careless, reckless, scatterbrained, shiftless, thoughtless, unreliable, untrustworthy

irreverent *adjective* <u>disrespectful</u>, cheeky (*informal*), flippant, iconoclastic, impertinent, impudent, mocking, tongue-in-cheek

irreversible *adjective* <u>irrevocable</u>, final, incurable, irreparable, unalterable

irrevocable *adjective* <u>fixed</u>, fated, immutable, irreversible, predestined, predetermined, settled, unalterable

irrigate *verb* <u>water</u>, flood, inundate, moisten, wet

irritability *noun* <u>bad temper</u>, ill humour, impatience, irascibility, prickliness, testiness, tetchiness, touchiness

irritable *adjective* <u>bad-tempered</u>, cantankerous, crotchety (*informal*), ill-tempered, irascible,

oversensitive, prickly, testy, tetchy, touchy

irritate *verb* **1** <u>annoy</u>, anger, bother, exasperate, get on one's nerves (*informal*), infuriate, needle (*informal*), nettle, rankle with, try one's patience **2** <u>rub</u>, chafe, inflame, pain

irritated *adjective* <u>annoyed</u>, angry, bothered, cross, exasperated, nettled, piqued, put out, vexed

irritating *adjective* <u>annoying</u>, disturbing, infuriating, irksome, maddening, nagging, troublesome, trying

irritation *noun* **1** <u>annoyance</u>, anger, displeasure, exasperation, indignation, resentment, testiness, vexation **2** <u>nuisance</u>, drag (*informal*), irritant, pain in the neck (*informal*), thorn in one's flesh

island *noun* <u>isle</u>, ait *or* eyot (*dialect*), atoll, cay *or* key, islet

isolate *verb* <u>separate</u>, cut off, detach, disconnect, insulate, segregate, set apart

isolated *adjective* <u>remote</u>, hidden, lonely, off the beaten track, outlying, out-of-the-way, secluded

isolation *noun* <u>separation</u>, detachment, remoteness, seclusion, segregation, solitude

issue *noun* **1** <u>topic</u>, bone of contention, matter, point, problem, question, subject **2** <u>outcome</u>, consequence, effect, end result, upshot **3** <u>edition</u>, copy, number, printing **4** <u>children</u>, descendants, heirs, offspring, progeny **5** **take issue** <u>disagree</u>, challenge, dispute, object, oppose, raise an objection, take exception ♦ *verb* **6** <u>publish</u>, announce, broadcast, circulate, deliver, distribute, give out, put out, release

isthmus *noun* <u>strip</u>, spit

itch *noun* **1** <u>irritation</u>, itchiness, prickling, tingling **2** <u>desire</u>, craving, hankering, hunger, longing, lust, passion, yearning, yen (*informal*) ♦ *verb* **3** <u>prickle</u>, irritate, tickle, tingle **4** <u>long</u>, ache, crave, hanker, hunger, lust, pine, yearn

itching *adjective* <u>longing</u>, avid, eager, impatient, mad keen (*informal*), raring, spoiling for

itchy *adjective* <u>impatient</u>, eager, edgy, fidgety, restive, restless, unsettled

item *noun* **1** <u>detail</u>, article, component, entry, matter, particular, point, thing **2** <u>report</u>, account, article, bulletin, dispatch, feature, note, notice, paragraph, piece

itinerant *adjective* <u>wandering</u>, migratory, nomadic, peripatetic, roaming, roving, travelling, vagrant

itinerary *noun* <u>schedule</u>, programme, route, timetable

J j

jab *verb, noun* <u>poke</u>, dig, lunge, nudge, prod, punch, stab, tap, thrust

jabber *verb* <u>chatter</u>, habble, blether, gabble, mumble, prate, rabbit (on) (*Brit. informal*), ramble, yap (*informal*)

jacket *noun* <u>covering</u>, case, casing, coat, sheath, skin, wrapper, wrapping

jackpot *noun* <u>prize</u>, award, bonanza, reward, winnings

jack up *verb* <u>raise</u>, elevate, hoist, lift, lift up

jaded *adjective* <u>tired</u>, exhausted, fatigued, spent, weary

jagged *adjective* <u>uneven</u>, barbed, craggy, indented, ragged, serrated, spiked, toothed

jail *noun* **1** <u>prison</u>, nick (*Brit. slang*), penitentiary (*U.S.*), reformatory, slammer (*slang*) ♦ *verb* **2** <u>imprison</u>, confine, detain, incarcerate, lock up, send down

jailer *noun* <u>guard</u>, keeper, warden, warder

jam *verb* **1** <u>pack</u>, cram, force, press, ram, squeeze, stuff, wedge **2** <u>crowd</u>, crush, throng **3** <u>congest</u>, block, clog, obstruct, stall, stick ♦ *noun* **4** <u>predicament</u>, deep water, fix (*informal*), hole (*slang*), hot water, pickle (*informal*), tight spot, trouble

jamboree *noun* <u>festival</u>, carnival, celebration, festivity, fête, revelry

jangle *verb* <u>rattle</u>, chime, clank, clash, clatter, jingle, vibrate

janitor *noun* <u>caretaker</u>, concierge, custodian, doorkeeper, porter

jar¹ *noun* <u>pot</u>, container, crock, jug, pitcher, urn, vase

jar² *verb* **1** <u>jolt</u>, bump, convulse, rattle, rock, shake, vibrate **2** <u>irritate</u>, annoy, get on one's nerves (*informal*), grate, irk, nettle, offend ♦ *noun* **3** <u>jolt</u>, bump, convulsion, shock, vibration

jargon noun <u>parlance</u>, argot, idiom, usage

jaundiced adjective 1 <u>cynical</u>, sceptical 2 <u>bitter</u>, envious, hostile, jealous, resentful, spiteful, suspicious

jaunt noun <u>outing</u>, airing, excursion, expedition, ramble, stroll, tour, trip

jaunty adjective <u>sprightly</u>, buoyant, carefree, high-spirited, lively, perky, self-confident, sparky

jaw verb <u>talk</u>, chat, chatter, gossip, spout

jaws plural noun <u>opening</u>, entrance, mouth

jazz up verb <u>enliven</u>, animate, enhance, improve

jazzy adjective <u>flashy</u>, fancy, gaudy, snazzy (informal)

jealous adjective 1 <u>envious</u>, covetous, desirous, green, grudging, resentful 2 <u>wary</u>, mistrustful, protective, suspicious, vigilant, watchful

jealousy noun <u>envy</u>, covetousness, mistrust, possessiveness, resentment, spite, suspicion

jeans plural noun <u>denims</u>, Levis (Trademark)

jeer verb 1 <u>scoff</u>, barrack, deride, gibe, heckle, mock, ridicule, taunt ♦ noun 2 <u>taunt</u>, abuse, boo, catcall, derision, gibe, ridicule

jell verb 1 <u>solidify</u>, congeal, harden, set, thicken 2 <u>take shape</u>, come together, crystallize, materialize

jeopardize verb <u>endanger</u>, chance, expose, gamble, imperil, risk, stake, venture

jeopardy noun <u>danger</u>, insecurity, peril, risk, vulnerability

jerk verb, noun <u>tug</u>, jolt, lurch, pull, thrust, twitch, wrench, yank

jerky adjective <u>bumpy</u>, convulsive, jolting, jumpy, shaky, spasmodic, twitchy

jerry-built adjective <u>ramshackle</u>, cheap, defective, flimsy, rickety, shabby, slipshod, thrown together

jest noun 1 <u>joke</u>, bon mot, crack (slang), jape, pleasantry, prank, quip, wisecrack (informal), witticism ♦ verb 2 <u>joke</u>, kid (informal), mock, quip, tease

jester noun <u>clown</u>, buffoon, fool, harlequin

jet¹ adjective <u>black</u>, coal-black, ebony, inky, pitch-black, raven, sable

jet² noun 1 <u>stream</u>, flow, fountain, gush, spout, spray, spring 2 <u>nozzle</u>, atomizer, sprayer, sprinkler ♦ verb 3 <u>fly</u>, soar, zoom

jettison verb <u>abandon</u>, discard, dump, eject, expel, scrap, throw overboard, unload

jetty noun <u>pier</u>, breakwater, dock, groyne, mole, quay, wharf

jewel noun 1 <u>gemstone</u>, ornament, rock (slang), sparkler (informal) 2 <u>rarity</u>, collector's item, find, gem, humdinger (slang), pearl, treasure, wonder

jewellery noun <u>jewels</u>, finery, gems, ornaments, regalia, treasure, trinkets

jib verb <u>refuse</u>, balk, recoil, retreat, shrink, stop short

jibe see GIBE

jig *verb* <u>skip</u>, bob, bounce, caper, prance, wiggle

jingle *noun* 1 <u>rattle</u>, clang, clink, reverberation, ringing, tinkle 2 <u>song</u>, chorus, ditty, melody, tune ♦ *verb* 3 <u>ring</u>, chime, clatter, clink, jangle, rattle, tinkle

jinx *noun* 1 <u>curse</u>, hex (*U.S. & Canad. informal*), hoodoo (*informal*), nemesis ♦ *verb* 2 <u>curse</u>, bewitch, hex (*U.S. & Canad. informal*)

jitters *plural noun* <u>nerves</u>, anxiety, butterflies (in one's stomach) (*informal*), cold feet (*informal*), fidgets, nervousness, the shakes (*informal*)

jittery *adjective* <u>nervous</u>, agitated, anxious, fidgety, jumpy, shaky, trembling, twitchy (*informal*)

job *noun* 1 <u>task</u>, assignment, chore, duty, enterprise, errand, undertaking, venture 2 <u>occupation</u>, business, calling, career, employment, livelihood, profession, vocation

jobless *adjective* <u>unemployed</u>, idle, inactive, out of work, unoccupied

jocular *adjective* <u>humorous</u>, amusing, droll, facetious, funny, joking, jovial, playful, sportive, teasing, waggish

jog *verb* 1 <u>nudge</u>, prod, push, shake, stir 2 <u>run</u>, canter, lope, trot

joie de vivre *noun* <u>enthusiasm</u>, ebullience, enjoyment, gusto, relish, zest

join *verb* 1 <u>connect</u>, add, append, attach, combine, couple, fasten, link, unite 2 <u>enrol</u>, enlist, enter, sign up

joint *adjective* 1 <u>shared</u>, collective, combined, communal, cooperative, joined, mutual, united ♦ *noun* 2 <u>junction</u>, connection, hinge, intersection, nexus, node ♦ *verb* 3 <u>divide</u>, carve, cut up, dissect, segment, sever

jointly *adverb* <u>collectively</u>, as one, in common, in conjunction, in league, in partnership, mutually, together

joke *noun* 1 <u>jest</u>, gag (*informal*), jape, prank, pun, quip, wisecrack (*informal*), witticism 2 <u>clown</u>, buffoon, laughing stock ♦ *verb* 3 <u>jest</u>, banter, kid (*informal*), mock, play the fool, quip, taunt, tease

joker *noun* <u>comedian</u>, buffoon, clown, comic, humorist, jester, prankster, trickster, wag, wit

jolly *adjective* <u>happy</u>, cheerful, chirpy (*informal*), genial, jovial, merry, playful, sprightly, upbeat (*informal*)

jolt *noun* 1 <u>jerk</u>, bump, jar, jog, jump, lurch, shake, start 2 <u>surprise</u>, blow, bolt from the blue, bombshell, setback, shock ♦ *verb* 3 <u>jerk</u>, jar, jog, jostle, knock, push, shake, shove 4 <u>surprise</u>, discompose, disturb, perturb, stagger, startle, stun

jostle *verb* <u>push</u>, bump, elbow, hustle, jog, jolt, shake, shove

jot *verb* 1 <u>note down</u>, list, record, scribble ♦ *noun* 2 <u>bit</u>, fraction, grain, morsel, scrap, speck

journal *noun* 1 <u>newspaper</u>, daily, gazette, magazine, monthly, periodical, weekly 2 <u>diary</u>, chronicle, log, record

journalist *noun* <u>reporter</u>,

broadcaster, columnist,
commentator, correspondent,
hack, journo (*slang*), newsman *or*
newswoman, pressman

journey *noun* 1 <u>trip</u>, excursion,
expedition, odyssey, pilgrimage,
tour, trek, voyage ♦ *verb* 2 <u>travel</u>,
go, proceed, roam, rove, tour,
traverse, trek, voyage, wander

jovial *adjective* <u>cheerful</u>,
animated, cheery, convivial,
happy, jolly, merry, mirthful

joy *noun* <u>delight</u>, bliss, ecstasy,
elation, gaiety, glee, pleasure,
rapture, satisfaction

joyful *adjective* <u>delighted</u>, elated,
enraptured, glad, gratified,
happy, jubilant, merry, pleased

joyless *adjective* <u>unhappy</u>,
cheerless, depressed, dismal,
dreary, gloomy, miserable, sad

joyous *adjective* <u>joyful</u>, festive,
merry, rapturous

jubilant *adjective* <u>overjoyed</u>,
elated, enraptured, euphoric,
exuberant, exultant, thrilled,
triumphant

jubilation *noun* <u>joy</u>, celebration,
ecstasy, elation, excitement,
exultation, festivity, triumph

jubilee *noun* <u>celebration</u>, festival,
festivity, holiday

judge *noun* 1 <u>referee</u>,
adjudicator, arbiter, arbitrator,
moderator, umpire 2 <u>critic</u>,
arbiter, assessor, authority,
connoisseur, expert
3 <u>magistrate</u>, beak (*Brit. slang*),
justice ♦ *verb* 4 <u>arbitrate</u>,
adjudicate, decide, mediate,
referee, umpire 5 <u>consider</u>,
appraise, assess, esteem,
estimate, evaluate, rate, value

judgment *noun* 1 <u>sense</u>,
acumen, discernment,
discrimination, prudence,
shrewdness, understanding,
wisdom 2 <u>verdict</u>, arbitration,
decision, decree, finding, ruling,
sentence 3 <u>opinion</u>, appraisal,
assessment, belief, diagnosis,
estimate, finding, valuation, view

judicial *adjective* <u>legal</u>, official

judicious *adjective* <u>sensible</u>,
astute, careful, discriminating,
enlightened, prudent, shrewd,
thoughtful, well-judged, wise

jug *noun* <u>container</u>, carafe, crock,
ewer, jar, pitcher, urn, vessel

juggle *verb* <u>manipulate</u>, alter,
change, manoeuvre, modify

juice *noun* <u>liquid</u>, extract, fluid,
liquor, nectar, sap

juicy *adjective* 1 <u>moist</u>, lush,
succulent 2 <u>interesting</u>,
colourful, provocative, racy,
risqué, sensational, spicy
(*informal*), suggestive, vivid

jumble *noun* 1 <u>muddle</u>, clutter,
confusion, disarray, disorder,
mess, mishmash, mixture ♦ *verb*
2 <u>mix</u>, confuse, disorder,
disorganize, mistake, muddle,
shuffle

jumbo *adjective* <u>giant</u>, gigantic,
huge, immense, large, oversized

jump *verb* 1 <u>leap</u>, bounce,
bound, hop, hurdle, skip, spring,
vault 2 <u>recoil</u>, flinch, jerk, start,
wince 3 <u>miss</u>, avoid, evade,
omit, skip 4 <u>increase</u>, advance,
ascend, escalate, rise, surge
♦ *noun* 5 <u>leap</u>, bound, hop, skip,
spring, vault 6 <u>interruption</u>,
break, gap, hiatus, lacuna, space
7 <u>rise</u>, advance, increase,
increment, upsurge, upturn

jumped-up *adjective* <u>conceited</u>, arrogant, insolent, overbearing, pompous, presumptuous

jumper *noun* <u>sweater</u>, jersey, pullover, woolly

jumpy *adjective* <u>nervous</u>, agitated, anxious, apprehensive, fidgety, jittery (*informal*), on edge, restless, tense

junction *noun* <u>connection</u>, coupling, linking, union

juncture *noun* <u>moment</u>, occasion, point, time

junior *adjective* <u>minor</u>, inferior, lesser, lower, secondary, subordinate, younger

junk *noun* <u>rubbish</u>, clutter, debris, litter, odds and ends, refuse, scrap, trash, waste

jurisdiction *noun* 1 <u>authority</u>, command, control, influence, power, rule 2 <u>range</u>, area, bounds, compass, field, province, scope, sphere

just *adverb* 1 <u>exactly</u>, absolutely, completely, entirely, perfectly, precisely 2 <u>recently</u>, hardly, lately, only now, scarcely 3 <u>merely</u>, by the skin of one's teeth, only, simply, solely ♦ *adjective* 4 <u>fair</u>, conscientious, equitable, fair-minded, good, honest, upright, virtuous 5 <u>proper</u>, appropriate, apt, deserved, due, fitting, justified, merited, rightful

justice *noun* 1 <u>fairness</u>, equity, honesty, integrity, law, legality, legitimacy, right 2 <u>judge</u>, magistrate

justifiable *adjective* <u>reasonable</u>, acceptable, defensible, excusable, legitimate, sensible, understandable, valid, warrantable

justification *noun* 1 <u>explanation</u>, defence, excuse, rationalization, vindication 2 <u>reason</u>, basis, grounds, warrant

justify *verb* <u>explain</u>, defend, exculpate, excuse, exonerate, support, uphold, vindicate, warrant

justly *adverb* <u>properly</u>, correctly, equitably, fairly, lawfully

jut *verb* <u>stick out</u>, bulge, extend, overhang, poke, project, protrude

juvenile *adjective* 1 <u>young</u>, babyish, callow, childish, immature, inexperienced, infantile, puerile, youthful ♦ *noun* 2 <u>child</u>, adolescent, boy, girl, infant, minor, youth

juxtaposition *noun* <u>proximity</u>, closeness, contact, nearness, propinquity, vicinity

K k

kamikaze *adjective* <u>self-destructive</u>, foolhardy, suicidal

keel over *verb* <u>collapse</u>, black out (*informal*), faint, pass out

keen *adjective* 1 <u>eager</u>, ardent, avid, enthusiastic, impassioned, intense, zealous 2 <u>sharp</u>, cutting, incisive, razor-like 3 <u>astute</u>, canny, clever, perceptive, quick, shrewd, wise

keenness *noun* <u>eagerness</u>, ardour, enthusiasm, fervour, intensity, passion, zeal, zest

keep *verb* 1 <u>retain</u>, conserve,

control, hold, maintain, possess, preserve 2 <u>store</u>, carry, deposit, hold, place, stack, stock 3 <u>look after</u>, care for, guard, maintain, manage, mind, protect, tend, watch over 4 <u>support</u>, feed, maintain, provide for, subsidize, sustain 5 <u>detain</u>, delay, hinder, hold back, keep back, obstruct, prevent, restrain ♦ noun 6 <u>board</u>, food, living, maintenance 7 <u>tower</u>, castle

keeper noun <u>guardian</u>, attendant, caretaker, curator, custodian, guard, preserver, steward, warden

keeping noun 1 <u>care</u>, charge, custody, guardianship, possession, protection, safekeeping 2 As in **in keeping with** <u>agreement</u>, accord, balance, compliance, conformity, correspondence, harmony, observance, proportion

keepsake noun <u>souvenir</u>, memento, relic, reminder, symbol, token

keep up verb <u>maintain</u>, continue, keep pace, preserve, sustain

keg noun <u>barrel</u>, cask, drum, vat

kernel noun <u>essence</u>, core, germ, gist, nub, pith, substance

key noun 1 <u>opener</u>, latchkey 2 <u>answer</u>, explanation, solution ♦ adjective 3 <u>essential</u>, crucial, decisive, fundamental, important, leading, main, major, pivotal, principal

key in verb <u>type</u>, enter, input, keyboard

keynote noun <u>heart</u>, centre, core, essence, gist, substance, theme

kick verb 1 <u>boot</u>, punt 2 Informal

<u>give up</u>, abandon, desist from, leave off, quit, stop ♦ noun 3 Informal <u>thrill</u>, buzz (slang), pleasure, stimulation

kick off verb Informal <u>begin</u>, commence, get the show on the road, initiate, open, start

kick out verb <u>dismiss</u>, eject, evict, expel, get rid of, remove, sack (informal)

kid[1] noun Informal <u>child</u>, baby, bairn, infant, teenager, tot, youngster, youth

kid[2] verb <u>tease</u>, delude, fool, hoax, jest, joke, pretend, trick, wind up (Brit. slang)

kidnap verb <u>abduct</u>, capture, hijack, hold to ransom, seize

kill verb 1 <u>slay</u>, assassinate, butcher, destroy, execute, exterminate, liquidate, massacre, murder, slaughter 2 <u>suppress</u>, extinguish, halt, quash, quell, scotch, smother, stifle, stop

killer noun <u>assassin</u>, butcher, cut-throat, executioner, exterminator, gunman, hit man (slang), murderer, slayer

killing adjective 1 Informal <u>tiring</u>, debilitating, exhausting, fatiguing, punishing 2 Informal <u>hilarious</u>, comical, ludicrous, uproarious ♦ noun 3 <u>slaughter</u>, bloodshed, carnage, extermination, homicide, manslaughter, massacre, murder, slaying 4 Informal <u>bonanza</u>, bomb (slang), cleanup (informal), coup, gain, profit, success, windfall

killjoy noun <u>spoilsport</u>, dampener, wet blanket (informal)

kin noun <u>family</u>, kindred, kinsfolk,

relations, relatives

kind[1] *adjective* <u>considerate</u>, benign, charitable, compassionate, courteous, friendly, generous, humane, kindly, obliging, philanthropic, tender-hearted

kind[2] *noun* <u>class</u>, brand, breed, family, set, sort, species, variety

kind-hearted *adjective* <u>sympathetic</u>, altruistic, compassionate, considerate, generous, good-natured, helpful, humane, kind, tender-hearted

kindle *verb* 1 <u>set fire to</u>, ignite, inflame, light 2 <u>arouse</u>, awaken, induce, inspire, provoke, rouse, stimulate, stir

kindliness *noun* <u>kindness</u>, amiability, benevolence, charity, compassion, friendliness, gentleness, humanity, kind-heartedness

kindly *adjective* 1 <u>good-natured</u>, benevolent, benign, compassionate, helpful, kind, pleasant, sympathetic, warm ♦ *adverb* 2 <u>politely</u>, agreeably, cordially, graciously, tenderly, thoughtfully

kindness *noun* <u>goodwill</u>, benevolence, charity, compassion, generosity, humanity, kindliness, philanthropy, understanding

kindred *adjective* 1 <u>similar</u>, akin, corresponding, like, matching, related ♦ *noun* 2 <u>family</u>, kin, kinsfolk, relations, relatives

king *noun* <u>ruler</u>, emperor, monarch, sovereign

kingdom *noun* <u>country</u>, nation, realm, state, territory

kink *noun* 1 <u>twist</u>, bend, coil, wrinkle 2 <u>quirk</u>, eccentricity, fetish, foible, idiosyncrasy, vagary, whim

kinky *adjective* 1 <u>weird</u>, eccentric, odd, outlandish, peculiar, queer, quirky, strange 2 <u>twisted</u>, coiled, curled, tangled

kinship *noun* 1 <u>relation</u>, consanguinity, kin, ties of blood 2 <u>similarity</u>, affinity, association, connection, correspondence, relationship

kiosk *noun* <u>booth</u>, bookstall, counter, newsstand, stall, stand

kiss *verb* 1 <u>osculate</u>, neck (*informal*), peck (*informal*) 2 <u>brush</u>, glance, graze, scrape, touch ♦ *noun* 3 <u>osculation</u>, peck (*informal*), smacker (*slang*)

kit *noun* <u>equipment</u>, apparatus, gear, paraphernalia, tackle, tools

kit out *verb* <u>equip</u>, accoutre, arm, deck out, fit out, fix up, furnish, provide with, supply

knack *noun* <u>skill</u>, ability, aptitude, capacity, expertise, facility, gift, propensity, talent, trick

knave *noun* <u>rogue</u>, blackguard, bounder (*old-fashioned Brit. slang*), rascal, rotter (*slang, chiefly Brit.*), scoundrel, villain

knead *verb* <u>squeeze</u>, form, manipulate, massage, mould, press, rub, shape, work

kneel *verb* <u>genuflect</u>, stoop

knell *noun* <u>ringing</u>, chime, peal, sound, toll

knickers *plural noun* <u>underwear</u>, bloomers, briefs, drawers, panties, smalls

knick-knack *noun* <u>trinket</u>, bagatelle, bauble, bric-a-brac, plaything, trifle

knife noun 1 blade, cutter ♦ verb
2 cut, lacerate, pierce, slash,
stab, wound

knit verb 1 join, bind, fasten,
intertwine, link, tie, unite, weave
2 wrinkle, crease, furrow, knot,
pucker

knob noun lump, bump, hump,
knot, projection, protrusion, stud

knock verb 1 hit, belt (informal),
cuff, punch, rap, smack, strike,
thump 2 Informal criticize, abuse,
belittle, censure, condemn,
denigrate, deprecate, disparage,
find fault, run down ♦ noun
3 blow, clip, clout (informal),
cuff, rap, slap, smack, thump
4 setback, defeat, failure, rebuff,
rejection, reversal

knockabout adjective boisterous,
farcical, riotous, rollicking,
slapstick

knock about or **around** verb
1 wander, ramble, range, roam,
rove, travel 2 hit, abuse, batter,
beat up (informal), maltreat,
manhandle, maul, mistreat, strike

knock down verb demolish,
destroy, fell, level, raze

knock off verb 1 stop work,
clock off, clock out, finish
2 steal, nick (slang, chiefly Brit.),
pinch, rob, thieve

knockout noun 1 killer blow,
coup de grâce, KO or K.O. (slang)
2 success, hit, sensation, smash,
smash hit, triumph, winner

knot noun 1 connection, bond,
joint, ligature, loop, tie 2 cluster,
bunch, clump, collection ♦ verb
3 tie, bind, loop, secure, tether

know verb 1 realize,
comprehend, feel certain, notice,
perceive, recognize, see,
understand 2 be acquainted
with, be familiar with, have
dealings with, have knowledge
of, recognize

know-how noun capability,
ability, aptitude, expertise,
ingenuity, knack, knowledge,
savoir-faire, skill, talent

knowing adjective meaningful,
expressive, significant

knowingly adverb deliberately,
consciously, intentionally, on
purpose, purposely, wilfully,
wittingly

knowledge noun 1 learning,
education, enlightenment,
erudition, instruction,
intelligence, scholarship, wisdom
2 acquaintance, familiarity,
intimacy

knowledgeable adjective
1 well-informed, au fait, aware,
clued-up (informal), cognizant,
conversant, experienced,
familiar, in the know (informal)
2 intelligent, educated, erudite,
learned, scholarly

known adjective famous,
acknowledged, avowed,
celebrated, noted, recognized,
well-known

L l

label noun 1 tag, marker, sticker,
ticket ♦ verb 2 mark, stamp, tag

laborious adjective hard,
arduous, backbreaking,
exhausting, onerous, strenuous,
tiring, tough, wearisome

labour *noun* **1** work, industry, toil **2** workers, employees, hands, labourers, workforce **3** childbirth, delivery, parturition ♦ *verb* **4** work, endeavour, slave, strive, struggle, sweat (*informal*), toil **5** *usually with* **under** be disadvantaged, be a victim of, be burdened by, suffer **6** overemphasize, dwell on, elaborate, overdo, strain

laboured *adjective* forced, awkward, difficult, heavy, stiff, strained

labourer *noun* worker, blue-collar worker, drudge, hand, manual worker, navvy (*Brit. informal*)

labyrinth *noun* maze, intricacy, jungle, tangle

lace *noun* **1** netting, filigree, openwork **2** cord, bootlace, shoelace, string, tie ♦ *verb* **3** fasten, bind, do up, thread, tie **4** mix in, add to, fortify, spike

lacerate *verb* tear, claw, cut, gash, mangle, rip, slash, wound

laceration *noun* cut, gash, rent, rip, slash, tear, wound

lack *noun* **1** shortage, absence, dearth, deficiency, need, scarcity, want ♦ *verb* **2** need, be deficient in, be short of, be without, miss, require, want

lackadaisical *adjective* **1** lethargic, apathetic, dull, half-hearted, indifferent, languid, listless **2** lazy, abstracted, dreamy, idle, indolent, inert

lackey *noun* **1** hanger-on, flatterer, minion, sycophant, toady, yes man **2** manservant, attendant, flunky, footman, valet

lacklustre *adjective* flat, drab, dull, leaden, lifeless, muted, prosaic, uninspired, vapid

laconic *adjective* terse, brief, concise, curt, monosyllabic, pithy, short, succinct

lad *noun* boy, fellow, guy (*informal*), juvenile, kid (*informal*), youngster, youth

laden *adjective* loaded, burdened, charged, encumbered, full, weighed down

lady *noun* **1** gentlewoman, dame **2** woman, female

lady-killer *noun* womanizer, Casanova, Don Juan, heartbreaker, ladies' man, libertine, philanderer, rake, roué

ladylike *adjective* refined, elegant, genteel, modest, polite, proper, respectable, sophisticated, well-bred

lag *verb* hang back, dawdle, delay, linger, loiter, straggle, tarry, trail

laggard *noun* straggler, dawdler, idler, loiterer, slowcoach (*Brit. informal*), sluggard, snail

laid-back *adjective* relaxed, casual, easy-going, free and easy, unflappable (*informal*), unhurried

lair *noun* nest, burrow, den, earth, hole

laissez faire *noun* nonintervention, free enterprise, free trade

lake *noun* pond, lagoon, loch (*Scot.*), lough (*Irish*), mere, reservoir, tarn

lame *adjective* **1** disabled, crippled, game, handicapped, hobbling, limping **2** unconvincing, feeble, flimsy, inadequate, pathetic, poor, thin, unsatisfactory, weak

lament verb 1 complain, bemoan, bewail, deplore, grieve, mourn, regret, sorrow, wail, weep ♦ noun 2 complaint, lamentation, moan, wailing 3 dirge, elegy, requiem, threnody

lamentable adjective regrettable, deplorable, distressing, grievous, mournful, tragic, unfortunate, woeful

lampoon noun 1 satire, burlesque, caricature, parody, send-up (Brit. informal), skit, takeoff (informal) ♦ verb 2 ridicule, caricature, make fun of, mock, parody, satirize, send up (Brit. informal), take off (informal)

land noun 1 ground, dry land, earth, terra firma 2 soil, dirt, ground, loam 3 countryside, farmland 4 property, estate, grounds, realty 5 country, district, nation, province, region, territory, tract ♦ verb 6 arrive, alight, come to rest, disembark, dock, touch down 7 end up, turn up, wind up 8 Informal obtain, acquire, gain, get, secure, win

landlord noun 1 innkeeper, host, hotelier 2 owner, freeholder, lessor, proprietor

landmark noun 1 feature, monument 2 milestone, turning point, watershed

landscape noun scenery, countryside, outlook, panorama, prospect, scene, view, vista

landslide noun 1 rockfall, avalanche, landslip ♦ adjective 2 overwhelming, conclusive,

decisive, runaway

lane noun road, alley, footpath, passageway, path, pathway, street, way

language noun 1 speech, communication, discourse, expression, parlance, talk 2 tongue, dialect, patois, vernacular

languid adjective 1 lazy, indifferent, lackadaisical, languorous, listless, unenthusiastic 2 lethargic, dull, heavy, sluggish, torpid

languish verb 1 weaken, decline, droop, fade, fail, faint, flag, wilt, wither 2 often with for pine, desire, hanker, hunger, long, yearn 3 be neglected, be abandoned, rot, suffer, waste away

lank adjective 1 limp, lifeless, straggling 2 thin, emaciated, gaunt, lean, scrawny, skinny, slender, slim, spare

lanky adjective gangling, angular, bony, gaunt, rangy, spare, tall

lap[1] noun circuit, circle, loop, orbit, tour

lap[2] verb 1 ripple, gurgle, plash, purl, splash, swish, wash 2 drink, lick, sip, sup

lapse noun 1 mistake, error, failing, fault, indiscretion, negligence, omission, oversight, slip 2 interval, break, breathing space, gap, intermission, interruption, lull, pause 3 drop, decline, deterioration, fall ♦ verb 4 drop, decline, degenerate, deteriorate, fall, sink, slide, slip 5 end, expire, run out, stop, terminate

lapsed *adjective* out of date, discontinued, ended, expired, finished, invalid, run out

large *adjective* **1** big, considerable, enormous, gigantic, great, huge, immense, massive, monumental, sizable *or* sizeable, substantial, vast **2 at large: a** free, at liberty, on the loose, on the run, unconfined **b** in general, as a whole, chiefly, generally, in the main, mainly **c** at length, exhaustively, greatly, in full detail

largely *adverb* mainly, as a rule, by and large, chiefly, generally, mostly, predominantly, primarily, principally, to a great extent

large-scale *adjective* wide-ranging, broad, extensive, far-reaching, global, sweeping, vast, wholesale, wide

lark *noun* **1** prank, caper, escapade, fun, game, jape, mischief ♦ *verb* **2 lark about** play, caper, cavort, have fun, make mischief

lash¹ *noun* **1** blow, hit, stripe, stroke, swipe (*informal*) ♦ *verb* **2** whip, beat, birch, flog, scourge, thrash **3** pound, beat, buffet, dash, drum, hammer, smack, strike **4** scold, attack, blast, censure, criticize, put down, slate (*informal, chiefly Brit.*), tear into (*informal*), upbraid

lash² *verb* fasten, bind, make fast, secure, strap, tie

lass *noun* girl, damsel, lassie (*informal*), maid, maiden, young woman

last¹ *adjective* **1** hindmost, at the end, rearmost **2** most recent, latest **3** final, closing, concluding, terminal, ultimate ♦ *adverb* **4** in the rear, after, behind, bringing up the rear, in *or* at the end

last² *verb* continue, abide, carry on, endure, keep on, persist, remain, stand up, survive

lasting *adjective* continuing, abiding, durable, enduring, long-standing, long-term, perennial, permanent

latch *noun* **1** fastening, bar, bolt, catch, hasp, hook, lock ♦ *verb* **2** fasten, bar, bolt, make fast, secure

late *adjective* **1** overdue, behind, behindhand, belated, delayed, last-minute, tardy **2** recent, advanced, fresh, modern, new **3** dead, deceased, defunct, departed, former, past ♦ *adverb* **4** belatedly, at the last minute, behindhand, behind time, dilatorily, tardily

lately *adverb* recently, in recent times, just now, latterly, not long ago, of late

lateness *noun* delay, belatedness, tardiness

latent *adjective* hidden, concealed, dormant, invisible, potential, undeveloped, unrealized

later *adverb* afterwards, after, by and by, in a while, in time, later on, subsequently, thereafter

lateral *adjective* sideways, edgeways, flanking

latest *adjective* up-to-date, current, fashionable, modern, most recent, newest, up-to-the-minute

lather *noun* **1** froth, bubbles,

foam, soapsuds, suds **2** *Informal* <u>fluster</u>, dither (*chiefly Brit.*), flap (*informal*), fuss, state (*informal*), sweat, tizzy (*informal*) ♦ *verb* **3** <u>froth</u>, foam, soap

latitude *noun* <u>scope</u>, elbowroom, freedom, laxity, leeway, liberty, licence, play

latter *adjective* <u>last-mentioned</u>, closing, concluding, last, second

latterly *adverb* <u>recently</u>, lately, of late

lattice *noun* <u>grid</u>, grating, grille, trellis

laudable *adjective* <u>praiseworthy</u>, admirable, commendable, creditable, excellent, meritorious, of note, worthy

laugh *verb* **1** <u>chuckle</u>, be in stitches, chortle, giggle, guffaw, snigger, split one's sides, titter ♦ *noun* **2** <u>chuckle</u>, chortle, giggle, guffaw, snigger, titter **3** *Informal* <u>clown</u>, card (*informal*), entertainer, hoot (*informal*), scream (*informal*) **4** *Informal* <u>joke</u>, hoot (*informal*), lark, scream (*informal*)

laughable *adjective* <u>ridiculous</u>, absurd, derisory, farcical, ludicrous, nonsensical, preposterous, risible

laughing stock *noun* <u>figure of fun</u>, Aunt Sally (*Brit.*), butt, target, victim

laugh off *verb* <u>disregard</u>, brush aside, dismiss, ignore, minimize, pooh-pooh, shrug off

laughter *noun* <u>amusement</u>, glee, hilarity, merriment, mirth

launch *verb* **1** <u>propel</u>, discharge, dispatch, fire, project, send off, set in motion **2** <u>begin</u>,

commence, embark upon, inaugurate, initiate, instigate, introduce, open, start

laurels *plural noun* <u>glory</u>, credit, distinction, fame, honour, praise, prestige, recognition, renown

lavatory *noun* <u>toilet</u>, bathroom, cloakroom (*Brit.*), latrine, loo (*Brit. informal*), powder room, (public) convenience, washroom, water closet, W.C.

lavish *adjective* **1** <u>plentiful</u>, abundant, copious, profuse, prolific **2** <u>generous</u>, bountiful, free, liberal, munificent, open-handed, unstinting **3** <u>extravagant</u>, exaggerated, excessive, immoderate, prodigal, unrestrained, wasteful, wild ♦ *verb* **4** <u>spend</u>, deluge, dissipate, expend, heap, pour, shower, squander, waste

law *noun* **1** <u>constitution</u>, charter, code **2** <u>rule</u>, act, command, commandment, decree, edict, order, ordinance, regulation, statute **3** <u>principle</u>, axiom, canon, precept

law-abiding *adjective* <u>obedient</u>, compliant, dutiful, good, honest, honourable, lawful, orderly, peaceable

law-breaker *noun* <u>criminal</u>, convict, crook (*informal*), culprit, delinquent, felon, miscreant, offender, villain, wrongdoer

lawful *adjective* <u>legal</u>, authorized, constitutional, legalized, legitimate, licit, permissible, rightful, valid, warranted

lawless *adjective* <u>disorderly</u>, anarchic, chaotic, rebellious, riotous, unruly, wild

lawlessness *noun* <u>anarchy</u>,

chaos, disorder, mob rule

lawsuit noun <u>case</u>, action, dispute, industrial tribunal, litigation, proceedings, prosecution, suit, trial

lawyer noun <u>legal adviser</u>, advocate, attorney, barrister, counsel, counsellor, solicitor

lax adjective <u>slack</u>, careless, casual, lenient, negligent, overindulgent, remiss, slapdash, slipshod

lay[1] verb **1** <u>place</u>, deposit, leave, plant, put, set, set down, spread **2** <u>arrange</u>, organize, position, set out **3** <u>produce</u>, bear, deposit **4** <u>put forward</u>, advance, bring forward, lodge, offer, present, submit **5** <u>attribute</u>, allocate, allot, ascribe, assign, impute **6** <u>devise</u>, concoct, contrive, design, hatch, plan, plot, prepare, work out **7** <u>bet</u>, gamble, give odds, hazard, risk, stake, wager

lay[2] adjective **1** <u>nonclerical</u>, secular **2** <u>nonspecialist</u>, amateur, inexpert, nonprofessional

layabout noun <u>idler</u>, couch potato (slang), good-for-nothing, loafer, lounger, ne'er-do-well, skiver (Brit. slang), wastrel

layer noun <u>tier</u>, row, seam, stratum, thickness

layman noun <u>amateur</u>, lay person, nonprofessional, outsider

lay-off noun <u>dismissal</u>, discharge, unemployment

lay off verb <u>dismiss</u>, discharge, let go, make redundant, pay off

lay on verb <u>provide</u>, cater (for), furnish, give, purvey, supply

layout noun <u>arrangement</u>,

design, formation, outline, plan

lay out verb **1** <u>arrange</u>, design, display, exhibit, plan, spread out **2** Informal <u>spend</u>, disburse, expend, fork out (slang), invest, pay, shell out (informal) **3** Informal <u>knock out</u>, knock for six (informal), knock unconscious, KO or K.O. (slang)

laziness noun <u>idleness</u>, inactivity, indolence, slackness, sloth, sluggishness

lazy adjective **1** <u>idle</u>, inactive, indolent, inert, slack, slothful, slow, workshy **2** <u>lethargic</u>, drowsy, languid, languorous, sleepy, slow-moving, sluggish, somnolent, torpid

leach verb <u>extract</u>, drain, filter, percolate, seep, strain

lead verb **1** <u>guide</u>, conduct, escort, pilot, precede, show the way, steer, usher **2** <u>persuade</u>, cause, dispose, draw, incline, induce, influence, prevail, prompt **3** <u>command</u>, direct, govern, head, manage, preside over, supervise **4** <u>be ahead (of)</u>, blaze a trail, come first, exceed, excel, outdo, outstrip, surpass, transcend **5** <u>live</u>, experience, have, pass, spend, undergo **6** <u>result in</u>, bring on, cause, contribute, produce ♦ noun **7** <u>first place</u>, precedence, primacy, priority, supremacy, vanguard **8** <u>advantage</u>, edge, margin, start **9** <u>example</u>, direction, guidance, leadership, model **10** <u>clue</u>, hint, indication, suggestion **11** <u>leading role</u>, principal, protagonist, title role ♦ adjective **12** <u>main</u>, chief, first, foremost, head, leading, premier, primary, prime, principal

leader noun <u>principal</u>, boss
(*informal*), captain, chief,
chieftain, commander, director,
guide, head, ringleader, ruler

leadership noun **1** <u>guidance</u>,
direction, domination,
management, running,
superintendency **2** <u>authority</u>,
command, control, influence,
initiative, pre-eminence,
supremacy

leading adjective <u>main</u>, chief,
dominant, first, foremost,
greatest, highest, primary,
principal

lead on verb <u>entice</u>, beguile,
deceive, draw on, lure, seduce,
string along (*informal*), tempt

lead up to verb <u>introduce</u>, pave
the way, prepare for

leaf noun **1** <u>frond</u>, blade **2** <u>page</u>,
folio, sheet ♦ verb **3 leaf through**
<u>browse</u>, flip, glance, riffle, skim,
thumb (through)

leaflet noun <u>booklet</u>, brochure,
circular, pamphlet

leafy adjective <u>green</u>, bosky
(*literary*), shaded, shady, verdant

league noun **1** <u>association</u>,
alliance, coalition, confederation,
consortium, federation,
fraternity, group, guild,
partnership, union **2** <u>class</u>,
category, level

leak noun **1** <u>hole</u>, aperture, chink,
crack, crevice, fissure, opening,
puncture **2** <u>drip</u>, leakage,
percolation, seepage
3 <u>disclosure</u>, divulgence ♦ verb
4 <u>drip</u>, escape, exude, ooze,
pass, percolate, seep, spill, trickle
5 <u>disclose</u>, divulge, give away,

let slip, make known, make
public, pass on, reveal, tell

leaky adjective <u>punctured</u>,
cracked, holey, leaking,
perforated, porous, split

lean¹ verb **1** <u>rest</u>, be supported,
prop, recline, repose **2** <u>bend</u>,
heel, incline, slant, slope, tilt, tip
3 <u>tend</u>, be disposed to, be prone
to, favour, prefer **4 lean on**
<u>depend on</u>, count on, have faith
in, rely on, trust

lean² adjective **1** <u>slim</u>, angular,
bony, gaunt, rangy, skinny,
slender, spare, thin, wiry
2 <u>unproductive</u>, barren, meagre,
poor, scanty, unfruitful

leaning noun <u>tendency</u>, bent,
bias, disposition, inclination,
partiality, penchant, predilection,
proclivity, propensity

leap verb **1** <u>jump</u>, bounce,
bound, hop, skip, spring ♦ noun
2 <u>jump</u>, bound, spring, vault
3 <u>increase</u>, escalation, rise,
surge, upsurge, upswing

learn verb **1** <u>master</u>, grasp, pick
up **2** <u>memorize</u>, commit to
memory, get off pat, learn by
heart **3** <u>discover</u>, ascertain,
detect, discern, find out, gather,
hear, understand

learned adjective <u>scholarly</u>,
academic, erudite, highbrow,
intellectual, versed,
well-informed, well-read

learner noun <u>beginner</u>,
apprentice, neophyte, novice,
tyro

learning noun <u>knowledge</u>,
culture, education, erudition,
information, lore, scholarship,
study, wisdom

lease *verb* hire, charter, let, loan, rent

leash *noun* lead, rein, tether

least *adjective* smallest, fewest, lowest, meanest, minimum, poorest, slightest, tiniest

leathery *adjective* tough, hard, rough

leave[1] *verb* 1 depart, decamp, disappear, exit, go away, make tracks, move, pull out, quit, retire, slope off, withdraw 2 forget, leave behind, mislay 3 cause, deposit, generate, produce, result in 4 give up, abandon, drop, relinquish, renounce, surrender 5 entrust, allot, assign, cede, commit, consign, give over, refer 6 bequeath, hand down, will

leave[2] *noun* 1 permission, allowance, authorization, concession, consent, dispensation, freedom, liberty, sanction 2 holiday, furlough, leave of absence, sabbatical, time off, vacation 3 parting, adieu, departure, farewell, goodbye, leave-taking, retirement, withdrawal

leave out *verb* omit, cast aside, disregard, exclude, ignore, neglect, overlook, reject

lecherous *adjective* lustful, lascivious, lewd, libidinous, licentious, prurient, randy (*informal, chiefly Brit.*), salacious

lecture *noun* 1 talk, address, discourse, instruction, lesson, speech 2 rebuke, dressing-down (*informal*), reprimand, reproof, scolding, talking-to (*informal*), telling off (*informal*) ♦ *verb* 3 talk, address, discourse, expound,

hold forth, speak, spout, teach 4 scold, admonish, berate, castigate, censure, reprimand, reprove, tell off (*informal*)

ledge *noun* shelf, mantle, projection, ridge, sill, step

leer *noun, verb* grin, gloat, goggle, ogle, smirk, squint, stare

lees *plural noun* sediment, deposit, dregs, grounds

leeway *noun* room, elbowroom, latitude, margin, play, scope, space

left *adjective* 1 left-hand, larboard (*Nautical*), port, sinistral 2 *Of politics* socialist, leftist, left-wing, radical

leftover *noun* remnant, oddment, scrap

left-wing *adjective* socialist, communist, radical, red (*informal*)

leg *noun* 1 limb, lower limb, member, pin (*informal*), stump (*informal*) 2 support, brace, prop, upright 3 stage, lap, part, portion, section, segment, stretch 4 **pull someone's leg** *Informal* tease, fool, kid (*informal*), make fun of, trick, wind up (*Brit. slang*)

legacy *noun* bequest, estate, gift, heirloom, inheritance

legal *adjective* 1 legitimate, allowed, authorized, constitutional, lawful, licit, permissible, sanctioned, valid 2 judicial, forensic, juridical

legality *noun* legitimacy, lawfulness, rightfulness, validity

legalize *verb* allow, approve, authorize, decriminalize, legitimate, legitimize, license, permit, sanction, validate

legation *noun* <u>delegation</u>, consulate, embassy, representation

legend *noun* 1 <u>myth</u>, fable, fiction, folk tale, saga, story, tale 2 <u>celebrity</u>, luminary, megastar (*informal*), phenomenon, prodigy 3 <u>inscription</u>, caption, motto

legendary *adjective* 1 <u>mythical</u>, apocryphal, fabled, fabulous, fictitious, romantic, traditional 2 <u>famous</u>, celebrated, famed, illustrious, immortal, renowned, well-known

legibility *noun* <u>clarity</u>, neatness, readability

legible *adjective* <u>clear</u>, decipherable, distinct, easy to read, neat, readable

legion *noun* 1 <u>army</u>, brigade, company, division, force, troop 2 <u>multitude</u>, drove, horde, host, mass, myriad, number, throng

legislation *noun* 1 <u>lawmaking</u>, enactment, prescription, regulation 2 <u>law</u>, act, bill, charter, measure, regulation, ruling, statute

legislative *adjective* <u>law-making</u>, judicial, law-giving

legislator *noun* <u>lawmaker</u>, lawgiver

legislature *noun* <u>parliament</u>, assembly, chamber, congress, senate

legitimate *adjective* 1 <u>legal</u>, authentic, authorized, genuine, kosher (*informal*), lawful, licit, rightful 2 <u>reasonable</u>, admissible, correct, justifiable, logical, sensible, valid, warranted, well-founded ♦ *verb* 3 <u>authorize</u>, legalize, legitimize, permit,

pronounce lawful, sanction

legitimize *verb* <u>legalize</u>, authorize, permit, sanction

leisure *noun* <u>spare time</u>, ease, freedom, free time, liberty, recreation, relaxation, rest

leisurely *adjective* <u>unhurried</u>, comfortable, easy, gentle, lazy, relaxed, slow

lend *verb* 1 <u>loan</u>, advance 2 <u>add</u>, bestow, confer, give, grant, impart, provide, supply 3 **lend itself to** <u>suit</u>, be appropriate, be serviceable

length *noun* 1 *Of linear extent* <u>distance</u>, extent, longitude, measure, reach, span 2 *Of time* <u>duration</u>, period, space, span, stretch, term 3 <u>piece</u>, measure, portion, section, segment 4 **at length: a** <u>in detail</u>, completely, fully, in depth, thoroughly, to the full **b** <u>for a long time</u>, for ages, for hours, interminably **c** <u>at last</u>, at long last, eventually, finally, in the end

lengthen *verb* <u>extend</u>, continue, draw out, elongate, expand, increase, prolong, protract, spin out, stretch

lengthy *adjective* <u>long</u>, drawn-out, extended, interminable, long-drawn-out, long-winded, prolonged, protracted, tedious

leniency *noun* <u>tolerance</u>, clemency, compassion, forbearance, indulgence, mercy, moderation, pity, quarter

lenient *adjective* <u>tolerant</u>, compassionate, forbearing, forgiving, indulgent, kind, merciful, sparing

lesbian adjective homosexual, gay, sapphic

less adjective 1 smaller, shorter ◆preposition 2 minus, excepting, lacking, subtracting, without

lessen verb reduce, contract, decrease, diminish, ease, lower, minimize, narrow, shrink

lesser adjective minor, inferior, less important, lower, secondary

lesson noun 1 class, coaching, instruction, period, schooling, teaching, tutoring 2 example, deterrent, message, moral

let¹ verb 1 allow, authorize, entitle, give permission, give the go-ahead, permit, sanction, tolerate 2 lease, hire, rent

let² noun hindrance, constraint, impediment, interference, obstacle, obstruction, prohibition, restriction

letdown noun disappointment, anticlimax, blow, comedown (informal), setback, washout (informal)

let down verb disappoint, disenchant, disillusion, dissatisfy, fail, fall short, leave in the lurch, leave stranded

lethal adjective deadly, dangerous, destructive, devastating, fatal, mortal, murderous, virulent

lethargic adjective sluggish, apathetic, drowsy, dull, languid, listless, sleepy, slothful

lethargy noun sluggishness, apathy, drowsiness, inertia, languor, lassitude, listlessness, sleepiness, sloth

let off verb 1 fire, detonate, discharge, explode 2 emit,

exude, give off, leak, release 3 excuse, absolve, discharge, exempt, exonerate, forgive, pardon, release, spare

let on verb reveal, admit, disclose, divulge, give away, let the cat out of the bag (informal), make known, say

let out verb 1 emit, give vent to, produce 2 release, discharge, free, let go, liberate

letter noun 1 character, sign, symbol 2 message, communication, dispatch, epistle, line, missive, note

let-up noun lessening, break, breathing space, interval, lull, pause, remission, respite, slackening

let up verb stop, abate, decrease, diminish, ease (up), moderate, relax, slacken, subside

level adjective 1 horizontal, flat 2 even, consistent, plain, smooth, uniform 3 equal, balanced, commensurate, comparable, equivalent, even, neck and neck, on a par, proportionate ◆verb 4 flatten, even off or out, plane, smooth 5 equalize, balance, even up 6 raze, bulldoze, demolish, destroy, devastate, flatten, knock down, pull down, tear down 7 direct, aim, focus, point, train ◆noun 8 position, achievement, degree, grade, rank, stage, standard, standing, status 9 **on the level** Informal honest, above board, fair, genuine, square, straight

level-headed adjective steady, balanced, calm, collected, composed, cool, sensible, unflappable (*informal*)

lever *noun* **1** <u>handle</u>, bar ♦ *verb* **2** <u>prise</u>, force

leverage *noun* <u>influence</u>, authority, clout (*informal*), pull (*informal*), weight

levity *noun* <u>light-heartedness</u>, facetiousness, flippancy, frivolity, silliness, skittishness, triviality

levy *verb* **1** <u>impose</u>, charge, collect, demand, exact **2** <u>conscript</u>, call up, mobilize, muster, raise ♦ *noun* **3** <u>imposition</u>, assessment, collection, exaction, gathering **4** <u>tax</u>, duty, excise, fee, tariff, toll

lewd *adjective* <u>indecent</u>, bawdy, lascivious, libidinous, licentious, lustful, obscene, pornographic, smutty, wanton

lewdness *noun* <u>indecency</u>, bawdiness, carnality, debauchery, depravity, lasciviousness, lechery, licentiousness, obscenity, pornography, wantonness

liability *noun* **1** <u>responsibility</u>, accountability, answerability, culpability **2** <u>debt</u>, debit, obligation **3** <u>disadvantage</u>, burden, drawback, encumbrance, handicap, hindrance, inconvenience, millstone, nuisance

liable *adjective* **1** <u>responsible</u>, accountable, answerable, obligated **2** <u>vulnerable</u>, exposed, open, subject, susceptible **3** <u>likely</u>, apt, disposed, inclined, prone, tending

liaise *verb* <u>link</u>, communicate, keep contact, mediate

liaison *noun* **1** <u>communication</u>, connection, contact, hook-up, interchange **2** <u>affair</u>, amour, entanglement, intrigue, love affair, romance

liar *noun* <u>falsifier</u>, fabricator, fibber, perjurer

libel *noun* **1** <u>defamation</u>, aspersion, calumny, denigration, smear ♦ *verb* **2** <u>defame</u>, blacken, malign, revile, slur, smear, vilify

libellous *adjective* <u>defamatory</u>, derogatory, false, injurious, malicious, scurrilous, untrue

liberal *adjective* **1** <u>progressive</u>, libertarian, radical, reformist **2** <u>generous</u>, beneficent, bountiful, charitable, kind, open-handed, open-hearted, unstinting **3** <u>tolerant</u>, broad-minded, indulgent, permissive **4** <u>abundant</u>, ample, bountiful, copious, handsome, lavish, munificent, plentiful, profuse, rich

liberality *noun* **1** <u>generosity</u>, beneficence, benevolence, bounty, charity, kindness, largesse *or* largess, munificence, philanthropy **2** <u>toleration</u>, broad-mindedness, latitude, liberalism, libertarianism, permissiveness

liberalize *verb* <u>relax</u>, ease, loosen, moderate, modify, slacken, soften

liberate *verb* <u>free</u>, deliver, emancipate, let loose, let out, release, rescue, set free

liberation *noun* <u>deliverance</u>, emancipation, freedom, freeing, liberty, release

liberator *noun* <u>deliverer</u>, emancipator, freer, redeemer, rescuer, saviour

libertine noun reprobate, debauchee, lecher, profligate, rake, roué, sensualist, voluptuary, womanizer

liberty noun 1 freedom, autonomy, emancipation, immunity, independence, liberation, release, self-determination, sovereignty 2 impertinence, impropriety, impudence, insolence, presumption 3 **at liberty** free, on the loose, unrestricted

libidinous adjective lustful, carnal, debauched, lascivious, lecherous, randy (informal, chiefly Brit.), sensual, wanton

licence noun 1 certificate, charter, permit, warrant 2 permission, authority, authorization, blank cheque, carte blanche, dispensation, entitlement, exemption, immunity, leave, liberty, right 3 latitude, freedom, independence, leeway, liberty 4 laxity, excess, immoderation, indulgence, irresponsibility

license verb permit, accredit, allow, authorize, certify, empower, sanction, warrant

licentious adjective promiscuous, abandoned, debauched, dissolute, immoral, lascivious, lustful, sensual, wanton

lick verb 1 taste, lap, tongue 2 Of flames flicker, dart, flick, play over, ripple, touch 3 Slang beat, defeat, master, outdo, outstrip, overcome, rout, trounce, vanquish ♦ noun 4 dab, bit, stroke, touch 5 Informal pace, clip (informal), rate, speed

lie¹ verb 1 falsify, dissimulate, equivocate, fabricate, fib, prevaricate, tell untruths ♦ noun 2 falsehood, deceit, fabrication, fib, fiction, invention, prevarication, untruth

lie² verb 1 recline, loll, lounge, repose, rest, sprawl, stretch out 2 be situated, be, be placed, exist, remain

life noun 1 being, sentience, vitality 2 existence, being, lifetime, span, time 3 biography, autobiography, confessions, history, life story, memoirs, story 4 behaviour, conduct, life style, way of life 5 liveliness, animation, energy, high spirits, spirit, verve, vigour, vitality, vivacity, zest

lifeless adjective 1 dead, deceased, defunct, extinct, inanimate 2 dull, colourless, flat, lacklustre, lethargic, listless, sluggish, wooden 3 unconscious, comatose, dead to the world (informal), insensible

lifelike adjective realistic, authentic, exact, faithful, natural, true-to-life, vivid

lifelong adjective long-standing, enduring, lasting, long-lasting, perennial, persistent

lifetime noun existence, career, day(s), span, time

lift verb 1 raise, draw up, elevate, hoist, pick up, uplift, upraise 2 revoke, annul, cancel, countermand, end, remove, rescind, stop, terminate 3 disappear, be dispelled, disperse, dissipate, vanish ♦ noun 4 ride, drive, run 5 boost, encouragement, fillip, pick-me-up, shot in the arm (*informal*) **6** <u>elevator</u> (*chiefly U.S.*)

light¹ *noun* **1** <u>brightness</u>, brilliance, glare, gleam, glint, glow, illumination, luminosity, radiance, shine **2** <u>lamp</u>, beacon, candle, flare, lantern, taper, torch **3** <u>aspect</u>, angle, context, interpretation, point of view, slant, vantage point, viewpoint **4** <u>match</u>, flame, lighter ♦ *adjective* **5** <u>bright</u>, brilliant, illuminated, luminous, lustrous, shining, well-lit **6** <u>pale</u>, bleached, blond, faded, fair, pastel ♦ *verb* **7** <u>ignite</u>, inflame, kindle **8** <u>illuminate</u>, brighten, light up

light² *adjective* **1** <u>insubstantial</u>, airy, buoyant, flimsy, portable, slight, underweight **2** <u>weak</u>, faint, gentle, indistinct, mild, moderate, slight, soft **3** <u>insignificant</u>, inconsiderable, inconsiderable, scanty, slight, small, trifling, trivial **4** <u>nimble</u>, agile, graceful, lithe, sprightly, sylphlike **5** <u>light-hearted</u>, amusing, entertaining, frivolous, funny, humorous, witty **6** <u>digestible</u>, frugal, modest ♦ *verb* **7** <u>settle</u>, alight, land, perch **8 light on** *or* **upon** <u>come across</u>, chance upon, discover, encounter, find, happen upon, hit upon, stumble on

lighten¹ *verb* <u>brighten</u>, become light, illuminate, irradiate, light up

lighten² *verb* **1** <u>ease</u>, allay, alleviate, ameliorate, assuage, lessen, mitigate, reduce, relieve **2** <u>cheer</u>, brighten, buoy up, lift, perk up, revive

light-headed *adjective* <u>faint</u>, dizzy, giddy, hazy, vertiginous, woozy (*informal*)

light-hearted *adjective* <u>carefree</u>, blithe, cheerful, happy-go-lucky, jolly, jovial, playful, upbeat (*informal*)

lightly *adverb* **1** <u>gently</u>, delicately, faintly, slightly, softly **2** <u>moderately</u>, sparingly, sparsely, thinly **3** <u>easily</u>, effortlessly, readily, simply **4** <u>carelessly</u>, breezily, flippantly, frivolously, heedlessly, thoughtlessly

lightweight *adjective* <u>unimportant</u>, inconsequential, insignificant, paltry, petty, slight, trifling, trivial, worthless

likable, likeable *adjective* <u>attractive</u>, agreeable, amiable, appealing, charming, engaging, nice, pleasant, sympathetic

like¹ *adjective* <u>similar</u>, akin, alike, analogous, corresponding, equivalent, identical, parallel, same

like² *verb* **1** <u>enjoy</u>, be fond of, be keen on, be partial to, delight in, go for, love, relish, revel in **2** <u>admire</u>, appreciate, approve, cherish, esteem, hold dear, prize, take to **3** <u>wish</u>, care to, choose, desire, fancy, feel inclined, prefer, want

likelihood *noun* <u>probability</u>, chance, possibility, prospect

likely *adjective* **1** <u>inclined</u>, apt, disposed, liable, prone, tending **2** <u>probable</u>, anticipated, expected, odds-on, on the cards, to be expected **3** <u>plausible</u>, believable, credible, feasible, possible, reasonable **4** <u>promising</u>, hopeful, up-and-coming

liken *verb* <u>compare</u>, equate, match, parallel, relate, set beside

likeness *noun* **1** <u>resemblance</u>, affinity, correspondence, similarity **2** <u>portrait</u>, depiction, effigy, image, picture, representation

likewise *adverb* <u>similarly</u>, in like manner, in the same way

liking *noun* <u>fondness</u>, affection, inclination, love, partiality, penchant, preference, soft spot, taste, weakness

limb *noun* **1** <u>part</u>, appendage, arm, extremity, leg, member, wing **2** <u>branch</u>, bough, offshoot, projection, spur

limelight *noun* <u>publicity</u>, attention, celebrity, fame, prominence, public eye, recognition, stardom, the spotlight

limit *noun* **1** <u>breaking point</u>, deadline, end, ultimate **2** <u>boundary</u>, border, edge, frontier, perimeter ♦ *verb* **3** <u>restrict</u>, bound, check, circumscribe, confine, curb, ration, restrain

limitation *noun* <u>restriction</u>, check, condition, constraint, control, curb, qualification, reservation, restraint

limited *adjective* <u>restricted</u>, bounded, checked, circumscribed, confined, constrained, controlled, curbed, finite

limitless *adjective* <u>infinite</u>, boundless, countless, endless, inexhaustible, unbounded, unlimited, untold, vast

limp¹ *verb* **1** <u>hobble</u>, falter, hop, shamble, shuffle ♦ *noun* **2** <u>lameness</u>, hobble

limp² *adjective* <u>floppy</u>, drooping, flabby, flaccid, pliable, slack, soft

line *noun* **1** <u>stroke</u>, band, groove, mark, score, scratch, streak, stripe **2** <u>wrinkle</u>, crease, crow's foot, furrow, mark **3** <u>boundary</u>, border, borderline, edge, frontier, limit **4** <u>string</u>, cable, cord, rope, thread, wire **5** <u>trajectory</u>, course, direction, path, route, track **6** <u>job</u>, area, business, calling, employment, field, occupation, profession, specialization, trade **7** <u>row</u>, column, file, procession, queue, rank **8 in line for** <u>due for</u>, in the running for ♦ *verb* **9** <u>mark</u>, crease, furrow, rule, score **10** <u>border</u>, bound, edge, fringe

lineaments *plural noun* <u>features</u>, countenance, face, physiognomy

lined *adjective* **1** <u>ruled</u>, feint **2** <u>wrinkled</u>, furrowed, wizened, worn

lines *plural noun* <u>words</u>, part, script

line-up *noun* <u>arrangement</u>, array, row, selection, team

linger *verb* **1** <u>stay</u>, hang around, loiter, remain, stop, tarry, wait **2** <u>delay</u>, dally, dawdle, drag one's feet *or* heels, idle, take one's time

link *noun* **1** <u>component</u>, constituent, element, member, part, piece **2** <u>connection</u>, affinity, association, attachment, bond, relationship, tie-up ♦ *verb* **3** <u>fasten</u>, attach, bind, connect, couple, join, tie, unite **4** <u>associate</u>, bracket, connect, identify, relate

lip noun **1** <u>edge</u>, brim, brink, margin, rim **2** *Slang* <u>impudence</u>, backchat (*informal*), cheek (*informal*), effrontery, impertinence, insolence

liquid noun **1** <u>fluid</u>, juice, solution ♦ *adjective* **2** <u>fluid</u>, aqueous, flowing, melted, molten, running, runny **3** *Of assets* <u>convertible</u>, negotiable

liquidate verb **1** <u>pay</u>, clear, discharge, honour, pay off, settle, square **2** <u>dissolve</u>, abolish, annul, cancel, terminate **3** <u>kill</u>, destroy, dispatch, eliminate, exterminate, get rid of, murder, wipe out (*informal*)

liquor noun **1** <u>alcohol</u>, booze (*informal*), drink, hard stuff (*informal*), spirits, strong drink **2** <u>juice</u>, broth, extract, liquid, stock

list[1] noun **1** <u>register</u>, catalogue, directory, index, inventory, record, roll, series, tally ♦ *verb* **2** <u>tabulate</u>, catalogue, enter, enumerate, itemize, record, register

list[2] verb **1** <u>lean</u>, careen, heel over, incline, tilt, tip ♦ *noun* **2** <u>tilt</u>, cant, leaning, slant

listen verb **1** <u>hear</u>, attend, lend an ear, prick up one's ears **2** <u>pay attention</u>, heed, mind, obey, observe, take notice

listless adjective <u>languid</u>, apathetic, indifferent, indolent, lethargic, sluggish

literacy noun <u>education</u>, knowledge, learning

literal adjective **1** <u>exact</u>, accurate, close, faithful, strict, verbatim, word for word **2** <u>actual</u>, bona fide, genuine, plain, real, simple, true, unvarnished

literally adverb <u>strictly</u>, actually, exactly, faithfully, precisely, really, to the letter, truly, verbatim, word for word

literary adjective <u>well-read</u>, bookish, erudite, formal, learned, scholarly

literate adjective <u>educated</u>, informed, knowledgeable

literature noun <u>writings</u>, letters, lore

lithe adjective <u>supple</u>, flexible, limber, lissom(e), loose-limbed, pliable

litigant noun <u>claimant</u>, party, plaintiff

litigate verb <u>sue</u>, go to court, press charges, prosecute

litigation noun <u>lawsuit</u>, action, case, prosecution

litter noun **1** <u>rubbish</u>, debris, detritus, garbage (*chiefly U.S.*), muck, refuse, trash **2** <u>brood</u>, offspring, progeny, young ♦ *verb* **3** <u>clutter</u>, derange, disarrange, disorder, mess up **4** <u>scatter</u>, strew

little adjective **1** <u>small</u>, diminutive, miniature, minute, petite, short, tiny, wee **2** <u>young</u>, babyish, immature, infant, junior, undeveloped ♦ *adverb* **3** <u>hardly</u>, barely **4** <u>rarely</u>, hardly ever, not often, scarcely, seldom ♦ *noun* **5** <u>bit</u>, fragment, hint, particle, speck, spot, touch, trace

live[1] verb **1** <u>exist</u>, be, be alive, breathe **2** <u>persist</u>, last, prevail **3** <u>dwell</u>, abide, inhabit, lodge, occupy, reside, settle **4** <u>survive</u>, endure, get along, make ends meet, subsist, support oneself **5** <u>thrive</u>, flourish, prosper

live² *adjective* **1** <u>living</u>, alive, animate, breathing **2** <u>topical</u>, burning, controversial, current, hot, pertinent, pressing, prevalent **3** <u>burning</u>, active, alight, blazing, glowing, hot, ignited, smouldering

livelihood *noun* <u>occupation</u>, bread and butter (*informal*), employment, job, living, work

liveliness *noun* <u>energy</u>, animation, boisterousness, dynamism, spirit, sprightliness, vitality, vivacity

lively *adjective* **1** <u>vigorous</u>, active, agile, alert, brisk, energetic, keen, perky, quick, sprightly **2** <u>animated</u>, cheerful, chirpy (*informal*), sparky, spirited, upbeat (*informal*), vivacious **3** <u>vivid</u>, bright, colourful, exciting, forceful, invigorating, refreshing, stimulating

liven up *verb* <u>stir</u>, animate, brighten, buck up (*informal*), enliven, perk up, rouse

liverish *adjective* **1** <u>sick</u>, bilious, queasy **2** <u>irritable</u>, crotchety (*informal*), crusty, disagreeable, grumpy, ill-humoured, irascible, splenetic, tetchy

livery *noun* <u>costume</u>, attire, clothing, dress, garb, regalia, suit, uniform

livid *adjective* **1** *Informal* <u>angry</u>, beside oneself, enraged, fuming, furious, incensed, indignant, infuriated, outraged **2** <u>discoloured</u>, black-and-blue, bruised, contused, purple

living *adjective* **1** <u>alive</u>, active, breathing, existing **2** <u>current</u>, active, contemporary, extant, in use ◆ *noun* **3** <u>existence</u>, being, existing, life, subsistence **4** <u>life style</u>, way of life

load *noun* **1** <u>cargo</u>, consignment, freight, shipment **2** <u>burden</u>, albatross, encumbrance, millstone, onus, trouble, weight, worry ◆ *verb* **3** <u>fill</u>, cram, freight, heap, pack, pile, stack, stuff **4** <u>burden</u>, encumber, oppress, saddle with, weigh down, worry **5** *Of firearms* <u>make ready</u>, charge, prime

loaded *adjective* **1** <u>weighted</u>, biased, distorted **2** <u>tricky</u>, artful, insidious, manipulative, prejudicial **3** *Slang* <u>rich</u>, affluent, flush (*informal*), moneyed, wealthy, well-heeled (*informal*), well off, well-to-do

loaf¹ *noun* **1** <u>lump</u>, block, cake, cube, slab **2** *Slang* <u>head</u>, gumption (*Brit. informal*), nous (*Brit. slang*), sense

loaf² *verb* <u>idle</u>, laze, lie around, loiter, lounge around, take it easy

loan *noun* **1** <u>advance</u>, credit ◆ *verb* **2** <u>lend</u>, advance, let out

loath, loth *adjective* <u>unwilling</u>, averse, disinclined, opposed, reluctant

loathe *verb* <u>hate</u>, abhor, abominate, despise, detest, dislike

loathing *noun* <u>hatred</u>, abhorrence, antipathy, aversion, detestation, disgust, repugnance, repulsion, revulsion

loathsome *adjective* <u>hateful</u>, abhorrent, detestable, disgusting, nauseating, obnoxious, odious, offensive, repugnant, repulsive, revolting, vile

lobby *noun* **1** <u>corridor</u>, entrance

hall, foyer, hallway, passage, porch, vestibule **2** <u>pressure group</u> ◆ *verb* **3** <u>campaign</u>, influence, persuade, press, pressure, promote, push, urge

local *adjective* **1** <u>regional</u>, provincial **2** <u>restricted</u> (*chiefly U.S.*), confined, limited ◆ *noun* **3** <u>resident</u>, inhabitant, native

locality *noun* **1** <u>neighbourhood</u>, area, district, neck of the woods (*informal*), region, vicinity **2** <u>site</u>, locale, location, place, position, scene, setting, spot

localize *verb* <u>restrict</u>, circumscribe, confine, contain, delimit, limit

locate *verb* **1** <u>find</u>, come across, detect, discover, pin down, pinpoint, track down, unearth **2** <u>place</u>, establish, fix, put, seat, set, settle, situate

location *noun* <u>position</u>, locale, place, point, site, situation, spot, venue

lock¹ *noun* **1** <u>fastening</u>, bolt, clasp, padlock ◆ *verb* **2** <u>fasten</u>, bolt, close, seal, secure, shut **3** <u>unite</u>, clench, engage, entangle, entwine, join, link **4** <u>embrace</u>, clasp, clutch, encircle, enclose, grasp, hug, press

lock² *noun* <u>strand</u>, curl, ringlet, tress, tuft

lockup *noun* <u>prison</u>, cell, jail *or* gaol

lock up *verb* <u>imprison</u>, cage, confine, detain, incarcerate, jail, put behind bars, shut up

lodge *noun* **1** <u>cabin</u>, chalet, cottage, gatehouse, hut, shelter **2** <u>society</u>, branch, chapter, club,

group ◆ *verb* **3** <u>stay</u>, board, room **4** <u>stick</u>, come to rest, imbed, implant **5** <u>register</u>, file, put on record, submit

lodger *noun* <u>tenant</u>, boarder, paying guest, resident

lodging *noun, often plural* <u>accommodation</u>, abode, apartments, digs (*Brit. informal*), quarters, residence, rooms, shelter

lofty *adjective* **1** <u>high</u>, elevated, raised, soaring, towering **2** <u>noble</u>, dignified, distinguished, elevated, exalted, grand, illustrious, renowned **3** <u>haughty</u>, arrogant, condescending, disdainful, patronizing, proud, supercilious

log *noun* **1** <u>stump</u>, block, chunk, trunk **2** <u>record</u>, account, journal, logbook ◆ *verb* **3** <u>chop</u>, cut, fell, hew **4** <u>record</u>, chart, note, register, set down

loggerheads *plural noun* **at loggerheads** <u>quarrelling</u>, at daggers drawn, at each other's throats, at odds, feuding, in dispute, opposed

logic *noun* <u>reason</u>, good sense, sense

logical *adjective* **1** <u>rational</u>, clear, cogent, coherent, consistent, sound, valid, well-organized **2** <u>reasonable</u>, plausible, sensible, wise

loiter *verb* <u>linger</u>, dally, dawdle, dilly-dally (*informal*), hang about *or* around, idle, loaf, skulk

loll *verb* **1** <u>lounge</u>, loaf, recline, relax, slouch, slump, sprawl **2** <u>droop</u>, dangle, drop, flap, flop, hang, sag

lone *adjective* <u>solitary</u>, one, only, single, sole, unaccompanied

loneliness *noun* <u>solitude</u>, desolation, isolation, seclusion

lonely *adjective* **1** <u>abandoned</u>, destitute, forlorn, forsaken, friendless, lonesome **2** <u>solitary</u>, alone, apart, companionless, isolated, lone, single, withdrawn **3** <u>remote</u>, deserted, desolate, godforsaken, isolated, out-of-the-way, secluded, unfrequented, uninhabited

loner *noun* <u>individualist</u>, lone wolf, maverick, outsider, recluse

lonesome *adjective* <u>lonely</u>, companionless, desolate, dreary, forlorn, friendless, gloomy

long¹ *adjective* **1** <u>elongated</u>, expanded, extended, extensive, far-reaching, lengthy, spread out, stretched **2** <u>prolonged</u>, interminable, lengthy, lingering, long-drawn-out, protracted, sustained

long² *verb* <u>desire</u>, crave, hanker, itch, lust, pine, want, wish, yearn

longing *noun* <u>desire</u>, ambition, aspiration, craving, hope, itch, thirst, urge, wish, yearning, yen (*informal*)

long-lived *adjective* <u>long-lasting</u>, enduring

long shot *noun* <u>outsider</u>, dark horse

long-standing *adjective* <u>established</u>, abiding, enduring, fixed, long-established, long-lasting, time-honoured

long-suffering *adjective* <u>uncomplaining</u>, easy-going, forbearing, forgiving, patient, resigned, stoical, tolerant

long-winded *adjective* <u>rambling</u>, lengthy, long-drawn-out, prolix, prolonged, repetitious, tedious, tiresome, verbose, wordy

look *verb* **1** <u>see</u>, contemplate, examine, eye, gaze, glance, observe, scan, study, survey, view, watch **2** <u>seem</u>, appear, look like, strike one as **3** <u>face</u>, front, overlook **4** <u>hope</u>, anticipate, await, expect, reckon on **5** <u>search</u>, forage, hunt, seek ♦ *noun* **6** <u>view</u>, examination, gaze, glance, glimpse, inspection, observation, peek, sight **7** <u>appearance</u>, air, aspect, bearing, countenance, demeanour, expression, manner, semblance

look after *verb* <u>take care of</u>, attend to, care for, guard, keep an eye on, mind, nurse, protect, supervise, take charge of, tend

look down on *verb* <u>disdain</u>, contemn, despise, scorn, sneer, spurn

look forward to *verb* <u>anticipate</u>, await, expect, hope for, long for, look for, wait for

lookout *noun* **1** <u>vigil</u>, guard, readiness, watch **2** <u>watchman</u>, guard, sentinel, sentry **3** <u>watchtower</u>, observation post, observatory, post **4** *Informal* <u>concern</u>, business, worry

look out *verb* <u>be careful</u>, beware, keep an eye out, pay attention, watch out

look up *verb* **1** <u>research</u>, find, hunt for, search for, seek out, track down **2** <u>improve</u>, get better, perk up, pick up, progress, shape up (*informal*) **3** <u>visit</u>, call on, drop in on

(*informal*), look in on **4 look up
to** <u>respect</u>, admire, defer to,
esteem, honour, revere

loom *verb* <u>appear</u>, bulk, emerge,
hover, impend, menace, take
shape, threaten

loop *noun* **1** <u>curve</u>, circle, coil,
curl, ring, spiral, twirl, twist,
whorl ♦ *verb* **2** <u>twist</u>, coil, curl,
knot, roll, spiral, turn, wind
round

loophole *noun* <u>let-out</u>, escape,
excuse

loose *adjective* **1** <u>untied</u>, free,
insecure, unattached, unbound,
unfastened, unfettered,
unrestricted **2** <u>slack</u>, easy,
relaxed, sloppy **3** <u>vague</u>,
ill-defined, imprecise, inaccurate,
indistinct, inexact, rambling,
random **4** <u>promiscuous</u>,
abandoned, debauched,
dissipated, dissolute, fast,
immoral, profligate ♦ *verb* **5** <u>free</u>,
detach, disconnect, liberate,
release, set free, unfasten,
unleash, untie

loosen *verb* **1** <u>untie</u>, detach,
separate, undo, unloose **2** <u>free</u>,
liberate, release, set free
3 loosen up <u>relax</u>, ease up *or*
off, go easy (*informal*), let up,
soften

loot *noun* **1** <u>plunder</u>, booty,
goods, haul, prize, spoils, swag
(*slang*) ♦ *verb* **2** <u>plunder</u>, despoil,
pillage, raid, ransack, ravage,
rifle, rob, sack

lopsided *adjective* <u>crooked</u>,
askew, asymmetrical, awry,
cockeyed, disproportionate,
skewwhiff (*Brit. informal*), squint,
unbalanced, uneven, warped

lord *noun* **1** <u>master</u>, commander,

governor, leader, liege, overlord,
ruler, superior **2** <u>nobleman</u>, earl,
noble, peer, viscount **3 Our Lord**
or **the Lord** <u>Jesus Christ</u>, Christ,
God, Jehovah, the Almighty
♦ *verb* **4 lord it over** <u>order
around</u>, boss around (*informal*),
domineer, pull rank, put on airs,
swagger

lordly *adjective* <u>proud</u>, arrogant,
condescending, disdainful,
domineering, haughty,
high-handed, imperious, lofty,
overbearing

lore *noun* <u>traditions</u>, beliefs,
doctrine, sayings, teaching,
wisdom

lose *verb* **1** <u>mislay</u>, be deprived
of, drop, forget, misplace
2 <u>forfeit</u>, miss, pass up (*informal*),
yield **3** <u>be defeated</u>, come to
grief, lose out

loser *noun* <u>failure</u>, also-ran, dud
(*informal*), flop (*informal*)

loss *noun* **1** <u>defeat</u>, failure,
forfeiture, mislaying,
squandering, waste **2** <u>damage</u>,
cost, destruction, harm, hurt,
injury, ruin **3** *sometimes plural*
<u>deficit</u>, debit, debt, deficiency,
depletion **4 at a loss** <u>confused</u>,
at one's wits' end, baffled,
bewildered, helpless,
nonplussed, perplexed, puzzled,
stumped

lost *adjective* **1** <u>missing</u>,
disappeared, mislaid, misplaced,
vanished, wayward **2** <u>off-course</u>,
adrift, astray, at sea, disoriented,
off-track

lot *noun* **1** <u>collection</u>, assortment,
batch, bunch (*informal*),
consignment, crowd, group,
quantity, set **2** <u>destiny</u>, accident,

chance, doom, fate, fortune **3 a lot** or **lots** <u>plenty</u>, abundance, a great deal, heap(s), load(s) (*informal*), masses (*informal*), piles (*informal*), scores, stack(s)

loth *see* LOATH

lotion *noun* <u>cream</u>, balm, embrocation, liniment, salve, solution

lottery *noun* **1** <u>raffle</u>, draw, sweepstake **2** <u>gamble</u>, chance, hazard, risk, toss-up (*informal*)

loud *adjective* **1** <u>noisy</u>, blaring, booming, clamorous, deafening, ear-splitting, forte (*Music*), resounding, thundering, tumultuous, vociferous **2** <u>garish</u>, brash, flamboyant, flashy, gaudy, glaring, lurid, showy

loudly *adverb* <u>noisily</u>, deafeningly, fortissimo (*Music*), lustily, shrilly, uproariously, vehemently, vigorously, vociferously

lounge *verb* <u>relax</u>, laze, lie about, loaf, loiter, loll, sprawl, take it easy

lout *noun* <u>oaf</u>, boor, dolt, lummox (*informal*), yob or yobbo (*Brit. slang*)

lovable, loveable *adjective* <u>endearing</u>, adorable, amiable, charming, cute, delightful, enchanting, likable or likeable, lovely, sweet

love *verb* **1** <u>adore</u>, cherish, dote on, hold dear, idolize, prize, treasure, worship **2** <u>enjoy</u>, appreciate, delight in, like, relish, savour, take pleasure in ♦ *noun* **3** <u>passion</u>, adoration, affection, ardour, attachment, devotion, infatuation, tenderness, warmth **4** <u>liking</u>, devotion, enjoyment, fondness, inclination, partiality,

relish, soft spot, taste, weakness **5** <u>beloved</u>, darling, dear, dearest, lover, sweetheart, truelove **6 in love** <u>enamoured</u>, besotted, charmed, enraptured, infatuated, smitten

love affair *noun* <u>romance</u>, affair, amour, intrigue, liaison, relationship

lovely *adjective* **1** <u>attractive</u>, adorable, beautiful, charming, comely, exquisite, graceful, handsome, pretty **2** <u>enjoyable</u>, agreeable, delightful, engaging, nice, pleasant, pleasing

lover *noun* <u>sweetheart</u>, admirer, beloved, boyfriend or girlfriend, flame (*informal*), mistress, suitor

loving *adjective* <u>affectionate</u>, amorous, dear, devoted, doting, fond, tender, warm-hearted

low *adjective* **1** <u>small</u>, little, short, squat, stunted **2** <u>inferior</u>, deficient, inadequate, poor, second-rate, shoddy **3** <u>coarse</u>, common, crude, disreputable, rough, rude, undignified, vulgar **4** <u>dejected</u>, depressed, despondent, disheartened, downcast, down in the dumps (*informal*), fed up, gloomy, glum, miserable **5** <u>ill</u>, debilitated, frail, stricken, weak **6** <u>quiet</u>, gentle, hushed, muffled, muted, soft, subdued, whispered

lowdown *noun* *Informal* <u>information</u>, gen (*Brit. informal*), info (*informal*), inside story, intelligence

lower *adjective* **1** <u>minor</u>, inferior, junior, lesser, secondary, second-class, smaller, subordinate **2** <u>reduced</u>, curtailed, decreased, diminished, lessened

♦ *verb* **3** drop, depress, fall, let down, sink, submerge, take down **4** lessen, cut, decrease, diminish, minimize, prune, reduce, slash

low-key *adjective* subdued, muted, quiet, restrained, toned down, understated

lowly *adjective* humble, meek, mild, modest, unassuming

low-spirited *adjective* depressed, dejected, despondent, dismal, down, down-hearted, fed up, low, miserable, sad

loyal *adjective* faithful, constant, dependable, devoted, dutiful, staunch, steadfast, true, trustworthy, trusty, unwavering

loyalty *noun* faithfulness, allegiance, constancy, dependability, devotion, fidelity, staunchness, steadfastness, trustworthiness

lubricate *verb* oil, grease, smear

lucid *adjective* **1** clear, comprehensible, explicit, intelligible, transparent **2** translucent, clear, crystalline, diaphanous, glassy, limpid, pellucid, transparent **3** clear-headed, all there, *compos mentis*, in one's right mind, rational, sane

luck *noun* **1** fortune, accident, chance, destiny, fate **2** good fortune, advantage, blessing, godsend, prosperity, serendipity, success, windfall

luckily *adverb* fortunately, favourably, happily, opportunely, propitiously, providentially

luckless *adjective* ill-fated, cursed, doomed, hapless, hopeless,

jinxed, unfortunate, unlucky

lucky *adjective* fortunate, advantageous, blessed, charmed, favoured, jammy (*Brit. slang*), serendipitous, successful

lucrative *adjective* profitable, advantageous, fruitful, productive, remunerative, well-paid

lucre *noun* money, gain, mammon, pelf, profit, riches, spoils, wealth

ludicrous *adjective* ridiculous, absurd, crazy, farcical, laughable, nonsensical, outlandish, preposterous, silly

luggage *noun* baggage, bags, cases, gear, impedimenta, paraphernalia, suitcases, things

lugubrious *adjective* gloomy, doleful, melancholy, mournful, sad, serious, sombre, sorrowful, woebegone

lukewarm *adjective* **1** tepid, warm **2** half-hearted, apathetic, cool, indifferent, unenthusiastic, unresponsive

lull *verb* **1** calm, allay, pacify, quell, soothe, subdue, tranquillize ♦ *noun* **2** respite, calm, hush, let-up (*informal*), pause, quiet, silence

lumber[1] *noun* **1** junk, clutter, jumble, refuse, rubbish, trash ♦ *verb* **2** *Informal* burden, encumber, land, load, saddle

lumber[2] *verb* plod, shamble, shuffle, stump, trudge, trundle, waddle

lumbering *adjective* awkward, clumsy, heavy, hulking, ponderous, ungainly

luminous *adjective* bright,

glowing, illuminated, luminescent, lustrous, radiant, shining

lump noun **1** <u>piece</u>, ball, chunk, hunk, mass, nugget **2** <u>swelling</u>, bulge, bump, growth, hump, protrusion, tumour ♦ verb **3** <u>group</u>, collect, combine, conglomerate, consolidate, mass, pool

lumpy adjective <u>bumpy</u>, knobbly, uneven

lunacy noun **1** <u>insanity</u>, dementia, derangement, madness, mania, psychosis **2** <u>foolishness</u>, absurdity, craziness, folly, foolhardiness, madness, stupidity

lunatic adjective **1** <u>irrational</u>, crackbrained, crackpot (informal), crazy, daft, deranged, insane, mad ♦ noun **2** <u>madman</u>, maniac, nutcase (slang), psychopath

lunge noun **1** <u>thrust</u>, charge, jab, pounce, spring, swing ♦ verb **2** <u>pounce</u>, charge, dive, leap, plunge, thrust

lurch verb **1** <u>tilt</u>, heave, heel, lean, list, pitch, rock, roll **2** <u>stagger</u>, reel, stumble, sway, totter, weave

lure verb **1** <u>tempt</u>, allure, attract, draw, ensnare, entice, invite, seduce ♦ noun **2** <u>temptation</u>, allurement, attraction, bait, carrot (informal), enticement, incentive, inducement

lurid adjective **1** <u>sensational</u>, graphic, melodramatic, shocking, vivid **2** <u>glaring</u>, intense

lurk verb <u>hide</u>, conceal oneself, lie in wait, prowl, skulk, slink, sneak

luscious adjective <u>delicious</u>, appetizing, juicy, mouth-watering, palatable, succulent, sweet, toothsome

lush adjective **1** <u>abundant</u>, dense, flourishing, green, rank, verdant **2** <u>luxurious</u>, elaborate, extravagant, grand, lavish, opulent, ornate, palatial, plush (informal), sumptuous

lust noun **1** <u>lechery</u>, lasciviousness, lewdness, sensuality **2** <u>appetite</u>, craving, desire, greed, longing, passion, thirst ♦ verb **3** <u>desire</u>, covet, crave, hunger for or after, want, yearn

lustre noun **1** <u>sparkle</u>, gleam, glint, glitter, gloss, glow, sheen, shimmer, shine **2** <u>glory</u>, distinction, fame, honour, prestige, renown

lusty adjective <u>vigorous</u>, energetic, healthy, hearty, powerful, robust, strong, sturdy, virile

luxurious adjective <u>sumptuous</u>, comfortable, expensive, lavish, magnificent, opulent, plush (informal), rich, splendid

luxury noun **1** <u>opulence</u>, affluence, hedonism, richness, splendour, sumptuousness **2** <u>extravagance</u>, extra, frill, indulgence, treat

lying noun **1** <u>dishonesty</u>, deceit, mendacity, perjury, untruthfulness ♦ adjective **2** <u>deceitful</u>, dishonest, false, mendacious, perfidious, treacherous, two-faced, untruthful

lyrical adjective <u>enthusiastic</u>, effusive, impassioned, inspired, poetic, rhapsodic

M m

macabre *adjective* <u>gruesome</u>, dreadful, eerie, frightening, ghastly, ghostly, ghoulish, grim, grisly, morbid

machiavellian *adjective* <u>scheming</u>, astute, crafty, cunning, cynical, double-dealing, opportunist, sly, underhand, unscrupulous

machine *noun* 1 <u>appliance</u>, apparatus, contraption, contrivance, device, engine, instrument, mechanism, tool 2 <u>system</u>, machinery, organization, setup (*informal*), structure

machinery *noun* <u>equipment</u>, apparatus, gear, instruments, tackle, tools

macho *adjective* <u>manly</u>, chauvinist, masculine, virile

mad *adjective* 1 <u>insane</u>, crazy (*informal*), demented, deranged, *non compos mentis*, nuts (*slang*), of unsound mind, out of one's mind, psychotic, raving, unhinged, unstable 2 <u>foolish</u>, absurd, asinine, daft (*informal*), foolhardy, irrational, nonsensical, preposterous, senseless, wild 3 *Informal* <u>angry</u>, berserk, enraged, furious, incensed, livid (*informal*), wild 4 <u>enthusiastic</u>, ardent, avid, crazy (*informal*), fanatical, impassioned, infatuated, wild 5 <u>frenzied</u>, excited, frenetic, uncontrolled, unrestrained, wild 6 **like mad** *Informal* <u>energetically</u>, enthusiastically, excitedly, furiously, rapidly, speedily, violently, wildly

madcap *adjective* <u>reckless</u>, crazy, foolhardy, hare-brained, imprudent, impulsive, rash, thoughtless

madden *verb* <u>infuriate</u>, annoy, derange, drive one crazy, enrage, incense, inflame, irritate, upset

madly *adverb* 1 <u>insanely</u>, crazily, deliriously, distractedly, frantically, frenziedly, hysterically 2 <u>foolishly</u>, absurdly, irrationally, ludicrously, senselessly, wildly 3 <u>energetically</u>, excitedly, furiously, like mad (*informal*), recklessly, speedily, wildly 4 *Informal* <u>passionately</u>, desperately, devotedly, intensely, to distraction

madman *or* **madwoman** *noun* <u>lunatic</u>, maniac, nutcase (*slang*), psycho (*slang*), psychopath

madness *noun* 1 <u>insanity</u>, aberration, craziness, delusion, dementia, derangement, distraction, lunacy, mania, mental illness, psychopathy, psychosis 2 <u>foolishness</u>, absurdity, daftness (*informal*), folly, foolhardiness, idiocy, nonsense, preposterousness, wildness

maelstrom *noun* 1 <u>whirlpool</u>, vortex 2 <u>turmoil</u>, chaos, confusion, disorder, tumult, upheaval

maestro *noun* <u>master</u>, expert, genius, virtuoso

magazine *noun* 1 <u>journal</u>, pamphlet, periodical 2 <u>storehouse</u>, arsenal, depot, store, warehouse

magic noun **1** <u>sorcery</u>, black art, enchantment, necromancy, witchcraft, wizardry **2** <u>conjuring</u>, illusion, legerdemain, prestidigitation, sleight of hand, trickery **3** <u>charm</u>, allurement, enchantment, fascination, glamour, magnetism, power ◆ adjective **4** Also **magical** <u>miraculous</u>, bewitching, charming, enchanting, entrancing, fascinating, marvellous, spellbinding

magician noun <u>sorcerer</u>, conjuror or conjuror, enchanter or enchantress, illusionist, necromancer, warlock, witch, wizard

magisterial adjective <u>authoritative</u>, commanding, lordly, masterful

magistrate noun <u>judge</u>, J.P., justice, justice of the peace

magnanimity noun <u>generosity</u>, benevolence, big-heartedness, largesse or largess, nobility, selflessness, unselfishness

magnanimous adjective <u>generous</u>, big-hearted, bountiful, charitable, kind, noble, selfless, unselfish

magnate noun <u>tycoon</u>, baron, captain of industry, mogul, plutocrat

magnetic adjective <u>attractive</u>, captivating, charismatic, charming, fascinating, hypnotic, irresistible, mesmerizing, seductive

magnetism noun <u>charm</u>, allure, appeal, attraction, charisma, drawing power, magic, pull, seductiveness

magnification noun <u>increase</u>, amplification, enhancement, enlargement, expansion, heightening, intensification

magnificence noun <u>splendour</u>, brilliance, glory, grandeur, majesty, nobility, opulence, stateliness, sumptuousness

magnificent adjective **1** <u>splendid</u>, glorious, gorgeous, imposing, impressive, majestic, regal, sublime, sumptuous **2** <u>excellent</u>, brilliant, fine, outstanding, splendid, superb

magnify verb **1** <u>enlarge</u>, amplify, blow up (informal), boost, dilate, expand, heighten, increase, intensify **2** <u>overstate</u>, exaggerate, inflate, overemphasize, overplay

magnitude noun **1** <u>importance</u>, consequence, greatness, moment, note, significance, weight **2** <u>size</u>, amount, amplitude, extent, mass, quantity, volume

maid noun **1** <u>girl</u>, damsel, lass, lassie (informal), maiden, wench **2** <u>servant</u>, housemaid, maidservant, serving-maid

maiden noun **1** <u>girl</u>, damsel, lass, lassie (informal), maid, virgin, wench ◆ adjective **2** <u>unmarried</u>, unwed **3** <u>first</u>, inaugural, initial, introductory

maidenly adjective <u>modest</u>, chaste, decent, decorous, demure, pure, virginal

mail noun **1** <u>post</u>, correspondence, letters ◆ verb **2** <u>post</u>, dispatch, forward, send

maim verb <u>cripple</u>, disable, hurt, injure, mutilate, wound

main adjective **1** <u>chief</u>, central,

essential, foremost, head, leading, pre-eminent, primary, principal ♦ *noun* **2** <u>conduit</u>, cable, channel, duct, line, pipe **3 in the main** <u>on the whole</u>, for the most part, generally, in general, mainly, mostly

mainly *adverb* <u>chiefly</u>, for the most part, in the main, largely, mostly, on the whole, predominantly, primarily, principally

mainstay *noun* <u>pillar</u>, anchor, backbone, bulwark, buttress, lynchpin, prop

mainstream *adjective* <u>conventional</u>, accepted, current, established, general, orthodox, prevailing, received

maintain *verb* **1** <u>keep up</u>, carry on, continue, perpetuate, preserve, prolong, retain, sustain **2** <u>support</u>, care for, look after, provide for, supply, take care of **3** <u>assert</u>, avow, claim, contend, declare, insist, profess, state

maintenance *noun* **1** <u>continuation</u>, carrying-on, perpetuation, prolongation **2** <u>upkeep</u>, care, conservation, keeping, nurture, preservation, repairs **3** <u>allowance</u>, alimony, keep, support

majestic *adjective* <u>grand</u>, grandiose, impressive, magnificent, monumental, regal, splendid, stately, sublime, superb

majesty *noun* <u>grandeur</u>, glory, magnificence, nobility, pomp, splendour, stateliness

major *adjective* **1** <u>main</u>, bigger, chief, greater, higher, leading, senior, supreme **2** <u>important</u>, critical, crucial, great, notable, outstanding, serious, significant

majority *noun* **1** <u>preponderance</u>, best part, bulk, greater number, mass, most **2** <u>adulthood</u>, manhood *or* womanhood, maturity, seniority

make *verb* **1** <u>create</u>, assemble, build, construct, fashion, form, manufacture, produce, put together, synthesize **2** <u>produce</u>, accomplish, bring about, cause, create, effect, generate, give rise to, lead to **3** <u>force</u>, cause, compel, constrain, drive, impel, induce, oblige, prevail upon, require **4** <u>amount to</u>, add up to, compose, constitute, form **5** <u>perform</u>, carry out, do, effect, execute **6** <u>earn</u>, clear, gain, get, net, obtain, win **7 make it** *Informal* <u>succeed</u>, arrive (*informal*), crack it (*informal*), get on, prosper ♦ *noun* **8** <u>brand</u>, kind, model, sort, style, type, variety

make-believe *noun* <u>fantasy</u>, imagination, play-acting, pretence, unreality

make for *verb* <u>head for</u>, aim for, be bound for, head towards

make off *verb* **1** <u>flee</u>, bolt, clear out (*informal*), run away *or* off, take to one's heels **2 make off with** <u>steal</u>, abduct, carry off, filch, kidnap, nick (*slang, chiefly Brit.*), pinch (*informal*), run away *or* off with

make out *verb* **1** <u>see</u>, detect, discern, discover, distinguish, perceive, recognize **2** <u>understand</u>, comprehend, decipher, fathom, follow, grasp, work out **3** <u>write out</u>, complete, draw up, fill in *or* out **4** <u>pretend</u>, assert, claim, let on, make as if or though **5** <u>fare</u>, get on, manage

maker *noun* <u>manufacturer</u>, builder, constructor, producer

makeshift *adjective* <u>temporary</u>, expedient, provisional, stopgap, substitute

make-up *noun* **1** <u>cosmetics</u>, face (*informal*), greasepaint (*Theatre*), paint (*informal*), powder **2** <u>structure</u>, arrangement, assembly, composition, configuration, constitution, construction, format, organization **3** <u>nature</u>, character, constitution, disposition, temperament

make up *verb* **1** <u>form</u>, compose, comprise, constitute **2** <u>invent</u>, coin, compose, concoct, construct, create, devise, dream up, formulate, frame, originate **3** <u>complete</u>, fill, supply **4** <u>settle</u>, bury the hatchet, call it quits, reconcile **5** <u>make up for</u> <u>compensate for</u>, atone for, balance, make amends for, offset, recompense

making *noun* <u>creation</u>, assembly, building, composition, construction, fabrication, manufacture, production

makings *plural noun* <u>beginnings</u>, capacity, ingredients, potential

maladjusted *adjective* <u>disturbed</u>, alienated, neurotic, unstable

maladministration *noun* <u>mismanagement</u>, corruption, dishonesty, incompetence, inefficiency, malpractice, misrule

maladroit *adjective* <u>clumsy</u>, awkward, cack-handed (*informal*), ham-fisted *or* ham-handed (*informal*), inept,

inexpert, unskilful

malady *noun* <u>disease</u>, affliction, ailment, complaint, disorder, illness, infirmity, sickness

malaise *noun* <u>unease</u>, anxiety, depression, disquiet, melancholy

malcontent *noun* <u>troublemaker</u>, agitator, mischief-maker, rebel, stirrer (*informal*)

male *adjective* <u>masculine</u>, manly, virile

malefactor *noun* <u>wrongdoer</u>, criminal, delinquent, evildoer, miscreant, offender, villain

malevolence *noun* <u>malice</u>, hate, hatred, ill will, rancour, spite, vindictiveness

malevolent *adjective* <u>spiteful</u>, hostile, ill-natured, malicious, malign, vengeful, vindictive

malformation *noun* <u>deformity</u>, distortion, misshapenness

malformed *adjective* <u>misshapen</u>, abnormal, crooked, deformed, distorted, irregular, twisted

malfunction *verb* **1** <u>break down</u>, fail, go wrong ♦ *noun* **2** <u>fault</u>, breakdown, defect, failure, flaw, glitch

malice *noun* <u>ill will</u>, animosity, enmity, evil intent, hate, hatred, malevolence, spite, vindictiveness

malicious *adjective* <u>spiteful</u>, ill-disposed, ill-natured, malevolent, rancorous, resentful, vengeful

malign *verb* **1** <u>disparage</u>, abuse, defame, denigrate, libel, run down, slander, smear, vilify ♦ *adjective* **2** <u>evil</u>, bad, destructive, harmful, hostile, injurious, malevolent, malignant, pernicious, wicked

malignant *adjective* **1** <u>harmful</u>, destructive, hostile, hurtful, malevolent, malign, pernicious, spiteful **2** *Medical* <u>uncontrollable</u>, cancerous, dangerous, deadly, fatal, irremediable

malleable *adjective* **1** <u>workable</u>, ductile, plastic, soft, tensile **2** <u>manageable</u>, adaptable, biddable, compliant, impressionable, pliable, tractable

malodorous *adjective* <u>smelly</u>, fetid, mephitic, nauseating, noisome, offensive, putrid, reeking, stinking

malpractice *noun* <u>misconduct</u>, abuse, dereliction, mismanagement, negligence

maltreat *verb* <u>abuse</u>, bully, harm, hurt, ill-treat, injure, mistreat

mammoth *adjective* <u>colossal</u>, enormous, giant, gigantic, huge, immense, massive, monumental, mountainous, prodigious

man *noun* **1** <u>male</u>, bloke (*Brit. informal*), chap (*informal*), gentleman, guy (*informal*) **2** <u>human</u>, human being, individual, person, soul **3** <u>mankind</u>, Homo sapiens, humanity, humankind, human race, people **4** <u>manservant</u>, attendant, retainer, servant, valet ◆ *verb* **5** <u>staff</u>, crew, garrison, occupy, people

manacle *noun* **1** <u>handcuff</u>, bond, chain, fetter, iron, shackle ◆ *verb* **2** <u>handcuff</u>, bind, chain, fetter, put in chains, shackle

manage *verb* **1** <u>administer</u>, be in charge (of), command, conduct, direct, handle, run, supervise **2** <u>succeed</u>, accomplish, arrange, contrive, effect, engineer

3 <u>handle</u>, control, manipulate, operate, use **4** <u>cope</u>, carry on, get by (*informal*), make do, muddle through, survive

manageable *adjective* <u>docile</u>, amenable, compliant, easy, submissive

management *noun* **1** <u>directors</u>, administration, board, employers, executive(s) **2** <u>administration</u>, command, control, direction, handling, operation, running, supervision

manager *noun* <u>supervisor</u>, administrator, boss (*informal*), director, executive, governor, head, organizer

mandate *noun* <u>command</u>, commission, decree, directive, edict, instruction, order

mandatory *adjective* <u>compulsory</u>, binding, obligatory, required, requisite

manfully *adverb* <u>bravely</u>, boldly, courageously, determinedly, gallantly, hard, resolutely, stoutly, valiantly

mangle *verb* <u>crush</u>, deform, destroy, disfigure, distort, mutilate, ruin, spoil, tear, wreck

mangy *adjective* <u>scruffy</u>, dirty, moth-eaten, seedy, shabby, shoddy, squalid

manhandle *verb* <u>rough up</u>, knock about *or* around, maul, paw (*informal*)

manhood *noun* <u>manliness</u>, masculinity, virility

mania *noun* **1** <u>madness</u>, delirium, dementia, derangement, insanity, lunacy **2** <u>obsession</u>, craze, fad (*informal*), fetish, fixation, passion, preoccupation, thing (*informal*)

maniac noun 1 <u>madman or madwoman</u>, headcase (*informal*), lunatic, psycho (*slang*), psychopath 2 <u>fanatic</u>, enthusiast, fan, fiend (*informal*), freak (*informal*)

manifest adjective 1 <u>obvious</u>, apparent, blatant, clear, conspicuous, evident, glaring, noticeable, palpable, patent ♦ *verb* 2 <u>display</u>, demonstrate, exhibit, expose, express, reveal, show

manifestation noun <u>display</u>, demonstration, exhibition, expression, indication, mark, show, sign, symptom

manifold adjective <u>numerous</u>, assorted, copious, diverse, many, multifarious, multiple, varied, various

manipulate verb 1 <u>work</u>, handle, operate, use 2 <u>influence</u>, control, direct, engineer, manoeuvre

mankind noun <u>people</u>, Homo sapiens, humanity, humankind, human race, man

manliness noun <u>virility</u>, boldness, bravery, courage, fearlessness, masculinity, valour, vigour

manly adjective <u>virile</u>, bold, brave, courageous, fearless, manful, masculine, strapping, strong, vigorous

man-made adjective <u>artificial</u>, ersatz, manufactured, mock, synthetic

manner noun 1 <u>behaviour</u>, air, aspect, bearing, conduct, demeanour 2 <u>style</u>, custom, fashion, method, mode, way 3 <u>type</u>, brand, category, form,

kind, sort, variety

mannered adjective <u>affected</u>, artificial, pretentious, stilted

mannerism noun <u>habit</u>, characteristic, foible, idiosyncrasy, peculiarity, quirk, trait, trick

manners plural noun 1 <u>behaviour</u>, conduct, demeanour 2 <u>politeness</u>, courtesy, decorum, etiquette, p's and q's, refinement

manoeuvre noun 1 <u>stratagem</u>, dodge, intrigue, machination, ploy, ruse, scheme, subterfuge, tactic, trick 2 <u>movement</u>, exercise, operation ♦ *verb* 3 <u>manipulate</u>, contrive, engineer, machinate, pull strings, scheme, wangle (*informal*) 4 <u>move</u>, deploy, exercise

mansion noun <u>residence</u>, hall, manor, seat, villa

mantle noun 1 <u>cloak</u>, cape, hood, shawl, wrap 2 <u>covering</u>, blanket, canopy, curtain, pall, screen, shroud, veil

manual adjective 1 <u>hand-operated</u>, human, physical ♦ *noun* 2 <u>handbook</u>, bible, instructions

manufacture verb 1 <u>make</u>, assemble, build, construct, create, mass-produce, produce, put together, turn out 2 <u>concoct</u>, cook up (*informal*), devise, fabricate, invent, make up, think up, trump up ♦ *noun* 3 <u>making</u>, assembly, construction, creation, production

manufacturer noun <u>maker</u>, builder, constructor, creator, industrialist, producer

manure *noun* <u>compost</u>, droppings, dung, excrement, fertilizer, muck, ordure

many *adjective* **1** <u>numerous</u>, abundant, countless, innumerable, manifold, myriad, umpteen (*informal*), various ♦ *noun* **2** <u>a lot</u>, heaps (*informal*), lots (*informal*), plenty, scores

mar *verb* <u>spoil</u>, blemish, damage, detract from, disfigure, hurt, impair, ruin, scar, stain, taint, tarnish

maraud *verb* <u>raid</u>, forage, loot, pillage, plunder, ransack, ravage

marauder *noun* <u>raider</u>, bandit, brigand, buccaneer, outlaw, plunderer

march *verb* **1** <u>walk</u>, file, pace, parade, stride, strut ♦ *noun* **2** <u>walk</u>, routemarch, trek **3** <u>progress</u>, advance, development, evolution, progression

margin *noun* <u>edge</u>, border, boundary, brink, perimeter, periphery, rim, side, verge

marginal *adjective* **1** <u>borderline</u>, bordering, on the edge, peripheral **2** <u>insignificant</u>, minimal, minor, negligible, slight, small

marijuana *noun* <u>cannabis</u>, dope (*slang*), grass (*slang*), hemp, pot (*slang*)

marine *adjective* <u>nautical</u>, maritime, naval, seafaring, seagoing

mariner *noun* <u>sailor</u>, salt, sea dog, seafarer, seaman

marital *adjective* <u>matrimonial</u>, conjugal, connubial, nuptial

maritime *adjective* **1** <u>nautical</u>, marine, naval, oceanic, seafaring **2** <u>coastal</u>, littoral, seaside

mark *noun* **1** <u>spot</u>, blemish, blot, line, scar, scratch, smudge, stain, streak **2** <u>sign</u>, badge, device, emblem, flag, hallmark, label, symbol, token **3** <u>criterion</u>, measure, norm, standard, yardstick **4** <u>target</u>, aim, goal, object, objective, purpose ♦ *verb* **5** <u>scar</u>, blemish, blot, scratch, smudge, stain, streak **6** <u>characterize</u>, brand, flag, identify, label, stamp **7** <u>distinguish</u>, denote, exemplify, illustrate, show **8** <u>observe</u>, attend, mind, note, notice, pay attention, pay heed, watch **9** <u>grade</u>, appraise, assess, correct, evaluate

marked *adjective* <u>noticeable</u>, blatant, clear, conspicuous, decided, distinct, obvious, patent, prominent, pronounced, striking

markedly *adverb* <u>noticeably</u>, clearly, considerably, conspicuously, decidedly, distinctly, obviously, strikingly

market *noun* **1** <u>fair</u>, bazaar, mart ♦ *verb* **2** <u>sell</u>, retail, vend

marketable *adjective* <u>sought after</u>, in demand, saleable, wanted

marksman, markswoman *noun* <u>sharpshooter</u>, crack shot (*informal*), good shot

maroon *verb* <u>abandon</u>, desert, leave, leave high and dry (*informal*), strand

marriage *noun* <u>wedding</u>, match, matrimony, nuptials, wedlock

marry *verb* **1** <u>wed</u>, get hitched (*slang*), tie the knot (*informal*)

2 unite, ally, bond, join, knit, link, merge, unify, yoke

marsh *noun* swamp, bog, fen, morass, quagmire, slough

marshal *verb* **1** arrange, align, array, deploy, draw up, group, line up, order, organize **2** conduct, escort, guide, lead, shepherd, usher

marshy *adjective* swampy, boggy, quaggy, waterlogged, wet

martial *adjective* military, bellicose, belligerent, warlike

martinet *noun* disciplinarian, stickler

martyrdom *noun* persecution, ordeal, suffering

marvel *verb* **1** wonder, be amazed, be awed, gape ◆ *noun* **2** wonder, miracle, phenomenon, portent, prodigy

marvellous *adjective* **1** amazing, astonishing, astounding, breathtaking, brilliant, extraordinary, miraculous, phenomenal, prodigious, spectacular, stupendous **2** excellent, fabulous (*informal*), fantastic (*informal*), great (*informal*), splendid, superb, terrific (*informal*), wonderful

masculine *adjective* male, manlike, manly, mannish, virile

mask *noun* **1** disguise, camouflage, cover, façade, front, guise, screen, veil ◆ *verb* **2** disguise, camouflage, cloak, conceal, cover, hide, obscure, screen, veil

masquerade *noun* **1** masked ball, fancy dress party, revel **2** pretence, cloak, cover-up,

deception, disguise, mask, pose, screen, subterfuge ◆ *verb* **3** pose, disguise, dissemble, dissimulate, impersonate, pass oneself off, pretend (to be)

mass *noun* **1** piece, block, chunk, hunk, lump **2** lot, bunch, collection, heap, load, pile, quantity, stack **3** size, bulk, greatness, magnitude ◆ *adjective* **4** large-scale, extensive, general, indiscriminate, wholesale, widespread ◆ *verb* **5** gather, accumulate, assemble, collect, congregate, rally, swarm, throng

massacre *noun* **1** slaughter, annihilation, blood bath, butchery, carnage, extermination, holocaust, murder ◆ *verb* **2** slaughter, butcher, cut to pieces, exterminate, kill, mow down, murder, wipe out

massage *noun* **1** rub-down, manipulation ◆ *verb* **2** rub down, knead, manipulate

massive *adjective* huge, big, colossal, enormous, gigantic, hefty, immense, mammoth, monumental, whopping (*informal*)

master *noun* **1** ruler, boss (*informal*), chief, commander, controller, director, governor, lord, manager **2** expert, ace (*informal*), doyen, genius, maestro, past master, virtuoso, wizard **3** teacher, guide, guru, instructor, tutor ◆ *adjective* **4** main, chief, foremost, leading, predominant, prime, principal ◆ *verb* **5** learn, get the hang of (*informal*), grasp **6** overcome, conquer, defeat, tame, triumph over, vanquish

masterful *adjective* **1** skilful, adroit, consummate, expert, fine, first-rate, masterly, superlative, supreme, world-class **2** domineering, arrogant, bossy (*informal*), high-handed, imperious, overbearing, overweening

masterly *adjective* skilful, adroit, consummate, crack (*informal*), expert, first-rate, masterful, supreme, world-class

mastermind *verb* **1** plan, conceive, devise, direct, manage, organize ♦ *noun* **2** organizer, architect, brain(s) (*informal*), director, engineer, manager, planner

masterpiece *noun* classic, jewel, magnum opus, *pièce de résistance, tour de force*

mastery *noun* **1** expertise, finesse, know-how (*informal*), proficiency, prowess, skill, virtuosity **2** control, ascendancy, command, domination, superiority, supremacy, upper hand, whip hand

match *noun* **1** game, bout, competition, contest, head-to-head, test, trial **2** equal, counterpart, peer, rival **3** marriage, alliance, pairing, partnership ♦ *verb* **4** correspond, accord, agree, fit, go with, harmonize, tally **5** rival, compare, compete, emulate, equal, measure up to

matching *adjective* identical, coordinating, corresponding, equivalent, like, twin

matchless *adjective* unequalled, incomparable, inimitable,

superlative, supreme, unmatched, unparalleled, unrivalled, unsurpassed

mate *noun* **1** partner, husband *or* wife, spouse **2** *Informal* friend, buddy (*informal*), chum (*informal*), comrade, crony, pal (*informal*) **3** colleague, associate, companion **4** assistant, helper, subordinate ♦ *verb* **5** pair, breed, couple

material *noun* **1** substance, matter, stuff **2** information, data, evidence, facts, notes **3** cloth, fabric ♦ *adjective* **4** physical, bodily, concrete, corporeal, palpable, substantial, tangible **5** important, essential, meaningful, momentous, serious, significant, vital, weighty **6** relevant, applicable, apposite, apropos, germane, pertinent

materialize *verb* occur, appear, come about, come to pass, happen, take shape, turn up

materially *adverb* significantly, essentially, gravely, greatly, much, seriously, substantially

maternal *adjective* motherly

maternity *noun* motherhood, motherliness

matey *adjective* friendly, chummy (*informal*), hail-fellow-well-met, intimate, pally (*informal*), sociable, thick (*informal*)

matrimonial *adjective* marital, conjugal, connubial, nuptial

matrimony *noun* marriage, nuptials, wedding ceremony, wedlock

matted *adjective* tangled, knotted, tousled, uncombed

matter *noun* **1** substance, body,

material, stuff **2** <u>situation</u>, affair, business, concern, event, incident, proceeding, question, subject, topic **3** As in **what's the matter?** <u>problem</u>, complication, difficulty, distress, trouble, worry ♦ verb **4** <u>be important</u>, carry weight, count, make a difference, signify

matter-of-fact adjective <u>unsentimental</u>, deadpan, down-to-earth, emotionless, mundane, plain, prosaic, sober, unimaginative

mature adjective **1** <u>grown-up</u>, adult, full-grown, fully fledged, mellow, of age, ready, ripe, seasoned ♦ verb **2** <u>develop</u>, age, bloom, blossom, come of age, grow up, mellow, ripen

maturity noun <u>adulthood</u>, experience, manhood or womanhood, ripeness, wisdom

maudlin adjective <u>sentimental</u>, mawkish, overemotional, slushy (informal), soppy (Brit. informal), tearful, weepy (informal)

maul verb **1** <u>ill-treat</u>, abuse, manhandle, molest, paw **2** <u>tear</u>, batter, claw, lacerate, mangle

maverick noun **1** <u>rebel</u>, dissenter, eccentric, heretic, iconoclast, individualist, nonconformist, protester, radical ♦ adjective **2** <u>rebel</u>, dissenting, eccentric, heretical, iconoclastic, individualistic, nonconformist, radical

mawkish adjective <u>sentimental</u>, emotional, maudlin, schmaltzy (slang), slushy (informal), soppy (Brit. informal)

maxim noun <u>saying</u>, adage, aphorism, axiom, dictum, motto, proverb, rule

maximum noun **1** <u>top</u>, ceiling, height, peak, pinnacle, summit, upper limit, utmost, zenith ♦ adjective **2** <u>greatest</u>, highest, most, paramount, supreme, topmost, utmost

maybe adverb <u>perhaps</u>, perchance (archaic), possibly

mayhem noun <u>chaos</u>, commotion, confusion, destruction, disorder, fracas, havoc, trouble, violence

maze noun **1** <u>labyrinth</u> **2** <u>web</u>, confusion, imbroglio, tangle

meadow noun <u>field</u>, grassland, lea (poetic), pasture

meagre adjective <u>insubstantial</u>, inadequate, measly, paltry, poor, puny, scanty, slight, small

mean[1] verb **1** <u>signify</u>, convey, denote, express, imply, indicate, represent, spell, stand for, symbolize **2** <u>intend</u>, aim, aspire, design, desire, plan, set out, want, wish

mean[2] adjective **1** <u>miserly</u>, mercenary, niggardly, parsimonious, penny-pinching, stingy, tight-fisted, ungenerous **2** <u>despicable</u>, callous, contemptible, hard-hearted, petty, shabby, shameful, sordid, vile

mean[3] noun **1** <u>average</u>, balance, compromise, happy medium, middle, midpoint, norm ♦ adjective **2** <u>average</u>, middle, standard

meander verb **1** <u>wind</u>, snake, turn, zigzag **2** <u>wander</u>, ramble, stroll ♦ noun **3** <u>curve</u>, bend, coil, loop, turn, twist, zigzag

meaning noun sense, connotation, drift, gist, message, significance, substance

meaningful adjective significant, important, material, purposeful, relevant, useful, valid, worthwhile

meaningless adjective pointless, empty, futile, inane, inconsequential, insignificant, senseless, useless, vain, worthless

meanness noun 1 miserliness, niggardliness, parsimony, selfishness, stinginess 2 pettiness, disgracefulness, ignobility, narrow-mindedness, shabbiness, shamefulness

means plural noun 1 method, agency, instrument, medium, mode, process, way 2 money, affluence, capital, fortune, funds, income, resources, wealth, wherewithal 3 by all means certainly, definitely, doubtlessly, of course, surely 4 by no means in no way, definitely not, not in the least, on no account

meantime, meanwhile adverb at the same time, concurrently, in the interim, simultaneously

measly adjective meagre, miserable, paltry, pathetic, pitiful, poor, puny, scanty, skimpy

measurable adjective quantifiable, assessable, perceptible, significant

measure noun 1 quantity, allotment, allowance, amount, portion, quota, ration, share 2 gauge, metre, rule, scale, yardstick 3 action, act, deed, expedient, manoeuvre, means, procedure, step 4 law, act, bill, resolution, statute 5 rhythm, beat, cadence, metre, verse ♦ verb 6 quantify, assess, calculate, calibrate, compute, determine, evaluate, gauge, weigh

measured adjective 1 steady, dignified, even, leisurely, regular, sedate, slow, solemn, stately, unhurried 2 considered, calculated, deliberate, reasoned, sober, studied, well-thought-out

measurement noun calculation, assessment, calibration, computation, evaluation, mensuration, valuation

measure up to verb fulfil the expectations, be equal to, be suitable, come up to scratch (informal), fit or fill the bill, make the grade (informal)

meat noun flesh

meaty adjective 1 brawny, beefy (informal), burly, heavily built, heavy, muscular, solid, strapping, sturdy 2 interesting, meaningful, profound, rich, significant, substantial

mechanical adjective 1 automatic, automated 2 unthinking, automatic, cursory, impersonal, instinctive, involuntary, perfunctory, routine, unfeeling

mechanism noun 1 machine, apparatus, appliance, contrivance, device, instrument, tool 2 process, agency, means, method, operation, procedure, system, technique

meddle verb interfere, butt in, intervene, intrude, pry, tamper

meddlesome adjective interfering, intrusive, meddling, mischievous, officious, prying

mediate *verb* <u>intervene</u>, arbitrate, conciliate, intercede, reconcile, referee, step in (*informal*), umpire

mediation *noun* <u>arbitration</u>, conciliation, intercession, intervention, reconciliation

mediator *noun* <u>negotiator</u>, arbiter, arbitrator, go-between, honest broker, intermediary, middleman, peacemaker, referee, umpire

medicinal *adjective* <u>therapeutic</u>, curative, healing, medical, remedial, restorative

medicine *noun* <u>remedy</u>, cure, drug, medicament, medication, nostrum

mediocre *adjective* <u>second-rate</u>, average, indifferent, inferior, middling, ordinary, passable, pedestrian, run-of-the-mill, so-so (*informal*), undistinguished

mediocrity *noun* <u>insignificance</u>, indifference, inferiority, ordinariness, unimportance

meditate *verb* 1 <u>reflect</u>, cogitate, consider, contemplate, deliberate, muse, ponder, ruminate, think 2 <u>plan</u>, have in mind, intend, purpose, scheme

meditation *noun* <u>reflection</u>, cogitation, contemplation, musing, pondering, rumination, study, thought

medium *adjective* 1 <u>middle</u>, average, fair, intermediate, mean, median, mediocre, middling, midway ♦ *noun* 2 <u>middle</u>, average, centre, compromise, mean, midpoint 3 <u>means</u>, agency, channel, instrument, mode, organ, vehicle, way 4 <u>environment</u>, atmosphere, conditions, milieu,

setting, surroundings 5 <u>spiritualist</u>

medley *noun* <u>mixture</u>, assortment, farrago, hotchpotch, jumble, *mélange*, miscellany, mishmash, mixed bag (*informal*), potpourri

meek *adjective* <u>submissive</u>, acquiescent, compliant, deferential, docile, gentle, humble, mild, modest, timid, unassuming, unpretentious

meekness *noun* <u>submissiveness</u>, acquiescence, compliance, deference, docility, gentleness, humility, mildness, modesty, timidity

meet *verb* 1 <u>encounter</u>, bump into, chance on, come across, confront, contact, find, happen on, run across, run into 2 <u>converge</u>, come together, connect, cross, intersect, join, link up, touch 3 <u>satisfy</u>, answer, come up to, comply with, discharge, fulfil, match, measure up to 4 <u>gather</u>, assemble, collect, come together, congregate, convene, muster 5 <u>experience</u>, bear, encounter, endure, face, go through, suffer, undergo

meeting *noun* 1 <u>encounter</u>, assignation, confrontation, engagement, introduction, rendezvous, tryst 2 <u>conference</u>, assembly, conclave, congress, convention, gathering, get-together (*informal*), reunion, session

melancholy *noun* 1 <u>sadness</u>, dejection, depression, despondency, gloom, low spirits, misery, sorrow, unhappiness ♦ *adjective* 2 <u>sad</u>, depressed, despondent, dispirited, downhearted, gloomy, glum, miserable, mournful, sorrowful

melee, mêlée noun <u>fight</u>, brawl, fracas, free-for-all (*informal*), rumpus, scrimmage, scuffle, set-to (*informal*), skirmish, tussle

mellifluous adjective <u>sweet</u>, dulcet, euphonious, honeyed, silvery, smooth, soft, soothing, sweet-sounding

mellow adjective 1 <u>soft</u>, delicate, full-flavoured, mature, rich, ripe, sweet ♦ verb 2 <u>mature</u>, develop, improve, ripen, season, soften, sweeten

melodious adjective <u>tuneful</u>, dulcet, euphonious, harmonious, melodic, musical, sweet-sounding

melodramatic adjective <u>sensational</u>, blood-and-thunder, extravagant, histrionic, overdramatic, overemotional, theatrical

melody noun 1 <u>tune</u>, air, music, song, strain, theme 2 <u>tunefulness</u>, euphony, harmony, melodiousness, musicality

melt verb 1 <u>dissolve</u>, fuse, liquefy, soften, thaw 2 *often with* **away** <u>disappear</u>, disperse, dissolve, evanesce, evaporate, fade, vanish 3 <u>soften</u>, disarm, mollify, relax

member noun 1 <u>representative</u>, associate, fellow 2 <u>limb</u>, appendage, arm, extremity, leg, part

membership noun 1 <u>members</u>, associates, body, fellows 2 <u>participation</u>, belonging, enrolment, fellowship

memento noun <u>souvenir</u>, keepsake, memorial, relic, remembrance, reminder, token, trophy

memoir noun <u>account</u>, biography, essay, journal, life, monograph, narrative, record

memoirs plural noun <u>autobiography</u>, diary, experiences, journals, life story, memories, recollections, reminiscences

memorable adjective <u>noteworthy</u>, celebrated, famous, historic, momentous, notable, remarkable, significant, striking, unforgettable

memorandum noun <u>note</u>, communication, jotting, memo, message, minute, reminder

memorial noun 1 <u>monument</u>, memento, plaque, record, remembrance, souvenir ♦ adjective 2 <u>commemorative</u>, monumental

memorize verb <u>remember</u>, commit to memory, learn, learn by heart, learn by rote

memory noun 1 <u>recall</u>, recollection, remembrance, reminiscence, retention 2 <u>commemoration</u>, honour, remembrance

menace noun 1 <u>threat</u>, intimidation, warning 2 *Informal* <u>nuisance</u>, annoyance, pest, plague, troublemaker ♦ verb 3 <u>threaten</u>, bully, frighten, intimidate, loom, lour or lower, terrorize

menacing adjective <u>threatening</u>, forbidding, frightening, intimidating, looming, louring or lowering, ominous

mend verb 1 <u>repair</u>, darn, fix, patch, refit, renew, renovate, restore, retouch 2 <u>improve</u>, ameliorate, amend, correct, emend, rectify, reform, revise 3 <u>heal</u>, convalesce, get better, recover, recuperate ♦ noun 4 <u>repair</u>, darn, patch, stitch 5 **on the mend** <u>convalescent</u>, getting better, improving, recovering, recuperating

mendacious adjective <u>lying</u>, deceitful, deceptive, dishonest, duplicitous, fallacious, false, fraudulent, insincere, untruthful

menial adjective 1 <u>unskilled</u>, boring, dull, humdrum, low-status, routine ♦ noun 2 <u>servant</u>, attendant, dogsbody (informal), drudge, flunky, lackey, skivvy (chiefly Brit.), underling

mental adjective 1 <u>intellectual</u>, cerebral 2 Informal <u>insane</u>, deranged, disturbed, mad, mentally ill, psychotic, unbalanced, unstable

mentality noun <u>attitude</u>, cast of mind, character, disposition, make-up, outlook, personality, psychology

mentally adverb <u>in the mind</u>, in one's head, intellectually, inwardly, psychologically

mention verb 1 <u>refer to</u>, bring up, declare, disclose, divulge, intimate, point out, reveal, state, touch upon ♦ noun 2 <u>acknowledgment</u>, citation, recognition, tribute 3 <u>reference</u>, allusion, indication, observation, remark

mentor noun <u>guide</u>, adviser, coach, counsellor, guru, instructor, teacher, tutor

menu noun <u>bill of fare</u>, carte du jour, tariff (chiefly Brit.)

mercantile adjective <u>commercial</u>, trading

mercenary adjective 1 <u>greedy</u>, acquisitive, avaricious, grasping, money-grubbing (informal), sordid, venal ♦ noun 2 <u>hireling</u>, soldier of fortune

merchandise noun <u>goods</u>, commodities, produce, products, stock, wares

merchant noun <u>tradesman</u>, broker, dealer, purveyor, retailer, salesman, seller, shopkeeper, supplier, trader, trafficker, vendor, wholesaler

merciful adjective <u>compassionate</u>, clement, forgiving, generous, gracious, humane, kind, lenient, sparing, sympathetic, tender-hearted

merciless adjective <u>cruel</u>, barbarous, callous, hard-hearted, harsh, heartless, pitiless, ruthless, unforgiving

mercurial adjective <u>lively</u>, active, capricious, changeable, impulsive, irrepressible, mobile, quicksilver, spirited, sprightly, unpredictable, volatile

mercy noun 1 <u>compassion</u>, clemency, forbearance, forgiveness, grace, kindness, leniency, pity 2 <u>blessing</u>, boon, godsend

mere adjective <u>simple</u>, bare, common, nothing more than, plain, pure, sheer

meretricious adjective <u>trashy</u>, flashy, garish, gaudy, gimcrack, showy, tawdry, tinsel

merge verb <u>combine</u>,

amalgamate, blend, coalesce,
converge, fuse, join, meet,
mingle, mix, unite

merger noun <u>union</u>,
amalgamation, coalition,
combination, consolidation,
fusion, incorporation

merit noun **1** <u>worth</u>, advantage,
asset, excellence, goodness,
integrity, quality, strong point,
talent, value, virtue ♦ verb
2 <u>deserve</u>, be entitled to, be
worthy of, earn, have a right to,
rate, warrant

meritorious adjective
<u>praiseworthy</u>, admirable,
commendable, creditable,
deserving, excellent, good,
laudable, virtuous, worthy

merriment noun <u>fun</u>,
amusement, festivity, glee,
hilarity, jollity, joviality, laughter,
mirth, revelry

merry adjective **1** <u>cheerful</u>, blithe,
carefree, convivial, festive,
happy, jolly, joyous **2** Brit.
informal <u>tipsy</u>, happy, mellow,
squiffy (Brit. informal), tiddly
(slang, chiefly Brit.)

mesh noun **1** <u>net</u>, netting,
network, tracery, web ♦ verb
2 <u>engage</u>, combine, connect,
coordinate, dovetail, harmonize,
interlock, knit

mesmerize verb <u>entrance</u>,
captivate, enthral, fascinate, grip,
hold spellbound, hypnotize

mess noun **1** <u>disorder</u>, chaos,
clutter, confusion, disarray,
disorganization, hotchpotch,
jumble, litter, shambles,
untidiness **2** <u>difficulty</u>, deep
water, dilemma, fix (informal),
jam (informal), muddle, pickle

(informal), plight, predicament,
tight spot ♦ verb **3** often with **up**
<u>dirty</u>, clutter, disarrange,
dishevel, muck up (Brit. slang),
muddle, pollute, scramble
4 often with **with** <u>interfere</u>, fiddle
(informal), meddle, play, tamper,
tinker

mess about or **around** verb
<u>potter</u>, amuse oneself, dabble,
fool (about or around), muck
about (informal), play about or
around, trifle

message noun
1 <u>communication</u>, bulletin,
communiqué, dispatch, letter,
memorandum, note, tidings,
word **2** <u>point</u>, idea, import,
meaning, moral, purport, theme

messenger noun <u>courier</u>, carrier,
delivery boy, emissary, envoy,
errand-boy, go-between, herald,
runner

messy adjective <u>untidy</u>, chaotic,
cluttered, confused, dirty,
dishevelled, disordered,
disorganized, muddled,
shambolic, sloppy (informal)

metamorphosis noun
<u>transformation</u>, alteration,
change, conversion, mutation,
transmutation

metaphor noun <u>figure of speech</u>,
allegory, analogy, image,
symbol, trope

metaphorical adjective <u>figurative</u>,
allegorical, emblematic, symbolic

mete verb <u>distribute</u>, administer,
apportion, assign, deal, dispense,
dole, portion

meteoric adjective <u>spectacular</u>,
brilliant, dazzling, fast,
overnight, rapid, speedy,
sudden, swift

method noun 1 manner, approach, mode, modus operandi, procedure, process, routine, style, system, technique, way 2 orderliness, order, organization, pattern, planning, purpose, regularity, system

methodical adjective orderly, businesslike, deliberate, disciplined, meticulous, organized, precise, regular, structured, systematic

meticulous adjective thorough, exact, fastidious, fussy, painstaking, particular, precise, punctilious, scrupulous, strict

mettle noun courage, bravery, fortitude, gallantry, life, nerve, pluck, resolution, spirit, valour, vigour

microbe noun microorganism, bacillus, bacterium, bug (informal), germ, virus

microscopic adjective tiny, imperceptible, infinitesimal, invisible, minuscule, minute, negligible

midday noun noon, noonday, twelve o'clock

middle adjective 1 central, halfway, intermediate, intervening, mean, median, medium, mid ♦ noun 2 centre, focus, halfway point, heart, midpoint, midsection, midst

middle-class adjective bourgeois, conventional, traditional

middling adjective 1 mediocre, indifferent, run-of-the-mill, so-so (informal), tolerable, unexceptional, unremarkable 2 moderate, adequate, all right, average, fair, medium, modest, O.K. or okay (informal), ordinary, passable, serviceable

midget noun dwarf, pygmy or pigmy, shrimp (informal), Tom Thumb

midnight noun twelve o'clock, dead of night, middle of the night, the witching hour

midst noun in the midst of among, amidst, during, in the middle of, in the thick of, surrounded by

midway adjective, adverb halfway, betwixt and between, in the middle

might noun 1 power, energy, force, strength, vigour 2 with might and main forcefully, lustily, manfully, mightily, vigorously

mightily adverb 1 very, decidedly, exceedingly, extremely, greatly, highly, hugely, intensely, much 2 powerfully, energetically, forcefully, lustily, manfully, strongly, vigorously

mighty adjective powerful, forceful, lusty, robust, strapping, strong, sturdy, vigorous

migrant noun 1 wanderer, drifter, emigrant, immigrant, itinerant, nomad, rover, traveller ♦ adjective 2 travelling, drifting, immigrant, itinerant, migratory, nomadic, roving, shifting, transient, vagrant, wandering

migrate verb move, emigrate, journey, roam, rove, travel, trek, voyage, wander

migration noun wandering, emigration, journey, movement, roving, travel, trek, voyage

migratory adjective nomadic,

itinerant, migrant, peripatetic, roving, transient

mild adjective 1 <u>gentle</u>, calm, docile, easy-going, equable, meek, peaceable, placid 2 <u>bland</u>, smooth 3 <u>calm</u>, balmy, moderate, temperate, tranquil, warm

mildness noun <u>gentleness</u>, calmness, clemency, docility, moderation, placidity, tranquillity, warmth

milieu noun <u>surroundings</u>, background, element, environment, locale, location, scene, setting

militant adjective <u>aggressive</u>, active, assertive, combative, vigorous

military adjective 1 <u>warlike</u>, armed, martial, soldierly ◆ noun 2 <u>armed forces</u>, army, forces, services

militate verb **militate against** <u>counteract</u>, be detrimental to, conflict with, counter, oppose, resist, tell against, weigh against

milk verb <u>exploit</u>, extract, pump, take advantage of

mill noun 1 <u>factory</u>, foundry, plant, works 2 <u>grinder</u>, crusher ◆ verb 3 <u>grind</u>, crush, grate, pound, powder 4 <u>swarm</u>, crowd, throng

millstone noun 1 <u>grindstone</u>, quernstone 2 <u>burden</u>, affliction, albatross, encumbrance, load, weight

mime verb <u>act out</u>, gesture, represent, simulate

mimic verb 1 <u>imitate</u>, ape, caricature, do (informal), impersonate, parody, take off

(informal) ◆ noun 2 <u>imitator</u>, caricaturist, copycat (informal), impersonator, impressionist

mimicry noun <u>imitation</u>, burlesque, caricature, impersonation, mimicking, mockery, parody, take-off (informal)

mince verb 1 <u>cut</u>, chop, crumble, grind, hash 2 As in **mince one's words** <u>tone down</u>, moderate, soften, spare, weaken

mincing adjective <u>affected</u>, camp (informal), dainty, effeminate, foppish, precious, pretentious, sissy

mind noun 1 <u>intelligence</u>, brain(s) (informal), grey matter (informal), intellect, reason, sense, understanding, wits 2 <u>memory</u>, recollection, remembrance 3 <u>intention</u>, desire, disposition, fancy, inclination, leaning, notion, urge, wish 4 <u>sanity</u>, judgment, marbles (informal), mental balance, rationality, reason, senses, wits 5 **make up one's mind** <u>decide</u>, choose, determine, resolve ◆ verb 6 **take offence**, be affronted, be bothered, care, disapprove, dislike, object, resent 7 <u>pay attention</u>, heed, listen to, mark, note, obey, observe, pay heed to, take heed 8 <u>guard</u>, attend to, keep an eye on, look after, take care of, tend, watch 9 <u>be careful</u>, be cautious, be on (one's) guard, be wary, take care, watch

mindful adjective <u>aware</u>, alert, alive to, careful, conscious, heedful, wary, watchful

mindless adjective <u>stupid</u>, foolish,

idiotic, inane, moronic, thoughtless, unthinking, witless

mine noun **1** pit, colliery, deposit, excavation, shaft **2** source, abundance, fund, hoard, reserve, stock, store, supply, treasury, wealth ♦ verb **3** dig up, dig for, excavate, extract, hew, quarry, unearth

miner noun coalminer, collier (Brit.), pitman (Brit.)

mingle verb **1** mix, blend, combine, intermingle, interweave, join, merge, unite **2** associate, consort, fraternize, hang about or around, hobnob, rub shoulders (informal), socialize

miniature adjective small, diminutive, little, minuscule, minute, scaled-down, tiny, toy

minimal adjective minimum, least, least possible, nominal, slightest, smallest, token

minimize verb **1** reduce, curtail, decrease, diminish, miniaturize, prune, shrink **2** play down, belittle, decry, deprecate, discount, disparage, make light or little of, underrate

minimum adjective **1** least, least possible, lowest, minimal, slightest, smallest ♦ noun **2** least, lowest, nadir

minion noun follower, flunky, hanger-on, henchman, hireling, lackey, underling, yes man

minister noun **1** clergyman, cleric, parson, pastor, preacher, priest, rector, vicar ♦ verb **2** attend, administer, cater to, pander to, serve, take care of, tend

ministry noun **1** department,

bureau, council, office, quango **2** the priesthood, holy orders, the church

minor adjective small, inconsequential, insignificant, lesser, petty, slight, trivial, unimportant

minstrel noun musician, bard, singer, songstress, troubadour

mint verb make, cast, coin, produce, punch, stamp, strike

minuscule adjective tiny, diminutive, infinitesimal, little, microscopic, miniature, minute

minute[1] noun moment, flash, instant, jiffy (informal), second, tick (Brit. informal), trice

minute[2] adjective **1** small, diminutive, infinitesimal, little, microscopic, miniature, minuscule, tiny **2** precise, close, critical, detailed, exact, exhaustive, meticulous, painstaking, punctilious

minutes plural noun record, memorandum, notes, proceedings, transactions, transcript

minutiae plural noun details, finer points, ins and outs, niceties, particulars, subtleties, trifles, trivia

minx noun flirt, coquette, hussy

miracle noun wonder, marvel, phenomenon, prodigy

miraculous adjective wonderful, amazing, astonishing, astounding, extraordinary, incredible, phenomenal, prodigious, unaccountable, unbelievable

mirage noun illusion, hallucination, optical illusion

mire noun **1** swamp, bog, marsh,

morass, quagmire **2** <u>mud</u>, dirt, muck, ooze, slime

mirror *noun* **1** <u>looking-glass</u>, glass, reflector ♦ *verb* **2** <u>reflect</u>, copy, echo, emulate, follow

mirth *noun* <u>merriment</u>, amusement, cheerfulness, fun, gaiety, glee, hilarity, jollity, joviality, laughter, revelry

mirthful *adjective* <u>merry</u>, blithe, cheerful, cheery, festive, happy, jolly, jovial, light-hearted, playful, sportive

misadventure *noun* <u>misfortune</u>, accident, bad luck, calamity, catastrophe, debacle, disaster, mishap, reverse, setback

misanthropic *adjective* <u>antisocial</u>, cynical, malevolent, unfriendly

misapprehend *verb* <u>misunderstand</u>, misconstrue, misinterpret, misread, mistake

misapprehension *noun* <u>misunderstanding</u>, delusion, error, fallacy, misconception, misinterpretation, mistake

misappropriate *verb* <u>steal</u>, embezzle, misspend, misuse, peculate, pocket

miscalculate *verb* <u>misjudge</u>, blunder, err, overestimate, overrate, slip up, underestimate, underrate

miscarriage *noun* <u>failure</u>, breakdown, error, mishap, perversion

miscarry *verb* <u>fail</u>, come to grief, fall through, go awry, go wrong, misfire

miscellaneous *adjective* <u>mixed</u>, assorted, diverse, jumbled, motley, sundry, varied, various

miscellany *noun* <u>assortment</u>, anthology, collection, hotchpotch, jumble, medley, *mélange*, mixed bag, mixture, potpourri, variety

mischance *noun* <u>misfortune</u>, accident, calamity, disaster, misadventure, mishap

mischief *noun* **1** <u>trouble</u>, impishness, misbehaviour, monkey business (*informal*), naughtiness, shenanigans (*informal*), waywardness **2** <u>harm</u>, damage, evil, hurt, injury, misfortune, trouble

mischievous *adjective* **1** <u>naughty</u>, impish, playful, puckish, rascally, roguish, sportive, troublesome, wayward **2** <u>malicious</u>, damaging, destructive, evil, harmful, hurtful, spiteful, vicious, wicked

misconception *noun* <u>delusion</u>, error, fallacy, misapprehension, misunderstanding

misconduct *noun* <u>immorality</u>, impropriety, malpractice, mismanagement, wrongdoing

miscreant *noun* <u>wrongdoer</u>, blackguard, criminal, rascal, reprobate, rogue, scoundrel, sinner, vagabond, villain

misdeed *noun* <u>offence</u>, crime, fault, misconduct, misdemeanour, sin, transgression, wrong

misdemeanour *noun* <u>offence</u>, fault, infringement, misdeed, peccadillo, transgression

miser *noun* <u>skinflint</u>, cheapskate (*informal*), niggard, penny-pincher (*informal*), Scrooge

miserable *adjective* **1** <u>unhappy</u>, dejected, depressed, despondent, disconsolate, forlorn, gloomy, sorrowful, woebegone, wretched **2** <u>squalid</u>, deplorable, lamentable, shameful, sordid, sorry, wretched

miserly adjective <u>mean</u>, avaricious, grasping, niggardly, parsimonious, penny-pinching (*informal*), stingy, tightfisted, ungenerous

misery noun **1** <u>unhappiness</u>, anguish, depression, desolation, despair, distress, gloom, grief, sorrow, suffering, torment, woe **2** *Brit. informal* <u>moaner</u>, killjoy, pessimist, prophet of doom, sourpuss (*informal*), spoilsport, wet blanket (*informal*)

misfire verb <u>fail</u>, fall through, go wrong, miscarry

misfit noun <u>nonconformist</u>, eccentric, fish out of water (*informal*), oddball (*informal*), square peg (in a round hole) (*informal*)

misfortune noun **1** <u>bad luck</u>, adversity, hard luck, ill luck, infelicity **2** <u>mishap</u>, affliction, calamity, disaster, reverse, setback, tragedy, tribulation, trouble

misgiving noun <u>unease</u>, anxiety, apprehension, distrust, doubt, qualm, reservation, suspicion, trepidation, uncertainty, worry

misguided adjective <u>unwise</u>, deluded, erroneous, ill-advised, imprudent, injudicious, misplaced, mistaken, unwarranted

mishandle verb <u>mismanage</u>, botch, bungle, make a mess of, mess up (*informal*), muff

mishap noun <u>accident</u>, calamity,

misadventure, mischance, misfortune

misinform verb <u>mislead</u>, deceive, misdirect, misguide

misinterpret verb <u>misunderstand</u>, distort, misapprehend, misconceive, misconstrue, misjudge, misread, misrepresent, mistake

misjudge verb <u>miscalculate</u>, overestimate, overrate, underestimate, underrate

mislay verb <u>lose</u>, lose track of, misplace

mislead verb <u>deceive</u>, delude, fool, hoodwink, misdirect, misguide, misinform, take in (*informal*)

misleading adjective <u>confusing</u>, ambiguous, deceptive, disingenuous, evasive, false

mismanage verb <u>mishandle</u>, botch, bungle, make a mess of, mess up, misconduct, misdirect, misgovern

misplace verb <u>lose</u>, lose track of, mislay

misprint noun <u>mistake</u>, corrigendum, erratum, literal, typo (*informal*)

misquote verb <u>misrepresent</u>, falsify, twist

misrepresent verb <u>distort</u>, disguise, falsify, misinterpret

misrule noun <u>disorder</u>, anarchy, chaos, confusion, lawlessness, turmoil

miss verb **1** <u>omit</u>, leave out, let go, overlook, pass over, skip **2** <u>avoid</u>, escape, evade **3** <u>long for</u>, pine for, yearn for ♦ *noun* **4** <u>mistake</u>, blunder, error, failure, omission, oversight

misshapen *adjective* <u>deformed</u>, contorted, crooked, distorted, grotesque, malformed, twisted, warped

missile *noun* <u>rocket</u>, projectile, weapon

missing *adjective* <u>absent</u>, astray, lacking, left out, lost, mislaid, misplaced, unaccounted-for

mission *noun* <u>task</u>, assignment, commission, duty, errand, job, quest, undertaking, vocation

missionary *noun* <u>evangelist</u>, apostle, preacher

missive *noun* <u>letter</u>, communication, dispatch, epistle, memorandum, message, note, report

misspent *adjective* <u>wasted</u>, dissipated, imprudent, profitless, squandered

mist *noun* <u>fog</u>, cloud, film, haze, smog, spray, steam, vapour

mistake *noun* 1 <u>error</u>, blunder, erratum, fault, faux pas, gaffe, howler (*informal*), miscalculation, oversight, slip ♦ *verb* 2 <u>misunderstand</u>, misapprehend, misconstrue, misinterpret, misjudge, misread 3 <u>confuse with</u>, mix up with, take for

mistaken *adjective* <u>wrong</u>, erroneous, false, faulty, inaccurate, incorrect, misguided, unsound, wide of the mark

mistakenly *adverb* <u>incorrectly</u>, by mistake, erroneously, fallaciously, falsely, inaccurately, misguidedly, wrongly

mistimed *adjective* <u>inopportune</u>, badly timed, ill-timed, untimely

mistreat *verb* <u>abuse</u>, harm, ill-treat, injure, knock about or around, maltreat, manhandle, misuse, molest

mistress *noun* <u>lover</u>, concubine, girlfriend, kept woman, paramour

mistrust *verb* 1 <u>doubt</u>, be wary of, distrust, fear, suspect ♦ *noun* 2 <u>suspicion</u>, distrust, doubt, misgiving, scepticism, uncertainty, wariness

mistrustful *adjective* <u>suspicious</u>, chary, cynical, distrustful, doubtful, fearful, hesitant, sceptical, uncertain, wary

misty *adjective* <u>foggy</u>, blurred, cloudy, dim, hazy, indistinct, murky, obscure, opaque, overcast

misunderstand *verb* <u>misinterpret</u>, be at cross-purposes, get the wrong end of the stick, misapprehend, misconstrue, misjudge, misread, mistake

misunderstanding *noun* <u>mistake</u>, error, misconception, misinterpretation, misjudgment, mix-up

misuse *noun* 1 <u>waste</u>, abuse, desecration, misapplication, squandering ♦ *verb* 2 <u>waste</u>, abuse, desecrate, misapply, prostitute, squander

mitigate *verb* <u>ease</u>, extenuate, lessen, lighten, moderate, soften, subdue, temper

mitigation *noun* <u>relief</u>, alleviation, diminution, extenuation, moderation, remission

mix *verb* 1 <u>combine</u>, blend, cross, fuse, intermingle, interweave, join, jumble, merge, mingle 2 <u>socialize</u>, associate, consort, fraternize, hang out (*informal*),

hobnob, mingle ♦ *noun*
3 <u>mixture</u>, alloy, amalgam,
assortment, blend, combination,
compound, fusion, medley

mixed *adjective* **1** <u>combined</u>,
amalgamated, blended,
composite, compound, joint,
mingled, united **2** <u>varied</u>,
assorted, cosmopolitan, diverse,
heterogeneous, miscellaneous,
motley

mixed-up *adjective* <u>confused</u>, at
sea, bewildered, distraught,
disturbed, maladjusted,
muddled, perplexed, puzzled,
upset

mixture *noun* <u>blend</u>, amalgam,
assortment, brew, compound,
fusion, jumble, medley, mix,
potpourri, variety

mix-up *noun* <u>confusion</u>, mess,
mistake, misunderstanding,
muddle, tangle

mix up *verb* **1** <u>combine</u>, blend,
mix **2** <u>confuse</u>, confound,
muddle

moan *noun* **1** <u>groan</u>, lament,
sigh, sob, wail, whine **2** *Informal*
<u>grumble</u>, complaint, gripe
(*informal*), grouch (*informal*),
grouse, protest, whine ♦ *verb*
3 <u>groan</u>, lament, sigh, sob,
whine **4** *Informal* <u>grumble</u>, bleat,
carp, complain, groan, grouse,
whine, whinge (*informal*)

mob *noun* **1** <u>crowd</u>, drove, flock,
horde, host, mass, multitude,
pack, swarm, throng **2** *Slang*
<u>gang</u>, crew (*informal*), group, lot,
set ♦ *verb* **3** <u>surround</u>, crowd
around, jostle, set upon, swarm
around

mobile *adjective* <u>movable</u>,
itinerant, moving, peripatetic,

portable, travelling, wandering

mobilize *verb* <u>prepare</u>, activate,
call to arms, call up, get *or* make
ready, marshal, organize, rally,
ready

mock *verb* **1** <u>laugh at</u>, deride,
jeer, make fun of, poke fun at,
ridicule, scoff, scorn, sneer,
taunt, tease **2** <u>mimic</u>, ape,
caricature, imitate, lampoon,
parody, satirize, send up (*Brit.
informal*) ♦ *adjective* **3** <u>imitation</u>,
artificial, dummy, fake, false,
feigned, phoney *or* phony
(*informal*), pretended, sham,
spurious

mockery *noun* **1** <u>derision</u>,
contempt, disdain, disrespect,
insults, jeering, ridicule, scoffing,
scorn **2** <u>farce</u>, apology (*informal*),
disappointment, joke, letdown

mocking *adjective* <u>scornful</u>,
contemptuous, derisive,
disdainful, disrespectful,
sarcastic, sardonic, satirical,
scoffing

mode *noun* **1** <u>method</u>, form,
manner, procedure, process,
style, system, technique, way
2 <u>fashion</u>, craze, look, rage,
style, trend, vogue

model *noun* **1** <u>representation</u>,
copy, dummy, facsimile, image,
imitation, miniature, mock-up,
replica **2** <u>pattern</u>, archetype,
example, ideal, original,
paradigm, paragon, prototype,
standard **3** <u>sitter</u>, poser, subject
♦ *verb* **4** <u>shape</u>, carve, design,
fashion, form, mould, sculpt
5 <u>show off</u>, display, sport
(*informal*), wear

moderate *adjective* **1** <u>mild</u>,
controlled, gentle, limited,

middle-of-the-road, modest, reasonable, restrained, steady **2** average, fair, indifferent, mediocre, middling, ordinary, passable, so-so (*informal*), unexceptional ♦ *verb* **3** regulate, control, curb, ease, modulate, restrain, soften, subdue, temper, tone down

moderately *adverb* reasonably, fairly, passably, quite, rather, slightly, somewhat, tolerably

moderation *noun* restraint, fairness, reasonableness, temperance

modern *adjective* current, contemporary, fresh, new, newfangled, novel, present-day, recent, up-to-date

modernity *noun* novelty, currency, freshness, innovation, newness

modernize *verb* update, make over, rejuvenate, remake, remodel, renew, renovate, revamp

modest *adjective* **1** unpretentious, bashful, coy, demure, diffident, reserved, reticent, retiring, self-effacing, shy **2** moderate, fair, limited, middling, ordinary, small, unexceptional

modesty *noun* reserve, bashfulness, coyness, demureness, diffidence, humility, reticence, shyness, timidity

modicum *noun* little, bit, crumb, drop, fragment, scrap, shred, touch

modification *noun* change, adjustment, alteration, qualification, refinement, revision, variation

modify *verb* **1** change, adapt, adjust, alter, convert, reform, remodel, revise, rework **2** tone down, ease, lessen, lower, moderate, qualify, restrain, soften, temper

modish *adjective* fashionable, contemporary, current, in, smart, stylish, trendy (*Brit. informal*), up-to-the-minute, voguish

modulate *verb* adjust, attune, balance, regulate, tune, vary

mogul *noun* tycoon, baron, big noise (*informal*), big shot (*informal*), magnate, V.I.P.

moist *adjective* damp, clammy, dewy, humid, soggy, wet

moisten *verb* dampen, damp, moisturize, soak, water, wet

moisture *noun* damp, dew, liquid, water, wetness

molecule *noun* particle, jot, speck

molest *verb* **1** annoy, badger, beset, bother, disturb, harass, persecute, pester, plague, torment, worry **2** abuse, attack, harm, hurt, ill-treat, interfere with, maltreat

mollify *verb* pacify, appease, calm, conciliate, placate, quiet, soothe, sweeten

mollycoddle *verb* pamper, baby, cosset, indulge, spoil

moment *noun* **1** instant, flash, jiffy (*informal*), second, split second, trice, twinkling **2** time, juncture, point, stage

momentarily *adverb* briefly, for a moment, temporarily

momentary *adjective* short-lived, brief, fleeting, passing, short, temporary, transitory

momentous *adjective* significant, critical, crucial, fateful, historic, important, pivotal, vital, weighty

momentum *noun* impetus, drive, energy, force, power, propulsion, push, strength, thrust

monarch *noun* ruler, emperor *or* empress, king, potentate, prince *or* princess, queen, sovereign

monarchy *noun* **1** sovereignty, autocracy, kingship, monocracy, royalism **2** kingdom, empire, principality, realm

monastery *noun* abbey, cloister, convent, friary, nunnery, priory

monastic *adjective* monkish, ascetic, cloistered, contemplative, hermit-like, reclusive, secluded, sequestered, withdrawn

monetary *adjective* financial, budgetary, capital, cash, fiscal, pecuniary

money *noun* cash, capital, coin, currency, hard cash, legal tender, readies (*informal*), riches, silver, wealth

mongrel *noun* **1** hybrid, cross, crossbreed, half-breed ♦ *adjective* **2** hybrid, crossbred

monitor *noun* **1** watchdog, guide, invigilator, prefect (*Brit.*), supervisor ♦ *verb* **2** check, follow, keep an eye on, keep tabs on, keep track of, observe, survey, watch

monk *noun* friar, brother

monkey *noun* **1** simian, primate **2** rascal, devil, imp, rogue, scamp ♦ *verb* **3** fool, meddle, mess, play, tinker

monolithic *adjective* huge, colossal, impenetrable, intractable, massive, monumental, solid

monologue *noun* speech, harangue, lecture, sermon, soliloquy

monopolize *verb* control, corner the market in, dominate, hog (*slang*), keep to oneself, take over

monotonous *adjective* tedious, boring, dull, humdrum, mind-numbing, repetitive, tiresome, unchanging, wearisome

monotony *noun* tedium, boredom, monotonousness, repetitiveness, routine, sameness, tediousness

monster *noun* **1** brute, beast, demon, devil, fiend, villain **2** freak, monstrosity, mutant **3** giant, colossus, mammoth, titan ♦ *adjective* **4** huge, colossal, enormous, gigantic, immense, mammoth, massive, stupendous, tremendous

monstrosity *noun* eyesore, freak, horror, monster

monstrous *adjective* **1** unnatural, fiendish, freakish, frightful, grotesque, gruesome, hideous, horrible **2** outrageous, diabolical, disgraceful, foul, inhuman, intolerable, scandalous, shocking **3** huge, colossal, enormous, immense, mammoth, massive, prodigious, stupendous, tremendous

monument *noun* memorial, cairn, cenotaph, commemoration, gravestone, headstone, marker, mausoleum, shrine, tombstone

monumental *adjective* **1** important, awesome, enormous, epoch-making,

historic, majestic, memorable, significant, unforgettable
2 *Informal* immense, colossal, great, massive, staggering

mood *noun* state of mind, disposition, frame of mind, humour, spirit, temper

moody *adjective* **1** sullen, gloomy, glum, ill-tempered, irritable, morose, sad, sulky, temperamental, touchy
2 changeable, capricious, erratic, fickle, flighty, impulsive, mercurial, temperamental, unpredictable, volatile

moon *noun* **1** satellite ♦ *verb*
2 idle, daydream, languish, mope, waste time

moor[1] *noun* moorland, fell (*Brit.*), heath

moor[2] *verb* tie up, anchor, berth, dock, lash, make fast, secure

moot *adjective* **1** debatable, arguable, contestable, controversial, disputable, doubtful, undecided, unresolved, unsettled ♦ *verb* **2** bring up, broach, propose, put forward, suggest

mop *noun* **1** squeegee, sponge, swab **2** mane, shock, tangle, thatch

mope *verb* brood, fret, languish, moon, pine, pout, sulk

mop up *verb* clean up, soak up, sponge, swab, wash, wipe

moral *adjective* **1** good, decent, ethical, high-minded, honourable, just, noble, principled, right, virtuous ♦ *noun*
2 lesson, meaning, message, point, significance

morale *noun* confidence, esprit

de corps, heart, self-esteem, spirit

morality *noun* **1** integrity, decency, goodness, honesty, justice, righteousness, virtue
2 standards, conduct, ethics, manners, morals, mores, philosophy, principles

morals *plural noun* morality, behaviour, conduct, ethics, habits, integrity, manners, mores, principles, scruples, standards

morass *noun* **1** marsh, bog, fen, quagmire, slough, swamp
2 mess, confusion, mix-up, muddle, tangle

moratorium *noun* postponement, freeze, halt, standstill, suspension

morbid *adjective* **1** unwholesome, ghoulish, gloomy, melancholy, sick, sombre, unhealthy
2 gruesome, dreadful, ghastly, grisly, hideous, horrid, macabre

mordant *adjective* sarcastic, biting, caustic, cutting, incisive, pungent, scathing, stinging, trenchant

more *adjective* **1** extra, added, additional, further, new, other, supplementary ♦ *adverb* **2** to a greater extent, better, further, longer

moreover *adverb* furthermore, additionally, also, as well, besides, further, in addition, too

morgue *noun* mortuary

moribund *adjective* declining, on its last legs, stagnant, waning, weak

morning *noun* dawn, a.m., break of day, daybreak, forenoon, morn (*poetic*), sunrise

moron noun <u>fool</u>, blockhead, cretin, dunce, dunderhead, halfwit, idiot, imbecile, oaf

moronic adjective <u>idiotic</u>, cretinous, foolish, halfwitted, imbecilic, mindless, stupid, unintelligent

morose adjective <u>sullen</u>, depressed, dour, gloomy, glum, ill-tempered, moody, sour, sulky, surly, taciturn

morsel noun <u>piece</u>, bit, bite, crumb, mouthful, part, scrap, soupçon, taste, titbit

mortal adjective 1 <u>human</u>, ephemeral, impermanent, passing, temporal, transient, worldly 2 <u>fatal</u>, deadly, death-dealing, destructive, killing, lethal, murderous, terminal ♦ noun 3 <u>human being</u>, being, earthling, human, individual, man, person, woman

mortality noun 1 <u>humanity</u>, impermanence, transience 2 <u>killing</u>, bloodshed, carnage, death, destruction, fatality

mortification noun 1 <u>humiliation</u>, annoyance, chagrin, discomfiture, embarrassment, shame, vexation 2 <u>discipline</u>, abasement, chastening, control, denial, subjugation 3 Medical <u>gangrene</u>, corruption, festering

mortified adjective <u>humiliated</u>, ashamed, chagrined, chastened, crushed, deflated, embarrassed, humbled, shamed

mortify verb 1 <u>humiliate</u>, chagrin, chasten, crush, deflate, embarrass, humble, shame 2 <u>discipline</u>, abase, chasten, control, deny, subdue 3 Of flesh

putrefy, deaden, die, fester

mortuary noun <u>morgue</u>, funeral parlour

mostly adverb <u>generally</u>, as a rule, chiefly, largely, mainly, on the whole, predominantly, primarily, principally, usually

moth-eaten adjective <u>decayed</u>, decrepit, dilapidated, ragged, shabby, tattered, threadbare, worn-out

mother noun 1 <u>parent</u>, dam, ma (informal), mater, mum (Brit. informal), mummy (Brit. informal) ♦ adjective 2 <u>native</u>, inborn, innate, natural ♦ verb 3 <u>nurture</u>, care for, cherish, nurse, protect, raise, rear, tend

motherly adjective <u>maternal</u>, affectionate, caring, comforting, loving, protective, sheltering

motif noun 1 <u>theme</u>, concept, idea, leitmotif, subject 2 <u>design</u>, decoration, ornament, shape

motion noun 1 <u>movement</u>, flow, locomotion, mobility, move, progress, travel 2 <u>proposal</u>, proposition, recommendation, submission, suggestion ♦ verb 3 <u>gesture</u>, beckon, direct, gesticulate, nod, signal, wave

motionless adjective <u>still</u>, fixed, frozen, immobile, paralysed, standing, static, stationary, stock-still, transfixed, unmoving

motivate verb <u>inspire</u>, arouse, cause, drive, induce, move, persuade, prompt, stimulate, stir

motivation noun <u>incentive</u>, incitement, inducement, inspiration, motive, reason, spur, stimulus

motive noun <u>reason</u>, ground(s),

incentive, inducement,
inspiration, object, purpose,
rationale, stimulus

motley *adjective* **1** <u>miscellaneous</u>,
assorted, disparate,
heterogeneous, mixed, varied
2 <u>multicoloured</u>, chequered,
variegated

mottled *adjective* <u>blotchy</u>,
dappled, flecked, piebald,
speckled, spotted, stippled,
streaked

motto *noun* <u>saying</u>, adage,
dictum, maxim, precept,
proverb, rule, slogan, watchword

mould¹ *noun* **1** <u>cast</u>, pattern,
shape **2** <u>design</u>, build,
construction, fashion, form,
format, kind, pattern, shape,
style **3** <u>nature</u>, calibre, character,
kind, quality, sort, stamp, type
♦ *verb* **4** <u>shape</u>, construct, create,
fashion, forge, form, make,
model, sculpt, work **5** <u>influence</u>,
affect, control, direct, form,
make, shape

mould² *noun* <u>fungus</u>, blight,
mildew

mouldy *adjective* <u>stale</u>, bad,
blighted, decaying, fusty,
mildewed, musty, rotten

mound *noun* **1** <u>heap</u>, drift, pile,
rick, stack **2** <u>hill</u>, bank, dune,
embankment, hillock, knoll, rise

mount *verb* **1** <u>climb</u>, ascend,
clamber up, go up, scale
2 <u>bestride</u>, climb onto, jump on
3 <u>increase</u>, accumulate, build,
escalate, grow, intensify,
multiply, pile up, swell ♦ *noun*
4 <u>backing</u>, base, frame, setting,
stand, support **5** <u>horse</u>, steed
(*literary*)

mountain *noun* **1** <u>peak</u>, alp, fell

(*Brit.*), mount **2** <u>heap</u>,
abundance, mass, mound, pile,
stack, ton

mountainous *adjective* **1** <u>high</u>,
alpine, highland, rocky, soaring,
steep, towering, upland **2** <u>huge</u>,
daunting, enormous, gigantic,
great, immense, mammoth,
mighty, monumental

mourn *verb* <u>grieve</u>, bemoan,
bewail, deplore, lament, rue,
wail, weep

mournful *adjective* **1** <u>sad</u>,
melancholy, piteous, plaintive,
sorrowful, tragic, unhappy,
woeful **2** <u>dismal</u>, disconsolate,
downcast, gloomy, grieving,
heavy-hearted, lugubrious,
miserable, rueful, sombre

mourning *noun* **1** <u>grieving</u>,
bereavement, grief, lamentation,
weeping, woe **2** <u>black</u>, sackcloth
and ashes, widow's weeds

mouth *noun* **1** <u>lips</u>, gob (*slang,
especially Brit.*), jaws, maw
2 <u>opening</u>, aperture, door,
entrance, gateway, inlet, orifice

mouthful *noun* <u>taste</u>, bit, bite,
little, morsel, sample, spoonful,
swallow

mouthpiece *noun* <u>spokesperson</u>,
agent, delegate, representative,
spokesman *or* spokeswoman

movable *adjective* <u>portable</u>,
detachable, mobile, transferable,
transportable

move *verb* **1** <u>go</u>, advance,
budge, proceed, progress, shift,
stir **2** <u>change</u>, shift, switch,
transfer, transpose **3** <u>leave</u>,
migrate, pack one's bags
(*informal*), quit, relocate, remove
4 <u>drive</u>, activate, operate,
propel, shift, start, turn **5** <u>touch</u>,

affect, excite, impress **6** <u>incite</u>, cause, induce, influence, inspire, motivate, persuade, prompt, rouse **7** <u>propose</u>, advocate, put forward, recommend, suggest, urge ♦ *noun* **8** <u>action</u>, manoeuvre, measure, ploy, step, stratagem, stroke, turn **9** <u>transfer</u>, relocation, removal, shift

movement *noun* **1** <u>motion</u>, action, activity, change, development, flow, manoeuvre, progress, stirring **2** <u>group</u>, campaign, crusade, drive, faction, front, grouping, organization, party **3** <u>workings</u>, action, machinery, mechanism, works **4** *Music* <u>section</u>, division, part, passage

movie *noun* <u>film</u>, feature, flick (*slang*), picture

moving *adjective* **1** <u>emotional</u>, affecting, inspiring, pathetic, persuasive, poignant, stirring, touching **2** <u>mobile</u>, movable, portable, running, unfixed

mow *verb* <u>cut</u>, crop, scythe, shear, trim

mow down *verb* <u>massacre</u>, butcher, cut down, cut to pieces, shoot down, slaughter

much *adjective* **1** <u>great</u>, abundant, a lot of, ample, considerable, copious, plenty of, sizable *or* sizeable, substantial ♦ *noun* **2** <u>a lot</u>, a good deal, a great deal, heaps (*informal*), loads (*informal*), lots (*informal*), plenty ♦ *adverb* **3** <u>greatly</u>, a great deal, a lot, considerably, decidedly, exceedingly

muck *noun* **1** <u>manure</u>, dung, ordure **2** <u>dirt</u>, filth, gunge

(*informal*), mire, mud, ooze, slime, sludge

muck up *verb* <u>ruin</u>, blow (*slang*), botch, bungle, make a mess of, make a pig's ear of (*informal*), mess up, muff, spoil

mucky *adjective* <u>dirty</u>, begrimed, filthy, grimy, messy, muddy

mud *noun* <u>dirt</u>, clay, mire, ooze, silt, slime, sludge

muddle *verb* **1** <u>jumble</u>, disarrange, disorder, disorganize, mess, scramble, spoil, tangle **2** <u>confuse</u>, befuddle, bewilder, confound, daze, disorient, perplex, stupefy ♦ *noun* **3** <u>confusion</u>, chaos, disarray, disorder, disorganization, jumble, mess, mix-up, predicament, tangle

muddy *adjective* **1** <u>dirty</u>, bespattered, grimy, mucky, mud-caked, soiled **2** <u>boggy</u>, marshy, quaggy, swampy

muffle *verb* **1** <u>wrap up</u>, cloak, cover, envelop, shroud, swaddle, swathe **2** <u>deaden</u>, muzzle, quieten, silence, soften, stifle, suppress

muffled *adjective* <u>indistinct</u>, faint, muted, stifled, strangled, subdued, suppressed

mug[1] *noun* <u>cup</u>, beaker, pot, tankard

mug[2] *noun* <u>face</u>, countenance, features, visage **1** <u>fool</u>, chump (*informal*), easy *or* soft touch (*slang*), simpleton, sucker (*slang*) ♦ *verb* **2** <u>attack</u>, assault, beat up, rob, set about *or* upon

muggy *adjective* <u>humid</u>, clammy, close, moist, oppressive, sticky, stuffy, sultry

mug up verb study, bone up on (*informal*), burn the midnight oil (*informal*), cram (*informal*), swot (*Brit. informal*)

mull verb ponder, consider, contemplate, deliberate, meditate, reflect on, ruminate, think over, weigh

multifarious adjective diverse, different, legion, manifold, many, miscellaneous, multiple, numerous, sundry, varied

multiple adjective many, manifold, multitudinous, numerous, several, sundry, various

multiply verb 1 increase, build up, expand, extend, proliferate, spread 2 reproduce, breed, propagate

multitude noun mass, army, crowd, horde, host, mob, myriad, swarm, throng

munch verb chew, champ, chomp, crunch

mundane adjective 1 ordinary, banal, commonplace, day-to-day, everyday, humdrum, prosaic, routine, workaday 2 earthly, mortal, secular, temporal, terrestrial, worldly

municipal adjective civic, public, urban

municipality noun town, borough, city, district, township

munificence noun generosity, beneficence, benevolence, bounty, largesse or largess, liberality, magnanimousness, philanthropy

munificent adjective generous, beneficent, benevolent, bountiful, lavish, liberal, magnanimous, open-handed, philanthropic, unstinting

murder noun 1 killing, assassination, bloodshed, butchery, carnage, homicide, manslaughter, massacre, slaying ♦ verb 2 kill, assassinate, bump off (*slang*), butcher, eliminate (*slang*), massacre, slaughter, slay

murderer noun killer, assassin, butcher, cut-throat, hit man (*slang*), homicide, slaughterer, slayer

murderous adjective deadly, bloodthirsty, brutal, cruel, cut-throat, ferocious, lethal, savage

murky adjective dark, cloudy, dim, dull, gloomy, grey, misty, overcast

murmur verb 1 mumble, mutter, whisper 2 grumble, complain, moan (*informal*) ♦ noun 3 drone, buzzing, humming, purr, rumble, whisper

muscle noun 1 tendon, sinew 2 strength, brawn, clout (*informal*), forcefulness, might, power, stamina, weight ♦ verb 3 **muscle in** Informal impose oneself, butt in, force one's way in

muscular adjective strong, athletic, powerful, robust, sinewy, strapping, sturdy, vigorous

muse verb ponder, brood, cogitate, consider, contemplate, deliberate, meditate, mull over, reflect, ruminate

mushy adjective 1 soft, pulpy, semi-solid, slushy, squashy, squelchy, squidgy (*informal*) 2 Informal sentimental, maudlin, mawkish, saccharine, schmaltzy (*slang*), sloppy (*informal*), slushy (*informal*)

musical *adjective* <u>melodious</u>, dulcet, euphonious, harmonious, lyrical, melodic, sweet-sounding, tuneful

must *noun* <u>necessity</u>, essential, fundamental, imperative, prerequisite, requirement, requisite, sine qua non

muster *verb* 1 <u>assemble</u>, call together, convene, gather, marshal, mobilize, rally, summon ♦ *noun* 2 <u>assembly</u>, collection, congregation, convention, gathering, meeting, rally, roundup

musty *adjective* <u>stale</u>, airless, dank, fusty, mildewed, mouldy, old, smelly, stuffy

mutability *noun* <u>change</u>, alteration, evolution, metamorphosis, transition, variation, vicissitude

mutable *adjective* <u>changeable</u>, adaptable, alterable, fickle, inconsistent, inconstant, unsettled, unstable, variable, volatile

mutation *noun* <u>change</u>, alteration, evolution, metamorphosis, modification, transfiguration, transformation, variation

mute *adjective* <u>silent</u>, dumb, mum, speechless, unspoken, voiceless, wordless

mutilate *verb* 1 <u>maim</u>, amputate, cut up, damage, disfigure, dismember, injure, lacerate, mangle 2 <u>distort</u>, adulterate, bowdlerize, censor, cut, damage, expurgate

mutinous *adjective* <u>rebellious</u>, disobedient, insubordinate, insurgent, refractory, riotous, subversive, unmanageable, unruly

mutiny *noun* 1 <u>rebellion</u>, disobedience, insubordination, insurrection, revolt, revolution, riot, uprising ♦ *verb* 2 <u>rebel</u>, disobey, resist, revolt, rise up

mutter *verb* <u>grumble</u>, complain, grouse, mumble, murmur, rumble

mutual *adjective* <u>shared</u>, common, interchangeable, joint, reciprocal, requited, returned

muzzle *noun* 1 <u>jaws</u>, mouth, nose, snout 2 <u>gag</u>, guard ♦ *verb* 3 <u>suppress</u>, censor, curb, gag, restrain, silence, stifle

myopic *adjective* <u>short-sighted</u>, near-sighted

myriad *adjective* 1 <u>innumerable</u>, countless, immeasurable, incalculable, multitudinous, untold ♦ *noun* 2 <u>multitude</u>, army, horde, host, swarm

mysterious *adjective* <u>strange</u>, arcane, enigmatic, inexplicable, inscrutable, mystifying, perplexing, puzzling, secret, uncanny, unfathomable, weird

mystery *noun* <u>puzzle</u>, conundrum, enigma, problem, question, riddle, secret, teaser

mystic, mystical *adjective* <u>supernatural</u>, inscrutable, metaphysical, mysterious, occult, otherworldly, paranormal, preternatural, transcendental

mystify *verb* <u>puzzle</u>, baffle, bewilder, confound, confuse, flummox, nonplus, perplex, stump

mystique *noun* <u>fascination</u>, awe, charisma, charm, glamour, magic, spell

myth *noun* 1 <u>legend</u>, allegory, fable, fairy story, fiction, folk tale, saga, story 2 <u>illusion</u>, delusion, fancy, fantasy, figment, imagination, superstition, tall story

mythical *adjective* 1 <u>legendary</u>, fabled, fabulous, fairy-tale, mythological 2 <u>imaginary</u>, fictitious, invented, made-up, make-believe, nonexistent, pretended, unreal, untrue

mythological *adjective* <u>legendary</u>, fabulous, mythic, mythical, traditional

mythology *noun* <u>legend</u>, folklore, lore, tradition

N n

nab *verb* <u>catch</u>, apprehend, arrest, capture, collar (*informal*), grab, seize, snatch

nadir *noun* <u>bottom</u>, depths, lowest point, minimum, rock bottom

naevus *noun* <u>birthmark</u>, mole

naff *adjective* <u>bad</u>, duff (*Brit. informal*), inferior, low-grade, poor, rubbishy, second-rate, shabby, shoddy, worthless

nag[1] *verb* 1 <u>scold</u>, annoy, badger, harass, hassle (*informal*), henpeck, irritate, pester, plague, upbraid, worry ♦ *noun* 2 <u>scold</u>, harpy, shrew, tartar, virago

nag[2] *noun* <u>horse</u>, hack

nagging *adjective* <u>irritating</u>, persistent, scolding, shrewish, worrying

nail *verb* <u>fasten</u>, attach, fix, hammer, join, pin, secure, tack

naive *adjective* 1 <u>gullible</u>, callow, credulous, green, unsuspicious, wet behind the ears (*informal*) 2 <u>innocent</u>, artless, guileless, ingenuous, open, simple, trusting, unsophisticated, unworldly

naivety, naïveté *noun* 1 <u>gullibility</u>, callowness, credulity 2 <u>innocence</u>, artlessness, guilelessness, inexperience, ingenuousness, naturalness, openness, simplicity

naked *adjective* <u>nude</u>, bare, exposed, starkers (*informal*), stripped, unclothed, undressed, without a stitch on (*informal*)

nakedness *noun* <u>nudity</u>, bareness, undress

namby-pamby *adjective* <u>feeble</u>, insipid, sentimental, spineless, vapid, weak, weedy (*informal*), wimpish *or* wimpy (*informal*), wishy-washy (*informal*)

name *noun* 1 <u>title</u>, designation, epithet, handle (*slang*), moniker *or* monicker (*slang*), nickname, sobriquet, term 2 <u>fame</u>, distinction, eminence, esteem, honour, note, praise, renown, repute ♦ *verb* 3 <u>call</u>, baptize, christen, dub, entitle, label, style, term 4 <u>nominate</u>, appoint, choose, designate, select, specify

named *adjective* 1 <u>called</u>, baptized, christened, dubbed, entitled, known as, labelled, styled, termed 2 <u>nominated</u>, appointed, chosen, designated, mentioned, picked, selected, singled out, specified

nameless *adjective*
1 <u>anonymous</u>, unnamed, untitled **2** <u>unknown</u>, incognito, obscure, undistinguished, unheard-of, unsung **3** <u>horrible</u>, abominable, indescribable, unmentionable, unspeakable, unutterable

namely *adverb* <u>specifically</u>, to wit, viz.

nap¹ *noun* **1** <u>sleep</u>, catnap, forty winks (*informal*), kip (*Brit. slang*), rest, siesta ♦ *verb* **2** <u>sleep</u>, catnap, doze, drop off (*informal*), kip (*Brit. slang*), nod off (*informal*), rest, snooze (*informal*)

nap² *noun* <u>weave</u>, down, fibre, grain, pile

napkin *noun* <u>serviette</u>, cloth

narcissism *noun* <u>egotism</u>, self-love, vanity

narcotic *noun* **1** <u>drug</u>, anaesthetic, analgesic, anodyne, opiate, painkiller, sedative, tranquillizer ♦ *adjective* **2** <u>sedative</u>, analgesic, calming, hypnotic, painkilling, soporific

nark *verb* <u>annoy</u>, bother, exasperate, get on one's nerves (*informal*), irritate, nettle

narrate *verb* <u>tell</u>, chronicle, describe, detail, recite, recount, relate, report

narration *noun* <u>telling</u>, description, explanation, reading, recital, relation

narrative *noun* <u>story</u>, account, chronicle, history, report, statement, tale

narrator *noun* <u>storyteller</u>, author, chronicler, commentator, reporter, writer

narrow *adjective* **1** <u>thin</u>, attenuated, fine, slender, slim, spare, tapering **2** <u>limited</u>, close, confined, constricted, contracted, meagre, restricted, tight **3** <u>insular</u>, dogmatic, illiberal, intolerant, narrow-minded, partial, prejudiced, small-minded ♦ *verb* **4** <u>tighten</u>, constrict, limit, reduce

narrowly *adverb* <u>just</u>, barely, by the skin of one's teeth, only just, scarcely

narrow-minded *adjective* <u>intolerant</u>, bigoted, hidebound, illiberal, opinionated, parochial, prejudiced, provincial, small-minded

nastiness *noun* <u>unpleasantness</u>, malice, meanness, spitefulness

nasty *adjective* **1** <u>objectionable</u>, disagreeable, loathsome, obnoxious, offensive, unpleasant, vile **2** <u>spiteful</u>, despicable, disagreeable, distasteful, malicious, mean, unpleasant, vicious, vile **3** <u>painful</u>, bad, critical, dangerous, serious, severe

nation *noun* <u>country</u>, people, race, realm, society, state, tribe

national *adjective* **1** <u>nationwide</u>, countrywide, public, widespread ♦ *noun* **2** <u>citizen</u>, inhabitant, native, resident, subject

nationalism *noun* <u>patriotism</u>, allegiance, chauvinism, jingoism, loyalty

nationality *noun* <u>race</u>, birth, nation

nationwide *adjective* <u>national</u>, countrywide, general, widespread

native *adjective* **1** <u>local</u>, domestic, home, indigenous **2** <u>inborn</u>, congenital, hereditary, inbred, ingrained, innate, instinctive, intrinsic, natural ♦ *noun* 3 <u>inhabitant</u>, aborigine, citizen, countryman, dweller, national, resident

natter *verb* 1 <u>gossip</u>, blether, chatter, gabble, jaw (*slang*), prattle, rabbit (on) (*Brit. informal*), talk ♦ *noun* 2 <u>gossip</u>, chat, chinwag (*Brit. informal*), chitchat, conversation, gab (*informal*), jaw (*slang*), prattle, talk

natty *adjective* <u>smart</u>, dapper, elegant, fashionable, neat, snazzy (*informal*), spruce, stylish, trim

natural *adjective* 1 <u>normal</u>, common, everyday, legitimate, logical, ordinary, regular, typical, usual 2 <u>unaffected</u>, genuine, ingenuous, open, real, simple, spontaneous, unpretentious, unsophisticated 3 <u>innate</u>, characteristic, essential, inborn, inherent, instinctive, intuitive, native 4 <u>pure</u>, organic, plain, unrefined, whole

naturalist *noun* <u>biologist</u>, botanist, ecologist, zoologist

naturalistic *adjective* <u>realistic</u>, lifelike, true-to-life

naturally *adverb* 1 <u>of course</u>, certainly 2 <u>genuinely</u>, normally, simply, spontaneously, typically, unaffectedly, unpretentiously

nature *noun* 1 <u>creation</u>, cosmos, earth, environment, universe, world 2 <u>make-up</u>, character, complexion, constitution, essence 3 <u>kind</u>, category, description, sort, species, style, type, variety 4 <u>temperament</u>, disposition, humour, mood,

outlook, temper

naughty *adjective* 1 <u>disobedient</u>, bad, impish, misbehaved, mischievous, refractory, wayward, wicked, worthless 2 <u>obscene</u>, improper, lewd, ribald, risqué, smutty, vulgar

nausea *noun* <u>sickness</u>, biliousness, queasiness, retching, squeamishness, vomiting

nauseate *verb* <u>sicken</u>, disgust, offend, repel, repulse, revolt, turn one's stomach

nauseous *adjective* <u>sickening</u>, abhorrent, disgusting, distasteful, nauseating, offensive, repugnant, repulsive, revolting

nautical *adjective* <u>maritime</u>, marine, naval

naval *adjective* <u>nautical</u>, marine, maritime

navigable *adjective* 1 <u>passable</u>, clear, negotiable, unobstructed 2 <u>sailable</u>, controllable, dirigible

navigate *verb* <u>sail</u>, drive, guide, handle, manoeuvre, pilot, steer, voyage

navigation *noun* <u>sailing</u>, helmsmanship, seamanship, voyaging

navigator *noun* <u>pilot</u>, mariner, seaman

navvy *noun* <u>labourer</u>, worker, workman

navy *noun* <u>fleet</u>, armada, flotilla

near *adjective* 1 <u>close</u>, adjacent, adjoining, nearby, neighbouring 2 <u>forthcoming</u>, approaching, imminent, impending, in the offing, looming, nigh, upcoming

nearby *adjective* <u>neighbouring</u>, adjacent, adjoining, convenient, handy

nearly adverb almost, approximately, as good as, just about, practically, roughly, virtually, well-nigh

nearness noun closeness, accessibility, availability, handiness, proximity, vicinity

near-sighted adjective short-sighted, myopic

neat adjective 1 tidy, orderly, shipshape, smart, spick-and-span, spruce, systematic, trim 2 elegant, adept, adroit, deft, dexterous, efficient, graceful, nimble, skilful, stylish 3 Of alcoholic drinks straight, pure, undiluted, unmixed

neatly adverb 1 tidily, daintily, fastidiously, methodically, smartly, sprucely, systematically 2 elegantly, adeptly, adroitly, deftly, dexterously, efficiently, expertly, gracefully, nimbly, skilfully

neatness noun 1 tidiness, daintiness, orderliness, smartness, spruceness, trimness 2 elegance, adroitness, deftness, dexterity, efficiency, grace, nimbleness, skill, style

nebulous adjective vague, confused, dim, hazy, imprecise, indefinite, indistinct, shadowy, uncertain, unclear

necessarily adverb certainly, automatically, compulsorily, incontrovertibly, inevitably, inexorably, naturally, of necessity, undoubtedly

necessary adjective 1 needed, compulsory, essential, imperative, indispensable, mandatory, obligatory, required,

requisite, vital 2 certain, fated, inescapable, inevitable, inexorable, unavoidable

necessitate verb compel, call for, coerce, constrain, demand, force, impel, oblige, require

necessities plural noun essentials, exigencies, fundamentals, needs, requirements

necessity noun 1 inevitability, compulsion, inexorableness, obligation 2 need, desideratum, essential, fundamental, prerequisite, requirement, requisite, sine qua non

necromancy noun magic, black magic, divination, enchantment, sorcery, witchcraft, wizardry

necropolis noun cemetery, burial ground, churchyard, graveyard

need verb 1 require, call for, demand, entail, lack, miss, necessitate, want ♦ noun 2 poverty, deprivation, destitution, inadequacy, insufficiency, lack, paucity, penury, shortage 3 requirement, demand, desideratum, essential, requisite 4 emergency, exigency, necessity, obligation, urgency, want

needed adjective necessary, called for, desired, lacked, required, wanted

needful adjective necessary, essential, indispensable, needed, required, requisite, stipulated, vital

needle verb irritate, annoy, get on one's nerves (informal), goad, harass, nag, pester, provoke, rile, taunt

needless adjective unnecessary,

gratuitous, groundless, pointless, redundant, superfluous, uncalled-for, unwanted, useless

needlework noun embroidery, needlecraft, sewing, stitching, tailoring

needy adjective poor, deprived, destitute, disadvantaged, impoverished, penniless, poverty-stricken, underprivileged

ne'er-do-well noun layabout, black sheep, good-for-nothing, idler, loafer, loser, skiver (Brit. slang), wastrel

nefarious adjective wicked, criminal, depraved, evil, foul, heinous, infernal, villainous

negate verb 1 invalidate, annul, cancel, countermand, neutralize, nullify, obviate, reverse, wipe out 2 deny, contradict, disallow, disprove, gainsay (archaic or literary), oppose, rebut, refute

negation noun 1 cancellation, neutralization, nullification 2 denial, contradiction, converse, disavowal, inverse, opposite, rejection, renunciation, reverse

negative adjective 1 contradictory, contrary, denying, dissenting, opposing, refusing, rejecting, resisting 2 pessimistic, cynical, gloomy, jaundiced, uncooperative, unenthusiastic, unwilling ◆ noun 3 contradiction, denial, refusal

neglect verb 1 disregard, disdain, ignore, overlook, rebuff, scorn, slight, spurn 2 forget, be remiss, evade, omit, pass over, shirk, skimp ◆ noun 3 disregard, disdain, inattention, indifference 4 negligence, carelessness,

dereliction, failure, laxity, oversight, slackness

neglected adjective 1 abandoned, derelict, overgrown 2 disregarded, unappreciated, underestimated, undervalued

neglectful adjective careless, heedless, inattentive, indifferent, lax, negligent, remiss, thoughtless, uncaring

negligence noun carelessness, dereliction, disregard, inattention, indifference, laxity, neglect, slackness, thoughtlessness

negligent adjective careless, forgetful, heedless, inattentive, neglectful, remiss, slack, slapdash, thoughtless, unthinking

negligible adjective insignificant, imperceptible, inconsequential, minor, minute, small, trifling, trivial, unimportant

negotiable adjective debatable, variable

negotiate verb 1 deal, arrange, bargain, conciliate, debate, discuss, mediate, transact, work out 2 get round, clear, cross, get over, get past, pass, surmount

negotiation noun bargaining, arbitration, debate, diplomacy, discussion, mediation, transaction, wheeling and dealing (informal)

negotiator noun mediator, ambassador, delegate, diplomat, honest broker, intermediary, moderator

neighbourhood noun district, community, environs, locale, locality, quarter, region, vicinity

neighbouring *adjective* nearby, adjacent, adjoining, bordering, connecting, near, next, surrounding

neighbourly *adjective* helpful, considerate, friendly, harmonious, hospitable, kind, obliging, sociable

nemesis *noun* retribution, destiny, destruction, fate, vengeance

nepotism *noun* favouritism, bias, partiality, patronage, preferential treatment

nerd, nurd *noun* bore, anorak (*informal*), dork (*slang*), drip (*informal*), geek (*informal*), obsessive, trainspotter (*informal*), wonk (*informal*)

nerve *noun* **1** bravery, bottle (*Brit. slang*), courage, daring, fearlessness, grit, guts (*informal*), pluck, resolution, will **2** impudence, audacity, boldness, brazenness, cheek (*informal*), impertinence, insolence, temerity ♦ *verb* **3 nerve oneself** brace oneself, fortify oneself, steel oneself

nerveless *adjective* calm, composed, controlled, cool, impassive, imperturbable, self-possessed, unemotional

nerve-racking *adjective* tense, difficult, distressing, frightening, harrowing, stressful, trying, worrying

nerves *plural noun* tension, anxiety, butterflies (in one's stomach) (*informal*), cold feet (*informal*), fretfulness, nervousness, strain, stress, worry

nervous *adjective* apprehensive, anxious, edgy, fearful, jumpy, on edge, tense, uneasy, uptight (*informal*), worried

nervousness *noun* anxiety, agitation, disquiet, excitability, fluster, tension, touchiness, worry

nervy *adjective* anxious, agitated, fidgety, jittery (*informal*), jumpy, nervous, on edge, tense, twitchy (*informal*)

nest *noun* refuge, den, haunt, hideaway, retreat

nest egg *noun* reserve, cache, deposit, fall-back, fund(s), savings, store

nestle *verb* snuggle, cuddle, curl up, huddle, nuzzle

nestling *noun* chick, fledgling

net¹ *noun* **1** mesh, lattice, netting, network, openwork, tracery, web ♦ *verb* **2** catch, bag, capture, enmesh, ensnare, entangle, trap

net², nett *adjective* **1** final, after taxes, clear, take-home ♦ *verb* **2** earn, accumulate, bring in, clear, gain, make, realize, reap

nether *adjective* lower, below, beneath, bottom, inferior, under, underground

nettled *adjective* irritated, annoyed, exasperated, galled, harassed, incensed, peeved, put out, riled, vexed

network *noun* system, arrangement, complex, grid, labyrinth, lattice, maze, organization, structure, web

neurosis *noun* obsession, abnormality, affliction, derangement, instability, maladjustment, mental illness, phobia

neurotic *adjective* unstable,

abnormal, compulsive,
disturbed, maladjusted, manic,
nervous, obsessive, unhealthy

neuter *verb* <u>castrate</u>, doctor
(*informal*), emasculate, fix
(*informal*), geld, spay

neutral *adjective* 1 <u>unbiased</u>,
disinterested, even-handed,
impartial, nonaligned,
nonpartisan, uncommitted,
uninvolved, unprejudiced
2 <u>indeterminate</u>, dull, indistinct,
intermediate, undefined

neutrality *noun* <u>impartiality</u>,
detachment, nonalignment,
noninterference,
noninvolvement, nonpartisanship

neutralize *verb* <u>counteract</u>,
cancel, compensate for,
counterbalance, frustrate,
negate, nullify, offset, undo

never *adverb* <u>at no time</u>, not at
all, on no account, under no
circumstances

nevertheless *adverb*
<u>nonetheless</u>, but, even so, (even)
though, however,
notwithstanding, regardless, still,
yet

new *adjective* 1 <u>modern</u>,
contemporary, current, fresh,
ground-breaking, latest, novel,
original, recent, state-of-the-art,
unfamiliar, up-to-date
2 <u>changed</u>, altered, improved,
modernized, redesigned,
renewed, restored 3 <u>extra</u>,
added, more, supplementary

newcomer *noun* <u>novice</u>, arrival,
beginner, Johnny-come-lately
(*informal*), parvenu

newfangled *adjective* <u>new</u>,
contemporary, fashionable,
gimmicky, modern, novel,

recent, state-of-the-art

newly *adverb* <u>recently</u>, anew,
freshly, just, lately, latterly

newness *noun* <u>novelty</u>,
freshness, innovation, oddity,
originality, strangeness,
unfamiliarity, uniqueness

news *noun* <u>information</u>, bulletin,
communiqué, exposé, gossip,
hearsay, intelligence, latest
(*informal*), report, revelation,
rumour, story

newsworthy *adjective*
<u>interesting</u>, important, notable,
noteworthy, remarkable,
significant, stimulating

next *adjective* 1 <u>following</u>,
consequent, ensuing, later,
subsequent, succeeding
2 <u>nearest</u>, adjacent, adjoining,
closest, neighbouring ♦ *adverb*
3 <u>afterwards</u>, following, later,
subsequently, thereafter

nibble *verb* 1 <u>bite</u>, eat, gnaw,
munch, nip, peck, pick at ♦ *noun*
2 <u>snack</u>, bite, crumb, morsel,
peck, soupçon, taste, titbit

nice *adjective* 1 <u>pleasant</u>,
agreeable, attractive, charming,
delightful, good, pleasurable
2 <u>kind</u>, courteous, friendly,
likable *or* likeable, polite,
well-mannered 3 <u>neat</u>, dainty,
fine, tidy, trim 4 <u>subtle</u>, careful,
delicate, fastidious, fine,
meticulous, precise, strict

nicely *adverb* 1 <u>pleasantly</u>,
acceptably, agreeably,
attractively, charmingly,
delightfully, pleasurably, well
2 <u>kindly</u>, amiably,
commendably, courteously,
politely 3 <u>neatly</u>, daintily, finely,
tidily, trimly

nicety noun <u>subtlety</u>, daintiness, delicacy, discrimination, distinction, nuance, refinement

niche noun 1 <u>alcove</u>, corner, hollow, nook, opening, recess 2 <u>position</u>, calling, pigeonhole (*informal*), place, slot (*informal*), vocation

nick verb 1 <u>cut</u>, chip, dent, mark, notch, scar, score, scratch, snick 2 <u>steal</u>, pilfer, pinch (*informal*), swipe (*slang*) ♦ noun 3 <u>cut</u>, chip, dent, mark, notch, scar, scratch

nickname noun <u>pet name</u>, diminutive, epithet, label, moniker or monicker (*slang*), sobriquet

nifty adjective <u>neat</u>, attractive, chic, deft, pleasing, smart, stylish

niggard noun <u>miser</u>, cheapskate (*informal*), Scrooge, skinflint

niggardly adjective <u>stingy</u>, avaricious, frugal, grudging, mean, miserly, parsimonious, tightfisted, ungenerous

niggle verb 1 <u>worry</u>, annoy, irritate, rankle 2 <u>criticize</u>, carp, cavil, find fault, fuss

niggling adjective 1 <u>persistent</u>, gnawing, irritating, troubling, worrying 2 <u>petty</u>, finicky, fussy, nit-picking (*informal*), pettifogging, picky (*informal*), quibbling

night noun <u>darkness</u>, dark, night-time

nightfall noun <u>evening</u>, dusk, sundown, sunset, twilight

nightly adjective 1 <u>nocturnal</u>, night-time ♦ adverb 2 <u>every night</u>, each night, night after night, nights (*informal*)

nightmare noun 1 <u>bad dream</u>, hallucination 2 <u>ordeal</u>, horror, torment, trial, tribulation

nil noun <u>nothing</u>, love, naught, none, zero

nimble adjective <u>agile</u>, brisk, deft, dexterous, lively, quick, sprightly, spry, swift

nimbly adverb <u>quickly</u>, briskly, deftly, dexterously, easily, readily, smartly, spryly, swiftly

nincompoop noun <u>idiot</u>, blockhead, chump, fool, nitwit (*informal*), numbskull or numskull, twit (*informal, chiefly Brit.*)

nip¹ verb <u>pinch</u>, bite, squeeze, tweak

nip² noun <u>dram</u>, draught, drop, mouthful, shot (*informal*), sip, snifter (*informal*)

nipper noun Informal <u>child</u>, baby, boy, girl, infant, kid (*informal*), tot

nippy adjective 1 <u>chilly</u>, biting, sharp 2 Informal <u>quick</u>, active, agile, fast, nimble, spry

nirvana noun <u>paradise</u>, bliss, joy, peace, serenity, tranquillity

nit-picking adjective <u>fussy</u>, captious, carping, finicky, hairsplitting, pedantic, pettifogging, quibbling

nitty-gritty noun <u>basics</u>, brass tacks (*informal*), core, crux, essentials, fundamentals, gist, substance

nitwit noun Informal <u>fool</u>, dimwit (*informal*), dummy (*slang*), halfwit, nincompoop, oaf, simpleton

no interjection 1 <u>never</u>, nay, not at all, no way ♦ noun 2 <u>refusal</u>, denial, negation

nob noun <u>aristocrat</u>, bigwig

(*informal*), toff (*Brit. slang*), V.I.P.

nobble *verb* <u>bribe</u>, get at, influence, intimidate, win over

nobility *noun* 1 <u>integrity</u>, honour, incorruptibility, uprightness, virtue 2 <u>aristocracy</u>, elite, lords, nobles, patricians, peerage, upper class

noble *adjective* 1 <u>worthy</u>, generous, honourable, magnanimous, upright, virtuous 2 <u>aristocratic</u>, blue-blooded, highborn, lordly, patrician, titled 3 <u>great</u>, dignified, distinguished, grand, imposing, impressive, lofty, splendid, stately ♦ *noun* 4 <u>lord</u>, aristocrat, nobleman, peer

nobody *pronoun* 1 <u>no-one</u> ♦ *noun* 2 <u>nonentity</u>, cipher, lightweight (*informal*), menial

nocturnal *adjective* <u>nightly</u>, night-time

nod *verb* 1 <u>acknowledge</u>, bow, gesture, indicate, signal 2 <u>sleep</u>, doze, drowse, nap ♦ *noun* 3 <u>gesture</u>, acknowledgment, greeting, indication, sign, signal

noggin *noun* 1 <u>cup</u>, dram, mug, nip, tot 2 *Informal* <u>head</u>, block (*informal*), nut (*slang*)

no go *adjective* <u>impossible</u>, futile, hopeless, not on (*informal*), vain

noise *noun* <u>sound</u>, clamour, commotion, din, hubbub, racket, row, uproar

noiseless *adjective* <u>silent</u>, hushed, inaudible, mute, quiet, soundless, still

noisome *adjective* 1 <u>poisonous</u>, bad, harmful, pernicious, pestilential, unhealthy, unwholesome 2 <u>offensive</u>, disgusting, fetid, foul, malodorous, noxious, putrid, smelly, stinking

noisy *adjective* <u>loud</u>, boisterous, cacophonous, clamorous, deafening, ear-splitting, strident, tumultuous, uproarious, vociferous

nomad *noun* <u>wanderer</u>, drifter, itinerant, migrant, rambler, rover, vagabond

nomadic *adjective* <u>wandering</u>, itinerant, migrant, peripatetic, roaming, roving, travelling, vagrant

nom de plume *noun* <u>pseudonym</u>, alias, assumed name, nom de guerre, pen name

nomenclature *noun* <u>terminology</u>, classification, codification, phraseology, taxonomy, vocabulary

nominal *adjective* 1 <u>so-called</u>, formal, ostensible, professed, puppet, purported, supposed, theoretical, titular 2 <u>small</u>, inconsiderable, insignificant, minimal, symbolic, token, trifling, trivial

nominate *verb* <u>name</u>, appoint, assign, choose, designate, elect, propose, recommend, select, suggest

nomination *noun* <u>choice</u>, appointment, designation, election, proposal, recommendation, selection, suggestion

nominee *noun* <u>candidate</u>, aspirant, contestant, entrant, protégé, runner

nonaligned *adjective* <u>neutral</u>, impartial, uncommitted, undecided

nonchalance noun <u>indifference</u>, calm, composure, equanimity, imperturbability, sang-froid, self-possession, unconcern

nonchalant adjective <u>casual</u>, blasé, calm, careless, indifferent, insouciant, laid-back (*informal*), offhand, unconcerned, unperturbed

noncombatant noun <u>civilian</u>, neutral, nonbelligerent

noncommittal adjective <u>evasive</u>, cautious, circumspect, equivocal, guarded, neutral, politic, temporizing, tentative, vague, wary

non compos mentis adjective <u>insane</u>, crazy, deranged, mentally ill, unbalanced, unhinged

nonconformist noun <u>maverick</u>, dissenter, eccentric, heretic, iconoclast, individualist, protester, radical, rebel

nonconformity noun <u>dissent</u>, eccentricity, heresy, heterodoxy

nondescript adjective <u>ordinary</u>, commonplace, dull, featureless, run-of-the-mill, undistinguished, unexceptional, unremarkable

none pronoun <u>not any</u>, nil, nobody, no-one, nothing, not one, zero

nonentity noun <u>nobody</u>, cipher, lightweight (*informal*), mediocrity, small fry

nonessential adjective <u>unnecessary</u>, dispensable, expendable, extraneous, inessential, peripheral, superfluous, unimportant

nonetheless adverb <u>nevertheless</u>, despite that, even so, however, in spite of that, yet

nonevent noun <u>flop</u> (*informal*), disappointment, dud (*informal*), failure, fiasco, washout

nonexistent adjective <u>imaginary</u>, chimerical, fictional, hypothetical, illusory, legendary, mythical, unreal

nonsense noun <u>rubbish</u>, balderdash, claptrap (*informal*), double Dutch (*Brit. informal*), drivel, gibberish, hot air (*informal*), stupidity, tripe (*informal*), twaddle

nonsensical adjective <u>senseless</u>, absurd, crazy, foolish, inane, incomprehensible, irrational, meaningless, ridiculous, silly

nonstarter noun <u>dead loss</u>, dud (*informal*), lemon (*informal*), loser, no-hoper (*informal*), turkey (*informal*), washout (*informal*)

nonstop adjective **1** <u>continuous</u>, constant, endless, incessant, interminable, relentless, unbroken, uninterrupted ♦ adverb **2** <u>continuously</u>, ceaselessly, constantly, endlessly, incessantly, interminably, perpetually, relentlessly

nook noun <u>niche</u>, alcove, corner, cubbyhole, hide-out, opening, recess, retreat

noon noun <u>midday</u>, high noon, noonday, noontide, twelve noon

norm noun <u>standard</u>, average, benchmark, criterion, par, pattern, rule, yardstick

normal adjective **1** <u>usual</u>, average, common, conventional, natural, ordinary, regular, routine, standard, typical **2** <u>sane</u>, rational, reasonable, well-adjusted

normality noun **1** regularity, conventionality, naturalness **2** sanity, balance, rationality, reason

normally adverb usually, as a rule, commonly, generally, habitually, ordinarily, regularly, typically

north adjective **1** northern, Arctic, boreal, northerly, polar ◆ adverb **2** northward(s), northerly

nose noun **1** snout, beak, bill, hooter (slang), proboscis ◆ verb **2** ease forward, nudge, nuzzle, push, shove **3** pry, meddle, snoop (informal)

nosegay noun posy, bouquet

nosey, nosy adjective inquisitive, curious, eavesdropping, interfering, intrusive, meddlesome, prying, snooping (informal)

nostalgia noun reminiscence, homesickness, longing, pining, regretfulness, remembrance, wistfulness, yearning

nostalgic adjective sentimental, emotional, homesick, longing, maudlin, regretful, wistful

nostrum noun medicine, cure, drug, elixir, panacea, potion, remedy, treatment

notability noun fame, celebrity, distinction, eminence, esteem, renown

notable adjective **1** remarkable, conspicuous, extraordinary, memorable, noteworthy, outstanding, rare, striking, uncommon, unusual ◆ noun **2** celebrity, big name, dignitary, personage, V.I.P.

notably adverb particularly, especially, outstandingly, strikingly

notation noun signs, characters, code, script, symbols, system

notch noun **1** cut, cleft, incision, indentation, mark, nick, score **2** Informal level, degree, grade, step ◆ verb **3** cut, indent, mark, nick, score, scratch

notch up verb register, achieve, gain, make, score

note noun **1** message, comment, communication, epistle, jotting, letter, memo, memorandum, minute, remark, reminder **2** symbol, indication, mark, sign, token ◆ verb **3** see, notice, observe, perceive **4** mark, denote, designate, indicate, record, register **5** mention, remark

notebook noun jotter, diary, exercise book, journal, notepad

noted adjective famous, acclaimed, celebrated, distinguished, eminent, illustrious, notable, prominent, renowned, well-known

noteworthy adjective remarkable, exceptional, extraordinary, important, notable, outstanding, significant, unusual

nothing noun nought, emptiness, nil, nothingness, nullity, void, zero

nothingness noun **1** oblivion, nonbeing, nonexistence, nullity **2** insignificance, unimportance, worthlessness

notice noun **1** observation, cognizance, consideration, heed, interest, note, regard

2 <u>attention</u>, civility, respect
3 <u>announcement</u>, advice, communication, instruction, intimation, news, notification, order, warning ♦ *verb* 4 <u>observe</u>, detect, discern, distinguish, mark, note, perceive, see, spot

noticeable *adjective* <u>obvious</u>, appreciable, clear, conspicuous, evident, manifest, perceptible, plain, striking

notification *noun* <u>announcement</u>, advice, declaration, information, intelligence, message, notice, statement, warning

notify *verb* <u>inform</u>, advise, alert, announce, declare, make known, publish, tell, warn

notion *noun* 1 <u>idea</u>, belief, concept, impression, inkling, opinion, sentiment, view
2 <u>whim</u>, caprice, desire, fancy, impulse, inclination, wish

notional *adjective* <u>speculative</u>, abstract, conceptual, hypothetical, imaginary, theoretical, unreal

notoriety *noun* <u>scandal</u>, dishonour, disrepute, infamy, obloquy, opprobrium

notorious *adjective* <u>infamous</u>, dishonourable, disreputable, opprobrious, scandalous

notoriously *adverb* <u>infamously</u>, dishonourably, disreputably, opprobriously, scandalously

notwithstanding *preposition* <u>despite</u>, in spite of

nought *noun* <u>zero</u>, nil, nothing

nourish *verb* 1 <u>feed</u>, nurse, nurture, supply, sustain, tend
2 <u>encourage</u>, comfort, cultivate, foster, maintain, promote, support

nourishing *adjective* <u>nutritious</u>, beneficial, nutritive, wholesome

nourishment *noun* <u>food</u>, nutriment, nutrition, sustenance

novel[1] *noun* <u>story</u>, fiction, narrative, romance, tale

novel[2] *adjective* <u>new</u>, different, fresh, innovative, original, strange, uncommon, unfamiliar, unusual

novelty *noun* 1 <u>newness</u>, freshness, innovation, oddity, originality, strangeness, surprise, unfamiliarity, uniqueness
2 <u>gimmick</u>, curiosity, gadget
3 <u>knick-knack</u>, bauble, memento, souvenir, trifle, trinket

novice *noun* <u>beginner</u>, amateur, apprentice, learner, newcomer, probationer, pupil, trainee

now *adverb* 1 <u>nowadays</u>, any more, at the moment
2 <u>immediately</u>, at once, instantly, promptly, straightaway
3 **now and then** *or* **again** <u>occasionally</u>, from time to time, infrequently, intermittently, on and off, sometimes, sporadically

nowadays *adverb* <u>now</u>, any more, at the moment, in this day and age, today

noxious *adjective* <u>harmful</u>, deadly, destructive, foul, hurtful, injurious, poisonous, unhealthy, unwholesome

nuance *noun* <u>subtlety</u>, degree, distinction, gradation, nicety, refinement, shade, tinge

nubile *adjective* <u>marriageable</u>, ripe (*informal*)

nucleus *noun* <u>centre</u>, basis, core,

focus, heart, kernel, nub, pivot

nude *adjective* <u>naked</u>, bare, disrobed, stark-naked, stripped, unclad, unclothed, undressed, without a stitch on (*informal*)

nudge *verb* <u>push</u>, bump, dig, elbow, jog, poke, prod, shove, touch

nudity *noun* <u>nakedness</u>, bareness, deshabille, nudism, undress

nugget *noun* <u>lump</u>, chunk, clump, hunk, mass, piece

nuisance *noun* <u>problem</u>, annoyance, bother, drag (*informal*), hassle (*informal*), inconvenience, irritation, pain in the neck, pest, trouble

null *adjective* **null and void** <u>invalid</u>, inoperative, useless, valueless, void, worthless

nullify *verb* <u>cancel</u>, counteract, invalidate, negate, neutralize, obviate, render null and void, veto

nullity *noun* <u>nonexistence</u>, invalidity, powerlessness, uselessness, worthlessness

numb *adjective* **1** <u>unfeeling</u>, benumbed, dead, deadened, frozen, immobilized, insensitive, paralysed, torpid ♦ *verb* **2** <u>deaden</u>, benumb, dull, freeze, immobilize, paralyse

number *noun* **1** <u>numeral</u>, character, digit, figure, integer **2** <u>quantity</u>, aggregate, amount, collection, crowd, horde, multitude, throng **3** <u>issue</u>, copy, edition, imprint, printing ♦ *verb* **4** <u>count</u>, account, add, calculate, compute, enumerate, include, reckon, total

numberless *adjective* <u>infinite</u>,

countless, endless, innumerable, multitudinous, myriad, unnumbered, untold

numbness *noun* <u>deadness</u>, dullness, insensitivity, paralysis, torpor

numbskull, numskull *noun* <u>fool</u>, blockhead, clot (*Brit. informal*), dolt, dummy (*slang*), dunce, oaf, twit (*informal*)

numeral *noun* <u>number</u>, digit, figure, integer

numerous *adjective* <u>many</u>, abundant, copious, plentiful, profuse, several, thick on the ground

nuncio *noun* <u>ambassador</u>, envoy, legate, messenger

nunnery *noun* <u>convent</u>, abbey, cloister, house

nuptial *adjective* <u>marital</u>, bridal, conjugal, connubial, matrimonial

nuptials *plural noun* <u>wedding</u>, marriage, matrimony

nurse *verb* **1** <u>look after</u>, care for, minister to, tend, treat **2** <u>breast-feed</u>, feed, nourish, nurture, suckle, wet-nurse **3** <u>foster</u>, cherish, cultivate, encourage, harbour, preserve, promote, succour, support

nursery *noun* <u>creche</u>, kindergarten, playgroup

nurture *noun* **1** <u>development</u>, discipline, education, instruction, rearing, training, upbringing ♦ *verb* **2** <u>develop</u>, bring up, discipline, educate, instruct, rear, school, train

nut *noun* **1** *Slang* <u>madman</u>, crank (*informal*), lunatic, maniac, nutcase (*slang*), psycho (*slang*) **2** *Slang* <u>head</u>, brain, mind, reason, senses

nutrition noun <u>food</u>, nourishment, nutriment, sustenance

nutritious adjective <u>nourishing</u>, beneficial, health-giving, invigorating, nutritive, strengthening, wholesome

nuzzle verb <u>snuggle</u>, burrow, cuddle, fondle, nestle, pet

nymph noun <u>sylph</u>, dryad, girl, maiden, naiad

O o

oaf noun <u>idiot</u>, blockhead, clod, dolt, dunce, fool, goon, lout, moron, numbskull or numskull

oafish adjective <u>moronic</u>, dense, dim-witted (informal), doltish, dumb (informal), loutish, stupid, thick

oath noun 1 <u>promise</u>, affirmation, avowal, bond, pledge, vow, word 2 <u>swearword</u>, blasphemy, curse, expletive, profanity

obdurate adjective <u>stubborn</u>, dogged, hard-hearted, immovable, implacable, inflexible, obstinate, pig-headed, unyielding

obedience noun <u>respect</u>, acquiescence, compliance, docility, observance, reverence, submissiveness, subservience

obedient adjective <u>respectful</u>, acquiescent, biddable, compliant, deferential, docile, dutiful, submissive, subservient, well-trained

obelisk noun <u>column</u>, monolith,

monument, needle, pillar, shaft

obese adjective <u>fat</u>, corpulent, gross, heavy, overweight, paunchy, plump, portly, rotund, stout, tubby

obesity noun <u>fatness</u>, bulk, corpulence, grossness, portliness, stoutness, tubbiness

obey verb <u>carry out</u>, abide by, act upon, adhere to, comply, conform, follow, heed, keep, observe

obfuscate verb <u>confuse</u>, befog, cloud, darken, muddy the waters, obscure, perplex

object¹ noun 1 <u>thing</u>, article, body, entity, item, phenomenon 2 <u>target</u>, focus, recipient, victim 3 <u>purpose</u>, aim, design, end, goal, idea, intention, objective, point

object² verb <u>protest</u>, argue against, demur, draw the line (at something), expostulate, oppose, take exception

objection noun <u>protest</u>, counter-argument, demur, doubt, opposition, remonstrance, scruple

objectionable adjective <u>unpleasant</u>, deplorable, disagreeable, intolerable, obnoxious, offensive, regrettable, repugnant, unseemly

objective noun 1 <u>purpose</u>, aim, ambition, end, goal, intention, mark, object, target ♦ adjective 2 <u>unbiased</u>, detached, disinterested, dispassionate, even-handed, fair, impartial, open-minded, unprejudiced

objectively adverb <u>impartially</u>, disinterestedly, dispassionately, even-handedly, with an open mind

objectivity noun impartiality, detachment, disinterestedness, dispassion

obligation noun duty, accountability, burden, charge, compulsion, liability, requirement, responsibility

obligatory adjective compulsory, binding, de rigueur, essential, imperative, mandatory, necessary, required, requisite, unavoidable

oblige verb 1 compel, bind, constrain, force, impel, make, necessitate, require 2 indulge, accommodate, benefit, gratify, please

obliged adjective 1 grateful, appreciative, beholden, indebted, in (someone's) debt, thankful 2 bound, compelled, forced, required

obliging adjective cooperative, accommodating, agreeable, considerate, good-natured, helpful, kind, polite, willing

oblique adjective 1 slanting, angled, aslant, sloping, tilted 2 indirect, backhanded, circuitous, implied, roundabout, sidelong

obliterate verb destroy, annihilate, blot out, efface, eradicate, erase, expunge, extirpate, root out, wipe out

obliteration noun annihilation, elimination, eradication, extirpation, wiping out

oblivion noun 1 neglect, abeyance, disregard, forgetfulness 2 unconsciousness,

insensibility, obliviousness, unawareness

oblivious adjective unaware, forgetful, heedless, ignorant, insensible, neglectful, negligent, regardless, unconcerned, unconscious, unmindful

obloquy noun 1 abuse, aspersion, attack, blame, censure, criticism, invective, reproach, slander, vilification 2 discredit, disgrace, dishonour, humiliation, ignominy, infamy, shame, stigma

obnoxious adjective offensive, disagreeable, insufferable, loathsome, nasty, nauseating, objectionable, odious, repulsive, revolting, unpleasant

obscene adjective 1 indecent, dirty, filthy, immoral, improper, lewd, offensive, pornographic, salacious 2 sickening, atrocious, disgusting, evil, heinous, loathsome, outrageous, shocking, vile, wicked

obscenity noun 1 indecency, coarseness, dirtiness, impropriety, lewdness, licentiousness, pornography, smut 2 swearword, four-letter word, profanity, vulgarism 3 outrage, abomination, affront, atrocity, blight, evil, offence, wrong

obscure adjective 1 vague, ambiguous, arcane, confusing, cryptic, enigmatic, esoteric, mysterious, opaque, recondite 2 indistinct, blurred, cloudy, dim, faint, gloomy, murky, shadowy 3 little-known, humble, lowly, out-of-the-way, remote, undistinguished, unheard-of, unknown ♦ *verb* **4** conceal, cover, disguise, hide, obfuscate, screen, veil

obscurity *noun* **1** darkness, dimness, dusk, gloom, haze, shadows **2** insignificance, lowliness, unimportance

obsequious *adjective* sycophantic, cringing, deferential, fawning, flattering, grovelling, ingratiating, servile, submissive, unctuous

observable *adjective* noticeable, apparent, detectable, discernible, evident, obvious, perceptible, recognizable, visible

observance *noun* honouring, carrying out, compliance, fulfilment, performance

observant *adjective* attentive, alert, eagle-eyed, perceptive, quick, sharp-eyed, vigilant, watchful, wide-awake

observation *noun* **1** study, examination, inspection, monitoring, review, scrutiny, surveillance, watching **2** remark, comment, note, opinion, pronouncement, reflection, thought, utterance

observe *verb* **1** see, detect, discern, discover, note, notice, perceive, spot, witness **2** watch, check, keep an eye on (*informal*), keep track of, look at, monitor, scrutinize, study, survey, view **3** remark, comment, mention, note, opine, say, state **4** honour, abide by, adhere to, comply, conform to, follow, heed, keep, obey, respect

observer *noun* spectator, beholder, bystander, eyewitness, fly on the wall, looker-on, onlooker, viewer, watcher, witness

obsessed *adjective* preoccupied, dominated, gripped, haunted, hung up on (*slang*), infatuated, troubled

obsession *noun* preoccupation, complex, fetish, fixation, hang-up (*informal*), infatuation, mania, phobia, thing (*informal*)

obsessive *adjective* compulsive, besetting, consuming, gripping, haunting

obsolescent *adjective* waning, ageing, declining, dying out, on the wane, on the way out, past its prime

obsolete *adjective* extinct, antiquated, archaic, discarded, disused, old, old-fashioned, outmoded, out of date, passé

obstacle *noun* difficulty, bar, barrier, block, hindrance, hitch, hurdle, impediment, obstruction, snag, stumbling block

obstinacy *noun* stubbornness, doggedness, inflexibility, intransigence, obduracy, persistence, pig-headedness, tenacity, wilfulness

obstinate *adjective* stubborn, determined, dogged, inflexible, intractable, intransigent, pig-headed, refractory, self-willed, strong-minded, wilful

obstreperous *adjective* unruly, disorderly, loud, noisy, riotous, rowdy, turbulent, unmanageable, wild

obstruct *verb* block, bar, barricade, check, hamper, hinder, impede, restrict, stop, thwart

obstruction noun obstacle, bar, barricade, barrier, blockage, difficulty, hindrance, impediment

obstructive adjective uncooperative, awkward, blocking, delaying, hindering, restrictive, stalling, unhelpful

obtain verb **1** get, achieve, acquire, attain, earn, gain, land, procure, secure **2** exist, be in force, be prevalent, be the case, hold, prevail

obtainable adjective available, achievable, attainable, on tap (informal), to be had

obtrusive adjective noticeable, blatant, obvious, prominent, protruding, protuberant, sticking out

obtuse adjective slow, dense, dull, stolid, stupid, thick, uncomprehending

obviate verb preclude, avert, prevent, remove

obvious adjective evident, apparent, clear, conspicuous, distinct, indisputable, manifest, noticeable, plain, self-evident, undeniable, unmistakable

obviously adverb clearly, manifestly, of course, palpably, patently, plainly, undeniably, unmistakably, unquestionably, without doubt

occasion noun **1** time, chance, moment, opening, opportunity, window **2** event, affair, celebration, experience, happening, occurrence **3** reason, call, cause, excuse, ground(s), justification, motive, prompting, provocation ◆ verb **4** cause, bring about, engender, generate, give rise to, induce, inspire, lead to, produce, prompt, provoke

occasional adjective infrequent, incidental, intermittent, irregular, odd, rare, sporadic, uncommon

occasionally adverb sometimes, at times, from time to time, irregularly, now and again, once in a while, periodically

occult adjective supernatural, arcane, esoteric, magical, mysterious, mystical

occupancy noun tenure, possession, residence, tenancy, use

occupant noun inhabitant, incumbent, indweller, inmate, lessee, occupier, resident, tenant

occupation noun **1** profession, business, calling, employment, job, line (of work), pursuit, trade, vocation, walk of life **2** possession, control, holding, occupancy, residence, tenancy, tenure **3** invasion, conquest, seizure, subjugation

occupied adjective **1** busy, employed, engaged, working **2** in use, engaged, full, taken, unavailable **3** inhabited, lived-in, peopled, settled, tenanted

occupy verb **1** often passive take up, divert, employ, engage, engross, involve, monopolize, preoccupy, tie up **2** live in, dwell in, inhabit, own, possess, reside in **3** fill, cover, permeate, pervade, take up **4** invade, capture, overrun, seize, take over

occur verb **1** happen, befall, come about, crop up (informal), take place, turn up (informal) **2** exist, appear, be found, be present, develop, manifest itself, show itself **3** occur to come to mind, cross one's mind, dawn on, enter one's head, spring to mind, strike one, suggest itself

occurrence noun **1** incident, adventure, affair, circumstance, episode, event, happening, instance **2** existence, appearance, development, manifestation, materialization

odd adjective **1** unusual, bizarre, extraordinary, freakish, irregular, peculiar, rare, remarkable, singular, strange **2** occasional, casual, incidental, irregular, periodic, random, sundry, various **3** spare, leftover, remaining, solitary, surplus, unmatched, unpaired

oddity noun **1** irregularity, abnormality, anomaly, eccentricity, freak, idiosyncrasy, peculiarity, quirk **2** misfit, crank (informal), maverick, oddball (informal)

oddment noun leftover, bit, fag end, fragment, off cut, remnant, scrap, snippet

odds plural noun **1** probability, chances, likelihood **2 at odds** in conflict, at daggers drawn, at loggerheads, at sixes and sevens, at variance, out of line

odds and ends plural noun scraps, bits, bits and pieces, debris, oddments, remnants

odious adjective offensive, detestable, horrid, loathsome, obnoxious, repulsive, revolting, unpleasant

odour noun smell, aroma, bouquet, essence, fragrance, perfume, redolence, scent, stench, stink

odyssey noun journey, crusade, pilgrimage, quest, trek, voyage

off adverb **1** away, apart, aside, elsewhere, out ♦ adjective **2** unavailable, cancelled, finished, gone, postponed **3** bad, mouldy, rancid, rotten, sour, turned

offbeat adjective unusual, eccentric, left-field (informal), novel, outré, strange, unconventional, unorthodox, way-out (informal)

off colour adjective ill, out of sorts, peaky, poorly (informal), queasy, run down, sick, under the weather (informal), unwell

offence noun **1** crime, fault, misdeed, misdemeanour, sin, transgression, trespass, wrongdoing **2** snub, affront, hurt, indignity, injustice, insult, outrage, slight **3** annoyance, anger, displeasure, indignation, pique, resentment, umbrage, wrath

offend verb insult, affront, annoy, displease, hurt (someone's) feelings, outrage, slight, snub, upset, wound

offended adjective resentful, affronted, disgruntled, displeased, outraged, piqued, put out (informal), smarting, stung, upset

offender noun criminal, crook, culprit, delinquent, lawbreaker, miscreant, sinner, transgressor, villain, wrongdoer

offensive adjective **1** insulting, abusive, discourteous, disrespectful, impertinent, insolent, objectionable, rude **2** disagreeable, disgusting, nauseating, obnoxious, odious, repellent, revolting, unpleasant, vile **3** <u>aggressive</u>, attacking, invading ♦ *noun* **4** <u>attack</u>, campaign, drive, onslaught, push (*informal*)

offer *verb* **1** <u>bid</u>, proffer, tender **2** <u>provide</u>, afford, furnish, present **3** <u>propose</u>, advance, submit, suggest **4** <u>volunteer</u>, come forward, offer one's services ♦ *noun* **5** <u>bid</u>, proposal, proposition, submission, suggestion, tender

offering *noun* <u>donation</u>, contribution, gift, hand-out, present, sacrifice, subscription

offhand *adjective* **1** <u>casual</u>, aloof, brusque, careless, curt, glib ♦ *adverb* **2** <u>impromptu</u>, ad lib, extempore, off the cuff (*informal*)

office *noun* <u>post</u>, function, occupation, place, responsibility, role, situation

officer *noun* <u>official</u>, agent, appointee, executive, functionary, office-holder, representative

official *adjective* **1** <u>authorized</u>, accredited, authentic, certified, formal, legitimate, licensed, proper, sanctioned ♦ *noun* **2** <u>officer</u>, agent, bureaucrat, executive, functionary, office bearer, representative

officiate *verb* <u>preside</u>, chair, conduct, manage, oversee, serve, superintend

officious *adjective* <u>interfering</u>, dictatorial, intrusive, meddlesome, obtrusive, overzealous, pushy (*informal*), self-important

offing *noun* **in the offing** <u>in prospect</u>, imminent, on the horizon, upcoming

off-putting *adjective* <u>discouraging</u>, daunting, disconcerting, dispiriting, disturbing, formidable, intimidating, unnerving, unsettling

offset *verb* <u>cancel out</u>, balance out, compensate for, counteract, counterbalance, make up for, neutralize

offshoot *noun* <u>by-product</u>, adjunct, appendage, development, spin-off

offspring *noun* **1** <u>child</u>, descendant, heir, scion, successor **2** <u>children</u>, brood, descendants, family, heirs, issue, progeny, young

often *adverb* <u>frequently</u>, generally, repeatedly, time and again

ogle *verb* <u>leer</u>, eye up (*informal*)

ogre *noun* <u>monster</u>, bogeyman, bugbear, demon, devil, giant, spectre

oil *verb* <u>lubricate</u>, grease

oily *adjective* <u>greasy</u>, fatty, oleaginous

ointment *noun* <u>lotion</u>, balm, cream, embrocation, emollient, liniment, salve, unguent

O.K., okay *interjection* **1** <u>all right</u>, agreed, right, roger, very good, very well, yes ♦ *adjective* **2** <u>all right</u>, acceptable, adequate, fine, good, in order, permitted, satisfactory, up to scratch (*informal*) ♦ *verb* **3** <u>approve</u>, agree to, authorize, endorse, give the green light, rubber-stamp (*informal*), sanction ♦ *noun* **4** <u>approval</u>, agreement, assent, authorization, consent, go-ahead (*informal*), green light, permission, sanction, say-so (*informal*), seal of approval

old *adjective* 1 senile, aged, ancient, decrepit, elderly, mature, venerable 2 antique, antediluvian, antiquated, dated, obsolete, superannuated, timeworn 3 former, earlier, erstwhile, one-time, previous

old-fashioned *adjective* out of date, behind the times, dated, obsolescent, obsolete, old hat, outdated, outmoded, passé, unfashionable

omen *noun* sign, foreboding, indication, portent, premonition, presage, warning

ominous *adjective* sinister, fateful, foreboding, inauspicious, portentous, threatening, unpromising, unpropitious

omission *noun* exclusion, failure, lack, neglect, oversight

omit *verb* leave out, drop, eliminate, exclude, forget, neglect, overlook, pass over, skip

omnipotence *noun* supremacy, invincibility, mastery

omnipotent *adjective* almighty, all-powerful, supreme

omniscient *adjective* all-knowing, all-wise

once *adverb* 1 formerly, at one time, long ago, once upon a time, previously 2 at once: a immediately, directly, forthwith, instantly, now, right away, straight away, this (very) minute b simultaneously, at the same time, together

oncoming *adjective* approaching, advancing, forthcoming, looming, onrushing

onerous *adjective* difficult, burdensome, demanding, exacting, hard, heavy, laborious, oppressive, taxing

one-sided *adjective* biased, lopsided, partial, partisan, prejudiced, unfair, unjust

ongoing *adjective* evolving, continuous, developing, progressing, unfinished, unfolding

onlooker *noun* observer, bystander, eyewitness, looker-on, spectator, viewer, watcher, witness

only *adjective* 1 sole, exclusive, individual, lone, single, solitary, unique ♦ *adverb* 2 merely, barely, just, purely, simply

onset *noun* beginning, inception, outbreak, start

onslaught *noun* attack, assault, blitz, charge, offensive, onrush, onset

onus *noun* burden, liability, load, obligation, responsibility, task

onward, onwards *adverb* ahead, beyond, forth, forward, in front, on

ooze¹ *verb* seep, drain, dribble, drip, escape, filter, leak

ooze² *noun* mud, alluvium, mire, silt, slime, sludge

opaque *adjective* cloudy, dim, dull, filmy, hazy, impenetrable, muddy, murky

open *adjective* 1 unfastened, agape, ajar, gaping, uncovered, unfolded, unfurled, unlocked, yawning 2 accessible, available, free, public, unoccupied,

unrestricted, vacant
3 <u>unresolved</u>, arguable,
debatable, moot, undecided,
unsettled **4** <u>frank</u>, candid,
guileless, honest, sincere,
transparent ♦ *verb* **5** <u>start</u>, begin,
commence, inaugurate, initiate,
kick off (*informal*), launch, set in
motion **6** <u>unfasten</u>, unblock,
uncork, uncover, undo, unlock,
untie, unwrap **7** <u>unfold</u>, expand,
spread (out), unfurl, unroll

open-air *adjective* <u>outdoor</u>,
alfresco

open-handed *adjective* <u>generous</u>,
bountiful, free, lavish, liberal,
munificent, unstinting

opening *noun* **1** <u>hole</u>, aperture,
chink, cleft, crack, fissure, gap,
orifice, perforation, slot, space
2 <u>opportunity</u>, chance, look-in
(*informal*), occasion, vacancy
3 <u>beginning</u>, commencement,
dawn, inception, initiation,
launch, outset, start ♦ *adjective*
4 <u>first</u>, beginning, inaugural,
initial, introductory, maiden,
primary

openly *adverb* <u>candidly</u>,
forthrightly, frankly, overtly,
plainly, unhesitatingly,
unreservedly

open-minded *adjective* <u>tolerant</u>,
broad-minded, impartial, liberal,
reasonable, receptive, unbiased,
undogmatic, unprejudiced

operate *verb* **1** <u>work</u>, act,
function, go, perform, run
2 <u>handle</u>, be in charge of,
manage, manoeuvre, use, work

operation *noun* <u>procedure</u>,
action, course, exercise, motion,
movement, performance, process

operational *adjective* <u>working</u>,

functional, going, operative,
prepared, ready, up and
running, usable, viable, workable

operative *adjective* **1** <u>in force</u>,
active, effective, functioning, in
operation, operational ♦ *noun*
2 <u>worker</u>, artisan, employee,
labourer

operator *noun* <u>worker</u>,
conductor, driver, handler,
mechanic, operative,
practitioner, technician

opinion *noun* <u>belief</u>, assessment,
feeling, idea, impression,
judgment, point of view,
sentiment, theory, view

opinionated *adjective* <u>dogmatic</u>,
bigoted, cocksure, doctrinaire,
overbearing, pig-headed,
prejudiced, single-minded

opponent *noun* <u>competitor</u>,
adversary, antagonist,
challenger, contestant, enemy,
foe, rival

opportune *adjective* <u>timely</u>,
advantageous, appropriate, apt,
auspicious, convenient,
favourable, fitting, suitable,
well-timed

opportunism *noun* <u>expediency</u>,
exploitation, pragmatism,
unscrupulousness

opportunity *noun* <u>chance</u>,
moment, occasion, opening,
scope, time

oppose *verb* <u>fight</u>, block,
combat, counter, defy, resist,
take issue with, take on, thwart,
withstand

opposed *adjective* <u>averse</u>,
antagonistic, clashing,
conflicting, contrary, dissentient,
hostile

opposing *adjective* hostile, conflicting, contrary, enemy, incompatible, opposite, rival

opposite *adjective* **1** facing, fronting **2** different, antithetical, conflicting, contrary, contrasted, reverse, unlike ♦ *noun* **3** reverse, antithesis, contradiction, contrary, converse, inverse

opposition *noun* **1** hostility, antagonism, competition, disapproval, obstruction, prevention, resistance, unfriendliness **2** opponent, antagonist, competition, foe, other side, rival

oppress *verb* **1** depress, afflict, burden, dispirit, harass, sadden, torment, vex **2** persecute, abuse, maltreat, subdue, subjugate, suppress, wrong

oppressed *adjective* downtrodden, abused, browbeaten, disadvantaged, harassed, maltreated, tyrannized, underprivileged

oppression *noun* persecution, abuse, brutality, cruelty, injury, injustice, maltreatment, subjection, tyranny

oppressive *adjective* **1** tyrannical, brutal, cruel, despotic, harsh, inhuman, repressive, severe, unjust **2** sultry, airless, close, muggy, stifling, stuffy

oppressor *noun* persecutor, autocrat, bully, despot, scourge, slave-driver, tormentor, tyrant

opt *verb, often with* for choose, decide (on), elect, go for, plump for, prefer

optimistic *adjective* hopeful, buoyant, cheerful, confident, encouraged, expectant, positive, rosy, sanguine

optimum *adjective* ideal, best, highest, optimal, peak, perfect, superlative

option *noun* choice, alternative, preference, selection

optional *adjective* voluntary, discretionary, elective, extra, open, possible

opulence *noun* **1** wealth, affluence, luxuriance, luxury, plenty, prosperity, riches **2** abundance, copiousness, cornucopia, fullness, profusion, richness, superabundance

opulent *adjective* **1** rich, affluent, lavish, luxurious, moneyed, prosperous, sumptuous, wealthy, well-off, well-to-do **2** abundant, copious, lavish, luxuriant, plentiful, profuse, prolific

opus *noun* work, brainchild, composition, creation, *oeuvre*, piece, production

oracle *noun* **1** prophecy, divination, prediction, prognostication, revelation **2** pundit, adviser, authority, guru, mastermind, mentor, wizard

oral *adjective* spoken, verbal, vocal

oration *noun* speech, address, discourse, harangue, homily, lecture

orator *noun* public speaker, declaimer, lecturer, rhetorician, speaker

oratorical *adjective* rhetorical, bombastic, declamatory, eloquent, grandiloquent, high-flown, magniloquent, sonorous

oratory *noun* eloquence,

declamation, elocution, grandiloquence, public speaking, rhetoric, speech-making

orb *noun* <u>sphere</u>, ball, circle, globe, ring

orbit *noun* 1 <u>path</u>, circle, course, cycle, revolution, rotation, trajectory 2 <u>sphere of influence</u>, ambit, compass, domain, influence, range, reach, scope, sweep ♦ *verb* 3 <u>circle</u>, circumnavigate, encircle, revolve around

orchestrate *verb* 1 <u>score</u>, arrange 2 <u>organize</u>, arrange, coordinate, put together, set up, stage-manage

ordain *verb* 1 <u>appoint</u>, anoint, consecrate, invest, nominate 2 <u>order</u>, decree, demand, dictate, fix, lay down, legislate, prescribe, rule, will

ordeal *noun* <u>hardship</u>, agony, anguish, baptism of fire, nightmare, suffering, test, torture, trial, tribulation(s)

order *noun* 1 <u>instruction</u>, command, decree, dictate, direction, directive, injunction, law, mandate, regulation, rule 2 <u>sequence</u>, arrangement, array, grouping, layout, line-up, progression, series, structure 3 <u>tidiness</u>, method, neatness, orderliness, organization, pattern, regularity, symmetry, system 4 <u>discipline</u>, calm, control, law, law and order, peace, quiet, tranquillity 5 <u>request</u>, application, booking, commission, requisition, reservation 6 <u>class</u>, caste, grade, position, rank, status 7 <u>kind</u>, class, family, genre, ilk, sort,

type 8 <u>society</u>, association, brotherhood, community, company, fraternity, guild, organization ♦ *verb* 9 <u>instruct</u>, bid, charge, command, decree, demand, direct, require 10 <u>request</u>, apply for, book, reserve, send away for 11 <u>arrange</u>, catalogue, classify, group, marshal, organize, sort out, systematize

orderly *adjective* 1 <u>well-organized</u>, businesslike, in order, methodical, neat, regular, scientific, shipshape, systematic, tidy 2 <u>well-behaved</u>, controlled, disciplined, law-abiding, peaceable, quiet, restrained

ordinarily *adverb* <u>usually</u>, as a rule, commonly, customarily, generally, habitually, in general, normally

ordinary *adjective* 1 <u>usual</u>, common, conventional, everyday, normal, regular, routine, standard, stock, typical 2 <u>commonplace</u>, banal, humble, humdrum, modest, mundane, plain, run-of-the-mill, unremarkable, workaday

organ *noun* 1 <u>part</u>, element, structure, unit 2 <u>mouthpiece</u>, forum, medium, vehicle, voice

organic *adjective* 1 <u>natural</u>, animate, biological, live, living 2 <u>systematic</u>, integrated, methodical, ordered, organized, structured

organism *noun* <u>creature</u>, animal, being, body, entity, structure

organization *noun* 1 <u>group</u>, association, body, company, confederation, corporation, institution, outfit (*informal*),

syndicate **2** management,
construction, coordination,
direction, organizing, planning,
running, structuring
3 arrangement, chemistry,
composition, format, make-up,
pattern, structure, unity

organize *verb* arrange, classify,
coordinate, group, marshal, put
together, run, set up,
systematize, take care of

orgy *noun* **1** revel, bacchanalia,
carousal, debauch, revelry,
Saturnalia **2** spree, binge
(*informal*), bout, excess,
indulgence, overindulgence,
splurge, surfeit

orient *verb* familiarize,
acclimatize, adapt, adjust, align,
get one's bearings, orientate

orientation *noun* **1** position,
bearings, direction, location
2 familiarization, acclimatization,
adaptation, adjustment,
assimilation, introduction,
settling in

orifice *noun* opening, aperture,
cleft, hole, mouth, pore, rent,
vent

origin *noun* **1** root, base, basis,
derivation, fount, fountainhead,
source, wellspring **2** beginning,
birth, creation, emergence,
foundation, genesis, inception,
launch, start

original *adjective* **1** first, earliest,
initial, introductory, opening,
primary, starting **2** new, fresh,
ground-breaking, innovative,
novel, seminal, unprecedented,
unusual **3** creative, fertile,
imaginative, ingenious,
inventive, resourceful ◆ *noun*
4 prototype, archetype, master,

model, paradigm, pattern,
precedent, standard

originality *noun* novelty,
creativity, freshness, imagination,
ingenuity, innovation,
inventiveness, newness,
unorthodoxy

originally *adverb* initially, at first,
first, in the beginning, to begin
with

originate *verb* **1** begin, arise,
come, derive, emerge, result,
rise, spring, start, stem
2 introduce, bring about, create,
formulate, generate, institute,
launch, pioneer

originator *noun* creator,
architect, author, father *or*
mother, founder, inventor,
maker, pioneer

ornament *noun* **1** decoration,
accessory, adornment, bauble,
embellishment, festoon,
knick-knack, trimming, trinket
◆ *verb* **2** decorate, adorn,
beautify, embellish, festoon,
grace, prettify

ornamental *adjective* decorative,
attractive, beautifying,
embellishing, for show, showy

ornamentation *noun*
decoration, adornment,
elaboration, embellishment,
embroidery, frills, ornateness

ornate *adjective* elaborate,
baroque, busy, decorated, fancy,
florid, fussy, ornamented,
overelaborate, rococo

orthodox *adjective* established,
accepted, approved,
conventional, customary, official,
received, traditional,
well-established

orthodoxy *noun* conformity, authority, conventionality, received wisdom, traditionalism

oscillate *verb* fluctuate, seesaw, sway, swing, vacillate, vary, vibrate, waver

oscillation *noun* swing, fluctuation, instability, vacillation, variation, wavering

ossify *verb* harden, fossilize, solidify, stiffen

ostensible *adjective* apparent, outward, pretended, professed, purported, seeming, so-called, superficial, supposed

ostensibly *adverb* apparently, on the face of it, professedly, seemingly, supposedly

ostentation *noun* display, affectation, exhibitionism, flamboyance, flashiness, flaunting, parade, pomp, pretentiousness, show, showing off (*informal*)

ostentatious *adjective* pretentious, brash, conspicuous, flamboyant, flashy, gaudy, loud, obtrusive, showy

ostracism *noun* exclusion, banishment, exile, isolation, rejection

ostracize *verb* exclude, banish, cast out, cold-shoulder, exile, give (someone) the cold shoulder, reject, send to Coventry, shun

other *adjective* 1 additional, added, alternative, auxiliary, extra, further, more, spare, supplementary 2 different, contrasting, dissimilar, distinct, diverse, separate, unrelated, variant

otherwise *conjunction* 1 or else, if not, or then ♦ *adverb* 2 differently, any other way, contrarily

ounce *noun* shred, atom, crumb, drop, grain, scrap, speck, trace

oust *verb* expel, depose, dislodge, displace, dispossess, eject, throw out, topple, turn out, unseat

out *adjective* 1 away, abroad, absent, elsewhere, gone, not at home, outside 2 extinguished, at an end, dead, ended, exhausted, expired, finished, used up

outbreak *noun* eruption, burst, epidemic, explosion, flare-up, outburst, rash, upsurge

outburst *noun* outpouring, eruption, explosion, flare-up, outbreak, paroxysm, spasm, surge

outcast *noun* pariah, castaway, exile, leper, *persona non grata*, refugee, vagabond, wretch

outclass *verb* surpass, eclipse, excel, leave standing (*informal*), outdo, outshine, outstrip, overshadow, run rings around (*informal*)

outcome *noun* result, conclusion, consequence, end, issue, payoff (*informal*), upshot

outcry *noun* protest, clamour, commotion, complaint, hue and cry, hullaballoo, outburst, uproar

outdated *adjective* old-fashioned, antiquated, archaic, obsolete, outmoded, out of date, passé, unfashionable

outdo *verb* surpass, beat, best, eclipse, exceed, get the better of, outclass, outmanoeuvre, overcome, top, transcend

outdoor *adjective* open-air, alfresco, out-of-door(s), outside

outer *adjective* external, exposed, exterior, outlying, outside, outward, peripheral, surface

outfit *noun* 1 costume, clothes, ensemble, garb, get-up (*informal*), kit, suit 2 *Informal* group, company, crew, organization, setup (*informal*), squad, team, unit

outgoing *adjective* 1 leaving, departing, former, retiring, withdrawing 2 sociable, approachable, communicative, expansive, extrovert, friendly, gregarious, open, warm

outgoings *plural noun* expenses, costs, expenditure, outlay, overheads

outing *noun* trip, excursion, expedition, jaunt, spin (*informal*)

outlandish *adjective* strange, bizarre, exotic, fantastic, far-out (*slang*), freakish, outré, preposterous, unheard-of, weird

outlaw *noun* 1 bandit, brigand, desperado, fugitive, highwayman, marauder, outcast, robber ♦ *verb* 2 forbid, ban, bar, disallow, exclude, prohibit, proscribe

outlay *noun* expenditure, cost, expenses, investment, outgoings, spending

outlet *noun* 1 release, avenue, channel, duct, exit, opening, vent 2 shop, market, store

outline *noun* 1 summary, recapitulation, résumé, rundown, synopsis, thumbnail sketch 2 shape, configuration, contour,

delineation, figure, form, profile, silhouette ♦ *verb* 3 summarize, adumbrate, delineate, draft, plan, rough out, sketch (in), trace

outlive *verb* survive, outlast

outlook *noun* 1 attitude, angle, frame of mind, perspective, point of view, slant, standpoint, viewpoint 2 prospect, expectations, forecast, future

outlying *adjective* remote, distant, far-flung, out-of-the-way, peripheral, provincial

outmoded *adjective* old-fashioned, anachronistic, antiquated, archaic, obsolete, out-of-date, outworn, passé, unfashionable

out-of-date *adjective* old-fashioned, antiquated, dated, expired, invalid, lapsed, obsolete, outmoded, outworn, passé

outpouring *noun* stream, cascade, effusion, flow, spate, spurt, torrent

output *noun* production, achievement, manufacture, productivity, yield

outrage *noun* 1 violation, abuse, affront, desecration, indignity, insult, offence, sacrilege, violence 2 indignation, anger, fury, hurt, resentment, shock, wrath ♦ *verb* 3 offend, affront, incense, infuriate, madden, scandalize, shock

outrageous *adjective* 1 offensive, atrocious, disgraceful, flagrant, heinous, iniquitous, nefarious, unspeakable, villainous, wicked 2 shocking, exorbitant, extravagant, immoderate, preposterous, scandalous, steep (*informal*), unreasonable

outré *adjective* <u>eccentric</u>, bizarre, fantastic, freakish, odd, off-the-wall (*slang*), outlandish, unconventional, weird

outright *adjective* 1 <u>absolute</u>, complete, out-and-out, perfect, thorough, thoroughgoing, total, unconditional, unmitigated, unqualified 2 <u>direct</u>, definite, flat, straightforward, unequivocal, unqualified ♦ *adverb* 3 <u>absolutely</u>, completely, openly, overtly, straightforwardly, thoroughly, to the full

outset *noun* <u>beginning</u>, commencement, inauguration, inception, kickoff (*informal*), onset, opening, start

outshine *verb* <u>overshadow</u>, eclipse, leave *or* put in the shade, outclass, outdo, outstrip, surpass, transcend, upstage

outside *adjective* 1 <u>external</u>, exterior, extraneous, outer, outward 2 *As in* **an outside chance** <u>unlikely</u>, distant, faint, marginal, remote, slight, slim, small ♦ *noun* 3 <u>surface</u>, exterior, façade, face, front, skin, topside

outsider *noun* <u>interloper</u>, incomer, intruder, newcomer, odd man out, stranger

outsize *adjective* <u>extra-large</u>, giant, gigantic, huge, jumbo (*informal*), mammoth, monster, oversized

outskirts *plural noun* <u>edge</u>, boundary, environs, periphery, suburbia, suburbs

outspoken *adjective* <u>forthright</u>, abrupt, blunt, explicit, frank, open, plain-spoken, unceremonious, unequivocal

outstanding *adjective* 1 <u>excellent</u>, exceptional, great, important, impressive, special, superior, superlative 2 <u>unpaid</u>, due, payable, pending, remaining, uncollected, unsettled

outstrip *verb* <u>surpass</u>, better, eclipse, exceed, excel, outdistance, outdo, overtake, transcend

outward *adjective* <u>apparent</u>, noticeable, observable, obvious, ostensible, perceptible, surface, visible

outwardly *adverb* <u>ostensibly</u>, apparently, externally, on the face of it, on the surface, seemingly, superficially, to all intents and purposes

outweigh *verb* <u>override</u>, cancel (out), compensate for, eclipse, prevail over, take precedence over, tip the scales

outwit *verb* <u>outthink</u>, cheat, dupe, get the better of, outfox, outmanoeuvre, outsmart (*informal*), put one over on (*informal*), swindle, take in (*informal*)

outworn *adjective* <u>outdated</u>, antiquated, discredited, disused, hackneyed, obsolete, outmoded, out-of-date, worn-out

oval *adjective* <u>elliptical</u>, egg-shaped, ovoid

ovation *noun* <u>applause</u>, acclaim, acclamation, big hand, cheers, clapping, plaudits, tribute

over *preposition* 1 <u>on</u>, above, on top of, upon 2 <u>exceeding</u>, above, in excess of, more than ♦ *adverb* 3 <u>above</u>, aloft, on high, overhead 4 <u>extra</u>, beyond, in addition, in excess, left over

♦ *adjective* **5** <u>finished</u>, bygone, closed, completed, concluded, done (with), ended, gone, past

overact *verb* <u>exaggerate</u>, ham *or* ham up (*informal*), overdo, overplay

overall *adjective* **1** <u>total</u>, all-embracing, blanket, complete, comprehensive, general, global, inclusive ♦ *adverb* **2** <u>in general</u>, on the whole

overawe *verb* <u>intimidate</u>, abash, alarm, daunt, frighten, scare, terrify

overbalance *verb* <u>overturn</u>, capsize, keel over, slip, tip over, topple over, tumble, turn turtle

overbearing *adjective* <u>arrogant</u>, bossy (*informal*), dictatorial, domineering, haughty, high-handed, imperious, supercilious, superior

overblown *adjective* <u>excessive</u>, disproportionate, immoderate, inflated, overdone, over the top, undue

overcast *adjective* <u>cloudy</u>, dismal, dreary, dull, grey, leaden, louring *or* lowering, murky

overcharge *verb* <u>cheat</u>, diddle (*informal*), fleece, rip off (*slang*), short-change, sting (*informal*), surcharge

overcome *verb* **1** <u>conquer</u>, beat, defeat, master, overpower, overwhelm, prevail, subdue, subjugate, surmount, triumph over, vanquish ♦ *adjective* **2** <u>affected</u>, at a loss for words, bowled over (*informal*), overwhelmed, speechless, swept off one's feet

overconfident *adjective* <u>brash</u>, cocksure, foolhardy, overweening, presumptuous

overcrowded *adjective* <u>congested</u>, bursting at the seams, choked, jam-packed, overloaded, overpopulated, packed (out), swarming

overdo *verb* **1** <u>exaggerate</u>, belabour, gild the lily, go overboard (*informal*), overindulge, overreach, overstate **2 overdo it** <u>overwork</u>, bite off more than one can chew, burn the candle at both ends (*informal*), overload, strain *or* overstrain oneself, wear oneself out

overdone *adjective* **1** <u>excessive</u>, exaggerated, fulsome, immoderate, inordinate, overelaborate, too much, undue, unnecessary **2** <u>overcooked</u>, burnt, charred, dried up, spoiled

overdue *adjective* <u>late</u>, behindhand, behind schedule, belated, owing, tardy, unpunctual

overeat *verb* <u>overindulge</u>, binge (*informal*), gorge, gormandize, guzzle, pig out (*slang*), stuff oneself

overemphasize *verb* <u>overstress</u>, belabour, blow up out of all proportion, make a mountain out of a molehill (*informal*), overdramatize

overflow *verb* **1** <u>spill</u>, brim over, bubble over, pour over, run over, well over ♦ *noun* **2** <u>surplus</u>, overabundance, spilling over

overhang *verb* <u>project</u>, extend, jut, loom, protrude, stick out

overhaul *verb* **1** <u>repair</u>, check, do up (*informal*), examine, inspect,

recondition, restore, service
2 <u>overtake</u>, catch up with, get
ahead of, pass ♦ *noun* 3 <u>checkup</u>,
check, examination, going-over
(*informal*), inspection,
reconditioning, service

overhead *adverb* 1 <u>above</u>, aloft,
in the sky, on high, skyward, up
above, upward ♦ *adjective*
2 <u>aerial</u>, overhanging, upper

overheads *plural noun* <u>running
costs</u>, operating costs

overindulgence *noun* <u>excess</u>,
immoderation, intemperance,
overeating, surfeit

overjoyed *adjective* <u>delighted</u>,
cock-a-hoop, elated, euphoric,
jubilant, on cloud nine (*informal*),
over the moon (*informal*), thrilled

overload *verb* <u>overburden</u>,
burden, encumber, oppress,
overtax, saddle (with), strain,
weigh down

overlook *verb* 1 <u>forget</u>,
disregard, miss, neglect, omit,
pass 2 <u>ignore</u>, condone,
disregard, excuse, forgive, make
allowances for, pardon, turn a
blind eye to, wink at 3 <u>have a
view of</u>, look over *or* out on

overpower *verb* <u>overwhelm</u>,
conquer, crush, defeat, master,
overcome, overthrow, quell,
subdue, subjugate, vanquish

overpowering *adjective*
<u>irresistible</u>, forceful, invincible,
irrefutable, overwhelming,
powerful, strong

overrate *verb* <u>overestimate</u>,
exaggerate, overvalue

override *verb* <u>overrule</u>, annul,
cancel, countermand, nullify,
outweigh, supersede

overriding *adjective* <u>ultimate</u>,
dominant, paramount,
predominant, primary, supreme

overrule *verb* <u>reverse</u>, alter,
annul, cancel, countermand,
override, overturn, repeal,
rescind, veto

overrun *verb* 1 <u>invade</u>, occupy,
overwhelm, rout 2 <u>infest</u>, choke,
inundate, permeate, ravage,
spread over, swarm over
3 <u>exceed</u>, go beyond, overshoot,
run over *or* on

overseer *noun* <u>supervisor</u>, boss
(*informal*), chief, foreman,
master, superintendent

overshadow *verb* 1 <u>outshine</u>,
dominate, dwarf, eclipse, leave
or put in the shade, surpass,
tower above 2 <u>spoil</u>, blight, mar,
put a damper on, ruin, temper

oversight *noun* <u>mistake</u>, blunder,
carelessness, error, fault, lapse,
neglect, omission, slip

overt *adjective* <u>open</u>, blatant,
manifest, observable, obvious,
plain, public, unconcealed,
undisguised

overtake *verb* 1 <u>pass</u>, catch up
with, get past, leave behind,
outdistance, outdo, outstrip,
overhaul 2 <u>befall</u>, engulf,
happen, hit, overwhelm, strike

overthrow *verb* 1 <u>defeat</u>, bring
down, conquer, depose,
dethrone, oust, overcome,
overpower, topple, unseat,
vanquish ♦ *noun* 2 <u>downfall</u>,
defeat, destruction,
dethronement, fall, ousting,
undoing, unseating

overtone *noun* <u>connotation</u>,
hint, implication, innuendo,
intimation, nuance, sense,

suggestion, undercurrent

overture noun 1 Music <u>introduction</u>, opening, prelude 2 **overtures** <u>approach</u>, advance, invitation, offer, proposal, proposition

overturn verb 1 <u>tip over</u>, capsize, keel over, overbalance, topple, upend, upturn 2 <u>overthrow</u>, bring down, depose, destroy, unseat

overweight adjective <u>fat</u>, bulky, chubby, chunky, corpulent, heavy, hefty, obese, plump, portly, stout, tubby (informal)

overwhelm verb 1 <u>devastate</u>, bowl over (informal), knock (someone) for six (informal), overcome, stagger, sweep (someone) off his or her feet, take (someone's) breath away 2 <u>destroy</u>, crush, cut to pieces, massacre, overpower, overrun, rout

overwhelming adjective <u>devastating</u>, breathtaking, crushing, irresistible, overpowering, shattering, stunning, towering

overwork verb 1 <u>strain</u>, burn the midnight oil, sweat (informal), work one's fingers to the bone 2 <u>overuse</u>, exhaust, exploit, fatigue, oppress, wear out, weary

overwrought adjective <u>agitated</u>, distracted, excited, frantic, keyed up, on edge, overexcited, tense, uptight (informal)

owe verb <u>be in debt</u>, be in arrears, be obligated or indebted

owing adjective <u>unpaid</u>, due, outstanding, overdue, owed, payable, unsettled

owing to preposition <u>because of</u>, as a result of, on account of

own adjective 1 <u>personal</u>, individual, particular, private ◆ pronoun 2 **hold one's own** <u>compete</u>, keep going, keep one's end up, keep one's head above water 3 **on one's own** <u>alone</u>, by oneself, independently, singly, unaided, unassisted, under one's own steam ◆ verb 4 <u>possess</u>, be in possession of, enjoy, have, hold, keep, retain 5 <u>acknowledge</u>, admit, allow, concede, confess, grant, recognize 6 **own up** <u>confess</u>, admit, come clean, make a clean breast, tell the truth

owner noun <u>possessor</u>, holder, landlord or landlady, proprietor

ownership noun <u>possession</u>, dominion, title

P p

pace noun 1 <u>step</u>, gait, stride, tread, walk 2 <u>speed</u>, rate, tempo, velocity ◆ verb 3 <u>stride</u>, march, patrol, pound 4 **pace out** <u>measure</u>, count, mark out, step

pacifist noun <u>peace lover</u>, conscientious objector, dove

pacify verb <u>calm</u>, allay, appease, assuage, mollify, placate, propitiate, soothe

pack verb 1 <u>package</u>, bundle, load, store, stow 2 <u>cram</u>, compress, crowd, fill, jam, press, ram, stuff 3 **pack off** <u>send away</u>, dismiss, send packing (informal) ◆ noun 4 <u>bundle</u>, back pack, burden, kitbag, knapsack, load,

parcel, rucksack **5** <u>packet</u>,
package **6** <u>group</u>, band, bunch,
company, crowd, flock, gang,
herd, mob, troop

package *noun* **1** <u>parcel</u>, box,
carton, container, packet **2** <u>unit</u>,
combination, whole ♦ *verb*
3 <u>pack</u>, box, parcel (up), wrap

packed *adjective* <u>full</u>,
chock-a-block, chock-full,
crammed, crowded, filled,
jammed, jam-packed

packet *noun* **1** <u>package</u>, bag,
carton, container, parcel **2** *Slang*
<u>fortune</u>, bomb (*Brit. slang*), king's
ransom (*informal*), pile (*informal*),
small fortune, tidy sum (*informal*)

pack in *verb Brit. informal* <u>stop</u>,
cease, chuck (*informal*), give up
or over, kick (*informal*)

pack up *verb* **1** <u>put away</u>, store
2 *Informal* <u>stop</u>, finish, give up,
pack in (*Brit. informal*) **3** <u>break
down</u>, conk out (*informal*), fail

pact *noun* <u>agreement</u>, alliance,
bargain, covenant, deal, treaty,
understanding

pad¹ *noun* **1** <u>cushion</u>, buffer,
protection, stuffing, wad
2 <u>notepad</u>, block, jotter, writing
pad **3** <u>paw</u>, foot, sole **4** *Slang*
<u>home</u>, apartment, flat, place
♦ *verb* **5** <u>pack</u>, cushion, fill,
protect, stuff **6 pad out**
<u>lengthen</u>, elaborate, fill out, flesh
out, protract, spin out, stretch

pad² *verb* <u>sneak</u>, creep, go
barefoot, steal

padding *noun* **1** <u>filling</u>, packing,
stuffing, wadding **2** <u>waffle</u>
(*informal, chiefly Brit.*), hot air
(*informal*), verbiage, verbosity,
wordiness

paddle¹ *noun* **1** <u>oar</u>, scull ♦ *verb*
2 <u>row</u>, propel, pull, scull

paddle² *verb* **1** <u>wade</u>, slop, splash
(about) **2** <u>dabble</u>, stir

pagan *adjective* **1** <u>heathen</u>,
idolatrous, infidel, polytheistic
♦ *noun* **2** <u>heathen</u>, idolater,
infidel, polytheist

page¹ *noun* <u>folio</u>, leaf, sheet, side

page² *noun* **1** <u>attendant</u>,
pageboy, servant, squire ♦ *verb*
2 <u>call</u>, send for, summon

pageant *noun* <u>show</u>, display,
parade, procession, spectacle,
tableau

pageantry *noun* <u>spectacle</u>,
display, grandeur, parade,
pomp, show, splendour,
theatricality

pain *noun* **1** <u>hurt</u>, ache,
discomfort, irritation, pang,
soreness, tenderness, throb,
twinge **2** <u>suffering</u>, agony,
anguish, distress, heartache,
misery, torment, torture ♦ *verb*
3 <u>hurt</u>, smart, sting, throb
4 <u>distress</u>, agonize, cut to the
quick, grieve, hurt, sadden,
torment, torture

pained *adjective* <u>distressed</u>,
aggrieved, hurt, injured,
offended, upset, wounded

painful *adjective* **1** <u>distressing</u>,
disagreeable, distasteful,
grievous, unpleasant **2** <u>sore</u>,
aching, agonizing, smarting,
tender **3** <u>difficult</u>, arduous, hard,
laborious, troublesome, trying

painfully *adverb* <u>distressingly</u>,
clearly, dreadfully, sadly,
unfortunately

painkiller *noun* <u>analgesic</u>,
anaesthetic, anodyne, drug

painless *adjective* <u>simple</u>, easy, effortless, fast, quick

pains *plural noun* <u>trouble</u>, bother, care, diligence, effort

painstaking *adjective* <u>thorough</u>, assiduous, careful, conscientious, diligent, meticulous, scrupulous

paint *noun* 1 <u>colouring</u>, colour, dye, pigment, stain, tint ♦ *verb* 2 <u>depict</u>, draw, picture, portray, represent, sketch 3 <u>coat</u>, apply, colour, cover, daub

pair *noun* 1 <u>couple</u>, brace, duo, twins ♦ *verb* 2 <u>couple</u>, bracket, join, match (up), team, twin

pal *noun* <u>friend</u>, buddy (*informal*), chum (*informal*), companion, comrade, crony, mate (*informal*)

palatable *adjective* <u>delicious</u>, appetizing, luscious, mouthwatering, tasty

palate *noun* <u>taste</u>, appetite, stomach

palatial *adjective* <u>magnificent</u>, grand, imposing, majestic, opulent, regal, splendid, stately

palaver *noun* <u>fuss</u>, business (*informal*), carry on (*informal, chiefly Brit.*), pantomime (*informal, chiefly Brit.*), performance (*informal*), rigmarole, song and dance (*Brit. informal*), to-do

pale *adjective* 1 <u>white</u>, ashen, bleached, colourless, faded, light, pallid, pasty, wan ♦ *verb* 2 <u>become pale</u>, blanch, go white, lose colour, whiten

pall¹ *noun* 1 <u>cloud</u>, mantle, shadow, shroud, veil 2 <u>gloom</u>, check, damp, damper

pall² *verb* <u>become boring</u>, become dull, become tedious, cloy, jade, sicken, tire, weary

pallid *adjective* <u>pale</u>, anaemic, ashen, colourless, pasty, wan

pallor *noun* <u>paleness</u>, lack of colour, pallidness, wanness, whiteness

palm off *verb* <u>fob off</u>, foist off, pass off

palpable *adjective* <u>obvious</u>, clear, conspicuous, evident, manifest, plain, unmistakable, visible

palpitate *verb* <u>beat</u>, flutter, pound, pulsate, throb, tremble

paltry *adjective* <u>insignificant</u>, contemptible, despicable, inconsiderable, meagre, mean, measly, minor, miserable, petty, poor, puny, slight, small, trifling, trivial, unimportant, worthless

pamper *verb* <u>spoil</u>, coddle, cosset, indulge, mollycoddle, pet

pamphlet *noun* <u>booklet</u>, brochure, circular, leaflet, tract

pan¹ *noun* 1 <u>pot</u>, container, saucepan ♦ *verb* 2 <u>sift out</u>, look for, search for 3 *Informal* <u>criticize</u>, censure, knock (*informal*), slam (*slang*), tear into (*informal*)

pan² *verb* <u>move</u>, follow, sweep, track

panacea *noun* <u>cure-all</u>, nostrum, universal cure

panache *noun* <u>style</u>, dash, élan, flamboyance

pandemonium *noun* <u>uproar</u>, bedlam, chaos, confusion, din, hullabaloo, racket, rumpus, turmoil

pander *verb* **pander to** <u>indulge</u>, cater to, gratify, play up to (*informal*), please, satisfy

pang *noun* <u>twinge</u>, ache, pain,

prick, spasm, stab, sting

panic noun **1** <u>fear</u>, alarm, fright, hysteria, scare, terror ♦ verb **2** <u>go to pieces</u>, become hysterical, lose one's nerve **3** <u>alarm</u>, scare, unnerve

panic-stricken adjective <u>frightened</u>, frightened out of one's wits, hysterical, in a cold sweat (informal), panicky, scared, scared stiff, terrified

panoply noun <u>array</u>, attire, dress, garb, regalia, trappings

panorama noun <u>view</u>, prospect, vista

panoramic adjective <u>wide</u>, comprehensive, extensive, overall, sweeping

pant verb <u>puff</u>, blow, breathe, gasp, heave, wheeze

pants plural noun **1** Brit. <u>underpants</u>, boxer shorts, briefs, drawers, knickers, panties **2** U.S. <u>trousers</u>, slacks

paper noun **1** <u>newspaper</u>, daily, gazette, journal **2** <u>essay</u>, article, dissertation, report, treatise **3 papers: a** <u>documents</u>, certificates, deeds, records **b** <u>letters</u>, archive, diaries, documents, dossier, file, records ♦ verb **4** <u>wallpaper</u>, hang

par noun <u>average</u>, level, mean, norm, standard, usual

parable noun <u>lesson</u>, allegory, fable, moral tale, story

parade noun **1** <u>procession</u>, array, cavalcade, march, pageant **2** <u>show</u>, display, spectacle ♦ verb **3** <u>flaunt</u>, display, exhibit, show off (informal) **4** <u>march</u>, process

paradigm noun <u>model</u>, example, ideal, pattern

paradise noun **1** <u>heaven</u>, Elysian fields, Happy Valley, Promised Land **2** <u>bliss</u>, delight, felicity, heaven, utopia

paradox noun <u>contradiction</u>, anomaly, enigma, oddity, puzzle

paradoxical adjective <u>contradictory</u>, baffling, confounding, enigmatic, puzzling

paragon noun <u>model</u>, epitome, exemplar, ideal, nonpareil, pattern, quintessence

paragraph noun <u>section</u>, clause, item, part, passage, subdivision

parallel adjective **1** <u>equidistant</u>, alongside, side by side **2** <u>matching</u>, analogous, corresponding, like, resembling, similar ♦ noun **3** <u>equivalent</u>, analogue, counterpart, equal, match, twin **4** <u>similarity</u>, analogy, comparison, likeness, resemblance

paralyse verb **1** <u>disable</u>, cripple, incapacitate, lame **2** <u>immobilize</u>, freeze, halt, numb, petrify, stun

paralysis noun **1** <u>immobility</u>, palsy **2** <u>standstill</u>, breakdown, halt, stoppage

paralytic adjective <u>paralysed</u>, crippled, disabled, incapacitated, lame, palsied

parameter noun Informal <u>limit</u>, framework, limitation, restriction, specification

paramount adjective <u>principal</u>, cardinal, chief, first, foremost, main, primary, prime, supreme

paranoid adjective **1** <u>mentally ill</u>, deluded, disturbed, manic, neurotic, paranoiac, psychotic **2** Informal <u>suspicious</u>, fearful, nervous, worried

paraphernalia noun equipment, apparatus, baggage, belongings, effects, gear, stuff, tackle, things, trappings

paraphrase noun 1 rewording, rephrasing, restatement ◆verb 2 reword, express in other words or one's own words, rephrase, restate

parasite noun sponger (informal), bloodsucker (informal), hanger-on, leech, scrounger (informal)

parasitic, parasitical adjective scrounging (informal), bloodsucking (informal), sponging (informal)

parcel noun 1 package, bundle, pack ◆verb 2 often with **up** wrap, do up, pack, package, tie up

parch verb dry up, dehydrate, desiccate, evaporate, shrivel, wither

parched adjective dried out or up, arid, dehydrated, dry, thirsty

pardon verb 1 forgive, absolve, acquit, excuse, exonerate, let off (informal), overlook ◆noun 2 forgiveness, absolution, acquittal, amnesty, exoneration

pardonable adjective forgivable, excusable, minor, understandable, venial

pare verb 1 peel, clip, cut, shave, skin, trim 2 cut back, crop, cut, decrease, dock, reduce

parent noun father or mother, procreator, progenitor, sire

parentage noun family, ancestry, birth, descent, lineage, pedigree, stock

pariah noun outcast, exile, undesirable, untouchable

parish noun community, church, congregation, flock

parity noun equality, consistency, equivalence, uniformity, unity

park noun parkland, estate, garden, grounds, woodland

parlance noun language, idiom, jargon, phraseology, speech, talk, tongue

parliament noun assembly, congress, convention, council, legislature, senate

parliamentary adjective governmental, law-making, legislative

parlour noun Old-fashioned sitting room, drawing room, front room, living room, lounge

parlous adjective Archaic or humorous dangerous, hazardous, risky

parochial adjective provincial, insular, limited, narrow, narrow-minded, petty, small-minded

parody noun 1 takeoff (informal), burlesque, caricature, satire, send-up (Brit. informal), skit, spoof (informal) ◆verb 2 take off (informal), burlesque, caricature, do a takeoff of (informal), satirize, send up (Brit. informal)

paroxysm noun outburst, attack, convulsion, fit, seizure, spasm

parrot verb repeat, copy, echo, imitate, mimic

parry verb 1 ward off, block, deflect, rebuff, repel, repulse 2 evade, avoid, dodge, sidestep

parsimonious adjective mean, close, frugal, miserly, niggardly, penny-pinching (informal), stingy, tightfisted

parson noun clergyman, churchman, cleric, minister, pastor, preacher, priest, vicar

part noun 1 piece, bit, fraction, fragment, portion, scrap, section, share 2 component, branch, constituent, division, member, unit 3 *Theatre* role, character, lines 4 side, behalf, cause, concern, interest 5 *often plural* region, area, district, neighbourhood, quarter, vicinity 6 **in good part** good-naturedly, cheerfully, well, without offence 7 **in part** partly, a little, in some measure, partially, somewhat ◆ *verb* 8 divide, break, come apart, detach, rend, separate, sever, split, tear 9 separate, depart, go, go away, leave, split up, withdraw

partake verb 1 **partake of** consume, eat, take 2 **partake in** participate in, engage in, share in, take part in

partial adjective 1 incomplete, imperfect, uncompleted, unfinished 2 biased, discriminatory, one-sided, partisan, prejudiced, unfair, unjust

partiality noun 1 bias, favouritism, preference, prejudice 2 liking, fondness, inclination, love, penchant, predilection, taste, weakness

partially adverb partly, fractionally, incompletely, in part, not wholly, somewhat

participant noun participator, contributor, member, player, stakeholder

participate verb take part, be involved in, join in, partake, perform, share

participation noun taking part, contribution, involvement, joining in, partaking, sharing in

particle noun bit, grain, iota, jot, mite, piece, scrap, shred, speck

particular adjective 1 specific, distinct, exact, peculiar, precise, special 2 special, especial, exceptional, marked, notable, noteworthy, remarkable, singular, uncommon, unusual 3 fussy, choosy (*informal*), demanding, fastidious, finicky, pernickety (*informal*), picky (*informal*) ◆ *noun* 4 *usually plural* detail, circumstance, fact, feature, item, specification 5 **in particular** especially, distinctly, exactly, particularly, specifically

particularly adverb 1 especially, exceptionally, notably, singularly, uncommonly, unusually 2 specifically, distinctly, especially, explicitly, expressly, in particular

parting noun 1 going, farewell, goodbye 2 division, breaking, rift, rupture, separation, split

partisan noun 1 supporter, adherent, devotee, upholder 2 underground fighter, guerrilla, resistance fighter ◆ *adjective* 3 prejudiced, biased, interested, one-sided, partial, sectarian

partition noun 1 screen, barrier, wall 2 division, segregation, separation 3 allotment, apportionment, distribution ◆ *verb* 4 separate, divide, screen

partly adverb partially, slightly, somewhat

partner noun 1 spouse, consort, husband *or* wife, mate,

significant other (*U.S. informal*)
2 <u>companion</u>, ally, associate,
colleague, comrade, helper, mate

partnership *noun* <u>company</u>,
alliance, cooperative, firm,
house, society, union

party *noun* 1 <u>get-together</u>
(*informal*), celebration, do
(*informal*), festivity, function,
gathering, reception, social
gathering 2 <u>group</u>, band,
company, crew, gang, squad,
team, unit 3 <u>faction</u>, camp,
clique, coterie, league, set, side
4 *Informal* <u>person</u>, individual,
someone

pass *verb* 1 <u>go by or past</u>, elapse,
go, lapse, move, proceed, run
2 <u>qualify</u>, do, get through,
graduate, succeed 3 <u>spend</u>, fill,
occupy, while away 4 <u>give</u>,
convey, deliver, hand, send,
transfer 5 <u>approve</u>, accept,
decree, enact, legislate, ordain,
ratify 6 <u>exceed</u>, beat, go
beyond, outdo, outstrip, surpass
7 <u>end</u>, blow over, cease, go
♦ *noun* 8 <u>gap</u>, canyon, gorge,
ravine, route 9 <u>licence</u>,
authorization, passport, permit,
ticket, warrant

passable *adjective* <u>adequate</u>,
acceptable, all right, average,
fair, mediocre, so-so (*informal*),
tolerable

passage *noun* 1 <u>way</u>, alley,
avenue, channel, course, path,
road, route 2 <u>corridor</u>, hall,
lobby, vestibule 3 <u>extract</u>,
excerpt, piece, quotation,
reading, section, text 4 <u>journey</u>,
crossing, trek, trip, voyage
5 <u>safe-conduct</u>, freedom,
permission, right

passageway *noun* <u>corridor</u>,
aisle, alley, hall, hallway, lane,
passage

pass away *verb Euphemistic* <u>die</u>,
expire, kick the bucket (*slang*),
pass on, pass over, shuffle off
this mortal coil, snuff it (*informal*)

passé *adjective* <u>out-of-date</u>,
dated, obsolete, old-fashioned,
old hat, outdated, outmoded,
unfashionable

passenger *noun* <u>traveller</u>, fare,
rider

passer-by *noun* <u>bystander</u>,
onlooker, witness

passing *adjective* 1 <u>momentary</u>,
brief, ephemeral, fleeting,
short-lived, temporary, transient,
transitory 2 <u>superficial</u>, casual,
cursory, glancing, quick, short

passion *noun* 1 <u>love</u>, ardour,
desire, infatuation, lust
2 <u>emotion</u>, ardour, excitement,
feeling, fervour, fire, heat,
intensity, warmth, zeal 3 <u>rage</u>,
anger, fit, frenzy, fury, outburst,
paroxysm, storm 4 <u>mania</u>, bug
(*informal*), craving, craze,
enthusiasm, fascination, obsession

passionate *adjective* 1 <u>loving</u>,
amorous, ardent, erotic, hot,
lustful 2 <u>emotional</u>, ardent,
eager, fervent, fierce, heartfelt,
impassioned, intense, strong

passive *adjective* <u>submissive</u>,
compliant, docile, inactive,
quiescent, receptive

pass off *verb* <u>fake</u>, counterfeit,
make a pretence of, palm off

pass out *verb Informal* <u>faint</u>,
become unconscious, black out
(*informal*), lose consciousness

pass over *verb* <u>disregard</u>, ignore,

overlook, take no notice of

pass up verb Informal miss, abstain, decline, forgo, give (something) a miss (informal), let slip, neglect

password noun signal, key word, watchword

past adjective 1 former, ancient, bygone, early, olden, previous 2 over, done, ended, finished, gone ◆ noun 3 background, history, life, past life 4 **the past** former times, days gone by, long ago, olden days ◆ preposition 5 after, beyond, later than 6 beyond, across, by, over

paste noun 1 adhesive, cement, glue, gum ◆ verb 2 stick, cement, glue, gum

pastel adjective pale, delicate, light, muted, soft

pastiche noun medley, blend, hotchpotch, mélange, miscellany, mixture

pastime noun activity, amusement, diversion, entertainment, game, hobby, recreation

pastor noun clergyman, churchman, ecclesiastic, minister, parson, priest, rector, vicar

pastoral adjective 1 rustic, bucolic, country, rural 2 ecclesiastical, clerical, ministerial, priestly

pasture noun grassland, grass, grazing, meadow

pasty adjective pale, anaemic, pallid, sickly, wan

pat verb 1 stroke, caress, fondle, pet, tap, touch ◆ noun 2 stroke, clap, tap

patch noun 1 reinforcement 2 spot, bit, scrap, shred, small piece 3 plot, area, ground, land, tract ◆ verb 4 mend, cover, reinforce, repair, sew up

patchwork noun mixture, hotchpotch, jumble, medley, pastiche

patchy adjective uneven, erratic, fitful, irregular, sketchy, spotty, variable

patent noun 1 copyright, licence ◆ adjective 2 obvious, apparent, clear, evident, glaring, manifest

paternal adjective fatherly, concerned, protective, solicitous

paternity noun 1 fatherhood 2 parentage, descent, extraction, family, lineage

path noun 1 way, footpath, road, track, trail 2 course, direction, road, route, way

pathetic adjective sad, affecting, distressing, heart-rending, moving, pitiable, plaintive, poignant, tender, touching

pathos noun sadness, pitifulness, plaintiveness, poignancy

patience noun 1 forbearance, calmness, restraint, serenity, sufferance, tolerance 2 endurance, constancy, fortitude, long-suffering, perseverance, resignation, stoicism, submission

patient adjective 1 long-suffering, calm, enduring, persevering, philosophical, resigned, stoical, submissive, uncomplaining 2 forbearing, even-tempered, forgiving, indulgent, lenient, mild, tolerant, understanding ◆ noun 3 sick person, case, invalid, sufferer

patriot noun <u>nationalist</u>, chauvinist, loyalist

patriotic adjective <u>nationalistic</u>, chauvinistic, jingoistic, loyal

patriotism noun <u>nationalism</u>, jingoism

patrol noun 1 <u>policing</u>, guarding, protecting, vigilance, watching 2 <u>guard</u>, patrolman, sentinel, watch, watchman ♦ verb 3 <u>police</u>, guard, inspect, keep guard, keep watch, safeguard

patron noun 1 <u>supporter</u>, backer, benefactor, champion, friend, helper, philanthropist, sponsor 2 <u>customer</u>, buyer, client, frequenter, habitué, shopper

patronage noun 1 <u>support</u>, aid, assistance, backing, help, promotion, sponsorship 2 <u>custom</u>, business, clientele, commerce, trade, trading, traffic

patronize verb 1 <u>talk down to</u>, look down on 2 <u>be a customer or client of</u>, do business with, frequent, shop at 3 <u>support</u>, back, fund, help, maintain, promote, sponsor

patronizing adjective <u>condescending</u>, disdainful, gracious, haughty, snobbish, supercilious, superior

patter¹ verb 1 <u>tap</u>, beat, pat, pitter-patter 2 <u>walk lightly</u>, scurry, scuttle, skip, trip ♦ noun 3 <u>tapping</u>, pattering, pitter-patter

patter² noun 1 <u>spiel</u> (informal), line, pitch 2 <u>chatter</u>, gabble, jabber, nattering, prattle 3 <u>jargon</u>, argot, cant, lingo (informal), patois, slang, vernacular ♦ verb 4 <u>chatter</u>,

jabber, prate, rattle on, spout (informal)

pattern noun 1 <u>design</u>, arrangement, decoration, device, figure, motif 2 <u>order</u>, method, plan, sequence, system 3 <u>plan</u>, design, diagram, guide, original, stencil, template ♦ verb 4 <u>model</u>, copy, follow, form, imitate, mould, style

paucity noun Formal <u>scarcity</u>, dearth, deficiency, lack, rarity, scantiness, shortage, sparseness

paunch noun <u>belly</u>, pot, potbelly, spare tyre (Brit. slang)

pauper noun <u>down-and-out</u>, bankrupt, beggar, mendicant, poor person

pause verb 1 <u>stop briefly</u>, break, cease, delay, halt, have a breather (informal), interrupt, rest, take a break, wait ♦ noun 2 <u>stop</u>, break, breather (informal), cessation, gap, halt, interlude, intermission, interval, lull, respite, rest, stoppage

pave verb <u>cover</u>, concrete, floor, surface, tile

paw verb Informal <u>manhandle</u>, grab, handle roughly, maul, molest

pawn¹ verb <u>hock</u> (informal, chiefly U.S.), deposit, mortgage, pledge

pawn² noun <u>tool</u>, cat's-paw, instrument, plaything, puppet, stooge (slang)

pay verb 1 <u>reimburse</u>, compensate, give, recompense, remit, remunerate, requite, reward, settle 2 <u>give</u>, bestow, extend, grant, hand out, present 3 <u>benefit</u>, be worthwhile, repay 4 <u>be profitable</u>, make a return, make money **5** <u>yield</u>, bring in, produce, return ♦ *noun* **6** <u>wages</u>, allowance, earnings, fee, income, payment, recompense, reimbursement, remuneration, reward, salary, stipend

payable *adjective* <u>due</u>, outstanding, owed, owing

pay back *verb* **1** <u>repay</u>, refund, reimburse, settle up, square **2** <u>get even with</u> (*informal*), get one's own back, hit back, retaliate

payment *noun* **1** <u>paying</u>, discharge, remittance, settlement **2** <u>remittance</u>, advance, deposit, instalment, premium **3** <u>wage</u>, fee, hire, remuneration, reward

pay off *verb* **1** <u>settle</u>, clear, discharge, pay in full, square **2** <u>succeed</u>, be effective, work

pay out *verb* <u>spend</u>, disburse, expend, fork out *or* over *or* up (*slang*), shell out (*informal*)

peace *noun* **1** <u>stillness</u>, calm, calmness, hush, quiet, repose, rest, silence, tranquillity **2** <u>serenity</u>, calm, composure, contentment, repose **3** <u>harmony</u>, accord, agreement, concord **4** <u>truce</u>, armistice, treaty

peaceable *adjective* <u>peace-loving</u>, conciliatory, friendly, gentle, mild, peaceful, unwarlike

peaceful *adjective* **1** <u>at peace</u>, amicable, friendly, harmonious, nonviolent **2** <u>calm</u>, placid, quiet, restful, serene, still, tranquil, undisturbed **3** <u>peace-loving</u>, conciliatory, peaceable, unwarlike

peacemaker *noun* <u>mediator</u>, arbitrator, conciliator, pacifier

peak *noun* **1** <u>point</u>, apex, brow, crest, pinnacle, summit, tip, top **2** <u>high point</u>, acme, climax, crown, culmination, zenith ♦ *verb* **3** <u>culminate</u>, climax, come to a head

peal *noun* **1** <u>ring</u>, blast, chime, clang, clap, crash, reverberation, roar, rumble ♦ *verb* **2** <u>ring</u>, chime, crash, resound, roar, rumble

peasant *noun* <u>rustic</u>, countryman

peccadillo *noun* <u>misdeed</u>, error, indiscretion, lapse, misdemeanour, slip

peck *verb, noun* <u>pick</u>, dig, hit, jab, poke, prick, strike, tap

peculiar *adjective* **1** <u>odd</u>, abnormal, bizarre, curious, eccentric, extraordinary, freakish, funny, offbeat, outlandish, outré, quaint, queer, singular, strange, uncommon, unconventional, unusual, weird **2** <u>specific</u>, characteristic, distinctive, particular, special, unique

peculiarity *noun* **1** <u>eccentricity</u>, abnormality, foible, idiosyncrasy, mannerism, oddity, quirk **2** <u>characteristic</u>, attribute, feature, mark, particularity, property, quality, trait

pedagogue *noun* <u>teacher</u>, instructor, master *or* mistress, schoolmaster *or* schoolmistress

pedant *noun* <u>hairsplitter</u>, nit-picker (*informal*), quibbler

pedantic *adjective* <u>hairsplitting</u>, academic, bookish, donnish, formal, fussy, nit-picking (*informal*), particular, precise, punctilious

pedantry *noun* <u>hairsplitting</u>, punctiliousness, quibbling

peddle verb <u>sell</u>, flog (slang), hawk, market, push (informal), trade

pedestal noun <u>support</u>, base, foot, mounting, plinth, stand

pedestrian noun 1 <u>walker</u>, foot-traveller ♦ adjective 2 <u>dull</u>, banal, boring, commonplace, humdrum, mediocre, mundane, ordinary, prosaic, run-of-the-mill, uninspired

pedigree noun 1 <u>lineage</u>, ancestry, blood, breed, descent, extraction, family, family tree, genealogy, line, race, stock ♦ adjective 2 <u>purebred</u>, full-blooded, thoroughbred

pedlar noun <u>seller</u>, door-to-door salesman, hawker, huckster, vendor

peek verb 1 <u>glance</u>, look, peep ♦ noun 2 <u>glance</u>, glimpse, look, look-see (slang), peep

peel verb 1 <u>skin</u>, flake off, pare, scale, strip off ♦ noun 2 <u>skin</u>, peeling, rind

peep[1] verb 1 <u>peek</u>, look, sneak a look, steal a look ♦ noun 2 <u>look</u>, glimpse, look-see (slang), peek

peep[2] verb, noun <u>tweet</u>, cheep, chirp, squeak

peephole noun <u>spyhole</u>, aperture, chink, crack, hole, opening

peer[1] noun 1 <u>noble</u>, aristocrat, lord, nobleman 2 <u>equal</u>, compeer, fellow, like

peer[2] verb <u>squint</u>, gaze, inspect, peep, scan, snoop, spy

peerage noun <u>aristocracy</u>, lords and ladies, nobility, peers

peerless adjective <u>unequalled</u>, beyond compare, excellent,

incomparable, matchless, outstanding, unmatched, unparalleled, unrivalled

peevish adjective <u>irritable</u>, cantankerous, childish, churlish, cross, crotchety (informal), fractious, fretful, grumpy, petulant, querulous, snappy, sulky, sullen, surly

peg verb <u>fasten</u>, attach, fix, join, secure

pejorative adjective <u>derogatory</u>, deprecatory, depreciatory, disparaging, negative, uncomplimentary, unpleasant

pelt[1] verb 1 <u>throw</u>, batter, bombard, cast, hurl, pepper, shower, sling, strike 2 <u>rush</u>, belt (slang), charge, dash, hurry, run fast, shoot, speed, tear 3 <u>pour</u>, bucket down (informal), rain cats and dogs (informal), rain hard, teem

pelt[2] noun <u>coat</u>, fell, hide, skin

pen[1] verb <u>write</u>, compose, draft, draw up, jot down

pen[2] noun 1 <u>enclosure</u>, cage, coop, fold, hutch, pound, sty ♦ verb 2 <u>enclose</u>, cage, confine, coop up, fence in, hedge, shut up or in

penal adjective <u>disciplinary</u>, corrective, punitive

penalize verb <u>punish</u>, discipline, handicap, impose a penalty on

penalty noun <u>punishment</u>, fine, forfeit, handicap, price

penance noun <u>atonement</u>, penalty, reparation, sackcloth and ashes

penchant noun <u>liking</u>, bent, bias, fondness, inclination, leaning, partiality, predilection, proclivity, propensity, taste, tendency

pending adjective undecided, awaiting, imminent, impending, in the balance, undetermined, unsettled

penetrate verb **1** pierce, bore, enter, go through, prick, stab **2** grasp, comprehend, decipher, fathom, figure out (informal), get to the bottom of, suss (out) (slang), work out

penetrating adjective **1** sharp, carrying, harsh, piercing, shrill **2** perceptive, acute, astute, incisive, intelligent, keen, perspicacious, quick, sharp, sharp-witted, shrewd

penetration noun **1** piercing, entrance, entry, incision, puncturing **2** perception, acuteness, astuteness, insight, keenness, sharpness, shrewdness

penitence noun repentance, compunction, contrition, regret, remorse, shame, sorrow

penitent adjective repentant, abject, apologetic, conscience-stricken, contrite, regretful, remorseful, sorry

pen name noun pseudonym, nom de plume

pennant noun flag, banner, ensign, pennon, streamer

penniless adjective poor, broke (informal), destitute, dirt-poor (informal), down and out, flat broke (informal), impecunious, impoverished, indigent, penurious, poverty-stricken, skint (Brit. slang), stony-broke (Brit. slang)

pension noun allowance, annuity, benefit, superannuation

pensioner noun senior citizen, O.A.P., retired person

pensive adjective thoughtful, contemplative, dreamy, meditative, musing, preoccupied, reflective, sad, serious, solemn, wistful

pent-up adjective suppressed, bottled up, curbed, held back, inhibited, repressed, smothered, stifled

penury noun poverty, beggary, destitution, indigence, need, privation, want

people plural noun **1** persons, humanity, mankind, men and women, mortals **2** nation, citizens, community, folk, inhabitants, population, public **3** family, clan, race, tribe ♦ verb **4** inhabit, colonize, occupy, populate, settle

pepper noun **1** seasoning, flavour, spice ♦ verb **2** sprinkle, dot, fleck, spatter, speck **3** pelt, bombard, shower

perceive verb **1** see, behold, discern, discover, espy, make out, note, notice, observe, recognize, spot **2** understand, comprehend, gather, grasp, learn, realize, see, suss (out) (slang)

perceptible adjective visible, apparent, appreciable, clear, detectable, discernible, evident, noticeable, observable, obvious, recognizable, tangible

perception noun understanding, awareness, conception, consciousness, feeling, grasp, idea, impression, notion, sensation, sense

perceptive adjective observant,

acute, alert, astute, aware, percipient, perspicacious, quick, sharp

perch noun 1 <u>resting place</u>, branch, pole, post ♦ verb 2 <u>sit</u>, alight, balance, land, rest, roost, settle

percussion noun <u>impact</u>, blow, bump, clash, collision, crash, knock, smash, thump

peremptory adjective 1 <u>imperative</u>, absolute, binding, compelling, decisive, final, obligatory 2 <u>imperious</u>, authoritative, bossy (informal), dictatorial, dogmatic, domineering, overbearing

perennial adjective <u>lasting</u>, abiding, constant, continual, enduring, incessant, persistent, recurrent

perfect adjective 1 <u>complete</u>, absolute, consummate, entire, finished, full, sheer, unmitigated, utter, whole 2 <u>faultless</u>, flawless, immaculate, impeccable, pure, spotless, unblemished 3 <u>excellent</u>, ideal, splendid, sublime, superb, superlative, supreme 4 <u>exact</u>, accurate, correct, faithful, precise, true, unerring ♦ verb 5 <u>improve</u>, develop, polish, refine 6 <u>accomplish</u>, achieve, carry out, complete, finish, fulfil, perform

perfection noun 1 <u>completeness</u>, maturity 2 <u>purity</u>, integrity, perfectness, wholeness 3 <u>excellence</u>, exquisiteness, sublimity, superiority 4 <u>exactness</u>, faultlessness, precision

perfectionist noun <u>stickler</u>, precisionist, purist

perfectly adverb 1 <u>completely</u>, absolutely, altogether, fully, quite, thoroughly, totally, utterly, wholly 2 <u>flawlessly</u>, faultlessly, ideally, impeccably, superbly, supremely, wonderfully

perfidious adjective Literary <u>treacherous</u>, disloyal, double-dealing, traitorous, two-faced, unfaithful

perforate verb <u>pierce</u>, bore, drill, penetrate, punch, puncture

perform verb 1 <u>carry out</u>, accomplish, achieve, complete, discharge, do, execute, fulfil, pull off, work 2 <u>present</u>, act, enact, play, produce, put on, represent, stage

performance noun 1 <u>carrying out</u>, accomplishment, achievement, act, completion, execution, fulfilment, work 2 <u>presentation</u>, acting, appearance, exhibition, gig (informal), play, portrayal, production, show

performer noun <u>artiste</u>, actor or actress, player, Thespian, trouper

perfume noun <u>fragrance</u>, aroma, bouquet, odour, scent, smell

perfunctory adjective <u>offhand</u>, cursory, heedless, indifferent, mechanical, routine, sketchy, superficial

perhaps adverb <u>maybe</u>, conceivably, feasibly, it may be, perchance (archaic), possibly

peril noun <u>danger</u>, hazard, jeopardy, menace, risk, uncertainty

perilous adjective <u>dangerous</u>, hazardous, precarious, risky, threatening, unsafe

perimeter noun <u>boundary</u>, ambit, border, bounds, circumference, confines, edge, limit, margin, periphery

period noun <u>time</u>, interval, season, space, span, spell, stretch, term, while

periodic adjective <u>recurrent</u>, cyclical, intermittent, occasional, regular, repeated, sporadic

periodical noun <u>publication</u>, journal, magazine, monthly, paper, quarterly, weekly

peripheral adjective 1 <u>incidental</u>, inessential, irrelevant, marginal, minor, secondary, unimportant 2 <u>outermost</u>, exterior, external, outer, outside

perish verb 1 <u>die</u>, be killed, expire, lose one's life, pass away 2 <u>be destroyed</u>, collapse, decline, disappear, fall, vanish 3 <u>rot</u>, decay, decompose, disintegrate, moulder, waste

perishable adjective <u>short-lived</u>, decaying, decomposable

perjure verb **perjure oneself** Criminal law <u>commit perjury</u>, bear false witness, forswear, give false testimony, lie under oath, swear falsely

perjury noun <u>lying under oath</u>, bearing false witness, false statement, forswearing, giving false testimony

perk noun Brit. informal <u>bonus</u>, benefit, extra, fringe benefit, perquisite, plus

permanence noun <u>continuity</u>, constancy, continuance, durability, endurance, finality, indestructibility, perpetuity, stability

permanent adjective <u>lasting</u>, abiding, constant, enduring, eternal, everlasting, immutable, perpetual, persistent, stable, steadfast, unchanging

permeate verb <u>pervade</u>, charge, fill, imbue, impregnate, infiltrate, penetrate, saturate, spread through

permissible adjective <u>permitted</u>, acceptable, allowable, all right, authorized, lawful, legal, legitimate, O.K. or okay (informal)

permission noun <u>authorization</u>, allowance, approval, assent, consent, dispensation, go-ahead (informal), green light, leave, liberty, licence, sanction

permissive adjective <u>tolerant</u>, easy-going, forbearing, free, indulgent, lax, lenient, liberal

permit verb 1 <u>allow</u>, authorize, consent, enable, entitle, give leave or permission, give the green light to, grant, let, license, sanction ♦ noun 2 <u>licence</u>, authorization, pass, passport, permission, warrant

permutation noun <u>transformation</u>, alteration, change, transposition

pernicious adjective Formal <u>wicked</u>, bad, damaging, dangerous, deadly, destructive, detrimental, evil, fatal, harmful, hurtful, malign, poisonous

pernickety adjective Informal <u>fussy</u>, exacting, fastidious, finicky, overprecise, particular, picky (informal)

perpendicular adjective <u>upright</u>, at right angles to, on end, plumb, straight, vertical

perpetrate verb <u>commit</u>, carry out, do, enact, execute, perform, wreak

perpetual adjective 1 <u>everlasting</u>, endless, eternal, infinite, lasting, never-ending, perennial, permanent, unchanging, unending 2 <u>continual</u>, constant, continuous, endless, incessant, interminable, never-ending, persistent, recurrent, repeated

perpetuate verb <u>maintain</u>, immortalize, keep going, preserve

perplex verb <u>puzzle</u>, baffle, bewilder, confound, confuse, mystify, stump

perplexing adjective <u>puzzling</u>, baffling, bewildering, complex, complicated, confusing, difficult, enigmatic, hard, inexplicable, mystifying

perplexity noun 1 <u>puzzlement</u>, bafflement, bewilderment, confusion, incomprehension, mystification 2 <u>puzzle</u>, difficulty, fix (informal), mystery, paradox

perquisite noun Formal <u>bonus</u>, benefit, dividend, extra, perk (Brit. informal), plus

persecute verb 1 <u>victimize</u>, afflict, ill-treat, maltreat, oppress, torment, torture 2 <u>harass</u>, annoy, badger, bother, hassle (informal), pester, tease

perseverance noun <u>persistence</u>, determination, diligence, doggedness, endurance, pertinacity, resolution, tenacity

persevere verb <u>keep going</u>, carry on, continue, go on, hang on, persist, remain, stick at or to

persist verb 1 <u>continue</u>, carry on, keep up, last, linger, remain

2 <u>persevere</u>, continue, insist, stand firm

persistence noun <u>determination</u>, doggedness, endurance, grit, perseverance, pertinacity, resolution, tenacity, tirelessness

persistent adjective 1 <u>continuous</u>, constant, continual, endless, incessant, never-ending, perpetual, repeated 2 <u>determined</u>, dogged, obdurate, obstinate, persevering, pertinacious, steadfast, steady, stubborn, tenacious, tireless, unflagging

person noun 1 <u>individual</u>, being, body, human, soul 2 **in person** <u>personally</u>, bodily, in the flesh, oneself

personable adjective <u>pleasant</u>, agreeable, amiable, attractive, charming, good-looking, handsome, likable or likeable, nice

personage noun <u>personality</u>, big shot (informal), celebrity, dignitary, luminary, megastar (informal), notable, public figure, somebody, V.I.P.

personal adjective 1 <u>private</u>, exclusive, individual, intimate, own, particular, peculiar, special 2 <u>offensive</u>, derogatory, disparaging, insulting, nasty

personality noun 1 <u>nature</u>, character, disposition, identity, individuality, make-up, temperament 2 <u>celebrity</u>, famous name, household name, megastar (informal), notable, personage, star

personally adverb 1 <u>by oneself</u>, alone, independently, on one's own, solely 2 <u>in one's opinion</u>, for one's part, from one's own viewpoint, in one's books, in one's own view **3** individually, individualistically, privately, specially, subjectively

personification noun embodiment, epitome, image, incarnation, portrayal, representation

personify verb embody, epitomize, exemplify, represent, symbolize, typify

personnel noun employees, helpers, human resources, people, staff, workers, workforce

perspective noun **1** outlook, angle, attitude, context, frame of reference **2** objectivity, proportion, relation, relative importance, relativity

perspicacious adjective Formal perceptive, acute, alert, astute, discerning, keen, percipient, sharp, shrewd

perspiration noun sweat, moisture, wetness

perspire verb sweat, exude, glow, pour with sweat, secrete, swelter

persuade verb **1** talk into, bring round (informal), coax, entice, impel, incite, induce, influence, sway, urge, win over **2** convince, cause to believe, satisfy

persuasion noun **1** urging, cajolery, enticement, inducement, wheedling **2** persuasiveness, cogency, force, potency, power, pull (informal) **3** creed, belief, conviction, credo, faith, opinion, tenet, views **4** faction, camp, denomination, party, school, school of thought, side

persuasive adjective convincing, cogent, compelling, credible, effective, eloquent, forceful, influential, plausible, sound, telling, valid, weighty

pert adjective impudent, bold, cheeky, forward, impertinent, insolent, sassy (U.S. informal), saucy

pertain verb relate, apply, befit, belong, be relevant, concern, refer, regard

pertinent adjective relevant, applicable, apposite, appropriate, apt, fit, fitting, germane, material, proper, to the point

pertness noun impudence, audacity, cheek (informal), cheekiness, effrontery, forwardness, front, impertinence, insolence, sauciness

perturb verb disturb, agitate, bother, disconcert, faze, fluster, ruffle, trouble, unsettle, vex, worry

perturbed adjective disturbed, agitated, anxious, disconcerted, flustered, shaken, troubled, uncomfortable, uneasy, worried

peruse verb read, browse, check, examine, inspect, scan, scrutinize, study

pervade verb spread through, charge, fill, imbue, infuse, penetrate, permeate, suffuse

pervasive adjective widespread, common, extensive, general, omnipresent, prevalent, rife, ubiquitous, universal

perverse adjective **1** abnormal, contrary, deviant, disobedient, improper, rebellious, refractory,

troublesome, unhealthy **2** <u>wilful</u>,
contrary, dogged, headstrong,
intractable, intransigent,
obdurate, wrong-headed
3 <u>stubborn</u>, contrary, cussed
(*informal*), mulish, obstinate,
pig-headed, stiff-necked,
wayward **4** <u>ill-natured</u>, churlish,
cross, fractious, ill-tempered,
peevish, stroppy (*Brit. slang*), surly

perversion *noun* **1** <u>deviation</u>,
aberration, abnormality,
debauchery, depravity,
immorality, kink (*Brit. informal*),
kinkiness (*slang*), unnaturalness,
vice **2** <u>distortion</u>, corruption,
falsification, misinterpretation,
misrepresentation, twisting

perversity *noun* <u>contrariness</u>,
contradictoriness, intransigence,
obduracy, refractoriness,
waywardness, wrong-headedness

pervert *verb* **1** <u>distort</u>, abuse,
falsify, garble, misrepresent,
misuse, twist, warp **2** <u>corrupt</u>,
debase, debauch, degrade,
deprave, lead astray ♦ *noun*
3 <u>deviant</u>, degenerate, sicko
(*informal*), weirdo *or* weirdie
(*informal*)

perverted *adjective* <u>unnatural</u>,
abnormal, corrupt, debased,
debauched, depraved, deviant,
kinky (*slang*), pervy (*slang*), sick,
twisted, unhealthy, warped

pessimism *noun* <u>gloominess</u>,
dejection, depression, despair,
despondency, distrust, gloom,
hopelessness, melancholy

pessimist *noun* <u>wet blanket</u>
(*informal*), cynic, defeatist, killjoy,
prophet of doom, worrier

pessimistic *adjective* <u>gloomy</u>,
bleak, cynical, dark, dejected,

depressed, despairing,
despondent, glum, hopeless,
morose

pest *noun* **1** <u>nuisance</u>,
annoyance, bane, bother, drag
(*informal*), irritation, pain
(*informal*), thorn in one's flesh,
trial, vexation **2** <u>infection</u>, blight,
bug, epidemic, pestilence,
plague, scourge

pester *verb* <u>annoy</u>, badger,
bedevil, be on one's back
(*slang*), bother, bug (*informal*),
harass, harry, hassle (*informal*),
nag, plague, torment

pestilence *noun* <u>plague</u>,
epidemic, visitation

pestilent *adjective* **1** <u>annoying</u>,
bothersome, irksome, irritating,
tiresome, vexing **2** <u>harmful</u>,
detrimental, evil, injurious,
pernicious **3** <u>contaminated</u>,
catching, contagious, diseased,
disease-ridden, infected,
infectious

pestilential *adjective* <u>deadly</u>,
dangerous, destructive,
detrimental, harmful, hazardous,
injurious, pernicious

pet *noun* **1** <u>favourite</u>, darling,
idol, jewel, treasure ♦ *adjective*
2 <u>favourite</u>, cherished, dearest,
dear to one's heart ♦ *verb*
3 <u>pamper</u>, baby, coddle, cosset,
mollycoddle, spoil **4** <u>fondle</u>,
caress, pat, stroke **5** *Informal*
<u>cuddle</u>, canoodle (*slang*), kiss,
neck (*informal*), smooch
(*informal*), snog (*Brit. slang*)

peter out *verb* <u>die out</u>, dwindle,
ebb, fade, fail, run out, stop,
taper off, wane

petite *adjective* <u>small</u>, dainty,
delicate, elfin, little, slight

petition noun **1** appeal, entreaty, plea, prayer, request, solicitation, suit, supplication ♦ verb **2** appeal, adjure, ask, beg, beseech, entreat, plead, pray, solicit, supplicate

petrify verb **1** terrify, horrify, immobilize, paralyse, stun, stupefy, transfix **2** fossilize, calcify, harden, turn to stone

petty adjective **1** trivial, contemptible, inconsiderable, insignificant, little, measly (informal), negligible, paltry, slight, small, trifling, unimportant **2** small-minded, mean, mean-minded, shabby, spiteful, ungenerous

petulance noun sulkiness, bad temper, ill humour, irritability, peevishness, pique, sullenness

petulant adjective sulky, bad-tempered, huffy, ill-humoured, moody, peevish, sullen

phantom noun **1** spectre, apparition, ghost, phantasm, shade (literary), spirit, spook (informal), wraith **2** illusion, figment of the imagination, hallucination, vision

phase noun stage, chapter, development, juncture, period, point, position, step, time

phase out verb wind down, close, ease off, eliminate, pull out, remove, run down, terminate, wind up, withdraw

phenomenal adjective extraordinary, exceptional, fantastic, marvellous, miraculous, outstanding, prodigious, remarkable, unusual

phenomenon noun

1 occurrence, circumstance, episode, event, fact, happening, incident **2** wonder, exception, marvel, miracle, prodigy, rarity, sensation

philanderer noun womanizer (informal), Casanova, Don Juan, flirt, ladies' man, lady-killer (informal), Lothario, playboy, stud (slang), wolf (informal)

philanthropic adjective humanitarian, beneficent, benevolent, charitable, humane, kind, kind-hearted, munificent, public-spirited

philanthropist noun humanitarian, benefactor, contributor, donor, giver, patron

philanthropy noun humanitarianism, almsgiving, beneficence, benevolence, brotherly love, charitableness, charity, generosity, kind-heartedness

philistine noun **1** boor, barbarian, ignoramus, lout, lowbrow, vulgarian, yahoo ♦ adjective **2** uncultured, boorish, ignorant, lowbrow, tasteless, uncultivated, uneducated, unrefined

philosopher noun thinker, logician, metaphysician, sage, theorist, wise man

philosophical, philosophic adjective **1** wise, abstract, logical, rational, sagacious, theoretical, thoughtful **2** stoical, calm, collected, composed, cool, serene, tranquil, unruffled

philosophy noun **1** thought, knowledge, logic, metaphysics, rationalism, reasoning, thinking, wisdom **2** outlook, beliefs, convictions, doctrine, ideology, principles, tenets, thinking, values, viewpoint, world view **3** <u>stoicism</u>, calmness, composure, equanimity, self-possession, serenity

phlegmatic adjective <u>unemotional</u>, apathetic, impassive, indifferent, placid, stoical, stolid, undemonstrative, unfeeling

phobia noun <u>terror</u>, aversion, detestation, dread, fear, hatred, horror, loathing, repulsion, revulsion, thing (informal)

phone noun **1** <u>telephone</u>, blower (informal) **2** <u>call</u>, ring (informal, chiefly Brit.), tinkle (Brit. informal) ♦ verb **3** <u>call</u>, get on the blower (informal), give someone a call, give someone a ring (informal, chiefly Brit.), give someone a tinkle (Brit. informal), make a call, ring (up) (informal, chiefly Brit.), telephone

phoney Informal ♦ adjective **1** <u>fake</u>, bogus, counterfeit, ersatz, false, imitation, pseudo (informal), sham ♦ noun **2** <u>fake</u>, counterfeit, forgery, fraud, impostor, pseud (informal), sham

photograph noun **1** <u>picture</u>, photo (informal), print, shot, snap (informal), snapshot, transparency ♦ verb **2** <u>take a picture of</u>, film, record, shoot, snap (informal), take (someone's) picture

photographic adjective **1** <u>lifelike</u>, graphic, natural, pictorial, realistic, visual, vivid **2** Of a person's memory <u>accurate</u>, exact, faithful, precise, retentive

phrase noun **1** <u>expression</u>, group

of words, idiom, remark, saying ♦ verb **2** <u>express</u>, put, put into words, say, voice, word

phraseology noun <u>wording</u>, choice of words, expression, idiom, language, parlance, phrase, phrasing, speech, style, syntax

physical adjective **1** <u>bodily</u>, corporal, corporeal, earthly, fleshly, incarnate, mortal **2** <u>material</u>, natural, palpable, real, solid, substantial, tangible

physician noun <u>doctor</u>, doc (informal), doctor of medicine, general practitioner, G.P., M.D., medic (informal), medical practitioner

physique noun <u>build</u>, body, constitution, figure, form, frame, shape, structure

pick verb **1** <u>select</u>, choose, decide upon, elect, fix upon, hand-pick, opt for, settle upon, single out **2** <u>gather</u>, collect, harvest, pluck, pull **3** <u>nibble</u>, have no appetite, peck at, play or toy with, push the food round the plate **4** <u>provoke</u>, incite, instigate, start **5** <u>open</u>, break into, break open, crack, force ♦ noun **6** <u>choice</u>, decision, option, preference, selection **7** <u>the best</u>, crème de la crème, elect, elite, the cream

picket noun **1** <u>protester</u>, demonstrator, picketer **2** <u>lookout</u>, guard, patrol, sentinel, sentry, watch **3** <u>stake</u>, pale, paling, post, stanchion, upright ♦ verb **4** <u>blockade</u>, boycott, demonstrate

pickle noun **1** Informal <u>predicament</u>, bind (informal), difficulty, dilemma, fix (informal), hot water (*informal*), jam (*informal*), quandary, scrape (*informal*), tight spot ♦ *verb* 2 <u>preserve</u>, marinade, steep

pick-me-up *noun Informal* <u>tonic</u>, bracer (*informal*), refreshment, restorative, shot in the arm (*informal*), stimulant

pick on *verb* <u>torment</u>, badger, bait, bully, goad, hector, tease

pick out *verb* <u>identify</u>, discriminate, distinguish, make out, perceive, recognize, tell apart

pick up *verb* 1 <u>lift</u>, gather, grasp, raise, take up, uplift 2 <u>obtain</u>, buy, come across, find, purchase 3 <u>recover</u>, be on the mend, get better, improve, mend, rally, take a turn for the better, turn the corner 4 <u>learn</u>, acquire, get the hang of (*informal*), master 5 <u>collect</u>, call for, get

pick-up *noun* <u>improvement</u>, change for the better, rally, recovery, revival, rise, strengthening, upswing, upturn

picnic *noun* <u>excursion</u>, outdoor meal, outing

pictorial *adjective* <u>graphic</u>, illustrated, picturesque, representational, scenic

picture *noun* 1 <u>representation</u>, drawing, engraving, illustration, image, likeness, painting, photograph, portrait, print, sketch 2 <u>description</u>, account, depiction, image, impression, report 3 <u>double</u>, carbon copy, copy, dead ringer (*slang*), duplicate, image, likeness, lookalike, replica, spitting image (*informal*), twin 4 <u>personification</u>, embodiment, epitome, essence

5 <u>film</u>, flick (*slang*), motion picture, movie (*U.S. informal*) ♦ *verb* 6 <u>imagine</u>, conceive of, envision, see, visualize 7 <u>represent</u>, depict, draw, illustrate, paint, photograph, show, sketch

picturesque *adjective* 1 <u>pretty</u>, attractive, beautiful, charming, quaint, scenic, striking 2 <u>vivid</u>, colourful, graphic

piebald *adjective* <u>pied</u>, black and white, brindled, dappled, flecked, mottled, speckled, spotted

piece *noun* 1 <u>bit</u>, chunk, fragment, morsel, part, portion, quantity, segment, slice 2 <u>work</u>, article, composition, creation, item, study, work of art

piecemeal *adverb* <u>bit by bit</u>, by degrees, gradually, little by little

pier *noun* 1 <u>jetty</u>, landing place, promenade, quay, wharf 2 <u>pillar</u>, buttress, column, pile, post, support, upright

pierce *verb* <u>penetrate</u>, bore, drill, enter, perforate, prick, puncture, spike, stab, stick into

piercing *adjective* 1 *Usually of sound* <u>penetrating</u>, ear-splitting, high-pitched, loud, sharp, shrill 2 <u>keen</u>, alert, penetrating, perceptive, perspicacious, quick-witted, sharp, shrewd 3 *Usually of weather* <u>cold</u>, arctic, biting, bitter, freezing, nippy, wintry 4 <u>sharp</u>, acute, agonizing, excruciating, intense, painful, severe, stabbing

piety *noun* <u>holiness</u>, faith, godliness, piousness, religion, reverence

pig *noun* 1 <u>hog</u>, boar, porker,

sow, swine **2** *Informal* slob
(*slang*), boor, brute, glutton,
swine

pigeonhole *noun*
1 compartment, cubbyhole,
locker, niche, place, section
♦ *verb* **2** classify, categorize,
characterize, compartmentalize,
ghettoize, label, slot (*informal*)
3 put off, defer, postpone, shelve

pig-headed *adjective* stubborn,
contrary, inflexible, mulish,
obstinate, self-willed,
stiff-necked, unyielding

pigment *noun* colour, colouring,
dye, paint, stain, tincture, tint

pile¹ *noun* **1** heap, accumulation,
collection, hoard, mass, mound,
mountain, stack **2** *often plural
Informal* a lot, great deal, ocean,
quantity, stacks **3** building,
edifice, erection, structure ♦ *verb*
4 collect, accumulate, amass,
assemble, gather, heap, hoard,
stack **5** crowd, crush, flock,
flood, jam, pack, rush, stream

pile² *noun* foundation, beam,
column, pillar, post, support,
upright

pile³ *noun* nap, down, fibre, fur,
hair, plush

pile-up *noun Informal* collision,
accident, crash, multiple
collision, smash, smash-up
(*informal*)

pilfer *verb* steal, appropriate,
embezzle, filch, knock off (*slang*),
lift (*informal*), nick (*slang, chiefly
Brit.*), pinch (*informal*), purloin,
snaffle (*Brit. informal*), swipe
(*slang*), take

pilgrim *noun* traveller, wanderer,
wayfarer

pilgrimage *noun* journey,
excursion, expedition, mission,
tour, trip

pill *noun* **1** tablet, capsule, pellet
2 the pill oral contraceptive

pillage *verb* **1** plunder, despoil,
loot, maraud, raid, ransack,
ravage, sack ♦ *noun* **2** plunder,
marauding, robbery, sack,
spoliation

pillar *noun* **1** support, column,
pier, post, prop, shaft,
stanchion, upright **2** supporter,
leader, leading light (*informal*),
mainstay, upholder

pillory *verb* ridicule, brand,
denounce, stigmatize

pilot *noun* **1** airman, aviator, flyer
2 helmsman, navigator,
steersman ♦ *adjective* **3** trial,
experimental, model, test ♦ *verb*
4 fly, conduct, direct, drive,
guide, handle, navigate, operate,
steer

pimple *noun* spot, boil, plook
(*Scot.*), pustule, zit (*slang*)

pin *verb* **1** fasten, affix, attach,
fix, join, secure **2** hold fast, fix,
hold down, immobilize, pinion

pinch *verb* **1** squeeze, compress,
grasp, nip, press **2** hurt, cramp,
crush, pain **3** *Informal* steal, filch,
knock off (*slang*), lift (*informal*),
nick (*slang, chiefly Brit.*), pilfer,
purloin, snaffle (*Brit. informal*),
swipe (*slang*) ♦ *noun* **4** squeeze,
nip **5** dash, bit, jot, mite,
soupçon, speck **6** hardship, crisis,
difficulty, emergency, necessity,
plight, predicament, strait

pinched *adjective* thin, drawn,
gaunt, haggard, peaky, worn

pin down *verb* **1** force, compel,

constrain, make, press, pressurize
2 <u>determine</u>, identify, locate,
name, pinpoint, specify

pine *verb* **1** *often with for* <u>long</u>,
ache, crave, desire, eat one's
heart out over, hanker, hunger
for, thirst for, wish for, yearn for
2 <u>waste</u>, decline, fade, languish,
sicken

pinion *verb* <u>immobilize</u>, bind,
chain, fasten, fetter, manacle,
shackle, tie

pink *adjective* <u>rosy</u>, flushed,
reddish, rose, roseate, salmon

pinnacle *noun* <u>peak</u>, apex, crest,
crown, height, summit, top,
vertex, zenith

pinpoint *verb* <u>identify</u>, define,
distinguish, locate

pioneer *noun* **1** <u>settler</u>, colonist,
explorer **2** <u>founder</u>, developer,
innovator, leader, trailblazer
♦ *verb* **3** <u>develop</u>, create,
discover, establish, initiate,
instigate, institute, invent,
originate, show the way, start

pious *adjective* <u>religious</u>, devout,
God-fearing, godly, holy,
reverent, righteous, saintly

pipe *noun* **1** <u>tube</u>, conduit, duct,
hose, line, main, passage,
pipeline ♦ *verb* **2** <u>whistle</u>, cheep,
peep, play, sing, sound, warble
3 <u>convey</u>, channel, conduct

pipe down *verb Informal* <u>be</u>
<u>quiet</u>, hold one's tongue, hush,
quieten down, shush, shut one's
mouth, shut up (*informal*)

pipeline *noun* <u>tube</u>, conduit,
duct, passage, pipe

piquant *adjective* **1** <u>spicy</u>, biting,
pungent, savoury, sharp, tangy,
tart, zesty **2** <u>interesting</u>, lively,

provocative, scintillating,
sparkling, stimulating

pique *noun* **1** <u>resentment</u>,
annoyance, displeasure, huff,
hurt feelings, irritation, offence,
umbrage, wounded pride ♦ *verb*
2 <u>displease</u>, affront, annoy, get
(*informal*), irk, irritate, nettle,
offend, rile, sting **3** <u>arouse</u>,
excite, rouse, spur, stimulate,
stir, whet

piracy *noun* <u>robbery</u>,
buccaneering, freebooting,
stealing, theft

pirate *noun* **1** <u>buccaneer</u>, corsair,
freebooter, marauder, raider
2 <u>plagiarist</u>, cribber (*informal*),
infringer, plagiarizer ♦ *verb*
3 <u>copy</u>, appropriate, crib
(*informal*), plagiarize, poach,
reproduce, steal

pit *noun* **1** <u>hole</u>, abyss, cavity,
chasm, crater, dent, depression,
hollow ♦ *verb* **2** <u>scar</u>, dent,
indent, mark, pockmark

pitch *verb* **1** <u>throw</u>, cast, chuck
(*informal*), fling, heave, hurl, lob
(*informal*), sling, toss **2** <u>set up</u>,
erect, put up, raise, settle **3** <u>fall</u>,
dive, drop, topple, tumble
4 <u>toss</u>, lurch, plunge, roll ♦ *noun*
5 <u>sports field</u>, field of play,
ground, park (*U.S. & Canad.*)
6 <u>level</u>, degree, height, highest
point, point, summit **7** <u>slope</u>,
angle, dip, gradient, incline, tilt
8 <u>tone</u>, modulation, sound,
timbre **9** <u>sales talk</u>, patter, spiel
(*informal*)

pitch-black *adjective* <u>jet-black</u>,
dark, inky, pitch-dark, unlit

pitch in *verb* <u>help</u>, chip in
(*informal*), contribute, cooperate,
do one's bit, join in, lend a

hand, participate

pitch into *verb Informal* <u>attack</u>, assail, assault, get stuck into (*informal*), tear into (*informal*)

piteous *adjective* <u>pathetic</u>, affecting, distressing, harrowing, heartbreaking, heart-rending, moving, pitiable, pitiful, plaintive, poignant, sad

pitfall *noun* <u>danger</u>, catch, difficulty, drawback, hazard, peril, snag, trap

pith *noun* <u>essence</u>, core, crux, gist, heart, kernel, nub, point, quintessence, salient point

pithy *adjective* <u>succinct</u>, brief, cogent, concise, epigrammatic, laconic, pointed, short, terse, to the point, trenchant

pitiful *adjective* 1 <u>pathetic</u>, distressing, grievous, harrowing, heartbreaking, heart-rending, piteous, pitiable, sad, wretched 2 <u>contemptible</u>, abject, base, low, mean, miserable, paltry, shabby, sorry

pitiless *adjective* <u>merciless</u>, callous, cold-blooded, cold-hearted, cruel, hardhearted, heartless, implacable, relentless, ruthless, unmerciful

pittance *noun* <u>peanuts</u> (*slang*), chicken feed (*slang*), drop, mite, slave wages, trifle

pity *noun* 1 <u>compassion</u>, charity, clemency, fellow feeling, forbearance, kindness, mercy, sympathy 2 <u>shame</u>, bummer (*slang*), crying shame, misfortune, sin ◆ *verb* 3 <u>feel sorry for</u>, bleed for, feel for, grieve for, have compassion for, sympathize with, weep for

pivot *noun* 1 <u>axis</u>, axle, fulcrum, spindle, swivel 2 <u>hub</u>, centre, heart, hinge, kingpin ◆ *verb* 3 <u>turn</u>, revolve, rotate, spin, swivel, twirl 4 <u>rely</u>, be contingent, depend, hang, hinge

pivotal *adjective* <u>crucial</u>, central, critical, decisive, vital

pixie *noun* <u>elf</u>, brownie, fairy, sprite

placard *noun* <u>notice</u>, advertisement, bill, poster

placate *verb* <u>calm</u>, appease, assuage, conciliate, humour, mollify, pacify, propitiate, soothe

place *noun* 1 <u>spot</u>, area, location, point, position, site, venue, whereabouts 2 <u>region</u>, district, locale, locality, neighbourhood, quarter, vicinity 3 <u>position</u>, grade, rank, station, status 4 <u>space</u>, accommodation, room 5 <u>home</u>, abode, domicile, dwelling, house, pad (*slang*), property, residence 6 <u>duty</u>, affair, charge, concern, function, prerogative, responsibility, right, role 7 <u>job</u>, appointment, employment, position, post 8 **take place** <u>happen</u>, come about, go on, occur, transpire (*informal*) ◆ *verb* 9 <u>put</u>, deposit, install, lay, locate, position, rest, set, situate, stand, station, stick (*informal*) 10 <u>classify</u>, arrange, class, grade, group, order, rank, sort 11 <u>identify</u>, know, put one's finger on, recognize, remember 12 <u>assign</u>, allocate, appoint, charge, entrust, give

placid *adjective* <u>calm</u>, collected, composed, equable, even-tempered, imperturbable, serene, tranquil, unexcitable, unruffled, untroubled

plagiarism *noun* <u>copying</u>, borrowing, cribbing (*informal*), infringement, piracy, theft

plagiarize *verb* <u>copy</u>, borrow, crib (*informal*), lift (*informal*), pirate, steal

plague *noun* 1 <u>disease</u>, epidemic, infection, pestilence 2 <u>affliction</u>, bane, blight, curse, evil, scourge, torment ♦ *verb* 3 <u>pester</u>, annoy, badger, bother, harass, harry, hassle (*informal*), tease, torment, torture, trouble, vex

plain *adjective* 1 <u>clear</u>, comprehensible, distinct, evident, manifest, obvious, overt, patent, unambiguous, understandable, unmistakable, visible 2 <u>honest</u>, blunt, candid, direct, downright, forthright, frank, open, outspoken, straightforward, upfront (*informal*) 3 <u>unadorned</u>, austere, bare, basic, severe, simple, Spartan, stark, unembellished, unfussy, unornamented 4 <u>ugly</u>, ill-favoured, no oil painting (*informal*), not beautiful, unattractive, unlovely, unprepossessing 5 <u>ordinary</u>, common, commonplace, everyday, simple, unaffected, unpretentious ♦ *noun* 6 <u>flatland</u>, grassland, plateau, prairie, steppe, veld

plain-spoken *adjective* <u>blunt</u>, candid, direct, downright, forthright, frank, outspoken

plaintive *adjective* <u>sorrowful</u>, heart-rending, mournful, pathetic, piteous, pitiful, sad

plan *noun* 1 <u>scheme</u>, design, method, plot, programme, proposal, strategy, suggestion, system 2 <u>diagram</u>, blueprint, chart, drawing, layout, map, representation, sketch ♦ *verb* 3 <u>devise</u>, arrange, contrive, design, draft, formulate, organize, outline, plot, scheme, think out 4 <u>intend</u>, aim, mean, propose, purpose

plane *noun* 1 <u>aeroplane</u>, aircraft, jet 2 <u>flat surface</u>, level surface 3 <u>level</u>, condition, degree, position ♦ *adjective* 4 <u>level</u>, even, flat, horizontal, regular, smooth ♦ *verb* 5 <u>skim</u>, glide, sail, skate

plant *noun* 1 <u>vegetable</u>, bush, flower, herb, shrub, weed 2 <u>factory</u>, foundry, mill, shop, works, yard 3 <u>machinery</u>, apparatus, equipment, gear ♦ *verb* 4 <u>sow</u>, put in the ground, scatter, seed, transplant 5 <u>place</u>, establish, fix, found, insert, put, set

plaster *noun* 1 <u>mortar</u>, gypsum, plaster of Paris, stucco 2 <u>bandage</u>, adhesive plaster, dressing, Elastoplast (*Trademark*), sticking plaster ♦ *verb* 3 <u>cover</u>, coat, daub, overlay, smear, spread

plastic *adjective* 1 <u>manageable</u>, docile, malleable, pliable, receptive, responsive, tractable 2 <u>pliant</u>, ductile, flexible, mouldable, pliable, soft, supple

plate *noun* 1 <u>platter</u>, dish, trencher (*archaic*) 2 <u>helping</u>, course, dish, portion, serving 3 <u>layer</u>, panel, sheet, slab 4 <u>illustration</u>, lithograph, print ♦ *verb* 5 <u>coat</u>, cover, gild, laminate, overlay

plateau *noun* 1 <u>upland</u>,

highland, table, tableland
2 <u>levelling off</u>, level, stability, stage

platform noun 1 <u>stage</u>, dais, podium, rostrum, stand 2 <u>policy</u>, manifesto, objective(s), party line, principle, programme

platitude noun <u>cliché</u>, banality, commonplace, truism

platoon noun <u>squad</u>, company, group, outfit (informal), patrol, squadron, team

platter noun <u>plate</u>, dish, salver, tray, trencher (archaic)

plaudits plural noun <u>approval</u>, acclaim, acclamation, applause, approbation, praise

plausible adjective 1 <u>reasonable</u>, believable, conceivable, credible, likely, persuasive, possible, probable, tenable 2 <u>glib</u>, smooth, smooth-talking, smooth-tongued, specious

play verb 1 <u>amuse oneself</u>, entertain oneself, fool, have fun, revel, romp, sport, trifle 2 <u>compete</u>, challenge, contend against, participate, take on, take part 3 <u>act</u>, act the part of, perform, portray, represent ♦ noun 4 <u>drama</u>, comedy, dramatic piece, farce, pantomime, piece, show, stage show, tragedy 5 <u>amusement</u>, diversion, entertainment, fun, game, pastime, recreation, sport 6 <u>fun</u>, humour, jest, joking, lark (informal), prank, sport 7 <u>space</u>, elbowroom, latitude, leeway, margin, room, scope

playboy noun <u>womanizer</u>, ladies' man, lady-killer (informal), philanderer, rake, roué

play down verb <u>minimize</u>, gloss over, make light of, make little of, soft-pedal (informal), underplay, underrate

player noun 1 <u>sportsman or sportswoman</u>, competitor, contestant, participant 2 <u>musician</u>, artist, instrumentalist, performer, virtuoso 3 <u>performer</u>, actor or actress, entertainer, Thespian, trouper

playful adjective <u>lively</u>, frisky, impish, merry, mischievous, spirited, sportive, sprightly, vivacious

playmate noun <u>friend</u>, chum (informal), companion, comrade, pal (informal), playfellow

play on or **upon** verb <u>take advantage of</u>, abuse, capitalize on, exploit, impose on, trade on

plaything noun <u>toy</u>, amusement, game, pastime, trifle

play up verb 1 <u>emphasize</u>, accentuate, highlight, stress, underline 2 Brit. informal <u>be awkward</u>, be disobedient, be stroppy (Brit. slang), give trouble, misbehave 3 Brit. informal <u>hurt</u>, be painful, be sore, bother, pain, trouble 4 Brit. informal <u>malfunction</u>, be on the blink (slang), not work properly

plea noun 1 <u>appeal</u>, entreaty, intercession, petition, prayer, request, suit, supplication 2 <u>excuse</u>, defence, explanation, justification

plead verb <u>appeal</u>, ask, beg, beseech, entreat, implore, petition, request

pleasant adjective 1 <u>pleasing</u>, agreeable, amusing, delightful, enjoyable, fine, lovely, nice,

pleasurable 2 nice, affable, agreeable, amiable, charming, congenial, engaging, friendly, genial, likable *or* likeable

pleasantry *noun* joke, badinage, banter, jest, quip, witticism

please *verb* delight, amuse, entertain, gladden, gratify, humour, indulge, satisfy, suit

pleased *adjective* happy, chuffed (*Brit. slang*), contented, delighted, euphoric, glad, gratified, over the moon (*informal*), satisfied, thrilled

pleasing *adjective* enjoyable, agreeable, charming, delightful, engaging, gratifying, likable *or* likeable, pleasurable, satisfying

pleasurable *adjective* enjoyable, agreeable, delightful, fun, good, lovely, nice, pleasant

pleasure *noun* happiness, amusement, bliss, delectation, delight, enjoyment, gladness, gratification, joy, satisfaction

plebeian *adjective* **1** common, base, coarse, low, lower-class, proletarian, uncultivated, unrefined, vulgar, working-class ♦ *noun* **2** commoner, common man, man in the street, pleb, prole (*derogatory slang, chiefly Brit.*), proletarian

pledge *noun* **1** promise, assurance, covenant, oath, undertaking, vow, warrant, word **2** guarantee, bail, collateral, deposit, pawn, security, surety ♦ *verb* **3** promise, contract, engage, give one's oath, give one's word, swear, vow

plentiful *adjective* abundant, ample, bountiful, copious, generous, lavish, liberal,

overflowing, plenteous, profuse

plenty *noun* **1** lots (*informal*), abundance, enough, great deal, heap(s) (*informal*), masses, pile(s) (*informal*), plethora, quantity, stack(s) **2** abundance, affluence, copiousness, fertility, fruitfulness, plenitude, profusion, prosperity, wealth

plethora *noun* excess, glut, overabundance, profusion, superabundance, surfeit, surplus

pliable *adjective* **1** flexible, bendable, bendy, malleable, plastic, pliant, supple **2** impressionable, adaptable, compliant, docile, easily led, pliant, receptive, responsive, susceptible, tractable

pliant *adjective* **1** flexible, bendable, bendy, plastic, pliable, supple **2** impressionable, biddable, compliant, easily led, pliable, susceptible, tractable

plight *noun* difficulty, condition, jam (*informal*), predicament, scrape (*informal*), situation, spot (*informal*), state, trouble

plod *verb* **1** trudge, clump, drag, lumber, tramp, tread **2** slog, grind (*informal*), labour, persevere, plough through, plug away (*informal*), soldier on, toil

plot¹ *noun* **1** plan, cabal, conspiracy, intrigue, machination, scheme, stratagem **2** story, action, narrative, outline, scenario, story line, subject, theme ♦ *verb* **3** plan, collude, conspire, contrive, intrigue, machinate, manoeuvre, scheme **4** devise, conceive, concoct, contrive, cook up (*informal*), design, hatch, lay

5 chart, calculate, locate, map, mark, outline

plot² *noun* patch, allotment, area, ground, lot, parcel, tract

plough *verb* **1** turn over, cultivate, dig, till **2** *usually with* **through** forge, cut, drive, plunge, press, push, wade

ploy *noun* tactic, device, dodge, manoeuvre, move, ruse, scheme, stratagem, trick, wile

pluck *verb* **1** pull out *or* off, collect, draw, gather, harvest, pick **2** tug, catch, clutch, jerk, pull at, snatch, tweak, yank **3** strum, finger, pick, twang ♦ *noun* **4** courage, backbone, boldness, bottle (*Brit. slang*), bravery, grit, guts (*informal*), nerve

plucky *adjective* courageous, bold, brave, daring, game, gutsy (*slang*), have-a-go (*informal*), intrepid

plug *noun* **1** stopper, bung, cork, spigot **2** *Informal* mention, advert (*Brit. informal*), advertisement, hype, publicity, push ♦ *verb* **3** seal, block, bung, close, cork, fill, pack, stop, stopper, stop up, stuff **4** *Informal* mention, advertise, build up, hype, promote, publicize, push **5** **plug away** *Informal* slog, grind (*informal*), labour, peg away, plod, toil

plum *adjective* choice, best, first-class, prize

plumb *verb* **1** delve, explore, fathom, gauge, go into, penetrate, probe, unravel ♦ *noun* **2** weight, lead, plumb bob, plummet ♦ *adverb* **3** exactly, bang, precisely, slap, spot-on

(*Brit. informal*)

plume *noun* feather, crest, pinion, quill

plummet *verb* plunge, crash, descend, dive, drop down, fall, nose-dive, tumble

plump *adjective* chubby, corpulent, dumpy, fat, podgy, roly-poly, rotund, round, stout, tubby

plunder *verb* **1** loot, pillage, raid, ransack, rifle, rob, sack, strip ♦ *noun* **2** loot, booty, ill-gotten gains, pillage, prize, spoils, swag (*slang*)

plunge *verb* **1** throw, cast, pitch **2** hurtle, career, charge, dash, jump, rush, tear **3** descend, dip, dive, drop, fall, nose-dive, plummet, sink, tumble ♦ *noun* **4** dive, descent, drop, fall, jump

plus *preposition* **1** and, added to, coupled with, with ♦ *adjective* **2** additional, added, add-on, extra, supplementary ♦ *noun* **3** *Informal* advantage, asset, benefit, bonus, extra, gain, good point

plush *adjective* luxurious, de luxe, lavish, luxury, opulent, rich, sumptuous

ply *verb* **1** work at, carry on, exercise, follow, practise, pursue **2** use, employ, handle, manipulate, wield

poach *verb* encroach, appropriate, infringe, intrude, trespass

pocket *noun* **1** pouch, bag, compartment, receptacle, sack ♦ *verb* **2** steal, appropriate, filch, lift (*informal*), pilfer, purloin, take ♦ *adjective* **3** small, abridged,

compact, concise, little,
miniature, portable

pod noun, verb <u>shell</u>, hull, husk,
shuck

podgy adjective <u>tubby</u>, chubby,
dumpy, fat, plump, roly-poly,
rotund, stout

podium noun <u>platform</u>, dais,
rostrum, stage

poem noun <u>verse</u>, lyric, ode,
rhyme, song, sonnet

poet noun <u>bard</u>, lyricist, rhymer,
versifier

poetic adjective <u>lyrical</u>, elegiac,
lyric, metrical

poetry noun <u>verse</u>, poems,
rhyme, rhyming

poignancy noun 1 <u>sadness</u>,
emotion, feeling, pathos,
sentiment, tenderness
2 <u>sharpness</u>, bitterness, intensity,
keenness

poignant adjective <u>moving</u>,
bitter, distressing, heart-rending,
intense, painful, pathetic, sad,
touching

point noun 1 <u>essence</u>, crux, drift,
gist, heart, import, meaning,
nub, pith, question, subject,
thrust 2 <u>aim</u>, end, goal, intent,
intention, motive, object,
objective, purpose, reason
3 <u>item</u>, aspect, detail, feature,
particular 4 <u>characteristic</u>,
aspect, attribute, quality,
respect, trait 5 <u>place</u>, location,
position, site, spot, stage 6 <u>full
stop</u>, dot, mark, period, stop
7 <u>end</u>, apex, prong, sharp end,
spike, spur, summit, tip, top
8 <u>headland</u>, cape, head,
promontory 9 <u>stage</u>,
circumstance, condition, degree,

extent, position 10 <u>moment</u>,
instant, juncture, time, very
minute 11 <u>unit</u>, score, tally ♦ verb
12 <u>indicate</u>, call attention to,
denote, designate, direct, show,
signify 13 <u>aim</u>, direct, level, train

point-blank adjective 1 <u>direct</u>,
blunt, downright, explicit,
express, plain ♦ adverb 2 <u>directly</u>,
bluntly, candidly, explicitly,
forthrightly, frankly, openly,
plainly, straight

pointed adjective 1 <u>sharp</u>, acute,
barbed, edged 2 <u>cutting</u>, acute,
biting, incisive, keen,
penetrating, pertinent, sharp,
telling

pointer noun 1 <u>hint</u>, advice,
caution, information,
recommendation, suggestion, tip
2 <u>indicator</u>, guide, hand, needle

pointless adjective <u>senseless</u>,
absurd, aimless, fruitless, futile,
inane, irrelevant, meaningless,
silly, stupid, useless

point out verb <u>mention</u>, allude
to, bring up, identify, indicate,
show, specify

poise noun <u>composure</u>, aplomb,
assurance, calmness, cool (slang),
dignity, presence, sang-froid,
self-possession

poised adjective 1 <u>ready</u>, all set,
prepared, standing by, waiting
2 <u>composed</u>, calm, collected,
dignified, self-confident,
self-possessed, together (informal)

poison noun 1 <u>toxin</u>, bane,
venom ♦ verb 2 <u>murder</u>, give
(someone) poison, kill
3 <u>contaminate</u>, infect, pollute
4 <u>corrupt</u>, defile, deprave,
pervert, subvert, taint,
undermine, warp

poisonous *adjective* **1** toxic, deadly, fatal, lethal, mortal, noxious, venomous, virulent **2** evil, baleful, corrupting, malicious, noxious, pernicious

poke *verb* **1** jab, dig, nudge, prod, push, shove, stab, stick, thrust ♦ *noun* **2** jab, dig, nudge, prod, thrust

poky *adjective* small, confined, cramped, narrow, tiny

pole *noun* rod, bar, mast, post, shaft, spar, staff, stick

police *noun* **1** the law (*informal*), boys in blue (*informal*), constabulary, fuzz (*slang*), police force, the Old Bill (*slang*) ♦ *verb* **2** control, guard, patrol, protect, regulate, watch

policeman *noun* cop (*slang*), bobby (*informal*), constable, copper (*slang*), fuzz (*slang*), officer

policy *noun* procedure, action, approach, code, course, custom, plan, practice, rule, scheme

polish *verb* **1** shine, brighten, buff, burnish, rub, smooth, wax **2** perfect, brush up, enhance, finish, improve, refine, touch up ♦ *noun* **3** varnish, wax **4** sheen, brightness, finish, glaze, gloss, lustre **5** style, breeding, class (*informal*), elegance, finesse, finish, grace, refinement

polished *adjective* **1** accomplished, adept, expert, fine, masterly, professional, skilful, superlative **2** shining, bright, burnished, gleaming, glossy, smooth **3** elegant, cultivated, polite, refined, sophisticated, well-bred

polite *adjective* **1** mannerly, civil, complaisant, courteous,

gracious, respectful, well-behaved, well-mannered **2** refined, civilized, cultured, elegant, genteel, polished, sophisticated, well-bred

politeness *noun* courtesy, civility, courteousness, decency, etiquette, mannerliness

politic *adjective* wise, advisable, diplomatic, expedient, judicious, prudent, sensible

political *adjective* governmental, parliamentary, policy-making

politician *noun* statesman, legislator, Member of Parliament, M.P., office bearer, public servant

politics *noun* statesmanship, affairs of state, civics, government, political science

poll *noun* **1** canvass, ballot, census, count, sampling, survey **2** vote, figures, returns, tally, voting ♦ *verb* **3** tally, register **4** question, ballot, canvass, interview, sample, survey

pollute *verb* **1** contaminate, dirty, foul, infect, poison, soil, spoil, stain, taint **2** defile, corrupt, debase, debauch, deprave, desecrate, dishonour, profane, sully

pollution *noun* contamination, corruption, defilement, dirtying, foulness, impurity, taint, uncleanness

pomp *noun* **1** ceremony, flourish, grandeur, magnificence, pageant, pageantry, splendour, state **2** show, display, grandiosity, ostentation

pomposity *noun* self-importance, affectation, airs, grandiosity,

pompousness, portentousness,
pretension, pretentiousness

pompous *adjective*
1 <u>self-important</u>, arrogant,
grandiose, ostentatious,
pretentious, puffed up, showy
2 <u>grandiloquent</u>, boastful,
bombastic, high-flown, inflated

pond *noun* <u>pool</u>, duck pond, fish
pond, millpond, small lake, tarn

ponder *verb* <u>think</u>, brood,
cogitate, consider, contemplate,
deliberate, meditate, mull over,
muse, reflect, ruminate

ponderous *adjective* 1 <u>dull</u>,
heavy, long-winded, pedantic,
tedious 2 <u>unwieldy</u>, bulky,
cumbersome, heavy, huge,
massive, weighty 3 <u>clumsy</u>,
awkward, heavy-footed,
lumbering

pontificate *verb* <u>expound</u>, hold
forth, lay down the law, preach,
pronounce, sound off

pool¹ *noun* 1 <u>pond</u>, lake, mere,
puddle, tarn 2 <u>swimming pool</u>,
swimming bath

pool² *noun* 1 <u>syndicate</u>, collective,
consortium, group, team, trust
2 <u>kitty</u>, bank, funds, jackpot, pot
♦ *verb* 3 <u>combine</u>, amalgamate,
join forces, league, merge, put
together, share

poor *adjective* 1 <u>impoverished</u>,
broke (*informal*), destitute, down
and out, hard up (*informal*),
impecunious, indigent, needy,
on the breadline, penniless,
penurious, poverty-stricken,
short, skint (*Brit. slang*),
stony-broke (*Brit. slang*)
2 <u>inadequate</u>, deficient,
incomplete, insufficient, lacking,
meagre, measly, scant, scanty,

skimpy 3 <u>inferior</u>, below par,
low-grade, mediocre, no great
shakes (*informal*), not much cop
(*Brit. slang*), rotten (*informal*),
rubbishy, second-rate,
substandard, unsatisfactory
4 <u>unfortunate</u>, hapless, ill-fated,
luckless, pitiable, unlucky,
wretched

poorly *adverb* 1 <u>badly</u>,
inadequately, incompetently,
inexpertly, insufficiently,
unsatisfactorily, unsuccessfully
♦ *adjective* 2 *Informal* ill, below
par, off colour, rotten (*informal*),
seedy (*informal*), sick, under the
weather (*informal*), unwell

pop *verb* 1 <u>burst</u>, bang, crack,
explode, go off, snap 2 <u>put</u>,
insert, push, shove, slip, stick,
thrust, tuck ♦ *noun* 3 <u>bang</u>,
burst, crack, explosion, noise,
report

pope *noun* <u>Holy Father</u>, Bishop of
Rome, pontiff, Vicar of Christ

populace *noun* <u>people</u>, general
public, hoi polloi, masses, mob,
multitude

popular *adjective* 1 <u>well-liked</u>,
accepted, approved, fashionable,
favourite, in, in demand, in
favour, liked, sought-after
2 <u>common</u>, conventional,
current, general, prevailing,
prevalent, universal

popularity *noun* <u>favour</u>,
acceptance, acclaim, approval,
currency, esteem, regard, vogue

popularize *verb* <u>make popular</u>,
disseminate, give currency to,
give mass appeal, make available
to all, spread, universalize

popularly *adverb* <u>generally</u>,
commonly, conventionally,

customarily, ordinarily, traditionally, universally, usually, widely

populate *verb* inhabit, colonize, live in, occupy, settle

population *noun* inhabitants, community, denizens, folk, natives, people, residents, society

populous *adjective* populated, crowded, heavily populated, overpopulated, packed, swarming, teeming

pore[1] *verb* pore over study, examine, peruse, ponder, read, scrutinize

pore[2] *noun* opening, hole, orifice, outlet

pornographic *adjective* obscene, blue, dirty, filthy, indecent, lewd, salacious, smutty

pornography *noun* obscenity, dirt, filth, indecency, porn (*informal*), smut

porous *adjective* permeable, absorbent, absorptive, penetrable, spongy

port *noun* harbour, anchorage, haven, seaport

portable *adjective* light, compact, convenient, easily carried, handy, manageable, movable

portend *verb* foretell, augur, betoken, bode, foreshadow, herald, indicate, predict, prognosticate, promise, warn of

portent *noun* omen, augury, forewarning, indication, prognostication, sign, warning

portentous *adjective*
1 significant, crucial, fateful, important, menacing, momentous, ominous
2 pompous, ponderous, self-important, solemn

porter[1] *noun* baggage attendant, bearer, carrier

porter[2] *noun* doorman, caretaker, concierge, gatekeeper, janitor

portion *noun* 1 part, bit, fragment, morsel, piece, scrap, section, segment 2 share, allocation, allotment, allowance, lot, measure, quantity, quota, ration 3 helping, piece, serving 4 destiny, fate, fortune, lot, luck ♦ *verb* 5 portion out divide, allocate, allot, apportion, deal, distribute, dole out, share out

portly *adjective* stout, burly, corpulent, fat, fleshy, heavy, large, plump

portrait *noun* 1 picture, image, likeness, painting, photograph, representation 2 description, characterization, depiction, portrayal, profile, thumbnail sketch

portray *verb* 1 represent, depict, draw, figure, illustrate, paint, picture, sketch 2 describe, characterize, depict, put in words 3 play, act the part of, represent

portrayal *noun* representation, characterization, depiction, interpretation, performance, picture

pose *verb* 1 position, model, sit 2 put on airs, posture, show off (*informal*) 3 pose as impersonate, masquerade as, pass oneself off as, pretend to be, profess to be ♦ *noun* 4 posture, attitude, bearing, position, stance 5 act, affectation, air, façade, front, mannerism, posturing, pretence

poser *noun* <u>puzzle</u>, enigma, problem, question, riddle

posh *adjective Informal* <u>upper-class</u>, classy (*slang*), grand, high-class, luxurious, ritzy (*slang*), smart, stylish, swanky (*informal*), swish (*informal, chiefly Brit.*), up-market

posit *verb* <u>put forward</u>, advance, assume, postulate, presume, propound, state

position *noun* 1 <u>place</u>, area, bearings, locale, location, point, post, situation, spot, station, whereabouts 2 <u>posture</u>, arrangement, attitude, pose, stance 3 <u>attitude</u>, belief, opinion, outlook, point of view, slant, stance, view, viewpoint 4 <u>status</u>, importance, place, prestige, rank, reputation, standing, station, stature 5 <u>job</u>, duty, employment, occupation, office, place, post, role, situation ◆ *verb* 6 <u>place</u>, arrange, lay out, locate, put, set, stand

positive *adjective* 1 <u>certain</u>, assured, confident, convinced, sure 2 <u>definite</u>, absolute, categorical, certain, clear, conclusive, decisive, explicit, express, firm, real 3 <u>helpful</u>, beneficial, constructive, practical, productive, progressive, useful 4 *Informal* <u>absolute</u>, complete, consummate, downright, out-and-out, perfect, thorough, utter

positively *adverb* <u>definitely</u>, absolutely, assuredly, categorically, certainly, emphatically, firmly, surely, unequivocally, unquestionably

possess *verb* 1 <u>have</u>, enjoy,

hold, own 2 <u>control</u>, acquire, dominate, hold, occupy, seize, take over

possessed *adjective* <u>crazed</u>, berserk, demented, frenzied, obsessed, raving

possession *noun* 1 <u>ownership</u>, control, custody, hold, occupation, tenure, title 2 **possessions** <u>property</u>, assets, belongings, chattels, effects, estate, things

possessive *adjective* <u>jealous</u>, controlling, covetous, dominating, domineering, overprotective, selfish

possibility *noun* 1 <u>feasibility</u>, likelihood, potentiality, practicability, workableness 2 <u>likelihood</u>, chance, hope, liability, odds, probability, prospect, risk 3 *often plural* <u>potential</u>, capabilities, potentiality, promise, prospects, talent

possible *adjective* 1 <u>conceivable</u>, credible, hypothetical, imaginable, likely, potential 2 <u>likely</u>, hopeful, potential, probable, promising 3 <u>feasible</u>, attainable, doable, practicable, realizable, viable, workable

possibly *adverb* <u>perhaps</u>, maybe, perchance (*archaic*)

post¹ *noun* 1 <u>mail</u>, collection, delivery, postal service ◆ *verb* 2 <u>send</u>, dispatch, mail, transmit 3 **keep someone posted** <u>notify</u>, advise, brief, fill in on (*informal*), inform, report to

post² *noun* 1 <u>support</u>, column, picket, pillar, pole, shaft, stake, upright ◆ *verb* 2 <u>put up</u>, affix, display, pin up

post³ noun **1** <u>job</u>, appointment, assignment, employment, office, place, position, situation **2** <u>station</u>, beat, place, position ♦ verb **3** <u>station</u>, assign, place, position, put, situate

poster noun <u>notice</u>, advertisement, announcement, bill, placard, public notice, sticker

posterity noun **1** <u>future</u>, succeeding generations **2** <u>descendants</u>, children, family, heirs, issue, offspring, progeny

postpone verb <u>put off</u>, adjourn, defer, delay, put back, put on the back burner (*informal*), shelve, suspend

postponement noun <u>delay</u>, adjournment, deferment, deferral, stay, suspension

postscript noun <u>P.S.</u>, addition, afterthought, supplement

postulate verb <u>presuppose</u>, assume, hypothesize, posit, propose, suppose, take for granted, theorize

posture noun **1** <u>bearing</u>, attitude, carriage, disposition, set, stance ♦ verb **2** <u>show off</u> (*informal*), affect, pose, put on airs

pot noun <u>container</u>, bowl, pan, vessel

potency noun <u>power</u>, effectiveness, force, influence, might, strength

potent adjective **1** <u>powerful</u>, authoritative, commanding, dominant, dynamic, influential **2** <u>strong</u>, forceful, mighty, powerful, vigorous

potential adjective **1** <u>possible</u>, dormant, future, hidden, inherent, latent, likely, promising ♦ noun **2** <u>ability</u>, aptitude, capability, capacity, possibility, potentiality, power, wherewithal

potion noun <u>concoction</u>, brew, dose, draught, elixir, mixture, philtre

potter verb <u>mess about</u>, dabble, footle (*informal*), tinker

pottery noun <u>ceramics</u>, earthenware, stoneware, terracotta

pouch noun <u>bag</u>, container, pocket, purse, sack

pounce verb **1** <u>spring</u>, attack, fall upon, jump, leap at, strike, swoop ♦ noun **2** <u>spring</u>, assault, attack, bound, jump, leap, swoop

pound¹ verb **1** <u>beat</u>, batter, belabour, clobber (*slang*), hammer, pummel, strike, thrash, thump **2** <u>crush</u>, powder, pulverize **3** <u>pulsate</u>, beat, palpitate, pulse, throb **4** <u>stomp</u> (*informal*), march, thunder, tramp

pound² noun <u>enclosure</u>, compound, pen, yard

pour verb **1** <u>flow</u>, course, emit, gush, run, rush, spew, spout, stream **2** <u>let flow</u>, decant, spill, splash **3** <u>rain</u>, bucket down (*informal*), pelt (down), teem **4** <u>stream</u>, crowd, swarm, teem, throng

pout verb **1** <u>sulk</u>, glower, look petulant, pull a long face ♦ noun **2** <u>sullen look</u>, glower, long face

poverty noun **1** <u>pennilessness</u>, beggary, destitution, hardship, indigence, insolvency, need, penury, privation, want **2** <u>scarcity</u>, dearth, deficiency, insufficiency, lack, paucity, shortage

poverty-stricken adjective penniless, broke (informal), destitute, down and out, flat broke (informal), impecunious, impoverished, indigent, poor

powder noun 1 dust, fine grains, loose particles, talc ♦ verb 2 dust, cover, dredge, scatter, sprinkle, strew

powdery adjective fine, crumbly, dry, dusty, grainy, granular

power noun 1 ability, capability, capacity, competence, competency, faculty, potential 2 control, ascendancy, authority, command, dominance, domination, dominion, influence, mastery, rule 3 authority, authorization, licence, prerogative, privilege, right, warrant 4 strength, brawn, energy, force, forcefulness, intensity, might, muscle, potency, vigour

powerful adjective 1 controlling, authoritative, commanding, dominant, influential, prevailing 2 strong, energetic, mighty, potent, strapping, sturdy, vigorous 3 persuasive, cogent, compelling, convincing, effectual, forceful, impressive, striking, telling, weighty

powerless adjective 1 defenceless, dependent, ineffective, subject, tied, unarmed, vulnerable 2 helpless, debilitated, disabled, feeble, frail, impotent, incapable, incapacitated, ineffectual, weak

practicability noun feasibility, advantage, possibility, practicality, use, usefulness, viability

practicable adjective feasible, achievable, attainable, doable, possible, viable

practical adjective 1 functional, applied, empirical, experimental, factual, pragmatic, realistic, utilitarian 2 sensible, businesslike, down-to-earth, hard-headed, matter-of-fact, ordinary, realistic 3 feasible, doable, practicable, serviceable, useful, workable 4 skilled, accomplished, efficient, experienced, proficient

practically adverb 1 almost, all but, basically, essentially, fundamentally, in effect, just about, nearly, very nearly, virtually, well-nigh 2 sensibly, clearly, matter-of-factly, rationally, realistically, reasonably

practice noun 1 custom, habit, method, mode, routine, rule, system, tradition, usage, way, wont 2 rehearsal, drill, exercise, preparation, repetition, study, training 3 profession, business, career, vocation, work 4 use, action, application, exercise, experience, operation

practise verb 1 rehearse, drill, exercise, go over, go through, prepare, repeat, study, train 2 do, apply, carry out, follow, observe, perform 3 work at, carry on, engage in, pursue

practised adjective skilled, able, accomplished, experienced, expert, proficient, seasoned, trained

pragmatic adjective practical, businesslike, down-to-earth, hard-headed, realistic, sensible, utilitarian

praise verb 1 <u>approve</u>, acclaim, admire, applaud, cheer, compliment, congratulate, eulogize, extol, honour, laud 2 <u>give thanks to</u>, adore, bless, exalt, glorify, worship ♦ noun 3 <u>approval</u>, acclaim, acclamation, approbation, commendation, compliment, congratulation, eulogy, plaudit, tribute 4 <u>thanks</u>, adoration, glory, homage, worship

praiseworthy adjective <u>creditable</u>, admirable, commendable, laudable, meritorious, worthy

prance verb 1 <u>dance</u>, caper, cavort, frisk, gambol, romp, skip 2 <u>strut</u>, parade, show off (informal), stalk, swagger, swank (informal)

prank noun <u>trick</u>, escapade, jape, lark (informal), practical joke

prattle verb <u>chatter</u>, babble, blather, blether, gabble, jabber, rabbit (on) (Brit. informal), waffle (informal, chiefly Brit.), witter (informal)

pray verb 1 <u>say one's prayers</u>, offer a prayer, recite the rosary 2 <u>beg</u>, adjure, ask, beseech, entreat, implore, petition, plead, request, solicit

prayer noun 1 <u>orison</u>, devotion, invocation, litany, supplication 2 <u>plea</u>, appeal, entreaty, petition, request, supplication

preach verb 1 <u>deliver a sermon</u>, address, evangelize 2 <u>lecture</u>, advocate, exhort, moralize, sermonize

preacher noun <u>clergyman</u>, evangelist, minister, missionary, parson

preamble noun <u>introduction</u>, foreword, opening statement or remarks, preface, prelude

precarious adjective <u>dangerous</u>, dodgy (Brit., Austral., & N.Z. informal), hazardous, insecure, perilous, risky, shaky, tricky, unreliable, unsafe, unsure

precaution noun 1 <u>safeguard</u>, insurance, protection, provision, safety measure 2 <u>forethought</u>, care, caution, providence, prudence, wariness

precede verb <u>go before</u>, antedate, come first, head, introduce, lead, preface

precedence noun <u>priority</u>, antecedence, pre-eminence, primacy, rank, seniority, superiority, supremacy

precedent noun <u>instance</u>, antecedent, example, model, paradigm, pattern, prototype, standard

preceding adjective <u>previous</u>, above, aforementioned, aforesaid, earlier, foregoing, former, past, prior

precept noun <u>rule</u>, canon, command, commandment, decree, instruction, law, order, principle, regulation, statute

precinct noun 1 <u>enclosure</u>, confine, limit 2 <u>area</u>, district, quarter, section, sector, zone

precious adjective 1 <u>valuable</u>, costly, dear, expensive, fine, invaluable, priceless, prized 2 <u>loved</u>, adored, beloved, cherished, darling, dear, prized, treasured 3 <u>affected</u>, artificial, overnice, overrefined, twee (Brit. informal)

precipice noun <u>cliff</u>, bluff, crag, height, rock face

precipitate verb 1 <u>quicken</u>, accelerate, advance, bring on, expedite, hasten, hurry, speed up, trigger 2 <u>throw</u>, cast, fling, hurl, launch, let fly ♦ adjective 3 <u>hasty</u>, heedless, impetuous, impulsive, precipitous, rash, reckless 4 <u>swift</u>, breakneck, headlong, rapid, rushing 5 <u>sudden</u>, abrupt, brief, quick, unexpected, without warning

precipitous adjective 1 <u>sheer</u>, abrupt, dizzy, high, perpendicular, steep 2 <u>hasty</u>, heedless, hurried, precipitate, rash, reckless

précis noun 1 <u>summary</u>, abridgment, outline, résumé, synopsis ♦ verb 2 <u>summarize</u>, abridge, outline, shorten, sum up

precise adjective 1 <u>exact</u>, absolute, accurate, correct, definite, explicit, express, particular, specific, strict 2 <u>strict</u>, careful, exact, fastidious, finicky, formal, meticulous, particular, punctilious, rigid, scrupulous, stiff

precisely adverb <u>exactly</u>, absolutely, accurately, correctly, just so, plumb (informal), smack (informal), square, squarely, strictly

precision noun <u>exactness</u>, accuracy, care, meticulousness, particularity, preciseness

preclude verb <u>prevent</u>, check, debar, exclude, forestall, inhibit, obviate, prohibit, rule out, stop

precocious adjective <u>advanced</u>, ahead, bright, developed, forward, quick, smart

preconceived adjective

presumed, forejudged, prejudged, presupposed

preconception noun <u>preconceived idea or notion</u>, bias, notion, predisposition, prejudice, presupposition

precursor noun 1 <u>herald</u>, forerunner, harbinger, vanguard 2 <u>forerunner</u>, antecedent, forebear, predecessor

predatory adjective <u>hunting</u>, carnivorous, predacious, raptorial

predecessor noun 1 <u>previous job holder</u>, antecedent, forerunner, precursor 2 <u>ancestor</u>, antecedent, forebear, forefather

predestination noun <u>fate</u>, destiny, foreordainment, foreordination, predetermination

predestined adjective <u>fated</u>, doomed, meant, preordained

predetermined adjective <u>prearranged</u>, agreed, fixed, preplanned, set

predicament noun <u>fix</u> (informal), dilemma, hole (slang), jam (informal), mess, pinch, plight, quandary, scrape (informal), situation, spot (informal)

predict verb <u>foretell</u>, augur, divine, forecast, portend, prophesy

predictable adjective <u>likely</u>, anticipated, certain, expected, foreseeable, reliable, sure

prediction noun <u>prophecy</u>, augury, divination, forecast, prognosis, prognostication

predilection noun <u>liking</u>, bias, fondness, inclination, leaning, love, partiality, penchant, preference, propensity, taste, weakness

predispose verb incline, affect, bias, dispose, influence, lead, prejudice, prompt

predisposed adjective inclined, given, liable, minded, ready, subject, susceptible, willing

predominant adjective main, ascendant, chief, dominant, leading, paramount, prevailing, prevalent, prime, principal

predominantly adverb mainly, chiefly, for the most part, generally, largely, mostly, primarily, principally

predominate verb prevail, be most noticeable, carry weight, hold sway, outweigh, overrule, overshadow

pre-eminence noun superiority, distinction, excellence, predominance, prestige, prominence, renown, supremacy

pre-eminent adjective outstanding, chief, distinguished, excellent, foremost, incomparable, matchless, predominant, renowned, superior, supreme

pre-empt verb anticipate, appropriate, assume, usurp

preen verb 1 Of birds clean, plume 2 smarten, dress up, spruce up, titivate 3 **preen oneself (on)** pride oneself, congratulate oneself

preface noun 1 introduction, foreword, preamble, preliminary, prelude, prologue ◆ verb 2 introduce, begin, open, prefix

prefer verb like better, be partial to, choose, desire, fancy, favour, go for, incline towards, opt for, pick

preferable adjective better, best, chosen, favoured, more desirable, superior

preferably adverb rather, by choice, first, in or for preference, sooner

preference noun 1 first choice, choice, desire, favourite, option, partiality, pick, predilection, selection 2 priority, favoured treatment, favouritism, first place, precedence

preferential adjective privileged, advantageous, better, favoured, special

preferment noun promotion, advancement, elevation, exaltation, rise, upgrading

pregnant adjective 1 expectant, big or heavy with child, expecting (informal), in the club (Brit. slang), with child 2 meaningful, charged, eloquent, expressive, loaded, pointed, significant, telling, weighty

prehistoric adjective earliest, early, primeval, primitive, primordial

prejudge verb jump to conclusions, anticipate, presume, presuppose

prejudice noun 1 bias, partiality, preconceived notion, preconception, prejudgment 2 discrimination, bigotry, chauvinism, injustice, intolerance, narrow-mindedness, unfairness ◆ verb 3 bias, colour, distort, influence, poison, predispose, slant 4 harm, damage, hinder, hurt, impair, injure, mar, spoil, undermine

prejudiced adjective biased,

bigoted, influenced, intolerant, narrow-minded, one-sided, opinionated, unfair

prejudicial *adjective* <u>harmful</u>, damaging, deleterious, detrimental, disadvantageous, hurtful, injurious, unfavourable

preliminary *adjective* 1 <u>first</u>, initial, introductory, opening, pilot, prefatory, preparatory, prior, test, trial ♦ *noun* 2 <u>introduction</u>, beginning, opening, overture, preamble, preface, prelude, start

prelude *noun* <u>introduction</u>, beginning, foreword, overture, preamble, preface, prologue, start

premature *adjective* 1 <u>early</u>, forward, unseasonable, untimely 2 <u>hasty</u>, ill-timed, overhasty, previous (*informal*), rash, too soon, untimely

premeditated *adjective* <u>planned</u>, calculated, conscious, considered, deliberate, intentional, wilful

premeditation *noun* <u>planning</u>, design, forethought, intention, plotting, prearrangement, predetermination, purpose

premier *noun* 1 <u>head of government</u>, chancellor, chief minister, P.M., prime minister ♦ *adjective* 2 <u>chief</u>, first, foremost, head, highest, leading, main, primary, prime, principal

premiere *noun* <u>first night</u>, debut, opening

premise *noun* <u>assumption</u>, argument, assertion, hypothesis, postulation, presupposition, proposition, supposition

premises *plural noun* <u>building</u>, establishment, place, property, site

premium *noun* 1 <u>bonus</u>, bounty, fee, perk (*Brit. informal*), perquisite, prize, reward 2 **at a premium** <u>in great demand</u>, hard to come by, in short supply, rare, scarce

premonition *noun* <u>feeling</u>, foreboding, hunch, idea, intuition, presentiment, suspicion

preoccupation *noun* 1 <u>obsession</u>, bee in one's bonnet, fixation 2 <u>absorption</u>, absent-mindedness, abstraction, daydreaming, engrossment, immersion, reverie, woolgathering

preoccupied *adjective* <u>absorbed</u>, absent-minded, distracted, engrossed, immersed, lost in, oblivious, rapt, wrapped up

preparation *noun* 1 <u>groundwork</u>, getting ready, preparing 2 *often plural* <u>arrangement</u>, measure, plan, provision 3 <u>mixture</u>, compound, concoction, medicine

preparatory *adjective* <u>introductory</u>, opening, prefatory, preliminary, primary

prepare *verb* <u>make *or* get ready</u>, adapt, adjust, arrange, practise, prime, train, warm up

prepared *adjective* 1 <u>ready</u>, arranged, in order, in readiness, primed, set 2 <u>willing</u>, disposed, inclined

preponderance *noun* <u>predominance</u>, dominance, domination, extensiveness, greater numbers, greater part, lion's share, mass, prevalence, supremacy

prepossessing adjective
<u>attractive</u>, appealing, charming, engaging, fetching, good-looking, handsome, likable or likeable, pleasing

preposterous adjective
<u>ridiculous</u>, absurd, crazy, incredible, insane, laughable, ludicrous, nonsensical, out of the question, outrageous, unthinkable

prerequisite noun
1 <u>requirement</u>, condition, essential, must, necessity, precondition, qualification, requisite, sine qua non ♦ adjective
2 <u>required</u>, essential, indispensable, mandatory, necessary, obligatory, requisite, vital

prerogative noun <u>right</u>, advantage, due, exemption, immunity, liberty, privilege

presage verb <u>portend</u>, augur, betoken, bode, foreshadow, foretoken, signify

prescience noun <u>foresight</u>, clairvoyance, foreknowledge, precognition, second sight

prescribe verb order, decree, dictate, direct, lay down, ordain, recommend, rule, set, specify, stipulate

prescription noun 1 <u>instruction</u>, direction, formula, recipe
2 <u>medicine</u>, drug, mixture, preparation, remedy

presence noun 1 <u>being</u>, attendance, existence, inhabitance, occupancy, residence 2 <u>personality</u>, air, appearance, aspect, aura, bearing, carriage, demeanour, poise, self-assurance

presence of mind noun

<u>level-headedness</u>, calmness, composure, cool (slang), coolness, self-possession, wits

present[1] adjective 1 <u>here</u>, at hand, near, nearby, ready, there 2 <u>current</u>, contemporary, existent, existing, immediate, present-day ♦ noun 3 **the present** <u>now</u>, here and now, the present moment, the time being, today 4 **at present** <u>just now</u>, at the moment, now, right now 5 **for the present** <u>for now</u>, for the moment, for the time being, in the meantime, temporarily

present[2] noun 1 <u>gift</u>, boon, donation, endowment, grant, gratuity, hand-out, offering, prezzie (informal) ♦ verb
2 <u>introduce</u>, acquaint with, make known 3 <u>put on</u>, display, exhibit, give, show, stage 4 <u>give</u>, award, bestow, confer, grant, hand out, hand over

presentable adjective <u>decent</u>, acceptable, becoming, fit to be seen, O.K. or okay (informal), passable, respectable, satisfactory, suitable

presentation noun 1 <u>giving</u>, award, bestowal, conferral, donation, offering 2 <u>production</u>, demonstration, display, exhibition, performance, show

presently adverb <u>soon</u>, anon (archaic), before long, by and by, shortly

preservation noun <u>protection</u>, conservation, maintenance, safeguarding, safekeeping, safety, salvation, support

preserve verb 1 <u>save</u>, care for, conserve, defend, keep, protect, safeguard, shelter, shield

2 <u>maintain</u>, continue, keep, keep up, perpetuate, sustain, uphold ♦ *noun* **3** <u>area</u>, domain, field, realm, sphere

preside *verb* <u>run</u>, administer, chair, conduct, control, direct, govern, head, lead, manage, officiate

press *verb* **1** <u>force down</u>, compress, crush, depress, jam, mash, push, squeeze **2** <u>hug</u>, clasp, crush, embrace, fold in one's arms, hold close, squeeze **3** <u>smooth</u>, flatten, iron **4** <u>urge</u>, beg, entreat, exhort, implore, petition, plead, pressurize **5** <u>crowd</u>, flock, gather, herd, push, seethe, surge, swarm, throng ♦ *noun* **6 the press: a** <u>newspapers</u>, Fleet Street, fourth estate, news media, the papers **b** <u>journalists</u>, columnists, correspondents, newsmen, pressmen, reporters

pressing *adjective* <u>urgent</u>, crucial, high-priority, imperative, important, importunate, serious, vital

pressure *noun* **1** <u>force</u>, compressing, compression, crushing, squeezing, weight **2** <u>power</u>, coercion, compulsion, constraint, force, influence, sway **3** <u>stress</u>, burden, demands, hassle (*informal*), heat, load, strain, urgency

prestige *noun* <u>status</u>, credit, distinction, eminence, fame, honour, importance, kudos, renown, reputation, standing

prestigious *adjective* <u>celebrated</u>, eminent, esteemed, great, illustrious, important, notable, prominent, renowned, respected

presumably *adverb* <u>it would seem</u>, apparently, in all likelihood, in all probability, on the face of it, probably, seemingly

presume *verb* **1** <u>believe</u>, assume, conjecture, guess (*informal, chiefly U.S. & Canad.*), infer, postulate, suppose, surmise, take for granted, think **2** <u>dare</u>, go so far, make so bold, take the liberty, venture

presumption *noun* **1** <u>cheek</u> (*informal*), audacity, boldness, effrontery, gall (*informal*), impudence, insolence, nerve (*informal*) **2** <u>probability</u>, basis, chance, likelihood

presumptuous *adjective* <u>pushy</u> (*informal*), audacious, bold, forward, insolent, overconfident, too big for one's boots, uppish (*Brit. informal*)

presuppose *verb* <u>presume</u>, assume, imply, posit, postulate, take as read, take for granted

presupposition *noun* <u>assumption</u>, belief, preconception, premise, presumption, supposition

pretence *noun* **1** <u>deception</u>, acting, charade, deceit, falsehood, feigning, sham, simulation, trickery **2** <u>show</u>, affectation, artifice, display, façade, veneer

pretend *verb* **1** <u>feign</u>, affect, allege, assume, fake, falsify, impersonate, profess, sham, simulate **2** <u>make believe</u>, act, imagine, make up, suppose

pretended *adjective* <u>feigned</u>, bogus, counterfeit, fake, false, phoney *or* phony (*informal*), pretend (*informal*), pseudo (*informal*), sham, so-called

pretender *noun* <u>claimant</u>, aspirant

pretension *noun* **1** <u>claim</u>, aspiration, assumption, demand, pretence, profession
2 <u>affectation</u>, airs, conceit, ostentation, pretentiousness, self-importance, show, snobbery, vanity

pretentious *adjective* <u>affected</u>, conceited, grandiloquent, grandiose, high-flown, inflated, mannered, ostentatious, pompous, puffed up, showy, snobbish

pretext *noun* <u>guise</u>, cloak, cover, excuse, ploy, pretence, ruse, show

pretty *adjective* **1** <u>attractive</u>, beautiful, bonny, charming, comely, fair, good-looking, lovely ♦ *adverb* **2** *Informal* <u>fairly</u>, kind of (*informal*), moderately, quite, rather, reasonably, somewhat

prevail *verb* **1** <u>win</u>, be victorious, overcome, overrule, succeed, triumph **2** <u>be widespread</u>, abound, be current, be prevalent, exist generally, predominate

prevailing *adjective*
1 <u>widespread</u>, common, current, customary, established, fashionable, general, in vogue, ordinary, popular, prevalent, usual **2** <u>predominating</u>, dominant, main, principal, ruling

prevalence *noun* <u>commonness</u>, currency, frequency, popularity, universality

prevalent *adjective* <u>common</u>, current, customary, established,

frequent, general, popular, universal, usual, widespread

prevaricate *verb* <u>evade</u>, beat about the bush, cavil, deceive, dodge, equivocate, flannel (*Brit. informal*), hedge

prevent *verb* <u>stop</u>, avert, avoid, foil, forestall, frustrate, hamper, hinder, impede, inhibit, obstruct, obviate, preclude, thwart

prevention *noun* <u>elimination</u>, avoidance, deterrence, precaution, safeguard, thwarting

preventive, preventative *adjective* **1** <u>hindering</u>, hampering, impeding, obstructive
2 <u>protective</u>, counteractive, deterrent, precautionary ♦ *noun*
3 <u>hindrance</u>, block, impediment, obstacle, obstruction
4 <u>protection</u>, deterrent, prevention, remedy, safeguard, shield

preview *noun* <u>advance showing</u>, foretaste, sneak preview, taster, trailer

previous *adjective* <u>earlier</u>, erstwhile, foregoing, former, past, preceding, prior

previously *adverb* <u>before</u>, beforehand, earlier, formerly, hitherto, in the past, once

prey *noun* **1** <u>quarry</u>, game, kill
2 <u>victim</u>, dupe, fall guy (*informal*), mug (*Brit. slang*), target

price *noun* **1** <u>cost</u>, amount, charge, damage (*informal*), estimate, expense, fee, figure, rate, value, worth
2 <u>consequences</u>, cost, penalty, toll ♦ *verb* **3** <u>evaluate</u>, assess, cost, estimate, rate, value

priceless *adjective* **1** <u>valuable</u>,

costly, dear, expensive,
invaluable, precious **2** *Informal*
hilarious, amusing, comic, droll,
funny, rib-tickling, side-splitting

pricey, pricy *adjective* expensive,
costly, dear, high-priced, steep
(*informal*)

prick *verb* **1** pierce, jab, lance,
perforate, punch, puncture, stab
2 sting, bite, itch, prickle, smart,
tingle ♦ *noun* **3** puncture, hole,
perforation, pinhole, wound

prickle *noun* **1** spike, barb,
needle, point, spine, spur, thorn
♦ *verb* **2** tingle, itch, smart, sting
3 prick, jab, stick

prickly *adjective* **1** spiny, barbed,
bristly, thorny **2** itchy, crawling,
scratchy, sharp, smarting,
stinging, tingling

pride *noun* **1** satisfaction, delight,
gratification, joy, pleasure
2 self-respect, dignity, honour,
self-esteem, self-worth **3** conceit,
arrogance, egotism, hubris,
pretension, pretentiousness,
self-importance, self-love,
superciliousness, vanity **4** gem,
jewel, pride and joy, treasure

priest *noun* clergyman, cleric,
curate, divine, ecclesiastic,
father, minister, pastor, vicar

prig *noun* goody-goody
(*informal*), prude, puritan, stuffed
shirt (*informal*)

priggish *adjective* self-righteous,
goody-goody (*informal*),
holier-than-thou, prim, prudish,
puritanical

prim *adjective* prudish, demure,
fastidious, fussy, priggish, prissy
(*informal*), proper, puritanical,
strait-laced

prima donna *noun* diva, leading
lady, star

primarily *adverb* **1** chiefly, above
all, essentially, fundamentally,
generally, largely, mainly,
mostly, principally **2** at first, at *or*
from the start, first and
foremost, initially, in the
beginning, in the first place,
originally

primary *adjective* **1** chief,
cardinal, first, greatest, highest,
main, paramount, prime,
principal **2** elementary,
introductory, rudimentary, simple

prime *adjective* **1** main, chief,
leading, predominant,
pre-eminent, primary, principal
2 best, choice, excellent,
first-class, first-rate, highest,
quality, select, top ♦ *noun*
3 peak, bloom, flower, height,
heyday, zenith ♦ *verb* **4** inform,
brief, clue in (*informal*), fill in
(*informal*), notify, tell **5** prepare,
coach, get ready, make ready,
train

primeval *adjective* earliest,
ancient, early, first, old,
prehistoric, primal, primitive,
primordial

primitive *adjective* **1** early,
earliest, elementary, first,
original, primary, primeval,
primordial **2** crude, rough,
rudimentary, simple, unrefined

prince *noun* ruler, lord, monarch,
sovereign

princely *adjective* **1** regal,
imperial, majestic, noble, royal,
sovereign **2** generous,
bounteous, gracious, lavish,
liberal, munificent, open-handed,
rich

principal *adjective* 1 main, cardinal, chief, essential, first, foremost, key, leading, paramount, pre-eminent, primary, prime ♦ *noun* 2 head (*informal*), dean, headmaster *or* headmistress, head teacher, master *or* mistress, rector 3 star, lead, leader 4 capital, assets, money

principally *adverb* mainly, above all, chiefly, especially, largely, mostly, predominantly, primarily

principle *noun* 1 rule, canon, criterion, doctrine, dogma, fundamental, law, maxim, precept, standard, truth 2 morals, conscience, integrity, probity, scruples, sense of honour 3 in principle in theory, ideally, theoretically

print *verb* 1 publish, engrave, impress, imprint, issue, mark, stamp ♦ *noun* 2 publication, book, magazine, newspaper, newsprint, periodical, printed matter 3 reproduction, copy, engraving, photo (*informal*), photograph, picture

prior *adjective* 1 earlier, foregoing, former, preceding, pre-existent, pre-existing, previous 2 prior to before, earlier than, preceding, previous to

priority *noun* precedence, pre-eminence, preference, rank, right of way, seniority

priory *noun* monastery, abbey, convent, nunnery, religious house

prison *noun* jail, clink (*slang*), confinement, cooler (*slang*), dungeon, jug (*slang*), lockup, nick (*Brit. slang*), penitentiary (*U.S.*), slammer (*slang*)

prisoner *noun* 1 convict, con (*slang*), jailbird, lag (*slang*) 2 captive, detainee, hostage, internee

prissy *adjective* prim, old-maidish (*informal*), prim and proper, prudish, strait-laced

pristine *adjective* new, immaculate, pure, uncorrupted, undefiled, unspoiled, unsullied, untouched, virginal

privacy *noun* seclusion, isolation, retirement, retreat, solitude

private *adjective* 1 exclusive, individual, intimate, own, personal, reserved, special 2 secret, clandestine, confidential, covert, hush-hush (*informal*), off the record, unofficial 3 secluded, isolated, secret, separate, sequestered, solitary

privilege *noun* right, advantage, claim, concession, due, entitlement, freedom, liberty, prerogative

privileged *adjective* special, advantaged, elite, entitled, favoured, honoured

privy *adjective* 1 privy to informed of, apprised of, aware of, cognizant of, in on, in the know about (*informal*), wise to (*slang*) ♦ *noun* 2 lavatory, latrine, outside toilet

prize¹ *noun* 1 reward, accolade, award, honour, trophy 2 winnings, haul, jackpot, purse, stakes ♦ *adjective* 3 champion, award-winning, best, first-rate, outstanding, top, winning

prize² *verb* value, cherish, esteem,

hold dear, treasure

probability noun <u>likelihood</u>, chance(s), expectation, liability, likeliness, odds, prospect

probable adjective <u>likely</u>, apparent, credible, feasible, plausible, possible, presumable, reasonable

probably adverb <u>likely</u>, doubtless, maybe, most likely, perchance (*archaic*), perhaps, possibly, presumably

probation noun <u>trial period</u>, apprenticeship, trial

probe verb 1 <u>examine</u>, explore, go into, investigate, look into, scrutinize, search 2 <u>explore</u>, feel around, poke, prod ♦ *noun* 3 <u>examination</u>, detection, exploration, inquiry, investigation, scrutiny, study

problem noun 1 <u>difficulty</u>, complication, dilemma, dispute, predicament, quandary, trouble 2 <u>puzzle</u>, conundrum, enigma, poser, question, riddle

problematic adjective <u>tricky</u>, debatable, doubtful, dubious, problematical, puzzling

procedure noun <u>method</u>, action, conduct, course, custom, modus operandi, policy, practice, process, routine, strategy, system

proceed verb 1 <u>go on</u>, carry on, continue, go ahead, move on, press on, progress 2 <u>arise</u>, come, derive, emanate, flow, issue, originate, result, spring, stem

proceeding noun 1 <u>action</u>, act, deed, measure, move, procedure, process, step 2 **proceedings** <u>business</u>, account, affairs, archives, doings, minutes, records, report, transactions

proceeds plural noun <u>income</u>, earnings, gain, products, profit, returns, revenue, takings, yield

process noun 1 <u>procedure</u>, action, course, manner, means, measure, method, operation, performance, practice, system 2 <u>development</u>, advance, evolution, growth, movement, progress, progression ♦ *verb* 3 <u>handle</u>, deal with, fulfil

procession noun <u>parade</u>, cavalcade, cortege, file, march, train

proclaim verb <u>declare</u>, advertise, announce, circulate, herald, indicate, make known, profess, publish

proclamation noun <u>declaration</u>, announcement, decree, edict, notice, notification, pronouncement, publication

procrastinate verb <u>delay</u>, dally, drag one's feet (*informal*), gain time, play for time, postpone, put off, stall, temporize

procure verb <u>obtain</u>, acquire, buy, come by, find, gain, get, pick up, purchase, score (*slang*), secure, win

prod verb 1 <u>poke</u>, dig, drive, jab, nudge, push, shove 2 <u>prompt</u>, egg on, goad, impel, incite, motivate, move, rouse, spur, stimulate, urge ♦ *noun* 3 <u>poke</u>, dig, jab, nudge, push, shove 4 <u>prompt</u>, cue, reminder, signal, stimulus

prodigal adjective <u>extravagant</u>, excessive, immoderate, improvident, profligate, reckless, spendthrift, wasteful

prodigious *adjective* **1** huge, colossal, enormous, giant, gigantic, immense, massive, monstrous, vast **2** wonderful, amazing, exceptional, extraordinary, fabulous, fantastic (*informal*), marvellous, phenomenal, remarkable, staggering

prodigy *noun* **1** genius, mastermind, talent, whizz (*informal*), wizard **2** wonder, marvel, miracle, phenomenon, sensation

produce *verb* **1** cause, bring about, effect, generate, give rise to **2** bring forth, bear, beget, breed, deliver **3** show, advance, demonstrate, exhibit, offer, present **4** make, compose, construct, create, develop, fabricate, invent, manufacture **5** present, direct, do, exhibit, mount, put on, show, stage ◆ *noun* **6** fruit and vegetables, crop, greengrocery, harvest, product, yield

producer *noun* **1** director, impresario **2** maker, farmer, grower, manufacturer

product *noun* **1** goods, artefact, commodity, creation, invention, merchandise, produce, work **2** result, consequence, effect, outcome, upshot

production *noun* **1** producing, construction, creation, fabrication, formation, making, manufacture, manufacturing **2** presentation, direction, management, staging

productive *adjective* **1** fertile, creative, fecund, fruitful, inventive, plentiful, prolific, rich **2** useful, advantageous, beneficial, constructive, effective, profitable, rewarding, valuable, worthwhile

productivity *noun* output, production, work rate, yield

profane *adjective* **1** sacrilegious, disrespectful, godless, impious, impure, irreligious, irreverent, sinful, ungodly, wicked **2** crude, blasphemous, coarse, filthy, foul, obscene, vulgar ◆ *verb* **3** desecrate, commit sacrilege, debase, defile, violate

profanity *noun* **1** sacrilege, blasphemy, impiety, profaneness **2** swearing, curse, cursing, irreverence, obscenity

profess *verb* **1** claim, allege, fake, feign, make out, pretend, purport **2** state, admit, affirm, announce, assert, avow, confess, declare, proclaim, vouch

professed *adjective* **1** supposed, alleged, ostensible, pretended, purported, self-styled, so-called, would-be **2** declared, avowed, confessed, confirmed, proclaimed, self-acknowledged, self-confessed

profession *noun* **1** occupation, business, calling, career, employment, office, position, sphere, vocation **2** declaration, affirmation, assertion, avowal, claim, confession, statement

professional *adjective* **1** expert, adept, competent, efficient, experienced, masterly, proficient, qualified, skilled ◆ *noun* **2** expert, adept, maestro, master, past master, pro (*informal*), specialist, virtuoso

professor *noun* don (*Brit.*), fellow

(*Brit.*), prof (*informal*)

proficiency noun <u>skill</u>, ability, aptitude, competence, dexterity, expertise, knack, know-how (*informal*), mastery

proficient adjective <u>skilled</u>, able, accomplished, adept, capable, competent, efficient, expert, gifted, masterly, skilful

profile noun 1 <u>outline</u>, contour, drawing, figure, form, side view, silhouette, sketch 2 <u>biography</u>, characterization, sketch, thumbnail sketch, vignette

profit noun 1 *often plural* <u>earnings</u>, gain, proceeds, receipts, return, revenue, takings, yield 2 <u>benefit</u>, advancement, advantage, gain, good, use, value ♦ *verb* 3 <u>benefit</u>, be of advantage to, gain, help, improve, promote, serve 4 <u>make money</u>, earn, gain

profitable adjective 1 <u>money-making</u>, commercial, cost-effective, fruitful, lucrative, paying, remunerative, worthwhile 2 <u>beneficial</u>, advantageous, fruitful, productive, rewarding, useful, valuable, worthwhile

profiteer noun 1 <u>racketeer</u>, exploiter ♦ *verb* 2 <u>racketeer</u>, exploit, make a quick buck (*slang*)

profligate adjective 1 <u>extravagant</u>, immoderate, improvident, prodigal, reckless, spendthrift, wasteful 2 <u>depraved</u>, debauched, degenerate, dissolute, immoral, licentious, shameless, wanton, wicked, wild ♦ *noun* 3 <u>spendthrift</u>, squanderer, waster, wastrel 4 <u>degenerate</u>, debauchee, libertine, rake,

reprobate, roué

profound adjective 1 <u>wise</u>, abstruse, deep, learned, penetrating, philosophical, sagacious, sage 2 <u>intense</u>, acute, deeply felt, extreme, great, heartfelt, keen

profuse adjective <u>plentiful</u>, abundant, ample, bountiful, copious, luxuriant, overflowing, prolific

profusion noun <u>abundance</u>, bounty, excess, extravagance, glut, plethora, quantity, surplus, wealth

progeny noun <u>children</u>, descendants, family, issue, lineage, offspring, race, stock, young

prognosis noun <u>forecast</u>, diagnosis, prediction, prognostication, projection

programme noun 1 <u>schedule</u>, agenda, curriculum, line-up, list, listing, order of events, plan, syllabus, timetable 2 <u>show</u>, broadcast, performance, presentation, production

progress noun 1 <u>development</u>, advance, breakthrough, gain, growth, headway, improvement 2 <u>movement</u>, advance, course, passage, way 3 **in progress** <u>going on</u>, being done, happening, occurring, proceeding, taking place, under way ♦ *verb* 4 <u>develop</u>, advance, gain, grow, improve 5 <u>move on</u>, advance, continue, go forward, make headway, proceed, travel

progression noun 1 <u>progress</u>, advance, advancement, furtherance, gain, headway, movement forward 2 <u>sequence</u>, chain, course, cycle, series, string, succession

progressive *adjective*
1 <u>enlightened</u>, advanced, avant-garde, forward-looking, liberal, modern, radical, reformist, revolutionary
2 <u>growing</u>, advancing, continuing, developing, increasing, ongoing

prohibit *verb* 1 <u>forbid</u>, ban, debar, disallow, outlaw, proscribe, veto 2 <u>prevent</u>, hamper, hinder, impede, restrict, stop

prohibition *noun* 1 <u>prevention</u>, constraint, exclusion, obstruction, restriction 2 <u>ban</u>, bar, boycott, embargo, injunction, interdict, proscription, veto

prohibitive *adjective* <u>exorbitant</u>, excessive, extortionate, steep (*informal*)

project *noun* 1 <u>scheme</u>, activity, assignment, enterprise, job, occupation, plan, task, undertaking, venture, work ♦ *verb* 2 <u>forecast</u>, calculate, estimate, extrapolate, gauge, predict, reckon 3 <u>stick out</u>, bulge, extend, jut, overhang, protrude, stand out

projectile *noun* <u>missile</u>, bullet, rocket, shell

projection *noun* 1 <u>protrusion</u>, bulge, ledge, overhang, protuberance, ridge, shelf 2 <u>forecast</u>, calculation, computation, estimate, estimation, extrapolation, reckoning

proletarian *adjective*
1 <u>working-class</u>, common,

plebeian ♦ *noun* 2 <u>worker</u>, commoner, man of the people, pleb, plebeian, prole (*derogatory slang, chiefly Brit.*)

proletariat *noun* <u>working class</u>, commoners, hoi polloi, labouring classes, lower classes, plebs, proles (*derogatory slang, chiefly Brit.*), the common people, the masses

proliferate *verb* <u>increase</u>, breed, expand, grow rapidly, multiply

proliferation *noun* <u>multiplication</u>, expansion, increase, spread

prolific *adjective* <u>productive</u>, abundant, copious, fecund, fertile, fruitful, luxuriant, profuse

prologue *noun* <u>introduction</u>, foreword, preamble, preface, prelude

prolong *verb* <u>lengthen</u>, continue, delay, drag out, draw out, extend, perpetuate, protract, spin out, stretch

promenade *noun* 1 <u>walkway</u>, esplanade, parade, prom 2 <u>stroll</u>, constitutional, saunter, turn, walk ♦ *verb* 3 <u>stroll</u>, perambulate, saunter, take a walk, walk

prominence *noun*
1 <u>conspicuousness</u>, markedness
2 <u>fame</u>, celebrity, distinction, eminence, importance, name, prestige, reputation

prominent *adjective* 1 <u>noticeable</u>, conspicuous, eye-catching, obtrusive, obvious, outstanding, pronounced 2 <u>famous</u>, distinguished, eminent, foremost, important, leading, main, notable, renowned, top, well-known

promiscuity noun licentiousness, debauchery, immorality, looseness, permissiveness, promiscuousness, wantonness

promiscuous adjective licentious, abandoned, debauched, fast, immoral, libertine, loose, wanton, wild

promise verb 1 guarantee, assure, contract, give an undertaking, give one's word, pledge, swear, take an oath, undertake, vow, warrant 2 seem likely, augur, betoken, indicate, look like, show signs of, suggest ♦ noun 3 guarantee, assurance, bond, commitment, oath, pledge, undertaking, vow, word 4 potential, ability, aptitude, capability, capacity, talent

promising adjective 1 encouraging, auspicious, bright, favourable, hopeful, likely, propitious, reassuring, rosy 2 talented, able, gifted, rising

promontory noun point, cape, foreland, head, headland

promote verb 1 help, advance, aid, assist, back, boost, encourage, forward, foster, support 2 raise, elevate, exalt, upgrade 3 advertise, hype, plug (informal), publicize, push, sell

promotion noun 1 rise, advancement, elevation, exaltation, honour, move up, preferment, upgrading 2 publicity, advertising, plugging (informal) 3 encouragement, advancement, boosting, furtherance, support

prompt verb 1 cause, elicit, give rise to, occasion, provoke 2 remind, assist, cue, help out

♦ adjective 3 immediate, early, instant, quick, rapid, speedy, swift, timely ♦ adverb 4 Informal exactly, on the dot, promptly, punctually, sharp

promptly adverb immediately, at once, directly, on the dot, on time, punctually, quickly, speedily, swiftly

promptness noun swiftness, briskness, eagerness, haste, punctuality, quickness, speed, willingness

promulgate verb make known, broadcast, circulate, communicate, disseminate, make public, proclaim, promote, publish, spread

prone adjective 1 liable, apt, bent, disposed, given, inclined, likely, predisposed, subject, susceptible, tending 2 face down, flat, horizontal, prostrate, recumbent

prong noun point, spike, tine

pronounce verb 1 say, accent, articulate, enunciate, sound, speak 2 declare, affirm, announce, decree, deliver, proclaim

pronounced adjective noticeable, conspicuous, decided, definite, distinct, evident, marked, obvious, striking

pronouncement noun announcement, declaration, decree, dictum, edict, judgment, proclamation, statement

pronunciation noun intonation, accent, articulation, diction, enunciation, inflection, speech, stress

proof noun 1 evidence,

authentication, confirmation, corroboration, demonstration, substantiation, testimony, verification ♦ *adjective*
2 impervious, impenetrable, repellent, resistant, strong

prop *verb* **1** support, bolster, brace, buttress, hold up, stay, sustain, uphold ♦ *noun*
2 support, brace, buttress, mainstay, stanchion, stay

propaganda *noun* information, advertising, disinformation, hype, promotion, publicity

propagate *verb* **1** spread, broadcast, circulate, disseminate, promote, promulgate, publish, transmit **2** reproduce, beget, breed, engender, generate, increase, multiply, procreate, produce

propel *verb* drive, force, impel, launch, push, send, shoot, shove, thrust

propensity *noun* tendency, bent, disposition, inclination, liability, penchant, predisposition, proclivity

proper *adjective* **1** suitable, appropriate, apt, becoming, befitting, fit, fitting, right **2** correct, accepted, conventional, established, formal, orthodox, precise, right **3** polite, decent, decorous, genteel, gentlemanly, ladylike, mannerly, respectable, seemly

properly *adverb* **1** suitably, appropriately, aptly, fittingly, rightly **2** correctly, accurately **3** politely, decently, respectably

property *noun* **1** possessions, assets, belongings, capital, effects, estate, goods, holdings,

riches, wealth **2** land, estate, freehold, holding, real estate **3** quality, attribute, characteristic, feature, hallmark, trait

prophecy *noun* prediction, augury, divination, forecast, prognostication, second sight, soothsaying

prophesy *verb* predict, augur, divine, forecast, foresee, foretell, prognosticate

prophet *noun* soothsayer, diviner, forecaster, oracle, prophesier, seer, sibyl

prophetic *adjective* predictive, oracular, prescient, prognostic, sibylline

propitious *adjective* favourable, auspicious, bright, encouraging, fortunate, happy, lucky, promising

proportion *noun* **1** relative amount, ratio, relationship **2** balance, congruity, correspondence, harmony, symmetry **3** part, amount, division, fraction, percentage, quota, segment, share **4** proportions dimensions, capacity, expanse, extent, size, volume

proportional, proportionate *adjective* balanced, commensurate, compatible, consistent, corresponding, equitable, even, in proportion

proposal *noun* suggestion, bid, offer, plan, presentation, programme, project, recommendation, scheme

propose *verb* **1** put forward, advance, present, submit, suggest **2** nominate, name, present, recommend **3** intend, aim, design, have in mind, mean, plan, scheme **4** offer marriage, ask for someone's hand (in marriage), pop the question (*informal*)

proposition *noun* **1** proposal, plan, recommendation, scheme, suggestion ◆ *verb* **2** make a pass at, accost, make an improper suggestion, solicit

propound *verb* put forward, advance, postulate, present, propose, submit, suggest

proprietor, proprietress *noun* owner, landlord *or* landlady, titleholder

propriety *noun* **1** correctness, aptness, fitness, rightness, seemliness **2** decorum, courtesy, decency, etiquette, manners, politeness, respectability, seemliness

propulsion *noun* drive, impetus, impulse, propelling force, push, thrust

prosaic *adjective* dull, boring, everyday, humdrum, matter-of-fact, mundane, ordinary, pedestrian, routine, trite, unimaginative

proscribe *verb* **1** prohibit, ban, embargo, forbid, interdict **2** outlaw, banish, deport, exclude, exile, expatriate, expel, ostracize

prosecute *verb Law* put on trial, arraign, bring to trial, indict, litigate, sue, take to court, try

prospect *noun* **1** expectation, anticipation, future, hope, odds, outlook, probability, promise **2** *sometimes plural* likelihood, chance, possibility **3** view,

landscape, outlook, scene, sight, spectacle, vista ◆ *verb* **4** look for, search for, seek

prospective *adjective* future, anticipated, coming, destined, expected, forthcoming, imminent, intended, likely, possible, potential

prospectus *noun* catalogue, list, outline, programme, syllabus, synopsis

prosper *verb* succeed, advance, do well, flourish, get on, progress, thrive

prosperity *noun* success, affluence, fortune, good fortune, luxury, plenty, prosperousness, riches, wealth

prosperous *adjective* **1** wealthy, affluent, moneyed, rich, well-heeled (*informal*), well-off, well-to-do **2** successful, booming, doing well, flourishing, fortunate, lucky, thriving

prostitute *noun* **1** whore, call girl, fallen woman, harlot, hooker (*U.S. slang*), loose woman, pro (*slang*), scrubber (*Brit. & Austral. slang*), streetwalker, strumpet, tart (*informal*), trollop ◆ *verb* **2** cheapen, debase, degrade, demean, devalue, misapply, pervert, profane

prostrate *adjective* **1** prone, flat, horizontal **2** exhausted, dejected, depressed, desolate, drained, inconsolable, overcome, spent, worn out ◆ *verb* **3** exhaust, drain, fatigue, sap, tire, wear out, weary **4** prostrate oneself bow down to, abase oneself, fall at (someone's) feet, grovel, kneel, kowtow

protagonist noun **1** supporter, advocate, champion, exponent **2** leading character, central character, hero or heroine, principal

protect verb keep safe, defend, guard, look after, preserve, safeguard, save, screen, shelter, shield, stick up for (*informal*), support, watch over

protection noun **1** safety, aegis, care, custody, defence, protecting, safeguard, safekeeping, security **2** safeguard, barrier, buffer, cover, guard, screen, shelter, shield

protective adjective protecting, defensive, fatherly, maternal, motherly, paternal, vigilant, watchful

protector noun defender, bodyguard, champion, guard, guardian, patron

protest noun **1** objection, complaint, dissent, outcry, protestation, remonstrance ♦ verb **2** object, complain, cry out, demonstrate, demur, disagree, disapprove, express disapproval, oppose, remonstrate **3** assert, affirm, attest, avow, declare, insist, maintain, profess

protestation noun declaration, affirmation, avowal, profession, vow

protester noun demonstrator, agitator, rebel

protocol noun code of behaviour, conventions, customs, decorum, etiquette, manners, propriety

prototype noun original, example, first, model, pattern, standard, type

protracted adjective extended, dragged out, drawn-out, long-drawn-out, prolonged, spun out

protrude verb stick out, bulge, come through, extend, jut, obtrude, project, stand out

protrusion noun projection, bulge, bump, lump, outgrowth, protuberance

protuberance noun bulge, bump, excrescence, hump, knob, lump, outgrowth, process, prominence, protrusion, swelling

proud adjective **1** satisfied, content, glad, gratified, pleased, well-pleased **2** conceited, arrogant, boastful, disdainful, haughty, imperious, lordly, overbearing, self-satisfied, snobbish, supercilious

prove verb **1** verify, authenticate, confirm, demonstrate, determine, establish, justify, show, substantiate **2** test, analyse, assay, check, examine, try **3** turn out, come out, end up, result

proven adjective established, attested, confirmed, definite, proved, reliable, tested, verified

proverb noun saying, adage, dictum, maxim, saw

proverbial adjective conventional, acknowledged, axiomatic, current, famed, famous, legendary, notorious, traditional, typical, well-known

provide verb **1** supply, cater, equip, furnish, outfit, purvey, stock up **2** <u>give</u>, add, afford, bring, impart, lend, present, produce, render, serve, yield **3 provide for** or **against** <u>take precautions</u>, anticipate, forearm, plan ahead, plan for, prepare for **4 provide for** <u>support</u>, care for, keep, maintain, sustain, take care of

providence noun <u>fate</u>, destiny, fortune

provident adjective **1** <u>thrifty</u>, economical, frugal, prudent **2** <u>foresighted</u>, careful, cautious, discreet, far-seeing, forearmed, shrewd, vigilant, well-prepared, wise

providential adjective <u>lucky</u>, fortuitous, fortunate, happy, heaven-sent, opportune, timely

provider noun **1** <u>supplier</u>, donor, giver, source **2** <u>breadwinner</u>, earner, supporter, wage earner

providing, provided conjunction <u>on condition that</u>, as long as, given

province noun **1** <u>region</u>, colony, department, district, division, domain, patch, section, zone **2** <u>area</u>, business, capacity, concern, duty, field, function, line, responsibility, role, sphere

provincial adjective **1** <u>rural</u>, country, hick (informal, chiefly U.S. & Canad.), homespun, local, rustic **2** <u>narrow-minded</u>, insular, inward-looking, limited, narrow, parochial, small-minded, small-town (chiefly U.S.), unsophisticated ♦ noun **3** <u>yokel</u>, country cousin, hayseed (U.S. & Canad. informal), hick (informal, chiefly U.S. & Canad.), rustic

provision noun **1** <u>supplying</u>, catering, equipping, furnishing, providing **2** <u>condition</u>, clause, demand, proviso, requirement, rider, stipulation, term

provisional adjective **1** <u>temporary</u>, interim **2** <u>conditional</u>, contingent, limited, qualified, tentative

provisions plural noun <u>food</u>, comestibles, eatables, edibles, fare, foodstuff, rations, stores, supplies, victuals

proviso noun <u>condition</u>, clause, qualification, requirement, rider, stipulation

provocation noun **1** <u>cause</u>, grounds, incitement, motivation, reason, stimulus **2** <u>offence</u>, affront, annoyance, challenge, dare, grievance, indignity, injury, insult, taunt

provocative adjective <u>offensive</u>, annoying, galling, goading, insulting, provoking, stimulating

provoke verb **1** <u>anger</u>, aggravate (informal), annoy, enrage, hassle (informal), incense, infuriate, irk, irritate, madden, rile **2** <u>cause</u>, bring about, elicit, evoke, incite, induce, occasion, produce, promote, prompt, rouse, stir

prowess noun **1** <u>skill</u>, accomplishment, adeptness, aptitude, excellence, expertise, genius, mastery, talent **2** <u>bravery</u>, courage, daring, fearlessness, heroism, mettle, valiance, valour

prowl verb <u>move stealthily</u>, skulk, slink, sneak, stalk, steal

proximity noun <u>nearness</u>, closeness

proxy noun <u>representative</u>, agent,

delegate, deputy, factor, substitute

prudence noun <u>common sense</u>, care, caution, discretion, good sense, judgment, vigilance, wariness, wisdom

prudent adjective 1 <u>sensible</u>, careful, cautious, discerning, discreet, judicious, politic, shrewd, vigilant, wary, wise 2 <u>thrifty</u>, canny, careful, economical, far-sighted, frugal, provident, sparing

prudish adjective <u>prim</u>, old-maidish (informal), overmodest, priggish, prissy (informal), proper, puritanical, starchy (informal), strait-laced, stuffy, Victorian

prune verb <u>cut</u>, clip, dock, reduce, shape, shorten, snip, trim

pry verb <u>be inquisitive</u>, be nosy (informal), interfere, intrude, meddle, poke, snoop (informal)

prying adjective <u>inquisitive</u>, curious, interfering, meddlesome, meddling, nosy (informal), snooping (informal), spying

psalm noun <u>hymn</u>, chant

pseudo- adjective <u>false</u>, artificial, fake, imitation, mock, phoney or phony (informal), pretended, sham, spurious

pseudonym noun <u>false name</u>, alias, assumed name, incognito, nom de plume, pen name

psyche noun <u>soul</u>, anima, individuality, mind, personality, self, spirit

psychiatrist noun <u>psychotherapist</u>, analyst, headshrinker (slang),

psychoanalyst, psychologist, shrink (slang), therapist

psychic adjective 1 <u>supernatural</u>, mystic, occult 2 <u>mental</u>, psychological, spiritual

psychological adjective 1 <u>mental</u>, cerebral, intellectual 2 <u>imaginary</u>, all in the mind, irrational, psychosomatic, unreal

psychology noun 1 <u>behaviourism</u>, science of mind, study of personality 2 Informal <u>way of thinking</u>, attitude, mental make-up, mental processes, thought processes, what makes one tick

psychopath noun <u>madman</u>, headbanger (informal), headcase (informal), lunatic, maniac, nutcase (slang), nutter (Brit. slang), psychotic, sociopath

psychotic adjective <u>mad</u>, certifiable, demented, deranged, insane, lunatic, mental (slang), non compos mentis, unbalanced

pub or **public house** noun <u>tavern</u>, bar, inn

puberty noun <u>adolescence</u>, pubescence, teens

public adjective 1 <u>general</u>, civic, common, national, popular, social, state, universal, widespread 2 <u>communal</u>, accessible, open, unrestricted 3 <u>well-known</u>, important, prominent, respected 4 <u>plain</u>, acknowledged, known, obvious, open, overt, patent ♦ noun 5 <u>people</u>, citizens, community, electorate, everyone, nation, populace, society

publication noun 1 <u>pamphlet</u>, brochure, issue, leaflet, magazine, newspaper, periodical, title **2** <u>announcement</u>, broadcasting, declaration, disclosure, notification, proclamation, publishing, reporting

publicity noun <u>advertising</u>, attention, boost, hype, plug (*informal*), press, promotion

publicize verb <u>advertise</u>, hype, make known, play up, plug (*informal*), promote, push

public-spirited adjective <u>altruistic</u>, charitable, humanitarian, philanthropic, unselfish

publish verb **1** <u>put out</u>, issue, print, produce **2** <u>announce</u>, advertise, broadcast, circulate, disclose, divulge, proclaim, publicize, reveal, spread

pucker verb **1** <u>wrinkle</u>, contract, crease, draw together, gather, knit, purse, screw up, tighten ♦ noun **2** <u>wrinkle</u>, crease, fold

pudding noun <u>dessert</u>, afters (*Brit. informal*), pud (*informal*), sweet

puerile adjective <u>childish</u>, babyish, foolish, immature, juvenile, silly, trivial

puff noun **1** <u>blast</u>, breath, draught, gust, whiff **2** <u>smoke</u>, drag (*slang*), pull ♦ verb **3** <u>blow</u>, breathe, exhale, gasp, gulp, pant, wheeze **4** <u>smoke</u>, drag (*slang*), draw, inhale, pull at *or* on, suck **5** *usually with* **up** <u>swell</u>, bloat, dilate, distend, expand, inflate

puffy adjective <u>swollen</u>, bloated, distended, enlarged, puffed up

pugilist noun <u>boxer</u>, fighter, prizefighter

pugnacious adjective <u>aggressive</u>, belligerent, combative, hot-tempered, quarrelsome

pull verb **1** <u>draw</u>, drag, haul, jerk, tow, trail, tug, yank **2** <u>strain</u>, dislocate, rip, sprain, stretch, tear, wrench **3** <u>extract</u>, draw out, gather, pick, pluck, remove, take out, uproot **4** *Informal* <u>attract</u>, draw, entice, lure, magnetize ♦ noun **5** <u>tug</u>, jerk, twitch, yank **6** <u>puff</u>, drag (*slang*), inhalation **7** *Informal* <u>influence</u>, clout (*informal*), muscle, power, weight

pull down verb <u>demolish</u>, bulldoze, destroy, raze, remove

pull off verb <u>succeed</u>, accomplish, carry out, do the trick, manage

pull out verb <u>withdraw</u>, depart, evacuate, leave, quit, retreat

pull through verb <u>survive</u>, get better, rally, recover

pull up verb **1** <u>stop</u>, brake, halt **2** <u>reprimand</u>, admonish, bawl out (*informal*), rap over the knuckles, read the riot act, rebuke, reprove, slap on the wrist, tear (someone) off a strip (*Brit. informal*), tell off (*informal*)

pulp noun **1** <u>paste</u>, mash, mush **2** <u>flesh</u>, soft part ♦ verb **3** <u>crush</u>, mash, pulverize, squash ♦ adjective **4** <u>cheap</u>, lurid, rubbishy, trashy

pulsate verb <u>throb</u>, beat, palpitate, pound, pulse, quiver, thump

pulse noun **1** <u>beat</u>, beating, pulsation, rhythm, throb, throbbing, vibration ♦ verb **2** <u>beat</u>, pulsate, throb, vibrate

pulverize verb **1** <u>crush</u>,

granulate, grind, mill, pound **2** <u>defeat</u>, annihilate, crush, demolish, destroy, flatten, smash, wreck

pummel *verb* <u>beat</u>, batter, hammer, pound, punch, strike, thump

pump *verb* **1** *often with* **into** <u>drive</u>, force, inject, pour, push, send, supply **2** <u>interrogate</u>, cross-examine, probe, quiz

pun *noun* <u>play on words</u>, double entendre, quip, witticism

punch¹ *verb* **1** <u>hit</u>, belt (*informal*), bop (*informal*), box, pummel, smash, sock (*slang*), strike ♦ *noun* **2** <u>blow</u>, bop (*informal*), hit, jab, sock (*slang*), wallop (*informal*) **3** *Informal* <u>effectiveness</u>, bite, drive, forcefulness, impact, verve, vigour

punch² *verb* <u>pierce</u>, bore, cut, drill, perforate, prick, puncture, stamp

punctilious *adjective* <u>particular</u>, exact, finicky, formal, fussy, meticulous, nice, precise, proper, strict

punctual *adjective* <u>on time</u>, exact, on the dot, precise, prompt, timely

punctuality *noun* <u>promptness</u>, promptitude, readiness

punctuate *verb* **1** <u>interrupt</u>, break, intersperse, pepper, sprinkle **2** <u>emphasize</u>, accentuate, stress, underline

puncture *noun* **1** <u>hole</u>, break, cut, damage, leak, nick, opening, slit **2** <u>flat tyre</u>, flat ♦ *verb* **3** <u>pierce</u>, bore, cut, nick, penetrate, perforate, prick, rupture

pungent *adjective* <u>strong</u>, acrid, bitter, hot, peppery, piquant, sharp, sour, spicy, tart

punish *verb* <u>discipline</u>, castigate, chasten, chastise, correct, penalize, sentence

punishable *adjective* <u>culpable</u>, blameworthy, criminal, indictable

punishing *adjective* <u>hard</u>, arduous, backbreaking, exhausting, gruelling, strenuous, taxing, tiring, wearing

punishment *noun* <u>penalty</u>, chastening, chastisement, correction, discipline, penance, retribution

punitive *adjective* <u>retaliatory</u>, in reprisal, retaliative

punt *verb* **1** <u>bet</u>, back, gamble, lay, stake, wager ♦ *noun* **2** <u>bet</u>, gamble, stake, wager

punter *noun* **1** <u>gambler</u>, backer, better **2** *Informal* <u>person</u>, man in the street

puny *adjective* <u>feeble</u>, frail, little, sickly, stunted, tiny, weak

pupil *noun* <u>learner</u>, beginner, disciple, novice, schoolboy *or* schoolgirl, student

puppet *noun* **1** <u>marionette</u>, doll **2** <u>pawn</u>, cat's-paw, instrument, mouthpiece, stooge, tool

purchase *verb* **1** <u>buy</u>, acquire, come by, gain, get, obtain, pay for, pick up, score (*slang*) ♦ *noun* **2** <u>buy</u>, acquisition, asset, gain, investment, possession, property **3** <u>grip</u>, foothold, hold, leverage, support

pure *adjective* **1** <u>unmixed</u>, authentic, flawless, genuine, natural, neat, real, simple, straight, unalloyed **2** <u>clean</u>, germ-free, sanitary, spotless, squeaky-clean, sterilized, uncontaminated, unpolluted, untainted, wholesome 3 <u>innocent</u>, blameless, chaste, impeccable, modest, uncorrupted, unsullied, virginal, virtuous 4 <u>complete</u>, absolute, outright, sheer, thorough, unmitigated, unqualified, utter

purely adverb <u>absolutely</u>, completely, entirely, exclusively, just, merely, only, simply, solely, wholly

purge verb 1 <u>get rid of</u>, do away with, eradicate, expel, exterminate, remove, wipe out ♦ noun 2 <u>removal</u>, ejection, elimination, eradication, expulsion

purify verb 1 <u>clean</u>, clarify, cleanse, decontaminate, disinfect, refine, sanitize, wash 2 <u>absolve</u>, cleanse, redeem, sanctify

purist noun <u>stickler</u>, formalist, pedant

puritan noun 1 <u>moralist</u>, fanatic, prude, rigorist, zealot ♦ adjective 2 <u>strict</u>, ascetic, austere, moralistic, narrow-minded, prudish, severe, strait-laced

puritanical adjective <u>strict</u>, ascetic, austere, narrow-minded, proper, prudish, puritan, severe, strait-laced

purity noun 1 <u>cleanness</u>, cleanliness, faultlessness, immaculateness, pureness, wholesomeness 2 <u>innocence</u>, chasteness, chastity, decency, honesty, integrity, virginity, virtue

purloin verb <u>steal</u>, appropriate, filch, nick (slang, chiefly Brit.),

pilfer, pinch (informal), swipe (slang), thieve

purport verb 1 <u>claim</u>, allege, assert, profess ♦ noun 2 <u>significance</u>, drift, gist, idea, implication, import, meaning

purpose noun 1 <u>reason</u>, aim, idea, intention, object, point 2 <u>aim</u>, ambition, desire, end, goal, hope, intention, object, plan, wish 3 <u>determination</u>, firmness, persistence, resolution, resolve, single-mindedness, tenacity, will 4 <u>on purpose</u> <u>deliberately</u>, designedly, intentionally, knowingly, purposely

purposeless adjective <u>pointless</u>, aimless, empty, motiveless, needless, senseless, uncalled-for, unnecessary

purposely adverb <u>deliberately</u>, consciously, expressly, intentionally, knowingly, on purpose, with intent

purse noun 1 <u>pouch</u>, money-bag, wallet 2 <u>money</u>, exchequer, funds, means, resources, treasury, wealth ♦ verb 3 <u>pucker</u>, contract, pout, press together, tighten

pursue verb 1 <u>follow</u>, chase, dog, hound, hunt, hunt down, run after, shadow, stalk, tail (informal), track 2 <u>try for</u>, aim for, desire, seek, strive for, work towards 3 <u>engage in</u>, carry on, conduct, perform, practise 4 <u>continue</u>, carry on, keep on, maintain, persevere in, persist in, proceed

pursuit noun 1 <u>pursuing</u>, chase, hunt, quest, search, seeking, trailing 2 <u>occupation</u>, activity, hobby, interest, line, pastime, pleasure

purvey verb supply, cater, deal in, furnish, provide, sell, trade in

push verb 1 shove, depress, drive, press, propel, ram, thrust 2 make or force one's way, elbow, jostle, move, shoulder, shove, squeeze, thrust 3 urge, encourage, hurry, impel, incite, persuade, press, spur ♦ noun 4 shove, butt, nudge, thrust 5 Informal drive, ambition, dynamism, energy, enterprise, go (informal), initiative, vigour, vitality 6 the push Informal, chiefly Brit. dismissal, discharge, one's cards (informal), the boot (slang), the sack (informal)

pushed adjective, often with for short of, hurried, pressed, rushed, under pressure

pushover noun 1 piece of cake (Brit. informal), breeze (U.S. & Canad. informal), child's play (informal), cinch (slang), doddle (Brit. slang), picnic (informal), plain sailing, walkover (informal) 2 sucker (slang), easy game (informal), easy or soft mark (informal), mug (Brit. slang), soft touch (slang), walkover (informal)

pushy adjective forceful, ambitious, assertive, bold, brash, bumptious, obtrusive, presumptuous, self-assertive

pussyfoot verb hedge, beat about the bush, be noncommittal, equivocate, flannel (Brit. informal), hum and haw, prevaricate, sit on the fence

put verb 1 place, deposit, lay, position, rest, set, settle, situate 2 express, phrase, state, utter,

word 3 throw, cast, fling, heave, hurl, lob, pitch, toss

put across or **over** verb communicate, convey, explain, get across, make clear, make oneself understood

put aside or **by** verb save, deposit, lay by, stockpile, store

put away verb 1 save, deposit, keep, put by 2 commit, certify, institutionalize, lock up 3 consume, devour, eat up, gobble, wolf down 4 put back, replace, tidy away

put down verb 1 record, enter, set down, take down, write down 2 stamp out, crush, quash, quell, repress, suppress 3 usually with to attribute, ascribe, impute, set down 4 put to sleep, destroy, do away with, put out of its misery 5 Slang humiliate, disparage, mortify, shame, slight, snub

put forward verb recommend, advance, nominate, propose, submit, suggest, tender

put off verb 1 postpone, defer, delay, hold over, put on the back burner (informal), take a rain check on (U.S. & Canad. informal) 2 disconcert, confuse, discomfit, dismay, faze, nonplus, perturb, throw (informal), unsettle 3 discourage, dishearten, dissuade

put on verb 1 don, change into, dress, get dressed in, slip into 2 fake, affect, assume, feign, pretend, sham, simulate 3 present, do, mount, produce, show, stage 4 add, gain, increase by

put out verb 1 annoy, anger,

exasperate, irk, irritate, nettle, vex **2** extinguish, blow out, douse, quench **3** inconvenience, bother, discomfit, discommode, impose upon, incommode, trouble

putrid adjective rotten, bad, decayed, decomposed, off, putrefied, rancid, rotting, spoiled

put up verb **1** erect, build, construct, fabricate, raise **2** accommodate, board, house, lodge, take in **3** recommend, nominate, offer, present, propose, put forward, submit **4** put up with Informal stand, abide, bear, endure, stand for, swallow, take, tolerate

puzzle verb **1** perplex, baffle, bewilder, confound, confuse, mystify, stump ♦ noun **2** problem, conundrum, enigma, mystery, paradox, poser, question, riddle

puzzled adjective perplexed, at a loss, at sea, baffled, bewildered, confused, lost, mystified

puzzlement noun perplexity, bafflement, bewilderment, confusion, doubt, mystification

puzzling adjective perplexing, abstruse, baffling, bewildering, enigmatic, incomprehensible, involved, mystifying

Q q

quack noun charlatan, fake, fraud, humbug, impostor, mountebank, phoney or phony (informal)

quaff verb drink, down, gulp,

imbibe, swallow, swig (informal)

quagmire noun bog, fen, marsh, mire, morass, quicksand, slough, swamp

quail verb shrink, blanch, blench, cower, cringe, falter, flinch, have cold feet (informal), recoil, shudder

quaint adjective **1** unusual, bizarre, curious, droll, eccentric, fanciful, odd, old-fashioned, peculiar, queer, rum (Brit. slang), singular, strange **2** old-fashioned, antiquated, old-world, picturesque

quake verb shake, move, quiver, rock, shiver, shudder, tremble, vibrate

qualification noun **1** attribute, ability, aptitude, capability, eligibility, fitness, quality, skill, suitability **2** condition, caveat, limitation, modification, proviso, requirement, reservation, rider, stipulation

qualified adjective **1** capable, able, adept, competent, efficient, experienced, expert, fit, practised, proficient, skilful, trained **2** restricted, bounded, conditional, confined, contingent, limited, modified, provisional, reserved

qualify verb **1** certify, empower, equip, fit, permit, prepare, ready, train **2** moderate, diminish, ease, lessen, limit, reduce, regulate, restrain, restrict, soften, temper

quality noun **1** excellence, calibre, distinction, grade, merit, position, rank, standing, status **2** characteristic, aspect, attribute, condition, feature, mark, property, trait **3** <u>nature</u>, character, kind, make, sort

qualm *noun* <u>misgiving</u>, anxiety, apprehension, compunction, disquiet, doubt, hesitation, scruple, twinge *or* pang of conscience, uneasiness

quandary *noun* <u>difficulty</u>, cleft stick, dilemma, impasse, plight, predicament, puzzle, strait

quantity *noun* **1** <u>amount</u>, lot, number, part, sum, total **2** <u>size</u>, bulk, capacity, extent, length, magnitude, mass, measure, volume

quarrel *noun* **1** <u>disagreement</u>, argument, brawl, breach, contention, controversy, dispute, dissension, feud, fight, row, squabble, tiff ♦ *verb* **2** <u>disagree</u>, argue, bicker, brawl, clash, differ, dispute, fall out (*informal*), fight, row, squabble

quarrelsome *adjective* <u>argumentative</u>, belligerent, combative, contentious, disputatious, pugnacious

quarry *noun* <u>prey</u>, aim, game, goal, objective, prize, victim

quarter *noun* **1** <u>district</u>, area, locality, neighbourhood, part, place, province, region, side, zone **2** <u>mercy</u>, clemency, compassion, forgiveness, leniency, pity ♦ *verb* **3** <u>accommodate</u>, billet, board, house, lodge, place, post, station

quarters *plural noun* <u>lodgings</u>, abode, barracks, billet, chambers, dwelling, habitation, residence, rooms

quash *verb* **1** <u>annul</u>, cancel, invalidate, overrule, overthrow, rescind, reverse, revoke

2 <u>suppress</u>, beat, crush, overthrow, put down, quell, repress, squash, subdue

quasi- *adjective* <u>pseudo-</u>, apparent, seeming, semi-, so-called, would-be

quaver *verb* **1** <u>tremble</u>, flicker, flutter, quake, quiver, shake, vibrate, waver ♦ *noun* **2** <u>trembling</u>, quiver, shake, tremble, tremor, vibration

queasy *adjective* **1** <u>sick</u>, bilious, green around the gills (*informal*), ill, nauseated, off colour, squeamish, upset **2** <u>uneasy</u>, anxious, fidgety, ill at ease, restless, troubled, uncertain, worried

queen *noun* **1** <u>sovereign</u>, consort, monarch, ruler **2** <u>ideal</u>, mistress, model, star

queer *adjective* **1** <u>strange</u>, abnormal, curious, droll, extraordinary, funny, odd, peculiar, uncommon, unusual, weird **2** <u>faint</u>, dizzy, giddy, light-headed, queasy

quell *verb* **1** <u>suppress</u>, conquer, crush, defeat, overcome, overpower, put down, quash, subdue, vanquish **2** <u>assuage</u>, allay, appease, calm, mollify, pacify, quiet, soothe

quench *verb* **1** <u>satisfy</u>, allay, appease, sate, satiate, slake **2** <u>put out</u>, crush, douse, extinguish, smother, stifle, suppress

querulous *adjective* <u>complaining</u>, captious, carping, critical, discontented, dissatisfied, fault-finding, grumbling, peevish, whining

query *noun* **1** <u>question</u>, doubt,

inquiry, objection, problem, suspicion ♦ *verb* **2** doubt, challenge, disbelieve, dispute, distrust, mistrust, suspect **3** ask, inquire *or* enquire, question

quest *noun* search, adventure, crusade, enterprise, expedition, hunt, journey, mission

question *noun* **1** issue, motion, point, point at issue, proposal, proposition, subject, theme, topic **2** difficulty, argument, contention, controversy, dispute, doubt, problem, query **3 in question** under discussion, at issue, in doubt, open to debate **4 out of the question** impossible, inconceivable, unthinkable ♦ *verb* **5** ask, cross-examine, examine, inquire, interrogate, interview, probe, quiz **6** dispute, challenge, disbelieve, doubt, mistrust, oppose, query, suspect

questionable *adjective* dubious, controversial, debatable, dodgy (*Brit., Austral., & N.Z. informal*), doubtful, iffy (*informal*), moot, suspect, suspicious

queue *noun* line, chain, file, sequence, series, string, train

quibble *verb* **1** split hairs, carp, cavil ♦ *noun* **2** objection, cavil, complaint, criticism, nicety, niggle

quick *adjective* **1** fast, brisk, express, fleet, hasty, rapid, speedy, swift **2** brief, cursory, hasty, hurried, perfunctory **3** sudden, prompt **4** intelligent, acute, alert, astute, bright (*informal*), clever, perceptive, quick-witted, sharp, shrewd, smart **5** deft, adept, adroit,

dexterous, skilful **6** excitable, irascible, irritable, passionate, testy, touchy

quicken *verb* **1** speed, accelerate, expedite, hasten, hurry, impel, precipitate **2** invigorate, arouse, energize, excite, incite, inspire, revive, stimulate, vitalize

quickly *adverb* swiftly, abruptly, apace, briskly, fast, hastily, hurriedly, promptly, pronto (*informal*), rapidly, soon, speedily

quick-tempered *adjective* hot-tempered, choleric, fiery, irascible, irritable, quarrelsome, ratty (*Brit. & N.Z. informal*), testy, tetchy

quick-witted *adjective* clever, alert, astute, bright (*informal*), keen, perceptive, sharp, shrewd, smart

quiet *adjective* **1** silent, hushed, inaudible, low, noiseless, peaceful, soft, soundless **2** calm, mild, peaceful, placid, restful, serene, smooth, tranquil **3** undisturbed, isolated, private, secluded, sequestered, unfrequented **4** reserved, gentle, meek, mild, retiring, sedate, shy ♦ *noun* **5** peace, calmness, ease, quietness, repose, rest, serenity, silence, stillness, tranquillity

quieten *verb* **1** silence, compose, hush, muffle, mute, quell, quiet, stifle, still, stop, subdue **2** soothe, allay, appease, blunt, calm, deaden, dull

quietly *adverb* **1** silently, in an undertone, inaudibly, in silence, mutely, noiselessly, softly **2** calmly, mildly, patiently, placidly, serenely

quietness *noun* peace, calm,

hush, quiet, silence, stillness, tranquillity

quilt noun <u>bedspread</u>, continental quilt, counterpane, coverlet, duvet, eiderdown

quintessence noun <u>essence</u>, distillation, soul, spirit

quintessential adjective <u>ultimate</u>, archetypal, definitive, prototypical, typical

quip noun <u>joke</u>, gibe, jest, pleasantry, retort, riposte, sally, wisecrack (informal), witticism

quirk noun <u>peculiarity</u>, aberration, characteristic, eccentricity, foible, habit, idiosyncrasy, kink, mannerism, oddity, trait

quirky adjective <u>odd</u>, eccentric, idiosyncratic, offbeat, peculiar, unusual

quit verb 1 <u>stop</u>, abandon, cease, discontinue, drop, end, give up, halt 2 <u>resign</u>, abdicate, go, leave, pull out, retire, step down (informal) 3 <u>depart</u>, go, leave, pull out

quite adverb 1 <u>somewhat</u>, fairly, moderately, rather, reasonably, relatively 2 <u>absolutely</u>, completely, entirely, fully, perfectly, totally, wholly 3 <u>truly</u>, in fact, in reality, in truth, really

quiver verb 1 <u>shake</u>, oscillate, quake, quaver, shiver, shudder, tremble, vibrate ◆ noun 2 <u>shake</u>, oscillation, shiver, shudder, tremble, tremor, vibration

quixotic adjective <u>unrealistic</u>, dreamy, fanciful, idealistic, impractical, romantic

quiz noun 1 <u>examination</u>, investigation, questioning, test ◆ verb 2 <u>question</u>, ask, examine,

interrogate, investigate

quizzical adjective <u>mocking</u>, arch, questioning, sardonic, teasing

quota noun <u>share</u>, allowance, assignment, part, portion, ration, slice, whack (informal)

quotation noun 1 <u>passage</u>, citation, excerpt, extract, quote (informal), reference 2 Commerce <u>estimate</u>, charge, cost, figure, price, quote (informal), rate, tender

quote verb <u>repeat</u>, cite, detail, instance, name, recall, recite, recollect, refer to

R r

rabble noun <u>mob</u>, canaille, crowd, herd, horde, swarm, throng

rabid adjective 1 <u>fanatical</u>, extreme, fervent, irrational, narrow-minded, zealous 2 <u>mad</u>, hydrophobic

race¹ noun 1 <u>contest</u>, chase, competition, dash, pursuit, rivalry ◆ verb 2 <u>run</u>, career, compete, contest, dart, dash, fly, gallop, hurry, speed, tear, zoom

race² noun <u>people</u>, blood, folk, nation, stock, tribe, type

racial adjective <u>ethnic</u>, ethnological, folk, genealogical, genetic, national, tribal

rack noun 1 <u>frame</u>, framework, stand, structure ◆ verb 2 <u>torture</u>, afflict, agonize, crucify, harrow, oppress, pain, torment

racket noun 1 <u>noise</u>, clamour, din, disturbance, fuss, outcry, pandemonium, row **2** <u>fraud</u>, scheme

racy *adjective* **1** <u>risqué</u>, bawdy, blue, naughty, near the knuckle (*informal*), smutty, suggestive **2** <u>lively</u>, animated, energetic, entertaining, exciting, sparkling, spirited

radiance *noun* **1** <u>happiness</u>, delight, gaiety, joy, pleasure, rapture, warmth **2** <u>brightness</u>, brilliance, glare, gleam, glow, light, lustre, shine

radiant *adjective* **1** <u>happy</u>, blissful, delighted, ecstatic, glowing, joyful, joyous, on cloud nine (*informal*), rapturous **2** <u>bright</u>, brilliant, gleaming, glittering, glowing, luminous, lustrous, shining

radiate *verb* **1** <u>spread out</u>, branch out, diverge, issue **2** <u>emit</u>, diffuse, give off *or* out, pour, scatter, send out, shed, spread

radical *adjective* **1** <u>fundamental</u>, basic, deep-seated, innate, natural, profound **2** <u>extreme</u>, complete, drastic, entire, extremist, fanatical, severe, sweeping, thorough ♦ *noun* **3** <u>extremist</u>, fanatic, militant, revolutionary

raffle *noun* <u>draw</u>, lottery, sweep, sweepstake

ragamuffin *noun* <u>urchin</u>, guttersnipe

rage *noun* **1** <u>fury</u>, anger, frenzy, ire, madness, passion, rampage, wrath **2** *As in* **all the rage** <u>craze</u>, enthusiasm, fad (*informal*), fashion, latest thing, vogue ♦ *verb* **3** <u>be furious</u>, blow one's top, blow up (*informal*), fly off

the handle (*informal*), fume, go ballistic (*slang, chiefly U.S.*), go up the wall (*slang*), lose the plot (*informal*), seethe, storm

ragged *adjective* **1** <u>tattered</u>, in rags, in tatters, shabby, tatty, threadbare, torn, unkempt **2** <u>rough</u>, jagged, rugged, serrated, uneven, unfinished

raging *adjective* <u>furious</u>, beside oneself, enraged, fuming, incensed, infuriated, mad, raving, seething

rags *plural noun* <u>tatters</u>, castoffs, old clothes, tattered clothing

raid *noun* **1** <u>attack</u>, foray, incursion, inroad, invasion, sally, sortie ♦ *verb* **2** <u>attack</u>, assault, foray, invade, pillage, plunder, sack

raider *noun* <u>attacker</u>, invader, marauder, plunderer, robber, thief

railing *noun* <u>fence</u>, balustrade, barrier, paling, rails

rain *noun* **1** <u>rainfall</u>, cloudburst, deluge, downpour, drizzle, fall, raindrops, showers ♦ *verb* **2** <u>pour</u>, bucket down (*informal*), come down in buckets (*informal*), drizzle, pelt (down), teem **3** <u>fall</u>, deposit, drop, shower, sprinkle

rainy *adjective* <u>wet</u>, damp, drizzly, showery

raise *verb* **1** <u>lift</u>, build, elevate, erect, heave, hoist, rear, uplift **2** <u>increase</u>, advance, amplify, boost, enhance, enlarge, heighten, inflate, intensify, magnify, strengthen **3** <u>collect</u>, assemble, form, gather, mass, obtain, rally, recruit **4** <u>cause</u>, create, engender, occasion, originate, produce, provoke, start **5** <u>bring up</u>, develop, nurture, rear **6** <u>suggest</u>, advance, broach, introduce, moot, put forward

rake¹ verb **1** <u>gather</u>, collect, remove **2** <u>search</u>, comb, scour, scrutinize

rake² noun <u>libertine</u>, debauchee, lecher, playboy, roué

rakish adjective <u>dashing</u>, dapper, debonair, devil-may-care, jaunty, natty (informal), raffish, smart

rally noun **1** <u>gathering</u>, assembly, congress, convention, meeting **2** <u>recovery</u>, improvement, recuperation, revival ♦ verb **3** <u>reassemble</u>, regroup, reorganize, unite **4** <u>gather</u>, assemble, collect, convene, marshal, muster, round up, unite **5** <u>recover</u>, get better, improve, recuperate, revive

ram verb **1** <u>hit</u>, butt, crash, dash, drive, force, impact, smash **2** <u>cram</u>, crowd, force, jam, stuff, thrust

ramble verb **1** <u>walk</u>, range, roam, rove, saunter, stray, stroll, wander **2** <u>babble</u>, rabbit (on) (Brit. informal), waffle (informal, chiefly Brit.), witter on (informal) ♦ noun **3** <u>walk</u>, hike, roaming, roving, saunter, stroll, tour

rambler noun <u>walker</u>, hiker, rover, wanderer, wayfarer

rambling adjective <u>long-winded</u>, circuitous, digressive, disconnected, discursive, disjointed, incoherent, wordy

ramification noun **ramifications** <u>consequences</u>, developments, results, sequel, upshot

ramp noun <u>slope</u>, gradient, incline, rise

rampage verb **1** <u>go berserk</u>, rage, run amok, run riot, storm ♦ noun **2 on the rampage** <u>berserk</u>, amok, out of control, raging, riotous, violent, wild

rampant adjective **1** <u>widespread</u>, prevalent, profuse, rife, spreading like wildfire, unchecked, uncontrolled, unrestrained **2** Heraldry <u>upright</u>, erect, rearing, standing

rampart noun <u>defence</u>, bastion, bulwark, fence, fortification, wall

ramshackle adjective <u>rickety</u>, crumbling, decrepit, derelict, flimsy, shaky, tumbledown, unsafe, unsteady

rancid adjective <u>rotten</u>, bad, fetid, foul, off, putrid, rank, sour, stale, strong-smelling, tainted

rancour noun <u>hatred</u>, animosity, bad blood, bitterness, hate, ill feeling, ill will

random adjective **1** <u>chance</u>, accidental, adventitious, casual, fortuitous, haphazard, hit or miss, incidental ♦ noun **2 at random** <u>haphazardly</u>, arbitrarily, by chance, randomly, unsystematically, willy-nilly

randy adjective Informal <u>aroused</u>, amorous, horny (slang), hot, lascivious, lustful, turned-on (slang)

range noun **1** <u>limits</u>, area, bounds, orbit, province, radius, reach, scope, sphere **2** <u>series</u>, assortment, collection, gamut, lot, selection, variety ♦ verb **3** <u>vary</u>, extend, reach, run, stretch **4** <u>roam</u>, ramble, rove, traverse, wander

rangy *adjective* <u>long-limbed</u>, gangling, lanky, leggy, long-legged

rank¹ *noun* 1 <u>status</u>, caste, class, degree, division, grade, level, order, position, sort, type 2 <u>row</u>, column, file, group, line, range, series, tier ♦ *verb* 3 <u>arrange</u>, align, array, dispose, line up, order, sort

rank² *adjective* 1 <u>absolute</u>, arrant, blatant, complete, downright, flagrant, gross, sheer, thorough, total, utter 2 <u>foul</u>, bad, disgusting, noisome, noxious, offensive, rancid, revolting, stinking 3 <u>abundant</u>, dense, lush, luxuriant, profuse

rank and file *noun* <u>general public</u>, majority, mass, masses

rankle *verb* <u>annoy</u>, anger, gall, get on one's nerves (*informal*), irk, irritate, rile

ransack *verb* 1 <u>search</u>, comb, explore, go through, rummage, scour, turn inside out 2 <u>plunder</u>, loot, pillage, raid, strip

ransom *noun* <u>payment</u>, money, payoff, price

rant *verb* <u>shout</u>, cry, declaim, rave, roar, yell

rap *verb* 1 <u>hit</u>, crack, knock, strike, tap ♦ *noun* 2 <u>blow</u>, clout (*informal*), crack, knock, tap 3 *Slang* <u>punishment</u>, blame, responsibility

rapacious *adjective* <u>greedy</u>, avaricious, grasping, insatiable, predatory, preying, voracious

rape *verb* 1 <u>sexually assault</u>, abuse, force, outrage, ravish, violate ♦ *noun* 2 <u>sexual assault</u>, outrage, ravishment, violation

3 <u>desecration</u>, abuse, defilement, violation

rapid *adjective* <u>quick</u>, brisk, express, fast, hasty, hurried, prompt, speedy, swift

rapidity *noun* <u>speed</u>, alacrity, briskness, fleetness, haste, hurry, promptness, quickness, rush, swiftness, velocity

rapidly *adverb* <u>quickly</u>, briskly, fast, hastily, hurriedly, in haste, promptly, pronto (*informal*), speedily, swiftly

rapport *noun* <u>bond</u>, affinity, empathy, harmony, link, relationship, sympathy, tie, understanding

rapprochement *noun* <u>reconciliation</u>, detente, reunion

rapt *adjective* <u>spellbound</u>, absorbed, engrossed, enthralled, entranced, fascinated, gripped

rapture *noun* <u>ecstasy</u>, bliss, delight, euphoria, joy, rhapsody, seventh heaven, transport

rapturous *adjective* <u>ecstatic</u>, blissful, euphoric, in seventh heaven, joyful, overjoyed, over the moon (*informal*), transported

rare *adjective* 1 <u>uncommon</u>, few, infrequent, scarce, singular, sparse, strange, unusual 2 <u>superb</u>, choice, excellent, fine, great, peerless, superlative

rarefied *adjective* <u>exalted</u>, elevated, high, lofty, noble, spiritual, sublime

rarely *adverb* <u>seldom</u>, hardly, hardly ever, infrequently

raring *adjective* As in **raring to** <u>eager</u>, desperate, enthusiastic, impatient, keen, longing, ready

rarity *noun* 1 <u>curio</u>, collector's

item, find, gem, treasure
2 <u>uncommonness</u>, infrequency, scarcity, shortage, sparseness, strangeness, unusualness

rascal *noun* <u>rogue</u>, blackguard, devil, good-for-nothing, imp, ne'er-do-well, scamp, scoundrel, villain

rash[1] *adjective* <u>reckless</u>, careless, foolhardy, hasty, heedless, ill-advised, impetuous, imprudent, impulsive, incautious

rash[2] *noun* **1** <u>outbreak</u>, eruption **2** <u>spate</u>, flood, outbreak, plague, series, wave

rashness *noun* <u>recklessness</u>, carelessness, foolhardiness, hastiness, heedlessness, indiscretion, thoughtlessness

rate *noun* **1** <u>speed</u>, pace, tempo, velocity **2** <u>degree</u>, proportion, ratio, scale, standard **3** <u>charge</u>, cost, fee, figure, price **4 at any rate** <u>in any case</u>, anyhow, anyway, at all events ♦ *verb* **5** <u>evaluate</u>, consider, count, estimate, grade, measure, rank, reckon, value **6** <u>deserve</u>, be entitled to, be worthy of, merit

rather *adverb* **1** <u>to some extent</u>, a little, fairly, moderately, quite, relatively, somewhat, to some degree **2** <u>preferably</u>, more readily, more willingly, sooner

ratify *verb* <u>approve</u>, affirm, authorize, confirm, endorse, establish, sanction, uphold

rating *noun* <u>position</u>, class, degree, grade, order, placing, rank, rate, status

ratio *noun* <u>proportion</u>, fraction, percentage, rate, relation

ration *noun* **1** <u>allowance</u>, allotment, helping, measure, part, portion, quota, share ♦ *verb* **2** <u>limit</u>, budget, control, restrict

rational *adjective* <u>sane</u>, intelligent, logical, lucid, realistic, reasonable, sensible, sound, wise

rationale *noun* <u>reason</u>, grounds, logic, motivation, philosophy, principle, *raison d'être*, theory

rationalize *verb* <u>justify</u>, account for, excuse, vindicate

rattle *verb* **1** <u>clatter</u>, bang, jangle **2** <u>shake</u>, bounce, jar, jolt, vibrate **3** *Informal* <u>fluster</u>, disconcert, disturb, faze, perturb, shake, upset

raucous *adjective* <u>harsh</u>, grating, hoarse, loud, noisy, rough, strident

raunchy *adjective Slang* <u>sexy</u>, coarse, earthy, lusty, sexual, steamy (*informal*)

ravage *verb* **1** <u>destroy</u>, demolish, despoil, devastate, lay waste, ransack, ruin, spoil ♦ *noun* **2 ravages** <u>damage</u>, destruction, devastation, havoc, ruin, ruination, spoliation

rave *verb* **1** <u>rant</u>, babble, be delirious, go mad (*informal*), rage, roar **2** *Informal* <u>enthuse</u>, be mad about (*informal*), be wild about (*informal*), gush, praise

ravenous *adjective* <u>starving</u>, famished, starved

ravine *noun* <u>canyon</u>, defile, gorge, gulch (*U.S.*), gully, pass

raving *adjective* <u>mad</u>, crazed, crazy, delirious, hysterical, insane, irrational, wild

ravish *verb* **1** <u>enchant</u>, captivate, charm, delight, enrapture, entrance, fascinate, spellbind

2 rape, abuse, force, sexually assault, violate

ravishing *adjective* enchanting, beautiful, bewitching, charming, entrancing, gorgeous, lovely

raw *adjective* **1** uncooked, fresh, natural **2** unrefined, basic, coarse, crude, natural, rough, unfinished, unprocessed **3** inexperienced, callow, green, immature, new **4** chilly, biting, bitter, cold, freezing, parky (*Brit. informal*), piercing

ray *noun* beam, bar, flash, gleam, shaft

raze *verb* destroy, demolish, flatten, knock down, level, pull down, ruin

re *preposition* concerning, about, apropos, regarding, with reference to, with regard to

reach *verb* **1** arrive at, attain, get to, make **2** touch, contact, extend to, grasp, stretch to **3** contact, communicate with, get hold of, get in touch with, get through to ◆ *noun* **4** range, capacity, distance, extension, extent, grasp, influence, power, scope, stretch

react *verb* **1** respond, answer, reply **2** act, behave, function, operate, proceed, work

reaction *noun* **1** response, answer, reply **2** recoil, counteraction **3** conservatism, the right

reactionary *adjective* **1** conservative, right-wing ◆ *noun* **2** conservative, die-hard, right-winger

read *verb* **1** look at, peruse, pore over, scan, study **2** interpret,

comprehend, construe, decipher, discover, see, understand **3** register, display, indicate, record, show

readable *adjective* **1** enjoyable, entertaining, enthralling, gripping, interesting **2** legible, clear, comprehensible, decipherable

readily *adverb* **1** willingly, eagerly, freely, gladly, promptly, quickly **2** easily, effortlessly, quickly, smoothly, speedily, unhesitatingly

readiness *noun* **1** willingness, eagerness, keenness **2** ease, adroitness, dexterity, facility, promptness

reading *noun* **1** perusal, examination, inspection, scrutiny, study **2** recital, lesson, performance, sermon **3** interpretation, grasp, impression, version **4** learning, education, erudition, knowledge, scholarship

ready *adjective* **1** prepared, arranged, fit, organized, primed, ripe, set **2** willing, agreeable, disposed, eager, glad, happy, inclined, keen, prone **3** prompt, alert, bright, clever, intelligent, keen, perceptive, quick, sharp, smart **4** available, accessible, convenient, handy, near, present

real *adjective* genuine, actual, authentic, factual, rightful, sincere, true, unfeigned, valid

realistic *adjective* **1** practical, common-sense, down-to-earth, level-headed, matter-of-fact, real, sensible **2** lifelike, authentic, faithful, genuine, natural, true, true to life

reality noun <u>truth</u>, actuality, fact, realism, validity, verity

realization noun 1 <u>awareness</u>, cognizance, comprehension, conception, grasp, perception, recognition, understanding 2 <u>achievement</u>, accomplishment, fulfilment

realize verb 1 <u>become aware of</u>, comprehend, get the message, grasp, take in, understand 2 <u>achieve</u>, accomplish, carry out or through, complete, do, effect, fulfil, perform

really adverb <u>truly</u>, actually, certainly, genuinely, in actuality, indeed, in fact, positively, surely

realm noun 1 <u>kingdom</u>, country, domain, dominion, empire, land 2 <u>sphere</u>, area, branch, department, field, province, territory, world

reap verb 1 <u>collect</u>, bring in, cut, garner, gather, harvest 2 <u>obtain</u>, acquire, derive, gain, get

rear[1] noun 1 <u>back</u>, end, rearguard, stern, tail, tail end ♦ adjective 2 <u>back</u>, following, hind, last

rear[2] verb 1 <u>bring up</u>, breed, educate, foster, nurture, raise, train 2 <u>rise</u>, loom, soar, tower

reason noun 1 <u>cause</u>, aim, goal, grounds, incentive, intention, motive, object, purpose 2 <u>sense(s)</u>, intellect, judgment, logic, mind, rationality, sanity, soundness, understanding ♦ verb 3 <u>deduce</u>, conclude, infer, make out, think, work out 4 <u>reason with</u> <u>persuade</u>, bring round (informal), prevail upon, talk into or out of, urge, win over

reasonable adjective 1 <u>sensible</u>,

logical, plausible, practical, sane, sober, sound, tenable, wise 2 <u>moderate</u>, equitable, fair, fit, just, modest, O.K. or okay (informal), proper, right

reasoned adjective <u>sensible</u>, clear, logical, well-thought-out

reasoning noun <u>thinking</u>, analysis, logic, thought

reassure verb <u>encourage</u>, comfort, hearten, put or set one's mind at rest, restore confidence to

rebate noun <u>refund</u>, allowance, bonus, deduction, discount, reduction

rebel verb 1 <u>revolt</u>, mutiny, resist, rise up 2 <u>defy</u>, disobey, dissent ♦ noun 3 <u>revolutionary</u>, insurgent, revolutionist, secessionist 4 <u>nonconformist</u>, apostate, dissenter, heretic, schismatic ♦ adjective 5 <u>rebellious</u>, insurgent, insurrectionary, revolutionary

rebellion noun 1 <u>resistance</u>, mutiny, revolt, revolution, rising, uprising 2 <u>nonconformity</u>, defiance, heresy, schism

rebellious adjective 1 <u>revolutionary</u>, disloyal, disobedient, disorderly, insurgent, mutinous, rebel, seditious, unruly 2 <u>defiant</u>, difficult, refractory, resistant, unmanageable

rebound verb 1 <u>bounce</u>, recoil, ricochet 2 <u>misfire</u>, backfire, boomerang, recoil

rebuff verb 1 <u>reject</u>, cold-shoulder, cut, knock back (slang), refuse, repulse, slight, snub, spurn, turn down ♦ noun 2 <u>rejection</u>, cold shoulder, kick in the teeth (*slang*), knock-back (*slang*), refusal, repulse, slap in the face (*informal*), slight, snub

rebuke *verb* 1 <u>scold</u>, admonish, castigate, censure, chide, dress down (*informal*), give a rocket (*Brit. & N.Z. informal*), haul (someone) over the coals (*informal*), reprimand, reprove, tear (someone) off a strip (*informal*), tell off (*informal*) ♦ *noun* 2 <u>scolding</u>, admonition, censure, dressing down (*informal*), reprimand, row, telling-off (*informal*)

rebut *verb* <u>disprove</u>, confute, invalidate, negate, overturn, prove wrong, refute

rebuttal *noun* <u>disproof</u>, confutation, invalidation, negation, refutation

recalcitrant *adjective* <u>disobedient</u>, defiant, insubordinate, refractory, unmanageable, unruly, wayward, wilful

recall *verb* 1 <u>recollect</u>, bring *or* call to mind, evoke, remember 2 <u>annul</u>, cancel, countermand, repeal, retract, revoke, withdraw ♦ *noun* 3 <u>recollection</u>, memory, remembrance 4 <u>annulment</u>, cancellation, repeal, rescindment, retraction, withdrawal

recant *verb* <u>withdraw</u>, disclaim, forswear, renege, repudiate, retract, revoke, take back

recapitulate *verb* <u>repeat</u>, outline, recap (*informal*), recount, restate, summarize

recede *verb* <u>fall back</u>, abate, ebb, regress, retire, retreat, return, subside, withdraw

receipt *noun* 1 <u>sales slip</u>, counterfoil, proof of purchase 2 <u>receiving</u>, acceptance, delivery, reception

receive *verb* 1 <u>get</u>, accept, acquire, be given, collect, obtain, pick up, take 2 <u>experience</u>, bear, encounter, suffer, sustain, undergo 3 <u>greet</u>, accommodate, admit, entertain, meet, welcome

recent *adjective* <u>new</u>, current, fresh, late, modern, novel, present-day, up-to-date

recently *adverb* <u>newly</u>, currently, freshly, lately, latterly, not long ago, of late

receptacle *noun* <u>container</u>, holder, repository

reception *noun* 1 <u>party</u>, function, levee, soirée 2 <u>welcome</u>, acknowledgment, greeting, reaction, response, treatment

receptive *adjective* <u>open</u>, amenable, interested, open-minded, open to suggestions, susceptible, sympathetic

recess *noun* 1 <u>alcove</u>, bay, corner, hollow, niche, nook 2 <u>break</u>, holiday, intermission, interval, respite, rest, vacation

recession *noun* <u>depression</u>, decline, drop, slump

recipe *noun* 1 <u>directions</u>, ingredients, instructions 2 <u>method</u>, formula, prescription, procedure, process, technique

reciprocal *adjective* <u>mutual</u>, alternate, complementary, correlative, corresponding, equivalent, exchanged, interchangeable

reciprocate verb return, exchange, reply, requite, respond, swap, trade

recital noun 1 performance, rehearsal, rendering 2 recitation, account, narrative, reading, relation, statement, telling

recitation noun recital, lecture, passage, performance, piece, reading

recite verb repeat, declaim, deliver, narrate, perform, speak

reckless adjective careless, hasty, headlong, heedless, imprudent, mindless, precipitate, rash, thoughtless, wild

reckon verb 1 think, assume, believe, guess (informal, chiefly U.S. & Canad.), imagine, suppose 2 consider, account, count, deem, esteem, judge, rate, regard 3 count, add up, calculate, compute, figure, number, tally, total

reckoning noun 1 count, addition, calculation, estimate 2 bill, account, charge, due, score

reclaim verb regain, recapture, recover, redeem, reform, retrieve, salvage

recline verb lean, lie (down), loll, lounge, repose, rest, sprawl

recluse noun hermit, anchoress, anchorite, monk, solitary

reclusive adjective solitary, hermit-like, isolated, retiring, withdrawn

recognition noun 1 identification, discovery, recollection, remembrance 2 acceptance, admission,

allowance, confession 3 appreciation, notice, respect

recognize verb 1 identify, know, notice, place, recall, recollect, remember, spot 2 accept, acknowledge, admit, allow, concede, grant 3 appreciate, notice, respect

recoil verb 1 jerk back, kick, react, rebound, spring back 2 draw back, falter, quail, shrink 3 backfire, boomerang, misfire, rebound ♦ noun 4 reaction, backlash, kick, rebound, repercussion

recollect verb remember, place, recall, summon up

recollection noun memory, impression, recall, remembrance, reminiscence

recommend verb 1 advise, advance, advocate, counsel, prescribe, propose, put forward, suggest 2 praise, approve, commend, endorse

recommendation noun 1 advice, counsel, proposal, suggestion 2 praise, advocacy, approval, commendation, endorsement, reference, sanction, testimonial

recompense verb 1 reward, pay, remunerate 2 compensate, make up for, pay for, redress, reimburse, repay, requite ♦ noun 3 compensation, amends, damages, payment, remuneration, reparation, repayment, requital, restitution 4 reward, payment, return, wages

reconcile verb 1 resolve, adjust, compose, put to rights, rectify, settle, square 2 reunite, appease, conciliate, make peace between, propitiate **3** <u>accept</u>, put up with (*informal*), resign oneself, submit, yield

reconciliation *noun* <u>reunion</u>, conciliation, pacification, reconcilement

recondite *adjective* <u>obscure</u>, arcane, concealed, dark, deep, difficult, hidden, mysterious, occult, profound, secret

recondition *verb* <u>restore</u>, do up (*informal*), overhaul, remodel, renew, renovate, repair, revamp

reconnaissance *noun* <u>inspection</u>, exploration, investigation, observation, recce (*slang*), scan, survey

reconnoitre *verb* <u>inspect</u>, case (*slang*), explore, investigate, observe, scan, spy out, survey

reconsider *verb* <u>rethink</u>, reassess, review, revise, think again

reconstruct *verb* **1** <u>rebuild</u>, recreate, regenerate, remake, remodel, renovate, restore **2** <u>deduce</u>, build up, piece together

record *noun* **1** <u>document</u>, account, chronicle, diary, entry, file, journal, log, register, report **2** <u>evidence</u>, documentation, testimony, trace, witness **3** <u>disc</u>, album, LP, single, vinyl **4** <u>background</u>, career, history, performance **5** **off the record** <u>confidential</u>, not for publication, private, unofficial ♦ *verb* **6** <u>write down</u>, chronicle, document, enter, log, minute, note, register, set down, take down **7** <u>tape</u>, make a recording of, tape-record, video, video-tape **8** <u>register</u>, give evidence of,

indicate, say, show

recorder *noun* <u>chronicler</u>, archivist, clerk, diarist, historian, scribe

recording *noun* <u>record</u>, disc, tape, video

recount *verb* <u>tell</u>, depict, describe, narrate, recite, relate, repeat, report

recoup *verb* **1** <u>regain</u>, recover, retrieve, win back **2** <u>compensate</u>, make up for, refund, reimburse, repay, requite

recourse *noun* <u>option</u>, alternative, choice, expedient, remedy, resort, resource, way out

recover *verb* **1** <u>get better</u>, convalesce, get well, heal, improve, mend, rally, recuperate, revive **2** <u>regain</u>, get back, recapture, reclaim, redeem, repossess, restore, retrieve

recovery *noun* **1** <u>improvement</u>, convalescence, healing, mending, recuperation, revival **2** <u>retrieval</u>, reclamation, repossession, restoration

recreation *noun* <u>pastime</u>, amusement, diversion, enjoyment, entertainment, fun, hobby, leisure activity, play, relaxation, sport

recrimination *noun* <u>bickering</u>, counterattack, mutual accusation, quarrel, squabbling

recruit *verb* **1** <u>enlist</u>, draft, enrol, levy, mobilize, muster, raise **2** <u>win (over)</u>, engage, obtain, procure ♦ *noun* **3** <u>beginner</u>, apprentice, convert, helper, initiate, learner, novice, trainee

rectify *verb* <u>correct</u>, adjust,

emend, fix, improve, redress, remedy, repair, right

rectitude noun morality, decency, goodness, honesty, honour, integrity, principle, probity, virtue

recuperate verb recover, convalesce, get better, improve, mend

recur verb happen again, come again, persist, reappear, repeat, return, revert

recurrent adjective periodic, continued, frequent, habitual, recurring

recycle verb reprocess, reclaim, reuse, salvage, save

red adjective 1 crimson, carmine, cherry, coral, ruby, scarlet, vermilion 2 Of hair chestnut, carroty, flame-coloured, reddish, sandy, titian 3 flushed, blushing, embarrassed, florid, shamefaced ♦ noun 4 in the red Informal in debt, in arrears, insolvent, overdrawn 5 see red Informal lose one's temper, blow one's top, crack up (informal), fly off the handle (informal), go ballistic (slang, chiefly U.S.), go mad (informal)

red-blooded adjective Informal vigorous, lusty, robust, strong, virile

redden verb flush, blush, colour (up), crimson, go red

redeem verb 1 make up for, atone for, compensate for, make amends for 2 reinstate, absolve, restore to favour 3 save, deliver, emancipate, free, liberate, ransom 4 buy back, reclaim, recover, regain, repurchase, retrieve

redemption noun
1 compensation, amends, atonement, reparation
2 salvation, deliverance, emancipation, liberation, release, rescue 3 repurchase, reclamation, recovery, repossession, retrieval

red-handed adjective in the act, bang to rights (slang), (in) flagrante delicto

redolent adjective 1 reminiscent, evocative, suggestive 2 scented, aromatic, fragrant, odorous, perfumed, sweet-smelling

redoubtable adjective formidable, fearful, fearsome, mighty, powerful, strong

redress verb 1 make amends for, compensate for, make up for 2 put right, adjust, balance, correct, even up, rectify, regulate ♦ noun 3 amends, atonement, compensation, payment, recompense, reparation

reduce verb 1 lessen, abate, curtail, cut down, decrease, diminish, lower, moderate, shorten, weaken 2 degrade, break, bring low, downgrade, humble

redundancy noun unemployment, joblessness, layoff, the axe (informal), the sack (informal)

redundant adjective superfluous, extra, inessential, supernumerary, surplus, unnecessary, unwanted

reek verb 1 stink, pong (Brit. informal), smell ♦ noun 2 stink, fetor, odour, pong (Brit. informal), smell, stench

reel verb 1 stagger, lurch, pitch,

rock, roll, sway **2** <u>whirl</u>, revolve, spin, swirl

refer verb **1** <u>allude</u>, bring up, cite, mention, speak of **2** <u>relate</u>, apply, belong, be relevant to, concern, pertain **3** <u>consult</u>, apply, go, look up, turn to **4** <u>direct</u>, guide, point, send

referee noun **1** <u>umpire</u>, adjudicator, arbiter, arbitrator, judge, ref (informal) ♦ verb **2** <u>umpire</u>, adjudicate, arbitrate, judge, mediate

reference noun **1** <u>citation</u>, allusion, mention, note, quotation **2** <u>testimonial</u>, character, credentials, endorsement, recommendation **3** <u>relevance</u>, applicability, bearing, connection, relation

referendum noun <u>public vote</u>, plebiscite, popular vote

refine verb **1** <u>purify</u>, clarify, cleanse, distil, filter, process **2** <u>improve</u>, hone, perfect, polish

refined adjective **1** <u>cultured</u>, civilized, cultivated, elegant, polished, polite, well-bred **2** <u>pure</u>, clarified, clean, distilled, filtered, processed, purified **3** <u>discerning</u>, delicate, discriminating, fastidious, fine, precise, sensitive

refinement noun **1** <u>sophistication</u>, breeding, civility, courtesy, cultivation, culture, discrimination, gentility, good breeding, polish, taste **2** <u>subtlety</u>, fine point, nicety, nuance **3** <u>purification</u>, clarification, cleansing, distillation, filtering, processing

reflect verb **1** <u>throw back</u>, echo, mirror, reproduce, return

2 <u>show</u>, demonstrate, display, indicate, manifest, reveal **3** <u>think</u>, cogitate, consider, meditate, muse, ponder, ruminate, wonder

reflection noun **1** <u>image</u>, echo, mirror image **2** <u>thought</u>, cogitation, consideration, contemplation, idea, meditation, musing, observation, opinion, thinking

reflective adjective <u>thoughtful</u>, contemplative, meditative, pensive

reform noun **1** <u>improvement</u>, amendment, betterment, rehabilitation ♦ verb **2** <u>improve</u>, amend, correct, mend, rectify, restore **3** <u>mend one's ways</u>, clean up one's act (informal), go straight (informal), pull one's socks up (Brit. informal), shape up (informal), turn over a new leaf

refractory adjective <u>unmanageable</u>, difficult, disobedient, headstrong, intractable, uncontrollable, unruly, wilful

refrain[1] verb <u>stop</u>, abstain, avoid, cease, desist, forbear, leave off, renounce

refrain[2] noun <u>chorus</u>, melody, tune

refresh verb **1** <u>revive</u>, brace, enliven, freshen, reinvigorate, revitalize, stimulate **2** <u>stimulate</u>, jog, prompt, renew

refreshing adjective **1** <u>stimulating</u>, bracing, fresh, invigorating **2** <u>new</u>, novel, original

refreshment noun **refreshments** <u>food and drink</u>, drinks, snacks, titbits

refrigerate verb cool, chill, freeze, keep cold

refuge noun shelter, asylum, haven, hide-out, protection, retreat, sanctuary

refugee noun exile, displaced person, émigré, escapee

refund verb 1 repay, pay back, reimburse, restore, return ♦ noun 2 repayment, reimbursement, return

refurbish verb renovate, clean up, do up (informal), mend, overhaul, repair, restore, revamp

refusal noun denial, knock-back (slang), rebuff, rejection

refuse[1] verb reject, decline, deny, say no, spurn, turn down, withhold

refuse[2] noun rubbish, garbage, junk (informal), litter, trash, waste

refute verb disprove, discredit, negate, overthrow, prove false, rebut

regain verb 1 recover, get back, recapture, recoup, retrieve, take back, win back 2 get back to, reach again, return to

regal adjective royal, kingly or queenly, magnificent, majestic, noble, princely

regale verb entertain, amuse, delight, divert

regalia plural noun emblems, accoutrements, decorations, finery, paraphernalia, trappings

regard verb 1 consider, believe, deem, esteem, judge, rate, see, suppose, think, view 2 look at, behold, check out (informal), clock (Brit. slang), eye, gaze at, observe, scrutinize, view, watch 3 heed, attend, listen to, mind, pay attention to, take notice of 4 as regards concerning, pertaining to, regarding, relating to ♦ noun 5 heed, attention, interest, mind, notice 6 respect, care, concern, consideration, esteem, thought 7 look, gaze, glance, scrutiny, stare

regarding preposition concerning, about, as regards, in or with regard to, on the subject of, re, respecting, with reference to

regardless adjective 1 heedless, inconsiderate, indifferent, neglectful, negligent, rash, reckless, unmindful ♦ adverb 2 anyway, in any case, in spite of everything, nevertheless

regards plural noun good wishes, best wishes, compliments, greetings, respects

regenerate verb renew, breathe new life into, invigorate, reawaken, reinvigorate, rejuvenate, restore, revive

regime noun government, leadership, management, reign, rule, system

regimented adjective controlled, disciplined, ordered, organized, regulated, systematized

region noun area, district, locality, part, place, quarter, section, sector, territory, tract, zone

regional adjective local, district, parochial, provincial, zonal

register noun 1 list, archives, catalogue, chronicle, diary, file, log, record, roll, roster ♦ verb 2 record, catalogue, chronicle, enlist, enrol, enter, list, note 3 show, display, exhibit, express, indicate, manifest, mark, reveal

regress verb <u>revert</u>, backslide, degenerate, deteriorate, fall away or off, go back, lapse, relapse, return

regret verb 1 <u>feel sorry about</u>, bemoan, bewail, deplore, grieve, lament, miss, mourn, repent, rue ♦ noun 2 <u>sorrow</u>, bitterness, compunction, contrition, penitence, remorse, repentance, ruefulness

regretful adjective <u>sorry</u>, apologetic, contrite, penitent, remorseful, repentant, rueful, sad, sorrowful

regrettable adjective <u>unfortunate</u>, disappointing, distressing, lamentable, sad, shameful

regular adjective 1 <u>normal</u>, common, customary, habitual, ordinary, routine, typical, usual 2 <u>even</u>, balanced, flat, level, smooth, straight, symmetrical, uniform 3 <u>systematic</u>, consistent, constant, even, fixed, ordered, set, stated, steady, uniform

regulate verb 1 <u>control</u>, direct, govern, guide, handle, manage, rule, run, supervise 2 <u>adjust</u>, balance, fit, moderate, modulate, tune

regulation noun 1 <u>rule</u>, decree, dictate, edict, law, order, precept, statute 2 <u>control</u>, direction, government, management, supervision 3 <u>adjustment</u>, modulation, tuning

regurgitate verb <u>vomit</u>, disgorge, puke (slang), sick up (informal), spew (out or up), throw up (informal)

rehabilitate verb 1 <u>reintegrate</u>, adjust 2 <u>redeem</u>, clear, reform, restore, save

rehash verb 1 <u>rework</u>, refashion, rejig (informal), reuse, rewrite ♦ noun 2 <u>reworking</u>, new version, rearrangement, rewrite

rehearsal noun <u>practice</u>, drill, preparation, rehearsing, run-through

rehearse verb <u>practise</u>, drill, go over, prepare, recite, repeat, run through, train

reign noun 1 <u>rule</u>, command, control, dominion, monarchy, power ♦ verb 2 <u>rule</u>, be in power, command, govern, influence 3 <u>be supreme</u>, hold sway, predominate, prevail

reimburse verb <u>pay back</u>, compensate, recompense, refund, remunerate, repay, return

rein verb 1 <u>control</u>, check, curb, halt, hold back, limit, restrain, restrict ♦ noun 2 <u>control</u>, brake, bridle, check, curb, harness, hold, restraint

reincarnation noun <u>rebirth</u>, transmigration of souls

reinforce verb <u>support</u>, bolster, emphasize, fortify, prop, strengthen, stress, supplement, toughen

reinforcement noun 1 <u>strengthening</u>, augmentation, fortification, increase 2 <u>support</u>, brace, buttress, prop, stay 3 **reinforcements** <u>reserves</u>, additional or fresh troops, auxiliaries, support

reinstate verb <u>restore</u>, recall, re-establish, replace, return

reiterate verb <u>repeat</u>, do again, restate, say again

reject verb 1 <u>deny</u>, decline, disallow, exclude, renounce, repudiate, veto **2** <u>rebuff</u>, jilt, refuse, repulse, say no to, spurn, turn down **3** <u>discard</u>, eliminate, jettison, scrap, throw away *or* out ♦ *noun* **4** <u>castoff</u>, discard, failure, second

rejection *noun* **1** <u>denial</u>, dismissal, exclusion, renunciation, repudiation, thumbs down, veto **2** <u>rebuff</u>, brushoff (*slang*), kick in the teeth (*slang*), knock-back (*slang*), refusal

rejig *verb* <u>rearrange</u>, alter, juggle, manipulate, reorganize, tweak

rejoice *verb* <u>be glad</u>, be happy, be overjoyed, celebrate, exult, glory

rejoicing *noun* <u>happiness</u>, celebration, elation, exultation, gladness, joy, jubilation, merrymaking

rejoin *verb* <u>reply</u>, answer, respond, retort, riposte

rejoinder *noun* <u>reply</u>, answer, comeback (*informal*), response, retort, riposte

rejuvenate *verb* <u>revitalize</u>, breathe new life into, refresh, regenerate, reinvigorate, renew, restore

relapse *verb* **1** <u>lapse</u>, backslide, degenerate, fail, regress, revert, slip back **2** <u>worsen</u>, deteriorate, fade, fail, sicken, sink, weaken ♦ *noun* **3** <u>lapse</u>, backsliding, regression, retrogression **4** <u>worsening</u>, deterioration, turn for the worse, weakening

relate *verb* **1** <u>connect</u>, associate, correlate, couple, join, link **2** <u>concern</u>, apply, be relevant to, have to do with, pertain, refer **3** <u>tell</u>, describe, detail, narrate, recite, recount, report

related *adjective* **1** <u>akin</u>, kindred **2** <u>associated</u>, affiliated, akin, connected, interconnected, joint, linked

relation *noun* **1** <u>connection</u>, bearing, bond, comparison, correlation, link **2** <u>relative</u>, kin, kinsman *or* kinswoman **3** <u>kinship</u>, affinity, kindred

relations *plural noun* **1** <u>dealings</u>, affairs, connections, contact, interaction, intercourse, relationship **2** <u>family</u>, clan, kin, kindred, kinsfolk, kinsmen, relatives, tribe

relationship *noun* **1** <u>association</u>, affinity, bond, connection, kinship, rapport **2** <u>affair</u>, liaison **3** <u>connection</u>, correlation, link, parallel, similarity, tie-up

relative *adjective* **1** <u>dependent</u>, allied, associated, comparative, contingent, corresponding, proportionate, related **2** <u>relevant</u>, applicable, apposite, appropriate, apropos, germane, pertinent ♦ *noun* **3** <u>relation</u>, kinsman *or* kinswoman, member of one's *or* the family

relatively *adverb* <u>comparatively</u>, rather, somewhat

relax *verb* **1** <u>be *or* feel at ease</u>, calm, chill out (*slang, chiefly U.S.*), lighten up (*slang*), rest, take it easy, unwind **2** <u>lessen</u>, abate, ease, ebb, let up, loosen, lower, moderate, reduce, relieve, slacken, weaken

relaxation *noun* <u>leisure</u>, enjoyment, fun, pleasure, recreation, rest

relaxed *adjective* <u>easy-going</u>, casual, comfortable, easy, free and easy, informal, laid-back (*informal*), leisurely

relay *noun* 1 <u>shift</u>, relief, turn
2 <u>message</u>, dispatch,
transmission ♦ *verb* 3 <u>pass on</u>,
broadcast, carry, communicate,
send, spread, transmit

release *verb* 1 <u>set free</u>,
discharge, drop, extricate, free,
liberate, loose, unbridle, undo,
unfasten 2 <u>acquit</u>, absolve,
exonerate, let go, let off 3 <u>issue</u>,
circulate, distribute, launch,
make known, make public,
publish, put out ♦ *noun*
4 <u>liberation</u>, deliverance,
discharge, emancipation,
freedom, liberty 5 <u>acquittal</u>,
absolution, exemption,
exoneration 6 <u>issue</u>,
proclamation, publication

relegate *verb* <u>demote</u>, downgrade

relent *verb* <u>be merciful</u>,
capitulate, change one's mind,
come round, have pity, show
mercy, soften, yield

relentless *adjective*
1 <u>unremitting</u>, incessant,
nonstop, persistent, unrelenting,
unrelieved 2 <u>merciless</u>, cruel,
fierce, implacable, pitiless,
remorseless, ruthless, unrelenting

relevant *adjective* <u>significant</u>,
apposite, appropriate, apt,
fitting, germane, pertinent,
related, to the point

reliable *adjective* <u>dependable</u>,
faithful, safe, sound, staunch,
sure, true, trustworthy

reliance *noun* <u>trust</u>, belief,
confidence, dependence, faith

relic *noun* <u>remnant</u>, fragment,
keepsake, memento, souvenir,
trace, vestige

relief *noun* 1 <u>ease</u>, comfort, cure,
deliverance, mitigation, release,
remedy, solace 2 <u>rest</u>, break,
breather (*informal*), relaxation,
respite 3 <u>aid</u>, assistance, help,
succour, support

relieve *verb* 1 <u>ease</u>, alleviate,
assuage, calm, comfort, console,
cure, mitigate, relax, soften,
soothe 2 <u>help</u>, aid, assist,
succour, support, sustain

religious *adjective* 1 <u>devout</u>,
devotional, faithful, godly, holy,
pious, sacred, spiritual
2 <u>conscientious</u>, faithful,
meticulous, punctilious, rigid,
scrupulous

relinquish *verb* <u>give up</u>,
abandon, abdicate, cede, drop,
forsake, leave, let go, renounce,
surrender

relish *verb* 1 <u>enjoy</u>, delight in,
fancy, like, revel in, savour
♦ *noun* 2 <u>enjoyment</u>, fancy,
fondness, gusto, liking, love,
partiality, penchant, predilection,
taste 3 <u>condiment</u>, sauce,
seasoning 4 <u>flavour</u>, piquancy,
smack, spice, tang, taste, trace

reluctance *noun* <u>unwillingness</u>,
aversion, disinclination, dislike,
distaste, loathing, repugnance

reluctant *adjective* <u>unwilling</u>,
disinclined, hesitant, loath,
unenthusiastic

rely *verb* <u>depend</u>, bank, bet,
count, trust

remain *verb* 1 <u>continue</u>, abide,
dwell, endure, go on, last,
persist, stand, stay, survive
2 <u>stay behind</u>, be left, delay,
linger, wait

remainder *noun* <u>rest</u>, balance,
excess, leavings, remains,

remnant, residue, surplus

remaining *adjective* left-over, lingering, outstanding, persisting, surviving, unfinished

remains *plural noun* **1** remnants, debris, dregs, leavings, leftovers, relics, residue, rest **2** body, cadaver, carcass, corpse

remark *verb* **1** comment, declare, mention, observe, pass comment, reflect, say, state **2** notice, espy, make out, mark, note, observe, perceive, see ♦ *noun* **3** comment, observation, reflection, statement, utterance

remarkable *adjective* extraordinary, notable, outstanding, rare, singular, striking, surprising, uncommon, unusual, wonderful

remedy *noun* **1** cure, medicine, nostrum, treatment ♦ *verb* **2** put right, correct, fix, rectify, set to rights

remember *verb* **1** recall, call to mind, commemorate, look back (on), recollect, reminisce, think back **2** bear in mind, keep in mind

remembrance *noun* **1** memory, recall, recollection, reminiscence, thought **2** souvenir, commemoration, keepsake, memento, memorial, monument, reminder, token

remind *verb* call to mind, jog one's memory, make (someone) remember, prompt

reminisce *verb* recall, hark back, look back, recollect, remember, think back

reminiscence *noun* recollection, anecdote, memoir, memory,

recall, remembrance

reminiscent *adjective* suggestive, evocative, similar

remiss *adjective* careless, forgetful, heedless, lax, neglectful, negligent, thoughtless

remission *noun* **1** pardon, absolution, amnesty, discharge, exemption, release, reprieve **2** lessening, abatement, alleviation, ebb, lull, relaxation, respite

remit *verb* **1** send, dispatch, forward, mail, post, transmit **2** cancel, halt, repeal, rescind, stop **3** postpone, defer, delay, put off, shelve, suspend ♦ *noun* **4** instructions, brief, guidelines, orders

remittance *noun* payment, allowance, fee

remnant *noun* remainder, end, fragment, leftovers, remains, residue, rest, trace, vestige

remonstrate *verb* argue, dispute, dissent, object, protest, take issue

remorse *noun* regret, anguish, compunction, contrition, grief, guilt, penitence, repentance, shame, sorrow

remorseful *adjective* regretful, apologetic, ashamed, conscience-stricken, contrite, guilty, penitent, repentant, sorry

remorseless *adjective* **1** pitiless, callous, cruel, inhumane, merciless, ruthless **2** relentless, inexorable

remote *adjective* **1** distant, far, inaccessible, in the middle of nowhere, isolated, out-of-the-way, secluded **2** aloof,

abstracted, cold, detached,
distant, reserved, standoffish,
uncommunicative, withdrawn
3 slight, doubtful, dubious, faint,
outside, slender, slim, small,
unlikely

removal *noun* **1** taking away or
off *or* out, dislodgment, ejection,
elimination, eradication,
extraction, uprooting,
withdrawal **2** dismissal, expulsion
3 move, departure, flitting (*Scot.
& Northern English dialect*),
relocation, transfer

remove *verb* **1** take away *or* off
or out, abolish, delete, detach,
displace, eject, eliminate, erase,
excise, extract, get rid of, wipe
from the face of the earth,
withdraw **2** dismiss, depose,
dethrone, discharge, expel, oust,
throw out **3** move, depart, flit
(*Scot. & Northern English dialect*),
relocate

remunerate *verb* pay,
compensate, recompense,
reimburse, repay, requite, reward

remuneration *noun* payment,
earnings, fee, income, pay,
return, reward, salary, stipend,
wages

remunerative *adjective*
profitable, economic, lucrative,
moneymaking, paying,
rewarding, worthwhile

renaissance, renascence *noun*
rebirth, reappearance,
reawakening, renewal,
restoration, resurgence, revival

rend *verb* tear, rip, rupture,
separate, wrench

render *verb* **1** make, cause to
become, leave **2** provide,
furnish, give, hand out, pay,

present, submit, supply, tender
3 portray, act, depict, do, give,
perform, play, represent

rendezvous *noun*
1 appointment, assignation,
date, engagement, meeting,
tryst (*archaic*) **2** meeting place,
gathering point, venue ♦ *verb*
3 meet, assemble, come
together, gather, join up

rendition *noun* **1** performance,
arrangement, interpretation,
portrayal, presentation, reading,
rendering, version **2** translation,
interpretation, reading,
transcription, version

renegade *noun* **1** deserter,
apostate, defector, traitor,
turncoat ♦ *adjective* **2** rebellious,
apostate, disloyal, traitorous,
unfaithful

renege *verb* break one's word,
back out, break a promise,
default, go back

renew *verb* **1** recommence,
continue, extend, reaffirm,
recreate, reopen, repeat, resume
2 restore, mend, modernize,
overhaul, refit, refurbish,
renovate, repair **3** replace,
refresh, replenish, restock

renounce *verb* give up, abjure,
deny, disown, forsake, forswear,
quit, recant, relinquish, waive

renovate *verb* restore, do up
(*informal*), modernize, overhaul,
recondition, refit, refurbish,
renew, repair

renown *noun* fame, distinction,
eminence, note, reputation,
repute

renowned *adjective* famous,
celebrated, distinguished,
eminent, esteemed, notable,

noted, well-known

rent[1] *verb* **1** <u>hire</u>, charter, lease, let ♦ *noun* **2** <u>hire</u>, fee, lease, payment, rental

rent[2] *noun* <u>tear</u>, gash, hole, opening, rip, slash, slit, split

renunciation *noun* <u>giving up</u>, abandonment, abdication, abjuration, denial, disavowal, forswearing, rejection, relinquishment, repudiation

reorganize *verb* <u>rearrange</u>, reshuffle, restructure

repair *verb* **1** <u>mend</u>, fix, heal, patch, patch up, renovate, restore ♦ *noun* **2** <u>mend</u>, darn, overhaul, patch, restoration **3** <u>condition</u>, form, shape (*informal*), state

reparation *noun* <u>compensation</u>, atonement, damages, recompense, restitution, satisfaction

repartee *noun* <u>wit</u>, badinage, banter, riposte, wittiness, wordplay

repast *noun* <u>meal</u>, food

repay *verb* **1** <u>pay back</u>, compensate, recompense, refund, reimburse, requite, return, square **2** <u>get even with</u> (*informal*), avenge, one's own back on (*informal*), hit back, reciprocate, retaliate, revenge

repeal *verb* **1** <u>abolish</u>, annul, cancel, invalidate, nullify, recall, reverse, revoke ♦ *noun* **2** <u>abolition</u>, annulment, cancellation, invalidation, rescindment

repeat *verb* **1** <u>reiterate</u>, echo, replay, reproduce, rerun, reshow, restate, retell ♦ *noun*

2 <u>repetition</u>, echo, reiteration, replay, rerun, reshowing

repeatedly *adverb* <u>over and over</u>, frequently, many times, often

repel *verb* **1** <u>disgust</u>, gross out (*U.S. slang*), nauseate, offend, revolt, sicken **2** <u>drive off</u>, fight, hold off, parry, rebuff, repulse, resist, ward off

repellent *adjective* **1** <u>disgusting</u>, abhorrent, hateful, horrid, loathsome, nauseating, noxious, offensive, repugnant, repulsive, revolting, sickening **2** <u>proof</u>, impermeable, repelling, resistant

repent *verb* <u>regret</u>, be sorry, feel remorse, rue

repentance *noun* <u>regret</u>, compunction, contrition, grief, guilt, penitence, remorse

repentant *adjective* <u>regretful</u>, contrite, penitent, remorseful, rueful, sorry

repercussion *noun* **repercussions** <u>consequences</u>, backlash, result, sequel, side effects

repertoire *noun* <u>range</u>, collection, list, repertory, stock, store, supply

repetition *noun* <u>repeating</u>, echo, recurrence, reiteration, renewal, replication, restatement, tautology

repetitious *adjective* <u>long-winded</u>, prolix, tautological, tedious, verbose, wordy

repetitive *adjective* <u>monotonous</u>, boring, dull, mechanical, recurrent, tedious, unchanging, unvaried

rephrase *verb* <u>reword</u>, paraphrase, put differently

repine verb <u>complain</u>, fret, grumble, moan

replace verb <u>take the place of</u>, follow, oust, substitute, succeed, supersede, supplant, take over from

replacement noun <u>successor</u>, double, proxy, stand-in, substitute, surrogate, understudy

replenish verb <u>refill</u>, fill, provide, reload, replace, restore, top up

replete adjective <u>full</u>, crammed, filled, full up, glutted, gorged, stuffed

replica noun <u>duplicate</u>, carbon copy (*informal*), copy, facsimile, imitation, model, reproduction

replicate verb <u>copy</u>, duplicate, mimic, recreate, reduplicate, reproduce

reply verb 1 <u>answer</u>, counter, reciprocate, rejoin, respond, retaliate, retort ♦ noun 2 <u>answer</u>, counter, counterattack, reaction, rejoinder, response, retaliation, retort

report verb 1 <u>communicate</u>, broadcast, cover, describe, detail, inform of, narrate, pass on, recount, relate, state, tell 2 <u>present oneself</u>, appear, arrive, come, turn up ♦ noun 3 <u>account</u>, communication, description, narrative, news, record, statement, word 4 <u>article</u>, piece, story, write-up 5 <u>rumour</u>, buzz, gossip, hearsay, talk 6 <u>bang</u>, blast, boom, crack, detonation, discharge, explosion, noise, sound

reporter noun <u>journalist</u>, correspondent, hack (*derogatory*), journo (*slang*), pressman, writer

repose noun 1 <u>peace</u>, ease, quietness, relaxation, respite, rest, stillness, tranquillity 2 <u>composure</u>, calmness, poise, self-possession 3 <u>sleep</u>, slumber ♦ verb 4 <u>rest</u>, lie, lie down, recline, rest upon

repository noun <u>store</u>, depository, storehouse, treasury, vault

reprehensible adjective <u>blameworthy</u>, bad, culpable, disgraceful, shameful, unworthy

represent verb 1 <u>stand for</u>, act for, betoken, mean, serve as, speak for, symbolize 2 <u>symbolize</u>, embody, epitomize, exemplify, personify, typify 3 <u>portray</u>, denote, depict, describe, illustrate, outline, picture, show

representation noun <u>portrayal</u>, account, depiction, description, illustration, image, likeness, model, picture, portrait

representative noun 1 <u>delegate</u>, agent, deputy, member, proxy, spokesman *or* spokeswoman 2 <u>salesman</u>, agent, commercial traveller, rep ♦ adjective 3 <u>typical</u>, archetypal, characteristic, exemplary, symbolic

repress verb 1 <u>inhibit</u>, bottle up, check, control, curb, hold back, restrain, stifle, suppress 2 <u>subdue</u>, quell, subjugate

repression noun <u>subjugation</u>, constraint, control, despotism, domination, restraint, suppression, tyranny

repressive adjective <u>oppressive</u>, absolute, authoritarian, despotic, dictatorial, tyrannical

reprieve verb 1 <u>grant a stay of</u>

execution to, let off the hook (*slang*), pardon **2** relieve, abate, allay, alleviate, mitigate, palliate ♦ *noun* **3** stay of execution, amnesty, deferment, pardon, postponement, remission **4** relief, alleviation, mitigation, palliation, respite

reprimand *verb* **1** blame, censure, dress down (*informal*), haul over the coals (*informal*), rap over the knuckles, rebuke, scold, tear (someone) off a strip (*Brit. informal*) ♦ *noun* **2** blame, censure, dressing-down (*informal*), rebuke, reproach, reproof, talking-to (*informal*)

reprisal *noun* retaliation, retribution, revenge, vengeance

reproach *noun* **1** blame, censure, condemnation, disapproval, opprobrium, rebuke ♦ *verb* **2** blame, censure, condemn, criticize, lambast(e), read the riot act, rebuke, reprimand, scold, upbraid

reproachful *adjective* critical, censorious, condemnatory, disapproving, fault-finding, reproving

reprobate *noun* **1** scoundrel, bad egg (*old-fashioned informal*), blackguard, degenerate, evildoer, miscreant, ne'er-do-well, profligate, rake, rascal, villain ♦ *adjective* **2** depraved, abandoned, bad, base, corrupt, degenerate, dissolute, immoral, sinful, wicked

reproduce *verb* **1** copy, duplicate, echo, imitate, match, mirror, recreate, repeat, replicate **2** breed, multiply, procreate, propagate, spawn

reproduction *noun* **1** breeding, generation, increase, multiplication **2** copy, duplicate, facsimile, imitation, picture, print, replica

reproof *noun* rebuke, blame, censure, condemnation, criticism, reprimand, scolding

reprove *verb* rebuke, berate, blame, censure, condemn, read the riot act, reprimand, scold, tear into (*informal*), tear (someone) off a strip (*Brit. informal*), tell off (*informal*)

repudiate *verb* reject, deny, disavow, disclaim, disown, renounce

repugnance *noun* distaste, abhorrence, aversion, disgust, dislike, hatred, loathing

repugnant *adjective* distasteful, abhorrent, disgusting, loathsome, nauseating, offensive, repellent, revolting, sickening, vile

repulse *verb* **1** drive back, beat off, fight off, rebuff, repel, ward off **2** rebuff, refuse, reject, snub, spurn, turn down

repulsion *noun* distaste, abhorrence, aversion, detestation, disgust, hatred, loathing, repugnance, revulsion

repulsive *adjective* disgusting, abhorrent, foul, loathsome, nauseating, repellent, revolting, sickening, vile

reputable *adjective* respectable, creditable, excellent, good, honourable, reliable, trustworthy, well-thought-of, worthy

reputation *noun* estimation, character, esteem, name, renown, repute, standing, stature

repute noun reputation, celebrity, distinction, eminence, fame, name, renown, standing, stature

reputed adjective supposed, alleged, believed, considered, deemed, estimated, held, reckoned, regarded

reputedly adverb supposedly, allegedly, apparently, seemingly

request verb 1 ask (for), appeal for, demand, desire, entreat, invite, seek, solicit ♦ noun 2 asking, appeal, call, demand, desire, entreaty, suit

require verb 1 need, crave, desire, lack, miss, want, wish 2 demand, ask, bid, call upon, command, compel, exact, insist upon, oblige, order

required adjective needed, called for, essential, necessary, obligatory, requisite

requirement noun necessity, demand, essential, lack, must, need, prerequisite, stipulation, want

requisite adjective 1 necessary, called for, essential, indispensable, needed, needful, obligatory, required ♦ noun 2 necessity, condition, essential, must, need, prerequisite, requirement

requisition verb 1 demand, call for, request ♦ noun 2 demand, call, request, summons

requital noun return, repayment

requite verb return, get even, give in return, pay (someone) back in his or her own coin, reciprocate, repay, respond, retaliate

rescind verb annul, cancel,

countermand, declare null and void, invalidate, repeal, set aside

rescue verb 1 save, deliver, get out, liberate, recover, redeem, release, salvage ♦ noun 2 liberation, deliverance, recovery, redemption, release, salvage, salvation, saving

research noun 1 investigation, analysis, examination, exploration, probe, study ♦ verb 2 investigate, analyse, examine, explore, probe, study

resemblance noun similarity, correspondence, kinship, likeness, parallel, sameness, similitude

resemble verb be like, bear a resemblance to, be similar to, look like, mirror, parallel

resent verb be bitter about, begrudge, grudge, object to, take exception to, take offence at

resentful adjective bitter, angry, embittered, grudging, indignant, miffed (informal), offended, piqued

resentment noun bitterness, animosity, bad blood, grudge, ill feeling, ill will, indignation, pique, rancour, umbrage

reservation noun 1 doubt, hesitancy, scruple 2 condition, proviso, qualification, rider, stipulation 3 reserve, preserve, sanctuary, territory

reserve verb 1 keep, hoard, hold, put by, retain, save, set aside, stockpile, store 2 book, engage, prearrange, secure ♦ noun 3 store, cache, fund, hoard, reservoir, savings, stock, supply 4 reservation, park, preserve, sanctuary, tract 5 shyness,

constraint, reservation, restraint, reticence, secretiveness, silence, taciturnity ♦ *adjective*
6 <u>substitute</u>, auxiliary, extra, fall-back, secondary, spare

reserved *adjective*
1 <u>uncommunicative</u>, restrained, reticent, retiring, secretive, shy, silent, standoffish, taciturn, undemonstrative 2 <u>set aside</u>, booked, engaged, held, kept, restricted, retained, spoken for, taken

reservoir *noun* 1 <u>lake</u>, basin, pond, tank 2 <u>store</u>, pool, reserves, source, stock, supply

reshuffle *noun* 1 <u>reorganization</u>, change, rearrangement, redistribution, regrouping, restructuring, revision ♦ *verb*
2 <u>reorganize</u>, change around, rearrange, redistribute, regroup, restructure, revise

reside *verb* <u>live</u>, abide, dwell, inhabit, lodge, stay

residence *noun* <u>home</u>, abode, domicile, dwelling, flat, habitation, house, lodging, place

resident *noun* <u>inhabitant</u>, citizen, local, lodger, occupant, tenant

residual *adjective* <u>remaining</u>, leftover, unconsumed, unused, vestigial

residue *noun* <u>remainder</u>, dregs, excess, extra, leftovers, remains, remnant, rest, surplus

resign *verb* 1 <u>quit</u>, abdicate, give in one's notice, leave, step down (*informal*), vacate 2 <u>give up</u>, abandon, forgo, forsake, relinquish, renounce, surrender, yield 3 **resign oneself** <u>accept</u>, acquiesce, give in, submit, succumb, yield

resignation *noun* 1 <u>leaving</u>, abandonment, abdication, departure 2 <u>endurance</u>, acceptance, acquiescence, compliance, nonresistance, passivity, patience, submission, sufferance

resigned *adjective* <u>stoical</u>, compliant, long-suffering, patient, subdued, unresisting

resilient *adjective* 1 <u>tough</u>, buoyant, hardy, irrepressible, strong 2 <u>flexible</u>, elastic, plastic, pliable, rubbery, springy, supple

resist *verb* 1 <u>oppose</u>, battle, combat, defy, hinder, stand up to 2 <u>refrain from</u>, abstain from, avoid, forbear, forgo, keep from 3 <u>withstand</u>, be proof against

resistance *noun* <u>fighting</u>, battle, defiance, fight, hindrance, impediment, obstruction, opposition, struggle

resistant *adjective* 1 <u>impervious</u>, hard, proof against, strong, tough, unaffected by 2 <u>opposed</u>, antagonistic, hostile, intractable, intransigent, unwilling

resolute *adjective* <u>determined</u>, dogged, firm, fixed, immovable, inflexible, set, steadfast, strong-willed, tenacious, unshakable, unwavering

resolution *noun*
1 <u>determination</u>, doggedness, firmness, perseverance, purpose, resoluteness, resolve, steadfastness, tenacity, willpower 2 <u>decision</u>, aim, declaration, determination, intent, intention, purpose, resolve

resolve *verb* 1 <u>decide</u>, agree, conclude, determine, fix, intend, purpose 2 <u>break down</u>, analyse,

reduce, separate **3** <u>work out</u>, answer, clear up, crack, fathom
♦ *noun* **4** <u>determination</u>, firmness, resoluteness, resolution, steadfastness, willpower **5** <u>decision</u>, intention, objective, purpose, resolution

resonant *adjective* <u>echoing</u>, booming, resounding, reverberating, ringing, sonorous

resort *verb* **1 resort to** <u>use</u>, employ, fall back on, have recourse to, turn to, utilize
♦ *noun* **2** <u>holiday centre</u>, haunt, retreat, spot, tourist centre **3** <u>recourse</u>, reference

resound *verb* <u>echo</u>, re-echo, resonate, reverberate, ring

resounding *adjective* <u>echoing</u>, booming, full, powerful, resonant, reverberating, ringing, sonorous

resource *noun* **1** <u>ingenuity</u>, ability, capability, cleverness, initiative, inventiveness **2** <u>means</u>, course, device, expedient, resort

resourceful *adjective* <u>ingenious</u>, able, bright, capable, clever, creative, inventive

resources *plural noun* <u>reserves</u>, assets, capital, funds, holdings, money, riches, supplies, wealth

respect *noun* **1** <u>regard</u>, admiration, consideration, deference, esteem, estimation, honour, recognition **2** <u>point</u>, aspect, characteristic, detail, feature, matter, particular, sense, way **3** <u>relation</u>, bearing, connection, reference, regard
♦ *verb* **4** <u>think highly of</u>, admire, defer to, esteem, have a good *or* high opinion of, honour, look up to, value **5** <u>show consideration</u>

<u>for</u>, abide by, adhere to, comply with, follow, heed, honour, obey, observe

respectable *adjective* **1** <u>honourable</u>, decent, estimable, good, honest, reputable, upright, worthy **2** <u>reasonable</u>, ample, appreciable, considerable, decent, fair, sizable *or* sizeable, substantial

respectful *adjective* <u>polite</u>, civil, courteous, deferential, mannerly, reverent, well-mannered

respective *adjective* <u>specific</u>, individual, own, particular, relevant

respite *noun* <u>pause</u>, break, cessation, halt, interval, lull, recess, relief, rest

resplendent *adjective* <u>brilliant</u>, bright, dazzling, glorious, radiant, shining, splendid

respond *verb* <u>answer</u>, counter, react, reciprocate, rejoin, reply, retort, return

response *noun* <u>answer</u>, counterattack, feedback, reaction, rejoinder, reply, retort, return

responsibility *noun* **1** <u>authority</u>, importance, power **2** <u>fault</u>, blame, culpability, guilt **3** <u>duty</u>, care, charge, liability, obligation, onus **4** <u>level-headedness</u>, conscientiousness, dependability, rationality, sensibleness, trustworthiness

responsible *adjective* **1** <u>in charge</u>, in authority, in control **2** <u>to blame</u>, at fault, culpable, guilty **3** <u>accountable</u>, answerable, liable **4** <u>sensible</u>, dependable, level-headed, rational, reliable, trustworthy

responsive adjective sensitive, alive, impressionable, open, reactive, receptive, susceptible

rest[1] noun 1 repose, calm, inactivity, leisure, relaxation, relief, stillness, tranquillity 2 pause, break, cessation, halt, interlude, intermission, interval, lull, respite, stop 3 support, base, holder, prop, stand ♦ verb 4 relax, be at ease, put one's feet up, sit down, take it easy 5 be supported, lean, lie, prop, recline, repose, sit

rest[2] noun remainder, balance, excess, others, remains, remnants, residue, surplus

restaurant noun bistro, café, cafeteria, diner (chiefly U.S. & Canad.), eatery, tearoom

restful adjective relaxing, calm, calming, peaceful, quiet, relaxed, serene, soothing, tranquil

restitution noun compensation, amends, recompense, reparation, requital

restive adjective restless, edgy, fidgety, impatient, jumpy, nervous, on edge

restless adjective 1 moving, nomadic, roving, transient, unsettled, unstable, wandering 2 unsettled, edgy, fidgeting, fidgety, jumpy, nervous, on edge, restive

restlessness noun 1 movement, activity, bustle, unrest, unsettledness 2 restiveness, edginess, jitters (informal), jumpiness, nervousness

restoration noun 1 repair, reconstruction, renewal, renovation, revitalization, revival 2 reinstatement,

re-establishment, replacement, restitution, return

restore verb 1 repair, fix, mend, rebuild, recondition, reconstruct, refurbish, renew, renovate 2 revive, build up, refresh, revitalize, strengthen 3 return, bring back, give back, hand back, recover, reinstate, replace, send back 4 reinstate, reintroduce

restrain verb hold back, check, constrain, contain, control, curb, curtail, hamper, hinder, inhibit, restrict

restrained adjective controlled, calm, mild, moderate, self-controlled, undemonstrative

restraint noun 1 self-control, control, inhibition, moderation, self-discipline, self-possession, self-restraint 2 limitation, ban, check, curb, embargo, interdict, limit, rein

restrict verb limit, bound, confine, contain, hamper, handicap, inhibit, regulate, restrain

restriction noun limitation, confinement, control, curb, handicap, inhibition, regulation, restraint, rule

result noun 1 consequence, effect, end, end result, outcome, product, sequel, upshot ♦ verb 2 happen, appear, arise, derive, develop, ensue, follow, issue, spring 3 result in end in, culminate in, finish with

resume verb begin again, carry on, continue, go on, proceed, reopen, restart

résumé noun summary, précis, recapitulation, rundown, synopsis

resumption noun <u>continuation</u>, carrying on, re-establishment, renewal, reopening, restart, resurgence

resurgence noun <u>revival</u>, rebirth, re-emergence, renaissance, resumption, resurrection, return

resurrect verb <u>revive</u>, bring back, reintroduce, renew

resurrection noun <u>revival</u>, reappearance, rebirth, renaissance, renewal, restoration, resurgence, return

resuscitate verb <u>revive</u>, bring round, resurrect, revitalize, save

retain verb 1 <u>keep</u>, hold, hold back, maintain, preserve, reserve, save 2 <u>hire</u>, commission, employ, engage, pay, reserve

retainer noun 1 <u>fee</u>, advance, deposit 2 <u>servant</u>, attendant, domestic

retaliate verb <u>pay (someone) back</u>, get even with (informal), get one's own back (informal), hit back, reciprocate, strike back, take revenge

retaliation noun <u>revenge</u>, an eye for an eye, counterblow, reciprocation, repayment, reprisal, requital, vengeance

retard verb <u>slow down</u>, arrest, check, delay, handicap, hinder, hold back or up, impede, set back

retch verb <u>gag</u>, be sick, heave, puke (slang), regurgitate, spew, throw up (informal), vomit

reticence noun <u>silence</u>, quietness, reserve, taciturnity

reticent adjective <u>uncommunicative</u>, close-lipped, quiet, reserved, silent, taciturn, tight-lipped, unforthcoming

retinue noun <u>attendants</u>, aides, entourage, escort, followers, servants

retire verb 1 <u>stop working</u>, give up work 2 <u>withdraw</u>, depart, exit, go away, leave 3 <u>go to bed</u>, hit the hay (slang), hit the sack (slang), turn in (informal)

retirement noun <u>withdrawal</u>, privacy, retreat, seclusion, solitude

retiring adjective <u>shy</u>, bashful, quiet, reserved, self-effacing, timid, unassertive, unassuming

retort verb 1 <u>reply</u>, answer, come back with, counter, respond, return, riposte ◆ noun 2 <u>reply</u>, answer, comeback (informal), rejoinder, response, riposte

retract verb 1 <u>withdraw</u>, deny, disavow, disclaim, eat one's words, recant, renege, renounce, revoke, take back 2 <u>draw in</u>, pull back, pull in, sheathe

retreat verb 1 <u>withdraw</u>, back away, back off, depart, draw back, fall back, go back, leave, pull back ◆ noun 2 <u>withdrawal</u>, departure, evacuation, flight, retirement 3 <u>refuge</u>, haven, hideaway, sanctuary, seclusion, shelter

retrench verb <u>cut back</u>, economize, make economies, save, tighten one's belt

retrenchment noun <u>cutback</u>, cost-cutting, cut, economy, tightening one's belt

retribution noun <u>punishment</u>, justice, Nemesis, reckoning, reprisal, retaliation, revenge, vengeance

retrieve verb get back, recapture, recoup, recover, redeem, regain, restore, save, win back

retrograde adjective declining, backward, degenerative, deteriorating, downward, regressive, retrogressive, worsening

retrogress verb decline, backslide, deteriorate, go back, go downhill (informal), regress, relapse, worsen

retrospect noun hindsight, re-examination, review

return verb 1 come back, go back, reappear, rebound, recur, retreat, revert, turn back 2 put back, re-establish, reinstate, replace, restore 3 give back, pay back, recompense, refund, reimburse, repay 4 reply, answer, respond, retort 5 elect, choose, vote in ♦ noun 6 restoration, re-establishment, reinstatement 7 reappearance, recurrence 8 retreat, rebound, recoil 9 profit, gain, income, interest, proceeds, revenue, takings, yield 10 report, account, form, list, statement, summary 11 reply, answer, comeback (informal), rejoinder, response, retort

revamp verb renovate, do up (informal), overhaul, recondition, refurbish, restore

reveal verb 1 make known, announce, disclose, divulge, give away, impart, let out, let slip, make public, proclaim, tell 2 show, display, exhibit, manifest, uncover, unearth, unmask, unveil

revel verb 1 celebrate, carouse, live it up (informal), make merry 2 revel in enjoy, delight in, indulge in, lap up, luxuriate in, relish, take pleasure in, thrive on ♦ noun 3 often plural merrymaking, carousal, celebration, festivity, party, spree

revelation noun disclosure, exhibition, exposé, exposure, news, proclamation, publication, uncovering, unearthing, unveiling

reveller noun carouser, partygoer

revelry noun festivity, carousal, celebration, fun, jollity, merrymaking, party, spree

revenge noun 1 retaliation, an eye for an eye, reprisal, retribution, vengeance ♦ verb 2 avenge, get even, get one's own back for (informal), hit back, repay, retaliate, take revenge for

revenue noun income, gain, proceeds, profits, receipts, returns, takings, yield

reverberate verb echo, re-echo, resound, ring, vibrate

revere verb be in awe of, exalt, honour, look up to, respect, reverence, venerate, worship

reverence noun awe, admiration, high esteem, honour, respect, veneration, worship

reverent adjective respectful, awed, deferential, humble, reverential

reverie noun daydream, abstraction, brown study, woolgathering

reverse verb 1 turn round, invert, transpose, turn back, turn over, turn upside down, upend 2 change, annul, cancel, countermand, invalidate, overrule, overthrow, overturn, quash, repeal, rescind, revoke, undo **3** go backwards, back, back up, move backwards, retreat ♦ *noun* **4** opposite, contrary, converse, inverse **5** back, other side, rear, underside, wrong side **6** misfortune, adversity, affliction, blow, disappointment, failure, hardship, misadventure, mishap, reversal, setback ♦ *adjective* **7** opposite, contrary, converse

revert *verb* return, come back, go back, resume

review *noun* **1** critique, commentary, criticism, evaluation, judgment, notice **2** magazine, journal, periodical **3** survey, analysis, examination, scrutiny, study **4** *Military* inspection, march past, parade ♦ *verb* **5** assess, criticize, evaluate, judge, study **6** reconsider, reassess, re-evaluate, re-examine, rethink, revise, think over **7** look back on, recall, recollect, reflect on, remember **8** inspect, examine

reviewer *noun* critic, commentator, judge

revile *verb* malign, abuse, bad-mouth (*slang, chiefly U.S. & Canad.*), denigrate, knock (*informal*), reproach, run down, slag (off) (*slang*), vilify

revise *verb* **1** change, alter, amend, correct, edit, emend, redo, review, rework, update **2** study, go over, run through, swot up (*Brit. informal*)

revision *noun* **1** change, amendment, correction, emendation, updating

2 studying, homework, swotting (*Brit. informal*)

revival *noun* renewal, reawakening, rebirth, renaissance, resurgence, resurrection, revitalization

revive *verb* revitalize, awaken, bring round, come round, invigorate, reanimate, recover, refresh, rekindle, renew, restore

revoke *verb* cancel, annul, countermand, disclaim, invalidate, negate, nullify, obviate, quash, repeal, rescind, retract, reverse, set aside, withdraw

revolt *noun* **1** uprising, insurgency, insurrection, mutiny, rebellion, revolution, rising ♦ *verb* **2** rebel, mutiny, resist, rise **3** disgust, gross out (*U.S. slang*), make one's flesh creep, nauseate, repel, repulse, sicken, turn one's stomach

revolting *adjective* disgusting, foul, horrible, horrid, nauseating, repellent, repugnant, repulsive, sickening, yucky or yukky (*slang*)

revolution *noun* **1** revolt, coup, insurgency, mutiny, rebellion, rising, uprising **2** transformation, innovation, reformation, sea change, shift, upheaval **3** rotation, circle, circuit, cycle, lap, orbit, spin, turn

revolutionary *adjective* **1** rebel, extremist, insurgent, radical, subversive **2** new, different, drastic, ground-breaking, innovative, novel, progressive, radical ♦ *noun* **3** rebel, insurgent, revolutionist

revolutionize *verb* transform, modernize, reform

revolve *verb* <u>rotate</u>, circle, go round, orbit, spin, turn, twist, wheel, whirl

revulsion *noun* <u>disgust</u>, abhorrence, detestation, loathing, repugnance, repulsion

reward *noun* 1 <u>payment</u>, bonus, bounty, premium, prize, recompense, repayment, return, wages 2 <u>punishment</u>, comeuppance (*slang*), just deserts, retribution ♦ *verb* 3 <u>pay</u>, compensate, recompense, remunerate, repay

rewarding *adjective* <u>worthwhile</u>, beneficial, enriching, fruitful, fulfilling, productive, profitable, satisfying, valuable

rhapsodize *verb* <u>enthuse</u>, go into ecstasies, gush, rave (*informal*)

rhetoric *noun* 1 <u>oratory</u>, eloquence 2 <u>hyperbole</u>, bombast, grandiloquence, magniloquence, verbosity, wordiness

rhetorical *adjective* <u>oratorical</u>, bombastic, declamatory, grandiloquent, high-flown, magniloquent, verbose

rhyme *noun* 1 <u>poetry</u>, ode, poem, song, verse ♦ *verb* 2 <u>sound like</u>, harmonize

rhythm *noun* <u>beat</u>, accent, cadence, lilt, metre, pulse, swing, tempo, time

rhythmic, rhythmical *adjective* <u>cadenced</u>, lilting, metrical, musical, periodic, pulsating, throbbing

ribald *adjective* <u>rude</u>, bawdy, blue, broad, coarse, earthy, naughty, near the knuckle

(*informal*), obscene, racy, smutty, vulgar

rich *adjective* 1 <u>wealthy</u>, affluent, loaded (*slang*), moneyed, prosperous, well-heeled (*informal*), well-off, well-to-do 2 <u>well-stocked</u>, full, productive, well-supplied 3 <u>abundant</u>, abounding, ample, copious, fertile, fruitful, lush, luxurious, plentiful, productive, prolific 4 <u>full-bodied</u>, creamy, fatty, luscious, succulent, sweet, tasty

riches *plural noun* <u>wealth</u>, affluence, assets, fortune, plenty, resources, substance, treasure

richly *adverb* 1 <u>elaborately</u>, elegantly, expensively, exquisitely, gorgeously, lavishly, luxuriously, opulently, splendidly, sumptuously 2 <u>fully</u>, amply, appropriately, properly, suitably, thoroughly, well

rickety *adjective* <u>shaky</u>, insecure, precarious, ramshackle, tottering, unsound, unsteady, wobbly

rid *verb* 1 <u>free</u>, clear, deliver, disburden, disencumber, make free, purge, relieve, unburden 2 **get rid of** <u>dispose of</u>, dump, eject, eliminate, expel, remove, throw away *or* out

riddle *noun* <u>puzzle</u>, conundrum, enigma, mystery, poser, problem

riddled *adjective* <u>filled</u>, damaged, infested, permeated, pervaded, spoilt

ride *verb* 1 <u>control</u>, handle, manage 2 <u>travel</u>, be carried, go, move ♦ *noun* 3 <u>trip</u>, drive, jaunt, journey, lift, outing

ridicule *noun* 1 <u>mockery</u>, chaff, derision, gibe, jeer, laughter, raillery, scorn ♦ *verb* 2 <u>laugh at</u>, chaff, deride, jeer, make fun of, mock, poke fun at, sneer

ridiculous adjective <u>laughable</u>, absurd, comical, farcical, funny, ludicrous, risible, silly, stupid

rife adjective <u>widespread</u>, common, frequent, general, prevalent, rampant, ubiquitous, universal

riffraff noun <u>rabble</u>, hoi polloi, ragtag and bobtail

rifle verb <u>ransack</u>, burgle, go through, loot, pillage, plunder, rob, sack, strip

rift noun 1 <u>breach</u>, disagreement, division, falling out (*informal*), quarrel, separation, split 2 <u>split</u>, break, cleft, crack, crevice, fault, fissure, flaw, gap, opening

rig verb 1 <u>fix</u> (*informal*), arrange, engineer, gerrymander, manipulate, tamper with 2 <u>equip</u>, fit out, furnish, kit out, outfit, supply ♦ noun 3 <u>apparatus</u>, equipment, fittings, fixtures, gear, tackle

right adjective 1 <u>just</u>, equitable, ethical, fair, good, honest, lawful, moral, proper 2 <u>correct</u>, accurate, exact, factual, genuine, precise, true, valid 3 <u>proper</u>, appropriate, becoming, desirable, done, fit, fitting, seemly, suitable ♦ adverb 4 <u>correctly</u>, accurately, exactly, genuinely, precisely, truly 5 <u>properly</u>, appropriately, aptly, fittingly, suitably 6 <u>straight</u>, directly, promptly, quickly, straightaway 7 <u>exactly</u>, precisely, squarely ♦ noun 8 <u>claim</u>, authority, business, due, freedom, liberty, licence, permission, power, prerogative,

privilege ♦ verb 9 <u>rectify</u>, correct, fix, put right, redress, settle, sort out, straighten

right away adverb <u>immediately</u>, at once, directly, forthwith, instantly, now, pronto (*informal*), straightaway

righteous adjective <u>virtuous</u>, ethical, fair, good, honest, honourable, just, moral, pure, upright

righteousness noun <u>virtue</u>, goodness, honesty, honour, integrity, justice, morality, probity, purity, rectitude, uprightness

rightful adjective <u>lawful</u>, due, just, legal, legitimate, proper, real, true, valid

rigid adjective 1 <u>strict</u>, exact, fixed, inflexible, rigorous, set, stringent, unbending, uncompromising 2 <u>stiff</u>, inflexible, unyielding

rigmarole noun <u>procedure</u>, bother, carry-on (*informal, chiefly Brit.*), fuss, hassle (*informal*), nonsense, palaver, pantomime (*informal*), performance (*informal*)

rigorous adjective <u>strict</u>, demanding, exacting, hard, harsh, inflexible, severe, stern, stringent, tough

rigour noun 1 <u>strictness</u>, harshness, inflexibility, rigidity, sternness, stringency 2 <u>hardship</u>, ordeal, privation, suffering, trial

rig-out noun <u>outfit</u>, costume, dress, garb, gear (*informal*), get-up (*informal*), togs

rig out verb 1 <u>dress</u>, array, attire, clothe, costume, kit out 2 <u>equip</u>, fit, furnish, kit out, outfit

rig up verb set up, arrange, assemble, build, construct, erect, fix up, improvise, put together, put up

rile verb anger, aggravate (informal), annoy, get or put one's back up, irk, irritate

rim noun edge, border, brim, brink, lip, margin, verge

rind noun skin, crust, husk, outer layer, peel

ring¹ verb 1 chime, clang, peal, reverberate, sound, toll 2 phone, buzz (informal), call, telephone ◆ noun 3 chime, knell, peal 4 call, buzz (informal), phone call

ring² noun 1 circle, band, circuit, halo, hoop, loop, round 2 arena, circus, enclosure, rink 3 gang, association, band, cartel, circle, group, mob, syndicate ◆ verb 4 encircle, enclose, gird, girdle, surround

rinse verb 1 wash, bathe, clean, cleanse, dip, splash ◆ noun 2 wash, bath, dip, splash

riot noun 1 disturbance, anarchy, confusion, disorder, lawlessness, strife, tumult, turbulence, turmoil, upheaval 2 revelry, carousal, festivity, frolic, high jinks, merrymaking 3 profusion, display, extravaganza, show, splash 4 run riot: a rampage, be out of control, go wild b grow profusely, spread like wildfire ◆ verb 5 rampage, go on the rampage, run riot

riotous adjective 1 unrestrained, boisterous, loud, noisy, uproarious, wild 2 unruly, anarchic, disorderly, lawless, rebellious, rowdy, ungovernable, violent

rip verb 1 tear, burst, claw, cut, gash, lacerate, rend, slash, slit, split ◆ noun 2 tear, cut, gash, hole, laceration, rent, slash, slit, split

ripe adjective 1 mature, mellow, ready, ripened, seasoned 2 suitable, auspicious, favourable, ideal, opportune, right, timely

ripen verb mature, burgeon, develop, grow ripe, season

rip-off noun swindle, cheat, con (informal), con trick (informal), fraud, scam (slang), theft

rip off verb Slang swindle, cheat, con (informal), defraud, fleece, rob, skin (slang)

riposte noun 1 retort, answer, comeback (informal), rejoinder, reply, response, sally ◆ verb 2 retort, answer, come back, reply, respond

rise verb 1 get up, arise, get to one's feet, stand up 2 go up, ascend, climb 3 advance, get on, progress, prosper 4 get steeper, ascend, go uphill, slope upwards 5 increase, go up, grow, intensify, mount 6 rebel, mutiny, revolt 7 originate, happen, issue, occur, spring ◆ noun 8 increase, upsurge, upswing, upturn 9 advancement, climb, progress, promotion 10 upward slope, ascent, elevation, incline 11 pay increase, increment, raise (U.S.) 12 give rise to cause, bring about, effect, produce, result in

risk noun 1 danger, chance, gamble, hazard, jeopardy, peril, pitfall, possibility ◆ verb 2 dare, chance, endanger, gamble, hazard, imperil, jeopardize, venture

risky *adjective* <u>dangerous</u>, chancy (*informal*), dicey (*informal, chiefly Brit.*), dodgy (*Brit., Austral., & N.Z. informal*), hazardous, perilous, uncertain, unsafe

risqué *adjective* <u>suggestive</u>, bawdy, blue, improper, indelicate, naughty, near the knuckle (*informal*), racy, ribald

rite *noun* <u>ceremony</u>, custom, observance, practice, procedure, ritual

ritual *noun* 1 <u>ceremony</u>, observance, rite 2 <u>custom</u>, convention, habit, practice, procedure, protocol, routine, tradition ♦ *adjective* 3 <u>ceremonial</u>, conventional, customary, habitual, routine

ritzy *adjective* <u>luxurious</u>, de luxe, grand, high-class, luxury, plush (*informal*), posh (*informal, chiefly Brit.*), sumptuous, swanky (*informal*)

rival *noun* 1 <u>opponent</u>, adversary, competitor, contender, contestant ♦ *adjective* 2 <u>competing</u>, conflicting, opposing ♦ *verb* 3 <u>equal</u>, be a match for, come up to, compare with, compete, match

rivalry *noun* <u>competition</u>, conflict, contention, contest, opposition

river *noun* 1 <u>stream</u>, brook, burn (*Scot.*), creek, tributary, waterway 2 <u>flow</u>, flood, rush, spate, torrent

riveting *adjective* <u>enthralling</u>, absorbing, captivating, engrossing, fascinating, gripping, hypnotic, spellbinding

road *noun* <u>way</u>, course, highway, lane, motorway, path, pathway, roadway, route, track

roam *verb* <u>wander</u>, prowl, ramble, range, rove, stray, travel, walk

roar *verb* 1 <u>cry</u>, bawl, bay, bellow, howl, shout, yell 2 <u>guffaw</u>, hoot, laugh heartily, split one's sides (*informal*) ♦ *noun* 3 <u>cry</u>, bellow, howl, outcry, shout, yell 4 <u>guffaw</u>, hoot

rob *verb* <u>steal from</u>, burgle, cheat, con (*informal*), defraud, deprive, dispossess, do out of (*informal*), hold up, loot, mug (*informal*), pillage, plunder, raid

robber *noun* <u>thief</u>, bandit, brigand, burglar, cheat, con man (*informal*), fraud, looter, mugger (*informal*), plunderer, raider

robbery *noun* <u>theft</u>, burglary, hold-up, larceny, mugging (*informal*), pillage, plunder, raid, rip-off (*slang*), stealing, stick-up (*slang, chiefly U.S.*), swindle

robe *noun* 1 <u>gown</u>, costume, habit ♦ *verb* 2 <u>clothe</u>, dress, garb

robot *noun* <u>machine</u>, android, automaton, mechanical man

robust *adjective* <u>strong</u>, fit, hale, hardy, healthy, muscular, powerful, stout, strapping, sturdy, tough, vigorous

rock¹ *noun* <u>stone</u>, boulder

rock² *verb* 1 <u>sway</u>, lurch, pitch, reel, roll, swing, toss 2 <u>shock</u>, astonish, astound, shake, stagger, stun, surprise

rocky¹ *adjective* <u>rough</u>, craggy, rugged, stony

rocky² *adjective* <u>unstable</u>, rickety,

shaky, unsteady, wobbly

rod *noun* <u>stick</u>, bar, baton, cane, pole, shaft, staff, wand

rogue *noun* <u>scoundrel</u>, blackguard, crook (*informal*), fraud, rascal, scally (*Northwest English dialect*), scamp, villain

role *noun* **1** <u>job</u>, capacity, duty, function, part, position, post, task **2** <u>part</u>, character, portrayal, representation

roll *verb* **1** <u>turn</u>, go round, revolve, rotate, spin, swivel, trundle, twirl, wheel, whirl **2** <u>wind</u>, bind, enfold, envelop, furl, swathe, wrap **3** <u>flow</u>, run, undulate **4** <u>level</u>, even, flatten, press, smooth **5** <u>tumble</u>, lurch, reel, rock, sway, toss ♦ *noun* **6** <u>turn</u>, cycle, reel, revolution, rotation, spin, twirl, wheel, whirl **7** <u>register</u>, census, index, list, record **8** <u>rumble</u>, boom, reverberation, roar, thunder

rollicking *adjective* <u>boisterous</u>, carefree, devil-may-care, exuberant, hearty, jaunty, lively, playful

roly-poly *adjective* <u>plump</u>, buxom, chubby, fat, podgy, rounded, tubby

romance *noun* **1** <u>love affair</u>, affair, amour, attachment, liaison, relationship **2** <u>excitement</u>, charm, colour, fascination, glamour, mystery **3** <u>story</u>, fairy tale, fantasy, legend, love story, melodrama, tale

romantic *adjective* **1** <u>loving</u>, amorous, fond, passionate, sentimental, tender **2** <u>idealistic</u>, dreamy, impractical, starry-eyed, unrealistic **3** <u>exciting</u>, colourful,

fascinating, glamorous, mysterious ♦ *noun* **4** <u>idealist</u>, dreamer, sentimentalist

romp *verb* **1** <u>frolic</u>, caper, cavort, frisk, gambol, have fun, sport **2** <u>win easily</u>, walk it (*informal*), win by a mile (*informal*), win hands down ♦ *noun* **3** <u>frolic</u>, caper, lark (*informal*)

room *noun* **1** <u>chamber</u>, apartment, office **2** <u>space</u>, area, capacity, expanse, extent, leeway, margin, range, scope **3** <u>opportunity</u>, chance, occasion, scope

roomy *adjective* <u>spacious</u>, ample, broad, capacious, commodious, extensive, generous, large, sizable *or* sizeable, wide

root¹ *noun* **1** <u>stem</u>, rhizome, tuber **2** <u>source</u>, base, bottom, cause, core, foundation, heart, nucleus, origin, seat, seed **3 roots** <u>sense of belonging</u>, birthplace, cradle, family, heritage, home, origins ♦ *verb* **4** <u>establish</u>, anchor, fasten, fix, ground, implant, moor, set, stick

root² *verb* <u>dig</u>, burrow, ferret

rooted *adjective* <u>deep-seated</u>, confirmed, deep, deeply felt, entrenched, established, firm, fixed, ingrained

root out *verb* <u>get rid of</u>, abolish, do away with, eliminate, eradicate, exterminate, extirpate, remove, weed out

rope *noun* **1** <u>cord</u>, cable, hawser, line, strand **2 know the ropes** <u>be experienced</u>, be an old hand, be knowledgeable

rope in *verb* <u>persuade</u>, engage, enlist, inveigle, involve, talk into

ropey, ropy *adjective Informal*
1 <u>inferior</u>, deficient, inadequate, of poor quality, poor, substandard 2 <u>unwell</u>, below par, off colour, under the weather (*informal*)

roster *noun* <u>rota</u>, agenda, catalogue, list, register, roll, schedule, table

rostrum *noun* <u>stage</u>, dais, platform, podium, stand

rosy *adjective* 1 <u>pink</u>, red 2 <u>glowing</u>, blooming, healthy-looking, radiant, ruddy 3 <u>promising</u>, auspicious, bright, cheerful, encouraging, favourable, hopeful, optimistic

rot *verb* 1 <u>decay</u>, crumble, decompose, deteriorate, go bad, moulder, perish, putrefy, spoil 2 <u>deteriorate</u>, decline, waste away ♦*noun* 3 <u>decay</u>, blight, canker, corruption, decomposition, mould, putrefaction 4 *Informal* <u>nonsense</u>, claptrap (*informal*), codswallop (*Brit. slang*), drivel, garbage (*chiefly U.S.*), hogwash, poppycock (*informal*), rubbish, stuff and nonsense, trash, tripe (*informal*), twaddle

rotary *adjective* <u>revolving</u>, rotating, spinning, turning

rotate *verb* 1 <u>revolve</u>, go round, gyrate, pivot, reel, spin, swivel, turn, wheel 2 <u>take turns</u>, alternate, switch

rotation *noun* 1 <u>revolution</u>, orbit, reel, spin, spinning, turn, turning, wheel 2 <u>sequence</u>, alternation, cycle, succession, switching

rotten *adjective* 1 <u>decaying</u>, bad, corrupt, crumbling, decomposing, festering, mouldy, perished, putrescent, rank, sour, stinking 2 <u>corrupt</u>, crooked (*informal*), dishonest, dishonourable, immoral, perfidious 3 *Informal* <u>despicable</u>, base, contemptible, dirty, mean, nasty 4 *Informal* <u>inferior</u>, crummy (*slang*), duff (*Brit. informal*), inadequate, lousy (*slang*), poor, substandard, unsatisfactory

rotter *noun* <u>scoundrel</u>, blackguard, bounder (*old-fashioned Brit. slang*), cad (*Brit. informal*), rat (*informal*)

rotund *adjective* 1 <u>round</u>, globular, rounded, spherical 2 <u>plump</u>, chubby, corpulent, fat, fleshy, podgy, portly, stout, tubby

rough *adjective* 1 <u>uneven</u>, broken, bumpy, craggy, irregular, jagged, rocky, stony 2 <u>ungracious</u>, blunt, brusque, coarse, impolite, rude, unceremonious, uncivil, uncouth, unmannerly 3 <u>approximate</u>, estimated, general, imprecise, inexact, sketchy, vague 4 <u>stormy</u>, choppy, squally, turbulent, wild 5 <u>nasty</u>, cruel, hard, harsh, tough, unfeeling, unpleasant, violent 6 <u>basic</u>, crude, imperfect, incomplete, rudimentary, sketchy, unfinished, unpolished, unrefined 7 <u>unpleasant</u>, arduous, hard, tough, uncomfortable ♦*verb* 8 <u>rough out</u> outline, draft, plan, sketch ♦*noun* 9 <u>outline</u>, draft, mock-up, preliminary sketch

rough-and-ready *adjective* <u>makeshift</u>, crude, improvised, provisional, sketchy, stopgap, unpolished, unrefined

round *adjective* **1** spherical, circular, curved, cylindrical, globular, rotund, rounded **2** plump, ample, fleshy, full, full-fleshed, rotund ♦ *verb* **3** go round, bypass, circle, encircle, flank, skirt, turn ♦ *noun* **4** sphere, ball, band, circle, disc, globe, orb, ring **5** stage, division, lap, level, period, session, turn **6** series, cycle, sequence, session, succession **7** course, beat, circuit, routine, schedule, series, tour

roundabout *adjective* indirect, circuitous, devious, discursive, evasive, oblique, tortuous

round off *verb* complete, close, conclude, finish off

roundup *noun* gathering, assembly, collection, herding, marshalling, muster, rally

round up *verb* gather, collect, drive, group, herd, marshal, muster, rally

rouse *verb* **1** wake up, awaken, call, rise, wake **2** excite, agitate, anger, animate, incite, inflame, move, provoke, stimulate, stir

rousing *adjective* lively, exciting, inspiring, moving, spirited, stimulating, stirring

rout *noun* **1** defeat, beating, debacle, drubbing, overthrow, pasting (*slang*), thrashing ♦ *verb* **2** defeat, beat, conquer, crush, destroy, drub, overthrow, thrash, wipe the floor with (*informal*)

route *noun* way, beat, circuit, course, direction, itinerary, journey, path, road

routine *noun* **1** procedure, custom, method, order, pattern, practice, programme ♦ *adjective* **2** usual, customary, everyday, habitual, normal, ordinary, standard, typical **3** boring, dull, humdrum, predictable, tedious, tiresome

rove *verb* wander, drift, ramble, range, roam, stray, traipse (*informal*)

row[1] *noun* line, bank, column, file, range, series, string

row[2] *noun* **1** dispute, brawl, quarrel, squabble, tiff, trouble **2** disturbance, commotion, noise, racket, rumpus, tumult, uproar ♦ *verb* **3** quarrel, argue, dispute, fight, squabble, wrangle

rowdy *adjective* **1** disorderly, loud, noisy, rough, unruly, wild ♦ *noun* **2** hooligan, lout, ruffian, tearaway (*Brit.*), yob *or* yobbo (*Brit. slang*)

royal *adjective* **1** regal, imperial, kingly, princely, queenly, sovereign **2** splendid, grand, impressive, magnificent, majestic, stately

rub *verb* **1** polish, clean, scour, shine, wipe **2** chafe, abrade, fray, grate, scrape ♦ *noun* **3** polish, shine, stroke, wipe **4** massage, caress, kneading

rubbish *noun* **1** waste, garbage (*chiefly U.S.*), junk (*informal*), litter, lumber, refuse, scrap, trash **2** nonsense, claptrap (*informal*), codswallop (*Brit. slang*), garbage (*chiefly U.S.*), hogwash, hot air (*informal*), rot, tommyrot, trash, tripe (*informal*), twaddle

rub out *verb* erase, cancel, delete, efface, obliterate, remove, wipe out

ructions *plural noun Informal* <u>uproar</u>, commotion, disturbance, fracas, fuss, hue and cry, row, trouble

ruddy *adjective* <u>rosy</u>, blooming, fresh, glowing, healthy, radiant, red, reddish, rosy-cheeked

rude *adjective* **1** <u>impolite</u>, abusive, cheeky, discourteous, disrespectful, ill-mannered, impertinent, impudent, insolent, insulting, uncivil, unmannerly **2** <u>vulgar</u>, boorish, brutish, coarse, graceless, loutish, oafish, rough, uncivilized, uncouth, uncultured **3** <u>unpleasant</u>, abrupt, harsh, sharp, startling, sudden **4** <u>roughly-made</u>, artless, crude, inartistic, inelegant, makeshift, primitive, raw, rough, simple

rudimentary *adjective* <u>basic</u>, early, elementary, fundamental, initial, primitive, undeveloped

rudiments *plural noun* <u>basics</u>, beginnings, elements, essentials, foundation, fundamentals

rue *verb* <u>regret</u>, be sorry for, kick oneself for, lament, mourn, repent

rueful *adjective* <u>regretful</u>, contrite, mournful, penitent, remorseful, repentant, sorrowful, sorry

ruffian *noun* <u>thug</u>, brute, bully, heavy (*slang*), hoodlum, hooligan, rough (*informal*), tough

ruffle *verb* **1** <u>disarrange</u>, dishevel, disorder, mess up, rumple, tousle **2** <u>annoy</u>, agitate, fluster, irritate, nettle, peeve (*informal*), upset

rugged *adjective* **1** <u>rough</u>, broken, bumpy, craggy, difficult, irregular, jagged, ragged, rocky, uneven **2** <u>strong-featured</u>,

rough-hewn, weather-beaten **3** <u>tough</u>, brawny, burly, husky (*informal*), muscular, robust, strong, sturdy, well-built

ruin *verb* **1** <u>destroy</u>, crush, defeat, demolish, devastate, lay waste, smash, wreck **2** <u>bankrupt</u>, impoverish, pauperize **3** <u>spoil</u>, blow (*slang*), botch, damage, make a mess of, mess up, screw up (*informal*) ♦ *noun* **4** <u>destruction</u>, breakdown, collapse, defeat, devastation, downfall, fall, undoing, wreck **5** <u>disrepair</u>, decay, disintegration, ruination, wreckage **6** <u>bankruptcy</u>, destitution, insolvency

ruinous *adjective* **1** <u>devastating</u>, calamitous, catastrophic, destructive, dire, disastrous, shattering **2** <u>extravagant</u>, crippling, immoderate, wasteful

rule *noun* **1** <u>regulation</u>, axiom, canon, decree, direction, guideline, law, maxim, precept, principle, tenet **2** <u>custom</u>, convention, habit, practice, procedure, routine, tradition **3** <u>government</u>, authority, command, control, dominion, jurisdiction, mastery, power, regime, reign **4 as a rule** <u>usually</u>, generally, mainly, normally, on the whole, ordinarily ♦ *verb* **5** <u>govern</u>, be in authority, be in power, command, control, direct, reign **6** <u>be prevalent</u>, be customary, predominate, preponderate, prevail **7** <u>decree</u>, decide, judge, pronounce, settle

rule out *verb* <u>exclude</u>, ban, debar, dismiss, disqualify, eliminate, leave out, preclude, prohibit, reject

ruler noun **1** <u>governor</u>, commander, controller, head of state, king or queen, leader, lord, monarch, potentate, sovereign **2** <u>measure</u>, rule, yardstick

ruling noun **1** <u>decision</u>, adjudication, decree, judgment, pronouncement, verdict
♦ adjective **2** <u>governing</u>, commanding, controlling, reigning **3** <u>predominant</u>, chief, dominant, main, pre-eminent, preponderant, prevailing, principal

ruminate verb <u>ponder</u>, cogitate, consider, contemplate, deliberate, mull over, muse, reflect, think, turn over in one's mind

rummage verb <u>search</u>, delve, forage, hunt, ransack, root

rumour noun <u>story</u>, buzz, dirt (U.S. slang), gossip, hearsay, news, report, talk, whisper, word

rump noun <u>buttocks</u>, backside (informal), bottom, bum (Brit. slang), buns (U.S. slang), butt (U.S. & Canad. informal), derrière (euphemistic), hindquarters, posterior, rear, rear end, seat

rumpus noun <u>commotion</u>, disturbance, furore, fuss, hue and cry, noise, row, uproar

run verb **1** <u>race</u>, bolt, dash, gallop, hare (Brit. informal), hurry, jog, leg it (informal), lope, rush, scurry, sprint **2** <u>flee</u>, beat a retreat, beat it (slang), bolt, do a runner (slang), escape, leg it (informal), make a run for it, take flight, take off (informal), take to one's heels **3** <u>move</u>, course, glide, go, pass, roll, skim **4** <u>work</u>, function, go, operate, perform

5 <u>manage</u>, administer, be in charge of, control, direct, handle, head, lead, operate **6** <u>continue</u>, extend, go, proceed, reach, stretch **7** <u>flow</u>, discharge, go, gush, leak, pour, spill, spout, stream **8** <u>melt</u>, dissolve, go soft, liquefy **9** <u>publish</u>, display, feature, print **10** <u>compete</u>, be a candidate, contend, put oneself up for, stand, take part **11** <u>smuggle</u>, bootleg, traffic in
♦ noun **12** <u>race</u>, dash, gallop, jog, rush, sprint, spurt **13** <u>ride</u>, drive, excursion, jaunt, outing, spin (informal), trip **14** <u>sequence</u>, course, period, season, series, spell, stretch, string **15** <u>enclosure</u>, coop, pen **16 in the long run** <u>eventually</u>, in the end, ultimately

run across verb <u>meet</u>, bump into, come across, encounter, run into

runaway noun **1** <u>fugitive</u>, deserter, escapee, refugee, truant ♦ adjective **2** <u>escaped</u>, fleeing, fugitive, loose, wild

run away verb <u>flee</u>, abscond, bolt, do a runner (slang), escape, fly the coop (U.S. & Canad. informal), make a run for it, scram (informal), take to one's heels

run-down adjective **1** <u>exhausted</u>, below par, debilitated, drained, enervated, unhealthy, weak, weary, worn-out **2** <u>dilapidated</u>, broken-down, decrepit, ramshackle, seedy, shabby, worn-out

run down verb **1** <u>criticize</u>, bad-mouth (slang, chiefly U.S. & Canad.), belittle, decry, denigrate, disparage, knock (*informal*), rubbish (*informal*), slag (off) (*slang*) **2** <u>reduce</u>, curtail, cut, cut back, decrease, downsize, trim **3** <u>knock down</u>, hit, knock over, run into, run over **4** <u>weaken</u>, debilitate, exhaust

run into *verb* **1** <u>meet</u>, bump into, come across *or* upon, encounter, run across **2** <u>hit</u>, collide with, strike

runner *noun* **1** <u>athlete</u>, jogger, sprinter **2** <u>messenger</u>, courier, dispatch bearer, errand boy

running *adjective* **1** <u>continuous</u>, constant, incessant, perpetual, unbroken, uninterrupted **2** <u>flowing</u>, moving, streaming ◆ *noun* **3** <u>management</u>, administration, control, direction, leadership, organization, supervision **4** <u>working</u>, functioning, maintenance, operation, performance

runny *adjective* <u>flowing</u>, fluid, liquefied, liquid, melted, watery

run off *verb* <u>flee</u>, bolt, do a runner (*slang*), escape, fly the coop (*U.S. & Canad. informal*), make off, run away, take flight, take to one's heels

run-of-the-mill *adjective* <u>ordinary</u>, average, bog-standard (*Brit. & Irish slang*), mediocre, middling, passable, tolerable, undistinguished, unexceptional

run out *verb* <u>be used up</u>, be exhausted, dry up, end, fail, finish, give out

run over *verb* **1** <u>knock down</u>, hit, knock over, run down **2** <u>go through</u>, check, go over, rehearse, run through

rupture *noun* **1** <u>break</u>, breach, burst, crack, fissure, rent, split, tear ◆ *verb* **2** <u>break</u>, burst, crack, separate, sever, split, tear

rural *adjective* <u>rustic</u>, agricultural, country, pastoral, sylvan

ruse *noun* <u>trick</u>, device, dodge, hoax, manoeuvre, ploy, stratagem, subterfuge

rush *verb* **1** <u>hurry</u>, bolt, career, dash, fly, hasten, race, run, shoot, speed, press **3** <u>attack</u>, charge, storm ◆ *noun* **4** <u>hurry</u>, charge, dash, haste, race, scramble, stampede, surge **5** <u>attack</u>, assault, charge, onslaught ◆ *adjective* **6** <u>hasty</u>, fast, hurried, quick, rapid, swift, urgent

rust *noun* **1** <u>corrosion</u>, oxidation **2** <u>mildew</u>, blight, mould, must, rot ◆ *verb* **3** <u>corrode</u>, oxidize

rustic *adjective* **1** <u>rural</u>, country, pastoral, sylvan **2** <u>uncouth</u>, awkward, coarse, crude, rough ◆ *noun* **3** <u>yokel</u>, boor, bumpkin, clod, clodhopper (*informal*), hick (*informal, chiefly U.S. & Canad.*), peasant

rustle *verb* **1** <u>crackle</u>, crinkle, whisper ◆ *noun* **2** <u>crackle</u>, crinkling, rustling, whisper

rusty *adjective* **1** <u>corroded</u>, oxidized, rust-covered, rusted **2** <u>reddish</u>, chestnut, coppery, reddish-brown, russet, rust-coloured **3** <u>out of practice</u>, stale, unpractised, weak

rut *noun* **1** <u>groove</u>, furrow, indentation, track, trough, wheel mark **2** <u>habit</u>, dead end, pattern, routine, system

ruthless adjective merciless, brutal, callous, cruel, harsh, heartless, pitiless, relentless, remorseless

S s

sabotage noun 1 damage, destruction, disruption, subversion, wrecking ◆ verb 2 damage, destroy, disable, disrupt, incapacitate, subvert, vandalize, wreck

saccharine adjective oversweet, cloying, honeyed, nauseating, sickly

sack[1] noun 1 the sack dismissal, discharge, the axe (informal), the boot (slang), the push (slang) ◆ verb 2 dismiss, axe (informal), discharge, fire (informal), give (someone) the push (informal)

sack[2] noun 1 plundering, looting, pillage ◆ verb 2 plunder, loot, pillage, raid, rob, ruin, strip

sacred adjective 1 holy, blessed, divine, hallowed, revered, sanctified 2 religious, ecclesiastical, holy 3 inviolable, protected, sacrosanct

sacrifice noun 1 surrender, loss, renunciation 2 offering, oblation ◆ verb 3 give up, forego, forfeit, let go, lose, say goodbye to, surrender 4 offer, immolate, offer up

sacrilege noun desecration, blasphemy, heresy, impiety, irreverence, profanation, violation

sacrilegious adjective profane, blasphemous, desecrating, impious, irreligious, irreverent

sacrosanct adjective inviolable, hallowed, inviolate, sacred, sanctified, set apart, untouchable

sad adjective 1 unhappy, blue, dejected, depressed, doleful, down, low, low-spirited, melancholy, mournful, woebegone 2 tragic, depressing, dismal, grievous, harrowing, heart-rending, moving, pathetic, pitiful, poignant, upsetting 3 deplorable, bad, lamentable, sorry, wretched

sadden verb upset, deject, depress, distress, grieve, make sad

saddle verb burden, encumber, load, lumber (Brit. informal)

sadistic adjective cruel, barbarous, brutal, ruthless, vicious

sadness noun unhappiness, dejection, depression, despondency, grief, melancholy, misery, poignancy, sorrow, the blues

safe adjective 1 secure, impregnable, in safe hands, out of danger, out of harm's way, protected, safe and sound 2 unharmed, all right, intact, O.K. or okay (informal), undamaged, unhurt, unscathed 3 risk-free, certain, impregnable, secure, sound ◆ noun 4 strongbox, coffer, deposit box, repository, safe-deposit box, vault

safeguard verb 1 protect, defend, guard, look after, preserve ◆ noun 2 protection, defence, guard, security

safely adverb in safety, in one piece, safe and sound, with impunity, without risk

safety noun 1 security,

impregnability, protection
2 <u>shelter</u>, cover, refuge, sanctuary

sag *verb* **1** <u>sink</u>, bag, dip, droop, fall, give way, hang loosely, slump **2** <u>tire</u>, droop, flag, wane, weaken, wilt

saga *noun* <u>tale</u>, epic, narrative, story, yarn

sage *noun* **1** <u>wise man</u>, elder, guru, master, philosopher
♦ *adjective* **2** <u>wise</u>, judicious, sagacious, sapient, sensible

sail *verb* **1** <u>embark</u>, set sail **2** <u>glide</u>, drift, float, fly, skim, soar, sweep, wing **3** <u>pilot</u>, steer

sailor *noun* <u>mariner</u>, marine, sea dog, seafarer, seaman

saintly *adjective* <u>virtuous</u>, godly, holy, pious, religious, righteous, saintlike

sake *noun* **1** <u>benefit</u>, account, behalf, good, interest, welfare **2** <u>purpose</u>, aim, end, motive, objective, reason

salacious *adjective* <u>lascivious</u>, carnal, erotic, lecherous, lewd, libidinous, lustful

salary *noun* <u>pay</u>, earnings, income, wage, wages

sale *noun* **1** <u>selling</u>, deal, disposal, marketing, transaction **2 for sale** <u>available</u>, obtainable, on the market

salient *adjective* <u>prominent</u>, conspicuous, important, noticeable, outstanding, pronounced, striking

sallow *adjective* <u>wan</u>, anaemic, pale, pallid, pasty, sickly, unhealthy, yellowish

salt *noun* **1** <u>seasoning</u>, flavour, relish, savour, taste **2 with a grain** *or* **pinch of salt** <u>sceptically</u>,

cynically, disbelievingly, suspiciously, with reservations
♦ *adjective* **3** <u>salty</u>, brackish, briny, saline

salty *adjective* <u>salt</u>, brackish, briny, saline

salubrious *adjective* <u>healthy</u>, beneficial, good for one, health-giving, wholesome

salutary *adjective* <u>beneficial</u>, advantageous, good for one, profitable, useful, valuable

salute *noun* **1** <u>greeting</u>, address, recognition, salutation ♦ *verb* **2** <u>greet</u>, acknowledge, address, hail, welcome **3** <u>honour</u>, acknowledge, pay tribute *or* homage to, recognize

salvage *verb* <u>save</u>, recover, redeem, rescue, retrieve

salvation *noun* <u>saving</u>, deliverance, escape, preservation, redemption, rescue

salve *noun* <u>ointment</u>, balm, cream, lotion

same *adjective* **1** <u>aforementioned</u>, aforesaid **2** <u>identical</u>, alike, corresponding, duplicate, equal, twin **3** <u>unchanged</u>, changeless, consistent, constant, invariable, unaltered, unvarying

sample *noun* **1** <u>specimen</u>, example, instance, model, pattern ♦ *verb* **2** <u>test</u>, experience, inspect, taste, try ♦ *adjective* **3** <u>test</u>, representative, specimen, trial

sanctify *verb* <u>consecrate</u>, cleanse, hallow

sanctimonious *adjective* <u>holier-than-thou</u>, hypocritical, pious, self-righteous, smug

sanction *noun* **1** <u>permission</u>,

approval, authority,
authorization, backing, O.K. *or*
okay (*informal*), stamp *or* seal of
approval **2** *often plural* ban,
boycott, coercive measures,
embargo, penalty ♦ *verb*
3 permit, allow, approve,
authorize, endorse

sanctity *noun* **1** sacredness,
inviolability **2** holiness, godliness,
goodness, grace, piety

sanctuary *noun* **1** shrine, altar,
church, temple **2** protection,
asylum, haven, refuge, retreat,
shelter **3** reserve, conservation
area, national park, nature reserve

sane *adjective* **1** rational, all there
(*informal*), *compos mentis*, in one's
right mind, mentally sound, of
sound mind **2** sensible,
balanced, judicious,
level-headed, reasonable, sound

sanguine *adjective* cheerful,
buoyant, confident, hopeful,
optimistic

sanitary *adjective* hygienic, clean,
germ-free, healthy, wholesome

sanity *noun* **1** mental health,
normality, rationality, reason,
saneness **2** good sense, common
sense, level-headedness,
rationality, sense

sap¹ *noun* **1** vital fluid, essence,
lifeblood **2** *Informal* fool, idiot,
jerk (*slang, chiefly U.S. & Canad.*),
ninny, simpleton, twit (*informal*),
wally (*slang*)

sap² *verb* weaken, deplete, drain,
exhaust, undermine

sarcasm *noun* irony, bitterness,
cynicism, derision, mockery,
satire

sarcastic *adjective* ironical, acid,

biting, caustic, cutting, cynical,
mocking, sardonic, sarky (*Brit.
informal*), satirical

sardonic *adjective* mocking,
cynical, derisive, dry, ironical,
sarcastic, sneering, wry

Satan *noun* The Devil, Beelzebub,
Lord of the Flies, Lucifer,
Mephistopheles, Old Nick
(*informal*), Prince of Darkness,
The Evil One

satanic *adjective* evil, black,
demonic, devilish, diabolic,
fiendish, hellish, infernal, wicked

satiate *verb* **1** glut, cloy, gorge,
jade, nauseate, overfill, stuff,
surfeit **2** satisfy, sate, slake

satire *noun* mockery, burlesque,
caricature, irony, lampoon,
parody, ridicule

satirical, satiric *adjective*
mocking, biting, caustic, cutting,
incisive, ironical

satirize *verb* ridicule, burlesque,
deride, lampoon, parody, pillory

satisfaction *noun*
1 contentment, comfort,
content, enjoyment, happiness,
pleasure, pride, repletion, satiety
2 fulfilment, achievement,
assuaging, gratification

satisfactory *adjective* adequate,
acceptable, all right, average,
fair, good enough, passable,
sufficient

satisfy *verb* **1** content, assuage,
gratify, indulge, pacify, pander
to, please, quench, sate, slake
2 fulfil, answer, do, meet, serve,
suffice **3** persuade, assure,
convince, reassure

saturate *verb* soak, drench,
imbue, souse, steep, suffuse,

waterlog, wet through

saturated *adjective* <u>soaked</u>, drenched, dripping, soaking (wet), sodden, sopping (wet), waterlogged, wet through

saturnine *adjective* <u>gloomy</u>, dour, glum, grave, morose, sombre

saucy *adjective* **1** <u>impudent</u>, cheeky (*informal*), forward, impertinent, insolent, pert, presumptuous, rude **2** <u>jaunty</u>, dashing, gay, natty (*informal*), perky

saunter *verb* **1** <u>stroll</u>, amble, meander, mosey (*informal*), ramble, roam, wander ♦ *noun* **2** <u>stroll</u>, airing, amble, ramble, turn, walk

savage *adjective* **1** <u>wild</u>, feral, undomesticated, untamed **2** <u>uncultivated</u>, rough, rugged, uncivilized **3** <u>cruel</u>, barbarous, bestial, bloodthirsty, brutal, ferocious, fierce, harsh, ruthless, sadistic, vicious **4** <u>primitive</u>, rude, unspoilt ♦ *noun* **5** <u>lout</u>, boor, yahoo, yob (*Brit. slang*) ♦ *verb* **6** <u>attack</u>, lacerate, mangle, maul

savagery *noun* <u>cruelty</u>, barbarity, brutality, ferocity, ruthlessness, viciousness

save *verb* **1** <u>rescue</u>, deliver, free, liberate, recover, redeem, salvage **2** <u>protect</u>, conserve, guard, keep safe, look after, preserve, safeguard **3** <u>keep</u>, collect, gather, hoard, hold, husband, lay by, put by, reserve, set aside, store

saving *noun* **1** <u>economy</u>, bargain, discount, reduction ♦ *adjective* **2** <u>redeeming</u>, compensatory, extenuating

savings *plural noun* <u>nest egg</u>, fund, reserves, resources, store

saviour *noun* <u>rescuer</u>, defender, deliverer, liberator, preserver, protector, redeemer

Saviour *noun* <u>Christ</u>, Jesus, Messiah, Redeemer

savoir-faire *noun* <u>social know-how</u> (*informal*), diplomacy, discretion, finesse, poise, social graces, tact, urbanity

savour *verb* **1** <u>enjoy</u>, appreciate, delight in, luxuriate in, relish, revel in **2** *often with* **of** <u>suggest</u>, be suggestive, show signs, smack ♦ *noun* **3** <u>flavour</u>, piquancy, relish, smack, smell, tang, taste

savoury *adjective* <u>spicy</u>, appetizing, full-flavoured, luscious, mouthwatering, palatable, piquant, rich, tasty

say *verb* **1** <u>speak</u>, affirm, announce, assert, declare, maintain, mention, pronounce, remark, state, utter, voice **2** <u>suppose</u>, assume, conjecture, estimate, guess, imagine, presume, surmise **3** <u>express</u>, communicate, convey, imply ♦ *noun* **4** <u>chance to speak</u>, voice, vote **5** <u>influence</u>, authority, clout (*informal*), power, weight

saying *noun* <u>proverb</u>, adage, aphorism, axiom, dictum, maxim

scale¹ *noun* <u>flake</u>, lamina, layer, plate

scale² *noun* **1** <u>graduation</u>, gradation, hierarchy, ladder, progression, ranking, sequence, series, steps **2** <u>ratio</u>, proportion **3** <u>degree</u>, extent, range, reach, scope ♦ *verb* **4** <u>climb</u>, ascend, clamber, escalade, mount, surmount 5 <u>adjust</u>, proportion, regulate

scamp noun <u>rascal</u>, devil, imp, monkey, rogue, scallywag (*informal*)

scamper verb <u>run</u>, dart, dash, hasten, hurry, romp, scoot, scurry, scuttle

scan verb 1 <u>glance over</u>, check, check out (*informal*), examine, eye, look through, run one's eye over, run over, skim 2 <u>scrutinize</u>, investigate, scour, search, survey, sweep

scandal noun 1 <u>crime</u>, disgrace, embarrassment, offence, sin, wrongdoing 2 <u>shame</u>, defamation, discredit, disgrace, dishonour, ignominy, infamy, opprobrium, stigma 3 <u>gossip</u>, aspersion, dirt, rumours, slander, talk, tattle

scandalize verb <u>shock</u>, affront, appal, horrify, offend, outrage

scandalous adjective 1 <u>shocking</u>, disgraceful, disreputable, infamous, outrageous, shameful, unseemly 2 <u>slanderous</u>, defamatory, libellous, scurrilous, untrue

scant adjective <u>meagre</u>, barely sufficient, little, minimal, sparse

scanty adjective <u>meagre</u>, bare, deficient, inadequate, insufficient, poor, scant, short, skimpy, sparse, thin

scapegoat noun <u>whipping boy</u>, fall guy (*informal*)

scar noun 1 <u>mark</u>, blemish, injury, wound ♦ verb 2 <u>mark</u>, damage, disfigure

scarce adjective <u>rare</u>, few, few and far between, infrequent, in short supply, insufficient, uncommon

scarcely adverb 1 <u>hardly</u>, barely 2 <u>definitely not</u>, hardly

scarcity noun <u>shortage</u>, dearth, deficiency, insufficiency, lack, paucity, rareness, want

scare verb 1 <u>frighten</u>, alarm, dismay, intimidate, panic, shock, startle, terrify ♦ noun 2 <u>fright</u>, panic, shock, start, terror

scared adjective <u>frightened</u>, fearful, panicky, panic-stricken, petrified, shaken, startled, terrified

scarper verb Slang <u>run away</u>, abscond, beat it (*slang*), clear off (*informal*), disappear, flee, run for it, scram (*informal*), take to one's heels

scary adjective <u>frightening</u>, alarming, chilling, creepy (*informal*), horrifying, spine-chilling, spooky (*informal*), terrifying

scathing adjective <u>critical</u>, biting, caustic, cutting, harsh, sarcastic, scornful, trenchant, withering

scatter verb 1 <u>throw about</u>, diffuse, disseminate, fling, shower, spread, sprinkle, strew 2 <u>disperse</u>, disband, dispel, dissipate

scatterbrain noun <u>featherbrain</u>, butterfly, flibbertigibbet

scenario noun <u>story line</u>, outline, résumé, summary, synopsis

scene noun 1 <u>site</u>, area, locality, place, position, setting, spot 2 <u>setting</u>, backdrop, background, location, set 3 <u>show</u>, display, drama, exhibition, pageant, picture, sight, spectacle **4** <u>act</u>, division, episode, part **5** <u>view</u>, landscape, panorama, prospect, vista **6** <u>fuss</u>, carry-on (*informal, chiefly Brit.*), commotion, exhibition, performance, row, tantrum, to-do **7** *Informal* <u>world</u>, arena, business, environment

scenery noun **1** <u>landscape</u>, surroundings, terrain, view, vista **2** *Theatre* <u>set</u>, backdrop, flats, setting, stage set

scenic adjective <u>picturesque</u>, beautiful, panoramic, spectacular, striking

scent noun **1** <u>fragrance</u>, aroma, bouquet, odour, perfume, smell **2** <u>trail</u>, spoor, track ♦ *verb* **3** <u>detect</u>, discern, nose out, sense, smell, sniff

scented adjective <u>fragrant</u>, aromatic, odoriferous, perfumed, sweet-smelling

sceptic noun <u>doubter</u>, cynic, disbeliever, doubting Thomas

sceptical adjective <u>doubtful</u>, cynical, disbelieving, dubious, incredulous, mistrustful, unconvinced

scepticism noun <u>doubt</u>, cynicism, disbelief, incredulity, unbelief

schedule noun **1** <u>plan</u>, agenda, calendar, catalogue, inventory, list, programme, timetable ♦ *verb* **2** <u>plan</u>, appoint, arrange, book, organize, programme

scheme noun **1** <u>plan</u>, programme, project, proposal, strategy, system, tactics **2** <u>diagram</u>, blueprint, chart, draft, layout, outline, pattern **3** <u>plot</u>, conspiracy, intrigue, manoeuvre, ploy, ruse, stratagem, subterfuge ♦ *verb* **4** <u>plan</u>, lay plans, project, work out **5** <u>plot</u>, collude, conspire, intrigue, machinate, manoeuvre

scheming adjective <u>calculating</u>, artful, conniving, cunning, sly, tricky, underhand, wily

schism noun <u>division</u>, breach, break, rift, rupture, separation, split

scholar noun **1** <u>intellectual</u>, academic, savant **2** <u>student</u>, disciple, learner, pupil, schoolboy *or* schoolgirl

scholarly adjective <u>learned</u>, academic, bookish, erudite, intellectual, lettered, scholastic

scholarship noun **1** <u>learning</u>, book-learning, education, erudition, knowledge **2** <u>bursary</u>, fellowship

scholastic adjective <u>learned</u>, academic, lettered, scholarly

school noun **1** <u>academy</u>, college, faculty, institute, institution, seminary **2** <u>group</u>, adherents, circle, denomination, devotees, disciples, faction, followers, set ♦ *verb* **3** <u>train</u>, coach, discipline, drill, educate, instruct, tutor

schooling noun **1** <u>teaching</u>, education, tuition **2** <u>training</u>, coaching, drill, instruction

science noun **1** <u>discipline</u>, body of knowledge, branch of knowledge **2** <u>skill</u>, art, technique

scientific adjective <u>systematic</u>, accurate, controlled, exact, mathematical, precise

scientist noun <u>inventor</u>, boffin (*informal*), technophile

scintillating adjective <u>brilliant</u>, animated, bright, dazzling, exciting, glittering, lively, sparkling, stimulating

scoff[1] *verb* <u>scorn</u>, belittle, deride, despise, jeer, knock (*informal*), laugh at, mock, pooh-pooh, ridicule, sneer

scoff[2] *verb* <u>gobble (up)</u>, bolt, devour, gorge oneself on, gulp down, guzzle, wolf

scold *verb* 1 <u>reprimand</u>, berate, castigate, censure, find fault with, give (someone) a dressing-down, lecture, rebuke, reproach, reprove, tell off (*informal*), tick off (*informal*), upbraid ♦ *noun* 2 <u>nag</u>, shrew, termagant (*rare*)

scolding *noun* <u>rebuke</u>, dressing-down (*informal*), lecture, row, telling-off (*informal*), ticking-off (*informal*)

scoop *noun* 1 <u>ladle</u>, dipper, spoon 2 <u>exclusive</u>, exposé, revelation, sensation ♦ *verb* 3 *often with* **up** <u>lift</u>, gather up, pick up, take up 4 *often with* **out** <u>hollow</u>, bail, dig, empty, excavate, gouge, shovel

scope *noun* 1 <u>opportunity</u>, freedom, latitude, liberty, room, space 2 <u>range</u>, area, capacity, orbit, outlook, reach, span, sphere

scorch *verb* <u>burn</u>, parch, roast, sear, shrivel, singe, wither

scorching *adjective* <u>burning</u>, baking, boiling, fiery, flaming, red-hot, roasting, searing

score *noun* 1 <u>points</u>, grade, mark, outcome, record, result, total 2 <u>grounds</u>, basis, cause, ground, reason 3 <u>grievance</u>, grudge, injury, injustice, wrong 4 **scores** <u>lots</u>, hundreds, masses, millions, multitudes, myriads, swarms ♦ *verb* 5 <u>gain</u>, achieve, chalk up (*informal*), make, notch up (*informal*), win 6 <u>keep count</u>, count, record, register, tally 7 <u>cut</u>, deface, gouge, graze, mark, scrape, scratch, slash 8 *with* **out** *or* **through** <u>cross out</u>, cancel, delete, obliterate, strike out 9 *Music* <u>arrange</u>, adapt, orchestrate, set

scorn *noun* 1 <u>contempt</u>, derision, disdain, disparagement, mockery, sarcasm ♦ *verb* 2 <u>despise</u>, be above, deride, disdain, flout, reject, scoff at, slight, spurn

scornful *adjective* <u>contemptuous</u>, derisive, disdainful, haughty, jeering, mocking, sarcastic, sardonic, scathing, scoffing, sneering

scoundrel *noun* <u>rogue</u>, bastard (*offensive*), blackguard, good-for-nothing, heel (*slang*), miscreant, ne'er-do-well, rascal, reprobate, rotter (*slang, chiefly Brit.*), scally (*Northwest English dialect*), scamp, swine, villain

scour[1] *verb* <u>rub</u>, abrade, buff, clean, polish, scrub, wash

scour[2] *verb* <u>search</u>, beat, comb, hunt, ransack

scourge *noun* 1 <u>affliction</u>, bane, curse, infliction, misfortune, pest, plague, terror, torment 2 <u>whip</u>, cat, lash, strap, switch, thong ♦ *verb* 3 <u>afflict</u>, curse, plague, terrorize, torment 4 <u>whip</u>, beat, cane, flog, horsewhip, lash, thrash

scout *noun* 1 <u>vanguard</u>, advance guard, lookout, outrider, precursor, reconnoitrer ♦ *verb*

2 <u>reconnoitre</u>, investigate, observe, probe, recce (*slang*), spy, survey, watch

scowl *verb* 1 <u>glower</u>, frown, lour or lower ♦ *noun* 2 <u>glower</u>, black look, dirty look, frown

scrabble *verb* <u>scrape</u>, claw, scramble, scratch

scraggy *adjective* <u>scrawny</u>, angular, bony, lean, skinny

scram *verb* <u>go away</u>, abscond, beat it (*slang*), clear off (*informal*), get lost (*informal*), leave, make oneself scarce (*informal*), make tracks, scarper (*Brit. slang*), vamoose (*slang, chiefly U.S.*)

scramble *verb* 1 <u>struggle</u>, climb, crawl, scrabble, swarm 2 <u>strive</u>, contend, jostle, push, run, rush, vie ♦ *noun* 3 <u>climb</u>, trek 4 <u>struggle</u>, commotion, competition, confusion, melee *or* mêlée, race, rush, tussle

scrap¹ *noun* 1 <u>piece</u>, bit, crumb, fragment, grain, morsel, part, particle, portion, sliver, snippet 2 <u>waste</u>, junk, off cuts 3 <u>scraps</u> leftovers, bits, leavings, remains ♦ *verb* 4 <u>discard</u>, abandon, ditch (*slang*), drop, jettison, throw away *or* out, write off

scrap² *Informal* ♦ *noun* 1 <u>fight</u>, argument, battle, disagreement, dispute, quarrel, row, squabble, wrangle ♦ *verb* 2 <u>fight</u>, argue, row, squabble, wrangle

scrape *verb* 1 <u>graze</u>, bark, rub, scratch, scuff, skin 2 <u>rub</u>, clean, erase, remove, scour 3 <u>grate</u>, grind, rasp, scratch, squeak 4 <u>scrimp</u>, pinch, save, skimp, stint 5 **scrape through** <u>get by</u> (*informal*), just make it, struggle

♦ *noun* 6 *Informal* <u>predicament</u>, awkward situation, difficulty, dilemma, fix (*informal*), mess, plight, tight spot

scrapheap *noun* **on the scrapheap** <u>discarded</u>, ditched (*slang*), jettisoned, put out to grass (*informal*), redundant, written off

scrappy *adjective* <u>fragmentary</u>, bitty, disjointed, incomplete, piecemeal, sketchy, thrown together

scratch *verb* 1 <u>mark</u>, claw, cut, damage, etch, grate, graze, lacerate, score, scrape 2 <u>withdraw</u>, cancel, delete, eliminate, erase, pull out ♦ *noun* 3 <u>mark</u>, blemish, claw mark, gash, graze, laceration, scrape 4 **up to scratch** <u>adequate</u>, acceptable, satisfactory, sufficient, up to standard ♦ *adjective* 5 <u>improvised</u>, impromptu, rough-and-ready

scrawl *verb* <u>scribble</u>, doodle, squiggle, writing

scrawny *adjective* <u>thin</u>, bony, gaunt, lean, scraggy, skin-and-bones (*informal*), skinny, undernourished

scream *verb* 1 <u>cry</u>, bawl, screech, shriek, yell ♦ *noun* 2 <u>cry</u>, howl, screech, shriek, yell, yelp

screech *noun, verb* <u>cry</u>, scream, shriek

screen *noun* 1 <u>cover</u>, awning, canopy, cloak, guard, partition, room divider, shade, shelter, shield 2 <u>mesh</u>, net ♦ *verb* 3 <u>cover</u>, cloak, conceal, hide, mask, shade, veil 4 <u>protect</u>, defend, guard, shelter, shield 5 <u>vet</u>, evaluate, examine, filter,

gauge, scan, sift, sort
6 broadcast, present, put on, show

screw *verb* **1** turn, tighten, twist
2 *Informal, often with* **out of** extort, extract, wrest, wring

screw up *verb* **1** *Informal* bungle, botch, make a hash of (*informal*), make a mess of (*slang*), mess up, mishandle, spoil **2** distort, contort, pucker, wrinkle

screwy *adjective* crazy, crackpot (*informal*), eccentric, loopy (*informal*), nutty (*slang*), odd, off-the-wall (*slang*), out to lunch (*informal*), round the bend (*Brit. slang*), weird

scribble *verb* scrawl, dash off, jot, write

scribe *noun* copyist, amanuensis, writer

scrimp *verb* economize, be frugal, save, scrape, skimp, stint, tighten one's belt

script *noun* **1** text, book, copy, dialogue, libretto, lines, words **2** handwriting, calligraphy, penmanship, writing

Scripture *noun* The Bible, Holy Bible, Holy Scripture, Holy Writ, The Good Book, The Gospels, The Scriptures

scrounge *verb Informal* cadge, beg, blag (*slang*), bum (*informal*), freeload (*slang*), sponge (*informal*)

scrounger *adjective* cadger, freeloader (*slang*), parasite, sponger (*informal*)

scrub *verb* **1** scour, clean, cleanse, rub **2** *Informal* cancel, abolish, call off, delete, drop, forget about, give up

scruffy *adjective* shabby,

ill-groomed, mangy, messy, ragged, run-down, seedy, tatty, unkempt, untidy

scrumptious *adjective Informal* delicious, appetizing, delectable, luscious, mouthwatering, succulent, yummy (*slang*)

scruple *noun* **1** misgiving, compunction, doubt, hesitation, qualm, reluctance, second thoughts, uneasiness ♦ *verb* **2** have misgivings about, demur, doubt, have qualms about, hesitate, think twice about

scrupulous *adjective* **1** moral, conscientious, honourable, principled, upright **2** careful, exact, fastidious, meticulous, precise, punctilious, rigorous, strict

scrutinize *verb* examine, explore, inspect, investigate, peruse, pore over, probe, scan, search, study

scrutiny *noun* examination, analysis, exploration, inspection, investigation, perusal, search, study

scuffle *verb* **1** fight, clash, grapple, jostle, struggle, tussle ♦ *noun* **2** fight, brawl, commotion, disturbance, fray, scrimmage, skirmish, tussle

sculpture *verb* sculpt, carve, chisel, fashion, form, hew, model, mould, shape

scum *noun* **1** impurities, dross, film, froth **2** rabble, dregs of society, riffraff, trash (*chiefly U.S. & Canad.*)

scupper *verb Brit. slang* destroy, defeat, demolish, put paid to, ruin, torpedo, wreck

scurrilous *adjective* slanderous,

abusive, defamatory, insulting, scandalous, vituperative

scurry verb 1 <u>hurry</u>, dart, dash, race, scamper, scoot, scuttle, sprint ◆ noun 2 <u>flurry</u>, scampering, whirl

scuttle verb <u>run</u>, bustle, hasten, hurry, rush, scamper, scoot, scurry

sea noun 1 <u>ocean</u>, main, the deep, the waves 2 <u>expanse</u>, abundance, mass, multitude, plethora, profusion 3 **at sea** <u>bewildered</u>, baffled, confused, lost, mystified, puzzled

seafaring adjective <u>nautical</u>, marine, maritime, naval

seal noun 1 <u>authentication</u>, confirmation, imprimatur, insignia, ratification, stamp ◆ verb 2 <u>close</u>, bung, enclose, fasten, plug, shut, stop, stopper, stop up 3 <u>authenticate</u>, confirm, ratify, stamp, validate 4 <u>settle</u>, clinch, conclude, consummate, finalize 5 **seal off** <u>isolate</u>, put out of bounds, quarantine, segregate

seam noun 1 <u>joint</u>, closure 2 <u>layer</u>, lode, stratum, vein 3 <u>ridge</u>, furrow, line, wrinkle

sear verb <u>scorch</u>, burn, sizzle

search verb 1 <u>look</u>, comb, examine, explore, hunt, inspect, investigate, ransack, scour, scrutinize ◆ noun 2 <u>look</u>, examination, exploration, hunt, inspection, investigation, pursuit, quest

searching adjective <u>keen</u>, close, intent, penetrating, piercing, probing, quizzical, sharp

season noun 1 <u>period</u>, spell, term, time ◆ verb 2 <u>flavour</u>,

enliven, pep up, salt, spice

seasonable adjective <u>appropriate</u>, convenient, fit, opportune, providential, suitable, timely, well-timed

seasoned adjective <u>experienced</u>, hardened, practised, time-served, veteran

seasoning noun <u>flavouring</u>, condiment, dressing, relish, salt and pepper, sauce, spice

seat noun 1 <u>chair</u>, bench, pew, settle, stall, stool 2 <u>centre</u>, capital, heart, hub, place, site, situation, source 3 <u>residence</u>, abode, ancestral hall, house, mansion 4 <u>membership</u>, chair, constituency, incumbency, place ◆ verb 5 <u>sit</u>, fix, install, locate, place, set, settle 6 <u>hold</u>, accommodate, cater for, contain, sit, take

seating noun <u>accommodation</u>, chairs, places, room, seats

secede verb <u>withdraw</u>, break with, leave, pull out, quit, resign, split from

secluded adjective <u>private</u>, cloistered, cut off, isolated, lonely, out-of-the-way, sheltered, solitary

seclusion noun <u>privacy</u>, isolation, shelter, solitude

second[1] adjective 1 <u>next</u>, following, subsequent, succeeding 2 <u>additional</u>, alternative, extra, further, other 3 <u>inferior</u>, lesser, lower, secondary, subordinate ◆ noun 4 <u>supporter</u>, assistant, backer, helper ◆ verb 5 <u>support</u>, approve, assist, back, endorse, go along with

second² noun <u>moment</u>, flash, instant, jiffy (*informal*), minute, sec (*informal*), trice

secondary *adjective*
1 <u>subordinate</u>, inferior, lesser, lower, minor, unimportant 2 <u>resultant</u>, contingent, derived, indirect 3 <u>backup</u>, auxiliary, fall-back, reserve, subsidiary, supporting

second-class *adjective* <u>inferior</u>, indifferent, mediocre, second-best, second-rate, undistinguished, uninspiring

second-hand *adjective* 1 <u>used</u>, hand-me-down (*informal*), nearly new ♦ *adverb* 2 <u>indirectly</u>

second in command *noun* <u>deputy</u>, number two, right-hand man

secondly *adverb* <u>next</u>, in the second place, second

second-rate *adjective* <u>inferior</u>, low-grade, low-quality, mediocre, poor, rubbishy, shoddy, substandard, tacky (*informal*), tawdry, two-bit (*U.S. & Canad. slang*)

secrecy *noun* 1 <u>mystery</u>, concealment, confidentiality, privacy, silence 2 <u>secretiveness</u>, clandestineness, covertness, furtiveness, stealth

secret *adjective* 1 <u>concealed</u>, close, disguised, furtive, hidden, undercover, underground, undisclosed, unknown, unrevealed 2 <u>stealthy</u>, secretive, sly, underhand 3 <u>mysterious</u>, abstruse, arcane, clandestine, cryptic, occult ♦ *noun* 4 <u>mystery</u>, code, enigma, key 5 **in secret** <u>secretly</u>, slyly, surreptitiously

secrete¹ *verb* <u>give off</u>, emanate, emit, exude

secrete² *verb* <u>hide</u>, cache, conceal, harbour, stash (*informal*), stow

secretive *adjective* <u>reticent</u>, close, deep, reserved, tight-lipped, uncommunicative

secretly *adverb* <u>in secret</u>, clandestinely, covertly, furtively, privately, quietly, stealthily, surreptitiously

sect *noun* <u>group</u>, camp, denomination, division, faction, party, schism

sectarian *adjective*
1 <u>narrow-minded</u>, bigoted, doctrinaire, dogmatic, factional, fanatical, limited, parochial, partisan ♦ *noun* 2 <u>bigot</u>, dogmatist, extremist, fanatic, partisan, zealot

section *noun* 1 <u>part</u>, division, fraction, instalment, passage, piece, portion, segment, slice 2 *Chiefly U.S.* <u>district</u>, area, region, sector, zone

sector *noun* <u>part</u>, area, district, division, quarter, region, zone

secular *adjective* <u>worldly</u>, civil, earthly, lay, nonspiritual, temporal

secure *adjective* 1 <u>safe</u>, immune, protected, unassailable 2 <u>sure</u>, assured, certain, confident, easy, reassured 3 <u>fixed</u>, fast, fastened, firm, immovable, stable, steady ♦ *verb* 4 <u>obtain</u>, acquire, gain, get, procure, score (*slang*) 5 <u>fasten</u>, attach, bolt, chain, fix, lock, make fast, tie up

security *noun* 1 <u>precautions</u>, defence, protection, safeguards, safety measures 2 <u>safety</u>, care,

sedate custody, refuge, safekeeping, sanctuary **3** <u>sureness</u>, assurance, certainty, confidence, conviction, positiveness, reliance **4** <u>pledge</u>, collateral, gage, guarantee, hostage, insurance, pawn, surety

sedate *adjective* <u>calm</u>, collected, composed, cool, dignified, serene, tranquil

sedative *adjective* **1** <u>calming</u>, anodyne, relaxing, soothing, tranquillizing ♦ *noun* **2** <u>tranquillizer</u>, anodyne, downer or down (*slang*)

sedentary *adjective* <u>inactive</u>, desk, desk-bound, seated, sitting

sediment *noun* <u>dregs</u>, deposit, grounds, lees, residue

sedition *noun* <u>rabble-rousing</u>, agitation, incitement to riot, subversion

seditious *adjective* <u>revolutionary</u>, dissident, mutinous, rebellious, refractory, subversive

seduce *verb* **1** <u>corrupt</u>, debauch, deflower, deprave, dishonour **2** <u>tempt</u>, beguile, deceive, entice, inveigle, lead astray, lure, mislead

seduction *noun* **1** <u>corruption</u> **2** <u>temptation</u>, enticement, lure, snare

seductive *adjective* <u>alluring</u>, attractive, bewitching, enticing, inviting, provocative, tempting

seductress *noun* <u>temptress</u>, enchantress, *femme fatale*, siren, vamp (*informal*)

see *verb* **1** <u>perceive</u>, behold, catch sight of, discern, distinguish, espy, glimpse, look, make out, notice, observe, sight, spot, witness **2** <u>understand</u>,

appreciate, comprehend, fathom, feel, follow, get, grasp, realize **3** <u>find out</u>, ascertain, determine, discover, learn **4** <u>make sure</u>, ensure, guarantee, make certain, see to it **5** <u>consider</u>, decide, deliberate, reflect, think over **6** <u>visit</u>, confer with, consult, interview, receive, speak to **7** <u>go out with</u>, court, date (*informal, chiefly U.S.*), go steady with (*informal*) **8** <u>accompany</u>, escort, lead, show, usher, walk

seed *noun* **1** <u>grain</u>, egg, embryo, germ, kernel, ovum, pip, spore **2** <u>origin</u>, beginning, germ, nucleus, source, start **3** <u>offspring</u>, children, descendants, issue, progeny **4 go** *or* **run to seed** <u>decline</u>, decay, degenerate, deteriorate, go downhill (*informal*), go to pot, let oneself go

seedy *adjective* **1** <u>shabby</u>, dilapidated, grotty (*slang*), grubby, mangy, run-down, scruffy, sleazy, squalid, tatty **2** *Informal* <u>unwell</u>, ill, off colour, out of sorts, poorly (*informal*), under the weather (*informal*)

seeing *conjunction* <u>since</u>, as, inasmuch as, in view of the fact that

seek *verb* **1** <u>look for</u>, be after, follow, hunt, pursue, search for **2** <u>try</u>, aim, aspire to, attempt, endeavour, essay, strive

seem *verb* <u>appear</u>, assume, give the impression, look

seemly *adjective* <u>fitting</u>, appropriate, becoming, decent, decorous, fit, proper, suitable

seep *verb* <u>ooze</u>, exude, leak,

permeate, soak, trickle, well

seer noun prophet, sibyl, soothsayer

seesaw verb alternate, fluctuate, oscillate, swing

seethe verb 1 be furious, be livid, fume, go ballistic (slang, chiefly U.S.), rage, see red (informal), simmer 2 boil, bubble, fizz, foam, froth

see through verb 1 be undeceived by, be wise to (informal), fathom, not fall for, penetrate 2 see (something) through persevere (with), keep at, persist, stick out (informal) 3 see (someone) through help out, stick by, support

segment noun section, bit, division, part, piece, portion, slice, wedge

segregate verb set apart, discriminate against, dissociate, isolate, separate

segregation noun separation, apartheid, discrimination, isolation

seize verb 1 grab, catch up, clutch, grasp, grip, lay hands on, snatch, take 2 confiscate, appropriate, commandeer, impound, take possession of 3 capture, apprehend, arrest, catch, take captive

seizure noun 1 attack, convulsion, fit, paroxysm, spasm 2 capture, apprehension, arrest 3 taking, annexation, commandeering, confiscation, grabbing

seldom adverb rarely, hardly ever, infrequently, not often

select verb 1 choose, opt for, pick, single out ◆ adjective 2 choice, excellent, first-class, hand-picked, special, superior, top-notch (informal) 3 exclusive, cliquish, elite, privileged

selection noun 1 choice, choosing, option, pick, preference 2 range, assortment, choice, collection, medley, variety

selective adjective particular, careful, discerning, discriminating

self-assurance noun confidence, assertiveness, positiveness, self-confidence, self-possession

self-centred adjective selfish, egotistic, narcissistic, self-seeking

self-confidence noun self-assurance, aplomb, confidence, nerve, poise

self-confident adjective self-assured, assured, confident, poised, sure of oneself

self-conscious adjective embarrassed, awkward, bashful, diffident, ill at ease, insecure, nervous, uncomfortable

self-control noun willpower, restraint, self-discipline, self-restraint

self-esteem noun self-respect, confidence, faith in oneself, pride, self-assurance, self-regard

self-evident adjective obvious, clear, incontrovertible, inescapable, undeniable

self-important adjective conceited, bigheaded, cocky, full of oneself, pompous, swollen-headed

self-indulgence noun intemperance, excess, extravagance

selfish adjective self-centred,

egoistic, egoistical, egotistic, egotistical, greedy, self-interested, ungenerous

selfless *adjective* <u>unselfish</u>, altruistic, generous, self-denying, self-sacrificing

self-possessed *adjective* <u>self-assured</u>, collected, confident, cool, poised, unruffled

self-reliant *adjective* <u>independent</u>, self-sufficient, self-supporting

self-respect *noun* <u>pride</u>, dignity, morale, self-esteem

self-restraint *noun* <u>self-control</u>, self-command, self-discipline, willpower

self-righteous *adjective* <u>sanctimonious</u>, complacent, holier-than-thou, priggish, self-satisfied, smug, superior

self-sacrifice *noun* <u>selflessness</u>, altruism, generosity, self-denial

self-satisfied *adjective* <u>smug</u>, complacent, pleased with oneself, self-congratulatory

self-seeking *adjective* <u>selfish</u>, careerist, looking out for number one (*informal*), out for what one can get, self-interested, self-serving

sell *verb* 1 <u>trade</u>, barter, exchange 2 <u>deal in</u>, handle, market, peddle, retail, stock, trade in, traffic in

seller *noun* <u>dealer</u>, agent, merchant, purveyor, retailer, salesman *or* saleswoman, supplier, vendor

selling *noun* <u>dealing</u>, business, trading, traffic

sell out *verb* 1 <u>dispose of</u>, be out of stock of, get rid of, run out of

2 *Informal* <u>betray</u>, double-cross (*informal*), sell down the river (*informal*), stab in the back

semblance *noun* <u>appearance</u>, aspect, façade, mask, pretence, resemblance, show, veneer

seminal *adjective* <u>influential</u>, formative, ground-breaking, important, innovative, original

send *verb* 1 <u>convey</u>, direct, dispatch, forward, remit, transmit 2 <u>propel</u>, cast, fire, fling, hurl, let fly, shoot

send for *verb* <u>summon</u>, call for, order, request

sendoff *noun* <u>farewell</u>, departure, leave-taking, start, valediction

send-up *noun* <u>imitation</u>, parody, satire, skit, spoof (*informal*), take-off (*informal*)

send up *verb* <u>imitate</u>, burlesque, lampoon, make fun of, mimic, mock, parody, satirize, spoof (*informal*), take off (*informal*)

senile *adjective* <u>doddering</u>, decrepit, doting, in one's dotage

senility *noun* <u>dotage</u>, decrepitude, infirmity, loss of one's faculties, senile dementia

senior *adjective* 1 <u>higher ranking</u>, superior 2 <u>older</u>, elder, major (*Brit.*)

senior citizen *noun* <u>pensioner</u>, O.A.P., old age pensioner, old *or* elderly person, retired person

seniority *noun* <u>superiority</u>, precedence, priority, rank

sensation *noun* 1 <u>feeling</u>, awareness, consciousness, impression, perception, sense 2 <u>excitement</u>, commotion, furore, stir, thrill

sensational *adjective* 1 <u>dramatic</u>,

amazing, astounding, exciting, melodramatic, shock-horror (*facetious*), shocking, thrilling 2 *Informal* excellent, fabulous (*informal*), impressive, marvellous, mean (*slang*), mind-blowing (*informal*), out of this world (*informal*), smashing (*informal*), superb

sense *noun* 1 faculty, feeling, sensation 2 feeling, atmosphere, aura, awareness, consciousness, impression, perception 3 *sometimes plural* intelligence, brains (*informal*), cleverness, common sense, judgment, reason, sagacity, sanity, sharpness, understanding, wisdom, wit(s) 4 meaning, drift, gist, implication, import, significance ♦ *verb* 5 perceive, be aware of, discern, feel, get the impression, pick up, realize, understand

senseless *adjective* 1 stupid, asinine, crazy, daft (*informal*), foolish, idiotic, illogical, inane, irrational, mad, mindless, nonsensical, pointless, ridiculous, silly 2 unconscious, insensible, out, out cold, stunned

sensibility *noun* 1 *often plural* feelings, emotions, moral sense, sentiments, susceptibilities 2 sensitivity, responsiveness, sensitiveness, susceptibility

sensible *adjective* 1 wise, canny, down-to-earth, intelligent, judicious, practical, prudent, rational, realistic, sage, sane, shrewd, sound 2 *usually with of* aware, conscious, mindful, sensitive to

sensitive *adjective* 1 easily hurt,

delicate, tender 2 susceptible, easily affected, impressionable, responsive, touchy-feely (*informal*) 3 touchy, easily offended, easily upset, thin-skinned 4 responsive, acute, fine, keen, precise

sensitivity *noun* sensitiveness, delicacy, receptiveness, responsiveness, susceptibility

sensual *adjective* 1 physical, animal, bodily, carnal, fleshly, luxurious, voluptuous 2 erotic, lascivious, lecherous, lewd, lustful, raunchy (*slang*), sexual

sensuality *noun* eroticism, carnality, lasciviousness, lecherousness, lewdness, sexiness (*informal*), voluptuousness

sensuous *adjective* pleasurable, gratifying, hedonistic, sybaritic

sentence *noun* 1 punishment, condemnation, decision, decree, judgment, order, ruling, verdict ♦ *verb* 2 condemn, doom, penalize

sententious *adjective* pompous, canting, judgmental, moralistic, preachifying (*informal*), sanctimonious

sentient *adjective* feeling, conscious, living, sensitive

sentiment *noun* 1 emotion, sensibility, tenderness 2 *often plural* feeling, attitude, belief, idea, judgment, opinion, view 3 sentimentality, emotionalism, mawkishness, romanticism

sentimental *adjective* romantic, emotional, maudlin, nostalgic, overemotional, schmaltzy (*slang*), slushy (*informal*), soft-hearted, touching, weepy (*informal*)

sentimentality noun
<u>romanticism</u>, corniness (*slang*),
emotionalism, mawkishness,
nostalgia, schmaltz (*slang*)

sentinel noun <u>guard</u>, lookout,
sentry, watch, watchman

separable adjective
<u>distinguishable</u>, detachable,
divisible

separate verb 1 <u>divide</u>, come
apart, come away, detach,
disconnect, disjoin, remove,
sever, split, sunder 2 <u>part</u>, break
up, disunite, diverge, divorce,
estrange, part company, split up
3 <u>isolate</u>, segregate, single out
♦ *adjective* 4 <u>unconnected</u>,
detached, disconnected, divided,
divorced, isolated, unattached
5 <u>individual</u>, alone, apart,
distinct, particular, single, solitary

separated adjective
<u>disconnected</u>, apart,
disassociated, disunited, divided,
parted, separate, sundered

separately adverb <u>individually</u>,
alone, apart, severally, singly

separation noun 1 <u>division</u>,
break, disconnection,
dissociation, disunion, gap
2 <u>split-up</u>, break-up, divorce,
parting, rift, split

septic adjective <u>infected</u>,
festering, poisoned, putrefying,
putrid, suppurating

sepulchre noun <u>tomb</u>, burial
place, grave, mausoleum, vault

sequel noun 1 <u>follow-up</u>,
continuation, development
2 <u>consequence</u>, conclusion, end,
outcome, result, upshot

sequence noun <u>succession</u>,
arrangement, chain, course,

cycle, order, progression, series

serene adjective <u>calm</u>, composed,
peaceful, tranquil, unruffled,
untroubled

serenity noun <u>calmness</u>, calm,
composure, peace, peacefulness,
quietness, stillness, tranquillity

series noun <u>sequence</u>, chain,
course, order, progression, run,
set, string, succession, train

serious adjective 1 <u>severe</u>, acute,
critical, dangerous 2 <u>important</u>,
crucial, fateful, grim,
momentous, no laughing
matter, pressing, significant,
urgent, worrying 3 <u>solemn</u>,
grave, humourless, sober,
unsmiling 4 <u>sincere</u>, earnest,
genuine, honest, in earnest

seriously adverb 1 <u>gravely</u>,
acutely, badly, critically,
dangerously, severely 2 <u>sincerely</u>,
gravely, in earnest

seriousness noun 1 <u>importance</u>,
gravity, significance, urgency
2 <u>solemnity</u>, earnestness,
gravitas, gravity

sermon noun 1 <u>homily</u>, address
2 <u>lecture</u>, harangue, talking-to
(*informal*)

servant noun <u>attendant</u>,
domestic, help, maid, retainer,
skivvy (*chiefly Brit.*), slave

serve verb 1 <u>work for</u>, aid, assist,
attend to, help, minister to, wait
on 2 <u>perform</u>, act, complete,
discharge, do, fulfil 3 <u>provide</u>,
deliver, dish up, present, set out,
supply 4 <u>be adequate</u>, answer
the purpose, be acceptable, do,
function as, satisfy, suffice, suit

service noun 1 <u>help</u>, assistance,
avail, benefit, use, usefulness

2 <u>work</u>, business, duty, employment, labour, office
3 <u>overhaul</u>, check, maintenance
4 <u>ceremony</u>, observance, rite, worship ♦*verb* 5 <u>overhaul</u>, check, fine tune, go over, maintain, tune (up)

serviceable *adjective* <u>useful</u>, beneficial, functional, helpful, operative, practical, profitable, usable, utilitarian

servile *adjective* <u>subservient</u>, abject, fawning, grovelling, obsequious, sycophantic, toadying

serving *noun* <u>portion</u>, helping

session *noun* <u>meeting</u>, assembly, conference, congress, discussion, hearing, period, sitting

set¹ *verb* 1 <u>put</u>, deposit, lay, locate, place, plant, position, rest, seat, situate, station, stick
2 <u>prepare</u>, arrange, lay, make ready, spread 3 <u>harden</u>, cake, congeal, crystallize, solidify, stiffen, thicken 4 <u>arrange</u>, appoint, decide (upon), determine, establish, fix, fix up, resolve, schedule, settle, specify
5 <u>assign</u>, allot, decree, impose, ordain, prescribe, specify 6 <u>go down</u>, decline, dip, disappear, sink, subside, vanish ♦*noun*
7 <u>position</u>, attitude, bearing, carriage, posture 8 <u>scenery</u>, scene, setting, stage set
♦*adjective* 9 <u>fixed</u>, agreed, appointed, arranged, decided, definite, established, prearranged, predetermined, scheduled, settled 10 <u>inflexible</u>, hard and fast, immovable, rigid, stubborn 11 <u>conventional</u>, stereotyped, traditional,

unspontaneous 12 **set on** or **upon** <u>determined</u>, bent, intent, resolute

set² *noun* 1 <u>series</u>, assortment, batch, collection, compendium
2 <u>group</u>, band, circle, clique, company, coterie, crowd, faction, gang

setback *noun* <u>hold-up</u>, blow, check, defeat, disappointment, hitch, misfortune, reverse

set back *verb* <u>hold up</u>, delay, hinder, impede, retard, slow

set off *verb* 1 <u>leave</u>, depart, embark, start out 2 <u>detonate</u>, explode, ignite

setting *noun* <u>background</u>, backdrop, context, location, scene, scenery, set, site, surroundings

settle *verb* 1 <u>put in order</u>, adjust, order, regulate, straighten out, work out 2 <u>land</u>, alight, come to rest, descend, light 3 <u>move to</u>, dwell, inhabit, live, make one's home, put down roots, reside, set up home, take up residence
4 <u>colonize</u>, people, pioneer, populate 5 <u>calm</u>, lull, pacify, quell, quiet, quieten, reassure, relax, relieve, soothe 6 <u>pay</u>, clear, discharge, square (up)
7 *often with* **on** *or* **upon** <u>decide</u>, agree, confirm, determine, establish, fix 8 <u>resolve</u>, clear up, decide, put an end to, reconcile

settlement *noun* 1 <u>agreement</u>, arrangement, conclusion, confirmation, establishment, working out 2 <u>payment</u>, clearing, discharge 3 <u>colony</u>, community, encampment, outpost

settler *noun* <u>colonist</u>,

frontiersman, immigrant, pioneer

setup noun <u>arrangement</u>, conditions, organization, regime, structure, system

set up verb 1 <u>build</u>, assemble, construct, erect, put together, put up, raise 2 <u>establish</u>, arrange, begin, found, initiate, institute, organize, prearrange, prepare

sever verb 1 <u>cut</u>, cut in two, detach, disconnect, disjoin, divide, part, separate, split 2 <u>break off</u>, dissociate, put an end to, terminate

several adjective <u>some</u>, different, diverse, manifold, many, sundry, various

severe adjective 1 <u>strict</u>, austere, cruel, drastic, hard, harsh, oppressive, rigid, unbending 2 <u>grim</u>, forbidding, grave, serious, stern, tight-lipped, unsmiling 3 <u>intense</u>, acute, extreme, fierce 4 <u>plain</u>, austere, classic, restrained, simple, Spartan, unadorned, unembellished, unfussy

severely adverb 1 <u>strictly</u>, harshly, sharply, sternly 2 <u>seriously</u>, acutely, badly, extremely, gravely

severity noun <u>strictness</u>, hardness, harshness, severeness, sternness, toughness

sex noun 1 <u>gender</u> 2 Informal (sexual) <u>intercourse</u>, coition, coitus, copulation, fornication, lovemaking, sexual relations

sexual adjective 1 <u>carnal</u>, erotic, intimate, sensual, sexy 2 <u>reproductive</u>, genital, procreative, sex

sexual intercourse noun <u>copulation</u>, bonking (informal), carnal knowledge, coition, coitus, sex (informal), union

sexuality noun <u>desire</u>, carnality, eroticism, lust, sensuality, sexiness (informal)

sexy adjective <u>erotic</u>, arousing, naughty, provocative, seductive, sensual, sensuous, suggestive, titillating

shabby adjective 1 <u>tatty</u>, dilapidated, mean, ragged, run-down, scruffy, seedy, tattered, threadbare, worn 2 <u>mean</u>, cheap, contemptible, despicable, dirty, dishonourable, low, rotten (informal), scurvy

shack noun <u>hut</u>, cabin, shanty

shackle noun 1 often plural <u>fetter</u>, bond, chain, iron, leg-iron, manacle ♦ verb 2 <u>fetter</u>, bind, chain, manacle, put in irons

shade noun 1 <u>dimness</u>, dusk, gloom, gloominess, semidarkness, shadow 2 <u>screen</u>, blind, canopy, cover, covering, curtain, shield, veil 3 <u>colour</u>, hue, tinge, tint, tone 4 <u>dash</u>, hint, suggestion, trace 5 Literary <u>ghost</u>, apparition, phantom, spectre, spirit 6 **put into the shade** <u>outshine</u>, eclipse, outclass, overshadow ♦ verb 7 <u>cover</u>, conceal, hide, obscure, protect, screen, shield, veil 8 <u>darken</u>, cloud, dim, shadow

shadow noun 1 <u>dimness</u>, cover, darkness, dusk, gloom, shade 2 <u>trace</u>, hint, suggestion, suspicion 3 <u>cloud</u>, blight, gloom, sadness ♦ verb 4 <u>shade</u>, darken, overhang, screen, shield 5 <u>follow</u>, stalk, tail (informal), trail

shadowy adjective 1 <u>dark</u>, dim, dusky, gloomy, murky, shaded, shady 2 <u>vague</u>, dim, dreamlike, faint, ghostly, nebulous, phantom, spectral, unsubstantial

shady adjective 1 <u>shaded</u>, cool, dim 2 Informal <u>crooked</u>, disreputable, dodgy (Brit., Austral., & N.Z. informal), dubious, questionable, shifty, suspect, suspicious, unethical

shaft noun 1 <u>handle</u>, pole, rod, shank, stem 2 <u>ray</u>, beam, gleam

shaggy adjective <u>unkempt</u>, hairy, hirsute, long-haired, rough, tousled, unshorn

shake verb 1 <u>vibrate</u>, bump, jar, jolt, quake, rock, shiver, totter, tremble 2 <u>wave</u>, brandish, flourish 3 <u>upset</u>, distress, disturb, frighten, rattle (informal), shock, unnerve ♦ noun 4 <u>vibration</u>, agitation, convulsion, jerk, jolt, quaking, shiver, shudder, trembling, tremor

shake up verb 1 <u>stir (up)</u>, agitate, churn (up), mix 2 <u>upset</u>, disturb, shock, unsettle

shaky adjective 1 <u>unsteady</u>, faltering, precarious, quivery, rickety, trembling, unstable, weak 2 <u>uncertain</u>, dubious, iffy (informal), questionable, suspect

shallow adjective 1 <u>superficial</u>, empty, slight, surface, trivial 2 <u>unintelligent</u>, foolish, frivolous, ignorant, puerile, simple

sham noun 1 <u>phoney or phony</u> (informal), counterfeit, forgery, fraud, hoax, humbug, imitation, impostor, pretence ♦ adjective 2 <u>false</u>, artificial, bogus, counterfeit, feigned, imitation, mock, phoney or phony

(informal), pretended, simulated ♦ verb 3 <u>fake</u>, affect, assume, feign, pretend, put on, simulate

shambles noun <u>chaos</u>, confusion, disarray, disorder, havoc, madhouse, mess, muddle

shame noun 1 <u>embarrassment</u>, abashment, humiliation, ignominy, mortification 2 <u>disgrace</u>, blot, discredit, dishonour, disrepute, infamy, reproach, scandal, smear ♦ verb 3 <u>embarrass</u>, abash, disgrace, humble, humiliate, mortify 4 <u>dishonour</u>, blot, debase, defile, degrade, smear, stain

shamefaced adjective <u>embarrassed</u>, abashed, ashamed, humiliated, mortified, red-faced, sheepish

shameful adjective 1 <u>embarrassing</u>, cringe-making (Brit. informal), humiliating, mortifying 2 <u>disgraceful</u>, base, dishonourable, low, mean, outrageous, scandalous, wicked

shameless adjective <u>brazen</u>, audacious, barefaced, flagrant, hardened, insolent, unabashed, unashamed

shanty noun <u>shack</u>, cabin, hut, shed

shape noun 1 <u>form</u>, build, configuration, contours, figure, lines, outline, profile, silhouette 2 <u>pattern</u>, frame, model, mould 3 <u>condition</u>, fettle, health, state, trim ♦ verb 4 <u>form</u>, create, fashion, make, model, mould, produce 5 <u>develop</u>, adapt, devise, frame, modify, plan

shapeless adjective <u>formless</u>, amorphous, irregular, misshapen, unstructured

shapely *adjective* well-formed, curvaceous, elegant, graceful, neat, trim, well-proportioned

share *noun* **1** part, allotment, allowance, contribution, due, lot, portion, quota, ration, whack (*informal*) ♦ *verb* **2** divide, assign, distribute, partake, participate, receive, split

sharp *adjective* **1** keen, acute, jagged, pointed, serrated, spiky **2** sudden, abrupt, distinct, extreme, marked **3** clear, crisp, distinct, well-defined **4** quick-witted, alert, astute, bright, clever, discerning, knowing, penetrating, perceptive, quick **5** dishonest, artful, crafty, cunning, sly, unscrupulous, wily **6** cutting, barbed, biting, bitter, caustic, harsh, hurtful **7** sour, acid, acrid, hot, piquant, pungent, tart **8** acute, intense, painful, piercing, severe, shooting, stabbing ♦ *adverb* **9** promptly, exactly, on the dot, on time, precisely, punctually

sharpen *verb* whet, edge, grind, hone

shatter *verb* **1** smash, break, burst, crack, crush, pulverize **2** destroy, demolish, ruin, torpedo, wreck

shattered *adjective Informal* **1** exhausted, all in (*slang*), dead beat (*informal*), done in (*informal*), drained, knackered (*slang*), ready to drop, tired out, worn out **2** devastated, crushed

shave *verb* trim, crop, pare, shear

shed[1] *noun* hut, outhouse, shack

shed[2] *verb* **1** give out, cast, drop, emit, give, radiate, scatter, shower, spill **2** cast off, discard, moult, slough

sheen *noun* shine, brightness, gleam, gloss, lustre, polish

sheepish *adjective* embarrassed, abashed, ashamed, mortified, self-conscious, shamefaced

sheer *adjective* **1** total, absolute, complete, downright, out-and-out, pure, unmitigated, utter **2** steep, abrupt, precipitous **3** fine, diaphanous, gauzy, gossamer, see-through, thin, transparent

sheet *noun* **1** coat, film, lamina, layer, overlay, stratum, surface, veneer **2** piece, panel, plate, slab **3** expanse, area, blanket, covering, stretch, sweep

shell *noun* **1** case, husk, pod **2** frame, framework, hull, structure ♦ *verb* **3** bomb, attack, blitz, bombard, strafe

shell out *verb* pay out, fork out (*slang*), give, hand over

shelter *noun* **1** protection, cover, defence, guard, screen **2** safety, asylum, haven, refuge, retreat, sanctuary, security ♦ *verb* **3** protect, cover, defend, guard, harbour, hide, safeguard, shield **4** take shelter, hide, seek refuge

sheltered *adjective* protected, cloistered, isolated, quiet, screened, secluded, shaded, shielded

shelve *verb* postpone, defer, freeze, put aside, put on ice, put on the back burner (*informal*), suspend, take a rain check on (*U.S. & Canad. informal*)

shepherd *verb* guide, conduct, herd, steer, usher

shield noun 1 <u>protection</u>, cover, defence, guard, safeguard, screen, shelter ♦ verb 2 <u>protect</u>, cover, defend, guard, safeguard, screen, shelter

shift verb 1 <u>move</u>, budge, displace, move around, rearrange, relocate, reposition ♦ noun 2 <u>move</u>, displacement, rearrangement, shifting

shiftless adjective <u>lazy</u>, aimless, good-for-nothing, idle, lackadaisical, slothful, unambitious, unenterprising

shifty adjective <u>untrustworthy</u>, deceitful, devious, evasive, furtive, slippery, sly, tricky, underhand

shimmer verb 1 <u>gleam</u>, glisten, scintillate, twinkle ♦ noun 2 <u>gleam</u>, iridescence

shine verb 1 <u>gleam</u>, beam, flash, glare, glisten, glitter, glow, radiate, sparkle, twinkle 2 <u>polish</u>, brush, buff, burnish 3 <u>stand out</u>, be conspicuous, excel ♦ noun 4 <u>brightness</u>, glare, gleam, light, radiance, shimmer, sparkle 5 <u>polish</u>, gloss, lustre, sheen

shining adjective <u>bright</u>, beaming, brilliant, gleaming, glistening, luminous, radiant, shimmering, sparkling

shiny adjective <u>bright</u>, gleaming, glistening, glossy, lustrous, polished

ship noun <u>vessel</u>, boat, craft

shipshape adjective <u>tidy</u>, neat, orderly, spick-and-span, trim, well-ordered, well-organized

shirk verb <u>dodge</u>, avoid, evade, get out of, skive (Brit. slang), slack

shirker noun <u>slacker</u>, clock-watcher, dodger, idler, skiver (Brit. slang)

shiver[1] verb 1 <u>tremble</u>, quake, quiver, shake, shudder ♦ noun 2 <u>trembling</u>, flutter, quiver, shudder, tremor

shiver[2] verb <u>splinter</u>, break, crack, fragment, shatter, smash, smash to smithereens

shivery adjective <u>shaking</u>, chilled, chilly, cold, quaking, quivery

shock verb 1 <u>horrify</u>, appal, disgust, nauseate, revolt, scandalize, sicken 2 <u>astound</u>, jolt, shake, stagger, stun, stupefy ♦ noun 3 <u>impact</u>, blow, clash, collision 4 <u>upset</u>, blow, bombshell, distress, disturbance, stupefaction, stupor, trauma, turn (informal)

shocking adjective <u>dreadful</u>, appalling, atrocious, disgraceful, disgusting, ghastly, horrifying, nauseating, outrageous, revolting, scandalous, sickening

shoddy adjective <u>inferior</u>, poor, rubbishy, second-rate, slipshod, tawdry, trashy

shoot verb 1 <u>hit</u>, blast (slang), bring down, kill, open fire, plug (slang) 2 <u>fire</u>, discharge, emit, fling, hurl, launch, project, propel 3 <u>speed</u>, bolt, charge, dart, dash, fly, hurtle, race, rush, streak, tear ♦ noun 4 <u>branch</u>, bud, offshoot, sprig, sprout

shop noun <u>store</u>, boutique, emporium, hypermarket, supermarket

shore noun <u>beach</u>, coast, sands, seashore, strand (poetic)

shore up verb <u>support</u>, brace, buttress, hold, prop, reinforce, strengthen, underpin

short *adjective* **1** <u>concise</u>, brief, compressed, laconic, pithy, succinct, summary, terse **2** <u>small</u>, diminutive, dumpy, little, petite, squat **3** <u>brief</u>, fleeting, momentary **4** *often with of* <u>lacking</u>, deficient, limited, low (on), scant, scarce, wanting **5** <u>abrupt</u>, brusque, curt, discourteous, impolite, sharp, terse, uncivil ♦ *adverb* **6** <u>abruptly</u>, suddenly, without warning

shortage *noun* <u>deficiency</u>, dearth, insufficiency, lack, paucity, scarcity, want

shortcoming *noun* <u>failing</u>, defect, fault, flaw, imperfection, weakness

shorten *verb* <u>cut</u>, abbreviate, abridge, curtail, decrease, diminish, lessen, reduce

shortly *adverb* <u>soon</u>, before long, in a little while, presently

short-sighted *adjective* **1** <u>near-sighted</u>, myopic **2** <u>unthinking</u>, ill-advised, ill-considered, impolitic, impractical, improvident, imprudent, injudicious

short-tempered *adjective* <u>quick-tempered</u>, hot-tempered, impatient, irascible, ratty (*Brit. & N.Z. informal*), testy

shot *noun* **1** <u>throw</u>, discharge, lob, pot shot **2** <u>pellet</u>, ball, bullet, lead, projectile, slug **3** <u>marksman</u>, shooter **4** *Slang* <u>attempt</u>, effort, endeavour, go (*informal*), stab (*informal*), try, turn

shoulder *verb* **1** <u>bear</u>, accept, assume, be responsible for, carry, take on **2** <u>push</u>, elbow, jostle, press, shove

shout *noun* **1** <u>cry</u>, bellow, call, roar, scream, yell ♦ *verb* **2** <u>cry (out)</u>, bawl, bellow, call (out), holler (*informal*), roar, scream, yell

shout down *verb* <u>silence</u>, drown, drown out, overwhelm

shove *verb* <u>push</u>, drive, elbow, impel, jostle, press, propel, thrust

shovel *verb* <u>move</u>, dredge, heap, ladle, load, scoop, toss

shove off *verb* <u>go away</u>, clear off (*informal*), depart, leave, push off (*informal*), scram (*informal*)

show *verb* **1** <u>be visible</u>, appear **2** <u>display</u>, exhibit, present **3** <u>prove</u>, clarify, demonstrate, elucidate, point out **4** <u>instruct</u>, demonstrate, explain, teach **5** <u>display</u>, indicate, manifest, register, reveal **6** <u>guide</u>, accompany, attend, conduct, escort, lead ♦ *noun* **7** <u>entertainment</u>, presentation, production **8** <u>exhibition</u>, array, display, fair, pageant, parade, sight, spectacle **9** <u>pretence</u>, affectation, air, appearance, display, illusion, parade, pose

showdown *noun* <u>confrontation</u>, clash, face-off (*slang*)

shower *noun* **1** <u>deluge</u>, barrage, stream, torrent, volley ♦ *verb* **2** <u>inundate</u>, deluge, heap, lavish, pour, rain

showman *noun* <u>performer</u>, entertainer

show-off *noun* <u>exhibitionist</u>, boaster, braggart, poseur

show off *verb* **1** <u>exhibit</u>, demonstrate, display, flaunt, parade **2** <u>boast</u>, blow one's own trumpet, brag, swagger

show up verb 1 <u>stand out</u>, appear, be conspicuous, be visible 2 <u>reveal</u>, expose, highlight, lay bare 3 Informal <u>embarrass</u>, let down, mortify, put to shame 4 Informal <u>arrive</u>, appear, come, turn up

showy adjective 1 <u>ostentatious</u>, brash, flamboyant, flash (informal), flashy, over the top (informal) 2 <u>gaudy</u>, garish, loud

shred noun 1 <u>strip</u>, bit, fragment, piece, scrap, sliver, tatter 2 <u>particle</u>, atom, grain, iota, jot, scrap, trace

shrew noun <u>nag</u>, harpy, harridan, scold, spitfire, vixen

shrewd adjective <u>clever</u>, astute, calculating, canny, crafty, cunning, intelligent, keen, perceptive, perspicacious, sharp, smart

shrewdness noun <u>astuteness</u>, canniness, discernment, judgment, perspicacity, quick wits, sharpness, smartness

shriek verb, noun <u>cry</u>, scream, screech, squeal, yell

shrill adjective <u>piercing</u>, high, penetrating, sharp

shrink verb 1 <u>decrease</u>, contract, diminish, dwindle, grow smaller, lessen, narrow, shorten 2 <u>recoil</u>, cower, cringe, draw back, flinch, quail

shrivel verb <u>wither</u>, dehydrate, desiccate, shrink, wilt, wizen

shroud noun 1 <u>winding sheet</u>, grave clothes 2 <u>covering</u>, mantle, pall, screen, veil ◆ verb 3 <u>conceal</u>, blanket, cloak, cover, envelop, hide, screen, veil

shudder verb 1 <u>shiver</u>, convulse, quake, quiver, shake, tremble ◆ noun 2 <u>shiver</u>, quiver, spasm, tremor

shuffle verb 1 <u>scuffle</u>, drag, scrape, shamble 2 <u>rearrange</u>, disarrange, disorder, jumble, mix

shun verb <u>avoid</u>, keep away from, steer clear of

shut verb <u>close</u>, fasten, seal, secure, slam

shut down verb 1 <u>stop</u>, halt, switch off 2 <u>close</u>, shut up

shut out verb <u>exclude</u>, bar, debar, keep out, lock out

shuttle verb <u>go back and forth</u>, alternate, commute, go to and fro

shut up verb 1 Informal <u>be quiet</u>, fall silent, gag, hold one's tongue, hush, silence 2 <u>confine</u>, cage, coop up, immure, imprison, incarcerate

shy[1] adjective 1 <u>timid</u>, bashful, coy, diffident, retiring, self-conscious, self-effacing, shrinking 2 <u>cautious</u>, chary, distrustful, hesitant, suspicious, wary ◆ verb 3 sometimes with **off** or **away** <u>recoil</u>, balk, draw back, flinch, start

shy[2] verb <u>throw</u>, cast, fling, hurl, pitch, sling, toss

shyness noun <u>timidness</u>, bashfulness, diffidence, lack of confidence, self-consciousness, timidity, timorousness

sick adjective 1 <u>nauseous</u>, ill, nauseated, queasy 2 <u>unwell</u>, ailing, diseased, indisposed, poorly (informal), under the weather 3 Informal <u>morbid</u>, black, ghoulish, macabre, sadistic 4 **sick of** <u>tired</u>, bored, fed up, jaded, weary

sicken verb **1** <u>disgust</u>, gross out (*U.S. slang*), nauseate, repel, revolt, turn one's stomach **2** <u>fall ill</u>, ail, take sick

sickening adjective <u>disgusting</u>, distasteful, foul, loathsome, nauseating, offensive, repulsive, revolting, stomach-turning (*informal*), yucky or yukky (*slang*)

sickly adjective **1** <u>unhealthy</u>, ailing, delicate, faint, feeble, infirm, pallid, peaky, wan, weak **2** <u>nauseating</u>, cloying, mawkish

sickness noun **1** <u>illness</u>, affliction, ailment, bug (*informal*), complaint, disease, disorder, malady **2** <u>nausea</u>, queasiness, vomiting

side noun **1** <u>border</u>, boundary, division, edge, limit, margin, perimeter, rim, sector, verge **2** <u>part</u>, aspect, face, facet, flank, hand, surface, view **3** <u>party</u>, camp, cause, faction, sect, team **4** <u>point of view</u>, angle, opinion, position, slant, stand, standpoint, viewpoint **5** *Brit. slang* <u>conceit</u>, airs, arrogance ♦ *adjective* **6** <u>subordinate</u>, ancillary, incidental, lesser, marginal, minor, secondary, subsidiary ♦ *verb* **7** *usually with* with <u>support</u>, ally with, favour, go along with, take the part of

sidelong adjective <u>sideways</u>, covert, indirect, oblique

sidestep verb <u>avoid</u>, circumvent, dodge, duck (*informal*), evade, skirt

sidetrack verb <u>divert</u>, deflect, distract

sideways adverb **1** <u>obliquely</u>, edgeways, laterally, sidelong, to the side ♦ *adjective* **2** <u>oblique</u>, sidelong

sidle verb <u>edge</u>, creep, inch, slink, sneak, steal

siesta noun <u>nap</u>, catnap, doze, forty winks (*informal*), sleep, snooze (*informal*)

sieve noun **1** <u>strainer</u>, colander ♦ *verb* **2** <u>sift</u>, separate, strain

sift verb **1** <u>sieve</u>, filter, separate **2** <u>examine</u>, analyse, go through, investigate, research, scrutinize, work over

sight noun **1** <u>vision</u>, eye, eyes, eyesight, seeing **2** <u>view</u>, appearance, perception, range of vision, visibility **3** <u>spectacle</u>, display, exhibition, pageant, scene, show, vista **4** *Informal* <u>eyesore</u>, mess, monstrosity **5** **catch sight of** <u>spot</u>, espy, glimpse ♦ *verb* **6** <u>spot</u>, behold, discern, distinguish, make out, observe, perceive, see

sign noun **1** <u>indication</u>, clue, evidence, hint, mark, proof, signal, symptom, token **2** <u>notice</u>, board, placard, warning **3** <u>symbol</u>, badge, device, emblem, logo, mark **4** <u>omen</u>, augury, auspice, foreboding, portent, warning ♦ *verb* **5** <u>autograph</u>, endorse, initial, inscribe **6** <u>gesture</u>, beckon, gesticulate, indicate, signal

signal noun **1** <u>sign</u>, beacon, cue, gesture, indication, mark, token ♦ *verb* **2** <u>gesture</u>, beckon, gesticulate, indicate, motion, sign, wave

significance noun **1** <u>importance</u>, consequence, moment, relevance, weight **2** <u>meaning</u>, force, implication(s), import, message, point, purport, sense

significant adjective 1 important, critical, material, momentous, noteworthy, serious, vital, weighty 2 meaningful, eloquent, expressive, indicative, suggestive

signify verb 1 indicate, be a sign of, betoken, connote, denote, imply, intimate, mean, portend, suggest 2 Informal matter, be important, carry weight, count

silence noun 1 quiet, calm, hush, lull, peace, stillness 2 muteness, dumbness, reticence, taciturnity ♦ verb 3 quieten, cut off, cut short, deaden, gag, muffle, quiet, stifle, still, suppress

silent adjective 1 quiet, hushed, muted, noiseless, soundless, still 2 mute, dumb, speechless, taciturn, voiceless, wordless

silently adjective quietly, inaudibly, in silence, mutely, noiselessly, soundlessly, without a sound, wordlessly

silhouette noun 1 outline, form, profile, shape ♦ verb 2 outline, etch, stand out

silky adjective smooth, silken, sleek, velvety

silly adjective foolish, absurd, asinine, fatuous, idiotic, inane, ridiculous, senseless, stupid, unwise

silt noun 1 sediment, alluvium, deposit, ooze, sludge ♦ verb 2 silt up clog, choke, congest

similar adjective alike, analogous, close, comparable, like, resembling

similarity noun resemblance, affinity, agreement, analogy, closeness, comparability, correspondence, likeness, sameness

simmer verb fume, be angry, rage, seethe, smoulder

simmer down verb calm down, control oneself, cool off or down

simper verb smile coyly, smile affectedly, smirk

simple adjective 1 easy, clear, intelligible, lucid, plain, straightforward, uncomplicated, understandable, uninvolved 2 plain, classic, natural, unembellished, unfussy 3 pure, elementary, unalloyed, uncombined, unmixed 4 artless, childlike, guileless, ingenuous, innocent, naive, natural, sincere, unaffected, unsophisticated 5 honest, bald, basic, direct, frank, naked, plain, sincere, stark 6 humble, homely, modest, unpretentious 7 feeble-minded, foolish, half-witted, moronic, slow, stupid

simple-minded adjective feeble-minded, backward, dim-witted, foolish, idiot, idiotic, moronic, retarded, simple, stupid

simpleton noun halfwit, dullard, fool, idiot, imbecile (informal), moron, numskull or numbskull

simplicity noun 1 ease, clarity, clearness, straightforwardness 2 plainness, lack of adornment, purity, restraint 3 artlessness, candour, directness, innocence, naivety, openness

simplify verb make simpler, abridge, disentangle, dumb down, reduce to essentials, streamline

simply adverb 1 plainly, clearly, directly, easily, intelligibly, naturally, straightforwardly, unpretentiously **2** just, merely, only, purely, solely **3** totally, absolutely, completely, really, utterly, wholly

simulate *verb* pretend, act, affect, feign, put on, sham

simultaneous *adjective* coinciding, at the same time, coincident, concurrent, contemporaneous, synchronous

simultaneously *adverb* at the same time, concurrently, together

sin *noun* **1** wrongdoing, crime, error, evil, guilt, iniquity, misdeed, offence, transgression ♦ *verb* **2** transgress, err, fall, go astray, lapse, offend

sincere *adjective* honest, candid, earnest, frank, genuine, guileless, heartfelt, real, serious, true, unaffected

sincerely *adverb* honestly, earnestly, genuinely, in earnest, seriously, truly, wholeheartedly

sincerity *noun* honesty, candour, frankness, genuineness, seriousness, truth

sinecure *noun* cushy number (*informal*), gravy train (*slang*), money for jam *or* old rope (*informal*), soft job (*informal*), soft option

sinful *adjective* guilty, bad, corrupt, criminal, erring, immoral, iniquitous, wicked

sing *verb* **1** warble, carol, chant, chirp, croon, pipe, trill, yodel **2** hum, buzz, purr, whine

singe *verb* burn, char, scorch, sear

singer *noun* vocalist, balladeer, chorister, crooner, minstrel, soloist

single *adjective* **1** one, distinct, individual, lone, only, separate, sole, solitary **2** individual, exclusive, separate, undivided, unshared **3** simple, unblended, unmixed **4** unmarried, free, unattached, unwed ♦ *verb* **5** *usually with* out pick, choose, distinguish, fix on, pick on *or* out, select, separate, set apart

single-handed *adverb* unaided, alone, by oneself, independently, on one's own, solo, unassisted, without help

single-minded *adjective* determined, dedicated, dogged, fixed, unswerving

singly *adverb* one by one, individually, one at a time, separately

singular *adjective* **1** single, individual, separate, sole **2** remarkable, eminent, exceptional, notable, noteworthy, outstanding **3** unusual, curious, eccentric, extraordinary, odd, peculiar, queer, strange

singularly *adverb* remarkably, especially, exceptionally, notably, outstandingly, particularly, uncommonly, unusually

sinister *adjective* threatening, dire, disquieting, evil, malign, menacing, ominous

sink *verb* **1** descend, dip, drop, fall, founder, go down, go under, lower, plunge, submerge, subside **2** fall, abate, collapse, drop, lapse, slip, subside **3** decline, decay, deteriorate, diminish, dwindle, fade, fail, flag, lessen, weaken, worsen **4** dig, bore, drill, drive, excavate

5 <u>stoop</u>, be reduced to, lower oneself

sink in *verb* <u>be understood</u>, get through to, penetrate, register (*informal*)

sinner *noun* <u>wrongdoer</u>, evildoer, malefactor, miscreant, offender, transgressor

sip *verb* **1** <u>drink</u>, sample, sup, taste ♦ *noun* **2** <u>swallow</u>, drop, taste, thimbleful

sissy *noun* **1** <u>wimp</u> (*informal*), coward, jessie (*Scot. slang*), milksop, mummy's boy, namby-pamby, softie (*informal*), weakling, wet (*Brit. informal*) ♦ *adjective* **2** <u>wimpish or wimpy</u> (*informal*), cowardly, effeminate, feeble, namby-pamby, soft (*informal*), unmanly, weak, wet (*Brit. informal*)

sit *verb* **1** <u>rest</u>, perch, settle **2** <u>convene</u>, assemble, deliberate, meet, officiate, preside

site *noun* **1** <u>location</u>, place, plot, position, setting, spot ♦ *verb* **2** <u>locate</u>, install, place, position, set, situate

situation *noun* **1** <u>state of affairs</u>, case, circumstances, condition, plight, state **2** <u>location</u>, place, position, setting, site, spot **3** <u>status</u>, rank, station **4** <u>job</u>, employment, office, place, position, post

sizable, sizeable *adjective* <u>large</u>, considerable, decent, goodly, largish, respectable, substantial

size *noun* <u>dimensions</u>, amount, bulk, extent, immensity, magnitude, mass, proportions, range, volume

size up *verb* <u>assess</u>, appraise, evaluate, take stock of

sizzle *verb* <u>hiss</u>, crackle, frizzle, fry, spit

skeleton *noun* <u>framework</u>, bare bones, draft, frame, outline, sketch, structure

sketch *noun* **1** <u>drawing</u>, delineation, design, draft, outline, plan ♦ *verb* **2** <u>draw</u>, delineate, depict, draft, outline, represent, rough out

sketchy *adjective* <u>incomplete</u>, cursory, inadequate, perfunctory, rough, scrappy, skimpy, superficial

skilful *adjective* <u>expert</u>, able, adept, adroit, clever, competent, dexterous, masterly, practised, professional, proficient, skilled

skill *noun* <u>expertise</u>, ability, art, cleverness, competence, craft, dexterity, facility, knack, proficiency, skilfulness, talent, technique

skilled *adjective* <u>expert</u>, able, masterly, professional, proficient, skilful

skim *verb* **1** <u>separate</u>, cream **2** <u>glide</u>, coast, float, fly, sail, soar **3** *usually with* **through** <u>scan</u>, glance, run one's eye over

skimp *verb* <u>stint</u>, be mean with, be sparing with, cut corners, scamp, scrimp

skin *noun* **1** <u>hide</u>, fell, pelt **2** <u>coating</u>, casing, crust, film, husk, outside, peel, rind ♦ *verb* **3** <u>peel</u>, flay, scrape

skinflint *noun* <u>miser</u>, meanie *or* meany (*informal, chiefly Brit.*), niggard, penny-pincher (*informal*), Scrooge

skinny *adjective* <u>thin</u>, emaciated,

lean, scrawny, undernourished

skip verb 1 hop, bob, bounce, caper, dance, flit, frisk, gambol, prance, trip 2 pass over, eschew, give (something) a miss, leave out, miss out, omit

skirmish noun 1 fight, battle, brush, clash, conflict, encounter, fracas, scrap (informal) ♦ verb 2 fight, clash, collide

skirt verb 1 border, edge, flank 2 often with **around** or **round** avoid, circumvent, evade, steer clear of

skit noun parody, burlesque, sketch, spoof (informal), takeoff (informal)

skittish adjective lively, excitable, fidgety, highly strung, jumpy, nervous, restive

skive verb slack, idle, malinger, shirk, swing the lead

skulduggery noun Informal trickery, double-dealing, duplicity, machinations, underhandedness

skulk verb lurk, creep, prowl, slink, sneak

sky noun heavens, firmament

slab noun piece, chunk, lump, portion, slice, wedge

slack adjective 1 loose, baggy, lax, limp, relaxed 2 negligent, idle, inactive, lax, lazy, neglectful, remiss, slapdash, slipshod 3 slow, dull, inactive, quiet, slow-moving, sluggish ♦ noun 4 room, excess, give (informal), leeway ♦ verb 5 shirk, dodge, idle, skive (Brit. slang)

slacken verb, often with **off** lessen, abate, decrease, diminish, drop off, moderate, reduce, relax

slacker noun layabout, dodger, idler, loafer, shirker, skiver (Brit. slang)

slag off verb Slang criticize, abuse, deride, insult, malign, mock, slander, slate

slake verb satisfy, assuage, quench, sate

slam verb bang, crash, dash, fling, hurl, smash, throw

slander noun 1 defamation, calumny, libel, scandal, smear ♦ verb 2 defame, blacken (someone's) name, libel, malign, smear

slanderous adjective defamatory, damaging, libellous, malicious

slant verb 1 slope, bend, bevel, cant, heel, incline, lean, list, tilt 2 bias, angle, colour, distort, twist ♦ noun 3 slope, camber, gradient, incline, tilt 4 bias, angle, emphasis, one-sidedness, point of view, prejudice

slanting adjective sloping, angled, at an angle, bent, diagonal, inclined, oblique, tilted, tilting

slap noun 1 smack, blow, cuff, spank ♦ verb 2 smack, clap, cuff, spank

slapdash adjective careless, clumsy, hasty, hurried, messy, slipshod, sloppy (informal)

slap-up adjective luxurious, lavish, magnificent, splendid, sumptuous, superb

slash verb 1 cut, gash, hack, lacerate, rend, rip, score, slit 2 reduce, cut, drop, lower ♦ noun 3 cut, gash, incision, laceration, rent, rip, slit

slate verb Informal criticize,

censure, rebuke, scold, tear into (*informal*)

slaughter *verb* 1 <u>murder</u>, butcher, kill, massacre, slay ♦ *noun* 2 <u>murder</u>, bloodshed, butchery, carnage, killing, massacre, slaying

slaughterhouse *noun* <u>abattoir</u>

slave *noun* 1 <u>servant</u>, drudge, serf, skivvy (*chiefly Brit.*), vassal ♦ *verb* 2 <u>toil</u>, drudge, slog

slavery *noun* <u>enslavement</u>, bondage, captivity, servitude, subjugation

slavish *adjective* 1 <u>servile</u>, abject, base, cringing, fawning, grovelling, obsequious, submissive, sycophantic 2 <u>imitative</u>, second-hand, unimaginative, unoriginal

slay *verb* <u>kill</u>, butcher, massacre, mow down, murder, slaughter

sleaze *noun* <u>corruption</u>, bribery, dishonesty, extortion, fraud, unscrupulousness, venality

sleazy *adjective* <u>sordid</u>, disreputable, low, run-down, seedy, squalid

sleek *adjective* <u>glossy</u>, lustrous, shiny, smooth

sleep *noun* 1 <u>slumber(s)</u>, doze, forty winks (*informal*), hibernation, nap, siesta, snooze (*informal*), zizz (*Brit. informal*) ♦ *verb* 2 <u>slumber</u>, catnap, doze, drowse, hibernate, snooze (*informal*), take a nap

sleepless *adjective* <u>wakeful</u>, insomniac, restless

sleepy *adjective* <u>drowsy</u>, dull, heavy, inactive, lethargic, sluggish

slender *adjective* 1 <u>slim</u>, lean,

narrow, slight, willowy 2 <u>faint</u>, poor, remote, slight, slim, tenuous, thin 3 <u>meagre</u>, little, scant, scanty, small

sleuth *noun* <u>detective</u>, private eye (*informal*), (private) investigator

slice *noun* 1 <u>share</u>, cut, helping, portion, segment, sliver, wedge ♦ *verb* 2 <u>cut</u>, carve, divide, sever

slick *adjective* 1 <u>glib</u>, plausible, polished, smooth, specious 2 <u>skilful</u>, adroit, deft, dexterous, polished, professional ♦ *verb* 3 <u>smooth</u>, plaster down, sleek

slide *verb* <u>slip</u>, coast, glide, skim, slither

slight *adjective* 1 <u>small</u>, feeble, insignificant, meagre, measly, minor, paltry, scanty, trifling, trivial, unimportant 2 <u>slim</u>, delicate, feeble, fragile, lightly-built, small, spare ♦ *verb* 3 <u>snub</u>, affront, disdain, ignore, insult, scorn ♦ *noun* 4 <u>snub</u>, affront, insult, neglect, rebuff, slap in the face (*informal*), (the) cold shoulder

slightly *adverb* <u>a little</u>, somewhat

slim *adjective* 1 <u>slender</u>, lean, narrow, slight, svelte, thin, trim 2 <u>slight</u>, faint, poor, remote, slender ♦ *verb* 3 <u>lose weight</u>, diet, reduce

slimy *adjective* 1 <u>viscous</u>, clammy, glutinous, oozy 2 <u>obsequious</u>, creeping, grovelling, oily, servile, smarmy (*Brit. informal*), unctuous

sling *verb* 1 <u>throw</u>, cast, chuck (*informal*), fling, heave, hurl, lob (*informal*), shy, toss 2 <u>hang</u>, dangle, suspend

slink verb <u>creep</u>, prowl, skulk, slip, sneak, steal

slinky adjective <u>figure-hugging</u>, clinging, close-fitting, skintight

slip verb 1 <u>fall</u>, skid 2 <u>slide</u>, glide, skate, slither 3 <u>sneak</u>, conceal, creep, hide, steal 4 *sometimes with* **up** <u>make a mistake</u>, blunder, err, miscalculate 5 **let slip** <u>give away</u>, disclose, divulge, leak, reveal ♦ *noun* 6 <u>mistake</u>, blunder, error, failure, fault, lapse, omission, oversight 7 **give (someone) the slip** <u>escape from</u>, dodge, elude, evade, get away from, lose (someone)

slippery adjective 1 <u>smooth</u>, glassy, greasy, icy, slippy (*informal or dialect*), unsafe 2 <u>devious</u>, crafty, cunning, dishonest, evasive, shifty, tricky, untrustworthy

slipshod adjective <u>careless</u>, casual, slapdash, sloppy (*informal*), slovenly, untidy

slit noun 1 <u>cut</u>, gash, incision, opening, rent, split, tear ♦ *verb* 2 <u>cut (open)</u>, gash, knife, lance, pierce, rip, slash

slither verb <u>slide</u>, glide, slink, slip, snake, undulate

sliver noun <u>shred</u>, fragment, paring, shaving, splinter

slobber verb <u>drool</u>, dribble, drivel, salivate, slaver

slobbish adjective <u>messy</u>, slovenly, unclean, unkempt, untidy

slog verb 1 <u>work</u>, labour, plod, plough through, slave, toil 2 <u>trudge</u>, tramp, trek 3 <u>hit</u>, punch, slug, sock (*slang*), strike, thump, wallop (*informal*) ♦ *noun*

4 <u>labour</u>, effort, exertion, struggle 5 <u>trudge</u>, hike, tramp, trek

slogan noun <u>catch phrase</u>, catchword, motto

slop verb <u>spill</u>, overflow, slosh (*informal*), splash

slope noun 1 <u>inclination</u>, gradient, incline, ramp, rise, slant, tilt ♦ *verb* 2 <u>slant</u>, drop away, fall, incline, lean, rise, tilt 3 **slope off** <u>slink away</u>, creep away, slip away

sloping adjective <u>slanting</u>, inclined, leaning, oblique

sloppy adjective 1 <u>careless</u>, messy, slipshod, slovenly, untidy 2 <u>sentimental</u>, gushing, mawkish, slushy (*informal*), soppy (*Brit. informal*)

slot noun 1 <u>opening</u>, aperture, groove, hole, slit, vent 2 *Informal* <u>place</u>, opening, position, space, time, vacancy ♦ *verb* 3 <u>fit in</u>, fit, insert

sloth noun <u>laziness</u>, idleness, inactivity, inertia, slackness, sluggishness, torpor

slothful adjective <u>lazy</u>, idle, inactive, indolent, skiving (*Brit. slang*), workshy

slouch verb <u>slump</u>, droop, loll, stoop

slovenly adjective <u>careless</u>, disorderly, negligent, slack, slapdash, slipshod, sloppy (*informal*), untidy

slow adjective 1 <u>prolonged</u>, gradual, lingering, long-drawn-out, protracted 2 <u>unhurried</u>, dawdling, lackadaisical, laggard, lazy, leisurely, ponderous, sluggish

3 <u>late</u>, backward, behind, delayed, tardy 4 <u>stupid</u>, braindead (*informal*), dense, dim, dozy (*Brit. informal*), dull-witted, obtuse, retarded, thick ◆ *verb* 5 *often with* **up** *or* **down** <u>reduce speed</u>, brake, decelerate, handicap, hold up, retard, slacken (off)

slowly *adverb* <u>gradually</u>, leisurely, unhurriedly

sludge *noun* <u>sediment</u>, mire, muck, mud, ooze, residue, silt, slime

sluggish *adjective* <u>inactive</u>, dull, heavy, indolent, inert, lethargic, slothful, slow, torpid

slum *noun* <u>hovel</u>, ghetto

slumber *verb* <u>sleep</u>, doze, drowse, nap, snooze (*informal*), zizz (*Brit. informal*)

slump *verb* 1 <u>fall</u>, collapse, crash, plunge, sink, slip 2 <u>sag</u>, droop, hunch, loll, slouch ◆ *noun* 3 <u>fall</u>, collapse, crash, decline, downturn, drop, reverse, trough 4 <u>recession</u>, depression

slur *noun* <u>insult</u>, affront, aspersion, calumny, innuendo, insinuation, smear, stain

slut *noun Offensive* <u>tart</u>, scrubber (*Brit. & Austral. slang*), slag (*Brit. slang*), slapper (*Brit. slang*), trollop

sly *adjective* 1 <u>cunning</u>, artful, clever, crafty, devious, scheming, secret, shifty, stealthy, subtle, underhand, wily 2 <u>roguish</u>, arch, impish, knowing, mischievous ◆ *noun* 3 **on the sly** <u>secretly</u>, covertly, on the quiet, privately, surreptitiously

smack *verb* 1 <u>slap</u>, clap, cuff, hit, spank, strike ◆ *noun* 2 <u>slap</u>, blow

◆ *adverb* 3 *Informal* <u>directly</u>, exactly, precisely, right, slap (*informal*), squarely, straight

small *adjective* 1 <u>little</u>, diminutive, mini, miniature, minute, petite, pygmy *or* pigmy, teeny, teeny-weeny, tiny, undersized, wee 2 <u>unimportant</u>, insignificant, minor, negligible, paltry, petty, trifling, trivial 3 <u>petty</u>, base, mean, narrow 4 <u>modest</u>, humble, unpretentious

small-minded *adjective* <u>petty</u>, bigoted, intolerant, mean, narrow-minded, ungenerous

small-time *adjective* <u>minor</u>, insignificant, of no account, petty, unimportant

smarmy *adjective Informal* <u>obsequious</u>, crawling, ingratiating, servile, smooth, suave, sycophantic, toadying, unctuous

smart *adjective* 1 <u>neat</u>, chic, elegant, natty (*informal*), snappy, spruce, stylish, trim 2 <u>clever</u>, acute, astute, bright, canny, ingenious, intelligent, keen, quick, sharp, shrewd 3 <u>brisk</u>, lively, quick, vigorous ◆ *verb* 4 <u>sting</u>, burn, hurt ◆ *noun* 5 <u>sting</u>, pain, soreness

smart aleck *noun Informal* <u>know-all</u> (*informal*), clever-clogs (*informal*), smarty pants (*informal*), wise guy (*informal*)

smarten *verb* <u>tidy</u>, groom, put in order, put to rights, spruce up

smash *verb* 1 <u>break</u>, crush, demolish, pulverize, shatter 2 <u>collide</u>, crash 3 <u>destroy</u>, lay waste, ruin, trash (*slang*), wreck ◆ *noun* 4 <u>destruction</u>, collapse, downfall, failure, ruin 5 <u>collision</u>, accident, crash

smashing adjective Informal <u>excellent</u>, awesome (slang), brilliant (informal), cracking (Brit. informal), fabulous (informal), fantastic (informal), great (informal), magnificent, marvellous, mean (slang), sensational (informal), super (informal), superb, terrific (informal), wonderful

smattering noun <u>modicum</u>, bit, rudiments

smear verb 1 <u>spread over</u>, bedaub, coat, cover, daub, rub on 2 <u>dirty</u>, smudge, soil, stain, sully 3 <u>slander</u>, besmirch, blacken, malign ◆ noun 4 <u>smudge</u>, blot, blotch, daub, splotch, streak 5 <u>slander</u>, calumny, defamation, libel

smell verb 1 <u>sniff</u>, scent 2 <u>stink</u>, pong (Brit. informal), reek ◆ noun 3 <u>odour</u>, aroma, bouquet, fragrance, perfume, scent 4 <u>stink</u>, fetor, pong (Brit. informal), stench

smelly adjective <u>stinking</u>, fetid, foul, foul-smelling, malodorous, noisome, reeking

smirk noun <u>smug look</u>, simper

smitten adjective 1 <u>afflicted</u>, laid low, plagued, struck 2 <u>infatuated</u>, beguiled, bewitched, captivated, charmed, enamoured

smooth adjective 1 <u>even</u>, flat, flush, horizontal, level, plane 2 <u>sleek</u>, glossy, polished, shiny, silky, soft, velvety 3 <u>easy</u>, effortless, well-ordered 4 <u>flowing</u>, regular, rhythmic, steady, uniform 5 <u>suave</u>, facile, glib, persuasive, slick, smarmy

(Brit. informal), unctuous, urbane 6 <u>mellow</u>, agreeable, mild, pleasant ◆ verb 7 <u>flatten</u>, iron, level, plane, press 8 <u>calm</u>, appease, assuage, ease, mitigate, mollify, soften

smother verb 1 <u>suffocate</u>, choke, stifle, strangle 2 <u>suppress</u>, conceal, hide, muffle, repress, stifle

smoulder verb <u>seethe</u>, boil, fume, rage, simmer

smudge verb 1 <u>smear</u>, daub, dirty, mark, smirch ◆ noun 2 <u>smear</u>, blemish, blot

smug adjective <u>self-satisfied</u>, complacent, conceited, superior

smuggler noun <u>trafficker</u>, bootlegger, runner

smutty adjective <u>obscene</u>, bawdy, blue, coarse, crude, dirty, indecent, indelicate, suggestive, vulgar

snack noun <u>light meal</u>, bite, refreshment(s)

snag noun 1 <u>difficulty</u>, catch, complication, disadvantage, downside, drawback, hitch, obstacle, problem ◆ verb 2 <u>catch</u>, rip, tear

snap verb 1 <u>break</u>, crack, separate 2 <u>crackle</u>, click, pop 3 <u>bite at</u>, bite, nip, snatch 4 <u>speak sharply</u>, bark, jump down (someone's) throat (informal), lash out at ◆ noun 5 <u>crackle</u>, pop 6 <u>bite</u>, grab, nip ◆ adjective 7 <u>instant</u>, immediate, spur-of-the-moment, sudden

snappy adjective 1 <u>irritable</u>, cross, edgy, ratty (Brit. & N.Z. informal), testy, tetchy, touchy 2 <u>smart</u>, chic, dapper, fashionable, natty (*informal*), stylish

snap up verb <u>seize</u>, grab, pounce upon, take advantage of

snare noun 1 <u>trap</u>, gin, net, noose, wire ♦ verb 2 <u>trap</u>, catch, entrap, net, seize, wire

snarl verb, often with up <u>tangle</u>, entangle, entwine, muddle, ravel

snarl-up noun <u>tangle</u>, confusion, entanglement, muddle

snatch verb 1 <u>seize</u>, clutch, grab, grasp, grip ♦ noun 2 <u>bit</u>, fragment, part, piece, snippet

sneak verb 1 <u>slink</u>, lurk, pad, skulk, slip, steal 2 <u>slip</u>, smuggle, spirit 3 *Informal* <u>inform on</u>, grass on (*Brit. slang*), shop (*slang, chiefly Brit.*), tell on (*informal*), tell tales ♦ noun 4 <u>informer</u>, telltale

sneaking adjective 1 <u>nagging</u>, persistent, uncomfortable, worrying 2 <u>secret</u>, hidden, private, undivulged, unexpressed, unvoiced

sneaky adjective <u>sly</u>, deceitful, devious, dishonest, double-dealing, furtive, low, mean, shifty, untrustworthy

sneer noun 1 <u>scorn</u>, derision, gibe, jeer, mockery, ridicule ♦ verb 2 <u>scorn</u>, deride, disdain, jeer, laugh, mock, ridicule

snide adjective <u>nasty</u>, cynical, disparaging, hurtful, ill-natured, malicious, sarcastic, scornful, sneering, spiteful

sniff verb <u>inhale</u>, breathe, smell

snigger noun, verb <u>laugh</u>, giggle, snicker, titter

snip verb 1 <u>cut</u>, clip, crop, dock, shave, trim ♦ noun 2 *Informal* <u>bargain</u>, giveaway, good buy, steal (*informal*) 3 <u>bit</u>, clipping,

fragment, piece, scrap, shred

snipe verb <u>criticize</u>, carp, denigrate, disparage, jeer, knock (*informal*), put down

snippet noun <u>piece</u>, fragment, part, scrap, shred

snivel verb <u>whine</u>, cry, grizzle (*informal, chiefly Brit.*), moan, sniffle, whimper, whinge (*informal*)

snob noun <u>elitist</u>, highbrow, prig

snobbery noun <u>arrogance</u>, airs, pretension, pride, snobbishness

snobbish adjective <u>superior</u>, arrogant, patronizing, pretentious, snooty (*informal*), stuck-up (*informal*)

snoop verb <u>pry</u>, interfere, poke one's nose in (*informal*), spy

snooper noun <u>nosy parker</u> (*informal*), busybody, meddler, snoop (*informal*)

snooze verb 1 <u>doze</u>, catnap, nap, take forty winks (*informal*) ♦ noun 2 <u>doze</u>, catnap, forty winks (*informal*), nap, siesta

snub verb 1 <u>put down</u>, cold-shoulder, cut (*informal*), humiliate, rebuff, slight ♦ noun 2 <u>insult</u>, affront, put-down, slap in the face

snug adjective <u>cosy</u>, comfortable, comfy (*informal*), warm

snuggle verb <u>nestle</u>, cuddle, nuzzle

soak verb 1 <u>wet</u>, bathe, damp, drench, immerse, moisten, saturate, steep 2 <u>penetrate</u>, permeate, seep 3 <u>soak up</u> <u>absorb</u>, assimilate

soaking adjective <u>soaked</u>, drenched, dripping, saturated, sodden, sopping, streaming, wet through, wringing wet

soar verb 1 <u>ascend</u>, fly, mount, rise, wing 2 <u>rise</u>, climb, escalate, rocket, shoot up

sob verb <u>cry</u>, howl, shed tears, weep

sober adjective 1 <u>abstinent</u>, abstemious, moderate, temperate 2 <u>serious</u>, composed, cool, grave, level-headed, rational, reasonable, sedate, solemn, staid, steady 3 <u>plain</u>, dark, drab, quiet, sombre, subdued

sobriety noun 1 <u>abstinence</u>, abstemiousness, moderation, nonindulgence, soberness, temperance 2 <u>seriousness</u>, gravity, level-headedness, solemnity, staidness, steadiness

so-called adjective <u>alleged</u>, pretended, professed, self-styled, supposed

sociable adjective <u>friendly</u>, affable, companionable, convivial, cordial, genial, gregarious, outgoing, social, warm

social adjective 1 <u>communal</u>, collective, common, community, general, group, public ♦ noun 2 <u>get-together</u> (informal), gathering, party

socialize verb <u>mix</u>, fraternize, get about or around, go out

society noun 1 <u>mankind</u>, civilization, humanity, people, the community, the public 2 <u>organization</u>, association, circle, club, fellowship, group, guild, institute, league, order, union 3 <u>upper classes</u>, beau monde, elite, gentry, high society 4 <u>companionship</u>,

company, fellowship, friendship

sodden adjective <u>soaked</u>, drenched, saturated, soggy, sopping, waterlogged

sofa noun <u>couch</u>, chaise longue, divan, settee

soft adjective 1 <u>pliable</u>, bendable, elastic, flexible, malleable, mouldable, plastic, supple 2 <u>yielding</u>, elastic, gelatinous, pulpy, spongy, squashy 3 <u>velvety</u>, downy, feathery, fleecy, silky, smooth 4 <u>quiet</u>, dulcet, gentle, murmured, muted, soft-toned 5 <u>pale</u>, bland, light, mellow, pastel, subdued 6 <u>dim</u>, dimmed, faint, restful 7 <u>mild</u>, balmy, temperate 8 <u>lenient</u>, easy-going, indulgent, lax, overindulgent, permissive, spineless 9 <u>out of condition</u>, effeminate, flabby, flaccid, limp, weak 10 Informal <u>easy</u>, comfortable, cushy (informal), undemanding 11 <u>kind</u>, compassionate, gentle, sensitive, sentimental, tenderhearted, touchy-feely (informal)

soften verb <u>lessen</u>, allay, appease, cushion, ease, mitigate, moderate, mollify, still, subdue, temper

softhearted adjective <u>kind</u>, charitable, compassionate, sentimental, sympathetic, tender, tenderhearted, warm-hearted

soggy adjective <u>sodden</u>, dripping, moist, saturated, soaked, sopping, waterlogged

soil[1] noun 1 <u>earth</u>, clay, dirt, dust, ground 2 <u>land</u>, country

soil[2] verb <u>dirty</u>, befoul, besmirch, defile, foul, pollute, spot, stain, sully, tarnish

solace noun 1 <u>comfort</u>, consolation, relief ♦ verb 2 <u>comfort</u>, console

soldier noun <u>fighter</u>, man-at-arms, serviceman, squaddie or squaddy (Brit. slang), trooper, warrior

sole adjective <u>only</u>, alone, exclusive, individual, one, single, solitary

solely adverb <u>only</u>, alone, completely, entirely, exclusively, merely

solemn adjective 1 <u>formal</u>, ceremonial, dignified, grand, grave, momentous, stately 2 <u>serious</u>, earnest, grave, sedate, sober, staid

solemnity noun 1 <u>seriousness</u>, earnestness, gravity 2 <u>formality</u>, grandeur, impressiveness, momentousness

solicitous adjective <u>concerned</u>, anxious, attentive, careful

solicitude noun <u>concern</u>, anxiety, attentiveness, care, consideration, regard

solid adjective 1 <u>firm</u>, compact, concrete, dense, hard 2 <u>strong</u>, stable, sturdy, substantial, unshakable 3 <u>sound</u>, genuine, good, pure, real, reliable 4 <u>reliable</u>, dependable, trusty, upright, upstanding, worthy

solidarity noun <u>unity</u>, accord, cohesion, concordance, like-mindedness, team spirit, unanimity, unification

solidify verb <u>harden</u>, cake, coagulate, cohere, congeal, jell, set

solitary adjective 1 <u>unsociable</u>, cloistered, isolated, reclusive, unsocial 2 <u>single</u>, alone, lone, sole 3 <u>lonely</u>, companionless, friendless, lonesome 4 <u>isolated</u>, hidden, out-of-the-way, remote, unfrequented

solitude noun <u>isolation</u>, loneliness, privacy, retirement, seclusion

solution noun 1 <u>answer</u>, explanation, key, result 2 Chemistry <u>mixture</u>, blend, compound, mix, solvent

solve verb <u>answer</u>, clear up, crack, decipher, disentangle, get to the bottom of, resolve, suss (out) (slang), unravel, work out

sombre adjective 1 <u>dark</u>, dim, drab, dull, gloomy, sober 2 <u>gloomy</u>, dismal, doleful, grave, joyless, lugubrious, mournful, sad, sober

somebody noun <u>celebrity</u>, dignitary, household name, luminary, megastar (informal), name, notable, personage, star

someday adverb <u>eventually</u>, one day, one of these (fine) days, sooner or later

somehow adverb <u>one way or another</u>, by fair means or foul, by hook or (by) crook, by some means or other, come hell or high water (informal), come what may

sometimes adverb <u>occasionally</u>, at times, now and then

song noun <u>ballad</u>, air, anthem, carol, chant, chorus, ditty, hymn, number, psalm, tune

soon adverb <u>before long</u>, in the near future, shortly

soothe verb 1 <u>calm</u>, allay,

appease, hush, lull, mollify, pacify, quiet, still **2** relieve, alleviate, assuage, ease

soothing adjective calming, emollient, palliative, relaxing, restful

soothsayer noun prophet, diviner, fortune-teller, seer, sibyl

sophisticated adjective
1 cultured, cosmopolitan, cultivated, refined, urbane, worldly **2** complex, advanced, complicated, delicate, elaborate, intricate, refined, subtle

sophistication noun savoir-faire, finesse, poise, urbanity, worldliness, worldly wisdom

soporific adjective
1 sleep-inducing, sedative, somnolent, tranquillizing ♦ noun
2 sedative, narcotic, opiate, tranquillizer

soppy adjective Informal sentimental, overemotional, schmaltzy (slang), slushy (informal), weepy (informal)

sorcerer noun magician, enchanter, necromancer, warlock, witch, wizard

sorcery noun black magic, black art, enchantment, magic, necromancy, witchcraft, wizardry

sordid adjective **1** dirty, filthy, foul, mean, seedy, sleazy, squalid, unclean **2** base, debauched, degenerate, low, shabby, shameful, vicious, vile **3** mercenary, avaricious, covetous, grasping, selfish

sore adjective **1** painful, angry, burning, inflamed, irritated, raw, sensitive, smarting, tender **2** annoying, severe, sharp,

troublesome **3** annoyed, aggrieved, angry, cross, hurt, irked, irritated, pained, resentful, stung, upset **4** urgent, acute, critical, desperate, dire, extreme, pressing

sorrow noun **1** grief, anguish, distress, heartache, heartbreak, misery, mourning, regret, sadness, unhappiness, woe **2** affliction, hardship, misfortune, trial, tribulation, trouble, woe ♦ verb **3** grieve, agonize, bemoan, be sad, bewail, lament, mourn

sorrowful adjective sad, dejected, dismal, doleful, grieving, miserable, mournful, sorry, unhappy, woebegone, woeful, wretched

sorry adjective **1** regretful, apologetic, conscience-stricken, contrite, penitent, remorseful, repentant, shamefaced **2** sympathetic, commiserative, compassionate, full of pity, moved **3** wretched, deplorable, mean, miserable, pathetic, pitiful, poor, sad

sort noun **1** kind, brand, category, class, ilk, make, nature, order, quality, style, type, variety ♦ verb **2** arrange, categorize, classify, divide, grade, group, order, put in order, rank

sort out verb **1** resolve, clarify, clear up **2** organize, tidy up

soul noun **1** spirit, essence, life, vital force **2** personification, embodiment, epitome, essence, quintessence, type **3** person, being, body, creature, individual, man or woman

sound[1] noun **1** noise, din, report,

reverberation, tone 2 <u>impression</u>, drift, idea, look ◆ *verb* 3 <u>resound</u>, echo, reverberate 4 <u>seem</u>, appear, look 5 <u>pronounce</u>, announce, articulate, declare, express, utter

sound² *adjective* 1 <u>perfect</u>, fit, healthy, intact, solid, unhurt, unimpaired, uninjured, whole 2 <u>sensible</u>, correct, logical, proper, prudent, rational, reasonable, right, trustworthy, valid, well-founded, wise 3 <u>deep</u>, unbroken, undisturbed, untroubled

sound³ *verb* <u>fathom</u>, plumb, probe

sound out *verb* <u>probe</u>, canvass, pump, question, see how the land lies

sour *adjective* 1 <u>sharp</u>, acetic, acid, bitter, pungent, tart 2 <u>gone off</u>, curdled, gone bad, turned 3 <u>ill-natured</u>, acrimonious, disagreeable, embittered, ill-tempered, peevish, tart, ungenerous, waspish

source *noun* 1 <u>origin</u>, author, beginning, cause, derivation, fount, originator 2 <u>informant</u>, authority

souvenir *noun* <u>keepsake</u>, memento, reminder

sovereign *noun* 1 <u>monarch</u>, chief, emperor *or* empress, king *or* queen, potentate, prince, ruler ◆ *adjective* 2 <u>supreme</u>, absolute, imperial, kingly *or* queenly, principal, royal, ruling 3 <u>excellent</u>, effectual, efficacious, efficient

sovereignty *noun* <u>supreme power</u>, domination, kingship,

primacy, supremacy

sow *verb* <u>scatter</u>, implant, plant, seed

space *noun* 1 <u>room</u>, capacity, elbowroom, expanse, extent, leeway, margin, play, scope 2 <u>gap</u>, blank, distance, interval, omission 3 <u>time</u>, duration, interval, period, span, while

spacious *adjective* <u>roomy</u>, ample, broad, capacious, commodious, expansive, extensive, huge, large, sizable *or* sizeable

spadework *noun* <u>preparation</u>, donkey-work, groundwork, labour

span *noun* 1 <u>extent</u>, amount, distance, length, reach, spread, stretch 2 <u>period</u>, duration, spell, term ◆ *verb* 3 <u>extend across</u>, bridge, cover, cross, link, traverse

spank *verb* <u>smack</u>, cuff, slap

spar *verb* <u>argue</u>, bicker, row, scrap (*informal*), squabble, wrangle

spare *adjective* 1 <u>extra</u>, additional, free, leftover, odd, over, superfluous, surplus, unoccupied, unused, unwanted 2 <u>thin</u>, gaunt, lean, meagre, wiry ◆ *verb* 3 <u>have mercy on</u>, be merciful to, go easy on (*informal*), leave, let off (*informal*), pardon, save from 4 <u>afford</u>, do without, give, grant, let (someone) have, manage without, part with

spare time *noun* <u>leisure</u>, free time, odd moments

sparing *adjective* <u>economical</u>, careful, frugal, prudent, saving, thrifty

spark *noun* 1 <u>flicker</u>, flare, flash,

gleam, glint **2** <u>trace</u>, atom, hint, jot, scrap, vestige ♦ *verb* **3** *often with* **off** <u>start</u>, inspire, precipitate, provoke, set off, stimulate, trigger (off)

sparkle *verb* **1** <u>glitter</u>, dance, flash, gleam, glint, glisten, scintillate, shimmer, shine, twinkle ♦ *noun* **2** <u>glitter</u>, brilliance, flash, flicker, gleam, glint, twinkle **3** <u>vivacity</u>, dash, élan, life, spirit, vitality

sparse *adjective* <u>scattered</u>, few and far between, meagre, scanty, scarce

spartan *adjective* <u>austere</u>, ascetic, disciplined, frugal, plain, rigorous, self-denying, severe, strict

spasm *noun* **1** <u>convulsion</u>, contraction, paroxysm, twitch **2** <u>burst</u>, eruption, fit, frenzy, outburst, seizure

spasmodic *adjective* <u>sporadic</u>, convulsive, erratic, fitful, intermittent, irregular, jerky

spate *noun* <u>flood</u>, deluge, flow, outpouring, rush, torrent

speak *verb* **1** <u>talk</u>, articulate, converse, express, pronounce, say, state, tell, utter **2** <u>lecture</u>, address, declaim, discourse, hold forth

speaker *noun* <u>lecturer</u>, orator, public speaker, spokesman *or* spokeswoman, spokesperson

speak out *or* **up** *verb* <u>speak one's mind</u>, have one's say, make one's position plain

spearhead *verb* <u>lead</u>, head, initiate, launch, pioneer, set in motion, set off

special *adjective* **1** <u>exceptional</u>,

extraordinary, important, memorable, significant, uncommon, unique, unusual **2** <u>particular</u>, appropriate, distinctive, individual, precise, specific

specialist *noun* <u>expert</u>, authority, buff (*informal*), connoisseur, consultant, master, professional

speciality *noun* <u>forte</u>, bag (*slang*), métier, *pièce de résistance*, specialty

species *noun* <u>kind</u>, breed, category, class, group, sort, type, variety

specific *adjective* **1** <u>particular</u>, characteristic, distinguishing, special **2** <u>definite</u>, clear-cut, exact, explicit, express, precise, unequivocal

specification *noun* <u>requirement</u>, condition, detail, particular, qualification, stipulation

specify *verb* <u>state</u>, define, designate, detail, indicate, mention, name, stipulate

specimen *noun* <u>sample</u>, example, exemplification, instance, model, pattern, representative, type

speck *noun* **1** <u>mark</u>, blemish, dot, fleck, mote, speckle, spot, stain **2** <u>particle</u>, atom, bit, grain, iota, jot, mite, shred

speckled *adjective* <u>flecked</u>, dappled, dotted, mottled, spotted, sprinkled

spectacle *noun* **1** <u>sight</u>, curiosity, marvel, phenomenon, scene, wonder **2** <u>show</u>, display, event, exhibition, extravaganza, pageant, performance

spectacular *adjective*

1 impressive, dazzling, dramatic, grand, magnificent, sensational, splendid, striking, stunning (*informal*) ♦ *noun* **2** show, display, spectacle

spectator *noun* onlooker, bystander, looker-on, observer, viewer, watcher

spectre *noun* ghost, apparition, phantom, spirit, vision, wraith

speculate *verb* **1** conjecture, consider, guess, hypothesize, suppose, surmise, theorize, wonder **2** gamble, hazard, risk, venture

speculation *noun* **1** guesswork, conjecture, hypothesis, opinion, supposition, surmise, theory **2** gamble, hazard, risk

speculative *adjective* hypothetical, academic, conjectural, notional, suppositional, theoretical

speech *noun* **1** communication, conversation, dialogue, discussion, talk **2** talk, address, discourse, homily, lecture, oration, spiel (*informal*) **3** language, articulation, dialect, diction, enunciation, idiom, jargon, parlance, tongue

speechless *adjective* **1** mute, dumb, inarticulate, silent, wordless **2** astounded, aghast, amazed, dazed, shocked

speed *noun* **1** swiftness, haste, hurry, pace, quickness, rapidity, rush, velocity ♦ *verb* **2** race, career, gallop, hasten, hurry, make haste, rush, tear, zoom **3** help, advance, aid, assist, boost, expedite, facilitate

speed up *verb* accelerate, gather momentum, increase the tempo

speedy *adjective* quick, express, fast, hasty, headlong, hurried, immediate, precipitate, prompt, rapid, swift

spell[1] *verb* indicate, augur, imply, mean, point to, portend, signify

spell[2] *noun* **1** incantation, charm **2** fascination, allure, bewitchment, enchantment, glamour, magic

spell[3] *noun* period, bout, course, interval, season, stretch, term, time

spellbound *adjective* entranced, bewitched, captivated, charmed, enthralled, fascinated, gripped, mesmerized, rapt

spend *verb* **1** pay out, disburse, expend, fork out (*slang*) **2** pass, fill, occupy, while away **3** use up, consume, dissipate, drain, empty, exhaust, run through, squander, waste

spendthrift *noun* **1** squanderer, big spender, profligate, spender, waster ♦ *adjective* **2** wasteful, extravagant, improvident, prodigal, profligate

spew *verb* vomit, disgorge, puke (*slang*), regurgitate, throw up (*informal*)

sphere *noun* **1** ball, circle, globe, globule, orb **2** field, capacity, department, domain, function, patch, province, realm, scope, territory, turf (*U.S. slang*)

spherical *adjective* round, globe-shaped, globular, rotund

spice *noun* **1** seasoning, relish, savour **2** excitement, colour, pep, piquancy, zest, zing (*informal*)

spicy *adjective* **1** hot, aromatic,

piquant, savoury, seasoned
2 *Informal* scandalous, hot
(*informal*), indelicate, racy, ribald,
risqué, suggestive, titillating

spike *noun* 1 point, barb, prong,
spine ♦ *verb* 2 impale, spear, spit,
stick

spill *verb* 1 pour, discharge,
disgorge, overflow, slop over
♦ *noun* 2 fall, tumble

spin *verb* 1 revolve, gyrate,
pirouette, reel, rotate, turn, twirl,
whirl 2 reel, swim, whirl ♦ *noun*
3 revolution, gyration, roll, whirl
4 *Informal* drive, joy ride
(*informal*), ride

spine *noun* 1 backbone, spinal
column, vertebrae, vertebral
column 2 barb, needle, quill,
ray, spike, spur

spine-chilling *adjective*
frightening, bloodcurdling, eerie,
horrifying, scary (*informal*),
spooky (*informal*), terrifying

spineless *adjective* weak,
cowardly, faint-hearted, feeble,
gutless (*informal*), lily-livered,
soft, weak-kneed (*informal*)

spin out *verb* prolong, amplify,
delay, drag out, draw out,
extend, lengthen

spiral *noun* 1 coil, corkscrew,
helix, whorl ♦ *adjective* 2 coiled,
helical, whorled, winding

spirit *noun* 1 life force, life, soul,
vital spark 2 feeling, atmosphere,
gist, tenor, tone 3 temperament,
attitude, character, disposition,
outlook, temper 4 liveliness,
animation, brio, energy,
enthusiasm, fire, force, life,
mettle, vigour, zest 5 courage,
backbone, gameness, grit, guts
(*informal*), spunk (*informal*)

6 essence, intention, meaning,
purport, purpose, sense,
substance 7 ghost, apparition,
phantom, spectre 8 spirits
mood, feelings, frame of mind,
morale ♦ *verb* 9 *with* away *or* off
remove, abduct, abstract, carry,
purloin, seize, steal, whisk

spirited *adjective* lively, active,
animated, energetic, feisty
(*informal, chiefly U.S. & Canad.*),
mettlesome, vivacious

spiritual *adjective* sacred,
devotional, divine, holy, religious

spit *verb* 1 eject, expectorate,
splutter, throw out ♦ *noun*
2 saliva, dribble, drool, slaver,
spittle

spite *noun* 1 malice, animosity,
hatred, ill will, malevolence,
spitefulness, spleen, venom 2 in
spite of despite, (even) though,
notwithstanding, regardless of
♦ *verb* 3 hurt, annoy, harm,
injure, vex

spiteful *adjective* malicious,
bitchy (*informal*), ill-natured,
malevolent, nasty, vindictive

splash *verb* 1 scatter, shower,
slop, spatter, spray, sprinkle, wet
2 publicize, broadcast, tout,
trumpet ♦ *noun* 3 dash, burst,
patch, spattering, touch
4 *Informal* display, effect, impact,
sensation, stir

splash out *verb Informal* spend,
be extravagant, push the boat
out (*Brit. informal*), spare no
expense, splurge

splendid *adjective* 1 excellent,
cracking (*Brit. informal*), fantastic
(*informal*), first-class, glorious,
great (*informal*), marvellous,
wonderful 2 magnificent, costly,

gorgeous, impressive, lavish, luxurious, ornate, resplendent, rich, sumptuous, superb

splendour noun <u>magnificence</u>, brightness, brilliance, display, glory, grandeur, pomp, richness, show, spectacle, sumptuousness

splinter noun **1** <u>sliver</u>, chip, flake, fragment ♦ verb **2** <u>shatter</u>, disintegrate, fracture, split

split verb **1** <u>break</u>, burst, come apart, come undone, crack, give way, open, rend, rip **2** <u>separate</u>, branch, cleave, disband, disunite, diverge, fork, part **3** <u>share out</u>, allocate, allot, apportion, distribute, divide, halve, partition ♦ noun **4** <u>crack</u>, breach, division, fissure, gap, rent, rip, separation, slit, tear **5** <u>division</u>, breach, break-up, discord, dissension, estrangement, rift, rupture, schism ♦ adjective **6** <u>divided</u>, broken, cleft, cracked, fractured, ruptured

split up verb <u>separate</u>, break up, divorce, part

spoil verb **1** <u>ruin</u>, damage, destroy, disfigure, harm, impair, injure, mar, mess up, trash (slang), wreck **2** <u>overindulge</u>, coddle, cosset, indulge, mollycoddle, pamper **3** <u>go bad</u>, addle, curdle, decay, decompose, go off (Brit. informal), rot, turn

spoils plural noun <u>booty</u>, loot, plunder, prey, swag (slang)

spoilsport noun <u>killjoy</u>, damper, dog in the manger, misery (Brit. informal), wet blanket (informal)

spoken adjective <u>said</u>, expressed, oral, told, unwritten, uttered,

verbal, viva voce, voiced

spokesperson noun <u>speaker</u>, mouthpiece, official, spin doctor (informal), spokesman or spokeswoman, voice

spongy adjective <u>porous</u>, absorbent

sponsor noun **1** <u>backer</u>, patron, promoter ♦ verb **2** <u>back</u>, finance, fund, patronize, promote, subsidize

spontaneous adjective <u>unplanned</u>, impromptu, impulsive, instinctive, natural, unprompted, voluntary, willing

spoof noun <u>parody</u>, burlesque, caricature, mockery, satire, send-up (Brit. informal), take-off (informal)

spooky adjective <u>eerie</u>, chilling, creepy (informal), frightening, scary (informal), spine-chilling, uncanny, unearthly, weird

sporadic adjective <u>intermittent</u>, irregular, occasional, scattered, spasmodic

sport noun **1** <u>game</u>, amusement, diversion, exercise, pastime, play, recreation **2** <u>fun</u>, badinage, banter, jest, joking, teasing ♦ verb **3** Informal <u>wear</u>, display, exhibit, show off

sporting adjective <u>fair</u>, game (informal), sportsmanlike

sporty adjective <u>athletic</u>, energetic, outdoor

spot noun **1** <u>mark</u>, blemish, blot, blotch, scar, smudge, speck, speckle, stain **2** <u>pimple</u>, pustule, zit (slang) **3** <u>place</u>, location, point, position, scene, site **4** Informal <u>predicament</u>, difficulty, hot water (informal), mess, plight, quandary, tight spot, trouble ♦ *verb* **5** see, catch sight of, detect, discern, espy, make out, observe, recognize, sight **6** mark, dirty, fleck, mottle, smirch, soil, spatter, speckle, splodge, splotch, stain

spotless *adjective* clean, flawless, gleaming, immaculate, impeccable, pure, shining, unblemished, unstained, unsullied, untarnished

spotlight *noun* **1** attention, fame, limelight, public eye ♦ *verb* **2** highlight, accentuate, draw attention to

spotted *adjective* speckled, dappled, dotted, flecked, mottled

spouse *noun* partner, consort, husband *or* wife, mate, significant other (*U.S. informal*)

spout *verb* stream, discharge, gush, shoot, spray, spurt, surge

sprawl *verb* loll, flop, lounge, slouch, slump

spray[1] *noun* **1** droplets, drizzle, fine mist **2** aerosol, atomizer, sprinkler ♦ *verb* **3** scatter, diffuse, shower, sprinkle

spray[2] *noun* sprig, branch, corsage, floral arrangement

spread *verb* **1** open (out), broaden, dilate, expand, extend, sprawl, stretch, unfold, unroll, widen **2** proliferate, escalate, multiply **3** circulate, broadcast, disseminate, make known, propagate ♦ *noun* **4** increase, advance, development, dispersal, dissemination, expansion, proliferation **5** extent, span, stretch, sweep

spree *noun* binge (*informal*),

bacchanalia, bender (*informal*), carousal, fling, orgy, revel

sprightly *adjective* lively, active, agile, brisk, energetic, nimble, spirited, spry, vivacious

spring *verb* **1** jump, bounce, bound, leap, vault **2** *often with* **from** originate, arise, come, derive, descend, issue, proceed, start, stem **3** *often with* **up** appear, develop, mushroom, shoot up ♦ *noun* **4** jump, bound, leap, vault **5** elasticity, bounce, buoyancy, flexibility, resilience

springy *adjective* elastic, bouncy, buoyant, flexible, resilient

sprinkle *verb* scatter, dredge, dust, pepper, powder, shower, spray, strew

sprinkling *noun* scattering, dash, dusting, few, handful, sprinkle

sprint *verb* race, dart, dash, hare (*Brit. informal*), shoot, tear

sprite *noun* spirit, brownie, elf, fairy, goblin, imp, pixie

sprout *verb* grow, bud, develop, shoot, spring

spruce *adjective* smart, dapper, natty (*informal*), neat, trim, well-groomed, well turned out

spruce up *verb* smarten up, tidy, titivate

spry *adjective* active, agile, nimble, sprightly, supple

spur *noun* **1** stimulus, impetus, impulse, incentive, incitement, inducement, motive **2** goad, prick **3 on the spur of the moment** on impulse, impromptu, impulsively, on the spot, without planning ♦ *verb* **4** incite, animate, drive, goad, impel, prick, prod, prompt, stimulate, urge

spurious *adjective* <u>false</u>, artificial, bogus, fake, phoney *or* phony (*informal*), pretended, sham, specious, unauthentic

spurn *verb* <u>reject</u>, despise, disdain, rebuff, repulse, scorn, slight, snub

spurt *verb* 1 <u>gush</u>, burst, erupt, shoot, squirt, surge ♦ *noun* 2 <u>burst</u>, fit, rush, spate, surge

spy *noun* 1 <u>undercover agent</u>, mole, nark (*Brit., Austral., & N.Z. slang*) ♦ *verb* 2 <u>catch sight of</u>, espy, glimpse, notice, observe, spot

squabble *verb* 1 <u>quarrel</u>, argue, bicker, dispute, fight, row, wrangle ♦ *noun* 2 <u>quarrel</u>, argument, disagreement, dispute, fight, row, tiff

squad *noun* <u>team</u>, band, company, crew, force, gang, group, troop

squalid *adjective* <u>dirty</u>, filthy, seedy, sleazy, slummy, sordid, unclean

squalor *noun* <u>filth</u>, foulness, sleaziness, squalidness

squander *verb* <u>waste</u>, blow (*slang*), expend, fritter away, misspend, misuse, spend

square *adjective* 1 <u>honest</u>, above board, ethical, fair, genuine, kosher (*informal*), on the level (*informal*), straight ♦ *verb* 2 <u>even up</u>, adjust, align, level 3 *sometimes with* up <u>pay off</u>, settle 4 *often with* with <u>agree</u>, correspond, fit, match, reconcile, tally

squash *verb* 1 <u>crush</u>, compress, distort, flatten, mash, press,

pulp, smash 2 <u>suppress</u>, annihilate, crush, humiliate, quell, silence

squashy *adjective* <u>soft</u>, mushy, pulpy, spongy, yielding

squawk *verb* <u>cry</u>, hoot, screech

squeak *verb* <u>peep</u>, pipe, squeal

squeal *noun, verb* <u>scream</u>, screech, shriek, wail, yell

squeamish *adjective* 1 <u>delicate</u>, fastidious, prudish, strait-laced 2 <u>sick</u>, nauseous, queasy

squeeze *verb* 1 <u>press</u>, clutch, compress, crush, grip, pinch, squash, wring 2 <u>cram</u>, crowd, force, jam, pack, press, ram, stuff 3 <u>hug</u>, clasp, cuddle, embrace, enfold 4 <u>extort</u>, milk, pressurize, wrest ♦ *noun* 5 <u>hug</u>, clasp, embrace 6 <u>crush</u>, congestion, crowd, jam, press, squash

squint *adjective* <u>crooked</u>, askew, aslant, awry, cockeyed, skew-whiff (*informal*)

squirm *verb* <u>wriggle</u>, twist, writhe

stab *verb* 1 <u>pierce</u>, impale, jab, knife, spear, stick, thrust, transfix, wound ♦ *noun* 2 <u>wound</u>, gash, incision, jab, puncture, thrust 3 <u>twinge</u>, ache, pang, prick 4 <u>make</u> *or* <u>have a stab at</u> *Informal* attempt, endeavour, have a go, try

stability *noun* <u>firmness</u>, solidity, soundness, steadiness, strength

stable *adjective* 1 <u>firm</u>, constant, established, fast, fixed, immovable, lasting, permanent, secure, sound, strong 2 <u>steady</u>, reliable, staunch, steadfast, sure

stack *noun* 1 <u>pile</u>, heap, load, mass, mound, mountain ♦ *verb* 2 <u>pile</u>, accumulate, amass, assemble, heap up, load

staff noun **1** <u>workers</u>, employees, personnel, team, workforce **2** <u>stick</u>, cane, crook, pole, rod, sceptre, stave, wand

stage noun <u>point</u>, division, juncture, lap, leg, level, period, phase, step

stagger verb **1** <u>totter</u>, lurch, reel, sway, wobble **2** <u>astound</u>, amaze, astonish, confound, overwhelm, shake, shock, stun, stupefy **3** <u>overlap</u>, alternate, step

stagnant adjective <u>stale</u>, quiet, sluggish, still

stagnate verb <u>vegetate</u>, decay, decline, idle, languish, rot, rust

staid adjective <u>sedate</u>, calm, composed, grave, serious, sober, solemn, steady

stain verb **1** <u>mark</u>, blemish, blot, dirty, discolour, smirch, soil, spot, tinge ◆ noun **2** <u>mark</u>, blemish, blot, discoloration, smirch, spot **3** <u>stigma</u>, disgrace, dishonour, shame, slur

stake¹ noun <u>pole</u>, pale, paling, palisade, picket, post, stick

stake² noun **1** <u>bet</u>, ante, pledge, wager **2** <u>interest</u>, concern, investment, involvement, share ◆ verb **3** <u>bet</u>, chance, gamble, hazard, risk, venture, wager

stale adjective **1** <u>old</u>, decayed, dry, flat, fusty, hard, musty, sour **2** <u>unoriginal</u>, banal, hackneyed, overused, stereotyped, threadbare, trite, worn-out

stalk verb <u>pursue</u>, follow, haunt, hunt, shadow, track

stall verb <u>play for time</u>, hedge, temporize

stalwart adjective <u>strong</u>,

staunch, stout, strapping, sturdy

stamina noun <u>staying power</u>, endurance, energy, force, power, resilience, strength

stammer verb <u>stutter</u>, falter, hesitate, pause, stumble

stamp noun **1** <u>imprint</u>, brand, earmark, hallmark, mark, signature ◆ verb **2** <u>trample</u>, crush **3** <u>identify</u>, brand, categorize, label, mark, reveal, show to be **4** <u>imprint</u>, impress, mark, print

stampede noun <u>rush</u>, charge, flight, rout

stamp out verb <u>eliminate</u>, crush, destroy, eradicate, put down, quell, scotch, suppress

stance noun **1** <u>attitude</u>, position, stand, standpoint, viewpoint **2** <u>posture</u>, bearing, carriage, deportment

stand verb **1** <u>be upright</u>, be erect, be vertical, rise **2** <u>put</u>, mount, place, position, set **3** <u>exist</u>, be valid, continue, hold, obtain, prevail, remain **4** <u>tolerate</u>, abide, allow, bear, brook, countenance, endure, handle, put up with (informal), stomach, take ◆ noun **5** <u>stall</u>, booth, table **6** <u>position</u>, attitude, determination, opinion, stance **7** <u>support</u>, base, bracket, dais, platform, rack, stage, tripod

standard noun **1** <u>benchmark</u>, average, criterion, gauge, grade, guideline, measure, model, norm, yardstick **2** often plural <u>principles</u>, ethics, ideals, morals **3** <u>flag</u>, banner, ensign ◆ adjective **4** <u>usual</u>, average, basic, customary, normal, orthodox, regular, typical **5** <u>accepted</u>, approved, authoritative, definitive, established, official, recognized

standardize verb <u>bring into line</u>, institutionalize, regiment

stand by verb **1** <u>be prepared</u>, wait **2** <u>support</u>, back, be loyal to, champion, take (someone's) part

stand for verb **1** <u>represent</u>, betoken, denote, indicate, mean, signify, symbolize **2** Informal <u>tolerate</u>, bear, brook, endure, put up with

stand-in noun <u>substitute</u>, deputy, locum, replacement, reserve, stopgap, surrogate, understudy

stand in for verb <u>be a substitute for</u>, cover for, deputize for, represent, take the place of

standing adjective **1** <u>permanent</u>, fixed, lasting, regular **2** <u>upright</u>, erect, vertical ♦ noun **3** <u>status</u>, eminence, footing, position, rank, reputation, repute **4** <u>duration</u>, continuance, existence

standoffish adjective <u>reserved</u>, aloof, cold, distant, haughty, remote, unapproachable, unsociable

stand out verb <u>be conspicuous</u>, be distinct, be obvious, be prominent

standpoint noun <u>point of view</u>, angle, position, stance, viewpoint

stand up for verb <u>support</u>, champion, defend, stick up for (informal), uphold

staple adjective <u>principal</u>, basic, chief, fundamental, key, main, predominant

star noun **1** <u>heavenly body</u> **2** <u>celebrity</u>, big name, luminary,

main attraction, megastar (informal), name ♦ adjective **3** <u>leading</u>, brilliant, celebrated, major, prominent, well-known

stare verb <u>gaze</u>, gape, gawk, gawp (Brit. slang), goggle, look, watch

stark adjective **1** <u>harsh</u>, austere, bare, barren, bleak, grim, hard, plain, severe **2** <u>absolute</u>, blunt, downright, out-and-out, pure, sheer, unmitigated, utter ♦ adverb **3** <u>absolutely</u>, altogether, completely, entirely, quite, utterly, wholly

start verb **1** <u>begin</u>, appear, arise, commence, issue, originate **2** <u>set about</u>, embark upon, make a beginning, take the first step **3** <u>set in motion</u>, activate, get going, initiate, instigate, kick-start, open, originate, trigger **4** <u>jump</u>, flinch, jerk, recoil, shy **5** <u>establish</u>, begin, create, found, inaugurate, initiate, institute, launch, pioneer, set up ♦ noun **6** <u>beginning</u>, birth, dawn, foundation, inception, initiation, onset, opening, outset **7** <u>advantage</u>, edge, head start, lead **8** <u>jump</u>, convulsion, spasm

startle verb <u>surprise</u>, frighten, make (someone) jump, scare, shock

starving adjective <u>hungry</u>, famished, ravenous, starved

state noun **1** <u>condition</u>, circumstances, position, predicament, shape, situation **2** <u>frame of mind</u>, attitude, humour, mood, spirits **3** <u>country</u>, commonwealth, federation, government, kingdom, land, nation, republic, territory **4** ceremony, display, glory, grandeur, majesty, pomp, splendour, style ♦ *verb* **5** express, affirm, articulate, assert, declare, expound, present, say, specify, utter, voice

stately *adjective* grand, august, dignified, lofty, majestic, noble, regal, royal

statement *noun* account, announcement, communication, communiqué, declaration, proclamation, report

state-of-the-art *adjective* latest, newest, up-to-date, up-to-the-minute

static *adjective* stationary, fixed, immobile, motionless, still, unmoving

station *noun* **1** headquarters, base, depot **2** place, location, position, post, seat, situation **3** position, post, rank, situation, standing, status ♦ *verb* **4** assign, establish, install, locate, post, set

stationary *adjective* motionless, fixed, parked, standing, static, stock-still, unmoving

statuesque *adjective* well-proportioned, imposing, Junoesque

stature *noun* importance, eminence, prestige, prominence, rank, standing

status *noun* position, condition, consequence, eminence, grade, prestige, rank, standing

staunch[1] *adjective* loyal, faithful, firm, sound, stalwart, steadfast, true, trusty

staunch[2] *verb* stop, check, dam, halt, stay, stem

stay *verb* **1** remain, abide, continue, halt, linger, loiter, pause, stop, tarry, wait ♦ *noun* **2** visit, holiday, sojourn, stop, stopover **3** postponement, deferment, delay, halt, stopping, suspension

steadfast *adjective* firm, faithful, fast, fixed, intent, loyal, resolute, stalwart, staunch, steady, unswerving, unwavering

steady *adjective* **1** firm, fixed, safe, stable **2** sensible, balanced, calm, dependable, equable, level-headed, reliable, sober **3** continuous, ceaseless, consistent, constant, incessant, nonstop, persistent, regular, unbroken, uninterrupted ♦ *verb* **4** stabilize, brace, secure, support

steal *verb* **1** take, appropriate, embezzle, filch, lift (*informal*), misappropriate, nick (*slang, chiefly Brit.*), pilfer, pinch (*informal*), purloin, thieve **2** sneak, creep, slink, slip, tiptoe

stealth *noun* secrecy, furtiveness, slyness, sneakiness, stealthiness, surreptitiousness, unobtrusiveness

stealthy *adjective* secret, furtive, secretive, sneaking, surreptitious

steep[1] *adjective* **1** sheer, abrupt, precipitous **2** *Informal* high, exorbitant, extortionate, extreme, overpriced, unreasonable

steep[2] *verb* **1** soak, drench, immerse, macerate, marinate (*Cookery*), moisten, souse, submerge **2** saturate, fill, imbue, infuse, permeate, pervade, suffuse

steer *verb* direct, conduct, control, guide, handle, pilot

stem[1] *noun* **1** stalk, axis, branch,

shoot, trunk ♦ *verb* 2 **stem from** <u>originate in</u>, arise from, be caused by, derive from

stem² *verb* <u>stop</u>, check, curb, dam, hold back, staunch

stench *noun* <u>stink</u>, foul smell, pong (*Brit. informal*), reek, whiff (*Brit. slang*)

step *noun* 1 <u>footstep</u>, footfall, footprint, pace, print, stride, track 2 <u>stage</u>, move, phase, point 3 <u>action</u>, act, deed, expedient, means, measure, move 4 <u>degree</u>, level, rank ♦ *verb* 5 <u>walk</u>, move, pace, tread

step in *verb* <u>intervene</u>, become involved, take action

step up *verb* <u>increase</u>, intensify, raise

stereotype *noun* 1 <u>formula</u>, pattern ♦ *verb* 2 <u>categorize</u>, pigeonhole, standardize, typecast

sterile *adjective* 1 <u>germ-free</u>, aseptic, disinfected, sterilized 2 <u>barren</u>, bare, dry, empty, fruitless, unfruitful, unproductive

sterilize *verb* <u>disinfect</u>, fumigate, purify

sterling *adjective* <u>excellent</u>, fine, genuine, sound, superlative, true

stern *adjective* <u>severe</u>, austere, forbidding, grim, hard, harsh, inflexible, rigid, serious, strict

stick¹ *noun* 1 <u>cane</u>, baton, crook, pole, rod, staff, twig 2 *Brit. slang* <u>abuse</u>, criticism, flak (*informal*)

stick² *verb* 1 <u>poke</u>, dig, jab, penetrate, pierce, prod, puncture, spear, stab, thrust, transfix 2 <u>fasten</u>, adhere, affix, attach, bind, bond, cling, fix, glue, hold, join, paste, weld 3 *with* **out, up,** *etc.* <u>protrude</u>,

bulge, extend, jut, obtrude, poke, project, show 4 *Informal* <u>put</u>, deposit, lay, place, set 5 <u>stay</u>, linger, persist, remain 6 *Slang* <u>tolerate</u>, abide, stand, stomach, take 7 **stick up for** *Informal* <u>defend</u>, champion, stand up for, support

stickler *noun* <u>perfectionist</u>, fanatic, fusspot (*Brit. informal*), purist

sticky *adjective* 1 <u>tacky</u>, adhesive, clinging, gluey, glutinous, gooey (*informal*), gummy, viscid, viscous 2 *Informal* <u>difficult</u>, awkward, delicate, embarrassing, nasty, tricky, unpleasant 3 <u>humid</u>, clammy, close, muggy, oppressive, sultry, sweltering

stiff *adjective* 1 <u>inflexible</u>, firm, hard, inelastic, rigid, solid, taut, tense, tight, unbending, unyielding 2 <u>awkward</u>, clumsy, graceless, inelegant, jerky (*informal*), ungainly, ungraceful 3 <u>difficult</u>, arduous, exacting, hard, tough 4 <u>severe</u>, drastic, extreme, hard, harsh, heavy, strict 5 <u>unrelaxed</u>, constrained, forced, formal, stilted, unnatural

stiffen *verb* 1 <u>brace</u>, reinforce, tauten, tense 2 <u>set</u>, congeal, crystallize, harden, jell, solidify, thicken

stifle *verb* 1 <u>suppress</u>, check, hush, repress, restrain, silence, smother, stop 2 <u>suffocate</u>, asphyxiate, choke, smother, strangle

stigma *noun* <u>disgrace</u>, dishonour, shame, slur, smirch, stain

still *adjective* 1 <u>motionless</u>, calm, peaceful, restful, serene, stationary, tranquil, undisturbed

2 silent, hushed, quiet ♦ *verb*
3 quieten, allay, calm, hush, lull,
pacify, quiet, settle, silence,
soothe ♦ *conjunction* 4 however,
but, nevertheless,
notwithstanding, yet

stilted *adjective* stiff, constrained,
forced, unnatural, wooden

stimulant *noun* pick-me-up
(*informal*), restorative, tonic,
upper (*slang*)

stimulate *verb* arouse,
encourage, fire, impel, incite,
prompt, provoke, rouse, spur

stimulating *adjective* exciting,
exhilarating, inspiring,
provocative, rousing, stirring

stimulus *noun* incentive,
encouragement, fillip, goad,
impetus, incitement,
inducement, spur

sting *verb* 1 hurt, burn, pain,
smart, tingle, wound 2 *Informal*
cheat, defraud, do (*slang*), fleece,
overcharge, rip off (*slang*),
swindle

stingy *adjective* mean, miserly,
niggardly, parsimonious,
penny-pinching (*informal*),
tightfisted, ungenerous

stink *noun* 1 stench, fetor, foul
smell, pong (*Brit. informal*) ♦ *verb*
2 reek, pong (*Brit. informal*)

stint *verb* 1 be mean, be frugal,
be sparing, hold back, skimp on
♦ *noun* 2 share, period, quota,
shift, spell, stretch, term, time,
turn

stipulate *verb* specify, agree,
contract, covenant, insist upon,
require, settle

stipulation *noun* specification,
agreement, clause, condition,

precondition, proviso,
qualification, requirement

stir *verb* 1 mix, agitate, beat,
shake 2 stimulate, arouse,
awaken, excite, incite, provoke,
rouse, spur ♦ *noun* 3 commotion,
activity, bustle, disorder,
disturbance, excitement, flurry,
fuss

stock *noun* 1 goods, array,
choice, commodities,
merchandise, range, selection,
variety, wares 2 supply, fund,
hoard, reserve, stockpile, store
3 property, assets, capital, funds,
investment 4 livestock, beasts,
cattle, domestic animals
♦ *adjective* 5 standard,
conventional, customary,
ordinary, regular, routine, usual
6 hackneyed, banal, overused,
trite ♦ *verb* 7 sell, deal in, handle,
keep, supply, trade in 8 provide
with, equip, fit out, furnish,
supply 9 stock up store (up),
accumulate, amass, gather,
hoard, lay in, put away, save

stocky *adjective* thickset, chunky,
dumpy, solid, stubby, sturdy

stodgy *adjective* 1 heavy, filling,
leaden, starchy 2 dull, boring,
fuddy-duddy (*informal*), heavy
going, staid, stuffy, tedious,
unexciting

stoical *adjective* resigned,
dispassionate, impassive,
long-suffering, philosophic,
phlegmatic, stoic, stolid

stoicism *noun* resignation,
acceptance, forbearance,
fortitude, impassivity,
long-suffering, patience, stolidity

stolid *adjective* apathetic, dull,
lumpish, unemotional, wooden

stomach noun 1 <u>belly</u>, abdomen, gut (*informal*), pot, tummy (*informal*) 2 <u>inclination</u>, appetite, desire, relish, taste ♦ *verb* 3 <u>bear</u>, abide, endure, swallow, take, tolerate

stony *adjective* <u>cold</u>, blank, chilly, expressionless, hard, hostile, icy, unresponsive

stoop *verb* 1 <u>bend</u>, bow, crouch, duck, hunch, lean 2 **stoop to** <u>sink to</u>, descend to, lower oneself by, resort to ♦ *noun* 3 <u>slouch</u>, bad posture, round-shoulderedness

stop *verb* 1 <u>halt</u>, cease, conclude, cut short, desist, discontinue, end, finish, pause, put an end to, quit, refrain, shut down, terminate 2 <u>prevent</u>, arrest, forestall, hinder, hold back, impede, repress, restrain 3 <u>plug</u>, block, obstruct, seal, staunch, stem 4 <u>stay</u>, lodge, rest ♦ *noun* 5 <u>end</u>, cessation, finish, halt, standstill 6 <u>stay</u>, break, rest 7 <u>station</u>, depot, terminus

stopgap noun <u>makeshift</u>, improvisation, resort, substitute

stoppage noun <u>stopping</u>, arrest, close, closure, cutoff, halt, hindrance, shutdown, standstill

store *verb* 1 <u>put by</u>, deposit, garner, hoard, keep, put aside, reserve, save, stockpile ♦ *noun* 2 <u>shop</u>, market, mart, outlet 3 <u>supply</u>, accumulation, cache, fund, hoard, quantity, reserve, stock, stockpile 4 <u>repository</u>, depository, storeroom, warehouse

storm noun 1 <u>tempest</u>, blizzard, gale, hurricane, squall 2 <u>outburst</u>, agitation, commotion, disturbance, furore,

outbreak, outcry, row, rumpus, strife, tumult, turmoil ♦ *verb* 3 <u>attack</u>, assail, assault, charge, rush 4 <u>rage</u>, bluster, rant, rave, thunder 5 <u>rush</u>, flounce, fly, stamp

stormy *adjective* <u>wild</u>, blustery, inclement, raging, rough, squally, turbulent, windy

story noun 1 <u>tale</u>, account, anecdote, history, legend, narrative, romance, yarn 2 <u>report</u>, article, feature, news, news item, scoop

stout *adjective* 1 <u>fat</u>, big, bulky, burly, corpulent, fleshy, heavy, overweight, plump, portly, rotund, tubby 2 <u>strong</u>, able-bodied, brawny, muscular, robust, stalwart, strapping, sturdy 3 <u>brave</u>, bold, courageous, fearless, gallant, intrepid, plucky, resolute, valiant

stow *verb* <u>pack</u>, bundle, load, put away, stash (*informal*), store

straight *adjective* 1 <u>direct</u>, near, short 2 <u>level</u>, aligned, even, horizontal, right, smooth, square, true 3 <u>upright</u>, erect, plumb, vertical 4 <u>honest</u>, above board, accurate, fair, honourable, just, law-abiding, trustworthy, upright 5 <u>frank</u>, blunt, bold, candid, forthright, honest, outright, plain, straightforward 6 <u>successive</u>, consecutive, continuous, nonstop, running, solid 7 <u>undiluted</u>, neat, pure, unadulterated, unmixed 8 <u>orderly</u>, arranged, in order, neat, organized, shipshape, tidy 9 *Slang* <u>conventional</u>, bourgeois, conservative ♦ *adverb* 10 <u>directly</u>, at once, immediately, instantly

straight away adverb <u>immediately</u>, at once, directly, instantly, now, right away

straighten verb <u>neaten</u>, arrange, order, put in order, tidy (up)

straightforward adjective
1 <u>honest</u>, candid, direct, forthright, genuine, open, sincere, truthful, upfront (informal) **2** <u>easy</u>, easy-peasy (slang), elementary, routine, simple, uncomplicated

strain¹ verb **1** <u>stretch</u>, distend, draw tight, tauten, tighten **2** <u>overexert</u>, injure, overtax, overwork, pull, sprain, tax, tear, twist, wrench **3** <u>strive</u>, bend over backwards (informal), endeavour, give one's best shot (informal), go for it (informal), knock oneself out (informal), labour, struggle **4** <u>sieve</u>, filter, purify, sift ♦ noun **5** <u>stress</u>, anxiety, burden, pressure, tension **6** <u>exertion</u>, effort, force, struggle **7** <u>injury</u>, pull, sprain, wrench

strain² noun **1** <u>breed</u>, ancestry, blood, descent, extraction, family, lineage, race **2** <u>trace</u>, streak, suggestion, tendency

strained adjective **1** <u>forced</u>, artificial, false, put on, unnatural **2** <u>tense</u>, awkward, difficult, embarrassed, stiff, uneasy

strait noun **1** often plural <u>channel</u>, narrows, sound **2 straits** <u>difficulty</u>, dilemma, extremity, hardship, plight, predicament

strait-laced adjective <u>strict</u>, moralistic, narrow-minded, prim, proper, prudish, puritanical

strand noun <u>filament</u>, fibre, string, thread

stranded adjective **1** <u>beached</u>, aground, ashore, grounded, marooned, shipwrecked **2** <u>helpless</u>, abandoned, high and dry

strange adjective **1** <u>odd</u>, abnormal, bizarre, curious, extraordinary, peculiar, queer, uncommon, weird, wonderful **2** <u>unfamiliar</u>, alien, exotic, foreign, new, novel, unknown, untried

stranger noun <u>newcomer</u>, alien, foreigner, guest, incomer, outlander, visitor

strangle verb **1** <u>throttle</u>, asphyxiate, choke, strangulate **2** <u>suppress</u>, inhibit, repress, stifle

strap noun **1** <u>belt</u>, thong, tie ♦ verb **2** <u>fasten</u>, bind, buckle, lash, secure, tie

strapping adjective <u>well-built</u>, big, brawny, husky (informal), powerful, robust, sturdy

stratagem noun <u>trick</u>, device, dodge, manoeuvre, plan, ploy, ruse, scheme, subterfuge

strategic adjective **1** <u>tactical</u>, calculated, deliberate, diplomatic, planned, politic **2** <u>crucial</u>, cardinal, critical, decisive, important, key, vital

strategy noun <u>plan</u>, approach, policy, procedure, scheme

stray verb **1** <u>wander</u>, drift, err, go astray **2** <u>digress</u>, deviate, diverge, get off the point ♦ adjective **3** <u>lost</u>, abandoned, homeless, roaming, vagrant **4** <u>random</u>, accidental, chance

streak noun **1** <u>band</u>, layer, line, slash, strip, stripe, stroke, vein **2** <u>trace</u>, dash, element, strain, touch, vein ◆ *verb* **3** speed, dart, flash, fly, hurtle, sprint, tear, whizz (*informal*), zoom

stream *noun* **1** river, bayou, beck, brook, burn (*Scot.*), rivulet, tributary **2** flow, course, current, drift, run, rush, surge, tide, torrent ◆ *verb* **3** flow, cascade, flood, gush, issue, pour, run, spill, spout

streamlined *adjective* efficient, organized, rationalized, slick, smooth-running

street *noun* road, avenue, lane, roadway, row, terrace

strength *noun* **1** might, brawn, courage, fortitude, muscle, robustness, stamina, sturdiness, toughness **2** intensity, effectiveness, efficacy, force, potency, power, vigour **3** advantage, asset, strong point

strengthen *verb* **1** fortify, brace up, consolidate, harden, invigorate, restore, stiffen, toughen **2** reinforce, augment, bolster, brace, build up, buttress, harden, intensify, support

strenuous *adjective* demanding, arduous, hard, laborious, taxing, tough, uphill

stress *noun* **1** strain, anxiety, burden, pressure, tension, trauma, worry **2** emphasis, force, significance, weight **3** accent, accentuation, beat, emphasis ◆ *verb* **4** emphasize, accentuate, dwell on, underline

stretch *verb* **1** extend, cover, put forth, reach, spread, unroll **2** pull, distend, draw out, elongate, expand, strain, tighten ◆ *noun* **3** expanse, area, distance, extent, spread, tract **4** period,

space, spell, stint, term, time

strict *adjective* **1** severe, authoritarian, firm, harsh, stern, stringent **2** exact, accurate, close, faithful, meticulous, precise, scrupulous, true **3** absolute, total, utter

strident *adjective* harsh, discordant, grating, jarring, raucous, screeching, shrill

strife *noun* conflict, battle, clash, discord, dissension, friction, quarrel

strike *verb* **1** walk out, down tools, mutiny, revolt **2** hit, beat, clobber (*slang*), clout (*informal*), cuff, hammer, knock, punch, slap, smack, thump, wallop (*informal*) **3** collide with, bump into, hit, run into **4** attack, assail, assault, hit **5** occur to, come to, dawn on *or* upon, hit, register (*informal*)

striking *adjective* impressive, conspicuous, dramatic, noticeable, outstanding

string *noun* **1** cord, fibre, twine **2** series, chain, file, line, procession, row, sequence, succession

stringent *adjective* strict, inflexible, rigid, rigorous, severe, tight, tough

stringy *adjective* fibrous, gristly, sinewy, tough

strip[1] *verb* **1** undress, disrobe, unclothe **2** plunder, despoil, divest, empty, loot, pillage, ransack, rob, sack

strip[2] *noun* piece, band, belt, shred

strive *verb* try, attempt, bend over backwards (*informal*), break one's neck (*informal*), do one's best, give it one's best shot (*informal*), go all out (*informal*), knock oneself out (*informal*), labour, make an all-out effort (*informal*), struggle, toil

stroke *verb* 1 <u>caress</u>, fondle, pet, rub ♦ *noun* 2 <u>apoplexy</u>, attack, collapse, fit, seizure 3 <u>blow</u>, hit, knock, pat, rap, thump

stroll *verb* 1 <u>walk</u>, amble, promenade, ramble, saunter ♦ *noun* 2 <u>walk</u>, breath of air, constitutional, promenade, ramble

strong *adjective* 1 <u>powerful</u>, athletic, brawny, burly, hardy, lusty, muscular, robust, strapping, sturdy, tough 2 <u>durable</u>, hard-wearing, heavy-duty, sturdy, substantial, well-built 3 <u>persuasive</u>, compelling, convincing, effective, potent, sound, telling, weighty, well-founded 4 <u>intense</u>, acute, deep, fervent, fervid, fierce, firm, keen, vehement, violent, zealous 5 <u>extreme</u>, drastic, forceful, severe 6 <u>bright</u>, bold, brilliant, dazzling

stronghold *noun* <u>fortress</u>, bastion, bulwark, castle, citadel, fort

stroppy *adjective Slang* <u>awkward</u>, bloody-minded (*Brit. informal*), difficult, obstreperous, quarrelsome, uncooperative

structure *noun* 1 <u>building</u>, construction, edifice, erection 2 <u>arrangement</u>, configuration, construction, design, form, formation, make-up, organization ♦ *verb* 3 <u>arrange</u>, assemble, build up, design, organize, shape

struggle *verb* 1 <u>strive</u>, exert oneself, give it one's best shot (*informal*), go all out (*informal*), knock oneself out (*informal*), labour, make an all-out effort (*informal*), strain, toil, work 2 <u>fight</u>, battle, compete, contend, grapple, wrestle ♦ *noun* 3 <u>effort</u>, exertion, labour, pains, scramble, toil, work 4 <u>fight</u>, battle, brush, clash, combat, conflict, contest, tussle

strut *verb* <u>swagger</u>, parade, peacock, prance

stub *noun* 1 <u>butt</u>, dog-end (*informal*), end, remnant, stump, tail, tail end 2 <u>counterfoil</u>

stubborn *adjective* <u>obstinate</u>, dogged, headstrong, inflexible, intractable, obdurate, persistent, pig-headed, recalcitrant, tenacious, unyielding

stubby *adjective* <u>stocky</u>, chunky, dumpy, short, squat, thickset

stuck *adjective* 1 <u>fastened</u>, cemented, fast, fixed, glued, joined 2 *Informal* <u>baffled</u>, beaten, stumped

stuck-up *adjective* <u>snobbish</u>, arrogant, bigheaded (*informal*), conceited, haughty, proud, snooty (*informal*), toffee-nosed (*slang, chiefly Brit.*)

stud *verb* <u>ornament</u>, bejewel, dot, spangle, spot

student *noun* <u>learner</u>, apprentice, disciple, pupil, scholar, trainee, undergraduate

studied *adjective* <u>planned</u>, conscious, deliberate, intentional, premeditated

studio *noun* <u>workshop</u>, atelier

studious *adjective* <u>scholarly</u>, academic, assiduous, bookish, diligent, hard-working, intellectual

study *verb* **1** <u>contemplate</u>, consider, examine, go into, ponder, pore over, read **2** <u>learn</u>, cram (*informal*), mug up (*Brit. slang*), read up, swot (up) (*Brit. informal*) **3** <u>examine</u>, analyse, investigate, look into, research, scrutinize, survey ♦ *noun* **4** <u>learning</u>, application, lessons, reading, research, school work, swotting (*Brit. informal*) **5** <u>examination</u>, analysis, consideration, contemplation, inquiry, inspection, investigation, review, scrutiny, survey

stuff *noun* **1** <u>things</u>, belongings, effects, equipment, gear, kit, objects, paraphernalia, possessions, tackle **2** <u>substance</u>, essence, matter **3** <u>material</u>, cloth, fabric, textile ♦ *verb* **4** <u>cram</u>, crowd, fill, force, jam, pack, push, ram, shove, squeeze

stuffing *noun* <u>filling</u>, packing, wadding

stuffy *adjective* **1** <u>airless</u>, close, frowsty, heavy, muggy, oppressive, stale, stifling, sultry, unventilated **2** *Informal* <u>staid</u>, dreary, dull, pompous, priggish, prim, stodgy

stumble *verb* **1** <u>trip</u>, fall, falter, lurch, reel, slip, stagger **2** *with* **across**, **on** *or* **upon** <u>discover</u>, chance upon, come across, find

stump *verb* <u>baffle</u>, bewilder, confuse, flummox, mystify, nonplus, perplex, puzzle

stumpy *adjective* <u>stocky</u>, dumpy, short, squat, stubby, thickset

stun *verb* <u>overcome</u>, astonish, astound, bewilder, confound, confuse, overpower, shock, stagger, stupefy

stunning *adjective* <u>wonderful</u>, beautiful, dazzling, gorgeous, impressive, lovely, marvellous, sensational (*informal*), spectacular, striking

stunt *noun* <u>feat</u>, act, deed, exploit, trick

stunted *adjective* <u>undersized</u>, diminutive, little, small, tiny

stupefy *verb* <u>astound</u>, amaze, daze, dumbfound, shock, stagger, stun

stupendous *adjective* **1** <u>wonderful</u>, amazing, astounding, breathtaking, marvellous, overwhelming, sensational (*informal*), staggering, superb **2** <u>huge</u>, colossal, enormous, gigantic, mega (*slang*), vast

stupid *adjective* **1** <u>unintelligent</u>, brainless, dense, dim, half-witted, moronic, obtuse, simple, simple-minded, slow, slow-witted, thick **2** <u>foolish</u>, asinine, daft (*informal*), idiotic, imbecilic, inane, nonsensical, pointless, rash, senseless, unintelligent **3** <u>dazed</u>, groggy, insensate, semiconscious, stunned, stupefied

stupidity *noun* **1** <u>lack of intelligence</u>, brainlessness, denseness, dimness, dullness, imbecility, obtuseness, slowness, thickness **2** <u>foolishness</u>, absurdity, fatuousness, folly, idiocy, inanity, lunacy, madness, silliness

stupor *noun* <u>daze</u>, coma,

insensibility, stupefaction, unconsciousness

sturdy *adjective* **1** <u>robust</u>, athletic, brawny, hardy, lusty, muscular, powerful **2** <u>well-built</u>, durable, solid, substantial, well-made

stutter *verb* <u>stammer</u>, falter, hesitate, stumble

style *noun* **1** <u>design</u>, cut, form, manner **2** <u>manner</u>, approach, method, mode, technique, way **3** <u>elegance</u>, chic, élan, flair, panache, polish, smartness, sophistication, taste **4** <u>type</u>, category, genre, kind, sort, variety **5** <u>fashion</u>, mode, rage, trend, vogue **6** <u>luxury</u>, affluence, comfort, ease, elegance, grandeur ♦ *verb* **7** <u>design</u>, adapt, arrange, cut, fashion, shape, tailor **8** <u>call</u>, designate, dub, entitle, label, name, term

stylish *adjective* <u>smart</u>, chic, dressy (*informal*), fashionable, modish, trendy (*Brit. informal*), voguish

suave *adjective* <u>smooth</u>, charming, courteous, debonair, polite, sophisticated, urbane

subconscious *adjective* <u>hidden</u>, inner, intuitive, latent, repressed, subliminal

subdue *verb* **1** <u>overcome</u>, break, conquer, control, crush, defeat, master, overpower, quell, tame, vanquish **2** <u>moderate</u>, mellow, quieten down, soften, suppress, tone down

subdued *adjective* **1** <u>quiet</u>, chastened, crestfallen, dejected, downcast, down in the mouth, sad, serious **2** <u>soft</u>, dim, hushed, muted, quiet, subtle, toned down, unobtrusive

subject *noun* **1** <u>topic</u>, affair, business, issue, matter, object, point, question, substance, theme **2** <u>citizen</u>, national, subordinate ♦ *adjective* **3** <u>subordinate</u>, dependent, inferior, obedient, satellite **4 subject to: a** <u>liable to</u>, exposed to, in danger of, open to, prone to, susceptible to, vulnerable to **b** <u>conditional on</u>, contingent on, dependent on ♦ *verb* **5** <u>put through</u>, expose, lay open, submit, treat

subjective *adjective* <u>personal</u>, biased, nonobjective, prejudiced

subjugate *verb* <u>conquer</u>, enslave, master, overcome, overpower, quell, subdue, suppress, vanquish

sublime *adjective* <u>noble</u>, elevated, exalted, glorious, grand, great, high, lofty

submerge *verb* <u>immerse</u>, deluge, dip, duck, engulf, flood, inundate, overflow, overwhelm, plunge, sink, swamp

submission *noun* **1** <u>surrender</u>, assent, capitulation, giving in, yielding **2** <u>presentation</u>, entry, handing in, tendering **3** <u>meekness</u>, compliance, deference, docility, obedience, passivity, resignation

submissive *adjective* <u>meek</u>, accommodating, acquiescent, amenable, compliant, docile, obedient, passive, pliant, tractable, unresisting, yielding

submit *verb* **1** <u>surrender</u>, accede, agree, capitulate, comply, endure, give in, succumb, tolerate, yield **2** <u>put forward</u>, hand in, present, proffer, table, tender

subordinate *adjective* **1** lesser, dependent, inferior, junior, lower, minor, secondary, subject ♦ *noun* **2** inferior, aide, assistant, attendant, junior, second

subordination *noun* inferiority, inferior *or* secondary status, servitude, subjection

subscribe *verb* **1** donate, contribute, give **2** support, advocate, endorse

subscription *noun* **1** membership fee, annual payment, dues **2** donation, contribution, gift

subsequent *adjective* following, after, ensuing, later, succeeding, successive

subsequently *adverb* later, afterwards

subservient *adjective* servile, abject, deferential, obsequious, slavish, submissive, sycophantic

subside *verb* **1** decrease, abate, diminish, ease, ebb, lessen, quieten, slacken, wane **2** sink, cave in, collapse, drop, lower, settle

subsidence *noun* **1** sinking, settling **2** decrease, abatement, easing off, lessening, slackening

subsidiary *adjective* lesser, ancillary, auxiliary, minor, secondary, subordinate, supplementary

subsidize *verb* fund, finance, promote, sponsor, support

subsidy *noun* aid, allowance, assistance, grant, help, support

substance *noun* **1** material, body, fabric, stuff **2** meaning, essence, gist, import, main point, significance **3** reality, actuality, concreteness **4** wealth, assets, estate, means, property, resources

substantial *adjective* big, ample, considerable, important, large, significant, sizable *or* sizeable

substantiate *verb* support, authenticate, confirm, establish, prove, verify

substitute *verb* **1** replace, change, exchange, interchange, swap, switch ♦ *noun* **2** replacement, agent, deputy, locum, proxy, reserve, sub, surrogate ♦ *adjective* **3** replacement, alternative, fall-back, proxy, reserve, second, surrogate

substitution *noun* replacement, change, exchange, swap, switch

subterfuge *noun* trick, deception, dodge, manoeuvre, ploy, ruse, stratagem

subtle *adjective* **1** sophisticated, delicate, refined **2** faint, delicate, implied, slight, understated **3** crafty, artful, cunning, devious, ingenious, shrewd, sly, wily

subtlety *noun* **1** sophistication, delicacy, refinement **2** cunning, artfulness, cleverness, craftiness, deviousness, ingenuity, slyness, wiliness

subtract *verb* take away, deduct, diminish, remove, take from, take off

subversive *adjective* **1** seditious, riotous, treasonous ♦ *noun* **2** dissident, fifth columnist, saboteur, terrorist, traitor

subvert *verb* overturn, sabotage, undermine

succeed *verb* **1** make it

(*informal*), be successful, crack it (*informal*), flourish, make good, make the grade (*informal*), prosper, thrive, triumph, work **2** follow, come next, ensue, result

success *noun* **1** luck, fame, fortune, happiness, prosperity, triumph **2** hit (*informal*), celebrity, megastar (*informal*), sensation, smash (*informal*), star, winner

successful *adjective* thriving, booming, flourishing, fortunate, fruitful, lucky, profitable, prosperous, rewarding, top, victorious

successfully *adverb* well, favourably, victoriously, with flying colours

succession *noun* **1** series, chain, course, cycle, order, progression, run, sequence, train **2** taking over, accession, assumption, inheritance

successive *adjective* consecutive, following, in succession

succinct *adjective* brief, compact, concise, laconic, pithy, terse

succour *noun* **1** help, aid, assistance ♦ *verb* **2** help, aid, assist

succulent *adjective* juicy, luscious, lush, moist

succumb *verb* **1** surrender, capitulate, give in, submit, yield **2** die, fall

sucker *noun* Slang fool, dupe, mug (*Brit. slang*), pushover (*slang*), victim

sudden *adjective* quick, abrupt, hasty, hurried, rapid, rash, swift, unexpected

suddenly *adverb* abruptly, all of a sudden, unexpectedly

sue *verb* Law take (someone) to court, charge, indict, prosecute, summon

suffer *verb* **1** undergo, bear, endure, experience, go through, sustain **2** tolerate, put up with (*informal*)

suffering *noun* pain, agony, anguish, discomfort, distress, hardship, misery, ordeal, torment

suffice *verb* be enough, be adequate, be sufficient, do, meet requirements, serve

sufficient *adjective* adequate, enough, satisfactory

suffocate *verb* choke, asphyxiate, smother, stifle

suggest *verb* **1** recommend, advise, advocate, prescribe, propose **2** bring to mind, evoke **3** hint, imply, indicate, intimate

suggestion *noun* **1** recommendation, motion, plan, proposal, proposition **2** hint, breath, indication, intimation, trace, whisper

suggestive *adjective* smutty, bawdy, blue, indelicate, provocative, racy, ribald, risqué, rude

suit *noun* **1** outfit, clothing, costume, dress, ensemble, habit **2** lawsuit, action, case, cause, proceeding, prosecution, trial ♦ *verb* **3** be acceptable to, do, gratify, please, satisfy **4** befit, agree, become, go with, harmonize, match, tally

suitability *noun* appropriateness, aptness, fitness, rightness

suitable *adjective* appropriate, apt, becoming, befitting, fit, fitting, proper, right, satisfactory

suite noun <u>rooms</u>, apartment

suitor noun Old-fashioned <u>admirer</u>, beau, young man

sulk verb <u>be sullen</u>, be in a huff, pout

sulky adjective <u>huffy</u>, cross, disgruntled, in the sulks, moody, petulant, querulous, resentful, sullen

sullen adjective <u>morose</u>, cross, dour, glowering, moody, sour, surly, unsociable

sully verb <u>defile</u>, besmirch, disgrace, dishonour, smirch, stain, tarnish

sultry adjective **1** <u>humid</u>, close, hot, muggy, oppressive, sticky, stifling **2** <u>seductive</u>, provocative, sensual, sexy (informal)

sum noun <u>total</u>, aggregate, amount, tally, whole

summarize verb <u>sum up</u>, abridge, condense, encapsulate, epitomize, précis

summary noun <u>synopsis</u>, abridgment, outline, précis, résumé, review, rundown

summit noun <u>peak</u>, acme, apex, head, height, pinnacle, top, zenith

summon verb **1** <u>send for</u>, bid, call, invite **2** often with **up** <u>gather</u>, draw on, muster

sumptuous adjective <u>luxurious</u>, gorgeous, grand, lavish, opulent, splendid, superb

sum up verb <u>summarize</u>, put in a nutshell, recapitulate, review

sunburnt adjective <u>tanned</u>, bronzed, brown, burnt, peeling, red

sundry adjective <u>various</u>, assorted, different, miscellaneous, several, some

sunken adjective **1** <u>hollow</u>, drawn, haggard **2** <u>lower</u>, buried, recessed, submerged

sunny adjective **1** <u>bright</u>, clear, fine, radiant, summery, sunlit, unclouded **2** <u>cheerful</u>, buoyant, cheery, happy, joyful, light-hearted

sunrise noun <u>dawn</u>, break of day, cockcrow, daybreak

sunset noun <u>nightfall</u>, close of (the) day, dusk, eventide

super adjective Slang <u>excellent</u>, cracking (Brit. informal), glorious, magnificent, marvellous, outstanding, sensational (informal), smashing (informal), superb, terrific (informal), wonderful

superb adjective <u>splendid</u>, excellent, exquisite, fine, first-rate, grand, magnificent, marvellous, superior, superlative, world-class

supercilious adjective <u>scornful</u>, arrogant, contemptuous, disdainful, haughty, lofty, snooty (Informal), stuck-up (informal)

superficial adjective **1** <u>hasty</u>, casual, cursory, desultory, hurried, perfunctory, sketchy, slapdash **2** <u>shallow</u>, empty-headed, frivolous, silly, trivial **3** <u>surface</u>, exterior, external, on the surface, slight

superfluous adjective <u>excess</u>, extra, left over, redundant, remaining, spare, supernumerary, surplus

superhuman adjective **1** <u>heroic</u>, phenomenal, prodigious

2 <u>supernatural</u>, paranormal

superintendence *noun*
<u>supervision</u>, charge, control,
direction, government,
management

superintendent *noun* <u>supervisor</u>,
chief, controller, director,
governor, inspector, manager,
overseer

superior *adjective* 1 <u>better</u>,
grander, greater, higher,
surpassing, unrivalled
2 <u>supercilious</u>, condescending,
disdainful, haughty, lofty, lordly,
patronizing, pretentious,
snobbish 3 <u>first-class</u>, choice, de
luxe, excellent, exceptional,
exclusive, first-rate ♦ *noun* 4 <u>boss</u>
(*informal*), chief, director,
manager, principal, senior,
supervisor

superiority *noun* <u>supremacy</u>,
advantage, ascendancy,
excellence, lead, predominance

superlative *adjective*
<u>outstanding</u>, excellent, supreme,
unparalleled, unrivalled,
unsurpassed

supernatural *adjective*
<u>paranormal</u>, ghostly, hidden,
miraculous, mystic, occult,
psychic, spectral, uncanny,
unearthly

supersede *verb* <u>replace</u>, displace,
oust, supplant, take the place of,
usurp

supervise *verb* <u>oversee</u>, control,
direct, handle, look after,
manage, run, superintend

supervision *noun*
<u>superintendence</u>, care, charge,
control, direction, guidance,
management

supervisor *noun* <u>boss</u> (*informal*),
administrator, chief, foreman,
inspector, manager, overseer

supplant *verb* <u>replace</u>, displace,
oust, supersede, take the place of

supple *adjective* <u>flexible</u>, limber,
lissom(e), lithe, pliable, pliant

supplement *noun* 1 <u>addition</u>,
add-on, appendix, extra, insert,
postscript, pull-out ♦ *verb* 2 <u>add</u>,
augment, extend, reinforce

supplementary *adjective*
<u>additional</u>, add-on, ancillary,
auxiliary, extra, secondary

supplication *noun* <u>plea</u>, appeal,
entreaty, petition, prayer, request

supply *verb* 1 <u>provide</u>,
contribute, endow, equip,
furnish, give, grant, produce,
stock, yield ♦ *noun* 2 <u>store</u>,
cache, fund, hoard, quantity,
reserve, source, stock 3 *usually
plural* <u>provisions</u>, equipment,
food, materials, necessities,
rations, stores

support *verb* 1 <u>bear</u>, brace,
buttress, carry, hold, prop,
reinforce, sustain 2 <u>provide for</u>,
finance, fund, keep, look after,
maintain, sustain 3 <u>help</u>, aid,
assist, back, champion, defend,
second, side with 4 <u>bear out</u>,
confirm, corroborate,
substantiate, verify ♦ *noun*
5 <u>help</u>, aid, assistance, backing,
encouragement, loyalty 6 <u>prop</u>,
brace, foundation, pillar, post
7 <u>supporter</u>, backer, mainstay,
prop, second, tower of strength
8 <u>upkeep</u>, keep, maintenance,
subsistence, sustenance

supporter *noun* <u>follower</u>,
adherent, advocate, champion,
fan, friend, helper, patron,

sponsor, well-wisher

supportive *adjective* <u>helpful</u>, encouraging, sympathetic, understanding

suppose *verb* 1 <u>presume</u>, assume, conjecture, expect, guess (*informal, chiefly U.S. & Canad.*), imagine, think 2 <u>imagine</u>, conjecture, consider, hypothesize, postulate, pretend

supposed *adjective* 1 <u>presumed</u>, accepted, alleged, assumed, professed 2 *usually with* **to** <u>meant</u>, expected, obliged, required

supposedly *adverb* <u>allegedly</u>, hypothetically, ostensibly, presumably, theoretically

supposition *noun* <u>guess</u>, conjecture, hypothesis, presumption, speculation, surmise, theory

suppress *verb* 1 <u>stop</u>, check, conquer, crush, overpower, put an end to, quash, quell, subdue 2 <u>restrain</u>, conceal, contain, curb, hold in *or* back, repress, silence, smother, stifle

suppression *noun* <u>elimination</u>, check, crushing, quashing, smothering

supremacy *noun* <u>domination</u>, mastery, predominance, primacy, sovereignty, supreme power, sway

supreme *adjective* <u>highest</u>, chief, foremost, greatest, head, leading, paramount, pre-eminent, prime, principal, top, ultimate

supremo *noun* <u>head</u>, boss (*informal*), commander, director, governor, leader, master, principal, ruler

sure *adjective* 1 <u>certain</u>, assured, confident, convinced, decided, definite, positive 2 <u>reliable</u>, accurate, dependable, foolproof, infallible, undeniable, undoubted, unerring, unfailing 3 <u>inevitable</u>, assured, bound, guaranteed, inescapable

surely *adverb* <u>undoubtedly</u>, certainly, definitely, doubtlessly, indubitably, unquestionably, without doubt

surface *noun* 1 <u>outside</u>, covering, exterior, face, side, top, veneer ♦ *verb* 2 <u>appear</u>, arise, come to light, come up, crop up (*informal*), emerge, materialize, transpire

surfeit *noun* <u>excess</u>, glut, plethora, superfluity

surge *noun* 1 <u>rush</u>, flood, flow, gush, outpouring 2 <u>wave</u>, billow, roller, swell ♦ *verb* 3 <u>rush</u>, gush, heave, rise, roll

surly *adjective* <u>ill-tempered</u>, churlish, cross, grouchy (*informal*), morose, sulky, sullen, uncivil, ungracious

surmise *verb* 1 <u>guess</u>, conjecture, imagine, presume, speculate, suppose ♦ *noun* 2 <u>guess</u>, assumption, conjecture, presumption, speculation, supposition

surpass *verb* <u>outdo</u>, beat, eclipse, exceed, excel, outshine, outstrip, transcend

surpassing *adjective* <u>supreme</u>, exceptional, extraordinary, incomparable, matchless, outstanding, unrivalled

surplus *noun* 1 <u>excess</u>, balance,

remainder, residue, surfeit
♦ *adjective* 2 excess, extra, odd, remaining, spare, superfluous

surprise *noun* 1 shock, bombshell, eye-opener (*informal*), jolt, revelation 2 amazement, astonishment, incredulity, wonder ♦ *verb* 3 amaze, astonish, stagger, stun, take aback 4 catch unawares or off-guard, discover, spring upon, startle

surprised *adjective* amazed, astonished, speechless, taken by surprise, thunderstruck

surprising *adjective* amazing, astonishing, extraordinary, incredible, remarkable, staggering, unexpected, unusual

surrender *verb* 1 give in, capitulate, give way, submit, succumb, yield 2 give up, abandon, cede, concede, part with, relinquish, renounce, waive, yield ♦ *noun* 3 submission, capitulation, relinquishment, renunciation, resignation

surreptitious *adjective* secret, covert, furtive, sly, stealthy, underhand

surrogate *noun* substitute, proxy, representative, stand-in

surround *verb* enclose, encircle, encompass, envelop, hem in, ring

surroundings *plural noun* environment, background, location, milieu, setting

surveillance *noun* observation, inspection, scrutiny, supervision, watch

survey *verb* 1 look over, contemplate, examine, inspect, observe, scan, scrutinize, view

2 estimate, appraise, assess, measure, plan, plot, size up ♦ *noun* 3 examination, inspection, scrutiny 4 study, inquiry, review

survive *verb* remain alive, endure, last, live on, outlast, outlive

susceptible *adjective* 1 *usually with* to liable, disposed, given, inclined, prone, subject, vulnerable 2 impressionable, receptive, responsive, sensitive, suggestible

suspect *verb* 1 believe, consider, feel, guess, speculate, suppose 2 distrust, doubt, mistrust ♦ *adjective* 3 dubious, doubtful, iffy (*informal*), questionable

suspend *verb* 1 hang, attach, dangle 2 postpone, cease, cut short, defer, discontinue, interrupt, put off, shelve

suspense *noun* uncertainty, anxiety, apprehension, doubt, expectation, insecurity, irresolution, tension

suspension *noun* postponement, abeyance, break, breaking off, deferment, discontinuation, interruption

suspicion *noun* 1 distrust, doubt, dubiety, misgiving, mistrust, qualm, scepticism, wariness 2 idea, guess, hunch, impression, notion 3 trace, hint, shade, *soupçon*, streak, suggestion, tinge, touch

suspicious *adjective* 1 distrustful, doubtful, sceptical, unbelieving, wary 2 suspect, dodgy (*Brit., Austral., & N.Z. informal*), doubtful, dubious, fishy (*informal*), questionable

sustain verb 1 <u>maintain</u>, continue, keep up, prolong, protract 2 <u>keep alive</u>, aid, assist, help, nourish 3 <u>withstand</u>, bear, endure, experience, feel, suffer, undergo 4 <u>support</u>, bear, uphold

sustained adjective <u>continuous</u>, constant, nonstop, perpetual, prolonged, steady, unremitting

swagger verb <u>show off</u> (informal), boast, brag, parade

swallow verb <u>gulp</u>, consume, devour, drink, eat, swig (informal)

swamp noun 1 <u>bog</u>, fen, marsh, mire, morass, quagmire, slough ♦ verb 2 <u>flood</u>, capsize, engulf, inundate, sink, submerge 3 <u>overwhelm</u>, flood, inundate, overload

swap, swop verb <u>exchange</u>, barter, interchange, switch, trade

swarm noun 1 <u>multitude</u>, army, crowd, flock, herd, horde, host, mass, throng ♦ verb 2 <u>crowd</u>, flock, mass, stream, throng 3 <u>teem</u>, abound, bristle, crawl

swarthy adjective <u>dark-skinned</u>, black, brown, dark, dark-complexioned, dusky

swashbuckling adjective <u>dashing</u>, bold, daredevil, flamboyant

swathe verb <u>wrap</u>, bundle up, cloak, drape, envelop, shroud

sway verb 1 <u>lean</u>, bend, rock, roll, swing 2 <u>influence</u>, affect, guide, induce, persuade ♦ noun 3 <u>power</u>, authority, clout (informal), control, influence

swear verb 1 <u>curse</u>, be foul-mouthed, blaspheme 2 <u>declare</u>, affirm, assert, attest, promise, testify, vow

swearing noun <u>bad language</u>, blasphemy, cursing, foul language, profanity

swearword noun <u>oath</u>, curse, expletive, four-letter word, obscenity, profanity

sweat noun 1 <u>perspiration</u> 2 Informal <u>labour</u>, chore, drudgery, toil 3 Informal <u>worry</u>, agitation, anxiety, distress, panic, strain ♦ verb 4 <u>perspire</u>, glow 5 Informal <u>worry</u>, agonize, fret, suffer, torture oneself

sweaty adjective <u>perspiring</u>, clammy, sticky

sweep verb 1 <u>clear</u>, brush, clean, remove 2 <u>sail</u>, fly, glide, pass, skim, tear, zoom ♦ noun 3 <u>arc</u>, bend, curve, move, stroke, swing 4 <u>extent</u>, range, scope, stretch

sweeping adjective 1 <u>wide-ranging</u>, all-embracing, all-inclusive, broad, comprehensive, extensive, global, wide 2 <u>indiscriminate</u>, blanket, exaggerated, overstated, unqualified, wholesale

sweet adjective 1 <u>sugary</u>, cloying, saccharine 2 <u>charming</u>, agreeable, appealing, cute, delightful, engaging, kind, likable or likeable, lovable, winning 3 <u>melodious</u>, dulcet, harmonious, mellow, musical 4 <u>fragrant</u>, aromatic, clean, fresh, pure ♦ noun 5 usually plural <u>confectionery</u>, bonbon, candy (U.S.) 6 <u>dessert</u>, pudding

sweeten verb 1 <u>sugar</u> 2 <u>mollify</u>, appease, pacify, soothe

sweetheart noun <u>lover</u>, beloved, boyfriend or girlfriend, darling, dear, love

swell verb 1 <u>expand</u>, balloon,

bloat, bulge, dilate, distend,
enlarge, grow, increase, rise
♦ *noun* 2 <u>wave</u>, billow, surge

swelling *noun* <u>enlargement</u>,
bulge, bump, distension,
inflammation, lump,
protuberance

sweltering *adjective* <u>hot</u>, boiling,
burning, oppressive, scorching,
stifling

swerve *verb* <u>veer</u>, bend, deflect,
deviate, diverge, stray, swing,
turn, turn aside

swift *adjective* <u>quick</u>, fast, hurried,
prompt, rapid, speedy

swiftly *adverb* <u>quickly</u>, fast,
hurriedly, promptly, rapidly,
speedily

swiftness *noun* <u>speed</u>,
promptness, quickness, rapidity,
speediness, velocity

swindle *verb* <u>cheat</u>, con,
defraud, do (*slang*), fleece, rip
(someone) off (*slang*), skin
(*slang*), sting (*informal*), trick
♦ *noun* 2 <u>fraud</u>, con trick
(*informal*), deception, fiddle (*Brit.
informal*), racket, rip-off (*slang*),
scam (*slang*)

swindler *noun* <u>cheat</u>, con man
(*informal*), fraud, rogue, shark,
trickster

swing *verb* 1 <u>sway</u>, oscillate,
rock, veer, wave 2 *usually with*
round <u>turn</u>, curve, pivot, rotate,
swivel 3 <u>hang</u>, dangle, suspend
♦ *noun* 4 <u>swaying</u>, oscillation

swingeing *adjective* <u>severe</u>,
drastic, excessive, harsh, heavy,
punishing, stringent

swipe *verb* 1 <u>hit</u>, lash out at,
slap, strike, wallop (*informal*)
2 *Slang* <u>steal</u>, appropriate, filch,

lift (*informal*), nick (*slang, chiefly
Brit.*), pinch (*informal*), purloin
♦ *noun* 3 <u>blow</u>, clout (*informal*),
cuff, slap, smack, wallop
(*informal*)

swirl *verb* <u>whirl</u>, churn, eddy,
spin, twist

switch *noun* 1 <u>change</u>, reversal,
shift 2 <u>exchange</u>, substitution,
swap ♦ *verb* 3 <u>change</u>, deflect,
deviate, divert, shift 4 <u>exchange</u>,
substitute, swap

swivel *verb* <u>turn</u>, pivot, revolve,
rotate, spin

swollen *adjective* <u>enlarged</u>,
bloated, distended, inflamed,
puffed up

swoop *verb* 1 <u>pounce</u>, descend,
dive, rush, stoop, sweep ♦ *noun*
2 <u>pounce</u>, descent, drop, lunge,
plunge, rush, stoop, sweep

swop *see* SWAP

swot *verb Informal* <u>study</u>, cram
(*informal*), mug up (*Brit. slang*),
revise

sycophant *noun* <u>crawler</u>,
bootlicker (*informal*), fawner,
flatterer, toady, yes man

sycophantic *adjective*
<u>obsequious</u>, crawling, fawning,
flattering, grovelling,
ingratiating, servile, smarmy
(*Brit. informal*), toadying,
unctuous

syllabus *noun* <u>course of study</u>,
curriculum

symbol *noun* <u>sign</u>, badge,
emblem, figure, image, logo,
mark, representation, token

symbolic *adjective* <u>representative</u>,
allegorical, emblematic, figurative

symbolize *verb* <u>represent</u>,
denote, mean, personify, signify,

stand for, typify

symmetrical *adjective* <u>balanced</u>, in proportion, regular

symmetry *noun* <u>balance</u>, evenness, order, proportion, regularity

sympathetic *adjective* 1 <u>caring</u>, compassionate, concerned, interested, kind, pitying, supportive, understanding, warm 2 <u>like-minded</u>, agreeable, companionable, compatible, congenial, friendly

sympathize *verb* 1 <u>feel for</u>, commiserate, condole, pity 2 <u>agree</u>, side with, understand

sympathizer *noun* <u>supporter</u>, partisan, well-wisher

sympathy *noun* 1 <u>compassion</u>, commiseration, pity, understanding 2 <u>agreement</u>, affinity, fellow feeling, rapport

symptom *noun* <u>sign</u>, expression, indication, mark, token, warning

symptomatic *adjective* <u>indicative</u>, characteristic, suggestive

synthetic *adjective* <u>artificial</u>, fake, man-made

system *noun* 1 <u>method</u>, practice, procedure, routine, technique 2 <u>arrangement</u>, classification, organization, scheme, structure

systematic *adjective* <u>methodical</u>, efficient, orderly, organized

T t

table *noun* 1 <u>counter</u>, bench, board, stand 2 <u>list</u>, catalogue, chart, diagram, record, register, roll, schedule, tabulation ◆ *verb* 3 <u>submit</u>, enter, move, propose, put forward, suggest

tableau *noun* <u>picture</u>, representation, scene, spectacle

taboo *noun* 1 <u>prohibition</u>, anathema, ban, interdict, proscription, restriction ◆ *adjective* 2 <u>forbidden</u>, anathema, banned, outlawed, prohibited, proscribed, unacceptable, unmentionable

tacit *adjective* <u>implied</u>, implicit, inferred, undeclared, understood, unexpressed, unspoken, unstated

taciturn *adjective* <u>uncommunicative</u>, quiet, reserved, reticent, silent, tight-lipped, unforthcoming, withdrawn

tack[1] *noun* 1 <u>nail</u>, drawing pin, pin ◆ *verb* 2 <u>fasten</u>, affix, attach, fix, nail, pin 3 <u>stitch</u>, baste 4 tack on <u>append</u>, add, attach, tag

tack[2] *noun* <u>course</u>, approach, direction, heading, line, method, path, plan, procedure, way

tackle *verb* 1 <u>deal with</u>, attempt, come *or* get to grips with, embark upon, get stuck into (*informal*), have a go at (*informal*), set about, undertake 2 <u>confront</u>, challenge, grab, grasp, halt, intercept, seize, stop ◆ *noun* 3 <u>challenge</u>, block 4 <u>equipment</u>, accoutrements, apparatus, gear, paraphernalia, tools, trappings

tacky[1] *adjective* <u>sticky</u>, adhesive, gluey, gummy, wet

tacky[2] *adjective Informal* <u>vulgar</u>, cheap, naff (*Brit. slang*), seedy, shabby, shoddy, sleazy, tasteless, tatty

tact noun <u>diplomacy</u>, consideration, delicacy, discretion, sensitivity, thoughtfulness, understanding

tactful adjective <u>diplomatic</u>, considerate, delicate, discreet, polite, politic, sensitive, thoughtful, understanding

tactic noun 1 <u>policy</u>, approach, manoeuvre, method, move, ploy, scheme, stratagem 2 **tactics** <u>strategy</u>, campaigning, generalship, manoeuvres, plans

tactical adjective <u>strategic</u>, cunning, diplomatic, shrewd, smart

tactician noun <u>strategist</u>, general, mastermind, planner

tactless adjective <u>insensitive</u>, impolite, impolitic, inconsiderate, indelicate, indiscreet, thoughtless, undiplomatic, unsubtle

tag noun 1 <u>label</u>, flap, identification, mark, marker, note, slip, tab, ticket ◆ verb 2 <u>label</u>, mark 3 **with along** or **on** <u>accompany</u>, attend, follow, shadow, tail (informal), trail

tail noun 1 <u>extremity</u>, appendage, end, rear end, tailpiece 2 **turn tail** <u>run away</u>, cut and run, flee, retreat, run off, take to one's heels ◆ verb 3 Informal <u>follow</u>, shadow, stalk, track, trail

tailor noun 1 <u>outfitter</u>, clothier, costumier, couturier, dressmaker, seamstress ◆ verb 2 <u>adapt</u>, adjust, alter, customize, fashion, modify, mould, shape, style

taint verb 1 <u>spoil</u>, blemish, contaminate, corrupt, damage, defile, pollute, ruin, stain, sully, tarnish ◆ noun 2 <u>stain</u>, black mark, blemish, blot, defect, demerit, fault, flaw, spot

take verb 1 <u>capture</u>, acquire, catch, get, grasp, grip, obtain, secure, seize 2 <u>accompany</u>, bring, conduct, convoy, escort, guide, lead, usher 3 <u>carry</u>, bear, bring, convey, ferry, fetch, haul, transport 4 <u>steal</u>, appropriate, misappropriate, pinch (informal), pocket, purloin 5 <u>require</u>, call for, demand, necessitate, need 6 <u>tolerate</u>, abide, bear, endure, put up with (informal), stand, stomach, withstand 7 <u>have room for</u>, accept, accommodate, contain, hold 8 <u>subtract</u>, deduct, eliminate, remove 9 <u>assume</u>, believe, consider, perceive, presume, regard, understand

take in verb 1 <u>understand</u>, absorb, assimilate, comprehend, digest, get the hang of (informal), grasp 2 <u>deceive</u>, cheat, con (informal), dupe, fool, hoodwink, mislead, swindle, trick

takeoff noun 1 <u>departure</u>, launch, liftoff 2 Informal <u>parody</u>, caricature, imitation, lampoon, satire, send-up (Brit. informal), spoof (informal)

take off verb 1 <u>remove</u>, discard, peel off, strip off 2 <u>lift off</u>, take to the air 3 Informal <u>depart</u>, abscond, decamp, disappear, go, leave, slope off 4 Informal <u>parody</u>, caricature, imitate, lampoon, mimic, mock, satirize, send up (Brit. informal)

takeover noun <u>merger</u>, coup, incorporation

take up verb 1 <u>occupy</u>, absorb, consume, cover, extend over, fill, use up 2 <u>start</u>, adopt, become involved in, engage in

taking adjective 1 <u>charming</u>, attractive, beguiling, captivating, enchanting, engaging, fetching (informal), likable or likeable, prepossessing ♦ noun 2 **takings** <u>revenue</u>, earnings, income, proceeds, profits, receipts, returns, take

tale noun <u>story</u>, account, anecdote, fable, legend, narrative, saga, yarn (informal)

talent noun <u>ability</u>, aptitude, capacity, flair, genius, gift, knack

talented adjective <u>gifted</u>, able, brilliant

talisman noun <u>charm</u>, amulet, fetish, lucky charm, mascot

talk verb 1 <u>speak</u>, chat, chatter, communicate, converse, gossip, natter, utter 2 <u>negotiate</u>, confabulate, confer, parley 3 <u>inform</u>, blab, give the game away, grass (Brit. slang), let the cat out of the bag, tell all ♦ noun 4 <u>speech</u>, address, discourse, disquisition, lecture, oration, sermon

talkative adjective <u>loquacious</u>, chatty, effusive, garrulous, gossipy, long-winded, mouthy, verbose, voluble, wordy

talker noun <u>speaker</u>, chatterbox, conversationalist, lecturer, orator

talking-to noun <u>reprimand</u>, criticism, dressing-down (informal), lecture, rebuke, reproach, reproof, scolding, telling-off (informal), ticking-off (informal)

tall adjective 1 <u>high</u>, big, elevated, giant, lanky, lofty, soaring, towering 2 As in **tall story** Informal <u>implausible</u>, absurd, cock-and-bull (informal), exaggerated, far-fetched, incredible, preposterous, unbelievable 3 As in **tall order** <u>difficult</u>, demanding, hard, unreasonable, well-nigh impossible

tally verb 1 <u>correspond</u>, accord, agree, coincide, concur, conform, fit, harmonize, match, square ♦ noun 2 <u>record</u>, count, mark, reckoning, running total, score, total

tame adjective 1 <u>domesticated</u>, amenable, broken, disciplined, docile, gentle, obedient, tractable 2 <u>submissive</u>, compliant, docile, manageable, meek, obedient, subdued, unresisting 3 <u>uninteresting</u>, bland, boring, dull, humdrum, insipid, unexciting, uninspiring, vapid ♦ verb 4 <u>domesticate</u>, break in, house train, train 5 <u>discipline</u>, bring to heel, conquer, humble, master, subdue, subjugate, suppress

tamper verb <u>interfere</u>, alter, fiddle (informal), fool about (informal), meddle, mess about, tinker

tangible adjective <u>definite</u>, actual, concrete, material, palpable, perceptible, positive, real

tangle noun 1 <u>knot</u>, coil, entanglement, jungle, twist, web 2 <u>confusion</u>, complication, entanglement, fix (informal), imbroglio, jam, mess, mix-up ♦ verb 3 <u>twist</u>, coil, entangle, interweave, knot, mat, mesh, ravel **4** *often with* **with** come into conflict, come up against, contend, contest, cross swords, dispute, lock horns

tangled *adjective* **1** twisted, entangled, jumbled, knotted, matted, messy, snarled, tousled **2** complicated, complex, confused, convoluted, involved, knotty, messy, mixed-up

tangy *adjective* sharp, piquant, pungent, spicy, tart

tantalize *verb* torment, frustrate, lead on, taunt, tease, torture

tantamount *adjective* equivalent, commensurate, equal, synonymous

tantrum *noun* outburst, fit, flare-up, hysterics, temper

tap¹ *verb* **1** knock, beat, drum, pat, rap, strike, touch ♦ *noun* **2** knock, pat, rap, touch

tap² *noun* **1** valve, stopcock **2 on tap: a** *Informal* available, at hand, in reserve, on hand, ready **b** on draught ♦ *verb* **3** listen in on, bug (*informal*), eavesdrop on **4** draw off, bleed, drain, siphon off

tape *noun* **1** strip, band, ribbon ♦ *verb* **2** record, tape-record, video **3** bind, seal, secure, stick, wrap

taper *verb* **1** narrow, come to a point, thin **2 taper off** lessen, decrease, die away, dwindle, fade, reduce, subside, wane, wind down

target *noun* **1** goal, aim, ambition, end, intention, mark, object, objective **2** victim, butt, scapegoat

tariff *noun* **1** tax, duty, excise, levy, toll **2** schedule, menu

tarnish *verb* **1** stain, blacken, blemish, blot, darken, discolour, sully, taint ♦ *noun* **2** stain, blemish, blot, discoloration, spot, taint

tart¹ *noun* pie, pastry, tartlet

tart² *adjective* sharp, acid, bitter, piquant, pungent, sour, tangy, vinegary

tart³ *noun* slut, call girl, floozy (*slang*), prostitute, trollop, whore

task *noun* **1** job, assignment, chore, duty, enterprise, exercise, mission, undertaking **2 take to task** criticize, blame, censure, reprimand, reproach, reprove, scold, tell off (*informal*), upbraid

taste *noun* **1** flavour, relish, savour, smack, tang **2** bit, bite, dash, morsel, mouthful, sample, *soupçon*, spoonful, titbit **3** liking, appetite, fancy, fondness, inclination, partiality, penchant, predilection, preference **4** refinement, appreciation, discernment, discrimination, elegance, judgment, sophistication, style ♦ *verb* **5** distinguish, differentiate, discern, perceive **6** sample, savour, sip, test, try **7** have a flavour of, savour of, smack of **8** experience, encounter, know, meet with, partake of, undergo

tasteful *adjective* refined, artistic, cultivated, cultured, discriminating, elegant, exquisite, in good taste, polished, stylish

tasteless *adjective* **1** insipid, bland, boring, dull, flat, flavourless, mild, thin, weak

2 <u>vulgar</u>, crass, crude, gaudy, gross, inelegant, naff (*Brit. slang*), tacky (*informal*), tawdry

tasty *adjective* <u>delicious</u>, appetizing, delectable, full-flavoured, luscious, palatable, savoury, scrumptious (*informal*), toothsome

tatters *noun* **in tatters** <u>ragged</u>, down at heel, in rags, in shreds, ripped, tattered, threadbare, torn

tatty *adjective* <u>ragged</u>, bedraggled, dilapidated, down at heel, neglected, run-down, scruffy, shabby, threadbare, worn

taunt *verb* **1** <u>tease</u>, deride, insult, jeer, mock, provoke, ridicule, torment ♦ *noun* **2** <u>jeer</u>, derision, dig, gibe, insult, provocation, ridicule, sarcasm, teasing

taut *adjective* <u>tight</u>, flexed, rigid, strained, stressed, stretched, tense

tavern *noun* <u>inn</u>, alehouse (*archaic*), bar, hostelry, pub (*informal, chiefly Brit.*), public house

tawdry *adjective* <u>vulgar</u>, cheap, gaudy, gimcrack, naff (*Brit. slang*), tacky (*Informal*), tasteless, tatty, tinselly

tax *noun* **1** <u>charge</u>, duty, excise, levy, tariff, tithe, toll ♦ *verb* **2** <u>charge</u>, assess, rate **3** <u>strain</u>, burden, exhaust, load, stretch, test, try, weaken, weary

taxing *adjective* <u>demanding</u>, exacting, onerous, punishing, sapping, stressful, tiring, tough, trying

teach *verb* <u>instruct</u>, coach, drill, educate, enlighten, guide, inform, show, train, tutor

teacher *noun* <u>instructor</u>, coach, educator, guide, lecturer, master *or* mistress, mentor, schoolteacher, trainer, tutor

team *noun* **1** <u>group</u>, band, body, bunch, company, gang, line-up, set, side, squad ♦ *verb* **2** *often with* **up** <u>join</u>, band together, cooperate, couple, get together, link, unite, work together

teamwork *noun* <u>cooperation</u>, collaboration, coordination, esprit de corps, fellowship, harmony, unity

tear *verb* **1** <u>rip</u>, claw, lacerate, mangle, mutilate, pull apart, rend, rupture, scratch, shred, split **2** <u>rush</u>, bolt, charge, dash, fly, hurry, race, run, speed, sprint, zoom ♦ *noun* **3** <u>hole</u>, laceration, rent, rip, rupture, scratch, split

tearaway *noun* <u>hooligan</u>, delinquent, good-for-nothing, rowdy, ruffian

tearful *adjective* <u>weeping</u>, blubbering, crying, in tears, lachrymose, sobbing, weepy (*informal*), whimpering

tears *plural noun* **1** <u>crying</u>, blubbering, sobbing, wailing, weeping **2** **in tears** <u>crying</u>, blubbering, distressed, sobbing, weeping

tease *verb* <u>mock</u>, goad, lead on, provoke, pull someone's leg (*informal*), tantalize, taunt, torment

technical *adjective* <u>scientific</u>, hi-tech *or* high-tech, skilled, specialist, specialized, technological

technique *noun* **1** <u>method</u>, approach, manner, means, mode, procedure, style, system, way **2** <u>skill</u>, artistry, craft, craftsmanship, execution, performance, proficiency, touch

tedious *adjective* <u>boring</u>, drab, dreary, dull, humdrum, irksome, laborious, mind-numbing, monotonous, tiresome, wearisome

tedium *noun* <u>boredom</u>, drabness, dreariness, dullness, monotony, routine, sameness, tediousness

teeming[1] *adjective* <u>full</u>, abundant, alive, brimming, bristling, bursting, crawling, overflowing, swarming, thick

teeming[2] *adjective* <u>pouring</u>, bucketing down (*informal*), pelting

teenager *noun* <u>youth</u>, adolescent, boy, girl, juvenile, minor

teeter *verb* <u>wobble</u>, rock, seesaw, stagger, sway, totter, waver

teetotaller *noun* <u>abstainer</u>, nondrinker

telepathy *noun* <u>mind-reading</u>, sixth sense

telephone *noun* **1** <u>phone</u>, handset, line ♦ *verb* **2** <u>call</u>, dial, phone, ring (*chiefly Brit.*)

telescope *noun* **1** <u>glass</u>, spyglass ♦ *verb* **2** <u>shorten</u>, abbreviate, abridge, compress, condense, contract, shrink

television *noun* <u>TV</u>, small screen (*informal*), telly (*Brit. informal*), the box (*Brit. informal*), the tube (*slang*)

tell *verb* **1** <u>inform</u>, announce, communicate, disclose, divulge, express, make known, notify, proclaim, reveal, state **2** <u>instruct</u>,

bid, call upon, command, direct, order, require, summon **3** <u>describe</u>, chronicle, depict, narrate, portray, recount, relate, report **4** <u>distinguish</u>, differentiate, discern, discriminate, identify **5** <u>carry weight</u>, count, have *or* take effect, make its presence felt, register, take its toll, weigh

telling *adjective* <u>effective</u>, considerable, decisive, forceful, impressive, influential, marked, powerful, significant, striking

telling-off *noun* <u>reprimand</u>, criticism, dressing-down (*informal*), lecture, rebuke, reproach, reproof, scolding, talking-to, ticking-off (*informal*)

tell off *verb* <u>reprimand</u>, berate, censure, chide, haul over the coals (*informal*), lecture, read the riot act, rebuke, reproach, scold

temerity *noun* <u>boldness</u>, audacity, chutzpah (*U.S. & Canad. informal*), effrontery, front, impudence, nerve (*informal*), rashness, recklessness

temper *noun* **1** <u>rage</u>, bad mood, fury, passion, tantrum **2** <u>irritability</u>, hot-headedness, irascibility, passion, petulance, resentment, surliness **3** <u>self-control</u>, calmness, composure, cool (*slang*), equanimity **4** <u>frame of mind</u>, constitution, disposition, humour, mind, mood, nature, temperament ♦ *verb* **5** <u>moderate</u>, assuage, lessen, mitigate, mollify, restrain, soften, soothe, tone down **6** <u>strengthen</u>, anneal, harden, toughen

temperament *noun* **1** <u>nature</u>,

bent, character, constitution, disposition, humour, make-up, outlook, personality, temper **2** excitability, anger, hot-headedness, moodiness, petulance, volatility

temperamental adjective **1** moody, capricious, emotional, excitable, highly strung, hypersensitive, irritable, sensitive, touchy, volatile **2** unreliable, erratic, inconsistent, inconstant, unpredictable

temperance noun **1** moderation, continence, discretion, forbearance, restraint, self-control, self-discipline, self-restraint **2** teetotalism, abstemiousness, abstinence, sobriety

temperate adjective **1** mild, calm, cool, fair, gentle, moderate, pleasant **2** self-restrained, calm, composed, dispassionate, even-tempered, mild, moderate, reasonable, self-controlled, sensible

tempest noun gale, cyclone, hurricane, squall, storm, tornado, typhoon

tempestuous adjective **1** stormy, blustery, gusty, inclement, raging, squally, turbulent, windy **2** violent, boisterous, emotional, furious, heated, intense, passionate, stormy, turbulent, wild

temple noun shrine, church, sanctuary

temporarily adverb briefly, fleetingly, for the time being, momentarily, pro tem

temporary adjective

impermanent, brief, ephemeral, fleeting, interim, momentary, provisional, short-lived, transitory

tempt verb entice, allure, attract, coax, invite, lead on, lure, seduce, tantalize

temptation noun enticement, allurement, inducement, lure, pull, seduction, tantalization

tempting adjective enticing, alluring, appetizing, attractive, inviting, mouthwatering, seductive, tantalizing

tenable adjective sound, arguable, believable, defensible, justifiable, plausible, rational, reasonable, viable

tenacious adjective **1** firm, clinging, forceful, immovable, iron, strong, tight, unshakable **2** stubborn, adamant, determined, dogged, obdurate, obstinate, persistent, resolute, steadfast, unswerving, unyielding

tenacity noun perseverance, application, determination, doggedness, obduracy, persistence, resolve, steadfastness, stubbornness

tenancy noun lease, occupancy, possession, renting, residence

tenant noun leaseholder, inhabitant, lessee, occupant, occupier, renter, resident

tend[1] verb **1** be inclined, be apt, be liable, gravitate, have a tendency, incline, lean **2** go, aim, bear, head, lead, make for, point

tend[2] verb take care of, attend, cultivate, keep, look after, maintain, manage, nurture, watch over

tendency noun inclination, disposition, leaning, liability, proclivity, proneness, propensity, susceptibility

tender[1] adjective 1 gentle, affectionate, caring, compassionate, considerate, kind, loving, sympathetic, tenderhearted, warm-hearted 2 vulnerable, immature, impressionable, inexperienced, raw, sensitive, young, youthful 3 sensitive, bruised, inflamed, painful, raw, sore

tender[2] verb 1 offer, give, hand in, present, proffer, propose, put forward, submit, volunteer ♦ noun 2 offer, bid, estimate, proposal, submission 3 As in legal tender currency, money, payment

tenderness noun 1 gentleness, affection, care, compassion, consideration, kindness, love, sentimentality, sympathy, warmth 2 soreness, inflammation, pain, sensitivity

tense adjective 1 nervous, anxious, apprehensive, edgy, jumpy, keyed up, on edge, on tenterhooks, strained, uptight (informal) 2 stressful, exciting, nerve-racking, worrying 3 tight, rigid, strained, stretched, taut ♦ verb 4 tighten, brace, flex, strain, stretch

tension noun 1 suspense, anxiety, apprehension, hostility, nervousness, pressure, strain, stress, unease 2 tightness, pressure, rigidity, stiffness, stress, stretching, tautness

tentative adjective 1 experimental, conjectural, indefinite, provisional, speculative, unconfirmed, unsettled 2 hesitant, cautious, diffident, doubtful, faltering, timid, uncertain, undecided, unsure

tenuous adjective slight, doubtful, dubious, flimsy, insubstantial, nebulous, shaky, sketchy, weak

tepid adjective 1 lukewarm, warmish 2 half-hearted, apathetic, cool, indifferent, lukewarm, unenthusiastic

term noun 1 word, expression, name, phrase, title 2 period, duration, interval, season, span, spell, time, while ♦ verb 3 call, designate, dub, entitle, label, name, style

terminal adjective 1 deadly, fatal, incurable, killing, lethal, mortal 2 final, concluding, extreme, last, ultimate, utmost ♦ noun 3 terminus, depot, end of the line, station

terminate verb end, abort, cease, close, complete, conclude, discontinue, finish, stop

termination noun ending, abortion, cessation, completion, conclusion, discontinuation, end, finish

terminology noun language, jargon, nomenclature, phraseology, terms, vocabulary

terminus noun end of the line, depot, garage, last stop, station

terms plural noun 1 conditions, particulars, provisions, provisos, qualifications, specifications, stipulations 2 relationship, footing, relations, standing, status

terrain noun <u>ground</u>, country, going, land, landscape, topography

terrestrial adjective <u>earthly</u>, global, worldly

terrible adjective 1 <u>serious</u>, dangerous, desperate, extreme, severe 2 Informal <u>bad</u>, abysmal, awful, dire, dreadful, poor, rotten (informal) 3 <u>fearful</u>, dreadful, frightful, horrendous, horrible, horrifying, monstrous, shocking, terrifying

terribly adverb <u>extremely</u>, awfully (informal), decidedly, desperately, exceedingly, seriously, thoroughly, very

terrific adjective 1 <u>great</u>, enormous, fearful, gigantic, huge, intense, tremendous 2 Informal <u>excellent</u>, amazing, brilliant, fantastic (informal), magnificent, marvellous, outstanding, sensational (informal), stupendous, superb, wonderful

terrified adjective <u>frightened</u>, alarmed, appalled, horrified, horror-struck, panic-stricken, petrified, scared

terrify verb <u>frighten</u>, alarm, appal, horrify, make one's hair stand on end, scare, shock, terrorize

territory noun <u>district</u>, area, country, domain, land, patch, province, region, zone

terror noun 1 <u>fear</u>, alarm, anxiety, dread, fright, horror, panic, shock 2 <u>scourge</u>, bogeyman, bugbear, devil, fiend, monster

terrorize verb <u>oppress</u>, browbeat, bully, coerce, intimidate, menace, threaten

terse adjective 1 <u>concise</u>, brief, condensed, laconic, monosyllabic, pithy, short, succinct 2 <u>curt</u>, abrupt, brusque, short, snappy

test verb 1 <u>check</u>, analyse, assess, examine, experiment, investigate, put to the test, research, try out ♦ noun 2 <u>examination</u>, acid test, analysis, assessment, check, evaluation, investigation, research, trial

testament noun 1 <u>proof</u>, demonstration, evidence, testimony, tribute, witness 2 <u>will</u>, last wishes

testify verb <u>bear witness</u>, affirm, assert, attest, certify, corroborate, state, swear, vouch

testimonial noun <u>tribute</u>, commendation, endorsement, recommendation, reference

testimony noun 1 <u>evidence</u>, affidavit, deposition, statement, submission 2 <u>proof</u>, corroboration, demonstration, evidence, indication, manifestation, support, verification

testing adjective <u>difficult</u>, arduous, challenging, demanding, exacting, rigorous, searching, strenuous, taxing, tough

tether noun 1 <u>rope</u>, chain, fetter, halter, lead, leash 2 **at the end of one's tether** <u>exasperated</u>, at one's wits' end, exhausted ♦ verb 3 <u>tie</u>, bind, chain, fasten, fetter, secure

text noun 1 <u>contents</u>, body 2 <u>words</u>, wording

texture *noun* feel, consistency, grain, structure, surface, tissue

thank *verb* say thank you, show one's appreciation

thankful *adjective* grateful, appreciative, beholden, indebted, obliged, pleased, relieved

thankless *adjective* unrewarding, fruitless, unappreciated, unprofitable, unrequited

thanks *plural noun* 1 gratitude, acknowledgment, appreciation, credit, gratefulness, recognition 2 **thanks to** because of, as a result of, due to, owing to, through

thaw *verb* melt, defrost, dissolve, liquefy, soften, unfreeze, warm

theatrical *adjective* 1 dramatic, Thespian 2 exaggerated, affected, dramatic, histrionic, mannered, melodramatic, ostentatious, showy, stagy

theft *noun* stealing, embezzlement, fraud, larceny, pilfering, purloining, robbery, thieving

theme *noun* 1 subject, idea, keynote, subject matter, topic 2 motif, leitmotif

theological *adjective* religious, doctrinal, ecclesiastical

theoretical *adjective* abstract, academic, conjectural, hypothetical, notional, speculative

theorize *verb* speculate, conjecture, formulate, guess, hypothesize, project, propound, suppose

theory *noun* supposition, assumption, conjecture, hypothesis, presumption, speculation, surmise, thesis

therapeutic *adjective* beneficial, corrective, curative, good, healing, remedial, restorative, salutary

therapist *noun* healer, physician

therapy *noun* remedy, cure, healing, treatment

therefore *adverb* consequently, accordingly, as a result, ergo, hence, so, then, thence, thus

thesis *noun* 1 dissertation, essay, monograph, paper, treatise 2 proposition, contention, hypothesis, idea, opinion, proposal, theory, view

thick *adjective* 1 wide, broad, bulky, fat, solid, substantial 2 dense, close, compact, concentrated, condensed, heavy, impenetrable, opaque 3 *Informal* stupid, brainless, dense, dopey (*informal*), moronic, obtuse, slow, thickheaded 4 *Informal* friendly, close, devoted, familiar, inseparable, intimate, pally (*informal*) 5 full, brimming, bristling, bursting, covered, crawling, packed, swarming, teeming 6 **a bit thick** unfair, unjust, unreasonable

thicken *verb* set, clot, coagulate, condense, congeal, jell

thicket *noun* wood, brake, coppice, copse, covert, grove

thickset *adjective* well-built, bulky, burly, heavy, muscular, stocky, strong, sturdy

thief *noun* robber, burglar, embezzler, housebreaker, pickpocket, pilferer, plunderer, shoplifter, stealer

thieve *verb* steal, filch, nick

(*slang, chiefly Brit.*), pilfer, pinch (*informal*), purloin, rob, swipe (*slang*)

thin *adjective* **1** <u>narrow</u>, attenuated, fine **2** <u>slim</u>, bony, emaciated, lean, scrawny, skeletal, skinny, slender, slight, spare, spindly **3** <u>meagre</u>, deficient, scanty, scarce, scattered, skimpy, sparse, wispy **4** <u>delicate</u>, diaphanous, filmy, fine, flimsy, gossamer, sheer, unsubstantial **5** <u>unconvincing</u>, feeble, flimsy, inadequate, lame, poor, superficial, weak

thing *noun* **1** <u>object</u>, article, being, body, entity, something, substance **2** *Informal* <u>obsession</u>, bee in one's bonnet, fetish, fixation, hang-up (*informal*), mania, phobia, preoccupation **3 things** <u>possessions</u>, belongings, clobber (*Brit. slang*), effects, equipment, gear, luggage, stuff

think *verb* **1** <u>believe</u>, consider, deem, estimate, imagine, judge, reckon, regard, suppose **2** <u>ponder</u>, cerebrate, cogitate, contemplate, deliberate, meditate, muse, reason, reflect, ruminate

thinker *noun* <u>philosopher</u>, brain (*informal*), intellect (*informal*), mastermind, sage, theorist, wise man

thinking *noun* **1** <u>reasoning</u>, conjecture, idea, judgment, opinion, position, theory, view ♦ *adjective* **2** <u>thoughtful</u>, contemplative, intelligent, meditative, philosophical, rational, reasoning, reflective

think up *verb* <u>devise</u>, come up

with, concoct, contrive, create, dream up, invent, visualize

thirst *noun* **1** <u>thirstiness</u>, drought, dryness **2** <u>craving</u>, appetite, desire, hankering, keenness, longing, passion, yearning

thirsty *adjective* **1** <u>parched</u>, arid, dehydrated, dry **2** <u>eager</u>, avid, craving, desirous, greedy, hungry, itching, longing, yearning

thorn *noun* <u>prickle</u>, barb, spike, spine

thorny *adjective* <u>prickly</u>, barbed, bristly, pointed, sharp, spiky, spiny

thorough *adjective* **1** <u>careful</u>, assiduous, conscientious, efficient, exhaustive, full, in-depth, intensive, meticulous, painstaking, sweeping **2** <u>complete</u>, absolute, out-and-out, outright, perfect, total, unmitigated, unqualified, utter

thoroughbred *adjective* <u>purebred</u>, pedigree

thoroughfare *noun* <u>road</u>, avenue, highway, passage, passageway, street, way

thoroughly *adverb* **1** <u>carefully</u>, assiduously, conscientiously, efficiently, exhaustively, from top to bottom, fully, intensively, meticulously, painstakingly, scrupulously **2** <u>completely</u>, absolutely, downright, perfectly, quite, totally, to the hilt, utterly

though *conjunction* **1** <u>although</u>, even if, even though, notwithstanding, while ♦ *adverb* **2** <u>nevertheless</u>, for all that, however, nonetheless, notwithstanding, still, yet

thought noun 1 <u>thinking</u>, brainwork, cogitation, consideration, deliberation, meditation, musing, reflection, rumination 2 <u>idea</u>, concept, judgment, notion, opinion, view 3 <u>consideration</u>, attention, heed, regard, scrutiny, study 4 <u>intention</u>, aim, design, idea, notion, object, plan, purpose 5 <u>expectation</u>, anticipation, aspiration, hope, prospect

thoughtful adjective 1 <u>considerate</u>, attentive, caring, helpful, kind, kindly, solicitous, unselfish 2 <u>well-thought-out</u>, astute, canny, prudent 3 <u>reflective</u>, contemplative, deliberative, meditative, pensive, ruminative, serious, studious

thoughtless adjective <u>inconsiderate</u>, impolite, insensitive, rude, selfish, tactless, uncaring, undiplomatic, unkind

thrash verb 1 <u>beat</u>, belt (informal), cane, flog, give (someone) a (good) hiding (informal), scourge, spank, whip 2 <u>defeat</u>, beat, crush, drub, rout, run rings around (informal), slaughter (informal), trounce, wipe the floor with (informal) 3 <u>thresh</u>, flail, jerk, toss and turn, writhe

thrashing noun 1 <u>beating</u>, belting (informal), flogging, hiding (informal), punishment, whipping 2 <u>defeat</u>, beating, drubbing, hammering (informal), hiding (informal), rout, trouncing

thrash out verb <u>settle</u>, argue out, debate, discuss, have out, resolve, solve, talk over

thread noun 1 <u>strand</u>, fibre, filament, line, string, yarn 2 <u>theme</u>, direction, drift, plot, story line, train of thought ♦ verb 3 <u>pass</u>, ease, pick (one's way), squeeze through

threadbare adjective 1 <u>shabby</u>, down at heel, frayed, old, ragged, scruffy, tattered, tatty, worn 2 <u>hackneyed</u>, commonplace, conventional, familiar, overused, stale, stereotyped, tired, trite, well-worn

threat noun 1 <u>warning</u>, foreboding, foreshadowing, omen, portent, presage, writing on the wall 2 <u>danger</u>, hazard, menace, peril, risk

threaten verb 1 <u>intimidate</u>, browbeat, bully, lean on (slang), menace, pressurize, terrorize 2 <u>endanger</u>, imperil, jeopardize, put at risk, put in jeopardy, put on the line 3 <u>foreshadow</u>, forebode, impend, portend, presage

threatening adjective 1 <u>menacing</u>, bullying, intimidatory 2 <u>ominous</u>, forbidding, grim, inauspicious, sinister

threshold noun 1 <u>entrance</u>, door, doorstep, doorway 2 <u>start</u>, beginning, brink, dawn, inception, opening, outset, verge 3 <u>minimum</u>, lower limit

thrift noun <u>frugality</u>, carefulness, economy, parsimony, prudence, saving, thriftiness

thrifty adjective <u>economical</u>, careful, frugal, parsimonious, provident, prudent, saving, sparing

thrill noun 1 <u>pleasure</u>, buzz

(*slang*), kick (*informal*),
stimulation, tingle, titillation
♦ *verb* 2 excite, arouse, electrify,
move, stimulate, stir, titillate

thrilling *adjective* exciting,
electrifying, gripping, riveting,
rousing, sensational, stimulating,
stirring

thrive *verb* prosper, boom,
develop, do well, flourish, get
on, grow, increase, succeed

thriving *adjective* prosperous,
blooming, booming,
burgeoning, flourishing, healthy,
successful, well

throb *verb* 1 pulsate, beat,
palpitate, pound, pulse, thump,
vibrate ♦ *noun* 2 pulse, beat,
palpitation, pounding, pulsating,
thump, thumping, vibration

throng *noun* 1 crowd, crush,
horde, host, mass, mob,
multitude, pack, swarm ♦ *verb*
2 crowd, congregate, converge,
flock, mill around, pack, swarm
around

throttle *verb* strangle, choke,
garrotte, strangulate

through *preposition* 1 between,
by, past 2 because of, by means
of, by way of, using, via
3 during, in, throughout
♦ *adjective* 4 finished, completed,
done, ended ♦ *adverb* 5 **through
and through** completely,
altogether, entirely, fully,
thoroughly, totally, utterly,
wholly

throughout *adverb* everywhere,
all over, from start to finish,
right through

throw *verb* 1 hurl, cast, chuck
(*informal*), fling, launch, lob
(*informal*), pitch, send, sling, toss

2 *Informal* confuse, astonish,
baffle, confound, disconcert,
dumbfound, faze ♦ *noun* 3 toss,
fling, heave, lob (*informal*), pitch,
sling

throwaway *adjective* casual,
careless, offhand, passing,
understated

throw away *verb* discard,
dispense with, dispose of, ditch
(*slang*), dump (*informal*), get rid
of, jettison, reject, scrap, throw
out

thrust *verb* 1 push, drive, force,
jam, plunge, propel, ram, shove
♦ *noun* 2 push, drive, lunge,
poke, prod, shove, stab
3 momentum, impetus

thud *noun, verb* thump, clunk,
crash, knock, smack

thug *noun* ruffian, bruiser
(*informal*), bully boy, gangster,
heavy (*slang*), hooligan, tough

thump *noun* 1 crash, bang,
clunk, thud, thwack 2 blow,
clout (*informal*), knock, punch,
rap, smack, wallop (*informal*),
whack ♦ *verb* 3 strike, beat,
clobber (*slang*), clout (*informal*),
hit, knock, pound, punch,
smack, wallop (*informal*), whack

thunder *noun* 1 rumble, boom,
crash, explosion ♦ *verb* 2 rumble,
boom, crash, peal, resound,
reverberate, roar 3 shout, bark,
bellow, roar, yell

thunderous *adjective* loud,
booming, deafening,
ear-splitting, noisy, resounding,
roaring, tumultuous

thunderstruck *adjective* amazed,
astonished, astounded,
dumbfounded, flabbergasted
(*informal*), open-mouthed,

shocked, staggered, stunned, taken aback

thus adverb **1** therefore, accordingly, consequently, ergo, for this reason, hence, on that account, so, then **2** in this way, as follows, like this, so

thwart verb frustrate, foil, hinder, obstruct, outwit, prevent, snooker, stymie

tick¹ noun **1** mark, dash, stroke **2** tapping, clicking, ticktock **3** Brit. informal moment, flash, instant, minute, second, split second, trice, twinkling ◆ verb **4** mark, check off, indicate **5** tap, click, ticktock

tick² noun credit, account, the slate (Brit. informal)

ticket noun **1** voucher, card, certificate, coupon, pass, slip, token **2** label, card, docket, marker, slip, sticker, tab, tag

tide noun **1** current, ebb, flow, stream, tideway, undertow **2** tendency, direction, drift, movement, trend

tidy adjective **1** neat, clean, methodical, orderly, shipshape, spruce, well-kept, well-ordered **2** Informal considerable, ample, generous, goodly, handsome, healthy, large, sizable or sizeable, substantial ◆ verb **3** neaten, clean, groom, order, spruce up, straighten

tie verb **1** fasten, attach, bind, connect, join, knot, link, secure, tether **2** restrict, bind, confine, hamper, hinder, limit, restrain **3** draw, equal, match ◆ noun **4** bond, affiliation, allegiance, commitment, connection, liaison, relationship **5** fastening, bond, cord, fetter, knot, ligature, link **6** draw, dead heat, deadlock, stalemate

tier noun row, bank, layer, level, line, rank, storey, stratum

tight adjective **1** stretched, close, constricted, cramped, narrow, rigid, snug, taut **2** Informal miserly, grasping, mean, niggardly, parsimonious, stingy, tightfisted **3** close, even, evenly-balanced, well-matched **4** Informal drunk, inebriated, intoxicated, paralytic (informal), plastered (slang), tipsy, under the influence (informal)

tighten verb squeeze, close, constrict, narrow

till¹ verb cultivate, dig, plough, work

till² noun cash register, cash box

tilt verb **1** slant, heel, incline, lean, list, slope, tip ◆ noun **2** slope, angle, inclination, incline, list, pitch, slant **3** Medieval history joust, combat, duel, fight, lists, tournament **4** (at) full tilt full speed, for dear life, headlong

timber noun wood, beams, boards, logs, planks, trees

timbre noun tone, colour, resonance, ring

time noun **1** period, duration, interval, season, space, span, spell, stretch, term **2** occasion, instance, juncture, point, stage **3** Music tempo, beat, measure, rhythm ◆ verb **4** schedule, set

timeless adjective eternal, ageless, changeless, enduring, everlasting, immortal, lasting, permanent

timely *adjective* <u>opportune</u>, appropriate, convenient, judicious, propitious, seasonable, suitable, well-timed

timetable *noun* <u>schedule</u>, agenda, calendar, curriculum, diary, list, programme

timid *adjective* <u>fearful</u>, apprehensive, bashful, coy, diffident, faint-hearted, shrinking, shy, timorous

timorous *adjective* <u>timid</u>, apprehensive, bashful, coy, diffident, faint-hearted, fearful, shrinking, shy

tinge *noun* 1 <u>tint</u>, colour, shade 2 <u>bit</u>, dash, drop, smattering, sprinkling, suggestion, touch, trace ♦ *verb* 3 <u>tint</u>, colour, imbue, suffuse

tingle *verb* 1 <u>prickle</u>, have goose pimples, itch, sting, tickle ♦ *noun* 2 <u>quiver</u>, goose pimples, itch, pins and needles (*informal*), prickling, shiver, thrill

tinker *verb* <u>meddle</u>, dabble, fiddle (*informal*), mess about, play, potter

tint *noun* 1 <u>shade</u>, colour, hue, tone 2 <u>dye</u>, rinse, tincture, tinge, wash ♦ *verb* 3 <u>dye</u>, colour

tiny *adjective* <u>small</u>, diminutive, infinitesimal, little, microscopic, miniature, minute, negligible, petite, slight

tip¹ *noun* 1 <u>end</u>, extremity, head, peak, pinnacle, point, summit, top ♦ *verb* 2 <u>cap</u>, crown, finish, surmount, top

tip² *noun* 1 <u>gratuity</u>, gift 2 <u>hint</u>, clue, pointer, suggestion, warning ♦ *verb* 3 <u>reward</u>, remunerate 4 <u>advise</u>, caution,

forewarn, suggest, warn

tip³ *verb* 1 <u>tilt</u>, incline, lean, list, slant 2 <u>dump</u>, empty, pour out, unload ♦ *noun* 3 <u>dump</u>, refuse heap, rubbish heap

tipple *verb* 1 <u>drink</u>, imbibe, indulge (*informal*), quaff, swig, tope ♦ *noun* 2 <u>alcohol</u>, booze (*informal*), drink, liquor

tirade *noun* <u>outburst</u>, diatribe, fulmination, harangue, invective, lecture

tire *verb* 1 <u>fatigue</u>, drain, exhaust, wear out, weary 2 <u>bore</u>, exasperate, irk, irritate, weary

tired *adjective* 1 <u>exhausted</u>, drained, drowsy, fatigued, flagging, jaded, sleepy, weary, worn out 2 <u>bored</u>, fed up, sick, weary 3 <u>hackneyed</u>, clichéd, corny (*slang*), old, outworn, stale, threadbare, trite, well-worn

tireless *adjective* <u>energetic</u>, indefatigable, industrious, resolute, unflagging, untiring, vigorous

tiresome *adjective* <u>boring</u>, dull, irksome, irritating, tedious, trying, vexatious, wearing, wearisome

tiring *adjective* <u>exhausting</u>, arduous, demanding, exacting, laborious, strenuous, tough, wearing

titbit *noun* <u>delicacy</u>, dainty, morsel, snack, treat

titillate *verb* <u>excite</u>, arouse, interest, stimulate, tantalize, tease, thrill

titillating *adjective* <u>exciting</u>, arousing, interesting, lurid, provocative, stimulating, suggestive, teasing

title noun 1 <u>name</u>, designation, handle (*slang*), moniker or monicker (*slang*), term 2 <u>championship</u>, crown 3 <u>ownership</u>, claim, entitlement, prerogative, privilege, right

titter verb <u>laugh</u>, chortle (*informal*), chuckle, giggle, snigger

toady noun 1 <u>sycophant</u>, bootlicker (*informal*), crawler (*slang*), creep (*slang*), flatterer, flunkey, hanger-on, lackey, minion, yes man ◆ verb 2 <u>flatter</u>, crawl, creep, cringe, fawn on, grovel, kowtow to, pander to, suck up to (*informal*)

toast[1] verb <u>warm</u>, brown, grill, heat, roast

toast[2] noun 1 <u>tribute</u>, compliment, health, pledge, salutation, salute 2 <u>favourite</u>, darling, hero or heroine ◆ verb 3 <u>drink to</u>, drink (to) the health of, salute

together adverb 1 <u>collectively</u>, as one, hand in glove, in concert, in unison, jointly, mutually, shoulder to shoulder, side by side 2 <u>at the same time</u>, at one fell swoop, concurrently, contemporaneously, simultaneously ◆ adjective 3 *Informal* <u>well-organized</u>, composed, well-adjusted, well-balanced

toil noun 1 <u>hard work</u>, application, drudgery, effort, elbow grease (*informal*), exertion, graft (*informal*), slog, sweat ◆ verb 2 <u>work</u>, drudge, graft (*informal*), labour, slave, slog, strive, struggle, sweat (*informal*), work one's fingers to the bone

toilet noun <u>lavatory</u>, bathroom, convenience, gents (*Brit. informal*), ladies' room, latrine, loo (*Brit. informal*), privy, urinal, water closet, W.C.

token noun 1 <u>symbol</u>, badge, expression, indication, mark, note, representation, sign ◆ adjective 2 <u>nominal</u>, hollow, minimal, perfunctory, superficial, symbolic

tolerable adjective 1 <u>bearable</u>, acceptable, allowable, endurable, sufferable, supportable 2 <u>fair</u>, acceptable, adequate, all right, average, O.K. or okay (*informal*), passable

tolerance noun 1 <u>broad-mindedness</u>, forbearance, indulgence, open-mindedness, permissiveness 2 <u>endurance</u>, fortitude, hardiness, resilience, resistance, stamina, staying power, toughness

tolerant adjective <u>broad-minded</u>, catholic, forbearing, liberal, long-suffering, open-minded, understanding, unprejudiced

tolerate verb <u>allow</u>, accept, brook, condone, endure, permit, put up with (*informal*), stand, stomach, take

toleration noun <u>acceptance</u>, allowance, endurance, indulgence, permissiveness, sanction

toll[1] verb 1 <u>ring</u>, chime, clang, knell, peal, sound, strike ◆ noun 2 <u>ringing</u>, chime, clang, knell, peal

toll[2] noun 1 <u>charge</u>, duty, fee, levy, payment, tariff, tax 2 <u>damage</u>, cost, loss, penalty

tomb noun <u>grave</u>, catacomb, crypt, mausoleum, sarcophagus, sepulchre, vault

tombstone noun <u>gravestone</u>, headstone, marker, memorial, monument

tomfoolery noun <u>foolishness</u>, buffoonery, clowning, fooling around (informal), horseplay, shenanigans (informal), silliness, skylarking (informal), stupidity

tone noun 1 <u>pitch</u>, inflection, intonation, modulation, timbre 2 <u>character</u>, air, attitude, feel, manner, mood, spirit, style, temper 3 <u>colour</u>, hue, shade, tinge, tint ♦ verb 4 <u>harmonize</u>, blend, go well with, match, suit

tone down verb <u>moderate</u>, play down, reduce, restrain, soften, subdue, temper

tongue noun <u>language</u>, dialect, parlance, speech

tonic noun <u>stimulant</u>, boost, fillip, pick-me-up (informal), restorative, shot in the arm (informal)

too adverb 1 <u>also</u>, as well, besides, further, in addition, likewise, moreover, to boot 2 <u>excessively</u>, extremely, immoderately, inordinately, overly, unduly, unreasonably, very

tool noun 1 <u>implement</u>, appliance, contraption, contrivance, device, gadget, instrument, machine, utensil 2 <u>puppet</u>, cat's-paw, creature, flunkey, hireling, lackey, minion, pawn, stooge (slang)

top noun 1 <u>peak</u>, apex, crest, crown, culmination, head, height, pinnacle, summit, zenith 2 <u>first place</u>, head, lead 3 <u>lid</u>, cap, cover, stopper ♦ adjective 4 <u>leading</u>, best, chief, elite, finest, first, foremost, head, highest, pre-eminent, principal, uppermost ♦ verb 5 <u>cover</u>, cap, crown, finish, garnish 6 <u>lead</u>, be first, head 7 <u>surpass</u>, beat, better, eclipse, exceed, excel, outstrip, transcend

topic noun <u>subject</u>, issue, matter, point, question, subject matter, theme

topical adjective <u>current</u>, contemporary, newsworthy, popular, up-to-date, up-to-the-minute

topmost adjective <u>highest</u>, dominant, foremost, leading, paramount, principal, supreme, top, uppermost

topple verb 1 <u>fall over</u>, collapse, fall, keel over, overbalance, overturn, totter, tumble 2 <u>overthrow</u>, bring down, bring low, oust, overturn, unseat

topsy-turvy adjective <u>confused</u>, chaotic, disorderly, disorganized, inside-out, jumbled, messy, mixed-up, upside-down

torment verb 1 <u>torture</u>, crucify, distress, rack 2 <u>tease</u>, annoy, bother, harass, hassle (informal), irritate, nag, pester, vex ♦ noun 3 <u>suffering</u>, agony, anguish, distress, hell, misery, pain, torture

torn adjective 1 <u>cut</u>, lacerated, ragged, rent, ripped, slit, split 2 <u>undecided</u>, in two minds (informal), irresolute, uncertain, unsure, vacillating, wavering

tornado noun <u>whirlwind</u>, cyclone, gale, hurricane, squall, storm, tempest, typhoon

torpor noun <u>inactivity</u>, apathy, drowsiness, indolence, laziness, lethargy, listlessness, sloth, sluggishness

torrent noun <u>stream</u>, cascade, deluge, downpour, flood, flow, rush, spate, tide

torrid adjective 1 <u>arid</u>, dried, parched, scorched 2 <u>passionate</u>, ardent, fervent, intense, steamy (*informal*)

tortuous adjective 1 <u>winding</u>, circuitous, convoluted, indirect, mazy, meandering, serpentine, sinuous, twisting, twisty 2 <u>complicated</u>, ambiguous, convoluted, devious, indirect, involved, roundabout, tricky

torture verb 1 <u>torment</u>, afflict, crucify, distress, persecute, put on the rack, rack ♦ noun 2 <u>agony</u>, anguish, distress, pain, persecution, suffering, torment

toss verb 1 <u>throw</u>, cast, fling, flip, hurl, launch, lob (*informal*), pitch, sling 2 <u>thrash</u>, rock, roll, shake, wriggle, writhe ♦ noun 3 <u>throw</u>, lob (*informal*), pitch

tot¹ noun 1 <u>infant</u>, baby, child, mite, toddler 2 <u>measure</u>, dram, finger, nip, shot (*informal*), slug, snifter (*informal*)

tot² verb <u>add up</u>, calculate, count up, reckon, tally, total

total noun 1 <u>whole</u>, aggregate, entirety, full amount, sum, totality ♦ adjective 2 <u>complete</u>, absolute, comprehensive, entire, full, gross, thoroughgoing, undivided, utter, whole ♦ verb 3 <u>amount to</u>, come to, mount up to, reach 4 <u>add up</u>, reckon, tot up

totalitarian adjective <u>dictatorial</u>, authoritarian, despotic, oppressive, tyrannous, undemocratic

totality noun <u>whole</u>, aggregate, entirety, sum, total

totally adverb <u>completely</u>, absolutely, comprehensively, entirely, fully, one hundred per cent, thoroughly, utterly, wholly

totter verb <u>stagger</u>, falter, lurch, reel, stumble, sway

touch verb 1 <u>handle</u>, brush, caress, contact, feel, finger, fondle, stroke, tap 2 <u>meet</u>, abut, adjoin, be in contact, border, contact, graze, impinge upon 3 <u>affect</u>, disturb, impress, influence, inspire, move, stir 4 <u>eat</u>, consume, drink, partake of 5 <u>match</u>, compare with, equal, hold a candle to (*informal*), parallel, rival 6 **touch on** <u>refer to</u>, allude to, bring in, cover, deal with, mention, speak of ♦ noun 7 <u>feeling</u>, handling, physical contact 8 <u>tap</u>, brush, contact, pat, stroke 9 <u>bit</u>, dash, drop, jot, small amount, smattering, *soupçon*, spot, trace 10 <u>style</u>, manner, method, technique, trademark, way

touch and go adjective <u>risky</u>, close, critical, near, nerve-racking, precarious

touching adjective <u>moving</u>, affecting, emotive, pathetic, pitiable, poignant, sad, stirring

touchstone noun <u>standard</u>, criterion, gauge, measure, norm, par, yardstick

touchy adjective <u>oversensitive</u>, irascible, irritable, querulous, quick-tempered, testy, tetchy, thin-skinned

tough *adjective* 1 <u>resilient</u>, durable, hard, inflexible, leathery, resistant, rugged, solid, strong, sturdy 2 <u>strong</u>, hardy, seasoned, stout, strapping, sturdy, vigorous 3 <u>rough</u>, hard-bitten, pugnacious, ruthless, violent 4 <u>strict</u>, hard, merciless, resolute, severe, stern, unbending 5 <u>difficult</u>, arduous, exacting, hard, laborious, strenuous, troublesome, uphill 6 *Informal* <u>unlucky</u>, lamentable, regrettable, unfortunate ♦ *noun* 7 <u>ruffian</u>, bruiser (*informal*), bully, hooligan, roughneck (*slang*), thug

tour *noun* 1 <u>journey</u>, excursion, expedition, jaunt, outing, trip ♦ *verb* 2 <u>visit</u>, explore, go round, journey, sightsee, travel through

tourist *noun* <u>traveller</u>, excursionist, globetrotter, holiday-maker, sightseer, tripper, voyager

tournament *noun* <u>competition</u>, contest, event, meeting, series

tow *verb* <u>drag</u>, draw, haul, lug, pull, tug

towards *preposition* 1 <u>in the direction of</u>, en route for, for, on the way to, to 2 <u>regarding</u>, about, concerning, for, with regard to, with respect to

tower *noun* <u>column</u>, belfry, obelisk, pillar, skyscraper, steeple, turret

towering *adjective* <u>high</u>, colossal, elevated, imposing, impressive, lofty, magnificent, soaring, tall

toxic *adjective* <u>poisonous</u>, deadly, harmful, lethal, noxious, pernicious, pestilential, septic

toy *noun* 1 <u>plaything</u>, doll, game

♦ *verb* 2 <u>play</u>, amuse oneself, dally, fiddle (*informal*), fool (about *or* around), trifle

trace *verb* 1 <u>find</u>, detect, discover, ferret out, hunt down, track, unearth 2 <u>copy</u>, draw, outline, sketch ♦ *noun* 3 <u>track</u>, footmark, footprint, footstep, path, spoor, trail 4 <u>bit</u>, drop, hint, shadow, suggestion, suspicion, tinge, touch, whiff 5 <u>indication</u>, evidence, mark, record, remnant, sign, survival, vestige

track *noun* 1 <u>path</u>, course, line, orbit, pathway, road, trajectory, way 2 <u>trail</u>, footmark, footprint, footstep, mark, path, spoor, trace, wake 3 <u>line</u>, permanent way, rails ♦ *verb* 4 <u>follow</u>, chase, hunt down, pursue, shadow, stalk, tail (*informal*), trace, trail

track down *verb* <u>find</u>, dig up, discover, hunt down, run to earth *or* ground, sniff out, trace, unearth

tract[1] *noun* <u>area</u>, district, expanse, extent, plot, region, stretch, territory

tract[2] *noun* <u>treatise</u>, booklet, dissertation, essay, homily, monograph, pamphlet

tractable *adjective* <u>manageable</u>, amenable, biddable, compliant, docile, obedient, submissive, tame, willing, yielding

traction *noun* <u>grip</u>, friction, pull, purchase, resistance

trade *noun* 1 <u>commerce</u>, barter, business, dealing, exchange, traffic, transactions, truck 2 <u>job</u>, business, craft, employment, line of work, métier, occupation, profession ♦ *verb* 3 <u>deal</u>, bargain, do business, have dealings, peddle, traffic, transact, truck 4 <u>exchange</u>, barter, swap, switch

trader noun <u>dealer</u>, merchant, purveyor, seller, supplier

tradesman noun 1 <u>craftsman</u>, artisan, journeyman, workman 2 <u>shopkeeper</u>, dealer, merchant, purveyor, retailer, seller, supplier, vendor

tradition noun <u>custom</u>, convention, folklore, habit, institution, lore, ritual

traditional adjective <u>customary</u>, accustomed, conventional, established, old, time-honoured, usual

traffic noun 1 <u>transport</u>, freight, transportation, vehicles 2 <u>trade</u>, business, commerce, dealings, exchange, peddling, truck ♦ verb 3 <u>trade</u>, bargain, deal, do business, exchange, have dealings, peddle

tragedy noun <u>disaster</u>, adversity, calamity, catastrophe, misfortune

tragic adjective <u>disastrous</u>, appalling, calamitous, catastrophic, deadly, dire, dreadful, miserable, pathetic, sad, unfortunate

trail noun 1 <u>path</u>, footpath, road, route, track, way 2 <u>tracks</u>, footprints, marks, path, scent, spoor, trace, wake ♦ verb 3 <u>drag</u>, dangle, draw, haul, pull, tow 4 <u>lag</u>, dawdle, follow, hang back, linger, loiter, straggle, traipse (informal) 5 <u>follow</u>, chase, hunt, pursue, shadow, stalk, tail (informal), trace, track

train verb 1 <u>instruct</u>, coach, drill, educate, guide, prepare, school, teach, tutor 2 <u>exercise</u>, prepare,

work out 3 <u>aim</u>, direct, focus, level, point ♦ noun 4 <u>sequence</u>, chain, progression, series, set, string, succession

trainer noun <u>coach</u>, handler

training noun 1 <u>instruction</u>, coaching, discipline, education, grounding, schooling, teaching, tuition 2 <u>exercise</u>, practice, preparation, working out

traipse verb <u>trudge</u>, drag oneself, footslog, slouch, trail, tramp

trait noun <u>characteristic</u>, attribute, feature, idiosyncrasy, mannerism, peculiarity, quality, quirk

traitor noun <u>betrayer</u>, apostate, back-stabber, defector, deserter, Judas, quisling, rebel, renegade, turncoat

trajectory noun <u>path</u>, course, flight path, line, route, track

tramp verb 1 <u>hike</u>, footslog, march, ramble, roam, rove, slog, trek, walk 2 <u>trudge</u>, plod, stump, toil, traipse (informal) ♦ noun 3 <u>vagrant</u>, derelict, down-and-out, drifter 4 <u>hike</u>, march, ramble, slog, trek 5 <u>tread</u>, footfall, footstep, stamp

trample verb <u>crush</u>, flatten, run over, squash, stamp, tread, walk over

trance noun <u>daze</u>, abstraction, dream, rapture, reverie, stupor, unconsciousness

tranquil adjective <u>calm</u>, peaceful, placid, quiet, restful, sedate, serene, still, undisturbed

tranquillity noun <u>calm</u>, hush, peace, placidity, quiet, repose, rest, serenity, stillness

tranquillize verb <u>calm</u>, lull, pacify, quell, quiet, relax, sedate, settle one's nerves, soothe

tranquillizer noun <u>sedative</u>, barbiturate, bromide, downer (*slang*), opiate

transaction noun <u>deal</u>, bargain, business, enterprise, negotiation, undertaking

transcend verb <u>surpass</u>, eclipse, exceed, excel, go beyond, outdo, outstrip, rise above

transcendent adjective <u>unparalleled</u>, consummate, incomparable, matchless, pre-eminent, sublime, unequalled, unrivalled

transcribe verb <u>write out</u>, copy out, reproduce, take down, transfer

transcript noun <u>copy</u>, duplicate, manuscript, record, reproduction, transcription

transfer verb 1 <u>move</u>, change, convey, hand over, pass on, relocate, shift, transplant, transport, transpose ♦ noun 2 <u>move</u>, change, handover, relocation, shift, transference, translation, transmission, transposition

transfix verb 1 <u>stun</u>, engross, fascinate, hold, hypnotize, mesmerize, paralyse 2 <u>pierce</u>, impale, puncture, run through, skewer, spear

transform verb <u>change</u>, alter, convert, remodel, revolutionize, transmute

transformation noun <u>change</u>, alteration, conversion, metamorphosis, revolution, sea change, transmutation

transgress verb <u>offend</u>, break the law, contravene, disobey, encroach, infringe, sin, trespass, violate

transgression noun <u>offence</u>, contravention, crime, encroachment, infraction, infringement, misdeed, misdemeanour, sin, trespass, violation

transgressor noun <u>offender</u>, criminal, culprit, lawbreaker, miscreant, sinner, trespasser, villain, wrongdoer

transient adjective <u>temporary</u>, brief, ephemeral, fleeting, impermanent, momentary, passing, short-lived, transitory

transit noun <u>movement</u>, carriage, conveyance, crossing, passage, transfer, transport, transportation

transition noun <u>change</u>, alteration, conversion, development, metamorphosis, passing, progression, shift, transmutation

transitional adjective <u>changing</u>, developmental, fluid, intermediate, passing, provisional, temporary, unsettled

transitory adjective <u>short-lived</u>, brief, ephemeral, fleeting, impermanent, momentary, passing, short, temporary, transient

translate verb <u>interpret</u>, construe, convert, decipher, decode, paraphrase, render

translation noun <u>interpretation</u>, decoding, paraphrase, rendering, rendition, version

transmission noun 1 <u>transfer</u>, conveyance, dissemination, sending, shipment, spread, transference 2 <u>broadcasting</u>, dissemination, putting out, relaying, sending, showing **3** programme, broadcast, show

transmit verb **1** pass on, bear, carry, convey, disseminate, hand on, impart, send, spread, transfer **2** broadcast, disseminate, radio, relay, send out

transparency noun **1** clarity, clearness, limpidity, pellucidness, translucence **2** photograph, slide

transparent adjective **1** clear, crystalline, diaphanous, limpid, lucid, see-through, sheer, translucent **2** plain, evident, explicit, manifest, obvious, patent, recognizable, unambiguous, undisguised

transpire verb **1** emerge, become known, come out, come to light **2** Informal happen, arise, befall, chance, come about, occur, take place

transplant verb transfer, displace, relocate, remove, resettle, shift, uproot

transport verb **1** convey, bear, bring, carry, haul, move, take, transfer **2** exile, banish, deport **3** enrapture, captivate, delight, enchant, entrance, move, ravish ♦ noun **4** vehicle, conveyance, transportation **5** transference, conveyance, shipment, transportation **6** ecstasy, bliss, delight, enchantment, euphoria, heaven, rapture, ravishment

transpose verb interchange, alter, change, exchange, move, reorder, shift, substitute, swap, switch, transfer

trap noun **1** snare, ambush, gin, net, noose, pitfall **2** trick,

ambush, deception, ruse, stratagem, subterfuge, wile ♦ verb **3** catch, corner, enmesh, ensnare, entrap, snare, take **4** trick, ambush, beguile, deceive, dupe, ensnare, inveigle

trappings plural noun accessories, accoutrements, equipment, finery, furnishings, gear, panoply, paraphernalia, things, trimmings

trash noun **1** nonsense, drivel, hogwash, moonshine, poppycock (informal), rot, rubbish, tripe (informal), twaddle **2** litter, dross, garbage, junk (informal), refuse, rubbish, waste

trashy adjective worthless, cheap, inferior, rubbishy, shabby, shoddy, tawdry

trauma noun suffering, agony, anguish, hurt, ordeal, pain, shock, torture

traumatic adjective shocking, agonizing, damaging, disturbing, hurtful, injurious, painful, scarring, upsetting, wounding

travel verb **1** go, journey, move, progress, roam, tour, trek, voyage, wander ♦ noun **2** usually plural wandering, excursion, expedition, globetrotting, journey, tour, trip, voyage

traveller noun wanderer, explorer, globetrotter, gypsy, holiday-maker, tourist, voyager, wayfarer

travelling adjective mobile, itinerant, migrant, nomadic, peripatetic, roaming, roving, touring, wandering, wayfaring

traverse verb cross, go over, span, travel over

travesty noun 1 <u>mockery</u>, burlesque, caricature, distortion, lampoon, parody, perversion ♦ verb 2 <u>mock</u>, burlesque, caricature, distort, lampoon, make a mockery of, parody, ridicule

treacherous adjective 1 <u>disloyal</u>, deceitful, double-dealing, duplicitous, faithless, false, perfidious, traitorous, unfaithful, untrustworthy 2 <u>dangerous</u>, deceptive, hazardous, icy, perilous, precarious, risky, slippery, unreliable, unsafe, unstable

treachery noun <u>betrayal</u>, disloyalty, double-dealing, duplicity, faithlessness, infidelity, perfidy, treason

tread verb 1 <u>step</u>, hike, march, pace, stamp, stride, walk 2 <u>trample</u>, crush underfoot, squash ♦ noun 3 <u>step</u>, footfall, footstep, gait, pace, stride, walk

treason noun <u>disloyalty</u>, duplicity, lese-majesty, mutiny, perfidy, sedition, traitorousness, treachery

treasonable adjective <u>disloyal</u>, mutinous, perfidious, seditious, subversive, traitorous, treacherous

treasure noun 1 <u>riches</u>, cash, fortune, gold, jewels, money, valuables, wealth 2 <u>darling</u>, apple of one's eye, gem, jewel, nonpareil, paragon, pride and joy ♦ verb 3 <u>prize</u>, adore, cherish, esteem, hold dear, idolize, love, revere, value

treasury noun <u>storehouse</u>, bank, cache, hoard, repository, store, vault

treat verb 1 <u>handle</u>, act towards, behave towards, consider, deal with, look upon, manage, regard, use 2 <u>attend to</u>, care for, nurse 3 <u>entertain</u>, lay on, provide, regale, stand (informal) ♦ noun 4 <u>entertainment</u>, banquet, celebration, feast, gift, party, refreshment 5 <u>pleasure</u>, delight, enjoyment, fun, joy, satisfaction, surprise, thrill

treatise noun <u>essay</u>, dissertation, monograph, pamphlet, paper, study, thesis, tract, work

treatment noun 1 <u>care</u>, cure, healing, medication, medicine, remedy, surgery, therapy 2 <u>handling</u>, action, behaviour, conduct, dealing, management, manipulation

treaty noun <u>pact</u>, agreement, alliance, compact, concordat, contract, convention, covenant, entente

trek noun 1 <u>journey</u>, expedition, hike, march, odyssey, safari, slog, tramp ♦ verb 2 <u>journey</u>, footslog, hike, march, rove, slog, traipse (informal), tramp, trudge

tremble verb 1 <u>shake</u>, quake, quiver, shiver, shudder, totter, vibrate, wobble ♦ noun 2 <u>shake</u>, quake, quiver, shiver, shudder, tremor, vibration, wobble

tremendous adjective 1 <u>huge</u>, colossal, enormous, formidable, gigantic, great, immense, stupendous, terrific 2 Informal <u>excellent</u>, amazing, brilliant, exceptional, extraordinary, fantastic (informal), great, marvellous, sensational (informal), wonderful

tremor noun 1 <u>shake</u>, quaking, quaver, quiver, shiver, trembling,

wobble 2 earthquake, quake
(*informal*), shock

trench noun ditch, channel,
drain, excavation, furrow, gutter,
trough

trenchant adjective 1 incisive,
acerbic, caustic, cutting,
penetrating, pointed, pungent,
scathing 2 effective, energetic,
forceful, potent, powerful,
strong, vigorous

trend noun 1 tendency, bias,
current, direction, drift, flow,
inclination, leaning 2 fashion,
craze, fad (*informal*), mode, rage,
style, thing, vogue

trendy adjective fashionable, in
fashion, in vogue, modish,
stylish, voguish, with it (*informal*)

trepidation noun anxiety, alarm,
apprehension, consternation,
disquiet, dread, fear,
nervousness, uneasiness, worry

trespass verb 1 intrude,
encroach, infringe, invade,
obtrude ◆ noun 2 intrusion,
encroachment, infringement,
invasion, unlawful entry

trespasser noun intruder,
interloper, invader, poacher

trial noun 1 hearing, litigation,
tribunal 2 test, audition, dry run
(*informal*), experiment,
probation, test-run 3 hardship,
adversity, affliction, distress,
ordeal, suffering, tribulation,
trouble

tribe noun race, clan, family,
people

tribunal noun hearing, court, trial

tribute noun 1 accolade,
commendation, compliment,
eulogy, panegyric, recognition,

testimonial 2 tax, charge,
homage, payment, ransom

trick noun 1 deception, fraud,
hoax, manoeuvre, ploy, ruse,
stratagem, subterfuge, swindle,
trap, wile 2 joke, antic, jape,
leg-pull (*Brit. informal*), practical
joke, prank, stunt 3 secret, hang
(*informal*), knack, know-how
(*informal*), skill, technique
4 mannerism, characteristic,
foible, habit, idiosyncrasy,
peculiarity, practice, quirk, trait
◆ verb 5 deceive, cheat, con
(*informal*), dupe, fool, hoodwink,
kid (*informal*), mislead, swindle,
take in (*informal*), trap

trickery noun deception,
cheating, chicanery, deceit,
dishonesty, guile, jiggery-pokery
(*informal, chiefly Brit.*), monkey
business (*informal*)

trickle verb 1 dribble, drip, drop,
exude, ooze, run, seep, stream
◆ noun 2 dribble, drip, seepage

tricky adjective 1 difficult,
complicated, delicate, knotty,
problematic, risky, thorny,
ticklish 2 crafty, artful, cunning,
deceitful, devious, scheming,
slippery, sly, wily

trifle noun 1 knick-knack,
bagatelle, bauble, plaything, toy
◆ verb 2 toy, dally, mess about,
play

trifling adjective insignificant,
measly, negligible, paltry, trivial,
unimportant, worthless

trigger verb set off, activate,
cause, generate, produce,
prompt, provoke, spark off, start

trim adjective 1 neat, dapper,
natty (*informal*), shipshape,
smart, spruce, tidy,

well-groomed 2 <u>slender</u>, fit, shapely, sleek, slim, streamlined, svelte, willowy ♦ *verb* 3 <u>cut</u>, clip, crop, even up, pare, prune, shave, tidy 4 <u>decorate</u>, adorn, array, beautify, deck out, dress, embellish, ornament ♦ *noun* 5 <u>decoration</u>, adornment, border, edging, embellishment, frill, ornamentation, piping, trimming 6 <u>condition</u>, fettle, fitness, health, shape (*informal*), state 7 <u>cut</u>, clipping, crop, pruning, shave, shearing, tidying up

trimming *noun* 1 <u>decoration</u>, adornment, border, edging, embellishment, frill, ornamentation, piping 2 **trimmings** <u>extras</u>, accessories, accompaniments, frills, ornaments, paraphernalia, trappings

trinity *noun* <u>threesome</u>, triad, trio, triumvirate

trinket *noun* <u>ornament</u>, bagatelle, bauble, knick-knack, toy, trifle

trio *noun* <u>threesome</u>, triad, trilogy, trinity, triumvirate

trip *noun* 1 <u>journey</u>, errand, excursion, expedition, foray, jaunt, outing, run, tour, voyage 2 <u>stumble</u>, fall, misstep, slip ♦ *verb* 3 <u>stumble</u>, fall, lose one's footing, misstep, slip, tumble 4 <u>catch out</u>, trap 5 <u>skip</u>, dance, gambol, hop

triple *adjective* 1 <u>threefold</u>, three-way, tripartite ♦ *verb* 2 <u>treble</u>, increase threefold

trite *adjective* <u>unoriginal</u>, banal, clichéd, commonplace, hackneyed, stale, stereotyped, threadbare, tired

triumph *noun* 1 <u>joy</u>, elation, exultation, happiness, jubilation, pride, rejoicing 2 <u>success</u>, accomplishment, achievement, attainment, conquest, coup, feat, victory ♦ *verb* 3 *often with* **over** <u>win</u>, overcome, prevail, prosper, succeed, vanquish 4 <u>rejoice</u>, celebrate, crow, exult, gloat, glory, revel

triumphant *adjective* <u>victorious</u>, celebratory, cock-a-hoop, conquering, elated, exultant, jubilant, proud, successful, winning

trivia *plural noun* <u>minutiae</u>, details, trifles, trivialities

trivial *adjective* <u>unimportant</u>, incidental, inconsequential, insignificant, meaningless, minor, petty, small, trifling, worthless

triviality *noun* <u>insignificance</u>, meaninglessness, pettiness, unimportance, worthlessness

trivialize *verb* <u>undervalue</u>, belittle, laugh off, make light of, minimize, play down, scoff at, underestimate, underplay

troop *noun* 1 <u>group</u>, band, body, company, crowd, horde, multitude, squad, team, unit 2 **troops** <u>soldiers</u>, armed forces, army, men, servicemen, soldiery ♦ *verb* 3 <u>flock</u>, march, stream, swarm, throng, traipse (*informal*)

trophy *noun* <u>prize</u>, award, booty, cup, laurels, memento, souvenir, spoils

tropical *adjective* <u>hot</u>, steamy, stifling, sultry, sweltering, torrid

trot *verb* 1 <u>run</u>, canter, jog, lope,

scamper ♦ *noun* 2 <u>run</u>, canter, jog, lope

trouble *noun* 1 <u>distress</u>, anxiety, disquiet, grief, misfortune, pain, sorrow, torment, woe, worry 2 <u>disease</u>, ailment, complaint, defect, disorder, failure, illness, malfunction 3 <u>disorder</u>, agitation, bother (*informal*), commotion, discord, disturbance, strife, tumult, unrest 4 <u>effort</u>, care, exertion, inconvenience, labour, pains, thought, work ♦ *verb* 5 <u>worry</u>, bother, disconcert, distress, disturb, pain, perturb, plague, sadden, upset 6 <u>take pains</u>, exert oneself, make an effort, take the time 7 <u>inconvenience</u>, bother, burden, disturb, impose upon, incommode, put out

troublesome *adjective* 1 <u>worrying</u>, annoying, demanding, difficult, inconvenient, irksome, taxing, tricky, trying, vexatious 2 <u>disorderly</u>, rebellious, rowdy, turbulent, uncooperative, undisciplined, unruly, violent

trough *noun* 1 <u>manger</u>, water trough 2 <u>channel</u>, canal, depression, ditch, duct, furrow, gully, gutter, trench

trounce *verb* <u>thrash</u>, beat, crush, drub, give a hiding (*informal*), hammer (*informal*), rout, slaughter (*informal*), wipe the floor with (*informal*)

troupe *noun* <u>company</u>, band, cast

truancy *noun* <u>absence</u>, absence without leave, malingering, shirking, skiving (*Brit. slang*)

truant *noun* <u>absentee</u>, malingerer, runaway, shirker, skiver (*Brit. slang*)

truce *noun* <u>ceasefire</u>, armistice, cessation, let-up (*informal*), lull, moratorium, peace, respite

truculent *adjective* <u>hostile</u>, aggressive, bellicose, belligerent, defiant, ill-tempered, obstreperous, pugnacious

trudge *verb* 1 <u>plod</u>, footslog, lumber, slog, stump, traipse (*informal*), tramp, trek ♦ *noun* 2 <u>hike</u>, footslog, march, slog, traipse (*informal*), tramp, trek

true *adjective* 1 <u>correct</u>, accurate, authentic, factual, genuine, precise, real, right, truthful, veracious 2 <u>faithful</u>, dedicated, devoted, dutiful, loyal, reliable, staunch, steady, trustworthy 3 <u>exact</u>, accurate, on target, perfect, precise, spot-on (*Brit. informal*), unerring

truism *noun* <u>cliché</u>, axiom, bromide, commonplace, platitude

truly *adverb* 1 <u>correctly</u>, authentically, exactly, factually, genuinely, legitimately, precisely, rightly, truthfully 2 <u>faithfully</u>, devotedly, dutifully, loyally, sincerely, staunchly, steadily 3 <u>really</u>, extremely, greatly, indeed, of course, very

trumpet *noun* 1 <u>horn</u>, bugle, clarion ♦ *verb* 2 <u>proclaim</u>, advertise, announce, broadcast, shout from the rooftops, tout (*informal*)

trump up *verb* <u>fabricate</u>, concoct, contrive, cook up (*informal*), create, fake, invent, make up

truncate *verb* <u>shorten</u>, abbreviate, curtail, cut short, dock, lop, pare, prune, trim

truncheon noun <u>club</u>, baton, cudgel, staff

trunk noun 1 <u>stem</u>, bole, stalk 2 <u>chest</u>, box, case, casket, coffer, crate 3 <u>body</u>, torso 4 <u>snout</u>, proboscis

truss verb 1 <u>tie</u>, bind, fasten, make fast, secure, strap, tether ♦ noun 2 <u>Medical support</u>, bandage 3 <u>joist</u>, beam, brace, buttress, prop, stanchion, stay, strut, support

trust verb 1 <u>believe in</u>, bank on, count on, depend on, have faith in, rely upon 2 <u>consign</u>, assign, commit, confide, delegate, entrust, give 3 <u>expect</u>, assume, hope, presume, suppose, surmise ♦ noun 4 <u>confidence</u>, assurance, belief, certainty, conviction, credence, credit, expectation, faith, reliance

trustful, trusting adjective <u>unwary</u>, credulous, gullible, naive, unsuspecting, unsuspicious

trustworthy adjective <u>honest</u>, dependable, honourable, principled, reliable, reputable, responsible, staunch, steadfast, trusty

trusty adjective <u>faithful</u>, dependable, reliable, solid, staunch, steady, strong, trustworthy

truth noun <u>truthfulness</u>, accuracy, exactness, fact, genuineness, legitimacy, precision, reality, validity, veracity

truthful adjective <u>honest</u>, candid, frank, precise, sincere, straight, true, trustworthy

try verb 1 <u>attempt</u>, aim, endeavour, have a go, make an effort, seek, strive, struggle

2 <u>test</u>, appraise, check out, evaluate, examine, investigate, put to the test, sample, taste ♦ noun 3 <u>attempt</u>, crack (informal), effort, go (informal), shot (informal), stab (informal), whack (informal)

trying adjective <u>annoying</u>, bothersome, difficult, exasperating, hard, stressful, taxing, tiresome, tough, wearisome

tubby adjective <u>fat</u>, chubby, corpulent, obese, overweight, plump, portly, stout

tuck verb 1 <u>push</u>, fold, gather, insert ♦ noun 2 <u>fold</u>, gather, pinch, pleat 3 Informal <u>food</u>, grub (slang), nosh (slang)

tuft noun <u>clump</u>, bunch, cluster, collection, knot, tussock

tug verb 1 <u>pull</u>, jerk, wrench, yank ♦ noun 2 <u>pull</u>, jerk, yank

tuition noun <u>training</u>, education, instruction, lessons, schooling, teaching, tutelage, tutoring

tumble verb 1 <u>fall</u>, drop, flop, plummet, stumble, topple ♦ noun 2 <u>fall</u>, drop, plunge, spill, stumble, trip

tumbledown adjective <u>dilapidated</u>, crumbling, decrepit, ramshackle, rickety, ruined

tumour noun <u>growth</u>, cancer, carcinoma (Pathology), lump, sarcoma (Medical), swelling

tumult noun <u>commotion</u>, clamour, din, hubbub, pandemonium, riot, row, turmoil, upheaval, uproar

tumultuous adjective <u>wild</u>, boisterous, excited, noisy, riotous, rowdy, turbulent, unruly, uproarious

tune noun **1** <u>melody</u>, air, song, strain, theme **2** <u>pitch</u>, concord, consonance, euphony, harmony ♦ verb **3** <u>adjust</u>, adapt, attune, harmonize, pitch, regulate

tuneful adjective <u>melodious</u>, catchy, euphonious, harmonious, mellifluous, melodic, musical, pleasant

tuneless adjective <u>discordant</u>, atonal, cacophonous, dissonant, harsh, unmusical

tunnel noun **1** <u>passage</u>, burrow, channel, hole, passageway, shaft, subway, underpass ♦ verb **2** <u>dig</u>, burrow, excavate, mine, scoop out

turbulence noun <u>confusion</u>, agitation, commotion, disorder, instability, tumult, turmoil, unrest, upheaval

turbulent adjective <u>agitated</u>, blustery, choppy, foaming, furious, raging, rough, tempestuous, tumultuous

turf noun **1** <u>grass</u>, sod, sward **2 the turf** <u>horse-racing</u>, racing, the flat

turmoil noun <u>confusion</u>, agitation, chaos, commotion, disarray, disorder, tumult, upheaval, uproar

turn verb **1** <u>change course</u>, move, shift, swerve, switch, veer, wheel **2** <u>rotate</u>, circle, go round, gyrate, pivot, revolve, roll, spin, twist, whirl **3** <u>change</u>, alter, convert, mould, mutate, remodel, shape, transform **4** <u>shape</u>, fashion, frame, make, mould **5** <u>go bad</u>, curdle, go off (Brit. informal), sour, spoil, taint ♦ noun **6** <u>rotation</u>, circle, cycle,

gyration, revolution, spin, twist, whirl **7** <u>shift</u>, departure, deviation **8** <u>opportunity</u>, chance, crack (informal), go, stint, time, try **9** <u>direction</u>, drift, heading, tendency, trend **10** As in **good turn** <u>act</u>, action, deed, favour, gesture, service

turncoat noun <u>traitor</u>, apostate, backslider, defector, deserter, renegade

turn down verb **1** <u>lower</u>, lessen, muffle, mute, quieten, soften **2** <u>refuse</u>, decline, rebuff, reject, repudiate, spurn

turn in verb **1** <u>go to bed</u>, go to sleep, hit the sack (slang) **2** <u>hand in</u>, deliver, give up, hand over, return, submit, surrender, tender

turning noun <u>junction</u>, bend, crossroads, curve, side road, turn, turn-off

turning point noun <u>crossroads</u>, change, crisis, crux, moment of truth

turn off verb <u>stop</u>, cut out, put out, shut down, switch off, turn out, unplug

turn on verb **1** <u>start</u>, activate, ignite, kick-start, start up, switch on **2** <u>attack</u>, assail, assault, fall on, round on **3** Informal <u>excite</u>, arouse, attract, please, stimulate, thrill, titillate

turnout noun <u>attendance</u>, assembly, audience, congregation, crowd, gate, number, throng

turnover noun **1** <u>output</u>, business, productivity **2** <u>movement</u>, change, coming and going

turn up verb **1** <u>arrive</u>, appear,

attend, come, put in an appearance, show one's face, show up (*informal*) **2** find, dig up, disclose, discover, expose, reveal, unearth **3** come to light, crop up (*informal*), pop up **4** increase, amplify, boost, enhance, intensify, raise

tussle *noun* **1** fight, battle, brawl, conflict, contest, scrap (*informal*), scuffle, struggle ♦ *verb* **2** fight, battle, grapple, scrap (*informal*), scuffle, struggle, vie, wrestle

tutor *noun* **1** teacher, coach, educator, guardian, guide, guru, instructor, lecturer, mentor ♦ *verb* **2** teach, coach, drill, educate, guide, instruct, school, train

twaddle *noun* nonsense, claptrap (*informal*), drivel, garbage (*informal*), gobbledegook (*informal*), poppycock (*informal*), rubbish, waffle (*informal, chiefly Brit.*)

tweak *verb, noun* twist, jerk, pinch, pull, squeeze

twig *noun* branch, shoot, spray, sprig, stick

twilight *noun* dusk, dimness, evening, gloaming (*Scot. or poetic*), gloom, half-light, sundown, sunset

twin *noun* **1** double, clone, counterpart, duplicate, fellow, likeness, lookalike, match, mate ♦ *verb* **2** pair, couple, join, link, match, yoke

twine *noun* **1** string, cord, yarn ♦ *verb* **2** coil, bend, curl, encircle, loop, spiral, twist, wind

twinge *noun* pain, pang, prick, spasm, stab, stitch

twinkle *verb* **1** sparkle, blink, flash, flicker, gleam, glint, glisten, glitter, shimmer, shine ♦ *noun* **2** flicker, flash, gleam, glimmer, shimmer, spark, sparkle

twirl *verb* **1** turn, pirouette, pivot, revolve, rotate, spin, twist, wheel, whirl, wind ♦ *noun* **2** turn, pirouette, revolution, rotation, spin, twist, wheel, whirl

twist *verb* **1** wind, coil, curl, screw, spin, swivel, wrap, wring **2** distort, contort, screw up ♦ *noun* **3** wind, coil, curl, spin, swivel **4** development, change, revelation, slant, surprise, turn, variation **5** curve, arc, bend, meander, turn, undulation, zigzag **6** distortion, defect, deformation, flaw, imperfection, kink, warp

twit *noun* fool, ass, chump (*informal*), halfwit, idiot, nincompoop, numbskull *or* numskull, prat (*slang*), twerp *or* twirp (*informal*)

twitch *verb* **1** jerk, flutter, jump, squirm ♦ *noun* **2** spasm, flutter, jerk, jump, tic

two-faced *adjective* hypocritical, deceitful, dissembling, duplicitous, false, insincere, treacherous, untrustworthy

tycoon *noun* magnate, baron, capitalist, fat cat (*slang, chiefly U.S.*), financier, industrialist, mogul, plutocrat

type *noun* category, class, genre, group, kind, order, sort, species, style, variety

typhoon *noun* storm, cyclone, squall, tempest, tornado

typical *adjective* characteristic, archetypal, average, model, normal, orthodox, representative, standard, stock, usual

typify *verb* symbolize, characterize, embody, epitomize, exemplify, illustrate, personify, represent, sum up

tyrannical *adjective* oppressive, authoritarian, autocratic, cruel, despotic, dictatorial, domineering, high-handed, imperious, overbearing, tyrannous

tyranny *noun* oppression, absolutism, authoritarianism, autocracy, cruelty, despotism, dictatorship, high-handedness, imperiousness

tyrant *noun* dictator, absolutist, authoritarian, autocrat, bully, despot, martinet, oppressor, slave-driver

U u

ubiquitous *adjective* everywhere, ever-present, omnipresent, pervasive, universal

ugly *adjective* 1 unattractive, homely (*chiefly U.S.*), ill-favoured, plain, unlovely, unprepossessing, unsightly 2 unpleasant, disagreeable, distasteful, horrid, objectionable, shocking, terrible 3 ominous, baleful, dangerous, menacing, sinister

ulcer *noun* sore, abscess, boil, gumboil, peptic ulcer, pustule

ulterior *adjective* hidden, concealed, covert, secret, undisclosed

ultimate *adjective* 1 final, end, last 2 supreme, extreme,

greatest, highest, paramount, superlative, utmost

ultimately *adverb* finally, after all, at last, eventually, in due time, in the end, sooner or later

umpire *noun* 1 referee, arbiter, arbitrator, judge ♦ *verb* 2 referee, adjudicate, arbitrate, judge

unabashed *adjective* unembarrassed, blatant, bold, brazen

unable *adjective* incapable, impotent, ineffectual, powerless, unfit, unqualified

unabridged *adjective* uncut, complete, full-length, unexpurgated, whole

unacceptable *adjective* unsatisfactory, displeasing, objectionable

unaccompanied *adjective* 1 alone, by oneself, lone, on one's own, solo, unescorted 2 *Music* a cappella

unaccountable *adjective* 1 inexplicable, baffling, mysterious, odd, puzzling, unexplainable, unfathomable 2 not answerable, exempt, not responsible

unaccustomed *adjective* 1 unfamiliar, new, strange, unwonted 2 **unaccustomed to** not used to, inexperienced at, unfamiliar with, unused to

unaffected[1] *adjective* natural, artless, genuine, plain, simple, sincere, unpretentious

unaffected[2] *adjective* impervious, proof, unmoved, unresponsive, untouched

unafraid *adjective* fearless, daring, dauntless, intrepid

unalterable *adjective* unchangeable, fixed, immutable, permanent

unanimity *noun* agreement, accord, assent, concord, concurrence, consensus, harmony, like-mindedness, unison

unanimous *adjective* agreed, common, concerted, harmonious, in agreement, like-minded, united

unanimously *adverb* without exception, nem. con., with one accord

unanswerable *adjective* conclusive, absolute, incontestable, incontrovertible, indisputable

unanswered *adjective* unresolved, disputed, open, undecided

unappetizing *adjective* unpleasant, distasteful, off-putting (*Brit. informal*), repulsive, unappealing, unattractive, unpalatable

unapproachable *adjective* 1 unfriendly, aloof, chilly, cool, distant, remote, reserved, standoffish 2 inaccessible, out of reach, remote

unarmed *adjective* defenceless, exposed, helpless, open, unprotected, weak

unassailable *adjective* impregnable, invincible, invulnerable, secure

unassuming *adjective* modest, humble, quiet, reserved, retiring, self-effacing, unassertive, unobtrusive, unpretentious

unattached *adjective* 1 free, independent 2 single, available,

not spoken for, unengaged, unmarried

unattended *adjective* 1 abandoned, unguarded, unwatched 2 alone, on one's own, unaccompanied

unauthorized *adjective* illegal, unlawful, unofficial, unsanctioned

unavoidable *adjective* inevitable, certain, fated, inescapable

unaware *adjective* ignorant, oblivious, unconscious, uninformed, unknowing

unawares *adverb* 1 by surprise, off guard, suddenly, unexpectedly 2 unknowingly, accidentally, by accident, inadvertently, unwittingly

unbalanced *adjective* 1 biased, one-sided, partial, partisan, prejudiced, unfair 2 shaky, lopsided, uneven, unstable, wobbly 3 deranged, crazy, demented, disturbed, eccentric, insane, irrational, mad, *non compos mentis*, not all there, unhinged, unstable

unbearable *adjective* intolerable, insufferable, too much (*informal*), unacceptable

unbeatable *adjective* invincible, indomitable

unbeaten *adjective* undefeated, triumphant, victorious

unbecoming *adjective* 1 unsightly, unattractive, unbefitting, unflattering, unsuitable 2 unseemly, discreditable, improper, offensive

unbelievable *adjective* incredible, astonishing, far-fetched, implausible, impossible, improbable, inconceivable, preposterous, unconvincing

unbending *adjective* inflexible, firm, intractable, resolute, rigid, severe, strict, stubborn, tough, uncompromising

unbiased *adjective* fair, disinterested, equitable, impartial, just, neutral, objective, unprejudiced

unblemished *adjective* spotless, flawless, immaculate, impeccable, perfect, pure, untarnished

unborn *adjective* expected, awaited, embryonic

unbreakable *adjective* indestructible, durable, lasting, rugged, strong

unbridled *adjective* unrestrained, excessive, intemperate, licentious, riotous, unchecked, unruly, wanton

unbroken *adjective* 1 intact, complete, entire, whole 2 continuous, constant, incessant, uninterrupted

unburden *verb* confess, confide, disclose, get (something) off one's chest (*informal*), reveal

uncalled-for *adjective* unjustified, gratuitous, needless, undeserved, unnecessary, unwarranted

uncanny *adjective* 1 weird, mysterious, strange, supernatural, unearthly, unnatural 2 extraordinary, astounding, exceptional, incredible, miraculous, remarkable, unusual

unceasing *adjective* continual, constant, continuous, endless, incessant, nonstop, perpetual

uncertain *adjective*

1 unpredictable, doubtful, indefinite, questionable, risky, speculative 2 unsure, dubious, hazy, irresolute, unclear, unconfirmed, undecided, vague

uncertainty *noun* doubt, ambiguity, confusion, dubiety, hesitancy, indecision, unpredictability

unchangeable *adjective* unalterable, constant, fixed, immutable, invariable, irreversible, permanent, stable

unchanging *adjective* constant, continuing, enduring, eternal, immutable, lasting, permanent, perpetual, unvarying

uncharitable *adjective* unkind, cruel, hardhearted, unfeeling, ungenerous

uncharted *adjective* unexplored, strange, undiscovered, unfamiliar, unknown

uncivil *adjective* impolite, bad-mannered, discourteous, ill-mannered, rude, unmannerly

uncivilized *adjective* 1 primitive, barbarian, savage, wild 2 uncouth, boorish, coarse, philistine, uncultivated, uneducated

unclean *adjective* dirty, corrupt, defiled, evil, filthy, foul, impure, polluted, soiled, stained

unclear *adjective* 1 indistinct, blurred, dim, faint, fuzzy, hazy, obscure, shadowy, undefined, vague 2 doubtful, ambiguous, indefinite, indeterminate, vague

uncomfortable *adjective* 1 awkward, cramped, painful, rough 2 uneasy, awkward, discomfited, disturbed, embarrassed, troubled

uncommitted *adjective*
<u>uninvolved</u>, floating, free,
neutral, nonaligned, not
involved, unattached

uncommon *adjective* **1** <u>rare</u>,
infrequent, novel, odd, peculiar,
queer, scarce, strange, unusual
2 <u>extraordinary</u>, distinctive,
exceptional, notable,
outstanding, remarkable, special

uncommonly *adverb* **1** <u>rarely</u>,
hardly ever, infrequently,
occasionally, seldom
2 <u>exceptionally</u>, particularly, very

uncommunicative *adjective*
<u>reticent</u>, close, reserved,
secretive, silent, taciturn,
tight-lipped, unforthcoming

uncompromising *adjective*
<u>inflexible</u>, firm, inexorable,
intransigent, rigid, strict, tough,
unbending

unconcern *noun* <u>indifference</u>,
aloofness, apathy, detachment,
lack of interest, nonchalance

unconcerned *adjective*
indifferent, aloof, apathetic, cool,
detached, dispassionate, distant,
uninterested, unmoved

unconditional *adjective* <u>absolute</u>,
complete, entire, full, outright,
positive, total, unlimited,
unqualified, unreserved

unconnected *adjective*
1 <u>separate</u>, detached, divided
2 <u>meaningless</u>, disjointed,
illogical, incoherent, irrelevant

unconscious *adjective*
1 <u>senseless</u>, insensible, knocked
out, out, out cold, stunned
2 <u>unaware</u>, ignorant, oblivious,
unknowing **3** <u>unintentional</u>,

accidental, inadvertent, unwitting

uncontrollable *adjective* <u>wild</u>,
frantic, furious, mad, strong,
unruly, violent

uncontrolled *adjective*
<u>unrestrained</u>, rampant, riotous,
unbridled, unchecked,
undisciplined

unconventional *adjective*
<u>unusual</u>, eccentric, individual,
irregular, nonconformist, odd,
offbeat, original, outré,
unorthodox

unconvincing *adjective*
<u>implausible</u>, dubious, feeble,
flimsy, improbable, lame,
questionable, suspect, thin,
unlikely, weak

uncooperative *adjective*
<u>unhelpful</u>, awkward, difficult,
disobliging, obstructive

uncoordinated *adjective* <u>clumsy</u>,
awkward, bungling, graceless,
lumbering, maladroit, ungainly,
ungraceful

uncouth *adjective* <u>coarse</u>,
boorish, crude, graceless,
ill-mannered, loutish, oafish,
rough, rude, vulgar

uncover *verb* **1** <u>reveal</u>, disclose,
divulge, expose, make known
2 <u>open</u>, bare, show, strip,
unwrap

uncritical *adjective*
<u>undiscriminating</u>, indiscriminate,
undiscerning

undecided *adjective* **1** <u>unsure</u>,
dithering (*chiefly Brit.*), hesitant,
in two minds, irresolute, torn,
uncertain **2** <u>unsettled</u>, debatable,
iffy (*informal*), indefinite, moot,
open, unconcluded,
undetermined

undefined *adjective*
1 underspecified, imprecise, inexact, unclear 2 indistinct, formless, indefinite, vague

undeniable *adjective* certain, clear, incontrovertible, indisputable, obvious, sure, unquestionable

under *preposition* 1 below, beneath, underneath 2 subject to, governed by, secondary to, subordinate to ♦ *adverb* 3 below, beneath, down, lower

underclothes *plural noun* underwear, lingerie, undergarments, undies (*informal*)

undercover *adjective* secret, concealed, covert, hidden, private

undercurrent *noun* 1 undertow, riptide 2 undertone, atmosphere, feeling, hint, overtone, sense, suggestion, tendency, tinge, vibes (*slang*)

underdog *noun* outsider, little fellow (*informal*)

underestimate *verb* underrate, belittle, minimize, miscalculate, undervalue

undergo *verb* experience, bear, endure, go through, stand, suffer, sustain

underground *adjective*
1 subterranean, buried, covered 2 secret, clandestine, covert, hidden ♦ *noun* 3 the underground: a the Resistance, partisans b the tube (*Brit.*), the metro, the subway

undergrowth *noun* scrub, bracken, briars, brush, underbrush

underhand *adjective* sly, crafty, deceitful, devious, dishonest, furtive, secret, sneaky, stealthy

underline *verb* 1 underscore, mark 2 emphasize, accentuate, highlight, stress

underlying *adjective* fundamental, basic, elementary, intrinsic, primary, prime

undermine *verb* weaken, disable, sabotage, sap, subvert

underprivileged *adjective* disadvantaged, deprived, destitute, impoverished, needy, poor

underrate *verb* underestimate, belittle, discount, undervalue

undersized *adjective* stunted, dwarfish, miniature, pygmy *or* pigmy, small

understand *verb* 1 comprehend, conceive, fathom, follow, get, grasp, perceive, realize, see, take in 2 believe, assume, gather, presume, suppose, think

understandable *adjective* reasonable, justifiable, legitimate, natural, to be expected

understanding *noun*
1 perception, appreciation, awareness, comprehension, discernment, grasp, insight, judgment, knowledge, sense 2 interpretation, belief, idea, judgment, notion, opinion, perception, view 3 agreement, accord, pact ♦ *adjective*
4 sympathetic, compassionate, considerate, kind, patient, sensitive, tolerant

understood *adjective* 1 implied, implicit, inferred, tacit, unspoken, unstated 2 assumed, accepted, taken for granted

understudy *noun* stand-in,

replacement, reserve, substitute

undertake verb <u>agree</u>, bargain, contract, engage, guarantee, pledge, promise

undertaking noun 1 <u>task</u>, affair, attempt, business, effort, endeavour, enterprise, operation, project, venture 2 <u>promise</u>, assurance, commitment, pledge, vow, word

undertone noun 1 <u>murmur</u>, whisper 2 <u>undercurrent</u>, hint, suggestion, tinge, touch, trace

undervalue verb <u>underrate</u>, depreciate, hold cheap, minimize, misjudge, underestimate

underwater adjective <u>submerged</u>, submarine, sunken

under way adjective <u>begun</u>, going on, in progress, started

underwear noun <u>underclothes</u>, lingerie, undergarments, underthings, undies (informal)

underweight adjective <u>skinny</u>, emaciated, half-starved, puny, skin and bone (informal), undernourished, undersized

underworld noun 1 <u>criminals</u>, gangland (informal), gangsters, organized crime 2 <u>nether world</u>, Hades, nether regions

underwrite verb 1 <u>finance</u>, back, fund, guarantee, insure, sponsor, subsidize 2 <u>sign</u>, endorse, initial

undesirable adjective <u>objectionable</u>, disagreeable, distasteful, unacceptable, unattractive, unsuitable, unwanted, unwelcome

undeveloped adjective <u>potential</u>, immature, latent

undignified adjective <u>unseemly</u>, improper, indecorous, inelegant, unbecoming, unsuitable

undisciplined adjective <u>uncontrolled</u>, obstreperous, unrestrained, unruly, wayward, wild, wilful

undisguised adjective <u>obvious</u>, blatant, evident, explicit, open, overt, patent, unconcealed

undisputed adjective <u>acknowledged</u>, accepted, certain, indisputable, recognized, unchallenged, undeniable, undoubted

undistinguished adjective <u>ordinary</u>, everyday, mediocre, run-of-the-mill, unexceptional, unimpressive, unremarkable

undisturbed adjective 1 <u>quiet</u>, tranquil 2 <u>calm</u>, collected, composed, placid, sedate, serene, tranquil, unfazed (informal), unperturbed, untroubled

undivided adjective <u>complete</u>, entire, exclusive, full, solid, thorough, undistracted, united, whole

undo verb 1 <u>open</u>, disentangle, loose, unbutton, unfasten, untie 2 <u>reverse</u>, annul, cancel, invalidate, neutralize, offset 3 <u>ruin</u>, defeat, destroy, overturn, quash, shatter, subvert, undermine, upset, wreck

undoing noun <u>downfall</u>, collapse, defeat, disgrace, overthrow, reversal, ruin, shame

undone adjective <u>unfinished</u>, left, neglected, omitted, unfulfilled, unperformed

undoubted adjective <u>certain</u>, acknowledged, definite, indisputable, indubitable, sure, undisputed, unquestioned

undoubtedly adverb certainly, assuredly, definitely, doubtless, surely, without doubt

undress verb 1 strip, disrobe, shed, take off one's clothes
♦ noun 2 nakedness, nudity

undue adjective excessive, extreme, improper, needless, uncalled-for, unnecessary, unwarranted

unduly adverb excessively, overly, unnecessarily, unreasonably

undying adjective eternal, constant, deathless, everlasting, infinite, permanent, perpetual, unending

unearth verb 1 discover, expose, find, reveal, uncover 2 dig up, dredge up, excavate, exhume

unearthly adjective eerie, ghostly, phantom, spectral, spooky (informal), strange, supernatural, uncanny, weird

uneasiness noun anxiety, disquiet, doubt, misgiving, qualms, trepidation, worry

uneasy adjective 1 anxious, disturbed, edgy, nervous, on edge, perturbed, troubled, twitchy (informal), uncomfortable, worried 2 awkward, insecure, precarious, shaky, strained, tense, uncomfortable

uneconomic adjective unprofitable, loss-making, nonpaying

uneducated adjective 1 ignorant, illiterate, unschooled, untaught 2 lowbrow, uncultivated, uncultured

unemotional adjective impassive, apathetic, cold, cool, phlegmatic, reserved, undemonstrative, unexcitable

unemployed adjective out of work, idle, jobless, laid off, redundant

unending adjective perpetual, continual, endless, eternal, everlasting, interminable, unceasing

unendurable adjective unbearable, insufferable, insupportable, intolerable

unenthusiastic adjective indifferent, apathetic, half-hearted, nonchalant

unenviable adjective unpleasant, disagreeable, uncomfortable, undesirable

unequal adjective 1 different, differing, disparate, dissimilar, unlike, unmatched, varying 2 disproportionate, asymmetrical, ill-matched, irregular, unbalanced, uneven

unequalled adjective incomparable, matchless, paramount, peerless, supreme, unparalleled, unrivalled

unequivocal adjective clear, absolute, certain, definite, explicit, incontrovertible, indubitable, manifest, plain, unambiguous

unerring adjective accurate, exact, infallible, perfect, sure, unfailing

unethical adjective dishonest, disreputable, illegal, immoral, improper, shady (informal), unprincipled, unscrupulous, wrong

uneven *adjective* 1 <u>rough</u>, bumpy
2 <u>variable</u>, broken, fitful,
irregular, jerky, patchy,
spasmodic 3 <u>unbalanced</u>,
lopsided, odd 4 <u>unequal</u>,
ill-matched, unfair

uneventful *adjective* <u>humdrum</u>,
boring, dull, ho-hum (*informal*),
monotonous, routine, tedious,
unexciting

unexceptional *adjective*
<u>ordinary</u>, commonplace,
conventional, mediocre, normal,
pedestrian, run-of-the-mill,
undistinguished, unremarkable

unexpected *adjective* <u>unforeseen</u>,
abrupt, chance, fortuitous,
sudden, surprising,
unanticipated, unlooked-for,
unpredictable

unfailing *adjective* 1 <u>continuous</u>,
boundless, endless, persistent,
unflagging 2 <u>reliable</u>, certain,
dependable, faithful, loyal,
staunch, sure, true

unfair *adjective* 1 <u>biased</u>, bigoted,
one-sided, partial, partisan,
prejudiced, unjust
2 <u>unscrupulous</u>, dishonest,
unethical, unsporting, wrongful

unfaithful *adjective* 1 <u>faithless</u>,
adulterous, two-timing
(*informal*), untrue 2 <u>disloyal</u>,
deceitful, faithless, false,
traitorous, treacherous,
untrustworthy

unfamiliar *adjective* <u>strange</u>,
alien, different, new, novel,
unknown, unusual

unfashionable *adjective* <u>passé</u>,
antiquated, dated, obsolete,
old-fashioned, old hat

unfasten *verb* <u>undo</u>, detach, let
go, loosen, open, separate, untie

unfathomable *adjective*
1 <u>baffling</u>, deep, impenetrable,
incomprehensible,
indecipherable, inexplicable,
profound 2 <u>immeasurable</u>,
bottomless, unmeasured

unfavourable *adjective*
1 <u>adverse</u>, contrary, inauspicious,
unfortunate, unlucky,
unpropitious 2 <u>hostile</u>, inimical,
negative, unfriendly

unfeeling *adjective*
1 <u>hardhearted</u>, apathetic,
callous, cold, cruel, heartless,
insensitive, pitiless, uncaring
2 <u>numb</u>, insensate, insensible

unfinished *adjective*
1 <u>incomplete</u>, half-done,
uncompleted, undone 2 <u>rough</u>,
bare, crude, natural, raw,
unrefined

unfit *adjective* 1 <u>incapable</u>,
inadequate, incompetent, no
good, unqualified, useless
2 <u>unsuitable</u>, inadequate,
ineffective, unsuited, useless
3 <u>out of shape</u>, feeble, flabby, in
poor condition, unhealthy

unflappable *adjective*
<u>imperturbable</u>, calm, collected,
composed, cool, impassive,
level-headed, self-possessed

unflattering *adjective* 1 <u>blunt</u>,
candid, critical, honest
2 <u>unattractive</u>, plain, unbecoming

unflinching *adjective* <u>determined</u>,
firm, immovable, resolute,
staunch, steadfast, steady,
unfaltering

unfold *verb* 1 <u>open</u>, expand,
spread out, undo, unfurl,
unravel, unroll, unwrap 2 <u>reveal</u>,
disclose, divulge, make known,
present, show, uncover

unforeseen *adjective*
<u>unexpected</u>, accidental, sudden, surprising, unanticipated, unpredicted

unforgettable *adjective*
<u>memorable</u>, exceptional, impressive, notable

unforgivable *adjective*
<u>inexcusable</u>, deplorable, disgraceful, shameful, unpardonable

unfortunate *adjective*
1 <u>disastrous</u>, adverse, calamitous, ill-fated 2 <u>unlucky</u>, cursed, doomed, hapless, unhappy, unsuccessful, wretched
3 <u>regrettable</u>, deplorable, lamentable, unsuitable

unfounded *adjective* <u>groundless</u>, baseless, false, idle, spurious, unjustified

unfriendly *adjective* 1 <u>hostile</u>, aloof, chilly, cold, distant, uncongenial, unsociable
2 <u>unfavourable</u>, alien, hostile, inhospitable

ungainly *adjective* <u>awkward</u>, clumsy, inelegant, lumbering, ungraceful

ungodly *adjective* 1 *Informal* <u>unreasonable</u>, dreadful, intolerable, outrageous, unearthly 2 <u>wicked</u>, corrupt, depraved, godless, immoral, impious, irreligious, profane, sinful

ungracious *adjective*
<u>bad-mannered</u>, churlish, discourteous, impolite, rude, uncivil, unmannerly

ungrateful *adjective*
<u>unappreciative</u>, unmindful, unthankful

unguarded *adjective*
1 <u>unprotected</u>, defenceless, undefended, vulnerable
2 <u>careless</u>, heedless, ill-considered, imprudent, incautious, rash, thoughtless, unthinking, unwary

unhappiness *noun* <u>sadness</u>, blues, dejection, depression, despondency, gloom, heartache, low spirits, melancholy, misery, sorrow, wretchedness

unhappy *adjective* 1 <u>sad</u>, blue, dejected, depressed, despondent, downcast, melancholy, miserable, mournful, sorrowful 2 <u>unlucky</u>, cursed, hapless, ill-fated, unfortunate, wretched

unharmed *adjective* <u>unhurt</u>, intact, safe, sound, undamaged, unscathed, whole

unhealthy *adjective* 1 <u>harmful</u>, detrimental, insalubrious, insanitary, unwholesome 2 <u>sick</u>, ailing, delicate, feeble, frail, infirm, invalid, sickly, unwell

unheard-of *adjective*
1 <u>unprecedented</u>, inconceivable, new, novel, singular, unique
2 <u>shocking</u>, disgraceful, outrageous, preposterous
3 <u>obscure</u>, unfamiliar, unknown

unhesitating *adjective* 1 <u>instant</u>, immediate, prompt, ready
2 <u>wholehearted</u>, resolute, unfaltering, unquestioning, unreserved

unholy *adjective* <u>evil</u>, corrupt, profane, sinful, ungodly, wicked

unhurried *adjective* <u>leisurely</u>, easy, sedate, slow

unidentified *adjective* <u>unnamed</u>, anonymous, nameless, unfamiliar, unrecognized

unification *noun* <u>union</u>, alliance, amalgamation, coalescence, coalition, confederation, federation, uniting

uniform *noun* 1 <u>outfit</u>, costume, dress, garb, habit, livery, regalia, suit ♦ *adjective* 2 <u>unvarying</u>, consistent, constant, even, regular, smooth, unchanging 3 <u>alike</u>, equal, like, same, similar

uniformity *noun* 1 <u>regularity</u>, constancy, evenness, invariability, sameness, similarity 2 <u>monotony</u>, dullness, flatness, sameness, tedium

unify *verb* <u>unite</u>, amalgamate, combine, confederate, consolidate, join, merge

unimaginable *adjective* <u>inconceivable</u>, fantastic, impossible, incredible, unbelievable

unimaginative *adjective* <u>unoriginal</u>, banal, derivative, dull, hackneyed, ordinary, pedestrian, predictable, prosaic, uncreative, uninspired

unimportant *adjective* <u>insignificant</u>, inconsequential, irrelevant, minor, paltry, petty, trifling, trivial, worthless

uninhabited *adjective* <u>deserted</u>, barren, desolate, empty, unpopulated, vacant

uninhibited *adjective* 1 <u>unselfconscious</u>, free, liberated, natural, open, relaxed, spontaneous, unrepressed, unreserved 2 <u>unrestrained</u>, free, unbridled, unchecked, unconstrained, uncontrolled, unrestricted

uninspired *adjective* <u>unimaginative</u>, banal, dull, humdrum, ordinary, prosaic, unexciting, unoriginal

unintelligent *adjective* <u>stupid</u>, braindead (*informal*), brainless, dense, dull, foolish, gormless (*Brit. informal*), obtuse, slow, thick

unintelligible *adjective* <u>incomprehensible</u>, inarticulate, incoherent, indistinct, jumbled, meaningless, muddled

unintentional *adjective* <u>accidental</u>, casual, inadvertent, involuntary, unconscious, unintended

uninterested *adjective* <u>indifferent</u>, apathetic, blasé, bored, listless, unconcerned

uninteresting *adjective* <u>boring</u>, drab, dreary, dry, dull, flat, humdrum, monotonous, tedious, unexciting

uninterrupted *adjective* <u>continuous</u>, constant, nonstop, steady, sustained, unbroken

union *noun* 1 <u>joining</u>, amalgamation, blend, combination, conjunction, fusion, mixture, uniting 2 <u>alliance</u>, association, coalition, confederacy, federation, league 3 <u>agreement</u>, accord, concord, harmony, unanimity, unison, unity

unique *adjective* 1 <u>single</u>, lone, only, solitary 2 <u>unparalleled</u>, incomparable, inimitable, matchless, unequalled, unmatched, unrivalled

unison *noun* <u>agreement</u>, accord, concert, concord, harmony, unity

unit *noun* 1 <u>item</u>, entity, whole

2 part, component, constituent, element, member, section, segment 3 section, detachment, group 4 measure, measurement, quantity

unite verb 1 join, amalgamate, blend, combine, couple, fuse, link, merge, unify 2 cooperate, ally, band, join forces, pool

united adjective 1 combined, affiliated, allied, banded together, collective, concerted, pooled, unified 2 in agreement, agreed, of one mind, of the same opinion, unanimous

unity noun 1 wholeness, entity, integrity, oneness, singleness, union 2 agreement, accord, assent, concord, consensus, harmony, solidarity, unison

universal adjective widespread, common, general, total, unlimited, whole, worldwide

universally adverb everywhere, always, invariably, without exception

universe noun cosmos, creation, macrocosm, nature

unjust adjective unfair, biased, one-sided, partial, partisan, prejudiced, wrong, wrongful

unjustifiable adjective inexcusable, indefensible, outrageous, unacceptable, unforgivable, unpardonable, wrong

unkempt adjective 1 uncombed, shaggy, tousled 2 untidy, dishevelled, disordered, messy, scruffy, slovenly, ungroomed

unkind adjective cruel, harsh, malicious, mean, nasty, spiteful, uncharitable, unfeeling,

unfriendly, unsympathetic

unknown adjective 1 hidden, concealed, dark, mysterious, secret, unrevealed 2 strange, alien, new 3 unidentified, anonymous, nameless, uncharted, undiscovered, unexplored, unnamed
4 obscure, humble, unfamiliar

unlawful adjective illegal, banned, criminal, forbidden, illicit, outlawed, prohibited

unleash verb release, free, let go, let loose

unlike adjective different, dissimilar, distinct, diverse, not alike, opposite, unequal

unlikely adjective 1 improbable, doubtful, faint, remote, slight 2 unbelievable, implausible, incredible, questionable

unlimited adjective 1 infinite, boundless, countless, endless, extensive, great, immense, limitless, unbounded, vast 2 complete, absolute, full, total, unqualified, unrestricted

unload verb empty, discharge, dump, lighten, relieve, unpack

unlock verb open, release, undo, unfasten, unlatch

unlooked-for adjective unexpected, chance, fortuitous, surprising, unanticipated, unforeseen, unpredicted

unloved adjective neglected, forsaken, loveless, rejected, spurned, unpopular, unwanted

unlucky adjective 1 unfortunate, cursed, hapless, luckless, miserable, unhappy, wretched 2 ill-fated, doomed, inauspicious, ominous, unfavourable

unmarried *adjective* <u>single</u>, bachelor, maiden, unattached, unwed

unmask *verb* <u>reveal</u>, disclose, discover, expose, lay bare, uncover

unmentionable *adjective* <u>taboo</u>, forbidden, indecent, obscene, scandalous, shameful, shocking, unspeakable

unmerciful *adjective* <u>merciless</u>, brutal, cruel, hard, implacable, pitiless, remorseless, ruthless

unmistakable *adjective* <u>clear</u>, certain, distinct, evident, manifest, obvious, plain, sure, unambiguous

unmitigated *adjective* 1 <u>unrelieved</u>, intense, persistent, unalleviated, unbroken, undiminished 2 <u>complete</u>, absolute, arrant, downright, outright, sheer, thorough, utter

unmoved *adjective* <u>unaffected</u>, cold, impassive, indifferent, unimpressed, unresponsive, untouched

unnatural *adjective* 1 <u>strange</u>, extraordinary, freakish, outlandish, queer 2 <u>abnormal</u>, anomalous, irregular, odd, perverse, perverted, unusual 3 <u>false</u>, affected, artificial, feigned, forced, insincere, phoney *or* phony (*informal*), stiff, stilted

unnecessary *adjective* <u>needless</u>, expendable, inessential, redundant, superfluous, unneeded, unrequired

unnerve *verb* <u>intimidate</u>, demoralize, discourage, dishearten, dismay, faze, fluster, frighten, psych out (*informal*),

rattle (*informal*), shake, upset

unnoticed *adjective* <u>unobserved</u>, disregarded, ignored, neglected, overlooked, unheeded, unperceived, unrecognized, unseen

unobtrusive *adjective* <u>inconspicuous</u>, low-key, modest, quiet, restrained, retiring, self-effacing, unassuming

unoccupied *adjective* <u>empty</u>, uninhabited, vacant

unofficial *adjective* <u>unauthorized</u>, informal, private, unconfirmed

unorthodox *adjective* <u>unconventional</u>, abnormal, irregular, off-the-wall (*slang*), unusual

unpaid *adjective* 1 <u>voluntary</u>, honorary, unsalaried 2 <u>owing</u>, due, outstanding, overdue, payable, unsettled

unpalatable *adjective* <u>unpleasant</u>, disagreeable, distasteful, horrid, offensive, repugnant, unappetizing, unsavoury

unparalleled *adjective* <u>unequalled</u>, incomparable, matchless, superlative, unique, unmatched, unprecedented, unsurpassed

unpardonable *adjective* <u>unforgivable</u>, deplorable, disgraceful, indefensible, inexcusable

unperturbed *adjective* <u>calm</u>, as cool as a cucumber, composed, cool, placid, unfazed (*informal*), unruffled, untroubled, unworried

unpleasant *adjective* <u>nasty</u>, bad, disagreeable, displeasing, distasteful, horrid, objectionable

unpopular *adjective* <u>disliked</u>,

rejected, shunned, unwanted, unwelcome

unprecedented *adjective*
<u>extraordinary</u>, abnormal, new, novel, original, remarkable, singular, unheard-of

unpredictable *adjective*
<u>inconstant</u>, chance, changeable, doubtful, erratic, random, unforeseeable, unreliable, variable

unprejudiced *adjective* <u>impartial</u>, balanced, fair, just, objective, open-minded, unbiased

unprepared *adjective* 1 <u>taken off guard</u>, surprised, unaware, unready 2 <u>improvised</u>, ad-lib, off the cuff (*informal*), spontaneous

unpretentious *adjective* <u>modest</u>, humble, plain, simple, straightforward, unaffected, unassuming, unostentatious

unprincipled *adjective* <u>dishonest</u>, amoral, crooked, devious, immoral, underhand, unethical, unscrupulous

unproductive *adjective* 1 <u>useless</u>, fruitless, futile, idle, ineffective, unprofitable, unrewarding, vain 2 <u>barren</u>, fruitless, sterile

unprofessional *adjective*
1 <u>unethical</u>, improper, lax, negligent, unprincipled
2 <u>amateurish</u>, cowboy (*informal*), incompetent, inefficient, inexpert

unprotected *adjective* <u>vulnerable</u>, defenceless, helpless, open, undefended

unqualified *adjective* 1 <u>unfit</u>, ill-equipped, incapable, incompetent, ineligible, unprepared 2 <u>total</u>, absolute, complete, downright, outright, thorough, utter

unquestionable *adjective*
<u>certain</u>, absolute, clear, conclusive, definite, incontrovertible, indisputable, sure, undeniable, unequivocal, unmistakable

unravel *verb* 1 <u>undo</u>, disentangle, free, separate, untangle, unwind 2 <u>solve</u>, explain, figure out (*informal*), resolve, work out

unreal *adjective* 1 <u>imaginary</u>, dreamlike, fabulous, fanciful, illusory, make-believe, visionary 2 <u>insubstantial</u>, immaterial, intangible, nebulous 3 <u>fake</u>, artificial, false, insincere, mock, pretended, sham

unrealistic *adjective* <u>impractical</u>, impracticable, improbable, romantic, unworkable

unreasonable *adjective*
1 <u>excessive</u>, extortionate, immoderate, undue, unfair, unjust, unwarranted 2 <u>biased</u>, blinkered, opinionated

unrelated *adjective* 1 <u>different</u>, unconnected, unlike 2 <u>irrelevant</u>, extraneous, inapplicable, inappropriate, unconnected

unreliable *adjective*
1 <u>undependable</u>, irresponsible, treacherous, untrustworthy 2 <u>uncertain</u>, deceptive, fallible, false, implausible, inaccurate, unsound

unrepentant *adjective*
<u>impenitent</u>, abandoned, callous, hardened, incorrigible, shameless, unremorseful

unreserved *adjective* 1 <u>total</u>, absolute, complete, entire, full, unlimited, wholehearted 2 <u>open</u>, demonstrative, extrovert, free,

outgoing, uninhibited,
unrestrained

unresolved *adjective* undecided,
doubtful, moot, unanswered,
undetermined, unsettled,
unsolved, vague

unrest *noun* discontent,
agitation, discord, dissension,
protest, rebellion, sedition, strife

unrestrained *adjective*
uncontrolled, abandoned, free,
immoderate, intemperate,
unbounded, unbridled,
unchecked, uninhibited

unrestricted *adjective*
1 unlimited, absolute, free,
open, unbounded, unregulated
2 open, public

unrivalled *adjective* unparalleled,
beyond compare, incomparable,
matchless, supreme, unequalled,
unmatched, unsurpassed

unruly *adjective* uncontrollable,
disobedient, mutinous,
rebellious, wayward, wild, wilful

unsafe *adjective* dangerous,
hazardous, insecure, perilous,
risky, unreliable

unsatisfactory *adjective*
unacceptable, deficient,
disappointing, inadequate,
insufficient, not good enough,
not up to scratch (*informal*), poor

unsavoury *adjective*
1 unpleasant, distasteful, nasty,
obnoxious, offensive, repellent,
repulsive, revolting
2 unappetizing, nauseating,
sickening, unpalatable

unscathed *adjective* unharmed,
safe, unhurt, uninjured,
unmarked, whole

unscrupulous *adjective*

unprincipled, corrupt, dishonest,
dishonourable, immoral,
improper, unethical

unseat *verb* 1 throw, unhorse,
unsaddle 2 depose, dethrone,
displace, oust, overthrow, remove

unseemly *adjective* improper,
inappropriate, indecorous,
unbecoming, undignified,
unsuitable

unseen *adjective* unobserved,
concealed, hidden, invisible,
obscure, undetected, unnoticed

unselfish *adjective* generous,
altruistic, kind, magnanimous,
noble, selfless, self-sacrificing

unsettle *verb* disturb, agitate,
bother, confuse, disconcert, faze,
fluster, perturb, ruffle, trouble,
upset

unsettled *adjective* 1 unstable,
disorderly, insecure, shaky,
unsteady 2 restless, agitated,
anxious, confused, disturbed,
flustered, restive, shaken, tense
3 changing, inconstant,
uncertain, variable

unshakable *adjective* firm,
absolute, fixed, immovable,
staunch, steadfast, sure,
unswerving, unwavering

unsightly *adjective* ugly,
disagreeable, hideous, horrid,
repulsive, unattractive

unskilled *adjective*
unprofessional, amateurish,
cowboy (*informal*),
inexperienced, unqualified,
untrained

unsociable *adjective* unfriendly,
chilly, cold, distant, hostile,
retiring, unforthcoming,
withdrawn

unsolicited *adjective*
unrequested, gratuitous, unasked
for, uncalled-for, uninvited,
unsought

unsophisticated *adjective*
1 natural, artless, childlike,
guileless, ingenuous, unaffected
2 simple, plain, uncomplicated,
unrefined, unspecialized

unsound *adjective* 1 unhealthy,
ailing, defective, diseased, ill,
unbalanced, unstable, unwell,
weak 2 unreliable, defective,
fallacious, false, flawed, illogical,
shaky, specious, weak

unspeakable *adjective*
1 indescribable, inconceivable,
unbelievable, unimaginable
2 dreadful, abominable,
appalling, awful, heinous,
horrible, monstrous, shocking

unspoiled, unspoilt *adjective*
1 perfect, intact, preserved,
unchanged, undamaged,
untouched 2 natural, artless,
innocent, unaffected

unspoken *adjective* tacit, implicit,
implied, understood,
unexpressed, unstated

unstable *adjective* 1 insecure,
precarious, shaky, tottering,
unsettled, unsteady, wobbly
2 changeable, fitful, fluctuating,
inconstant, unpredictable,
variable, volatile 3 unpredictable,
capricious, changeable, erratic,
inconsistent, irrational,
temperamental

unsteady *adjective* 1 unstable,
infirm, insecure, precarious,
shaky, unsafe, wobbly
2 changeable, erratic,
inconstant, temperamental,
unsettled, volatile

unsuccessful *adjective* 1 useless,
failed, fruitless, futile, unavailing,
unproductive, vain 2 unlucky,
hapless, luckless, unfortunate

unsuitable *adjective*
inappropriate, improper,
inapposite, inapt, ineligible,
unacceptable, unbecoming,
unfit, unfitting, unseemly

unsure *adjective* 1 unconfident,
insecure, unassured 2 doubtful,
distrustful, dubious, hesitant,
mistrustful, sceptical, suspicious,
unconvinced

unsuspecting *adjective* trusting,
credulous, gullible, trustful,
unwary

unswerving *adjective* constant,
firm, resolute, single-minded,
staunch, steadfast, steady, true,
unwavering

unsympathetic *adjective* hard,
callous, cold, cruel, harsh,
heartless, insensitive, unfeeling,
unkind, unmoved

untangle *verb* disentangle,
extricate, unravel, unsnarl

untenable *adjective*
unsustainable, groundless,
illogical, indefensible,
insupportable, shaky, unsound,
weak

unthinkable *adjective*
1 impossible, absurd, out of the
question, unreasonable
2 inconceivable, implausible,
incredible, unimaginable

untidy *adjective* messy, chaotic,
cluttered, disarrayed, disordered,
jumbled, littered, muddled,
shambolic, unkempt

untie *verb* undo, free, loosen,
release, unbind, unfasten, unlace

untimely *adjective* **1** early, premature **2** ill-timed, awkward, inappropriate, inconvenient, inopportune, mistimed

untiring *adjective* tireless, constant, determined, dogged, persevering, steady, unflagging, unremitting

untold *adjective* **1** indescribable, inexpressible, undreamed of, unimaginable, unthinkable, unutterable **2** countless, incalculable, innumerable, myriad, numberless, uncountable

untouched *adjective* unharmed, intact, undamaged, unhurt, uninjured, unscathed

untoward *adjective* **1** annoying, awkward, inconvenient, irritating, troublesome, unfortunate **2** unlucky, adverse, inauspicious, inopportune, unfavourable

untrained *adjective* amateur, green, inexperienced, raw, uneducated, unqualified, unschooled, unskilled, untaught

untroubled *adjective* undisturbed, calm, cool, peaceful, placid, tranquil, unfazed (*informal*), unperturbed, unworried

untrue *adjective* **1** false, deceptive, dishonest, erroneous, inaccurate, incorrect, lying, mistaken, wrong **2** unfaithful, deceitful, disloyal, faithless, false, inconstant, treacherous, untrustworthy

untrustworthy *adjective* unreliable, deceitful, devious, dishonest, disloyal, false, slippery, treacherous, tricky

untruth *noun* lie, deceit, falsehood, fib, pork pie (*Brit. slang*), porky (*Brit. slang*), story

untruthful *adjective* dishonest, deceitful, deceptive, false, lying, mendacious

unusual *adjective* extraordinary, curious, different, exceptional, odd, queer, rare, remarkable, singular, strange, uncommon, unconventional

unveil *verb* reveal, disclose, divulge, expose, make known, uncover

unwanted *adjective* undesired, outcast, rejected, uninvited, unneeded, unsolicited, unwelcome

unwarranted *adjective* unnecessary, gratuitous, groundless, indefensible, inexcusable, uncalled-for, unjustified, unprovoked

unwavering *adjective* steady, consistent, determined, immovable, resolute, staunch, steadfast, unshakable, unswerving

unwelcome *adjective* **1** unwanted, excluded, rejected, unacceptable, undesirable **2** disagreeable, displeasing, distasteful, undesirable, unpleasant

unwell *adjective* ill, ailing, sick, sickly, under the weather (*informal*), unhealthy

unwholesome *adjective* **1** harmful, deleterious, noxious, poisonous, unhealthy **2** wicked, bad, corrupting, degrading, demoralizing, evil, immoral

unwieldy *adjective* **1** awkward, cumbersome, inconvenient, unmanageable **2** bulky, clumsy, hefty, massive, ponderous

unwilling *adjective* <u>reluctant</u>, averse, disinclined, grudging, indisposed, loath, resistant, unenthusiastic

unwind *verb* **1** <u>unravel</u>, slacken, uncoil, undo, unroll, untwine, untwist **2** <u>relax</u>, loosen up, take it easy, wind down

unwise *adjective* <u>foolish</u>, foolhardy, improvident, imprudent, inadvisable, injudicious, rash, reckless, senseless, silly, stupid

unwitting *adjective* **1** <u>unintentional</u>, accidental, chance, inadvertent, involuntary, unplanned **2** <u>unknowing</u>, ignorant, innocent, unaware, unconscious, unsuspecting

unworldly *adjective* **1** <u>spiritual</u>, metaphysical, nonmaterialistic **2** <u>naive</u>, idealistic, innocent, unsophisticated

unworthy *adjective* **1** <u>undeserving</u>, not fit for, not good enough **2** <u>dishonourable</u>, base, contemptible, degrading, discreditable, disgraceful, disreputable, ignoble, shameful **3** **unworthy of** <u>unbefitting</u>, beneath, inappropriate, unbecoming, unfitting, unseemly, unsuitable

unwritten *adjective* **1** <u>oral</u>, vocal **2** <u>customary</u>, accepted, tacit, understood

unyielding *adjective* <u>firm</u>, adamant, immovable, inflexible, obdurate, obstinate, resolute, rigid, stiff-necked, stubborn, tough, uncompromising

upbeat *adjective Informal* <u>cheerful</u>, cheery, encouraging, hopeful, optimistic, positive

upbraid *verb* <u>scold</u>, admonish, berate, rebuke, reprimand, reproach, reprove

upbringing *noun* <u>education</u>, breeding, raising, rearing, training

update *verb* <u>revise</u>, amend, bring up to date, modernize, renew

upgrade *verb* <u>promote</u>, advance, better, elevate, enhance, improve, raise

upheaval *noun* <u>disturbance</u>, disorder, disruption, revolution, turmoil

uphill *adjective* **1** <u>ascending</u>, climbing, mounting, rising **2** <u>arduous</u>, difficult, exhausting, gruelling, hard, laborious, strenuous, taxing, tough

uphold *verb* <u>support</u>, advocate, aid, back, champion, defend, endorse, maintain, promote, sustain

upkeep *noun* **1** <u>maintenance</u>, keep, repair, running, subsistence **2** <u>overheads</u>, expenditure, expenses, running costs

uplift *verb* **1** <u>raise</u>, elevate, hoist, lift up **2** <u>improve</u>, advance, better, edify, inspire, raise, refine ◆ *noun* **3** <u>improvement</u>, advancement, edification, enhancement, enlightenment, enrichment, refinement

upper *adjective* **1** <u>higher</u>, high, loftier, top, topmost **2** <u>superior</u>, eminent, greater, important

upper-class *adjective* <u>aristocratic</u>, blue-blooded, highborn, high-class, noble, patrician

upper hand *noun* <u>control</u>,

advantage, ascendancy, edge, mastery, supremacy

uppermost *adjective* 1 <u>top</u>, highest, loftiest, topmost 2 <u>supreme</u>, chief, dominant, foremost, greatest, leading, main, principal

uppity *adjective Informal* <u>conceited</u>, bumptious, cocky, full of oneself, impertinent, self-important, uppish (*Brit. informal*)

upright *adjective* 1 <u>vertical</u>, erect, perpendicular, straight 2 <u>honest</u>, conscientious, ethical, good, honourable, just, principled, righteous, virtuous

uprising *noun* <u>rebellion</u>, disturbance, insurgence, insurrection, mutiny, revolt, revolution, rising

uproar *noun* <u>commotion</u>, din, furore, mayhem, noise, outcry, pandemonium, racket, riot, turmoil

uproarious *adjective* 1 <u>hilarious</u>, hysterical, killing (*informal*), rib-tickling, rip-roaring (*informal*), side-splitting, very funny 2 <u>loud</u>, boisterous, rollicking, unrestrained

uproot *verb* 1 <u>pull up</u>, dig up, rip up, root out, weed out 2 <u>displace</u>, exile

upset *adjective* 1 <u>sick</u>, ill, queasy 2 <u>distressed</u>, agitated, bothered, dismayed, disturbed, grieved, hurt, put out, troubled, worried 3 <u>disordered</u>, chaotic, confused, disarrayed, in disarray, muddled 4 <u>overturned</u>, capsized, spilled, upside down ♦ *verb* 5 <u>tip over</u>, capsize, knock over, overturn, spill 6 <u>mess up</u>, change,

disorder, disorganize, disturb, spoil 7 <u>distress</u>, agitate, bother, disconcert, disturb, faze, fluster, grieve, perturb, ruffle, trouble ♦ *noun* 8 <u>reversal</u>, defeat, shake-up (*informal*) 9 <u>illness</u>, bug (*informal*), complaint, disorder, malady, sickness 10 <u>distress</u>, agitation, bother, disturbance, shock, trouble, worry

upshot *noun* <u>result</u>, culmination, end, end result, finale, outcome, sequel

upside down *adjective* 1 <u>inverted</u>, overturned, upturned 2 *Informal* <u>confused</u>, chaotic, disordered, higgledy-piggledy (*informal*), muddled, topsy-turvy

upstanding *adjective* <u>honest</u>, ethical, good, honourable, incorruptible, moral, principled, upright

upstart *noun* <u>social climber</u>, arriviste, *nouveau riche*, parvenu

uptight *adjective Informal* <u>tense</u>, anxious, edgy, on edge, uneasy, wired (*slang*)

up-to-date *adjective* <u>modern</u>, current, fashionable, in vogue, stylish, trendy (*Brit. informal*), up-to-the-minute

upturn *noun* <u>rise</u>, advancement, improvement, increase, recovery, revival, upsurge, upswing

urban *adjective* <u>civic</u>, city, metropolitan, municipal, town

urbane *adjective* <u>sophisticated</u>, courteous, cultivated, cultured, debonair, polished, refined, smooth, suave, well-bred

urchin *noun* <u>ragamuffin</u>, brat, gamin, waif

urge *noun* 1 <u>impulse</u>,

compulsion, desire, drive, itch, longing, thirst, wish, yearning ♦ *verb* 2 beg, beseech, entreat, exhort, implore, plead 3 advocate, advise, counsel, recommend, support 4 drive, compel, force, goad, impel, incite, induce, press, push, spur

urgency *noun* importance, extremity, gravity, hurry, necessity, need, pressure, seriousness

urgent *adjective* crucial, compelling, critical, immediate, imperative, important, pressing

usable *adjective* serviceable, available, current, functional, practical, utilizable, valid, working

usage *noun* 1 use, control, employment, handling, management, operation, running 2 practice, convention, custom, habit, method, mode, procedure, regime, routine

use *verb* 1 employ, apply, exercise, exert, operate, practise, utilize, work 2 take advantage of, exploit, manipulate 3 consume, exhaust, expend, run through, spend ♦ *noun* 4 usage, application, employment, exercise, handling, operation, practice, service 5 good, advantage, avail, benefit, help, point, profit, service, usefulness, value 6 purpose, end, object, reason

used *adjective* second-hand, cast-off, nearly new, shopsoiled

used to *adjective* accustomed to, familiar with

useful *adjective* helpful, advantageous, beneficial, effective, fruitful, practical, profitable, serviceable, valuable, worthwhile

usefulness *noun* helpfulness, benefit, convenience, effectiveness, efficacy, practicality, use, utility, value, worth

useless *adjective* 1 worthless, fruitless, futile, impractical, ineffectual, pointless, unproductive, vain, valueless 2 *Informal* inept, hopeless, incompetent, ineffectual, no good

use up *verb* consume, absorb, drain, exhaust, finish, run through

usher *noun* 1 attendant, doorkeeper, doorman, escort, guide ♦ *verb* 2 escort, conduct, direct, guide, lead

usual *adjective* normal, common, customary, everyday, general, habitual, ordinary, regular, routine, standard, typical

usually *adverb* normally, as a rule, commonly, generally, habitually, mainly, mostly, on the whole

usurp *verb* seize, appropriate, assume, commandeer, take, take over, wrest

utility *noun* usefulness, benefit, convenience, efficacy, practicality, serviceableness

utilize *verb* use, avail oneself of, employ, make use of, put to use, take advantage of, turn to account

utmost *adjective* 1 greatest, chief, highest, maximum, paramount, pre-eminent, supreme 2 farthest, extreme, final, last ♦ *noun* 3 greatest, best, hardest, highest

Utopia *noun* paradise, bliss, Eden, Garden of Eden, heaven, Shangri-la

Utopian *adjective* perfect, dream, fantasy, ideal, idealistic, imaginary, romantic, visionary

utter[1] *verb* express, articulate, pronounce, say, speak, voice

utter[2] *adjective* absolute, complete, downright, outright, sheer, thorough, total, unmitigated

utterance *noun* speech, announcement, declaration, expression, remark, statement, words

utterly *adverb* totally, absolutely, completely, entirely, extremely, fully, perfectly, thoroughly

V v

vacancy *noun* job, opening, opportunity, position, post, situation

vacant *adjective* 1 unoccupied, available, empty, free, idle, unfilled, untenanted, void 2 vague, absent-minded, abstracted, blank, dreamy, idle, inane, vacuous

vacate *verb* leave, evacuate, quit

vacuous *adjective* unintelligent, blank, inane, stupid, uncomprehending, vacant

vacuum *noun* emptiness, gap, nothingness, space, vacuity, void

vagabond *noun* beggar, down-and-out, itinerant, rover, tramp, vagrant

vagrant *noun* 1 tramp, drifter, hobo (*U.S.*), itinerant, rolling stone, wanderer ♦ *adjective* 2 itinerant, nomadic, roaming, rootless, roving, unsettled, vagabond

vague *adjective* unclear, hazy, ill-defined, imprecise, indefinite, indeterminate, indistinct, loose, nebulous, uncertain, unspecified

vain *adjective* proud, arrogant, conceited, egotistical, narcissistic, self-important, swaggering 2 futile, abortive, fruitless, idle, pointless, senseless, unavailing, unprofitable, useless, worthless ♦ *noun* 3 **in vain** to no avail, fruitless(ly), ineffectual(ly), unsuccessful(ly), useless(ly), vain(ly)

valiant *adjective* brave, bold, courageous, fearless, gallant, heroic, intrepid, lion-hearted

valid *adjective* 1 logical, cogent, convincing, good, sound, telling, well founded, well-grounded 2 legal, authentic, bona fide, genuine, lawful, legitimate, official

validate *verb* confirm, authenticate, authorize, certify, corroborate, endorse, ratify, substantiate

validity *noun* 1 soundness, cogency, force, power, strength, weight 2 legality, authority, lawfulness, legitimacy, right

valley *noun* hollow, dale, dell, depression, glen, vale

valour *noun* bravery, boldness, courage, fearlessness, gallantry, heroism, intrepidity, spirit

valuable *adjective* **1** precious, costly, dear, expensive, high-priced **2** useful, beneficial, helpful, important, prized, profitable, worthwhile ♦ *noun* **3 valuables** treasures, heirlooms

value *noun* **1** importance, advantage, benefit, desirability, merit, profit, usefulness, utility, worth **2** cost, market price, rate **3 values** principles, ethics, (moral) standards ♦ *verb* **4** evaluate, appraise, assess, estimate, price, rate, set at **5** respect, appreciate, cherish, esteem, hold dear, prize, regard highly, treasure

vandal *noun* hooligan, delinquent, rowdy, yob *or* yobbo (*Brit. slang*)

vanguard *noun* forerunners, cutting edge, forefront, front line, leaders, spearhead, trailblazers, trendsetters, van

vanish *verb* disappear, dissolve, evanesce, evaporate, fade (away), melt (away)

vanity *noun* pride, arrogance, conceit, conceitedness, egotism, narcissism

vanquish *verb Literary* defeat, beat, conquer, crush, master, overcome, overpower, overwhelm, triumph over

vapid *adjective* dull, bland, boring, flat, insipid, tame, uninspiring, uninteresting, weak, wishy-washy (*informal*)

vapour *noun* mist, exhalation, fog, haze, steam

variable *adjective* changeable, flexible, fluctuating, inconstant, mutable, shifting, temperamental, uneven,

unstable, unsteady

variance *noun* **at variance** in disagreement, at loggerheads, at odds, at sixes and sevens (*informal*), conflicting, out of line

variant *adjective* **1** different, alternative, divergent, modified ♦ *noun* **2** variation, alternative, development, modification

variation *noun* difference, change, departure, deviation, diversity, innovation, modification, novelty, variety

varied *adjective* different, assorted, diverse, heterogeneous, miscellaneous, mixed, motley, sundry, various

variety *noun* **1** diversity, change, difference, discrepancy, diversification, multifariousness, variation **2** range, array, assortment, collection, cross section, medley, miscellany, mixture **3** type, brand, breed, category, class, kind, sort, species, strain

various *adjective* different, assorted, disparate, distinct, diverse, miscellaneous, several, sundry, varied

varnish *noun, verb* polish, glaze, gloss, lacquer

vary *verb* change, alter, differ, disagree, diverge, fluctuate

vast *adjective* huge, boundless, colossal, enormous, gigantic, great, immense, massive, monumental, wide

vault[1] *noun* **1** strongroom, depository, repository **2** crypt, catacomb, cellar, charnel house, mausoleum, tomb, undercroft

vault[2] *verb* jump, bound, clear,

hurdle, leap, spring

vaulted *adjective* <u>arched</u>, cavernous, domed

veer *verb* <u>swerve</u>, change course, change direction, sheer, shift, turn

vegetate *verb* <u>stagnate</u>, deteriorate, go to seed, idle, languish, loaf

vehemence *noun* <u>forcefulness</u>, ardour, emphasis, energy, fervour, force, intensity, passion, vigour

vehement *adjective* <u>strong</u>, ardent, emphatic, fervent, fierce, forceful, impassioned, intense, passionate, powerful

vehicle *noun* 1 <u>transport</u>, conveyance, transportation 2 <u>medium</u>, apparatus, channel, means, mechanism, organ

veil *noun* 1 <u>cover</u>, blind, cloak, curtain, disguise, film, mask, screen, shroud ♦ *verb* 2 <u>cover</u>, cloak, conceal, disguise, hide, mask, obscure, screen, shield

veiled *adjective* <u>disguised</u>, concealed, covert, hinted at, implied, masked, suppressed

vein *noun* 1 <u>blood vessel</u> 2 <u>seam</u>, course, current, lode, stratum, streak, stripe 3 <u>mood</u>, mode, note, style, temper, tenor, tone

velocity *noun* <u>speed</u>, pace, quickness, rapidity, swiftness

velvety *adjective* <u>smooth</u>, delicate, downy, soft

vendetta *noun* <u>feud</u>, bad blood, quarrel

veneer *noun* <u>mask</u>, appearance, façade, front, guise, pretence, semblance, show

venerable *adjective* <u>respected</u>, august, esteemed, honoured, revered, sage, wise, worshipped

venerate *verb* <u>respect</u>, adore, esteem, honour, look up to, revere, reverence, worship

vengeance *noun* <u>revenge</u>, reprisal, requital, retaliation, retribution

venom *noun* 1 <u>malice</u>, acrimony, bitterness, hate, rancour, spite, spleen, virulence 2 <u>poison</u>, bane, toxin

venomous *adjective* 1 <u>malicious</u>, hostile, malignant, rancorous, savage, spiteful, vicious, vindictive 2 <u>poisonous</u>, mephitic, noxious, toxic, virulent

vent *noun* 1 <u>outlet</u>, aperture, duct, opening, orifice ♦ *verb* 2 <u>express</u>, air, discharge, emit, give vent to, pour out, release, utter, voice

venture *noun* 1 <u>undertaking</u>, adventure, endeavour, enterprise, gamble, hazard, project, risk ♦ *verb* 2 <u>risk</u>, chance, hazard, speculate, stake, wager 3 <u>dare</u>, hazard, make bold, presume, take the liberty, volunteer 4 <u>go</u>, embark on, plunge into, set out

verbal *adjective* <u>spoken</u>, oral, unwritten, word-of-mouth

verbatim *adverb* <u>exactly</u>, precisely, to the letter, word for word

verbose *adjective* <u>long-winded</u>, circumlocutory, diffuse, periphrastic, prolix, tautological, windy, wordy

verbosity *noun* <u>long-windedness</u>, loquaciousness, prolixity, verboseness, wordiness

verdant *adjective* <u>green</u>, flourishing, fresh, grassy, leafy, lush

verdict *noun* <u>decision</u>, adjudication, conclusion, finding, judgment, opinion, sentence

verge *noun* 1 <u>border</u>, boundary, brim, brink, edge, limit, margin, threshold ♦ *verb* 2 **verge on** <u>border</u>, approach, come near

verification *noun* <u>proof</u>, authentication, confirmation, corroboration, substantiation, validation

verify *verb* <u>check</u>, authenticate, bear out, confirm, corroborate, prove, substantiate, support, validate

vernacular *noun* <u>dialect</u>, idiom, parlance, patois, speech

versatile *adjective* <u>adaptable</u>, adjustable, all-purpose, all-round, flexible, multifaceted, resourceful, variable

versed *adjective* <u>knowledgeable</u>, acquainted, conversant, experienced, familiar, practised, proficient, seasoned, well informed

version *noun* 1 <u>form</u>, design, model, style, variant 2 <u>account</u>, adaptation, interpretation, portrayal, rendering

vertical *adjective* <u>upright</u>, erect, on end, perpendicular

vertigo *noun* <u>dizziness</u>, giddiness, light-headedness

verve *noun* <u>enthusiasm</u>, animation, energy, gusto, liveliness, sparkle, spirit, vitality

very *adverb* 1 <u>extremely</u>, acutely, decidedly, deeply, exceedingly, greatly, highly, profoundly, uncommonly, unusually ♦ *adjective* 2 <u>exact</u>, precise, selfsame

vessel *noun* 1 <u>ship</u>, boat, craft 2 <u>container</u>, pot, receptacle, utensil

vest *verb*, *with* **in** *or* **with** <u>place</u>, bestow, confer, consign, endow, entrust, invest, settle

vestibule *noun* <u>hall</u>, anteroom, foyer, lobby, porch, portico

vestige *noun* <u>trace</u>, glimmer, indication, remnant, scrap, suspicion

vet *verb* <u>check</u>, appraise, examine, investigate, review, scrutinize

veteran *noun* 1 <u>old hand</u>, old stager, past master, warhorse (*informal*) ♦ *adjective* 2 <u>long-serving</u>, battle-scarred, old, seasoned

veto *noun* 1 <u>ban</u>, boycott, embargo, interdict, prohibition ♦ *verb* 2 <u>ban</u>, boycott, disallow, forbid, prohibit, reject, rule out, turn down

vex *verb* <u>annoy</u>, bother, distress, exasperate, irritate, plague, trouble, upset, worry

vexation *noun* 1 <u>annoyance</u>, chagrin, displeasure, dissatisfaction, exasperation, frustration, irritation, pique 2 <u>problem</u>, bother, difficulty, hassle (*informal*), headache (*informal*), nuisance, trouble, worry

viable *adjective* <u>workable</u>, applicable, feasible, operable, practicable, usable

vibrant *adjective* <u>energetic</u>, alive, animated, dynamic, sparkling, spirited, vigorous, vivacious, vivid

vibrate verb shake, fluctuate, judder (informal), oscillate, pulsate, quiver, reverberate, sway, throb, tremble

vibration noun tremor, judder (informal), oscillation, pulsation, quiver, reverberation, shake, throbbing, trembling

vicarious adjective indirect, delegated, substituted, surrogate

vice noun 1 wickedness, corruption, depravity, evil, immorality, iniquity, sin, turpitude 2 fault, blemish, defect, failing, imperfection, shortcoming, weakness

vice versa adverb conversely, contrariwise, in reverse, the other way round

vicinity noun neighbourhood, area, district, environs, locality, neck of the woods (informal), proximity

vicious adjective 1 violent, barbarous, cruel, ferocious, savage, wicked 2 malicious, cruel, mean, spiteful, venomous, vindictive

victim noun casualty, fatality, martyr, sacrifice, scapegoat, sufferer

victimize verb persecute, discriminate against, have it in for (someone) (informal), pick on

victor noun winner, champion, conqueror, prizewinner, vanquisher

victorious adjective winning, champion, conquering, first, prizewinning, successful, triumphant, vanquishing

victory noun win, conquest, success, triumph

vie verb compete, contend, strive, struggle

view noun 1 sometimes plural opinion, attitude, belief, conviction, feeling, impression, point of view, sentiment 2 scene, landscape, outlook, panorama, perspective, picture, prospect, spectacle, vista 3 vision, sight ♦ verb 4 regard, consider, deem, look on

viewer noun watcher, observer, onlooker, spectator

vigilance noun watchfulness, alertness, attentiveness, carefulness, caution, circumspection, observance

vigilant adjective watchful, alert, attentive, careful, cautious, circumspect, on one's guard, on the lookout, wakeful

vigorous adjective energetic, active, dynamic, forceful, lively, lusty, powerful, spirited, strenuous, strong

vigorously adverb energetically, forcefully, hard, lustily, strenuously, strongly

vigour noun energy, animation, dynamism, forcefulness, gusto, liveliness, power, spirit, strength, verve, vitality

vile adjective 1 wicked, corrupt, degenerate, depraved, evil, nefarious, perverted 2 disgusting, foul, horrid, nasty, nauseating, offensive, repugnant, repulsive, revolting, sickening

vilify verb malign, abuse, berate, denigrate, disparage, revile, slander, smear

villain noun 1 evildoer,

blackguard, criminal, miscreant, reprobate, rogue, scoundrel, wretch 2 <u>antihero</u>, baddy (*informal*)

villainous *adjective* <u>wicked</u>, bad, cruel, degenerate, depraved, evil, fiendish, nefarious, vicious, vile

villainy *noun* <u>wickedness</u>, delinquency, depravity, devilry, iniquity, turpitude, vice

vindicate *verb* 1 <u>clear</u>, absolve, acquit, exculpate, exonerate, rehabilitate 2 <u>justify</u>, defend, excuse

vindication *noun* 1 <u>exoneration</u>, exculpation, rehabilitation 2 <u>justification</u>, defence, excuse

vindictive *adjective* <u>vengeful</u>, implacable, malicious, resentful, revengeful, spiteful, unforgiving, unrelenting

vintage *adjective* <u>best</u>, choice, classic, prime, select, superior

violate *verb* 1 <u>break</u>, contravene, disobey, disregard, encroach upon, infringe, transgress 2 <u>desecrate</u>, abuse, befoul, defile, dishonour, pollute, profane 3 <u>rape</u>, abuse, assault, debauch, ravish

violation *noun* 1 <u>infringement</u>, abuse, breach, contravention, encroachment, infraction, transgression, trespass 2 <u>desecration</u>, defilement, profanation, sacrilege, spoliation

violence *noun* 1 <u>force</u>, bloodshed, brutality, cruelty, ferocity, fighting, savagery, terrorism 2 <u>intensity</u>, abandon, fervour, force, severity, vehemence

violent *adjective* <u>destructive</u>, brutal, cruel, hot-headed, murderous, riotous, savage, uncontrollable, unrestrained, vicious

V.I.P. *noun* <u>celebrity</u>, big name, luminary, somebody, star

virgin *noun* 1 <u>maiden</u>, girl ♦ *adjective* 2 <u>pure</u>, chaste, immaculate, uncorrupted, undefiled, vestal, virginal

virginity *noun* <u>chastity</u>, maidenhood

virile *adjective* <u>manly</u>, lusty, macho, manlike, masculine, red-blooded, strong, vigorous

virility *noun* <u>masculinity</u>, machismo, manhood, vigour

virtual *adjective* <u>practical</u>, essential, in all but name

virtually *adverb* <u>practically</u>, almost, as good as, in all but name, in effect, in essence, nearly

virtue *noun* 1 <u>goodness</u>, incorruptibility, integrity, morality, probity, rectitude, righteousness, uprightness, worth 2 <u>merit</u>, advantage, asset, attribute, credit, good point, plus (*informal*), strength

virtuosity *noun* <u>mastery</u>, brilliance, craft, expertise, flair, panache, polish, skill

virtuoso *noun* <u>master</u>, artist, genius, maestro, magician

virtuous *adjective* <u>good</u>, ethical, honourable, incorruptible, moral, praiseworthy, righteous, upright, worthy

virulent *adjective* <u>poisonous</u>, deadly, lethal, pernicious, toxic, venomous

viscous *adjective* <u>thick</u>,

gelatinous, sticky, syrupy

visible *adjective* apparent, clear, discernible, evident, in view, manifest, observable, perceptible, unconcealed

vision *noun* 1 sight, eyesight, perception, seeing, view 2 image, concept, conception, daydream, dream, fantasy, idea, ideal 3 hallucination, apparition, chimera, delusion, illusion, mirage, revelation 4 foresight, discernment, farsightedness, imagination, insight, intuition, penetration, prescience

visionary *adjective* 1 prophetic, mystical 2 impractical, idealistic, quixotic, romantic, speculative, starry-eyed, unrealistic, unworkable, utopian ◆ *noun* 3 prophet, mystic, seer

visit *verb* 1 call on, drop in on (*informal*), look (someone) up, stay with, stop by ◆ *noun* 2 call, sojourn, stay, stop

visitation *noun* 1 inspection, examination, visit 2 catastrophe, blight, calamity, cataclysm, disaster, ordeal, punishment, scourge

visitor *noun* guest, caller, company

vista *noun* view, panorama, perspective, prospect

visual *adjective* 1 optical, ocular, optic 2 observable, discernible, perceptible, visible

visualize *verb* picture, conceive of, envisage, imagine

vital *adjective* 1 essential, basic, fundamental, imperative, indispensable, necessary, requisite 2 important, critical,

crucial, decisive, key, life-or-death, significant, urgent 3 lively, animated, dynamic, energetic, spirited, vibrant, vigorous, vivacious, zestful

vitality *noun* energy, animation, exuberance, life, liveliness, strength, vigour, vivacity

vitriolic *adjective* bitter, acerbic, caustic, envenomed, sardonic, scathing, venomous, virulent, withering

vivacious *adjective* lively, bubbling, ebullient, high-spirited, sparkling, spirited, sprightly, upbeat (*informal*), vital

vivacity *noun* liveliness, animation, ebullience, energy, gaiety, high spirits, sparkle, spirit, sprightliness

vivid *adjective* 1 bright, brilliant, clear, colourful, glowing, intense, rich 2 lifelike, dramatic, graphic, memorable, powerful, realistic, stirring, telling, true to life

vocabulary *noun* words, dictionary, glossary, language, lexicon

vocal *adjective* 1 spoken, oral, said, uttered, voiced 2 outspoken, articulate, eloquent, expressive, forthright, frank, plain-spoken, strident, vociferous

vocation *noun* profession, calling, career, job, mission, pursuit, trade

vociferous *adjective* noisy, clamorous, loud, outspoken, strident, uproarious, vehement, vocal

vogue *noun* 1 fashion, craze,

custom, mode, style, trend, way
2 *As in* **in vogue** <u>popularity</u>,
acceptance, currency, favour,
prevalence, usage, use

voice *noun* 1 <u>sound</u>, articulation,
tone, utterance 2 <u>say</u>, view,
vote, will, wish ♦ *verb* 3 <u>express</u>,
air, articulate, declare, enunciate,
utter

void *noun* 1 <u>emptiness</u>,
blankness, gap, lack, space,
vacuity, vacuum ♦ *adjective*
2 <u>invalid</u>, ineffective, inoperative,
null and void, useless, vain,
worthless 3 <u>empty</u>, bare, free,
tenantless, unfilled, unoccupied,
vacant ♦ *verb* 4 <u>invalidate</u>,
cancel, nullify, rescind 5 <u>empty</u>,
drain, evacuate

volatile *adjective* 1 <u>changeable</u>,
explosive, inconstant, unsettled,
unstable, unsteady, variable
2 <u>temperamental</u>, erratic, fickle,
mercurial, up and down (*informal*)

volition *noun* <u>free will</u>, choice,
choosing, discretion, preference,
will

volley *noun* <u>barrage</u>, blast,
bombardment, burst,
cannonade, fusillade, hail, salvo,
shower

voluble *adjective* <u>talkative</u>,
articulate, fluent, forthcoming,
glib, loquacious

volume *noun* 1 <u>capacity</u>,
compass, dimensions 2 <u>amount</u>,
aggregate, body, bulk, mass,
quantity, total 3 <u>book</u>,
publication, title, tome, treatise

voluminous *adjective* <u>large</u>,
ample, capacious, cavernous,
roomy, vast

voluntarily *adverb* <u>willingly</u>, by
choice, freely, off one's own bat,

of one's own accord

voluntary *adjective* <u>unforced</u>,
discretionary, free, optional,
spontaneous, willing

volunteer *verb* <u>offer</u>, step forward.

voluptuous *adjective* 1 <u>buxom</u>,
ample, curvaceous (*informal*),
enticing, seductive, shapely
2 <u>sensual</u>, epicurean, hedonistic,
licentious, luxurious,
self-indulgent, sybaritic

vomit *verb* <u>be sick</u>, disgorge,
emit, heave, regurgitate, retch,
spew out *or* up, throw up
(*informal*)

voracious *adjective* 1 <u>gluttonous</u>,
greedy, hungry, insatiable,
omnivorous, ravenous 2 <u>avid</u>,
hungry, insatiable, rapacious,
uncontrolled, unquenchable

vortex *noun* <u>whirlpool</u>, eddy,
maelstrom

vote *noun* 1 <u>poll</u>, ballot,
franchise, plebiscite, referendum,
show of hands ♦ *verb* 2 <u>elect</u>,
cast one's vote, opt

voucher *noun* <u>ticket</u>, coupon,
token

vouch for *verb* 1 <u>guarantee</u>,
answer for, certify, give
assurance of, stand witness,
swear to 2 <u>confirm</u>, affirm,
assert, attest to, support, uphold

vow *noun* 1 <u>promise</u>, oath,
pledge ♦ *verb* 2 <u>promise</u>, affirm,
pledge, swear

voyage *noun* <u>journey</u>, crossing,
cruise, passage, trip

vulgar *adjective* <u>crude</u>, coarse,
common, impolite, indecent,
ribald, risqué, rude, tasteless,
uncouth, unrefined

vulgarity *noun* <u>crudeness</u>, bad

taste, coarseness, indelicacy, ribaldry, rudeness, tastelessness

vulnerable *adjective* 1 <u>weak</u>, sensitive, susceptible, tender, thin-skinned 2 <u>exposed</u>, accessible, assailable, defenceless, unprotected, wide open

W w

wad *noun* <u>mass</u>, bundle, hunk, roll

waddle *verb* <u>shuffle</u>, sway, toddle, totter, wobble

wade *verb* 1 <u>walk through</u>, ford, paddle, splash 2 **wade through** <u>plough through</u>, drudge at, labour at, peg away at, toil at, work one's way through

waffle *verb* 1 <u>prattle</u>, blather, jabber, prate, rabbit (on) (*Brit. informal*), witter on (*informal*) ♦ *noun* 2 <u>verbosity</u>, padding, prolixity, verbiage, wordiness

waft *verb* <u>carry</u>, bear, convey, drift, float, transport

wag *verb* 1 <u>wave</u>, bob, nod, quiver, shake, stir, vibrate, waggle, wiggle ♦ *noun* 2 <u>wave</u>, bob, nod, quiver, shake, vibration, waggle, wiggle

wage *noun* 1 *Also* **wages** <u>payment</u>, allowance, emolument, fee, pay, recompense, remuneration, reward, stipend ♦ *verb* 2 <u>engage in</u>, carry on, conduct, practise, proceed with, prosecute, pursue, undertake

wager *noun* 1 <u>bet</u>, flutter (*Brit. informal*), gamble, punt (*chiefly Brit.*) ♦ *verb* 2 <u>bet</u>, chance,

gamble, lay, risk, speculate, stake, venture

waggle *verb* <u>wag</u>, flutter, oscillate, shake, wave, wiggle, wobble

waif *noun* <u>stray</u>, foundling, orphan

wail *verb* 1 <u>cry</u>, bawl, grieve, howl, lament, weep, yowl ♦ *noun* 2 <u>cry</u>, complaint, howl, lament, moan, weeping, yowl

wait *verb* 1 <u>remain</u>, hang fire, hold back, linger, pause, rest, stay, tarry ♦ *noun* 2 <u>delay</u>, halt, hold-up, interval, pause, rest, stay

waiter, waitress *noun* <u>attendant</u>, server, steward *or* stewardess

wait on *or* **upon** *verb* <u>serve</u>, attend, minister to, tend

waive *verb* <u>set aside</u>, abandon, dispense with, forgo, give up, relinquish, remit, renounce

wake[1] *verb* 1 <u>awaken</u>, arise, awake, bestir, come to, get up, rouse, stir 2 <u>activate</u>, animate, arouse, excite, fire, galvanize, kindle, provoke, stimulate, stir up ♦ *noun* 3 <u>vigil</u>, deathwatch, funeral, watch

wake[2] *noun* <u>slipstream</u>, aftermath, backwash, path, track, trail, train, wash, waves

wakeful *adjective* 1 <u>sleepless</u>, insomniac, restless 2 <u>watchful</u>, alert, alive, attentive, observant, on guard, vigilant, wary

waken *verb* <u>awaken</u>, activate, arouse, awake, rouse, stir

walk *verb* 1 <u>go</u>, amble, hike, march, move, pace, step, stride, stroll 2 <u>escort</u>, accompany, convoy, take ♦ *noun* 3 <u>stroll</u>, hike, march, promenade,

ramble, saunter, trek, trudge
4 gait, carriage, step **5 path**,
alley, avenue, esplanade,
footpath, lane, promenade, trail
6 walk of life profession, calling,
career, field, line, trade, vocation

walker *noun* <u>pedestrian</u>, hiker,
rambler, wayfarer

walkout *noun* <u>strike</u>, industrial
action, protest, stoppage

walkover *noun* <u>pushover</u> (*slang*),
breeze (*U.S. & Canad. informal*),
cakewalk (*informal*), child's play
(*informal*), doddle (*Brit. slang*),
picnic (*informal*), piece of cake
(*informal*)

wall *noun* **1** <u>partition</u>, enclosure,
screen **2** <u>barrier</u>, fence, hedge,
impediment, obstacle,
obstruction

wallet *noun* <u>holder</u>, case,
pocketbook, pouch, purse

wallop *verb* **1** <u>hit</u>, batter, beat,
clobber (*slang*), pound, pummel,
strike, thrash, thump, whack
♦ *noun* **2** <u>blow</u>, bash, punch,
slug, smack, thump, thwack,
whack

wallow *verb* **1** <u>revel</u>, bask,
delight, glory, luxuriate, relish,
take pleasure **2** <u>roll about</u>, splash
around

wan *adjective* <u>pale</u>, anaemic,
ashen, pallid, pasty, sickly,
washed out, white

wand *noun* <u>stick</u>, baton, rod

wander *verb* **1** <u>roam</u>, drift,
meander, ramble, range, rove,
stray, stroll **2** <u>deviate</u>, depart,
digress, diverge, err, go astray,
swerve, veer ♦ *noun* **3** <u>excursion</u>,
cruise, meander, ramble

wanderer *noun* <u>traveller</u>, drifter,

gypsy, nomad, rambler, rover,
vagabond, voyager

wandering *adjective* <u>nomadic</u>,
itinerant, migratory, peripatetic,
rootless, roving, travelling,
vagrant, wayfaring

wane *verb* **1** <u>decline</u>, decrease,
diminish, dwindle, ebb, fade,
fail, lessen, subside, taper off,
weaken ♦ *noun* **2 on the wane**
<u>declining</u>, dwindling, ebbing,
fading, obsolescent, on the
decline, tapering off, weakening

wangle *verb* <u>contrive</u>, arrange,
engineer, fiddle (*informal*), fix
(*informal*), manipulate,
manoeuvre, pull off

want *verb* **1** <u>desire</u>, covet, crave,
hanker after, hope for, hunger
for, long for, thirst for, wish,
yearn for **2** <u>need</u>, call for,
demand, lack, miss, require
♦ *noun* **3** <u>wish</u>, appetite, craving,
desire, longing, need,
requirement, yearning **4** <u>lack</u>,
absence, dearth, deficiency,
famine, insufficiency, paucity,
scarcity, shortage **5** <u>poverty</u>,
destitution, neediness, penury,
privation

wanting *adjective* **1** <u>lacking</u>,
absent, incomplete, missing,
short, shy **2** <u>inadequate</u>,
defective, deficient, faulty,
imperfect, poor, substandard,
unsound

wanton *adjective* **1** <u>unprovoked</u>,
arbitrary, gratuitous, groundless,
motiveless, needless, senseless,
uncalled-for, unjustifiable, wilful
2 <u>promiscuous</u>, dissipated,
dissolute, immoral, lecherous,
libidinous, loose, lustful,
shameless, unchaste

war noun 1 <u>fighting</u>, battle, combat, conflict, enmity, hostilities, struggle, warfare ♦ verb 2 <u>fight</u>, battle, campaign against, clash, combat, take up arms, wage war

warble verb <u>sing</u>, chirp, trill, twitter

ward noun 1 <u>room</u>, apartment, cubicle 2 <u>district</u>, area, division, precinct, quarter, zone 3 <u>dependant</u>, charge, minor, protégé, pupil

warden noun <u>keeper</u>, administrator, caretaker, curator, custodian, guardian, ranger, superintendent

warder, wardress noun <u>jailer</u>, custodian, guard, prison officer, screw (slang)

ward off verb <u>repel</u>, avert, avoid, deflect, fend off, parry, stave off

wardrobe noun 1 <u>clothes cupboard</u>, closet 2 <u>clothes</u>, apparel, attire

warehouse noun <u>store</u>, depository, depot, stockroom, storehouse

wares plural noun <u>goods</u>, commodities, merchandise, produce, products, stock, stuff

warfare noun <u>war</u>, arms, battle, combat, conflict, fighting, hostilities

warily adverb <u>cautiously</u>, carefully, charily, circumspectly, distrustfully, gingerly, suspiciously, vigilantly, watchfully, with care

warlike adjective <u>belligerent</u>, aggressive, bellicose, bloodthirsty, hawkish, hostile, martial, warmongering

warlock noun <u>magician</u>, conjuror, enchanter, sorcerer, wizard

warm adjective 1 <u>heated</u>, balmy, lukewarm, pleasant, sunny, tepid, thermal 2 <u>affectionate</u>, amorous, cordial, friendly, hospitable, kindly, loving, tender ♦ verb 3 <u>heat</u>, heat up, melt, thaw, warm up

warmonger noun <u>hawk</u>, belligerent, militarist, sabre-rattler

warmth noun 1 <u>heat</u>, hotness, warmness 2 <u>affection</u>, amorousness, cordiality, heartiness, kindliness, love, tenderness

warn verb <u>notify</u>, advise, alert, apprise, caution, forewarn, give notice, inform, make (someone) aware, tip off

warning noun <u>caution</u>, advice, alarm, alert, notification, omen, sign, tip-off

warp verb 1 <u>twist</u>, bend, contort, deform, distort ♦ noun 2 <u>twist</u>, bend, contortion, distortion, kink

warrant noun 1 <u>authorization</u>, authority, licence, permission, permit, sanction ♦ verb 2 <u>call for</u>, demand, deserve, excuse, justify, license, necessitate, permit, require, sanction 3 <u>guarantee</u>, affirm, attest, certify, declare, pledge, vouch for

warranty noun <u>guarantee</u>, assurance, bond, certificate, contract, covenant, pledge

warrior noun <u>soldier</u>, combatant, fighter, gladiator, man-at-arms

wary adjective <u>cautious</u>, alert, careful, chary, circumspect, distrustful, guarded, suspicious, vigilant, watchful

wash verb 1 <u>clean</u>, bathe, cleanse, launder, rinse, scrub 2 <u>sweep away</u>, bear away, carry off, move 3 *Informal* <u>be plausible</u>, bear scrutiny, be convincing, carry weight, hold up, hold water, stand up, stick ♦ *noun* 4 <u>cleaning</u>, cleansing, laundering, rinse, scrub 5 <u>coat</u>, coating, film, layer, overlay 6 <u>swell</u>, surge, wave

washout noun <u>failure</u>, disappointment, disaster, dud (*informal*), fiasco, flop (*informal*)

waste verb 1 <u>misuse</u>, blow (*slang*), dissipate, fritter away, lavish, squander, throw away 2 **waste away** <u>decline</u>, atrophy, crumble, decay, dwindle, fade, wane, wear out, wither ♦ *noun* 3 <u>misuse</u>, dissipation, extravagance, frittering away, prodigality, squandering, wastefulness 4 <u>rubbish</u>, debris, dross, garbage, leftovers, litter, refuse, scrap, trash 5 **wastes** <u>desert</u>, wasteland, wilderness ♦ *adjective* 6 <u>unwanted</u>, leftover, superfluous, supernumerary, unused, useless, worthless 7 <u>uncultivated</u>, bare, barren, desolate, empty, uninhabited, unproductive, wild

wasteful adjective <u>extravagant</u>, lavish, prodigal, profligate, spendthrift, thriftless, uneconomical

waster noun <u>layabout</u>, good-for-nothing, idler, loafer, ne'er-do-well, shirker, skiver (*Brit. slang*), wastrel

watch verb 1 <u>look at</u>, contemplate, eye, observe, regard, see, view 2 <u>guard</u>, keep, look after, mind, protect, superintend, take care of, tend ♦ *noun* 3 <u>wristwatch</u>, chronometer, timepiece 4 <u>lookout</u>, observation, surveillance, vigil

watchdog noun 1 <u>guard dog</u> 2 <u>guardian</u>, custodian, monitor, protector, scrutineer

watchful adjective <u>alert</u>, attentive, observant, on the lookout, suspicious, vigilant, wary, wide awake

watchman noun <u>guard</u>, caretaker, custodian, security guard

watchword noun <u>motto</u>, battle cry, byword, catch phrase, catchword, maxim, rallying cry, slogan

water noun 1 <u>liquid</u>, H_2O ♦ *verb* 2 <u>moisten</u>, dampen, douse, drench, hose, irrigate, soak, spray

water down verb <u>dilute</u>, thin, water, weaken

waterfall noun <u>cascade</u>, cataract, fall

watertight adjective 1 <u>waterproof</u> 2 <u>foolproof</u>, airtight, flawless, impregnable, sound, unassailable

watery adjective 1 <u>wet</u>, aqueous, damp, fluid, liquid, moist, soggy 2 <u>diluted</u>, runny, thin, washy, watered-down, weak

wave verb 1 <u>signal</u>, beckon, direct, gesticulate, gesture, indicate, sign 2 <u>flap</u>, brandish, flourish, flutter, oscillate, shake, stir, swing, wag ♦ *noun* 3 <u>ripple</u>, billow, breaker, ridge, roller, swell, undulation 4 <u>outbreak</u>, flood, rash, rush, stream, surge, upsurge

waver *verb* 1 <u>hesitate</u>, dither (*chiefly Brit.*), falter, fluctuate, hum and haw, seesaw, vacillate 2 <u>tremble</u>, flicker, quiver, shake, totter, wobble

wax *verb* <u>increase</u>, develop, enlarge, expand, grow, magnify, swell

way *noun* 1 <u>method</u>, fashion, manner, means, mode, procedure, process, system, technique 2 <u>style</u>, custom, habit, manner, nature, personality, practice, wont 3 <u>route</u>, channel, course, direction, path, pathway, road, track, trail 4 <u>journey</u>, approach, march, passage 5 <u>distance</u>, length, stretch

wayfarer *noun* <u>traveller</u>, gypsy, itinerant, nomad, rover, voyager, wanderer

wayward *adjective* <u>erratic</u>, capricious, inconstant, ungovernable, unmanageable, unpredictable, unruly

weak *adjective* 1 <u>feeble</u>, debilitated, effete, fragile, frail, infirm, puny, sickly, unsteady 2 <u>unsafe</u>, defenceless, exposed, helpless, unguarded, unprotected, vulnerable 3 <u>unconvincing</u>, feeble, flimsy, hollow, lame, pathetic, unsatisfactory 4 <u>tasteless</u>, diluted, insipid, runny, thin, watery

weaken *verb* 1 <u>lessen</u>, diminish, dwindle, fade, flag, lower, moderate, reduce, sap, undermine, wane 2 <u>dilute</u>, thin out, water down

weakling *noun* <u>sissy</u>, drip

(*informal*), wet (*Brit. informal*), wimp (*informal*)

weakness *noun* 1 <u>frailty</u>, decrepitude, feebleness, fragility, infirmity, powerlessness, vulnerability 2 <u>failing</u>, blemish, defect, deficiency, fault, flaw, imperfection, lack, shortcoming 3 <u>liking</u>, fondness, inclination, partiality, passion, penchant, soft spot

wealth *noun* 1 <u>riches</u>, affluence, capital, fortune, money, opulence, prosperity 2 <u>plenty</u>, abundance, copiousness, cornucopia, fullness, profusion, richness

wealthy *adjective* <u>rich</u>, affluent, flush (*informal*), moneyed, opulent, prosperous, well-heeled (*informal*), well-off, well-to-do

wear *verb* 1 <u>be dressed in</u>, don, have on, put on, sport (*informal*) 2 <u>show</u>, display, exhibit 3 <u>deteriorate</u>, abrade, corrode, erode, fray, grind, rub ♦ *noun* 4 <u>clothes</u>, apparel, attire, costume, dress, garb, garments, gear (*informal*), things 5 <u>damage</u>, abrasion, attrition, corrosion, deterioration, erosion, wear and tear

weariness *noun* <u>tiredness</u>, drowsiness, exhaustion, fatigue, languor, lassitude, lethargy, listlessness

wearing *adjective* <u>tiresome</u>, exasperating, fatiguing, irksome, oppressive, trying, wearisome

wearisome *adjective* <u>tedious</u>, annoying, boring, exhausting, fatiguing, irksome, oppressive, tiresome, troublesome, trying, wearing

wear off verb subside, decrease, diminish, disappear, dwindle, fade, peter out, wane

weary adjective **1** tired, done in (informal), drained, drowsy, exhausted, fatigued, flagging, jaded, sleepy, worn out **2** tiring, arduous, laborious, tiresome, wearisome ◆ verb **3** tire, drain, enervate, fatigue, sap, take it out of (informal), tax, tire out, wear out

weather noun **1** climate, conditions ◆ verb **2** withstand, brave, come through, endure, overcome, resist, ride out, stand, survive

weave verb **1** knit, braid, entwine, interlace, intertwine, plait **2** create, build, construct, contrive, fabricate, make up, put together, spin **3** zigzag, crisscross, wind

web noun **1** spider's web, cobweb **2** network, lattice, tangle

wed verb **1** marry, get married, take the plunge (informal), tie the knot (informal) **2** unite, ally, blend, combine, interweave, join, link, merge

wedding noun marriage, nuptials, wedlock

wedge noun **1** block, chunk, lump ◆ verb **2** squeeze, cram, crowd, force, jam, lodge, pack, ram, stuff, thrust

wedlock noun marriage, matrimony

weed out verb eliminate, dispense with, eradicate, get rid of, remove, root out, uproot

weedy adjective weak, feeble, frail, ineffectual, namby-pamby, puny, skinny, thin

weep verb cry, blubber, lament, mourn, shed tears, snivel, sob, whimper

weigh verb **1** have a weight of, tip the scales at (informal) **2** consider, contemplate, deliberate upon, evaluate, examine, meditate upon, ponder, reflect upon, think over **3** matter, carry weight, count

weight noun **1** heaviness, load, mass, poundage, tonnage **2** importance, authority, consequence, impact, import, influence, power, value ◆ verb **3** load, freight **4** bias, load, slant, unbalance

weighty adjective **1** important, consequential, crucial, grave, momentous, portentous, serious, significant, solemn **2** heavy, burdensome, cumbersome, hefty (informal), massive, ponderous

weird adjective strange, bizarre, creepy (informal), eerie, freakish, mysterious, odd, queer, spooky (informal), unnatural

welcome verb **1** greet, embrace, hail, meet, receive ◆ noun **2** greeting, acceptance, hospitality, reception, salutation ◆ adjective **3** acceptable, agreeable, appreciated, delightful, desirable, gratifying, pleasant, refreshing **4** free, under no obligation

weld verb join, bind, bond, connect, fuse, link, solder, unite

welfare noun wellbeing, advantage, benefit, good, happiness, health, interest, prosperity

well¹ adverb **1** satisfactorily,

agreeably, nicely, pleasantly, smoothly, splendidly, successfully **2** <u>skilfully</u>, ably, adeptly, adequately, admirably, correctly, efficiently, expertly, proficiently, properly **3** <u>prosperously</u>, comfortably **4** <u>suitably</u>, fairly, fittingly, justly, properly, rightly **5** <u>intimately</u>, deeply, fully, profoundly, thoroughly **6** <u>favourably</u>, approvingly, glowingly, highly, kindly, warmly **7** <u>considerably</u>, abundantly, amply, fully, greatly, heartily, highly, substantially, thoroughly, very much ♦ *adjective* **8** <u>healthy</u>, fit, in fine fettle, sound **9** <u>satisfactory</u>, agreeable, fine, pleasing, proper, right, thriving

well² *noun* **1** <u>hole</u>, bore, pit, shaft ♦ *verb* **2** <u>flow</u>, gush, jet, pour, spout, spring, spurt, surge

well-known *adjective* <u>famous</u>, celebrated, familiar, noted, popular, renowned

well-off *adjective* <u>rich</u>, affluent, comfortable, moneyed, prosperous, wealthy, well-heeled (*informal*), well-to-do

well-to-do *adjective* <u>rich</u>, affluent, comfortable, moneyed, prosperous, wealthy, well-heeled (*informal*), well-off

well-worn *adjective* <u>stale</u>, banal, commonplace, hackneyed, overused, stereotyped, trite

welt *noun* <u>mark</u>, contusion, streak, stripe, wale, weal

welter *noun* <u>jumble</u>, confusion, hotchpotch, mess, muddle, tangle, web

wet *adjective* **1** <u>damp</u>, dank, moist, saturated, soaking, sodden, soggy, sopping,

waterlogged, watery **2** <u>rainy</u>, drizzling, pouring, raining, showery, teeming **3** *Informal* <u>feeble</u>, effete, ineffectual, namby-pamby, soft, spineless, timorous, weak, weedy (*informal*) ♦ *noun* **4** <u>rain</u>, drizzle **5** *Informal* <u>weakling</u>, drip (*informal*), weed (*informal*), wimp (*informal*) **6** <u>moisture</u>, condensation, damp, dampness, humidity, liquid, water, wetness ♦ *verb* **7** <u>moisten</u>, dampen, douse, irrigate, saturate, soak, spray, water

whack *verb* **1** <u>strike</u>, bang, belt (*informal*), clobber (*slang*), hit, smack, thrash, thump, thwack, wallop (*informal*) ♦ *noun* **2** <u>blow</u>, bang, belt (*informal*), hit, smack, stroke, thump, thwack, wallop (*informal*) **3** *Informal* <u>share</u>, bit, cut (*informal*), part, portion, quota **4** *As in* **have a whack** <u>attempt</u>, bash (*informal*), crack (*informal*), go (*informal*), shot (*informal*), stab (*informal*), try, turn

wharf *noun* <u>dock</u>, jetty, landing stage, pier, quay

wheedle *verb* <u>coax</u>, cajole, entice, inveigle, persuade

wheel *noun* **1** <u>circle</u>, gyration, pivot, revolution, rotation, spin, turn ♦ *verb* **2** <u>turn</u>, gyrate, pirouette, revolve, rotate, spin, swing, swivel, twirl, whirl

wheeze *verb* **1** <u>gasp</u>, cough, hiss, rasp, whistle ♦ *noun* **2** <u>gasp</u>, cough, hiss, rasp, whistle **3** *Brit. slang* <u>trick</u>, idea, plan, ploy, ruse, scheme, stunt

whereabouts *noun* <u>position</u>, location, site, situation

wherewithal *noun* <u>resources</u>,

capital, funds, means, money, supplies

whet verb 1 *As in* whet someone's appetite stimulate, arouse, awaken, enhance, excite, kindle, quicken, rouse, stir 2 sharpen, hone

whiff noun smell, aroma, hint, odour, scent, sniff

whim noun impulse, caprice, fancy, notion, urge

whimper verb 1 cry, moan, snivel, sob, weep, whine, whinge (*informal*) ♦ noun 2 sob, moan, snivel, whine

whimsical adjective fanciful, curious, eccentric, freakish, funny, odd, playful, quaint, unusual

whine noun 1 cry, moan, sob, wail, whimper 2 complaint, gripe (*informal*), grouch (*informal*), grouse, grumble, moan

whinge Informal ♦ verb 1 complain, bleat, carp, gripe (*informal*), grouse, grumble, moan ♦ noun 2 complaint, gripe (*informal*), grouch, grouse, grumble, moan, whine

whip noun 1 lash, birch, cane, cat-o'-nine-tails, crop, scourge ♦ verb 2 lash, beat, birch, cane, flagellate, flog, scourge, spank, strap, thrash 3 *Informal* dash, dart, dive, fly, rush, shoot, tear, whisk 4 beat, whisk 5 incite, agitate, drive, foment, goad, spur, stir, work up

whirl verb 1 spin, pirouette, revolve, roll, rotate, swirl, turn, twirl, twist 2 feel dizzy, reel, spin ♦ noun 3 revolution, pirouette, roll, rotation, spin, swirl, turn, twirl, twist 4 bustle, flurry, merry-go-round, round, series, succession 5 confusion, daze, dither (*chiefly Brit.*), giddiness, spin

whirlwind noun 1 tornado, waterspout ♦ adjective 2 rapid, hasty, quick, short, speedy, swift

whisk verb 1 flick, brush, sweep, whip 2 beat, fluff up, whip ♦ noun 3 flick, brush, sweep, whip 4 beater

whisper verb 1 murmur, breathe 2 rustle, hiss, sigh, swish ♦ noun 3 murmur, undertone 4 *Informal* rumour, gossip, innuendo, insinuation, report 5 rustle, hiss, sigh, swish

white adjective pale, ashen, pallid, pasty, wan

white-collar adjective clerical, nonmanual, professional, salaried

whiten verb pale, blanch, bleach, fade

whitewash noun 1 cover-up, camouflage, concealment, deception ♦ verb 2 cover up, camouflage, conceal, gloss over, suppress

whittle verb 1 carve, cut, hew, pare, shape, shave, trim 2 whittle down *or* away reduce, consume, eat away, erode, wear away

whole adjective 1 complete, entire, full, total, unabridged, uncut, undivided 2 undamaged, in one piece, intact, unbroken, unharmed, unscathed, untouched ♦ noun 3 totality, ensemble, entirety 4 on the whole: a all in all, all things considered, by and large b generally, as a rule, in general, in the main, mostly, predominantly

wholehearted *adjective* sincere, committed, dedicated, determined, devoted, enthusiastic, unstinting, zealous

wholesale *adjective* **1** extensive, broad, comprehensive, far-reaching, indiscriminate, mass, sweeping, wide-ranging ♦ *adverb* **2** extensively, comprehensively, indiscriminately

wholesome *adjective*
1 beneficial, good, healthy, nourishing, nutritious, salubrious **2** moral, decent, edifying, improving, respectable

wholly *adverb* completely, altogether, entirely, fully, in every respect, perfectly, thoroughly, totally, utterly

whopper *noun* **1** giant, colossus, crackerjack (*informal*), jumbo (*informal*), leviathan, mammoth, monster **2** big lie, fabrication, falsehood, tall story (*informal*), untruth

whopping *adjective* gigantic, big, enormous, giant, great, huge, mammoth, massive

whore *noun* prostitute, call girl, streetwalker, tart (*informal*)

wicked *adjective* **1** bad, corrupt, depraved, devilish, evil, fiendish, immoral, sinful, vicious, villainous **2** mischievous, impish, incorrigible, naughty, rascally, roguish

wide *adjective* **1** broad, expansive, extensive, far-reaching, immense, large, sweeping, vast **2** spacious, baggy, capacious, commodious, full, loose, roomy **3** expanded,

dilated, distended, outspread, outstretched **4** distant, off course, off target, remote ♦ *adverb* **5** fully, completely **6** off target, astray, off course, off the mark, out

widen *verb* broaden, dilate, enlarge, expand, extend, spread, stretch

widespread *adjective* common, broad, extensive, far-reaching, general, pervasive, popular, universal

width *noun* breadth, compass, diameter, extent, girth, scope, span, thickness

wield *verb* **1** brandish, employ, flourish, handle, manage, manipulate, ply, swing, use **2** *As in* **wield power** exert, exercise, have, maintain, possess

wife *noun* spouse, better half (*humorous*), bride, mate, partner

wiggle *verb, noun* jerk, jiggle, shake, shimmy, squirm, twitch, wag, waggle, writhe

wild *adjective* **1** untamed, feral, ferocious, fierce, savage, unbroken, undomesticated **2** uncultivated, free, natural **3** uncivilized, barbaric, barbarous, brutish, ferocious, fierce, primitive, savage **4** uncontrolled, disorderly, riotous, rowdy, turbulent, undisciplined, unfettered, unmanageable, unrestrained, unruly, wayward **5** stormy, blustery, choppy, raging, rough, tempestuous, violent **6** excited, crazy (*informal*), enthusiastic, hysterical, raving ♦ *noun* **7 wilds** wilderness, back of beyond (*informal*), desert, middle of nowhere (*informal*), wasteland

wilderness noun <u>desert</u>, jungle, wasteland, wilds

wiles plural noun <u>trickery</u>, artfulness, chicanery, craftiness, cunning, guile, slyness

wilful adjective 1 <u>obstinate</u>, determined, headstrong, inflexible, intransigent, obdurate, perverse, pig-headed, stubborn, uncompromising 2 <u>intentional</u>, conscious, deliberate, intended, purposeful, voluntary

will noun 1 <u>determination</u>, purpose, resolution, resolve, willpower 2 <u>wish</u>, desire, fancy, inclination, mind, preference, volition 3 <u>testament</u>, last wishes ♦ verb 4 <u>wish</u>, desire, prefer, see fit, want 5 <u>bequeath</u>, confer, give, leave, pass on, transfer

willing adjective <u>ready</u>, agreeable, amenable, compliant, consenting, game (*informal*), inclined, prepared

willingly adverb <u>readily</u>, by choice, cheerfully, eagerly, freely, gladly, happily, of one's own accord, voluntarily

willingness noun <u>inclination</u>, agreement, consent, volition, will, wish

willowy adjective <u>slender</u>, graceful, lithe, slim, supple, svelte, sylphlike

willpower noun <u>self-control</u>, determination, drive, grit, resolution, resolve, self-discipline, single-mindedness

wilt verb 1 <u>droop</u>, sag, shrivel, wither 2 <u>weaken</u>, fade, flag, languish, wane

wily adjective <u>cunning</u>, artful, astute, crafty, guileful, sharp, shrewd, sly, tricky

wimp noun Informal <u>weakling</u>, coward, drip (*informal*), mouse, sissy, softy or softie

win verb 1 <u>triumph</u>, come first, conquer, overcome, prevail, succeed, sweep the board 2 <u>gain</u>, achieve, acquire, attain, earn, get, land, obtain, procure, secure ♦ noun 3 <u>victory</u>, conquest, success, triumph

wince verb 1 <u>flinch</u>, blench, cower, cringe, draw back, quail, recoil, shrink, start ♦ noun 2 <u>flinch</u>, cringe, start

wind¹ noun 1 <u>air</u>, blast, breeze, draught, gust, zephyr 2 <u>breath</u>, puff, respiration 3 <u>flatulence</u>, gas 4 <u>talk</u>, babble, blather, bluster, boasting, hot air, humbug 5 As in get wind of <u>hint</u>, inkling, notice, report, rumour, suggestion, warning, whisper

wind² verb 1 <u>coil</u>, curl, encircle, loop, reel, roll, spiral, twist 2 <u>meander</u>, bend, curve, ramble, snake, turn, twist, zigzag

windfall noun <u>godsend</u>, bonanza, find, jackpot, manna from heaven

wind up verb 1 <u>end</u>, close, conclude, finalize, finish, settle, terminate, wrap up 2 <u>end up</u>, be left, finish up 3 Informal <u>excite</u>, put on edge, work up

windy adjective <u>breezy</u>, blowy, blustery, gusty, squally, stormy, wild, windswept

wing noun 1 <u>faction</u>, arm, branch, group, section ♦ verb 2 <u>fly</u>, glide, soar 3 <u>wound</u>, clip, hit

wink verb 1 <u>blink</u>, bat, flutter
2 <u>twinkle</u>, flash, gleam, glimmer,
sparkle ♦ noun 3 <u>blink</u>, flutter

winkle out verb <u>extract</u>, dig out,
dislodge, draw out, extricate,
force out, prise out

winner noun <u>victor</u>, champ
(informal), champion, conqueror,
master

winning adjective 1 <u>victorious</u>,
conquering, successful,
triumphant 2 <u>charming</u>, alluring,
attractive, cute, disarming,
enchanting, endearing,
engaging, likable or likeable,
pleasing

winnings plural noun <u>spoils</u>,
gains, prize, proceeds, profits,
takings

winnow verb <u>separate</u>, divide,
select, sift, sort out

win over verb <u>convince</u>, bring or
talk round, convert, influence,
persuade, prevail upon, sway

wintry adjective <u>cold</u>, chilly,
freezing, frosty, frozen, icy,
snowy

wipe verb 1 <u>clean</u>, brush, mop,
rub, sponge, swab 2 <u>erase</u>,
remove ♦ noun 3 <u>rub</u>, brush

wipe out verb <u>destroy</u>,
annihilate, eradicate, erase,
expunge, exterminate, massacre,
obliterate

wiry adjective <u>lean</u>, sinewy,
strong, tough

wisdom noun <u>understanding</u>,
discernment, enlightenment,
erudition, insight, intelligence,
judgment, knowledge, learning,
sense

wise adjective <u>sensible</u>, clever,
discerning, enlightened, erudite,

intelligent, judicious, perceptive,
prudent, sage

wisecrack noun 1 <u>joke</u>, jest, jibe,
quip, witticism ♦ verb 2 <u>joke</u>, jest,
jibe, quip

wish verb 1 <u>want</u>, aspire, crave,
desire, hanker, hope, long, yearn
♦ noun 2 <u>desire</u>, aspiration, hope,
intention, urge, want, whim, will

wispy adjective <u>thin</u>, attenuated,
delicate, fine, flimsy, fragile, frail

wistful adjective <u>melancholy</u>,
contemplative, dreamy, longing,
meditative, pensive, reflective,
thoughtful

wit noun 1 <u>humour</u>, badinage,
banter, drollery, jocularity,
raillery, repartee, wordplay
2 <u>humorist</u>, card (informal),
comedian, joker, wag
3 <u>cleverness</u>, acumen, brains,
common sense, ingenuity,
intellect, sense, wisdom

witch noun <u>enchantress</u>, crone,
hag, magician, sorceress

witchcraft noun <u>magic</u>,
enchantment, necromancy,
occultism, sorcery, the black art,
voodoo, wizardry

withdraw verb <u>remove</u>, draw
back, extract, pull out, take
away, take off

withdrawal noun <u>removal</u>,
extraction

withdrawn adjective
<u>uncommunicative</u>, distant,
introverted, reserved, retiring,
shy, taciturn, unforthcoming

wither verb <u>wilt</u>, decay, decline,
disintegrate, fade, perish, shrivel,
waste

withering adjective <u>scornful</u>,
devastating, humiliating, hurtful,

mortifying, snubbing

withhold verb <u>keep back</u>, conceal, hide, hold back, refuse, reserve, retain, suppress

withstand verb <u>resist</u>, bear, cope with, endure, hold off, oppose, stand up to, suffer, tolerate

witless adjective <u>foolish</u>, halfwitted, idiotic, inane, moronic, senseless, silly, stupid

witness noun 1 <u>observer</u>, beholder, bystander, eyewitness, looker-on, onlooker, spectator, viewer, watcher 2 <u>testifier</u>, corroborator ♦ verb 3 <u>see</u>, note, notice, observe, perceive, view, watch 4 <u>sign</u>, countersign, endorse

wits plural noun <u>intelligence</u>, acumen, brains (informal), cleverness, comprehension, faculties, ingenuity, reason, sense, understanding

witter verb <u>chatter</u>, babble, blather, chat, gabble, jabber, prate, prattle, waffle (informal, chiefly Brit.)

witticism noun <u>quip</u>, bon mot, one-liner (slang), pun, riposte

witty adjective <u>humorous</u>, amusing, clever, droll, funny, piquant, sparkling, waggish, whimsical

wizard noun <u>magician</u>, conjuror, magus, necromancer, occultist, shaman, sorcerer, warlock, witch

wizardry noun <u>magic</u>, sorcery, voodoo, witchcraft

wizened adjective <u>wrinkled</u>, dried up, gnarled, lined, shrivelled, shrunken, withered

wobble verb 1 <u>shake</u>, rock, sway, teeter, totter, tremble ♦ noun

2 <u>unsteadiness</u>, shake, tremble, tremor

wobbly adjective <u>unsteady</u>, rickety, shaky, teetering, tottering, uneven

woe noun <u>grief</u>, agony, anguish, distress, gloom, misery, sadness, sorrow, unhappiness, wretchedness

woeful adjective 1 <u>sad</u>, deplorable, dismal, distressing, grievous, lamentable, miserable, pathetic, tragic, wretched 2 <u>pitiful</u>, abysmal, appalling, bad, deplorable, dreadful, feeble, pathetic, poor, sorry

woman noun <u>lady</u>, female, girl

womanizer noun <u>philanderer</u>, Casanova, Don Juan, lady-killer, lecher, seducer

womanly adjective <u>feminine</u>, female, ladylike, matronly, motherly, tender, warm

wonder verb 1 <u>think</u>, conjecture, meditate, ponder, puzzle, query, question, speculate 2 <u>be amazed</u>, be astonished, gape, marvel, stare ♦ noun 3 <u>phenomenon</u>, curiosity, marvel, miracle, prodigy, rarity, sight, spectacle 4 <u>amazement</u>, admiration, astonishment, awe, bewilderment, fascination, surprise, wonderment

wonderful adjective 1 <u>excellent</u>, brilliant, fabulous (informal), fantastic (informal), great (informal), magnificent, marvellous, outstanding, superb, terrific, tremendous 2 <u>remarkable</u>, amazing, astonishing, extraordinary, incredible, miraculous, phenomenal, staggering, startling, unheard-of

wonky adjective <u>shaky</u>, unsteady, wobbly

woo verb <u>court</u>, cultivate, pursue

wood noun 1 <u>timber</u>
2 <u>woodland</u>, coppice, copse, forest, grove, thicket

wooded adjective <u>tree-covered</u>, forested, sylvan (poetic), timbered, tree-clad

wooden adjective 1 <u>woody</u>, ligneous, timber
2 <u>expressionless</u>, deadpan, lifeless, unresponsive

wool noun <u>fleece</u>, hair, yarn

woolly adjective 1 <u>fleecy</u>, hairy, shaggy, woollen 2 <u>vague</u>, confused, hazy, ill-defined, indefinite, indistinct, muddled, unclear

word noun 1 <u>term</u>, expression, name 2 <u>chat</u>, confab (informal), consultation, discussion, talk, tête-à-tête 3 <u>remark</u>, comment, utterance 4 <u>message</u>, communiqué, dispatch, information, intelligence, news, notice, report 5 <u>promise</u>, assurance, guarantee, oath, pledge, vow 6 <u>command</u>, bidding, decree, mandate, order ♦ verb 7 <u>express</u>, couch, phrase, put, say, state, utter

wording noun <u>phraseology</u>, language, phrasing, terminology, words

wordy adjective <u>long-winded</u>, diffuse, prolix, rambling, verbose, windy

work noun 1 <u>effort</u>, drudgery, elbow grease (facetious), exertion, industry, labour, sweat, toil 2 <u>employment</u>, business,

duty, job, livelihood, occupation, profession, trade 3 <u>task</u>, assignment, chore, commission, duty, job, stint, undertaking 4 <u>creation</u>, achievement, composition, handiwork, opus, piece, production ♦ verb 5 <u>labour</u>, drudge, exert oneself, peg away, slave, slog (away), sweat, toil 6 <u>be employed</u>, be in work 7 <u>operate</u>, control, drive, handle, manage, manipulate, move, use 8 <u>function</u>, go, operate, run 9 <u>cultivate</u>, dig, farm, till 10 <u>manipulate</u>, fashion, form, knead, mould, shape

workable adjective <u>viable</u>, doable, feasible, possible, practicable, practical

worker noun <u>employee</u>, artisan, craftsman, hand, labourer, tradesman, workman

working adjective 1 <u>employed</u>, active, in work 2 <u>functioning</u>, going, operative, running

workman noun <u>labourer</u>, artisan, craftsman, employee, hand, journeyman, mechanic, operative, tradesman, worker

workmanship noun <u>skill</u>, artistry, craftsmanship, expertise, handiwork, technique

work out verb 1 <u>solve</u>, calculate, figure out, find out 2 <u>happen</u>, develop, evolve, result, turn out 3 <u>exercise</u>, practise, train, warm up

works plural noun 1 <u>factory</u>, mill, plant, workshop 2 <u>writings</u>, canon, oeuvre, output 3 <u>mechanism</u>, action, machinery, movement, parts, workings

workshop noun <u>studio</u>, factory,

mill, plant, workroom

world noun 1 <u>earth</u>, globe 2 <u>mankind</u>, everybody, everyone, humanity, humankind, man, the public 3 <u>sphere</u>, area, domain, environment, field, realm

worldly adjective 1 <u>earthly</u>, physical, profane, secular, temporal, terrestrial 2 <u>materialistic</u>, grasping, greedy, selfish 3 <u>worldly-wise</u>, blasé, cosmopolitan, experienced, knowing, sophisticated, urbane

worldwide adjective <u>global</u>, general, international, omnipresent, pandemic, ubiquitous, universal

worn adjective <u>ragged</u>, frayed, shabby, tattered, tatty, the worse for wear, threadbare

worn-out adjective 1 <u>run-down</u>, on its last legs, ragged, shabby, threadbare, used-up, useless, worn 2 <u>exhausted</u>, all in (slang), done in (informal), fatigued, fit to drop, spent, tired out, weary

worried adjective <u>anxious</u>, afraid, apprehensive, concerned, fearful, frightened, nervous, perturbed, tense, troubled, uneasy

worry verb 1 <u>be anxious</u>, agonize, brood, fret 2 <u>trouble</u>, annoy, bother, disturb, perturb, pester, unsettle, upset, vex ♦ noun 3 <u>anxiety</u>, apprehension, concern, fear, misgiving, trepidation, trouble, unease 4 <u>problem</u>, bother, care, hassle (informal), trouble

worsen verb 1 <u>aggravate</u>, damage, exacerbate 2 <u>deteriorate</u>, decay, decline, degenerate, get worse, go

downhill (informal), sink

worship verb 1 <u>praise</u>, adore, exalt, glorify, honour, pray to, revere, venerate 2 <u>love</u>, adore, idolize, put on a pedestal ♦ noun 3 <u>praise</u>, adoration, adulation, devotion, glory, honour, regard, respect, reverence

worth noun 1 <u>value</u>, cost, price, rate, valuation 2 <u>excellence</u>, goodness, importance, merit, quality, usefulness, value, worthiness

worthless adjective 1 <u>useless</u>, ineffectual, rubbishy, unimportant, valueless 2 <u>good-for-nothing</u>, contemptible, despicable, vile

worthwhile adjective <u>useful</u>, beneficial, constructive, expedient, helpful, productive, profitable, valuable

worthy adjective <u>praiseworthy</u>, admirable, creditable, deserving, laudable, meritorious, valuable, virtuous, worthwhile

would-be adjective <u>budding</u>, self-appointed, self-styled, unfulfilled, wannabe (informal)

wound noun 1 <u>injury</u>, cut, gash, hurt, laceration, lesion, trauma (Pathology) 2 <u>insult</u>, offence, slight ♦ verb 3 <u>injure</u>, cut, gash, hurt, lacerate, pierce, wing 4 <u>offend</u>, annoy, cut (someone) to the quick, hurt, mortify, sting

wrangle verb 1 <u>argue</u>, bicker, contend, disagree, dispute, fight, quarrel, row, squabble ♦ noun 2 <u>argument</u>, altercation, bickering, dispute, quarrel, row, squabble, tiff

wrap verb 1 <u>cover</u>, bind, bundle up, encase, enclose, enfold,

pack, package, shroud, swathe
♦ *noun* 2 <u>cloak</u>, cape, mantle, shawl, stole

wrapper *noun* <u>cover</u>, case, envelope, jacket, packaging, wrapping

wrap up *verb* 1 <u>giftwrap</u>, bundle up, pack, package 2 *Informal* <u>end</u>, conclude, finish off, polish off, round off, terminate, wind up

wrath *noun* <u>anger</u>, displeasure, fury, indignation, ire, rage, resentment, temper

wreath *noun* <u>garland</u>, band, chaplet, crown, festoon, ring

wreck *verb* 1 <u>destroy</u>, break, demolish, devastate, ruin, shatter, smash, spoil ♦ *noun* 2 <u>shipwreck</u>, hulk

wreckage *noun* <u>remains</u>, debris, fragments, pieces, rubble, ruin

wrench *verb* 1 <u>twist</u>, force, jerk, pull, rip, tear, tug, yank 2 <u>sprain</u>, rick, strain ♦ *noun* 3 <u>twist</u>, jerk, pull, rip, tug, yank 4 <u>sprain</u>, strain, twist 5 <u>blow</u>, pang, shock, upheaval 6 <u>spanner</u>, adjustable spanner

wrest *verb* <u>seize</u>, extract, force, take, win, wrench

wrestle *verb* <u>fight</u>, battle, combat, grapple, scuffle, struggle, tussle

wretch *noun* <u>scoundrel</u>, good-for-nothing, miscreant, rascal, rogue, swine, worm

wretched *adjective* 1 <u>unhappy</u>, dejected, depressed, disconsolate, downcast, forlorn, hapless, miserable, woebegone 2 <u>worthless</u>, inferior, miserable, paltry, pathetic, poor, sorry

wriggle *verb* 1 <u>twist</u>, jerk, jiggle,

squirm, turn, waggle, wiggle, writhe 2 <u>crawl</u>, slink, snake, worm, zigzag 3 *As in* **wriggle out of** <u>manoeuvre</u>, dodge, extricate oneself ♦ *noun* 4 <u>twist</u>, jerk, jiggle, squirm, turn, waggle, wiggle

wring *verb* <u>twist</u>, extract, force, screw, squeeze

wrinkle *noun* 1 <u>crease</u>, corrugation, crinkle, crow's-foot, crumple, fold, furrow, line ♦ *verb* 2 <u>crease</u>, corrugate, crumple, fold, furrow, gather, pucker, rumple

writ *noun* <u>summons</u>, court order, decree, document

write *verb* <u>record</u>, draft, draw up, inscribe, jot down, pen, scribble, set down

writer *noun* <u>author</u>, hack, novelist, penpusher, scribbler, scribe, wordsmith

writhe *verb* <u>squirm</u>, jerk, struggle, thrash, thresh, toss, twist, wiggle, wriggle

writing *noun* 1 <u>script</u>, calligraphy, hand, handwriting, penmanship, scrawl, scribble 2 <u>document</u>, book, composition, opus, publication, work

wrong *adjective* 1 <u>incorrect</u>, erroneous, fallacious, false, inaccurate, mistaken, untrue, wide of the mark 2 <u>bad</u>, criminal, dishonest, evil, illegal, immoral, sinful, unjust, unlawful, wicked, wrongful 3 <u>inappropriate</u>, incongruous, incorrect, unacceptable, unbecoming, undesirable, unseemly, unsuitable 4 <u>defective</u>, amiss, askew, awry, faulty ♦ *adverb* 5 <u>incorrectly</u>, badly, erroneously, inaccurately, mistakenly, wrongly **6** <u>amiss</u>, askew, astray, awry ◆ *noun* **7** <u>offence</u>, crime, error, injury, injustice, misdeed, sin, transgression, wickedness ◆ *verb* **8** <u>mistreat</u>, abuse, cheat, dishonour, harm, hurt, malign, oppress, take advantage of

wrongdoer *noun* <u>offender</u>, criminal, culprit, delinquent, lawbreaker, miscreant, sinner, villain

wrongful *adjective* <u>improper</u>, criminal, evil, illegal, illegitimate, immoral, unethical, unjust, unlawful, wicked

wry *adjective* **1** <u>ironic</u>, droll, dry, mocking, sarcastic, sardonic **2** <u>contorted</u>, crooked, twisted, uneven

Xmas *noun* <u>Christmas</u>, Noel, Yule (*archaic*), Yuletide (*archaic*)
X-rays *plural noun* <u>Röntgen rays</u> (*old name*)

Y y

yank *verb, noun* <u>pull</u>, hitch, jerk, snatch, tug, wrench
yardstick *noun* <u>standard</u>, benchmark, criterion, gauge, measure, par, touchstone
yarn *noun* **1** <u>thread</u>, fibre **2** *Informal* <u>story</u>, anecdote, cock-and-bull story (*informal*), fable, tale, tall story

yawning *adjective* <u>gaping</u>, cavernous, vast, wide
yearly *adjective* **1** <u>annual</u> ◆ *adverb* **2** <u>annually</u>, every year, once a year, per annum
yearn *verb* <u>long</u>, ache, covet, crave, desire, hanker, hunger, itch
yell *verb* **1** <u>scream</u>, bawl, holler (*informal*), howl, screech, shout, shriek, squeal ◆ *noun* **2** <u>scream</u>, cry, howl, screech, shriek, whoop
yelp *verb* <u>cry</u>, yap, yowl
yen *noun* <u>longing</u>, ache, craving, desire, hankering, hunger, itch, passion, thirst, yearning
yes man *noun* <u>sycophant</u>, bootlicker (*informal*), crawler (*slang*), minion, timeserver, toady
yet *conjunction* **1** <u>nevertheless</u>, however, notwithstanding, still ◆ *adverb* **2** <u>so far</u>, as yet, thus far, until now, up to now **3** <u>still</u>, besides, in addition, into the bargain, to boot **4** <u>now</u>, just now, right now, so soon
yield *verb* **1** <u>produce</u>, bear, bring forth, earn, generate, give, net, provide, return, supply **2** <u>surrender</u>, bow, capitulate, give in, relinquish, resign, submit, succumb ◆ *noun* **3** <u>profit</u>, crop, earnings, harvest, income, output, produce, return, revenue, takings
yielding *adjective* **1** <u>submissive</u>, accommodating, acquiescent, biddable, compliant, docile, flexible, obedient, pliant **2** <u>soft</u>, elastic, pliable, spongy, springy, supple, unresisting
yob, yobbo *noun* <u>thug</u>, hooligan, lout, roughneck

(slang), ruffian

yokel noun <u>peasant</u>, (country) bumpkin, countryman, hick (informal, chiefly U.S. & Canad.), hillbilly, rustic

young adjective 1 <u>immature</u>, adolescent, callow, green, infant, junior, juvenile, little, youthful 2 <u>new</u>, early, fledgling, recent, undeveloped ◆ plural noun 3 <u>offspring</u>, babies, brood, family, issue, litter, progeny

youngster noun <u>youth</u>, boy, girl, juvenile, kid (informal), lad, lass, teenager

youth noun 1 <u>immaturity</u>, adolescence, boyhood, girlhood, salad days 2 <u>boy</u>, adolescent, kid (informal), lad, stripling, teenager, young man, youngster

youthful adjective <u>young</u>, boyish, childish, girlish, immature, inexperienced, juvenile

Z z

zany adjective <u>comical</u>, clownish, crazy, eccentric, goofy (informal), madcap, wacky (slang)

zeal noun <u>enthusiasm</u>, ardour, eagerness, fanaticism, fervour, gusto, keenness, passion, spirit, verve, zest

zealot noun <u>fanatic</u>, bigot, enthusiast, extremist, militant

zealous adjective <u>enthusiastic</u>, ardent, devoted, eager, fanatical, fervent, impassioned, keen, passionate

zenith noun <u>height</u>, acme, apex, apogee, climax, crest, high point, peak, pinnacle, summit, top

zero noun 1 <u>nothing</u>, nil, nought 2 <u>bottom</u>, nadir, rock bottom

zest noun 1 <u>enjoyment</u>, appetite, gusto, keenness, relish, zeal 2 <u>flavour</u>, charm, interest, piquancy, pungency, relish, spice, tang, taste

zip noun 1 Informal <u>energy</u>, drive, gusto, liveliness, verve, vigour, zest ◆ verb 2 <u>speed</u>, flash, fly, shoot, whizz (informal), zoom

zone noun <u>area</u>, belt, district, region, section, sector, sphere

zoom verb <u>speed</u>, dash, flash, fly, hurtle, pelt, rush, shoot, whizz (Informal)

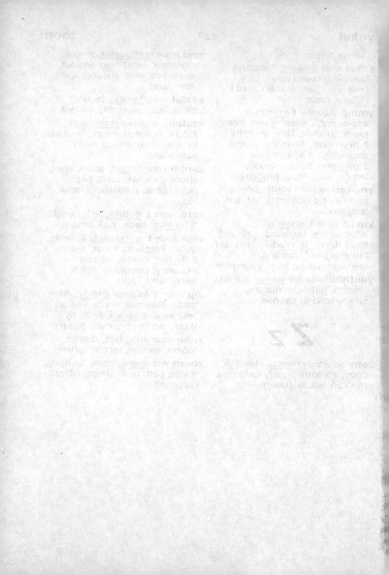